The EY Tax Guide 2015

Years of critical acclaim for America's no. 1 tax guide...

"This is the best tax guide of the bunch...the most up-to-date guide."
USA Today

"Hard to beat...[EY professionals] elucidate each point, giving examples, definitions and strategies that you won't learn about from the IRS."
Money

"This book...has more up-to-date information on tax changes than its competitors—or even the IRS."
Chicago Sun-Times

"Best of the commercially available guides."
New York Daily News

"Destined to become the 'old standard,' all written in plain English....If you can afford just one tax book, this could be the one."
Seattle Post-Intelligencer

"The text-with-commentary approach makes the book both authoritative and easy-to-use."
People

"The simplest tax guide to understand."
CBS This Morning

"The explanations, examples, and planning advice are top-drawer."
Orlando Sentinel

"Exceptionally detailed."
The Sunday Denver Post

"An excellent book, full of clear explanations, planning hints, tax savers and sample forms."
Atlanta Journal Constitution

"Our brand-name choice for filers with lots of questions for filing and planning situations."
Fort Worth Star-Telegram

"...a veritable fountain of information."
Milwaukee Sentinel

"...the best of the bunch for return preparation."
Des Moines Register

2015 tax calendar

Date in 2015   Action required

January

15   ☐ Final estimated tax payment for 2014 due if you did not pay your income tax (or enough of your income tax) for that year through withholding. Use Form 1040-ES.

February

2   ☐ If you did not pay your last installment of estimated tax by January 15, file your income tax return for 2014 on this date, thereby avoiding any penalty for late payment of the last installment. Use Form 1040 or 1040A.

17   ☐ File a new Form W-4 if you can claim exemption from withholding.

March

2   ☐ Farmers and fishermen must file their 2014 income tax return (Form 1040) to avoid an underpayment penalty for the last quarter of 2014 if they were required to but did not pay estimated tax on January 15.

April

15   ☐ File your income tax return for 2014 (Forms 1040, 1040A, or 1040EZ) and pay any tax due.

    ☐ Make your 2014 IRA contribution.

    ☐ If you are not extending your return, make your Keogh or SEP-IRA contribution if you have self-employment income.

    ☐ For an automatic 6-month extension, file Form 4868 and pay any tax that you estimate will be due. Then file Form 1040 or 1040A by October 15. If you get an extension, you can't file Form 1040EZ. (You can use one Form 4868 to file for both your income tax and gift tax extensions.)

    ☐ Pay the first installment of your 2015 estimated tax if you are not paying your 2015 income tax (or enough of it) through withholding tax.

    ☐ If you made any taxable gifts during 2014 (more than $14,000 per donee), file a gift tax return for that year (Form 709 or 709-A) and pay any tax due.

June

15   ☐ Pay the second installment of 2015 estimated tax.

    ☐ If you are a U.S. citizen or resident alien living and working (or on military duty) outside the United States and Puerto Rico, file Form 1040 and pay any tax, interest, and penalties due. Otherwise, see April 15.

30   ☐ Individuals who have signature authority or other authority over certain bank, securities, or other financial accounts in a foreign country must file Form TD F 90-22.1. The form must be received on or before June 30.

September

15   ☐ Pay the third installment of your 2015 estimated tax.

    ☐ Last day to make a required minimum contribution to a defined benefit or money purchase Keogh plan.

October

15   ☐ If you requested an automatic 6-month extension to file your 2014 income tax return, file Form 1040 or Form 1040A and pay any tax, interest, and penalty due, and file any gift tax return if due.

    ☐ Last day to make a Keogh or SEP-IRA contribution deductible for calendar year 2014 if you requested a 6-month extension of time to file your tax return.

December

31   ☐ Last day to establish a Keogh plan for 2015.

The EY Tax Guide 2015

By the Tax Partners and Professionals of Ernst & Young LLP

EY
Building a better
working world

WILEY

The EY Tax Guide Editorial Board 2015

Special thanks to:

Mark Weinberger, Global Chairman and CEO; Stephen R. Howe, Americas Area Managing Partner; Gary L. Belske, Americas Deputy Managing Partner, Kathryn J. Barton, Americas Vice Chair–Tax Services; Eric Solomon and Michael Mundaca, Co-Directors of National Tax; Marnix vin Rij, Global Director of Private Client Services; Steven L. Shultz, Americas Director of Private Client Services.

Special awards and acknowledgments:

The EY Tax Guide is a proud recipient of a Communications Concept, Inc. 2013 Apex Grand Award for Electronic Media; a 2012 Apex Grand Award for Content Excellence for Content and Design (Brochures, Manuals & Reports category); and, an Independent Publisher 2012 Axiom award for Best Business Reference Book.

Thanks to Amy Koeppl, Ellen Lee, Ingrid McGuire, Peter McKinley, and Lizzie McWilliams.

The Ernst & Young global network of member firms has more than 35,000 tax practitioners worldwide, with more than 12,300 practitioners in the United States. This book draws upon the experience of many of those professionals for its content.

SUSTAINABLE FORESTRY INITIATIVE

Certified Chain of Custody
Promoting Sustainable Forestry
www.sfiprogram.org
SFI-01054

Published by John Wiley & Sons, Inc.

Notice: In the preparation of this book, every effort has been made to offer the most current, correct, and clearly expressed information available prior to publication: the Internal Revenue Code as of September 2014, the 2013 version of Internal Revenue Service Publication 17, *Your Federal Income Tax* (rev. Jan. 2013), updated by the author for 2014, and portions of other pertinent Internal Revenue Service publications. Readers may obtain the 2014 version of Publication 17 at *www.irs.gov.* Note also that inadvertent errors can occur, and tax rules and regulations often change.

Limit of Liability/Disclaimer of Warranty: The information in the text is intended to afford general guidelines on matters of interest to taxpayers. The application and impact of tax laws can vary widely, from case to case, based upon the specific or unique facts involved. Readers are encouraged to consult with professional advisors for advice concerning specific matters before making any decision, and the author and publisher disclaim any responsibility for positions taken by taxpayers in their individual cases or for any misunderstanding on the part of readers. While the publisher and author have used their best efforts in preparing this book, they make no representations or warranties with respect to the accuracy or completeness of the contents of this book and specifically disclaim any implied warranties of merchantability or fitness for a particular purpose. No warranty may be created or extended by sales representatives or written sales materials. Neither the publisher nor author shall be liable for any loss of profit or any other damages, including but not limited to direct, indirect, special, incidental, consequential, or other damages.

For general information on Ernst & Young LLP's other products and services or for technical support, please contact our Customer Care Department within the United States at (800) 762-2974, outside the United States at (317) 572-3993 or fax (317) 572-4002.

Wiley publishes in a variety of print and electronic formats and by print-on-demand. Some material included with standard print versions of this book may not be included in e-books or in print-on-demand. If this book refers to media such as a CD or DVD that is not included in the version you purchased, you may download this material at http://booksupport.wiley.com. For more information about Wiley products, visit www.wiley.com.

ISBN
978-1-118-86698-6 (paper); 978-1-118-86683-2 (epdf); 978-1-118-86696-2 (epub)

ISSN
1059-809X

Printed in the United States of America

10 9 8 7 6 5 4 3 2 1

How to use this guide

The *EY Tax Guide 2015* is an easy-to-use, step-by-step guide to preparing your own tax return. It has been designed with you in mind, and its format should help highlight information to save you time and money.

The book explains, in clear and simple English, important aspects of the tax laws that affect you. It covers what you need to know about your taxes—from how to file your return to how to lower the tax you'll pay next year. Throughout the book, you will find hundreds of examples illustrating how the tax laws work. Sample tax forms and schedules show you how to fill out your return line by line. Here are some of the book's special features and how to use them:

- **Two Books in One** The *EY Tax Guide 2015* is really two books. The first book is the 2013 version of the official Internal Revenue Service tax guide, Publication 17, *Your Federal Income Tax*, which is reproduced here. Published annually, it contains the IRS's position on many of the tax questions taxpayers face. To make the *EY Tax Guide 2015* available to the public as quickly as possible, we have updated the text of the 2013 version of IRS Publication 17 to take into account developments during 2014. These updates are noted throughout the text. Upon release, the 2014 IRS Publication 17 can be found at *www.irs.gov*. The second book is the Ernst & Young guide. Here are comments, explanations, and tax-saving tips on what the IRS tells you—and doesn't tell you. It's no surprise that the IRS doesn't tell you everything, and what it does say often favors the U.S. government. Courts and tax professionals frequently differ with IRS opinions. The Ernst & Young text provides you this additional material. The two books have been spliced together to give you the most well-rounded tax guide on the market. To distinguish between the two perspectives, the original IRS text appears in black throughout the book, our updates of the IRS text are underlined, and Ernst & Young's comments appear in the green boxes.

- **TaxSavers, TaxPlanners, TaxAlerts, and TaxOrganizers** Among this book's biggest attractions are the more than 400 *TaxSavers, TaxPlanners, TaxAlerts*, and *TaxOrganizers* that you'll find appropriately placed throughout the text. *TaxSavers* are tips that help you slash your tax bill this year and next—legally. *TaxPlanners* outline ideas that help you plan better for the upcoming year. *TaxAlerts* point out tax rules and regulations that have just changed or may change in the near future; they give you important current filing advice about issues you will want to consider as you prepare your return. *TaxOrganizers* point out steps you can take now to make it easier to file your taxes later.

- **Tax Breaks and Deductions You Can Use Checklists** You will find a checklist of key tax breaks and deductions for which you may be eligible at the beginning of each chapter, immediately following the Introduction. You should review each checklist to make sure you are taking all the deductions and tax breaks that you deserve.

- **Companion Website** Purchase of this guide includes access throughout the 2014 tax return filing season to *ey.com/EYTaxGuide*. This website contains up-to-date information you need about changes in the tax laws that occur throughout the year.

- **Special Contents** We've taken great pains to ensure that this book is clearly organized for easy access. If you can't find the section you want in the regular Contents, check the *Special Contents*. All told, there are eight of these—one each for families, homeowners, investors in stocks and bonds, investors in real estate, self-employed entrepreneurs, business executives, senior citizens, and members of the Armed Forces. Each *Special Contents* section contains a listing of the major tax issues for members of that group and tells where you can find the answers in the book. In addition, we have a table of contents at the beginning of each chapter to help you find what you need.

We have drawn from the tax experience of scores of Ernst & Young LLP partners, professionals, and staff from all parts of the United States to create this tax guide. Among the major accounting firms, only Ernst & Young LLP publishes a complete tax guide that is available to the general public. It provides the most complete and up-to-date tax information of any tax guide published.

Contents

vi   Contents

Special contents

Real estate investors' tax guide

Self-employed entrepreneurs' tax guide

Business executives' tax guide

Senior citizens' tax guide

Members of the Armed Forces' tax guide (Including Veterans)

Changes in the tax law you should know about

For those who like to plan ahead, 2014 is a challenging tax year. Uncertainty dominates the federal tax landscape, and taxpayers may not get clear answers on several outstanding tax issues until close-to year-end . . . or even later.

At the time this book went to press, the fate of "tax extenders," a group of 55 individual and business tax provisions that expired at the end of 2013 was still uncertain. In years past, Congress has extended these provisions temporarily–sometimes retroactively. This may happen again after the November elections if Congress decides to address tax extenders in a "lame duck" session. There are no guarantees, however, and the House and Senate have so far taken different approaches to the issue.

In the meantime, the lack of resolution means taxpayers may not know until late this year or early 2015 whether they will be able to use many exclusions, deductions and credits that have been available in the past. Among them are the itemized deduction for state and local sales tax, the exclusion from gross income of IRA funds distributed to charity, and higher expensing limits for small businesses.

Because the landscape may shift before income tax returns are due, taxpayers need to monitor late-breaking legislative developments and be ready to adjust accordingly. For updated information on tax legislation enacted after this book is published, see our website, ey.com/EYTaxGuide.

Tax Changes Effective for 2014

Personal Exemption Limitation

Under the American Taxpayer Relief Act (ATRA), the personal exemption phaseout rules were fully reinstated, effective in 2013. With this limitation, taxpayers lose 2% of their total personal exemption amount for each $2,500 (or portion thereof) of adjusted gross income (AGI) in excess of an applicable threshold amount based on their tax filing status. For 2014, the phaseout begins and ends at the following amounts of AGI:

Filing status	Phaseout begins	Phaseout ends
Single	$254,200	$376,700
Married filing jointly and qualifying widow(er)	305,050	427,550
Married filing separately	152,525	213,775
Head of household	279,650	402,150

Itemized Deductions Limitation

The limitation on certain itemized deductions was fully reinstated under ATRA. Under this rule, the amount of itemized deductions you can claim is reduced by 3% of the amount of your adjusted gross income (AGI) in excess of the applicable thresholds; although no more than 80% of these otherwise allowable deductions will be eliminated. The thresholds are $254,200 for individual filers, $279,650 for heads of households, $305,050 for married couples filing jointly, and $152,525 for married couples filing separately.

Itemized deductions that are subject to this limitation include taxes, home mortgage interest, charitable contributions, and most miscellaneous itemized deductions. This limitation will be applied after you have used any other limitations that specifically apply with respect to affected itemized deductions, such as the AGI limitation for charitable contributions and the mortgage interest expense limitations. Medical expenses, casualty and theft losses, investment interest expense, and deductible gambling losses are not subject to this overall limitation.

Standard Mileage Rates

The standard mileage rate for the cost of operating your car decreased slightly to 56 cents a mile for all business miles driven for 2014. See chapter 27, *Car expenses and other employee business expenses.*

The standard mileage rate allowed for the use of your car for medical reasons or a qualified move is 23.5 cents per mile for 2014. See chapter 22, *Medical and dental expenses*, and chapter 20, *Moving expenses.*

The standard mileage rate allowed for charitable purposes remains at 14 cents per mile for 2014. See chapter 25, *Contributions.*

Itemized Deduction for State and Local General Sales Tax Expired

ATRA retroactively extended for 2012 and 2013 the provision allowing a taxpayer to elect to take an itemized deduction for state and local general sales taxes instead of the itemized deduction for state and local income taxes paid. However, this provision expired at the end of 2013. Congress may act late this year to retroactively extend it, but unless that happens, taxpayers will not be able to deduct state and local general sales taxes for 2014. For updated information on tax law changes that occur after this book was published, see our website, *ey.com/EYTaxGuide.*

This provision particularly benefitted residents of states with no state income tax such as Alaska, Florida, Nevada, South Dakota, Texas, Washington, and Wyoming. (New Hampshire and Tennessee tax interest and dividend income but otherwise do not tax income.) Because it was available to all taxpayers as an option, however, it had the potential to benefit other taxpayers whose sales tax bill for the year exceeded their state income tax; e.g., in low-tax jurisdictions or in years when large taxable expenditures were incurred.

Alternative Minimum Tax (AMT)

AMT exemption permanently "patched." The tax laws give preferential treatment to certain kinds of income and allow special deductions and credits for certain kinds of expenses. The AMT attempts to ensure that anyone who benefits from these tax advantages pays at least a minimum amount of tax. The AMT is a separately computed tax that eliminates many deductions and credits that are allowed in computing your regular tax liability.

The AMT is the government's mechanism through which taxpayers with a large amount of deductions still pay some income tax. The tentative minimum tax rates on ordinary income are 26% and 28%. ATRA permanently "patched" the AMT and indexes the exemption and phaseout amounts for inflation. For 2014, the exemption amounts increased to $52,800 for single taxpayers, $82,100 for married couples filing jointly, and $41,050 for married filing separately. The exemption phases out at higher levels of alternative minimum taxable income (AMTI). For 2014, a taxpayer's exemption amount is reduced (but not below zero) by 25 percent of the amount by which alternative minimum taxable income exceeds the following: $117,300 (singles), $156,500 (married filing jointly), and $78,250 (married filing separately).

The 20% maximum tax rate (0% for those taxpayers who are otherwise in the 10% and 15% marginal tax brackets for ordinary income in 2014 and 15% for those in the 25% to 35% brackets) on qualified dividends and long-term capital gains for regular tax purposes also applies when calculating the AMT. If your taxable income for regular tax purposes, plus any adjustments and preference items you have, total more than the exemption amount, then you may have to pay the AMT.

For an explanation of the AMT, see chapter 31, *How to figure your tax.*

AMT relief for nonrefundable personal credits. Under ATRA, taxpayers can continue to offset their entire regular tax and AMT liabilities with personal nonrefundable tax credits. These credits include the dependent care credit, the credit for the elderly and disabled, the adoption credit, the child tax credit, the credit for interest on certain home mortgages, the Lifetime Learning and American Opportunity credits (except for the refundable portion of the American Opportunity credit), the savers credit for elective deferrals and IRA contributions by certain individuals, the credit for residential energy efficient property, and the credits for certain plug-in electric drive motor and alternative motor vehicles. These credits are described in the section on _Nonrefundable Credits_, in chapter 37, _Other credits including the earned income credit_.

Exclusion from Gross Income for IRA Distributions Contributed Directly to Charity Expired

The provision that allowed the exclusion from gross income for distributions from an IRA directly contributed to charity by individuals over age 70½ (called Qualified Charitable Distributions or QCDs), expired at the end of 2013. Congress may yet extend this provision retroactively, but unless it does so, such donations are not excludable from gross income for 2014.

If the provision is extended, it could benefit many taxpayers. Under the expired provision, distributions eligible for the exclusion may not exceed $100,000 per taxpayer per tax year. Spouses filing a joint return can each make a qualified charitable distribution of up to $100,000. Distributions in excess of $100,000 that otherwise meet the requirements for a qualified charitable distribution could not be carried over to future years.

Qualifying IRA owners could recognize significantly greater tax benefits from utilizing this provision to fund charitable donations than they would from making contributions from other accounts or property. The amount distributed as a QCD would not be taxable to the account holder and counted towards the minimum required distributions the IRA account holder had for the year. Excluding IRA distributions that satisfied the QCD requirements reduced adjusted gross income (AGI), which, in turn reduced the percentage limitations based on AGI that apply to various deductions and credits. On the other hand, a charitable deduction could not be claimed for the QCD.

For more information, see _Qualified charitable distributions (QCD)_ in chapter 17, _Individual retirement arrangements (IRAs)_. For updated information on tax law changes that occur after this book was published, see our website, _ey.com/EYTaxGuide_.

Increased Contribution Limits and Carryforward Period for Qualified Conservation Contributions Expired

Through the end of 2013, the charitable deduction limit for qualified conservation contributions of real property (including partial interests in real estate) was 50% of the excess of your adjusted gross income (AGI) over the amount of all other allowable charitable contributions. If you were a qualified farmer or rancher when you made the contribution, the limitation was further increased to 100%. You were also allowed to carry over any qualified conservation contributions that exceed the 50% limitation for up to 15 years. For more information, see _Qualified Conservation Contribution_, in chapter 25, _Contributions_.

These higher deduction limits for qualified conservation contributions expired at the end of 2013. Unless Congress acts to extend them, the limit for qualified conservation contributions made after 2013 drops to 30% and the carryover period is reduced from 15 years to 5 years. For updated information on this and any other tax law changes that occur after this book was published, see our website, _ey.com/EYTaxGuide_.

Adjustment to S Corporation Shareholder's Stock Basis for Contributions of Property to Charity Expired

ATRA extended to the end of 2013 the adjustment of an S corporation shareholder's stock basis by a pro rata share of the adjusted basis of appreciated property donated by the corporation to charity. Unless

Congress acts to retroactively extend this provision, the tax treatment will revert to prior law, which required that when an S corporation donated appreciated property that qualified for a fair market value deduction, the shareholder's basis in the S corporation stock be reduced by the full fair market value of the deduction. Due to this reduction in basis, when the S corporation shareholder ultimately sells shares, the shareholder will effectively pay tax on the appreciated value of the property that had been contributed to charity. This result differs from what the shareholder would have realized had he or she personally donated that appreciated property. In that case, the shareholder would not recognize the gain attributable to the appreciation. For updated information on tax law changes that occur after this book was published, see our website, _ey.com/EYTaxGuide_.

Exclusion from Gross Income of Certain Discharged Mortgage Debt Expired

ATRA extended through 2013 the exclusion from gross income of income realized from the discharge of qualified principal residence indebtedness. But, unless Congress acts to retroactively extend the provision, the exclusion is not available for tax years after 2013. Under the expired provision, up to $2 million ($1 million if married filing separately) of qualified principal residence indebtedness could be forgiven, and no income would have to be recognized related to the cancellation of debt. However, your basis in your principal residence would be reduced by the amount excluded from income.

Qualified principal residence indebtedness is defined as acquisition indebtedness with respect to your principal residence. Acquisition indebtedness generally means debt you incurred in the acquisition, construction, or substantial improvement of your principal residence that is secured by the residence. It also includes the refinancing of such debt to the extent the new loan balance is attributable to qualified principal residence indebtedness.

Some Education-Related Adjustments Continue; Others Expired

ATRA extended certain education-related adjustments you can deduct to calculate your adjusted gross income (AGI). These provisions can reduce the amount of your income subject to tax, regardless of whether you itemize deductions. While some were extended permanently, others have since expired.

Expanded student loan interest deduction permanently extended. You may be able to claim a deduction for calculating your adjusted gross income (AGI)—typically called an "above-the-line" deduction—of up to $2,500 in interest you pay on a qualified student loan used for higher education. The amount of your student loan interest deduction is gradually reduced (phased out) if your modified adjusted gross income (MAGI) is between $65,000 and $80,000 ($130,000 and $160,000 if you file a joint return). You cannot take a deduction if your MAGI is $80,000 or more ($160,000 or more if you file a joint return). For more information, see _Student Loan Interest Deduction_ in chapter 19, _Education-related adjustments_.

Above-the-line deduction for qualified tuition-related expenses expired. Under the deduction, which at the time of this writing was not available for 2014, you could claim an adjustment in figuring your AGI of up to $4,000 for qualified education expenses you paid during the year for tuition and fees at a college, university, or other qualifying postsecondary education institution. For more information, see _Tuition and Fees Deduction_ in chapter 19, _Education-related adjustments_. For updated information on tax law changes that occur after this book was published, see our website, _ey.com/EYTaxGuide_.

Deduction for educator expenses expired. ATRA extended the availability of the "above-the-line" deduction for up to $250 in expenses paid or incurred in 2013 for books, qualifying supplies, and equipment (including computer equipment, software, and service) by elementary and secondary school teachers and other eligible school professionals. But unless Congress acts, the educator expense adjustment is not available after 2013. Instead, you will only be able to deduct ordinary and necessary educator expenses as a miscellaneous itemized deduction subject to the 2% limitation. For more information, see *Educator Expenses*, in chapter 29, *Miscellaneous deductions*. For updated information on tax law changes that occur after this book was published, see our website, *ey.com/EYTaxGuide*.

Section 179 Small Business Expensing Amounts

Section 179 of the tax code allows you to elect to deduct all or part of the cost–up to specified yearly limits–of certain qualifying property in the year in which the property is purchased and placed in service, rather than capitalizing the cost and depreciating it over its life. This means that you can deduct all or part of the cost up front in one year rather than take depreciation deductions spread out over many years. You must decide for each item of qualifying property whether to deduct, subject to the yearly limit, or capitalize and depreciate its cost. Qualifying property is property purchased for use in your trade or business and property that would have qualified for the investment tax credit.

Specified limits. Unless Congress acts, the maximum amount you can elect to deduct for most Section 179 property placed into service in 2014 is $25,000, with an investment ceiling of $200,000. This is a sharp decline from the maximum $500,000 deduction allowed ($535,000 for qualified enterprise zone property) and investment ceiling of $2 million for 2013. In early 2014, both the House and Senate were considering legislation to extend higher limits for small business expensing, but at the time this was written, legislation had not been passed. For updated information on tax law changes that occur after this book was published, see our website, *ey.com/EYTaxGuide*.

Special Depreciation Allowance

Unless Congress acts, companies will not be able to use the so-called "bonus depreciation" allowance in 2014. The Small Business Jobs Act of 2010 provided that qualified property placed in service after September 8, 2010, and before January 1, 2012, was eligible for 100% first-year depreciation. For 2012, the bonus depreciation allowed for investments placed into service dropped from 100% to 50% of the depreciable basis of qualified property. ATRA extended 50% bonus depreciation through 2013. Bonus depreciation applied to qualified property acquired between 2008 and 2013 and placed in service prior to January 1, 2014. The types of property that qualified for the 50% special depreciation allowance were Section 168 (tangible) property with a recovery period of 20 years or less, off-the-shelf computer software, water utility property, and qualified leasehold improvement property. For updated information on tax law changes that occur after this book was published, see our website, *ey.com/EYTaxGuide*. The rules for claiming the special depreciation allowance are complex. See Publication 946, *How to Depreciate Property*, for more information.

100% Exclusion of Small Business Capital Gains Expired

For 2014, unless Congress acts, taxpayers will be able to exclude 50% of the gain realized from the sale or exchange of qualified small business stock (QSBS) held for more than 5 years. This is down from the 100% exclusion allowed in 2013 under ATRA. For updated information on tax law changes that occur after this book was published, see our website, *ey.com/EYTaxGuide*, and for more information on the exclusion of gain on qualified small business stock, see *Gain on Qualified Small Business Stock*, in chapter 14, *Sale of Property*.

Temporary Reduction in Recognition Period for S Corporation Built-In Gains Expired

When a C corporation elects to become an S corporation, the conversion is not a taxable event. However, following such a conversion, an S corporation must hold on to its assets for a certain period of time. If the S corporation sells an asset sooner, then any built-in gain in such asset that existed at the time of the conversion is taxed to the S corporation at the existing highest marginal tax rate applicable to corporations; currently, 35%. Generally, the minimum required holding period is 10 years. Under

ATRA, the holding period had been reduced to 5 years for sales of assets in 2013 or 2012. (Earlier tax laws reduced the holding period to 7 years for sales during 2009 and 2010 and 5 years for sales occurring in 2011.) Unless Congress acts, the holding period rises back to 10 years for sales of assets occurring in 2014 and thereafter. For updated information on tax law changes that occur after this book was published, see our website, *ey.com/EYTaxGuide*.

Tax Benefits for Adoption

The adoption credit and the maximum exclusion from income of benefits under an employer's adoption assistance program increased to $13,190 for 2014. These benefits are phased out for taxpayers with AGI between $197,880 and $237,880. See *Adoption Credit* in chapter 37, *Other credits including the earned income credit*.

Other ATRA Provisions That Have Expired

Unless Congress acts, the following individual tax provisions that ATRA had extended do not apply for 2014. For updated information on tax legislation that is enacted after this book is published, see our website, *ey.com/EYTaxGuide*.

- The itemized deduction for the cost of mortgage insurance on a qualified personal residence is no longer available. See *Mortgage insurance premiums* in chapter 24, *Interest expense,* for more information.
- Parity for exclusion from income for employer-provided mass transit and parking benefits has expired. Accordingly, the monthly exclusion for employer-provided transit and vanpool benefits is $130 per month for 2014, down from $245 per month at the end of 2013, while the monthly exclusion for employer-provided parking benefits is $250 for 2014.
- The credit for nonbusiness energy property to existing homes is not available for 2014. For 2013, it was limited to 10% of the cost of qualified energy efficiency improvements to existing homes. The maximum credit for a taxpayer was $500, and no more than $200 of such credit could be attributable to expenditures on windows.
- The credit for alternative fuel vehicle refueling property is not available for 2013 except for hydrogen refueling property. See *Hydrogen refueling property credit* in chapter 37, *Other credits including the earned income credit,* for further information.
- The credit for plug-in electric drive motor vehicles is not available for electric motorcycles and three-wheeled vehicles placed into service after 2013. Vehicles that qualify for the credit in 2014 are: those with at least four wheels; are propelled to a significant extent by an electric motor that draws electricity from a battery that has a capacity of not less than 4 kilowatt hours and is capable of being recharged from an external source of electricity; and, has a gross vehicle weight of less than 14,000 pounds.

Recapture of First-Time Homebuyer Credit for Homes Purchased in 2008

If you claimed the first-time homebuyer credit for a home you bought in 2008, you were required to begin repaying the credit in 2010. Your fifth installment will be due with your 2014 tax return. You generally must repay the credit over a 15-year period in 15 equal installments. Each installment is reported as additional tax on your tax return. However, if you sold or stopped using your home as your principal residence before the 15-year period is up, you must include all remaining annual installments as additional tax on the return for the tax year that happened. See *Recapturing (Paying Back) the First-Time Homebuyer Credit* in chapter 37, *Other credits including the earned income credit*, for additional information.

2014 Disaster Area Tax Relief

You may be eligible for tax relief if you were the victim of various storms that occurred during 2014. The IRS website, *IRS.gov* (click on "Disaster Relief" under "Resolve an issue"), contains links to related news releases for the victims of the affected areas. A list of the 2014 Federal Disaster Declarations is available on the FEMA website at *fema.gov/news/disasters.fema*.

Estate, Gift, and Generation-Skipping Transfer Taxes

ATRA reunified the estate and gift taxes with a single graduated rate schedule for both, while permanently setting the estate, gift, and generation-skipping transfer (GST) tax exemption at $5 million. The exemption is indexed annually for inflation. For 2014, the exemption amount is $5.34 million. The maximum tax rate on transfers of property subject to gift, estate, and GST tax is 40%. For more information on estate and gift tax, see chapter 44, *Estate and gift tax planning*.

Gift tax applicable for 2014. The annual exclusion remains $14,000 for 2014 per donee for gifts. As described above, ATRA reunified the gift and estate taxes. The gift tax exemption for 2014 is therefore $5.34 million and the maximum tax rate on taxable gifts made during 2014 is 40%. See *The Fundamentals of the Gift Tax* in chapter 44, *Estate and gift tax planning*.

Inflation Adjustments for 2014

Each year a number of tax benefits and income limitations for tax benefits are adjusted for inflation. In recent years these changes, if any, were very small due to the low rate of inflation—and this holds true for 2014. The adjustments for 2014 are as follows:

- Tax Rate Tables: The income brackets for each tax rate have been increased slightly. See chapter 48, *Tax rate schedules*.
- Personal Exemption: The personal exemption amount increased from $3,900 to $3,950 in 2014. See chapter 3, *Personal exemptions and dependents*.
- Standard Deduction: The standard deduction increased for 2013 to $12,400 (up from $12,200) for married individuals filing joint returns and surviving spouses, $9,100 (up from $8,950) for heads of household, and $6,200 (up from $6,100) for unmarried individuals and married individuals filing separate returns. The additional standard deduction for blind people and senior citizens is $1,200 for married individuals or surviving spouse, and $1,550 for unmarried and not a surviving spouse. See chapter 21, *Standard deduction*.
- Pension Plan Limitations: Most of the contribution limits and income limitations increased slightly for 2014. The primary changes include:
  1. The elective contribution limit for employees who participate in 401(k), 403(b), most 457 plans, and the federal government's Thrift Savings Plan is $17,500 for 2014, unchanged from 2013.
  2. For married couples filing jointly, in which the spouse who makes the IRA contribution is an active participant in an employer-sponsored retirement plan, the income phaseout range is $96,000 to $116,000 for 2014, up from $95,000 to $115,000; for singles and heads of household, the income phaseout range is $60,000 to $70,000, up from $59,000 to $69,000 in 2013.
  3. For an IRA contributor who is not an active participant in an employer-sponsored retirement plan, but who either lives with his/her spouse or files jointly, and the spouse is an active participant, the deduction is phased out if the couple's income is between $181,000 and $191,000 for 2014, up from $178,000 and $188,000.
  4. The AGI phaseout range for 2014 for taxpayers making contributions to a Roth IRA is $181,000 to $191,000 for married couples filing jointly or a qualifying widow(er), up from $178,000 to $188,000; for singles, heads of household, or married filing separately who did not live with his/her spouse at any time during 2014, the income phaseout range is $114,000 to $129,000, up from $112,000 to $127,000; and the phaseout range for married taxpayers filing separately who lived with their spouse at any time during the year remains unchanged at $0 to $10,000. See chapter 17, *Individual retirement arrangements (IRAs)*.

- Saver's Credit Limitations: The AGI limit for the saver's credit (also known as the retirement savings contributions credit) in 2014 is $60,000 for married couples filing jointly, up from $59,000. For heads of household, the AGI limit is $45,000, up from $44,250, and for married individuals filing separately and for singles, the AGI limit is $30,000, up from $29,500. See chapter 37, *Other credits including the earned income credit*.
- Earned Income Credit: The maximum earned income credit (EIC) rises to $6,143 for 2013, up from $6,044 in 2013. The maximum income limit for the EIC rises to $52,427 for 2014, up from $51,567 in 2013. The credit varies by family size, filing status, and other factors, with the maximum credit going to joint filers with three or more qualifying children. See chapter 37, *Other credits including the earned income credit*.
- Lifetime Learning Credit Limitation: The modified AGI threshold at which the lifetime learning credit begins to phase out in 2014 is $108,000 for joint filers, up from $107,000, and $54,000 for singles and heads of household, up from $53,000. The modified AGI threshold at which the American opportunity credit begins to phase out for 2014 is $80,000 for married individuals filing separately and singles, and $160,000 for married couples filing jointly. See chapter 36, *Education credits and other education tax benefits*.
- AMT Exemption for a Child Subject to the Kiddie Tax: For purposes of determining the AMT tax on a child subject to the "kiddie tax," the exemption amount increased for 2014 to the sum of the child's earned income for the tax year, plus $7,250 (up from $7,150). See chapter 31, *How to figure your tax*.
- Education Savings Bond Program Limitations: The exclusion of interest income from savings bonds for taxpayers who pay qualified higher education expenses begins to phase out in 2014 for modified adjusted gross income (MAGI) above $113,950 (up from $112,050) for married filing jointly or qualifying widow(er), and $76,000 (up from $74,700) for other returns. The exclusion is completely phased out for MAGI of $143,950 (up from $142,050) or more for joint returns or qualifying widow(er), and $91,000 (up from $89,700) or more for other returns. See *Education Savings Bond Program* in chapter 7, *Interest income*.
- Long-Term Care Premium Deduction: The long-term care premium deduction has increased slightly in 2014 for each age group. For taxpayers age 40 or less, the amount that can be claimed as a medical expense deduction is $370 (up from $360); for taxpayers age 41–50, the deduction is $700 (up from $680); for taxpayers age 51-60, the deduction is $1,400 (up from $1,360); for taxpayers age 61-70, the deduction is $3,720 (up from $3,640); and for taxpayers more than 70 years old, the deduction is $4,660 (up from $4,550). See chapter 22, *Medical and dental expenses*.
- Medical Savings Account Limitations: The minimum and maximum annual deductible for self-only and family coverage, and the annual out-of-pocket expenses required to be paid for covered benefits has been increased slightly. See IRS Publication 969, *Health Savings Accounts and Other Tax-Favored Health Plans*, for more information on these limits.

Planning Ahead for 2015 and Beyond

See chapter 47 for a discussion of tax developments and issues in 2015 and after.

Important 2014 tax reminders

Listed below are important reminders and other items that may help you file your 2014 tax return. Many of these items are explained in more detail later in this publication.

- **Enter your social security number (SSN).**
  Enter your SSN in the space provided on your tax form. If you filed a joint return for 2013 and are filing a joint return for 2014 with the same spouse, enter your names and SSNs in the same order as on your 2013 return. See chapter 1.

- **Taxpayer identification numbers.**
  You must provide the taxpayer identification number for each person for whom you claim certain tax benefits. This applies even if the person was born in 2014. Generally, this number is the person's social security number (SSN). See chapter 1.

- **Individual retirement arrangements (IRAs).**
  For purposes of taking an IRA deduction, earned income includes any nontaxable combat pay received by a member of the U.S. Armed Forces.

- **Qualified joint venture.**
  A qualified joint venture conducted by you and your spouse may not be treated as a partnership if you file a joint return for the tax year. See chapters 12 and 38.

- **Recordkeeping requirements for cash contributions.**
  You cannot deduct a cash contribution, regardless of the amount, unless you keep as a record of the contribution a bank record (such as a canceled check, a bank copy of a canceled check, or a bank statement containing the name of the charity, the date, and amount) or a written communication from the charity. The written communication must include the name of the charity and the date and amount of the contribution. See chapter 25.

- **Foreign source income.**
  If you are a U.S. citizen with income from sources outside the United States (foreign income), you must report all such income on your tax return unless it is exempt by U.S. law. This is true whether you reside inside or outside the United States and whether or not you receive a Form W-2 or 1099 from the foreign payer. This applies to earned income (such as wages and tips) as well as unearned income (such as interest, dividends, capital gains, pensions, rents, and royalties). If you reside outside the United States, you may be able to exclude part or all of your foreign source earned income. For details, see chapter 41, *U.S. citizens working abroad: Tax treatment of foreign earned income,* and IRS Publication 54, *Tax Guide for U.S. Citizens and Resident Aliens Abroad.*

- **Foreign financial assets.**
  If you had foreign financial assets in 2014, you may have to file Form 8938 with your return. Check *www.IRS.gov/form8938* for details.

- **Automatic six-month extension to file tax return.**
  You can use Form 4868, Application for Automatic Extension of Time To File U.S. Individual Income Tax Return, to obtain an automatic 6-month extension of time to file your tax return. See chapter 1.

- **Tax Computation Worksheet.**
  If your taxable income is $100,000 or more, figure your tax using the Tax Computation Worksheet, which can be found at the IRS website (*www.irs.gov*). The Tax Rate Schedules in chapter 48 are shown so you can see the tax rate that applies to all levels of taxable income. Do not use the Tax Rate Schedules to figure your tax. Instead, see chapter 31.

- **Joint return responsibility.**
  Generally, both spouses are responsible for the tax and any interest or penalties on a joint tax return. In some cases, one spouse may be relieved of that responsibility for items of the other spouse that were incorrectly reported on the joint return. See chapter 2.

- **Include your phone number on your return.**
  To promptly resolve any questions the IRS has in processing your tax return, they would like to be able to call you. Please enter your daytime telephone number on your tax form next to your signature and occupation. If you are filing a joint return, you can enter either your or your spouse's daytime phone number.

- **Third party designee.**
  You can check the "Yes" box in the "Third Party Designee" area of your return to authorize the IRS to discuss your return with a friend, family member, or any other person you choose. This allows the IRS to call the person you identified as your designee to answer any questions that may arise during the processing of your return. It also allows your designee to perform certain actions. See chapter 1.

- **Frivolous tax submissions.**
  The IRS has published a list of positions that are identified as frivolous. The penalty for filing a frivolous tax return is $5,000. See chapter 1.

- **Filing erroneous claim for refund or credit.**
  You may have to pay a penalty if you file an erroneous claim for refund or credit. See chapter 1.

- **Payment of taxes.**
  You can pay your taxes online, by phone, or by check or money order. You can make a direct transfer from your bank account or use a credit or debit card. If you *e-file*, you can schedule an electronic payment. See chapter 1.

- **Faster ways to file your return.**
  The IRS offers fast, accurate ways to file your tax return information without filing a paper tax return. You can use IRS *e-file* (electronic filing). See chapter 1.

- **Free electronic filing.**
  You may be able to file your 2014 taxes online for free. See chapter 1.

- **Change of address.**
  If you change your address, you should notify the IRS. See *Change of Address* in chapter 1.

- **Private delivery services.**
  You may be able to use a designated private delivery service to mail your tax returns and payments. See chapter 1.

- **Refund on a late filed return.**
  If you were due a refund but you did not file a return, you generally must file your return within 3 years from the date the return was due (including extensions) to get that refund. See chapter 1.

- **Customer service for taxpayers.**
  You can set up a personal appointment at the most convenient Taxpayer Assistance Center, on the most convenient business day.

- **Preparer *e-file* mandate.**
  Most paid preparers must *e-file* returns they prepare and file. Your preparer may make you aware of this requirement and the options available to you.

- **Secure your tax records from identity theft.**

  Identity theft occurs when someone uses your personal information such as your name, SSN, or other identifying information, without your permission, to commit fraud or other crimes. An identity thief may use your SSN to get a job or may file a tax return using your SSN to receive a refund. For more information about identity theft and how to reduce your risk from it, see chapter 1.

- **Protect yourself from suspicious emails or phishing schemes.**

  Phishing is the creation and use of email and websites designed to mimic legitimate business emails and websites. The most common form is the act of sending an email to a user falsely claiming to be an established legitimate enterprise in an attempt to scam the user into surrendering private information that will be used for identity theft. The IRS does not initiate contacts with taxpayers via emails. Also, the IRS does not request detailed personal information through email or ask taxpayers for the PIN numbers, passwords, or similar secret access information for their credit card, bank, or other financial accounts. If you receive an unsolicited email claiming to be from the IRS, forward the message to: _phishing@irs.gov_. You may also report misuse of the IRS name, logo, forms, or other IRS property to the Treasury Inspector General for Tax Administration toll-free at 1-800-366-4484. You can forward suspicious emails to the Federal Trade Commission at: _spam@uce.gov_ or contact them at _www.ftc.gov/idtheft_ or 1-877-IDTHEFT (1-877-438-4338). Visit _www.irs.gov_ and enter "identity theft" in the search box to learn more about identity theft and how to reduce your risk.

- **Tax questions.**

  If you have a tax question, visit _www.irs.gov_ or call 1-800-829-1040. For TTY/TDD, call 1-800-829-4059.

How to avoid 25 common errors

1. Most importantly, check your math.

2. Double-check that your social security number has been correctly written on the return. If you are married, check that your spouse's social security number is properly listed, whether filing a joint or separate return.

3. Include your social security number on each page of the return so that if a page is misplaced by the IRS, it can be reattached.

4. Check that you have claimed all of your dependents, such as elderly parents who may not live with you. See chapter 3, *Personal exemptions and dependents*.

5. Include on the return the social security numbers for all dependents, including those born during 2014. In addition, for each child under age 17 who is a qualifying child for the child tax credit, make sure you checked the box beside the child's name indicating the child is a qualifying child for the child tax credit.

6. If you are single and have a dependent who lives with you, check to see if you qualify for the lower tax rates available to a head of household or surviving spouse.

7. You may be eligible for the earned income credit if you do NOT file as married filing separately. If you have one qualifying child and your earned income and modified adjusted gross income for 2014 are less than $38,511 ($43,941 if married filing jointly), you may qualify. If you have two qualifying children, you may qualify for the earned income credit if your earned income and modified adjusted gross income for 2014 are less than $43,756 ($49,186 if married filing jointly). If you have three or more qualifying children, you may qualify for the earned income credit if your earned income and modified adjusted gross income for 2014 are less than $46,997 ($52,427 if married filing jointly). If you do not have a qualifying child, but are over age 24 and under age 65, and your earned income for 2014 and modified adjusted gross income are less than $14,590 ($20,020 if married filing jointly), you may qualify as well. See chapter 37, *Other credits including the earned income credit*.

8. If you are married, check to see if filing separate returns rather than a joint return is more beneficial.

9. Attach all copies B of your W-2 forms to your return in order to avoid correspondence with the IRS. If you received a Form 1099-R showing federal income tax withheld, attach copy B of that form as well.

10. You may be eligible to claim the additional standard deductions if you are blind or 65 years of age or older.

11. Be sure to sign your check and write your social security number, the form number, and the tax year on the face of any checks made out to the United States Treasury. (Example: "000-00-000-2014 Form 1040.")

12. Be sure that your Form W-2 and all Form 1099s are correct. If they're wrong, have them corrected as soon as possible so that the IRS's records agree with the amounts you show on your return.

13. If you worked for more than one employer, be sure to claim a credit for any overpaid social security taxes withheld from your wages.

14. If you received a state tax refund or a refund of interest you paid on a mortgage in an earlier year, make sure you have not included too much of your refund in your income. These refunds may not be taxable if you did not get a tax benefit from deducting them. If, for example, you used the standard deduction in the year in which the taxes or interest were paid, you do not have to include the refund in income this year. In addition, if you were subject to the alternative minimum tax in the prior year, a portion, or all, of your state income tax refund may not be taxable.

15. Deductible real property taxes should be distinguished from assessments paid for local benefits, such as repair of streets, sidewalks, sewers, curbs, gutters, and other improvements that tend to benefit specific properties. Assessments of this type generally are not deductible.

16. Make sure that you sign and date your return and enter your occupation. If you are filing a joint return, be sure that your spouse also signs as required.

17. Only a portion of your social security benefits may be taxable. If your income does not exceed a certain amount, none of it may be taxable.

18. Check last year's tax return to see if there are any items that carry over to this year, such as charitable contributions or capital losses that exceeded the amount you were previously able to deduct.

19. If you can be claimed as a dependent on someone else's return, do not claim a personal exemption on your return. Your standard deduction may be limited as well. See chapter 21, *Standard deduction*.

20. Fill out Form 8606, Nondeductible IRA Contributions, for your contributions to an IRA account, if you don't claim any deduction for the contribution.

21. Recheck your basis in the securities that you sold during the year, particularly shares of a mutual fund. Income and capital gains dividends that were automatically reinvested in the fund over the years increase your basis in the mutual fund and thus reduce a gain or increase a loss that you have to report. Also, any "front-end" or purchase fees are still considered part of your cost basis for tax purposes, even though they reduce your investment in a mutual fund.

22. Recheck that you have used the correct column in the Tax Rate Table or the right Tax Rate Schedule for your filing status.

23. Don't miss deadlines: December 31—set up a Keogh plan; April 15—make your IRA contribution; April 15—file your return or request an extension. Check the tax calendar periodically. See the *2015 Tax Calendar*.

24. If you regularly get large refunds, you're having too much withheld and, in effect, giving the IRS an interest-free loan. Increasing the number of allowances you claim on Form W-4 will increase your take-home pay.

25. Keep copies of all documents you send to the IRS. Use certified mail for all important correspondence to the IRS. Don't forget to keep your records in good shape so that you can find answers to any IRS questions about your return.

50 of the most easily overlooked deductions

The following list will serve as a reminder of some deductions you can easily overlook when you prepare your return. It is not intended to be all-inclusive, nor applicable to everyone. The circumstances of your situation will determine whether you qualify. See the Chapter reference following each item for a complete explanation.

1. Accounting fees for tax preparation services and IRS audits (chapter 29)
2. Alcoholism and drug abuse treatment (chapter 22)
3. Amortization of premium on taxable bonds (chapter 29)
4. Appraisal fees for charitable donations or casualty losses (chapters 25 and 26)
5. Appreciation on property donated to a charity (chapter 25)
6. Casualty or theft losses (chapter 26)
7. Cellular telephones (chapter 29)
8. Cleaning and laundering services when traveling (chapter 27)
9. Commissions and closing costs on sale of property (chapter 14)
10. Contact lenses, eyeglasses, and hearing devices (chapter 22)
11. Contraceptives, if bought with a prescription (chapter 22)
12. Costs associated with looking for a new job in your present occupation, including fees for résumé preparation and employment of outplacement agencies (chapter 29)
13. Depreciation of home computers (chapter 29)
14. Dues to labor unions (chapter 29)
15. Education expenses to the extent required by law or your employer or needed to maintain or improve your skills (chapters 28 and 29)
16. Employee contributions to a state disability fund (chapter 23)
17. Employee's moving expenses (chapter 20)
18. Federal estate tax on income with respect to a decedent (chapter 29)
19. Fees for a safe deposit box to hold investments (e.g., stock certificate) (chapter 29)
20. Fees paid for childbirth preparation classes if instruction relates to obstetrical care (chapter 22)
21. Fifty percent of self-employment tax (chapter 38)
22. Foreign taxes paid (chapter 23)
23. Foster child care expenditures (chapter 25)
24. Gambling losses to the extent of gambling winnings (chapter 29)
25. Hospital services fees (laboratory work, therapy, nursing services, and surgery) (chapter 22)
26. Impairment-related work expenses for a disabled individual (chapter 22)
27. Breast pumps and lactation supplies (chapter 22)
28. Investment advisory fees (chapter 29)
29. IRA trustee's administrative fees billed separately (chapter 29)
30. Lead paint removal (chapter 22)
31. Legal fees incurred in connection with obtaining or collecting alimony (chapter 29)
32. Long-term care insurance premiums (chapter 22)
33. Margin account interest expense (chapter 24)
34. Medical transportation, including standard mileage deduction (chapter 22) and lodging expenses incurred for medical reasons while away from home (chapter 22)
35. Mortgage prepayment penalties and late fees (chapter 24)
36. Out-of-pocket expenses relating to charitable activities, including the standard mileage deduction (chapter 25)
37. Health insurance premiums if self-employed (chapter 38)
38. Penalty on early withdrawal of savings (chapter 7)
39. Personal liability insurance for wrongful acts as an employee (chapter 29)
40. Points on a home mortgage and certain refinancings (chapter 24)
41. Protective clothing required at work (chapter 29)
42. Real estate taxes associated with the purchase or sale of property (chapter 23)
43. Seller-paid points on the purchase of a home (chapter 24)
44. Special equipment for the disabled (chapter 22)
45. Special schools and separately stated fees for medical care included in tuition (chapter 22)
46. State personal property taxes on cars and boats (chapter 23)
47. Subscriptions to professional journals (chapter 29)
48. Theft or embezzlement losses (chapter 26)
49. Trade or business tools with life of 1 year or less (chapter 29)
50. Worthless stock or securities (chapter 16)

Individual tax organizer

The following schedules should help you organize the data you need to prepare your 2014 federal income tax return. They are intended only to provide general guidelines and should not be regarded as all-inclusive.

Taxpayer information

Personal data

Your name:	
Your spouse's name:	
Social security number:	Spouse's social security number:

Marital status at year end: ☐ Married ☐ Single ☐ Widowed after 2012 with qualifying child ☐ Divorced ☐ Married but separated

Dependent children

Qualifying children: Children age 18 or younger (age 19-23 if attending school full time for at least five months during the year) who lived with you more than half the year and who did not provide more than half of their own support (or a permanently and totally disabled child).

(Qualifying children) Name (address if different from yours)	Social security number	Date of birth	Married filing a joint return?[1]

[1] Dependent must be unmarried (or if married, does not file a joint return).

Other dependents

(Qualifying relative) Name (address if different from yours)	Social security number	Relationship	Months lived in your home	Is dependent's income over $3,950?	Did you provide more than half of support?

Payments and refunds of income taxes

	FEDERAL		STATE		CITY	
	Date paid	Amount	Date paid	Amount	Date paid	Amount
2014 estimated payments, including overpayment credited from 2013 return						
Tax refunds received in 2014[1]						

[1] Do not include interest received on refunds. Detail these amounts in the interest income section of this organizer.

Compensation

Indicate recipient: H=Husband; W=Wife

H W	Employer name	Gross earnings	Federal income tax withheld	Social security tax withheld	Medicare tax withheld	State tax withheld	City tax withheld

Interest income

Indicate ownership: H=Husband; W=Wife; J=Joint.

Report all interest received by you or for your account on Forms 1099-INT or other statements of total interest received. Failure to record any such income could result in a notice from the IRS.

If the amount of interest reported on Forms 1099-INT includes interest accrued on bonds at the time of purchase, adjustments can be made. If you invested in a tax-exempt municipal bond fund, note the fund's schedule of percentage of income related to each state.

H W J		Amount
	Savings accounts, credit unions, and certificates of deposit	$
	U.S. savings bonds and other U.S. government securities	$
	Corporate bonds	$
	Other interest[1]	$
	Tax-exempt interest	$
	Interest received on tax refunds	$

[1] If you received interest income from seller-financed mortgages, you will need the payer's name, address, and social security number.

Dividend income

Indicate ownership: H=Husband; W=Wife; J=Joint.

Report all dividends received by you for your account on Forms 1099-DIV or other information statements received. Failure to record any such income could result in a notice from the IRS.

H W J	Name of corporation [identify foreign corporation with (F)]	Indicate: T (taxable) C (capital gain distribution) N (nondividend distribution) U (U.S. obligation) X (exempt) Q (qualified)	Dividends received	U.S. taxes withheld

Sale of residence

Did you sell your residence during the year or within the last two years? If you answered "Yes," see chapter 15, Selling your home.	☐ Yes	☐ No

Sale of stocks and bonds

Indicate ownership: H=Husband; W=Wife; J=Joint.

Note: Gross proceeds from sales reported here should reconcile with Forms 1099-B received from your broker. You should explain any discrepancies to prevent an IRS inquiry stemming from their matching program.

H W J	Description (including numbers of shares, common or preferred, and par value of bonds)	Date Acq.	Date Sold	Gross sales price[1]	Cost or other basis plus expenses of sale[2]	Gain or (loss)[3]	Covered security[4]
							☐

[1] List proceeds of sale or cash received in lieu of fractions on receipt of stock rights or stock dividends.

[2] The basis of stock should be decreased by all nontaxable dividends and increased by any reinvested dividends. See chapter 13, Basis of property.

[3] Have you acquired stock, securities, contracts, or options to sell or acquire stock or securities substantially identical to stock or securities sold at a loss within a period beginning 30 days prior to and ending 30 days after the date of sale? ☐ Yes ☐ No

If "Yes," see the discussion of "Wash Sale" in chapter 14, Sale of property.

[4] Transactions reported on Form 1099-B with basis reported to the IRS and box 6b checked.

Other transactions

Did you exchange securities for other securities or exchange any investment property for any other property? Did any security held by you or any amounts due to you become worthless during the year? Did you sell your vacation home or other property during the year? Did you realize a gain or a loss on property, in whole or part, by destruction, theft, seizure, or condemnation (including the threat or imminence thereof)? Did you engage in any commodity transactions (including open positions on December 31) during the year? Did you engage in any transactions involving traded options?

If you answered "Yes" to any of these questions, read the applicable portions of this book.

Sale of other property

H W J	Description	Date		Gross sales price	Cost or other basis plus expenses of sale	Depreciation or depletion	Gain or (loss)
		Acq.	Sold				

Installment sales

Did you make sales during the year for which the receipt of all or part of the sales price was deferred until future years?	☐ Yes	☐ No
If "Yes," discuss with your tax advisor.		
Did you collect on any installment obligations from sales made prior to 2014?	☐ Yes	☐ No
For more information, see chapter 14, *Sale of property*.		

Rent and royalty income

Location/Description of property	Active participation[1]	Rent/Royalty income received	Expenses	Fair rental days	Personal use days

Did you make any payments (generally over $600) requiring Form 1099 to be filed?   ☐ Yes   ☐ No
If yes, these forms are required to be filed by March 2, 2015, if filing by paper, or March 31, 2015, if filing electronically.

[1] *For more information on active participation, see chapter 9, Rental income and expenses.*

Partnerships (P), small business corporations (S), and estates and trusts (E/T)

Retain all Forms K-1 or other information relating to entity listed below.

P S E/T	H W J	Name	Tax shelter registration number	I.D. number	Income or (loss)

Pension and annuity income

Did you receive any payments from a retirement plan?	☐ Yes ☐ No
If yes, write in the amount received during the year and any taxes withheld.	$
Did you roll over a profit-sharing or retirement plan distribution into another plan?	☐ Yes ☐ No
What was the starting date of your annuity?	
What is the amount received in the current taxable year?	$
Did you receive any IRA distributions during the year?	☐ Yes ☐ No
Retain all Forms 1099-R or other information relating to each distribution.	
Did you convert all or any part of a regular IRA into a Roth IRA during 2014?	☐ Yes ☐ No
If yes, write in the amount converted.	$

Other income

Description	Amount
Alimony or legal separation payments received	$
Disability payments	$
Other tax refunds not shown elsewhere	$
Unemployment insurance compensation	$
Social security benefits	$
Other[1] (describe)	$

[1] The types of other income include, but are not limited to, net income from self-employment, director's fees, prizes, cancellation of debts, gambling winnings, jury fees, punitive damages (unless awarded in a wrongful death action where state law so provides), and receiver's fees. Also, include gross income from oil and gas working interests, as well as any expenses relating to them. For more information see chapter 12, Other income.

			Amount
Did you receive any income from a foreign source?	☐ Yes	☐ No	$
Did you own shares in a mutual fund that retained your share of capital gains and paid the tax on it?	☐ Yes	☐ No	$
Did you have any income from farm property?	☐ Yes	☐ No	$
Did you have any bartering income?	☐ Yes	☐ No	$

Deductions

Adjustments to income

			Amount
Alimony or legal separation payment made in current year			
Recipient's last name _____ Social security no. _____			
Penalties for early withdrawal of savings			$ _____
Education-related expenses			
☐ Student loan interest			$ _____
Individual retirement arrangements (IRAs)[1]			
Did you contribute to your own IRA?	☐ Yes	☐ No	$ _____
Type:			
☐ Regular			$ _____
☐ Roth			$ _____
Did you participate in a retirement plan maintained by your employer?	☐ Yes	☐ No	$ _____
Did your spouse contribute to his/her own IRA?	☐ Yes	☐ No	$ _____
Did your spouse participate in a retirement plan maintained by his/her employer?	☐ Yes	☐ No	
Did you and your spouse contribute to a spousal IRA?	☐ Yes	☐ No	$ _____

	Yours	Spouse's
Self-employed Keogh (HR-10) plan		
Amount contributed	$ _____	$ _____
Self-employed health insurance[2]	$ _____	$ _____

Have you incurred moving expenses in connection with starting work at a new permanent location? See chapter 20, Moving expenses.	☐ Yes	☐ No	
Health Savings Account (amount contributed)			$ _____

[1] Depending on your (and your spouse's) income level and whether you (or your spouse) are an active participant in an employer-maintained retirement plan, your IRA deduction may be limited.

[2] If you were self-employed and had a net profit for the year, were a general partner (or a limited partner receiving guaranteed payments), or if you received wages from an S corporation in which you were a more than 2% shareholder, you may be able to deduct the amount paid for health insurance on behalf of yourself, your spouse, and dependents.

Medical expenses

Note: You will qualify for a federal deduction only if your total unreimbursed medical expenses exceed 10% (7.5% if you or your spouse are age 65 or older by the end of the year) of your adjusted gross income.

List even if reimbursed	Amount
Medical or health insurance premiums (including amounts paid by payroll deductions)	$
Medicare premiums	$
Premiums paid for long-term health care[1]	
For you	$
For your spouse	$
Prescription drugs and insulin	$
Doctors and dentists	$
Hospitals	$
Other medical expenses (eyeglasses, contact lenses, hearing aids, travel and lodging expenses)	$
Reimbursements for medical expenses through insurance or other sources	( )

Note: If you are divorced or separated, have a child, and paid medical expenses for that child, include these amounts whether or not you are entitled to the dependency exemption. For more information, see chapter 22, Medical and dental expenses.

[1] *See chapter 22 for limitations on deduction.*

Taxes

Item	Amount
Real estate taxes	$
Personal property	$
Vehicle licenses (allowed in some states). State of:	$
State or local income taxes	$
State and local sales taxes	$
State disability tax	$
Foreign income taxes[1]	$

[1] *Generally, you can take either a deduction or a credit for income taxes imposed on you by a foreign country or a U.S. possession. For more information on deducting foreign income taxes, see Foreign Income Taxes in chapter 23, Taxes you may deduct. For more information on claiming a credit for such taxes paid, see Foreign Tax Credit in chapter 37, Other credits including the earned income credit.*

Interest expenses

Item	Payee	Amount
Home mortgage paid to financial institutions		$
Home mortgage paid to individuals[1]		$
Mortgage points on principal residence[2]		$
Mortgage insurance premiums on qualified residence[3]		$
Prepayment penalty on loans		$
Brokerage accounts		$
Investment interest		$
Other (itemize)		$

[1] *You need name(s) and social security number(s).*

[2] *Include only points, including loan organization fees, on the purchase or improvement of your principal residence. If you paid points to refinance your mortgage, see chapter 24, Interest expense.*

[3] *Premiums you paid or accrued during 2014 for qualified mortgage insurance may be deductible. See chapter 24, Interest expense.*

Charitable contributions

In addition to outright gifts of cash or property, deductible contributions also include out-of-pocket expenses incurred for charity; for example, transportation, meals, and lodging away from home, and cost and upkeep of special uniforms and equipment required in the performance of donated services. Contributions of cash, regardless of the amount, are allowed only if you have appropriate substantiation such as a canceled check, credit card statement, or receipt from the charity. In addition, you need a contemporaneous written acknowledgment from the charity to which a contribution or contributions of $250 or more was made during the year. A canceled check does not constitute adequate substantiation for contributions in excess of $250. If you have sold any property to a charity for less than the property's fair market value, you will need details. For more information, see chapter 25, *Contributions*.

Cash Contributions

Recipient	Amount

If total noncash contributions have a value in excess of $500, you may need the following information:

The name and address of the donee; the date of the gift; a description of the property; how it was acquired by you, and when it was acquired by you; your tax basis; its value at the time of the donation and how the value was ascertained. Indicate (☐) if any property was held by you one year or less.

If you made noncash contributions of property in excess of $5,000 in value, use Form 8283, Noncash Charitable Contributions, with Section B, *Appraisal Summary*, completed.   ☐ Yes   ☐ No

If you contributed a motor vehicle to charity, see chapter 25, *Contributions*.

Casualty losses

Note: You will qualify for a deduction for a personal casualty loss only if it exceeds 10% of your adjusted gross income and only for the amount not covered by insurance reimbursements. However, special rules apply if you are in a federally declared disaster area. See chapter 26, *Casualty and theft losses*, for details.

Casualty losses include such items as losses from automobile collisions; damage from storms, fires, and floods; and damage from vandalism, theft, and other casualties.

A disaster loss is a loss that occurred in an area determined by the President of the United States to warrant federal disaster assistance. See chapter 26, *Casualty and theft losses*.

Describe the casualty and loss and its approximate date and location:

Indicate (✓) type of property: ☐ business   ☐ investment   ☐ personal

Other deductions

Note: In general, you will qualify for a federal deduction only if your total other miscellaneous deductions exceed 2% of your adjusted gross income.

Item	Amount	Item	Amount
Investment expenses		Educational expense (to maintain or improve skills required by employer)	
Investment counsel fees		Meals and entertainment[1]	
Safe deposit box		Tax advice/return fees	
Subscriptions		Union dues	
Telephone		Dues for professional organizations	
IRA fees		Business publications	
Other		Office-in-home expenses[2]	

[1] *Generally, only 50% of meals and entertainment expenses are deductible.*
[2] *See chapter 29, Miscellaneous deductions.*

Employee business expenses

Were you reimbursed for any business expenses incurred in connection with the performance of services for your employer?	☐ Yes	☐ No

If yes, answer the following questions:

A. Are you required to return reimbursement to the extent it exceeds expenses?	☐ Yes	☐ No
B. Are you required to submit itemized supporting documentation to your employer?	☐ Yes	☐ No

If you answered "Yes" to the above questions and your reimbursement does not exceed your expenses, you are generally not required to report the reimbursement and expenses on your return. However, if your reimbursement does not equal your expenses, or if you answered "No" to questions A and/or B, report below the total reimbursements and expenses for the year. Certain other business expenses, even if not reimbursed, may also be deductible.

Does your employer have an accountable reimbursement plan? See chapter 27, *Car Expenses and Other Employee Business Expenses*.	☐ Yes	☐ No

Employee business expenses:	Amount
	$
	$
Total amount reimbursed. (Do not include any amounts that were reported to you as wages in box 1 of Form W-2.)	$

Do you have substantiation (described below) for travel and entertainment expenses?	☐ Yes	☐ No

Information that must be available includes:

- Amounts spent
- Dates of departure and return for each trip and the number of days spent on business
- Dates of entertainment
- Places of entertainment or travel
- Dates and descriptions of business gifts
- Business purposes of the travel, entertainment, or business gifts
- Business relationships with the persons entertained or to whom gifts were made

Automobile expenses

Mileage	Automobile 1	Automobile 2
Number of months used for business during the year	$	$
Total mileage (include personal miles)	$	$
Business mileage portion of the total mileage	$	$
Commuting mileage portion of the total mileage	$	$
Original cost	$	$
Annual lease payments	$	$
Total actual expenses (business and personal for months used for business)		

Automobile Depreciation		
Year, make, model	Cost	Date Acquired
Automobile:	$	$
Do you have adequate or sufficient evidence to justify the deduction for the vehicles?	☐ Yes ☐ No	
If yes, is the evidence written?	☐ Yes ☐ No	

Child care credit

If you incurred any expenses for child or dependent care so that you and your spouse could be gainfully employed or attend an educational institution as a full-time student, complete the table below.

Did your employer provide or reimburse you for the cost of child or dependent care?	☐ Yes	☐ No

If so, the qualifying expenses for calculating the credit must be reduced by the amount excluded from your income through your employer's dependent care assistance program. See chapter 33, *Child and dependent care credit*.

Name of child or dependent	Name, address, and social security number or FEIN of person or organization providing care	Relationship, if any	Period of care		Amount paid
			From	To	

Foreign taxes

List foreign source income and foreign income taxes paid or withheld[1]

Country	Income		Taxes Paid	
	Type	Amount	Date Paid	Amount

Did you or your spouse have a financial interest in, or signature authority over, one or more foreign financial accounts (such as bank or securities accounts) at any time during 2014?	☐ Yes	☐ No
Did you receive a distribution from, or were you the grantor of, or a transferor to, a foreign trust?	☐ Yes	☐ No
Do you have financial accounts maintained by a foreign (non-U.S.) bank or financial institution that totaled more than $50,000 on the last day of the year or more than $75,000 at any time during the year ($100,000 and $150,000, respectively, if married filing a joint return)?[2]	☐ Yes	☐ No

[1] *Generally, you can take either a credit or a deduction for income taxes imposed on you by a foreign country or a U.S. possession. For more information on claiming a credit for such taxes paid, see* Foreign Tax Credit *in chapter 37,* Other credits including the earned income credit. *For more information on deducting foreign income taxes, see* Foreign Income Taxes *in chapter 23,* Taxes you may deduct.

[2] For more information on foreign filing requirements, see chapter 7, Interest income.

Employing domestic help

Did you employ domestic help?	☐ Yes	☐ No
Did you pay more than $1,800 during the year to an individual for services provided in your home?	☐ Yes	☐ No
If so, you may be required to pay employment taxes (see chapter 40, *What to do if you employ domestic help*).		

Income and expense records you should keep in addition to your income tax return

Some Suggestions That Could Come in Handy

Income	Records
☐ Wages, salaries	✓ Form W-2
☐ Interest income	✓ 1099-INT, 1099-OID, or Substitute 1099, such as broker statement or year-end account summary
☐ Dividend income	✓ 1099-DIV or Substitute 1099, such as broker statement or year-end account summary
☐ State tax refunds	✓ Form 1099-G, state income tax return
☐ Self-employment income	✓ Sales slips, invoices, receipts, sales tax reports, business books and records, 1099-MISC
☐ Capital gains and losses	✓ 1099-B or Substitute 1099, such as broker statement or year-end account summary showing proceeds from sales of securities or other capital assets. Records must also show your cost or other basis and the expenses of the sale. Your records must show when and how an asset was acquired (including property received as a gift or inheritance), how the asset was used, and when and how it was disposed of. To support the basis of securities, you should keep old account statements, buy/sell execution records, stock dividend and stock split information, and dividend reinvestment records (see chapter 14, *Sale of property*).
☐ IRA distributions	✓ 1099-R, year-end account summary, Form 8606
☐ Pension and annuities	✓ 1099-R, records of contributions
☐ Rents	✓ Checkbook, receipts and canceled checks, and other books and records, 1099-MISC
☐ Partnerships, S corporations	✓ Schedule K-1, record of unused passive activity losses
☐ Estates, trusts	✓ Schedule K-1, copies of last will and testament including codicils, Form 56-Notice Concerning Fiduciary Relationship, Form 1310-Statement of Person Claiming Refund Due a Deceased Taxpayer, including death certificate or letters of office, Form 4810-Request for Prompt Assessment Under IRC Section 6501(d), Tax Worksheets showing pre- and post-death income allocation, including copies of all 1099s received for the year of death, copies of prior three years' Forms 1040, and copies of all prior-year gift tax returns
☐ Social security benefits	✓ Form SSA-1099
☐ Royalties	✓ 1099-MISC
☐ Unemployment compensation	✓ 1099-G
☐ Alimony	✓ Divorce settlement papers
☐ Miscellaneous income	✓ 1099-MISC and other records of amounts received

Expense	Records
☐ Domestic employee expense	✓ Canceled checks, state unemployment tax payments; see chapter 40, *What to do if you employ domestic help*
☐ Self-employment expense	✓ Bills, canceled checks, receipts, bank statements, all business books and records
☐ IRA contribution	✓ Year-end account summary, deposit receipt
☐ Keogh contribution	✓ Year-end account summary, deposit receipt
☐ Alimony	✓ Divorce settlement papers, canceled alimony checks
☐ Medical and dental expense	✓ Bills, canceled checks, receipts, pay stubs if employer withholds medical insurance from wages
☐ Taxes	✓ Canceled checks, mortgage statements, receipts, Form W-2
☐ Interest expense	✓ Bank statements, mortgage statements (Form 1098), canceled checks
☐ Charitable contributions	✓ Canceled checks, receipts, detailed description of noncash property contributed (see chapter 25)
☐ Miscellaneous deductions	✓ Receipts, canceled checks, or other documentary evidence (see chapters 27 through 29)
☐ Casualty and theft losses	✓ Description of property, photograph of damaged property, receipts, canceled checks, policy and insurance reports
☐ Exemptions	✓ Birth certificates, social security numbers, signed Form 8332, divorce decree

Credits	Records
☐ Child and dependent care	✓ Receipts, canceled checks, and name, address, and identification number of care provider
☐ Estimated taxes	✓ Canceled checks
☐ Foreign taxes	✓ Form 1099-DIV or Substitute 1099 such as broker statement or year-end account summary
☐ Withheld taxes	✓ Forms W-2 and 1099 (including SSA-1099)

Part 1

The income tax return

ey.com/EYTaxGuide

The four chapters in this part provide basic information on the tax system. They take you through the first steps of filling out a tax return—such as deciding what your filing status is, how many exemptions you can take, and what form to file. They also discuss recordkeeping requirements, IRS *e-file* (electronic filing), certain penalties, and the two methods used to pay tax during the year: withholding and estimated tax.

You can find additional information about electronic filing in chapter 45, *Everything you need to know about e-filing*.

Chapter 1	Filing information
Chapter 2	Filing status
Chapter 3	Personal exemptions and dependents
Chapter 4	Tax withholding and estimated tax

Chapter 1
Filing information

Note

IRS Publication 17 (*Your Federal Income Tax*) has been updated by Ernst & Young LLP for 2014. Dates and dollar amounts shown are for 2014. Underlined type is used to indicate where IRS text has been updated. Places where text has been removed are indicated by the sentence: *Text intentionally omitted.*

ey.com/EYTaxGuide

Ernst & Young LLP will update the *EY Tax Guide 2015* website with relevant taxpayer information as it becomes available. You can also sign up for email alerts to let you know when changes have been made.

Introduction

This chapter provides the basic framework you need to know for filing your federal income tax return. It explains when you must file your tax return and what to do if you are unable to get it prepared on time. The chapter also answers many of the most frequently asked questions about procedures and calculations used to determine your income tax.

    The chapter discusses such items as who is required to file a return and who should file a return even though he or she is not required to do so. It tells you which tax forms to use, how to go about preparing your tax return once you have obtained the correct forms, and where to mail your tax return once it has been completed. In addition, the chapter reviews the penalties that may be imposed if you do not pay your taxes on time and instructs you on what to do if you discover that a previous tax return contains errors. It also explains what the different accounting methods are and which method may be used in preparing your return.

What's New

Text intentionally omitted.

Who must file. Generally, the amount of income you can receive before you must file a return has been increased. See Table 1-1, Table 1-2, and Table 1-3 for the specific amounts.

A Special Note About the Affordable Care Act and Your 2014 Tax Return. When you file your 2014 tax return in 2015, you and your family will have to document that you had health care coverage throughout 2014. Under certain circumstances, you may be entitled to an exemption if you did not maintain coverage in 2014. Otherwise, you may need to make a payment with the 2014 return. For more information on the payment or exemptions, visit www.IRS.gov/aca. If you currently have qualifying health care coverage, you will not need to do anything more than maintain that coverage throughout 2014. If you buy insurance through the Health Insurance Marketplace, you may be eligible for an advance payment of the Premium Tax Credit to help pay for your insurance coverage. If you are receiving an advance payment of the Premium Tax Credit during 2014, you should report changes in your income or family size to your Marketplace. By reporting changes promptly, you can make adjustments that will help you get the correct amount. Receiving too much or too little in advance will affect your refund or balance due when you file your 2014 tax return in 2015. Visit www.IRS.gov/aca for information on the tax provisions of the Affordable Care Act and www.HealthCare.gov for Marketplace information.

TAXALERT

For more information, see *Premium Tax Credit* in chapter 37, *Other credits including the earned income credit.*

Table 1-1. **2014 Filing Requirements for Most Taxpayers**

IF your filing status is...	AND at the end of 2014 you were...*	THEN file a return if your gross income was at least...**
single	under 65	$10,150
	65 or older	$11,700
married filing jointly***	under 65 (both spouses)	$20,300
	65 or older (one spouse)	$21,500
	65 or older (both spouses)	$22,700
married filing separately	any age	$ 3,950
head of household	under 65	$13,050
	65 or older	$14,600
qualifying widow(er) with dependent child	under 65	$16,350
	65 or older	$17,550

* If you were born on January 1, 1950, you are considered to be age 65 at the end of 2014.

** Gross income means all income you received in the form of money, goods, property, and services that is not exempt from tax, including any income from sources outside the United States or from the sale of your main home (even if you can exclude part or all of it). Do not include any social security benefits unless (a) you are married filing a separate return and you lived with your spouse at any time during 2014 or (b) one-half of your social security benefits plus your other gross income and any tax-exempt interest is more than $25,000 ($32,000 if married filing jointly). If (a) or (b) applies, see the Instructions for Form 1040 or 1040A or Publication 915 to figure the taxable part of social security benefits you must include in gross income. Gross income includes gains, but not losses, reported on Form 8949 or Schedule D. Gross income from a business means, for example, the amount on Schedule C, line 7, or Schedule F, line 9. But, in figuring gross income, do not reduce your income by any losses, including any loss on Schedule C, line 7, or Schedule F, line 9.

*** If you did not live with your spouse at the end of 2014 (or on the date your spouse died) and your gross income was at least $3,950, you must file a return regardless of your age.

Table 1-2. 2014 Filing Requirements for Dependents

See chapter 3 to find out if someone can claim you as a dependent.

If your parents (or someone else) can claim you as a dependent, use this table to see if you must file a return. (See Table 1-3 for other situations when you must file.)

In this table, earned income includes salaries, wages, tips, and professional fees. It also includes taxable scholarship and fellowship grants. (See Scholarships and fellowships in chapter 12.) Unearned income includes investment-type income such as taxable interest, ordinary dividends, and capital gain distributions. It also includes unemployment compensation, taxable social security benefits, pensions, annuities, cancellation of debt, and distributions of unearned income from a trust. Gross income is the total of your earned and unearned income.

Single dependents—Were you **either** age 65 or older **or** blind?

☐ **No.** You must file a return if **any** of the following apply.
- Your unearned income was more than $1,000.
- Your earned income was more than $6,200.
- Your gross income was more than the **larger** of:
  - $1,000, or
  - Your earned income (up to $5,850) plus $350.

☐ **Yes.** You must file a return if **any** of the following apply.
- Your unearned income was more than $2,550 ($4,100 if 65 or older **and** blind).
- Your earned income was more than $7,750 ($9,300 if 65 or older **and** blind).
- Your gross income was more than the **larger** of:
  - $2,550 ($4,100 if 65 or older **and** blind), or
  - Your earned income (up to $5,850) plus $1,900 ($3,450 if 65 or older **and** blind).

Married dependents—Were you **either** age 65 or older **or** blind?

☐ **No.** You must file a return if **any** of the following apply.
- Your unearned income was more than $1,000.
- Your earned income was more than $6,200.
- Your gross income was at least $5 and your spouse files a separate return and itemizes deductions.
- Your gross income was more than the **larger** of:
  - $1,000, or
  - Your earned income (up to $5,850) plus $350.

☐ **Yes.** You must file a return if **any** of the following apply.
- Your unearned income was more than $2,200 ($3,400 if 65 or older **and** blind).
- Your earned income was more than $7,400 ($8,600 if 65 or older **and** blind).
- Your gross income was at least $5 and your spouse files a separate return and itemizes deductions.
- Your gross income was more than the **larger** of:
  - $2,200 ($3,400 if 65 or older **and** blind), or
  - Your earned income (up to $5,850) plus $1,550 ($2,750 if 65 or older **and** blind).

Table 1-3. Other Situations When You Must File a 2014 Return

You must file a return if any of the four conditions below apply for 2014.

1. You owe any special taxes, including any of the following.
   a. Alternative minimum tax.
   b. Additional tax on a qualified plan, including an individual retirement arrangement (IRA), or other tax-favored account. But if you are filing a return only because you owe this tax, you can file **Form 5329** by itself.
   c. Household employment taxes. But if you are filing a return only because you owe this tax, you can file **Schedule H** by itself.
   d. Social security and Medicare tax on tips you did not report to your employer or on wages you received from an employer who did not withhold these taxes.
   e. Recapture of first-time homebuyer credit.
   f. Write-in taxes, including uncollected social security and Medicare or RRTA tax on tips you reported to your employer or on group term life insurance and additional taxes on health savings accounts.
   g. Recapture taxes.
2. You (or your spouse, if filing jointly) received HSA, Archer MSA, or Medicare Advantage MSA distributions.
3. You had net earnings from self-employment of at least $400.
4. You had wages of $108.28 or more from a church or qualified church-controlled organization that is exempt from employer social security and Medicare taxes.

Reminders

File online. Rather than filing a return on paper, you may be able to file electronically using IRS *e-file*. Create your own personal identification number (PIN) and file a completely paperless tax return. For more information, see *Does My Return Have To Be on Paper*, later.

Change of address. If you change your address, you should notify the IRS. You can use Form 8822 to notify the IRS of the change. See *Change of Address*, later, under *What Happens After I File*.

Enter your social security number. You must enter your social security number (SSN) in the spaces provided on your tax return. If you file a joint return, enter the SSNs in the same order as the names.

Direct deposit of refund. Instead of getting a paper check, you may be able to have your refund deposited directly into your account at a bank or other financial institution. See *Direct Deposit* under *Refunds*, later. If you choose direct deposit of your refund, you may be able to split the refund among two or three accounts.

Pay online or by phone. If you owe additional tax, you may be able to pay online or by phone. See *How To Pay*, later.

Installment agreement. If you cannot pay the full amount due with your return, you may ask to make monthly installment payments. See *Installment Agreement*, later, under *Amount You Owe*. You may be able to apply online for a payment agreement if you owe federal tax, interest, and penalties.

Automatic 6-month extension. You can get an automatic 6-month extension to file your tax return if, no later than the date your return is due, you file Form 4868, Application for Automatic Extension of Time To File U.S. Individual Income Tax Return. See *Automatic Extension*, later.

Service in combat zone. You are allowed extra time to take care of your tax matters if you are a member of the Armed Forces who served in a combat zone, or if you served in the combat zone in support of the Armed Forces. See *Individuals Serving in Combat Zone*, later, under *When Do I Have To File*.

Adoption taxpayer identification number. If a child has been placed in your home for purposes of legal adoption and you will not be able to get a social security number for the child in time to file your return, you may be able to get an adoption taxpayer identification number (ATIN). For more information, see *Social Security Number (SSN)*, later.

Taxpayer identification number for aliens. If you or your dependent is a nonresident or resident alien who does not have and is not eligible to get a social security number, file Form W-7, Application for IRS Individual Taxpayer Identification Number, with the IRS. For more information, see *Social Security Number (SSN)*, later.

Frivolous tax submissions. The IRS has published a list of positions that are identified as frivolous. The penalty for filing a frivolous tax return is $5,000. Also, the $5,000 penalty will apply to other specified frivolous submissions. For more information, see *Civil Penalties*, later.

TAXALERT

For all federal tax purposes for which marriage is a factor, including the subject matter covered in this chapter, same-sex couples who legally married in a state (including the District of Columbia) or foreign jurisdiction that recognizes same-sex marriages are treated as married for U.S. federal tax purposes-even if they reside in a jurisdiction that does not recognize same-sex marriage. If you meet certain requirements, you may be able to file amended returns to change your filing status for some earlier years. However, registered domestic partners and individuals who enter into a civil union or other similar formal relationship are not treated as a married couple for federal tax purposes. See Publication 501 for more information.

Introduction

This chapter discusses the following topics.
- Whether you have to file a return.
- Which form to use.
- How to file electronically.
- When, how, and where to file your return.

- What happens if you pay too little or too much tax.
- What records you should keep and how long you should keep them.
- How you can change a return you have already filed.

Do I Have To File a Return?

You must file a federal income tax return if you are a citizen or resident of the United States or a resident of Puerto Rico and you meet the filing requirements for any of the following categories that apply to you.

1. Individuals in general. (There are special rules for surviving spouses, executors, administrators, legal representatives, U.S. citizens and residents living outside the United States, residents of Puerto Rico, and individuals with income from U.S. possessions.)
2. Dependents.
3. Certain children under age 19 or full-time students.
4. Self-employed persons.
5. Aliens.

The filing requirements for each category are explained in this chapter.
The filing requirements apply even if you do not owe tax.

Individuals—In General

If you are a U.S. citizen or resident, whether you must file a return depends on three factors:

1. Your gross income,
2. Your filing status, and
3. Your age.

To find out whether you must file, see Table 1-1, Table 1-2, and Table 1-3. Even if no table shows that you must file, you may need to file to get money back. (See *Who Should File*, later.)

Gross income. This includes all income you receive in the form of money, goods, property, and services that is not exempt from tax. It also includes income from sources outside the United States or from the sale of your main home (even if you can exclude all or part of it). Include part of your social security benefits if:

1. You were married, filing a separate return, and you lived with your spouse at any time during 2014; or
2. Half of your social security benefits plus your other gross income and any tax-exempt interest is more than $25,000 ($32,000 if married filing jointly).

If either (1) or (2) applies, see the instructions for Form 1040 or 1040A, or Publication 915, Social Security and Equivalent Railroad Retirement Benefits, to figure the social security benefits you must include in gross income.

Common types of income are discussed in *Part Two* of this publication.

Community income. If you are married and your permanent home is in a community property state, half of any income described by state law as community income may be considered yours. This affects your federal taxes, including whether you must file if you do not file a joint return with your spouse. See Publication 555, Community Property, for more information.

> ### Tip
> *Even if you do not have to file a return, it may be to your advantage to do so. See* Who Should File, *later.*

> ### Caution
> *File only one federal income tax return for the year regardless of how many jobs you had, how many Forms W-2 you received, or how many states you lived in during the year. Do not file more than one original return for the same year, even if you have not gotten your refund or have not heard from the IRS since you filed.*

TAXALERT
For all federal tax purposes for which marriage is a factor, same-sex couples who legally married in a state (including the District of Columbia) or foreign jurisdiction that recognizes same-sex marriages are treated as married for U.S. federal tax purposes—even if they reside in a jurisdiction that does not recognize same-sex marriage. See Publication 501 for more information.

Nevada, Washington, and California domestic partners. A registered domestic partner in Nevada, Washington, or California generally must report half the combined community income of the individual and his or her domestic partner. See Publication 555.

EXPLANATION
Individuals of the same sex and opposite sex who are in registered domestic partnerships, civil unions, or other similar formal relationships that are not marriages under state law are not considered as married or spouses for federal tax purposes. Such couples may not file a federal return using a married filing separately or jointly filing status. Generally, they must each report half the combined community income earned by the partners. In addition to half of the community income, a partner who has income that is not community income must report that separate income.

Self-employed individuals. If you are self-employed, your gross income includes the amount on line 7 of Schedule C (Form 1040), Profit or Loss From Business; line 1 of Schedule C-EZ (Form 1040), Net Profit From Business; and line 9 of Schedule F (Form 1040), Profit or Loss From Farming. See *Self-Employed Persons*, later, for more information about your filing requirements.

Filing status. Your filing status depends on whether you are single or married and on your family situation. Your filing status is determined on the last day of your tax year, which is December 31 for most taxpayers. See chapter 2 for an explanation of each filing status.

Age. If you are 65 or older at the end of the year, you generally can have a higher amount of gross income than other taxpayers before you must file. See Table 1-1. You are considered 65 on the day before your 65th birthday. For example, if your 65th birthday is on January 1, 2015, you are considered 65 for 2014.

EXAMPLE

You are 65 years old and earned $12,000 of taxable income last year. Your husband, who is 66 years old, received a pension of $6,000, all of which was taxable income. You and your husband legally separated under a decree of divorce or separate maintenance on December 28. As a result, you are considered unmarried for the whole year. If you had been married at the end of the year, you would not have had to file an income tax return, because your combined income was less than $22,700. But, because you are legally separated and your gross income was more than $11,700, you must file a return.

Surviving Spouses, Executors, Administrators, and Legal Representatives

You must file a final return for a decedent (a person who died) if both of the following are true.
- You are the surviving spouse, executor, administrator, or legal representative.
- The decedent met the filing requirements at the date of death.

For more information on rules for filing a decedent's final return, see Publication 559, Survivors, Executors, and Administrators.

U.S. Citizens and Resident Aliens Living Abroad

To determine whether you must file a return, include in your gross income any income you received abroad, including any income you can exclude under the foreign earned income exclusion. For information on special tax rules that may apply to you, see Publication 54, Tax Guide for U.S. Citizens and Resident Aliens Abroad. It is available online and at most U.S. embassies and consulates. See *How To Get Tax Help* in the back of this publication.

EXPLANATION

For more information about U.S. citizens living abroad, see chapter 41, *U.S. citizens working abroad: Tax treatment of foreign earned income.*

Residents of Puerto Rico

If you are a U.S. citizen and also a bona fide resident of Puerto Rico, you generally must file a U.S. income tax return for any year in which you meet the income requirements. This is in addition to any legal requirement you may have to file an income tax return with Puerto Rico.

If you are a bona fide resident of Puerto Rico for the entire year, your U.S. gross income does not include income from sources within Puerto Rico. It does, however, include any income you received for your services as an employee of the United States or a U.S. agency. If you receive income from Puerto Rican sources that is not subject to U.S. tax, you must reduce your standard deduction. As a result, the amount of income you must have before you are required to file a U.S. income tax return is lower than the applicable amount in Table 1-1 or Table 1-2. For more information, see Publication 570, Tax Guide for Individuals With Income From U.S. Possessions.

Individuals With Income From U.S. Possessions

If you had income from Guam, the Commonwealth of the Northern Mariana Islands, American Samoa, or the U.S. Virgin Islands, special rules may apply when determining whether you must file a U.S. federal income tax return. In addition, you may have to file a return with the individual island government. See Publication 570 for more information.

Dependents

If you are a dependent (one who meets the dependency tests in chapter 3), see Table 1-2 to find out whether you must file a return. You also must file if your situation is described in Table 1-3.

Responsibility of parent. Generally, a child is responsible for filing his or her own tax return and for paying any tax on the return. If a dependent child must file an income tax return but cannot file due to age or any other reason, then a parent, guardian, or other legally responsible person must file it for the child. If the child cannot sign the return, the parent or guardian must sign the child's name followed by the words "By (your signature), parent for minor child."

Child's earnings. Amounts a child earns by performing services are included in his or her gross income and not the gross income of the parent. This is true even if under local law the child's parent has the right to the earnings and may actually have received them. But if the child does not pay the tax due on this income, the parent is liable for the tax.

EXPLANATION
For more details about dependents, see chapter 3, *Personal exemptions and dependents.*

Certain Children Under Age 19 or Full-Time Students

If a child's only income is interest and dividends (including capital gain distributions and Alaska Permanent Fund dividends), the child was under age 19 at the end of 2014 or was a full-time student under age 24 at the end of 2014, and certain other conditions are met, a parent can elect to include the child's income on the parent's return. If this election is made, the child does not have to file a return. See *Parent's Election To Report Child's Interest and Dividends* in chapter 32.

TAXALERT
The unearned income of children under age 19, or under age 24 if a full-time student, is taxed at the parent's rate. Unearned income includes interest, dividends, and capital gains.

If a child's interest, dividends, capital gains distributions, and other unearned income total more than $2,000, part of that income is taxed at the marginal tax rate to which the child's parent is subject, rather than the child's own marginal rate. In effect, such income is treated as if the parent had received the income.

A child who is either age 18 by the end of 2014, or a full-time student between the ages of 19 and 23 by the end of 2014, is not subject to the so-called kiddie tax if he or she has earned income that exceeds one-half of the amount of support they receive. IRS Publication 501 provides a worksheet for determining support. See chapter 32, *Tax on investment income of certain minor children,* for more information.

Self-Employed Persons

You are self-employed if you:
- Carry on a trade or business as a sole proprietor,
- Are an independent contractor,
- Are a member of a partnership, or
- Are in business for yourself in any other way.

Self-employment can include work in addition to your regular full-time business activities, such as certain part-time work you do at home or in addition to your regular job.

EXAMPLE
A person who delivers newspapers would be subject to self-employment tax. A person working at home in a cottage industry—woodworking or furniture making, for example—would be subject to self-employment tax. In some instances, it is to your advantage to report income from self-employment, because if you do not already qualify, you will then become eligible for social security benefits. For more information on self-employed persons, see chapter 38, *Self-employment income: How to file Schedule C.*

You must file a return if your gross income is at least as much as the filing requirement amount for your filing status and age (shown in Table 1-1). Also, you must file Form 1040 and Schedule SE (Form 1040), Self-Employment Tax, if:

1. Your net earnings from self-employment (excluding church employee income) were $400 or more, or
2. You had church employee income of $108.28 or more. (See Table 1-3.)

Use Schedule SE (Form 1040) to figure your self-employment tax. Self-employment tax is comparable to the social security and Medicare tax withheld from an employee's wages. For more information about this tax, see Publication 334, Tax Guide for Small Business.

TAXSAVER
You are able to deduct approximately one-half of your self-employment tax for the year in calculating your adjusted gross income. For details see chapter 23, *Taxes you may deduct.*

TAXALERT
Self-employment tax has two parts: old age, survivor, and disability insurance (OASDI) and Medicare hospital insurance (HI). (The comparable social security tax withheld on an employee's wages consists of these same two parts.) In 2014, the cap on self-employment income subject to OASDI is $117,000. There is no limit on the amount of self-employment income subject to the HI portion of the self-employment tax. More information about the social security contribution and benefit base is available at www.socialsecurity.gov/OACT/COLA/cbb.html.

Employees of foreign governments or international organizations. If you are a U.S. citizen who works in the United States for an international organization, a foreign government, or a wholly owned instrumentality of a foreign government, and your employer is not required to withhold social security and Medicare taxes from your wages, you must include your earnings from services performed in the United States when figuring your net earnings from self-employment.

Ministers. You must include income from services you performed as a minister when figuring your net earnings from self-employment, unless you have an exemption from self-employment tax. This also applies to Christian Science practitioners and members of a religious order who have not taken a vow of poverty. For more information, see Publication 517, Social Security and Other Information for Members of the Clergy and Religious Workers.

Aliens
Your status as an alien—resident, nonresident, or dual-status—determines whether and how you must file an income tax return.

The rules used to determine your alien status are discussed in Publication 519, U.S. Tax Guide for Aliens.

Resident alien. If you are a resident alien for the entire year, you must file a tax return following the same rules that apply to U.S. citizens. Use the forms discussed in this publication.

Nonresident alien. If you are a nonresident alien, the rules and tax forms that apply to you are different from those that apply to U.S. citizens and resident aliens. See Publication 519 to find out if U.S. income tax laws apply to you and which forms you should file.

TAXSAVER
Certain compensation paid to a nonresident alien by a foreign employer is not included in gross income. For more information, see chapter 3 of IRS Publication 519.

Dual-status taxpayer. If you are a resident alien for part of the tax year and a nonresident alien for the rest of the year, you are a dual-status taxpayer. Different rules apply for each part of the year. For information on dual-status taxpayers, see Publication 519.

EXPLANATION
For more information about foreign citizens living in the United States, see chapter 42, *Foreign citizens living in the United States.*

Who Should File

Even if you do not have to file, you should file a federal income tax return to get money back if any of the following conditions apply.

1. You had federal income tax withheld or made estimated tax payments.
2. You qualify for the earned income credit. See chapter 37 for more information.
3. You qualify for the additional child tax credit. See chapter 35 for more information.
4. You qualify for the health coverage tax credit. See chapter 37 for more information.
5. You qualify for the American opportunity credit. See chapter 36 for more information.
6. You qualify for the credit for federal tax on fuels. See chapter 37 for more information.

Which Form Should I Use?

You must use one of three forms to file your return: Form 1040EZ, Form 1040A, or Form 1040. (But also see *Does My Return Have To Be on Paper*, later.)

Form 1040EZ

Form 1040EZ is the simplest form to use.

You can use Form 1040EZ if all of the following apply.

1. Your filing status is single or married filing jointly. If you were a nonresident alien at any time in 2014, your filing status must be married filing jointly.
2. You (and your spouse if married filing a joint return) were under age 65 and not blind at the end of 2014. If you were born on January 1, 1950, you are considered to be age 65 at the end of 2014.
3. You do not claim any dependents.
4. Your taxable income is less than $100,000.
5. Your income is only from wages, salaries, tips, unemployment compensation, Alaska Permanent Fund dividends, taxable scholarship and fellowship grants, and taxable interest of $1,500 or less.
6. You do not claim any adjustments to income, such as a deduction for IRA contributions or student loan interest.
7. You do not claim any credits other than the earned income credit.
8. You do not owe any household employment taxes on wages you paid to a household employee.
9. If you earned tips, they are included in boxes 5 and 7 of your Form W-2.
10. You are not a debtor in a Chapter 11 bankruptcy case filed after October 16, 2005.

You must meet all of these requirements to use Form 1040EZ. If you do not, you must use Form 1040A or Form 1040.

> ### TAXPLANNER
> Even though it might be easier for you to file Form 1040EZ, you should carefully review your situation before doing so, especially if your income is close to the Form 1040EZ maximum level of $100,000. Check what deductions you may be able to claim if you itemize. (You cannot claim itemized deductions on Form 1040EZ.) If you have deductions that can be itemized and you do not claim them, you could be significantly overpaying your tax.

Figuring tax. On Form 1040EZ, you can use only the tax table to figure your income tax. You cannot use Form 1040EZ to report any other tax.

Form 1040A

If you do not qualify to use Form 1040EZ, you may be able to use Form 1040A.

You can use Form 1040A if all of the following apply.

1. Your income is only from:
    a. Wages, salaries, and tips,
    b. Interest,
    c. Ordinary dividends (including Alaska Permanent Fund dividends),
    d. Capital gain distributions,
    e. IRA distributions,
    f. Pensions and annuities,
    g. Unemployment compensation,
    h. Taxable social security and railroad retirement benefits, and
    i. Taxable scholarship and fellowship grants.

If you receive a capital gain distribution that includes un-recaptured Section 1250 gain, Section 1202 gain, or collectibles (28%) gain, you cannot use Form 1040A. You must use Form 1040.

2. Your taxable income is less than $100,000.
3. Your adjustments to income are for only the following items.
    a. Educator expenses.
    b. IRA deduction.
    c. Student loan interest deduction.
    d. Tuition and fees.
4. You do not itemize your deductions.
5. You claim only the following tax credits.
    a. The credit for child and dependent care expenses. (See chapter 33.)
    b. The credit for the elderly or the disabled. (See chapter 34.)
    c. The education credits. (See chapter 36.)
    d. The retirement savings contribution credit. (See chapter 37.)
    e. The child tax credit. (See chapter 35.)
    f. The earned income credit. (See chapter 37.)
    g. The additional child tax credit. (See chapter 35.)
6. You did not have an alternative minimum tax adjustment on stock you acquired from the exercise of an incentive stock option. (See Publication 525, Taxable and Nontaxable Income.)

You can also use Form 1040A if you received employer-provided dependent care benefits or if you owe tax from the recapture of an education credit or the alternative minimum tax.

You must meet all these requirements to use Form 1040A. If you do not, you must use Form 1040.

> ### TAXALERT
> Form 1040A lets you report most retirement income, including pension and annuity payments, taxable social security and railroad retirement benefits, and payments from your IRA. Furthermore, it allows you to claim the credit for the elderly or the disabled and report your estimated tax payments. If you have been filing a Form 1040 because of these items, you can qualify for the easier-to-file Form 1040A. Be aware that you still cannot claim itemized deductions on Form 1040A. If you have deductions that can be itemized, you may be better off continuing to file a Form 1040.

Form 1040

If you cannot use Form 1040EZ or Form 1040A, you must use Form 1040. You can use Form 1040 to report all types of income, deductions, and credits.

You may pay less tax by filing Form 1040 because you can take itemized deductions, some adjustments to income, and credits you cannot take on Form 1040A or Form 1040EZ.

You must use Form 1040 if any of the following apply.

1. Your taxable income is $100,000 or more.
2. You itemize your deductions on Schedule A.
3. You had income that cannot be reported on Form 1040EZ or Form 1040A, including tax-exempt interest from private activity bonds issued after August 7, 1986.
4. You claim any adjustments to gross income other than the adjustments listed earlier under *Form 1040A.*
5. Your Form W-2, box 12, shows uncollected employee tax (social security and Medicare tax) on tips (see chapter 6) or group-term life insurance (see chapter 5).
6. You received $20 or more in tips in any 1 month and did not report all of them to your employer. (See chapter 6.)
7. You were a bona fide resident of Puerto Rico and exclude income from sources in Puerto Rico.
8. You claim any credits other than the credits listed earlier under *Form 1040A.*
9. You owe the excise tax on insider stock compensation from an expatriated corporation.
10. Your Form W-2 shows an amount in box 12 with a code Z.
11. You had a qualified health savings account funding distribution from your IRA.
12. You are an employee and your employer did not withhold social security and Medicare tax.
13. You have to file other forms with your return to report certain exclusions, taxes, or transactions, such as Form 8959 or Form 8960.
14. You are a debtor in a bankruptcy case filed after October 16, 2005.
15. You must repay the first-time homebuyer credit.
16. You have adjusted gross income of more than $152,525 and must reduce the dollar amount of your exemptions.

Does My Return Have To Be on Paper?

You may be able to file a paperless return using IRS *e-file* (electronic filing). If your 2014 adjusted gross income (AGI) is less than a certain amount, you are eligible for *Free File*. See your tax return instructions for details. If you do not qualify for Free File, then you should check out IRS.gov for low-cost *e-file* options or Free File Fillable Forms.

TAXPLANNER
As of the date this book went to press, the maximum amount of adjusted gross income (AGI) that qualified for free filing had not yet been announced. In 2013, the maximum AGI was $58,000. For more information about e-filing and the IRS's Free File program, see chapter 45, *Everything you need to know about e-filing.*

IRS *e-file*

Table 1-4 lists the benefits of IRS *e-file*. IRS *e-file* uses automation to replace most of the manual steps needed to process paper returns. As a result, the processing of *e-file* returns is faster and more accurate than the processing of paper returns. However, as with a paper return, you are responsible for making sure your return contains accurate information and is filed on time.

EXPLANATION
For a detailed discussion about e-filing, see chapter 45, *Everything you need to know about e-filing.*

EXPLANATION
Composition of an Electronic Return
In total, an electronic return contains the same information as a comparable return filed entirely on paper documents. An electronic return consists of:
1. Electronic portion of return—Data transmitted to the IRS electronically
2. Non-electronic portion of return—Paper documents (filed with the IRS within three days of the IRS acceptance of the electronic portion of the return) that contain information that cannot be electronically transmitted, such as documents prepared by third parties

Electronic Portion of Return
For 2014 returns, most forms and schedules, including Form 1040 and Form 1040A, can be transmitted electronically and are considered the "electronic portion" of the return.

Non-electronic Portion of Return
If you have portions of your tax return that cannot be submitted electronically, you will need to mail them in with Form 8453, U.S. Individual Income Tax Transmittal for an IRS e-file Return. See chapter 45, *Everything you need to know about e-filing,* for more information.

Using *e-file* does not affect your chances of an IRS examination of your return.

TAXPLANNER
There are many variables that impact the speed of a tax refund. Using e-file with direct deposit is the fastest option. By doing so, your refund could be deposited into your designated account in as few as ten days. Filing an electronic return could allow you to receive a refund sooner and invest the amount you receive. However, some companies charge a separate fee for electronically filing a return, so you will need to weigh the advantage of investing your refund earlier against additional costs you may incur.

Free File Fillable Forms. If you do not need the help of a tax preparer, then Free File Fillable Forms may be for you. These forms:
- Do not have an income requirement so everyone is eligible,
- Are easy to use,
- Perform basic math calculations,
- Are available only at IRS.gov, and
- Apply only to a federal tax return.

Table 1-4. **Benefits of IRS *e-file***

- Free File allows qualified taxpayers to prepare and *e-file* their own tax returns for free.
- Free File is available in English and Spanish.
- Free File is available online 24 hours a day, 7 days a week.
- Get your refund faster by *e-filing* using Direct Deposit.
- Sign electronically with a secure self-selected PIN and file a completely paperless return.
- Receive an acknowledgement that your return was received and accepted.
- If you owe, you can *e-file* and pay electronically either online or by phone, using your bank account or a credit or debit card. You can also file a return early and pay the amount you owe by the due date of your return.
- Save time by preparing and *e-filing* federal and state returns together.
- IRS computers quickly and automatically check for errors or other missing information.
- Help the environment, use less paper, and save taxpayer money—it costs less to process an *e-filed* return than a paper return.

Electronic return signatures. To file your return electronically, you must sign the return electronically using a personal identification number (PIN). If you are filing online, you must use a Self-Select PIN. If you are filing electronically using a tax practitioner, you can use a Self-Select PIN or a Practitioner PIN.

Self-Select PIN. The Self-Select PIN method allows you to create your own PIN. If you are married filing jointly, you and your spouse will each need to create a PIN and enter these PINs as your electronic signatures.

A PIN is any combination of five digits you choose except five zeros. If you use a PIN, there is nothing to sign and nothing to mail—not even your Forms W-2.

To verify your identity, you will be prompted to enter your adjusted gross income (AGI) from your originally filed 2013 federal income tax return, if applicable. Do not use your AGI from an amended return (Form 1040X) or a math error correction made by the IRS. AGI is the amount shown on your 2013 Form 1040, line 38; Form 1040A, line 22; or Form 1040EZ, line 4. If you do not have your 2013 income tax return, you can quickly request a transcript by using our automated self-service tool. Visit us at IRS.gov and click on *Order a Return or Account Transcript* or call 1-800-908-9946 to get a free transcript of your return. (If you filed electronically last year, you may use your prior year PIN to verify your identity instead of your prior year AGI. The prior year PIN is the five digit PIN you used to electronically sign your 2013 return.) You will also be prompted to enter your date of birth.

Practitioner PIN. The Practitioner PIN method allows you to authorize your tax practitioner to enter or generate your PIN. The practitioner can provide you with details.

Form 8453. You must send in a paper Form 8453 if you have to attach certain forms or other documents that cannot be electronically filed. For details, see Form 8453.

For more details, visit www.irs.gov/efile and click on *"Individuals."*

Identity Protection PIN. If the IRS gave you an identity protection personal identification number (PIN) because you were a victim of identity theft, enter it in the spaces provided on your tax form. If the IRS has not given you this type of number, leave these spaces blank. For more information, see the Instructions for Form 1040A or Form 1040.

Power of attorney. If an agent is signing your return for you, a power of attorney (POA) must be filed. Attach the POA to Form 8453 and file it using that form's instructions. See *Signatures*, later, for more information on POAs.

State returns. In most states, you can file an electronic state return simultaneously with your federal return. For more information, check with your local IRS office, state tax agency, tax professional, or the IRS website at www.irs.gov/efile.

Refunds. You can have a refund check mailed to you, or you can have your refund deposited directly to your checking or savings account or split among two or three accounts. With *e-file*, your refund will be issued faster than if you filed on paper.

As with a paper return, you may not get all of your refund if you owe certain past-due amounts, such as federal tax, state income tax, state unemployment compensation debts, child support, spousal support, or certain other federal nontax debts, such as student loans. See *Offset against debts* under *Refunds*, later.

TAXALERT
The IRS will allow you to deposit your refund into up to three different accounts or financial institutions. For instance, a refund could be split between a savings account, a checking account, or an Individual Retirement Account (IRA). See Form 8888, Allocation of Refund (including Savings Bond Purchases), for more information.

TAXPLANNER
Some banks do not allow a joint refund to be deposited into an individual account. You should check with your bank to make sure your direct deposit will be accepted.

EXPLANATION

Direct Deposit Refunds
Direct deposit refunds will be issued in as few as ten days from the date the electronic return is accepted. However, the Treasury Department does not guarantee that a refund will be issued by a specific date or for the anticipated amount. Direct deposit is quickest when used in conjunction with *e-filing*; however, it can be used regardless of the method used to file your return.

TAXALERT
You can use the "Where's My Refund?" feature at www.irs.gov to determine the status of your return. This service is available 72 hours after e-filing your return or four weeks after you mail your paper return.

   The following conditions may delay refunds and/or change refund amounts. Direct deposit elections generally will not be honored in these cases:
1. You owe back taxes, either individual or business.
2. You owe delinquent child support.
3. You have certain delinquent debts, such as student loans.
4. The last name and social security number of the primary taxpayer are not the same as on last year's return. If this is the case, the return will be delayed at least 1 week for re-matching.
5. The estimated tax payments reported on the return do not match the estimated tax payments recorded on the IRS master file. This generally occurs when:
    a. The spouse made separate payments and filed a joint return, or vice versa; or
    b. The return was filed before the last estimated tax payment was credited to the taxpayer's account (i.e., before January 15, 2015).
6. You have a Schedule E claiming a deduction for a questionable tax shelter.
7. You are claiming a blatantly unallowable deduction.

TAXSAVER
If you are consistently receiving large refunds, you should consider adjusting your annual withholding adjusted during the year by filing a Form W-4. This could enable you to keep more of your income throughout the year, instead of waiting to receive a large refund after filing your tax return. See chapter 4, *Tax withholding and estimated tax*.

Refund inquiries. Information about your return will generally be available within 24 hours after the IRS receives your *e-filed* return. See *Refund Information*, later.

Amount you owe. To avoid late-payment penalties and interest, pay your taxes in full by April 15, 2015. See *How To Pay*, later, for information on how to pay the amount you owe.

Using Your Personal Computer

You can file your tax return in a fast, easy, and convenient way using your personal computer. A computer with Internet access and tax preparation software are all you need. Best of all, you can *e-file* from the comfort of your home 24 hours a day, 7 days a week.

IRS approved tax preparation software is available for online use on the Internet, for download from the Internet, and in retail stores. For information, visit www.irs.gov/efile.

Through Employers and Financial Institutions

Some businesses offer free *e-file* to their employees, members, or customers. Others offer it for a fee. Ask your employer or financial institution if they offer IRS *e-file* as an employee, member, or customer benefit.

Free Help With Your Return

Free help in preparing your return is available nationwide from IRS-trained volunteers. The Volunteer Income Tax Assistance (VITA) program is designed to help low to moderate income taxpayers and the Tax Counseling for the Elderly (TCE) program is designed to assist taxpayers age 60 or older with their tax returns. Many VITA sites offer free electronic filing and all volunteers will let you know about the credits and deductions you may be entitled to claim. To find a site near you, call 1-800-906-9887. Or to find the nearest AARP TaxAide site, visit AARP's website at www.aarp.org/taxaide or call 1-888-227-7669. For more information on these programs, go to IRS.gov and enter keyword "VITA" in the search box.

> ### TAXPLANNER
> VITA sites are generally located at community and neighborhood centers, libraries, schools, shopping malls, and other convenient locations.

> ### TAXPLANNER
> Free help is also available through the Tax Counseling for the Elderly (TCE) program. TCE is designed to assist taxpayers age 60 or older with their tax returns. Volunteers are specially trained to assist with questions about pensions and retirement issues unique to seniors.

> ### TAXPLANNER
> The U.S. military also has a strong Volunteer Income Tax Assistance (VITA) program to provide free tax advice, tax preparation, and assistance to Army, Air Force, Navy, Marine Corps, and Coast Guard personnel. This special worldwide tax program is overseen by the Armed Forces Tax Council (AFTC). The AFTC, in coordination with the IRS, trains and equips volunteers for serving military-specific tax issues, such as combat zone tax benefits and the Earned Income Tax Credit. More information can be found via www.irs.gov by entering the keyword "AFTC" in the upper right-hand corner.

Using a Tax Professional

Many tax professionals electronically file tax returns for their clients. You may personally enter your PIN or complete Form 8879, IRS *e-file* Signature Authorization, to authorize the tax professional to enter your PIN on your return.

Note. Tax professionals may charge a fee for IRS *e-file*. Fees can vary depending on the professional and the specific services rendered.

When Do I Have To File?

April 15, 2015, is the due date for filing your 2014 income tax return if you use the calendar year. For a quick view of due dates for filing a return with or without an extension of time to file (discussed later), see Table 1-5.

Table 1-5. When To File Your 2014 Return

For U.S. citizens and residents who file returns on a calendar year.

	For Most Taxpayers	For Certain Taxpayers Outside the U.S.
No extension requested	April 15, 2015	June 15, 2015
Automatic extension	October 15, 2015	October 15, 2015

TAXPLANNER

Certain taxpayers outside the U.S. qualify for a two-month automatic extension time to file their income tax return; e.g., their Form 1040 would be due June 15, 2015. This extension gives the taxpayer an extra 2 months to file <u>and</u> pay the tax. However interest will be charged on the unpaid tax liability from April 15, 2015, until paid. If you expect a balance will be due with your return, you may want to consider paying it by April 15, 2015, to minimize the interest. Refer to *When and Where Should You File?* in Form 1040 instructions for more details.

If you use a fiscal year (a year ending on the last day of any month except December, or a 52–53-week year), your income tax return is due by the 15th day of the 4th month after the close of your fiscal year.

When the due date for doing any act for tax purposes—filing a return, paying taxes, etc.—falls on a Saturday, Sunday, or legal holiday, the due date is delayed until the next business day.

Filing paper returns on time. Your paper return is filed on time if it is mailed in an envelope that is properly addressed, has enough postage, and is postmarked by the due date. If you send your return by registered mail, the date of the registration is the postmark date. The registration is evidence that the return was delivered. If you send a return by certified mail and have your receipt postmarked by a postal employee, the date on the receipt is the postmark date. The postmarked certified mail receipt is evidence that the return was delivered.

Private delivery services. If you use a private delivery service designated by the IRS to send your return, the postmark date generally is the date the private delivery service records in its database or marks on the mailing label. The private delivery service can tell you how to get written proof of this date.

For the IRS mailing address to use if you are using a private delivery service, go to IRS.gov and enter "private delivery service" in the search box.

The following are designated private delivery services.

- DHL Express (DHL): Same Day Service.
- Federal Express (FedEx): FedEx Priority Overnight, FedEx Standard Overnight, FedEx 2Day, FedEx International Priority, and FedEx International First.
- United Parcel Service (UPS): UPS Next Day Air, UPS Next Day Air Saver, UPS 2nd Day Air, UPS 2nd Day Air A.M., UPS Worldwide Express Plus, and UPS Worldwide Express.

TAXPLANNER

Private Delivery Services cannot deliver to post office boxes. If you need to locate information on the specific address for mailing go to www.irs.gov and enter the keyword "Private Delivery Service" in the upper right-hand corner search box and click on "Search." Then, choose the link for Submission Processing Center Street Addresses for Private Delivery Service (PDS).

Filing electronic returns on time. If you use IRS *e-file*, your return is considered filed on time if the authorized electronic return transmitter postmarks the transmission by the due date. An authorized electronic return transmitter is a participant in the IRS *e-file* program that transmits electronic tax return information directly to the IRS.

The electronic postmark is a record of when the authorized electronic return transmitter received the transmission of your electronically filed return on its host system. The date and time in your time zone controls whether your electronically filed return is timely.

Filing late. If you do not file your return by the due date, you may have to pay a failure-to-file penalty and interest. For more information, see *Penalties*, later. Also see *Interest* under *Amount You Owe*.

If you were due a refund but you did not file a return, you generally must file within 3 years from the date the return was due (including extensions) to get that refund.

Nonresident alien. If you are a nonresident alien and earn wages subject to U.S. income tax withholding, your 2014 U.S. income tax return (Form 1040NR or Form 1040NR-EZ) is due by:

- April 15, 2015, if you use a calendar year, or
- The 15th day of the 4th month after the end of your fiscal year if you use a fiscal year.

If you do not earn wages subject to U.S. income tax withholding, your return is due by:

- June 15, 2015, if you use a calendar year, or
- The 15th day of the 6th month after the end of your fiscal year, if you use a fiscal year.

See Publication 519 for more filing information.

Filing for a decedent. If you must file a final income tax return for a taxpayer who died during the year (a decedent), the return is due by the 15th day of the 4th month after the end of the decedent's normal tax year. See Publication 559.

Extensions of Time To File

You may be able to get an extension of time to file your return. There are three types of situations where you may qualify for an extension:

- Automatic extensions,
- You are outside the United States, or
- You are serving in a combat zone.

Automatic Extension

If you cannot file your 2014 return by the due date, you may be able to get an automatic 6-month extension of time to file.

Example. If your return is due on April 15, 2015, you will have until October 15, 2015, to file.

How to get the automatic extension. You can get the automatic extension by:

1. Using IRS *e-file* (electronic filing), or
2. Filing a paper form.

E-file options. There are two ways you can use *e-file* to get an extension of time to file. Complete Form 4868, Application for Automatic Extension of Time To File U.S. Individual Income Tax Return, to use as a worksheet. If you think you may owe tax when you file your return, use *Part II* of the form to estimate your balance due. If you *e-file* Form 4868 to the IRS, do not also send a paper Form 4868.

E-file using your personal computer or a tax professional. You can use a tax software package with your personal computer or a tax professional to file Form 4868 electronically. You will need to provide certain information from your tax return for 2013. If you wish to make a payment by direct transfer from your bank account, see *Pay online*, under *How To Pay*, later in this chapter.

E-file and pay by credit or debit card or by direct transfer from your bank account. You can get an extension by paying part or all of your estimate of tax due by using a credit or debit card or by direct transfer from your bank account. You can do this by phone or over the Internet. You do not file Form 4868. See *Pay online*, under *How To Pay*, later in this chapter.

Filing a paper Form 4868. You can get an extension of time to file by filing a paper Form 4868. Mail it to the address shown in the form instructions.

If you want to make a payment with the form, make your check or money order payable to "United States Treasury." Write your SSN, daytime phone number, and "2014 Form 4868" on your check or money order.

Caution

If you do not pay the tax due by the regular due date (generally, April 15), you will owe interest. You may also be charged penalties, discussed later.

TAXPLANNER

The IRS offers some relief to taxpayers unable to pay the amount owed with the filing of Form 4868. The IRS permits Form 4868 to be filed and an automatic 6-month extension obtained even though the tax properly estimated to be due is not paid in full when the form is filed. No late filing penalty will be assessed under these circumstances. However, it is still required that the tax liability shown on Form 4868 be properly estimated based on the information available to the taxpayer. Furthermore, unless at least 90% of the taxpayer's actual tax liability was paid prior to the original due date of the return through withholding or estimated payments, a late payment penalty of 0.5% per month will be assessed for each month from the original due date to the date of payment plus the regular rate of interest on underpayments.

When to file. You must request the automatic extension by the due date for your return. You can file your return any time before the 6-month extension period ends.

> ### TAXSAVER
> An extension of time to file will not be valid if it does not show a "proper" estimate of tax liability. A proper estimate is based on all the facts and information you have at the time of filing. If your estimate is found to be improper, your extension will be invalid and you will be subject to failure-to-file penalties. See _Penalties_, later. Some tax experts contend that you should request an extension to file your return, arguing that your chances of an audit are reduced, because IRS field agents will have less time to conduct the audit. Other tax experts contend that you're better off filing on April 15, because that way you get lost in the crowd. Both theories are gross over-simplifications of IRS procedures.

When you file your return. Enter any payment you made related to the extension of time to file on Form 1040, line 68. If you file Form 1040EZ or Form 1040A, include that payment in your total payments on Form 1040EZ, line 9, or Form 1040A, line 41. Also enter "Form 4868" and the amount paid in the space to the left of line 9 or line 41.

> ### TAXPLANNER
> An extension of time to file is not an extension of time to pay. If you are unable to pay the full amount of tax due with your tax return because of financial hardship, you should still file the tax return along with a "good faith" payment of as much of the tax due as you can afford to pay. If you can pay in full within 120 days, you should call 1-800-829-1040 to establish the request. Alternatively, you can apply online by going to www.irs.gov and entering the keyword "OPA" in the upper right-hand corner to locate the link for the "Online Payment Agreement Application." If you cannot pay within 120 days, you should complete Form 9465 or Form 9465-FS to request the privilege of paying the remaining tax in installments. For more information about this topic see _Installment Agreements_ later in this chapter.

Individuals Outside the United States

You are allowed an automatic 2-month extension, without filing Form 4868 (until June 15, 2015, if you use the calendar year), to file your 2014 return and pay any federal income tax due if:

1. You are a U.S. citizen or resident, and
2. On the due date of your return:
   a. You are living outside the United States and Puerto Rico, and your main place of business or post of duty is outside the United States and Puerto Rico, or
   b. You are in military or naval service on duty outside the United States and Puerto Rico.

However, if you pay the tax due after the regular due date (generally, April 15), interest will be charged from that date until the date the tax is paid.

If you served in a combat zone or qualified hazardous duty area, you may be eligible for a longer extension of time to file. See _Individuals Serving in Combat Zone_, later, for special rules that apply to you.

Married taxpayers. If you file a joint return, only one spouse has to qualify for this automatic extension. If you and your spouse file separate returns, this automatic extension applies only to the spouse who qualifies.

How to get the extension. To use this automatic extension, you must attach a statement to your return explaining what situation qualified you for the extension. (See the situations listed under (2), earlier.)

Extensions beyond 2 months. If you cannot file your return within the automatic 2-month extension period, you may be able to get an additional 4-month extension, for a total of 6 months. File Form 4868 and check the box on line 8.

No further extension. An extension of more than 6 months will generally not be granted. However, if you are outside the United States and meet certain tests, you may be granted a longer extension. For more information, see _When To File and Pay_ in Publication 54.

Individuals Serving in Combat Zone

The deadline for filing your tax return, paying any tax you may owe, and filing a claim for refund is automatically extended if you serve in a combat zone. This applies to members of the Armed Forces, as well as merchant marines serving aboard vessels under the operational control of the Department of Defense, Red Cross personnel, accredited correspondents, and civilians under the direction of the Armed Forces in support of the Armed Forces.

Combat zone. For purposes of the automatic extension, the term "combat zone" includes the following areas.

1. The Arabian peninsula area, effective January 17, 1991.
2. The Kosovo area, effective March 24, 1999.
3. Afghanistan area, effective September 19, 2001.

See Publication 3, Armed Forces' Tax Guide, for more detailed information on the locations comprising each combat zone. The publication also has information about other tax benefits available to military personnel serving in a combat zone.

Extension period. The deadline for filing your return, paying any tax due, and filing a claim for refund is extended for at least 180 days after the later of:

1. The last day you are in a combat zone or the last day the area qualifies as a combat zone, or
2. The last day of any continuous qualified hospitalization for injury from service in the combat zone.

In addition to the 180 days, your deadline is also extended by the number of days you had left to take action with the IRS when you entered the combat zone. For example, you have 3½ months (January 1 – April 15) to file your tax return. Any days left in this period when you entered the combat zone (or the entire 3½ months if you entered it before the beginning of the year) are added to the 180 days. See *Extension of Deadlines* in Publication 3 for more information.

The rules on the extension for filing your return also apply when you are deployed outside the United States (away from your permanent duty station) while participating in a designated contingency operation.

TAXPLANNER

In addition to the three combat zones listed above, certain areas that support active military operations receive the same combat zone tax benefits (for example, Qualified Hazardous Duty Areas). These areas are listed at www.irs.gov and can be found by entering the keyword "Combat Zone" in the upper right-hand corner. Military operations that are part of Operation Enduring Freedom and Operation Iraqi Freedom are included on the list.

EXPLANATION

You may obtain tax forms via the Internet by visiting the IRS site at www.irs.gov.

How Do I Prepare My Return?

This section explains how to get ready to fill in your tax return and when to report your income and expenses. It also explains how to complete certain sections of the form. You may find Table 1-6 helpful when you prepare your paper return.

Table 1-6. **Six Steps for Preparing Your Paper Return**

1 – Get your records together for income and expenses.
2 – Get the forms, schedules, and publications you need.
3 – Fill in your return.
4 – Check your return to make sure it is correct.
5 – Sign and date your return.
6 – Attach all required forms and schedules.

Electronic returns. For information you may find useful in preparing a paperless return, see *Does My Return Have To Be on Paper*, earlier.

Substitute tax forms. You cannot use your own version of a tax form unless it meets the requirements explained in Publication 1167, General Rules and Specifications for Substitute Forms and Schedules.

Form W-2. If you were an employee, you should receive Form W-2 from your employer. You will need the information from this form to prepare your return. See *Form W-2* under *Credit for Withholding and Estimated Tax* in chapter 4.

Your employer is required to provide or send Form W-2 to you no later than February 2, 2015. If it is mailed, you should allow adequate time to receive it before contacting your employer. If you still do not get the form by February 17, the IRS can help you by requesting the form from your employer. When you request IRS help, be prepared to provide the following information.
- Your name, address (including ZIP code), and phone number.
- Your SSN.
- Your dates of employment.
- Your employer's name, address (including ZIP code), and phone number.

Form 1099. If you received certain types of income, you may receive a Form 1099. For example, if you received taxable interest of $10 or more, the payer is required to provide or send Form 1099 to you no later than February 2, 2015 (or by February 17, 2015, if furnished by a broker). If it is mailed, you should allow adequate time to receive it before contacting the payer. If you still do not get the form by February 17 (or by March 5, 2015, if furnished by a broker), call the IRS for help.

When Do I Report My Income and Expenses?

You must figure your taxable income on the basis of a tax year. A "tax year" is an annual accounting period used for keeping records and reporting income and expenses. You must account for your income and expenses in a way that clearly shows your taxable income. The way you do this is called an accounting method. This section explains which accounting periods and methods you can use.

Accounting Periods

Most individual tax returns cover a calendar year the 12 months from January 1 through December 31. If you do not use a calendar year, your accounting period is a fiscal year. A regular fiscal year is a 12-month period that ends on the last day of any month except December. A 52–53-week fiscal year varies from 52 to 53 weeks and always ends on the same day of the week.

You choose your accounting period (tax year) when you file your first income tax return. It cannot be longer than 12 months.

TAXPLANNER

To operate on a fiscal year accounting basis, you must keep your books and records based on that fiscal year. Because most individual taxpayers keep their personal financial records on a calendar year basis, it is easier to use a calendar year period. It is virtually impossible for an individual to obtain approval from the IRS to change to a fiscal year accounting period without justification. Usually, the justification must be that you are involved in a cyclical business from which self-employment or partnership income flows. Furthermore, in most cases, that income has to be your sole or principal source of income.

More information. For more information on accounting periods, including how to change your accounting period, see Publication 538, Accounting Periods and Methods.

Accounting Methods

Your accounting method is the way you account for your income and expenses. Most taxpayers use either the cash method or an accrual method. You choose a method when you file your first income tax return. If you want to change your accounting method after that, you generally must get IRS approval.

Cash method. If you use this method, report all items of income in the year in which you actually or constructively receive them. Generally, you deduct all expenses in the year you actually pay them. This is the method most individual taxpayers use.

EXPLANATION

Accounting methods are important because they determine when you recognize income and when you deduct expenses for tax purposes. The cash method allows you more flexibility and control over your tax liability. Individuals who do not own and operate their own business must use the cash method. However, the IRS generally will not permit you to use the cash method if you own your own business and cash method accounting doesn't clearly show your income. The cash method is generally not permitted if your business maintains inventory, or production materials are on hand at the end of the year. See IRS Publication 538, *Accounting Periods and Methods*, for more information.

TAXALERT

IRS officials have expressed the view that you may not use the cash method for any substantial business activity, even one providing only personal or professional services. The law does not support this view. Nevertheless, in conducting audits, the IRS has been aggressive in urging taxpayers to change to the accrual method of accounting.

TAXPLANNER

Generally, most taxpayers who expect to be in the same tax bracket from one year to the next and who want to reduce their current tax bill as much as possible should attempt to defer income to a subsequent year and to take deductions in the current year. If you suspect you might be in a higher tax bracket in a subsequent year, however, you would want to do just the opposite.

If you find yourself facing higher tax rates next year, it may make sense for you to rethink traditional tax strategies. For such taxpayers, it may be beneficial to accelerate and recognize income in an earlier year, while deferring deductions to a later year. This approach may allow you to pay tax on the accelerated income at a lower tax rate. Deductions deferred until future years could produce a greater tax benefit for you. When deciding to accelerate income/deductions into 2014, or defer them until 2015, keep in mind the following:

a. In some states and cities, you may pay property, state, and local income taxes in either December or January, giving you the opportunity to pay 2 years' worth of these taxes in a single calendar year.

b. You can control when you make charitable contributions.

c. To some extent, you can control when you make interest payments on a mortgage.

d. You can chose when to sell assets with unrealized gains or losses in order to recognize the gain or loss.

e. Contributions to an IRA for the tax year 2014 may be made as late April 15, 2015.

For more information about tax law changes that are scheduled to take effect in 2015 and thereafter, see chapter 47, *Planning ahead for 2014 and beyond*. We also recommend that you consult your tax advisor for planning assistance in anticipation of forthcoming tax law changes.

Constructive receipt. Generally, you constructively receive income when it is credited to your account or set apart in any way that makes it available to you. You do not need to have physical possession of it. For example, interest credited to your bank account on December 31, 2014, is taxable income to you in 2014 if you could have withdrawn it in 2014 (even if the amount is not entered in your records or withdrawn until 2015).

TAXALERT

Profits from a brokerage account, or similar account, are fully taxable in the year you earn them. This is true even if:

1. You do not withdraw the earnings,
2. You automatically reinvest your earnings (i.e., a dividend reinvestment plan),
3. The credit balance in the account may be reduced or eliminated by losses in later years, or
4. Current profits are used to reduce or eliminate a debit balance from a prior year.

Example

You sold your ABC Company stock on December 16, 2014, realizing a gain of $5,000. You did not withdraw the cash in your account until January 7, 2015. The gain is taxable income to you for 2014.

Garnisheed wages. If your employer uses your wages to pay your debts, or if your wages are attached or garnisheed, the full amount is constructively received by you. You must include these wages in income for the year you would have received them.

Debts paid for you. If another person cancels or pays your debts (but not as a gift or loan), you have constructively received the amount and generally must include it in your gross income for the year. See *Canceled Debts* in chapter 12 for more information.

> ## EXAMPLE
> Your new employer pays the balance of the mortgage due on your home that is not covered by the selling price so you can move to Florida to work for him. The payments are not intended to be a gift or a loan to you. The amount your employer pays on the mortgage is income to you in the year that it is paid off.

Payment to third party. If a third party is paid income from property you own, you have constructively received the income. It is the same as if you had actually received the income and paid it to the third party.

Payment to an agent. Income an agent receives for you is income you constructively received in the year the agent receives it. If you indicate in a contract that your income is to be paid to another person, you must include the amount in your gross income when the other person receives it.

> ## EXPLANATION
> The IRS considers you to have received income in the year that your agent receives it, but if a person who is not your agent or creditor receives your income, you do not have to consider that amount as income until you personally receive it. The key question is whether you can control the receipt of the income during the year. If you can, the income is taxable to you in that year. In general, when you receive income, or incur deductions right before or after year-end, you should be careful to document the circumstances related to the receipt or payment of the item. The IRS document-matching program will be used to identify income reported on a 2014 Form 1099 as having been paid to you in 2014.
>
> ### Example
> ABC Company mailed you a $500 dividend check on December 10, 2014. The post office inadvertently delivered the check on December 31 to Mr. Wheat on the other side of town. You didn't receive the check until January 7, 2015. The $500 in dividends is taxable to you in 2015, because Mr. Wheat was not your agent and you were not in control of the income. You should carefully explain this turn of events when you prepare your return because the IRS document-matching program will have a Form 1099 from ABC Company on file that lists the $500 as having been paid to you in 2014.
>
> By contrast, suppose ABC Company mailed you a $500 dividend check on December 12, 2014, and you received but *did not cash or deposit* the check until January 7, 2015. The $500 in dividends is taxable to you in 2014, because you were in control of the income, even though you chose not to cash the check until 2015.

Check received or available. A valid check that was made available to you before the end of the tax year is constructively received by you in that year. A check that was "made available to you" includes a check you have already received, but not cashed or deposited. It also includes, for example, your last paycheck of the year that your employer made available for you to pick up at the office before the end of the year. It is constructively received by you in that year whether or not you pick it up before the end of the year or wait to receive it by mail after the end of the year.

No constructive receipt. There may be facts to show that you did not constructively receive income.

Example. Alice Johnson, a teacher, agreed to her school board's condition that, in her absence, she would receive only the difference between her regular salary and the salary of a substitute teacher hired by the school board. Therefore, Alice did not constructively receive the amount by which her salary was reduced to pay the substitute teacher.

Accrual method. If you use an accrual method, you generally report income when you earn it, rather than when you receive it. You generally deduct your expenses when you incur them, rather than when you pay them.

Income paid in advance. An advance payment of income is generally included in gross income in the year you receive it. Your method of accounting does not matter as long as the income is available to you. An advance payment may include rent or interest you receive in advance and pay for services you will perform later.

A limited deferral until the next tax year may be allowed for certain advance payments. See Publication 538 for specific information.

Additional information. For more information on accounting methods, including how to change your accounting method, see Publication 538.

Social Security Number (SSN)

You must enter your SSN on your return. If you are married, enter the SSNs for both you and your spouse, whether you file jointly or separately.

If you are filing a joint return, include the SSNs in the same order as the names. Use this same order in submitting other forms and documents to the IRS.

Check that both the name and SSN on your Form 1040, W-2, and 1099 agree with your social security card. If they do not, certain deductions and credits on your Form 1040 may be reduced or disallowed and you may not receive credit for your social security earnings. If your Form W-2 shows an incorrect SSN or name, notify your employer or the form-issuing agent as soon as possible to make sure your earnings are credited to your social security record. If the name or SSN on your social security card is incorrect, call the SSA at 1-800-772-1213.

Name change. If you changed your name because of marriage, divorce, etc., be sure to report the change to your local Social Security Administration (SSA) office before filing your return. This prevents delays in processing your return and issuing refunds. It also safeguards your future social security benefits.

Dependent's SSN. You must provide the SSN of each dependent you claim, regardless of the dependent's age. This requirement applies to all dependents (not just your children) claimed on your tax return.

Exception. If your child was born and died in 2014 and did not have an SSN, enter "DIED" in column (2) of line 6c (Form 1040 or 1040A) and include a copy of the child's birth certificate, death certificate, or hospital records. The document must show that the child was born alive.

No SSN. File Form SS-5, Application for a Social Security Card, with your local SSA office to get an SSN for yourself or your dependent. It usually takes about 2 weeks to get an SSN. If you or your dependent is not eligible for an SSN, see *Individual taxpayer identification number (ITIN)*, later.

If you are a U.S. citizen or resident alien, you must show proof of age, identity, and citizenship or alien status with your Form SS-5. If you are 12 or older and have never been assigned an SSN, you must appear in person with this proof at an SSA office.

Form SS-5 is available at any SSA office, on the Internet at www.socialsecurity.gov, or by calling 1-800-772-1213. If you have any questions about which documents you can use as proof of age, identity, or citizenship, contact your SSA office.

If your dependent does not have an SSN by the time your return is due, you may want to ask for an extension of time to file, as explained earlier under *When Do I Have To File*.

If you do not provide a required SSN or if you provide an incorrect SSN, your tax may be increased and any refund may be reduced.

Adoption taxpayer identification number (ATIN). If you are in the process of adopting a child who is a U.S. citizen or resident and cannot get an SSN for the child until the adoption is final, you can apply for an ATIN to use instead of an SSN.

File Form W-7A, Application for Taxpayer Identification Number for Pending U.S. Adoptions, with the IRS to get an ATIN if all of the following are true.

- You have a child living with you who was placed in your home for legal adoption.
- You cannot get the child's existing SSN even though you have made a reasonable attempt to get it from the birth parents, the placement agency, and other persons.
- You cannot get an SSN for the child from the SSA because, for example, the adoption is not final.
- You are eligible to claim the child as a dependent on your tax return.

After the adoption is final, you must apply for an SSN for the child. You cannot continue using the ATIN.

See Form W-7A for more information.

Nonresident alien spouse. If your spouse is a nonresident alien, your spouse must have either an SSN or an ITIN if:

- You file a joint return,
- You file a separate return and claim an exemption for your spouse, or
- Your spouse is filing a separate return.

If your spouse is not eligible for an SSN, see the following discussion on ITINs.

Individual taxpayer identification number (ITIN). The IRS will issue you an ITIN if you are a nonresident or resident alien and you do not have and are not eligible to get an SSN. This also applies to an alien spouse or dependent. To apply for an ITIN, file Form W-7 with the IRS. It usually takes about 6 to 10 weeks to get an ITIN. Enter the ITIN on your tax return wherever an SSN is requested.

> **Tip**
>
> *If you are applying for an ITIN for yourself, your spouse, or a dependent in order to file your tax return, attach your completed tax return to your Form W-7. See the Form W-7 instructions for how and where to file.*

TAXALERT

On June 30, 2014, the IRS announced that it changed its expiration policy for ITINs. A taxpayer's ITIN will not expire as long as they continue to file tax returns. However, if the taxpayer fails to file tax returns for five consecutive years, the ITIN will expire. Previously, all ITINs expired automatically after five years.

ITIN for tax use only. An ITIN is for tax use only. It does not entitle you or your dependent to social security benefits or change the employment or immigration status of either of you under U.S. law.

Penalty for not providing social security number. If you do not include your SSN or the SSN of your spouse or dependent as required, you may have to pay a penalty. See the discussion on *Penalties*, later, for more information.

SSN on correspondence. If you write to the IRS about your tax account, be sure to include your SSN (and the name and SSN of your spouse, if you filed a joint return) in your correspondence. Because your SSN is used to identify your account, this helps the IRS respond to your correspondence promptly.

> **Caution**
>
> *You cannot e-file a return using an ITIN in the calendar year the ITIN is issued; however, you can e-file returns in the following years.*

Presidential Election Campaign Fund

This fund helps pay for Presidential election campaigns. If you want $3 to go to this fund, check the box. If you are filing a joint return, your spouse can also have $3 go to the fund. If you check a box, your tax or refund will not change.

Computations

The following information may be useful in making the return easier to complete.

Rounding off dollars. You can round off cents to whole dollars on your return and schedules. If you do round to whole dollars, you must round all amounts. To round, drop amounts under 50 cents and increase amounts from 50 to 99 cents to the next dollar. For example, $1.39 becomes $1 and $2.50 becomes $3.

If you have to add two or more amounts to figure the amount to enter on a line, include cents when adding the amounts and round off only the total.

Example. You receive two Forms W-2: one showing wages of $5,000.55 and one showing wages of $18,500.73. On Form 1040, line 7, you would enter $23,501 ($5,000.55 + $18,500.73 = $23,501.28), not $23,502 ($5,001 + $18,501).

Equal amounts. If you are asked to enter the smaller or larger of two equal amounts, enter that amount.

Example. Line 1 is $500. Line 3 is $500. Line 5 asks you to enter the smaller of line 1 or 3. Enter $500 on line 5.

Negative amounts. If you file a paper return and you need to enter a negative amount, put the amount in parentheses rather than using a minus sign. To combine positive and negative amounts, add all the positive amounts together and then subtract the negative amounts.

Attachments

Tip

You may be able to file a paperless return using IRS e-file. There's nothing to attach or mail, not even your Forms W-2. See Does My Return Have To Be on Paper, *earlier.*

Depending on the form you file and the items reported on your return, you may have to complete additional schedules and forms and attach them to your paper return.

Form W-2. Form W-2 is a statement from your employer of wages and other compensation paid to you and taxes withheld from your pay. You should have a Form W-2 from each employer. If you file a paper return, be sure to attach a copy of Form W-2 in the place indicated on the front page of your return. Attach it to the front page of your paper return, not to any attachments. For more information, see *Form W-2* in chapter 4.

If you received a Form 1099-R, Distributions From Pensions, Annuities, Retirement or Profit-Sharing Plans, IRAs, Insurance Contracts, etc., showing federal income tax withheld, and you file a paper return, attach a copy of that form in the place indicated on the front page of your return.

Form 1040EZ. There are no additional schedules to file with Form 1040EZ.

Form 1040A. If you file a paper return, attach any forms and schedules behind Form 1040A in order of the "Attachment Sequence Number" shown in the upper right corner of the form or schedule. Then arrange all other statements or attachments in the same order as the forms and schedules they relate to and attach them last. Do not attach items unless required to do so.

Form 1040. If you file a paper return, attach any forms and schedules behind Form 1040 in order of the "Attachment Sequence Number" shown in the upper right corner of the form or schedule. Then arrange all other statements or attachments in the same order as the forms and schedules they relate to and attach them last. Do not attach items unless required to do so.

TAXPLANNER

If you fail to organize your return according to the prescribed sequence numbers, the IRS, upon receipt of your return, will disassemble it and put it back together in the proper order. This procedure may result in the loss of a page of your return, causing some delay in its processing. To avoid this problem, you can electronically file your return. See chapter 45, *Everything you need to know about e-filing.*

Third Party Designee

You can authorize the IRS to discuss your return with your preparer, a friend, family member, or any other person you choose. If you check the "Yes" box in the *Third party designee* area of your 2014 tax return and provide the information required, you are authorizing:

1. The IRS to call the designee to answer any questions that arise during the processing of your return, and
2. The designee to:
   a. Give information that is missing from your return to the IRS,
   b. Call the IRS for information about the processing of your return or the status of your refund or payments,
   c. Receive copies of notices or transcripts related to your return, upon request, and
   d. Respond to certain IRS notices about math errors, offsets (see *Refunds*, later), and return preparation.

The authorization will automatically end no later than the due date (without any extensions) for filing your 2015 tax return. This is April 15, 2016, for most people.

See your form instructions for more information.

Signatures

You must sign and date your return. If you file a joint return, both you and your spouse must sign the return, even if only one of you had income.

If you are due a refund, it cannot be issued unless you have signed your return.

Enter your occupation. If you file a joint return, enter both your occupation and your spouse's occupation. Entering your daytime phone number may help speed the processing of your return.

When someone can sign for you. You can appoint an agent to sign your return if you are:

1. Unable to sign the return because of disease or injury,
2. Absent from the United States for a continuous period of at least 60 days before the due date for filing your return, or
3. Given permission to do so by the IRS office in your area.

Power of attorney. A return signed by an agent in any of these cases must have a power of attorney (POA) attached that authorizes the agent to sign for you. You can use a POA that states that the agent is granted authority to sign the return, or you can use Form 2848, Power of Attorney and Declaration of Representative. Part I of Form 2848 must state that the agent is granted authority to sign the return.

Court-appointed conservator or other fiduciary. If you are a court-appointed conservator, guardian, or other fiduciary for a mentally or physically incompetent individual who has to file a tax return, sign your name for the individual. File Form 56.

Unable to sign. If the taxpayer is mentally competent but physically unable to sign the return or POA, a valid "signature" is defined under state law. It can be anything that clearly indicates the taxpayer's intent to sign. For example, the taxpayer's "X" with the signatures of two witnesses might be considered a valid signature under a state's law.

Spouse unable to sign. If your spouse is unable to sign for any reason, see *Signing a joint return* in chapter 2.

Child's return. If a child has to file a tax return but cannot sign the return, the child's parent, guardian, or another legally responsible person must sign the child's name, followed by the words "By (your signature), parent for minor child."

Paid Preparer

Generally, anyone you pay to prepare, assist in preparing, or review your tax return must sign it and fill in the other blanks, including their Preparer Tax Identification Number (PTIN), in the paid preparer's area of your return.

Many preparers are required to *e-file* the tax returns they prepare. They sign these e-filed returns using their tax preparation software. However, you can choose to have your return completed on paper if you prefer. In that case, the paid preparer can sign the paper return manually or use a rubber stamp or mechanical device. The preparer is personally responsible for affixing his or her signature to the return.

If the preparer is self-employed (that is, not employed by any person or business to prepare the return), he or she should check the self-employed box in the *Paid Preparer Use Only* space on the return.

Caution

If you file a joint return, both spouses are generally liable for the tax, and the entire tax liability may be assessed against either spouse. See chapter 2.

Tip

If you e-file *your return, you can use an electronic signature to sign your return. See* Does My Return Have To Be on Paper, *earlier.*

The preparer must give you a copy of your return in addition to the copy filed with the IRS.

If you prepare your own return, leave this area blank. If another person prepares your return and does not charge you, that person should not sign your return.

If you have questions about whether a preparer must sign your return, contact any IRS office.

Refunds

When you complete your return, you will determine if you paid more income tax than you owed. If so, you can get a refund of the amount you overpaid or, if you file Form 1040 or Form 1040A, you can choose to apply all or part of the overpayment to your next year's (2015) estimated tax. You cannot have your overpayment applied to your 2015 estimated tax if you file Form 1040EZ.

Follow the form instructions to complete the entries to claim your refund and/or to apply your overpayment to your 2015 estimated tax.

DIRECT DEPOSIT: _Simple. Safe. Secure._ Instead of getting a paper check, you may be able to have your refund deposited directly into your checking or savings account, including an individual retirement arrangement. Follow the form instructions to request direct deposit.

If the direct deposit cannot be done, the IRS will send a check instead.

TreasuryDirect®. You can request a deposit of your refund to a TreasuryDirect® online account to buy U.S. Treasury marketable securities and savings bonds. For more information, go to www.treasurydirect.gov.

Split refunds. If you choose direct deposit, you may be able to split the refund and have it deposited among two or three accounts or buy up to $5,000 in paper series I savings bonds. Complete Form 8888, Allocation of Refund (Including Savings Bond Purchases), and attach it to your return.

Overpayment less than one dollar. If your overpayment is less than one dollar, you will not get a refund unless you ask for it in writing.

Cashing your refund check. Cash your tax refund check soon after you receive it. Checks expire the last business day of the 12th month of issue.

If your check has expired, you can apply to the IRS to have it reissued.

Refund more or less than expected. If you receive a check for a refund you are not entitled to, or for an overpayment that should have been credited to estimated tax, do not cash the check. Call the IRS.

If you receive a check for more than the refund you claimed, do not cash the check until you receive a notice explaining the difference.

If your refund check is for less than you claimed, it should be accompanied by a notice explaining the difference. Cashing the check does not stop you from claiming an additional amount of refund.

If you did not receive a notice and you have any questions about the amount of your refund, you should wait 2 weeks. If you still have not received a notice, call the IRS.

Offset against debts. If you are due a refund but have not paid certain amounts you owe, all or part of your refund may be used to pay all or part of the past-due amount. This includes past-due federal income tax, other federal debts (such as student loans), state income tax, child and spousal support payments, and state unemployment compensation debt. You will be notified if the refund you claimed has been offset against your debts.

Joint return and injured spouse. When a joint return is filed and only one spouse owes a past-due amount, the other spouse can be considered an injured spouse. An injured spouse should file Form 8379, Injured Spouse Allocation, if both of the following apply and the spouse wants a refund of his or her share of the overpayment shown on the joint return.

1. You are not legally obligated to pay the past-due amount.
2. You made and reported tax payments (such as federal income tax withheld from your wages or estimated tax payments), or claimed a refundable tax credit (see the credits listed under *Who Should File*, earlier).

Note. If the injured spouse's residence was in a community property state at any time during the tax year, special rules may apply. See the Instructions for Form 8379.

If you have not filed your joint return and you know that your joint refund will be offset, file Form 8379 with your return. You should receive your refund within 14 weeks from the date the paper return is filed or within 11 weeks from the date the return is filed electronically.

If you filed your joint return and your joint refund was offset, file Form 8379 by itself. When filed after offset, it can take up to 8 weeks to receive your refund. Do not attach the previously filed tax return, but do include copies of all Forms W-2 and W-2G for both spouses and any Forms 1099 that show income tax withheld. The processing of Form 8379 may be delayed if these forms are not attached, or if the form is incomplete when filed.

A separate Form 8379 must be filed for each tax year to be considered.

Amount You Owe

When you complete your return, you will determine if you have paid the full amount of tax that you owe. If you owe additional tax, you should pay it with your return.

If the IRS figures your tax for you, you will receive a bill for any tax that is due. You should pay this bill within 30 days (or by the due date of your return, if later). See *Tax Figured by IRS* in chapter 31.

How To Pay

You can pay online, by phone, or by check or money order. Do not include any estimated tax payment for 2015 in this payment. Instead, make the estimated tax payment separately.

Caution

An injured spouse claim is different from an innocent spouse relief request. An injured spouse uses Form 8379 to request the division of the tax overpayment attributed to each spouse. An innocent spouse uses Form 8857, Request for Innocent Spouse Relief, to request relief from joint liability for tax, interest, and penalties on a joint return for items of the other spouse (or former spouse) that were incorrectly reported on the joint return. For information on innocent spouses, see Relief from joint responsibility under Filing a Joint Return in chapter 2.

Tip

You do not have to pay if the amount you owe is under $1.

Caution

If you do not pay your tax when due, you may have to pay a failure-to-pay penalty. See Penalties, later. For more information about your balance due, see Publication 594, The IRS Collection Process.

Bad check or payment. The penalty for writing a bad check to the IRS is $25 or 2% of the check, whichever is more. This penalty also applies to other forms of payment if the IRS does not receive the funds.

Pay online. Paying online is convenient and secure and helps make sure we get your payments on time.

You can pay using either of the following electronic payment methods.
- Direct transfer from your bank account.
- Credit or debit card.

To pay your taxes online or for more information, go to www.irs.gov/e-pay.

Pay by phone. Paying by phone is another safe and secure method of paying electronically. Use one of the following methods.
- Direct transfer from your bank account.
- Credit or debit card.

To pay by direct transfer from your bank account, call 1-800-555-4477 (English) or 1-800-244-4829 (Espanol). People who are deaf, hard of hearing, or have a speech disability and have access to TTY/TDD equipment can call 1-800-733-4829.

To pay using a credit or debit card, you can call one of the following service providers. There is a convenience fee charged by these providers that varies by provider, card type, and payment amount.

WorldPay
1-888-9-PAY-TAX™ (1-888-972-9829)
www.payUSAtax.com

Official Payments Corporation
1-888-UPAY-TAX™ (1-888-872-9829)
www.officialpayments.com

Link2Gov Corporation
1-888-PAY-1040™ (1-888-729-1040)
www.PAY1040.com

For the latest details on how to pay by phone, go to www.irs.gov/e-pay.

Pay by check or money order. Make your check or money order payable to "United States Treasury" for the full amount due. Do not send cash. Do not attach the payment to your return. Show your correct name, address, SSN, daytime phone number, and the tax year and form number on the front of your check or money order. If you are filing a joint return, enter the SSN shown first on your tax return.

Estimated tax payments. Do not include any 2015 estimated tax payment in the payment for your 2014 income tax return. See chapter 4 for information on how to pay estimated tax.

TAXPLANNER
Be careful about paying your taxes by credit card. Most of the payment options demand that you pay a "convenience fee" for using your card. Also, use caution if you won't be paying off your balance right away. The interest your credit card charges may be much higher than the interest the IRS charges for late payment. The IRS e-pay service providers are WorldPay US, Inc., Official Payments Corporation, and Link2Gov Corporation. As of the date this book went to press, the convenience fee for paying by credit card for both Link2Gov and Official Payments Corporation was 2.35% of the payment made, and the fee for WorldPayUS was 1.87% of the payment made. If you choose to pay your tax liability with a debit card, each provider charges a flat fee per transaction rather than a convenience fee. This flat fee ranges from $2.49 to $3.95 per transaction. Since both the convenience fee and the flat fee are subject to change, you should contact the service providers for the most up-to-date information before deciding if paying by credit or debit card makes sense for you. The fees above are based on paper filing. The fees are different when you e-file. For additional information, go to the IRS website at www.irs.gov and type in "pay taxes by credit or debit card" in the search box in the upper right-hand corner of the screen.

Interest
Interest is charged on tax you do not pay by the due date of your return. Interest is charged even if you get an extension of time for filing.

Interest on penalties. Interest is charged on the failure-to-file penalty, the accuracy-related penalty, and the fraud penalty from the due date of the return (including extensions) to the date of payment. Interest on other penalties starts on the date of notice and demand, but is not charged on penalties paid within 21 calendar days from the date of the notice (or within 10 business days if the notice is for $100,000 or more).

Interest due to IRS error or delay. All or part of any interest you were charged can be forgiven if the interest is due to an unreasonable error or delay by an officer or employee of the IRS in performing a ministerial or managerial act.

A ministerial act is a procedural or mechanical act that occurs during the processing of your case. A managerial act includes personnel transfers and extended personnel training. A decision concerning the proper application of federal tax law is not a ministerial or managerial act.

The interest can be forgiven only if you are not responsible in any important way for the error or delay and the IRS has notified you in writing of the deficiency or payment. For more information, see Publication 556, Examination of Returns, Appeal Rights, and Claims for Refund.

Interest and certain penalties may also be suspended for a limited period if you filed your return by the due date (including extensions) and the IRS does not provide you with a notice specifically stating your liability and the basis for it before the close of the 36-month period beginning on the later of:

- The date the return is filed, or
- The due date of the return without regard to extensions.

For more information, see Publication 556.

Tip

If the IRS figures your tax for you, to avoid interest for late payment, you must pay the bill within 30 days of the date of the bill or by the due date of your return, whichever is later. For information, see Tax Figured by IRS *in chapter 30.*

TAXPLANNER

If you owe additional tax, it is not a good idea to paper file your return by January 31. As long as you have planned well and have paid enough in estimated taxes to avoid a penalty, you would be better off keeping any other tax you owe in your savings account, where it will earn interest for 2½ months, rather than paying your tax bill early. If you *e-file* your return, you can prepare and submit it before the due date and authorize an electronic funds withdrawal on April 15th.

Installment Agreement

If you cannot pay the full amount due with your return, you can ask to make monthly installment payments for the full or a partial amount. However, you will be charged interest and may be charged a late payment penalty on the tax not paid by the date your return is due, even if your request to pay in installments is granted. If your request is granted, you must also pay a fee. To limit the interest and penalty charges, pay as much of the tax as possible with your return. But before requesting an installment agreement, you should consider other less costly alternatives, such as a bank loan or credit card payment.

To ask for an installment agreement, you can apply online or use Form 9465.

In addition to paying by check or money order, you can use a credit or debit card or direct payment from your bank account to make installment agreement payments. See *How To Pay*, earlier.

To apply online, go to IRS.gov and click on "Tools" and then *Online Payment Agreement*.

TAXPLANNER

An extension of time to file is not an extension of time to pay. If you are unable to pay the full amount of tax due with your tax return because of financial hardship, you should still file the tax return along with a "good faith" payment of as much of the tax due as you can afford to pay. If you can pay in full within 120 days, you should call 1-800-829-1040 to establish the request. Alternatively, you can apply online by going to www.irs.gov and entering the keyword "OPA" in the upper right-hand corner to locate the link for the "Online Payment Agreement Application." If you cannot pay within 120 days, you should complete Form 9465 or Form 9465-FS to request the privilege of paying the remaining tax in installments. This form should be attached to the front of the return when it is filed. However, the IRS will impose a fee of $105 ($52 if you make your payments by electronic funds withdrawal) for entering into an installment agreement. (If your income is below a certain level, you may qualify to pay a reduced fee of $43.) You can expect a decision back from the IRS within 30 days regarding your installment request, but **you still will be subject to interest and the failure-to-pay penalty on the unpaid tax.**

The IRS will continue to send you a bill for the unpaid tax, interest, and penalty until the total amount is paid. After the tax is completely paid, you can request in writing that the penalty be waived due to reasonable cause because of financial hardship. The IRS has total discretion in waiving penalties and may require you to prove your financial hardship.

If your tax return is already in the formal collection process (i.e., you have been contacted by an IRS official regarding a delinquent tax liability) and you are unable to pay the tax due, you may request an installment agreement with the IRS officer. If he or she agrees, the installment agreement is made using Form 433-D, and you will be required to provide financial information. You may need to seek professional tax advice if this is the case.

Gift To Reduce Debt Held by the Public

You can make a contribution (gift) to reduce debt held by the public. If you wish to do so, make a separate check payable to "Bureau of the Public Debt."

Send your check to:

Bureau of the Public Debt
ATTN: Department G
P.O. Box 2188
Parkersburg, WV 26106-2188

Or, enclose your separate check in the envelope with your income tax return. Do not add this gift to any tax you owe.

Go to www.publicdebt.treas.gov for information on how to make this type of gift online.

You may be able to deduct this gift as a charitable contribution on next year's tax return if you itemize your deductions on Schedule A (Form 1040).

Name and Address

After you have completed your return, fill in your name and address in the appropriate area of the Form 1040, Form 1040A, or Form 1040EZ.

P.O. box. If your post office does not deliver mail to your street address and you have a P.O. box, enter your P.O. box number on the line for your present home address instead of your street address.

Foreign address. If your address is outside the United States or its possessions or territories, enter the city name on the appropriate line of your return. Do not enter any other information on that line, but also complete the line listing:

1. Foreign country name,
2. Foreign province/state/county, and
3. Foreign postal code.

Follow the country's practice for entering the postal code and the name of the province, county, or state.

TAXALERT

You are not excused from filing a return because you have not received the proper forms from the IRS. The IRS has free tax forms and publications on a wide variety of topics. If you need IRS forms or information, try one of these easy options:

- **Internet.** You can access forms and publications on the IRS website 24 hours a day, 7 days a week, at www.irs.gov.
- **Phone.** Call 1-800-TAX-FORM (800-829-3676) to order current year forms, instructions, and publications, and prior year forms and instructions. You should receive your order within 10 days.
- **Locations in your community.** During the tax-filing season, many libraries and post offices offer free tax forms to taxpayers. Some libraries also have copies of commonly requested publications. Braille materials may also be available. Many large grocery stores, copy centers, and office supply stores have forms you can photocopy or print from a CD.
- **Mail.** Order your tax forms and publications from the Internal Revenue Service, 1201 N. Mitsubishi Motorway, Bloomington, IL, 61705-6613. You should receive your products 10 days after receipt of your order.

Where Do I File?

After you complete your return, you must send it to the IRS. You can mail it or you may be able to file it electronically. See *Does My Return Have To Be on Paper*, earlier.

Mailing your paper return. Mail your paper return to the address shown in your instructions.

What Happens After I File?

After you send your return to the IRS, you may have some questions. This section discusses concerns you may have about recordkeeping, your refund, and what to do if you move.

What Records Should I Keep?

This part discusses why you should keep records, what kinds of records you should keep, and how long you should keep them.

Records

You must keep records so that you can prepare a complete and accurate income tax return. The law does not require any special form of records. However, you should keep all receipts, canceled checks or other proof of payment, and any other records to support any deductions or credits you claim.

> ### TAXPLANNER
> See the detailed listing of tax records to keep at the end of the EY Individual Tax Organizer in the front of this book.

If you file a claim for refund, you must be able to prove by your records that you have overpaid your tax.

This part does not discuss the records you should keep when operating a business. For information on business records, see Publication 583, Starting a Business and Keeping Records.

Why Keep Records?

Good records help you:
- **Identify sources of income.** Your records can identify the sources of your income to help you separate business from nonbusiness income and taxable from nontaxable income.
- **Keep track of expenses.** You can use your records to identify expenses for which you can claim a deduction. This helps you determine if you can itemize deductions on your tax return.
- **Keep track of the basis of property.** You need to keep records that show the basis of your property. This includes the original cost or other basis of the property and any improvements you made.
- **Prepare tax returns.** You need records to prepare your tax return.
- **Support items reported on tax returns.** The IRS may question an item on your return. Your records will help you explain any item and arrive at the correct tax. If you cannot produce the correct documents, you may have to pay additional tax and be subject to penalties.

Kinds of Records to Keep

The IRS does not require you to keep your records in a particular way. Keep them in a manner that allows you and the IRS to determine your correct tax.

You can use your checkbook to keep a record of your income and expenses. You also need to keep documents, such as receipts and sales slips, that can help prove a deduction.

In this section you will find guidance about basic records that everyone should keep. The section also provides guidance about specific records you should keep for certain items.

Electronic records. All requirements that apply to hard copy books and records also apply to electronic storage systems that maintain tax books and records. When you replace hard copy books and records, you must maintain the electronic storage systems for as long as they are material to the administration of tax law.

For details on electronic storage system requirements, see Rev. Proc. 97-22, which is on page 9 of Internal Revenue Bulletin 1997-13 at www.irs.gov/pub/irs-irbs/irb97-13.pdf.

Copies of tax returns. You should keep copies of your tax returns as part of your tax records. They can help you prepare future tax returns, and you will need them if you file an amended return or are audited. Copies of your returns and other records can be helpful to your survivor or the executor or administrator of your estate.

If necessary, you can request a copy of a return and all attachments (including Form W-2) from the IRS by using Form 4506, Request for Copy of Tax Return. There is a charge for a copy of a return. For information on the cost and where to file, see the Form 4506 instructions.

If you just need information from your return, you can order a transcript in one of the following ways.
- Visit IRS.gov and click on *Order a Return or Account Transcript*.
- Call 1-800-908-9946.
- Use Form 4506-T, Request for Transcript of Tax Return, or Form 4506T-EZ, Short Form Request for Individual Tax Return Transcript.

There is no fee for a transcript. For more information, see Form 4506-T.

TAXORGANIZER

Disaster Preparedness. In addition to the IRS rules for documentation and records, taxpayers should take into consideration disaster preparedness to help prevent their loss. The IRS encourages taxpayers to back-up their records electronically and store them separately from the originals. It is also important to document your valuables to support any insurance or casualty loss claims. Taking photographs of your home and valuables is also an easy, yet effective, aid to help prove the value of items, should you ever have to. Affected taxpayers that need assistance with handling disaster-related issues can call 1-866-562-5227 to speak with an IRS specialist.

Basic Records

Basic records are documents that everybody should keep. These are the records that prove your income and expenses. If you own a home or investments, your basic records should contain documents related to those items.

Income. Your basic records prove the amounts you report as income on your tax return. Your income may include wages, dividends, interest, and partnership or S corporation distributions. Your records also can prove that certain amounts are not taxable, such as tax-exempt interest.

Note. If you receive a Form W-2, keep Copy C until you begin receiving social security benefits. This will help protect your benefits in case there is a question about your work record or earnings in a particular year.

Expenses. Your basic records prove the expenses for which you claim a deduction (or credit) on your tax return. Your deductions may include alimony, charitable contributions, mortgage interest, and real estate taxes. You also may have child care expenses for which you can claim a credit.

Home. Your basic records should enable you to determine the basis or adjusted basis of your home. You need this information to determine if you have a gain or loss when you sell your home or to figure depreciation if you use part of your home for business purposes or for rent. Your records should show the purchase price, settlement or closing costs, and the cost of any improvements. They also may show any casualty losses deducted and insurance reimbursements for casualty losses. Your records also should include a copy of Form 2119, Sale of Your Home, if you sold your previous home before May 7, 1997, and postponed tax on the gain from that sale.

For detailed information on basis, including which settlement or closing costs are included in the basis of your home, see chapter 13.

When you sell your home, your records should show the sales price and any selling expenses, such as commissions. For information on selling your home, see chapter 15.

Investments. Your basic records should enable you to determine your basis in an investment and whether you have a gain or loss when you sell it. Investments include stocks, bonds, and mutual funds. Your records should show the purchase price, sales price, and commissions. They may also show any reinvested dividends, stock splits and dividends, load charges, and original issue discount (OID).

For information on stocks, bonds, and mutual funds, see chapters 8, 13, 14, and 16.

Proof of Payment

One of your basic records is proof of payment. You should keep these records to support certain amounts shown on your tax return. Proof of payment alone is not proof that the item claimed on your return is allowable. You also should keep other documents that will help prove that the item is allowable.

Generally, you prove payment with a cash receipt, financial account statement, credit card statement, canceled check, or substitute check. If you make payments in cash, you should get a dated and signed receipt showing the amount and the reason for the payment.

If you make payments using your bank account, you may be able to prove payment with an account statement.

Account statements. You may be able to prove payment with a legible financial account statement prepared by your bank or other financial institution.

Pay statements. You may have deductible expenses withheld from your paycheck, such as union dues or medical insurance premiums. You should keep your year-end or final pay statements as proof of payment of these expenses.

How Long to Keep Records

You must keep your records as long as they may be needed for the administration of any provision of the Internal Revenue Code. Generally, this means you must keep records that support items shown on your return until the period of limitations for that return runs out.

The period of limitations is the period of time in which you can amend your return to claim a credit or refund or the IRS can assess additional tax. Table 1-7 contains the periods of limitations that apply to income tax returns. Unless otherwise stated, the years refer to the period beginning after the return was filed. Returns filed before the due date are treated as being filed on the due date.

Property. Keep records relating to property until the period of limitations expires for the year in which you dispose of the property in a taxable disposition. You must keep these records to figure your basis for computing gain or loss when you sell or otherwise dispose of the property.

Generally, if you received property in a nontaxable exchange, your basis in that property is the same as the basis of the property you gave up. You must keep the records on the old property, as well as the new property, until the period of limitations expires for the year in which you dispose of the new property in a taxable disposition.

TAXORGANIZER

It would be wise to keep your income tax returns permanently. You should keep documents showing your basis in a piece of property for as long as you own that piece of property. If you sell a piece of property, you should keep your records showing your basis in the old property for at least 6 years after the sale. And, if you still receive canceled checks from your bank, we recommend that you keep them for 6 years.

If you do not keep the requisite records, it may be impossible for you to prove that you incurred deductible expenses or to establish your basis for gain or loss. Without such proof the IRS can deny you a deduction.

If you acquire property from an estate or by gift, it is advisable to secure a copy of the valuation of the estate or of the gift tax return so that you can determine the donor's basis in the property that you have been given. When acquiring property from an estate, the basis in the property is generally the fair market value at the date of the decedent's death if the decedent passed away before January 1, 2010, or after December 31, 2010. If the decedent passed away in 2010, your basis in the inherited property will generally be the lesser of the fair market value of the property on the decedent's date of death or the decedent's adjusted basis in the property.

Special rules allow for basis to be stepped up to specified limits on certain property inherited from a decedent who died during 2010. When receiving property as a gift, the taxpayer must know the donor's adjusted basis as well as the fair market value at the time of the gift in order to properly determine the basis used in calculating the gain or loss upon disposition. For more information, see chapter 44, *Estate and gift tax planning*.

Knowing the donor's basis, you can easily determine your gain or loss when you sell the property. See chapter 13, *Basis of property*, for more details on determining gains and losses from the sale of property.

Example

Your parents buy a house for you as a wedding present. You sell the house 10 years later. The only record of the initial transaction is in the county real estate records. You believe there were other costs associated with the purchase but you cannot find any records of them. If you claim the additional unsupported costs and the IRS examines your return for the year of the sale, it's likely that those costs will not be allowed. If you claim the additional costs and do not disclose on your return the lack of records to substantiate them, you could be subject to a penalty.

Table 1-7. **Period of Limitations**

IF you...	THEN the period is...
1 Owe additional tax and (2), (3), and (4) do not apply to you	3 years
2 Do not report income that you should and it is more than 25% of the gross income shown on your return	6 years
3 File a fraudulent return	No limit
4 Do not file a return	No limit
5 File a claim for credit or refund after you filed your return	The later of 3 years or 2 years after tax was paid.
6 File a claim for a loss from worthless securities	7 years

Refund Information

You can go online to check the status of your 2014 refund 24 hours after the IRS receives your e-filed return, or 4 weeks after you mail a paper return. If you filed Form 8379 with your return, allow 14 weeks (11 weeks if you filed electronically) before checking your refund status. Be sure to have a copy of your 2014 tax return handy because you will need to know the filing status, the first SSN shown on the return, and the exact whole-dollar amount of the refund. To check on your refund, do one of the following.

- Go to IRS.gov, and click on "Where's My Refund."
- Download the free IRS2GO app by visiting the iTunes app store or Google Play.
- Call 1-800-829-4477 24 hours a day, 7 days a week for automated refund information.

Interest on Refunds

If you are due a refund, you may get interest on it. The interest rates are adjusted quarterly.

If the refund is made within 45 days after the due date of your return, no interest will be paid. If you file your return after the due date (including extensions), no interest will be paid if the refund is made within 45 days after the date you filed. If the refund is not made within this 45-day period, interest will be paid from the due date of the return or from the date you filed, whichever is later.

Accepting a refund check does not change your right to claim an additional refund and interest. File your claim within the period of time that applies. See _Amended Returns and Claims for Refund_, later. If you do not accept a refund check, no more interest will be paid on the overpayment included in the check.

Interest on erroneous refund. All or part of any interest you were charged on an erroneous refund generally will be forgiven. Any interest charged for the period before demand for repayment was made will be forgiven unless:

1. You, or a person related to you, caused the erroneous refund in any way, or
2. The refund is more than $50,000.

For example, if you claimed a refund of $100 on your return, but the IRS made an error and sent you $1,000, you would not be charged interest for the time you held the $900 difference. You must, however, repay the $900 when the IRS asks.

Change of Address

If you have moved, file your return using your new address.

If you move after you filed your return, you should give the IRS clear and concise notification of your change of address. The notification may be written, electronic, or oral. Send written notification to the Internal Revenue Service Center serving your old address. You can use Form 8822, Change of Address. If you are expecting a refund, also notify the post office serving your old address. This will help in forwarding your check to your new address (unless you chose direct deposit of your refund). For more information, see Revenue Procedure 2010-16, 2010-19 I.R.B. 664, available at www.irs.gov/irb/2010-19_IRB/ar07.html.

Be sure to include your SSN (and the name and SSN of your spouse, if you filed a joint return) in any correspondence with the IRS.

What If I Made a Mistake?

Errors may delay your refund or result in notices being sent to you. If you discover an error, you can file an amended return or claim for refund.

Amended Returns and Claims for Refund

You should correct your return if, after you have filed it, you find that:

1. You did not report some income,
2. You claimed deductions or credits you should not have claimed,
3. You did not claim deductions or credits you could have claimed, or
4. You should have claimed a different filing status. (Once you file a joint return, you cannot choose to file separate returns for that year after the due date of the return. However, an executor may be able to make this change for a deceased spouse.)

If you need a copy of your return, see *Copies of tax returns* under *Kinds of Records to Keep*, earlier in this chapter.

Form 1040X. Use Form 1040X, Amended U.S. Individual Income Tax Return, to correct a return you have already filed. An amended tax return cannot be filed electronically.

Completing Form 1040X. On Form 1040X, enter your income, deductions, and credits as you originally reported them on your return, the changes you are making, and the corrected amounts. Then figure the tax on the corrected amount of taxable income and the amount you owe or your refund.

If you owe tax, pay the full amount with Form 1040X. The tax owed will not be subtracted from any amount you had credited to your estimated tax.

If you cannot pay the full amount due with your return, you can ask to make monthly installment payments. See *Installment Agreement*, earlier.

If you overpaid tax, you can have all or part of the overpayment refunded to you, or you can apply all or part of it to your estimated tax. If you choose to get a refund, it will be sent separately from any refund shown on your original return.

Filing Form 1040X. When completing Form 1040X, do not forget to show the year of your original return and explain all changes you made. Be sure to attach any forms or schedules needed to explain your changes. Mail your Form 1040X to the Internal Revenue Service Center serving the area where you now live (as shown in the instructions to the form). However, if you are filing Form 1040X in response to a notice you received from the IRS, mail it to the address shown on the notice.

File a separate form for each tax year involved.

Time for filing a claim for refund. Generally, you must file your claim for a credit or refund within 3 years after the date you filed your original return or within 2 years after the date you paid the tax, whichever is later. Returns filed before the due date (without regard to extensions) are considered filed on the due date (even if the due date was a Saturday, Sunday, or legal holiday). These time periods are suspended while you are <u>financially disabled</u>, discussed later.

If the last day for claiming a credit or refund is a Saturday, Sunday, or legal holiday, you can file the claim on the next business day.

If you do not file a claim within this period, you may not be entitled to a credit or a refund.

Protective claim for refund. Generally, a protective claim is a formal claim or amended return for credit or refund normally based on current litigation or expected changes in tax law or other legislation. You file a protective claim when your right to a refund is contingent on future events and may not be determinable until after the statute of limitations expires. A valid protective claim does not have to list a particular dollar amount or demand an immediate refund. However, a valid protective claim must:

- Be in writing and signed,
- Include your name, address, SSN or ITIN, and other contact information,
- Identify and describe the contingencies affecting the claim,
- Clearly alert the IRS to the essential nature of the claim, and
- Identify the specific year(s) for which a refund is sought.

Mail your protective claim for refund to the address listed in the instructions for Form 1040X, under *Where To File.*

Generally, the IRS will delay action on the protective claim until the contingency is resolved.

Limit on amount of refund. If you file your claim within 3 years after the date you filed your return, the credit or refund cannot be more than the part of the tax paid within the 3-year period (plus any extension of time for filing your return) immediately before you filed the claim. This time period is suspended while you are <u>financially disabled</u>, discussed later.

Tax paid. Payments, including estimated tax payments, made before the due date (without regard to extensions) of the original return are considered paid on the due date. For example, income tax withheld during the year is considered paid on the due date of the return, April 15 for most taxpayers.

Example 1. You made estimated tax payments of $500 and got an automatic extension of time to October 15, 2011, to file your 2010 income tax return. When you filed your return on that date, you paid an additional $200 tax. On October 15, 2014, you filed an amended return and claimed a refund of $700. Because you filed your claim within 3 years after you filed your original return, you can get a refund of up to $700, the tax paid within the 3 years plus the 6-month extension period immediately before you filed the claim.

Example 2. The situation is the same as in *Example 1*, except you filed your return on October 30, 2011, 2 weeks after the extension period ended. You paid an additional $200 on that date. On October 31, 2014, you filed an amended return and claimed a refund of $700. Although you filed your claim within 3 years from the date you filed your original return, the refund was limited to $200, the tax paid within the 3 years plus the 6-month extension period immediately before you filed the claim. The estimated tax of $500 paid before that period cannot be refunded or credited.

If you file a claim more than 3 years after you file your return, the credit or refund cannot be more than the tax you paid within the 2 years immediately before you file the claim.

Example. You filed your 2010 tax return on April 15, 2011. You paid taxes of $500. On November 5, 2012, after an examination of your 2010 return, you had to pay an additional tax of $200. On May 12, 2014, you file a claim for a refund of $300. However, because you filed your claim more than 3 years after you filed your return, your refund will be limited to the $200 you paid during the 2 years immediately before you filed your claim.

Financially disabled. The time periods for claiming a refund are suspended for the period in which you are financially disabled. For a joint income tax return, only one spouse has to be financially disabled for the time period to be suspended. You are financially disabled if you are unable to manage your financial affairs because of a medically determinable physical or mental impairment which can be expected to result in death or which has lasted or can be expected to last for a continuous period of not less than 12 months. However, you are not treated as financially disabled during any period your spouse or any other person is authorized to act on your behalf in financial matters.

To claim that you are financially disabled, you must send in the following written statements with your claim for refund.

1. A statement from your qualified physician that includes:
   a. The name and a description of your physical or mental impairment,
   b. The physician's medical opinion that the impairment prevented you from managing your financial affairs,
   c. The physician's medical opinion that the impairment was or can be expected to result in death, or that its duration has lasted, or can be expected to last, at least 12 months,
   d. The specific time period (to the best of the physician's knowledge), and
   e. The following certification signed by the physician: "I hereby certify that, to the best of my knowledge and belief, the above representations are true, correct, and complete."
2. A statement made by the person signing the claim for credit or refund that no person, including your spouse, was authorized to act on your behalf in financial matters during the period of disability (or the exact dates that a person was authorized to act for you).

Exceptions for special types of refunds. If you file a claim for one of the items in the following list, the dates and limits discussed earlier may not apply. These items, and where to get more information, are as follows.

- Bad debt. (See *Nonbusiness Bad Debts* in chapter 14.)
- Worthless security. (See *Worthless securities* in chapter 14.)
- Foreign tax paid or accrued. (See Publication 514, Foreign Tax Credit for Individuals.)
- Net operating loss carryback. (See Publication 536, Net Operating Losses (NOLs) for Individuals, Estates, and Trusts.)
- Carryback of certain business tax credits. (See Form 3800, General Business Credit.)
- Claim based on an agreement with the IRS extending the period for assessment of tax.

Processing claims for refund. Claims are usually processed 8–12 weeks after they are filed. Your claim may be accepted as filed, disallowed, or subject to examination. If a claim is examined, the procedures are the same as in the examination of a tax return.

If your claim is disallowed, you will receive an explanation of why it was disallowed.

Taking your claim to court. You can sue for a refund in court, but you must first file a timely claim with the IRS. If the IRS disallows your claim or does not act on your claim within 6 months after you file it, you can then take your claim to court. For information on the burden of proof in a court proceeding, see Publication 556.

The IRS provides a direct method to move your claim to court if:

- You are filing a claim for a credit or refund based solely on contested income tax or on estate tax or gift tax issues considered in your previously examined returns, and
- You want to take your case to court instead of appealing it within the IRS.

When you file your claim with the IRS, you get the direct method by requesting in writing that your claim be immediately rejected. A notice of claim disallowance will be sent to you.

You have 2 years from the date of mailing of the notice of claim disallowance to file a refund suit in the United States District Court having jurisdiction or in the United States Court of Federal Claims.

Interest on refund. If you receive a refund because of your amended return, interest will be paid on it from the due date of your original return or the date you filed your original return, whichever is later, to the date you filed the amended return. However, if the refund is not made within 45 days after you file the amended return, interest will be paid up to the date the refund is paid.

Reduced refund. Your refund may be reduced by an additional tax liability that has been assessed against you.

Also, your refund may be reduced by amounts you owe for past-due federal tax, state income tax, state unemployment compensation debts, child support, spousal support, or certain other federal nontax debts, such as student loans. If your spouse owes these debts, see *Offset against debts*, under *Refunds*, earlier, for the correct refund procedures to follow.

Effect on state tax liability. If your return is changed for any reason, it may affect your state income tax liability. This includes changes made as a result of an examination of your return by the IRS. Contact your state tax agency for more information.

TAXPLANNER

The IRS routinely shares information with most states that have state income taxes. If you file an amended federal tax return showing a balance due, you may avoid interest on tax due to the state and any penalties by taking the initiative and filing amended state tax returns when that is appropriate.

Penalties

The law provides penalties for failure to file returns or pay taxes as required.

Civil Penalties

If you do not file your return and pay your tax by the due date, you may have to pay a penalty. You may also have to pay a penalty if you substantially understate your tax, understate a reportable transaction, file an erroneous claim for refund or credit, file a frivolous tax submission, or fail to supply your SSN or individual taxpayer identification number. If you provide fraudulent information on your return, you may have to pay a civil fraud penalty.

Filing late. If you do not file your return by the due date (including extensions), you may have to pay a failure-to-file penalty. The penalty is usually 5% for each month or part of a month that a return is late, but not more than 25%. The penalty is based on the tax not paid by the due date (without regard to extensions).

Fraud. If your failure to file is due to fraud, the penalty is 15% for each month or part of a month that your return is late, up to a maximum of 75%.

Return over 60 days late. If you file your return more than 60 days after the due date or extended due date, the minimum penalty is the smaller of $135 or 100% of the unpaid tax.

Exception. You will not have to pay the penalty if you show that you failed to file on time because of reasonable cause and not because of willful neglect.

Paying tax late. You will have to pay a failure-to-pay penalty of ½ of 1% (.50%) of your unpaid taxes for each month, or part of a month, after the due date that the tax is not paid. This penalty does not apply during the automatic 6-month extension of time to file period if you paid at least 90% of your actual tax liability on or before the due date of your return and pay the balance when you file the return.

The monthly rate of the failure-to-pay penalty is half the usual rate (.25% instead of .50%) if an installment agreement is in effect for that month. You must have filed your return by the due date (including extensions) to qualify for this reduced penalty.

If a notice of intent to levy is issued, the rate will increase to 1% at the start of the first month beginning at least 10 days after the day that the notice is issued. If a notice and demand for immediate payment is issued, the rate will increase to 1% at the start of the first month beginning after the day that the notice and demand is issued.

This penalty cannot be more than 25% of your unpaid tax. You will not have to pay the penalty if you can show that you had a good reason for not paying your tax on time.

Combined penalties. If both the failure-to-file penalty and the failure-to-pay penalty (discussed earlier) apply in any month, the 5% (or 15%) failure-to-file penalty is reduced by the failure-to-pay penalty. However, if you file your return more than 60 days after the due date or extended due date, the minimum penalty is the smaller of $135 or 100% of the unpaid tax.

Accuracy-related penalty. You may have to pay an accuracy-related penalty if you underpay your tax because:

1. You show negligence or disregard of the rules or regulations,
2. You substantially understate your income tax,
3. You claim tax benefits for a transaction that lacks economic substance, or
4. You fail to disclose a foreign financial asset.

The penalty is equal to 20% of the underpayment. The penalty is 40% of any portion of the underpayment that is attributable to an undisclosed noneconomic substance transaction or an undisclosed foreign financial asset transaction. The penalty will not be figured on any part of an underpayment on which the fraud penalty (discussed later) is charged.

Negligence or disregard. The term "negligence" includes a failure to make a reasonable attempt to comply with the tax law or to exercise ordinary and reasonable care in preparing a return. Negligence also includes failure to keep adequate books and records. You will not have to pay a negligence penalty if you have a reasonable basis for a position you took.

The term "disregard" includes any careless, reckless, or intentional disregard.

TAXPLANNER

The IRS has a comprehensive program to compare the amounts of income reported as paid by payers on Form 1099 series information returns with the amounts of income reported by the payees on their income tax returns. If this document-matching program discloses apparently underreported income, you will receive a notice of additional tax due that may include imposition of a 20% negligence penalty. If you receive an information return showing income paid to you that, through no fault of your own, you did not receive in 2014 or that for some reason is not taxable to you, you should nevertheless report as income on your return the entire amount shown by the information return and subtract from that the amount you believe to be erroneous. Following this procedure usually will avoid automatic generation of the IRS notice and the inconvenience and frustration of corresponding with the IRS to get the matter resolved.

TAXALERT

The penalty in the case of a gross valuation misstatement is 40% of the portion of the underpayment attributable to the misstatement. A gross valuation misstatement is a misstatement with respect to which either the value or adjusted basis claimed on the return for any property is 200% or more of the correct value or adjusted basis. You should keep the necessary documentation in order to avoid the valuation misstatement penalty.

Example

Ted and Joan contributed property to a charity and claimed a charitable contribution deduction of $120,000 on their joint return. The property is actually worth only $54,000. Since the value of the property claimed on the return is more than 150% of the correct value, they are subject to a penalty of 40% on the difference between the amount of tax they should have paid if they claimed only $54,000 as a charitable contribution and the amount of tax they actually paid.

Adequate disclosure. You can avoid the penalty for disregard of rules or regulations if you adequately disclose on your return a position that has at least a reasonable basis. See *Disclosure statement*, later.

This exception will not apply to an item that is attributable to a tax shelter. In addition, it will not apply if you fail to keep adequate books and records, or substantiate items properly.

Substantial understatement of income tax. You understate your tax if the tax shown on your return is less than the correct tax. The understatement is substantial if it is more than the larger of 10% of the correct tax or $5,000. However, the amount of the understatement may be reduced to the extent the understatement is due to:

1. Substantial authority, or
2. Adequate disclosure and a reasonable basis.

If an item on your return is attributable to a tax shelter, there is no reduction for an adequate disclosure. However, there is a reduction for a position with substantial authority, but only if you reasonably believed that your tax treatment was more likely than not the proper treatment.

Substantial authority. Whether there is or was substantial authority for the tax treatment of an item depends on the facts and circumstances. Some of the items that may be considered are court opinions, Treasury regulations, revenue rulings, revenue procedures, and notices and announcements issued by the IRS and published in the Internal Revenue Bulletin that involve the same or similar circumstances as yours.

Disclosure statement. To adequately disclose the relevant facts about your tax treatment of an item, use Form 8275, Disclosure Statement. You must also have a reasonable basis for treating the item the way you did.

In cases of substantial understatement only, items that meet the requirements of Revenue Procedure 2012-51 (or later update) are considered adequately disclosed on your return without filing Form 8275.

Use Form 8275-R, Regulation Disclosure Statement, to disclose items or positions contrary to regulations.

Transaction lacking economic substance. For more information on economic substance, see Section 7701(o).

Foreign financial asset. For more information on undisclosed foreign financial assets, see Section 6662(j).

Reasonable cause. You will not have to pay a penalty if you show a good reason (reasonable cause) for the way you treated an item. You must also show that you acted in good faith. This does not apply to a transaction that lacks economic substance.

EXPLANATION

The IRS's explanation of the penalty for substantial understatement and how to avoid it oversimplifies a very complex situation.

Under regulations issued by the IRS, the following items may generally be considered substantial authority:

- Internal Revenue Code and other statutory provisions
- Temporary and final IRS regulations
- Court cases
- Administrative pronouncements (including revenue rulings and revenue procedures)
- Tax treaties and regulations issued as a result of a treaty
- Congressional intent as reflected in committee reports, joint explanatory statements of managers included in conference committee reports, and statements made in Congress by one of a bill's managers prior to enactment of a bill
- General explanations of tax legislation prepared by the Joint Committee on Taxation (the Blue Book)
- Proposed IRS regulations
- Information or press releases, notices, announcements, and any other similar documents published by the IRS in the Internal Revenue Bulletin
- Private letter rulings, technical advice memoranda, actions on decisions, and general counsel memoranda after they have been released to the public, if they are dated after March 12, 1981

TAXALERT

There is a 20% penalty on refund claims filed after May 25, 2007, that are filed without a reasonable basis. Under previous law, penalties applied to understatements of income tax but not to claims for refund.

Filing erroneous claim for refund or credit. You may have to pay a penalty if you file an erroneous claim for refund or credit. The penalty is equal to 20% of the disallowed amount of the claim, unless you can show a reasonable basis for the way you treated an item. However, any disallowed amount due to a transaction that lacks economic substance will not be treated as having a reasonable basis. The penalty will not be figured on any part of the disallowed amount of the claim that relates to the earned income credit or on which the accuracy-related or fraud penalties are charged.

Frivolous tax submission. You may have to pay a penalty of $5,000 if you file a frivolous tax return or other frivolous submissions. A frivolous tax return is one that does not include enough information to figure the correct tax or that contains information clearly showing that the tax you reported is substantially incorrect. For more information on frivolous returns, frivolous submissions, and a list of positions that are identified as frivolous, see Notice 2010-33, 2010-17 I.R.B. 609, available at www.irs.gov/irb/2010-17_IRB/ar13.html.

> ### *TAXALERT*
> You can also refer to the 2014 version of "The Truth about Frivolous Tax Arguments" (http://www.irs.gov/pub/irs-utl/friv_tax.pdf) for more information on frivolous tax arguments made by taxpayers.

You will have to pay the penalty if you filed this kind of return or submission based on a frivolous position or a desire to delay or interfere with the administration of federal tax laws. This includes altering or striking out the preprinted language above the space provided for your signature.

This penalty is added to any other penalty provided by law.

> ### *EXPLANATION*
> Congress enacted this penalty to attack a great variety of tax protest activities, including:
> 1. Irregular tax forms that cannot be processed
> 2. References to spurious constitutional arguments as a basis for not completing tax forms
> 3. Unallowable deductions claimed as a protest against military expenses
> 4. Deliberate use of incorrect Tax Tables
> 5. Presentation of clearly inconsistent information, such as a taxpayer who lists only two dependents while claiming 99 exemptions for withholding purposes

> ### *TAXALERT*
> Unlike most other penalties, the penalty for filing a frivolous return is not based on your tax liability. The penalty for filing a frivolous return will be assessed immediately and added to any other penalties.

Fraud. If there is any underpayment of tax on your return due to fraud, a penalty of 75% of the underpayment due to fraud will be added to your tax.

Joint return. The fraud penalty on a joint return does not apply to a spouse unless some part of the underpayment is due to the fraud of that spouse.

Failure to supply SSN. If you do not include your SSN or the SSN of another person where required on a return, statement, or other document, you will be subject to a penalty of $50 for each failure. You will also be subject to a penalty of $50 if you do not give your SSN to another person when it is required on a return, statement, or other document.

For example, if you have a bank account that earns interest, you must give your SSN to the bank. The number must be shown on the Form 1099-INT or other statement the bank sends you. If you do not give the bank your SSN, you will be subject to the $50 penalty. (You also may be subject to "backup" withholding of income tax. See chapter 4.)

You will not have to pay the penalty if you are able to show that the failure was due to reasonable cause and not willful neglect.

Criminal Penalties

You may be subject to criminal prosecution (brought to trial) for actions such as:

1. Tax evasion,
2. Willful failure to file a return, supply information, or pay any tax due,
3. Fraud and false statements,
4. Preparing and filing a fraudulent return, or
5. Identity theft.

TAXALERT

In addition to any of the other penalties discussed in this section, you can be charged a penalty for paying your tax with a bad check. The penalty may not be imposed if you submit a bad check in good faith and with reasonable cause to believe that it will be paid. The penalty is 2% of the amount of the check or, if the check is less than $1,250, the lesser of $25 or the amount of the check.

Identity Theft

Identity theft occurs when someone uses your personal information such as your name, SSN, or other identifying information, without your permission, to commit fraud or other crimes. An identity thief may use your SSN to get a job or may file a tax return using your SSN to receive a refund.

To reduce your risk:

- Protect your SSN,
- Ensure your employer is protecting your SSN, and
- Be careful when choosing a tax preparer.

If your tax records are affected by identity theft and you receive a notice from the IRS, respond right away to the name and phone number printed on the IRS notice or letter.

If your tax records are not currently affected by identity theft but you think you are at risk due to a lost or stolen purse or wallet, questionable credit card activity or credit report, etc., contact the IRS Identity Protection Specialized Unit at 1-800-908-4490 or submit Form 14039.

For more information, see Publication 4535, Identity Theft Prevention and Victim Assistance.

Victims of identity theft who are experiencing economic harm or a systemic problem, or are seeking help in resolving tax problems that have not been resolved through normal channels, may be eligible for Taxpayer Advocate Service (TAS) assistance. You can reach TAS by calling the National Taxpayer Advocate helpline at 1-877-777-4778 or TTY/TDD 1-800-829-4059. Deaf or hard-of-hearing individuals can also contact the IRS through relay services such as the Federal Relay Service available at www.gsa.gov/fedrelay.

TAXALERT

To keep up to date on the latest scams, go to *www.irs.gov* and enter "scam" in the search box. Additionally, the IRS releases its annual "Dirty Dozen" list of tax scams to help alert taxpayers about these schemes.

Protect yourself from suspicious emails or phishing schemes. Phishing is the creation and use of email and websites designed to mimic legitimate business emails and websites. The most common form is the act of sending an email to a user falsely claiming to be an established legitimate enterprise in an attempt to scam the user into surrendering private information that will be used for identity theft.

The IRS does not initiate contacts with taxpayers via emails. Also, the IRS does not request detailed personal information through email or ask taxpayers for the PIN numbers, passwords, or similar secret access information for their credit card, bank, or other financial accounts.

If you receive an unsolicited email claiming to be from the IRS, forward the message to: *phishing@irs.gov*. You may also report misuse of the IRS name, logo, forms or other IRS property to the Treasury Inspector General for Tax Administration toll-free at 1-800-366-4484. You can forward suspicious emails to the Federal Trade Commission at: *spam@uce.gov* or contact them at www.ftc.gov/idtheft or 1-877-ID-THEFT (1-877-438-4338).

Visit IRS.gov and enter "identity theft" in the search box to learn more about identity theft and how to reduce your risk.

Using social media can help you keep up to date on the latest news from the IRS. The centerpiece of IRS social media efforts is YouTube, where viewers can watch three different channels for short, informative videos in English, Spanish, and American Sign Language (ASL). The channels include more than 100 videos and have been viewed more than 7.5 million times. Videos are also featured on the IRS Facebook and Tumblr sites.

In addition, more than 95,500 people follow the IRS Twitter feeds. The latest tax information is available at @IRSnews and @IRSenEspanol. @IRStaxpros provides news and guidance for tax professionals. @RecruitmentIRS provides updates for job seekers, and the Taxpayer Advocate Service has information available @YourVoiceAtIRS.

Over 5.5 million people have downloaded the free IRS2Go phone app, which is available in both English and Spanish for Apple and Android devices. The totally redesigned IRS2Go 4.0 provides features to help taxpayers check on the status of their tax refunds, obtain tax records, find free tax preparation providers and stay connected with the IRS through social media channels such as YouTube and Twitter.

To protect taxpayer privacy, the IRS only uses social media tools to share public information, not to answer personal tax or account questions. It advises taxpayers to never post confidential information, like a Social Security number, on social media sites.

Chapter 2
Filing status

Note

IRS Publication 17 (*Your Federal Income Tax*) has been updated by Ernst & Young LLP for 2014. Dates and dollar amounts shown are for 2014. Underlined type is used to indicate where IRS text has been updated. Places where text has been removed are indicated by the sentence: *Text intentionally omitted.*

ey.com/EYTaxGuide
Ernst & Young LLP will update the *EY Tax Guide 2015* website with relevant taxpayer information as it becomes available. You can also sign up for email alerts to let you know when changes have been made.

Tip

If more than one filing status applies to you, choose the one that will give you the lowest tax.

Introduction
One of the first things to determine in preparing your income tax return is your filing status. There are five possible choices: single, married filing jointly, married filing separately, unmarried head of household, and qualifying widow or widower with a dependent child. Your choice of filing status dictates which Tax Table or Tax Rate Schedule to use in calculating your tax liability; whether you may claim an exemption for a dependent; whether you may be claimed as a dependent; and how much income you can have before you are taxed at all.

This chapter helps you determine which filing status to use. There are five filing statuses.
- Single.
- Married Filing Jointly.
- Married Filing Separately.
- Head of Household.
- Qualifying Widow(er) With Dependent Child

EXPLANATION
If your filing status changes during the year, you may not file under one status for one part of that year and under a second status for the remainder of the year. The law requires that your filing status for the entire year be determined by your status on the last day of the tax year. For example, even if you get married on December 31, you are treated as married for the entire year and you may either file as married filing jointly or married filing separately. Choose the one that will produce the lowest tax. (Note: If your spouse or a qualifying person died during the year, see the IRS explanation below under *Spouse died during the year*.)

You must determine your filing status before you can determine whether you must file a tax return (chapter 1), your standard deduction (chapter 21), and your tax (chapter 31). You also use your filing status to determine whether you are eligible to claim certain deductions and credits.

Useful Items
You may want to see:

Publication
- ☐ **501** Exemptions, Standard Deduction, and Filing Information
- ☐ **519** U.S. Tax Guide for Aliens
- ☐ **555** Community Property

Marital Status

In general, your filing status depends on whether you are considered unmarried or married.

Unmarried persons. You are considered unmarried for the whole year if, on the last day of your tax year, you are unmarried or legally separated from your spouse under a divorce or separate maintenance decree. State law governs whether you are married or legally separated under a divorce or separate maintenance decree.

Divorced persons. If you are divorced under a final decree by the last day of the year, you are considered unmarried for the whole year.

Divorce and remarriage. If you obtain a divorce for the sole purpose of filing tax returns as unmarried individuals, and at the time of divorce you intend to and do, in fact, remarry each other in the next tax year, you and your spouse must file as married individuals in both years.

Annulled marriages. If you obtain a court decree of annulment, which holds that no valid marriage ever existed, you are considered unmarried even if you filed joint returns for earlier years. You must file Form 1040X, Amended U.S. Individual Income Tax Return, claiming single or head of household status for all tax years that are affected by the annulment and are not closed by the statute of limitations for filing a tax return. Generally, for a credit or refund, you must file Form 1040X within 3 years (including extensions) after the date you filed your original return or within 2 years after the date you paid the tax, whichever is later. If you filed your original return early (for example, March 1), your return is considered filed on the due date (generally April 15). However, if you had an extension to file (for example, until October 15) but you filed earlier and we received it on July 1, your return is considered filed on July 1.

EXPLANATION

Invalid divorces. This is a very confusing subject because courts in different geographic locations disagree with each other. Furthermore, the courts and the IRS have interpreted the law differently.

Generally, the law in your state of residence determines whether you are legally married. The marital laws in every state require you to be unmarried before being allowed to get married. Therefore, you may not file a joint return with your second spouse unless the marital relationship with your first spouse has been severed. Only a few states recognize common-law marriage, and only residents of those states may file as married filing jointly if they are in a common-law marriage relationship.

While terminating a marriage is usually a matter of obtaining a divorce from a domestic or foreign court, it is not always that straightforward. When a particular state's law does not recognize the validity of a divorce decree acquired in another jurisdiction, the IRS and the courts disagree over the status of the divorce.

The Second and Third Circuit Courts of Appeals adhere to the so-called rule of validation. Basically, this rule specifies that a divorce in any court's jurisdiction must be recognized for the purposes of tax law. Consequently, under the rule of validation, a valid joint return may be filed with a second spouse. However, the IRS, the Tax Court, and the Ninth Circuit Court of Appeals do not support the rule of validation. Instead, they maintain that a second court possessing jurisdiction may declare a prior divorce invalid. Thus, a return filed jointly by a party of the invalid divorce and a subsequent marriage partner may not be valid. Nevertheless, neither these courts nor the IRS will challenge the validity of a divorce decree until a court of competent jurisdiction has declared the divorce invalid.

Prisoners of war. You are still considered to be married if your spouse is a prisoner of war (POW) or is listed as missing in action (MIA). Even if you subsequently discover that your spouse died in action or in captivity in a prior year, you cannot alter your married filing status on prior income tax returns.

TAXSAVER

When to get divorced. December is the better month to get divorced if spouses have similar incomes. In this way, you can file single returns for the entire year. January is the better month to get divorced if one spouse has considerably more income than the other and you both want to save on taxes.

The IRS contends that actions that are designed to control an individual's marital status at the close of the year for tax purposes, such as a year-end tax-motivated divorce followed by immediate remarriage, are shams and should be disregarded for tax purposes. According to the IRS, individuals retain their married status when:

1. A divorce under the laws of a foreign jurisdiction is obtained late in the year.
2. At the time of the divorce the parties intend to remarry.
3. The remarriage occurs in January of the next year.

However, a divorce followed by cohabitation is not necessarily a sham. The IRS has recognized such arrangements and has allowed individuals to claim single filing status as long as they say that they intend to remain divorced and not remarry each other.

TAXPLANNER

If you are getting a divorce, you should consider the impact of the alternative minimum tax (AMT) on special types of income. Accelerating these types of income or deferring related deductions may provide a greater benefit while still filing as married filing jointly. See chapter 31, *How to figure your tax*, for additional discussion of the AMT.

Head of household or qualifying widow(er) with dependent child. If you are considered unmarried, you may be able to file as a head of household or as a qualifying widow(er) with a dependent child. *See Head of Household* and *Qualifying Widow(er) With Dependent Child* to see if you qualify.

Married persons. If you are considered married, you and your spouse can file a joint return or separate returns.

Considered married. You are considered married for the whole year if, on the last day of your tax year, you and your spouse meet any one of the following tests.

1. You are married and living together as a married couple.
2. You are living together in a common-law marriage recognized in the state where you now live or in the state where the common-law marriage began.
3. You are married and living apart, but not legally separated under a decree of divorce or separate maintenance.
4. You are separated under an interlocutory (not final) decree of divorce.

Same-sex marriage. For federal tax purposes, individuals of the same sex are considered married if they were lawfully married in a state (or foreign country) whose laws authorize the marriage of two individuals of the same sex, even if the state (or foreign country) in which they now live does not recognize same-sex marriage. The term "spouse" includes an individual married to a person of the same sex if the couple is lawfully married under state (or foreign) law. However, individuals who have entered into a registered domestic partnership, civil union, or other similar relationship that is not considered a marriage under state (or foreign) law are not considered married for federal tax purposes. For more details, see Publication 501.

may also be eligible to file a joint return for two tax years following the death of their spouse if certain requirements are met.

Head of household. A special filing status called "Head of Household" can save you a significant amount of taxes. If you qualify, you can use the lower rates and other benefits available for this status, such as potential eligibility for the earned income credit, a higher standard deduction than single or married filing separately, and additional personal exemptions that reduce your taxable income.

In order to qualify you must meet these requirements:

1. You must be unmarried or "considered unmarried" on the last day of the year,
2. You paid more than half the cost of keeping up a home for the year, and
3. A "qualifying person" lived with you in the home for more than half the year (except for temporary absences, such as school). If the "qualifying person," however, is your dependent parent, he or she does not have to live with you.

EXPLANATION

Registered domestic partnerships and civil unions. Individuals of the same sex and opposite sex who are in registered domestic partnerships (RDP), civil unions, or other similar formal relationships that are not marriages under state law are not considered as married or spouses for federal tax purposes. Such couples may not file a federal return using a married filing separately or jointly filing status. Instead, each partner can only select single filing status, or if qualified, the head of household filing status when filing their own federal income tax return.

In addition, an RDP in Nevada, Washington, or California generally must follow state community property laws and report half the combined community income of the individual and his or her RDP on their individual federal income tax returns, according to the IRS (see IRS Publication 555, *Community Property*, or a series of FAQs posted to the IRS website at "http://www.irs.gov/uac/Answers-to-Frequently-Asked-Questions-for-Registered-Domestic-Partners-and-Individuals-in-Civil-Unions" for more details). Each taxpayer is also entitled to half of any taxes withheld since the RDP is the recipient of one-half of the couple's community property income. These rules apply to RDPs in Nevada, Washington, and California because they have full community property rights in 2010 and following years. RDPs in California attained these rights as of January 1, 2007. Nevada RDPs attained them as of October 1, 2009, and Washington RDPs attained them as of June 12, 2008.

If you are in a registered domestic partnership, civil union, or other similar formal relationship that is not marriage under state law, you should consult with a professional tax advisor for advice on preparing your federal and state tax returns, as these rules are complex and are constantly evolving.

Example

John and Mark are RDPs in California. In 2014, John earned wages of $20,000 and Mark earned wages of $100,000. When applying the community property rules discussed above, John and Mark file separate Federal income tax returns; however, their income is split equally with each reporting income of $60,000 (one-half of their community income of $120,000), rather than John reporting income of $20,000 and Mark reporting income of $100,000 on their respective 2013-2014 Federal income tax returns. Each is also entitled to claim credit for half of the income tax withheld on their combined wages of $120,000.

Spouse died during the year. If your spouse died during the year, you are considered married for the whole year for filing status purposes.

If you did not remarry before the end of the tax year, you can file a joint return for yourself and your deceased spouse. For the next 2 years, you may be entitled to the special benefits described later under *Qualifying Widow(er) With Dependent Child.*

If you remarried before the end of the tax year, you can file a joint return with your new spouse. Your deceased spouse's filing status is married filing separately for that year.

Married persons living apart. If you live apart from your spouse and meet certain tests, you may be able to file as head of household even if you are not divorced or legally separated. If you qualify to file as head of household instead of married filing separately, your standard deduction will be higher. Also, your tax may be lower, and you may be able to claim the earned income credit. See *Head of Household*, later.

Single

Your filing status is single if you are considered unmarried and you do not qualify for another filing status. To determine your marital status, see *Marital Status*, earlier.

Widow(er). Your filing status may be single if you were widowed before January 1, 2014, and did not remarry before the end of 2014. You may, however, be able to use another filing status that will give you a lower tax. See *Head of Household* and *Qualifying Widow(er) With Dependent Child*, later, to see if you qualify.

How to file. You can file Form 1040. If you have taxable income of less than $100,000, you may be able to file Form 1040A. If, in addition, you have no dependents, and are under 65 and not blind, and meet other requirements, you can file Form 1040EZ. If you file Form 1040A or Form 1040, show your filing status as single by checking the box on line 1. Use the Single column of the Tax Table or Section A of the Tax Computation Worksheet to figure your tax.

Married Filing Jointly

You can choose married filing jointly as your filing status if you are considered married and both you and your spouse agree to file a joint return. On a joint return, you and your spouse report your combined income and deduct your combined allowable expenses. You can file a joint return even if one of you had no income or deductions.

If you and your spouse decide to file a joint return, your tax may be lower than your combined tax for the other filing statuses. Also, your standard deduction (if you do not itemize deductions) may be higher, and you may qualify for tax benefits that do not apply to other filing statuses.

EXPLANATION

Marriage tax penalty. Married taxpayers who earn approximately the same income may pay more tax if they file a joint return or file separate married returns than they would if they filed two single returns. This is known as the "marriage penalty."

Tax legislation enacted in 2013 included provisions to reduce the marriage penalty. Specifically, the basic standard deduction for joint returns is twice the amount of the standard deduction available to single filers. Also, the size of the 15% tax bracket (i.e., the range of taxable income subject to the 15% tax rate) for taxpayers who are married filing jointly is set at twice the size of the 15% bracket for single filers. Despite this relief, the marriage penalty can still impact married taxpayers who file jointly or even as married filing separately. This is because the size of the tax brackets for tax rates over 15% that apply to married taxpayers is smaller than the size of the corresponding rate bracket for an unmarried individual filing a single return. As a result, higher tax rates kick in at lower levels of taxable income for married taxpayers than for single taxpayers.

On the other hand, married couples with a large disparity in earnings and other taxable income may find that their combined taxes when filing a joint return is lower than the sum of the tax liabilities each would have had, had they been been unmarried with each filing as single. This is referred to as a "marriage bonus."

TAXPLANNER

Singles' tax penalty. A single person earning the same taxable income as a married person whose spouse has comparatively little taxable income will pay substantially more income tax than the married person. In other words, if you marry someone with little or no taxable income, your tax decreases. This is known as "the singles' tax penalty."

Example

Mary had a total income of $30,000, all from wages for 2014. John had a total income of $300 from interest income for 2014. If John and Mary marry on or before December 31, 2014, their joint tax liability on their gross income of $30,300, less standard deductions and exemptions, would be $1,000. If they wait until 2015 to marry, their combined tax liabilities in 2014, filing as single taxpayers, would be as follows:

Mary's tax:	$2,524
John's tax:	0
Total:	$2,524

Thus there is a singles' tax penalty of $1,524. One possible solution would be to get married quickly.

TAXSAVER

When to get married. If you are contemplating a winter marriage and one of you has more income than the other, choose December instead of January if you want to save on your taxes.

How to file. If you file as married filing jointly, you can use Form 1040. If you and your spouse have taxable income of less than $100,000, you may be able to file Form 1040A. If, in addition, you and your spouse have no dependents, are both under 65 and not blind, and meet other requirements, you can file Form 1040EZ. If you file Form 1040 or Form 1040A, show this filing status by checking the box on line 2. Use the *Married filing jointly* column of the Tax Table or Section B of the Tax Computation Worksheet to figure your tax.

Spouse died. If your spouse died during the year, you are considered married for the whole year and can choose married filing jointly as your filing status. See *Spouse died during the year* under Marital Status, earlier, for more information.

If your spouse died in 2015 before filing a 2014 return, you can choose married filing jointly as your filing status on your 2014 return.

Divorced persons. If you are divorced under a final decree by the last day of the year, you are considered unmarried for the whole year and you cannot choose married filing jointly as your filing status.

Tip

If you and your spouse each have income, you may want to figure your tax both on a joint return and on separate returns (using the filing status of married filing separately). You can choose the method that gives the two of you the lower combined tax.

Filing a Joint Return

Both you and your spouse must include all of your income, exemptions, and deductions on your joint return.

Accounting period. Both of you must use the same accounting period, but you can use different accounting methods. See *Accounting Periods* and *Accounting Methods* in chapter 1.

Joint responsibility. Both of you may be held responsible, jointly and individually, for the tax and any interest or penalty due on your joint return. This means that if one spouse does not pay the tax due, the other may have to. Or, if one spouse does not report the correct tax, both spouses may be responsible for any additional taxes assessed by the IRS. One spouse may be held responsible for all the tax due even if all the income was earned by the other spouse.

You may want to file separately if:

- You believe your spouse is not reporting all of his or her income, or
- You do not want to be responsible for any taxes due if your spouse does not have enough tax withheld or does not pay enough estimated tax.

Divorced taxpayer. You may be held jointly and individually responsible for any tax, interest, and penalties due on a joint return filed before your divorce. This responsibility may apply even if your divorce decree states that your former spouse will be responsible for any amounts due on previously filed joint returns.

Relief from joint responsibility. In some cases, one spouse may be relieved of joint responsibility for tax, interest, and penalties on a joint return for items of the other spouse that were incorrectly reported on the joint return. You can ask for relief no matter how small the liability.

There are three types of relief available.

1. Innocent spouse relief.
2. Separation of liability (available only to joint filers who are divorced, widowed, legally separated, or have not lived together for the 12 months ending on the date the election for this relief is filed).
3. Equitable relief.

You must file Form 8857, Request for Innocent Spouse Relief, to request relief from joint responsibility. Publication 971, Innocent Spouse Relief, explains these kinds of relief and who may qualify for them.

Signing a joint return. For a return to be considered a joint return, both spouses generally must sign the return.

Spouse died before signing. If your spouse died before signing the return, the executor or administrator must sign the return for your spouse. If neither you nor anyone else has yet been appointed as executor or administrator, you can sign the return for your spouse and enter "Filing as surviving spouse" in the area where you sign the return.

Spouse away from home. If your spouse is away from home, you should prepare the return, sign it, and send it to your spouse to sign so that it can be filed on time.

Injury or disease prevents signing. If your spouse cannot sign because of disease or injury and tells you to sign for him or her, you can sign your spouse's name in the proper space on the return followed by the words "By (your name), Husband (or Wife)." Be sure to also sign in the space provided for your signature. Attach a dated statement, signed by you, to the return. The statement should include the form number of the return you are filing, the tax year, and the reason your spouse cannot sign, and should state that your spouse has agreed to your signing for him or her.

Signing as guardian of spouse. If you are the guardian of your spouse who is mentally incompetent, you can sign the return for your spouse as guardian.

Spouse in combat zone. You can sign a joint return for your spouse if your spouse cannot sign because he or she is serving in a combat zone (such as the Persian Gulf Area, Serbia, Montenegro, Albania, or Afghanistan), even if you do not have a power of attorney or other statement. Attach a signed statement to your return explaining that your spouse is serving in a combat zone. For more information on special tax rules for persons who are serving in a combat zone, or who are in missing status as a result of serving in a combat zone, see Publication 3, Armed Forces' Tax Guide.

Other reasons spouse cannot sign. If your spouse cannot sign the joint return for any other reason, you can sign for your spouse only if you are given a valid power of attorney (a legal document giving you permission to act for your spouse). Attach the power of attorney (or a copy of it) to your tax return. You can use Form 2848, Power of Attorney and Declaration of Representative.

Nonresident alien or dual-status alien. Generally, a married couple cannot file a joint return if either one is a nonresident alien at any time during the tax year. However, if one spouse was a nonresident alien or dual-status alien who was married to a U.S. citizen or resident alien at the end of the year, the spouses can choose to file a joint return. If you do file a joint return, you and your spouse are both treated as U.S. residents for the entire tax year. See chapter 1 of Publication 519.

Married Filing Separately

You can choose married filing separately as your filing status if you are married. This filing status may benefit you if you want to be responsible only for your own tax or if it results in less tax than filing a joint return.

If you and your spouse do not agree to file a joint return, you must use this filing status unless you qualify for head of household status, discussed later.

You may be able to choose head of household filing status if you are considered unmarried because you live apart from your spouse and meet certain tests (explained later, under *Head of Household*). This can apply to you even if you are not divorced or legally separated. If you qualify to file as head of household, instead of as married filing separately, your tax may be lower, you may be able to claim the earned income credit and certain other credits, and your standard deduction will be higher. The head of household filing status allows you to choose the standard deduction even if your spouse chooses to itemize deductions. See *Head of Household*, later, for more information.

How to file. If you file a separate return, you generally report only your own income, exemptions, credits, and deductions. You can claim an exemption for your spouse only if your spouse had no gross income, is not filing a return, and was not the dependent of another person.

You can file Form 1040. If your taxable income is less than $100,000, you may be able to file Form 1040A. Select this filing status by checking the box on line 3 of either form. Enter your spouse's full name and SSN or ITIN in the spaces provided. If your spouse does not have and is not required to have an SSN or ITIN, enter "NRA" in the space for your spouse's SSN. Use the *Married filing separately* column of the Tax Table or Section C of the Tax Computation Worksheet to figure your tax.

Tip

You will generally pay more combined tax on separate returns than you would on a joint return for the reasons listed under Special Rules, later. However, unless you are required to file separately, you should figure your tax both ways (on a joint return and on separate returns). This way you can make sure you are using the filing status that results in the lowest combined tax. When figuring the combined tax of a married couple, you may want to consider state taxes as well as federal taxes.

Special Rules

If you choose married filing separately as your filing status, the following special rules apply. Because of these special rules, you usually pay more tax on a separate return than if you use another filing status you qualify for.

1. Your tax rate generally is higher than on a joint return.
2. Your exemption amount for figuring the alternative minimum tax is half that allowed on a joint return.
3. You cannot take the credit for child and dependent care expenses in most cases, and the amount you can exclude from income under an employer's dependent care assistance program is limited to $2,500 (instead of $5,000). If you are legally separated or living apart from your spouse, you may be able to file a separate return and still take the credit. For more information about these expenses, the credit, and the exclusion, see chapter 33.
4. You cannot take the earned income credit.
5. You cannot take the exclusion or credit for adoption expenses in most cases.
6. You cannot take the education credits (the American opportunity credit and lifetime learning credit), or the deduction for student loan interest. *Text intentionally omitted*.
7. You cannot exclude any interest income from qualified U.S. savings bonds you used for higher education expenses.
8. If you lived with your spouse at any time during the tax year:
   a. You cannot claim the credit for the elderly or the disabled, and
   b. You must include in income a greater percentage (up to 85%) of any social security or equivalent railroad retirement benefits you received.
9. The following credits and deductions are reduced at income levels half those for a joint return:
   a. The child tax credit,
   b. The retirement savings contributions credit,
   c. The deduction for personal exemptions, and
   d. Itemized deductions.
10. Your capital loss deduction limit is $1,500 (instead of $3,000 on a joint return).
11. If your spouse itemizes deductions, you cannot claim the standard deduction. If you can claim the standard deduction, your basic standard deduction is half the amount allowed on a joint return.

> ### TAXALERT
> If you choose married filing separately as your filing status, your home acquisition debt limit for purposes of determining your deductible home mortgage interest expense is reduced from $1 million to $500,000. Your home equity debt limit is also reduced from $100,000 to $50,000. Therefore, total mortgage interest deduction limitations are reduced from $1.1 million to $550,000 for married filing separate taxpayers.
>
> In 2012, the U.S. Tax Court ruled that a taxpayer electing married filing separately status is still subject to the "halved" mortgage interest deduction limitations (total of $550,000) even if his or her spouse claims no such deduction. This ruling clarified any confusion that the $1.1 million may be applied on a per-couple basis regardless of filing status.
>
> For more information on the deductibility of home mortgage interest paid, see chapter 24, *Interest expense*.

Adjusted gross income (AGI) limits. If your AGI on a separate return is lower than it would have been on a joint return, you may be able to deduct a larger amount for certain deductions that are limited by AGI, such as medical expenses.

> ### TAXSAVER
> Consider filing separate returns:
> 1. If you suspect that your spouse owes the IRS money. If you file a joint return, you will both be liable for any tax due.
> 2. If you can obtain a larger benefit from a deduction for a net operating loss against separate rather than joint income.

3. If you or your spouse has significant medical or miscellaneous expenses or casualty losses. A larger deduction may be obtained because only medical expenses exceeding 10% (7.5% if you or your spouse are age 65 or older by the end of the year), miscellaneous expenses exceeding 2%, and personal casualty losses exceeding 10% of adjusted gross income are deductible. Thus, the lower your adjusted gross income, the more medical, miscellaneous expenses, or casualty losses will be deductible.
4. If you are getting divorced. Overall tax savings will result from filing separately when, during the legal separation period, a high-bracket taxpayer deducts his or her alimony payment and an ex-spouse includes that alimony payment in his or her income at a lower marginal rate.
5. If both husband and wife have similar income and deductions.
6. If a spouse wishes to be responsible for only his or her tax liability.
   Consider filing a joint return:
1. If only one spouse has income.
2. If, as of the close of the tax year, you are a nonresident alien married to a citizen or resident of the United States, or you are a nonresident alien at the beginning of the tax year but a resident of the United States at the close of the year and you are married to a U.S. citizen or resident of the United States at the end of the year.

Individual retirement arrangements (IRAs). You may not be able to deduct all or part of your contributions to a traditional IRA if you or your spouse were covered by an employee retirement plan at work during the year. Your deduction is reduced or eliminated if your income is more than a certain amount. This amount is much lower for married individuals who file separately and lived together at any time during the year. For more information, see *How Much Can You Deduct* in chapter 17.

Rental activity losses. If you actively participated in a passive rental real estate activity that produced a loss, you generally can deduct the loss from your nonpassive income, up to $25,000. This is called a special allowance. However, married persons filing separate returns who lived together at any time during the year cannot claim this special allowance. Married persons filing separate returns who lived apart at all times during the year are each allowed a $12,500 maximum special allowance for losses from passive real estate activities. See *Limits on Rental Losses* in chapter 9.

Community property states. If you live in Arizona, California, Idaho, Louisiana, Nevada, New Mexico, Texas, Washington, or Wisconsin and file separately, your income may be considered separate income or community income for income tax purposes. See Publication 555.

Joint Return After Separate Returns

You can change your filing status from a separate return to a joint return by filing an amended return using Form 1040X.

You generally can change to a joint return any time within 3 years from the due date of the separate return or returns. This does not include any extensions. A separate return includes a return filed by you or your spouse claiming married filing separately, single, or head of household filing status.

Separate Returns After Joint Return

Once you file a joint return, you cannot choose to file separate returns for that year after the due date of the return.

EXPLANATION

If a husband and wife fail to file for a particular year, they may still file a joint return for that period, even if the return is as much as 3 years overdue. However, once the IRS has notified each spouse individually that he or she has not filed a return that is more than 3 years overdue, they cannot file a joint return.

Exception. A personal representative for a decedent can change from a joint return elected by the surviving spouse to a separate return for the decedent. The personal representative has 1 year from the due date of the return (including extensions) to make the change. See Publication 559, Survivors, Executors, and Administrators, for more information on filing a return for a decedent.

Head of Household

You may be able to file as head of household if you meet all the following requirements.

1. You are unmarried or "considered unmarried" on the last day of the year. See *Marital Status*, earlier, and *Considered Unmarried*, later.
2. You paid more than half the cost of keeping up a home for the year.
3. A qualifying person lived with you in the home for more than half the year (except for temporary absences, such as school). However, if the qualifying person is your dependent parent, he or she does not have to live with you. See *Special rule for parent*, later, under *Qualifying Person*.

Kidnapped child. A child may qualify you to file as head of household even if the child has been kidnapped. For more information, see Publication 501.

How to file. If you file as head of household, you can use Form 1040. If your taxable income is less than $100,000, you may be able to file Form 1040A. Indicate your choice of this filing status by checking the box on line 4 of either form. Use the *Head of a household* column of the Tax Table or Section D of the Tax Computation Worksheet to figure your tax.

Considered Unmarried

To qualify for head of household status, you must be either unmarried or considered unmarried on the last day of the year. You are considered unmarried on the last day of the tax year if you meet all the following tests.

1. You file a separate return (defined earlier under *Joint Return After Separate Returns*).
2. You paid more than half the cost of keeping up your home for the tax year.
3. Your spouse did not live in your home during the last 6 months of the tax year. Your spouse is considered to live in your home even if he or she is temporarily absent due to special circumstances. See *Temporary absences*, under *Qualifying Person*, later.
4. Your home was the main home of your child, stepchild, or foster child for more than half the year. (See *Home of qualifying person*, under *Qualifying Person*, later, for rules applying to a child's birth, death, or temporary absence during the year.)
5. You must be able to claim an exemption for the child. However, you meet this test if you cannot claim the exemption only because the noncustodial parent can claim the child using the rules described in *Children of divorced or separated parents (or parents who live apart)* under Qualifying Child in chapter 3, or in *Support Test for Children of Divorced or Separated Parents (or Parents Who Live Apart)* under Qualifying Relative in chapter 3. The general rules for claiming an exemption for a dependent are explained under *Exemptions for Dependents* in chapter 3.

Nonresident alien spouse. You are considered unmarried for head of household purposes if your spouse was a nonresident alien at any time during the year and you do not choose to treat your nonresident spouse as a resident alien. However, your spouse is not a qualifying person for head of household purposes. You must have another qualifying person and meet the other tests to be eligible to file as a head of household.

Choice to treat spouse as resident. You are considered married if you choose to treat your spouse as a resident alien. See Publication 519.

Keeping Up a Home

To qualify for head of household status, you must pay more than half of the cost of keeping up a home for the year. You can determine whether you paid more than half of the cost of keeping up a home by using Worksheet 2–1.

Costs you include. Include in the cost of keeping up a home expenses such as rent, mortgage interest, real estate taxes, insurance on the home, repairs, utilities, and food eaten in the home.

If the total amount you paid is more than the amount others paid, you meet the requirement of paying more than half the cost of keeping up the home.

If you used payments you received under Temporary Assistance for Needy Families (TANF) or other public assistance programs to pay part of the cost of keeping up your home, you cannot count them as money you paid. However, you must include them in the total cost of keeping up your home to figure if you paid over half the cost.

Costs you do not include. Do not include the costs of clothing, education, medical treatment, vacations, life insurance, or transportation. Also, do not include the rental value of a home you own or the value of your services or those of a member of your household.

	Amount You Paid	Total Cost
Property taxes	$ _____	$ _____
Mortgage interest expense	_____	_____
Rent	_____	_____
Utility charges	_____	_____
Repairs/maintenance	_____	_____
Property insurance	_____	_____
Food consumed on the premises	_____	_____
Other household expenses	_____	_____
Totals	$ _____	$ _____
Minus total amount you paid		(_____)
Amount others paid		$ _____

TAXPLANNER

If you are providing some support for your parents—but less than half of their total support—you should investigate targeting your support payments so that you can qualify as a head of household by establishing one of your parents as a dependent. For example, when you are providing funds to your parents for their support, some type of notation should be made on your check that specifically states for whom the money is being provided. In this fashion, you can clearly demonstrate that the 50% support requirement has been satisfied for at least one of your parents.

Qualifying Person

See Table 2-1 to see who is a qualifying person. Any person not described in Table 2-1 is not a qualifying person.

Example 1—child. Your unmarried son lived with you all year and was 18 years old at the end of the year. He did not provide more than half of his own support and does not meet the tests to be a qualifying child of anyone else. As a result, he is your qualifying child (see *Qualifying Child* in chapter 3) and, because he is single, your qualifying person for you to claim head of household filing status.

Example 2—child who is not qualifying person. The facts are the same as in Example 1 except your son was 25 years old at the end of the year and his gross income was $5,000. Because he does not meet the age test (explained under *Qualifying Child* in chapter 3), your son is not your qualifying child. Because he does not meet the gross income test (explained later under *Qualifying Relative* in chapter 3), he is not your qualifying relative. As a result, he is not your qualifying person for head of household purposes.

Example 3—girlfriend. Your girlfriend lived with you all year. Even though she may be your qualifying relative if the gross income and support tests (explained in chapter 3) are met, she is not your qualifying person for head of household purposes because she is not related to you in one of the ways listed under *Relatives who do not have to live with you* in chapter 3. See Table 2-1.

Example 4—girlfriend's child. The facts are the same as in *Example 3* except your girlfriend's 10-year-old son also lived with you all year. He is not your qualifying child and, because he is your girlfriend's qualifying child, he is not your qualifying relative (see *Not a Qualifying Child Test* in chapter 3). As a result, he is not your qualifying person for head of household purposes.

Home of qualifying person. Generally, the qualifying person must live with you for more than half of the year.

Special rule for parent. If your qualifying person is your father or mother, you may be eligible to file as head of household even if your father or mother does not live with you. However, you must be able to claim an exemption for your father or mother. Also, you must pay more than half the cost of keeping up a home that was the main home for the entire year for your father or mother.

You are keeping up a main home for your father or mother if you pay more than half the cost of keeping your parent in a rest home or home for the elderly.

Caution

See the text of this chapter for the other requirements you must meet to claim head of household filing status.

Table 2-1. Who Is a Qualifying Person Qualifying You To File as Head of Household?[1]

IF the person is your...	AND...	THEN that person is...
qualifying child (such as a son, daughter, or grandchild who lived with you more than half the year and meets certain other tests)[2]	he or she is single	a qualifying person, whether or not you can claim an exemption for the person.
	he or she is married **and** you can claim an exemption for him or her	a qualifying person.
	he or she is married **and** you cannot claim an exemption for him or her	not a qualifying person.[3]
qualifying relative[4] who is your father or mother	you can claim an exemption for him or her[5]	a qualifying person.[6]
	you cannot claim an exemption for him or her	not a qualifying person.
qualifying relative[4] other than your father or mother (such as a grandparent, brother, or sister who meets certain tests)	he or she lived with you more than half the year, **and** he or she is related to you in one of the ways listed under _Relatives who do not have to live with you_ in chapter 3 **and** you can claim an exemption for him or her[5]	a qualifying person.
	he or she did not live with you more than half the year	not a qualifying person.
	he or she is not related to you in one of the ways listed under _Relatives who do not have to live with you_ in chapter 3 **and** is your qualifying relative only because he or she lived with you all year as a member of your household	not a qualifying person.
	you cannot claim an exemption for him or her	not a qualifying person.

[1] A person cannot qualify more than one taxpayer to use the head of household filing status for the year.
[2]The term "qualifying child" is defined in chapter 3. **Note.** If you are a noncustodial parent, the term "qualifying child" for head of household filing status does not include a child who is your qualifying child for exemption purposes only because of the rules described under _Children of divorced or separated parents (or parents who live apart)_ under _Qualifying Child_ in chapter 3. If you are the custodial parent and those rules apply, the child generally is your qualifying child for head of household filing status even though the child is not a qualifying child for whom you can claim an exemption.
[3]This person is a qualifying person if the only reason you cannot claim the exemption is that you can be claimed as a dependent on someone else's return.
[4]The term "qualifying relative" is defined in chapter 3.
[5]If you can claim an exemption for a person only because of a multiple support agreement, that person is not a qualifying person. See _Multiple Support Agreement_ in chapter 3.
[6]See _Special rule for parent_.

TAXALERT

Married child. Your child who is married at the end of the year generally cannot be your qualifying person unless you can claim the child as a dependent. However, the child is a qualifying person if all three of the following requirements are met.

- The child is your qualifying child (as defined under Exemptions for Dependents in chapter 3, _Personal exemptions and dependents_).
- The child does not file a joint return, unless the return is filed only as a claim for refund and no tax liability would exist for either spouse if they had filed separate returns.
- The child is a U.S. citizen or resident, or a resident of Canada or Mexico. (This requirement is met if you are a U.S. citizen and the child is an adopted child who lived with you all year as a member of your household.)

**Death or birth.** You may be eligible to file as head of household even if the individual who qualifies you for this filing status is born or dies during the year. If the individual is your qualifying child, the child must have lived with you for more than half the part of the year he or she was alive. If the individual is anyone else, see Publication 501.

Temporary absences. You and your qualifying person are considered to live together even if one or both of you are temporarily absent from your home due to special circumstances such as illness, education, business, vacation, or military service. It must be reasonable to assume the absent person will return to the home after the temporary absence. You must continue to keep up the home during the absence.

EXAMPLES

One court has held that a man still qualified for head of household status even though he temporarily moved out of his home after becoming legally separated. The court believed that the man had always intended to return to his home (and, in fact, he did return). The court was also aware that he had been awarded custody of his child.

Another court has held that a man could not claim that he was the head of the household that he maintained for his son where he himself did not live because of fear of his son.

Note: If your child or stepchild is absent from the home less than 6 months under a custody agreement, the absence is considered temporary.

EXPLANATION

Except when you are supporting and maintaining your parents, who do not have to live with you, the IRS says that you cannot qualify as head of household unless you live in the home that you are supporting and maintaining. However, some courts have said that you can maintain more than one home and still claim head of household status. The household that qualifies you as a head of household need not be your principal place of abode, but it must be the home where you and members of your household live for an adequate period of time.

Example 1

A woman who owned two homes, hundreds of miles apart, could still claim to be head of household at the home that was the principal place of residence of her adopted son, though she spent only 40% of her time there. For both homes, however, she paid more than half the cost of upkeep.

Example 2

A man could not claim to be head of household, although he paid 80%-90% of the household expenses and was a member of a nearby church, because he did not spend a substantial amount of time at the house. He only visited his sisters at the house, either when he was in town on business during the week or when he stopped by for Sunday dinner. The house was owned by his sisters.

Example 3

A woman who spent 85% of her time in one house and 15% in another house that was the principal residence of her daughter and grandchildren was not allowed to claim head of household status. In this case, the houses were less than 2 miles apart and the woman stayed over at her daughter's only when either she or her daughter were ill. Besides, the daughter, not her mother, rented the house, although the daughter used money given to her by her mother to pay the rent.

Example 4

The case of the two-family house. In this case, a husband, wife, and their children lived in one of the house's units and the wife's mother and unwed sister lived in the other unit. The home contained some common areas but also some partitioned areas for the private use of each family unit. A court upheld the wife's mother's claim of head of household status based on her support of her unwed daughter. Even though the mother paid less than half of the total household expenses, she did pay more than half of the expenses attributable to her and her daughter.

Qualifying Widow(er) With Dependent Child

If your spouse died in 2014, you can use married filing jointly as your filing status for 2014 if you otherwise qualify to use that status. The year of death is the last year for which you can file jointly with your deceased spouse. See *Married Filing Jointly*, earlier.

You may be eligible to use qualifying widow(er) with dependent child as your filing status for 2 years following the year your spouse died. For example, if your spouse died in 2013, and you have not remarried, you may be able to use this filing status for 2014 and 2015.

This filing status entitles you to use joint return tax rates and the highest standard deduction amount (if you do not itemize deductions). It does not entitle you to file a joint return.

How to file. If you file as qualifying widow(er) with dependent child, you can use Form 1040. If you also have taxable income of less than $100,000 and meet certain other conditions, you may be able to file Form 1040A. Check the box on line 5 of either form. Use the *Married filing jointly* column of the Tax Table or Section B of the Tax Computation Worksheet to figure your tax.

Eligibility rules. You are eligible to file your 2014 return as a qualifying widow(er) with dependent child if you meet all of the following tests.

- You were entitled to file a joint return with your spouse for the year your spouse died. It does not matter whether you actually filed a joint return.
- Your spouse died in 2012 or 2013 and you did not remarry before the end of 2014.
- You have a child or stepchild for whom you can claim an exemption. This does not include a foster child.
- This child lived in your home all year, except for temporary absences. See *Temporary absences*, earlier, under *Head of Household*. There are also exceptions, described later, for a child who was born or died during the year and for a kidnapped child.
- You paid more than half the cost of keeping up a home for the year. See *Keeping Up a Home*, earlier, under *Head of Household*.

Example. John's wife died in 2012. John has not remarried. During 2013 and 2014, he continued to keep up a home for himself and his child, who lives with him and for whom he can claim an exemption. For 2012 he was entitled to file a joint return for himself and his deceased wife. For 2013 and 2014, he can file as qualifying widower with a dependent child. After 2014 he can file as head of household if he qualifies.

Death or birth. You may be eligible to file as a qualifying widow(er) with dependent child if the child who qualifies you for this filing status is born or dies during the year. You must have provided more than half of the cost of keeping up a home that was the child's main home during the entire part of the year he or she was alive.

Kidnapped child. A child may qualify you for qualifying widow(er) with dependent child, even if the child has been kidnapped. See Publication 501.

Caution

As mentioned earlier, this filing status is available for only 2 years following the year your spouse died.

Chapter 3
Personal exemptions and dependents

Exemptions...61
    Personal Exemptions 61
    Exemptions for Dependents 62
    Qualifying Child 64
    Joint Return Test (To Be a Qualifying Child).......................................69
    Qualifying Relative 74
Phaseout of Exemptions 85
Social Security Numbers for Dependents 86

Note

IRS Publication 17 (*Your Federal Income Tax*) has been updated by Ernst & Young LLP for 2014. Dates and dollar amounts shown are for 2014. Underlined type is used to indicate where IRS text has been updated. Places where text has been removed are indicated by the sentence: *Text intentionally omitted*.

ey.com/EYTaxGuide

Ernst & Young LLP will update the *EY Tax Guide 2015* website with relevant taxpayer information as it becomes available. You can also sign up for email alerts to let you know when changes have been made.

Introduction

In 2014, you are entitled to a $3,950 deduction for yourself, your spouse, and each person you support who otherwise qualifies as a dependent. This is a $50 increase over the personal exemption amount of $3,900 that was effective for 2013. The amount of the personal exemption generally increases over time because of the statutory requirement to adjust the amount annually for inflation. This chapter tells you what specific qualifications you have to meet to take this deduction. This chapter also informs you about the special rules and procedures that apply to divorced and separated couples with children, widows and widowers, and residents of community property states. Perhaps most important, this chapter suggests when it might not be a good idea to take a deduction, even though you could qualify for it.

There are two types of dependents: a qualifying child and a qualifying relative.

First, a word about a qualifying child. A uniform definition of a "qualifying child" applies to all of the following tax benefits:

1. Dependency exemption
2. Child tax credit
3. Earned income credit
4. Child and dependent care credit
5. Head of household filing status
6. The exclusion from income for dependent care benefits

In order to claim an exemption for a qualifying child, the following four tests must be met:

1. Relationship test
2. Residency test
3. Age test
4. Support test

In addition to these four tests, the child must not file a joint return, unless the return was filed only as a claim for refund. In addition, special rules apply if the child is a qualifying child of more than one person. These tests are discussed in greater detail later in this chapter. You should be aware, however, that a child who is not a qualifying child might still be a dependent as a qualifying relative. Other rules apply in determining whether someone is a "qualifying relative." These rules are also discussed in detail in this chapter.

The original intent of personal *exemptions* for dependents was to provide tax relief so that even the poorest citizen would be left with enough money after taxes to support themselves and their family. Obviously, a $3,950 deduction can save the taxpayer only a small portion of the income necessary to live. Ironically, the higher your income level and the higher your marginal tax rate, the greater economic benefit you derive from these deductions. A $3,950 deduction is worth $593 to a married couple filing a joint return with a taxable income of up to $73,800 and a marginal tax rate of 15%. The same $3,950 deduction is worth $1,106 to a married couple filing a joint return with a taxable income over $148,850 and a marginal tax rate of 28%. Figuring out who should claim whom as a dependent can be a difficult matter. For example, when parents are divorced, the custodial parent may sign a declaration permitting the noncustodial parent to claim the exemption for the dependent child. Consequently, if the noncustodial parent is in a higher tax bracket, a greater tax benefit can be obtained. However,

59

Personal exemption. You can claim a deduction for yourself, called a personal exemption. You can claim a deduction for your spouse on a joint return. You can also claim a deduction for each of your dependents. In 2014, the exemption amount is $3,950 (each year it is indexed for inflation). The amount of the personal exemption is not prorated. That means if your dependent was born or died in 2014, you are still entitled to the full $3,950 exemption for the dependent even though he or she did not live with you for the full year. The amount of your allowable deduction is phased out once your adjusted gross income goes above a certain level for your filing status. See Phaseout of Exemptions for details.

Personal exemption for dependent. You can claim an exemption for each dependent who meets the definition of either a "qualifying child" or a "qualifying relative" and who also meets certain additional tests as explained in detail later in this chapter. Below are some helpful hints regarding planning and the personal exemption for dependents:

(1) If you claim your child as a dependent, only you may claim the education credit for the child's qualified tuition and related expenses. If, however, you are eligible to claim your child as a dependent but choose not to do so, your child may claim the education credit for his or her qualified tuition and related expenses even if the tuition and expenses were paid by you, the parent. It is important to note,

if the noncustodial parent has an income over $305,050 and a filing status of married filing jointly, he or she will have a reduction in the tax benefit received due to the fact that the exemption is phased out for high income earners. The exemption is fully phased out and there is no tax benefit if you have an income above $427,550 and a filing status of married filing jointly. Either parent is entitled to claim the medical expenses paid for the child, even if that parent cannot claim the child as a dependent.

What's New

Exemption amount. The amount you can deduct for each exemption has increased. It was $3,900 for 2013. It is $3,950 for 2014.

Reminders

Exemption phaseout. You lose at least part of the benefit of your exemptions if your adjusted gross income is more than a certain amount. For 2014, this amount is $152,525 for a married individual filing a separate return; $254,200 for a single individual; $279,650 for a head of household; and $305,050 for married individuals filing jointly or a qualifying widow(er). See *Phaseout of Exemptions*, later.

TAXPLANNER

In 2014, the amount of your allowable deduction for personal exemptions is phased out once your adjusted gross income goes above a certain level for your filing status. See the chart below for details.

Filing status	AGI-Beginning of phaseout	AGI-Phaseout completed
Married filing jointly and qualifying widow(er)s	$305,050	$427,550
Head of household	$279,650	$402,150
Single (other than qualifying widow(er)s and head of household)	$254,200	$376,700
Married filing separately	$152,525	$213,775

This chapter discusses the following topics.
- Personal exemptions—You generally can take one for yourself and, if you are married, one for your spouse.
- Exemptions for dependents—You generally can take an exemption for each of your dependents. A dependent is your qualifying child or qualifying relative. If you are entitled to claim an exemption for a dependent, that dependent cannot claim a personal exemption on his or her own tax return.
- Phaseout of exemptions—Your deduction is reduced if your adjusted gross income is more than a certain amount.
- Social security number (SSN) requirement for dependents—You must list the SSN of any dependent for whom you claim an exemption.

Deduction. Exemptions reduce your taxable income. You can deduct $3,950 for each exemption you claim in 2014. But you may lose at least part of the dollar amount of your exemptions if your adjusted gross income is more than a certain amount. See *Phaseout of Exemptions*, later.

How to claim exemptions. How you claim an exemption on your tax return depends on which form you file.

If you file Form 1040EZ, the exemption amount is combined with the standard deduction amount and entered on line 5.

If you file Form 1040A, complete lines 6a through 6d. The total number of exemptions you can claim is the total in the box on line 6d. Also complete line 26.

If you file Form 1040, complete lines 6a through 6d. The total number of exemptions you can claim is the total in the box on line 6d. Also complete line 42.

Useful Items

You may want to see:

Publication

☐ **501**   Exemptions, Standard Deduction, and Filing Information

Form (and Instructions)

☐ **2120**   Multiple Support Declaration

☐ **8332**   Release/Revocation of Release of Claim to Exemption for Child by Custodial Parent

Exemptions

There are two types of exemptions you may be able to take:

- Personal exemptions for yourself and your spouse, and
- Exemptions for dependents (dependency exemptions).

While each is worth the same amount ($3,950 for 2014), different rules apply to each type.

Personal Exemptions

You are generally allowed one exemption for yourself. If you are married, you may be allowed one exemption for your spouse. These are called personal exemptions.

Your Own Exemption

You can take one exemption for yourself unless you can be claimed as a dependent by another taxpayer. If another taxpayer is entitled to claim you as a dependent, you cannot take an exemption for yourself even if the other taxpayer does not actually claim you as a dependent.

Your Spouse's Exemption

Your spouse is never considered your dependent.

> ### TAXPLANNER
> An exemption for your spouse is available only if you are married to that person on the last day of your tax year. See chapter 2, *Filing status*, for discussion of the marriage tax penalty, the singles' tax penalty, and the best time to marry for tax purposes.
>
> A common-law marriage is recognized for federal tax purposes if it is recognized by the state. Legal advice may be needed to determine if you have a common-law marriage.
>
> Same-sex couples who legally married in a state (including the District of Columbia) or foreign jurisdiction that recognizes same-sex marriages are treated as married for U.S. federal tax purposes—even if they reside in a jurisdiction that does not recognize same-sex marriage. However, registered domestic partners and individuals who enter into a civil union or other similar formal relationship are not treated as a married couple for federal tax purposes.

Joint return. On a joint return you can claim one exemption for yourself and one for your spouse.

> ### EXPLANATION
> Filing a joint return with your spouse will prevent anyone else from claiming him or her as a dependent, even if that person was otherwise entitled to do so. However, filing as married, filing separately, can allow someone else to claim your spouse as a dependent.
>
> #### Example
> Jake and Elena attended college for 6 months during 2014 and were married in November of that year. Jake earned $12,000 and Elena earned $3,000 during 2014. If the newlyweds file a joint income tax return, they will owe $0 in taxes. However, Elena's parents will then be unable to claim their daughter as a dependent, even though they provided more than half her support that year.
>
> If Jake and Elena file as married, filing separately, Elena will owe no tax and Jake will owe $185. In addition, Elena's parents, who are in the 28% tax bracket, will be entitled to claim Elena as a dependent, giving them a tax benefit of $1,106. Thus, if the newlyweds file separate returns, their overall tax liability combined with that of Elena's parents will be reduced by $921 (the $1,106 tax savings to Elena's parents less the additional $185 tax Jake and Elena incur by filing separate returns). If Jake's parents also provided half of his support in 2014 and can claim him as a dependent, the combined tax liability for everybody involved will be even lower.

Separate return. If you file a separate return, you can claim an exemption for your spouse only if your spouse had no gross income, is not filing a return, and was not the dependent of another

---

however, that if a parent who is eligible to claim a dependency exemption for a student does not do so, the student is not allowed to take a personal exemption for himself or herself on his or her own return. As a result, the exemption for the student may be lost. If you are subject to the income phaseout limitation of the education credits, you should review the overall tax effect of not claiming an exemption for your child and allowing your child to claim the education credits. You should not claim your child as your dependent if the education tax credit will provide a greater tax benefit for your child than your tax benefit from the $3,950 exemption amount. The maximum tax benefit for a married couple, in the 28% tax bracket, to claim a child as a dependent is $1,106. For further information, see chapter 36, *Education credits and other education tax benefits*.

(2) Generally, the parent in the higher tax bracket should be designated as the parent to claim the dependency exemption for a child, assuming that (1) the parent meets all the tests for claiming the dependency deduction and (2) the parent is not subject to the exemption phaseout for higher income taxpayers. If one parent's exemptions are partially or fully phased out, the other parent, although at a lower tax bracket, may receive a higher tax benefit by claiming the dependency exemption. Also, you need to consider if the person with the highest tax bracket is subject to alternative minimum tax (AMT) to maximize your tax savings. A taxpayer subject to the AMT receives no tax benefit from claiming a dependency deduction.

In that case, it will be more beneficial for the parent in the lower tax bracket to claim the child as a dependent. See chapter 31, *How to figure your tax*, for further discussion regarding the AMT.

taxpayer. This is true even if the other taxpayer does not actually claim your spouse as a dependent. You can claim an exemption for your spouse even if he or she is a nonresident alien; in that case, your spouse must have no gross income for U.S. tax purposes, must not be filing a return, and must not be the dependent of another taxpayer.

Death of spouse. If your spouse died during the year and you file a joint return for yourself and your deceased spouse, you generally can claim your spouse's exemption under the rules just explained in *Joint return*. If you file a separate return for the year, you may be able to claim your spouse's exemption under the rules just described in *Separate return*.

If you remarried during the year, you cannot take an exemption for your deceased spouse.

If you are a surviving spouse without gross income and you remarry in the year your spouse died, you can be claimed as an exemption on both the final separate return of your deceased spouse and the separate return of your new spouse for that year. If you file a joint return with your new spouse, you can be claimed as an exemption only on that return.

Divorced or separated spouse. If you obtained a final decree of divorce or separate maintenance during the year, you cannot take your former spouse's exemption. This rule applies even if you provided all of your former spouse's support.

TAXPLANNER
If you're getting divorced near the end of 2014, it may be better to postpone the divorce until January of 2015. In that way, you can claim an exemption for your spouse as well as use the married filing jointly tax rates when you file your 2014 tax return. However, the amount of the tax benefit from claiming an exemption for your spouse in 2014 will be reduced, and may even be completely eliminated to the extent your combined adjusted gross income exceeds $305,050. See Phaseout of Exemptions near the end of this chapter for more information.

Exemptions for Dependents
You are allowed one exemption for each person you can claim as a dependent. You can claim an exemption for a dependent even if your dependent files a return.

The term "dependent" means:
- A qualifying child, or
- A qualifying relative.

The terms "qualifying child" and "qualifying relative" are defined later.

EXPLANATION
Oddly enough, a qualifying child does not have to be your child and your child may be a qualifying relative and not a qualifying child.

You can claim an exemption for a qualifying child or qualifying relative only if these three tests are met.

1. Dependent taxpayer test.
2. Joint return test.
3. Citizen or resident test.

These three tests are explained in detail later.

All the requirements for claiming an exemption for a dependent are summarized in Table 3-1.

Caution

Dependent not allowed a personal exemption. If you can claim an exemption for your dependent, the dependent cannot claim his or her own personal exemption on his or her own tax return. This is true even if you do not claim the dependent's exemption on your return. It is also true if the dependent's exemption on your return is reduced or eliminated under the phaseout rule described under Phaseout of Exemptions, later.

TAXALERT
You are allowed only one exemption for each person who meets the qualifications listed above for a dependent. If your dependent is age 65 or older and/or blind, you can only deduct a $3,950 personal exemption for the dependent on your tax return and are not eligible to claim the additional standard deductions as discussed in chapter 21, *Standard deduction*. The additional standard deduction is only available with respect to you and/or your spouse to the extent you each qualify.

Housekeepers, maids, or servants. If these people work for you, you cannot claim exemptions for them.

Table 3-1. **Overview of the Rules for Claiming an Exemption for a Dependent**

Caution. This table is only an overview of the rules. For details, see the rest of this chapter.

• You cannot claim any dependents if you (or your spouse, if filing jointly) could be claimed as a dependent by another taxpayer.
• You cannot claim a married person who files a joint return as a dependent unless that joint return is filed only to claim a refund of withheld income tax or estimated tax paid.
• You cannot claim a person as a dependent unless that person is a U.S. citizen, U.S. resident alien, U.S. national, or a resident of Canada or Mexico.[1]
• You cannot claim a person as a dependent unless that person is your **qualifying child** or **qualifying relative**.

Tests To Be a Qualifying Child	Tests To Be a Qualifying Relative
1. The child must be your son, daughter, stepchild, foster child, brother, sister, half brother, half sister, stepbrother, stepsister, or a descendant of any of them.	1. The person cannot be your qualifying child or the qualifying child of any other taxpayer.
2. The child must be (a) under age 19 at the end of the year and younger than you (or your spouse, if filing jointly), (b) under age 24 at the end of the year, a student, and younger than you (or your spouse, if filing jointly), or (c) any age if permanently and totally disabled.	2. The person either (a) must be related to you in one of the ways listed under _Relatives who do not have to live with you_, or (b) must live with you all year as a member of your household[2] (and your relationship must not violate local law).
3. The child must have lived with you for more than half of the year.[2]	3. The person's gross income for the year must be less than $3,950.[3]
4. The child must not have provided more than half of his or her own support for the year.	4. You must provide more than half of the person's total support for the year.[4]
5. The child is not filing a joint return for the year (unless that return is filed only to get a refund of income tax withheld or estimated tax paid). If the child meets the rules to be a qualifying child of more than one person, only one person can actually treat the child as a qualifying child. See the _Special Rule for Qualifying Child of More Than One Person_ to find out which person is the person entitled to claim the child as a qualifying child.	

[1]There is an exception for certain adopted children.
[2]There are exceptions for temporary absences, children who were born or died during the year, children of divorced or separated parents (or parents who live apart), and kidnapped children.
[3]There is an exception if the person is disabled and has income from a sheltered workshop.
[4]There are exceptions for multiple support agreements, children of divorced or separated parents (or parents who live apart), and kidnapped children.

Child tax credit. You may be entitled to a child tax credit for each qualifying child who was under age 17 at the end of the year if you claimed an exemption for that child. For more information, see chapter 35.

Dependent Taxpayer Test
If you can be claimed as a dependent by another person, you cannot claim anyone else as a dependent. Even if you have a qualifying child or qualifying relative, you cannot claim that person as a dependent.

If you are filing a joint return and your spouse can be claimed as a dependent by someone else, you and your spouse cannot claim any dependents on your joint return.

Joint Return Test
You generally cannot claim a married person as a dependent if he or she files a joint return.

Exception. You can claim an exemption for a person who files a joint return if that person and his or her spouse file the joint return only to claim a refund of income tax withheld or estimated tax paid.

Example 1—child files joint return. You supported your 18-year-old daughter, and she lived with you all year while her husband was in the Armed Forces. He earned $25,000 for the year. The couple files a joint return. You cannot take an exemption for your daughter.

Example 2—child files joint return only as claim for refund of withheld tax. Your 18-year-old son and his 17-year-old wife had $800 of wages from part-time jobs and no other income. Neither is required to file a tax return. They do not have a child. Taxes were taken out of their pay so they filed a joint return only to get a refund of the withheld taxes. The exception to the joint return test applies, so you are not disqualified from claiming an exemption for each of them just because they file a joint return. You can claim exemptions for each of them if all the other tests to do so are met.

Example 3—child files joint return to claim American opportunity credit. The facts are the same as in Example 2 except no taxes were taken out of your son's pay. He and his wife are not required to file a tax return. However, they file a joint return to claim an American opportunity credit of $124 and get a refund of that amount. Because claiming the American opportunity credit is their reason for filing the return, they are not filing it only to get a refund of income tax withheld or estimated tax paid. The exception to the joint return test does not apply, so you cannot claim an exemption for either of them.

Citizen or Resident Test

You cannot claim a person as a dependent unless that person is a U.S. citizen, U.S. resident alien, U.S. national, or a resident of Canada or Mexico. However, there is an exception for certain adopted children, as explained next.

EXPLANATION
Residents of Puerto Rico do not meet the citizenship test unless they are also U.S. citizens.

Exception for adopted child. If you are a U.S. citizen or U.S. national who has legally adopted a child who is not a U.S. citizen, U.S. resident alien, or U.S. national, this test is met if the child lived with you as a member of your household all year. This exception also applies if the child was lawfully placed with you for legal adoption.

Child's place of residence. Children usually are citizens or residents of the country of their parents.

If you were a U.S. citizen when your child was born, the child may be a U.S. citizen and meet this test even if the other parent was a nonresident alien and the child was born in a foreign country.

EXAMPLE
The IRS has ruled that a U.S. citizen living in England since the age of 9, who subsequently married an Englishwoman, could not claim their son, who was born in England, as a dependent. The foreign-born child of a U.S. citizen and a nonresident alien is not a citizen or resident of the United States unless the American parent lived in the United States for 10 years before the child's birth. At least 5 of those 10 years must have been subsequent to age 14.

Foreign students' place of residence. Foreign students brought to this country under a qualified international education exchange program and placed in American homes for a temporary period generally are not U.S. residents and do not meet this test. You cannot claim an exemption for them. However, if you provided a home for a foreign student, you may be able to take a charitable contribution deduction. See *Expenses Paid for Student Living With You* in chapter 25.

EXPLANATION
For more information about taxes for aliens, see chapter 42, *Foreign citizens living in the United States* and IRS Publication 519, *U.S. Tax Guide for Aliens.*

U.S. national. A U.S. national is an individual who, although not a U.S. citizen, owes his or her allegiance to the United States. U.S. nationals include American Samoans and Northern Mariana Islanders who chose to become U.S. nationals instead of U.S. citizens.

Qualifying Child

Five tests must be met for a child to be your qualifying child. The five tests are:
1. Relationship,
2. Age,
3. Residency,
4. Support, and
5. Joint return.

These tests are explained next.

Relationship Test

To meet this test, a child must be:
- Your son, daughter, stepchild, foster child, or a descendant (for example, your grandchild) of any of them, or
- Your brother, sister, half brother, half sister, stepbrother, stepsister, or a descendant (for example, your niece or nephew) of any of them.

Adopted child. An adopted child is always treated as your own child. The term "adopted child" includes a child who was lawfully placed with you for legal adoption.

Foster child. A foster child is an individual who is placed with you by an authorized placement agency or by judgment, decree, or other order of any court of competent jurisdiction.

Age Test

To meet this test, a child must be:
- Under age 19 at the end of the year and younger than you (or your spouse, if filing jointly),
- A student under age 24 at the end of the year and younger than you (or your spouse, if filing jointly), or
- Permanently and totally disabled at any time during the year, regardless of age.

Example. Your son turned 19 on December 10. Unless he was permanently and totally disabled or a student, he does not meet the age test because, at the end of the year, he was not **under** age 19.

Child must be younger than you or spouse. To be your qualifying child, a child who is not permanently and totally disabled must be younger than you. However, if you are married filing jointly, the child must be younger than you or your spouse but does not have to be younger than both of you.

Example 1—child not younger than you or spouse. Your 23-year-old brother, who is a student and unmarried, lives with you and your spouse. He is not disabled. Both you and your spouse are 21 years old, and you file a joint return. Your brother is not your qualifying child because he is not younger than you or your spouse.

Example 2—child younger than your spouse but not younger than you. The facts are the same as in Example 1 except your spouse is 25 years old. Because your brother is younger than your spouse, and you and your spouse are filing a joint return, your brother is your qualifying child, even though he is not younger than you.

Student defined. To qualify as a student, your child must be, during some part of each of any 5 calendar months of the year:
1. A full-time student at a school that has a regular teaching staff, course of study, and a regularly enrolled student body at the school, or
2. A student taking a full-time, on-farm training course given by a school described in (1), or by a state, county, or local government agency.

The 5 calendar months do not have to be consecutive.

Full-time student. A full-time student is a student who is enrolled for the number of hours or courses the school considers to be full-time attendance.

School defined. A school can be an elementary school, junior or senior high school, college, university, or technical, trade, or mechanical school. However, an on-the-job training course, correspondence school, or school offering courses only through the Internet does not count as a school.

Vocational high school students. Students who work on "co-op" jobs in private industry as a part of a school's regular course of classroom and practical training are considered full-time students.

Permanently and totally disabled. Your child is permanently and totally disabled if both of the following apply.

- He or she cannot engage in any substantial gainful activity because of a physical or mental condition.
- A doctor determines the condition has lasted or can be expected to last continuously for at least a year or can lead to death.

Residency Test

To meet this test, your child must have lived with you for more than half the year. There are exceptions for temporary absences, children who were born or died during the year, kidnapped children, and children of divorced or separated parents.

Temporary absences. Your child is considered to have lived with you during periods of time when one of you, or both, are temporarily absent due to special circumstances such as:

- Illness,
- Education,
- Business,
- Vacation, or
- Military service.

Your child is also considered to have lived with you during any required hospital stay following birth, as long as the child would have lived with you during that time but for the hospitalization.

Death or birth of child. A child who was born or died during the year is treated as having lived with you more than half of the year if your home was the child's home more than half of the time he or she was alive during the year.

Child born alive. You may be able to claim an exemption for a child born alive during the year, even if the child lived only for a moment. State or local law must treat the child as having been born alive. There must be proof of a live birth shown by an official document, such as a birth certificate. The child must be your qualifying child or qualifying relative, and all the other tests to claim an exemption for a dependent must be met.

TAXPLANNER
You can take a dependency exemption for 2014 for a child born on or before December 31, 2014, but not for a baby born January 1, 2015. Plan accordingly!

TAXPLANNER
In addition to the personal exemption, a tax credit may be available for each qualifying child under age 17. The maximum per child credit for 2014 is $1,000. See chapter 35, *Child tax credit*, for additional information.

Stillborn child. You cannot claim an exemption for a stillborn child.

Kidnapped child. You may be able to treat your child as meeting the residency test even if the child has been kidnapped. See Publication 501 for details.

Children of divorced or separated parents (or parents who live apart). In most cases, because of the residency test, a child of divorced or separated parents is the qualifying child of the custodial parent. However, the child will be treated as the qualifying child of the noncustodial parent if all four of the following statements are true.

1. The parents:
   a. Are divorced or legally separated under a decree of divorce or separate maintenance,
   b. Are separated under a written separation agreement, or
   c. Lived apart at all times during the last 6 months of the year, whether or not they are or were married.
2. The child received over half of his or her support for the year from the parents.
3. The child is in the custody of one or both parents for more than half of the year.
4. Either of the following statements is true.
   a. The custodial parent signs a written declaration, discussed later, that he or she will not claim the child as a dependent for the year, and the noncustodial parent attaches this written declaration to his or her return. (If the decree or agreement went into effect after 1984 and before 2009, see *Post-1984 and pre-2009 divorce decree or separation agreement*, later. If the decree or agreement went into effect after 2008, see *Post-2008 divorce decree or separation agreement*, later.)
   b. A pre-1985 decree of divorce or separate maintenance or written separation agreement that applies to 2014 states that the noncustodial parent can claim the child as a dependent, the decree or agreement was not changed after 1984 to say the noncustodial parent cannot claim the child as a dependent, and the noncustodial parent provides at least $600 for the child's support during the year.

Custodial parent and noncustodial parent. The custodial parent is the parent with whom the child lived for the greater number of nights during the year. The other parent is the noncustodial parent.

If the parents divorced or separated during the year and the child lived with both parents before the separation, the custodial parent is the one with whom the child lived for the greater number of nights during the rest of the year.

A child is treated as living with a parent for a night if the child sleeps:
- At that parent's home, whether or not the parent is present, or
- In the company of the parent, when the child does not sleep at a parent's home (for example, the parent and child are on vacation together).

Equal number of nights. If the child lived with each parent for an equal number of nights during the year, the custodial parent is the parent with the higher adjusted gross income (AGI).

December 31. The night of December 31 is treated as part of the year in which it begins. For example, December 31, 2014, is treated as part of 2014.

Emancipated child. If a child is emancipated under state law, the child is treated as not living with either parent. See Examples 5 and 6.

Absences. If a child was not with either parent on a particular night (because, for example, the child was staying at a friend's house), the child is treated as living with the parent with whom the child normally would have lived for that night, except for the absence. But if it cannot be determined with which parent the child normally would have lived or if the child would not have lived with either parent that night, the child is treated as not living with either parent that night.

Parent works at night. If, due to a parent's nighttime work schedule, a child lives for a greater number of days, but not nights, with the parent who works at night, that parent is treated as the custodial parent. On a school day, the child is treated as living at the primary residence registered with the school.

Example 1—child lived with one parent for a greater number of nights. You and your child's other parent are divorced. In 2014, your child lived with you 210 nights and with the other parent 155 nights. You are the custodial parent.

Example 2—child is away at camp. In 2014, your daughter lives with each parent for alternate weeks. In the summer, she spends 6 weeks at summer camp. During the time she is at camp, she is treated as living with you for 3 weeks and with her other parent, your ex-spouse, for 3 weeks because this is how long she would have lived with each parent if she had not attended summer camp.

Example 3—child lived same number of nights with each parent. Your son lived with you 180 nights during the year and lived the same number of nights with his other parent, your ex-spouse. Your AGI is $40,000. Your ex-spouse's AGI is $25,000. You are treated as your son's custodial parent because you have the higher AGI.

Example 4—child is at parent's home but with other parent. Your son normally lives with you during the week and with his other parent, your ex-spouse, every other weekend. You become ill and are hospitalized. The other parent lives in your home with your son for 10 consecutive days while you are in the hospital. Your son is treated as living with you during this 10-day period because he was living in your home.

Example 5—child emancipated in May. When your son turned age 18 in May 2014, he became emancipated under the law of the state where he lives. As a result, he is not considered in the custody of his parents for more than half of the year. The special rule for children of divorced or separated parents does not apply.

Example 6—child emancipated in August. Your daughter lives with you from January 1, 2014, until May 31, 2014, and lives with her other parent, your ex-spouse, from June 1, 2014, through the end of the year. She turns 18 and is emancipated under state law on August 1, 2014. Because she is treated as not living with either parent beginning on August 1, she is treated as living with you the greater number of nights in 2014. You are the custodial parent.

Written declaration. The custodial parent may use either Form 8332 or a similar statement (containing the same information required by the form) to make the written declaration to release the exemption to the noncustodial parent. The noncustodial parent must attach a copy of the form or statement to his or her tax return.

The exemption can be released for 1 year, for a number of specified years (for example, alternate years), or for all future years, as specified in the declaration.

Post-1984 and pre-2009 divorce decree or separation agreement. If the divorce decree or separation agreement went into effect after 1984 and before 2009, the noncustodial parent may be able to attach certain pages from the decree or agreement instead of Form 8332. The decree or agreement must state all three of the following.

1. The noncustodial parent can claim the child as a dependent without regard to any condition, such as payment of support.
2. The custodial parent will not claim the child as a dependent for the year.
3. The years for which the noncustodial parent, rather than the custodial parent, can claim the child as a dependent.

The noncustodial parent must attach all of the following pages of the decree or agreement to his or her tax return.

- The cover page (write the other parent's social security number on this page).
- The pages that include all of the information identified in items (1) through (3) above.
- The signature page with the other parent's signature and the date of the agreement.

Post-2008 divorce decree or separation agreement. The noncustodial parent cannot attach pages from the decree or agreement instead of Form 8332 if the decree or agreement went into effect after 2008. The custodial parent must sign either Form 8332 or a similar statement whose only purpose is to release the custodial parent's claim to an exemption for a child, and the noncustodial parent must attach a copy to his or her return. The form or statement must release the custodial parent's claim to the child without any conditions. For example, the release must not depend on the noncustodial parent paying support.

Revocation of release of claim to an exemption. The custodial parent can revoke a release of claim to exemption that he or she previously released to the noncustodial parent on Form 8332 (or a similar statement). For the revocation to be effective for 2014, the custodial parent must have given (or made reasonable efforts to give) written notice of the revocation to the noncustodial parent in 2013 or earlier. The custodial parent can use Part III of Form 8332 for this purpose and must attach a copy of the revocation to his or her return for each tax year he or she claims the child as a dependent as a result of the revocation.

Remarried parent. If you remarry, the support provided by your new spouse is treated as provided by you.

Parents who never married. This special rule for divorced or separated parents also applies to parents who never married, and who lived apart at all times during the last 6 months of the year.

Support Test (To Be a Qualifying Child)

To meet this test, the child cannot have provided more than half of his or her own support for the year.

This test is different from the support test to be a qualifying relative, which is described later. However, to see what is or is not support, see *Support Test (To Be a Qualifying Relative)*, later. If you are not sure whether a child provided more than half of his or her own support, you may find Worksheet 3-1 helpful.

Example. You provided $4,000 toward your 16-year-old son's support for the year. He has a part-time job and provided $6,000 to his own support. He provided more than half of his own support for the year. He is not your qualifying child.

Foster care payments and expenses. Payments you receive for the support of a foster child from a child placement agency are considered support provided by the agency. Similarly, payments you receive for the support of a foster child from a state or county are considered support provided by the state or county.

If you are not in the trade or business of providing foster care and your unreimbursed out-of-pocket expenses in caring for a foster child were mainly to benefit an organization qualified to receive deductible charitable contributions, the expenses are deductible as charitable contributions but are not considered support you provided. For more information about the deduction for charitable contributions, see chapter 25. If your unreimbursed expenses are not deductible as charitable contributions, they may qualify as support you provided.

If you are in the trade or business of providing foster care, your unreimbursed expenses are not considered support provided by you.

Example 1. Lauren, a foster child, lived with Mr. and Mrs. Smith for the last 3 months of the year. The Smiths cared for Lauren because they wanted to adopt her (although she had not been placed with them for adoption). They did not care for her as a trade or business or to benefit the agency that placed her in their home. The Smiths' unreimbursed expenses are not deductible as charitable contributions but are considered support they provided for Lauren.

Example 2. You provided $3,000 toward your 10-year-old foster child's support for the year. The state government provided $4,000, which is considered support provided by the state, not by the child. See *Support provided by the state (welfare, food stamps, housing, etc.)*, later. Your foster child did not provide more than half of her own support for the year.

EXPLANATION
Unlike prior law, the current tax law does not consider the person who provides over half the support of the child as relevant for determining who is a qualifying child. What is relevant is that the child cannot provide over half of his or her own support during the year.

Scholarships. A scholarship received by a child who is a student is not taken into account in determining whether the child provided more than half of his or her own support.

Joint Return Test (To Be a Qualifying Child)
To meet this test, the child cannot file a joint return for the year.

Funds Belonging to the Person You Supported

1. Enter the total funds belonging to the person you supported, including income received (taxable and nontaxable) and amounts borrowed during the year, plus the amount in savings and other accounts at the beginning of the year. Do not include funds provided by the state; include those amounts on line 23 instead .... **1.** _____

2. Enter the amount on line 1 that was used for the person's support..................................... **2.** _____

3. Enter the amount on line 1 that was used for other purposes.. **3.** _____

4. Enter the total amount in the person's savings and other accounts at the end of the year................. **4.** _____

5. Add lines 2 through 4. (This amount should equal line 1.) .... **5.** _____

Expenses for Entire Household (where the person you supported lived)

6. Lodging (complete line 6a or 6b):...

    a. Enter the total rent paid.. **6a.** _____

    b. Enter the fair rental value of the home. If the person you supported owned the home, also include this amount in line 21 .... **6b.** _____

7. Enter the total food expenses.. **7.** _____

8. Enter the total amount of utilities (heat, light, water, etc. not included in line 6a or 6b) .... **8.** _____

9. Enter the total amount of repairs (not included in line 6a or 6b)... **9.** _____

10. Enter the total of other expenses. Do not include expenses of maintaining the home, such as mortgage interest, real estate taxes, and insurance.. **10.** _____

11. Add lines 6a through 10. These are the total household expenses .... **11.** _____

12. Enter total number of persons who lived in the household... **12.** _____

Expenses for the Person You Supported

13. Divide line 11 by line 12. This is the person's share of the household expenses .... **13.** _____

14. Enter the person's total clothing expenses .... **14.** _____

15. Enter the person's total education expenses .... **15.** _____

16. Enter the person's total medical and dental expenses not paid for or reimbursed by insurance .... **16.** _____

17. Enter the person's total travel and recreation expenses .... **17.** _____

18. Enter the total of the person's other expenses.. **18.** _____

19. Add lines 13 through 18. This is the total cost of the person's support for the year .... **19.** _____

Did the Person Provide More Than Half of His or Her Own Support?

20. Multiply line 19 by 50% (.50) .... **20.** _____

21. Enter the amount from line 2, plus the amount from line 6b if the person you supported owned the home. This is the amount the person provided for his or her own support .... **21.** _____

22. Is line 21 more than line 20?

    ☐ **No.** You meet the support test for this person to be your qualifying child. If this person also meets the other tests to be a qualifying child, stop here; do not complete lines 23-26. Otherwise, go to line 23 and fill out the rest of the worksheet to determine if this person is your qualifying relative.

    ☐ **Yes.** You do not meet the support test for this person to be either your qualifying child or your qualifying relative. **Stop here.**

Did You Provide More Than Half?

23. Enter the amount others provided for the person's support. Include amounts provided by state, local, and other welfare societies or agencies. Do not include any amounts included on line 1...........**23.** _____

24. Add lines 21 and 23..**24.** _____

25. Subtract line 24 from line 19. This is the amount you provided for the person's support ....**25.** _____

26. Is line 25 more than line 20?

    ☐ **Yes.** You meet the support test for this person to be your qualifying relative.

    ☐ **No.** You do not meet the support test for this person to be your qualifying relative. You cannot claim an exemption for this person unless you can do so under a multiple support agreement, the support test for children of divorced or separated parents, or the special rule for kidnapped children. See *Multiple Support Agreement* or *Support Test for Children of Divorced or Separated Parents (or Parents Who Live Apart)*, or *Kidnapped child* under *Qualifying Relative*.

Exception. An exception to the joint return test applies if your child and his or her spouse file a joint return only to claim a refund of income tax withheld or estimated tax paid.

Example 1—child files joint return. You supported your 18-year-old daughter, and she lived with you all year while her husband was in the Armed Forces. He earned $25,000 for the year. The couple files a joint return. Because your daughter and her husband file a joint return, she is not your qualifying child.

Example 2—child files joint return only as a claim for refund of withheld tax. Your 18-year-old son and his 17-year-old wife had $800 of wages from part-time jobs and no other income. Neither is required to file a tax return. They do not have a child. Taxes were taken out of their pay so they filed a joint return only to get a refund of the withheld taxes. The exception to the joint return test applies, so your son may be your qualifying child if all the other tests are met.

Example 3—child files joint return to claim American opportunity credit. The facts are the same as in Example 2 except no taxes were taken out of your son's pay. He and his wife were not required to file a tax return. However, they file a joint return to claim an American opportunity credit of $124 and get a refund of that amount. Because claiming the American opportunity credit is their reason for filing the return, they are not filing it only to get a refund of income tax withheld or estimated tax paid. The exception to the joint return test does not apply, so your son is not your qualifying child.

Special Rule for Qualifying Child of More Than One Person

TAXALERT

Children of divorced or separated parents. If a parent may claim the child as a qualifying child then no other person may claim such child as a qualifying child unless (1) the parents do not claim the child as a qualifying child, (2) the other person is eligible to claim the child as a qualifying child, and (3) the adjusted gross income of the other person is higher than the highest adjusted gross income of any parent of the child.

Sometimes, a child meets the relationship, age, residency, support, and joint return tests to be a qualifying child of more than one person. Although the child is a qualifying child of each of these persons, only one person can actually treat the child as a qualifying child to take all of the following tax benefits (provided the person is eligible for each benefit).

1. The exemption for the child.
2. The child tax credit.
3. Head of household filing status.
4. The credit for child and dependent care expenses.
5. The exclusion from income for dependent care benefits.
6. The earned income credit.

The other person cannot take any of these benefits based on this qualifying child. In other words, you and the other person cannot agree to divide these benefits between you. The other person cannot take any of these tax benefits for a child unless he or she has a different qualifying child.

Tiebreaker rules. To determine which person can treat the child as a qualifying child to claim these six tax benefits, the following tiebreaker rules apply.

- If only one of the persons is the child's parent, the child is treated as the qualifying child of the parent.
- If the parents file a joint return together and can claim the child as a qualifying child, the child is treated as the qualifying child of the parents.
- If the parents do not file a joint return together but both parents claim the child as a qualifying child, the IRS will treat the child as the qualifying child of the parent with whom the child lived for the longer period of time during the year. If the child lived with each parent for the same amount of time, the IRS will treat the child as the qualifying child of the parent who had the higher adjusted gross income (AGI) for the year.
- If no parent can claim the child as a qualifying child, the child is treated as the qualifying child of the person who had the highest AGI for the year.
- If a parent can claim the child as a qualifying child but no parent does so claim the child, the child is treated as the qualifying child of the person who had the highest AGI for the year, but only if that person's AGI is higher than the highest AGI of any of the child's parents who can claim the child. If the child's parents file a joint return with each other, this rule can be applied by dividing the parents' combined AGI equally between the parents. See *Example 6*.

Subject to these tiebreaker rules, you and the other person may be able to choose which of you claims the child as a qualifying child.

Tip

If your qualifying child is not a qualifying child of anyone else, this special rule does not apply to you and you do not need to read about it. This is also true if your qualifying child is not a qualifying child of anyone else except your spouse with whom you file a joint return.

Caution

If a child is treated as the qualifying child of the non-custodial parent under the rules for children of divorced or separated parents (or parents who live apart) described earlier, see Applying this special rule to divorced or separated parents (or parents who live apart), *later.*

EXPLANATION

The table below summarizes the tiebreaker rules:

When More Than One Person Files a Return Claiming the Same Qualifying Child (Tiebreaker Rule)

Caution. *if a child is treated as the qualifying child of the noncustodial parent under the rules for children of divorced or separated parents, see Applying this special test to divorced or separated parents or parents who live apart.*

IF more than one person files a return claiming the same qualifying child and...	THEN the child will be treated as the qualifying child of the...
only one of the persons is the child's parent,	parent.
two of the persons are parents of the child and they do not file a joint return together,	parent with whom the child lived for the longer period of time during the year.
two of the persons are parents of the child, they do not file a joint return together, and the child lived with each parent the same amount of time during the year,	parent with the higher adjusted gross income (AGI).
none of the persons are the child's parent,	person with the highest AGI.
the parents of the child can claim the child as a qualifying child, but no parent claims the child.	person whose AGI is higher than the highest AGI of any parent of the child, otherwise, no one else can claim the child as a qualifying child.*

*If the child's parents file a joint return with each other, this rule can be applied by dividing the parents' combined AGI equally between the parents.

Example 1—child lived with parent and grandparent. You and your 3-year-old daughter Jane lived with your mother all year. You are 25 years old, unmarried, and your AGI is $9,000. Your mother's AGI is $15,000. Jane's father did not live with you or your daughter. You have not signed Form 8332 (or a similar statement) to release the child's exemption to the noncustodial parent.

Jane is a qualifying child of both you and your mother because she meets the relationship, age, residency, support, and joint return tests for both you and your mother. However, only one of you can claim her. Jane is not a qualifying child of anyone else, including her father. You agree to let your mother claim Jane. This means your mother can claim Jane as a qualifying child for all of the six tax benefits listed earlier, if she qualifies (and if you do not claim Jane as a qualifying child for any of those tax benefits).

Example 2—parent has higher AGI than grandparent. The facts are the same as in *Example 1* except your AGI is $18,000. Because your mother's AGI is not higher than yours, she cannot claim Jane. Only you can claim Jane.

Example 3—two persons claim same child. The facts are the same as in *Example 1* except that you and your mother both claim Jane as a qualifying child. In this case, you, as the child's parent, will be the only one allowed to claim Jane as a qualifying child. The IRS will disallow your mother's claim to the six tax benefits listed earlier unless she has another qualifying child.

Example 4—qualifying children split between two persons. The facts are the same as in *Example 1* except you also have two other young children who are qualifying children of both you and your mother. Only one of you can claim each child. However, if your mother's AGI is higher than yours, you can allow your mother to claim one or more of the children. For example, if you claim one child, your mother can claim the other two.

Example 5—taxpayer who is a qualifying child. The facts are the same as in *Example 1* except you are only 18 years old and did not provide more than half of your own support for the year. This means you are your mother's qualifying child. If she can claim you as a dependent, then you cannot claim your daughter as a dependent because of the *Dependent Taxpayer Test* explained earlier.

Example 6—child lived with both parents and grandparent. The facts are the same as in *Example 1* except you are married to your daughter's father. The two of you live together with your daughter and your mother, and have an AGI of $20,000 on a joint return. If you and your husband do not claim your daughter as a qualifying child, your mother can claim her instead. Even though the AGI on your joint return, $20,000, is more than your mother's AGI of $15,000, for this purpose each parent's AGI can be treated as $10,000, so your mother's $15,000 AGI is treated as higher than the highest AGI of any of the child's parents who can claim the child.

Example 7—separated parents. You, your husband, and your 10-year-old son lived together until August 1, 2014, when your husband moved out of the household. In August and September, your son lived with you. For the rest of the year, your son lived with your husband, the boy's father. Your son is a qualifying child of both you and your husband because your son lived with each of you for more than half the year and because he met the relationship, age, support, and joint return tests for both of you. At the end of the year, you and your husband still were not divorced, legally separated, or separated under a written separation agreement, so the rule for children of divorced or separated parents (or parents who live apart) does not apply.

You and your husband will file separate returns. Your husband agrees to let you treat your son as a qualifying child. This means, if your husband does not claim your son as a qualifying child, you can claim your son as a qualifying child for the dependency exemption, child tax credit, and exclusion for dependent care benefits (if you qualify for each of those tax benefits). However, you cannot claim head of household filing status because you and your husband did not live apart for the last 6 months of the year. As a result, your filing status is married filing separately, so you cannot claim the earned income credit or the credit for child and dependent care expenses.

Example 8—separated parents claim same child. The facts are the same as in Example 7 except that you and your husband both claim your son as a qualifying child. In this case, only your husband will be allowed to treat your son as a qualifying child. This is because, during 2014, the boy lived with him longer than with you. If you claimed an exemption or the child tax credit for your son, the IRS will disallow your claim to both these tax benefits. If you do not have another qualifying child or dependent, the IRS will also disallow your claim to the exclusion for dependent care benefits. In addition, because you and your husband did not live apart for the last 6 months of the year, your husband cannot claim head of household filing status. As a result, his filing status is married filing separately, so he cannot claim the earned income credit or the credit for child and dependent care expenses.

Example 9—unmarried parents. You, your 5-year-old son, and your son's father lived together all year. You and your son's father are not married. Your son is a qualifying child of both you and his father because he meets the relationship, age, residency, support, and joint return tests for both you and his father. Your AGI is $12,000 and your son's father's AGI is $14,000. Your son's father agrees to let you claim the child as a qualifying child. This means you can claim him as a qualifying child for the dependency exemption, child tax credit, head of household filing status, credit for child and dependent care expenses, exclusion for dependent care benefits, and the earned income credit, if you qualify for each of those tax benefits (and if your son's father does not, in fact, claim your son as a qualifying child for any of those tax benefits).

Example 10—unmarried parents claim same child. The facts are the same as in Example 9 except that you and your son's father both claim your son as a qualifying child. In this case, only your son's father will be allowed to treat your son as a qualifying child. This is because his AGI, $14,000, is more than your AGI, $12,000. If you claimed an exemption or the child tax credit for your son, the IRS will disallow your claim to both these tax benefits. If you do not have another qualifying child or dependent, the IRS will also disallow your claim to the earned income credit, head of household filing status, the credit for child and dependent care expenses, and the exclusion for dependent care benefits.

Example 11—child did not live with a parent. You and your 7-year-old niece, your sister's child, lived with your mother all year. You are 25 years old, and your AGI is $9,300. Your mother's AGI is $15,000. Your niece's parents file jointly, have an AGI of less than $9,000, and do not live with you or their child. Your niece is a qualifying child of both you and your mother because she meets the relationship, age, residency, support, and joint return tests for both you and your mother. However, only your mother can treat her as a qualifying child. This is because your mother's AGI, $15,000, is more than your AGI, $9,300.

Applying this special rule to divorced or separated parents (or parents who live apart). If a child is treated as the qualifying child of the noncustodial parent under the rules described earlier for children of divorced or separated parents (or parents who live apart), only the noncustodial parent can claim an exemption and the child tax credit for the child. However, the custodial parent, if eligible, or other eligible person can claim the child as a qualifying child for head of household filing status, the credit for child and dependent care expenses, the exclusion for dependent care benefits, and the earned income credit. If the child is the qualifying child of more than one person for these benefits, then the tiebreaker rules just explained determine which person can treat the child as a qualifying child.

Example 1. You and your 5-year-old son lived all year with your mother, who paid the entire cost of keeping up the home. Your AGI is $10,000. Your mother's AGI is $25,000. Your son's father did not live with you or your son.

Under the rules explained earlier for children of divorced or separated parents (or parents who live apart), your son is treated as the qualifying child of his father, who can claim an exemption and the child tax credit for him. Because of this, you cannot claim an exemption or the child tax credit for your son. However, your son's father cannot claim your son as a qualifying child for head of household filing status, the credit for child and dependent care expenses, the exclusion for dependent care benefits, or the earned income credit.

You and your mother did not have any child care expenses or dependent care benefits, so neither of you can claim the credit for child and dependent care expenses or the exclusion for dependent care benefits. But the boy is a qualifying child of both you and your mother for head of household filing status and the earned income credit because he meets the relationship, age, residency, support, and joint return tests for both you and your mother. (Note: The support test does not apply for the earned income credit.) However, you agree to let your mother claim your son. This means she can claim him for head of household filing status and the earned income credit if she qualifies for each and if you do not claim him as a qualifying child for the earned income credit. (You cannot claim head of household filing status because your mother paid the entire cost of keeping up the home.)

Example 2. The facts are the same as in *Example 1* except your AGI is $25,000 and your mother's AGI is $21,000. Your mother cannot claim your son as a qualifying child for any purpose because her AGI is not higher than yours.

Example 3. The facts are the same as in *Example 1* except you and your mother both claim your son as a qualifying child for the earned income credit. Your mother also claims him as a qualifying child for head of household filing status. You, as the child's parent, will be the only one allowed to claim your son as a qualifying child for the earned income credit. The IRS will disallow your mother's claim to the earned income credit and head of household filing status unless she has another qualifying child.

Qualifying Relative
Four tests must be met for a person to be your qualifying relative. The four tests are:
1. Not a qualifying child test,
2. Member of household or relationship test,
3. Gross income test, and
4. Support test.

Age. Unlike a qualifying child, a qualifying relative can be any age. There is no age test for a qualifying relative.

Kidnapped child. You may be able to treat a child as your qualifying relative even if the child has been kidnapped. See Publication 501 for details.

Not a Qualifying Child Test
A child is not your qualifying relative if the child is your qualifying child or the qualifying child of any other taxpayer.

Example 1. Your 22-year-old daughter, who is a student, lives with you and meets all the tests to be your qualifying child. She is not your qualifying relative.

Example 2. Your 2-year-old son lives with your parents and meets all the tests to be their qualifying child. He is not your qualifying relative.

Example 3. Your son lives with you but is not your qualifying child because he is 30 years old and does not meet the age test. He may be your qualifying relative if the gross income test and the support test are met.

Example 4. Your 13-year-old grandson lived with his mother for 3 months, with his uncle for 4 months, and with you for 5 months during the year. He is not your qualifying child because he does not meet the residency test. He may be your qualifying relative if the gross income test and the support test are met.

Child of person not required to file a return. A child is not the qualifying child of any other taxpayer and so may qualify as your qualifying relative if the child's parent (or other person for whom the child is defined as a qualifying child) is not required to file an income tax return and either:
- Does not file an income tax return, or
- Files a return only to get a refund of income tax withheld or estimated tax paid.

Example 1—return not required. You support an unrelated friend and her 3-year-old child, who lived with you all year in your home. Your friend has no gross income, is not required to file a 2014 tax return, and does not file a 2014 tax return. Both your friend and her child are your qualifying relatives if the support test is met.

Example 2—return filed to claim refund. The facts are the same as in *Example 1* except your friend had wages of $1,500 during the year and had income tax withheld from her wages. She files a return only to get a refund of the income tax withheld and does not claim the earned income credit or any other tax credits or deductions. Both your friend and her child are your qualifying relatives if the support test is met.

Example 3—earned income credit claimed. The facts are the same as in *Example 2* except your friend had wages of $8,000 during the year and claimed the earned income credit on her return. Your friend's child is the qualifying child of another taxpayer (your friend), so you cannot claim your friend's child as your qualifying relative.

Child in Canada or Mexico. You may be able to claim your child as a dependent even if the child lives in Canada or Mexico. If the child does not live with you, the child does not meet the residency test to be your qualifying child. However, the child may still be your qualifying relative. If the persons the child does live with are not U.S. citizens and have no U.S. gross income, those persons are not "taxpayers," so the child is not the qualifying child of any other taxpayer. If the child is not the qualifying child of any other taxpayer, the child is your qualifying relative as long as the gross income test and the support test are met.

You cannot claim as a dependent a child who lives in a foreign country other than Canada or Mexico, unless the child is a U.S. citizen, U.S. resident alien, or U.S. national. There is an exception for certain adopted children who lived with you all year. See *Citizen or Resident Test*, earlier.

Example. You provide all the support of your children, ages 6, 8, and 12, who live in Mexico with your mother and have no income. You are single and live in the United States. Your mother is not a U.S. citizen and has no U.S. income, so she is not a "taxpayer." Your children are not your qualifying children because they do not meet the residency test. But since they are not the qualifying children of any other taxpayer, they are your qualifying relatives and you can claim them as dependents. You may also be able to claim your mother as a dependent if the gross income and support tests are met.

Member of Household or Relationship Test

To meet this test, a person must either:

1. Live with you all year as a member of your household, or
2. Be related to you in one of the ways listed under *Relatives who do not have to live with you*.

If at any time during the year the person was your spouse, that person cannot be your qualifying relative. However, see *Personal Exemptions*, earlier.

EXPLANATION

For an unrelated person to qualify as your dependent, he or she must live with you in your principal place of residence not merely in a house that you maintain for the entire year.

Relatives who do not have to live with you. A person related to you in any of the following ways does not have to live with you all year as a member of your household to meet this test.

- Your child, stepchild, foster child, or a descendant of any of them (for example, your grandchild). (A legally adopted child is considered your child.)
- Your brother, sister, half brother, half sister, stepbrother, or stepsister.
- Your father, mother, grandparent, or other direct ancestor, but not foster parent.
- Your stepfather or stepmother.
- A son or daughter of your brother or sister.
- A son or daughter of your half brother or half sister.
- A brother or sister of your father or mother.
- Your son-in-law, daughter-in-law, father-in-law, mother-in-law, brother-in-law, or sister-in-law.

Any of these relationships that were established by marriage are not ended by death or divorce.

Example. You and your wife began supporting your wife's father, a widower, in 2006. Your wife died in 2013. Despite your wife's death, your father-in-law continues to meet this test, even if he does not live with you. You can claim him as a dependent if all other tests are met, including the gross income test and support test.

Foster child. A foster child is an individual who is placed with you by an authorized placement agency or by judgment, decree, or other order of any court of competent jurisdiction.

Joint return. If you file a joint return, the person can be related to either you or your spouse. Also, the person does not need to be related to the spouse who provides support.

For example, your spouse's uncle who receives more than half of his support from you may be your qualifying relative, even though he does not live with you. However, if you and your spouse file separate returns, your spouse's uncle can be your qualifying relative only if he lives with you all year as a member of your household.

Temporary absences. A person is considered to live with you as a member of your household during periods of time when one of you, or both, are temporarily absent due to special circumstances such as:

- Illness,
- Education,
- Business,
- Vacation, or
- Military service.

If the person is placed in a nursing home for an indefinite period of time to receive constant medical care, the absence may be considered temporary.

Death or birth. A person who died during the year, but lived with you as a member of your household until death, will meet this test. The same is true for a child who was born during the year and lived with you as a member of your household for the rest of the year. The test is also met if a child lived with you as a member of your household except for any required hospital stay following birth.

If your dependent died during the year and you otherwise qualify to claim an exemption for the dependent, you can still claim the exemption.

Example. Your dependent mother died on January 15. She met the tests to be your qualifying relative. The other tests to claim an exemption for a dependent were also met. You can claim an exemption for her on your return.

Local law violated. A person does not meet this test if at any time during the year the relationship between you and that person violates local law.

Example. Your girlfriend lived with you as a member of your household all year. However, your relationship with her violated the laws of the state where you live, because she was married to someone else. Therefore, she does not meet this test and you cannot claim her as a dependent.

Adopted child. An adopted child is always treated as your own child. The term "adopted child" includes a child who was lawfully placed with you for legal adoption.

Cousin. Your cousin meets this test only if he or she lives with you all year as a member of your household. A cousin is a descendant of a brother or sister of your father or mother.

EXPLANATION

A dependent must be either a relative as described above or a full-time resident in your principal residence. Your child qualifies as a relative, even if you are not married to the child's other parent.

While your stepchild, stepfather, and stepmother all qualify as relatives, their blood relations do not. Even so, their blood relations may qualify as your dependents if they are full-time residents in your home.

While your spouse's brother and/or sister qualify as relatives to you, their spouses do not.

Example

Amy is married to Oliver. Amy's sister Laura, along with Laura's husband, Stephen, are relatives of Amy, but only Laura is a relative of Oliver. If Amy and Oliver file a joint tax return, Laura and Stephen may both be claimed as dependents (as relatives) if they otherwise qualify. But if Amy and Oliver file as married filing separately, Stephen would not be considered a relative of Oliver and could only be claimed as a dependent by Oliver if Stephen was a full-time resident in Oliver's personal residence.

Gross Income Test

To meet this test, a person's gross income for the year must be less than $3,950.

Gross income defined. Gross income is all income in the form of money, property, and services that is not exempt from tax.

In a manufacturing, merchandising, or mining business, gross income is the total net sales minus the cost of goods sold, plus any miscellaneous income from the business.

Gross receipts from rental property are gross income. Do not deduct taxes, repairs, or other expenses, to determine the gross income from rental property.

Gross income includes a partner's share of the gross (not a share of the net) partnership income.

EXAMPLE

Jamal's father retired 5 years ago and receives over half of his support from Jamal. The father is a partner in a real estate partnership, and his share of gross rental income from the partnership is $4,000 before expenses. After expenses, his net rental income is $200. Jamal may not claim his father as a dependent because his father's share of the partnership's gross rental income exceeds the $3,950 exemption amount.

Gross income also includes all taxable unemployment compensation and certain scholarship and fellowship grants. Scholarships received by degree candidates and used for tuition, fees, supplies, books, and equipment required for particular courses generally are not included in gross income. For more information about scholarships, see chapter 12.

Tax-exempt income, such as certain social security benefits, is not included in gross income.

EXPLANATION

Gross income also includes (1) gross profit from self-employment, (2) the full gain from the sale of stock or real estate, and (3) the gain on the sale of a personal residence.

Gross income does not include (1) tax-free municipal bond interest and (2) gifts received from others.

TAXSAVER

Because tax-free municipal bond interest is not included in gross income, a person who may possibly be claimed by another as a dependent may be better off holding municipal bonds rather than taxable bonds.

Example

Widower Nick, 63 years old, lives with his son and daughter-in-law. His only source of income is earnings from the $60,000 he has to invest. If he invests in a bond yielding 7%, he would receive $4,200 of taxable income. Because that is less than his $6,200 standard deduction, Nick would not have any tax liability. However, Nick's son would not be able to claim his father as a dependent because Nick would have more than $3,950 in gross income.

If Nick invests $50,000 in the 7% bond and $10,000 in a 4% tax-free municipal bond, his annual income would be $3,900 ($3,500 + $400), $300 less than if he put all his money in a taxable bond. His son would now be able to claim his father as a dependent, because Nick's gross income of $3,500 (gross income does not include the $400 of interest received from the municipal bond since that income is exempt from federal income tax). would be less than $3,950. However,

> Nick would now have to file a tax return because his total income is more than $1,000, the filing requirement threshold for dependents (see chapter 1, *Filing information*). If Nick is claimed as a dependent by his son, his standard deduction would also drop from $6,200 to $1,000 (see chapter 21, *Standard deduction*).
>
> The tax benefit to his son, which would vary based on his marginal tax rate, should be compared with Nick's lower yield and increased tax to see which is more beneficial.

Disabled dependent working at sheltered workshop. For purposes of the gross income test, the gross income of an individual who is permanently and totally disabled at any time during the year does not include income for services the individual performs at a sheltered workshop. The availability of medical care at the workshop must be the main reason for the individual's presence there. Also, the income must come solely from activities at the workshop that are incident to this medical care.

A "sheltered workshop" is a school that:

- Provides special instruction or training designed to alleviate the disability of the individual, and
- Is operated by certain tax-exempt organizations, or by a state, a U.S. possession, a political subdivision of a state or possession, the United States, or the District of Columbia.

"Permanently and totally disabled" has the same meaning here as under *Qualifying Child*, earlier.

Support Test (To Be a Qualifying Relative)

To meet this test, you generally must provide more than half of a person's total support during the calendar year.

However, if two or more persons provide support, but no one person provides more than half of a person's total support, see *Multiple Support Agreement*, later.

How to determine if support test is met. You figure whether you have provided more than half of a person's total support by comparing the amount you contributed to that person's support with the entire amount of support that person received from all sources. This includes support the person provided from his or her own funds.

You may find Worksheet 3-1 helpful in figuring whether you provided more than half of a person's support.

> ### EXPLANATION
> You may be able to claim someone as a dependent even though you provide support for less than half the year. Support depends on the amount spent, not the length of time over which it is spent. As long as you provide over 50% of the total amount of a person's support for a year, you may claim that person as a dependent.

Person's own funds not used for support. A person's own funds are not support unless they are actually spent for support.

Example. Your mother received $2,400 in social security benefits and $300 in interest. She paid $2,000 for lodging and $400 for recreation. She put $300 in a savings account.

Even though your mother received a total of $2,700 ($2,400 + $300), she spent only $2,400 ($2,000 + $400) for her own support. If you spent more than $2,400 for her support and no other support was received, you have provided more than half of her support.

Child's wages used for own support. You cannot include in your contribution to your child's support any support paid for by the child with the child's own wages, even if you paid the wages.

> ### EXPLANATION
> The gross income of a married couple residing in a community property state is generally split equally between each spouse for the purposes of the dependency deduction. Similarly, support for dependents is generally split equally between each spouse.
>
> #### Example
> Henry Smith provides more than 50% of the support for his son Jim and his daughter-in-law Jan, both of whom are over 19. Jim has no income and is not a student during 2014. Jan earns $8,000. Assuming that the other dependency tests are met, Henry Smith may claim his son Jim as a dependent in a common-law state. In a community property state, however, Henry could not claim Jim as a dependent, because each spouse is treated as having gross income of $4,000 (half of $8,000).

Year support is provided. The year you provide the support is the year you pay for it, even if you do so with borrowed money that you repay in a later year.

If you use a fiscal year to report your income, you must provide more than half of the dependent's support for the calendar year in which your fiscal year begins.

Armed Forces dependency allotments. The part of the allotment contributed by the government and the part taken out of your military pay are both considered provided by you in figuring whether you provide more than half of the support. If your allotment is used to support persons other than those you name, you can take the exemptions for them if they otherwise qualify.

Example. You are in the Armed Forces. You authorize an allotment for your widowed mother that she uses to support herself and her sister. If the allotment provides more than half of each person's support, you can take an exemption for each of them, if they otherwise qualify, even though you authorize the allotment only for your mother.

Tax-exempt military quarters allowances. These allowances are treated the same way as dependency allotments in figuring support. The allotment of pay and the tax-exempt basic allowance for quarters are both considered as provided by you for support.

Tax-exempt income. In figuring a person's total support, include tax-exempt income, savings, and borrowed amounts used to support that person. Tax-exempt income includes certain social security benefits, welfare benefits, nontaxable life insurance proceeds, Armed Forces family allotments, nontaxable pensions, and tax-exempt interest.

Example 1. You provide $4,000 toward your mother's support during the year. She has earned income of $600, nontaxable social security benefits of $4,800, and tax-exempt interest of $200. She uses all these for her support. You cannot claim an exemption for your mother because the $4,000 you provide is not more than half of her total support of $9,600 ($4,000 + $600 + $4,800 + $200).

Example 2. Your niece takes out a student loan of $2,500 and uses it to pay her college tuition. She is personally responsible for the loan. You provide $2,000 toward her total support. You cannot claim an exemption for her because you provide less than half of her support.

Social security benefits. If a married couple receives benefits that are paid by one check made out to both of them, half of the total paid is considered to be for the support of each spouse, unless they can show otherwise.

If a child receives social security benefits and uses them toward his or her own support, the benefits are considered as provided by the child.

Support provided by the state (welfare, food stamps, housing, etc.). Benefits provided by the state to a needy person generally are considered support provided by the state. However, payments based on the needs of the recipient will not be considered as used entirely for that person's support if it is shown that part of the payments were not used for that purpose.

Foster care. Payments you receive for the support of a foster child from a child placement agency are considered support provided by the agency. See *Foster care payments and expenses*, earlier.

Home for the aged. If you make a lump-sum advance payment to a home for the aged to take care of your relative for life and the payment is based on that person's life expectancy, the amount of support you provide each year is the lump-sum payment divided by the relative's life expectancy. The amount of support you provide also includes any other amounts you provided during the year.

EXAMPLE
Selena's mother resides in a senior citizens' home that is supported and operated by a church. It cost the church $6,000 last year to support Selena's mother. For Selena to claim her mother as a dependent, she must prove that she has provided more than $6,000 additional support for her mother, over and above the $6,000 provided by the church.

Total Support
To figure if you provided more than half of a person's support, you must first determine the total support provided for that person. Total support includes amounts spent to provide food, lodging, clothing, education, medical and dental care, recreation, transportation, and similar necessities.

EXPLANATION
Money that is not included in gross income, such as certain social security benefits, veterans' benefits, and so on, must be considered in determining support. For example, an amount borrowed by the person, or by you, and spent for support must be included in total support.

EXPLANATION
Generally, the IRS maintains that only expenditures necessary for essential support—basic food, housing, clothing, education, health, and transportation—qualify toward the 50% support test. Here is a quick list of broad areas in which expenditures will generally constitute support:
• Lodging, including utilities and telephone
• Room and board at a college or private school
• Clothing, laundry, and dry cleaning
• Education, including tuition, books, and supplies
• Medical expenses, including doctor, dentist, and health insurance premiums

- Transportation, including purchase of a car, its maintenance, and gas
- Child care, including babysitters and nursery school
- Charitable contributions on behalf of a dependent
- Payments to an institution for the care of an elderly parent

Courts, however, have been more lenient and allowed these additional types of expenditures to count as support:

- Music and drama lessons
- Summer camp
- Wedding costs, including receptions
- Entertainment, including movies, theater, spending money, toys, and vacations

EXPLANATION

Funding for education by contributing to education savings accounts and qualified tuition programs, such as 529 plans, are considered gifts made to the student and are considered the student's own funds. In the year tuition payments are made, withdrawals from the accounts are considered funds provided by the student for their own support–not support provided by the person who originally contributed the funds.

Generally, the amount of an item of support is the amount of the expense incurred in providing that item. For lodging, the amount of support is the fair rental value of the lodging.

Expenses not directly related to any one member of a household, such as the cost of food for the household, must be divided among the members of the household.

Example 1. Grace Brown, mother of Mary Miller, lives with Frank and Mary Miller and their two children. Grace gets social security benefits of $2,400, which she spends for clothing, transportation, and recreation. Grace has no other income. Frank and Mary's total food expense for the household is $5,200. They pay Grace's medical and drug expenses of $1,200. The fair rental value of the lodging provided for Grace is $1,800 a year, based on the cost of similar rooming facilities. Figure Grace's total support as follows:

Fair rental value of lodging	$1,800
Clothing, transportation, and recreation	2,400
Medical expenses	1,200
Share of food (1/5 of $5,200)	1,040
Total support	**$6,440**

The support Frank and Mary provide, $4,040 ($1,800 lodging + $1,200 medical expenses + $1,040 food), is more than half of Grace's $6,440 total support.

Example 2. Your parents live with you, your spouse, and your two children in a house you own. The fair rental value of your parents' share of the lodging is $2,000 a year ($1,000 each), which includes furnishings and utilities. Your father receives a nontaxable pension of $4,200, which he spends equally between your mother and himself for items of support such as clothing, transportation, and recreation. Your total food expense for the household is $6,000. Your heat and utility bills amount to $1,200. Your mother has hospital and medical expenses of $600, which you pay during the year. Figure your parents' total support as follows:

Support provided	Father	Mother
Fair rental value of lodging	$1,000	$1,000
Pension spent for their support	2,100	2,100
Share of food (1/6 of $6,000)	1,000	1,000
Medical expenses for mother		600
Parents' total support	$4,100	$4,700

You must apply the support test separately to each parent. You provide $2,000 ($1,000 lodging + $1,000 food) of your father's total support of $4,100–less than half. You provide $2,600 to your mother ($1,000 lodging + $1,000 food + $600 medical)–more than half of her total support of $4,700. You meet the support test for your mother, but not your father. Heat and utility costs are included in the fair rental value of the lodging, so these are not considered separately.

Lodging. If you provide a person with lodging, you are considered to provide support equal to the fair rental value of the room, apartment, house, or other shelter in which the person lives. Fair rental value includes a reasonable allowance for the use of furniture and appliances, and for heat and other utilities that are provided.

Fair rental value defined. Fair rental value is the amount you could reasonably expect to receive from a stranger for the same kind of lodging. It is used instead of actual expenses such as taxes, interest, depreciation, paint, insurance, utilities, and the cost of furniture and appliances. In some cases, fair rental value may be equal to the rent paid.

If you provide the total lodging, the amount of support you provide is the fair rental value of the room the person uses, or a share of the fair rental value of the entire dwelling if the person has use of your entire home. If you do not provide the total lodging, the total fair rental value must be divided depending on how much of the total lodging you provide. If you provide only a part and the person supplies the rest, the fair rental value must be divided between both of you according to the amount each provides.

Example. Your parents live rent free in a house you own. It has a fair rental value of $5,400 a year furnished, which includes a fair rental value of $3,600 for the house and $1,800 for the furniture. This does not include heat and utilities. The house is completely furnished with furniture belonging to your parents. You pay $600 for their utility bills. Utilities are not usually included in rent for houses in the area where your parents live. Therefore, you consider the total fair rental value of the lodging to be $6,000 ($3,600 fair rental value of the unfurnished house + $1,800 allowance for the furnishings provided by your parents + $600 cost of utilities) of which you are considered to provide $4,200 ($3,600 + $600).

Person living in his or her own home. The total fair rental value of a person's home that he or she owns is considered support contributed by that person.

Living with someone rent free. If you live with a person rent free in his or her home, you must reduce the amount you provide for support of that person by the fair rental value of lodging he or she provides you.

TAXSAVER

If your dependent is living in his or her own home, it may be to your mutual advantage for you to acquire a partial interest in the home and thereby become jointly liable for the mortgage and real estate taxes. By doing this, you can include 50% of the mortgage expense and real estate taxes you incur as part of your support calculation.

TAXPLANNER

If your mother lives alone in her own home and you pay the mortgage and real estate taxes for her, no one is entitled to the deduction for mortgage interest expenses or real estate taxes. You pay them, but because you are not personally liable for them, you may not deduct them. Conversely, your mother is personally responsible for them, but she does not pay them and so she may not deduct them.

If you give your mother the cash and she pays the mortgage interest expenses and real estate taxes, she would be entitled to the deductions. However, if you are in a higher tax bracket than your mother, it would be more advantageous for you to take the deductions than for your mother to do so. The higher your tax bracket, the more a deduction is worth.

If the house were transferred into joint ownership and you also became obligated for the mortgage, you could deduct the mortgage interest and real estate taxes you paid. In addition, you could claim your mother as a dependent. Arranging things in this manner may realize the greatest tax savings. To take full advantage of the deduction for mortgage interest, you would have to meet the special rules for qualified residence mortgages. See *chapter 24*, *Interest expense*.

Property. Property provided as support is measured by its fair market value. Fair market value is the price that property would sell for on the open market. It is the price that would be agreed upon between a willing buyer and a willing seller, with neither being required to act, and both having reasonable knowledge of the relevant facts.

Capital expenses. Capital items, such as furniture, appliances, and cars, bought for a person during the year can be included in total support under certain circumstances.

The following examples show when a capital item is or is not support.

Example 1. You buy a $200 power lawn mower for your 13-year-old child. The child is given the duty of keeping the lawn trimmed. Because the lawn mower benefits all members of the household, do not include the cost of the lawn mower in the support of your child.

Example 2. You buy a $150 television set as a birthday present for your 12-year-old child. The television set is placed in your child's bedroom. You can include the cost of the television set in the support of your child.

Example 3. You pay $5,000 for a car and register it in your name. You and your 17-year-old daughter use the car equally. Because you own the car and do not give it to your daughter but merely let her use it, do not include the cost of the car in your daughter's total support. However, you can include in your daughter's support your out-of-pocket expenses of operating the car for her benefit.

Example 4. Your 17-year-old son, using personal funds, buys a car for $4,500. You provide the rest of your son's support–$4,000. Because the car is bought and owned by your son, the car's fair market value ($4,500) must be included in his support. Your son has provided more than half of his own total support of $8,500 ($4,500 + $4,000), so he is not your qualifying child. You did not provide more than half of his total support, so he is not your qualifying relative. You cannot claim an exemption for your son.

TAXSAVER

In Example 4 above, the parents were not able to claim their son as a dependent because the son paid the entire $4,500 to buy the car. However, if the parents had contributed $251 toward the car's purchase, they would then have contributed more than half of their son's support and could claim the son as a dependent and get a $3,950 deduction. Assuming that the parents were in the 28% tax bracket, the deduction was worth $1,106 to them. The moral of the story is: Contributing to the purchase of a car or a trip in the year in which your child graduates from school may make good tax sense if the contribution assures you of one more year in which you can claim your child as a dependent.

Medical insurance premiums. Medical insurance premiums you pay, including premiums for supplementary Medicare coverage, are included in the support you provide.

Medical insurance benefits. Medical insurance benefits, including basic and supplementary Medicare benefits, are not part of support.

Tuition payments and allowances under the GI Bill. Amounts veterans receive under the GI Bill for tuition payments and allowances while they attend school are included in total support.

Example. During the year, your son receives $2,200 from the government under the GI Bill. He uses this amount for his education. You provide the rest of his support– $2,000. Because GI benefits are included in total support, your son's total support is $4,200 ($2,200 + $2,000). You have not provided more than half of his support.

Child care expenses. If you pay someone to provide child or dependent care, you can include these payments in the amount you provided for the support of your child or disabled dependent, even if you claim a credit for the payments. For information on the credit, see chapter 33.

Other support items. Other items may be considered as support depending on the facts in each case.

TAXPLANNER

If you contribute support to a household other than the one in which you live and that household includes more than one person who may qualify as your dependent, you may earmark portions of your support funds for specific persons. This enables you to prove that you have provided more than 50% of the support for a certain member or members of the household. Without written corroboration, it is likely that the monies contributed will be prorated among all the members of the household, which could result in your losing a dependency exemption.

EXAMPLE

You provide $5,000 of support for your parents. They live in their own apartment and spend $6,000 annually on their joint support.

Unless you specify how much support is designated for each parent, the IRS assumes that half of the money was intended for each parent. Therefore, you won't meet the more than 50% test for either parent.

If you establish in writing that over $3,000 of your funds is support for one of your parents and the balance is for the other, you can claim one dependency deduction.

Do Not Include in Total Support

The following items are not included in total support.

1. Federal, state, and local income taxes paid by persons from their own income.
2. Social security and Medicare taxes paid by persons from their own income.
3. Life insurance premiums.
4. Funeral expenses.
5. Scholarships received by your child if your child is a student.
6. Survivors' and Dependents' Educational Assistance payments used for the support of the child who receives them.

> ### EXAMPLE
> If a child puts his or her entire after-tax earnings from a part-time job in a savings account or purchases common stock, the child is not considered to have spent any earnings toward self-support.
>
> This is an important point to remember in the year in which a child graduates from school and gets a job for the rest of the year. Whether or not the parents may claim the child as a dependent hinges on whether or not their support payments—tuition, room and board, graduation presents, and so on—exceed the child's earnings that are not put into savings or used to pay taxes.

Multiple Support Agreement

Sometimes no one provides more than half of the support of a person. Instead, two or more persons, each of whom would be able to take the exemption but for the support test, together provide more than half of the person's support.

When this happens, you can agree that any one of you who individually provides more than 10% of the person's support, but only one can claim an exemption for that person as a qualifying relative. Each of the others must sign a statement agreeing not to claim the exemption for that year. The person who claims the exemption must keep these signed statements for his or her records. A multiple support declaration identifying each of the others who agreed not to claim the exemption must be attached to the return of the person claiming the exemption. Form 2120, Multiple Support Declaration, can be used for this purpose.

You can claim an exemption under a multiple support agreement for someone related to you or for someone who lived with you all year as a member of your household.

Example 1. You, your sister, and your two brothers provide the entire support of your mother for the year. You provide 45%, your sister 35%, and your two brothers each provide 10%. Either you or your sister can claim an exemption for your mother. The other must sign a statement agreeing not to take an exemption for your mother. The one who claims the exemption must attach Form 2120, or a similar declaration, to his or her return and must keep the statement signed by the other for his or her records. Because neither brother provides more than 10% of the support, neither can take the exemption and neither has to sign a statement.

Example 2. You and your brother each provide 20% of your mother's support for the year. The remaining 60% of her support is provided equally by two persons who are not related to her. She does not live with them. Because more than half of her support is provided by persons who cannot claim an exemption for her, no one can take the exemption.

Example 3. Your father lives with you and receives 25% of his support from social security, 40% from you, 24% from his brother (your uncle), and 11% from a friend. Either you or your uncle can take the exemption for your father if the other signs a statement agreeing not to. The one who takes the exemption must attach Form 2120, or a similar declaration, to his return and must keep for his records the signed statement from the one agreeing not to take the exemption.

> ### TAXPLANNER
> The multiple support agreement provides a tax-planning opportunity that should not be overlooked. If more than one individual provides over 10% of the support of a dependent, and if no one individual provides over 50% support, an individual in a higher tax bracket may take the deduction, even if that individual did not provide the most support for the dependent.
>
> #### Example
> Four adult children jointly furnish all of the support for their elderly father. The marginal tax rate for three of the children is 15%, but the fourth child is in the 28% bracket. Therefore, the fourth child should be designated as the one to claim the dependency deduction under the multiple support agreement, even if he or she is providing less support than the other three. The $3,950 deduction is worth $1,106 to the fourth child but is worth only $593 to any of the other children, because they are taxed at 15%.

Support Test for Children of Divorced or Separated Parents (or Parents Who Live Apart)

In most cases, a child of divorced or separated parents (or parents who live apart) will be a qualifying child of one of the parents. See *Children of divorced or separated parents (or parents who live apart)* under *Qualifying Child*, earlier. However, if the child does not meet the requirements to be a qualifying child of either parent, the child may be a qualifying relative of one of the parents. If you think this might apply to you, see Publication 501.

TAXPLANNER

Due to the education credits (see chapter 36, *Education credits and other education tax benefits*, for information about the American Opportunity Tax Credit and the Lifetime Learning Credit), there are situations where the parent may not want to claim an eligible dependent. These education credits phase out for higher income taxpayers. For example, under the provisions of the American opportunity credit, education credits phase out for single taxpayers with modified adjusted gross income between $80,000 and $90,000 and for couples filing jointly with modified adjusted gross income between $160,000 and $180,000. The credits are not available to married taxpayers filing separately.

The student may claim the credits, even if the parents paid the expenses, but no one may claim the student as a dependent. The parent must not include the student on his or her tax return, and if the parent is allowed to take a dependency exemption for the student, the student may not claim a dependency exemption on his or her own tax return.

You should not claim your child as your dependent if the education tax credit will provide a greater tax benefit for your child than your tax benefit from the $3,950 exemption amount. The maximum tax benefit for a married couple, in the 28% tax bracket, to claim a child as a dependent is $1,106.

TAXPLANNER

Generally, the parent in the higher tax bracket should be designated as the parent to claim the dependency exemption for a child, assuming that the parent meets all the tests for claiming the dependency deduction. However, if the person with the highest tax bracket is subject to the phaseout of the personal exemption, it may be more beneficial for the parent in the lower tax bracket to claim the child as a dependent since the taxpayer in the lower bracket may recognize a larger tax benefit. Similarly, where a person in the highest tax bracket for regular tax purposes becomes subject to the alternative minimum tax, that person receives no tax benefit for claiming a dependency deduction while the person in the lower tax bracket would receive a tax benefit from claiming the child as a dependent.

Note: The child and dependent care credit and medical expense deductions may be claimed whether or not you can claim the child as a dependent. For more information on the child and dependent care credit, see chapter 33, *Child and dependent care credit*. For more information on the medical expense deduction, see chapter 22, *Medical and dental expenses*.

Phaseout of Exemptions

You lose at least part of the benefit of your exemptions if your adjusted gross income (AGI) is above a certain amount. For 2014, the phaseout begins at the following amounts.

Filing Status	AGI Level Which Reduces Exemption Amount
Married filing separately	$152,525
Single	254,200
Head of household	279,650
Married filing jointly	305,050
Qualifying widow(er)	305,050

You must reduce the dollar amount of your exemptions by 2% for each $2,500, or part of $2,500 ($1,250 if you are married filing separately), that your AGI exceeds the amount shown above for your filing status. If your AGI exceeds the amount shown above by more than $122,500 ($61,250 if married filing separately), the amount of your deduction for exemptions is reduced to zero.

If your AGI exceeds the level for your filing status, use Worksheet 3-2 to figure the amount of your deduction for exemptions.

1. Is the amount on Form 1040, line 38, more than the amount on line 4 below for your filing status?...**1.** _____

   ☐ **No.** Stop. Multiply $3,950 by the total number of exemptions claimed on line 6d of Form 1040 and enter the result on Form 1040, line 42.

   ☐ **Yes.** Continue.

2. Multiply $3,950 by the total number of exemptions claimed on line 6d of Form 1040 ....**2.** _____

3. Enter the amount from Form 1040, line 38...**3.** _____

4. Enter the amount shown below for your filing status:
   * Married filing separately—$152,525
   * Single—$254,200 ....**4.** _____
   * Head of household—$279,650
   * Married filing jointly or Qualifying widow(er)—$305,050

5. Subtract line 4 from line 3. If the result is more than $122,500 ($61,250 if married filing separately), **stop here.** You cannot take a deduction for exemptions..**5.** _____

6. Divide line 5 by $2,500 ($1,250 if married filing separately). If the result is not a whole number, round it up to the next higher whole number (for example, increase .00004 to 1) ....**6.** _____

7. Multiply line 6 by 2% (.02) and enter the result as a decimal (rounded to at least three places).........**7.** _____

8. Multiply line 2 by line 7 ....**8.** _____

9. Deduction for exemptions. Subtract line 8 from line 2. Enter the result here and on Form 1040, line 42...**9.** _____

Caution

If you do not show the dependent's SSN when required or if you show an incorrect SSN, the exemption may be disallowed.

Social Security Numbers for Dependents

You must show the social security number (SSN) of any dependent for whom you claim an exemption in column (2) of line 6c of your Form 1040 or Form 1040A.

No SSN. If a person for whom you expect to claim an exemption on your return does not have an SSN, either you or that person should apply for an SSN as soon as possible by filing Form SS-5, Application for a Social Security Card, with the Social Security Administration (SSA). You can get Form SS-5 online at *www.socialsecurity.gov* or at your local SSA office.

It usually takes about 2 weeks to get an SSN once the SSA has all the information it needs. If you do not have a required SSN by the filing due date, you can file Form 4868 for an extension of time to file.

Born and died in 2014. If your child was born and died in 2014, and you do not have an SSN for the child, you may attach a copy of the child's birth certificate, death certificate, or hospital records instead. The document must show the child was born alive. If you do this, enter "DIED" in column (2) of line 6c of your Form 1040 or Form 1040A.

Alien or adoptee with no SSN. If your dependent does not have and cannot get an SSN, you must list the individual taxpayer identification number (ITIN) or adoption taxpayer identification number (ATIN) instead of an SSN.

Taxpayer identification numbers for aliens. If your dependent is a resident or nonresident alien who does not have and is not eligible to get an SSN, your dependent must apply for an individual taxpayer identification number (ITIN). For details on how to apply, see Form W-7, Application for IRS Individual Taxpayer Identification Number.

Taxpayer identification numbers for adoptees. If you have a child who was placed with you by an authorized placement agency, you may be able to claim an exemption for the child. However, if you cannot get an SSN or an ITIN for the child, you must get an adoption taxpayer identification number (ATIN) for the child from the IRS. See Form W-7A, Application for Taxpayer Identification Number for Pending U.S. Adoptions, for details.

TAXORGANIZER
Records you should keep:

- Social security card
- Support test calculations, if your dependent has sufficient income that might jeopardize your claiming him or her as a dependent. This includes documenting all amounts that you and your dependent spend during the year toward the dependent's support.
- Form 8332, Release of Claim to Exemption for Child by Custodial Parent
- Multiple support agreements as to who can claim the dependency exemption including Form 2120, Multiple Support Declaration, and signed statement from others agreeing not to claim the exemption
- Divorce decree or separation agreement

Chapter 4

Tax withholding and estimated tax

Note

IRS Publication 17 (*Your Federal Income Tax*) has been updated by Ernst & Young LLP for 2014. Dates and dollar amounts shown are for 2014. Underlined type is used to indicate where IRS text has been updated. Places where text has been removed are indicated by the sentence: *Text intentionally omitted.*

ey.com/EYTaxGuide

Ernst & Young LLP will update the *EY Tax Guide 2015* website with relevant taxpayer information as it becomes available. You can also sign up for email alerts to let you know when changes have been made.

Introduction

April 15 is the date by which most people file their income tax return for the previous year, but it is not the day most people actually pay their taxes. The bulk of your tax liability is paid during the year, either through money withheld from your paycheck by your employer or through payment of estimated taxes every quarter. The tax system operates on a pay-as-you-go policy, which generally requires that at least 90% of your tax liability be paid during the year.

The tax law imposes severe penalties if you underwithhold or underpay your estimated taxes. Yet, it is clearly not in your best interest to overwithhold or overpay estimated taxes, as the U.S. government does not pay interest on such overpayments. Therefore, it is essential that you estimate your tax liability as accurately as possible so you neither underpay nor overpay your taxes. This chapter helps you do just that.

Salaries and wages are subject to withholding by your employer regardless of the amount you are paid, the frequency of payment, or the form of payment. Nevertheless, you are entitled to reduce the amount of withholding by filing a completed Form W-4 with your employer. This form takes into account not only your marital status, personal exemptions, and dependents, but also your estimated deductions and tax credits. Form W-4 may prove especially beneficial if you have large itemized deductions.

Estimated tax payments cover sources of income not subject to withholding; for example, income from partnerships, S-corporations, rental property, royalties, self-employment, trusts and estates, interest, dividends, and capital gains. While generally your tax withholding and estimated payments have to cover 90% of your tax liability for you to avoid paying some stiff penalties, this is not always the case. This chapter discusses all the important exceptions.

TAXPLANNER

The Affordable Care Act (ACA) imposes two permanent taxes on income that started in 2013. Taxpayers are still learning how these taxes may impact their tax liability and tax returns.

Additional Medicare tax on wages and compensation. The ACA imposes an additional Medicare tax of 0.9% on earned income in excess of $200,000 ($250,000 for married filing jointly, $125,000 for married taxpayers filing separately). For married couples filing jointly, the additional 0.9% tax applies to the couple's combined wages in excess of $250,000. (These thresholds not adjusted annually for inflation.) This 0.9% tax is assessed in addition to the basic 1.45% Medicare tax employees already pay. Earned income includes wages and other compensation, as well as self-employment income. There is, however, no corresponding employer portion of the Additional Medicare Tax.

Employers are required to withhold the 0.9% Additional Medicare Tax on wages paid to an employee in excess of $200,000 regardless of the tax filing status (married or single) of the individual indicated on the Form W-4 that you submit to your employer and without regard to any other earned income on which the 0.9% Additional Medicare Tax may be owed. So, you may see this additional tax being withheld even though you may not even be liable for it because, for example, your wages or other compensation together with those of your spouse (when filing a joint return) does not exceed the $250,000 threshold that would make you liable for the 0.9% additional tax. If this is the case, any Additional Medicare Tax withheld from you can be credited against your total tax liability—including income taxes—shown on your income tax return (Form 1040).

On the other hand, since an employer is only allowed to withhold the 0.9% Additional Medicare Tax on wages paid in excess of $200,000, married employees who file separately may have too little of this additional tax withheld. This is because the threshold at which the 0.9% tax kicks in is only $125,000 for married taxpayers filing separately. If this is your situation, you may need to make quarterly estimated tax payment to the IRS to make up the difference and avoid a tax underpayment penalty.

Net investment income tax (NIIT). The other tax enacted by the ACA is the 3.8% Net Investment Income Tax (NIIT) on unearned income. It is assessed on the lesser of your net investment income or the excess of your modified adjusted gross income over $200,000 ($250,000 if you are married filing jointly or a qualifying widow(er) with dependent child; $125,000 if married filing separately). Income subject to the 0.9% Additional Medicare Tax is specifically exempted from the 3.8% NIIT, and certain allocable deductions are permitted in arriving at net investment income.

The NIIT falls broadly into three categories:
- Investment income including interest, dividends, rents, and annuities not derived in the ordinary course of a trade or business
- Trade or business income from passive activities or from trading in financial instruments or commodities
- Net gains from the disposition of property not used in a trade or business

TAXPLANNER

Although, as previously explained, compensation income subject to the 0.9% Additional Medicare Tax is specifically exempted from the 3.8% NIIT, such earned income does figure into a taxpayer's modified adjusted gross income for purposes of determining the amount of unearned, net investment income subject to the 3.8% NIIT.

Example

A single employee receives wages of $150,000 and $50,000 in earnings from her employer's nonqualified deferred compensation (NQDC). Although these wages aren't subject to the 0.9% additional Medicare tax, the 3.8% NIIT will be owed on any net investment income received for the year because her earnings reached the $200,000 threshold.

TAXPLANNER

When employers provide investment-type benefits, which ACA tax do employees pay?

A challenge arises when employers award employees compensation under stock, nonqualified deferred compensation (NQDC), or similar investment-type plans. As explained above, compensation provided by employers to their employees is subject to the 0.9% Additional Medicare Tax while unearned income is subject to the NIIT of 3.8%. But which of the two taxes will apply, since the 3.8% NIIT is assessed at a substantially higher rate than the 0.9% Additional Medicare Tax?

Tax withholding. Most people pay their tax liability through withholding from their wages. But there are a number of other items of income which are subject to withholding (either mandatory or at your election). These items include pension distributions, IRA distributions, gambling winnings, and social security benefits. If you don't want to have to make quarterly estimated tax payments, you can ask that taxes be withheld from some of these payments. And no matter when the withholding takes place during the year, the IRS will treat it as being withheld equally throughout the year, unless you ask otherwise.

Tax refunds. Some people like getting a large refund when they file their tax return. But a refund isn't necessarily a good thing—it means you overpaid your taxes during the year. And, because the IRS doesn't pay you interest on that overpayment, you've essentially made an interest-free loan to Uncle Sam. From a financial perspective, you're probably better off breaking even or paying a balance when you file. Of course, some people treat overwithholding as forced savings, because they're afraid they'll spend the money if it's included in their paycheck.

Estimated taxes. For people receiving income not subject to withholding, such as income from self-employment, partnerships, S corporations, rental property, royalties, trusts and estates, interest, dividends, and capital

Following are two examples where this question may arise:
- *Qualified retirement and NQDC plans.* Compensation deferred from current ordinary federal income tax under qualified retirement plans (e.g., 401(k)) and NQDC plans is subject to the additional Medicare tax of 0.9% tax when FICA tax—i.e., Social Security and 1.45% Medicare tax—is due. Subsequent distributions of contributions and earnings from such plans previously subject to FICA tax are exempt from both the Additional Medicare Tax and the NIIT.

  An amount paid by an employer to an employee that is treated as wages subject to federal income tax withholding is not considered investment income. So, for example, amounts paid to an employee under an NQDC plan that includes interest credited or other earnings on the deferred amounts are included in wages, and, therefore, are not subject to the 3.8% NIIT.
- *Restricted stock awards.* Under normal federal income tax withholding rules, an employee is taxed when a restricted stock award vests. Upon vesting, federal income tax withholding is required on the excess of the fair market value of the stock award price over the grant price. This amount is also subject to FICA tax, including the new 0.9% Additional Medicare Tax. Subsequent dividends received on the restricted stock award and any capital gains generated if the employee subsequently sells the shares are not subject to the 0.9% Additional Medicare Tax. On the other hand, these dividends and capital gains are considered investment income subject to the 3.8% NIIT.

What's New for 2015

Tax law changes for 2015. When you figure how much income tax you want withheld from your pay and when you figure your estimated tax, consider tax law changes effective in 2015. For more information, see Publication 505.

TAXPLANNER

When calculating how much income tax to withhold from your wages or other sources, or computing your estimated tax payments each quarter, it is important to keep in mind any changes in the tax law. For more information on tax law changes impacting 2015, see chapter 47, *Planning ahead for 2015 and beyond*.

Reminders

Estimated tax safe harbor for higher income taxpayers. If your 2014 adjusted gross income was more than $150,000 ($75,000 if you are married filing a separate return), you must pay the smaller of 90% of your expected tax for 2015 or 110% of the tax shown on your 2014 return to avoid an estimated tax penalty.

This chapter discusses how to pay your tax as you earn or receive income during the year. In general, the federal income tax is a pay-as-you-go tax. There are two ways to pay as you go.
- *Withholding.* If you are an employee, your employer probably withholds income tax from your pay. Tax also may be withheld from certain other income, such as pensions, bonuses, commissions, and gambling winnings. The amount withheld is paid to the IRS in your name.
- *Estimated tax.* If you do not pay your tax through withholding, or do not pay enough tax that way, you may have to pay estimated tax. People who are in business for themselves generally will have to pay their tax this way. Also, you may have to pay estimated tax if you receive income such as dividends, interest, capital gains, rent, and royalties. Estimated tax is used to pay not only income tax, but self-employment tax and alternative minimum tax as well.

This chapter explains these methods. In addition, it also explains the following.
- *Credit for withholding and estimated tax.* When you file your 2014 income tax return, take credit for all the income tax withheld from your salary, wages, pensions, etc., and for the estimated tax you paid for 2014. Also take credit for any excess social security or railroad retirement tax withheld (discussed in chapter 37).
- *Underpayment penalty.* If you did not pay enough tax during the year, either through withholding or by making estimated tax payments, you may have to pay a penalty. In most cases, the IRS can figure this penalty for you. See *Underpayment Penalty for 2014* at the end of this chapter.

Useful Items

You may want to see:

Publication

☐ **505** Tax Withholding and Estimated Tax

Form (and Instructions)

☐ **W-4** Employee's Withholding Allowance Certificate
☐ **W-4P** Withholding Certificate for Pension or Annuity Payments
☐ **W-4S** Request for Federal Income Tax Withholding From Sick Pay
☐ **W-4V** Voluntary Withholding Request
☐ **1040-ES** Estimated Tax for Individuals
☐ **2210** Underpayment of Estimated Tax by Individuals, Estates, and Trusts
☐ **2210-F** Underpayment of Estimated Tax by Farmers and Fishermen

Tax Withholding for 2015

This section discusses income tax withholding on:

- Salaries and wages,
- Tips,
- Taxable fringe benefits,
- Sick pay,
- Pensions and annuities,
- Gambling winnings,
- Unemployment compensation, and
- Certain federal payments.

This section explains the rules for withholding tax from each of these types of income.

This section also covers backup withholding on interest, dividends, and other payments.

gains, the tax liability associated with such income is generally covered through quarterly estimated tax payments. Because many individuals don't know what their tax liability will be in the coming year, the law allows them to base their estimated tax payments on the previous year's tax liability. See this chapter for more details on how to calculate the amount of estimated taxes you need to pay in order to avoid underpayment penalties.

TAXPLANNER

The IRS created a page on IRS.gov for information about Publication 505 and future developments at *irs.gov/pub505*.

Salaries and Wages

Income tax is withheld from the pay of most employees. Your pay includes your regular pay, bonuses, commissions, and vacation allowances. It also includes reimbursements and other expense allowances paid under a nonaccountable plan. See *Supplemental Wages*, later, for more information about reimbursements and allowances paid under a nonaccountable plan.

If your income is low enough that you will not have to pay income tax for the year, you may be exempt from withholding. This is explained under *Exemption From Withholding*, later.

You can ask your employer to withhold income tax from noncash wages and other wages not subject to withholding. If your employer does not agree to withhold tax, or if not enough is withheld, you may have to pay estimated tax, as discussed later under *Estimated Tax for 2015*.

Military retirees. Military retirement pay is treated in the same manner as regular pay for income tax withholding purposes, even though it is treated as a pension or annuity for other tax purposes.

Household workers. If you are a household worker, you can ask your employer to withhold income tax from your pay. A household worker is an employee who performs household work in a private home, local college club, or local fraternity or sorority chapter.

Tax is withheld only if you want it withheld and your employer agrees to withhold it. If you do not have enough income tax withheld, you may have to pay estimated tax, as discussed later under *Estimated Tax for 2015*.

Farmworkers. Generally, income tax is withheld from your cash wages for work on a farm unless your employer does both of these:

- Pays you cash wages of less than $150 during the year, and
- Has expenditures for agricultural labor totaling less than $2,500 during the year.

You must specify a filing status and a number of withholding allowances on Form W-4. You cannot specify only a dollar amount of withholding.

EXPLANATION
Generally, withholding is required on wages, regardless of the amount of wages paid, the frequency of payment, the form of payment (cash, check, stock, or other property), or the manner in which the wage is computed (hourly, weekly, yearly, or even as a percentage of employer profits).

For more information about household workers, see chapter 40, *What to do if you employ domestic help.*

Differential wage payments. When employees are on leave from employment for military duty, some employers make up the difference between the military pay and civilian pay. Payments to an employee who is on active duty for a period of more than 30 days will be subject to income tax withholding, but not subject to social security or Medicare taxes. The wages and withholding will be reported on Form W-2, Wage and Tax Statement.

Text intentionally omitted.

Determining Amount of Tax Withheld Using Form W-4
The amount of income tax your employer withholds from your regular pay depends on two things.
- The amount you earn in each payroll period.
- The information you give your employer on Form W-4.

Form W-4 includes four types of information that your employer will use to figure your withholding.
- Whether to withhold at the single rate or at the lower married rate.
- How many withholding allowances you claim (each allowance reduces the amount withheld).
- Whether you want an additional amount withheld.
- Whether you are claiming an exemption from withholding in 2015. See *Exemption From Withholding*, later.

Note. You must specify a filing status and a number of withholding allowances on Form W-4. You cannot specify only a dollar amount of withholding.

New Job
When you start a new job, you must fill out Form W-4 and give it to your employer. Your employer should have copies of the form. If you need to change the information later, you must fill out a new form.

If you work only part of the year (for example, you start working after the beginning of the year), too much tax may be withheld. You may be able to avoid overwithholding if your employer agrees to use the part-year method. See *Part-Year Method* in chapter 1 of Publication 505 for more information.

Employee also receiving pension income. If you receive pension or annuity income and begin a new job, you will need to file Form W-4 with your new employer. However, you can choose to split your withholding allowances between your pension and job in any manner.

Changing Your Withholding
During the year changes may occur to your marital status, exemptions, adjustments, deductions, or credits you expect to claim on your tax return. When this happens, you may need to give your employer a new Form W-4 to change your withholding status or your number of allowances.

If the changes reduce the number of allowances you are allowed to claim or changes your marital status from married to single, you must give your employer a new Form W-4 within 10 days.

Generally, you can submit a new Form W-4 whenever you wish to change the number of your withholding allowances for any other reason.

Changing your withholding for 2016. If events in 2015 will decrease the number of your withholding allowances for 2016, you must give your employer a new Form W-4 by December 1, 2015. If the event occurs in December 2015, submit a new Form W-4 within 10 days.

EXPLANATION
You must file a new Form W-4 when it becomes reasonable for you to expect that the estimated deductions or credits you claim on your existing Form W-4 will be less than you anticipated. Conversely, you may file a new Form W-4 when it becomes reasonable to expect that your estimated deductions or credits will be more than you claim on your existing form. Examples of situations that might warrant that you file a new Form W-4 include: (1) buying or selling a house, (2) refinancing or paying off a home mortgage, (3) moving to a different city, (4) a substantial increase in medical costs, (5) change in filing status, or (6) change in number of dependents.

Checking Your Withholding

After you have given your employer a Form W-4, you can check to see whether the amount of tax withheld from your pay is too little or too much. If too much or too little tax is being withheld, you should give your employer a new Form W-4 to change your withholding. You should try to have your withholding match your actual tax liability. If not enough tax is withheld, you will owe tax at the end of the year and may have to pay interest and a penalty. If too much tax is withheld, you will lose the use of that money until you get your refund. Always check your withholding if there are personal or financial changes in your life or changes in the law that might change your tax liability.

Note. You cannot give your employer a payment to cover withholding on salaries and wages for past pay periods or a payment for estimated tax.

Completing Form W-4 and Worksheets

Form W-4 has worksheets to help you figure how many withholding allowances you can claim. The worksheets are for your own records. Do not give them to your employer.

Multiple jobs. If you have income from more than one job at the same time, complete only one set of Form W-4 worksheets. Then split your allowances between the Forms W-4 for each job. You cannot claim the same allowances with more than one employer at the same time. You can claim all your allowances with one employer and none with the other(s), or divide them any other way.

EXAMPLE

Brian and Sheri are married. Both are employed and expect to file a joint return. When they combine their expected salary and other income and then total their expected deductions and credits on a Form W-4 worksheet, they determine that they are entitled to claim 26 allowances. Brian and Sheri must both file separate W-4 forms with their respective employers, but may allocate the 26 allowances any way they like. Brian could claim 24 allowances and Sheri could claim 2, for example, or each could claim 13 allowances.

Married individuals. If both you and your spouse are employed and expect to file a joint return, figure your withholding allowances using your combined income, adjustments, deductions, exemptions, and credits. Use only one set of worksheets. You can divide your total allowances any way, but you cannot claim an allowance that your spouse also claims.

If you and your spouse expect to file separate returns, figure your allowances using separate worksheets based on your own individual income, adjustments, deductions, exemptions, and credits.

Alternative method of figuring withholding allowances. You do not have to use the Form W-4 worksheets if you use a more accurate method of figuring the number of withholding allowances. For more information, see *Alternative method of figuring withholding allowances* under *Completing Form W-4 and Worksheets* in Publication 505, chapter 1.

Personal Allowances Worksheet. Use the Personal Allowances Worksheet on Form W-4 to figure your withholding allowances based on exemptions and any special allowances that apply.

EXAMPLE

Ray and Bev are married and plan to file a joint return. Ray's wages from his only employer are $55,000. Bev's wages from her only employer are $1,000. Because Bev's wages are $1,000 or less, Ray may claim a special allowance.

Deduction and Adjustments Worksheet. Use the Deduction and Adjustments Worksheet on Form W-4 if you plan to itemize your deductions, claim certain credits, or claim adjustments to the income on your 2015 tax return and you want to reduce your withholding. Also, complete this worksheet when you have changes to these items to see if you need to change your withholding.

Two-Earners/Multiple Jobs Worksheet. You may need to complete the Two-Earners/Multiple Jobs Worksheet on Form W-4 if you have more than one job, a working spouse, or are also receiving a pension. Also, on this worksheet you can add any additional withholding necessary to cover any amount you expect to owe other than income tax, such as self-employment tax.

Getting the Right Amount of Tax Withheld

In most situations, the tax withheld from your pay will be close to the tax you figure on your return if you follow these two rules.

- You accurately complete all the Form W-4 worksheets that apply to you.
- You give your employer a new Form W-4 when changes occur.

But because the worksheets and withholding methods do not account for all possible situations, you may not be getting the right amount withheld. This is most likely to happen in the following situations.

- You are married and both you and your spouse work.
- You have more than one job at a time.
- You have nonwage income, such as interest, dividends, alimony, unemployment compensation, or self-employment income.
- You will owe additional amounts with your return, such as self-employment tax.
- Your withholding is based on obsolete Form W-4 information for a substantial part of the year.
- Your earnings are more than the amount shown under *Check your withholding* in the instructions at the top of page 1 of Form W-4.
- You work only part of the year.
- You change the number of your withholding allowances during the year.

EXAMPLE

Ashley is single living in an apartment. Her annual income is $35,000, and she claims the standard deduction when she files her income tax return. She is currently claiming two allowances on her Form W-4. In March 2015, Ashley buys a house. As a result of the increased deductions resulting from the purchase, she will itemize her deductions on her 2015 federal income tax return. She estimates that the deductions will total $13,200 and will be made up of mortgage interest, points, real estate tax, and state income tax. She revises her Form W-4 to reflect the change in her status to claim four allowances for the remainder of the year.

Cumulative wage method. If you change the number of your withholding allowances during the year, too much or too little tax may have been withheld for the period before you made the change. You may be able to compensate for this if your employer agrees to use the cumulative wage withholding method for the rest of the year. You must ask your employer in writing to use this method.

To be eligible, you must have been paid for the same kind of payroll period (weekly, biweekly, etc.) since the beginning of the year.

TAXPLANNER

The tax withheld from your salary or wages based on the revised Form W-4 that you file with your employer should be appropriate for your circumstances on an annual basis. However, the new withholding is effective only for pay periods after you file the form, and the total tax withheld for any given year may be significantly less than your actual tax liability. You should estimate your annual tax, as explained later in this chapter, and compare that estimate to the year-to-date tax withheld plus the amounts expected to be withheld based on your revised Form W-4. If that comparison shows a substantial gap, it would be appropriate to file a new Form W-4, claiming fewer allowances or requesting a larger additional amount to be withheld in order to narrow that gap.

TAXPLANNER

You are liable for severe penalties if you complete a Form W-4 with false information in an attempt to reduce your withholding below the amount you are legally allowed. The form should be filled out carefully and accurately so that the amount of your withholding is the least you are legally allowed but enough to avoid underpayment penalties.

On the other hand, contrary to the belief of many taxpayers, there is not a penalty for over-withholding.

So much emphasis has been put on the accuracy of various worksheets that some taxpayers may have increased their withholding more than they actually want. If you are more comfortable claiming fewer exemptions than you are entitled to so that you can get a nice refund when you file your return, feel free to do so, but remember, it is like giving the government an interest-free loan during the year.

TAXPLANNER

Your Form W-4 should be reviewed periodically as your sources and levels of income change and as your deductible expenses and credits increase or decrease.

Example 1

You have an estimated net loss from a partnership of $2,000, which you would report on Schedule E of your Form 1040. You are not required to make any payments of estimated tax. You may use your $2,000 partnership loss to figure the number of withholding allowances you may claim on your Form W-4.

Example 2

In addition to wages, you have alimony income of $5,000 and an estimated net loss from business of $3,000, which you would report on Schedule C. If you did not have the estimated business loss, you would have been required to make payments of estimated tax on your alimony income of $5,000. The business loss can be netted against the alimony income in order to figure the amount of net income on which you would be required to pay estimated tax—$2,000 in this case. You may not use your business loss to figure your withholding allowances since the loss is already used to offset the alimony income.

Example 3

You have an estimated net loss from your farm of $5,000, which you would report on Schedule F. You would otherwise be required to make payments of estimated tax on rental income of $4,000. To figure your withholding allowances, you may include only $1,000 of your farm loss ($5,000 estimated net loss minus $4,000 income subject to estimated tax).

Example 4

You expect to have itemized deductions of $15,000, which you would report on Schedule A. You also expect to have $9,000 of self-employment income on which you would otherwise have to pay estimated tax. To figure your withholding allowances for Form W-4, you should include only $6,000 of your itemized deductions ($15,000 total itemized deductions minus the $9,000 self-employment income subject to estimated tax). This will, in effect, allow you to withhold through your salary any estimated tax due on your self-employment income. However, you will still be subject to self-employment tax on the $9,000 income.

Rules relating to when you may properly claim withholding allowances. For the purpose of figuring your withholding allowances for estimated deductions and estimated tax credits, estimated means the dollar amount of each item you reasonably expect to claim on your 2015 return. That dollar amount should be no more than the sum of the following:

1. The amount of each item shown or expected to be shown on your 2014 return that you also reasonably expect to show on your 2015 return
2. Additional amounts that you can determine for each item for 2015

   Additional amounts that can be determined. These are amounts that are not included in (1) and that can be shown to result from identifiable events in 2014 or 2015. Amounts can be shown to result from identifiable events if the amounts relate to payments already made during 2015, to binding obligations to make payments (including payments of taxes) during 2015, and to other events or transactions that have been started and that you can prove at the time you file your Form W-4.

   Amounts disallowed by the Internal Revenue Service. Generally, to figure your withholding allowances for 2015, you should not include any amount shown on your 2014 return that has been disallowed by the IRS. If you have not yet filed your 2014 return, you should not include any amount shown on your 2013 return that has been disallowed by the IRS.

Publication 505

To make sure you are getting the right amount of tax withheld, get Publication 505. It will help you compare the total tax to be withheld during the year with the tax you can expect to figure on your return. It also will help you determine how much, if any, additional withholding is needed each payday to avoid owing tax when you file your return. If you do not have enough tax withheld, you may have to pay estimated tax, as explained under *Estimated Tax for 2015*, later.

You can use the IRS Withholding Calculator at www.irs.gov/Individuals, instead of Publication 505 or the worksheets included with Form W-4, to determine whether you need to have your withholding increased or decreased.

Rules Your Employer Must Follow

It may be helpful for you to know some of the withholding rules your employer must follow. These rules can affect how to fill out your Form W-4 and how to handle problems that may arise.

New Form W-4. When you start a new job, your employer should have you complete a Form W-4. Beginning with your first payday, your employer will use the information you give on the form to figure your withholding.

If you later fill out a new Form W-4, your employer can put it into effect as soon as possible. The deadline for putting it into effect is the start of the first payroll period ending 30 or more days after you turn it in.

No Form W-4. If you do not give your employer a completed Form W-4, your employer must withhold at the highest rate, as if you were single and claimed no withholding allowances.

Repaying withheld tax. If you find you are having too much tax withheld because you did not claim all the withholding allowances you are entitled to, you should give your employer a new Form W-4. Your employer cannot repay any of the tax previously withheld. Instead, claim the full amount withheld when you file your tax return.

However, if your employer has withheld more than the correct amount of tax for the Form W-4 you have in effect, you do not have to fill out a new Form W-4 to have your withholding lowered to the correct amount. Your employer can repay the amount that was withheld incorrectly. If you are not repaid, your Form W-2 will reflect the full amount actually withheld, which you would claim when you file your tax return.

Exemption From Withholding

If you claim exemption from withholding, your employer will not withhold federal income tax from your wages. The exemption applies only to income tax, not to social security or Medicare tax.

You can claim exemption from withholding for 2015 only if both of the following situations apply.
- For 2014 you had a right to a refund of all federal income tax withheld because you had no tax liability.
- For 2015 you expect a refund of all federal income tax withheld because you expect to have no tax liability.

Students. If you are a student, you are not automatically exempt. See chapter 1 to find out if you must file a return. If you work only part time or only during the summer, you may qualify for exemption from withholding.

Age 65 or older or blind. If you are 65 or older or blind, use Worksheet 1-3 or 1-4 in chapter 1 of Publication 505, to help you decide if you qualify for exemption from withholding. Do not use either worksheet if you will itemize deductions, claim exemptions for dependents, or claim tax credits on your 2015 return. Instead, see *Itemizing deductions or claiming exemptions or credits* in chapter 1 of Publication 505.

Claiming exemption from withholding. To claim exemption, you must give your employer a Form W-4. Do not complete lines 5 and 6. Enter "Exempt" on line 7.

If you claim exemption, but later your situation changes so that you will have to pay income tax after all, you must file a new Form W-4 within 10 days after the change. If you claim exemption in 2015, but you expect to owe income tax for 2016, you must file a new Form W-4 by December 1, 2015.

Your claim of exempt status may be reviewed by the IRS.

An exemption is good for only 1 year. You must give your employer a new Form W-4 by February 15 each year to continue your exemption.

> ### TAXALERT
> You must generally give your employer a new Form W-4 by February 15 each year to continue your exemption. However, if February 15 is not a business day, the date is extended until the next business day. Consequently, your 2014 Form W-4 will expire on February 17, 2015, because February 15 is a Sunday, and February 16 is a legal holiday (President's Day). Similarly, your 2015 Form W-4 will expire on February 16, 2016, because Monday, February 15, is President's Day, a legal holiday.

Supplemental Wages

Supplemental wages include bonuses, commissions, overtime pay, vacation allowances, certain sick pay, and expense allowances under certain plans. The payer can figure withholding on supplemental wages using the same method used for your regular wages. However, if these payments are identified separately from your regular wages, your employer or other payer of supplemental wages can withhold income tax from these wages at a flat rate.

> ### EXPLANATION
> The IRS has issued regulations to clarify that supplemental wages include any payments by an employer other than regular wages. In the case that an employee receives only one type of compensation from an employer, that type of compensation will be regular wages even if the type of compensation is something that would normally be classified as supplemental wages. For example, if an employee receives only stock options as compensation with no other fringe benefits includible as wages, the income on the exercise of the option would generally be regular wages, rather than supplemental wages. For more information, see IRS Publication 15 (Circular E) and Publication 15-B.

> ### TAXALERT
> The current flat rate of withholding on supplemental wages is 25%. However, once annual supplemental wage payments to an employee exceed $1 million, any additional supplemental wage payments in that year would be subject to withholding at the highest individual regular income tax rate, which is 39.6%. IRS regulations provide that mandatory withholding at the highest individual income tax rate on supplemental wage payments in excess of $1 million applies regardless of the withholding method used by the employer for regular wages, and even if the employee has a Form W-4 asserting either exempt status or claiming a reduced rate of withholding.
>
> #### Example
> Jillian works as an employee of Corporation R. She receives regular wage payments of $200,000 per month in 2015 from Corporation R and income tax is withheld from those wages. In addition, Jillian receives the following payments:
>
> | | |
> |---|---|
> | June 30, 2015 | $3,000,000 (bonus from Corporation R) |
> | October 31, 2015 | $50,000 (sick pay from Corporation U, one of the subsidiaries of Corporation R) |
> | December 31, 2015 | $100,000 (bonus from Corporation T, another subsidiary of Corporation R) |

All payments would be treated as made by one employer. The withholding on the regular monthly wage payment would be based upon Jillian's withholding allowances claimed on Form W-4. For the first $1,000,000 of the $3,000,000 bonus paid on June 30, 2015, income tax may be withheld using the same method used for regular wages. Alternatively, Jillian can elect to withhold income tax at the flat rate of 25% or $250,000. For the rest of the supplemental payments, including the remaining $2,000,000 of the bonus paid on June 30, income tax withheld is required to be calculated at the highest individual income tax rate (39.6% for 2015).

TAXPLANNER

The mandatory withholding for excess supplemental payments may be problematic for individuals who have substantial deductions, losses, and credits, which could otherwise have been taken into account by claiming additional withholding allowances on their Form W-4. Such individuals will have to wait for a refund when they file their return for the year of payment. Alternatively, they may be able to adjust withholding on other compensation or their quarterly estimated tax payments to take into account any excess withholding.

Expense allowances. Reimbursements or other expense allowances paid by your employer under a nonaccountable plan are treated as supplemental wages.

Reimbursements or other expense allowances paid under an accountable plan that are more than your proven expenses are treated as paid under a nonaccountable plan if you do not return the excess payments within a reasonable period of time.

For more information about accountable and nonaccountable expense allowance plans, see *Reimbursements* in chapter 27.

Penalties

You may have to pay a penalty of $500 if both of the following apply.
- You make statements or claim withholding allowances on your Form W-4 that reduce the amount of tax withheld.
- You have no reasonable basis for those statements or allowances at the time you prepare your Form W-4.

There is also a criminal penalty for willfully supplying false or fraudulent information on your Form W-4 or for willfully failing to supply information that would increase the amount withheld. The penalty upon conviction can be either a fine of up to $1,000 or imprisonment for up to 1 year, or both.

These penalties will apply if you deliberately and knowingly falsify your Form W-4 in an attempt to reduce or eliminate the proper withholding of taxes. A simple error or an honest mistake will not result in one of these penalties. For example, a person who has tried to figure the number of withholding allowances correctly, but claims seven when the proper number is six, will not be charged a W-4 penalty.

Tips

The tips you receive while working on your job are considered part of your pay. You must include your tips on your tax return on the same line as your regular pay. However, tax is not withheld directly from tip income, as it is from your regular pay. Nevertheless, your employer will take into account the tips you report when figuring how much to withhold from your regular pay.

See chapter 6 for information on reporting your tips to your employer. For more information on the withholding rules for tip income, see Publication 531, Reporting Tip Income.

How employer figures amount to withhold. The tips you report to your employer are counted as part of your income for the month you report them. Your employer can figure your withholding in either of two ways.
- By withholding at the regular rate on the sum of your pay plus your reported tips.
- By withholding at the regular rate on your pay plus a percentage of your reported tips.

Not enough pay to cover taxes. If your regular pay is not enough for your employer to withhold all the tax (including income tax and social security and Medicare taxes (or the equivalent railroad retirement tax)) due on your pay plus your tips, you can give your employer money to cover the shortage. See *Giving your employer money for taxes* in chapter 6.

Allocated tips. Your employer should not withhold income tax, Medicare tax, social security tax, or railroad retirement tax on any allocated tips.

Withholding is based only on your pay plus your reported tips. Your employer should refund to you any incorrectly withheld tax. See *Allocated Tips* in chapter 6 for more information.

TAXSAVER

Many students and retired persons who expect to have no federal income tax liability work part time in occupations in which they receive tips. To avoid unnecessary income tax withholding, you may file a Form W-4 with your employer, certifying that you had no federal income tax liability last year and expect to have none this year as well. Keep in mind that the exemption only applies to income tax withholding, not to social security or Medicare tax.

Taxable Fringe Benefits

The value of certain noncash fringe benefits you receive from your employer is considered part of your pay. Your employer generally must withhold income tax on these benefits from your regular pay.

For information on fringe benefits, see *Fringe Benefits* under *Employee Compensation* in chapter 5.

Although the value of your personal use of an employer-provided car, truck, or other highway motor vehicle is taxable, your employer can choose not to withhold income tax on that amount. Your employer must notify you if this choice is made.

For more information on withholding on taxable fringe benefits, see chapter 1 of Publication 505.

Sick Pay

Sick pay is a payment to you to replace your regular wages while you are temporarily absent from work due to sickness or personal injury. To qualify as sick pay, it must be paid under a plan to which your employer is a party.

If you receive sick pay from your employer or an agent of your employer, income tax must be withheld. An agent who does not pay regular wages to you may choose to withhold income tax at a flat rate.

However, if you receive sick pay from a third party who is not acting as an agent of your employer, income tax will be withheld only if you choose to have it withheld. See *Form W-4S*, later.

If you receive payments under a plan in which your employer does not participate (such as an accident or health plan where you paid all the premiums), the payments are not sick pay and usually are not taxable.

Union agreements. If you receive sick pay under a collective bargaining agreement between your union and your employer, the agreement may determine the amount of income tax withholding. See your union representative or your employer for more information.

Form W-4S. If you choose to have income tax withheld from sick pay paid by a third party, such as an insurance company, you must fill out Form W-4S. Its instructions contain a worksheet you can use to figure the amount you want withheld. They also explain restrictions that may apply.

Give the completed form to the payer of your sick pay. The payer must withhold according to your directions on the form.

Estimated tax. If you do not request withholding on Form W-4S, or if you do not have enough tax withheld, you may have to make estimated tax payments. If you do not pay enough tax, either through estimated tax or withholding, or a combination of both, you may have to pay a penalty. See *Underpayment Penalty for 2014* at the end of this chapter.

Pensions and Annuities

Income tax usually will be withheld from your pension or annuity distributions unless you choose not to have it withheld. This rule applies to distributions from:

- A traditional individual retirement arrangement (IRA);
- A life insurance company under an endowment, annuity, or life insurance contract;
- A pension, annuity, or profit-sharing plan;
- A stock bonus plan; and
- Any other plan that defers the time you receive compensation.

The amount withheld depends on whether you receive payments spread out over more than 1 year (periodic payments), within 1 year (nonperiodic payments), or as an eligible rollover distribution (ERD). Income tax withholding from an ERD is mandatory.

EXPLANATION

A part of your pension or annuity may not be taxable. See chapter 10, *Retirement plans, pensions, and annuities*, for information on figuring the nontaxable part. Income tax will not be withheld from the part of your pension or annuity that is nontaxable. Therefore, the tax withheld will be figured on, and cannot be more than the taxable part.

TAXALERT

A distribution that is eligible for direct rollover treatment (see chapter 10, *Retirement plans, pensions, and annuities*) but is not directly rolled over is subject to mandatory 20% withholding, unless the participant's eligible rollover distributions for the year are expected to be less than $200.

If a participant elects to have a portion of a distribution transferred in a direct rollover and the remainder distributed to him or her, only the portion that is distributed to him or her will be subject to the 20% withholding. A plan administrator will not be liable for tax, interest, or penalties for failure to withhold if he or she reasonably relied on information about the participant's plan received from the participant.

TAXALERT

Under normal federal income tax withholding rules, an employee is taxed when a restricted stock award vests. Upon vesting, federal income tax withholding is required on the excess of the fair market value of the stock award price over the grant price. This amount is also subject to FICA tax (i.e., Social Security and 1.45% Medicare tax), plus the 0.9% Additional Medicare Tax (for taxpayers with total wages, compensation, or self-employment income above specified thresholds) that took effect beginning 2013 under the ACA. Subsequent dividends received on the restricted stock award and any capital gains generated if the employee subsequently sells the shares are not, however, subject to the 0.9% Additional Medicare Tax. On the other hand, these dividends and capital gains are considered investment income subject to the new 3.8% Net Investment Income Tax (NIIT) that also took effect under the ACA.

TAXPLANNER

If *property other than cash* is distributed, such property is subject to 20% withholding. If all of the property distributed is company stock, no withholding is actually due. However, if, in addition to company stock, the distribution consists of cash or other property, the actual amount withheld need not exceed the sum of the cash and fair market value of such other property received, though the 20% withholding factor will be applied to the entire distribution including the value of company stock distributed.

TAXALERT

A written explanation of the direct rollover option and related rules (including the rules governing withholding) must generally be provided to participants not more than 90 days and not less than 30 days before the distribution date. For a series of periodic payments that are eligible for direct rollover, an initial timely notice must be given and an additional notice must be provided at least annually for as long as the payments continue.

Failure to provide such notice could cause the plan to become disqualified under the Internal Revenue Code. The IRS has issued a model notice that plan administrators are allowed to customize by deleting any portions that do not apply to the plan and adding additional information that is not inconsistent with the model notice.

Periodic Payments

Withholding from periodic payments of a pension or annuity is figured in the same way as withholding from salaries and wages. To tell the payer of your pension or annuity how much you want withheld, fill out Form W-4P, Withholding Certificate for Pension or Annuity Payments, or a similar form provided by the payer. Follow the rules on withholding discussed under *Salaries and Wages*, earlier, to fill out your Form W-4P.

The withholding rules for pensions and annuities differ from those for salaries and wages in the following ways:

1. If you do not fill out a withholding certificate, tax will be withheld as if you were married and were claiming three withholding allowances.
2. Your certificate will not be sent to the IRS regardless of the number of allowances you claim on it.
3. You can choose not to have tax withheld, regardless of how much tax you owed last year or expect to owe this year. You do not have to qualify for exemption. See *Choosing Not to Have Income Tax Withheld*, later.
4. Tax will be withheld as if you were single and claiming no withholding allowances if:
   a. You do not give the payer your social security number (in the required manner), or
   b. The IRS notifies the payer, before any payment or distribution is made, that you gave it an incorrect social security number.

Note: Military retirement pay generally is treated in the same manner as wages and not as a pension or annuity for income tax withholding purposes. Military retirees should use Form W-4, not Form W-4P.

TAXALERT

If a series of periodic payments began prior to January 1, 1993, you determine whether post-December 31, 1992, payments are a series of substantially equal periodic payments over a specified period by taking into account all payments, including payments made before January 1, 1993. If the post-December 31, 1992, payments are not a series of substantially equal periodic payments, they will be subject to the direct rollover rules, including mandatory 20% withholding.

Nonperiodic Payments

Tax will be withheld at a 10% rate on any nonperiodic payments you receive.

Because withholding on nonperiodic payments does not depend on withholding allowances or whether you are married or single, you cannot use Form W-4P to tell the payer how much to withhold. However, you can use Form W-4P to specify that an additional amount be withheld. You can also use Form W-4P to choose not to have tax withheld or to revoke a choice not to have tax withheld. See *Choosing Not to Have Income Tax Withheld*, later.

Eligible Rollover Distributions (ERDs)

Distributions you receive that are eligible to be rolled over tax-free into qualified retirement or annuity plans are subject to a 20% withholding tax.

An eligible rollover distribution (ERD) is any distribution of all or any part of the balance to your credit in a qualified retirement plan except:

1. Any of a series of substantially equal distributions paid at least once a year over:
   a. Your lifetime or life expectancy,
   b. The joint lives or life expectancies of you and your beneficiary, or
   c. A period of 10 years or more.
2. A required minimum distribution (discussed in Publication 575, *Pension and Annuity Income*, under *Tax on Excess Accumulation*),
3. Hardship distributions,
4. Corrective distributions of excess contributions or excess deferrals, and any income allocable to these distributions, or of excess annual additions and any allocable gains (see *Corrective distributions of excess plan contributions*, at the beginning of *Taxation of Nonperiodic Payments* in Publication 575),
5. A loan treated as a distribution because it does not satisfy certain requirements either when made or later (such as upon default), unless the participant's accrued benefits are reduced (offset) to repay the loan (see *Loans Treated as Distributions*, in Publication 575),
6. Dividends paid on employer securities, and
7. The cost of life insurance coverage.

In addition, a distribution to the plan participant's beneficiary generally is not treated as an eligible rollover distribution. However, see *Qualified domestic relations order, Rollover by surviving spouse*, and *Rollovers by nonspouse beneficiary*, later.

For more information about eligible rollover distributions, see Publication 575, Pension and Annuity Income.

EXPLANATION

The withholding rules for non-ERD distributions are discussed earlier under Periodic Payments and Nonperiodic Payments.

A distribution is subject to withholding if it is not substantially equal to the periodic payments.

For example, upon retirement you receive 30% of your accrued pension benefits in the form of a single sum distribution with the balance payable in annuity form. The 30% distribution is an ERD subject to 20% withholding. The annuity payments are periodic payments subject to withholding only if you choose to have withholding taken out.

The payer of a distribution must withhold at a 20% rate on any part of an ERD that is not rolled over directly to another qualified plan. You cannot elect not to have withholding on these distributions.

If tax is withheld on the ERD, it will be withheld only on the taxable portion of the distribution. You must either:

1. Contribute to the new plan (within 60 days from the date of the distribution) an amount equal to the taxable part of the total ERD, including the amount withheld, to avoid including the distribution as taxable income on your 2015 tax return or
2. Include in your income for the year of the distribution any amount withheld for which you did not make a matching contribution to the new plan.

The matching contribution to cover the withheld amount, as explained in 1 above, must be in addition to the rollover of the net amount that you actually received. If all or any portion of an amount equal to the amount withheld is not contributed as a rollover, it must be included in your income to the extent of the difference between the taxable part of the distribution and the actual rollover amount.

Exception to withholding rule. The only way to avoid withholding on an ERD is to have it directly rolled over from the employer's plan to a qualified plan or IRA. This direct rollover is made only at your direction. You must first make sure that the receiving trustee agrees to accept a direct rollover. The transferor or trustee must allow you to make such a rollover and provide to you, within a reasonable period of time, written instructions on how to do so. You must also follow spousal consent and other participant and beneficiary protection rules.

TAXSAVER

If you receive an eligible rollover distribution from which the mandatory 20% withholding tax has been withheld, and you then decide you wish to roll the distribution over to an IRA within the allowed 60 days, you must come up with the 20% that was withheld from other funds within the 60-day period in order to roll the entire balance over. Otherwise the 20% that has been withheld will be treated as a taxable distribution and ineligible for rollover.

Choosing Not to Have Income Tax Withheld

You can choose not to have income tax withheld from your pension or annuity, whether the payments are periodic or nonperiodic. This rule does not apply to eligible rollover distributions. The payer will tell you how to make this choice. If you use Form W-4P, check the box on line 1 to make this election. Your choice will stay in effect until you decide you want withholding. The payer will ignore your request not to have income tax withheld if:

1. You do not give the payer your social security number (in the required manner), or
2. The IRS notifies the payer, before any payment or distribution is made, that you gave it an incorrect social security number.

TAXPLANNER

You should choose to have no tax withheld from nonperiodic payments (total distributions within 1 year) from an employer pension or profit-sharing plan if you intend to defer taxation by putting the money directly into an individual retirement arrangement (IRA).

If you choose not to have any income tax withheld from your pension or annuity, or if you do not have enough withheld, you may have to make estimated tax payments. See _Estimated Tax_, later.

If you do not pay enough tax through either estimated tax or withholding, you may have to pay a penalty. See _Underpayment Penalty_, later in this chapter.

Outside United States. If you are a U.S. citizen or resident alien and you choose not to have tax withheld from pension or annuity benefits, you must give the payer of the benefits a home address in the United States or in a U.S. possession. Otherwise, the payer must withhold tax. For example, the payer would have to withhold tax if you provide a U.S. address for a nominee, trustee, or agent to whom the benefits are to be delivered but do not provide your own home address in the United States or in a U.S. possession.

Revoking a choice not to have tax withheld. If you want to revoke your choice not to have tax withheld, the payer of your pension or annuity will tell you how. If the payer gives you Form W-4P, write "Revoked" by the checkbox on line 1 of the form.

If you get periodic payments and do not complete the rest of the form, the payer will withhold tax as if you were married and claiming three allowances. If you want tax withheld at a different rate, you must complete the rest of the form.

Notice required of payer. The payer of your pension or annuity is required to send you a notice telling you about your right to choose not to have tax withheld.

More information. For more information on taxation of annuities and distributions (including ERDs) from qualified retirement plans, see chapter 10. For information on IRAs, see chapter 17. For more information on withholding on pensions and annuities, including a discussion of Form W-4P, see *Pensions and Annuities* in chapter 1 of Publication 505.

Gambling Winnings

Income tax is withheld at a flat 25% rate from certain kinds of gambling winnings.

Gambling winnings of more than $5,000 from the following sources are subject to income tax withholding.

- Any sweepstakes; wagering pool, including payments made to winners of poker tournaments; or lottery.
- Any other wager, if the proceeds are at least 300 times the amount of the bet.

It does not matter whether your winnings are paid in cash, in property, or as an annuity. Winnings not paid in cash are taken into account at their fair market value.

Exception. Gambling winnings from bingo, keno, and slot machines generally are not subject to income tax withholding. However, you may need to provide the payer with a social security number to avoid withholding. See *Backup withholding on gambling winnings* in chapter 1 of Publication 505. If you receive gambling winnings not subject to withholding, you may need to pay estimated tax. See *Estimated Tax for 2015*, later.

If you do not pay enough tax, either through withholding or estimated tax, or a combination of both, you may have to pay a penalty. See *Underpayment Penalty for 2014* at the end of this chapter.

Form W-2G. If a payer withholds income tax from your gambling winnings, you should receive a Form W-2G, Certain Gambling Winnings, showing the amount you won and the amount withheld. Report the tax withheld on line 62 of Form 1040.

TAXPLANNER
Gambling losses are deductible, but only to the extent that you have gambling winnings to offset the losses and only if you itemize your deductions. It is very important to keep accurate records to document both your winnings and your losses.

Unemployment Compensation

You can choose to have income tax withheld from unemployment compensation. To make this choice, fill out Form W-4V (or a similar form provided by the payer) and give it to the payer.

All unemployment compensation is taxable. So, if you do not have income tax withheld, you may have to pay estimated tax. See *Estimated Tax for 2015*, later.

If you do not pay enough tax, either through withholding or estimated tax, or a combination of both, you may have to pay a penalty. For information, see *Underpayment Penalty for 2014* at the end of this chapter.

Federal Payments

You can choose to have income tax withheld from certain federal payments you receive. These payments are:

1. Social security benefits,
2. Tier 1 railroad retirement benefits,

3. Commodity credit corporation loans you choose to include in your gross income,
4. Payments under the Agricultural Act of 1949 (7 U.S.C. 1421 et. seq.), as amended, or title II of the Disaster Assistance Act of 1988, that are treated as insurance proceeds and that you receive because:
    a. Your crops were destroyed or damaged by drought, flood, or any other natural disaster, or
    b. You were unable to plant crops because of a natural disaster described in (a), and
5. Any other payment under Federal law as determined by the Secretary.

To make this choice, fill out Form W-4V (or a similar form provided by the payer) and give it to the payer.

If you do not choose to have income tax withheld, you may have to pay estimated tax. See _Estimated Tax for 2015_, later.

If you do not pay enough tax, either through withholding or estimated tax, or a combination of both, you may have to pay a penalty. For information, see _Underpayment Penalty for 2014_ at the end of this chapter.

More information. For more information about the tax treatment of social security and railroad retirement benefits, see chapter 11. Get Publication 225, Farmer's Tax Guide, for information about the tax treatment of commodity credit corporation loans or crop disaster payments.

Backup Withholding

Banks or other businesses that pay you certain kinds of income must file an information return (Form 1099) with the IRS. The information return shows how much you were paid during the year. It also includes your name and taxpayer identification number (TIN). TINs are explained in chapter 1 under _Social Security Number (SSN)._

These payments generally are not subject to withholding. However, "backup" withholding is required in certain situations. Backup withholding can apply to most kinds of payments that are reported on Form 1099.

The payer must withhold at a flat 28% rate in the following situations.
- You do not give the payer your TIN in the required manner.
- The IRS notifies the payer that the TIN you gave is incorrect.
- You are required, but fail, to certify that you are not subject to backup withholding.
- The IRS notifies the payer to start withholding on interest or dividends because you have underreported interest or dividends on your income tax return. The IRS will do this only after it has mailed you four notices over at least a 210-day period.

See _Backup Withholding_ in chapter 1 of Publication 505 for more information.

Penalties. There are civil and criminal penalties for giving false information to avoid backup withholding. The civil penalty is $500. The criminal penalty, upon conviction, is a fine of up to $1,000 or imprisonment of up to 1 year, or both.

Estimated Tax for 2015

Estimated tax is the method used to pay tax on income that is not subject to withholding. This includes income from self-employment, interest, dividends, alimony, rent, gains from the sale of assets, prizes, and awards. You also may have to pay estimated tax if the amount of income tax being withheld from your salary, pension, or other income is not enough.

Estimated tax is used to pay both income tax and self-employment tax, as well as other taxes and amounts reported on your tax return. If you do not pay enough tax, either through withholding or estimated tax, or a combination of both, you may have to pay a penalty. If you do not pay enough by the due date of each payment period (see _When To Pay Estimated Tax_, later), you may be charged a penalty even if you are due a refund when you file your tax return. For information on when the penalty applies, see _Underpayment Penalty for 2014_ at the end of this chapter.

Who Does Not Have To Pay Estimated Tax

If you receive salaries or wages, you can avoid having to pay estimated tax by asking your employer to take more tax out of your earnings. To do this, give a new Form W-4 to your employer. See chapter 1 of Publication 505.

Estimated tax not required. You do not have to pay estimated tax for 2015 if you meet all three of the following conditions.
- You had no tax liability for 2014.
- You were a U.S. citizen or resident alien for the whole year.
- Your 2014 tax year covered a 12-month period.

Figure 4-A. Do You Have To Pay Estimated Tax?

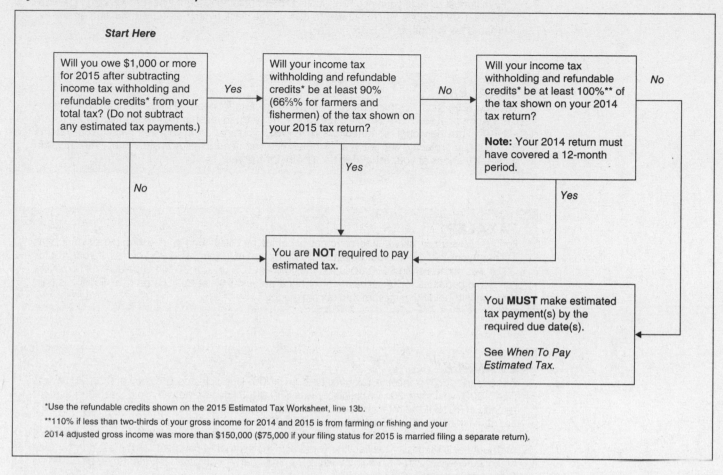

*Use the refundable credits shown on the 2015 Estimated Tax Worksheet, line 13b.

**110% if less than two-thirds of your gross income for 2014 and 2015 is from farming or fishing and your

2014 adjusted gross income was more than $150,000 ($75,000 if your filing status for 2015 is married filing a separate return).

You had no tax liability for 2014 if your total tax was zero or you did not have to file an income tax return. For the definition of "total tax" for 2014, see Publication 505, chapter 2.

Who Must Pay Estimated Tax
If you owe additional tax for 2014, you may have to pay estimated tax for 2015.

You can use the following general rule as a guide during the year to see if you will have enough withholding, or if you should increase your withholding or make estimated tax payments.

General rule. In most cases, you must pay estimated tax for 2015 if both of the following apply.
1. You expect to owe at least $1,000 in tax for 2015, after subtracting your withholding and refundable credits.
2. You expect your withholding plus your refundable credits to be less than the smaller of:
   a. 90% of the tax to be shown on your 2015 tax return, or
   b. 100% of the tax shown on your 2014 tax return (but see *Special rules for farmers, fishermen, and higher income taxpayers*, later). Your 2014 tax return must cover all 12 months.

TAXPLANNER
If you receive a considerable amount of taxable income on which no tax is withheld, you might need to make quarterly estimated tax payments to the IRS.

Some of the most common sources of income not subject to withholding are:
1. Income from self-employment
2. Alimony
3. Interest, dividends, and capital gains
4. Rent

Even if most or all of your income is subject to withholding, you may not have enough tax withheld to satisfy the IRS. You may need to pick up the slack by increasing withholding or making estimated tax payments, or both.

TAXALERT

The new 3.8% Net Investment Income Tax (NIIT) on certain unearned investment income and the 0.9% Additional Medicare Tax on wages and other earned income that took effect in 2013 are subject to the individual estimated tax provisions. If you are basing your estimated tax payments for 2015 on projected current year income, then you need to also consider these new taxes in your calculations of your estimated tax liability for the year.

TAXALERT

For 2015, you can avoid underpayment penalties by calculating your estimated payments as 100% of your 2014 tax if your adjusted gross income (AGI) was $150,000 or less. If your AGI for 2014 was greater than $150,000, you must have 110% of your 2014 tax paid in. All taxpayers can avoid penalties for underpayment of tax if at least 90% of their current tax liability is paid through withholding and estimated tax payments.

EXAMPLE

Anne-Marie's 2015 income tax liability is $45,000. Her adjusted gross income in 2014 was $140,000, while her 2014 tax liability was $30,000. Anne-Marie will avoid an underpayment penalty in 2015 if the total amount of tax withheld and estimated tax payments made for 2015 are at least 100% of her 2014 liability, or $30,000.

Each quarter, the calculation for estimated payment purposes may differ depending on which method yields the lesser tax liability. Therefore, the estimated payment for the 1st quarter may be based on your 2014 tax liability while the 2nd quarter estimated payment may be based on 90% of your current year tax liability.

<table>
<tr><td>**Caution**</td></tr>
</table>

If the result from using the general rule above suggests that you will not have enough withholding, complete the 2015 Estimated Tax Worksheet in Publication 505 for a more accurate calculation.

Special rules for farmers, fishermen, and higher income taxpayers. If at least two-thirds of your gross income for tax year 2014 or 2015 is from farming or fishing, substitute 66⅔% for 90% in (2a) under the *General rule*, earlier. If your AGI for 2014 was more than $150,000 ($75,000 if your filing status for 2015 is married filing a separate return), substitute 110% for 100% in (2b) under *General rule*, earlier. See Figure 4-A and Publication 505, chapter 2 for more information.

Aliens. Resident and nonresident aliens also may have to pay estimated tax. Resident aliens should follow the rules in this chapter unless noted otherwise. Nonresident aliens should get Form 1040-ES (NR), U.S. Estimated Tax for Nonresident Alien Individuals.

You are an alien if you are not a citizen or national of the United States. You are a resident alien if you either have a green card or meet the substantial presence test. For more information about the substantial presence test, see Publication 519, U.S. Tax Guide for Aliens.

Married taxpayers. If you qualify to make joint estimated tax payments, apply the rules discussed here to your joint estimated income.

You and your spouse can make joint estimated tax payments even if you are not living together. However, you and your spouse cannot make joint estimated tax payments if:
- You are legally separated under a decree of divorce or separate maintenance,
- You and your spouse have different tax years, or
- Either spouse is a nonresident alien (unless that spouse elected to be treated as a resident alien for tax purposes (see chapter 1 of Publication 519)).

If you do not qualify to make joint estimated tax payments, apply these rules to your separate estimated income. Making joint or separate estimated tax payments will not affect your choice of filing a joint tax return or separate returns for 2015.

2014 separate returns and 2015 joint return. If you plan to file a joint return with your spouse for 2015, but you filed separate returns for 2014, your 2014 tax is the total of the tax shown on your separate returns. You filed a separate return if you filed as single, head of household, or married filing separately.

2014 joint return and 2015 separate returns. If you plan to file a separate return for 2015 but you filed a joint return for 2014, your 2014 tax is your share of the tax on the joint return. You file a separate return if you file as single, head of household, or married filing separately.

To figure your share of the tax on the joint return, first figure the tax both you and your spouse would have paid had you filed separate returns for 2014 using the same filing status as for 2015. Then multiply the tax on the joint return by the following fraction.

$$\frac{\text{The tax you would have paid had you filed a separate return}}{\text{The total tax you and your spouse would have paid had you filed separate returns}}$$

Example. Joe and Heather filed a joint return for 2014 showing taxable income of $48,500 and a tax of $6,386. Of the $48,500 taxable income, $40,100 was Joe's and the rest was Heather's. For 2015, they plan to file married filing separately. Joe figures his share of the tax on the 2014 joint return as follows.

Tax on $40,100 based on a separate return	$5,960
Tax on $8,400 based on a separate return	843
Total	$6,803
Joe's percentage of total ($5,960 ÷ $6,803)	87.6%
Joe's share of tax on joint return ($6,386 × 87.6%)	$5,594

How To Figure Estimated Tax

To figure your estimated tax, you must figure your expected adjusted gross income (AGI), taxable income, taxes, deductions, and credits for the year.

When figuring your 2015 estimated tax, it may be helpful to use your income, deductions, and credits for 2014 as a starting point. Use your 2014 federal tax return as a guide. You can use Form 1040-ES and Publication 505 to figure your estimated tax. Nonresident aliens use Form 1040-ES (NR) and Publication 505 to figure estimated tax (see chapter 8 of Publication 519 for more information).

You must make adjustments both for changes in your own situation and for recent changes in the tax law. For a discussion of these changes, visit IRS.gov.

For more complete information on how to figure your estimated tax for 2015, see chapter 2 of Publication 505.

TAXPLANNER

A convenient way to figure your estimated tax is to list all your sources of income from last year. Then enter the estimated income from each source for this year. Add to this list all new sources of income that you expect this year. Repeat this procedure for all deductions and exemptions. If your itemized deductions are more than the standard deduction, use your itemized deductions. Then compute your estimated tax liability for 2015 based on your estimated taxable income.

After you have calculated your estimated tax liability, add any additional taxes, including self-employment taxes, household employment taxes, and alternative minimum taxes, that you expect to pay for the current year. Then subtract the various tax credits you expect to claim for the current year, and also subtract the income tax you expect to have withheld. The remaining tax liability is your estimated tax.

If your estimated tax exceeds $1,000, equal estimated tax payments generally have to be made on April 15, June 15, September 15, and January 15. Special exceptions, described later in this chapter, may reduce or eliminate this requirement.

When To Pay Estimated Tax

For estimated tax purposes, the tax year is divided into four payment periods. Each period has a specific payment due date. If you do not pay enough tax by the due date of each payment period, you may be charged a penalty even if you are due a refund when you file your income tax return. The payment periods and due dates for estimated tax payments are shown next.

For the period:	Due date:*
Jan. 1 – March 31	April 15
April 1 – May 31	June 15
June 1 – August 31	Sept. 15
Sept. 1 – Dec. 31	Jan. 15, next year

*See *Saturday, Sunday, holiday rule* and *January payment*.

Saturday, Sunday, holiday rule. If the due date for an estimated tax payment falls on a Saturday, Sunday, or legal holiday, the payment will be on time if you make it on the next day that is not a Saturday, Sunday, or legal holiday.

January payment. If you file your 2015 Form 1040 or Form 1040A by February 1, 2016, and pay the rest of the tax you owe, you do not need to make the payment due on January 15, 2016.

Fiscal year taxpayers. If your tax year does not start on January 1, see the Form 1040-ES instructions for your payment due dates.

When To Start

You do not have to make estimated tax payments until you have income on which you will owe income tax. If you have income subject to estimated tax during the first payment period, you must make your first payment by the due date for the first payment period. You can pay all your estimated tax at that time, or you can pay it in installments. If you choose to pay in installments, make your first payment by the due date for the first payment period. Make your remaining installment payments by the due dates for the later periods.

No income subject to estimated tax during first period. If you do not have income subject to estimated tax until a later payment period, you must make your first payment by the due date for that period. You can pay your entire estimated tax by the due date for that period or you can pay it in installments by the due date for that period and the due dates for the remaining periods. The following chart shows when to make installment payments.

> ### EXAMPLE
> In April 2015, Maura figured that her estimated tax for 2015 would be $12,000. Accordingly, she made her first 2015 quarterly estimated payment of $3,000 on April 15, 2015, and her second quarterly estimated payment of $3,000 on June 15, 2015. In August, Maura purchased a new home, and her monthly mortgage payments increased dramatically. Because Maura could deduct her mortgage interest payments, she reduced her third and fourth quarterly estimated payments due on September 15, 2015, and January 15, 2016, respectively.

If you first have income on which you must pay estimated tax:	Make a payment by:*	Make later installments by:*
Before April 1	April 15	June 15 Sept. 15 Jan. 15 next year
April 1–May 31	June 15	Sept. 15 Jan. 15 next year
June 1–Aug. 31	Sept. 15	Jan. 15 next year
After Aug. 31	Jan. 15 next year	(None)

*See Saturday, Sunday, holiday rule and January payment.

How much to pay to avoid a penalty. To determine how much you should pay by each payment due date, see *How To Figure Each Payment*, next.

EXPLANATION

The discussion that follows shows in detail how to compute your annualized income installment.

Figure your installment for each payment period as follows:

1. Figure your adjusted gross income (AGI), alternative minimum taxable income (AMTI), and adjusted self-employment income (SEI) for the months in 2015 ending before the due date of the payment period. (Your AGI is your actual total income minus your actual adjustments to income for the months in the period.) See <u>chapter 31</u>, *How to figure your tax*, for more information on AMTI. Also, see <u>chapter 38</u>, *Self-employment income*: How to file Schedule C, for more information on SEI.

2. Multiply each of the amounts in step (1) by
   a. 4, if the payment due date is April 15.
   b. 2.4, if the payment due date is June 15.
   c. 1.5, if the payment due date is September 15.
   d. 1, if the payment due date is January 15, 2016. These amounts are your annualized AGI, AMTI, and SEI.

3. Determine the greater of your
   a. Actual allowable itemized deductions for the months in the period multiplied by the same figure used in step (2), or
   b. Standard deduction for the year.

4. Multiply your exemptions by the 2015 exemption amount (see <u>chapter 3</u>, *Personal exemptions and dependents*).

5. Add the amounts from steps (3) and (4), and subtract the total from your annualized AGI determined in step (2). This amount is your annualized taxable income.

6. Figure the appropriate tax on your annualized taxable income [from step (5)], the alternative minimum tax on your annualized AMTI, and self-employment tax on SEI [from step (2)].

7. Total the amounts figured in step (6).

8. Add any additional taxes that you may owe because of events that occurred during the months in 2015 ending before the due date of the payment period. "Other Taxes" are the ones listed on lines 56–60 of the 2014 Form 1040.

9. Subtract from this total any nonrefundable credits that you may be able to claim because of events that occurred during the months in 2015 ending before the due date of the payment period. These are the credits that make up the total on line 54 of the 2014 Form 1040. If these credits are more than the total of step (7) plus additional taxes figured in step (8), use zero as the result and go on to the next step.

10. Add to the result of step (9) any of the taxes listed below that you may owe because of events that occurred during the months in 2015 ending before the due date of the payment period:
    a. Uncollected social security and Medicare tax or RRTA tax on tips or group-term life insurance.
    b. Excise tax on golden parachute payments.
    c. Plus the tax from Form 4952, Tax on Lump Sum Distributions, Form 8814, Parent's Election to Report Child's Interest and Dividends, and alternative minimum tax.

11. Subtract the following credits that apply to your situation for the months in 2015 ending before the due date of the payment period:
    a. Earned income credit.
    b. Adoption credit.
    c. Etc.

12. Multiply the result of step (11) by
    a. 22.5%, if the payment due date is April 15.
    b. 45%, if the payment due date is June 15.
    c. 67.5%, if the payment due date is September 15.
    d. 90%, if the payment due date is January 15, 2016.

13. Figure the total estimated tax you had to pay by the due date of each of the preceding payment periods. This is the total of the lower of the required installment or the annualized income installment for each payment period.

14. Subtract the step (13) amount from the step (12) amount.

If the annualized income installment for the payment period is less than the required installment, you only need to pay the annualized income installment.

When you pay the annualized income installment for the next payment period, you must add the difference between the required installment for that subsequent payment period (as increased) and the annualized income installment for the previous payment period to the required installment for the next payment period.

How To Figure Each Payment

You should pay enough estimated tax by the due date of each payment period to avoid a penalty for that period. You can figure your required payment for each period by using either the regular installment method or the annualized income installment method. These methods are described in chapter 2 of Publication 505. If you do not pay enough during each payment period, you may be charged a penalty even if you are due a refund when you file your tax return.

If the earlier discussion of *No income subject to estimated tax during first period* or the later discussion of *Change in estimated tax* applies to you, you may benefit from reading *Annualized Income Installment Method* in chapter 2 of Publication 505 for information on how to avoid a penalty.

Underpayment penalty. Under the regular installment method, if your estimated tax payment for any period is less than one-fourth of your estimated tax, you may be charged a penalty for underpayment of estimated tax for that period when you file your tax return. Under the annualized income installment method, your estimated tax payments vary with your income, but the amount required must be paid each period. See chapter 4 of Publication 505 for more information.

Change in estimated tax. After you make an estimated tax payment, changes in your income, adjustments, deductions, credits, or exemptions may make it necessary for you to refigure your estimated tax. Pay the unpaid balance of your amended estimated tax by the next payment due date after the change or in installments by that date and the due dates for the remaining payment periods.

Estimated Tax Payments Not Required

You do not have to pay estimated tax if your withholding in each payment period is at least as much as:
- One-fourth of your required annual payment, or
- Your required annualized income installment for that period.

You also do not have to pay estimated tax if you will pay enough through withholding to keep the amount you owe with your return under $1,000.

How To Pay Estimated Tax

There are several ways to pay estimated tax.
- Credit an overpayment on your 2014 return to your 2015 estimated tax.
- Pay by direct transfer from your bank account, or pay by credit or debit card using a pay-by-phone system or the Internet.
- Send in your payment (check or money order) with a payment voucher from Form 1040-ES.

Credit an Overpayment

If you show an overpayment of tax after completing your Form 1040 or Form 1040A for 2014, you can apply part or all of it to your estimated tax for 2015. On line 75 of Form 1040, or line 44 of Form 1040A, enter the amount you want credited to your estimated tax rather than refunded. Take the amount you have credited into account when figuring your estimated tax payments.

You cannot have any of the amount you credited to your estimated tax refunded to you until you file your tax return for the following year. You also cannot use that overpayment in any other way.

EXPLANATION

An overpayment that is applied to your estimated tax payment for the current year is considered to have been paid on time even if you are granted an extension and file your previous year's tax return after April 15.

Example

If you get a legal extension on your tax return from April 15 to October 15 and you actually file your return in July, you can apply any overpayment you may have made in the previous year to your estimated tax payments that were due first on April 15 and then on June 15.

Pay Online

Paying online is convenient and secure and helps make sure we get your payments on time. You can pay using either of the following electronic payment methods.
- Direct transfer from your bank account.
- Credit or debit card.

To pay your taxes online or for more information, go to *www.irs.gov/e-pay*.

Pay by Phone

Paying by phone is another safe and secure method of paying electronically. Use one of the following methods.

- Direct transfer from your bank account.
- Credit or debit card.

To pay by direct transfer from your bank account, call 1-800-555-4477 (English), 1-800-244-4829 (Espanol). People who are deaf, hard of hearing, or have a speech disability and who have access to TTY/TDD can call 1-800-733-4829.

To pay using a credit or debit card, you can call one of the following service providers. There is a convenience fee charged by these providers that varies by provider, card type, and payment amount.

WorldPay 1-888-9-PAY-TAX™ (1-888-972-9829) *www.payUSAtax.com*
Official Payments Corporation 1-888-UPAY-TAX™ (1-888-872-9829) *www.officialpayments.com*
Link2Gov Corporation 1-888-PAY-1040™ (1-888-729-1040) *www.PAY1040.com*
For the latest details on how to pay by phone, go to *www.irs.gov/e-pay*.

Pay by Check or Money Order Using the Estimated Tax Payment Voucher

Each payment of estimated tax by check or money order must be accompanied by a payment voucher from Form 1040-ES.

During 2014, if you:

- made at least one estimated tax payment but not by electronic means,
- did not use software or a paid preparer to prepare or file your return,

then you should receive a copy of the 2014 Form 1040-ES/V.

The enclosed payment vouchers will be preprinted with your name, address, and social security number. Using the preprinted vouchers will speed processing, reduce the chance of error, and help save processing costs.

Use the window envelopes that came with your Form 1040-ES package. If you use your own envelopes, make sure you mail your payment vouchers to the address shown in the Form 1040-ES instructions for the place where you live.

Note. These criteria can change without notice. If you do not receive a Form 1040-ES/V package and you are required to make an estimated tax payment, you should go to *www.irs.gov* and print a copy of Form 1040-ES which includes four blank payment vouchers. Complete one of these and make your payment timely to avoid penalties for paying late.

If you did not pay estimated tax last year, you can order Form 1040-ES from the IRS (see inside back cover of this publication) or download it from IRS.gov. Follow the instructions to make sure you use the vouchers correctly.

Joint estimated tax payments. If you file a joint return and are making joint estimated tax payments, enter the names and social security numbers on the payment voucher in the same order as they will appear on the joint return.

Change of address. You must notify the IRS if you are making estimated tax payments and you changed your address during the year. Complete Form 8822, Change of Address, and mail it to the address shown in the instructions for that form.

> **Caution**
> *Do not use the address shown in the Form 1040 or Form 1040A instructions for your estimated tax payments.*

Credit for Withholding and Estimated Tax for 2014

When you file your 2014 income tax return, take credit for all the income tax and excess social security or railroad retirement tax withheld from your salary, wages, pensions, etc. Also take credit for the estimated tax you paid for 2014. These credits are subtracted from your total tax. Because these credits are refundable, you should file a return and claim these credits, even if you do not owe tax.

Two or more employers. If you had two or more employers in 2014 and were paid wages of more than $117,000, too much social security or tier 1 railroad retirement tax may have been withheld from your pay. You may be able to claim the excess as a credit against your income tax when you file your return. See *Credit for Excess Social Security Tax or Railroad Retirement Tax Withheld* in chapter 37.

Withholding

If you had income tax withheld during 2014, you should be sent a statement by February 2, 2015, showing your income and the tax withheld. Depending on the source of your income, you should receive:

- Form W-2, Wage and Tax Statement,
- Form W-2G, Certain Gambling Winnings, or
- A form in the 1099 series.

Forms W-2 and W-2G. If you file a paper return, always file Form W-2 with your income tax return. File Form W-2G with your return only if it shows any federal income tax withheld from your winnings.

You should get at least two copies of each form. If you file a paper return, attach one copy to the front of your federal income tax return. Keep one copy for your records. You also should receive copies to file with your state and local returns.

> ### EXAMPLE
>
> Eric Jones is employed by ABC Company, Inc. His Form W-2, box 2, reflects that he had $10,675.00 in federal tax withheld by ABC Company on wages of $46,958.
>
> His state income tax of $2,817.48 withheld for the state of Georgia is reflected in box 17 on the same amount of wages. Box 12 (Code D—code definitions can be found on the back of the W-2 form) indicates that Eric contributed $2,546.21 to his company's 401(k) plan. That amount of income was not included in the federal or state wages, but it is included in determining how much was withheld from Eric's income for social security and Medicare purposes. Refer to boxes 3 and 5. The social security tax withheld is in box 4, and the Medicare tax withheld is in box 6. The retirement plan box is checked in box 13 and lets Eric (and the IRS) know that he is covered by a retirement plan and therefore may be limited in his ability to make deductible IRA contributions.

22222	a Employee's social security number	OMB No. 1545-0008	Safe, accurate, FAST! Use	IRS e-file	Visit the IRS website at www.irs.gov/efile

b Employer identification number (EIN)	1 Wages, tips, other compensation 46,958.00	2 Federal income tax withheld 10,675.00
c Employer's name, address, and ZIP code ABC Company, Inc.	3 Social security wages 49,504.21	4 Social security tax withheld 2,079.18
	5 Medicare wages and tips 49,504.21	6 Medicare tax withheld 717.81
	7 Social security tips	8 Allocated tips
d Control number	9	10 Dependent care benefits
e Employee's first name and initial Last name Suff. Eric Jones 1983 Emory Lane Conyers, GA 30013	11 Nonqualified plans	12a See instructions for box 12 D 2,546.21
	13 Statutory employee ☐ Retirement plan ☒ Third-party sick pay ☐	12b
	14 Other	12c
		12d
f Employee's address and ZIP code		

15 State Employer's state ID number GA	16 State wages, tips, etc. 46,958.00	17 State income tax 2,817.48	18 Local wages, tips, etc.	19 Local income tax	20 Locality name

Form W-2 Wage and Tax Statement **2014** Department of the Treasury—Internal Revenue Service

Copy B—To Be Filed With Employee's FEDERAL Tax Return.
This information is being furnished to the Internal Revenue Service.

Form W-2

Your employer is required to provide or send Form W-2 to you no later than February 2, 2015. You should receive a separate Form W-2 from each employer you worked for.

If you stopped working before the end of 2014, your employer could have given you your Form W-2 at any time after you stopped working. However, your employer must provide or send it to you by February 2, 2015.

If you ask for the form, your employer must send it to you within 30 days after receiving your written request or within 30 days after your final wage payment, whichever is later.

If you have not received your Form W-2 by February 2, you should ask your employer for it. If you do not receive it by February 17, call the IRS.

Form W-2 shows your total pay and other compensation and the income tax, social security tax, and Medicare tax that was withheld during the year. Include the federal income tax withheld (as shown in box 2 of Form W-2) on:

- Line 62 if you file Form 1040,
- Line 36 if you file Form 1040A, or
- Line 7 if you file Form 1040EZ.

In addition, Form W-2 is used to report any taxable sick pay you received and any income tax withheld from your sick pay.

Form W-2G

If you had gambling winnings in 2014, the payer may have withheld income tax. If tax was withheld, the payer will give you a Form W-2G showing the amount you won and the amount of tax withheld.

Report the amounts you won on line 21 of Form 1040. Take credit for the tax withheld on line 62 of Form 1040. If you had gambling winnings, you must use Form 1040; you cannot use Form 1040A or Form 1040EZ.

The 1099 Series

Most forms in the 1099 series are not filed with your return. These forms should be furnished to you by February 2, 2015 (or, for Forms 1099-B, 1099-S, and certain Forms 1099-MISC, by February 17, 2015). Unless instructed to file any of these forms with your return, keep them for your records. There are several different forms in this series, including:

- Form 1099-B, Proceeds From Broker and Barter Exchange Transactions;
- Form 1099-DIV, Dividends and Distributions;
- Form 1099-G, Certain Government Payments;
- Form 1099-INT, Interest Income;
- Form 1099-K, Payment Card and Third Party Network Transactions;
- Form 1099-MISC, Miscellaneous Income;
- Form 1099-OID, Original Issue Discount;
- Form 1099-PATR, Taxable Distributions Received from Cooperatives;
- Form 1099-Q, Payments From Qualified Education Programs;
- Form 1099-R, Distributions From Pensions, Annuities, Retirement or Profit-Sharing Plans, IRAs, Insurance Contracts, etc.;
- Form 1099-S, Proceeds From Real Estate Transactions;
- Form RRB-1099, Payments by the Railroad Retirement Board.

If you received the types of income reported on some forms in the 1099 series, you may not be able to use Form 1040A or Form 1040EZ. See the instructions to these forms for details.

Form 1099-R. Attach Form 1099-R to your paper return if box 4 shows federal income tax withheld. Include the amount withheld in the total on line 62 of Form 1040 or line 36 of Form 1040A. You cannot use Form 1040EZ if you received payments reported on Form 1099-R.

Backup withholding. If you were subject to backup withholding on income you received during 2014, include the amount withheld, as shown on your Form 1099, in the total on line 62 of Form 1040, line 36 of Form 1040A, or line 7 of Form 1040EZ.

Form Not Correct

If you receive a form with incorrect information on it, you should ask the payer for a corrected form. Call the telephone number or write to the address given for the payer on the form. The corrected Form W-2G or Form 1099 you receive will have an "X" in the "CORRECTED" box at the top of the form. A special form, Form W-2c, Corrected Wage and Tax Statement, is used to correct a Form W-2.

In certain situations, you will receive two forms in place of the original incorrect form. This will happen when your taxpayer identification number is wrong or missing, your name and address are wrong, or you received the wrong type of form (for example, a Form 1099-DIV instead of a Form 1099-INT). One new form you receive will be the same incorrect form or have the same incorrect information, but all money amounts will be zero. This form will have an "X" in the "CORRECTED" box at the top of the form. The second new form should have all the correct information, prepared as though it is the original (the "CORRECTED" box will not be checked).

Form Received After Filing

If you file your return and you later receive a form for income that you did not include on your return, you should report the income and take credit for any income tax withheld by filing Form 1040X, Amended U.S. Individual Income Tax Return.

Separate Returns

If you are married but file a separate return, you can take credit only for the tax withheld from your own income. Do not include any amount withheld from your spouse's income. However, different rules may apply if you live in a community property state.

Community property states are listed in chapter 2. For more information on these rules, and some exceptions, see Publication 555, Community Property.

Fiscal Years

If you file your tax return on the basis of a fiscal year (a 12-month period ending on the last day of any month except December), you must follow special rules to determine your credit for federal income tax withholding. For a discussion of how to take credit for withholding on a fiscal year return, see *Fiscal Years (FY)* in chapter 3 of Publication 505.

EXPLANATION

Employees on a fiscal year may suffer a delay in utilizing their credit from withheld taxes. See chapter 42, *Foreign citizens living in the United States,* for an example.

Estimated Tax

Take credit for all your estimated tax payments for 2014 on line 63 of Form 1040 or line 37 of Form 1040A. Include any overpayment from 2013 that you had credited to your 2014 estimated tax. You must use Form 1040 or Form 1040A if you paid estimated tax. You cannot use Form 1040EZ.

Name changed. If you changed your name, and you made estimated tax payments using your old name, attach a brief statement to the front of your paper tax return indicating:

- When you made the payments,
- The amount of each payment,
- Your name when you made the payments, and
- Your social security number.

The statement should cover payments you made jointly with your spouse as well as any you made separately.

Be sure to report the change to the Social Security Administration. This prevents delays in processing your return and issuing any refunds.

Separate Returns

If you and your spouse made separate estimated tax payments for 2014 and you file separate returns, you can take credit only for your own payments.

If you made joint estimated tax payments, you must decide how to divide the payments between your returns. One of you can claim all of the estimated tax paid and the other none, or you can divide it in any other way you agree on. If you cannot agree, you must divide the payments in proportion to each spouse's individual tax as shown on your separate returns for 2014.

Divorced Taxpayers

If you made joint estimated tax payments for 2014, and you were divorced during the year, either you or your former spouse can claim all of the joint payments, or you each can claim part of them. If you cannot agree on how to divide the payments, you must divide them in proportion to each spouse's individual tax as shown on your separate returns for 2014.

If you claim any of the joint payments on your tax return, enter your former spouse's social security number (SSN) in the space provided on the front of Form 1040 or Form 1040A. If you divorced and remarried in 2014, enter your present spouse's SSN in that space and write your former spouse's SSN, followed by "DIV," to the left of Form 1040, line 63, or Form 1040A, line 37.

Underpayment Penalty for 2014

If you did not pay enough tax, either through withholding or by making timely estimated tax payments, you will have an underpayment of estimated tax and you may have to pay a penalty.

Generally, you will not have to pay a penalty for 2014 if any of the following apply.

- The total of your withholding and estimated tax payments was at least as much as your 2013 tax (or 110% of your 2013 tax if your AGI was more than $150,000, $75,000 if your 2014 filing status is married filing separately) and you paid all required estimated tax payments on time.
- The tax balance due on your 2014 return is no more than 10% of your total 2014 tax, and you paid all required estimated tax payments on time.
- Your total 2014 tax minus your withholding and refundable credits is less than $1,000.
- You did not have a tax liability for 2013 and your 2013 tax year was 12 months, or
- You did not have any withholding taxes and your current year tax less any household employment taxes is less than $1,000.

See Publication 505, chapter 4, for a definition of "total tax" for 2013 and 2014.

Farmers and fishermen. Special rules apply if you are a farmer or fisherman. See *Farmers and Fishermen* in chapter 4 of Publication 505 for more information.

IRS can figure the penalty for you. If you think you owe the penalty but you do not want to figure it yourself when you file your tax return, you may not have to. Generally, the IRS will figure the penalty for you and send you a bill. However, if you think you are able to lower or eliminate your penalty, you must complete Form 2210 or Form 2210-F and attach it to your paper return. See chapter 4 of Publication 505.

TAXPLANNER

The safest method of paying enough estimated tax and withholding, and thereby avoiding underpayment penalties, is to use last year's tax. The tax shown on your previous year's tax return less the tax that is expected to be withheld during the current year must be paid in estimated installments throughout the year.

Example

Laercio's 2014 tax return indicates that his 2014 tax liability (including self-employment tax and alternative minimum tax) was $14,000. In 2015, Laercio estimates that his tax liability will jump to $24,000 due to several contemplated stock sales that should result in a substantial capital gain. Laercio's withholding on his 2015 salary is expected to be $13,000.

Because his withholding of $13,000 during 2015 is not expected to exceed her 2014 tax of $14,000, he should increase his withholding by $1,000 during the year. Even though he will have paid less than 90% of his tax liability for 2015, he will avoid an underpayment penalty because he has paid an amount at least equal to his 2014 tax. If he made this determination early enough in the year, he could accomplish the same result by making four quarterly estimated tax payments of $250.

However, Laercio will have to pay an additional $10,000 ($24,000 − $14,000) when he files his 2015 tax return by April 15, 2016. Nevertheless, he will have had the use of this money from the time he sold his stock until the time he filed his 2015 tax return.

Explanation

Underpayment penalties. You may be penalized for not paying enough tax for a particular installment period. The amount subject to the penalty is the amount by which the required installment, defined as the lesser of items 1 or 2 below, exceeds the amount paid for the quarterly period:

1. 90% of the tax shown on the return (after certain adjustments), allocated evenly to each of the quarterly periods; or
2. 100% of the 2014 tax, allocated evenly to each of the quarterly periods (provided the prior year comprised 12 months and a return was filed for such year); if your 2014 adjusted gross income exceeded $150,000, you must have paid 110% of the 2014 tax liability to avoid underpayment penalties for 2015. Note: 100% of prior year tax is the tax liability as shown on the 2014 original return. The tax liability on an amended return is not used for purposes of quarterly estimated payments.

Example

Laura's adjusted gross income in 2013 was $175,000, while her 2013 tax liability was $40,000. Her 2014 income tax liability is $55,000. Laura will avoid an underpayment penalty in 2014 if the total amount of tax withheld and estimated tax payments exceeds 110% of her 2013 tax liability, or $44,000. To avoid a penalty in 2015, she would have to pay in $60,500 (110% of $55,000), since her adjusted gross income also exceeded $150,000 in 2014.

The underpayment penalty may also be avoided by using a special rule based on your annualized income. Under the special rule, no penalty is imposed for a quarter if the cumulative amount paid by the installment date equals or exceeds 90% of the cumulative estimated tax as computed on annualized income.

In general, the annualized method allows you to calculate your quarterly payment based on taxable income received up to the end of the latest quarter, annualized to a 12-month period. You can usually benefit from the annualized method if you do not receive your taxable income evenly throughout the year (e.g., if you are the owner of a ski shop that receives most of its revenue during the winter months).

The use of the methods for determining the underpaid amount, described previously, may vary from quarter to quarter to provide the minimum underpayment amount by quarter. Remember, however, that if you pay the annualized income installment, you must add the difference between the amount you pay and the required installment to the required installment for the next period if the annualized income method is not used for the next period.

The tax computed for purposes of determining the quarterly payment required to avoid the underpayment penalty includes the self-employment tax and all other taxes (including the alternative minimum tax), minus any allowable credits.

If the amount paid for a quarterly period is greater than the amount required to avoid penalty, the excess is applied first against underpayments in prior quarters, and then against subsequent underpayments. Any penalty is assessed from the installment due date to the date paid or the original due date of the return, whichever is earlier. The rate of the penalty is the same as the rate of interest for underpayments of tax. However, the penalty is not compounded daily, whereas the interest is.

Special requirements and exceptions are provided for farmers, fishermen, and nonresident aliens

TAXALERT

The underpayment of estimated tax penalty is not imposed where the total tax liability for the year, reduced by any withheld tax and estimated tax payments, is less than $1,000.

TAXPLANNER

You may avoid an underpayment penalty before the end of the year by taking a distribution from your IRA account and having enough taxes withheld to cover your underpayment. It is important to remember to repay the entire amount of the distribution, including taxes withheld, within 60 days after the distribution. Otherwise, the distribution is subject to taxes as well as a 10% early withdrawal penalty if you are under age 59½.

Part 2
Income

ey.com/EYTaxGuide

The eight chapters in this part discuss many kinds of income. They explain which income is and is not taxed. See Part Three for information on gains and losses you report on Form 8949 and Schedule D (Form 1040) and for information on selling your home.

INCOME

INCOME GENERALLY INCLUDES:

Alimony (chapter 18, *Alimony*)

Bartering income (chapter 12, *Other income*)

Canceled debt income (chapter 12, *Other income*)

Dividends (chapter 8, *Dividends and other corporate distributions*)

Gain on the sale of personal items, such as a car (chapter 12, *Other income*)

Gambling winnings (chapter 12, *Other income*)

Income from an activity not for profit (chapter 12, *Other income*)

Interest (chapter 7, *Interest income*)

Part of social security benefits and equivalent railroad retirement benefits (chapter 11, *Social security and equivalent railroad retirement benefits*)

Pensions and annuities (chapter 10, *Retirement plans, pensions, and annuities*)

Recoveries of amounts previously deducted (chapter 12, *Other income*)

Rental income (chapter 9, *Rental income and expenses*)

Royalties (chapter 12, *Other income*)

Tips (chapter 6, *Tip income*)

Wages, salaries, and other earnings (chapter 5, *Wages, salaries, and other earnings*)

Your share of estate and trust income (chapter 12, *Other income*)

Your share of partnership and S corporation income (chapter 12, *Other income*)

INCOME GENERALLY DOES NOT INCLUDE:

Accident and health insurance proceeds (chapter 12, *Other income*)

Gifts and inheritances (chapter 12, *Other income*)

Housing allowance for members of the clergy (chapter 5, *Wages, salaries, and other earnings*)

Interest on state and local government obligations (chapter 7, *Interest income*)

Life insurance proceeds (chapter 12, *Other income*)

Military allowances (chapter 5, *Wages, salaries, and other earnings*)

Part of scholarship and fellowship grants (chapter 12, *Other income*)

Part of social security benefits and equivalent railroad retirement benefits (chapter 11, *Social security and equivalent railroad retirement benefits*)

Veterans' benefits (chapter 5, *Wages, salaries, and other earnings*)

Welfare and other public assistance benefits (chapter 12, *Other income*)

Workers' compensation and similar payments for sickness and injury (chapter 12, *Other income*)

Chapter 5
Wages, salaries, and other earnings

Note

IRS Publication 17 (*Your Federal Income Tax*) has been updated by Ernst & Young LLP for 2014. Dates and dollar amounts shown are for 2014. Underlined type is used to indicate where IRS text has been updated. Places where text has been removed are indicated by the sentence: *Text intentionally omitted*.

ey.com/EYTaxGuide

Ernst & Young LLP will update the *EY Tax Guide 2015* website with relevant taxpayer information as it becomes available. You can also sign up for email alerts to let you know when changes have been made.

Introduction

Ask most people how much they get paid, and, if they are willing to admit anything, they'll tell you what their salary is. Usually, there's more to income than that.

The way the IRS sees it, "gross income means all income from whatever source derived." That means not only is your salary subject to tax, but so are many of the fringe benefits provided by your employer that you might receive—everything from country club memberships and employer-provided discounts to a company car. This chapter spells out in greater detail items of compensation that are taxable.

Some fringe benefits you receive from your employer are tax-free. For example, the cost of the first $50,000 of coverage in a group-term life insurance plan will be tax-free if all employees in the plan are treated in the same way. But, if your employer, in a moment of detached and disinterested generosity, presents you with a Rolls-Royce as a gift, you will probably have to pay taxes on it. This chapter prepares you—in a tax sense—for whatever lies ahead.

What's New

TAXPLANNER
Limit on elective deferrals. The maximum amount of elective deferrals under a salary reduction agreement that can be contributed to a qualified plan (such as a Section 401(k) or 403(b) plan) in 2014 is $17,500 ($23,000 if you were age 50 or older). For more information, see the TaxPlanner regarding elective deferrals in chapter 10, *Retirement plans, pensions, and annuities*.

Reminder

Foreign income. If you are a U.S. citizen or resident alien, you must report income from sources outside the United States (foreign income) on your tax return unless it is exempt by U.S. law. This is true whether you reside inside or outside the United States and whether or not you receive a Form W-2, Wage and Tax Statement, or Form 1099 from the foreign payer. This applies to earned income (such as wages and tips) as well as unearned income (such as interest, dividends, capital gains, pensions, rents, and royalties).

Tax Breaks and Deductions You Can Use Checklist

Withholding on wages. If you're getting a very large refund when you file your return, remember that you can claim withholding allowances based on your expected deductions for 2015. Claiming more allowances will increase the amount of your take-home pay. For more details, see *Getting the Right Amount of Tax Withheld* in chapter 4, *Tax withholding and estimated tax.*

Health Flexible Spending Arrangements (FSAs). If your employer provides you with an FSA (also known as a cafeteria plan), consider taking advantage of it. You can contribute part of your salary to the arrangement on a pre-tax basis (not subject to income, social security, or Medicare taxes). You can then pay for qualified health care expenses (including prescription medication and insurance co-payments) tax-free. FSA coverage and reimbursement are now allowed for your children who are under age 27 as of the end of your tax year. For more details, see *Cafeteria Plans* in chapter 22, *Medical and dental expenses.*

401(k) and 403(b) plan contributions. You can reduce your taxable wages (and your tax bill) by contributing on a pre-tax basis to a 401(k) or 403(b) plan sponsored by your employer. In 2014, you can contribute up to $17,500 ($23,000 if you are 50 or older by the end of the year). For more details, see chapter 10, *Retirement plans, pensions, and annuities.*

If you reside outside the United States, you may be able to exclude part or all of your foreign source earned income. For details, see Publication 54, Tax Guide for U.S. Citizens and Resident Aliens Abroad.

TAXALERT

Foreign earned income exclusion. If you qualify, you may elect to exclude a maximum of $99,200 in foreign earned income from your U.S. taxable income in 2014. The amount of the exclusion is indexed annually for inflation. For more information on the foreign earned income exclusion, see *The Foreign Earned Income Exclusion* in chapter 41.

Introduction

This chapter discusses compensation received for services as an employee, such as wages, salaries, and fringe benefits. The following topics are included.

- Bonuses and awards.
- Special rules for certain employees.
- Sickness and injury benefits.

The chapter explains what income is included in the employee's gross income and what is not included.

EXPLANATION

One of the most important decisions you have to make in determining your correct taxable income is what payments to include. A taxable payment is not limited to cash. It may be property, stock, or other assets. Also, you must include in your gross income the fair market value of payments in kind.

Example 1
Your employer provides you with a car that is used for both personal and business purposes. The value of the personal use of the car is included in earnings and it is taxable to you.

Example 2
You assist a group of investors in purchasing a piece of real estate. In consideration of your services, the investors award you an unconditional percentage of ownership in the acquired asset. You have invested none of your personal funds. The fair market value of your ownership interest is considered as compensation taxable to you in the year the transfer is completed.

Example 3
A farmer receives 50 bushels of wheat as a payment in kind. Unless specifically excluded under a government program, the farmer has income to the extent of the fair market value of the wheat.

Useful Items

You may want to see:

Publication
- ☐ **463** Travel, Entertainment, Gift, and Car Expenses
- ☐ **525** Taxable and Nontaxable Income

EXPLANATION

Other useful publications and references include:
- **Publication 15, Circular E,** Employer's Tax Guide; chapter 5, Wages and Other Compensation
- **Publication 15-B,** Employer's Tax Guide to Fringe Benefits; chapter 1, Fringe Benefit Overview

These and other IRS publications are available online at *www.irs.gov*.

Employee Compensation

This section discusses various types of employee compensation including fringe benefits, retirement plan contributions, stock options, and restricted property.

EXPLANATION

All compensation for personal services, no matter what the form of payment, must be included in gross income. Such compensation is subject to taxes in the year received, unless the taxpayer reports income on the accrual basis.

If you perform services and decide that payment for them should be made to another person, the monies remitted to the third party are taxable to you. The IRS and the courts have long held that "fruits" of a taxpayer's labor are attributable to the "tree" that grew them. Furthermore, you may not render services and then ask your employer to hold the funds in an attempt to artificially control when the wages will be included in your taxable income.

Example

You are due compensation for work you performed. You advise the payer to hold the money because you will not require the funds immediately. The payer credits the payment due to you on the company books. You do not request the money until after the close of the tax year in which the services were rendered.

The IRS may hold that you were in constructive receipt of the funds before year's end. The compensation may have to be included in your income for the year in which the payment could have been received, even though you were not actually paid until later.

TAXPLANNER

You will have a problem with the IRS if you ask your employer after you have performed the work to withhold funds in an attempt to artificially control when the wages will be included in your taxable income. If you make arrangements to defer receipt of income prior to commencing work, you may not have a problem as long as the arrangement meets the requirements of the law. However, if your employer requires you to take your bonus in a later year, then it is not taxable to you until the year in which you receive it.

EXAMPLE

If you arrange to have your employer pay your year-end bonus over a 5-year period, the IRS will not claim that you were in constructive receipt of the entire bonus at the end of the first year if the deferral of your bonus is within the strict nonqualified deferred compensation rules. (These rules are complex. Your employer will likely provide you with guidelines if you are eligible to participate in such a plan. Also, consider consulting with your tax advisor.) You may even arrange to have your employer add interest to your deferred bonus. You must make these arrangements prior to performance of the work for which the bonus will be paid. Keep in mind these types of arrangements must meet a complicated set of requirements, which have been in place since 2004. (You should consider consulting your tax advisor for specific guidance.)

Form W-2. If you are an employee, you should receive Form W-2 from your employer showing the pay you received for your services. Include your pay on line 7 of Form 1040 or Form 1040A, or on line 1 of Form 1040EZ, even if you do not receive a Form W-2.

If you performed services, other than as an independent contractor, and your employer did not withhold social security and Medicare taxes from your pay, you must file Form 8919, Uncollected Social Security and Medicare Tax on Wages, with your Form 1040. These wages must be included on line 7 of Form 1040. See Form 8919 for more information.

EXPLANATION

For 2014, your employer is required to furnish your W-2 to you no later than February 2, 2015. If a Form W-2 is not received from your employer by the tax filing deadline, Form 4852, the substitute for W-2, should be attached to the return. If you leave your job prior to December 31, 2014, and are not expecting to return to it prior to the calendar year-end, you can request a copy of your W-2 in writing from your employer and they are required to provide a copy to you within 30 days of the request if the 30-day period ends before February 2, 2015.

Childcare providers. If you provide childcare, either in the child's home or in your home or other place of business, the pay you receive must be included in your income. If you are not an employee, you are probably self-employed and must include payments for your services on Schedule C (Form 1040), Profit or Loss From Business, or Schedule C-EZ (Form 1040), Net Profit From

Disability Income. If you become disabled, any benefits paid to you while you can't work are usually taxable income. But if an insurance company pays the benefits, and the premium payments were originally taxable to you, those benefits will not be taxable. Check to see how your employer treats those premium payments. For more details, see *Disability Pensions* in chapter 10, *Retirement plans, pensions, and annuities.*

Health Savings Accounts (HSAs). If you are covered by a health plan with a high deductible amount (HDHP) and meet other certain requirements, you may want to consider establishing a health savings account (HSA). Contributions made by you would be a deduction from your adjusted gross income, and contributions by your employer are excluded from your income and are not subject to employment taxes. Similar to FSAs, HSA's coverage and reimbursement are now allowed for your children under age 27 as of the end of your tax year. For frequently asked questions related to HSAs, see Publication 969, *Health Savings Accounts and Other Tax-Favored Health Plans*, and additional information included in this chapter.

Business. You generally are not an employee unless you are subject to the will and control of the person who employs you as to what you are to do and how you are to do it.

Babysitting. If you babysit for relatives or neighborhood children, whether on a regular basis or only periodically, the rules for childcare providers apply to you.

Miscellaneous Compensation

This section discusses different types of employee compensation.

Advance commissions and other earnings. If you receive advance commissions or other amounts for services to be performed in the future and you are a cash-method taxpayer, you must include these amounts in your income in the year you receive them.

If you repay unearned commissions or other amounts in the same year you receive them, reduce the amount included in your income by the repayment. If you repay them in a later tax year, you can deduct the repayment as an itemized deduction on your Schedule A (Form 1040), or you may be able to take a credit for that year. See *Repayments* in chapter 12.

EXPLANATION

In some cases, an advance payment of a commission or salary may be considered a loan, thus permitting you to delay paying tax on that amount. If the loan is repaid, you will not have to recognize any taxable income. If the loan is forgiven, you will recognize the amount of the loan as compensation in the year in which it was forgiven. See *Canceled Debts* in chapter 12, *Other income*, for a complete discussion. Commissions and salaries are considered to be income when they are paid to you or when they are applied as a reduction to your loan account.

The key question is: When may a payment be characterized as a loan? Generally, for a transaction to be considered a loan, a debtor-creditor relationship must exist from the beginning. In other words, the lending party expects and will eventually receive monetary repayment. Payment in return for a future obligation to render services is not a loan. Thus, an advance on your wages is not a loan. Whether a payment is or is not a loan is usually a question of fact, requiring a review of each case's unique circumstances.

Example

If you receive an advance of your January 2015 salary on December 31, 2014, you will have taxable income in 2015.

TAXSAVER

Generally, you should take advantage of your employer's 401(k) plan or 403(b) plan. Your contribution to the plan will not be included in your taxable wages. See chapter 10, *Retirement plans, pensions, and annuities*, for more information about these plans.

TAXPLANNER

You may wish to consider a loan from your employer's qualified pension or annuity plan rather than an advance on your next year's salary. Loans are not considered taxable income to the borrower under most circumstances. See chapter 10, *Retirement plans, pensions, and annuities*, for rules regarding loans from an employer's qualified pension or annuity plan.

TAXALERT

Owner-employees, such as S corporation shareholders, partners, and sole proprietors, are able to borrow from their pension plans without being subject to a penalty tax.

Allowances and reimbursements. If you receive travel, transportation, or other business expense allowances or reimbursements from your employer, see Publication 463. If you are reimbursed for moving expenses, see Publication 521, Moving Expenses.

Back pay awards. Include in income amounts you are awarded in a settlement or judgment for back pay. These include payments made to you for damages, unpaid life insurance premiums, and unpaid health insurance premiums. They should be reported to you by your employer on Form W-2.

Bonuses and awards. Bonuses or awards you receive for outstanding work are included in your income and should be shown on your Form W-2. These include prizes such as vacation trips for meeting sales goals. If the prize or award you receive is goods or services, you must include the fair market value of the goods or services in your income. However, if your employer merely promises to pay you a bonus or award at some future time, it is not taxable until you receive it or it is made available to you.

Employee achievement award. If you receive tangible personal property (other than cash, a gift certificate, or an equivalent item) as an award for length of service or safety achievement, you generally can exclude its value from your income. However, the amount you can exclude is limited to your employer's cost and cannot be more than $1,600 ($400 for awards that are not qualified plan awards) for all such awards you receive during the year. Your employer can tell you whether your award is a qualified plan award. Your employer must make the award as part of a meaningful presentation, under conditions and circumstances that do not create a significant likelihood of it being disguised pay.

However, the exclusion does not apply to the following awards:

- A length-of-service award if you received it for less than 5 years of service or if you received another length-of-service award during the year or the previous 4 years.
- A safety achievement award if you are a manager, administrator, clerical employee, or other professional employee or if more than 10% of eligible employees previously received safety achievement awards during the year.

Example. Ben Green received three employee achievement awards during the year: a nonqualified plan award of a watch valued at $250, and two qualified plan awards of a stereo valued at $1,000 and a set of golf clubs valued at $500. Assuming that the requirements for qualified plan awards are otherwise satisfied, each award by itself would be excluded from income. However, because the $1,750 total value of the awards is more than $1,600, Ben must include $150 ($1,750 − $1,600) in his income.

Differential wage payments. This is any payment made to you by an employer for any period during which you are, for a period of more than 30 days, an active duty member of the uniformed services and represents all or a portion of the wages you would have received from the employer during that period. These payments are treated as wages and are subject to income tax withholding, but not FICA or FUTA taxes. The payments are reported as wages on Form W-2.

Government cost-of-living allowances. Most payments received by U.S. Government civilian employees for working abroad are taxable. However, certain cost-of-living allowances are tax free. Publication 516, U. S. Government Civilian Employees Stationed Abroad, explains the tax treatment of allowances, differentials, and other special pay you receive for employment abroad.

Nonqualified deferred compensation plans. Your employer will report to you the total amount of deferrals for the year under a nonqualified deferred compensation plan. This amount is shown on Form W-2, box 12, using code Y. This amount is not included in your income.

However, if at any time during the tax year, the plan fails to meet certain requirements, or is not operated under those requirements, all amounts deferred under the plan for the tax year and all preceding tax years are included in your income for the current year. This amount is included in your wages shown on Form W-2, box 1. It is also shown on Form W-2, box 12, using code Z.

> ### TAXALERT
> Under a change made by a 2008 tax act, nonqualified deferred compensation paid for services performed after 2008 by an offshore corporation or partnership situated in a low or no-tax jurisdiction (a so-called tax-indifferent corporation or partnership) is included in the income of the employee or service provider when there is no substantial risk of forfeiture. Substantial risk of forfeiture exists if a person's rights to compensation are conditioned on the future performance of substantial services. These rules are complex. See your tax advisor for more information if this may affect you.

Note received for services. If your employer gives you a secured note as payment for your services, you must include the fair market value (usually the discount value) of the note in your income for the year you receive it. When you later receive payments on the note, a proportionate part of each payment is the recovery of the fair market value that you previously included in your income. Do not include that part again in your income. Include the rest of the payment in your income in the year of payment.

If your employer gives you a nonnegotiable unsecured note as payment for your services, payments on the note that are credited toward the principal amount of the note are compensation income when you receive them.

Severance pay. You must include in income amounts you receive as severance pay and any payment for the cancellation of your employment contract.

Accrued leave payment. If you are a federal employee and receive a lump-sum payment for accrued annual leave when you retire or resign, this amount will be included as wages on your Form W-2.

If you resign from one agency and are reemployed by another agency, you may have to repay part of your lump-sum annual leave payment to the second agency. You can reduce gross wages by the amount you repaid in the same tax year in which you received it. Attach to your tax return a copy of the receipt or statement given to you by the agency you repaid to explain the difference between the wages on the return and the wages on your Forms W-2.

Outplacement services. If you choose to accept a reduced amount of severance pay so that you can receive outplacement services (such as training in résumé writing and interview techniques), you must include the unreduced amount of the severance pay in income.

However, you can deduct the value of these outplacement services (up to the difference between the severance pay included in income and the amount actually received) as a miscellaneous deduction (subject to the 2%-of-adjusted-gross-income (AGI) limit) on Schedule A (Form 1040).

Sick pay. Pay you receive from your employer while you are sick or injured is part of your salary or wages. In addition, you must include in your income sick pay benefits received from any of the following payers:

- A welfare fund.
- A state sickness or disability fund.
- An association of employers or employees.
- An insurance company, if your employer paid for the plan.

However, if you paid the premiums on an accident or health insurance policy, the benefits you receive under the policy are not taxable. For more information, see Publication 525.

Social security and Medicare taxes paid by employer. If you and your employer have an agreement that your employer pays your social security and Medicare taxes without deducting them from your gross wages, you must report the amount of tax paid for you as taxable wages on your tax return. The payment also is treated as wages for figuring your social security and Medicare taxes and your social security and Medicare benefits. However, these payments are not treated as social security and Medicare wages if you are a household worker or a farm worker.

Stock appreciation rights. Do not include a stock appreciation right granted by your employer in income until you exercise (use) the right. When you use the right, you are entitled to a cash payment equal to the fair market value of the corporation's stock on the date of use minus the fair market value on the date the right was granted. You include the cash payment in your income in the year you use the right.

Fringe Benefits

Fringe benefits received in connection with the performance of your services are included in your income as compensation unless you pay fair market value for them or they are specifically excluded by law. Abstaining from the performance of services (for example, under a covenant not to compete) is treated as the performance of services for purposes of these rules.

Accounting period. You must use the same accounting period your employer uses to report your taxable noncash fringe benefits. Your employer has the option to report taxable noncash fringe benefits by using either of the following rules.

- The general rule: benefits are reported for a full calendar year (January 1–December 31).
- The special accounting period rule: benefits provided during the last 2 months of the calendar year (or any shorter period) are treated as paid during the following calendar year. For example, each year your employer reports the value of benefits provided during the last 2 months of the prior year and the first 10 months of the current year.

Your employer does not have to use the same accounting period for each fringe benefit, but must use the same period for all employees who receive a particular benefit.

You must use the same accounting period that you use to report the benefit to claim an employee business deduction (for use of a car, for example).

Form W-2. Your employer must include all taxable fringe benefits in box 1 of Form W-2 as wages, tips, and other compensation and, if applicable, in boxes 3 and 5 as social security and Medicare wages. Although not required, your employer may include the total value of fringe benefits in box 14 (or on a separate statement). However, if your employer provided you with a vehicle and included 100% of its annual lease value in your income, the employer must separately report this value to you in box 14 (or on a separate statement).

TAXALERT

Your employer is required to provide in Form W-2, box 12, code DD, the "aggregate cost of employer-sponsored health coverage." This reporting is for information purposes only.

Accident or Health Plan

In most cases, the value of accident or health plan coverage provided to you by your employer is not included in your income. Benefits you receive from the plan may be taxable, as explained later under *Sickness and Injury Benefits.*

For information on the items covered in this section, other than *Long-term care coverage*, see Publication 969, Health Savings Accounts and Other Tax-Favored Health Plans.

EXPLANATION

This exclusion applies to coverage provided to the taxpayer and the taxpayer's spouse, dependents, and children under age 27 as of the calendar year-end.

Long-term care coverage. Contributions by your employer to provide coverage for long-term care services generally are not included in your income. However, contributions made through a flexible spending or similar arrangement (such as a cafeteria plan) must be included in your income. This amount will be reported as wages in box 1 of your Form W-2.

Contributions you make to the plan are discussed in Publication 502, Medical and Dental Expenses.

Archer MSA contributions. Contributions by your employer to your Archer MSA generally are not included in your income. Their total will be reported in box 12 of Form W-2 with code R. You must report this amount on Form 8853, Archer MSAs and Long-Term Care Insurance Contracts. File the form with your return.

Health flexible spending arrangement (health FSA). If your employer provides a health FSA that qualifies as an accident or health plan, the amount of your salary reduction, and reimbursements of your medical care expenses, in most cases, are not included in your income.

Note. Health FSAs are subject to a $2,500 limit on salary reduction contributions for plan years beginning after 2012. The $2,500 limit is subject to an inflation adjustment for plan years beginning after 2013. <u>For 2014, the annual limit on employee contributions to employer-sponsored health FSAs remains unchanged at $2,500.</u> For more information, see Notice 2012-40, 2012-26 I.R.B. 1046, available at *www.irs.gov/irb/2012-26 IRB/ar09.html.*

Health reimbursement arrangement (HRA). If your employer provides an HRA that qualifies as an accident or health plan, coverage and reimbursements of your medical care expenses generally are not included in your income.

Health savings accounts (HSA). If you are an eligible individual, you and any other person, including your employer or a family member, can make contributions to your HSA. Contributions, other than employer contributions, are deductible on your return whether or not you itemize deductions. Contributions made by your employer are not included in your income. Distributions from your HSA that are used to pay qualified medical expenses are not included in your income. Distributions not used for qualified medical expenses are included in your income. See Publication 969 for the requirements of an HSA.

EXPLANATION

The contributions you make to your HSA grow tax-free. The funds in the HSA account are used to pay qualified medical expenses. Only eligible individuals can qualify for an HSA. Some of the requirements for eligibility are that you must be covered under a high deductible health plan, you cannot be enrolled in Medicare, and you cannot be claimed as a dependent on someone else's tax return. HSAs offer both tax and non-tax benefits:

- Your current year taxable income is reduced when you make pretax contributions through payroll deductions to your HSA.
- If you or your family members make contributions to your HSA, you can deduct them on your federal income tax return, even if you do not itemize your deductions.
- If your employer contributes to your HSA, the funds contributed are not taxable income to you.
- Contributions do not have to be distributed from your HSA. The funds remain in your account until used for the payment of your medical expenses.
- The earnings on your account grow tax-free.
- Distributions from your HSA are tax-free if used to pay qualified medical expenses.

TAXALERT

In 2014, the maximum amount that can be contributed to an HSA is $3,250 for self-only coverage and $6,550 for family coverage. In 2015, the maximum contribution amounts increase to $3,350 for self-only coverage and $6,650 for family coverage.

In addition to the maximum contribution amount, an annual catch-up contribution of $1,000 may be made by or on behalf of individuals age 55 and older, who are not enrolled in Medicare.

Qualified medical expenses no longer include over the counter medications unless they are prescribed. Doctor-prescribed drugs and insulin are qualified medical expenses.

Distributions not used for qualified medical expenses that are included in your income are also subject to an additional 20% tax with certain exceptions.

TAXALERT

File Form 8889, Health Savings Accounts, with your income tax return to report contributions to the HSA, even if only your employer made the contributions. In addition to contributions, the form is used to report distributions from your HSA, the calculation of your HSA deduction, and the calculation of any income that is taxable to you if you are no longer an eligible individual.

Contributions by a partnership to a *bona fide* partner's HSA are not contributions by an employer. The contributions are treated as a distribution of money and are not included in the partner's gross income. Contributions by a partnership to a partner's HSA for services rendered are treated as guaranteed payments that are includible in the partner's gross income. In both situations, the partner can deduct the contribution made to the partner's HSA.

Contributions by an S corporation to a 2% shareholder-employee's HSA for services rendered are treated as guaranteed payments and are includible in the shareholder-employee's gross income. The shareholder-employee can deduct the contribution made to the shareholder-employee's HSA.

Qualified HSA funding distribution. You can make a one-time distribution from your individual retirement account (IRA) to an HSA and you generally will not include any of the distribution in your income. See Publication 590 for the requirements for these qualified HSA funding distributions.

Failure to maintain eligibility. If your HSA received qualified HSA distributions from a health FSA or HRA (discussed earlier) or a qualified HSA funding distribution, you must be an eligible individual for HSA purposes for the period beginning with the month in which the qualified distribution was made and ending on the last day of the 12th month following that month. If you fail to be an eligible individual during this period, other than because of death or disability, you must include the distribution in your income for the tax year in which you become ineligible. This income is also subject to an additional 10% tax.

TAXALERT

Generally, you are not an eligible individual for an HSA if you have health coverage other than a High Deductible Health Plan (HDHP). For tax years beginning after 2006, coverage under an FSA for the period immediately following the health FSA's plan year during which unused benefits or contributions remaining at the end of the year may be paid or reimbursed to you for qualifying expenses incurred during that period does not disqualify you from being an eligible individual. The coverage does not disqualify you if the balance in the health FSA at the end of the plan year is zero or the entire remaining balance in the health FSA is transferred to your HSA as described previously.

Adoption Assistance

You may be able to exclude from your income amounts paid or expenses incurred by your employer for qualified adoption expenses in connection with your adoption of an eligible child. See the Instructions for Form 8839, Qualified Adoption Expenses, for more information.

Adoption benefits are reported by your employer in box 12 of Form W-2 with code T. They also are included as social security and Medicare wages in boxes 3 and 5. However, they are not included as wages in box 1. To determine the taxable and nontaxable amounts, you must complete Part III of Form 8839. File the form with your return.

EXPLANATION

Employer-provided adoption benefits are amounts your employer paid directly to either you or a third party for qualified adoption expenses under a qualified adoption assistance program. Generally, a qualified adoption assistance program is a separate written plan set up by an employer to provide adoption assistance to its employees. For more details, see Publication 15-B, *Employer's Tax Guide to Fringe Benefits*.

Qualified adoption expenses are reasonable and necessary expenses directly related to, and for the principal purpose of, the legal adoption of an eligible child. Such expenses include:
- Adoption fees,
- Attorney costs,
- Court costs,
- Travel expenses (including meals and lodging) while away from home, and
- Re-adoption expenses relating to the adoption of a foreign child.
  Qualified adoption expenses do not include expenses:
- For which you received funds under any state, local, or federal program;
- That violate state or federal law;
- For carrying out a surrogate parenting arrangement;
- For the adoption of your spouse's child;
- Paid or reimbursed by your employer or any other person or organization;
- Paid before 1997; or
- Allowed as a credit or deduction under any other provision of federal income tax law.

De Minimis (Minimal) Benefits

If your employer provides you with a product or service and the cost of it is so small that it would be unreasonable for the employer to account for it, the value is not included in your income. In most cases, the value of benefits such as discounts at company cafeterias, cab fares home when working overtime, and company picnics are not included in your income.

Holiday gifts. If your employer gives you a turkey, ham, or other item of nominal value at Christmas or other holidays, do not include the value of the gift in your income. However, if your employer gives you cash, a gift certificate, or a similar item that you can easily exchange for cash, you include the value of that gift as extra salary or wages regardless of the amount involved.

Educational Assistance

You can exclude from your income up to $5,250 of qualified employer-provided educational assistance. For more information, see Publication 970, Tax Benefits for Education.

Group-Term Life Insurance

In most cases, the cost of up to $50,000 of group-term life insurance coverage provided to you by your employer (or former employer) is not included in your income. However, you must include in income the cost of employer-provided insurance that is more than the cost of $50,000 of coverage reduced by any amount you pay toward the purchase of the insurance.

For exceptions, see *Entire cost excluded*, and *Entire cost taxed*, later.

If your employer provided more than $50,000 of coverage, the amount included in your income is reported as part of your wages in box 1 of your Form W-2. Also, it is shown separately in box 12 with code C.

EXAMPLE

Your employer, ABC Company, pays the premiums on your $150,000 group-term life insurance policy. You are 40 years old. Every $1,000 worth of coverage costs $0.10 per month. Because under the law only $50,000 worth of coverage may be excluded from your income, the cost of the additional $100,000 of life insurance, or $120 [($0.10 x 12 months) x $100], has to be included in your income, even though your employer covers the cost.

If you pay any amount of the $120 directly, you may reduce, dollar for dollar, the amount of the premium that would otherwise be included in your income. Thus, if you paid $50, only $70 ($120 – $50) of the premium would be included in your income.

Group-term life insurance. This insurance is term life insurance protection (insurance for a fixed period of time) that:
- Provides a general death benefit,
- Is provided to a group of employees,
- Is provided under a policy carried by the employer, and
- Provides an amount of insurance to each employee based on a formula that prevents individual selection.

Permanent benefits. If your group-term life insurance policy includes permanent benefits, such as a paid-up or cash surrender value, you must include in your income, as wages, the cost of the permanent benefits minus the amount you pay for them. Your employer should be able to tell you the amount to include in your income.

Accidental death benefits. Insurance that provides accidental or other death benefits but does not provide general death benefits (travel insurance, for example) is not group-term life insurance.

Former employer. If your former employer provided more than $50,000 of group-term life insurance coverage during the year, the amount included in your income is reported as wages in box 1 of Form W-2. Also, it is shown separately in box 12 with code C. Box 12 also will show the amount of uncollected social security and Medicare taxes on the excess coverage, with codes M and N. You must pay these taxes with your income tax return. Include them on line 60, Form 1040, and follow the instructions for line 60. For more information, see the Instructions for Form 1040.

Table 5-1. Cost of $1,000 of Group-Term Life Insurance for One Month

Age	Cost
Under 25	$.05
25 through 29	.06
30 through 34	.08
35 through 39	.09
40 through 44	.10
45 through 49	.15
50 through 54	.23
55 through 59	.43
60 through 64	.66
65 through 69	1.27
70 and older	2.06

Two or more employers. Your exclusion for employer-provided group-term life insurance coverage cannot exceed the cost of $50,000 of coverage, whether the insurance is provided by a single employer or multiple employers. If two or more employers provide insurance coverage that totals more than $50,000, the amounts reported as wages on your Forms W-2 will not be correct. You must figure how much to include in your income. Reduce the amount you figure by any amount reported with code C in box 12 of your Forms W-2, add the result to the wages reported in box 1, and report the total on your return.

Figuring the taxable cost. Use the following worksheet to figure the amount to include in your income.

Worksheet 5-1.   Figuring the Cost of Group-Term Life Insurance To Include in Income   *Keep for Your Records*

1.	Enter the total amount of your insurance coverage from your employer(s)	1.	_____
2.	Limit on exclusion for employer-provided group-term life insurance coverage	2.	**_50,000_**
3.	Subtract line 2 from line 1	3.	_____
4.	Divide line 3 by $1,000. Figure to the nearest tenth	4.	_____
5.	Go to Table 5-1. Using your age on the last day of the tax year, find your age group in the left column, and enter the cost from the column on the right for your age group	5.	_____
6.	Multiply line 4 by line 5	6.	_____
7.	Enter the number of full months of coverage at this cost	7.	_____
8.	Multiply line 6 by line 7	8.	_____
9.	Enter the premiums you paid per month	9.	_____
10.	Enter the number of months you paid the premiums	10.	_____
11.	Multiply line 9 by line 10	11.	_____
12.	Subtract line 11 from line 8. **Include this amount in your income as wages**	12.	_____

Example. You are 51 years old and work for employers A and B. Both employers provide group-term life insurance coverage for you for the entire year. Your coverage is $35,000 with employer A and $45,000 with employer B. You pay premiums of $4.15 a month under the employer B group plan. You figure the amount to include in your income as shown in <u>Worksheet 5-1. Figuring the Cost of Group-Term Life Insurance to Include in Income—Illustrated</u>.

Worksheet 5-1.	**Figuring the Cost of Group-Term Life Insurance to Include in Income–Illustrated**	*Keep for Your Records*	

1.	Enter the total amount of your insurance coverage from your employer(s)	1.	**80,000**
2.	Limit on exclusion for employer-provided group-term life insurance coverage	2.	**50,000**
3.	Subtract line 2 from line 1..	3.	**30,000**
4.	Divide line 3 by $1,000. Figure to the nearest tenth.....................................	4.	**30.0**
5.	Go to Table 5-1. Using your age on the last day of the tax year, find your age group in the left column, and enter the cost from the column on the right for your age group	5.	**23**
6.	Multiply line 4 by line 5...	6.	**6.90**
7.	Enter the number of full months of coverage at this cost	7.	**12**
8.	Multiply line 6 by line 7...	8.	**82.80**
9.	Enter the premiums you paid per month...	9.	**4.15**
10.	Enter the number of months you paid the premiums	10.	**12**
11.	Multiply line 9 by line 10...	11.	**49.80**
12.	Subtract line 11 from line 8. **Include this amount in your income as wages**	12.	**33.00**

Entire cost excluded. You are not taxed on the cost of group-term life insurance if any of the following circumstances apply.
1. You are permanently and totally disabled and have ended your employment.
2. Your employer is the beneficiary of the policy for the entire period the insurance is in force during the tax year.
3. A charitable organization (defined in <u>chapter 25</u>) to which contributions are deductible is the only beneficiary of the policy for the entire period the insurance is in force during the tax year. (You are not entitled to a deduction for a charitable contribution for naming a charitable organization as the beneficiary of your policy.)
4. The plan existed on January 1, 1984, and
    a. You retired before January 2, 1984, and were covered by the plan when you retired, or
    b. You reached age 55 before January 2, 1984, and were employed by the employer or its predecessor in 1983.

Entire cost taxed. You are taxed on the entire cost of group-term life insurance if either of the following circumstances apply:
*   The insurance is provided by your employer through a qualified employees' trust, such as a pension trust or a qualified annuity plan.
*   You are a key employee and your employer's plan discriminates in favor of key employees.

Retirement Planning Services
If your employer has a qualified retirement plan, qualified retirement planning services provided to you (and your spouse) by your employer are not included in your income. Qualified services include retirement planning advice, information about your employer's retirement plan, and information about how the plan may fit into your overall individual retirement income plan. You cannot exclude the value of any tax preparation, accounting, legal, or brokerage services provided by your employer.

Transportation

If your employer provides you with a qualified transportation fringe benefit, it can be excluded from your income, up to certain limits. A qualified transportation fringe benefit is:

- Transportation in a commuter highway vehicle (such as a van) between your home and work place,
- A transit pass,
- Qualified parking, or
- Qualified bicycle commuting reimbursement.

Cash reimbursement by your employer for these expenses under a *bona fide* reimbursement arrangement is also excludable. However, cash reimbursement for a transit pass is excludable only if a voucher or similar item that can be exchanged only for a transit pass is not readily available for direct distribution to you.

Exclusion limit. The exclusion for commuter vehicle transportation and transit pass fringe benefits cannot be more than $130 month.

TAXALERT

Before 2014, the monthly exclusion for employer-provided transit and vanpool benefits was the same amount as the exclusion for employer-provided parking benefits. This "parity" expired at the end of 2013, thereby causing the maximum exclusion of monthly commuter vehicle transportation and transit passes to decline from $245 in 2013 to $130 for 2014. As of the date this book was published in October 2014, Congress had been considering legislation that would restore this parity through 2014; however, no extension had yet been passed. If parity is restored, then the monthly exclusion for exclusion for commuter vehicle transportation and transit passes would be $250 in 2014. For updated information on this and any other tax law changes that occur after this book was published, see our website, *ey.com/EYTaxGuide*.

The exclusion for the qualified parking fringe benefit cannot be more than $250 a month.

TAXALERT

An exclusion from gross income is allowed for an employee whose employer offers the choice between cash or employer-provided parking, and the employee chooses parking. If you choose cash, the amount offered is includable in your income.

The exclusion for qualified bicycle commuting in a calendar year is $20 multiplied by the number of qualified bicycle commuting months that year.

If the benefits have a value that is more than these limits, the excess must be included in your income. You are not entitled to these exclusions if the reimbursements are made under a compensation reduction agreement.

Commuter highway vehicle. This is a highway vehicle that seats at least six adults (not including the driver). At least 80% of the vehicle's mileage must reasonably be expected to be:

- For transporting employees between their homes and work place, and
- On trips during which employees occupy at least half of the vehicle's adult seating capacity (not including the driver).

Transit pass. This is any pass, token, fare-card, voucher, or similar item entitling a person to ride mass transit (whether public or private) free or at a reduced rate or to ride in a commuter highway vehicle operated by a person in the business of transporting persons for compensation.

Qualified parking. This is parking provided to an employee at or near the employer's place of business. It also includes parking provided on or near a location from which the employee commutes to work by mass transit, in a commuter highway vehicle, or by carpool. It does not include parking at or near the employee's home.

Qualified bicycle commuting. This is reimbursement based on the number of qualified bicycle commuting months for the year. A qualified bicycle commuting month is any month you use the bicycle regularly for a substantial portion of the travel between your home and place of employment and you do not receive any of the other qualified transportation fringe benefits. The reimbursement can be for expenses you incurred during the year for the purchase of a bicycle and bicycle improvements, repair, and storage.

Retirement Plan Contributions

Your employer's contributions to a qualified retirement plan for you are not included in income at the time contributed. (Your employer can tell you whether your retirement plan is qualified.) However, the cost of life insurance coverage included in the plan may have to be included. See *Group-Term Life Insurance*, earlier, under *Fringe Benefits*.

   If your employer pays into a nonqualified plan for you, you generally must include the contributions in your income as wages for the tax year in which the contributions are made. However, if your interest in the plan is not transferable or is subject to a substantial risk of forfeiture (you have a good chance of losing it) at the time of the contribution, you do not have to include the value of your interest in your income until it is transferable or is no longer subject to a substantial risk of forfeiture.

> **Tip**
>
> *For information on distributions from retirement plans, see Publication 575, Pension and Annuity Income (or Publication 721, Tax Guide to U.S. Civil Service Retirement Benefits, if you are a federal employee or retiree).*

EXPLANATION

Under a *qualified plan*, participating employees may defer taxation on an employer's contributions into their individual accounts or for their vested benefits in qualified plans until some future date of distribution. Additionally, the tax on the income the account generates may be deferred until the money is distributed to the employee. The same deferred taxation is allowed under a *nonqualified plan* as long as the employee's interest in the plan is simply an unfunded promise by the employer to pay the employee. Additionally, the plan needs to meet all the requirements under the 2004 tax law change. (Whether a plan is qualified or nonqualified depends on whether or not certain statutory requirements are satisfied.) See chapter 10, *Retirement plans, pensions, and annuities*, for suggestions about what to do when you receive distributions from qualified plans.

Elective deferrals. If you are covered by certain kinds of retirement plans, you can choose to have part of your compensation contributed by your employer to a retirement fund, rather than have it paid to you. The amount you set aside (called an elective deferral) is treated as an employer contribution to a qualified plan. An elective deferral, other than a designated Roth contribution (discussed later), is not included in wages subject to income tax at the time contributed. However, it is included in wages subject to social security and Medicare taxes.

   Elective deferrals include elective contributions to the following retirement plans.

1. Cash or deferred arrangements (Section 401(k) plans).
2. The Thrift Savings Plan for federal employees.
3. Salary reduction simplified employee pension plans (SARSEP).
4. Savings incentive match plans for employees (SIMPLE plans).
5. Tax-sheltered annuity plans (403(b) plans).
6. Section 501(c)(18)(D) plans.
7. Section 457 plans.

Qualified automatic contribution arrangements. Under a qualified automatic contribution arrangement, your employer can treat you as having elected to have a part of your compensation contributed to a Section 401(k) plan. You are to receive written notice of your rights and obligations under the qualified automatic contribution arrangement. The notice must explain:

- Your rights to elect not to have elective contributions made, or to have contributions made at a different percentage, and
- How contributions made will be invested in the absence of any investment decision by you.

You must be given a reasonable period of time after receipt of the notice and before the first elective contribution is made to make an election with respect to the contributions.

Overall limit on deferrals. For 2014, in most cases, you should not have deferred more than a total of $17,500 of contributions to the plans listed in (1) through (3) and (5) above. The limit for

SIMPLE plans is $12,000. The limit for Section 501(c)(18)(D) plans is the lesser of $7,000 or 25% of your compensation. The limit for Section 457 plans is the lesser of your includible compensation or $17,500. Amounts deferred under specific plan limits are part of the overall limit on deferrals.

Designated Roth contributions. Employers with Section 401(k) and Section 403(b) plans can create qualified Roth contribution programs so that you may elect to have part or all of your elective deferrals to the plan designated as after-tax Roth contributions. Designated Roth contributions are treated as elective deferrals, except that they are included in income.

TAXPLANNER
Roth 401(k) Plans
Designated Roth contributions. Employers with Section 401(k) and Section 403(b) plans can create qualified Roth contribution programs so that you may elect to have part or all of your elective deferrals to the plan designated as after-tax Roth contributions. If your employer's plan allows it, you are able to designate part or all of your 401(k) contributions as "Roth 401(k)" contributions. As with a Roth IRA, your contributions to a Roth 401(k) are nondeductible, but all of the income in the plan will be tax-free to you when distributed if you meet the same requirements that apply to Roth IRAs—5 years of participation and distribution after age 59½, death, disability, or for up to $10,000 for a first-time home purchase. For more information on Roth IRAs, see chapter 17, Individual retirement arrangements (IRAs).

TAXPLANNER
In-plan rollovers to designated Roth accounts. Deferral plans under Section 401(k) (including the Thrift Savings Plan), 403(b), or 457(b) also have the option to permit participants to roll their pre-tax account balances into a designated Roth account within the same plan. (Not all plans offer this rollover option, so you need to check with your employer.) Before 2013, plans that offered this rollover option could allow participants to convert their pre-tax accounts to Roth accounts, but only with respect to money they otherwise had a right to take out of the plan; usually because they either reached age 59½ or separated from service from an employer. After 2012, any amount in a non-Roth account is allowed to be converted to a Roth account in the same plan, whether or not the amount is otherwise eligible for distribution.

Just like a conversion to a Roth IRA (discussed in chapter 17, *Individual retirement arrangements (IRAs)*, the amount rolled over is includible in taxable income except to the extent it includes a return of after-tax contributions.

Excess deferrals. Your employer or plan administrator should apply the proper annual limit when figuring your plan contributions. However, you are responsible for monitoring the total you defer to ensure that the deferrals are not more than the overall limit.

If you set aside more than the limit, the excess generally must be included in your income for that year, unless you have an excess deferral of a designated Roth contribution. See Publication 525 for a discussion of the tax treatment of excess deferrals.

Catch-up contributions. You may be allowed catch-up contributions (additional elective deferral) if you are age 50 or older by the end of your tax year.

TAXALERT
The dollar limitation for 2014 catch-up contributions for participants age 50 or over in 401(k), 403(b), and 457 plans is $5,500. The limitation for catch-up contributions to SIMPLE plans is $2,500.

Stock Options

If you receive a nonstatutory option to buy or sell stock or other property as payment for your services, you usually will have income when you receive the option, when you exercise the option (use it to buy or sell the stock or other property), or when you sell or otherwise dispose of the option. However, if your option is a statutory stock option, you will not have any income until you sell or exchange your stock. Your employer can tell you which kind of option you hold. For more information, see Publication 525.

EXPLANATION

A stock option gives you the right to buy a company's stock at a specified price within a designated time period. The price is generally equal to the stock's value on the day you get the option. Generally, stock options are awarded to you by your employer as an alternative method of compensation. The option itself is generally not taxed when it is granted to you. The amount of income and the year when it is included in your taxable income depend on the type of option granted. There are two basic types of stock options: nonqualified (nonstatutory) stock options and incentive stock options.

Nonqualified stock options (NSOs or NQSOs). Nonqualified stock options do not have some of the favorable tax attributes that incentive stock options (ISOs) have (see *Incentive stock options* in the next section).

A nonqualified stock option is not taxable to you at the time the option is granted, unless the option is traded through a public stock exchange. Rather, you are taxed when the option is exercised on the difference between the fixed option price (the exercise price) and the fair market value of the stock on the date you exercise your option. This amount is taxed at ordinary income rates. The basis of the stock received is generally its fair market value on the date you exercise the option. If the stock appreciates thereafter, that gain will be taxable as a capital gain when you sell it.

An advantage of the nonqualified stock option is that you do not have to invest any personal funds when the option is granted or while the option is outstanding. However, if you exercise the option, you will need funds to pay the option price and the income tax that will be due on the option spread, the difference between the fair market value on the exercise date and the exercise price.

Incentive stock options (ISOs). Generally, incentive stock options let you take advantage of a specific provision of the Internal Revenue Code that gives favorable tax treatment to this type of stock option.

Incentive stock options are not taxable to you at the time the option is granted, nor do you pay tax when the option is exercised. Furthermore, if you do not dispose of the stock within 2 years after the option is granted, and you hold the stock for over 12 months after you exercise the option, any gain will be taxed as a long-term capital gain.

However, if you sell the stock within 1 year after the date you exercised the option, or 2 years from the date of grant, the option loses its preferential treatment and the difference between the exercise price and the value at date of exercise is taxed to you as ordinary income.

The spread between the option price and the fair market value of the stock upon exercise of the incentive stock option may be taxed indirectly if you are subject to alternative minimum tax. For a discussion of the alternative minimum tax, see chapter 31, *How to figure your tax*. For a further discussion of stock options, see chapter 13, *Basis of property*.

TAXPLANNER

The top income tax rate on net capital gains from sales of most types of assets held more than 1 year is 15% for taxpayers that are in the 25%, 28%, 33%, or 35% tax brackets. For higher income taxpayers who are otherwise in the 39.6% income tax bracket (i.e., taxable income over $406,750 for single filers, $432,200 for head of household, $457,600 married filing jointly, and $228,800 for married filing separately), the maximum income tax rate on net capital gains is 20%. Net capital gains received by taxpayers in the 10% and 15% tax brackets are not subject to federal income tax; i.e., they are taxed at a 0% rate. These net capital gains tax rates apply to both the regular tax and the alternative minimum tax. For more information on tax rates on net capital gains, see chapter 16, *Reporting gains and losses*.

TAXPLANNER

Some employers allow you to use employer stock already owned to finance the exercise of stock options. This exercise method is called a stock swap and allows you to use the stock value without recognizing the gain that would result if you sold the stock and used the proceeds to exercise the stock options. Certain stock holding periods and other restrictions can apply, which should be stipulated in your employer's stock option plan.

Restricted Property

In most cases, if you receive property for your services, you must include its fair market value in your income in the year you receive the property. However, if you receive stock or other property that has certain restrictions that affect its value, you do not include the value of the property in your income until it has substantially vested. (You can choose to include the value of the property in your income in the year it is transferred to you.) For more information, see *Restricted Property* in Publication 525.

Dividends received on restricted stock. Dividends you receive on restricted stock are treated as compensation and not as dividend income. Your employer should include these payments on your Form W-2.

Stock you chose to include in income. Dividends you receive on restricted stock you chose to include in your income in the year transferred are treated the same as any other dividends. Report them on your return as dividends. For a discussion of dividends, see chapter 8.

For information on how to treat dividends reported on both your Form W-2 and Form 1099-DIV, see *Dividends received on restricted stock* in Publication 525.

Special Rules for Certain Employees

This section deals with special rules for people in certain types of employment: members of the clergy, members of religious orders, people working for foreign employers, military personnel, and volunteers.

Clergy

Generally, if you are a member of the clergy, you must include in your income offerings and fees you receive for marriages, baptisms, funerals, masses, etc., in addition to your salary. If the offering is made to the religious institution, it is not taxable to you.

If you are a member of a religious organization and you give your outside earnings to the religious organization, you still must include the earnings in your income. However, you may be entitled to a charitable contribution deduction for the amount paid to the organization. See chapter 25.

Pension. A pension or retirement pay for a member of the clergy usually is treated as any other pension or annuity. It must be reported on lines 16a and 16b of Form 1040 or on lines 12a and 12b of Form 1040A.

Housing. Special rules for housing apply to members of the clergy. Under these rules, you do not include in your income the rental value of a home (including utilities) or a designated housing allowance provided to you as part of your pay. However, the exclusion cannot be more than the reasonable pay for your service. If you pay for the utilities, you can exclude any allowance designated for utility cost, up to your actual cost. The home or allowance must be provided as compensation for your services as an ordained, licensed, or commissioned minister. However, you must include the rental value of the home or the housing allowance as earnings from self-employment on Schedule SE (Form 1040) if you are subject to the self-employment tax. For more information, see Publication 517, Social Security and Other Information for Members of the Clergy and Religious Workers.

Sham churches. The IRS has been cracking down on individuals who declare themselves clergy of newly established churches, arrange to have all their income paid to the church, and then have the church pay their living expenses. The object of such individuals is to take advantage of a church's tax-exempt status and shield income from taxation. Individuals who set up sham churches may be subject to criminal sanctions.

EXPLANATION

Designation requirement. The church or organization that employs you must officially designate the payment as a housing allowance before the payment is made. A definite amount must be designated; the amount of the housing allowance cannot be determined at a later date.

If you are employed and paid by a local congregation, a resolution by a national church agency of your denomination does not effectively designate a housing allowance for you. The local congregation must officially designate the part of your salary that is to be a housing allowance. However, a resolution of a national church agency can designate your housing allowance if you are directly employed by the agency. If no part has been officially designated, you must include your total salary in your income.

Homeownership. If you own your home or are buying it, you can exclude your housing allowance from your income if you spend it for the down payment on the home, for mortgage payments, or for interest, taxes, utilities, repairs, etc. However, you cannot exclude more than the fair rental value of the home plus the cost of utilities, even if a larger amount is designated as a housing allowance. The fair rental value of a home includes the fair rental value of the furnishings in it.

You can deduct on Schedule A (Form 1040) the qualified mortgage interest and real estate taxes you pay on your home even if you use nontaxable housing allowance funds to make the payments. See chapter 23, *Taxes you may deduct*, and chapter 24, *Interest expense*.

Teachers or administrators. If you are a minister employed as a teacher or administrator by a church school, college, or university, you are performing ministerial services for purposes of the housing exclusion.

However, if you perform services as a teacher or administrator on the faculty of a nonchurch college, you cannot exclude from your income a housing allowance or the value of a home that is provided to you.

If you serve as a minister of music or minister of education or serve in an administrative or other function of your religious organization, but are not authorized to perform substantially all of the religious duties of an ordained minister in your church (even if you are commissioned as a minister of the gospel), the housing exclusion does not apply to you.

Theological students. The housing exclusion does not apply if you are a theological student serving a required internship as an assistant pastor, unless you are ordained, commissioned, or licensed as a minister.

Traveling evangelists. If you are an ordained minister and are providing evangelistic services, you can exclude amounts received from out-of-town churches that are designated as a housing allowance, provided you actually use them to maintain your permanent home.

Retired members of the clergy. The rental value of a home provided rent free by your church for your past services is not income if you are a retired minister. In addition, the amount of your housing allowance that you spend for utilities, maintenance, repairs, and similar expenses that are directly related to providing a home is not income to you. These amounts are also not included in net earnings from self-employment.

The general convention of a national religious denomination can designate a housing allowance for retired ministers that can be excluded from income. This applies if the local congregations authorize the general convention to establish and maintain a unified pension system for all retired clergy members of the denomination for their past services to the local churches. A surviving spouse of a retired minister cannot exclude a housing allowance from income.

Members of Religious Orders

If you are a member of a religious order who has taken a vow of poverty, how you treat earnings that you renounce and turn over to the order depends on whether your services are performed for the order.

Services performed for the order. If you are performing the services as an agent of the order in the exercise of duties required by the order, do not include in your income the amounts turned over to the order.

If your order directs you to perform services for another agency of the supervising church or an associated institution, you are considered to be performing the services as an agent of the order. Any wages you earn as an agent of an order that you turn over to the order are not included in your income.

Example. You are a member of a church order and have taken a vow of poverty. You renounce any claims to your earnings and turn over to the order any salaries or wages you earn. You are a registered nurse, so your order assigns you to work in a hospital that is an associated institution of the church. However, you remain under the general direction and control of the order. You are considered to be an agent of the order and any wages you earn at the hospital that you turn over to your order are not included in your income.

Services performed outside the order. If you are directed to work outside the order, your services are not an exercise of duties required by the order unless they meet both of the following requirements:

- They are the kind of services that are ordinarily the duties of members of the order.
- They are part of the duties that you must exercise for, or on behalf of, the religious order as its agent.

If you are an employee of a third party, the services you perform for the third party will not be considered directed or required of you by the order. Amounts you receive for these services are included in your income, even if you have taken a vow of poverty.

Example. Mark Brown is a member of a religious order and has taken a vow of poverty. He renounces all claims to his earnings and turns over his earnings to the order.

Mark is a schoolteacher. He was instructed by the superiors of the order to get a job with a private tax-exempt school. Mark became an employee of the school, and, at his request, the school made the salary payments directly to the order.

Because Mark is an employee of the school, he is performing services for the school rather than as an agent of the order. The wages Mark earns working for the school are included in his income.

Foreign Employer
Special rules apply if you work for a foreign employer.

U.S. citizen. If you are a U.S. citizen who works in the United States for a foreign government, an international organization, a foreign embassy, or any foreign employer, you must include your salary in your income.

Social security and Medicare taxes. You are exempt from social security and Medicare employee taxes if you are employed in the United States by an international organization or a foreign government. However, you must pay self-employment tax on your earnings from services performed in the United States, even though you are not self-employed. This rule also applies if you are an employee of a qualifying wholly owned instrumentality of a foreign government.

Employees of international organizations or foreign governments. Your compensation for official services to an international organization is exempt from federal income tax if you are not a citizen of the United States or you are a citizen of the Philippines (whether or not you are a citizen of the United States).

Your compensation for official services to a foreign government is exempt from federal income tax if all of the following are true.

- You are not a citizen of the United States or you are a citizen of the Philippines (whether or not you are a citizen of the United States).
- Your work is like the work done by employees of the United States in foreign countries.
- The foreign government gives an equal exemption to employees of the United States in its country.

Waiver of alien status. If you are an alien who works for a foreign government or international organization and you file a waiver under Section 247(b) of the Immigration and Nationality Act to keep your immigrant status, different rules may apply. See *Foreign Employer* in Publication 525.

Employment abroad. For information on the tax treatment of income earned abroad, see Publication 54.

Military
Payments you receive as a member of a military service generally are taxed as wages except for retirement pay, which is taxed as a pension. Allowances generally are not taxed. For more information on the tax treatment of military allowances and benefits, see Publication 3, Armed Forces' Tax Guide.

Differential wage payments. Any payments made to you by an employer during the time you are performing service in the uniformed services are treated as compensation. These wages are subject to income tax withholding and are reported on a Form W-2. See the discussion under *Miscellaneous Compensation*, earlier.

Military retirement pay. If your retirement pay is based on age or length of service, it is taxable and must be included in your income as a pension on lines 16a and 16b of Form 1040 or on lines 12a and 12b of Form 1040A. Do not include in your income the amount of any reduction in retirement or retainer pay to provide a survivor annuity for your spouse or children under the Retired Serviceman's Family Protection Plan or the Survivor Benefit Plan.

For more detailed discussion of survivor annuities, see chapter 10.

Disability. If you are retired on disability, see *Military and Government Disability Pensions* under *Sickness and Injury Benefits*, later.

Veterans' benefits. Do not include in your income any veterans' benefits paid under any law, regulation, or administrative practice administered by the Department of Veterans Affairs (VA). The following amounts paid to veterans or their families are not taxable.

- Education, training, and subsistence allowances.
- Disability compensation and pension payments for disabilities paid either to veterans or their families.
- Grants for homes designed for wheelchair living.
- Grants for motor vehicles for veterans who lost their sight or the use of their limbs.
- Veterans' insurance proceeds and dividends paid either to veterans or their beneficiaries, including the proceeds of a veteran's endowment policy paid before death.
- Interest on insurance dividends you leave on deposit with the VA.
- Benefits under a dependent-care assistance program.
- The death gratuity paid to a survivor of a member of the Armed Forces who died after September 10, 2001.
- Payments made under the compensated work therapy program.
- Any bonus payment by a state or political subdivision because of service in a combat zone.

Volunteers

The tax treatment of amounts you receive as a volunteer worker for the Peace Corps or similar agency is covered in the following discussions.

Peace Corps. Living allowances you receive as a Peace Corps volunteer or volunteer leader for housing, utilities, household supplies, food, and clothing are exempt from tax.

Taxable allowances. The following allowances must be included in your income and reported as wages:

- Allowances paid to your spouse and minor children while you are a volunteer leader training in the United States.
- Living allowances designated by the Director of the Peace Corps as basic compensation. These are allowances for personal items such as domestic help, laundry and clothing maintenance, entertainment and recreation, transportation, and other miscellaneous expenses.
- Leave allowances.
- Readjustment allowances or termination payments. These are considered received by you when credited to your account.

Example. Gary Carpenter, a Peace Corps volunteer, gets $175 a month as a readjustment allowance during his period of service, to be paid to him in a lump sum at the end of his tour of duty. Although the allowance is not available to him until the end of his service, Gary must include it in his income on a monthly basis as it is credited to his account.

Volunteers in Service to America (VISTA). If you are a VISTA volunteer, you must include meal and lodging allowances paid to you in your income as wages.

EXPLANATION
VISTA volunteers do not benefit from the same gross income exclusions as do members of the Peace Corps.

National Senior Services Corps programs. Do not include in your income amounts you receive for supportive services or reimbursements for out-of-pocket expenses from the following programs.
- Retired Senior Volunteer Program (RSVP).
- Foster Grandparent Program.
- Senior Companion Program.

Service Corps of Retired Executives (SCORE). If you receive amounts for supportive services or reimbursements for out-of-pocket expenses from SCORE, do not include these amounts in income.

Volunteer tax counseling. Do not include in your income any reimbursements you receive for transportation, meals, and other expenses you have in training for, or actually providing, volunteer federal income tax counseling for the elderly (TCE).

You can deduct as a charitable contribution your unreimbursed out-of-pocket expenses in taking part in the volunteer income tax assistance (VITA) program. See chapter 25.

Sickness and Injury Benefits

This section discusses sickness and injury benefits including disability pensions, long-term care insurance contracts, workers' compensation, and other benefits.

> **TAXALERT**
> Holocaust restitution payments paid to eligible individuals or their heirs are exempt from taxable income. The restitution payments are also not considered in computations that include tax-exempt income (e.g., the calculation of taxable social security payments.)

In most cases, you must report as income any amount you receive for personal injury or sickness through an accident or health plan that is paid for by your employer. If both you and your employer pay for the plan, only the amount you receive that is due to your employer's payments is reported as income. However, certain payments may not be taxable to you. Your employer should be able to give you specific details about your pension plan and tell you the amount you paid for your disability pension. In addition to disability pensions and annuities, you may be receiving other payments for sickness and injury.

Cost paid by you. If you pay the entire cost of a health or accident insurance plan, do not include any amounts you receive from the plan for personal injury or sickness as income on your tax return. If your plan reimbursed you for medical expenses you deducted in an earlier year, you may have to include some, or all, of the reimbursement in your income. See *Reimbursement in a later year* in chapter 22.

Cafeteria plans. In most cases, if you are covered by an accident or health insurance plan through a cafeteria plan, and the amount of the insurance premiums was not included in your income, you are not considered to have paid the premiums and you must include any benefits you receive in your income. If the amount of the premiums was included in your income, you are considered to have paid the premiums, and any benefits you receive are not taxable.

> **EXPLANATION**
> If you paid disability premiums with after-tax dollars, the value of any disability benefits you receive will not be taxable. If you paid the premiums with pre-tax dollars or your employer paid the premiums and you did not elect to treat these premiums as taxable, the value of benefits you receive will be taxable.

Disability Pensions

If you retired on disability, you must include in income any disability pension you receive under a plan that is paid for by your employer. You must report your taxable disability payments as wages on line 7 of Form 1040 or Form 1040A, until you reach minimum retirement age. Minimum retirement age generally is the age at which you can first receive a pension or annuity if you are not disabled.

Beginning on the day after you reach minimum retirement age, payments you receive are taxable as a pension or annuity. Report the payments on lines 16a and 16b of Form 1040 or on lines 12a and 12b of Form 1040A. The rules for reporting pensions are explained in *How To Report* in chapter 10.

Tip

Do not report as income any amounts paid to reimburse you for medical expenses you incurred after the plan was established.

Tip

You may be entitled to a tax credit if you were permanently and totally disabled when you retired. For information on this credit and the definition of permanent and total disability, see chapter 33.

For information on disability payments from a governmental program provided as a substitute for unemployment compensation, see chapter 12.

Retirement and profit-sharing plans. If you receive payments from a retirement or profit-sharing plan that does not provide for disability retirement, do not treat the payments as a disability pension. The payments must be reported as a pension or annuity. For more information on pensions, see chapter 10.

Accrued leave payment. If you retire on disability, any lump-sum payment you receive for accrued annual leave is a salary payment. The payment is not a disability payment. Include it in your income in the tax year you receive it.

Military and Government Disability Pensions
Certain military and government disability pensions are not taxable.

Service-connected disability. You may be able to exclude from income amounts you receive as a pension, annuity, or similar allowance for personal injury or sickness resulting from active service in one of the following government services.
- The armed forces of any country.
- The National Oceanic and Atmospheric Administration.
- The Public Health Service.
- The Foreign Service.

Conditions for exclusion. Do not include the disability payments in your income if any of the following conditions apply.
1. You were entitled to receive a disability payment before September 25, 1975.
2. You were a member of a listed government service or its reserve component, or were under a binding written commitment to become a member, on September 24, 1975.
3. You receive the disability payments for a combat-related injury. This is a personal injury or sickness that
   a. Results directly from armed conflict,
   b. Takes place while you are engaged in extra-hazardous service,
   c. Takes place under conditions simulating war, including training exercises such as maneuvers, or
   d. Is caused by an instrumentality of war.
4. You would be entitled to receive disability compensation from the Department of Veterans Affairs (VA) if you filed an application for it. Your exclusion under this condition is equal to the amount you would be entitled to receive from the VA.

Pension based on years of service. If you receive a disability pension based on years of service, in most cases you must include it in your income. However, if the pension qualifies for the exclusion for a service-connected disability (discussed earlier), do not include in income the part of your pension that you would have received if the pension had been based on a percentage of disability. You must include the rest of your pension in your income.

Retroactive VA determination. If you retire from the armed services based on years of service and are later given a retroactive service-connected disability rating by the VA, your retirement pay for the retroactive period is excluded from income up to the amount of VA disability benefits you would have been entitled to receive. You can claim a refund of any tax paid on the excludable amount (subject to the statute of limitations) by filing an amended return on Form 1040X for each previous year during the retroactive period. You must include with each Form 1040X a copy of the official VA Determination letter granting the retroactive benefit. The letter must show the amount withheld and the effective date of the benefit.

If you receive a lump-sum disability severance payment and are later awarded VA disability benefits, exclude 100% of the severance benefit from your income. However, you must include in your income any lump-sum readjustment or other nondisability severance payment you received on release from active duty, even if you are later given a retroactive disability rating by the VA.

Special statute of limitations. In most cases, under the statute of limitations a claim for credit or refund must be filed within 3 years from the time a return was filed. However, if you receive a retroactive service-connected disability rating determination, the statute of limitations is extended by a 1-year period beginning on the date of the determination. This 1-year extended period applies to claims for credit or refund filed after June 17, 2008, and does not apply to any tax year that began more than 5 years before the date of the determination.

Example. You retired in 2008 and receive a pension based on your years of service. On July 1, 2014, you receive a determination of service-connected disability retroactive to 2008. Generally, you could claim a refund for the taxes paid on your pension for 2011, 2012, and 2013. However, under the special limitation period, you can also file a claim for 2010 as long as you file the claim by July 1, 2015. You cannot file a claim for 2008 and 2009 because those tax years began more than 5 years before the determination.

Terrorist attack or military action. Do not include in your income disability payments you receive for injuries resulting directly from a terrorist or military action.

Long-Term Care Insurance Contracts

Long-term care insurance contracts in most cases are treated as accident and health insurance contracts. Amounts you receive from them (other than policyholder dividends or premium refunds) in most cases are excludable from income as amounts received for personal injury or sickness. To claim an exclusion for payments made on a *per diem* or other periodic basis under a long-term care insurance contract, you must file Form 8853 with your return.

A long-term care insurance contract is an insurance contract that only provides coverage for qualified long-term care services. The contract must:

- Be guaranteed renewable,
- Not provide for a cash surrender value or other money that can be paid, assigned, pledged, or borrowed,
- Provide that refunds, other than refunds on the death of the insured or complete surrender or cancellation of the contract, and dividends under the contract may be used only to reduce future premiums or increase future benefits, and
- In most cases, not pay or reimburse expenses incurred for services or items that would be reimbursed under Medicare, except where Medicare is a secondary payer or the contract makes per diem or other periodic payments without regard to expenses.

Qualified long-term care services. Qualified long-term care services are:

- Necessary diagnostic, preventive, therapeutic, curing, treating, mitigating, and rehabilitative services, and maintenance and personal care services, and
- Required by a chronically ill individual and provided pursuant to a plan of care as prescribed by a licensed health care practitioner.

Chronically ill individual. A chronically ill individual is one who has been certified by a licensed health care practitioner within the previous 12 months as one of the following:

- An individual who, for at least 90 days, is unable to perform at least two activities of daily living without substantial assistance due to loss of functional capacity. Activities of daily living are eating, toileting, transferring, bathing, dressing, and continence.
- An individual who requires substantial supervision to be protected from threats to health and safety due to severe cognitive impairment.

Limit on exclusion. You generally can exclude from gross income up to $370 a day for 2014. See *Limit on exclusion*, under *Long-Term Care Insurance Contracts*, under *Sickness and Injury Benefits* in Publication 525 for more information.

Workers' Compensation

Amounts you receive as workers' compensation for an occupational sickness or injury are fully exempt from tax if they are paid under a workers' compensation act or a statute in the nature of a workers' compensation act. The exemption also applies to your survivors. The exemption, however, does not apply to retirement plan benefits you receive based on your age, length of service, or prior contributions to the plan, even if you retired because of an occupational sickness or injury.

Return to work. If you return to work after qualifying for workers' compensation, salary payments you receive for performing light duties are taxable as wages.

Other Sickness and Injury Benefits

In addition to disability pensions and annuities, you may receive other payments for sickness or injury.

Railroad sick pay. Payments you receive as sick pay under the Railroad Unemployment Insurance Act are taxable and you must include them in your income. However, do not include them in your income if they are for an on-the-job injury.

If you received income because of a disability, see *Disability Pensions*, earlier.

> **Caution**
>
> *If part of your workers' compensation reduces your social security or equivalent railroad retirement benefits received, that part is considered social security (or equivalent railroad retirement) benefits and may be taxable. For more information, see Publication 915, Social Security and Equivalent Railroad Retirement Benefits.*

> **Caution**
>
> *If part of the payments you receive under FECA reduces your social security or equivalent railroad retirement benefits received, that part is considered social security (or equivalent railroad retirement) benefits and may be taxable. For a discussion of the taxability of these benefits, see Social security and equivalent railroad retirement benefits under Other Income, in Publication 525.*

Federal Employees' Compensation Act (FECA). Payments received under this Act for personal injury or sickness, including payments to beneficiaries in case of death, are not taxable. However, you are taxed on amounts you receive under this Act as continuation of pay for up to 45 days while a claim is being decided. Report this income on line 7 of Form 1040 or Form 1040A or on line 1 of Form 1040-EZ. Also, pay for sick leave while a claim is being processed is taxable and must be included in your income as wages.

You can deduct the amount you spend to buy back sick leave for an earlier year to be eligible for nontaxable FECA benefits for that period. It is a miscellaneous deduction subject to the 2%-of-AGI limit on Schedule A (Form 1040). If you buy back sick leave in the same year you used it, the amount reduces your taxable sick leave pay. Do not deduct it separately.

Other compensation. Many other amounts you receive as compensation for sickness or injury are not taxable. These include the following amounts.

- Compensatory damages you receive for physical injury or physical sickness, whether paid in a lump sum or in periodic payments.
- Benefits you receive under an accident or health insurance policy on which either you paid the premiums or your employer paid the premiums but you had to include them in your income.
- Disability benefits you receive for loss of income or earning capacity as a result of injuries under a no-fault car insurance policy.
- Compensation you receive for permanent loss or loss of use of a part or function of your body, or for your permanent disfigurement. This compensation must be based only on the injury and not on the period of your absence from work. These benefits are not taxable even if your employer pays for the accident and health plan that provides these benefits.

Reimbursement for medical care. A reimbursement for medical care is generally not taxable. However, it may reduce your medical expense deduction. For more information, see chapter 22.

Chapter 6
Tip income

Note

IRS Publication 17 (*Your Federal Income Tax*) has been updated by Ernst & Young LLP for 2014. Dates and dollar amounts shown are for 2014. Underlined type is used to indicate where IRS text has been updated. Places where text has been removed are indicated by the sentence: *Text intentionally omitted.*

ey.com/EYTaxGuide

Ernst & Young LLP will update the EY Tax Guide 2015 website with relevant taxpayer information as it becomes available. You can also sign up for email alerts to let you know when changes have been made.

Introduction

Tips are one of the least-reported types of income and the IRS has been trying to do something about that. Since 2000, it has been undertaking a controversial audit program under which it conducts employer-only tip examinations and assessments for FICA in cases of "flagrant violations" of tip reporting rules. This audit program focuses on cases of serious noncompliance at businesses in which tipping is customary. As an alternative to audit examinations, the IRS also established voluntary compliance agreements for industries, such as the restaurant industry, where tipping is customary. These agreements are designed to enhance tax compliance among tipped employees through taxpayer education, instead of through traditional enforcement actions, such as tip examinations. Nevertheless, employee reporting requirements and employer withholding requirements have not changed. This chapter spells out the details of reporting tip income.

This chapter is for employees who receive tips.

All tips you receive are income and are subject to federal income tax. You must include in gross income all tips you receive directly, charged tips paid to you by your employer, and your share of any tips you receive under a tip-splitting or tip-pooling arrangement.

The value of noncash tips, such as tickets, passes, or other items of value, is also income and subject to tax.

EXPLANATION

Self-employed individuals may receive cash tips or other income from clients. This additional income is not considered income from tips. It is, however, considered self-employment income and must be reported to the IRS on Schedule C. See chapter 38, *Self-Employment Income: How to File Schedule C*, for more information.

Reporting your tip income correctly is not difficult. You must do three things.
1. Keep a daily tip record.
2. Report tips to your employer.
3. Report all your tips on your income tax return.

This chapter will explain these three things and show you what to do on your tax return if you have not done the first two. This chapter will also show you how to treat allocated tips.

For information on special tip programs and agreements, see Publication 531.

Useful Items

You may want to see:

Publication

☐ **531** Reporting Tip Income
☐ **1244** Employee's Daily Record of Tips and Report to Employer

Form (and Instructions)

☐ **4137** Social Security and Medicare Tax on Unreported Tip Income
☐ **4070** Employee's Report of Tips to Employer

Tax Breaks and Deductions You Can Use Checklist

Tip income. If you work in a business where tips are common, make sure you read this chapter. Tips must be reported as income, but there are special rules on how much tip income you must report and what records you must keep. Keeping good records will keep you from having to pay more tax than required.

Keeping a Daily Tip Record

Why keep a daily tip record. You must keep a daily tip record so you can:
- Report your tips accurately to your employer,
- Report your tips accurately on your tax return, and
- Prove your tip income if your return is ever questioned.

How to keep a daily tip record. There are two ways to keep a daily tip record. You can either:
- Write information about your tips in a tip diary, or
- Keep copies of documents that show your tips, such as restaurant bills and credit or debit card charge slips.

You should keep your daily tip record with your tax or other personal records. You must keep your records for as long as they are important for administration of the federal tax law. For information on how long to keep records, see *How long to keep records* in chapter 1.

If you keep a tip diary, you can use Form 4070A, Employee's Daily Record of Tips. To get Form 4070A, ask the Internal Revenue Service (IRS) or your employer for Publication 1244. Also, Publication 1244 is available online at *www.irs.gov/pub/irs-pdf/p1244.pdf*. Publication 1244 includes a 1-year supply of Form 4070A. Each day, write in the information asked for on the form.

In addition to the information asked for on Form 4070A, you also need to keep a record of the date and value of any noncash tips you get, such as tickets, passes, or other items of value. Although you do not report these tips to your employer, you must report them on your tax return.

TAXPLANNER
You are not required to complete Form 4070A as long as you have an alternative method of recording your tips. The IRS issues the form merely to help employees keep track of their income from tips.

Complete written records are essential, particularly if you must later substantiate a claim that you did not receive all the tips your employer alleges were allocated to you.

Examples of documentary evidence are copies of restaurant bills, credit card charges, or charges under any other arrangement containing amounts added by the customer as a tip.

If you do not use Form 4070A, start your records by writing your name, your employer's name, and the name of the business (if it is different from your employer's name). Then, each workday, write the date and the following information.
- Cash tips you get directly from customers or from other employees.
- Tips from credit and debit card charge customers that your employer pays you.
- The value of any noncash tips you get, such as tickets, passes, or other items of value.
- The amount of tips you paid out to other employees through tip pools or tip splitting, or other arrangements, and the names of the employees to whom you paid the tips.

EXPLANATION
An arbitrary fixed charge that your employer adds to the customer's bill is not a tip or gratuity subject to tip reporting and withholding requirements. Even if it is called a tip, the amount an employee is guaranteed from his or her employer is additional wage compensation.

Example
A club does not permit its members to tip its employees, but adds 10% to each member's restaurant charges. This additional amount is set aside in a fund and is disbursed monthly to all employees.

Because the employer controls the allocation of the funds, they are additional wages, not tips.

However, if a headwaiter receives one lump-sum payment to be distributed to all waiters and waitresses, then the payment is income from tips. The headwaiter would include in his income only the amount he retained, not the total he distributed.

Electronic tip record. You can use an electronic system provided by your employer to record your daily tips. If you do, you must receive and keep a paper copy of this record.

Service charges. Do not write in your tip diary the amount of any service charge that your employer adds to a customer's bill and then pays to you and treats as wages. This is part of your wages, not a tip. See examples below.

Example 1. Good Food Restaurant adds an 18% charge to the bill for parties of 6 or more customers. Jane's bill for food and beverages for her party of 8 includes an amount on the tip line equal to 18% of the charges for food and beverages, and the total includes this amount. Because Jane did not have an unrestricted right to determine the amount on the "tip line," the 18% charge is considered a service charge. Do not include the 18% charge in your tip diary. Service charges that are paid to you are considered wages, not tips.

Example 2. Good Food Restaurant also includes sample calculations of tip amounts at the bottom of its bills for food and beverages provided to customers. David's bill includes a blank "tip line," with sample tip calculations of 15%, 18%, and 20% of his charges for food and beverages at the bottom of the bill beneath the signature line. Because David is free to enter any amount on the "tip line" or leave it blank, any amount he includes is considered a tip. Be sure to include this amount in your tip diary.

Reporting Tips to Your Employer

Why report tips to your employer. You must report tips to your employer so that:
- Your employer can withhold federal income tax and social security, Medicare, Additional Medicare, or railroad retirement taxes,
- Your employer can report the correct amount of your earnings to the Social Security Administration or Railroad Retirement Board (which affects your benefits when you retire or if you become disabled, or your family's benefits if you die), and
- You can avoid the <u>penalty for not reporting tips</u> to your employer (explained later).

TAXSAVER
Your employer usually deducts the withholding due on tips from your regular wages. However, you do not have to have income tax withheld if you can claim exemption from withholding. You can claim an exemption only if you had no income tax liability last year and expect none this year. See *Exemption from Withholding* in chapter 4, *Tax withholding and estimated tax*, for more information.

Example
Many students and retired persons who expect to have no federal income tax liability work part-time in occupations in which they receive tips. To avoid unnecessary income tax withholding, you may file a Form W-4 with your employer, certifying that you had no federal income tax liability last year and expect to have none this year as well.

What tips to report. Report to your employer only cash, check, and debit and credit card tips you receive.

If your total tips for any 1 month from any one job are less than $20, do not report the tips for that month to that employer.

If you participate in a tip-splitting or tip-pooling arrangement, report only the tips you receive and retain. Do not report to your employer any portion of the tips you receive that you pass on to other employees. However, you must report tips you receive from other employees.

Do not report the value of any noncash tips, such as tickets or passes, to your employer. You do not pay social security, Medicare, Additional Medicare or railroad retirement taxes on these tips.

EXAMPLE
If you earn only $15 in tips in October, you do not have to report anything to your employer. However, you must still pay federal income tax on the tips when you report them on your tax return. The $15 is never subject to social security and Medicare taxes.

How to report. If your employer does not give you any other way to report tips, you can use Form 4070. Fill in the information asked for on the form, sign and date the form, and give it to your employer. To get a 1-year supply of the form, ask the IRS or your employer for Publication 1244.

If you do not use Form 4070, give your employer a statement with the following information.

- Your name, address, and social security number.
- Your employer's name, address, and business name (if it is different from your employer's name).
- The month (or the dates of any shorter period) in which you received tips.
- The total tips required to be reported for that period.

You must sign and date the statement. Be sure to keep a copy with your tax or other personal records.

Your employer may require you to report your tips more than once a month. However, the statement cannot cover a period of more than 1 calendar month.

Electronic tip statement. Your employer can have you furnish your tip statements electronically.

When to report. Give your report for each month to your employer by the 10th of the next month. If the 10th falls on a Saturday, Sunday, or legal holiday, give your employer the report by the next day that is not a Saturday, Sunday, or legal holiday.

Example. You must report your tips received in September 2015 by October 13, 2015 (October 10, 2015, falls on Saturday and Monday, October 12, 2015, is Columbus Day, a federal holiday. The next day that is not a Saturday, Sunday, or legal holiday is Tuesday, October 13th).

Final report. If your employment ends during the month, you can report your tips when your employment ends.

Penalty for not reporting tips. If you do not report tips to your employer as required, you may be subject to a penalty equal to 50% of the social security, Medicare, and Additional Medicare taxes or railroad retirement tax you owe on the unreported tips. (For information about these taxes, see *Reporting social security, Medicare, Additional Medicare, or railroad retirement taxes on tips not reported to your employer* under *Reporting Tips on Your Tax Return*, later.) The penalty amount is in addition to the taxes you owe.

You can avoid this penalty if you can show reasonable cause for not reporting the tips to your employer. To do so, attach a statement to your return explaining why you did not report them.

TAXALERT

Since 1995, the IRS has had in place a voluntary program for tip reporting by food and beverage establishments, known as the Tip Reporting Alternative Commitment (TRAC). This program is intended to increase tip reporting and compliance levels by both employees and employers. Under TRAC, an employer agrees to (1) maintain quarterly educational programs that will instruct new employees and update existing employees as to their reporting obligations; (2) comply with all federal tax requirements regarding the maintaining of records, filing of returns, and depositing of taxes; and (3) set up procedures to ensure the accurate recording of all tips. In return, the IRS agrees to base the restaurant's liability for employment taxes solely on reported tips and any unreported tips discovered during an IRS audit of an employee.

During 2000, the IRS announced that it was simplifying its voluntary income from tip compliance agreements and expanding them to all industries where tipping is customary. Under the Tip Rate Determination Agreement (TRDA), the IRS and the employer work together to determine the amount of tips that employees generally receive and should report. Unlike the TRAC, the TRDA does not have any specific education requirements.

Previously, only the gaming, food and beverage, and cosmetology and barber industries were able to make TRDAs with the IRS. The IRS has now developed a TRDA and TRAC for other industries in which tipping is customary. Employers that can participate include taxicab and limousine companies, airport skycap companies, and car wash operations.

In September 2004, the IRS announced that it would indefinitely extend its Tip Rate Determination and Education Program (TRD/EP). Originally, the TRD/EP program was due to expire in 2005, but due to its success it will continue indefinitely. The program offers employers several voluntary agreement options that assist both employers and employees to comply with tip reporting laws. These options include the TRDA, TRAC, and Employer-designed TRAC (EmTRAC). Each agreement educates employers and employees on federal tax laws regarding tips, simplifies the process for employees to calculate and report their tips and pay taxes, and reduces the likelihood and burden associated with a tip examination.

The IRS has issued draft forms of TRAC agreements that can be used as a model for various industries. Employers considering entering into TRAC agreements with the IRS should carefully determine if such an agreement is in their best interest. Consult your tax advisors for more information.

Giving your employer money for taxes. Your regular pay may not be enough for your employer to withhold all the taxes you owe on your regular pay plus your reported tips. If this happens, you can give your employer money until the close of the calendar year to pay the rest of the taxes.

If you do not give your employer enough money, your employer will apply your regular pay and any money you give in the following order.
1. All taxes on your regular pay.
2. Social security, Medicare, and Additional Medicare taxes or railroad retirement taxes on your reported tips.
3. Federal, state, and local income taxes on your reported tips.

Any taxes that remain unpaid can be collected by your employer from your next paycheck. If withholding taxes remain uncollected at the end of the year, you may be subject to a penalty for underpayment of estimated taxes. See Publication 505, Tax Withholding and Estimated Tax, for more information.

Reporting Tips on Your Tax Return

How to report tips. Report your tips with your wages on Form 1040, line 7; Form 1040A, line 7; or Form 1040EZ, line 1.

What tips to report. You must report all tips you received in 2014 on your tax return, including both cash tips and noncash tips. Any tips you reported to your employer for 2014 are included in the wages shown in box 1 of your Form W-2. Add to the amount in box 1 only the tips you did not report to your employer.

If you kept a daily tip record and reported tips to your employer as required under the rules explained earlier, add the following tips to the amount in box 1 of your Form W-2.
- Cash and charge tips you received that totaled less than $20 for any month.
- The value of noncash tips, such as tickets, passes, or other items of value.

Example. Ben Smith began working at the Blue Ocean Restaurant (his only employer in 2014) on June 30 and received $10,000 in wages during the year. Ben kept a daily tip record showing that his tips for June were $18 and his tips for the rest of the year totaled $7,000. He was not required to report his June tips to his employer, but he reported all of the rest of his tips to his employer as required.

Ben's Form W-2 from Blue Ocean Restaurant shows $17,000 ($10,000 wages plus $7,000 reported tips) in box 1. He adds the $18 unreported tips to that amount and reports $17,018 as wages on his tax return.

Reporting social security, Medicare, Additional Medicare, or railroad retirement taxes on tips not reported to your employer. If you received $20 or more in cash and charge tips in a month from any one job and did not report all of those tips to your employer, you must report the social security, Medicare, and Additional Medicare taxes on the unreported tips as additional tax on your return. To report these taxes, you must file a return even if you would not otherwise have to file. You must use Form 1040. (You cannot file Form 1040EZ or Form 1040A.)

> ### TAXSAVER
> **Limit on social security and railroad retirement tax.** There are limits on the amount of social security and railroad retirement tax that your employer withholds from your wages and reported tips. If you worked for two or more employers in 2014, you may have overpaid one or more of these taxes. You may be eligible for a credit for excess social security tax or railroad retirement tax, discussed in chapter 37, *Other credits including the earned income credit*.

> ### TAXALERT
> There is currently no limit on the amount of wages and reported tips subject to Medicare tax. The Medicare tax rate is 1.45%. (For self-employed individuals the Medicare tax rate is 2.9%). Higher income individuals are also subject to a 0.9% Additional Medicare Tax on wages and self-employment income received in excess of specified threshold amounts ($250,000 for a joint return; $125,000 for a married individual filing a separate return; and $200,000 for single, head of household, and qualifying widow(er) with dependent child filers).
> However, only the first $117,000 of wages and tips are subject to social security tax in 2014. The social security tax rate is 6.2%. (For self-employed individuals, the tax rate is 12.4% on their self-employment income for 2014.)

Use Form 4137 to figure social security and Medicare taxes. Enter the tax on your return as instructed, and attach the completed Form 4137 to your return. Use Form 8959 to figure Additional Medicare Tax.

Reporting uncollected social security, Medicare, or railroad retirement taxes on tips reported to your employer. You may have uncollected taxes if your regular pay was not enough for your employer to withhold all the taxes you owe and you did not give your employer enough money to pay the rest of the taxes. For more information, see *Giving your employer money for taxes*, under *Reporting Tips to Your Employer*, earlier.

If your employer could not collect all the social security and Medicare taxes or railroad retirement tax you owe on tips reported for 2014, the uncollected taxes will be shown in box 12 of your Form W-2 (codes A and B). You must report these amounts as additional tax on your return. Unlike the uncollected portion of the regular (1.45%) Medicare tax, the uncollected Additional Medicare Tax is not reported in box 12 of Form W-2 with code B.

To report these uncollected taxes, you must file a return even if you would not otherwise have to file. You must report these taxes on Form 1040, line 58. See the instructions for Form 1040, line 58. (You cannot file Form 1040EZ or Form 1040A.)

> **Caution**
> *If you are subject to the Railroad Retirement Tax Act, you cannot use Form 4137 to pay railroad retirement tax on unreported tips. To get railroad retirement credit, you must report tips to your employer.*

> ### TAXSAVER
> Tips received while working at a job covered by the Railroad Retirement Tax Act or while working for most state or local governments or for some nonprofit organizations are not subject to social security tax and should not be included on Form 4137.

Allocated Tips

If your employer allocated tips to you, they are shown separately in box 8 of your Form W-2. They are not included in box 1 with your wages and reported tips. If box 8 is blank, this discussion does not apply to you.

What are allocated tips. These are tips that your employer assigned to you in addition to the tips you reported to your employer for the year. Your employer will have done this only if:

- You worked in an establishment (restaurant, cocktail lounge, or similar business) that must allocate tips to employees, and
- The tips you reported to your employer were less than your share of 8% of food and drink sales.

No income, social security, Medicare, Additional Medicare or railroad retirement taxes are withheld on allocated tips.

EXPLANATION

Large food or beverage establishments must report tip allocations to the IRS. A large food or beverage establishment is defined as one where the employer normally employed 10 or more employees on a typical day during the preceding calendar year and where tipping is customary.

How were your allocated tips figured. The tips allocated to you are your share of an amount figured by subtracting the reported tips of all employees from 8% (or an approved lower rate) of food and drink sales (other than carry-out sales and sales with a service charge of 10% or more). Your share of that amount was figured using either a method provided by an employer-employee agreement or a method provided by IRS regulations based on employees' sales or hours worked. For information about the exact allocation method used, ask your employer.

EXAMPLE

The following example shows how a food and beverage establishment might determine what amount to include in the special box provided on each employee's Form W-2.

Lee's is a large food and beverage establishment that for one payroll period had gross receipts of $100,000 and reported tips of $6,200. Directly tipped employees reported $5,700, while indirectly tipped employees reported $500.

Directly tipped employees	Gross receipts for payroll period	Tips reported
Amos	$18,000	$1,080
Michaela	16,000	880
Charlie	23,000	1,810
Robin	17,000	800
Guilherme	12,000	450
Kenji	14,000	680
	$100,000	$5,700

The allocation computations would be as follows:
1. Total tips to be allocated: $100,000 (gross receipts) × 0.08 = $8,000.
2. Tips reported by indirectly tipped employees = $500.
3. Tips to be allocated to directly tipped employees: $8,000 − $500 (indirect employees' tips) = $7,500.
4. Allocation of tips to directly tipped employees:

	Directly tipped employees' share of 8% gross	×	Gross receipts ratio	=	Employee share of 8% gross
Amos	$7,500	×	18,000/100,000	=	$1,350
Michaela	7,500	×	16,000/100,000	=	1,200
Charlie	7,500	×	23,000/100,000	=	1,725
Robin	7,500	×	17,000/100,000	=	1,275
Guilherme	7,500	×	12,000/100,000	=	900
Kenji	7,500	×	14,000/100,000	=	1,050
				=	$7,500

5. Calculation of tip shortfall of directly tipped employees:

	Employee share of 8% gross	×	Tips reported	=	Employees' shortfall
Amos	$1,350	−	$1,080	=	$270
Michaela	1,200	−	880	=	320
Charlie	1,725	−	1,810	=	−
Robin	1,275	−	800	=	475
Guilherme	450	−	450	=	450
Kenji	1,050	−	680	=	370
			Total Shortfall	=	$1,885

Because Charlie has no reporting shortfall, there is no allocation to him.

6. Total tips reported, including reported tips of indirectly tipped employees: $8,000 − $6,200 (total tips reported) = $1,800 (amount allocable among shortfall employees).

7. Allocation of tip shortfall among directly tipped employees:

	Allocable amount	×	Shortfall ratio	=	Amount of allocation
Amos	$1,800	×	270/1,885	=	$258
Michaela	1,800	×	320/1,885	=	305
Robin	1,800	×	475/1,885	=	454
Guilherme	1,800	×	450/1,885	=	430
Kenji	1,800	×	370/1,885	=	353
			Total	=	$1,800

These allocated amounts must be reported by the employer on the employees' W-2s in box 8. For example, Amos would have allocated tip income of $258.

TAXPLANNER

The reporting requirements for employers are only guidelines and apply only to large food or beverage establishments. Nevertheless, the courts have imposed industry averages on taxpayers who had no records or inadequate records.

Example

In a series of cases, the courts held that average tips for taxi drivers come to 10% of gross income. A court was willing to accept a 2% figure for tips only when the driver produced daily logs that showed the amounts of fares and tips. The court believed that the records were true and accurate.

The courts have held that the average tips for barbers and hairdressers range from 2% to 8%.

To estimate the tip income of waiters and waitresses, the IRS has used various methods, based on the total sales of the restaurant. While the courts often adjust the IRS determination, they usually accept any reasonable method the IRS uses. Recent Federal Appeals case law has held that the IRS can assess the restaurant owners for FICA taxes without attempting to first determine the unreported income of each individual employee.

Our advice is: Maintain adequate records of all amounts that you actually receive.

TAXPLANNER

If the employee or employer would like to request a tip rate lower than 8%, he or she must file a petition with the district director for the IRS district in which the business is located. The petition must include specific information to justify the lower rate. An employee petition can only be filed with the consent of the majority of the directly tipped employees. The petition must state the total number of directly tipped employees and the number of employees consenting to the petition. The employer must also be notified immediately, and the employer must promptly give the district director a copy of any Form 8027, Employer's Annual Information Return of Tip Income and Allocated Tips, filed by the employer for the prior 3 years.

Must you report your allocated tips on your tax return? You must report all tips you received in 2014 on your tax return, including both cash tips and noncash tips. Any tips you reported to your employer for 2014 are included in the wages shown in box 1 of your Form W-2. Add to the amount in box 1 only the tips you did not report to your employer. This should include any allocated tips shown in box 8 on your Form(s) W-2, unless you have adequate records to show that you received less tips in the year than the allocated figures.

See *What tips to report* under *Reporting Tips on Your Tax Return*, and *Keeping a Daily Tip Record*, earlier.

How to report allocated tips. Report the amount in box 1 and the allocated tips in box 8 of your Form(s) W-2 as wages on Form 1040, line 7; Form 1040NR, line 8; or Form 1040NR-EZ, line 3. (You cannot file Form 1040A or Form 1040EZ when you have allocated tips.)

Because social security, Medicare, and Additional Medicare taxes were not withheld from the allocated tips, you must report those taxes as additional tax on your return. Complete Form 4137, and include the allocated tips on line 1 of the form. See *Reporting social security, Medicare, Additional Medicare, or railroad retirement taxes on tips not reported to your employer* under *Reporting Tips on Your Tax Return*, earlier.

TAXORGANIZER
Records you should keep:
- Daily tip record/journal
- Copies of bills and credit card charge slips
- Copies of reports provided to employers related to tip income
- Summary of money given to employers to pay any of your taxes on tips not covered by withholding, and receipts from your employer or canceled checks to evidence these payments

Chapter 7
Interest income

Note

IRS Publication 17 (*Your Federal Income Tax*) has been updated by Ernst & Young LLP for 2014. Dates and dollar amounts shown are for 2014. Underlined type is used to indicate where IRS text has been updated. Places where text has been removed are indicated by the sentence: *Text intentionally omitted.*

ey.com/EYTaxGuide

Ernst & Young LLP will update the *EY Tax Guide 2015* website with relevant taxpayer information as it becomes available. You can also sign up for email alerts to let you know when changes have been made.

Introduction

Interest income is a significant portion of all income earned by many Americans. The government takes pains to make sure that all such income is reported by taxpayers. That's why payers of interest, like banks, are required to report to the government the amounts of interest they pay out and to whom. If you do not supply your proper tax identification number–usually your social security number–to a payer of interest, tax will automatically be withheld.

Some investments permit you to defer reporting interest income. Such investments may boost the after-tax rate of return on your money, because you may pay tax on the income in a year-a retirement year, for example-when your tax rate is lower. This chapter outlines several tax planning ideas for deferring taxes on interest income.

What's New

Income limits for excluding education savings bond interest increased. In order to exclude interest, your modified adjusted gross income (MAGI) must be less than $91,000 ($143,950 if married filing jointly or qualifying widow(er)).

TAXPLANNER

For 2014, the amount of your Education Savings Bond Program interest exclusion is phased out if your modified adjusted gross income (MAGI) is between $76,000 and $91,000 (between $113,950 and $143,950 if your filing status is married filing jointly or qualifying widow(er)). See *Education Savings Bond Program*, later in this chapter for more information.

Reminder

Foreign-source income. If you are a U.S. citizen with interest income from sources outside the United States (foreign income), you must report that income on your tax return unless it is exempt by U.S. law. This is true whether you reside inside or outside the United States and whether or not you receive a Form 1099 from the foreign payer.

TAXALERT

Form 8938, Statement of Specified Foreign Financial Assets, must be filed with your annual income tax return if you have an interest in specified foreign financial assets with an aggregate value of over $50,000. If a specified foreign financial asset was sold during the year, you must take the asset sold into consideration when calculating the aggregate value of specified foreign financial assets you held during the year.

While most tax forms report income you receive, Form 8938 is different; it is an informational disclosure that is not used to calculate any part of your tax liability. It is used to provide information to the IRS on a range of foreign accounts and assets that may or may not actually generate taxable income.

Reportable specified foreign financial assets include, but are not limited to, financial accounts located at foreign financial institutions; interests in foreign mutual funds, hedge funds, and private equity funds; directly owned foreign stock or foreign partnership interests; and beneficial interests in foreign trusts or estates. Reportable assets also include financial instruments or contracts with a foreign issuer or counterparty, a category which may include derivatives offered by non-U.S. persons, foreign deferred compensation, or pension plans and insurance contracts purchased from a foreign insurance company.

If you fail to report foreign financial assets on Form 8938, you may be subject to a penalty of $10,000, and potentially an additional $50,000 penalty for continued failure to report after receiving IRS notification to file. In addition, underpayments of tax attributable to nondisclosed foreign financial assets are subject to a substantial understatement penalty of 40%.

You may also have a U.S. Treasury Department filing obligation to report your financial interest in or signature authority over any financial accounts in a foreign country, if the aggregate value of these financial accounts exceeds $10,000 at any time during the calendar year. It is important to note that this rule applies to any financial accounts that you hold as an individual or through a partnership in which you have a greater than 50% ownership interest. You must report that relationship each calendar year by electronically filing a Financial Crimes Enforcement Network (FinCEN) Form 114, Report of Foreign Bank and Financial Accounts (often referred to as the "FBAR"). FinCEN Form 114 supersedes TD F 90-22.1 (the FBAR form that was used in prior years) and is only available online through the BSA E-Filing System website. The system allows the filer to enter the calendar year reported, including past years, on the online FinCEN Form 114. It also offers an option to "explain a late filing," or to select "Other" to enter up to 750-characters within a text box where the filer can provide a further explanation of the late filing or indicate whether the filing is made in conjunction with an IRS compliance program.

On July 29, 2013, FinCEN posted a notice on their internet site that introduced a new form to filers who submit FBARs jointly with spouses or who wish to have a third-party preparer file their FBARs on their behalf. The new FinCEN Form 114a, *Record of Authorization to Electronically File FBARs*, is not submitted with the filing but, instead, is maintained with the FBAR records by the filer and the account owner, and made available to FinCEN or the IRS on request.

Previous IRS guidance clarified that, although foreign mutual funds remain reportable financial accounts for the purpose of this reporting obligation, interests in private equity funds, hedge funds, and other "commingled funds" are not subject to reporting.

The FBAR is not filed with your income tax return. Rather, this form must be electronically filed separately with the Department of the Treasury on or before June 30 of the succeeding year. A substantial penalty may apply if you fail to completely disclose your foreign accounts or file the FBAR on time. Therefore, you should file a complete and accurate FBAR as early in June as possible in order to allow adequate time for electronic submission.

This chapter discusses the following topics.
- Different types of interest income.
- What interest is taxable and what interest is nontaxable.
- When to report interest income.
- How to report interest income on your tax return.

In general, any interest you receive or that is credited to your account and can be withdrawn is taxable income. Exceptions to this rule are discussed later in this chapter.

You may be able to deduct expenses you have in earning this income on Schedule A (Form 1040) if you itemize your deductions. See *Money borrowed to invest in certificate of deposit*, later, and chapter 29.

TAXALERT
Expenses you incur in earning interest income (reported on Schedule A) are miscellaneous itemized deductions. Your available deduction is reduced by 2% of your adjusted gross income. See *Deductions Subject to the 2% Limit* in chapter 29, *Miscellaneous Deductions*.

Any miscellaneous itemized deductions you claim must be added back to the amount of income that may be subject to alternative minimum tax. For more information, see *Adjustments And Tax Preferences Items* within the *Alternative Minimum Tax* section of chapter 31, *How to figure your tax.*

Useful Items

You may want to see:

Publication

- ☐ **537** Installment Sales
- ☐ **550** Investment Income and Expenses
- ☐ **1212** Guide to Original Issue Discount (OID) Instruments

Form (and Instructions)

- ☐ **Schedule B (Form 1040A or 1040)** Interest and Ordinary Dividends
- ☐ **8815** Exclusion of Interest From Series EE and I U.S. Savings Bonds Issued After 1989
- ☐ **8818** Optional Form To Record Redemption of Series EE and I U.S. Savings Bonds Issued After 1989
- ☐ **8960** Net Investment Income Tax—Individuals, Estates, and Trusts

General Information

A few items of general interest are covered here.

� TAXALERT

Net Investment Income Tax (NIIT). The NIIT applies at a rate of 3.8% on the lesser of certain "Net Investment Income" (NII) of individuals or (2) the excess of modified adjusted gross income (MAGI) over $200,000 ($250,000 if married filing jointly or qualifying widow(er) with dependent child; $125,000 if married filing separately). Generally, NII includes interest income.

NII subject to the tax is defined as investment income reduced by allocable deductions. Investment income generally includes interest income, as well as dividends and other items. The NIIT is assessed in addition to income taxes due on interest and other net investment income, and is payable regardless of whether you otherwise pay any regular income tax or are subject to the alternative minimum tax on your income. For more information, see *Net Investment Income Tax (NIIT)* in chapter 31, *How to figure your tax,* and Form 8960.

Recordkeeping. You should keep a list showing sources and interest amounts received during the year. Also, keep the forms you receive showing your interest income (Forms 1099-INT, for example) as an important part of your records.

▶ TAXORGANIZER

Keep the following records for at least 3 years: 1099-INT, 1099-OID, or Substitute 1099, such as a broker statement or year-end account summary. You should also keep a written record of Series EE and Series I U.S. savings bonds issued after 1989. This includes serial numbers, issue dates, face values, and redemption proceeds of each bond. Form 8818 may also be used. If you have foreign financial accounts reported on FinCEN Form 114 or 114a, as explained above, you must retain detailed records of account ownership and balances for 5 years from the applicable filing deadline.

Tax on unearned income of certain children. Part of a child's 2014 unearned income may be taxed at the parent's tax rate. If so, Form 8615, Tax for Certain Children Who Have Unearned Income, must be completed and attached to the child's tax return. If not, Form 8615 is not required and the child's income is taxed at his or her own tax rate.

the United States and the nonresident alien's home country that may reduce the withholding to a lower rate.

Government bond interest. Interest on federal bonds is subject to federal taxation but not to state and local tax. Although the interest on most municipal bonds is not subject to federal income taxation, the amount of that interest earned must be reported on page 1, Line 8b, of your Form 1040. Interest on municipal "private activity" bonds is not subject to regular federal income tax but is subject to the alternative minimum tax.

Family loans. If you make a loan to a member of your family (or anyone else) without charging interest, you may have to recognize interest income anyway. There are exceptions based on the size of the loan and other factors, so make sure you check out the discussion in this chapter before you make such a loan.

Series E, Series EE, and Series I bonds. If you own these bonds, and are a cash method taxpayer, you can choose whether or not to report the increase in value of the bonds as income each year or instead report the interest income when the bonds are cashed in or when they reach final maturity (whichever is earlier). This enables you to control when the income is recognized. If you decide to hold off on recognizing interest earned until you redeem your bonds, consider cashing them in a year when you are subject to a low tax rate in order to minimize the tax you'll need to pay on the bonds.

EXPLANATION

The investment income of a child under age 19 (or under age 24 if the child is a full-time student) may be taxed at the parent's rate if the child does not have earned income that is more than one-half of his support. A child's support includes amounts spent to provide your child with food, lodging, medical and dental care, recreation, transportation, and similar necessities. These rules for taxing a child's investment income at their parent's rate are commonly known as the "kiddie tax." Children whose earned income exceeds one-half of the amount of support they receive are not subject to the kiddie tax under this provision.

TAXPLANNER

To avoid paying the "kiddie tax," you should consider investments for your child that generate little or no taxable income until your child "grows out" of the reach of the kiddie tax.

Some parents can choose to include the child's interest and dividends on the parent's return. If you can, use Form 8814, Parents' Election To Report Child's Interest and Dividends, for this purpose.

For more information about the tax on unearned income of children and the parents' election, see chapter 32.

EXPLANATION

You may elect to include your child's income on your return only if (1) your child's income consists solely of interest and dividends, including capital gain distributions and Alaska Permanent Fund dividends, and is between $1,000 and $10,000 in 2014, (2) your child made no estimated tax payments, (3) your child had no backup withholding, (4) your child did not have any overpayment of tax shown on his or her 2013 return applied to the 2014 return, and (5) your child is not required to file his or her own return. You may still need to file a state income tax return for your child.

TAXPLANNER

Amounts of Net Investment Income that are included on your own tax return by reason of Form 8814 are included in calculating the 3.8% Net Investment Income Tax (NIIT) that you may owe.

If you may be subject to the NIIT and have children subject to the "kiddie tax," you may consider having your children file their own tax returns to reduce the amount of income potentially subject to the NIIT.

Beneficiary of an estate or trust. Interest you receive as a beneficiary of an estate or trust is generally taxable income. You should receive a Schedule K-1 (Form 1041), Beneficiary's Share of Income, Deductions, Credits, etc., from the fiduciary. Your copy of Schedule K-1 (Form 1041) and its instructions will tell you where to report the income on your Form 1040.

Social security number (SSN). You must give your name and SSN or individual tax identification number (ITIN) to any person required by federal tax law to make a return, statement, or other document that relates to you. This includes payers of interest. If you do not give your SSN or ITIN to the payer of interest, you may have to pay a penalty.

SSN for joint account. If the funds in a joint account belong to one person, list that person's name first on the account and give that person's SSN to the payer. (For information on who owns the funds in a joint account, see *Joint accounts*, later.) If the joint account contains combined funds, give the SSN of the person whose name is listed first on the account. This is because only one name and SSN can be shown on Form 1099.

These rules apply both to joint ownership by a married couple and to joint ownership by other individuals. For example, if you open a joint savings account with your child using funds belonging to the child, list the child's name first on the account and give the child's SSN.

Custodian account for your child. If your child is the actual owner of an account that is recorded in your name as custodian for the child, give the child's SSN to the payer. For example, you must give your child's SSN to the payer of interest on an account owned by your child, even though the interest is paid to you as custodian.

Penalty for failure to supply SSN. If you do not give your SSN to the payer of interest, you may have to pay a penalty. See *Failure to supply SSN under Penalties* in chapter 1. Backup withholding also may apply.

Backup withholding. Your interest income is generally not subject to regular withholding. However, it may be subject to backup withholding to ensure that income tax is collected on the income. Under backup withholding, the payer of interest must withhold, as income tax, on the amount you are paid, applying the appropriate withholding rate.

Backup withholding may also be required if the IRS has determined that you underreported your interest or dividend income. For more information, see _Backup Withholding_ in chapter 4.

Reporting backup withholding. If backup withholding is deducted from your interest income, the payer must give you a Form 1099-INT for the year indicating the amount withheld. The Form 1099-INT will show any backup withholding as "Federal income tax withheld."

Joint accounts. If two or more persons hold property (such as a savings account or bond) as joint tenants, tenants by the entirety, or tenants in common, each person's share of any interest from the property is determined by local law.

Income from property given to a child. Property you give as a parent to your child under the Model Gifts of Securities to Minors Act, the Uniform Gifts to Minors Act, or any similar law becomes the child's property.

Income from the property is taxable to the child, except that any part used to satisfy a legal obligation to support the child is taxable to the parent or guardian having that legal obligation.

Savings account with parent as trustee. Interest income from a savings account opened for a minor child, but placed in the name and subject to the order of the parents as trustees, is taxable to the child if, under the law of the state in which the child resides, both of the following are true.
- The savings account legally belongs to the child.
- The parents are not legally permitted to use any of the funds to support the child.

Form 1099-INT. Interest income is generally reported to you on Form 1099-INT, or a similar statement, by banks, savings and loans, and other payers of interest. This form shows you the interest you received during the year. Keep this form for your records. You do not have to attach it to your tax return.

Report on your tax return the total interest income you receive for the tax year.

2014, you should not have to pay income tax on this amount. Therefore, on Schedule B (Form 1040 or Form 1040A), you should report as follows:

XYZ Corporation interest	$3,000
Less amount of purchased interest	($1,000)

See *Bonds Sold Between Interest Dates*, later in this chapter.

TAXORGANIZER
You should keep copies of each Form 1099-INT you receive for a minimum of 3 years. See chapter 1, *Filing information*, for more information on recordkeeping.

Interest not reported on Form 1099-INT. Even if you do not receive Form 1099-INT, you must still report all of your interest income. For example, you may receive distributive shares of interest from partnerships or S corporations. This interest is reported to you on Schedule K-1 (Form 1065), Partner's Share of Income, Deduction, Credits, etc., or Schedule K-1 (Form 1120S), Shareholder's Share of Income, Deductions, Credits, etc.

Nominees. Generally, if someone receives interest as a nominee for you, that person must give you a Form 1099-INT showing the interest received on your behalf.

If you receive a Form 1099-INT that includes amounts belonging to another person, see the discussion on nominee distributions under *How To Report Interest Income* in chapter 1 of Publication 550, or Schedule B (Form 1040A or 1040) instructions.

Incorrect amount. If you receive a Form 1099-INT that shows an incorrect amount (or other incorrect information), you should ask the issuer for a corrected form. The new Form 1099-INT you receive will be marked "Corrected."

Form 1099-OID. Reportable interest income also may be shown on Form 1099-OID, Original Issue Discount. For more information about amounts shown on this form, see *Original Issue Discount (OID)*, later in this chapter.

TAXORGANIZER
You should keep copies of each Form 1099-OID you receive for a minimum of 3 years. See chapter 1, *Filing information*, for more information on record keeping.

Exempt-interest dividends. Exempt-interest dividends you receive from a mutual fund or other regulated investment company, including those received from a qualified fund of funds in any tax year beginning after December 22, 2010, are not included in your taxable income. (However, see *Information reporting requirement*, next.) Exempt-interest dividends should be shown in box 10 of Form 1099-DIV. You do not reduce your basis for distributions that are exempt-interest dividends.

Information reporting requirement. Although exempt-interest dividends are not taxable, you must show them on your tax return if you have to file. This is an information reporting requirement and does not change the exempt-interest dividends into taxable income.

Note. Exempt-interest dividends paid from specified private activity bonds may be subject to the alternative minimum tax. See *Alternative Minimum Tax (AMT)* in chapter 31 for more information. Chapter 1 of Publication 550 contains a discussion on private activity bonds under *State or Local Government Obligations*.

TAXSAVER
Investment income that is exempt from federal tax may still be taxable on your state tax return. This includes interest and dividends paid or accrued to you on state, municipal, or any other type of debt obligation. However, in most states, there are certain federally tax-exempt bonds that are not taxable at the state level. Be sure to check your state filing requirements before you invest in federally tax-exempt obligations. Lastly, be aware that interest from certain private activity bonds will result in an adjustment for the alternative minimum tax, even though the interest is not taxable for regular tax. See chapter 31, *How to figure your tax*, for more information on the alternative minimum tax.

Interest on VA dividends. Interest on insurance dividends left on deposit with the Department of Veterans Affairs (VA) is not taxable. This includes interest paid on dividends on converted United States Government Life Insurance and on National Service Life Insurance policies.

Individual retirement arrangements (IRAs). Interest on a Roth IRA generally is not taxable. Interest on a traditional IRA is tax deferred. You generally do not include it in your income until you make withdrawals from the IRA. See chapter 17.

Taxable Interest

Taxable interest includes interest you receive from bank accounts, loans you make to others, and other sources. The following are some sources of taxable interest.

Dividends that are actually interest. Certain distributions commonly called dividends are actually interest. You must report as interest so-called "dividends" on deposits or on share accounts in:
- Cooperative banks,
- Credit unions,
- Domestic building and loan associations,
- Domestic savings and loan associations,
- Federal savings and loan associations, and
- Mutual savings banks.

The "dividends" will be shown as interest income on Form 1099-INT.

Money market funds. Money market funds pay dividends and are offered by nonbank financial institutions, such as mutual funds and stock brokerage houses. Generally, amounts you receive from money market funds should be reported as dividends, not as interest.

Certificates of deposit and other deferred interest accounts. If you open any of these accounts, interest may be paid at fixed intervals of 1 year or less during the term of the account. You generally must include this interest in your income when you actually receive it or are entitled to receive it without paying a substantial penalty. The same is true for accounts that mature in 1 year or less and pay interest in a single payment at maturity. If interest is deferred for more than 1 year, see *Original Issue Discount (OID)*, later.

Interest subject to penalty for early withdrawal. If you withdraw funds from a deferred interest account before maturity, you may have to pay a penalty. You must report the total amount of interest paid or credited to your account during the year, without subtracting the penalty. See *Penalty on early withdrawal of savings* in chapter 1 of Publication 550 for more information on how to report the interest and deduct the penalty.

Money borrowed to invest in certificate of deposit. The interest you pay on money borrowed from a bank or savings institution to meet the minimum deposit required for a certificate of deposit from the institution and the interest you earn on the certificate are two separate items. You must report the total interest you earn on the certificate in your income. If you itemize deductions, you can deduct the interest you pay as investment interest, up to the amount of your net investment income. See *Interest Expenses* in chapter 3 of Publication 550.

Example. You deposited $5,000 with a bank and borrowed $5,000 from the bank to make up the $10,000 minimum deposit required to buy a 6-month certificate of deposit. The certificate earned $575 at maturity in 2014, but you received only $265, which represented the $575 you earned minus $310 interest charged on your $5,000 loan. The bank gives you a Form 1099-INT for 2014 showing the $575 interest you earned. The bank also gives you a statement showing that you paid $310 interest for 2014. You must include the $575 in your income. If you itemize your deductions on Schedule A (Form 1040), you can deduct $310, subject to the net investment income limit.

TAXPLANNER

Note in the previous example, the $310 of interest is deductible only if you itemize your deductions and may be further limited if you do not have net investment income (see chapter 24, *Interest expense*). If you are not able to fully deduct the interest you pay, you may want to reconsider the investment arrangement.

Example

Assuming the same facts as in the previous example, if you are in the top tax bracket, paying 43.4% (39.6% top marginal rate plus 3.8% Net Investment Income tax), $250 of the $575 interest you earned will go to the IRS, leaving you with only $325. Since you paid $310 in interest charges (for which you receive no tax benefit if you do not itemize) to earn that $325, you have only $15 of after-tax gain on your $5,000 investment, for an after-tax rate of return of 0.3% on this investment. The impact of state income taxes should also be factored to calculate your overall after-tax rate of return.

Gift for opening account. If you receive noncash gifts or services for making deposits or for opening an account in a savings institution, you may have to report the value as interest.

For deposits of less than $5,000, gifts or services valued at more than $10 must be reported as interest. For deposits of $5,000 or more, gifts or services valued at more than $20 must be reported as interest. The value is determined by the cost to the financial institution.

Example. You open a savings account at your local bank and deposit $800. The account earns $20 interest. You also receive a $15 calculator. If no other interest is credited to your account during the year, the Form 1099-INT you receive will show $35 interest for the year. You must report $35 interest income on your tax return.

Interest on insurance dividends. Interest on insurance dividends left on deposit with an insurance company that can be withdrawn annually is taxable to you in the year it is credited to your account. However, if you can withdraw it only on the anniversary date of the policy (or other specified date), the interest is taxable in the year that date occurs.

Prepaid insurance premiums. Any increase in the value of prepaid insurance premiums, advance premiums, or premium deposit funds is interest if it is applied to the payment of premiums due on insurance policies or made available for you to withdraw.

U.S. obligations. Interest on U.S. obligations, such as U.S. Treasury bills, notes, and bonds, issued by any agency or instrumentality of the United States is taxable for federal income tax purposes.

Interest on tax refunds. Interest you receive on tax refunds is taxable income.

Interest on condemnation award. If the condemning authority pays you interest to compensate you for a delay in payment of an award, the interest is taxable.

Installment sale payments. If a contract for the sale or exchange of property provides for deferred payments, it also usually provides for interest payable with the deferred payments. That interest is taxable when you receive it. If little or no interest is provided for in a deferred payment contract, part of each payment may be treated as interest. See *Unstated Interest and Original Issue Discount* in Publication 537, Installment Sales.

Interest on annuity contract. Accumulated interest on an annuity contract you sell before its maturity date is taxable.

Usurious interest. Usurious interest is interest charged at an illegal rate. This is taxable as interest unless state law automatically changes it to a payment on the principal.

Interest income on frozen deposits. Exclude from your gross income interest on frozen deposits. A deposit is frozen if, at the end of the year, you cannot withdraw any part of the deposit because:

- The financial institution is bankrupt or insolvent, or
- The state where the institution is located has placed limits on withdrawals because other financial institutions in the state are bankrupt or insolvent.

The amount of interest you must exclude is the interest that was credited on the frozen deposits minus the sum of:

- The net amount you withdrew from these deposits during the year, and
- The amount you could have withdrawn as of the end of the year (not reduced by any penalty for premature withdrawals of a time deposit).

If you receive a Form 1099-INT for interest income on deposits that were frozen at the end of 2014, see *Frozen deposits* under *How To Report Interest Income* in chapter 1 of Publication 550, for information about reporting this interest income exclusion on your tax return.

The interest you exclude is treated as credited to your account in the following year. You must include it in income in the year you can withdraw it.

Example. $100 of interest was credited on your frozen deposit during the year. You withdrew $80 but could not withdraw any more as of the end of the year. You must include $80 in your income and exclude $20 from your income for the year. You must include the $20 in your income for the year you can withdraw it.

Bonds traded flat. If you buy a bond at a discount when interest has been defaulted or when the interest has accrued but has not been paid, the transaction is described as trading a bond flat. The defaulted or unpaid interest is not income and is not taxable as interest if paid later. When you receive a payment of that interest, it is a return of capital that reduces the remaining cost basis of your bond. Interest that accrues after the date of purchase, however, is taxable interest income for the year it is received or accrued. See <u>Bonds Sold Between Interest Dates</u>, later, for more information.

Below-market loans. In general, a below-market loan is a loan on which no interest is charged or on which interest is charged at a rate below the applicable federal rate. See *Below-Market Loans* in chapter 1 of Publication 550 for more information.

EXPLANATION

If you make a below-market loan, you must report as interest income any forgone interest (defined next) arising from that loan. How you should report the income as well as the application of the below-market loan rules and exceptions are described in this section.

If you receive a below-market loan, you may be able to claim a deduction for interest expense in excess of the interest that you actually paid–but only if you use the funds to buy investment property.

Forgone interest. For any period, forgone interest is:

1. The amount of interest that would be payable for that period if interest accrued on the loan at the applicable federal rate and was payable annually on December 31, *minus*
2. Any interest actually payable on the loan for the period.

The applicable federal rate is set by the IRS each month and is published in the *Internal Revenue Bulletin*. You can also contact an IRS office to get these rates.

Below-market loans. A below-market loan is a loan on which no interest is charged or on which interest is charged at a rate below the applicable federal rate. A below-market loan is generally recharacterized as an arm's length transaction in which the lender is treated as having made:

1. A loan to the borrower in exchange for a note that requires the payment of interest at the applicable federal rate, and
2. An additional payment to the borrower.

The lender's additional payment to the borrower is treated as a gift, dividend, contribution to capital, payment of compensation, or other payment, depending on the substance of the transaction. The borrower may have to report this payment as taxable income depending on its classification.

Loans subject to the rules. The rules for below-market loans apply to:

- Gift loans
- Compensation-related loans
- Corporation-shareholder loans
- Tax avoidance loans
- Certain loans to qualified continuing care facilities (made after October 11, 1985)
- Certain other below-market loans

Exceptions

The rules for below-market loans do not apply to certain loans on days on which the total outstanding amount of loans between the borrower and lender is $10,000 or less. The rules do not apply on those days to:

1. Gift loans between individuals if the gift loan is not directly used to purchase or carry income-producing assets
2. Compensation-related loans or corporation-shareholder loans if the avoidance of federal tax is not a principal purpose of the loan

A compensation-related loan is any below-market loan between an employer and an employee or between an independent contractor and a person for whom the contractor provided services.

Other loans not subject to the rules. Other loans are excluded from the below-market loan rules, including:

1. Loans made available by the lender to the general public on the same terms and conditions and that are consistent with the lender's customary business practice.
2. Loans subsidized by a federal, state, or municipal government that are made available under a program of general application to the public.
3. Certain employee-relocation loans.
4. Loans to or from a foreign person, unless the interest income would be effectively connected with the conduct of a U.S. trade or business and would not be exempt from U.S. tax under an income tax treaty.
5. Gift loans to a charitable organization, contributions to which are deductible, if the total outstanding amount of the loans between the organization and the lender is $250,000 or less at all times during the tax year.
6. Other loans on which the interest arrangement can be shown to have no significant effect on the federal tax liability of the lender or the borrower.
7. Certain refundable loans to a qualified continuing care facility under a continuing care contract. The reporting of interest income from loans to continuing care facilities is subject to the rules for below-market loans unless certain requirements are met. However, there is no dollar limit on the total outstanding loan balance for these loans if the lender or the lender's spouse is at least 62 years old and is to receive services under the continuing care service contract. It is important to understand the definition of a qualified continuing care facility and the type of services allowed for purposes of this loan type. Facilities which are of a type traditionally considered as nursing homes are not considered continuing care facilities. A continuing care facility which falls under this exception must: (1) provide service under a continuing care contract, (2) include an independent living unit, plus an assisted living or nursing facility, or both, and (3) substantially all of the independent living unit residents living there must be covered by continuing care contracts. For more information, see Publication 550, *Investment Income and Expenses,* and consult your tax advisor.

If a taxpayer structures a transaction to be a loan not subject to the below-market loan rules, and one of the principal purposes of structuring the transaction in such a way is to avoid federal tax, then the IRS may consider the loan to be a tax-avoidance scheme and, as such, subject the loan to the rules for below-market loans.

All the facts and circumstances are used to determine if the interest arrangement of a loan has a significant effect on the federal tax liability of the lender or borrower. Some factors to be considered are:

- Whether income and deduction items generated by the loan offset each other
- The amount of such items
- The cost to the taxpayer of complying with the below-market loan provisions, if they applied
- Any reasons other than tax-avoidance purposes for structuring the transaction as a below-market loan

Gift and demand loans. A gift loan is any below-market loan where the forgone interest is in the nature of a gift. A demand loan is a loan payable in full at any time upon demand by the lender. A lender who makes a gift loan or demand loan is treated as transferring an additional payment to the borrower (as a gift, dividend, etc.) in an amount equal to the forgone interest. The borrower is treated as transferring the forgone interest to the lender and may be entitled to an interest expense deduction depending on the use of the monies borrowed. The lender must report that amount as interest income. These transfers are considered to occur annually, generally on December 31.

Example 1

Jill's grandmother makes an interest-free loan to Jill on July 1 for $50,000. Jill has net investment income from outside sources of $5,000. The applicable federal interest rate is 5% at this time. This loan will be treated as a gift loan. On December 31, Jill will be treated as having paid her grandmother $1,250 in interest and her grandmother must report $1,250 of interest income and as a gift, even though no money has changed hands.

Special rules for gift loans between individuals that do not exceed $100,000. For gift loans that do not exceed $100,000, the amount of forgone interest that is treated as transferred by the borrower to the lender is limited. This limit is the borrower's net investment income for the year, unless one of the principal purposes of the loan is the avoidance of federal tax. Also, if a borrower has net investment income of $1,000 or less for the year, the borrower's net investment income is considered to be zero and the borrower will have no interest expense deduction.

Example 2
Using the same facts in Example 1, assume Jill has $1,100 in net investment income for the year. On December 31, Jill will be treated as having paid her grandmother $1,100 in interest (not $1,250) because of the net investment income limitation. Jill's grandmother would include the $1,100 as interest income.

Term loans. A lender who makes a below-market term loan (a loan that is not a demand loan) is treated as transferring, as a gift, dividend, etc., an additional lump-sum cash payment to the borrower on the date the loan is made. The amount of this payment is the amount of the loan minus the present value of all payments due under the loan. An amount equal to this excess is treated as an original issue discount (OID). Accordingly, the OID rules of Section 1272 of the Internal Revenue Code apply. The lender must report the annual part of the OID as interest income. The borrower may be able to deduct some or all of the excess as interest expense depending on the use of the monies borrowed. The OID rules are discussed in greater detail later in this chapter.

Effective dates. These rules apply to term loans made after June 6, 1984, as well as to demand loans outstanding after that date.

U.S. Savings Bonds
This section provides tax information on U.S. savings bonds. It explains how to report the interest income on these bonds and how to treat transfers of these bonds.

For other information on U.S. savings bonds, write to:

For series EE and I paper savings bonds: Bureau of the Public Debt Division of Customer Assistance P.O. Box 7012 Parkersburg, WV 26106-7012

For series EE and I electronic bonds: Bureau of the Public Debt Division of Customer Assistance P.O. Box 7015 Parkersburg, WV 26106-7015

For series HH/H: Bureau of the Public Debt Division of Customer Assistance P.O. Box 2186 Parkersburg, WV 26106-2186

Or, on the Internet, visit: www.treasurydirect.gov/indiv/indiv.htm.

Accrual method taxpayers. If you use an accrual method of accounting, you must report interest on U.S. savings bonds each year as it accrues. You cannot postpone reporting interest until you receive it or until the bonds mature. Accrual methods of accounting are explained in chapter 1 under *Accounting Methods*.

Cash method taxpayers. If you use the cash method of accounting, as most individual taxpayers do, you generally report the interest on U.S. savings bonds when you receive it. The cash method of accounting is explained in chapter 1 under *Accounting Methods*. But see *Reporting options for cash method taxpayers*, later.

Series HH bonds. These bonds were issued at face value. Interest is paid twice a year by direct deposit to your bank account. If you are a cash method taxpayer, you must report interest on these bonds as income in the year you receive it.

Series HH bonds were first offered in 1980 and last offered in August 2004. Before 1980, series H bonds were issued. Series H bonds are treated the same as series HH bonds. If you are a cash method taxpayer, you must report the interest when you receive it.

Series H bonds have a maturity period of 30 years. Series HH bonds mature in 20 years. The last series H bonds matured in 2009.

Series EE and series I bonds. Interest on these bonds is payable when you redeem the bonds. The difference between the purchase price and the redemption value is taxable interest.

Series EE bonds. Series EE bonds were first offered in January 1980 and have a maturity period of 30 years.

Before July 1980, series E bonds were issued. The original 10-year maturity period of series E bonds has been extended to 40 years for bonds issued before December 1965 and 30 years for bonds issued after November 1965. Paper series EE and series E bonds are issued at a discount. The face value is payable to you at maturity. Electronic series EE bonds are issued at their face value. The face value plus accrued interest is payable to you at maturity. As of January 1, 2012, paper savings bonds were no longer sold at financial institutions.

Owners of paper series EE bonds can convert them to electronic bonds. These converted bonds do not retain the denomination listed on the paper certificate but are posted at their purchase price (with accrued interest).

Series I bonds. Series I bonds were first offered in 1998. These are inflation-indexed bonds issued at their face amount with a maturity period of 30 years. The face value plus all accrued interest is payable to you at maturity.

Reporting options for cash method taxpayers. If you use the cash method of reporting income, you can report the interest on series EE, series E, and series I bonds in either of the following ways.

1. *Method 1.* Postpone reporting the interest until the earlier of the year you cash or dispose of the bonds or the year they mature. (However, see *Savings bonds traded*, later.)

    Note. Series EE bonds issued in 1984 matured in 2014. If you have used method 1, you generally must report the interest on these bonds on your 2014 return. The last series E bonds were issued in 1980 and matured in 2010. If you used method 1, you generally should have reported the interest on these bonds on your 2010 return.

2. *Method 2.* Choose to report the increase in redemption value as interest each year.

You must use the same method for all series EE, series E, and series I bonds you own. If you do not choose method 2 by reporting the increase in redemption value as interest each year, you must use method 1.

Change from method 1. If you want to change your method of reporting the interest from method 1 to method 2, you can do so without permission from the IRS. In the year of change you must report all interest accrued to date and not previously reported for all your bonds.

Once you choose to report the interest each year, you must continue to do so for all series EE, series E, and series I bonds you own and for any you get later, unless you request permission to change, as explained next.

Change from method 2. To change from method 2 to method 1, you must request permission from the IRS. Permission for the change is automatically granted if you send the IRS a statement that meets all the following requirements.

1. You have typed or printed the following number at the top: "131."
2. It includes your name and social security number under "131."
3. It includes the year of change (both the beginning and ending dates).
4. It identifies the savings bonds for which you are requesting this change.
5. It includes your agreement to:
    a. Report all interest on any bonds acquired during or after the year of change when the interest is realized upon disposition, redemption, or final maturity, whichever is earliest, and
    b. Report all interest on the bonds acquired before the year of change when the interest is realized upon disposition, redemption, or final maturity, whichever is earliest, with the exception of the interest reported in prior tax years.

You must attach this statement to your tax return for the year of change, which you must file by the due date (including extensions).

You can have an automatic extension of 6 months from the due date of your return for the year of change (excluding extensions) to file the statement with an amended return. On the statement, type or print "Filed pursuant to section 301.9100-2." To get this extension, you must have filed your original return for the year of the change by the due date (including extensions).

TAXALERT

By the date you file the original statement with your return, you must also send a signed copy to the address below.

Internal Revenue Service
Attention: CC:IT&A (Automatic Rulings Branch)
P.O. Box 7604 Benjamin Franklin Station
Washington, DC 20044

If you use a private delivery service, send the signed copy to the address below.

Internal Revenue Service
Attention: CC:IT&A (Automatic Rulings Branch)
Room 5336 1111 Constitution Avenue,
NW Washington, DC 20224

Instead of filing this statement, you can request permission to change from method 2 to method 1 by filing Form 3115, Application for Change in Accounting Method. In that case, follow the form instructions for an automatic change. No user fee is required.

EXPLANATION

Series E, Series EE, and Series I bonds are unique investments from a tax viewpoint. Since you, as a cash method taxpayer, may decide not to report the increase in value of the bonds as income each year and instead may decide to report the interest income when the bonds are cashed in or when they reach final maturity (whichever is earlier), you can–to an unusual extent–control when the income is recognized. The best time to redeem the bonds is a year in which you have low taxable income and a low tax rate.

Few people choose to report income annually rather than at sale or maturity, but if you do, you would report as income the increase in the redemption value of each bond each year. All you must do is report the income on your tax return. It would be advantageous to report the income annually only if you had an income so low that your personal exemption and itemized deductions or standard deduction might otherwise be wasted. The most likely people to choose this option are retired people and children over 18 years old in 2014 (or, if a full-time student, over age 23), both of whom may have low taxable income. (Income received by children under age 19 or, if a full-time student, under age 24, may be taxed at their parents' rate.) Remember, once you choose to report the income each year, you must obtain permission from the IRS to change your reporting method.

Example

A 70-year-old unmarried man with only $1,500 of other income might wish to report his savings bond interest each year, since his first $11,500 of income (his standard deduction and exemption) is tax-free in 2014. If he holds the bonds and reports all the income in the year they mature, his taxable income in that year might be more than $11,500, and he would therefore pay taxes he could have otherwise avoided by reporting a smaller amount of interest each year over the life of the bond.

Explanation

The interest rate on Series EE bonds varies depending upon when the bonds were purchased. The method of calculating the interest rate is different for bonds purchased prior to May 1, 1995, between May 1, 1995, and April 30, 1997, and after May 1, 1997. The interest rate on Series I bonds, the value of which is adjusted with inflation, also changes periodically. The Treasury site at *www.publicdebt.treas.gov* has more details.

Millions of Series E and H bonds continue to be held by the public. Most are still earning interest due to extended maturity rates. Some, however, have reached their final maturity and should be exchanged or redeemed.

Prior to September 1, 2004, Series HH bonds could be obtained in exchange for outstanding eligible Series EE bonds and Series E bonds having a combined redemption value of $500 or more. Owners who deferred reporting interest earned on the bonds that they exchange can continue to defer the interest until the year in which the Series HH bonds received in the exchange are redeemed, reach final maturity, or are otherwise disposed of.

Although Series H bonds cannot be exchanged for Series HH bonds (nor can Series E bonds be exchanged for Series EE bonds), the redemption proceeds can be reinvested in new series bonds. However, any previously tax-deferred interest must be reported for federal income tax purposes in the year of redemption.

TAXPLANNER

For most bonds issued prior to May 1997, interest is credited to U.S. savings bonds at specified dates (i.e., there is no proration of interest for bonds cashed during the middle of an interest period). Thus, you should plan ahead to cash in your bonds just after (versus just before) an interest credit date.

Co-owners. If a U.S. savings bond is issued in the names of co-owners, such as you and your child or you and your spouse, interest on the bond is generally taxable to the co-owner who bought the bond.

One co-owner's funds used. If you used your funds to buy the bond, you must pay the tax on the interest. This is true even if you let the other co-owner redeem the bond and keep all the proceeds. Under these circumstances, the co-owner who redeemed the bond will receive a Form 1099-INT at the time of redemption and must provide you with another Form 1099-INT showing the amount of interest from the bond taxable to you. The co-owner who redeemed the bond is a "nominee." See *Nominee distributions* under *How To Report Interest Income* in chapter 1 of Publication 550 for more information about how a person who is a nominee reports interest income belonging to another person.

Both co-owners' funds used. If you and the other co-owner each contribute part of the bond's purchase price, the interest is generally taxable to each of you, in proportion to the amount each of you paid.

Community property. If you and your spouse live in a community property state and hold bonds as community property, one-half of the interest is considered received by each of you. If you file separate returns, each of you generally must report one-half of the bond interest. For more information about community property, see Publication 555.

Table 7-1. These rules are also shown in Table 7-1.

Ownership transferred. If you bought series E, series EE, or series I bonds entirely with your own funds and had them reissued in your co-owner's name or beneficiary's name alone, you must include in your gross income for the year of reissue all interest that you earned on these bonds and have not previously reported. But, if the bonds were reissued in your name alone, you do not have to report the interest accrued at that time.

This same rule applies when bonds (other than bonds held as community property) are transferred between spouses or incident to divorce.

EXPLANATION

If you make a gift of Series E, Series EE, or Series I bonds to a child, remember that it is not possible to transfer the obligation of reporting the interest income that has already accumulated. The interest that has accumulated through the date of the gift must be reported by the donor in the year of the gift. Interest that accumulates from the date of the gift until maturity is reported by the individual receiving the gift.

Purchased jointly. If you and a co-owner each contributed funds to buy series E, series EE, or series I bonds jointly and later have the bonds reissued in the co-owner's name alone, you must include in your gross income for the year of reissue your share of all the interest earned on the bonds that you have not previously reported. The former co-owner does not have to include in gross income at the time of reissue his or her share of the interest earned that was not reported before the transfer. This interest, however, as well as all interest earned after the reissue, is income to the former co-owner.

Table 7-1. **Who Pays the Tax on U.S. Savings Bond Interest**

IF ...	THEN the interest must be reported by ...
you buy a bond in your name and the name of another person as co-owners, using only your own funds	you.
you buy a bond in the name of another person, who is the sole owner of the bond	the person for whom you bought the bond.
you and another person buy a bond as co-owners, each contributing part of the purchase price	both you and the other co-owner, in proportion to the amount each paid for the bond.
you and your spouse, who live in a community property state, buy a bond that is community property	you and your spouse. If you file separate returns, both you and your spouse generally report one-half of the interest.

This income-reporting rule also applies when the bonds are reissued in the name of your former co-owner and a new co-owner. But the new co-owner will report only his or her share of the interest earned after the transfer.

If bonds that you and a co-owner bought jointly are reissued to each of you separately in the same proportion as your contribution to the purchase price, neither you nor your co-owner has to report at that time the interest earned before the bonds were reissued.

Example 1. You and your spouse each spent an equal amount to buy a $1,000 series EE savings bond. The bond was issued to you and your spouse as co-owners. You both postpone reporting interest on the bond. You later have the bond reissued as two $500 bonds, one in your name and one in your spouse's name. At that time neither you nor your spouse has to report the interest earned to the date of reissue.

Example 2. You bought a $1,000 series EE savings bond entirely with your own funds. The bond was issued to you and your spouse as co-owners. You both postpone reporting interest on the bond. You later have the bond reissued as two $500 bonds, one in your name and one in your spouse's name. You must report half the interest earned to the date of reissue.

Transfer to a trust. If you own series E, series EE, or series I bonds and transfer them to a trust, giving up all rights of ownership, you must include in your income for that year the interest earned to the date of transfer if you have not already reported it. However, if you are considered the owner of the trust and if the increase in value both before and after the transfer continues to be taxable to you, you can continue to defer reporting the interest earned each year. You must include the total interest in your income in the year you cash or dispose of the bonds or the year the bonds finally mature, whichever is earlier.

The same rules apply to previously unreported interest on series EE or series E bonds if the transfer to a trust consisted of series HH or series H bonds you acquired in a trade for the series EE or series E bonds. See *Savings bonds traded*, later.

TAXSAVER
If you transfer the bonds to a revocable trust, of which you are considered the owner, you may continue to defer reporting the income. Many individuals use a revocable trust as a substitute for a will. A revocable trust is not required to pay federal income tax on income earned in the trust. Instead, all income (and deductions) is reported on your individual tax return, as if the revocable trust did not exist. In essence, you are treated as if you owned the assets outright. For more details, consult your tax advisor.

Decedents. The manner of reporting interest income on series E, series EE, or series I bonds, after the death of the owner (decedent), depends on the accounting and income-reporting methods previously used by the decedent. This is explained in chapter 1 of Publication 550.

EXPLANATION
Income that the decedent had a right to receive at the time of death, but which is included on another's tax return (or the estate tax return), is called "income in respect of the decedent." See chapter 43, *Decedents: Dealing with the death of a family member,* for more information.

TAXPLANNER
If the final income tax return of the decedent shows a low amount of taxable income, it would be better to include the interest income from the date of purchase of the bonds through the date of death, the choice described in Example 1. Otherwise, the IRS says that the interest income must be reported by the person who receives the bonds, the choice described in Example 2.

However, there is a third option. If the bonds are in the name of the decedent alone, their ownership passes to the estate. The estate is a separate taxable entity that files its own income tax return. If the estate has a low amount of taxable income, it might be advisable for the executor to redeem the bonds.

A point to remember is this: The unique method by which interest from U.S. savings bonds is taxed gives you an opportunity to reduce income tax by selecting the person or entity with the lowest tax rate to receive the income.

Example 1

Your uncle, a cash method taxpayer, died near the end of 2013 and left you a $1,000 Series E bond. He bought the bond for $750 and chose not to report the interest each year. At the date of death, interest of $200 had accrued on the bond and its value of $950 was included in your uncle's estate. Your uncle's executor did not choose to include the $200 accrued interest in your uncle's final income tax return.

You are a cash method taxpayer and do not choose to report the interest each year as it is earned. If you cash the bond when it reaches its maturity value of $1,000, you will report $250 of interest income-the difference between the maturity value of $1,000 and the original cost of $750. Also, you may deduct (as a miscellaneous deduction not subject to the 2% AGI limit) in that year any federal estate tax that was paid on the $200 of interest that was included in your uncle's estate. For more information on this subject, see chapter 43, *Decedents: Dealing with the death of a family member.*

Example 2

If, in Example 1, the executor had chosen to include the $200 accrued interest in your uncle's final tax return, you would report only $50 as interest when you cashed the bond at maturity. This $50 is the interest earned after your uncle's death.

Example 3

Your aunt died owning Series H bonds that she got in a trade for Series E bonds. (See *Savings bonds traded,* in the next section.) You were the beneficiary of these bonds. Your aunt used the cash method and did not choose to report the interest on the Series E bonds each year as it accrued. Your aunt's executor did not choose to include on her final tax return any interest earned before her death.

The income in respect of a decedent is the sum of the unreported interest on the Series E bonds and the interest, if any, payable on the Series H bonds but not received as of the date of your aunt's death. You must report any interest received during the year as income on your return. The part of the interest that was payable but not received before your aunt's death is income in respect of the decedent and may qualify for the estate tax deduction. For when to report the interest on the Series E bonds traded, see *Savings bonds traded*, in the next section.

TAXPLANNER

There is an annual limitation on the purchase of Series EE and Series I bonds. Over-the-counter sales of paper bonds at financial institutions ended December 31, 2012, however, an individual may purchase a total of up to $20,000 (face amount), each, of Series EE and Series I bonds electronically per year. Because bonds are sold for one-half their face value, this means you can spend no more than $10,000 on electronic Series EE or Series I bonds per year. In addition, you may buy an additional $10,000 of Series I paper bonds each year with up to $5,000 of your federal income tax refund by checking the appropriate box (Form 1040EZ, line 11a; Form 1040A, line 43a; or Form 1040, line 74a) and attaching Form 8888, Allocation of Refund (Including Savings Bond Purchases) to your income tax return.

Savings bonds traded. If you postponed reporting the interest on your series EE or series E bonds, you did not recognize taxable income when you traded the bonds for series HH or series H bonds, unless you received cash in the trade. (You cannot trade series I bonds for series HH bonds. After August 31, 2004, you cannot trade any other series of bonds for series HH bonds.) Any cash you received is income up to the amount of the interest earned on the bonds traded. When your series HH or series H bonds mature, or if you dispose of them before maturity, you report as interest the difference between their redemption value and your cost. Your cost is the sum of the amount you paid for the traded series EE or series E bonds plus any amount you had to pay at the time of the trade.

Example. You traded series EE bonds (on which you postponed reporting the interest) for $2,500 in series HH bonds and $223 in cash. You reported the $223 as taxable income on your tax return. At the time of the trade, the series EE bonds had accrued interest of $523 and a redemption value of $2,723. You hold the series HH bonds until maturity, when you receive $2,500. You must report $300 as interest income in the year of maturity. This is the difference between their redemption value, $2,500, and your cost, $2,200 (the amount you paid for the series EE bonds). (It is also the difference between the accrued interest of $523 on the series EE bonds and the $223 cash received on the trade.)

Choice to report interest in year of trade. You could have chosen to treat all of the previously unreported accrued interest on the series EE or series E bonds traded for series HH bonds as income in the year of the trade. If you made this choice, it is treated as a change from method 1. See *Change from method 1* under *Series EE and series I bonds*, earlier.

Form 1099-INT for U.S. savings bonds interest. When you cash a bond, the bank or other payer that redeems it must give you a Form 1099-INT if the interest part of the payment you receive is $10 or more. Box 3 of your Form 1099-INT should show the interest as the difference between the amount you received and the amount paid for the bond. However, your Form 1099-INT may show more interest than you have to include on your income tax return. For example, this may happen if any of the following are true.

- You chose to report the increase in the redemption value of the bond each year. The interest shown on your Form 1099-INT will not be reduced by amounts previously included in income.
- You received the bond from a decedent. The interest shown on your Form 1099-INT will not be reduced by any interest reported by the decedent before death, or on the decedent's final return, or by the estate on the estate's income tax return.
- Ownership of the bond was transferred. The interest shown on your Form 1099-INT will not be reduced by interest that accrued before the transfer.
- You were named as a co-owner, and the other co-owner contributed funds to buy the bond. The interest shown on your Form 1099-INT will not be reduced by the amount you received as nominee for the other co-owner. (See *Co-owners*, earlier in this chapter, for more information about the reporting requirements.)
- You received the bond in a taxable distribution from a retirement or profit-sharing plan. The interest shown on your Form 1099-INT will not be reduced by the interest portion of the amount taxable as a distribution from the plan and not taxable as interest. (This amount is generally shown on Form 1099-R, Distributions From Pensions, Annuities, Retirement or Profit-Sharing Plans, IRAs, Insurance Contracts, etc., for the year of distribution.)

For more information on including the correct amount of interest on your return, see *How To Report Interest Income*, later. Publication 550 includes examples showing how to report these amounts.

EXPLANATION

When you redeem U.S. savings bonds, the government assumes that the difference between the issue price and the redemption amount is interest paid to you entirely at that time, even though some of the interest may already have been reported by you or someone else. The government will therefore issue a Form 1099-INT to you for the full amount.

If you should not be taxed on the full amount of interest, you should show the full amount as reported on the Form 1099-INT issued by the government on Schedule B (Form 1040 or Form 1040A) and also show a subtraction for the amount that is not taxable to you. This will help you to avoid IRS matching notices.

Education Savings Bond Program

You may be able to exclude from income all or part of the interest you receive on the redemption of qualified U.S. savings bonds during the year if you pay qualified higher educational expenses during the same year. This exclusion is known as the Education Savings Bond Program.

You do not qualify for this exclusion if your filing status is married filing separately.

TAXPLANNER

For 2014, the amount of your Education Savings Bond Program interest exclusion is phased out if your modified adjusted gross income (MAGI) is between $76,000 and $91,000 (between $113,950 and $143,950 if your filing status is married filing jointly or qualifying widow(er)).

Form 8815. Use Form 8815 to figure your exclusion. Attach the form to your Form 1040 or Form 1040A.

Qualified U.S. savings bonds. A qualified U.S. savings bond is a series EE bond issued after 1989 or a series I bond. The bond must be issued either in your name (sole owner) or in your and your spouse's names (co-owners). You must be at least 24 years old before the bond's issue date. For example, a bond bought by a parent and issued in the name of his or her child under age 24 does not qualify for the exclusion by the parent or child.

Beneficiary. You can designate any individual (including a child) as a beneficiary of the bond.

Verification by IRS. If you claim the exclusion, the IRS will check it by using bond redemption information from the Department of the Treasury.

Qualified expenses. Qualified higher educational expenses are tuition and fees required for you, your spouse, or your dependent (for whom you claim an exemption) to attend an eligible educational institution.

Qualified expenses include any contribution you make to a qualified tuition program or to a Coverdell education savings account.

Qualified expenses do not include expenses for room and board or for courses involving sports, games, or hobbies that are not part of a degree or certificate granting program.

Eligible educational institutions. These institutions include most public, private, and nonprofit universities, colleges, and vocational schools that are accredited and eligible to participate in student aid programs run by the U.S. Department of Education.

Reduction for certain benefits. You must reduce your qualified higher educational expenses by all of the following tax-free benefits.

1. Tax-free part of scholarships and fellowships (see *Scholarships and fellowships* in chapter 12).
2. Expenses used to figure the tax-free portion of distributions from a Coverdell ESA.
3. Expenses used to figure the tax-free portion of distributions from a qualified tuition program.
4. Any tax-free payments (other than gifts or inheritances) received for educational expenses, such as
   a. Veterans' educational assistance benefits,
   b. Qualified tuition reductions, or
   c. Employer-provided educational assistance.
5. Any expense used in figuring the American Opportunity and lifetime learning credits.

EXPLANATION
These reductions help you arrive at your "adjusted qualified higher educational expenses."

TAXORGANIZER
You should keep bills, receipts, canceled checks, and other documentation that show you paid qualified higher education expenses.

Amount excludable. If the total proceeds (interest and principal) from the qualified U.S. savings bonds you redeem during the year are not more than your adjusted qualified higher educational expenses for the year, you may be able to exclude all of the interest. If the proceeds are more than the expenses, you may be able to exclude only part of the interest.

To determine the excludable amount, multiply the interest part of the proceeds by a fraction. The numerator of the fraction is the qualified higher educational expenses you paid during the year. The denominator of the fraction is the total proceeds you received during the year.

Example. In February 2014, Mark and Joan, a married couple, cashed a qualified series EE U.S. savings bond they bought in April 1998. They received proceeds of $8,372 representing principal of $5,000 and interest of $3,372. In 2014, they paid $4,000 of their daughter's college tuition. They are not claiming an education credit for that amount, and their daughter does not have any tax-free educational assistance. They can exclude $1,611 ($3,372 × ($4,000 ÷ $8,372)) of interest in 2014. They must pay tax on the remaining $1,761 ($3,372 – $1,611) interest.

Modified adjusted gross income limit. The interest exclusion is limited if your modified adjusted gross income (modified AGI) is:

- $76,000 to $91,000 for taxpayers filing single or head of household, and
- $113,950 to $143,950 for married taxpayers filing jointly or for a qualifying widow(er) with dependent child.

You do not qualify for the interest exclusion if your modified AGI is equal to or more than the upper limit for your filing status.

Modified AGI, for purposes of this exclusion, is adjusted gross income (Form 1040, line 37, or Form 1040A, line 21) figured before the interest exclusion, and modified by adding back any:

1. Foreign earned income exclusion,
2. Foreign housing exclusion and deduction,
3. Exclusion of income for *bona fide* residents of American Samoa,
4. Exclusion for income from Puerto Rico,
5. Exclusion for adoption benefits received under an employer's adoption assistance program,
6. *Text intentionally omitted.*
7. Deduction for student loan interest, and
8. Deduction for domestic production activities.

Use the Line 9 Worksheet in the Form 8815 instructions to figure your modified AGI. If you claim any of the exclusion or deduction items listed above (except items 6, 7, and 8), add the amount of the exclusion or deduction (except items 6, 7, and 8) to the amount on line 5 of the worksheet, and enter the total on Form 8815, line 9, as your modified AGI.

If you have investment interest expense incurred to earn royalties and other investment income, see *Education Savings Bond Program* in chapter 1 of Publication 550.

U.S. Treasury Bills, Notes, and Bonds

Treasury bills, notes, and bonds are direct debts (obligations) of the U.S. Government.

Taxation of interest. Interest income from Treasury bills, notes, and bonds is subject to federal income tax but is exempt from all state and local income taxes. You should receive Form 1099-INT showing the interest (in box 3) paid to you for the year.

Payments of principal and interest generally will be credited to your designated checking or savings account by direct deposit through the TreasuryDirect® system.

Treasury bills. These bills generally have a 4-week, 13-week, 26-week, or 52-week maturity period. They are generally issued at a discount in the amount of $100 and multiples of $100. The difference between the discounted price you pay for the bills and the face value you receive at maturity is interest income. Generally, you report this interest income when the bill is paid at maturity. If you paid a premium for a bill (more than the face value), you generally report the premium as a Section 171 deduction when the bill is paid at maturity.

Treasury notes and bonds. Treasury notes have maturity periods of more than 1 year, ranging up to 10 years. Maturity periods for Treasury bonds are longer than 10 years. Both generally are issued in denominations of $100 to $1 million and generally pay interest every 6 months. Generally, you report this interest for the year paid. For more information, see *U.S. Treasury Bills, Notes, and Bonds* in chapter 1 of Publication 550.

For other information on Treasury notes or bonds, write to:

Bureau of the Public Debt

P.O. Box 7015

Parkersburg, WV 26106-7015

Or, on the Internet, visit: *www.treasurydirect.gov/indiv/indiv.htm.*

For information on series EE, series I, and series HH savings bonds, see *U.S. Savings Bonds,* earlier.

Treasury inflation-protected securities (TIPS). These securities pay interest twice a year at a fixed rate, based on a principal amount adjusted to take into account inflation and deflation. For the tax treatment of these securities, see *Inflation-Indexed Debt Instruments* under *Original Issue Discount (OID)*, in Publication 550.

EXPLANATION

The paragraph above discusses interest income only when a Treasury bill is held until maturity. When a Treasury bill is sold before maturity, the difference between the purchase price and the selling price may be part interest and part short-term capital gain or loss.

Example

You buy a $10,000 Treasury bill for $9,760 exactly 100 days before maturity. Thirty days later, you sell the bill for $9,850.

For tax purposes, you have earned a pro rata portion of the discount as interest income for the time you held the bill: $30/100 \times (\$10,000 - \$9,760) = \$72$. The other $18 you receive over and above the purchase price is a short-term capital gain.

TAXSAVER

U.S. Treasury bills are relatively short-term investments. Their maturity dates vary from a few days to 26 weeks. Since the interest income in most cases is reported at maturity (unless the bill is sold beforehand), purchasing Treasury bills with a maturity date falling in the following year offers cash basis taxpayers an opportunity to postpone interest income from one year to the next. However, if you borrow money to acquire Treasury bills, your interest expense deduction may also be deferred. See chapter 24, *Interest expense*, for an explanation.

Bonds Sold Between Interest Dates

If you sell a bond between interest payment dates, part of the sales price represents interest accrued to the date of sale. You must report that part of the sales price as interest income for the year of sale.

If you buy a bond between interest payment dates, part of the purchase price represents interest accrued before the date of purchase. When that interest is paid to you, treat it as a return of your capital investment, rather than interest income, by reducing your basis in the bond. See *Accrued interest on bonds* under *How To Report Interest Income* in chapter 1 of Publication 550 for information on reporting the payment.

EXPLANATION

Usually, interest on a bond is paid every 6 months. When a bond is sold between interest payment dates, the seller is entitled to payment from the buyer for the interest earned since the issuer's last interest payment, in addition to payment for the bond itself. This extra payment-often called "purchased interest" on a broker's statement-is interest income to the seller of the bond, reportable for tax purposes as of the date of the sale. The buyer of the bond should record the purchased interest separately from the price of the bond in his or her records. The purchased interest partially offsets the first interest payment made to the buyer.

If the purchased interest is paid in 2014 but the first interest payment is not received until 2015, the buyer should report the purchased interest as an adjustment to interest income in 2015, not in 2014.

Example 1

On April 1, 2014, Cindy bought from Michelle a $10,000 bond yielding 10%. Interest on the bond is paid on January 1 and July 1 of each year. Cindy paid $10,250, representing $10,000 in principal plus $250 for interest earned from January 1 to April 1. Thus, Michelle received $250 of interest income on April 1, 2014. Cindy received her first interest check on July 1, 2014. Half of the $500 Cindy received on July 1 represented a payment of purchased interest, and the other half represented interest income. In order to avoid any IRS matching notices, Cindy should report the full $500 on Schedule B (Form 1040 or Form 1040A) and also show a subtraction for $250 of interest that she purchased.

Example 2

Assume the same facts as in Example 1, except that Cindy bought the bond from Michelle on October 1, 2014. Cindy received her interest check for $500 on January 1, 2015. Half of it represented repayment of purchased interest, and the other half represented interest income. However, Cindy may not deduct the $250 of purchased interest in 2014, but must wait until 2015. On the other hand, Michelle will report $250 of interest income on her 2014 return, since she received it on October 1, 2014.

Insurance

Life insurance proceeds paid to you as beneficiary of the insured person are usually not taxable. But if you receive the proceeds in installments, you must usually report a part of each installment payment as interest income.

For more information about insurance proceeds received in installments, see Publication 525, Taxable and Nontaxable Income.

EXPLANATION

For more information on life insurance proceeds, see chapter 12, *Other income.*

Annuity. If you buy an annuity with life insurance proceeds, the annuity payments you receive are taxed as pension and annuity income from a nonqualified plan, not as interest income. See chapter 10 for information on pension and annuity income from nonqualified plans.

State or Local Government Obligations

Interest on a bond used to finance government operations generally is not taxable if the bond is issued by a state, the District of Columbia, a possession of the United States, or any of their political subdivisions.

Bonds issued after 1982 (including tribal economic development bonds issued after February 17, 2009) by an Indian tribal government are treated as issued by a state. Interest on these bonds is generally tax exempt if the bonds are part of an issue of which substantially all proceeds are to be used in the exercise of any essential government function.

EXPLANATION

While the interest accrued on municipal bonds is generally tax-exempt for federal income tax purposes, any accretion of gain recognized on the bond's sale or upon the maturity of a bond purchased at a market discount is subject to tax as interest up to the amount of the market discount. The balance is taxed as capital gain.

To illustrate, assume that tax-exempt municipal bonds were previously sold to the public at par (face value) at an interest rate lower than the rate demanded by today's investors. Since the interest rate on these bonds is lower than the rate demanded by today's investors, the bonds are trading in the marketplace at a substantial discount from par. This is a market discount. If you buy these bonds now and subsequently realize a gain either when you sell them or when they reach maturity, you must report the gain as taxable interest income up to the amount of the bonds' accrued market discount and the remaining portion as capital gain if the bond was a capital asset. Similarly, if you realize a capital loss on municipal bonds, it is deductible.

The rule with regard to bonds bought at a premium is different. If you buy a bond for $11,000 that will mature for $10,000 and you hold it until maturity, you may not claim a capital loss or any kind of deduction because the tax law requires that you amortize the premium over the life of the bond. The annual amortization of the premium is deducted from the cost basis of the bond so that at the bond's maturity date, its cost basis is equal to the proceeds received.

TAXSAVER

If you are considering selling a tax-exempt bond and purchasing another tax-exempt bond, keep in mind that for bonds purchased before May 1, 1993, you will not have to treat accrued market discount as ordinary income, but rather as a capital gain. Depending on your tax bracket, this may be a significant consideration, since currently the top capital gains tax rate is 20%, while the top marginal rate is 39.6%. When considering the 3.8% Net Investment Income Tax, these tax rates become 23.8% and 43.4% respectively. Further, while most municipal bond interest is not subject to federal tax, capital gain income and accretion of market discount are. You should take these differences into account when you are deciding which bonds to buy.

Example

A $10,000, 10-year tax-exempt municipal bond, yielding 8% purchased at par, will provide $800 of tax-free interest each year, and there will be no capital gain on maturity. The total earned for the 10 years is $8,000.

Similarly, a $12,000, 10-year tax-exempt municipal bond with a 5.2% coupon ($624 interest per year) purchased on May 1, 2004, at $10,000 will yield a total of $8,240 over the life of the bond: $624 of tax-free interest each year plus $200 of taxable interest income each year if the bond is held to maturity. The $200 represents the annual market discount accretion. But the taxable interest income will be subject to tax of up to 43.4%, so the net earnings for the 10 years may be reduced to $7,108.

TAXPLANNER

When you are determining whether to invest in tax-exempt securities, compare the net after-tax income from a tax-exempt investment with a similar taxable investment.

Tax-Exempt Yield	27%	30%	33%	35%	38.6%	42%	44%	50%	55%
3.50	4.79	5.00	5.22	5.38	5.70	6.03	6.25	7.00	7.78
4.00	5.48	5.71	5.97	6.15	6.51	6.90	7.14	8.00	8.89
4.50	6.16	6.43	6.72	6.92	7.33	7.76	8.04	9.00	10.00
5.00	6.85	7.14	7.46	7.69	8.14	8.62	8.93	10.00	11.11
5.50	7.53	7.86	8.21	8.46	8.96	9.48	9.82	11.00	12.22
6.00	8.22	8.57	8.96	9.23	9.77	10.34	10.71	12.00	13.33
6.50	8.90	9.29	9.70	10.00	10.59	11.21	11.61	13.00	14.44
7.00	9.59	10.00	10.45	10.77	11.40	12.07	12.50	14.00	15.56

For information on federally guaranteed bonds, mortgage revenue bonds, arbitrage bonds, private activity bonds, qualified tax credit bonds, and Build America bonds, see *State or Local Government Obligations* in chapter 1 of Publication 550.

Information reporting requirement. If you must file a tax return, you are required to show any tax-exempt interest you received on your return. This is an information reporting requirement only. It does not change tax-exempt interest to taxable interest.

Original Issue Discount (OID)

Original issue discount (OID) is a form of interest. You generally include OID in your income as it accrues over the term of the debt instrument, whether or not you receive any payments from the issuer.

A debt instrument generally has OID when the instrument is issued for a price that is less than its stated redemption price at maturity. OID is the difference between the stated redemption price at maturity and the issue price.

All debt instruments that pay no interest before maturity are presumed to be issued at a discount. Zero coupon bonds are one example of these instruments.

The OID accrual rules generally do not apply to short-term obligations (those with a fixed maturity date of 1 year or less from date of issue). See *Discount on Short-Term Obligations* in chapter 1 of Publication 550.

De minimis OID. You can treat the discount as zero if it is less than one-fourth of 1% (.0025) of the stated redemption price at maturity multiplied by the number of full years from the date of original issue to maturity. This small discount is known as *"de minimis"* OID.

Example 1. You bought a 10-year bond with a stated redemption price at maturity of $1,000, issued at $980 with OID of $20. One-fourth of 1% of $1,000 (stated redemption price) times 10 (the number of full years from the date of original issue to maturity) equals $25. Because the $20 discount is less than $25, the OID is treated as zero. (If you hold the bond at maturity, you will recognize $20 ($1,000–$980) of capital gain.)

Example 2. The facts are the same as in *Example 1*, except that the bond was issued at $950. The OID is $50. Because the $50 discount is more than the $25 figured in *Example 1*, you must include the OID in income as it accrues over the term of the bond.

Debt instrument bought after original issue. If you buy a debt instrument with *de minimis* OID at a premium, the discount is not includible in income. If you buy a debt instrument with *de minimis* OID at a discount, the discount is reported under the market discount rules. See *Market Discount Bonds* in chapter 1 of Publication 550.

Exceptions to reporting OID. The OID rules discussed in this chapter do not apply to the following debt instruments.

1. Tax-exempt obligations. (However, see *Stripped tax-exempt obligations* under *Stripped Bonds and Coupons* in chapter 1 of Publication 550).
2. U.S. savings bonds.
3. Short-term debt instruments (those with a fixed maturity date of not more than 1 year from the date of issue).
4. Obligations issued by an individual before March 2, 1984.
5. Loans between individuals if all the following are true.
   a. The lender is not in the business of lending money.
   b. The amount of the loan, plus the amount of any outstanding prior loans between the same individuals, is $10,000 or less.
   c. Avoiding any federal tax is not one of the principal purposes of the loan.

Form 1099-OID. The issuer of the debt instrument (or your broker if you held the instrument through a broker) should give you Form 1099-OID, or a similar statement, if the total OID for the calendar year is $10 or more. Form 1099-OID will show, in box 1, the amount of OID for the part of the year that you held the bond. It also will show, in box 2, the stated interest you must include in your income. A copy of Form 1099-OID will be sent to the IRS. Do not file your copy with your return. Keep it for your records.

In most cases, you must report the entire amount in boxes 1 and 2 of Form 1099-OID as interest income. But see *Refiguring OID shown on Form 1099-OID,* later in this discussion, for more information.

Form 1099-OID not received. If you had OID for the year but did not receive a Form 1099-OID, you can find tables on IRS.gov that list total OID on certain debt instruments and have information that will help you figure OID. For the latest OID tables, go to *www.irs.gov* and enter "OID tables" in the Search box. If your debt instrument is not listed, consult the issuer for further information about the accrued OID for the year.

Nominee. If someone else is the holder of record (the registered owner) of an OID instrument belonging to you and receives a Form 1099-OID on your behalf, that person must give you a Form 1099-OID.

Refiguring OID shown on Form 1099-OID. You must refigure the OID shown in box 1 or box 8 of Form 1099-OID if either of the following apply.

- You bought the debt instrument after its original issue and paid a premium or an acquisition premium.
- The debt instrument is a stripped bond or a stripped coupon (including certain zero coupon instruments).

For information about figuring the correct amount of OID to include in your income, see *Figuring OID on Long-Term Debt Instruments* in Publication 1212.

EXPLANATION

Stripped coupon bonds are coupon bonds that have been separated into component parts. The coupons represent claims for interest payments, which are paid on a periodic basis. The bond itself represents the claim for the repayment of the principal, which occurs at some future time.

Example

A 10-year $10,000, 9% bond (interest paid semiannually) was issued on January 1, 2014, for $10,000. On April 1, 2014, when the bond had a market price of $9,900, the coupons were stripped from the bond so that they and the bond became separate assets that could be bought and sold in the marketplace. In other words, the holder could have sold the right to receive $450 semiannually for the next 9¾ years and could have independently sold the right to receive the $10,000 on January 1, 2024.

Assume that the right to receive 20 semiannual payments is worth $4,100 and the right to receive $10,000 on January 1, 2024, is worth $5,800. The tax treatment to buyer and to seller is as follows:

The seller:

1. Include the accrued interest income of $225 from January 1, 2014, through April 1, 2014, in income.
2. Increase your basis by the $225 to $10,225.
3. Allocate the basis, using fair market value, to the coupons [($4,100 ÷ $9,900) × $10,225 = $4,235] and the bond [($5,800 ÷ $9,900) × $10,225 = $5,990].
4. Compare the proceeds for what you sell–either the coupons or the bond–with the basis figured above to determine if you've had a gain or a loss.
5. The difference between the basis of what is not sold and the amount that will be received over time is considered an original issue discount (OID). That amount is treated as earned over the life of the asset. Thus, if the coupons were retained, the difference between their basis ($4,235) and the amount that will be received over time ($450 semiannually for 10 years, or $9,000) would be the original issue discount.

In this example, $4,765 in interest income must be included on your returns over the 10 years. The amount to be included in your income for each year is figured by performing a complicated computation, for which you will probably require professional assistance.

Similarly, if the bond were retained, the difference between its basis ($5,990) and the proceeds ($10,000) would be its original issue discount. Again, complicated computations are required to determine the amount included in your income each year.

The buyer: The difference between what you pay and what you will receive over time is the original issue discount. A special computation is necessary to figure how much you should include in income each year.

Refiguring periodic interest shown on Form 1099-OID. If you disposed of a debt instrument or acquired it from another holder during the year, see _Bonds Sold Between Interest Dates_, earlier, for information about the treatment of periodic interest that may be shown in box 2 of Form 1099-OID for that instrument.

EXPLANATION

These rules also apply to debt instruments issued by individuals after March 1, 1984. This will affect individuals who borrow and lend at a discounted rate.

The current law also makes original issue discount the general rule with regard to obligations issued after July 18, 1984, and purchased in the open market. (This law also applies to bonds issued before July 19, 1984, and purchased after April 30, 1993.) If you sell property after December 31, 1984, or buy a bond in the marketplace that was issued after July 18, 1984, or a bond issued prior to July 19, 1984, and purchased after April 30, 1993, you must determine whether there is original issue discount and, if so, how much. Some of that amount will be included in your ordinary income each year. You will likely need professional help to make this calculation. For more information, see _Market discount bonds_, later in this chapter.

Example

Assume that Jorge purchases a publicly traded 6% $1 million bond that was issued after December 31, 1984, for $900,000. The bond has a maturity of 10 years at the time of purchase. Jorge will also receive $60,000 in interest each year.

The computation of the amount of original issue discount to be included is as follows:

Face value	$1,000,000
Purchase price	$900,000
Length of term	10
Coupon rate	6%

Period	Beginning basis	Total interest income	OID portion	Interest portion	Ending basis
1	$900,000	$69,533	9,533	$60,000	$909,533
2	909,533	69,634	9,634	60,000	919,166
3	919,166	69,736	9,736	60,000	928,902
4	928,902	69,839	9,839	60,000	938,740
5	938,740	69,943	9,943	60,000	948,683
6	948,683	70,048	10,048	60,000	958,732
7	958,732	70,155	10,155	60,000	968,866
8	968,886	70,262	10,262	60,000	979,148
9	979,148	70,371	70,371	60,000	989,519
10	989,519	70,481	70,481	60,000	1,000,000
		$700,000	$100,000	$600,000	

The total interest income recognized for the first year will be $69,533 ($60,000 interest and $9,533 of OID). Further special computations will be required if the obligation is sold prior to maturity. Professional advice is absolutely essential for anyone who needs to make special OID computations.

TAXPLANNER

A zero-coupon bond is one that is purchased at a substantial discount and pays no interest during its life.

If you buy a zero-coupon bond, you do not bear the investment risk entailed in reinvesting interest payments received over the life of the bond because there are no such payments. Moreover, since the issue price and the maturity value have been derived from compound interest tables, you may figure what the precise return on your investment will be if the bond is held until it matures. This is true only of zero-coupon bonds.

Note: Because you do not receive the interest until a zero-coupon bond matures, the market value of the bond during the holding period can be very volatile as market interest rates change. The longer the maturity is, the more volatile is the price.

Even though the interest on a zero-coupon bond is not paid until maturity, it is included in income each year. Consequently, an individual must pay tax on income that he or she has not yet received. However, if the bonds are owned in your IRA or Keogh plan, this income is not currently taxable. (See chapter 17, *Individual retirement arrangements [IRAs]*.) The advantage, however, is that you lock in an interest rate.

On the other hand, nontaxable zero-coupon bonds, such as zero-coupon municipal bonds, may be attractive to individuals in a high tax bracket for the obvious reasons that interest rates are locked in and the increase in value each year is not taxable. In this case, you increase your cost basis on the bonds each year by the amount of the original issue discount applicable to that year, even though you don't pay any federal tax on the income. You may, however, have to pay state income taxes. You will need to check your state tax rules.

Avoid holding municipal bonds in your IRA or Keogh plan as all distributions from the account, including the interest earned on the bonds, will be treated as federal and state taxable income when you make a withdrawal from your account and will be taxed at ordinary income rates.

Example 1

Assume that Jennifer purchases a 10-year $100,000, nontaxable zero-coupon bond on June 30, 2014, for $50,000. The chart below illustrates how the basis of the bond increases over the life of the bond.

Face value	$100,000
Purchase price	$50,000
Length of term	10

Period	Beginning basis	OID	Ending basis
1	$50,000	$3,589	$53,589
2	53,589	3,846	57,435
3	57,435	4,122	61,557
4	61,557	4,418	65,975
5	65,975	4,735	70,711
6	70,711	5,075	75,786
7	75,786	5,439	81,225
8	81,225	5,830	87,055
9	87,055	6,248	93,303
10	93,303	6,697	100,000
		$50,000	

The method for determining original issue discount illustrated in this example is applicable to tax-exempt bonds. The annual increase in basis is determined accordingly. However, the original issue discount computation is not the method used for a tax-exempt bond issued before September 4, 1982, and acquired before March 2, 1984. Instead, a rule is used that allocates the discount proportionately over the life of the bond.

Certificates of deposit (CDs). If you buy a CD with a maturity of more than 1 year, you must include in income each year a part of the total interest due and report it in the same manner as other OID.

This also applies to similar deposit arrangements with banks, building and loan associations, etc., including:

- Time deposits,
- Bonus plans,
- Savings certificates,
- Deferred income certificates,
- Bonus savings certificates, and
- Growth savings certificates.

Bearer CDs. CDs issued after 1982 generally must be in registered form. Bearer CDs are CDs not in registered form. They are not issued in the depositor's name and are transferable from one individual to another.

Banks must provide the IRS and the person redeeming a bearer CD with a Form 1099-INT.

More information. See chapter 1 of Publication 550 for more information about OID and related topics, such as market discount bonds.

When To Report Interest Income

When to report your interest income depends on whether you use the cash method or an accrual method to report income.

Cash method. Most individual taxpayers use the cash method. If you use this method, you generally report your interest income in the year in which you actually or constructively receive it. However, there are special rules for reporting the discount on certain debt instruments. See *U.S. Savings Bonds* and *Original Issue Discount (OID)*, earlier.

Example. On September 1, 2012, you loaned another individual $2,000 at 12%, compounded annually. You are not in the business of lending money. The note stated that principal and interest would be due on August 31, 2014. In 2014, you received $2,508.80 ($2,000 principal and $508.80 interest). If you use the cash method, you must include in income on your 2014 return the $508.80 interest you received in that year.

Constructive receipt. You constructively receive income when it is credited to your account or made available to you. You do not need to have physical possession of it. For example, you are considered to receive interest, dividends, or other earnings on any deposit or account in a bank, savings and loan, or similar financial institution, or interest on life insurance policy dividends left to accumulate, when they are credited to your account and subject to your withdrawal. This is true even if they are not yet entered in your passbook.

You constructively receive income on the deposit or account even if you must:
- Make withdrawals in multiples of even amounts,
- Give a notice to withdraw before making the withdrawal,
- Withdraw all or part of the account to withdraw the earnings, or
- Pay a penalty on early withdrawals, unless the interest you are to receive on an early withdrawal or redemption is substantially less than the interest payable at maturity.

Accrual method. If you use an accrual method, you report your interest income when you earn it, whether or not you have received it. Interest is earned over the term of the debt instrument.

Example. If, in the previous example, you use an accrual method, you must include the interest in your income as you earn it. You would report the interest as follows: 2012, $80; 2013, $249.60; and 2014, $179.20.

Coupon bonds. Interest on coupon bonds is taxable in the year the coupon becomes due and payable. It does not matter when you mail the coupon for payment.

How To Report Interest Income

Generally, you report all your taxable interest income on Form 1040, line 8a; Form 1040A, line 8a; or Form 1040EZ, line 2.

You cannot use Form 1040EZ if your taxable interest income is more than $1,500. Instead, you must use Form 1040A or Form 1040.

Form 1040A. You must complete Schedule B (Form 1040A or 1040), Part I, if you file Form 1040A and any of the following are true.
1. Your taxable interest income is more than $1,500.
2. You are claiming the interest exclusion under the Education Savings Bond Program (discussed earlier).
3. You received interest from a seller-financed mortgage, and the buyer used the property as a home.
4. You received a Form 1099-INT for U.S. savings bond interest that includes amounts you reported before 2014.
5. You received, as a nominee, interest that actually belongs to someone else.
6. You received a Form 1099-INT for interest on frozen deposits.
7. You are reporting OID in an amount less than the amount shown on Form 1099-OID.
8. You received a Form 1099-INT for interest on a bond you bought between interest payment dates.
9. You acquired taxable bonds after 1987 and choose to reduce interest income from the bonds by any amortizable bond premium (see *Bond Premium Amortization* in chapter 3 of Publication 550).

List each payer's name and the amount of interest income received from each payer on line 1. If you received a Form 1099-INT or Form 1099-OID from a brokerage firm, list the brokerage firm as the payer.

You cannot use Form 1040A if you must use Form 1040, as described next.

Form 1040. You must use Form 1040 instead of Form 1040A or Form 1040EZ if:
1. You forfeited interest income because of the early withdrawal of a time deposit;
2. You acquired taxable bonds after 1987, you choose to reduce interest income from the bonds by any amortizable bond premium, and you are deducting the excess of bond premium amortization for the accrual period over the qualified stated interest for the period (see *Bond Premium Amortization* in chapter 3 of Publication 550); or
3. You received tax-exempt interest from private activity bonds issued after August 7, 1986.
Schedule B (Form 1040A or 1040). You must complete Schedule B (Form 1040A or 1040), Part I, if you file Form 1040 and any of the following apply.
1. Your taxable interest income is more than $1,500.
2. You are claiming the interest exclusion under the Education Savings Bond Program (discussed earlier).
3. You received interest from a seller-financed mortgage, and the buyer used the property as a home.
4. You received a Form 1099-INT for U.S. savings bond interest that includes amounts you reported before 2014.
5. You received, as a nominee, interest that actually belongs to someone else.
6. You received a Form 1099-INT for interest on frozen deposits.
7. You received a Form 1099-INT for interest on a bond you bought between interest payment dates.

8. You are reporting OID in an amount less than the amount shown on Form 1099-OID.

9. Statement (2) in the preceding list under Form 1040 is true.

In Part I, line 1, list each payer's name and the amount received from each. If you received a Form 1099-INT or Form 1099-OID from a brokerage firm, list the brokerage firm as the payer.

Reporting tax-exempt interest. Total your tax-exempt interest (such as interest or accrued OID on certain state and municipal bonds, including tax-exempt interest on zero coupon municipal bonds) and exempt-interest dividends from a mutual fund as shown on Form 1099-INT, box 8, and on Form 1099-DIV, box 10. Add these amounts to any other tax-exempt interest you received. Report the total on line 8b of Form 1040A or 1040.

If you file Form 1040EZ, enter "TEI" and the amount in the space to the left of line 2. Do not add tax-exempt interest in the total on Form 1040EZ, line 2.

Form 1099-INT, box 9, and Form 1099-DIV, box 11, show the tax-exempt interest subject to the alternative minimum tax on Form 6251. These amounts are already included in the amounts on Form 1099-INT, box 8, and Form 1099-DIV, box 10. Do not add the amounts in Form 1099-INT, box 9 and Form 1099-DIV, box 11 to, or subtract them from, the amounts on Form 1099-INT, box 8, and Form 1099-DIV, box 10.

Form 1099-INT. Your taxable interest income, except for interest from U.S. savings bonds and Treasury obligations, is shown in box 1 of Form 1099-INT. Add this amount to any other taxable interest income you received. You must report all of your taxable interest income even if you do not receive a Form 1099-INT. Generally, contact your financial institution if you do not receive a Form 1099-INT by February 15. Your identifying number may be truncated on any paper Form 1099-INT you receive.

If you forfeited interest income because of the early withdrawal of a time deposit, the deductible amount will be shown on Form 1099-INT in box 2. See *Penalty on early withdrawal of savings* in chapter 1 of Publication 550.

Box 3 of Form 1099-INT shows the interest income you received from U.S. savings bonds, Treasury bills, Treasury notes, and Treasury bonds. Add the amount shown in box 3 to any other taxable interest income you received, unless part of the amount in box 3 was previously included in your interest income. If part of the amount shown in box 3 was previously included in your interest income, see *U.S. savings bond interest previously reported*, later.

Box 4 of Form 1099-INT will contain an amount if you were subject to backup withholding. Report the amount from box 4 on Form 1040EZ, line 7; on Form 1040A, line 36; or Form 1040, line 62 (federal income tax withheld).

Box 5 of Form 1099-INT shows investment expenses you may be able to deduct as an itemized deduction. See chapter 29 for more information about investment expenses.

If there are entries in boxes 6 and 7 of Form 1099-INT, you must file Form 1040. You may be able to take a credit for the amount shown in box 6 unless you deduct this amount on line 8 of Schedule A (Form 1040). To take the credit, you may have to file Form 1116, Foreign Tax Credit. For more information, see Publication 514, Foreign Tax Credit for Individuals.

Caution

Do not report interest from an individual retirement account (IRA) as tax-exempt interest.

TAXALERT

If you receive a Form 1099-INT that includes an amount of foreign tax paid in box 6, it is likely that the interest was generated by some foreign asset you owned during the year. As noted previously in this chapter, starting in 2011, Form 8938, Statement of Specified Foreign Financial Assets, may be required to be filed with your income tax return if you have an interest in specified foreign financial assets that have an aggregate value in excess of certain threshold amounts. The threshold amounts are based on your filing category and whether you reside in the United States or overseas. Because the measurement of account value is based on the combined total of the highest value of each of your foreign assets and financial accounts during the calendar year, it is important to consider all of your assets that are invested outside of the United States, including all interests in foreign corporations or partnerships, and all contracts with non-U.S. counterparties including foreign employers, insurance companies, and other issuers of financial instruments.

Even accounts holding inconsequential amounts or assets you disposed of during 2014 may be subject to reporting if the total value of all account "maximum balances" and other specified foreign financial assets exceeds the applicable threshold amount for your filing category and residency status at any time during the calendar year. It is important to note that the thresholds are higher for U.S. persons who reside abroad. The instructions to Form 8938 describe in detail the threshold amounts that apply to each filing category both within and without the United States.

U.S. savings bond interest previously reported. If you received a Form 1099-INT for U.S. savings bond interest, the form may show interest you do not have to report. See *Form 1099-INT for U.S. savings bonds interest*, earlier, under *U.S. Savings Bonds.*

On Schedule B (Form 1040A or 1040), Part I, line 1, report all the interest shown on your Form 1099-INT. Then follow these steps.

1. Several lines above line 2, enter a subtotal of all interest listed on line 1.
2. Below the subtotal enter "U.S. Savings Bond Interest Previously Reported" and enter amounts previously reported or interest accrued before you received the bond.
3. Subtract these amounts from the subtotal and enter the result on line 2.

More information. For more information about how to report interest income, see chapter 1 of Publication 550 or the instructions for the form you must file.

TAXORGANIZER

Records you should keep:
Keep a list of the sources and amounts of interest income received during the year. In particular, keep the following forms that report interest you received for at least 3 years:
- Form 1099-INT
- Form 1099-OID
- Any substitute 1099, such as a broker statement or year-end account summary
  You should also keep a written record of Series EE and Series I U.S. savings bonds issued after 1989. Include the serial number, issue date, face value, and amount of redemption proceeds of each bond. You may also use Form 8818.

Chapter 8
Dividends and other corporate distributions

IRS Publication 17 (*Your Federal Income Tax*) has been updated by Ernst & Young LLP for 2014. Dates and dollar amounts shown are for 2014. Underlined type is used to indicate where IRS text has been updated. Places where text has been removed are indicated by the sentence: *Text intentionally omitted.*

ey.com/EYTaxGuide

Ernst & Young LLP will update the *EY Tax Guide 2015* website with relevant taxpayer information as it becomes available. You can also sign up for email alerts to let you know when changes have been made.

Introduction

Most people think they know what dividends are. The problem is that the term is commonly used to describe a large number of items that the IRS does not consider to be dividends. "Dividends" paid by an insurance company to its policyholders are considered by the IRS to be a return of premiums, not dividends. "Dividends" paid by a savings and loan association to its depositors are considered to be interest, not dividends.

So what is a dividend? A dividend is a share of a corporation's profits that is distributed to shareholders. This chapter discusses how these distributions, as well as other corporate distributions, are taxed.

If you own stock in a company or shares in a mutual fund or real estate investment trust (REIT), you may receive dividend distributions. The distributing company or mutual fund will send you a Form 1099-DIV just after year-end with the total amount of dividends you must report to the IRS on your income tax return. This chapter explains the difference between the various tax forms you may receive and which forms to keep in your records or attach to your income tax return.

This chapter also discusses dividend reinvestment plans (DRPs) that reinvest the dividends in the stock generating them. These plans are provided by companies for all their shareholders and should not be confused with retirement plans run by employers for the benefit of their employees.

Certain dividend income (but not interest income), referred to as "qualified dividend income," is taxed at a maximum rate of 20% for high income taxpayers who are otherwise in the 39.6% regular income tax bracket (i.e., taxable incomes over $406,750 for individual filers, $432,200 for heads of households, $457,600 married filing jointly, and $228,800 if married filing separately). Qualified dividends received by taxpayers in the 10% and 15% tax brackets are taxed at a zero rate. For all others, the tax rate on qualified is 15%. These preferential tax rates on qualified dividend income apply to both the regular tax and the alternative minimum tax.

Under the Affordable Care Act, the 3.8% Net Investment Income Tax (NIIT) on unearned income—including dividends—took effect for tax years beginning in 2013 and thereafter. For individuals, the tax is 3.8% of the lesser of: (1) "net investment income" or (2) the excess of modified adjusted gross income (MAGI) over $200,000 ($250,000 if married filing jointly or a qualifying widow(er) with dependent child; $125,000 if married filing separately). The NIIT is payable regardless of whether or not you otherwise pay any regular income tax or are subject to alternative minimum tax on your income.

Tax Breaks and Deductions You Can Use Checklist

Qualified dividend income. Taxpayers in the highest regular tax bracket of 39.6% are subject to a maximum tax rate of 20% on qualified dividend income. On the other hand, taxpayers who are in the 10% and 15% tax brackets have a zero percent tax rate applied to qualified dividend income. For taxpayers in the other regular tax brackets, the top rate on qualified dividends is 15%. (The top tax rates on long-term capital gains are the same as those for qualified dividends. See chapter 16, *Reporting gains and losses*, for more information.) The twist is that not all dividend income is "qualified," so look carefully before you invest. For example, most income from money market funds is not qualified dividend income. Dividends from foreign corporations, on the other hand, may be qualified.

Foreign dividends. If you received dividends on foreign corporation stock that you own, it's likely that the corporation withheld foreign tax on those payments. Don't report the net amount on your tax return. Instead, you should report the full amount of the dividend (before withholding) and claim the foreign tax withheld either as a credit or as a deduction on your return. See chapter 23, *Taxes you may deduct*, and chapter 37, *Other credits including the earned income credit*.

Life insurance dividends. "Dividends" paid out on life insurance policies are not taxable income. They

Reminder

Foreign-source income. If you are a U.S. citizen with dividend income from sources outside the United States (foreign-source income), you must report that income on your tax return unless it is exempt by U.S. law. This is true whether you reside inside or outside the United States and whether or not you receive a Form 1099 from the foreign payer.

TAXSAVER

Foreign dividends. Foreign governments often withhold tax on dividends from foreign corporations before you receive them. For example, if you are a stockholder in a Canadian company that declares a $100 dividend, you might receive only $85 because of a $15 Canadian withholding tax. Nevertheless, the $100 must be reported on your U.S. income tax return. The $15 of foreign taxes may be claimed either as a foreign tax credit using Form 1116 or as an itemized deduction on Schedule A (Form 1040). It is generally preferable to take the tax credit. For more on this subject, see chapter 23, *Taxes you may deduct*, and chapter 37, *Other credits including the earned income credit*.

TAXSAVER

Individuals with $300 or less of foreign taxes paid ($600 for joint filers) are able to take a foreign tax credit for that entire amount. This is an exemption from the limitation of offsetting foreign tax credits against U.S. tax liability, which applies to taxes paid in excess of $300 ($600 married filing jointly). The exemption must be elected each year and is only available if all foreign source income is qualified passive income.

Example
You are a single individual who invests in a mutual fund that holds foreign securities. During 2014, your share of foreign taxes paid by this mutual fund is $250. When you prepare your 2014 tax return, you can claim an exemption from the foreign tax credit limitation and credit the full $250 against your U.S. tax liability.

TAXALERT

Dividends paid on foreign corporation stocks that are readily tradable on U.S. securities markets are eligible for the preferential federal tax rate applicable to qualified dividend income. For this purpose, a share will be treated as so traded if an American Depository Receipt (ADR) backed by such a share is readily tradable on an established securities market in the United States. Moreover, dividends from corporations incorporated in a U.S. possession, or those eligible for benefits under a comprehensive income tax treaty with the United States, are generally eligible for the lower rate. Dividends paid by foreign personal holding companies, foreign investment companies, and passive foreign investment companies do not qualify for the reduced tax rates.

TAXALERT

Dividends received by an individual shareholder from domestic corporations and "qualified foreign corporations" are eligible for the same reduced federal tax rate as net capital gain income. These reduced rates apply for both the regular tax and the alternative minimum tax.

Thus, these dividends are taxed at a maximum rate of 20% for taxpayers who are in the top 39.6% tax bracket (i.e., taxable incomes over $406,750 for individual filers, $432,200 for heads of households, $457,600 married filing jointly, and $228,800 if married filing separately). Qualified dividends received by taxpayers subject to tax brackets of 15% or lower are taxed at 0%. Qualified dividends received by taxpayers in the other regular income tax brackets (i.e., 25%, 28%, 33%, or 35%) are taxed at 15%.

This reduced tax rate only applies to dividends from common shares held for more than 60 days during the 121-day period beginning 60 days before the ex-dividend period. (The ex-dividend date is the date that determines whether the seller, rather than the buyer, receives the announced dividend.) Hence, this provision combined with the 20% top rate on long-term capital gains makes short-term investing less tax-efficient.

TAXALERT

You only need to attach Schedule B and report individual dividends if your total dividend income exceeds $1,500.

are actually considered to be a return of your premiums. You should not report them on your return unless their total is more than your accumulated premiums.

Dividends used to buy more stock. If you invest in stock and choose to have the dividends reinvested to purchase additional stock, your basis in the stock is increased by the amount of dividends reinvested. The dividends are taxable to you even though you did not receive the cash, but the basis of your stock is increased by the amount of the dividends reinvested. When the stock is sold, don't forget to increase your basis by the amount of the dividends reinvested.

This chapter discusses the tax treatment of:
- Ordinary dividends,
- Capital gain distributions,
- Nondividend distributions, and
- Other distributions you may receive from a corporation or a mutual fund.

This chapter also explains how to report dividend income on your tax return.

Dividends are distributions of money, stock, or other property paid to you by a corporation or by a mutual fund. You also may receive dividends through a partnership, an estate, a trust, or an association that is taxed as a corporation. However, some amounts you receive that are called dividends are actually interest income. (See *Dividends that are actually interest* under *Taxable Interest* in chapter 7.)

EXPLANATION

There are generally two different types of corporations: S corporations and C corporations. The treatment of distributions from S corporations to shareholders differs from that of C corporations to their shareholders.

In this chapter, the IRS is referring to C corporations only, because S corporations do not technically pay dividends. See chapter 12, *Other income*, for information on distributions from S corporations.

Most distributions are paid in cash (or check). However, distributions can consist of more stock, stock rights, other property, or services.

EXPLANATION

Any distribution to a shareholder from earnings and profits is generally a dividend. However, a distribution is not a taxable dividend if it is a return of capital to the shareholder. Most distributions are in the form of money, but they may also be in stock or other property.

An interest-free loan or below-market rate loan by a corporation to a stockholder may result in taxable dividend income to the stockholder.

Additionally, if you are a stockholder who uses company property for personal use, you are considered to be in constructive receipt of a dividend that will be taxable to you and disallowed as a tax deduction to the company. The value of a constructive dividend is the fair market value of the benefit provided to the shareholder.

Example 1
A shareholder's use of a condominium maintained by his solely owned corporation resulted in his receipt of constructive dividends because he maintained the unit as his residence. The taxpayer benefited from the corporation's payments because he did not have to pay any housing costs. The Tax Court determined the portion of the condominium expenses that was allocable to business use and permitted the corporation to deduct that amount. The balance of the expenses was treated as constructive dividends received by the shareholder.

Example 2
A corporation sold real property to its sole shareholder at a price lower than the property's fair market value. The result is a constructive dividend to the shareholder of the difference between the fair market value and the purchase price, and is treated as a gain for the corporation.

TAXPLANNER
All personal loans from corporations should have written documentation and charge market interest rates. If the corporation does not charge appropriate interest on the personal loans, and if the corporation has sufficient earnings and profits, the unpaid interest will be treated as a constructive dividend of ordinary income to the borrower (individual taxpayer). Failure to correctly report this transaction may subject the borrower to penalties and interest on the underpaid tax.

Useful Items
You may want to see:

Publication
☐ **514** Foreign Tax Credit for Individuals
☐ **550** Investment Income and Expenses

Form (and Instructions)
☐ **Schedule B (Form 1040A or 1040)** Interest and Ordinary Dividends
☐ **8960** Net Investment Income Tax—Individuals, Estates, and Trusts

TAXPLANNER
Records you should keep. The following is a list of records that you should keep to substantiate your dividend figures in the event of an IRS or state examination. Generally, we recommend that you retain these records for at least 6 years. However, you should keep records related to dividend reinvestment programs for 6 years after you fully exit the program.
- 1099-DIV, Dividends and Distributions
- Dividend Reinvestment Plan Records
- Form 2439, Notice to Shareholders of Undistributed Long-Term Capital Gains
- 1099s with backup withholding for attachment to your tax return
- Form 1096, Annual Summary and Transmittal of U.S. Information Returns
- Schedule K-1 (Form 1041), Beneficiary's Share of Income, Deductions, Credits, etc.
- Schedule K-1 (Form 1065), Partner's Share of Income, Credits, Deductions, etc.
- Schedule K-1 (Form 1120S), Shareholder's Share of Income, Credits, Deductions, etc.

General Information
This section discusses general rules for dividend income.

Tax on unearned income of certain children. Part of a child's 2014 unearned income may be taxed at the parent's tax rate. If it is, Form 8615, Tax for Certain Children Who Have Unearned Income, must be completed and attached to the child's tax return. If not, Form 8615 is not required and the child's income is taxed at his or her own tax rate.

Some parents can choose to include the child's interest and dividends on the parent's return if certain requirements are met. Use Form 8814, Parents' Election To Report Child's Interest and Dividends, for this purpose.

For more information about the tax on unearned income of children and the parents' election, see chapter 32.

TAXALERT

The rules for taxing a child's investment income at their parent's rate are commonly known as the "kiddie tax" rules.

Form 8615, *Tax for Certain Children Who Have Investment Income of More than $2,000*, is required to figure the tax for a child with investment income of more than $2,000 if the child:

1. Was under age 18 at the end of 2014,
2. Was age 18 at the end of 2014 and did not have earned income that was more than half of the child's support, or
3. Was a full-time student over age 18 and under age 24 at the end of 2014 and did not have earned income that was more than half of the child's support.

Children whose earned income exceeds one-half of the amount of the support they receive are not subject to the kiddie tax under this provision.

The election to report a child's investment income on a parent's return and the special rule for when a child must file Form 6251, Alternative Minimum Tax–Individuals, also applies to the children listed above.

For more information, see chapter 32, *Tax on investment income of certain children*.

TAXPLANNER

To avoid paying the "kiddie tax," you should consider investments for your child that generate little or no taxable income until your child "grows out" of the reach of the kiddie tax.

Explanation

A parent may elect on Form 8814 to include on his or her return the unearned income of a child under the age of 19 whose income is less than $10,000 in 2014 and consists solely of interest, dividends, or Alaska Permanent Fund dividends. The election cannot be made if estimated payments were made in your child's name, if your child had an overpayment on his or her 2013 tax return which was applied to 2014, or if your child is subject to backup withholding. (See explanation of backup withholding, later.) The election must be made by the due date (including extensions) of the parent's tax return. A separate election must be made for each child whose income the parents choose to report.

If a child (under age 19) had income in 2014 over $2,000, it would be taxed on Form 8814 as follows: the first $1,000 would be tax-free, the next $1,000 would be taxed at 10% (0% for qualified dividends), and the amount of income over $2,000 would be taxed at the parent's tax rate. If the child files his own return, the child is required to attach Form 8615 to his or her return, which can be complicated if there is more than one child under age 19 required to file a return.

TAXPLANNER

Amounts of Net Investment Income that are included on your own tax return by reason of Form 8814 are included in calculating the 3.8% Net Investment Income Tax (NIIT) that you may owe.

If you may be subject to the NIIT and have children subject to the "kiddie tax," you may consider having your children file their own tax returns to reduce the amount of income potentially subject to the NIIT.

Beneficiary of an estate or trust. Dividends and other distributions you receive as a beneficiary of an estate or trust are generally taxable income. You should receive a Schedule K-1 (Form 1041), Beneficiary's Share of Income, Deductions, Credits, etc., from the fiduciary. Your copy of Schedule K-1 (Form 1041) and its instructions will tell you where to report the income on your Form 1040.

Social security number (SSN) or individual taxpayer identification number (ITIN). You must give your SSN or ITIN to any person required by federal tax law to make a return, statement, or other document that relates to you. This includes payers of dividends. If you do not give your SSN or ITIN to the payer of dividends, you may have to pay a penalty.

For more information on SSNs and ITINs, see *Social Security Number (SSN)* in chapter 1.

Backup withholding. Your dividend income is generally not subject to regular withholding. However, it may be subject to backup withholding to ensure that income tax is collected on the income. Under backup withholding, the payer of dividends must withhold, as income tax, on the amount you are paid, applying the appropriate withholding rate.

Backup withholding may also be required if the IRS has determined that you underreported your interest or dividend income. For more information, see *Backup Withholding* in chapter 4.

Stock certificate in two or more names. If two or more persons hold stock as joint tenants, tenants by the entirety, or tenants in common, each person's share of any dividends from the stock is determined by local law.

Form 1099-DIV. Most corporations and mutual funds use Form 1099-DIV, Dividends and Distributions, to show you the distributions you received from them during the year. Keep this form with your records. You do not have to attach it to your tax return.

Dividends not reported on Form 1099-DIV. Even if you do not receive Form 1099-DIV, you must still report all your taxable dividend income. For example, you may receive distributive shares of dividends from partnerships or S corporations. These dividends are reported to you on Schedule K-1 (Form 1065), Partner's Share of Income, Deductions, Credits, etc., and Schedule K-1 (Form 1120S), Shareholder's Share of Income, Deductions, Credits, etc.

Reporting tax withheld. If tax is withheld from your dividend income, the payer must give you a Form 1099-DIV that indicates the amount withheld.

Nominees. If someone receives distributions as a nominee for you, that person should give you a Form 1099-DIV, which will show distributions received on your behalf.

Form 1099-MISC. Certain substitute payments in lieu of dividends or tax-exempt interest received by a broker on your behalf must be reported to you on Form 1099-MISC, Miscellaneous Income, or a similar statement. See _Reporting Substitute Payments_ under _Short Sales_ in chapter 4 of Publication 550 for more information about reporting these payments.

Incorrect amount shown on a Form 1099. If you receive a Form 1099 that shows an incorrect amount (or other incorrect information), you should ask the issuer for a corrected form. The new Form 1099 you receive will be marked "Corrected."

Dividends on stock sold. If stock is sold, exchanged, or otherwise disposed of after a dividend is declared but before it is paid, the owner of record (usually the payee shown on the dividend check) must include the dividend in income.

The following timeline illustrates when you are entitled to receive dividend payments:

Declaration Date	**Ex-Dividend Date**	**Record Date**	**Payment Date**
The company decides to pay a dividend at some point in the future.	On or after this date, the stock trades without its dividend. If you sell your stock prior to this date, the new owner will generally receive the dividend; if you sell on or after this date, you will generally receive the dividend.	The owner as of the record date is entitled to the declared dividend.	The owner as of the record date receives payment of the dividend whether or not he or she still owns the stock

TAXPLANNER

If you buy stock on or near the date a dividend is declared, make sure you receive all amounts due. The transaction of the sale may not be recorded in time by the corporation paying the dividend, and the former stock owner may receive payment. If you do not receive a dividend due to you, check with your broker as soon as possible.

If you receive a dividend to which you were not entitled in one year and pay it back in another, it is counted as income in the year received and a deduction in the year repaid. Show the deduction as a negative amount of dividend income on Schedule B (Form 1040 or Form 1040A). If the repayment is greater than $3,000, see the calculations for lowering your tax under *Repayments* in chapter 12, *Other income*, and the further information on this topic in IRS Publication 525, *Taxable and Nontaxable Income*. Consult your tax advisor.

Dividends received in January. If a mutual fund (or other regulated investment company) or real estate investment trust (REIT) declares a dividend (including any exempt-interest dividend or capital gain distribution) in October, November, or December, payable to shareholders of record on a date in one of those months but actually pays the dividend during January of the next calendar year, you are considered to have received the dividend on December 31. You report the dividend in the year it was declared.

TAXSAVER

You should pay close attention to the timing of your purchase of a mutual fund. For example, if you invest in a fund near the end of the year and the fund shortly thereafter makes a year-end distribution, you will have to pay tax on the distribution even though from your point of view you are simply getting back the capital you just invested in the fund. In effect, all you've done is "bought" taxable income that the fund earned earlier in the year but had not yet paid out to shareholders. Typically, the fund's share price drops by the amount of the distribution. However, your cost basis in the mutual fund will be the predistribution price you paid for the shares.

There is one consolation: Your higher basis will reduce any capital gain on a later sale, or if you sell the fund at a loss, it will increase your capital loss. If you want to limit your tax liability and lower your basis in the shares, you should delay your purchase of fund shares until after the record date for the distribution. Usually a fund can tell you when distributions, if any, for the year are expected. Alternatively, you can consult investment publications or websites, which indicate distribution dates for the previous year. They are usually a pretty good guide to future distribution dates.

Example

ABC Fund declares and distributes a $1 dividend on October 1. If you purchased 1,000 shares at $10 per share on September 30, you will have to report $1,000 of income for 2013. If you bought the shares on October 2, after the record date, you will pay $9 per share and have no taxable income to report. Of course, for the shares bought on September 30, your basis would be $10 per share instead of $9.

Ordinary Dividends

Ordinary (taxable) dividends are the most common type of distribution from a corporation or a mutual fund. They are paid out of earnings and profits and are ordinary income to you. This means they are not capital gains. You can assume that any dividend you receive on common or preferred stock is an ordinary dividend unless the paying corporation or mutual fund tells you otherwise. Ordinary dividends will be shown in box 1a of the Form 1099-DIV you receive.

Qualified Dividends

Qualified dividends are the ordinary dividends subject to the same 0%, 15%, or 20% maximum tax rate that applies to net capital gain. They should be shown in box 1b of the Form 1099-DIV you receive.

The maximum rate of tax on qualified dividends is:

- 0% on any amount that otherwise would be taxed at a 10% or 15% rate.
- 15% on any amount that otherwise would be taxed at rates greater than 15% but less than 39.6%.
- 20% on any amount that otherwise would be taxed at a 39.6% rate.

To qualify for the maximum rate, all of the following requirements must be met.

- The dividends must have been paid by a U.S. corporation or a qualified foreign corporation. (See *Qualified foreign corporation*, later.)
- The dividends are not of the type listed later under *Dividends that are not qualified dividends*.
- You meet the holding period (discussed next).

Holding period. You must have held the stock for more than 60 days during the 121-day period that begins 60 days before the ex-dividend date. The ex-dividend date is the first date following the declaration of a dividend on which the buyer of a stock is not entitled to receive the next dividend payment. Instead, the seller will get the dividend.

When counting the number of days you held the stock, include the day you disposed of the stock, but not the day you acquired it. See the examples later.

Exception for preferred stock. In the case of preferred stock, you must have held the stock more than 90 days during the 181-day period that begins 90 days before the ex-dividend date if the dividends are due to periods totaling more than 366 days. If the preferred dividends are due to periods totaling less than 367 days, the holding period in the previous paragraph applies.

Example 1. You bought 5,000 shares of XYZ Corp. common stock on July 9, 2014. XYZ Corp. paid a cash dividend of 10 cents per share. The ex-dividend date was July 16, 2014. Your Form 1099-DIV from XYZ Corp. shows $500 in box 1a (ordinary dividends) and in box 1b (qualified dividends). However, you sold the 5,000 shares on August 12, 2014. You held your shares of XYZ Corp. for only 34 days of the 121-day period (from July 10, 2014, through August 12, 2014). The 121-day period began on May 17, 2014 (60 days before the ex-dividend date), and ended on September 14, 2014. You have no qualified dividends from XYZ Corp. because you held the XYZ stock for less than 61 days.

Example 2. Assume the same facts as in Example 1 except that you bought the stock on July 15, 2014 (the day before the ex-dividend date), and you sold the stock on September 16, 2014. You held the stock for 63 days (from July 16, 2014, through September 16, 2014). The $500 of qualified dividends shown in box 1b of your Form 1099-DIV are all qualified dividends because you held the stock for 61 days of the 121-day period (from July 16, 2014, through September 14, 2014).

Example 3. You bought 10,000 shares of ABC Mutual Fund common stock on July 9, 2014. ABC Mutual Fund paid a cash dividend of 10 cents a share. The ex-dividend date was July 16, 2014. The

ABC Mutual Fund advises you that the portion of the dividend eligible to be treated as qualified dividends equals 2 cents per share. Your Form 1099-DIV from ABC Mutual Fund shows total ordinary dividends of $1,000 and qualified dividends of $200. However, you sold the 10,000 shares on August 12, 2014. You have no qualified dividends from ABC Mutual Fund because you held the ABC Mutual Fund stock for less than 61 days.

Holding period reduced where risk of loss is diminished. When determining whether you met the minimum holding period discussed earlier, you cannot count any day during which you meet any of the following conditions.

1. You had an option to sell, were under a contractual obligation to sell, or had made (and not closed) a short sale of substantially identical stock or securities.
2. You were grantor (writer) of an option to buy substantially identical stock or securities.
3. Your risk of loss is diminished by holding one or more other positions in substantially similar or related property.

For information about how to apply condition (3), see Regulations section 1.246-5.

Qualified foreign corporation. A foreign corporation is a qualified foreign corporation if it meets any of the following conditions.

1. The corporation is incorporated in a U.S. possession.
2. The corporation is eligible for the benefits of a comprehensive income tax treaty with the United States that the Treasury Department determines is satisfactory for this purpose and that includes an exchange of information program. For a list of those treaties, see Table 8-1.
3. The corporation does not meet (1) or (2) above, but the stock for which the dividend is paid is readily tradable on an established securities market in the United States. See *Readily tradable stock*, later.

Exception. A corporation is not a qualified foreign corporation if it is a passive foreign investment company during its tax year in which the dividends are paid or during its previous tax year.

Readily tradable stock. Any stock (such as common, ordinary, or preferred) or an American depositary receipt in respect of that stock is considered to satisfy requirement (3) under *Qualified foreign corporation*, if it is listed on a national securities exchange that is registered under Section 6 of the Securities Exchange Act of 1934 or on the Nasdaq Stock Market. For a list of the exchanges that meet these requirements, see *www.sec.gov/divisions/marketreg/mrexchanges.shtml*.

Dividends that are not qualified dividends. The following dividends are not qualified dividends. They are not qualified dividends even if they are shown in box 1b of Form 1099-DIV.

- Capital gain distributions.
- Dividends paid on deposits with mutual savings banks, cooperative banks, credit unions, U.S. building and loan associations, U.S. savings and loan associations, federal savings

Table 8-1. **Income Tax Treaties**

Income tax treaties the United States has with the following countries satisfy requirement (2) under *Qualified foreign corporation*.		
Australia	India	Philippines
Austria	Indonesia	Poland
Bangladesh	Ireland	Portugal
Barbados	Israel	Romania
Belgium	Italy	Russian Federation
Bulgaria	Jamaica	Slovak Republic
Canada	Japan	Slovenia
China	Kazakhstan	South Africa
Cyprus	Korea	Spain
Czech Republic	Latvia	Sri Lanka
Denmark	Lithuania	Sweden
Egypt	Luxembourg	Switzerland
Estonia	Malta	Thailand
Finland	Mexico	Trinidad and Tobago
France	Morocco	Tunisia
Germany	Netherlands	Turkey
Greece	New Zealand	Ukraine
Hungary	Norway	United Kingdom
Iceland	Pakistan	Venezuela

and loan associations, and similar financial institutions. (Report these amounts as interest income.)

- Dividends from a corporation that is a tax-exempt organization or farmer's cooperative during the corporation's tax year in which the dividends were paid or during the corporation's previous tax year.
- Dividends paid by a corporation on employer securities held on the date of record by an employee stock ownership plan (ESOP) maintained by that corporation.
- Dividends on any share of stock to the extent you are obligated (whether under a short sale or otherwise) to make related payments for positions in substantially similar or related property.
- Payments in lieu of dividends, but only if you know or have reason to know the payments are not qualified dividends.
- Payments shown in Form 1099-DIV, box 1b, from a foreign corporation to the extent you know or have reason to know the payments are not qualified dividends.

TAXPLANNER

When purchasing stock, you should consider whether the dividends received will be qualified dividends that are taxed at the 0%, 15%, or 20% maximum rate or ordinary dividends taxed at your higher regular income tax bracket.

TAXALERT

Regardless of whether dividends you receive are qualified dividends that are taxed at the lower 0%, 15%, or 20% preferential tax rates or are ordinary dividends subject to the higher regular income tax rates that apply to ordinary income, under the Affordable Care Act, dividends, along with certain other investment income, are subject to the 3.8% Net Investment Income Tax (NIIT) that took effect for tax years beginning in 2013. For individuals, the tax is 3.8% of the lesser of: (1) "net investment income" or (2) the excess of modified adjusted gross income (MAGI) over $200,000 ($250,000 if married filing jointly or a qualifying widow(er) with dependent child; $125,000 if married filing separately). These threshold dollar amounts are not indexed each year for inflation.

Net investment income subject to the NIIT is defined as investment income reduced by allocable deductions.

The NIIT is payable regardless of whether or not you otherwise pay any regular income tax or are subject to alternative minimum tax on your income.

Dividends Used to Buy More Stock

The corporation in which you own stock may have a dividend reinvestment plan. This plan lets you choose to use your dividends to buy (through an agent) more shares of stock in the corporation instead of receiving the dividends in cash. Most mutual funds also permit shareholders to automatically reinvest distributions in more shares in the fund, instead of receiving cash. If you use your dividends to buy more stock at a price equal to its fair market value, you still must report the dividends as income.

EXPLANATION

Many large publicly held companies allow stockholders to use their dividends to buy more shares of stock directly from the company. This type of program eliminates the need to use or pay commissions to an agent or broker. You should keep this cost savings in mind when considering a particular dividend reinvestment plan.

If you are a member of a dividend reinvestment plan that lets you buy more stock at a price less than its fair market value, you must report as dividend income the fair market value of the additional stock on the dividend payment date.

You also must report as dividend income any service charge subtracted from your cash dividends before the dividends are used to buy the additional stock. But you may be able to deduct the service charge. See chapter 29 for more information about deducting expenses of producing income.

In some dividend reinvestment plans, you can invest more cash to buy shares of stock at a price less than fair market value. If you choose to do this, you must report as dividend income the difference between the cash you invest and the fair market value of the stock you buy. When figuring this amount, use the fair market value of the stock on the dividend payment date.

EXPLANATION

Dividend reinvestment plans (often called DRPs)—even those in which employees may make voluntary contributions—should not be confused with retirement plans that invest in company stock. DRPs are open to all stockholders, not just employees. Dividends are immediately reinvested to buy more shares of that company's stock. DRPs are also subject to income taxes annually, whereas income in employee retirement plans is typically tax deferred.

DRPs may cause confusion because some plans permit you to reinvest in shares at a discount, usually about 5%. The discount is included in the amount of dividend taxable to you.

Example

Stock of Company X is selling for $10. You are entitled to $20 in dividends on the stock you hold. Because you are in a DRP that includes a 5% discount, your dividends will buy 2.105 shares of stock. You will report $21.05 of dividend income.

TAXALERT

The IRS has privately ruled (PLR 9750033) that shareholders who purchase stock solely through a cash purchase plan will not be treated as having received a distribution of the discount amount. However, if the shareholders participate in both a DRP and the cash purchase aspects of the plan, they will be treated as having received a taxable distribution of the discount amount of the stock.

TAXPLANNER

Unless you're very careful, you're likely to get an IRS deficiency notice when you take advantage of a dividend reinvestment plan if you hold the shares that are producing the dividends. Problems can occur if you receive two Forms 1099. One will report the dividends paid on shares you hold.

The other Form 1099 will report the discount and the dividends paid on the shares held in the plan. Be sure to reconcile the amounts and report the correct total.

Any service charge paid on a dividend reinvestment plan may be taken as an itemized deduction on Schedule A of Form 1040 (subject to the 2% of adjusted gross income limitation explained in chapter 29, *Miscellaneous deductions*). You should not offset your dividend income with the service charge. If you do, you may receive a notice from the IRS.

TAXPLANNER

When you sell shares acquired in a dividend reinvestment plan, you compute the gain or loss in the same way that you normally would by subtracting your cost basis from the proceeds of the sale. Your cost basis includes the amount of dividends that have been reinvested. Usually your only record of the shares' cost is the annual statement issued by the administrator of the dividend reinvestment plan. It is imperative to keep these statements as a permanent part of your records. If you don't have this information, you can contact the transfer agent who handles the company's dividend reinvestment plan. You can obtain the name from the company's investor relations office. However, some dividend reinvestment plans charge a fee for re-creating records. Alternatively, you can look up a company's dividend history in Standard & Poor's.

Example

You have accumulated 14 shares of ABC Mutual Fund through a purchase and dividend reinvestments.

Method	Shares	Cost Basis	Date
Purchase	10 shares	$100	4/30/10
Dividend Reinvestments	1 share	$10	12/30/11
	1 share	$15	12/28/12
	2 shares	$25	12/31/13
	14 shares	**$150**	

If you sold all 14 shares on January 15, 2014, for $15 per share, your gain would be $60 ($210 proceeds less $150 cost basis). Without proof of your dividend reinvestments, however, the IRS could argue that your basis was only the original $100 and your gain was actually $110 ($210 proceeds less $100 cost of original purchase).

Note that a portion of your $60 gain would be long-term, but the gain attributable to the 2 shares purchased on December 31, 2013, through the DRP would be short-term, because you would not have owned these shares for more than 12 months. The short-term gain would be $5 of the total gain ($30 proceeds on 2 shares less $25 cost basis).

See chapter 16, *Reporting gains and losses*, to determine how to calculate your gain or loss if you did not sell all 14 shares of ABC Mutual Fund at once.

TAXPLANNER

Beginning January 1, 2011, shares acquired through a dividend reinvestment plan may use the average method for computing basis, provided the written plan documents require that at least 10% of every dividend is reinvested in identical stock. Under the new basis reporting rules, brokers are required to track adjusted cost basis for mutual fund and DRP (dividend reinvestment plan) shares acquired on or after January 1, 2012. Brokers must track adjusted cost basis in accordance with their default method unless a taxpayer notifies the broker in writing to elect the average basis method. The taxpayer may revoke that election within one year of making the election, or, if the earlier, by the date of the first stock disposition. Once the election is revoked, the basis of the stock reverts to the cost basis for the election.

EXPLANATION

For further discussion, see chapter 13, *Basis of property*, and chapter 16, *Reporting gains and losses*.

TAXSAVER

Dividend reinvestment plans that permit you to invest at less than market price (e.g., whether by discount or reduction in commissions on purchase) may be a very good deal. In effect, you earn a higher yield because you are receiving "extra" shares. Consider making an average basis method election with your broker for newly acquired shares because in a rising stock market, the average basis method election may result in tax savings, rather than if the broker's default method is utilized.

Money Market Funds

Report amounts you receive from money market funds as dividend income. Money market funds are a type of mutual fund and should not be confused with bank money market accounts that pay interest.

TAXPLANNER

Dividends paid from money market funds are reported as dividends–not interest–even though they represent income the money market fund received on certificates of deposit and other interest-bearing investments. Dividends from money market funds are not eligible for the lower dividend rate. These dividends must be shown in the dividend section of Schedule B (Form 1040). If they are not, you're likely to receive a notice from the IRS requesting an explanation.

However, dividends paid or credited by a mutual savings bank, building and loan association, savings and loan association, cooperative bank, or credit union are considered *interest*–not dividends–for income tax reporting purposes. The Form 1099 that you receive from these organizations tells you which type of income to report and generally instructs you on how to report the income.

Capital Gain Distributions

Capital gain distributions (also called capital gain dividends) are paid to you or credited to your account by mutual funds (or other regulated investment companies) and real estate investment trusts (REITs). They will be shown in box 2a of the Form 1099-DIV you receive from the mutual fund or REIT.

Report capital gain distributions as long-term capital gains, regardless of how long you owned your shares in the mutual fund or REIT.

EXPLANATION

For 2014, capital gain distributions are reported on Schedule D, line 13. For more information, see chapter 16, *Reporting gains and losses*.

TAXALERT

Although qualifying dividends are taxed at the same rate as capital gains, a taxpayer who has net capital losses and dividend income may not offset those losses against dividends. Net capital losses can be offset against capital gain distributions, however.

Undistributed capital gains of mutual funds and REITs. Some mutual funds and REITs keep their long-term capital gains and pay tax on them. You must treat your share of these gains as distributions, even though you did not actually receive them. However, they are not included on Form 1099-DIV. Instead, they are reported to you in box 1a of Form 2439.

Report undistributed capital gains (box 1a of Form 2439) as long-term capital gains on Schedule D (Form 1040), column (h), line 11.

The tax paid on these gains by the mutual fund or REIT is shown in box 2 of Form 2439. You take credit for this tax by including it on Form 1040, line 71, and checking box a on that line. Attach Copy B of Form 2439 to your return, and keep Copy C for your records.

Basis adjustment. Increase your basis in your mutual fund, or your interest in a REIT, by the difference between the gain you report and the credit you claim for the tax paid.

Additional information. For more information on the treatment of distributions from mutual funds, see Publication 550.

EXPLANATION

An investment company or mutual fund that realizes capital gains during the year has the option of whether or not to distribute the capital gains to shareholders of the mutual fund. The two different treatments are reported by shareholders as follows:

Distributed capital gains are reported to shareholders on Form 1099-DIV box 2a. You will receive this amount in cash and must include the entire amount of the distributed capital gains in your calculation of taxable income.

Undistributed capital gains are reported to shareholders on Form 2439. You will not receive this amount in cash. Rather, the mutual fund or real estate investment trust (REIT) has retained the capital gains and paid your proportionate share of the tax due. You will include the entire amount of the undistributed capital gains in your calculation of taxable income, but you will also be credited for the tax that the mutual fund paid on your behalf. In addition, you will increase your basis in the stock by the net amount not distributed to you.

Nondividend Distributions

A nondividend distribution is a distribution that is not paid out of the earnings and profits of a corporation or a mutual fund. You should receive a Form 1099-DIV or other statement showing the nondividend distribution. On Form 1099-DIV, a nondividend distribution will be shown in box 3. If you do not receive such a statement, you report the distribution as an ordinary dividend.

Basis adjustment. A nondividend distribution reduces the basis of your stock. It is not taxed until your basis in the stock is fully recovered. This nontaxable portion is also called a return of capital; it is a return of your investment in the stock of the company. If you buy stock in a corporation in different lots at different times, and you cannot definitely identify the shares subject to the nondividend distribution, reduce the basis of your earliest purchases first.

When the basis of your stock has been reduced to zero, report any additional nondividend distribution you receive as a capital gain. Whether you report it as a long-term or short-term capital gain depends on how long you have held the stock. See *Holding Period* in chapter 14.

Example. You bought stock in 2001 for $100. In 2004, you received a nondividend distribution of $80. You did not include this amount in your income, but you reduced the basis of your stock to $20. You received a nondividend distribution of $30 in 2014. The first $20 of this amount reduced your basis to zero. You report the other $10 as a long-term capital gain for 2014. You must report as a long-term capital gain any nondividend distribution you receive on this stock in later years.

EXPLANATION

Some mutual fund dividends may be treated as a tax-free return of capital. This occurs when the mutual fund does not have enough current or accumulated earnings and profits to cover the distribution. In this situation, the distribution is considered to be a "return of capital" (the amount you originally invested) and is nontaxable to the extent of the basis in your shares. (Your basis is generally the price at which you bought the shares plus or minus any adjustments. See chapter 13, *Basis of property*.) This amount will be shown in box 3 of Form 1099-DIV.

Although the distribution is tax-free, it will reduce your basis in the mutual fund shares. To the extent the distribution is greater than your basis in your shares, you will be treated as having a gain from the sale or exchange of the shares. This gain must be reported on Schedule D (Form 1040). (See the IRS example directly preceding this explanation.)

TAXORGANIZER

It is extremely important to keep accurate records of nontaxable dividends. Most people do not realize that a nontaxable dividend is usually considered a return of purchase price and then a capital gain once your cost has been recovered. Keep in mind that even nontaxable dividends can become subject to tax at some point.

Liquidating Distributions

Liquidating distributions, sometimes called liquidating dividends, are distributions you receive during a partial or complete liquidation of a corporation. These distributions are, at least in part, one form of a return of capital. They may be paid in one or more installments. You will receive Form 1099-DIV from the corporation showing you the amount of the liquidating distribution in box 8 or 9.

For more information on liquidating distributions, see chapter 1 of Publication 550.

TAXSAVER

If the total liquidating distributions you receive are less than the basis of your stock, you may have a capital loss. You can report a capital loss only after you have received the final distribution in liquidation that results in the redemption or cancellation of the stock. Whether you report the loss as a long-term or short-term capital loss depends on how long you held the stock. See *Holding Period* in chapter 14, *Sale of property*.

Example

You own stock in XYZ Corporation with a basis of $100. You received liquidating distributions of $90: $60 in 2013 and $30 in 2014. You report the $10 loss in 2014.

Distributions of Stock and Stock Rights

Distributions by a corporation of its own stock are commonly known as stock dividends. Stock rights (also known as "stock options") are distributions by a corporation of rights to acquire the corporation's stock. Generally, stock dividends and stock rights are not taxable to you, and you do not report them on your return.

Taxable stock dividends and stock rights. Distributions of stock dividends and stock rights are taxable to you if any of the following apply.

1. You or any other shareholder have the choice to receive cash or other property instead of stock or stock rights.
2. The distribution gives cash or other property to some shareholders and an increase in the percentage interest in the corporation's assets or earnings and profits to other shareholders.
3. The distribution is in convertible preferred stock and has the same result as in (2).
4. The distribution gives preferred stock to some common stock shareholders and common stock to other common stock shareholders.
5. The distribution is on preferred stock. (The distribution, however, is not taxable if it is an increase in the conversion ratio of convertible preferred stock made solely to take into account a stock dividend, stock split, or similar event that would otherwise result in reducing the conversion right.)

EXPLANATION

Any transaction having the effect of increasing your proportionate interest in a corporation's assets or earnings and profits may be taxable to you, even though no stock or stock rights are actually distributed.

A number of transactions, for example, a change in the conversion ratio on certain classes of stock or a change in the redemption price of certain securities, have the effect of increasing your proportionate interest in a corporation. If such a transaction occurs, you will be informed by the corporation.

The term "stock" includes rights to acquire stock, and the term "shareholder" includes a holder of rights or of convertible securities.

If you receive taxable stock dividends or stock rights, include their fair market value at the time of distribution in your income.

EXAMPLE

ABC Company gives its shareholders the option of receiving a dividend as $10 cash or as stock (thus, the distribution will be taxable to all shareholders). On February 15, the date of distribution, the value of 1 share of stock is $5. A shareholder who chooses stock in lieu of cash will receive 2 additional shares of stock on February 15. This shareholder will be taxed on $10, the fair market value of the stock, even though no cash was received with which to pay the tax. A shareholder who chooses cash will also be taxed on $10, but this shareholder will have the cash in hand to pay the tax.

Preferred stock redeemable at a premium. If you hold preferred stock having a redemption price higher than its issue price, the difference (the redemption premium) generally is taxable as a constructive distribution of additional stock on the preferred stock. For more information, see chapter 1 of Publication 550.

Basis. Your basis in stock or stock rights received in a taxable distribution is their fair market value when distributed. If you receive stock or stock rights that are not taxable to you, see *Stocks and Bonds* under *Basis of Investment Property* in chapter 4 of Publication 550 for information on how to figure their basis.

Fractional shares. You may not own enough stock in a corporation to receive a full share of stock if the corporation declares a stock dividend. However, with the approval of the shareholders, the corporation may set up a plan in which fractional shares are not issued but instead are sold, and the cash proceeds are given to the shareholders. Any cash you receive for fractional shares under such a plan is treated as an amount realized on the sale of the fractional shares. Report this transaction on Form 8949, Sales and Other Dispositions of Capital Assets. Enter your gain or loss, the difference between the cash you receive and the basis of the fractional shares sold, in column (h) of Schedule D (Form 1040) in Part I or Part II, whichever is appropriate.

Tip

Report these transactions on Form 8949 with the correct box checked.

For more information on Form 8949 and Schedule D (Form 1040), see chapter 4 of Publication 550. Also see the Instructions for Form 8949 and the Instructions for Schedule D (Form 1040).

Example. You own one share of common stock that you bought on January 3, 2005, for $100. The corporation declared a common stock dividend of 5% on June 30, 2014. The fair market value of the stock at the time the stock dividend was declared was $200. You were paid $10 for the fractional-share stock dividend under a plan described in the discussion above. You figure your gain or loss as follows:

Fair market value of old stock	$200.00
Fair market value of stock dividend (cash received)	+10.00
Fair market value of old stock and stock dividend	$210.00
Basis (cost) of old stock after the stock dividend (($200 ÷ $210) × $100)	$95.24
Basis (cost) of stock dividend (($10 ÷ $210) × $100)	+ 4.76
Total	$100.00
Cash received	$10.00
Basis (cost) of stock dividend	4.76
Gain	$5.24

Because you had held the share of stock for more than 1 year at the time the stock dividend was declared, your gain on the stock dividend is a long-term capital gain.

EXPLANATION

It is *not* true that all amounts received with regard to fractional shares are treated as capital gains, as described in the IRS text.

A distinction is made when shareholders have the *option* of receiving cash or other property instead of fractional shares. If shareholders have this option and receive cash in lieu of fractional shares, the value received is treated as dividend income. If the corporation issues cash in lieu of fractional shares of stock for the purpose of saving the trouble, expense, and inconvenience of issuing fractional shares, then the capital gain treatment described earlier applies. The transaction will be treated as though fractional shares had been received by the shareholders and were then redeemed by the corporation.

Scrip dividends. A corporation that declares a stock dividend may issue you a scrip certificate that entitles you to a fractional share. The certificate is generally nontaxable when you receive it. If you choose to have the corporation sell the certificate for you and give you the proceeds, your gain or loss is the difference between the proceeds and the portion of your basis in the corporation's stock allocated to the certificate.

However, if you receive a scrip certificate that you can choose to redeem for cash instead of stock, the certificate is taxable when you receive it. You must include its fair market value in income on the date you receive it.

Other Distributions

You may receive any of the following distributions during the year.

Exempt-interest dividends. Exempt-interest dividends you receive from a mutual fund or other regulated investment company, including those received from a qualified fund of funds in any tax year beginning after December 22, 2010, are not included in your taxable income. Exempt-interest dividends should be shown in box 10 of Form 1099-DIV.

EXPLANATION

Exempt-interest dividends are reported on line 8b of Form 1040 as tax-exempt interest. While exempt-interest dividends are exempt from federal income taxes, they may be considered an "add-back" for state and local tax purposes. This treatment depends on which state returns you are required to file. Generally, your state may require that you add back to federal adjusted gross income either all or some portion of the amount you entered on line 8b of your 1040. See your state income tax forms and instructions for guidance.

Information reporting requirement. Although exempt-interest dividends are not taxable, you must show them on your tax return if you have to file a return. This is an information reporting requirement and does not change the exempt-interest dividends to taxable income.

Alternative minimum tax treatment. Exempt-interest dividends paid from specified private activity bonds may be subject to the alternative minimum tax. See *Alternative Minimum Tax (AMT)* in chapter 31 for more information.

Dividends on insurance policies. Insurance policy dividends the insurer keeps and uses to pay your premiums are not taxable. However, you must report as taxable interest income the interest that is paid or credited on dividends left with the insurance company.

If dividends on an insurance contract (other than a modified endowment contract) are distributed to you, they are a partial return of the premiums you paid. Do not include them in your gross income until they are more than the total of all net premiums you paid for the contract. Report any taxable distributions on insurance policies on Form 1040, line 21.

Dividends on veterans' insurance. Dividends you receive on veterans' insurance policies are not taxable. In addition, interest on dividends left with the Department of Veterans Affairs is not taxable.

Patronage dividends. Generally, patronage dividends you receive in money from a cooperative organization are included in your income.

Do not include in your income patronage dividends you receive on:
- Property bought for your personal use, or
- Capital assets or depreciable property bought for use in your business. But you must reduce the basis (cost) of the items bought. If the dividend is more than the adjusted basis of the assets, you must report the excess as income.

These rules are the same whether the cooperative paying the dividend is a taxable or tax-exempt cooperative.

EXPLANATION

Patronage dividends are amounts paid by a cooperative organization to one of its patrons (1) on the basis of the quantity or quality of business done with the patron, (2) pursuant to a written obligation in existence before the cooperative received the amounts paid into it by the patron, and (3) determined by reference to net earnings. In other words, patronage dividends amount to a return of some of the amounts a patron spent with a cooperative. Patronage dividends usually occur with farm cooperatives. Any "refund" or "discount" to the patron is income.

However, if the purchase leading to receipt of the dividend was neither deductible nor considered a capital expense, the dividend really amounts to a discount or a rebate, which is not considered income.

Alaska Permanent Fund dividends. Do not report these amounts as dividends. Instead, report these amounts on Form 1040, line 21; Form 1040A, line 13; or Form 1040EZ, line 3.

How To Report Dividend Income

Generally, you can use either Form 1040 or Form 1040A to report your dividend income. Report the total of your ordinary dividends on line 9a of Form 1040 or Form 1040A. Report qualified dividends on line 9b of Form 1040 or Form 1040A.

If you receive capital gain distributions, you may be able to use Form 1040A or you may have to use Form 1040. See *Exceptions to filing Form 8949 and Schedule D (Form 1040)* in chapter 16. If you receive nondividend distributions required to be reported as capital gains, you must use Form 1040. You cannot use Form 1040EZ if you receive any dividend income.

Form 1099-DIV. If you owned stock on which you received $10 or more in dividends and other distributions, you should receive a Form 1099-DIV. Even if you do not receive Form 1099-DIV, you must report all your dividend income.

See Form 1099-DIV for more information on how to report dividend income.

Form 1040A or 1040. You must complete Schedule B (Form 1040A or 1040), Part II, and attach it to your Form 1040A or 1040, if:

- Your ordinary dividends (Form 1099-DIV, box 1a) are more than $1,500, or
- You received, as a nominee, dividends that actually belong to someone else.

If your ordinary dividends are more than $1,500, you must also complete Schedule B (Form 1040A or 1040), Part III.

List on Schedule B (Form 1040A or 1040), Part II, line 5, each payer's name and the ordinary dividends you received. If your securities are held by a brokerage firm (in "street name"), list the name of the brokerage firm shown on Form 1099-DIV as the payer. If your stock is held by a nominee who is the owner of record, and the nominee credited or paid you dividends on the stock, show the name of the nominee and the dividends you received or for which you were credited.

Enter on line 6 the total of the amounts listed on line 5. Also enter this total on line 9a of Form 1040A or 1040.

Qualified dividends. Report qualified dividends (Form 1099-DIV, box 1b) on line 9b of Form 1040 or Form 1040A. The amount in box 1b is already included in box 1a. Do not add the amount in box 1b to, or subtract it from, the amount in box 1a.

Do not include any of the following on line 9b.

- Qualified dividends you received as a nominee. See *Nominees* under *How to Report Dividend Income* in chapter 1 of Publication 550.
- Dividends on stock for which you did not meet the holding period. See *Holding period*, earlier under *Qualified Dividends*.
- Dividends on any share of stock to the extent you are obligated (whether under a short sale or otherwise) to make related payments for positions in substantially similar or related property.
- Payments in lieu of dividends, but only if you know or have reason to know the payments are not qualified dividends.
- Payments shown in Form 1099-DIV, box 1b, from a foreign corporation to the extent you know or have reason to know the payments are not qualified dividends.

If you have qualified dividends, you must figure your tax by completing the Qualified Dividends and Capital Gain Tax Worksheet in the Form 1040 or 1040A instructions or the Schedule D Tax Worksheet in the Schedule D (Form 1040) instructions, whichever applies. Enter qualified dividends on line 2 of the worksheet.

Investment interest deducted. If you claim a deduction for investment interest, you may have to reduce the amount of your qualified dividends that are eligible for the 0%, 15%, or 20% tax rate. Reduce it by the qualified dividends you choose to include in investment income when figuring the limit on your investment interest deduction. This is done on the Qualified Dividends and Capital Gain Tax Worksheet or the Schedule D Tax Worksheet. For more information about the limit on investment interest, see *Investment expenses* in chapter 24.

Expenses related to dividend income. You may be able to deduct expenses related to dividend income if you itemize your deductions on Schedule A (Form 1040). See chapter 29 for general information about deducting expenses of producing income.

EXPLANATION

Expenses that may be deducted include custody fees, investment advisory fees, depository fees (which are usually applicable to foreign dividends), and service charges relating to dividend income. A more complete discussion of these items appears in chapter 29, *Miscellaneous deductions*.

Explanation

Stock sold short. If you borrow stock to make a short sale, you may have to pay the lender an amount to replace the dividends distributed while you maintain your short position. Your treatment of the payment depends on the kind of distribution for which you are reimbursing the lender of the stock.

TAXALERT

Owners whose shares are lent in short sales do not receive the lower capital gains rate on "payments in lieu of dividends," which are often called "substitute" dividends. Brokerages commonly lend stock held in margin accounts to short sellers, but may need to accommodate investors who do not want to receive the unfavorable dividend treatment. If this pertains to your investments, your Form 1099-DIV should indicate the status of your dividends.

See chapter 14, *Sale of property*, for an explanation of a short sale.

TAXPLANNER

If you borrow stock to make a short sale, and you pay the lender in lieu of the dividends distributed while you maintain your short position, you can deduct these payments provided you hold the short sale open at least 46 days (more than 1 year in the case of an extraordinary dividend as defined later) and you itemize your deductions. You deduct these expenses as investment interest on Schedule A (Form 1040).

If you close the short sale on or before the 45th day after the date of the short sale (1 year or less in the case of an extraordinary dividend), you cannot deduct the payments made. Instead you must increase the basis of the stock used to close the short sale by that amount.

Exception

The IRS allows a deduction for amounts you pay in place of dividends to the extent of ordinary income received from the lender of the stock for the use of collateral with the short sale. However, this special rule does not apply to payments in place of extraordinary dividends, discussed next.

Explanation

Extraordinary dividends. If the amount of any dividend you receive on a share of preferred stock equals or exceeds 5% (10% in the case of other stock) of the amount realized on the short sale, the dividend you receive is an extraordinary dividend.

If your payment is made for a liquidating distribution or nontaxable stock distribution, or if you buy more shares equal to a stock distribution issued on the borrowed stock during your short position, you have a capital expense. You must add the payment to the cost of the stock sold short.

See *Short Sales* in Publication 550 for more information about the tax treatment of short sales.

If an individual receives an extraordinary dividend eligible for the capital gain rates with respect to any share of stock, any loss on the sale of the stock is treated as a long-term capital loss to the extent of the dividend. A dividend is treated as investment income for purposes of determining the amount of deductible investment interest only if the taxpayer elects to treat the dividend as not eligible for the capital gain rates.

Example

Ben feels that the market value of XYZ Corporation stock is going to decline, so he sells XYZ stock to Sally. However, Ben does not hold any XYZ stock so, to effect the transaction, Ben's broker borrows XYZ stock from another customer, Robert, to deliver to Sally. Sally is now the stockholder of record.

XYZ Corporation will pay any and all dividends on this stock directly to Sally. However, Robert is entitled to the money, because he merely lent his shares to Ben. Ben, not XYZ Corporation, will pay Robert the amount of the dividend. Ben may deduct the payment as an itemized deduction on Schedule A if he borrows the stock for more than 45 days and has not diminished his risk of loss by, for example, holding an option to buy substantially similar stock. Robert enters that amount on page 1 (Form 1040) as income from Ben.

If Ben returns the stock within 45 days, he will not be able to claim a deduction. The amount paid to Robert increases the basis of the stock sold.

More information. For more information about how to report dividend income, see chapter 1 of Publication 550 or the instructions for the form you must file.

TAXORGANIZER

Records you should keep:
- Annual statements from brokerage accounts and mutual funds
- All Forms 1099
- All Forms K-1 (partnership, trust, S corporation)
- All information on purchase of investments and sale of investments
- All Forms 2439

Chapter 9
Rental income and expenses

Note

IRS Publication 17 (*Your Federal Income Tax*) has been updated by Ernst & Young LLP for 2014. Dates and dollar amounts shown are for 2014. Underlined type is used to indicate where IRS text has been updated. Places where text has been removed are indicated by the sentence: *Text intentionally omitted.*

ey.com/EYTaxGuide

Ernst & Young LLP will update the *EY Tax Guide 2015* website with relevant taxpayer information as it becomes available. You can also sign up for email alerts to let you know when changes have been made.

Introduction

Rent is the income received for allowing another person to use property that you own. This income is customarily received in cash. If, in lieu of paying all or part of the rent in cash, a tenant provides you with certain services, the value of those services is rental income to you.

You may deduct expenses incurred to repair or to maintain your rental property. However, certain other expenses may not be deducted in the year in which you pay for them; rather, they must be *capitalized* and deducted over a period of years. You may also deduct any *depreciation* taken on your rental property. Depreciation is a noncash expense claimed in order to deduct each year a small part of what you originally paid for the property. There are a variety of methods by which you may depreciate property and calculate your tax deduction. These methods are explained in this chapter.

Rental real estate activities are generally considered passive activities, and the amount of any loss you can deduct is limited unless you have income from other passive activities or you "materially" or "actively" participate in your rental activity. This chapter explains the rules for figuring rental income, expenses, depreciation, and allowable losses.

In addition to paying regular income tax or alternative minimum tax on rental income, a 3.8% Net Investment Income Tax (NIIT) is assessed on unearned Net Investment Income (NII). For individuals, the NIIT is 3.8% of the lesser of: (1) NII or (2) the excess of modified adjusted gross income (MAGI) over $200,000 ($250,000 if married filing jointly; $125,000 if married filing separately). Net investment income includes income from passive activities. For most taxpayers, rental activities are treated as passive, and any net rental income is subject to the NIIT. On the other hand, rental income derived in the ordinary course of a trade or business by certain real estate professionals is considered to be nonpassive, and therefore is not subject to the NIIT. For more information, see *Passive Activity Limits*, later in this chapter.

Introduction

This chapter discusses rental income and expenses. It also covers the following topics.

- Personal use of dwelling unit (including vacation home).
- Depreciation.
- Limits on rental losses.
- How to report your rental income and expenses.

If you sell or otherwise dispose of your rental property, see Publication 544, Sales and Other Dispositions of Assets.

If you have a loss from damage to, or theft of, rental property, see Publication 547, Casualties, Disasters, and Thefts.

If you rent a condominium or a cooperative apartment, some special rules apply to you even though you receive the same tax treatment as other owners of rental property. See Publication 527, Residential Rental Property, for more information.

Useful Items

You may want to see:

Publication
- ☐ **527** Residential Rental Property
- ☐ **534** Depreciating Property Placed in Service Before 1987
- ☐ **535** Business Expenses
- ☐ **925** Passive Activity and At-Risk Rules
- ☐ **946** How To Depreciate Property

Form (and Instructions)
- ☐ **4562** Depreciation and Amortization
- ☐ **6251** Alternative Minimum Tax—Individuals
- ☐ **8582** Passive Activity Loss Limitations
- ☐ **Schedule E (Form 1040)** Supplemental Income and Loss

Rental Income

In most cases, you must include in your gross income all amounts you receive as rent. Rental income is any payment you receive for the use or occupation of property. In addition to amounts you receive as normal rent payments, there are other amounts that may be rental income.

When to report. If you are a cash-basis taxpayer, you report rental income on your return for the year you actually or constructively receive it. You are a cash-basis taxpayer if you report income in the year you receive it, regardless of when it was earned. You constructively receive income when it is made available to you, for example, by being credited to your bank account.

For more information about when you constructively receive income, see *Accounting Methods* in chapter 1.

Advance rent. Advance rent is any amount you receive before the period that it covers. Include advance rent in your rental income in the year you receive it regardless of the period covered or the method of accounting you use.

Example. You sign a 10-year lease to rent your property. In the first year, you receive $5,000 for the first year's rent and $5,000 as rent for the last year of the lease. You must include $10,000 in your income in the first year.

EXPLANATION

Some taxpayers have attempted to circumvent the rule requiring advance rent to be included in current income by structuring the payment as a "loan." The courts have generally disallowed this technique and examine this type of transaction with close scrutiny. As a general rule, if such a loan is to be repaid out of future rental proceeds, the loan will probably be considered advance rent.

However, the courts have held that an up-front payment for an option to purchase the property is not considered advance rent and, as such, does not have to be included in income where the agreement provides no provision for returning the money to the renter or applying it to the rent.

Even if a promissory note is written to support the "loan," the courts will look to the parties' intent, as well as to other factors such as interest charged, whether the loan is secured, and whether the loan payment and rental dates are identified.

EXPLANATION

Generally, the distinction between advance rent and security deposits depends on the nature of the rights and obligations that are assumed when the deposit is made. If, for example, the landlord has the option either to refund a security deposit or to apply it to a future year's rent, the courts have held that the landlord has unrestricted use of the money and that it is considered advance rent.

In cases in which the landlord is required by law to pay interest on the security deposit, the deposit generally is not considered advance rent.

TAXPLANNER

Landlords may forget whether they have treated a security deposit as a true security deposit or as advance rent. If this happens, the landlord may not be sure how to treat the refund and/or application of the security deposit at the end of the term of the lease. Be sure to note in your records exactly how you are treating the amount for tax purposes so that the tax returns for the year in which the security deposit is returned and/or applied will be easy to prepare.

TAXSAVER

Advice for landlords. When drawing up a rental agreement, it is helpful to include language specifying that the security deposit is not to be used for the last month's rent. This helps ensure deferred recognition of the security deposit as income until such time as you determine it should not be refunded.

Canceling a lease. If your tenant pays you to cancel a lease, the amount you receive is rent. Include the payment in your income in the year you receive it regardless of your method of accounting.

EXPLANATION

The courts have ruled that any payments you receive as consideration for modifying the terms of an existing lease must be treated as ordinary income. However, certain expenses incurred as a result of the cancellation or modification of a lease may be deductible currently. For example, attorney fees attributable to the lessee's forfeiture and termination of a lease would be deductible currently. On the other hand, if the lessor caused the termination, the expense usually would be amortized over a period of time. You should consult your tax advisor.

TAXSAVER

A payment for cancellation of a lease may be very large, depending on the time left on the lease and the agreement of the parties. As with most types of income to cash basis taxpayers, arranging for the receipt of this payment in a year in which you have a lower marginal tax rate may save you taxes.

Expenses paid by tenant. If your tenant pays any of your expenses, the payments are rental income. Because you must include this amount in income, you can deduct the expenses if they are deductible rental expenses. See *Rental Expenses*, later, for more information.

EXPLANATION

When a tenant pays to have capital improvements constructed on the landlord's property and these improvements are not made in lieu of rent or other required payments, the value of these improvements is not income to the landlord, either when made or on termination of the lease, even though the landlord keeps the improvements at the end of the lease. However, the landlord will have no basis in the improvements and, therefore, cannot depreciate the improvements.

of property, prolongs its useful life, or adapts the property to new uses. For more details, see *Repairs and Improvements*, later.

Exclusion of rental income from a home rented for less than 15 days during the year. If a dwelling unit is used as a personal home and you rent it for less than 15 days during the year, you can exclude all of the rental income received from your taxable income. You are also not permitted to deduct any rental expenses paid. Note, however, that you can continue to deduct qualified residence interest, real estate taxes, and casualty and theft losses if you itemize deductions. For details, see *Exception for Minimal Rental Use*, later.

Passive rental losses allowed as a deduction. There is an exception to the general rule that disallows a deduction for passive rental losses. If you actively participate in a passive rental real estate activity (you actively participate if you and your spouse owned at least 10% of the rental property and you made significant management decisions—such as approving new tenants, deciding on rental terms, and approving expenditures for the property), you can deduct up to $25,000 of your losses from the activity from your nonpassive income. However, if your modified adjusted gross income is $150,000 or more ($75,000 or more if you are married filing separately), this exception to the passive loss deduction rules is not available. For more details, see *Losses From Rental Real Estate Activities*, later.

TAXPLANNER

It would be unusual for an expense that is the responsibility of the landlord not to be deductible by the landlord when the tenant pays the expense. But such expenses do exist. Consider, for example, a building code violation fine incurred for some change made in the tenant's space by the tenant without the landlord's consent. The fine is imposed on the landlord, but the violation is the tenant's fault. The tenant pays the penalty, but the landlord still has to declare that amount as income. Since most penalties are not deductible, the landlord probably will not be able to deduct the amount of the fine as an expense. If this is a possibility, a clause in the lease making the payment of such a penalty the responsibility of the tenant when the tenant is at fault would probably keep the payment by the tenant from being income to the landlord.

Property or services. If you receive property or services, instead of money, as rent, include the fair market value of the property or services in your rental income.

EXAMPLE

Denise rents a home to a licensed contractor for $700 per month. The home needed repairs to the kitchen flooring, and the contractor agreed to make the repairs in exchange for living in the home rent-free for 2 months. Denise must report the fair market value of the repairs as rental income (presumably the fair market value would be equal to 2 months' rent, or $1,400). Denise may be able to claim a deduction for the repair of the kitchen floor.

EXPLANATION

Examples of other types of income treated as rental income include the following:
1. Amounts received from an insurance company under a policy that reimburses a property owner for rent lost because of a fire or other casualty affecting the rental property.
2. Amounts received by subletting a property to another individual. If you did receive such income, you would be able to deduct the rent you are paying to the landlord as an expense. However, you are still not the owner and therefore would not be able to depreciate the property.

   If the services are provided at an agreed upon or specified price, that price is the fair market value unless there is evidence to the contrary.

Security deposits. Do not include a security deposit in your income when you receive it if you plan to return it to your tenant at the end of the lease. But if you keep part or all of the security deposit during any year because your tenant does not live up to the terms of the lease, include the amount you keep in your income in that year.

   If an amount called a security deposit is to be used as a final payment of rent, it is advance rent. Include it in your income when you receive it.

Part interest. If you own a part interest in rental property, you must report your part of the rental income from the property.

Rental of property also used as your home. If you rent property that you also use as your home and you rent it less than 15 days during the tax year, do not include the rent you receive in your income and do not deduct rental expenses. However, you can deduct on Schedule A (Form 1040) the interest, taxes, and casualty and theft losses that are allowed for nonrental property. See *Personal Use of Dwelling Unit (Including Vacation Home)*, later.

TAXALERT

If you plan to convert your rental property into your principal residence, the amount of gain you may be able to exclude from a future sale of that home may be limited. Generally, you are allowed to exclude up to $250,000 ($500,000 if married filing a joint return) of gain realized on the sale or exchange of a principal residence. The sale of a home will qualify for this exclusion if the home is a taxpayer's principal residence for at least two of the five years ending on the date of the sale or exchange. Under this law, the period of time you rented the residence after 2008 and before you converted it into your principal residence will figure into a formula that reduces the maximum exclusion ($250,000 or $500,000 if married filing a joint return) you can apply to offset gains realized when you ultimately sell that home. See chapter 15, *Selling your home*, for more information.

Rental Expenses

This part discusses expenses of renting property that you ordinarily can deduct from your rental income. It includes information on the expenses you can deduct if you rent part of your property, or if you change your property to rental use. *Depreciation*, which you can also deduct from your rental income, is discussed later.

TAXSAVER

You may deduct expenses on your rental property during a period in which it is not being rented as long as it is actively being held out for rent. This applies to a period between rentals, as well as to the period during which a property is being marketed as a rental property for the first time. The IRS can disallow these deductions if you are unable to show you were actively seeking a profit and had a reasonable expectation of achieving one. The deduction cannot be disallowed just because your property is difficult to rent.

Personal use of rental property. If you sometimes use your rental property for personal purposes, you must divide your expenses between rental and personal use. Also, your rental expense deductions may be limited. See *Personal Use of Dwelling Unit (Including Vacation Home)*, later.

Part interest. If you own a part interest in rental property, you can deduct expenses that you paid according to your percentage of ownership.

When to deduct. If you are a cash-basis taxpayer, you generally deduct your rental expenses in the year you pay them.

Depreciation. You can begin to depreciate rental property when it is ready and available for rent. See *Placed-in-Service* under *When Does Depreciation Begin and End* in chapter 2 of Publication 527.

Pre-rental expenses. You can deduct your ordinary and necessary expenses for managing, conserving, or maintaining rental property from the time you make it available for rent.

Uncollected rent. If you are a cash-basis taxpayer, do not deduct uncollected rent. Because you have not included it in your income, it is not deductible.

Vacant rental property. If you hold property for rental purposes, you may be able to deduct your ordinary and necessary expenses (including depreciation) for managing, conserving, or maintaining the property while the property is vacant. However, you cannot deduct any loss of rental income for the period the property is vacant.

Vacant while listed for sale. If you sell property you held for rental purposes, you can deduct the ordinary and necessary expenses for managing, conserving, or maintaining the property until it is sold. If the property is not held out and available for rent while listed for sale, the expenses are not deductible rental expenses.

Repairs and Improvements

Generally, an expense for repairing or maintaining your rental property may be deducted if you are not required to capitalize the expense.

Improvements. You must capitalize any expense you pay to improve your rental property. An expense is for an improvement if it results in a betterment to your property, restores your property, or adapts your property to a new or different use.

Betterments. Expenses that may result in a betterment to your property include expenses for fixing a pre-existing defect or condition, enlarging or expanding your property, or increasing the capacity, strength, or quality of your property.

Restoration. Expenses that may be for restoration include expenses for replacing a substantial structural part of your property, repairing damage to your property after you properly adjusted the basis of your property as a result of a casualty loss, or rebuilding your property to a like-new condition.

Adaptation. Expenses that may be for adaptation include expenses for altering your property to a use that is not consistent with the intended ordinary use of your property when you began renting the property.

The expenses you capitalize for improving your property can generally be depreciated as if the improvement were separate property.

Other Expenses

Other expenses you can deduct from your rental income include advertising, cleaning and maintenance, utilities, fire and liability insurance, taxes, interest, commissions for the collection of rent, ordinary and necessary travel and transportation, and other expenses, discussed next.

Insurance premiums paid in advance. If you pay an insurance premium for more than one year in advance, for each year of coverage you can deduct the part of the premium payment that will apply to that year. You cannot deduct the total premium in the year you pay it.

Legal and other professional fees. You can deduct, as a rental expense, legal and other professional expenses, such as tax return preparation fees you paid to prepare Schedule E (Form 1040), Part I. For example, on your 2014 Schedule E, you can deduct fees paid in 2014 to prepare your 2013 Schedule E, Part I. You can also deduct, as a rental expense, any expense (other than federal taxes and penalties) you paid to resolve a tax underpayment related to your rental activities.

Local benefit taxes. In most cases, you cannot deduct charges for local benefits that increase the value of your property, such as charges for putting in streets, sidewalks, or water and sewer systems. These charges are nondepreciable capital expenditures, and must be added to the basis of your property. However, you can deduct local benefit taxes that are for maintaining, repairing, or paying interest charges for the benefits.

Local transportation expenses. You may be able to deduct your ordinary and necessary local transportation expenses if you incur them to collect rental income or to manage, conserve, or maintain your rental property. However, transportation expenses incurred to travel between your home and a rental property generally constitute nondeductible commuting costs unless you use your home as your principal place of business. See Publication 587, Business Use of Your Home, for information on determining if your home office qualifies as a principal place of business.

Generally, if you use your personal car, pickup truck, or light van for rental activities, you can deduct the expenses using one of two methods: actual expenses or the standard mileage rate. For 2014, the standard mileage rate for business use is 56 cents per mile. For more information, see chapter 27.

Rental of equipment. You can deduct the rent you pay for equipment that you use for rental purposes. However, in some cases, lease contracts are actually purchase contracts. If so, you cannot deduct these payments. You can recover the cost of purchased equipment through depreciation.

Rental of property. You can deduct the rent you pay for property that you use for rental purposes. If you buy a leasehold for rental purposes, you can deduct an equal part of the cost each year over the term of the lease.

Travel expenses. You can deduct the ordinary and necessary expenses of traveling away from home if the primary purpose of the trip is to collect rental income or to manage, conserve, or maintain your rental property. You must properly allocate your expenses between rental and nonrental activities. You cannot deduct the cost of traveling away from home if the primary purpose of the trip was to improve your property. You recover the cost of improvements by taking depreciation. For information on travel expenses, see chapter 27.

See *Rental Expenses* in Publication 527 for more information.

Property Changed to Rental Use

If you change your home or other property (or a part of it) to rental use at any time other than the beginning of your tax year, you must divide yearly expenses, such as taxes and insurance, between rental use and personal use.

You can deduct as rental expenses only the part of the expense that is for the part of the year the property was used or held for rental purposes.

You cannot deduct depreciation or insurance for the part of the year the property was held for personal use. However, you can include the home mortgage interest, qualified mortgage insurance premiums, and real estate tax expenses for the part of the year the property was held for personal use as an itemized deduction on Schedule A (Form 1040).

Example. Your tax year is the calendar year. You moved from your home in May and started renting it out on June 1. You can deduct as rental expenses seven-twelfths of your yearly expenses, such as taxes and insurance.

Starting with June, you can deduct as rental expenses the amounts you pay for items generally billed monthly, such as utilities.

Renting Part of Property

If you rent part of your property, you must divide certain expenses between the part of the property used for rental purposes and the part of the property used for personal purposes, as though you actually had two separate pieces of property.

You can deduct the expenses related to the part of the property used for rental purposes, such as home mortgage interest, qualified mortgage insurance premiums, and real estate taxes, as rental expenses on Schedule E (Form 1040). You can also deduct as rental expenses a portion of other expenses that normally are nondeductible personal expenses, such as expenses for electricity or painting the outside of your house.

There is no change in the types of expenses deductible for the personal-use part of your property. Generally, these expenses may be deducted only if you itemize your deductions on Schedule A (Form 1040).

You cannot deduct any part of the cost of the first phone line even if your tenants have unlimited use of it.

You do not have to divide the expenses that belong only to the rental part of your property. For example, if you paint a room that you rent, or if you pay premiums for liability insurance in connection with renting a room in your home, your entire cost is a rental expense. If you install a second phone line strictly for your tenants' use, all of the cost of the second line is deductible as a rental expense. You can deduct depreciation, discussed later, on the part of the house used for rental purposes as well as on the furniture and equipment you use for rental purposes.

How to divide expenses. If an expense is for both rental use and personal use, such as mortgage interest or heat for the entire house, you must divide the expense between the rental use and the personal use. You can use any reasonable method for dividing the expense. It may be reasonable to divide the cost of some items (for example, water) based on the number of people using them. The two most common methods for dividing an expense are based on (1) the number of rooms in your home, and (2) the square footage of your home.

> ### TAXPLANNER
> As there are various methods of dividing expenses, you should use whichever "reasonable" method provides the best result. For more information, see *How to Divide Expenses*, later in this chapter.

Not Rented for Profit

If you do not rent your property to make a profit, you can deduct your rental expenses only up to the amount of your rental income. You cannot deduct a loss or carry forward to the next year any rental expenses that are more than your rental income for the year. For more information about the rules for an activity not engaged in for profit, see *Not-for-Profit Activities* in chapter 1 of Publication 535.

Where to report. Report your not-for-profit rental income on Form 1040, line 21. For example, you can include your mortgage interest and any qualified mortgage insurance premiums (if you use the property as your main home or second home), real estate taxes, and casualty losses on the appropriate lines of Schedule A (Form 1040) if you itemize your deductions.

If you itemize your deductions, claim your other rental expenses, subject to the rules explained in chapter 1 of Publication 535, as miscellaneous itemized deductions on Form 1040, Schedule A, line 23. You can deduct these expenses only if they, together with certain other miscellaneous itemized deductions, total more than 2% of your adjusted gross income.

> ### TAXPLANNER
> If you move out of your personal residence and rent it, your deductions for real estate tax and mortgage interest are shifted from itemized deductions on Schedule A to rental deductions on Schedule E of Form 1040. The only additional deductions you become entitled to are those for operating expenses and depreciation. Since the rental income is included in your gross income, and the amount of additional deductions you are entitled to may be small, renting out your personal residence could increase your taxable income. If you rent out your personal residence with the intention of returning to live in it in the future, a special rule governing the deduction of mortgage interest may benefit you. See *Passive Activity Limits* later in this chapter.

Personal Use of Dwelling Unit (Including Vacation Home)

If you have any personal use of a dwelling unit (including a vacation home) that you rent, you must divide your expenses between rental use and personal use. In general, your rental expenses will be no more than your total expenses multiplied by a fraction; the denominator of which is the total number of days the dwelling unit is used and the numerator of which is the total number of days actually rented at a fair rental price. Only your rental expenses may be deducted on Schedule E (Form 1040). Some of your personal expenses may be deductible if you itemize your deductions on Schedule A (Form 1040).

You must also determine if the dwelling unit is considered a home. The amount of rental expenses that you can deduct may be limited if the dwelling unit is considered a home. Whether a dwelling unit is considered a home depends on how many days during the year are considered to be days of personal use. There is a special rule if you used the dwelling unit as a home and you rented it for less than 15 days during the year.

> ### TAXSAVER
> This is one of the very few instances in which the IRS considers income to be nontaxable. You should be on the lookout for opportunities to rent property for less than 15 days to take advantage of this tax loophole. Residents of Augusta, Georgia, for example, have an annual opportunity to rent their houses for a short period during the Masters golf tournament.

In general, the tax rules governing the rental of vacation homes and other dwelling units are the same as those governing any rental property. The allowable methods of depreciation, the types of deductible expenditures, and the types of expenditures that should be capitalized are all determined in the same way for both categories of rental property. However, if you or a member of your family uses the vacation home or dwelling unit during the year, the amount of deductible expenses may be limited by special rules.

Here's an easy way to figure out whether or not you have to follow the special rules for reporting rental income outlined later:

Step 1. Determine the number of days the property was rented at fair market value during the year. If this number is less than 15, STOP. You may not deduct any rental expenses, and you do not report any rental income. (Note: You may always deduct qualified residence interest, taxes, casualty losses, and theft losses if you itemize deductions. To do so, simply take the deduction for the entire amount of these items on Schedule A of Form 1040.) If the number of days rented is 15 or more, you must report rental income. Proceed to Step 2.

Step 2. Determine the number of days you personally use the property. If this number does not exceed the greater of (a) 14 days or (b) 10% of the number of days for which the property was rented at fair market value, you are not subject to any special rules. After completing Step 3, you determine your rental income or loss in the same way you would for any type of rental property.

If your personal use of the property exceeds the limits described earlier, you are subject to special rules limiting the amount of deductible expenses. After completing Step 3, you determine your rental income or loss using the rules discussed in this section.

Step 3. Allocate all expenses between the rental period and the period in which you use the property personally, using the method described in the following section. Expenses allocated to the period of personal use are not deductible, except for interest, taxes, and casualty and theft losses (see Step 1). Then determine your rental income or loss, using either the general rules for rental property or the special rules regarding the personal use of vacation homes, whichever is appropriate.

Note: See _What Is a Day of Personal Use?_, later, regarding use of a home before or after renting.

Dwelling unit. A dwelling unit includes a house, apartment, condominium, mobile home, boat, vacation home, or similar property. It also includes all structures or other property belonging to the dwelling unit. A dwelling unit has basic living accommodations, such as sleeping space, a toilet, and cooking facilities.

A dwelling unit does not include property used solely as a hotel, motel, inn, or similar establishment. Property is used solely as a hotel, motel, inn, or similar establishment if it is regularly available for occupancy by paying customers and is not used by an owner as a home during the year.

Example. You rent a room in your home that is always available for short-term occupancy by paying customers. You do not use the room yourself, and you allow only paying customers to use the room. The room is used solely as a hotel, motel, inn, or similar establishment and is not a dwelling unit.

EXPLANATION

A dwelling unit must provide basic living accommodations, such as sleeping space, a rest room, and cooking facilities.

The Tax Court has ruled that a mini-motor home qualifies as a dwelling unit.

An outbuilding used in conjunction with the main building to provide living accommodations, such as a garage, a barn, or a greenhouse, constitutes part of the main dwelling unit. When renting one of these outbuildings, you may deduct expenses only to the extent you have income. You may not deduct a rental loss because the outbuilding is not considered separate from the main building that is being used as a personal residence or vacation home.

Rental pools and time-shares. Rental pools are agreements under which two or more vacation homes are made available for rent by their owners, who agree to share "at least substantially part of the rental income from the homes regardless [of] which of the vacation homes are actually rented." Under proposed IRS regulations, special rules apply when you are computing income, expense, and personal use days.

Also, under proposed IRS regulations, individuals owning a time-share that they rent are to treat their rental income and expense separately with respect to their unit. Consult your tax advisor.

Dividing Expenses

If you use a dwelling unit for both rental and personal purposes, divide your expenses between the rental use and the personal use based on the number of days used for each purpose.

When dividing your expenses, follow these rules.

- Any day that the unit is rented at a fair rental price is a day of rental use even if you used the unit for personal purposes that day. This rule does not apply when determining whether you used the unit as a home.
- Any day that the unit is available for rent but not actually rented is not a day of rental use.

Example. Your beach cottage was available for rent from June 1 through August 31 (92 days). During that time, except for the first week in August (7 days) when you were unable to find a renter, you rented the cottage at a fair rental price. The person who rented the cottage for July allowed you to use it over the weekend (2 days) without any reduction in or refund of rent. Your family also used the cottage during the last 2 weeks of May (14 days). The cottage was not used at all before May 17 or after August 31.

You figure the part of the cottage expenses to treat as rental expenses as follows.

- The cottage was used for rental a total of 85 days (92 − 7). The days it was available for rent but not rented (7 days) are not days of rental use. The July weekend (2 days) you used it is rental use because you received a fair rental price for the weekend.
- You used the cottage for personal purposes for 14 days (the last 2 weeks in May).
- The total use of the cottage was 99 days (14 days personal use + 85 days rental use).
- Your rental expenses are 85/99 (86%) of the cottage expenses.

Note. When determining whether you used the cottage as a home, the July weekend (2 days) you used it is considered personal use even though you received a fair rental price for the weekend. Therefore, you had 16 days of personal use and 83 days of rental use for this purpose. Because you used the cottage for personal purposes more than 14 days and more than 10% of the days of rental use (8 days), you used it as a home. If you have a net loss, you may not be able to deduct all of the rental expenses. See *Dwelling Unit Used as a Home*, next.

TAXSAVER

The Tax Court allows you to use a different allocation formula for interest and taxes than the one the IRS describes. Under the Tax Court formula, interest and taxes are allocated in the ratio of days rented to days in the year instead of in the ratio of days rented to days used. Using the Tax Court ratio results in a smaller amount of interest and taxes being allocated to the rental property, which creates the potential for you to deduct a larger amount of your other rental expenses.

Example

You own a cabin, which you rented for June and July, lived in for 1 month, and tried to rent the rest of the year. Your rental income for the 2 months was $2,800. Your total expenses for the cabin were as follows:

Interest	$1,500
Taxes	900
Utilities	750
Maintenance	300
Depreciation	1,200

	IRS method	Tax Court method
1) Gross rental income	$2,800	$2,800
2) Minus:		
a) Part of interest for rental use		
($1,500 × 61/91)	(1,005)	
($1,500 × 61/365)		(251)
b) Part of taxes for rental use		
($900 × 61/91)	(603)	
($900 × 61/365)		(150)
3) Gross rental income that is more than the interest and taxes for rental	$1,192	$2,399

4) Minus:		
a) Part of utilities for rental use (61/91)	(503)	(503)
b) Part of maintenance for rental use (61/91)	(201)	(201)
5) Gross rental income that is more than the interest, taxes, and operating expenses for rental use	$488	$1,695
6) Minus: Depreciation limited to the part for rental use ($1,200 × 61/91 = $804) or line 5, whichever is less	(488)	(804)
7) Net rental income	$ -0-	$ 891

Both the IRS method and the Tax Court method allocate interest expense and real estate taxes partly to Schedule E (for determining net rental income) and partly to Schedule A (for personal itemized deductions). But examine how these allocations affect Schedule A.

Total interest paid is $1,500. Since the IRS method allocates $1,005 to the rental activity, the $495 balance is allocated to Schedule A. The Tax Court method allocates only $251 to the rental activity, leaving $1,249 for a deduction on Schedule A. Similarly, the IRS method allocates $603 of the $900 in real estate taxes to the rental activity, leaving $297 for Schedule A. The Tax Court method allocates only $150 to the rental activity, leaving $750 for Schedule A.

	Schedule A Deduction		
	Tax Court method	IRS method	Additional itemized per Tax Court method
Interest	$1,249	$495	$754
Real estate taxes	750	297	453
			$1,207

Under the Tax Court method, you end up with additional deductions of $1,207, but you also have an additional net rental income of $891. The difference is that you reduce your taxable income by $316 more than under the IRS method. This conclusion assumes that you had enough other itemized deductions to make itemizing worthwhile and that your itemized deductions are not being limited.

The concept illustrated here is also important because rental income is considered to be passive income and, as such, can be used to offset passive losses. For more details, see chapter 24, *Interest expense*.

Dwelling Unit Used as a Home

If you use a dwelling unit for both rental and personal purposes, the tax treatment of the rental expenses you figured earlier under *Dividing Expenses* and rental income depends on whether you are considered to be using the dwelling unit as a home.

You use a dwelling unit as a home during the tax year if you use it for personal purposes more than the greater of:

1. 14 days, or
2. 10% of the total days it is rented to others at a fair rental price.

See *What is a day of personal use?*, later.

Fair rental price. A fair rental price for your property generally is the amount of rent that a person who is not related to you would be willing to pay. The rent you charge is not a fair rental price if it is substantially less than the rents charged for other properties that are similar to your property in your area.

If a dwelling unit is used for personal purposes on a day it is rented at a fair rental price, do not count that day as a day of rental use in applying (2) above. Instead, count it as a day of personal use in applying both (1) and (2) above.

EXPLANATION

Determining a fair rental price. According to IRS Publication 527, *Residential Rental Property (Including Rental of Vacation Homes)*, you should ask yourself the following questions to determine if another property is similar and the rent you charge is fair: (1) are they used for the same purpose? (2) are they approximately the same size? (3) are they in approximately the same condition? (4) do they have similar furnishings? and (5) are they in similar locations?

What Is a Day of Personal Use?

What is a day of personal use? A day of personal use of a dwelling unit is any day that the unit is used by any of the following persons.

1. You or any other person who has an interest in the unit, unless you rent it to another owner as his or her main home under a shared equity financing agreement (defined later). However, see *Days used as a main home before or after renting*, later.
2. A member of your family or a member of the family of any other person who owns an interest in the unit, unless the family member uses the dwelling unit as his or her main home and pays a fair rental price. Family includes only your spouse, brothers and sisters, half-brothers and half-sisters, ancestors (parents, grandparents, etc.), and lineal descendants (children, grandchildren, etc.).
3. Anyone under an arrangement that lets you use some other dwelling unit.
4. Anyone at less than a fair rental price.

> ### TAXSAVER
> The rule relating to personal use does not apply to use by an in-law of the taxpayer who owns the property. Thus, a son-in-law could lease property at a fair market value to his mother-in-law, and it would not be treated as personal use.

Main home. If the other person or member of the family in (1) or (2) above has more than one home, his or her main home is ordinarily the one he or she lived in most of the time.

Shared equity financing agreement. This is an agreement under which two or more persons acquire undivided interests for more than 50 years in an entire dwelling unit, including the land, and one or more of the co-owners is entitled to occupy the unit as his or her main home upon payment of rent to the other co-owner or owners.

Donation of use of property. You use a dwelling unit for personal purposes if:

- You donate the use of the unit to a charitable organization,
- The organization sells the use of the unit at a fund-raising event, and
- The "purchaser" uses the unit.

> ### TAXPLANNER
> Although donating your rental property for a certain time period to a charitable organization is considered personal use, you still may be allowed to deduct certain expenses during that time on Schedule A as a charitable contribution. See chapter 25, *Contributions*, for further details on donating your property. You cannot deduct the value of the personal use, or lost rental income, as a charitable deduction.

Examples. The following examples show how to determine days of personal use.

Example 1. You and your neighbor are co-owners of a condominium at the beach. Last year, you rented the unit to vacationers whenever possible. The unit was not used as a main home by anyone. Your neighbor used the unit for 2 weeks last year; you did not use it at all.

Because your neighbor has an interest in the unit, both of you are considered to have used the unit for personal purposes during those 2 weeks.

Example 2. You and your neighbors are co-owners of a house under a shared equity financing agreement. Your neighbors live in the house and pay you a fair rental price.

Even though your neighbors have an interest in the house, the days your neighbors live there are not counted as days of personal use by you. This is because your neighbors rent the house as their main home under a shared equity financing agreement.

Example 3. You own a rental property that you rent to your son. Your son does not own any interest in this property. He uses it as his main home and pays you a fair rental price.

Your son's use of the property is not personal use by you because your son is using it as his main home, he owns no interest in the property, and he is paying you a fair rental price.

Example 4. You rent your beach house to Joshua. Joshua rents his cabin in the mountains to you. You each pay a fair rental price.

You are using your house for personal purposes on the days that Joshua uses it because your house is used by Joshua under an arrangement that allows you to use his house.

Days used for repairs and maintenance. Any day that you spend working substantially full time repairing and maintaining (not improving) your property is not counted as a day of personal use. Do not count such a day as a day of personal use even if family members use the property for recreational purposes on the same day.

> ## EXPLANATION
> If the dwelling unit is rented and you are a guest of the occupant for a brief visit, this will not constitute personal use. Of course, the longer the visit is, the more likely the IRS is to claim you were an occupant rather than a visitor. Certainly, 1 or 2 days should be no problem.

Days used as a main home before or after renting. For purposes of determining whether a dwelling unit was used as a home, you may not have to count days you used the property as your main home before or after renting it or offering it for rent as days of personal use. Do not count them as days of personal use if:
- You rented or tried to rent the property for 12 or more consecutive months.
- You rented or tried to rent the property for a period of less than 12 consecutive months and the period ended because you sold or exchanged the property.

However, this special rule does not apply when dividing expenses between rental and personal use.

Examples. The following examples show how to determine whether you used your rental property as a home.

Example 1. You converted the basement of your home into an apartment with a bedroom, a bathroom, and a small kitchen. You rented the basement apartment at a fair rental price to college students during the regular school year. You rented to them on a 9-month lease (273 days). You figured 10% of the total days rented to others at a fair rental price is 27 days.

During June (30 days), your brothers stayed with you and lived in the basement apartment rent free.

Your basement apartment was used as a home because you used it for personal purposes for 30 days. Rent-free use by your brothers is considered personal use. Your personal use (30 days) is more than the greater of 14 days or 10% of the total days it was rented (27 days).

Example 2. You rented the guest bedroom in your home at a fair rental price during the local college's homecoming, commencement, and football weekends (a total of 27 days). Your sister-in-law stayed in the room, rent free, for the last 3 weeks (21 days) in July. You figured 10% of the total days rented to others at a fair rental price is 3 days.

The room was used as a home because you used it for personal purposes for 21 days. That is more than the greater of 14 days or 10% of the 27 days it was rented (3 days).

Example 3. You own a condominium apartment in a resort area. You rented it at a fair rental price for a total of 170 days during the year. For 12 of those days, the tenant was not able to use the apartment and allowed you to use it even though you did not refund any of the rent. Your family actually used the apartment for 10 of those days. Therefore, the apartment is treated as having been rented for 160 (170 − 10) days. You figured 10% of the total days rented to others at a fair rental price is 16 days. Your family also used the apartment for 7 other days during the year.

You used the apartment as a home because you used it for personal purposes for 17 days. That is more than the greater of 14 days or 10% of the 160 days it was rented (16 days).

Minimal rental use. If you use the dwelling unit as a home and you rent it less than 15 days during the year, that period is not treated as rental activity. See *Used as a home but rented less than 15 days*, later, for more information.

Limit on deductions. Renting a dwelling unit that is considered a home is not a passive activity. Instead, if your rental expenses are more than your rental income, some or all of the excess expenses cannot be used to offset income from other sources. The excess expenses that cannot be used to offset income from other sources are carried forward to the next year and treated as rental expenses for the same property. Any expenses carried forward to the next year will be subject to any limits that apply for that year. This limitation will apply to expenses carried forward to another year even if you do not use the property as your home for that subsequent year.

To figure your deductible rental expenses for this year and any carryover to next year, use Worksheet 9-1.

Reporting Income and Deductions
Property not used for personal purposes. If you do not use a dwelling unit for personal purposes, see *How To Report Rental Income and Expenses*, later, for how to report your rental income and expenses.

Property used for personal purposes. If you do use a dwelling unit for personal purposes, then how you report your rental income and expenses depends on whether you used the dwelling unit as a home.

Not used as a home. If you use a dwelling unit for personal purposes, but not as a home, report all the rental income in your income. Since you used the dwelling unit for personal purposes, you must divide your expenses between the rental use and the personal use as described earlier in *Dividing Expenses*. The expenses for personal use are not deductible as rental expenses.

Your deductible rental expenses can be more than your gross rental income; however, see *Limits on Rental Losses*, later.

Used as a home but rented less than 15 days. If you use a dwelling unit as a home and you rent it less than 15 days during the year, its primary function is not considered to be rental and it should not be reported on Schedule E (Form 1040). You are not required to report the rental income and rental expenses from this activity. The expenses, including qualified mortgage interest, property taxes, and any qualified casualty loss will be reported as normally allowed on Schedule A (Form 1040). See the Instructions for Schedule A (Form 1040) for more information on deducting these expenses.

Used as a home and rented 15 days or more. If you use a dwelling unit as a home and rent it 15 days or more during the year, include all your rental income in your income. Since you used the dwelling unit for personal purposes, you must divide your expenses between the rental use and the personal use as described earlier in *Dividing Expenses*. The expenses for personal use are not deductible as rental expenses.

If you had a net profit from renting the dwelling unit for the year (that is, if your rental income is more than the total of your rental expenses, including depreciation), deduct all of your rental expenses. You do not need to use Worksheet 9-1.

However, if you had a net loss from renting the dwelling unit for the year, your deduction for certain rental expenses is limited. To figure your deductible rental expenses and any carryover to next year, use Worksheet 9-1.

EXPLANATION

The IRS explanation on reporting income and deductions for property used for personal purposes is correct as far as it goes. However, four areas require clarification:

1. The starting point in determining your rental income is gross rental income, which is defined by the IRS as the gross rent received less expenses incurred to obtain tenants, such as advertising and real estate agents' fees. This definition is important because it enables you to deduct this type of expense *before* taking deductions for interest, taxes, and casualty losses, which might be enough to reduce your rental income to zero. The result may be a larger total deduction. The key point is: Start with gross rent received, deduct your expenses to obtain tenants, and then proceed through the deduction process described earlier.

2. The total amount of a casualty or theft loss allocated to the rental period is deductible. Ordinarily, a personal casualty or theft loss is deductible only to the extent that it is more than $100 and more than 10% of your adjusted gross income, but this is not the case when you are dealing with rental property. Your loss in this case would not be subject to the $100 or 10% floor limitation. (See chapter 26, *Casualty and theft losses*, for further details.)

3. Your basis in the vacation home or other dwelling unit is reduced only by the amount of depreciation actually allowed as a deduction, not by the amount of depreciation allocated to the rental period. This, in effect, decreases any gain you have to recognize if you subsequently sell the property. For more details on sales of depreciable assets, see *Depreciation*, later in this chapter.

4. Although the deductions for operating expenses and depreciation may not reduce income below zero, the deductions for interest and real estate taxes may.

TAXSAVER

When you personally use a dwelling unit for more than 14 days or more than 10% of the number of days it is rented at fair market value, it is generally to your advantage to use the Tax Court formula, described earlier in *Dividing Expenses*, for computing the amount of interest and taxes allocable to the rental period. Doing so usually allows you a greater total deduction, because interest, taxes, and casualty losses may be deducted on Schedule A, even if they are disallowed on Schedule E.

However, when your personal use of the dwelling is less than both 15 days and 10% of the number of days it is rented at fair market value, it is to your advantage to use the IRS method of allocating interest and taxes, described earlier in *Dividing Expenses*, because the net loss on the rental property will be allowed if your personal use is not substantial. (This assumes that the passive loss rules will not limit your net loss.) In this case, the IRS method does not reduce your total deduction; instead, it decreases your rental income (or increases your rental loss) and hence decreases your adjusted gross income.

Decreasing your adjusted gross income can be important, for the following reasons:

1. The amounts of certain itemized deductions, such as medical expenses, casualty losses, and most miscellaneous itemized deductions, are determined by reference to your adjusted gross income. Decreasing your adjusted gross income potentially increases your itemized deductions for these items.
2. Many states use adjusted gross income as the starting point in computing state taxable income. Using the IRS method may reduce your state tax liability.
3. If you are subject to alternative minimum tax, this method will reduce your alternative minimum taxable income.
4. A reduction in adjusted gross income may reduce the taxable amount of social security payments.
5. If you are a participant in a qualified pension plan, a decrease in your adjusted gross income may allow you to deduct contributions to an IRA.

Depreciation

You recover the cost of income-producing property through yearly tax deductions. You do this by depreciating the property; that is, by deducting some of the cost each year on your tax return.

Three factors determine how much depreciation you can deduct each year: (1) your basis in the property, (2) the recovery period for the property, and (3) the depreciation method used. You cannot simply deduct your mortgage or principal payments, or the cost of furniture, fixtures, and equipment, as an expense.

You can deduct depreciation only on the part of your property used for rental purposes. Depreciation reduces your basis for figuring gain or loss on a later sale or exchange.

You may have to use Form 4562 to figure and report your depreciation. See *How To Report Rental Income and Expenses*, later.

Alternative minimum tax (AMT). If you use accelerated depreciation, you may be subject to the AMT. Accelerated depreciation allows you to deduct more depreciation earlier in the recovery period than you could deduct using a straight line method (same deduction each year).

EXPLANATION

Form 6251 is the tax form used to determine if you are subject to alternative minimum tax (AMT). The depreciation method and the useful life for depreciating property used as a rental property may be different for AMT purposes. As a result, if you own rental property and are depreciating the property, more than likely you will have an adjustment to make for AMT purposes. See chapter 31, *How to figure your tax*, and the IRS instructions for Form 6251 for more information.

Claiming the correct amount of depreciation. You should claim the correct amount of depreciation each tax year. If you did not claim all the depreciation you were entitled to deduct, you must still reduce your basis in the property by the full amount of depreciation that you could have deducted.

EXAMPLE

Barbara makes improvements in the amount of $10,000 to her rental property. These improvements are capitalized and depreciated over time. In the first year the improvements are put in service, Barbara does not deduct the correct amount of depreciation. She deducts $100 and reduces her basis by that amount, when the actual depreciation amount allowable is $200. If Barbara sells the property at the beginning of the next year, her basis in the property would be $9,800 (not $9,900). This is because even though Barbara only deducted $100 as depreciation, she was allowed to take a depreciation deduction of $200 and her adjusted basis should reflect the correct amount of depreciation that should have been taken.

If you deducted an incorrect amount of depreciation for property in any year, you may be able to make a correction by filing Form 1040X, Amended U.S Individual Income Tax Return. If you are not allowed to make the correction on an amended return, you can change your accounting method to claim the correct amount of depreciation. See *Claiming the correct amount of depreciation* in chapter 2 of Publication 527 for more information.

    Changing your accounting method to deduct unclaimed depreciation. To change your accounting method, you generally must file Form 3115, Application for Change in Accounting Method, to get the consent of the IRS. In some instances, that consent is automatic. For more information, see chapter 1 of Publication 946.

Land. You cannot depreciate the cost of land because land generally does not wear out, become obsolete, or get used up. The costs of clearing, grading, planting, and landscaping are usually all part of the cost of land and cannot be depreciated.

EXPLANATION

When calculating your depreciation expense, be sure to separate out the cost of land from the cost of the building because land is not depreciable. Taxpayers often forget to separate these costs, and, therefore, the true adjusted basis of the building is often not reflected. These amounts are normally not allocated on your purchase agreement so you must get an estimate of the value of the land by a real estate broker or by your county. For further details, consult your tax advisor.

More information. See Publication 527 for more information about depreciating rental property and see Publication 946 for more information about depreciation.

EXPLANATION

Depreciation may perhaps be best understood as a way of deducting the cost of an expenditure over many years. Depreciation is calculated in the same way whether you report income on the cash or the accrual method.

    The period of time over which you depreciate your property has long been the subject of controversy. Different taxpayers, often in the same business, have depreciated the same type of property over widely different periods. Efforts to bring more uniformity to the write-off period resulted in the introduction of the Accelerated Cost Recovery System (ACRS). ACRS was replaced with MACRS (Modified ACRS) by the Tax Reform Act of 1986. Most tangible personal property can be depreciated. Artwork is an exception. It cannot be depreciated because no useful life can be established.

    Under current law, leasehold improvements must be depreciated under MACRS. You generally must depreciate an addition or improvement to nonresidential real property placed in service over a 39-year period using the straight-line method beginning in the month the addition or improvement is placed in service for assets placed in service after May 12, 1993. Leasehold improvements must be depreciated over the MACRS recovery period even if it exceeds the term of the lease.

    Under a tax provision first enacted in 2004 and subsequently extended, qualified leasehold improvements placed in service after October 22, 2004, and before January 1, 2014, are depreciated using the straight-line method over a 15-year recovery period. The availability of this provision expired at the end of 2013 and is not available for 2014. As of the date this book was published, Congress had been considering legislation that would extend its availability, but no such extension had yet been passed. For updated information on this and any other tax law changes that occur after this book was published, see our website, *ey.com/EYTaxGuide*.

    Qualified improvements are any improvements to an interior portion of a building that is nonresidential real property provided:

- The improvement is made under a lease either by the lessee (or sub-lessee), or by the lessor, of that portion of the building to be occupied exclusively by the lessee (or sub-lessee);
- The improvement is placed in service more than 3 years after the date the building was first placed in service; and
- The improvement is not attributable to the enlargement of the building, any elevator or escalator, any structural component benefiting a common area, or the internal structural framework of the building.

TAXORGANIZER

Make sure to keep track of all assets acquired and improvements made related to your rental properties. You should keep records of cost, depreciation method, and amount of depreciation already taken. Therefore, if any of these assets are sold, it will be easier to calculate the gain and depreciation recapture amount, if necessary.

Limits on Rental Losses

If you have a loss from your rental real estate activity, two sets of rules may limit the amount of loss you can deduct. You must consider these rules in the order shown below.

1. At-risk rules. These rules are applied first if there is investment in your rental real estate activity for which you are not at risk. This applies only if the real property was placed in service after 1986.
2. Passive activity limits. Generally, rental real estate activities are considered passive activities and losses are not deductible unless you have income from other passive activities to offset them. However, there are exceptions.

At-Risk Rules

You may be subject to the at-risk rules if you have:

- A loss from an activity carried on as a trade or business or for the production of income, and
- Amounts invested in the activity for which you are not fully at risk.

Losses from holding real property (other than mineral property) placed in service before 1987 are not subject to the at-risk rules.

In most cases, any loss from an activity subject to the at-risk rules is allowed only to the extent of the total amount you have at risk in the activity at the end of the tax year. You are considered at risk in an activity to the extent of cash and the adjusted basis of other property you contributed to the activity and certain amounts borrowed for use in the activity. See Publication 925 for more information.

Passive Activity Limits

In most cases, all rental real estate activities (except those of certain real estate professionals, discussed later) are passive activities. For this purpose, a rental activity is an activity from which you receive income mainly for the use of tangible property, rather than for services.

Limits on passive activity deductions and credits. Deductions or losses from passive activities are limited. You generally cannot offset income, other than passive income, with losses from passive activities. Nor can you offset taxes on income, other than passive income, with credits resulting from passive activities. Any excess loss or credit is carried forward to the next tax year.

For a detailed discussion of these rules, see Publication 925.

You may have to complete Form 8582 to figure the amount of any passive activity loss for the current tax year for all activities and the amount of the passive activity loss allowed on your tax return.

TAXSAVER

Note that any passive losses disallowed and carried forward can generally be taken in the year the property is sold. Any passive loss carryforward that has not been utilized at your death is only deductible to the extent that the carryforward loss exceeds the spread between the cost basis of the property that produced the loss and its fair market value on date of death (or alternate valuation date, if so elected by the executor).

Real estate professionals. Rental activities in which you materially participated during the year are not passive activities if, for that year, you were a real estate professional. For a detailed discussion of the requirements, see Publication 527. For a detailed discussion of material participation, see Publication 925.

EXPLANATION

A rental activity is considered a passive activity unless you are considered a real estate professional. An activity is a rental activity if:
1. Tangible property is used by customers.
2. Income received is principally for the use of the property whether or not there is a lease, service contract, or other arrangement.

An activity is not considered a rental activity if:
1. The average time the customer uses the property is 7 days or less.
2. The average time the customer uses the property is 30 days or less and personal services have been provided by the owner in connection with the rental.
3. Extraordinary personal services are provided by the owner in connection with the rental.
4. The rental of the activity is incidental to the nonrental.
5. The property is associated with a partnership, S corporation, or joint venture.

Example

Amy owns a time-share condo and rents it to a third party for a week each year. Amy paid for no additional services except for weekly cleaning of the unit through condominium dues. This property is not considered a rental activity.

Exception for Personal Use of Dwelling Unit

If you used the rental property as a home during the year, any income, deductions, gain, or loss allocable to such use shall not be taken into account for purposes of the passive activity loss limitation. Instead, follow the rules explained in Personal Use of Dwelling Unit (Including Vacation Home), earlier.

Exception for Rental Real Estate Activities With Active Participation

If you or your spouse actively participated in a passive rental real estate activity, you may be able to deduct up to $25,000 of loss from the activity from your nonpassive income. This special allowance is an exception to the general rule disallowing losses in excess of income from passive activities. Similarly, you may be able to offset credits from the activity against the tax on up to $25,000 of nonpassive income after taking into account any losses allowed under this exception.

Active participation. You actively participated in a rental real estate activity if you (and your spouse) owned at least 10% of the rental property and you made management decisions or arranged for others to provide services (such as repairs) in a significant and *bona fide* sense. Management decisions that may count as active participation include approving new tenants, deciding on rental terms, approving expenditures, and similar decisions.

Maximum special allowance. The maximum special allowance is:

- $25,000 for single individuals and married individuals filing a joint return for the tax year,
- $12,500 for married individuals who file separate returns for the tax year and lived apart from their spouses at all times during the tax year, and
- $25,000 for a qualifying estate reduced by the special allowance for which the surviving spouse qualified.

If your modified adjusted gross income (MAGI) is $100,000 or less ($50,000 or less if married filing separately), you can deduct your loss up to the amount specified above. If your MAGI is more than $100,000 (more than $50,000 if married filing separately), your special allowance is limited to 50% of the difference between $150,000 ($75,000 if married filing separately) and your MAGI.

Generally, if your MAGI is $150,000 or more ($75,000 or more if you are married filing separately), there is no special allowance.

More information. See Publication 925 for more information on the passive loss limits, including information on the treatment of unused disallowed passive losses and credits and the treatment of gains and losses realized on the disposition of a passive activity.

TAXSAVER

If you rent out your personal residence with the intention of returning to it (say, for example, you are transferred overseas for several years), the mortgage interest on the property may not be subject to the passive loss limitation rules. This can result in significant tax savings.

Example

Rental of a dwelling unit

Rent income	$15,000
Mortgage interest	(7,000)
Real estate tax	(3,000)
Other expenses	(1,000)
Depreciation	(9,000)
Net loss subject to passive loss rules	($5,000)

This loss may be deductible on your tax return, under the active participation $25,000 limitation mentioned earlier.

Rental of a personal residence with intention of returning

Rent income	$15,000
Real estate tax	(3,000)
Other expenses	(1,000)
Depreciation	(9,000)
Net rental (passive) income	$2,000
Mortgage interest (loss not subject to passive loss rules)	(7,000)
Net loss from property allowed on tax return	($5,000)

Of this loss, $7,000 (the portion representing qualified residence mortgage interest) may be deductible against nonpassive income. In addition, the $2,000 net passive income may offset passive losses from other passive activities.

Be aware that the depreciation deduction reduces the cost basis of your property, thereby increasing the gain upon sale of the property.

Explanation

You must meet the active participation standards both in the year in which the loss arose and in the year in which the loss is allowed. Losses that exceed $25,000 carried over from an active participation year can be used in a later year if the taxpayer continues to actively participate.

The $25,000 offset rule does not apply to the losses carried over from prior years where the taxpayer did not actively participate in the rental.

How To Report Rental Income and Expenses

The basic form for reporting residential rental income and expenses is Schedule E (Form 1040). However, do not use that schedule to report a not-for-profit activity. See *Not Rented for Profit,* earlier.

Providing substantial services. If you provide substantial services that are primarily for your tenant's convenience, such as regular cleaning, changing linen, or maid service, report your rental income and expenses on Schedule C (Form 1040), Profit or Loss From Business, or Schedule C-EZ (Form 1040), Net Profit From Business (Sole Proprietorship). Substantial services do not include the furnishing of heat and light, cleaning of public areas, trash collection, etc. For information, see Publication 334, Tax Guide for Small Business. You also may have to pay self-employment tax on your rental income using Schedule SE (Form 1040), Self-Employment Tax.

Use Form 1065, U.S. Return of Partnership Income, if your rental activity is a partnership (including a partnership with your spouse unless it is a qualified joint venture).

Qualified joint venture. If you and your spouse each materially participate as the only members of a jointly owned and operated real estate business, and you file a joint return for the tax year, you can make a joint election to be treated as a qualified joint venture instead of a partnership. This election, in most cases, will not increase the total tax owed on the joint return, but it does give each of you credit for social security earnings on which retirement benefits are based and for Medicare coverage if your rental income is subject to self-employment tax. For more information, see Publication 527.

Form 1098, Mortgage Interest Statement. If you paid $600 or more of mortgage interest on your rental property to any one person, you should receive a Form 1098, or similar statement showing the interest you paid for the year. If you and at least one other person (other than your spouse if you file a joint return) were liable for, and paid interest on the mortgage, and the other person received the Form 1098, report your share of the interest on Schedule E (Form 1040), line 13. Attach a statement to your return showing the name and address of the other person. In the left margin of Schedule E, next to line 13, enter "See attached."

Schedule E (Form 1040)

If you rent buildings, rooms, or apartments, and provide basic services such as heat and light, trash collection, etc., you normally report your rental income and expenses on Schedule E, Part I.

List your total income, expenses, and depreciation for each rental property. Be sure to enter the number of fair rental and personal use days on line 2.

If you have more than three rental or royalty properties, complete and attach as many Schedules E as are needed to list the properties. Complete lines 1 and 2 for each property. However, fill in lines 23a through 26 on only one Schedule E.

On Schedule E, page 1, line 18, enter the depreciation you are claiming for each property. To find out if you need to attach Form 4562, see *Form 4562*, in chapter 3 of Publication 527.

If you have a loss from your rental real estate activity, you also may need to complete one or both of the following forms.

- Form 6198, At-Risk Limitations. See *At-Risk Rules*, earlier. Also see Publication 925.
- Form 8582, Passive Activity Loss Limitations. See *Passive Activity Limits*, earlier.

Page 2 of Schedule E is used to report income or loss from partnerships, S corporations, estates, trusts, and real estate mortgage investment conduits. If you need to use page 2 of Schedule E, be sure to use page 2 of the same Schedule E you used to enter your rental activity on page 1. Also, include the amount from line 26 (Part I) in the "Total income or (loss)" on line 41 (Part V).

TAXORGANIZER
Records you should keep:

- Rental agreement
- Records of tenant-paid improvements, real estate taxes, mortgage payments, etc.
- A log of how many days a property is rented, used for personal purposes, or vacant
- Proof of advertising vacant properties in newspapers, magazines, websites, etc.
- Lists distinguishing the nature of each repair or improvement
- Receipts for each repair and improvement including date and amount paid
- A log of travel expenses allocating between rental and nonrental purposes
- A schedule showing method of division of expenses if part of property is rented
- Schedule listing depreciable assets with respect to the rental property including amount, date purchased, life of asset, method of depreciation, and depreciation already taken
- Carryforward of passive activity losses not utilized in prior years
- Carryforward of rental losses in excess of $25,000 when actively participating in rental activity
- Form 1098 or other form indicating mortgage interest paid
- Property tax forms and receipts
- Proof of tax preparation fees paid in relation to rental property
- Security deposit information

Use this worksheet only if you answer "yes" to all of the following questions.
- Did you use the dwelling unit as a home this year? (See *Dwelling Unit Used as a Home*.)
- Did you rent the dwelling unit at a fair rental price 15 days or more this year?
- Is the total of your rental expenses and depreciation more than your rental income?

PART I. Rental Use Percentage

A.	Total days available for rent at fair rental price...	**A.** _____
B.	Total days available for rent (line A) but not rented...	**B.** _____
C.	**Total days of rental use.** Subtract line B from line A......................................	**C.** _____
D.	**Total days of personal use** (including days rented at less than fair rental price)	**D.** _____
E.	**Total days of rental and personal use.** Add lines C and D................................	**E.** _____
F.	**Percentage of expenses allowed for rental.** Divide line C by line E	**F.** _____

PART II. Allowable Rental Expenses

1.	Enter rents received	**1.** _____
2a.	Enter the rental portion of deductible home mortgage interest and qualified mortgage insurance premiums (see instructions)	**2a.** _____
b.	Enter the rental portion of real estate taxes..	**b.** _____
c.	Enter the rental portion of deductible casualty and theft losses (see instructions)......................................	**c.** _____
d.	Enter direct rental expenses (see instructions)...	**d.** _____
e.	**Fully deductible rental expenses.** Add lines 2a–2d. Enter here and on the appropriate lines on Schedule E (see instructions)	**2e.** _____
3.	Subtract line 2e from line 1. If zero or less, enter -0-	**3.** _____
4a.	Enter the rental portion of expenses directly related to operating or maintaining the dwelling unit (such as repairs, insurance, and utilities)..	**4a.** _____
b.	Enter the rental portion of excess mortgage interest and qualified mortgage insurance premiums (see instructions)	**b.** _____
c.	Carryover of operating expenses from 2013 worksheet	**c.** _____
d.	Add lines 4a–4c..	**d.** _____
e.	**Allowable expenses.** Enter the **smaller** of line 3 or line 4d (see instructions)	**4e.** _____
5.	Subtract line 4e from line 3. If zero or less, enter -0-	**5.** _____
6a.	Enter the rental portion of excess casualty and theft losses (see instructions)..	**6a.** _____
b.	Enter the rental portion of depreciation of the dwelling unit.................................	**b.** _____
c.	Carryover of excess casualty losses and depreciation from 2013 worksheet	**c.** _____
d.	Add lines 6a–6c...	**d.** _____
e.	**Allowable excess casualty and theft losses and depreciation.** Enter the **smaller** of line 5 or line 6d (see instructions)	**6e.** _____

PART III. Carryover of Unallowed Expenses to Next Year

7a.	**Operating expenses to be carried over to next year.** Subtract line 4e from line 4d	**7a.** _____
b.	**Excess casualty and theft losses and depreciation to be carried over to next year.** Subtract line 6e from line 6d..	**b.** _____

Caution. Use the percentage determined in Part I, line F, to figure the rental portions to enter on lines 2a–2c, 4a–4b, and 6a–6b of Part II.

Line 2a. Figure the mortgage interest on the dwelling unit that you could deduct on Schedule A as if you had not rented the unit. Do not include interest on a loan that did not benefit the dwelling unit. For example, do not include interest on a home equity loan used to pay off credit cards or other personal loans, buy a car, or pay college tuition. Include interest on a loan used to buy, build, or improve the dwelling unit, or to refinance such a loan. Include the rental portion of this interest in the total you enter on line 2a of the worksheet.

Figure the qualified mortgage insurance premiums on the dwelling unit that you could deduct on line 13 of Schedule A as if you had not rented the unit. See the Schedule A instructions. However, figure your adjusted gross income (Form 1040, line 38) without your rental income and expenses from the dwelling unit. See *Line 4b* to deduct the part of the qualified mortgage insurance premiums not allowed because of the adjusted gross income limit. Include the rental portion of the amount from Schedule A, line 13, in the total you enter on line 2a of the worksheet.

Note. Do not file this Schedule A or use it to figure the amount to deduct on line 13 of that schedule. Instead, figure the personal portion on a separate Schedule A. If you have deducted mortgage interest or qualified mortgage insurance premiums on the dwelling unit on other forms, such as Schedule C or F, remember to reduce your Schedule A deduction by that amount.

Line 2c. Figure the casualty and theft losses related to the dwelling unit that you could deduct on Schedule A as if you had not rented the dwelling unit. To do this, complete Section A of Form 4684, Casualties and Thefts, treating the losses as personal losses. If any of the loss is due to a federally declared disaster, see the Instructions for Form 4684. On Form 4684, line 17, enter 10% of your adjusted gross income figured without your rental income and expenses from the dwelling unit. Enter the rental portion of the result from Form 4684, line 18, on line 2c of this worksheet.

Note. Do not file this Form 4684 or use it to figure your personal losses on Schedule A. Instead, figure the personal portion on a separate Form 4684.

Line 2d. Enter the total of your rental expenses that are directly related only to the rental activity. These include interest on loans used for rental activities other than to buy, build, or improve the dwelling unit. Also include rental agency fees, advertising, office supplies, and depreciation on office equipment used in your rental activity.

Line 2e. You can deduct the amounts on lines 2a, 2b, 2c, and 2d as rental expenses on Schedule E even if your rental expenses are more than your rental income. Enter the amounts on lines 2a, 2b, 2c, and 2d on the appropriate lines of Schedule E.

Line 4b. On line 2a, you entered the rental portion of the mortgage interest and qualified mortgage insurance premiums you could deduct on Schedule A if you had not rented the dwelling unit. If you had additional mortgage interest and qualified mortgage insurance premiums that would not be deductible on Schedule A because of limits imposed on them, enter on line 4b of this worksheet the rental portion of those excess amounts. Do not include interest on a loan that did not benefit the dwelling unit (as explained in the line 2a instructions).

Line 4e. You can deduct the amounts on lines 4a, 4b, and 4c as rental expenses on Schedule E only to the extent they are not more than the amount on line 4e.*

Line 6a. To find the rental portion of excess casualty and theft losses, use the Form 4684 you prepared for line 2c of this worksheet.

    A. Enter the amount from Form 4684, line 10 .... _____

    B. Enter the rental portion of line A .... _____

    C. Enter the amount from line 2c of this worksheet .... _____

    D. Subtract line C from line B. Enter the result here and on line 6a of this worksheet .... _____

Line 6e. You can deduct the amounts on lines 6a, 6b, and 6c as rental expenses on Schedule E only to the extent they are not more than the amount on line 6e.*

---

*Allocating the limited deduction.** If you cannot deduct all of the amount on line 4d or 6d this year, you can allocate the allowable deduction in any way you wish among the expenses included on line 4d or 6d. Enter the amount you allocate to each expense on the appropriate line of Schedule E, Part I.

Chapter 10

Retirement plans, pensions, and annuities

ey.com/EYTaxGuide

Introduction

No matter how welcome retirement may be, you're likely to encounter a host of challenging tax dilemmas that you've never before faced. For starters, chances are good that you will have some difficulty projecting your tax liabilities. Your income will most likely be different from what it has been, and the way in which you calculate your tax will be different, too. You'll have to puzzle over the complicated withdrawal requirements from 401(k) and other retirement accounts. You may also be faced with the decision of whether to withdraw certain funds as an annuity, or in one lump-sum distribution. If you are entitled to any lump-sum distributions, you will have to make the difficult decision as to whether to roll over the funds and defer the tax or to pay the tax currently. If your pension payments are not subject to mandatory withholding rules, you may have to start making estimated tax payments or elect to have income taxes withheld from your pension payments. This chapter helps guide you through this maze of complicated decisions.

Reminder

For purposes of the Net Investment Income Tax (NIIT), net investment income does not include distributions from a qualified retirement plan (for example, 401(a), 403(a), 403(b), 408, 408A, or 457(b) plans). However, these distributions are taken into account when determining the modified adjusted gross income threshold. Distributions from a nonqualified retirement plan are included in net investment income. See Form 8960, Net Investment Income Tax—Individuals, Estates, and Trusts, and its instructions for more information.

Starting in 2013, the American Taxpayer Relief Act of 2012 (ATRA) expanded the rules for in-plan Roth rollovers to include more taxpayers. For more information, see *Designated Roth accounts* discussed later.

TAXALERT

Roth conversions expanded for retirement plans. A deferral plan under section 401(k) (including the Thrift Savings Plan), 403(b), or 457(b) governmental plan can have Roth accounts. This means that participants can designate a portion or even all of any elective deferrals they make as contributions to their Roth account. Deferrals so designated are currently taxable to the participant, but qualified distributions subsequently received from the Roth account are received tax-free.

Note

IRS Publication 17 (*Your Federal Income Tax*) has been updated by Ernst & Young LLP for 2014. Dates and dollar amounts shown are for 2014. Underlined type is used to indicate where IRS text has been updated. Places where text has been removed are indicated by the sentence: *Text intentionally omitted*.

ey.com/EYTaxGuide
Ernst & Young LLP will update the *EY Tax Guide* 2015 website with relevant taxpayer information as it becomes available. You can also sign up for email alerts to let you know when changes have been made.

Tax Breaks and Deductions You Can Use Checklist

Excluding a rollover distribution from current taxes. If you withdraw all or a part of your balance in a qualified plan or tax-sheltered annuity arrangement, and such distribution is eligible to be rolled over to the qualified retirement plan of an employer or an IRA, you can defer tax on the distribution by contributing it to an eligible retirement plan. For more information, see *Rollovers*, later.

Avoiding mandatory 20% withholding on eligible rollover distributions. Payers of benefits from your pension, profit-sharing, annuity, stock bonus, or other qualified deferred compensation plans are generally required to withhold 20%

These plans also have the option to permit participants to roll their pre-tax account balances into a designated Roth account within the same plan. (Not all plans offer this rollover option, so you need to check with your employer.) Before 2013, plans that offered this rollover option could allow participants to convert their pre-tax accounts to Roth accounts, but only with respect to money they otherwise had a right to take out of the plan; usually because they either reached age 59½ or separated from their employer. After 2012, any amount in a non-Roth account is allowed to be converted to a Roth account in the same plan, whether or not the amount is otherwise eligible for distribution. Any amount converted to the Roth account is subject to regular income tax at the time of the conversion.

This chapter discusses the tax treatment of distributions you receive from:
- An employee pension or annuity from a qualified plan,
- A disability retirement, and
- A purchased commercial annuity.

What is not covered in this chapter. The following topics are not discussed in this chapter.

The General Rule. This is the method generally used to determine the tax treatment of pension and annuity income from nonqualified plans (including commercial annuities). For a qualified plan, you generally cannot use the General Rule unless your annuity starting date is before November 19, 1996. For more information about the General Rule, see Publication 939, General Rule for Pensions and Annuities.

Individual retirement arrangements (IRAs). Information on the tax treatment of amounts you receive from an IRA is in chapter 17.

Civil service retirement benefits. If you are retired from the federal government (regular, phased, or disability retirement), see Publication 721, Tax Guide to U.S. Civil Service Retirement Benefits. Publication 721 also covers the information that you need if you are the survivor or beneficiary of a federal employee or retiree who died.

Useful Items

You may want to see:

Publication

- ☐ **575** Pension and Annuity Income
- ☐ **721** Tax Guide to U.S. Civil Service Retirement Benefits
- ☐ **939** General Rule for Pensions and Annuities

Form (and Instructions)

- ☐ **W-4P** Withholding Certificate for Pension or Annuity Payments
- ☐ **1099-R** Distributions From Pensions, Annuities, Retirement or Profit-Sharing Plans, IRAs, Insurance Contracts, etc.
- ☐ **4972** Tax on Lump-Sum Distributions
- ☐ **5329** Additional Taxes on Qualified Plans (Including IRAs) and Other Tax-Favored Accounts

General Information

Designated Roth accounts. A designated Roth account is a separate account created under a qualified Roth contribution program to which participants may elect to have part or all of their elective deferrals to a 401(k), 403(b), or 457(b) plan designated as Roth contributions. Elective deferrals that are designated as Roth contributions are included in your income. However, qualified distributions are not included in your income. See Publication 575 for more information.

TAXPLANNER

Your contributions to a Roth 401(k) are nondeductible, but all of the income in the plan will be tax-free to you when distributed if you meet the same requirements that apply to Roth IRAs: 5 years of participation and distribution after age 59½, death, disability, or up to $10,000 for a first-time home purchase. Unlike Roth IRAs, the ability to contribute to a Roth 401(k) is not limited by the amount of your income.

of distributions from such plans. However, withholding is not required on an eligible rollover distribution if you elect to have it paid directly to an IRA or qualified retirement plan of an employer. For more information, see *Withholding and Estimated Tax*, later.

401(k) and 403(b) plan contributions. You can reduce your taxable wages (and your tax bill) by contributing on a pretax basis to a 401(k) or 403(b) plan sponsored by your employer. In 2014, you could contribute up to $17,500 ($23,000 if you were 50 or older by the end of 2014). For more details, see *Elective deferrals*, later.

Roth 401(k) plans. If your employer plan allows it, you may be able to designate part or all of your contributions to your employer's 401(k) plan as "Roth 401(k)" contributions. Unlike contributions made to a "traditional" 401(k) plan that reduce your taxable wages, contributions to a Roth 401(k) do not reduce the amount of your earnings currently subject to tax. However, if certain requirements are met, your entire plan account can be distributed to you completely tax-free. For more details, see *General Information*.

Taxation of appreciated employer securities received as part of a lump-sum distribution. If a lump-sum distribution includes shares of stock in your employer that have appreciated in value, this "net unrealized appreciation" (NUA), which is determined upon the distribution, will not be subject to tax until you subsequently sell the shares. If the shares are sold, then the gain will be taxed as a

In-plan rollovers to designated Roth accounts. If you are a participant in a 401(k), 403(b), or 457(b) plan, your plan may permit you to roll over amounts in those plans to a designated Roth account within the same plan. The rollover of any untaxed amounts must be included in income. See Publication 575 for more information.

TAXPLANNER

Not all plans offer this rollover option, so you need to check with your employer.

TAXALERT

Before 2013, rollovers from a pre-tax account to a Roth account within a plan were allowed only with respect to funds the individual plan participants otherwise had a right to withdraw from the plan; usually because the participant either reached age 59½ or separated from service from his or her employer. Beginning in 2013, the American Taxpayer Relief Act of 2012 allows any amount in a non-Roth account to be converted to a Roth account in the same plan, whether or not the amount is otherwise eligible for distribution. This tax law change significantly expands the population of taxpayers who can take advantage of this option for converting pre-tax amounts held inside their 401(k), 403(b), and/or 457(b) plans to a Roth account.

Just like a conversion to a Roth IRA (discussed in chapter 17, *Individual retirement arrangements (IRAs)*), the amount rolled over is includible in taxable income except to the extent it includes a return of after-tax contributions.

More than one program. If you receive benefits from more than one program under a single trust or plan of your employer, such as a pension plan and a profit-sharing plan, you may have to figure the taxable part of each pension or annuity contract separately. Your former employer or the plan administrator should be able to tell you if you have more than one pension or annuity contract.

Section 457 deferred compensation plans. If you work for a state or local government or for a tax-exempt organization, you may be able to participate in a section 457 deferred compensation plan. If your plan is an eligible plan, you are not taxed currently on pay that is deferred under the plan or on any earnings from the plan's investment of the deferred pay. You are generally taxed on amounts deferred in an eligible state or local government plan only when they are distributed from the plan. You are taxed on amounts deferred in an eligible tax-exempt organization plan when they are distributed or otherwise made available to you.

Your 457(b) plan may have a designated Roth account option. If so, you may be able to roll over amounts to the designated Roth account or make contributions. Elective deferrals to a designated Roth account are included in your income. Qualified distributions from a designated Roth account are not subject to tax.

This chapter covers the tax treatment of benefits under eligible section 457 plans, but it does not cover the treatment of deferrals. For information on deferrals under section 457 plans, see *Retirement Plan Contributions* under *Employee Compensation* in Publication 525, Taxable and Nontaxable Income.

For general information on these deferred compensation plans, see *Section 457 Deferred Compensation Plans* in Publication 575.

Disability pensions. If you retired on disability, you generally must include in income any disability pension you receive under a plan that is paid for by your employer. You must report your taxable disability payments as wages on line 7 of Form 1040 or Form 1040A until you reach minimum retirement age. Minimum retirement age generally is the age at which you can first receive a pension or annuity if you are not disabled.

Beginning on the day after you reach minimum retirement age, payments you receive are taxable as a pension or annuity. Report the payments on Form 1040, lines 16a and 16b, or on Form 1040A, lines 12a and 12b.

For more information on how to report disability pensions, including military and certain government disability pensions, see chapter 5.

Retired public safety officers. An eligible retired public safety officer can elect to exclude from income distributions of up to $3,000 made directly from a government retirement plan to the provider of accident, health, or long-term disability insurance. See *Insurance Premiums for Retired Public Safety Officers* in Publication 575 for more information.

Caution

You may be entitled to a tax credit if you were permanently and totally disabled when you retired. For information on the credit for the elderly or the disabled, see chapter 34.

Caution

Disability payments for injuries incurred as a direct result of a terrorist attack directed against the United States (or its allies) are not included in income. For more information about payments to survivors of terrorist attacks, see Publication 3920, Tax Relief for Victims of Terrorist Attacks.

Railroad retirement benefits. Part of any railroad retirement benefits you receive is treated for tax purposes as social security benefits, and part is treated as an employee pension. For information about railroad retirement benefits treated as social security benefits, see Publication 915, Social Security and Equivalent Railroad Retirement Benefits. For information about railroad retirement benefits treated as an employee pension, see *Railroad Retirement Benefits* in Publication 575.

EXPLANATION

Unless you elect to have your distribution paid *directly* to an eligible retirement plan, the payer of benefits from your pension, profit-sharing, stock bonus, annuity, or other qualified deferred compensation plan is required to withhold an amount equal to 20% of any designated distribution that is an eligible rollover distribution. An eligible rollover distribution is any distribution of all or a portion of an employee's balance in a qualified plan or tax-sheltered annuity arrangement other than (1) any distribution that is one of a series of substantially equal periodic payments made over the life or life expectancy of the employee (or the joint lives or joint life expectancies of the employee and the employee's designated beneficiary) or made over a period of 10 years or more, (2) required minimum distributions, and (3) certain corrective and deemed distributions. An eligible retirement plan is generally another qualified retirement plan, an individual retirement account, an individual retirement annuity, a governmental Section 457 plan, or a 403(b) tax-sheltered annuity.

If the payment made to you is not an eligible rollover distribution, the payer will withhold income tax on the taxable amounts paid to you. However, withholding from these payments is not mandatory and you can tell the payer how to withhold by filing Form W-4P, Withholding Certificate for Pension or Annuity Payments. If you choose not to have tax withheld, you may have to pay estimated tax.

Withholding and estimated tax. The payer of your pension, profit-sharing, stock bonus, annuity, or deferred compensation plan will withhold income tax on the taxable parts of amounts paid to you. You can tell the payer how much to withhold, or not to withhold, by filing Form W-4P. If you choose not to have tax withheld, or you do not have enough tax withheld, you may have to pay estimated tax.

If you receive an eligible rollover distribution, you cannot choose not to have tax withheld. Generally, 20% will be withheld, but no tax will be withheld on a direct rollover of an eligible rollover distribution. See *Direct rollover option* under *Rollovers,* later.

For more information, see *Pensions and Annuities* under *Tax Withholding for 2014* in chapter 4.

Qualified plans for self-employed individuals. Qualified plans set up by self-employed individuals are sometimes called Keogh or H.R. 10 plans. Qualified plans can be set up by sole proprietors, partnerships (but not a partner), and corporations. They can cover self-employed persons, such as the sole proprietor or partners, as well as regular (common-law) employees.

Distributions from a qualified plan are usually fully taxable because most recipients have no cost basis. If you have an investment (cost) in the plan, however, your pension or annuity payments from a qualified plan are taxed under the Simplified Method. For more information about qualified plans, see Publication 560, Retirement Plans for Small Business.

Purchased annuities. If you receive pension or annuity payments from a privately purchased annuity contract from a commercial organization, such as an insurance company, you generally must use the General Rule to figure the tax-free part of each annuity payment. For more information about the General Rule, get Publication 939. Also, see *Variable Annuities* in Publication 575 for the special provisions that apply to these annuity contracts.

Loans. If you borrow money from your retirement plan, you must treat the loan as a nonperiodic distribution from the plan unless certain exceptions apply. This treatment also applies to any loan under a contract purchased under your retirement plan, and to the value of any part of your interest in the plan or contract that you pledge or assign. This means that you must include in income all or part of the amount borrowed. Even if you do not have to treat the loan as a nonperiodic distribution, you may not be able to deduct the interest on the loan in some situations. For details, see *Loans Treated as Distributions* in Publication 575. For information on the deductibility of interest, see chapter 24.

EXCEPTION

A loan will not be considered a distribution to the extent that the loan (when added to the outstanding balance of all other loans maintained by the employer) does not exceed the lesser of (1) $50,000 or (2) the greater of either $10,000 or one-half of the participant's vested accrued

---

benefits under the plan. The $50,000 limit is reduced by the excess of the participant's highest outstanding loan balance during the preceding 12-month period, over the outstanding balance at the date of the new loan.

In addition, the exception does not apply unless the loan by its terms must be repaid within 5 years and requires level repayments made not less frequently than quarterly over the term of the loan.

The 5-year rule does not generally apply to loans made in connection with the purchase of a principal residence of a participant.

TAXALERT

Interest on a loan from an employee plan is only deductible under the general loan interest rules (discussed in chapter 24, *Interest expense*). Even if the interest is otherwise deductible under the general rules, it will not be deductible if the loan was made to a key employee or secured by amounts attributable to an employee's salary reduction amounts. It should also be noted that personal loan interest is not deductible.

TAXPLANNER

Loans from a retirement plan may be an option to provide for your children's college expenses, a housing down payment, or any other family need. The interest you pay on the loan helps your account grow at an attractive rate if the plan credits interest paid on the loan to your account. But there are some significant risks to consider before taking such a loan. One downside is that you may earn less in your plan from this interest than you would have had you left the money in other investments. Another drawback is that any loan that is not paid back within 5 years is subject to income tax and penalties, and perhaps above all, your retirement plan is depleted. Saving for education through a 529 plan and even taking out student loans may be preferable.

Elective deferrals. Some retirement plans allow you to elect to have your employer contribute part of your compensation to a retirement fund, rather than have it paid to you. You do not pay income tax on this money until you receive it in a distribution from the plan. Generally, you may not defer more than a total of $17,500 ($23,000 for individuals who have attained at least age 50 by year-end) for all qualified plans by which you are covered in 2014.

Elective deferrals generally include elective contributions to cash or deferred arrangements (known as *401(k) plans*) and elective contributions to Section 501(c)(18)(D) plans, salary reduction simplified employee pension (SARSEP) plans, SIMPLE plans, and 403(b) tax-sheltered annuities. Some employers offer a Roth 401(k) account as an alternative to the traditional 401(k) plan. The difference is that instead of your elective contributions being excluded from taxable wages up front and earnings on the 401(k) account being taxed upon withdrawal, your contributions to the Roth 401(k) are included as part of your taxable wages but distributions—if certain requirements are met—of both your contributions and all future earnings are completely tax-free.

Certain deferrals (such as cafeteria plan contributions and qualified transportation fringe benefits) that are not included in your gross income are still included in your compensation for purposes of determining your base amount for your 401(k) contributions. For example, the amounts contributed to a cafeteria plan will not decrease the tax-deferred amount that can be contributed by the employer at the election of the employee to his or her 401(k) plan.

TAXPLANNER

There are several special rules used to determine the limit on employee elective deferrals. If the deferrals are otherwise permitted under these special rules, there is an annual limit on elective deferrals—$17,500 for 2014 (plus an additional $5,500 for persons who have attained at least age 50 by the end of the year). This is an aggregate limit for each individual. It takes into consideration all deferrals by that individual during the year to all 401(k) plans (including Roth 401(k) accounts), 403(b) tax-sheltered annuities, SIMPLE plans, and salary reduction simplified employee pension (SARSEP) plans. (Employers that established SEPs were prohibited in 1996 from establishing any new SARSEPs—which are salary reduction SEPs—after December 31, 1996). A SEP is a special type of IRA established by an employer for all its employees.

The limit on contributions to a SIMPLE plan is $12,000; so if the employee has access to only a SIMPLE plan, the employee can defer only $12,000 because the SIMPLE limit cuts off the permissible $17,500. However, if the employee moves mid-year to another employer that has a 401(k) plan, then the combined $17,500 limit applies (as long as not more than $12,000 was deferred to the SIMPLE). The limit applies even if the employee makes deferrals to plans sponsored by different employers or to different types of plans (elective contributions to Section 457 plans for government and non-profit employees are not included in this aggregation). Note that this limit is an elective contribution limit. There is also a limit on total employer contributions to qualified defined contribution plans of $52,000 in 2014; for this limit, elective deferrals are treated as employer contributions. Thus, if you are under age 50 and make the maximum deferral of $17,500 in 2014, you only have $34,500 left for other employer contributions.

The dollar limit is indexed annually for inflation in $500 increments.

Example

Assume Steve works for Employer A from January 2014 to April 2014 and defers $5,000 to Employer A's 401(k) plan during this time. If Steve leaves in May 2014 to work for Employer B for the remainder of the year, the most Steve could defer to Employer B's 401(k) plan for the remainder of 2014 is $12,500.

Alternatively, assume Steve works for Employer A from January 2014 to August 2014 and defers $7,500 to Employer A's 401(k) plan. In September, Steve leaves to work for Employer B, which sponsors a SIMPLE IRA for its employees. Steve will only be allowed to defer $10,000 to the SIMPLE IRA for 2014—$17,500 aggregate limit less $7,500 already deferred to Employer A's 401(k) plan. If instead Steve had deferred only $2,500 in Employer A's 401(k) plan, then because the elective deferral limit for a SIMPLE is $12,000, Steve would only be able to defer an additional $12,000 even though the total amount of his elective deferrals for the year is only $14,500.

TAXALERT

If you are at least 50 years old by the end of the taxable year, you can elect to defer even more to a 401(k) plan, a 403(b) tax-sheltered annuity, a SARSEP, a SIMPLE plan, or a governmental Section 457 plan. The additional amount of elective contributions that may be made is the lesser of (1) the applicable dollar amount (as described) or (2) your compensation for the year reduced by any other elective deferrals you made for the year. The applicable dollar amount for age 50 catch-up contributions under a 401(k) plan, a 403(b) tax-sheltered annuity, a SARSEP, or a governmental Section 457 plan is $5,500 for 2014. The applicable dollar amount for the age 50 catch-up contributions under a SIMPLE plan is $2,500 for 2014.

TAXALERT

If you realize that you made excess elective deferrals (the limit is $17,500 or, if you have attained age 50, $23,000 for 2014) in any given calendar year, be certain to notify your plan administrator(s) as soon as possible. The excess deferral amount will be taxable to you in the year of the deferral. In addition, if this excess deferral (plus earnings for the year) is not distributed to you by the following April 15, the excess deferral amount will again be taxed to you when it is ultimately distributed to you upon your retirement or separation from your employer. If the excess deferral is distributed to you by the following April 15, however, it will not be taxed a second time when distributed (although the income attributable to the excess deferral will be taxed to you in the year of distribution). Excess deferrals (with earnings or losses attributable to such excess deferrals) in 2014 must be distributed by April 15, 2015. Any earnings or losses on the excess deferral occurring after December 31 of the deferral year do not impact the amount of the distribution if the excess is distributed by April 15 of the following year; only earnings or losses on the excess deferral through December 31 of the year of deferral are distributed at this time.

TAXPLANNER

The benefits of 401(k) plans are substantial. The elective deferrals are not subject to federal, most state, and most local income taxes until they are withdrawn. (They are subject to social security and Medicare taxes at the time of deferral, though.) Earnings on elective deferrals are also not subject to income tax until they are withdrawn. An employer matching contribution program (which is deductible to the employer within certain limits and not taxable to the employee until distributed) can encourage employees to make elective deferrals. Finally, on withdrawal, a lump-sum distribution can escape immediate income tax or excise tax if it is deposited into a rollover account. For more information, see _Rollovers_ later in this chapter.

Since 2006, the law also allows employers to offer "Roth 401(k)" plans to their employees. Under a Roth 401(k), contributions are nondeductible but all the income in the plan is tax-free if certain requirements are met at distribution. (The regular 401(k) dollar limitation applies to the combination of regular and Roth 401(k) contributions.) These requirements are similar to those that apply to Roth IRAs, which are discussed in chapter 17, *Individual retirement arrangements (IRAs)*. However, unlike with Roth IRAs, the ability to contribute to a Roth 401(k) is not limited to those with income below certain limits.

TAXPLANNER

403(b) plans (tax-sheltered annuity, or TSA plans), which are available to employees of certain tax-exempt organizations, to employees of educational organizations and of state and local governments, and to certain church employees, offer many of the same benefits that 401(k) plans offer. The elective deferrals are not subject to federal income tax, most state income taxes, and most local income taxes, until they are withdrawn. Earnings on elective deferrals are also not subject to income tax until they are withdrawn. Rollovers are permitted for qualifying distributions, which avoid immediate income tax or excise taxes, if applicable. Effective for distributions made after December 31, 2001, eligible rollover distributions from a TSA plan can be rolled over into a qualified retirement plan, another TSA plan, or an IRA, including a Roth IRA. Under a 2010 tax law, if the TSA has a designated Roth contribution program, amounts held inside a pre-tax account can be rolled over to a designated Roth account within the plan. (Distributions rolled over to either a designated Roth account within the TSA or to a Roth IRA are subject to special rules for rollovers to Roth IRAs from non-Roth accounts.)

State and local governments (other than rural cooperative plans and, for certain employees, Indian tribal governments) cannot provide 401(k) plans to their employees, although they may offer a TSA plan for employees of certain educational organizations and they may offer Section 457 plans.

For information about tax-sheltered annuities, see Publication 571, *Tax-Sheltered Annuity Programs for Employees of Public Schools and Certain Tax-Exempt Organizations*. For information on Section 457 plans, see Publication 4484, *Choose a Retirement Plan for Employees of Tax Exempt and Government Entities*.

TAXSAVER

Individuals earning limited amounts of self-employment income may be able to shelter all or a substantial portion of their income by utilizing a SIMPLE IRA. (Note: Unless you are self-employed, other than as a partner, SIMPLE IRAs may only be established by your employer.) Although an individual may only defer $12,000 in 2014 to a SIMPLE IRA, these deferrals are not limited to a certain percentage of an individual's compensation as is the case with other plans. For example, in 2014 an individual with $12,500 in self-employment income (e.g., director's fees) could defer $12,000 (or 96%) of the income into a SIMPLE IRA. In addition to the $12,000 employee deferral, either a 3% matching contribution or a 2% employer contribution would be required to satisfy the SIMPLE IRA rules. On the other hand, the same individual could contribute only 25% of the income (after reduction for the 25% contribution itself) into a SEP, or $2,500. (An even better alternative would be a Keogh/401(k) plan combination. Under that type of plan, you could contribute up to the full 401(k) limit of $17,500.) See the discussion in chapter 17, *Individual retirement arrangements (IRAs)*, for more details on the requirements for SIMPLE IRAs.

TAXALERT

A nonrefundable tax saver's credit is available for eligible individuals, in an amount equal to a percentage (see the following table) of their qualified retirement savings contribution, not to exceed $2,000. Only individuals with a joint return with adjusted gross income of less than $60,000, a head-of-household return of less than $45,000, or a single or married filing separate return of less than $30,000 are eligible for the credit. The credit is available with respect to elective deferrals to a 401(k) plan, a 403(b) tax-sheltered annuity, or a governmental Section 457 plan, a SIMPLE plan, or a SEP, and with respect to contributions to a traditional or Roth IRA, and voluntary after-tax employee contributions to a qualified retirement plan or a 403(b) tax-sheltered annuity.

Adjusted Gross Income						
Joint Return		Head of Household		All Other Cases		Applicable Percentage
Over	Not Over	Over	Not Over	Over	Not Over	
$0	$36,000	$0	$27,000	$0	$18,000	50%
$36,001	$39,000	$27,001	$29,250	$18,001	$19,500	20%
$39,001	$60,000	$29,251	$45,000	$19,501	$30,000	10%
$60,000		$45,000		$30,000		0%

Tax-free exchange. No gain or loss is recognized on an exchange of an annuity contract for another annuity contract if the insured or annuitant remains the same. However, if an annuity contract is exchanged for a life insurance or endowment contract, any gain due to interest accumulated on the contract is ordinary income. See *Transfers of Annuity Contracts* in Publication 575 for more information about exchanges of annuity contracts.

How To Report

If you file Form 1040, report your total annuity on line 16a and the taxable part on line 16b. If your pension or annuity is fully taxable, enter it on line 16b; do not make an entry on line 16a.

If you file Form 1040A, report your total annuity on line 12a and the taxable part on line 12b. If your pension or annuity is fully taxable, enter it on line 12b; do not make an entry on line 12a.

More than one annuity. If you receive more than one annuity and at least one of them is not fully taxable, enter the total amount received from all annuities on Form 1040, line 16a, or Form 1040A, line 12a, and enter the taxable part on Form 1040, line 16b, or Form 1040A, line 12b. If all the annuities you receive are fully taxable, enter the total of all of them on Form 1040, line 16b, or Form 1040A, line 12b.

Joint return. If you file a joint return and you and your spouse each receive one or more pensions or annuities, report the total of the pensions and annuities on Form 1040, line 16a, or Form 1040A, line 12a, and report the taxable part on Form 1040, line 16b, or Form 1040A, line 12b.

Cost (Investment in the Contract)

Before you can figure how much, if any, of a distribution from your pension or annuity plan is taxable, you must determine your cost (your investment in the contract) in the pension or annuity. Your total cost in the plan includes the total premiums, contributions, or other amounts you paid. This includes the amounts your employer contributed that were taxable to you when paid. Cost does not include any amounts you deducted or were excluded from your income.

From this total cost, subtract any refunds of premiums, rebates, dividends, unrepaid loans that were not included in your income, or other tax-free amounts that you received by the later of the annuity starting date or the date on which you received your first payment.

Your annuity starting date is the later of the first day of the first period for which you received a payment or the date the plan's obligations became fixed.

TAXSAVER

You may or may not have any cost (investment) in your plan for unrepaid loans. If you received a loan from a plan but did not repay the loan according to the repayment schedule (a default), the amount of the loan that was in default was probably reported to you as taxable income in the year you failed to make the required payments. The amount of the unrepaid loan that has already been taxed to you reduces the amount that can be distributed to you and should not be included in your cost. However, if you repay all or part of the loan to the plan after the loan has been taxed to you because of a default, your repayments will increase your cost in the plan. Your plan administrator should properly track your loan repayments and determine your cost in the plan.

Designated Roth accounts. Your cost in these accounts is your designated Roth contributions that were included in your income as wages subject to applicable withholding requirements. Your cost will also include any in-plan Roth rollovers you included in income.

Foreign employment contributions. If you worked in a foreign country and contributions were made to your retirement plan, special rules apply in determining your cost. See *Foreign employment contributions* under *Cost (Investment in the Contract)* in Publication 575.

Taxation of Periodic Payments

Fully taxable payments. Generally, if you did not pay any part of the cost of your employee pension or annuity and your employer did not withhold part of the cost from your pay while you worked, the amounts you receive each year are fully taxable. You must report them on your income tax return.

Partly taxable payments. If you paid part of the cost of your pension or annuity, you are not taxed on the part of the pension or annuity you receive that represents a return of your cost. The rest of the amount you receive is generally taxable. You figure the tax-free part of the payment using either the Simplified Method or the General Rule. Your annuity starting date and whether or not your plan is qualified determine which method you must or may use.

If your annuity starting date is after November 18, 1996, and your payments are from a qualified plan, you must use the Simplified Method. Generally, you must use the General Rule if your annuity is paid under a nonqualified plan, and you cannot use this method if your annuity is paid under a qualified plan.

If you had more than one partly taxable pension or annuity, figure the tax-free part and the taxable part of each separately.

If your annuity is paid under a qualified plan and your annuity starting date is after July 1, 1986, and before November 19, 1996, you could have chosen to use either the General Rule or the Simplified Method.

Exclusion limit. Your annuity starting date determines the total amount of annuity payments that you can exclude from your taxable income over the years. Once your annuity starting date is determined, it does not change. If you calculate the taxable portion of your annuity payments using the simplified method worksheet, the annuity starting date determines the recovery period for your cost. That recovery period begins on your annuity starting date and is not affected by the date you first complete the worksheet.

Exclusion limited to cost. If your annuity starting date is after 1986, the total amount of annuity income that you can exclude over the years as a recovery of the cost cannot exceed your total cost. Any unrecovered cost at your (or the last annuitant's) death is allowed as a miscellaneous itemized deduction on the final return of the decedent. This deduction is not subject to the 2%-of-adjusted-gross-income limit.

Exclusion not limited to cost. If your annuity starting date is before 1987, you can continue to take your monthly exclusion for as long as you receive your annuity. If you chose a joint and survivor annuity, your survivor can continue to take the survivor's exclusion figured as of the annuity starting date. The total exclusion may be more than your cost.

> ### TAXALERT
> Your cost includes contributions by your employer if you were required to include the amounts in your gross income.
> For distributions on or after October 22, 2004, your cost will include only amounts that have been previously taxed either in the U.S. or in a foreign jurisdiction.

Simplified Method

Under the Simplified Method, you figure the tax-free part of each annuity payment by dividing your cost by the total number of anticipated monthly payments. For an annuity that is payable for the lives of the annuitants, this number is based on the annuitants' ages on the annuity starting date and is determined from a table. For any other annuity, this number is the number of monthly annuity payments under the contract.

Who must use the Simplified Method. You must use the Simplified Method if your annuity starting date is after November 18, 1996, and you both:

1. Receive pension or annuity payments from a qualified employee plan, qualified employee annuity, or a tax-sheltered annuity (403(b)) plan, and
2. On your annuity starting date, you were either under age 75, or entitled to less than 5 years of guaranteed payments.

Guaranteed payments. Your annuity contract provides guaranteed payments if a minimum number of payments or a minimum amount (for example, the amount of your investment) is payable even if you and any survivor annuitant do not live to receive the minimum. If the minimum amount is less than the total amount of the payments you are to receive, barring death, during the first 5 years after payments begin (figured by ignoring any payment increases), you are entitled to less than 5 years of guaranteed payments.

How to use the Simplified Method. Complete the Simplified Method Worksheet in Publication 575 to figure your taxable annuity for 2014.

Single-life annuity. If your annuity is payable for your life alone, use Table 1 at the bottom of the worksheet to determine the total number of expected monthly payments. Enter on line 3 the number shown for your age at the annuity starting date.

Multiple-lives annuity. If your annuity is payable for the lives of more than one annuitant, use Table 2 at the bottom of the worksheet to determine the total number of expected monthly payments. Enter on line 3 the number shown for the combined ages of you and the youngest survivor annuitant at the annuity starting date.

However, if your annuity starting date is before 1998, do not use Table 2 and do not combine the annuitants' ages. Instead you must use Table 1 and enter on line 3 the number shown for the primary annuitant's age on the annuity starting date.

Example. Bill Smith, age 65, began receiving retirement benefits in 2014, under a joint and survivor annuity. Bill's annuity starting date is January 1, 2014. The benefits are to be paid for the joint lives of Bill and his wife Kathy, age 65. Bill had contributed $31,000 to a qualified plan and had received no distributions before the annuity starting date. Bill is to receive a retirement benefit of $1,200 a month, and Kathy is to receive a monthly survivor benefit of $600 upon Bill's death.

Bill must use the Simplified Method to figure his taxable annuity because his payments are from a qualified plan and he is under age 75. Because his annuity is payable over the lives of more than one annuitant, he uses his and Kathy's combined ages and Table 2 at the bottom of the worksheet in completing line 3 of the worksheet. His completed worksheet is shown in Worksheet 10-A.

Bill's tax-free monthly amount is $100 ($31,000 ÷ 310) as shown on line 4 of the worksheet. Upon Bill's death, if Bill has not recovered the full $31,000 investment, Kathy will also exclude $100 from her $600 monthly payment. The full amount of any annuity payments received after 310 payments are paid must be included in gross income.

If Bill and Kathy die before 310 payments are made, a miscellaneous itemized deduction will be allowed for the unrecovered cost on the final income tax return of the last to die. This deduction is not subject to the 2%-of-adjusted-gross-income limit.

Who must use the General Rule. You must use the General Rule if you receive pension or annuity payments from:
- A nonqualified plan (such as a private annuity, a purchased commercial annuity, or a nonqualified employee plan), or
- A qualified plan if you are age 75 or older on your annuity starting date and your annuity payments are guaranteed for at least 5 years.

Annuity starting before November 19, 1996. If your annuity starting date is after July 1, 1986, and before November 19, 1996, you had to use the General Rule for either circumstance just described. You also had to use it for any fixed-period annuity. If you did not have to use the General Rule, you could have chosen to use it. If your annuity starting date is before July 2, 1986, you had to use the General Rule unless you could use the Three-Year Rule.

If you had to use the General Rule (or chose to use it), you must continue to use it each year that you recover your cost.

Who cannot use the General Rule. You cannot use the General Rule if you receive your pension or annuity from a qualified plan and none of the circumstances described in the preceding discussions apply to you. See *Who must use the Simplified Method*, earlier.

Records

Be sure to keep a copy of the completed worksheet; it will help you figure your taxable annuity next year.

More information. For complete information on using the General Rule, including the actuarial tables you need, see Publication 939.

Worksheet 10-A. **Simplified Method Worksheet for Bill Smith**   *Keep for Your Records*

1. Enter the total pension or annuity payments received this year. Also, add this amount to the total for Form 1040, line 16a, or Form 1040A, line 12a	**1.** 14,400
2. Enter your cost in the plan (contract) at the annuity starting date plus any death benefit exclusion*. See *Cost (Investment in the Contract)*, earlier	**2.** 31,000

Note: *If your annuity starting date was **before this year** and you completed this worksheet last year, skip line 3 and enter the amount from line 4 of last year's worksheet on line 4 below (even if the amount of your pension or annuity has changed). Otherwise, go to line 3.*

3. Enter the appropriate number from Table 1 below. **But** if your annuity starting date was **after** 1997 **and** the payments are for your life and that of your beneficiary, enter the appropriate number from Table 2 below	**3.** 310
4. Divide line 2 by the number on line 3	**4.** 100
5. Multiply line 4 by the number of months for which this year's payments were made. If your annuity starting date was **before** 1987, enter this amount on line 8 below and skip lines 6, 7, 10, and 11. Otherwise, go to line 6	**5.** 1,200
6. Enter any amounts previously recovered tax free in years after 1986. This is the amount shown on line 10 of your worksheet for last year	**6.** -0-
7. Subtract line 6 from line 2	**7.** 31,000
8. Enter the ***smaller*** of line 5 or line 7	**8.** 1,200
9. **Taxable amount for year.** Subtract line 8 from line 1. Enter the result, but not less than zero. Also, add this amount to the total for Form 1040, line 16b, or Form 1040A, line 12b	**9.** 13,200

Note: *If your Form 1099-R shows a larger taxable amount, use the amount figured on this line instead. If you are a retired public safety officer, see Insurance Premiums for Retired Public Safety Officers in Publication 575 before entering an amount on your tax return.*

10. Was your annuity starting date before 1987?	
☐ Yes. **STOP.** Do not complete the rest of this worksheet.	
☑ No. Add lines 6 and 8. This is the amount you have recovered tax free through 2013. You will need this number if you need to fill out this worksheet next year	**10.** 1,200
11. **Balance of cost to be recovered**. Subtract line 10 from line 2. If zero, you will not have to complete this worksheet next year. The payments you receive next year will generally be fully taxable	**11.** 29,800

TABLE 1 FOR LINE 3 ABOVE

	AND your annuity starting date was–	
IF the age at annuity starting date was...	before November 19, 1996, enter on line 3...	after November 18, 1996, enter on line 3...
55 or under	300	360
56-60	260	310
61-65	240	260
66-70	170	210
71 or older	120	160

TABLE 2 FOR LINE 3 ABOVE

IF the combined ages at annuity starting date were...	THEN enter on line 3...
110 or under	410
111-120	360
121-130	310
131-140	260
141 or older	210

*A death benefit exclusion (up to $5,000) applied to certain benefits received by employees who died before August 21, 1996.

Taxation of Nonperiodic Payments

Nonperiodic distributions are also known as amounts not received as an annuity. They include all payments other than periodic payments and corrective distributions. Examples of nonperiodic payments are cash withdrawals, distributions of current earnings, certain loans, and the value of annuity contracts transferred without full and adequate consideration.

Corrective distributions of excess plan contributions. Generally, if the contributions made for you during the year to certain retirement plans exceed certain limits, the excess is taxable to you. To correct an excess, your plan may distribute it to you (along with any income earned on the excess). For information on plan contribution limits and how to report corrective distributions of excess contributions, see *Retirement Plan Contributions* under *Employee Compensation* in Publication 525.

Figuring the taxable amount of nonperiodic payments. How you figure the taxable amount of a nonperiodic distribution depends on whether it is made before the annuity starting date, or on or after the annuity starting date. If it is made before the annuity starting date, its tax treatment also depends on whether it is made under a qualified or nonqualified plan. If it is made under a nonqualified plan, its tax treatment depends on whether it fully discharges the contract, is received under certain life insurance or endowment contracts, or is allocable to an investment you made before August 14, 1982.

Annuity starting date. The annuity starting date is either the first day of the first period for which you receive an annuity payment under the contract or the date on which the obligation under the contract becomes fixed, whichever is later.

Distribution on or after annuity starting date. If you receive a nonperiodic payment from your annuity contract on or after the annuity starting date, you generally must include all of the payment in gross income.

Distribution before annuity starting date. If you receive a nonperiodic distribution before the annuity starting date from a qualified retirement plan, you generally can allocate only part of it to the cost of the contract. You exclude from your gross income the part that you allocate to the cost. You include the remainder in your gross income.

If you receive a nonperiodic distribution before the annuity starting date from a plan other than a qualified retirement plan (nonqualified plan), it is allocated first to earnings (the taxable part) and then to the cost of the contract (the tax-free part). This allocation rule applies, for example, to a commercial annuity contract you bought directly from the issuer.

For more information, see *Figuring the Taxable Amount* under *Taxation of Nonperiodic Payments* in Publication 575.

EXPLANATION

If you receive a distribution and, to avoid the current tax, decide to roll it over into another retirement vehicle such as an IRA, you still are required to show the total amount received on line 16a (or line 12a, Form 1040A). However, on line 16b (or line 12b, Form 1040A) show the taxable amount as zero. Also, enter "Rollover" next to line 16b (or line 12b, Form 1040A).

Lump-Sum Distributions

A lump-sum distribution is the distribution or payment in one tax year of a plan participant's entire balance from all of the employer's qualified plans of one kind (for example, pension, profit-sharing, or stock bonus plans). A distribution from a nonqualified plan (such as a privately purchased commercial annuity or a section 457 deferred compensation plan of a state or local government or tax-exempt organization) cannot qualify as a lump-sum distribution.

The participant's entire balance from a plan does not include certain forfeited amounts. It also does not include any deductible voluntary employee contributions allowed by the plan after 1981 and before 1987. For more information about distributions that do not qualify as lump-sum distributions, see *Distributions that do not qualify* under *Lump-Sum Distributions* in Publication 575.

TAXALERT

A plan may not distribute your vested accrued benefit to you without your consent (and the consent of your spouse if the qualified joint and survivor annuity rules apply) unless the present value of your accrued benefit is $5,000 or less. Effective for distributions made after December 31, 2001, in determining your accrued benefit for purposes of the $5,000 limitation on involuntary distributions, employers may disregard benefits and related earnings, which are attributable to rollover contributions. Involuntary distributions that exceed $1,000 must be rolled over automatically to a designated IRA, unless you affirmatively elect to have the distribution transferred to a different IRA or qualified plan, or to receive it directly.

> ### TAXPLANNER
>
> If you change jobs and plan to participate in your new employer's plan, you may want to consider a "plan-to-plan" transfer to the new plan, if your new employer allows. If an amount is transferred from one qualified plan to another, no amount will be required to be withheld on the amount transferred from your old employer's plan. While there is nothing in the law that requires your new employer to accept transferred amounts, some employers may do this as an accommodation to new employees.
>
> Plan-to-plan transfers have certain advantages over rollovers. See _Rollovers_, later in this chapter.

If you receive a lump-sum distribution from a qualified employee plan or qualified employee annuity and the plan participant was born before January 2, 1936, you may be able to elect optional methods of figuring the tax on the distribution. The part from active participation in the plan before 1974 may qualify as capital gain subject to a 20% tax rate. The part from participation after 1973 (and any part from participation before 1974 that you do not report as capital gain) is ordinary income. You may be able to use the 10-year tax option, discussed later, to figure tax on the ordinary income part.

Use Form 4972 to figure the separate tax on a lump-sum distribution using the optional methods. The tax figured on Form 4972 is added to the regular tax figured on your other income. This may result in a smaller tax than you would pay by including the taxable amount of the distribution as ordinary income in figuring your regular tax.

How to treat the distribution. If you receive a lump-sum distribution, you may have the following options for how you treat the taxable part.

- Report the part of the distribution from participation before 1974 as a capital gain (if you qualify) and the part from participation after 1973 as ordinary income.
- Report the part of the distribution from participation before 1974 as a capital gain (if you qualify) and use the 10-year tax option to figure the tax on the part from participation after 1973 (if you qualify).
- Use the 10-year tax option to figure the tax on the total taxable amount (if you qualify).
- Roll over all or part of the distribution. See _Rollovers_, later. No tax is currently due on the part rolled over. Report any part not rolled over as ordinary income.
- Report the entire taxable part of the distribution as ordinary income on your tax return.

The first three options are explained in the following discussions.

Electing optional lump-sum treatment. You can choose to use the 10-year tax option or capital gain treatment only once after 1986 for any plan participant. If you make this choice, you cannot use either of these optional treatments for any future distributions for the participant.

Taxable and tax-free parts of the distribution. The taxable part of a lump-sum distribution is the employer's contributions and income earned on your account. You may recover your cost in the lump sum and any net unrealized appreciation (NUA) in employer securities tax free.

Cost. In general, your cost is the total of:

- The plan participant's nondeductible contributions to the plan,
- The plan participant's taxable costs of any life insurance contract distributed,
- Any employer contributions that were taxable to the plan participant, and
- Repayments of any loans that were taxable to the plan participant.

You must reduce this cost by amounts previously distributed tax free.

**Net unrealized appreciation (NUA).** The NUA in employer securities (box 6 of Form 1099-R) received as part of a lump-sum distribution is generally tax free until you sell or exchange the securities. (For more information, see _Distributions of employer securities_ under _Taxation of Non-periodic Payments_ in Publication 575.)

EXPLANATION

Employer securities distributed as part of a lump-sum distribution may have increased in value after they were purchased by the trust that is making the distribution. This increase is called "net unrealized appreciation." It is not taxed at the time of the lump-sum distribution.

If you later sell these securities, any gain is taxed as a long-term capital gain (i.e., as if held for more than 12 months)—up to the amount of your net unrealized appreciation (NUA). Any gain above this amount is a long-term capital gain only if the employee holds the stock after distribution for more than 12 months prior to selling it.

You may also elect not to use this treatment on your tax return and instead treat the NUA as part of your lump-sum distribution. This may be desirable if you have tax losses that can offset the amount of NUA.

You may not claim a loss if you receive stock that is worth less than your total contributions to the plan. You may claim a loss when you sell the stock if it is sold for less than the amount of your own after-tax employee contributions allocated to the shares of stock sold.

Example

Assume that Widget Company's pension trust used the company's contribution for Sarah Jones to purchase 100 shares of Widget Company common stock at $10 per share on January 10, 2001. These securities were given to Sarah Jones as part of a lump-sum distribution on January 3, 2014, when their value had risen to $15 per share. Sarah is taxed on the $10 per share that was contributed by Widget, but she is not taxed on the NUA of $5 per share on January 3, 2014.

If Sarah sold the 100 shares of Widget Company stock on January 10, 2014, for $25 per share, $500 of the gain [($15 − $10) × 100 shares] attributed to NUA would be taxed as long-term capital gain. The balance of the gain, $1,000 [($25 − $5 − $10) × 100 shares], would be taxed as a short-term capital gain, since Sarah did not hold the securities for more than 12 months from the distribution date.

If Sarah had made her own after-tax contributions of $1,700 to the pension trust and received Widget Company stock valued at only $1,000 at the time of the lump-sum distribution, she could not have claimed a loss at that time. However, if she later sold the stock, she would compare her proceeds with $1,700 to determine if she had a gain or a loss on the sale.

TAXPLANNER

If you receive only employer securities in an eligible rollover distribution (or employer securities and less than $200 in cash), there is no mandatory 20% withholding requirement. See *Rollovers*, on the next page. Therefore, it may be beneficial under some circumstances for you to receive an eligible rollover distribution consisting solely of employer securities and up to $200 in cash rather than all cash or a mix of cash (greater than $200) and employer securities.

Capital Gain Treatment

Capital gain treatment applies only to the taxable part of a lump-sum distribution resulting from participation in the plan before 1974. The amount treated as capital gain is taxed at a 20% rate. You can elect this treatment only once for any plan participant, and only if the plan participant was born before January 2, 1936.

Complete Part II of Form 4972 to choose the 20% capital gain election. For more information, see *Capital Gain Treatment* under *Lump-Sum Distributions* in Publication 575.

10-Year Tax Option

The 10-year tax option is a special formula used to figure a separate tax on the ordinary income part of a lump-sum distribution. You pay the tax only once, for the year in which you receive the distribution, not over the next 10 years. You can elect this treatment only once for any plan participant, and only if the plan participant was born before January 2, 1936.

The ordinary income part of the distribution is the amount shown in box 2a of the Form 1099-R given to you by the payer, minus the amount, if any, shown in box 3. You also can treat the capital gain part of the distribution (box 3 of Form 1099-R) as ordinary income for the 10-year tax option if you do not choose capital gain treatment for that part.

Complete Part III of Form 4972 to choose the 10-year tax option. You must use the special Tax Rate Schedule shown in the instructions for Part III to figure the tax. Publication 575 illustrates how to complete Form 4972 to figure the separate tax.

Rollovers

If you withdraw cash or other assets from a qualified retirement plan in an eligible rollover distribution, you can defer tax on the distribution by rolling it over to another qualified retirement plan or a traditional IRA.

For this purpose, the following plans are qualified retirement plans.
- A qualified employee plan.
- A qualified employee annuity.
- A tax-sheltered annuity plan (403(b) plan).
- An eligible state or local government section 457 deferred compensation plan.

TAXSAVER
The distribution from a qualified plan is includible in the taxpayer's gross income subject to tax, except to the extent the distribution consists of a return of after-tax contributions or is rolled over. (See *Can You Move Amounts Into a Roth IRA?* in chapter 17, *Individual retirement arrangements (IRAs)*, for more information.)

TAXSAVER
Distributions from a qualified retirement plan can be rolled over directly to a Roth IRA regardless of the amount of a taxpayer's adjusted gross income. Section 401(k), 403(b), and governmental 457(b) plans also have the option, if they so choose, to permit participants to roll their pre-tax account balances into a designated Roth account within the same plan.

TAXSAVER
If you want to roll over the taxable portion of your income to a traditional IRA (so it is not currently taxed) and your basis to a Roth IRA so the earnings on the basis won't be taxed when eventually distributed, the safest way to do that is to have the plan distribute the full amount to you (withholding the necessary 20%). Then within 60 days of the distribution, (in this order) roll over the taxable amount plus other funds equal to the amount withheld to a traditional IRA, and then on the next day (or after the first rollover and before 60 days from the date of the distribution), roll the remaining amount (all basis) to the Roth IRA. In this way, you will pay no tax on the distribution now and the earnings on the basis will not be taxed on eventual distribution.

Eligible rollover distributions. Generally, an eligible rollover distribution is any distribution of all or any part of the balance to your credit in a qualified retirement plan. For information about exceptions to eligible rollover distributions, see Publication 575.

Rollover of nontaxable amounts. You may be able to roll over the nontaxable part of a distribution (such as your after-tax contributions) made to another qualified retirement plan that is a qualified employee plan or a 403(b) plan, or to a traditional or Roth IRA. The transfer must be made either through a direct rollover to a qualified plan or 403(b) plan that separately accounts for the taxable and nontaxable parts of the rollover or through a rollover to a traditional or Roth IRA.

If you roll over only part of a distribution that includes both taxable and nontaxable amounts, the amount you roll over is treated as coming first from the taxable part of the distribution.

Any after-tax contributions that you roll over into your traditional IRA become part of your basis (cost) in your IRAs. To recover your basis when you take distributions from your IRA, you must complete Form 8606 for the year of the distribution. For more information, see the Form 8606 instructions.

TAXALERT
Distributions of after-tax contributions from a qualified retirement plan can be rolled over to either a defined contribution or defined benefit plan or to a tax-sheltered annuity that accepts such rollovers of after-tax contributions. A rollover must be done directly from the trustee of the old plan to the trustee of the new plan, and the plan to which the rollover is made must separately account for the after-tax contributions and earnings thereon. (There is no requirement that a plan accept rollovers of after-tax contributions.)

Direct rollover option. You can choose to have any part or all of an eligible rollover distribution paid directly to another qualified retirement plan that accepts rollover distributions or to a traditional or Roth IRA. If you choose the direct rollover option, or have an automatic rollover, no tax will be withheld from any part of the distribution that is directly paid to the trustee of the other plan.

Payment to you option. If an eligible rollover distribution is paid to you, 20% generally will be withheld for income tax. However, the full amount is treated as distributed to you even though you actually receive only 80%. You generally must include in income any part (including the part withheld) that you do not roll over within 60 days to another qualified retirement plan or to a traditional or Roth IRA. (See *Pensions and Annuities* under *Tax Withholding for 2014* in chapter 4.)

Time for making rollover. You generally must complete the rollover of an eligible rollover distribution paid to you by the 60th day following the day on which you receive the distribution from your employer's plan. (If an amount distributed to you becomes a frozen deposit in a financial institution during the 60-day period after you receive it, the rollover period is extended for the period during which the distribution is in a frozen deposit in a financial institution.)

The IRS may waive the 60-day requirement where the failure to do so would be against equity or good conscience, such as in the event of a casualty, disaster, or other event beyond your reasonable control.

The administrator of a qualified plan must give you a written explanation of your distribution options within a reasonable period of time before making an eligible rollover distribution.

Qualified domestic relations order (QDRO). You may be able to roll over tax free all or part of a distribution from a qualified retirement plan that you receive under a QDRO. If you receive the distribution as an employee's spouse or former spouse (not as a nonspousal beneficiary), the rollover rules apply to you as if you were the employee. You can roll over the distribution from the plan into a traditional IRA or to another eligible retirement plan. See *Rollovers* in Publication 575 for more information on benefits received under a QDRO.

Rollover by surviving spouse. You may be able to roll over tax free all or part of a distribution from a qualified retirement plan you receive as the surviving spouse of a deceased employee. The rollover rules apply to you as if you were the employee. You can roll over a distribution into a qualified retirement plan or a traditional or Roth IRA. For a rollover to a Roth IRA, see *Rollovers to Roth IRAs*, later.

A distribution paid to a beneficiary other than the employee's surviving spouse is generally not an eligible rollover distribution. However, see *Rollovers by nonspouse beneficiary* next.

Rollovers by nonspouse beneficiary. If you are a designated beneficiary (other than a surviving spouse) of a deceased employee, you may be able to roll over tax free all or a portion of a distribution you receive from an eligible retirement plan of the employee. The distribution must be a direct trustee-to-trustee transfer to your traditional or Roth IRA that was set up to receive the distribution. The transfer will be treated as an eligible rollover distribution and the receiving plan will be treated as an inherited IRA. For information on inherited IRAs, see *What if You Inherit an IRA?* in chapter 1 of Publication 590, Individual Retirement Arrangements (IRAs).

> **Caution**
>
> *If you decide to roll over an amount equal to the distribution before withholding, your contribution to the new plan or IRA must include other money (for example, from savings or amounts borrowed) to replace the amount withheld.*

EXPLANATION

An inherited IRA is still subject to the minimum required distribution rules (MRD) that would have otherwise applied. See chapter 17, *Individual retirement arrangements (IRAs)*, for more details on MRDs.

Any distribution attributable to an employee that is paid to the employee's surviving spouse is treated in the same manner as if the spouse were the employee. The same rule applies if any distribution attributable to an employee is paid to a spouse or a former spouse as an "alternate payee" under a QDRO. A distribution made to the surviving spouse of an employee (or an alternate payee under a QDRO) is an eligible rollover distribution if it meets the requirements explained earlier. For further details, consult your tax advisor.

TAXPLANNER

Be certain to inform your plan administrator if you wish to change the beneficiary of your qualified retirement plan. Generally, the designated beneficiary on file with your plan administrator will be treated as the beneficiary of your plan even if you have subsequently changed the beneficiary under other agreements, such as a divorce settlement. It is a good idea to review your

ey.com/EYTaxGuide   Chapter 10 | Retirement plans, pensions, and annuities   249

Retirement bonds. If you redeem retirement bonds purchased under a qualified bond purchase plan, you can roll over the proceeds that exceed your basis tax free into an IRA (as discussed in Publication 590) or a qualified employer plan.

Designated Roth accounts. You can roll over an eligible rollover distribution from a designated Roth account into another designated Roth account or a Roth IRA. If you want to roll over the part of the distribution that is not included in income, you must make a direct rollover of the entire distribution or you can roll over the entire amount (or any portion) to a Roth IRA. For more information on rollovers from designated Roth accounts, see *Rollovers* in Publication 575.

   In-plan rollovers to designated Roth accounts. If you are a plan participant in a 401(k), 403(b), or 457(b) plan, your plan may permit you to roll over amounts in those plans to a designated Roth account within the same plan. The rollover of any untaxed amounts must be included in income. See *Designated Roth accounts* under *Rollovers* in Publication 575 for more information.

TAXPLANNER

Not all plans offer this rollover option, so you need to check with your employer.

TAXALERT

Before 2013, rollovers from a pre-tax account to a Roth account within a plan were allowed only with respect to funds the individual plan participants otherwise had a right to withdraw from the plan; usually because the participant either reached age 59½ or separated from service. Due to a 2012 tax law change, beginning in 2013, any amount in a non-Roth account can be converted to a Roth account in the same plan, whether or not the amount is otherwise eligible for distribution. This tax law significantly expanded the population of taxpayers who can take advantage of this option for converting pre-tax amounts held inside their 401(k), 403(b), and/or 457(b) plans to a Roth account.

   Just like a conversion to a Roth IRA (discussed in chapter 17, *Individual retirement arrangements (IRAs)*, the amount rolled over is includible in taxable income except to the extent it includes a return of after-tax contributions.

Rollovers to Roth IRAs. You can roll over distributions directly from a qualified retirement plan (other than a designated Roth account) to a Roth IRA.

   You must include in your gross income distributions from a qualified retirement plan (other than a designated Roth account) that you would have had to include in income if you had not rolled them over into a Roth IRA. You do not include in gross income any part of a distribution from a qualified retirement plan that is a return of contributions to the plan that were taxable to you when paid. In addition, the 10% tax on early distributions does not apply.

More information. For more information on the rules for rolling over distributions, see *Rollovers* in Publication 575.

TAXALERT

Distributions of after-tax contributions from a qualified retirement plan can be rolled over to either a defined contribution or defined benefit plan or to a tax-sheltered annuity that accepts such rollovers of after-tax contributions. A rollover must be done directly from the trustee of the old plan to the trustee of the new plan, and the plan to which the rollover is made must separately account for the after-tax contributions and earnings thereon. (There is no requirement that a plan accept rollovers of after-tax contributions.)

TAXPLANNER

Hardship distributions are not considered eligible rollover distributions. While they are subject to withholding, they are not subject to the mandatory 20% withholding rules that apply to eligible rollover distributions. If you are receiving a hardship distribution, you can elect to reduce the amount withheld from the distribution and retain more cash to satisfy the need giving rise to the hardship by filing a Form W-4P with your plan administrator. See the earlier discussion in this chapter on *Withholding and Estimated Tax*.

TAXPLANNER

If you receive a hardship distribution and another event occurs, such as separation from your employer or attainment of age 59½, so that the distribution is permitted without regard to hardship, you should consult your plan administrator to determine proper treatment of the distribution under your plan. Plans have two alternatives. First, the amount distributed after that event may be treated as eligible for rollover treatment. Alternatively, the distribution may be treated as *ineligible* for rollover even though another event, such as termination of employment, has occurred, which could entitle the recipient to a distribution without regard to hardship. Plans must be consistent in the treatment of all distributions.

Plans also have alternatives with respect to allocation of basis. If a segment of a distribution that includes a hardship distribution is not includible in gross income (e.g., after-tax contributions), that piece may be allocated to either the portion ineligible for rollover or the portion eligible for rollover (or between the two portions) using any reasonable method. Again, plans must be consistent in the treatment of the distributions. Consult your plan administrator for additional information.

TAXPLANNER

Remember, if you receive property (such as stock) as part of a rollover distribution, you cannot roll over cash in place of the property received unless the actual property is sold first. The proceeds from the bona fide sale may then be included in the rollover.

Explanation

Generally, an eligible rollover distribution means any distribution of all or any portion of an employee's balance in a qualified plan. Eligible rollover distributions do not include the following:

- Required minimum distributions (e.g., distributions at the later of age 70½ or retirement from the employer maintaining the plan—except 5% owners do not have the retirement-delay option). Distributions that are part of a series of substantially equal payments received at least annually over the life or life expectancy of the employee (or the joint lives or joint life expectancies of the employee and the employee's designated beneficiary), or over a period of at least 10 years;
- Certain corrective distributions made because of the plan's violation of the Internal Revenue Code's limitations. For example, excess contributions returned to highly compensated employees, because the plan fails the 401(k) nondiscrimination (ADP) test for a year;
- Loans treated as distributions because they violate the Internal Revenue Code's plan loan rules;
- Certain dividends paid on employer securities;
- Hardship distributions;
- The cost of life insurance.

TAXALERT

A qualified plan must allow participants the option of a direct rollover to other qualified plans or an IRA. However, there is nothing in the law that requires your new employer to accept these amounts. If the new employer's plan will not accept these amounts, they could be transferred directly from your old employer's plan to an IRA.

TAXPLANNER

Direct rollover. A direct rollover may be accomplished by the trustee making a wire transfer or mailing a check to the trustee of the recipient plan or IRA. The trustee may even provide you with a check and instruct you to deliver it to an eligible retirement plan or IRA. However, the check must be made payable only to the trustee or custodian of the eligible retirement plan, not to you. If you do a direct rollover, you can also roll over after-tax contributions to another qualified plan.

Explanation

You cannot be precluded from dividing an eligible rollover distribution into a portion you roll over and a portion you receive. However, your employer may not allow you to directly roll over any portion that is less than $500. Further, if there is basis in the qualified plan, the basis will be allocated pro rata between the direct rollover and the distribution to you.

TAXPLANNER

Employers may, but need not, exclude eligible rollover distributions that are less than $200 from the direct rollover option if the administrator reasonably believes that total eligible rollover distributions from the plan during the year will be less than $200. In addition, employers are not required to withhold from distributions of less than $200 if the administrator reasonably believes that total eligible rollover distributions from the plan during the year will be less than $200. It should be noted, however, that amounts of $200 or less that constitute an eligible rollover distribution are still eligible for rollover by you within 60 days after receipt (see discussion later).

An employer is not required to allow employees to have a direct rollover paid to more than one recipient plan. Therefore, if you wish to diversify an IRA investment, for example, you can subsequently roll over a distribution to another IRA or utilize an IRA trustee-to-trustee transfer. If an amount is subsequently transferred to a second IRA, it cannot be rolled over again for one year. However, there is no limit on direct IRA trustee-to-trustee transfers.

The withholding requirement on eligible rollover distributions from a qualified plan can be avoided on a distribution received currently simply by having amounts transferred directly to an IRA and then immediately withdrawing them from the IRA.

TAXALERT

Plan administrators are required to give plan participants a written notice explaining the rollover rules, including the direct rollover option and related tax rules. You may consider whether to have your benefits paid in a direct rollover or paid directly to you for at least 30 days after you receive this notice, unless you waive this right.

Explanation

There is a second way amounts can be rolled over. If your funds are paid out to you rather than transferred in a direct rollover, you may still roll over some or all of your eligible rollover distribution to an eligible retirement plan. You must complete the rollover by the 60th day following the day on which you receive the distribution. In this case, the plan administrator making the distribution will withhold 20% of the taxable part of the distribution as income tax, and in order to roll over the full distribution, you will have to use other funds to make up the 20% withheld. If you do not make up the amount withheld, you will be taxed on the amount withheld and may also owe a 10% early distribution tax on such amount. See *Tax on Early Distributions*, later in this chapter. In this type of rollover, after-tax contributions can only be rolled into an IRA but not into a qualified plan.

TAXPLANNER

One of the most difficult decisions you have to make when you near retirement is what to do with the amounts held in your qualified pension or profit-sharing plan. There are usually four choices:

1. **Retention in the plan.** If you have more than $5,000 vested in the plan when you terminate employment, the plan must permit you to leave your accrued benefit or account balance in the qualified plan until you reach the later of age 62 or the plan's normal retirement age. (If you have $5,000 or less vested in the plan, the plan may require that you receive your account balance in a lump sum whether or not you consent. However, the $5,000 just affects whether you have a choice about getting a distribution. It neither limits the tax consequences, such as the 10% excise tax on premature distribution, nor affects your ability to roll over the money to a traditional or Roth IRA.)
2. **Lump-sum distribution.** While virtually all defined contribution plans offer lump-sum payments of benefits, many defined benefit pension plans do not offer lump-sum payments. Other defined benefit pension plans pay lump sums only if the value of benefits is de minimis ($5,000 or less). If you receive a lump-sum from either type of plan, the tax rules are the same. You must roll the distribution over to another qualified plan or to an IRA within 60 days, or the lump-sum distribution (other than the return of after-tax contributions) generally will be taxed to you as ordinary income; the after-tax balance will not be taxed. If you were born before 1936, you may be eligible to pay tax based on 10-year income averaging (discussed earlier).

3. **Annuity.** Defined benefit pension plans and money purchase plans must provide benefits in the form of a joint and survivor annuity. However, an employee, with spousal consent if the employee is married, may agree to receive the money as a lump sum (if the plan so provides). In a defined benefit pension plan, the normal form of payment is described as a single life annuity and is converted into a joint and survivor annuity. You will receive that amount (generally monthly) while you survive and your spouse usually will receive a reduced benefit monthly if he or she survives you. Larger plans pay the annuity from their assets; smaller plans will normally buy the annuity from an insurance company. In the case of a money purchase plan or other individual account plan, the participant has an account and the monthly annuity will be dependent on the annuity the account can purchase from the insurance company when you commence payments. Annuities directly from a plan typically pay more than annuities purchased in the individual insurance market. This is because of "adverse selection," the idea that only the healthiest persons with the best genetic history will choose to use their lump sum to purchase an annuity. Income paid from an annuity is treated as ordinary regardless of whether the earnings actually resulted from qualified dividends and/or long-term capital gains.

4. **Rollover to an IRA or other eligible retirement plan.** There is no income tax required to be withheld on any portion of an eligible rollover distribution that is rolled over directly to a traditional IRA or other eligible retirement plan. The principal continues to earn income without tax until it is withdrawn. Withdrawals are taxed at ordinary income rates and are required to begin not later than April 1 of the calendar year following the calendar year in which the employee attains age 70½, or following the calendar year of retirement in the case of an employer plan where the employee is not a 5% owner. Withdrawals from the plan or IRA are required to be made over the life of such employee or over the lives of such employee and a designated beneficiary (or over a period not extending beyond the life expectancy of such employee or the joint life expectancy of such employee and a designated beneficiary). If the rollover is to a Roth IRA, discussed in the next paragraph, there are no required mandatory distributions while the participant is alive.

Beginning in 2010, taxpayers at all income levels, including those who are married filing separately, are permitted to roll over ("convert") a distribution from an employer qualified retirement plan and/or a traditional IRA into a Roth IRA. Also, a 2010 tax law allows 401(k), 403(b), and governmental 457(b) plans, if they so choose, to permit participants to roll their pre-tax account balances into a designated Roth account within the same plan. The amount distributed is taxable income at the time of the distribution, except to the extent it includes nontaxable amounts (e.g., after-tax contributions). Contributions and earnings in an employer qualified retirement plan or traditional IRA grow tax-free. However, when funds are ultimately withdrawn, they are taxable to the participant. Contributions to a Roth IRA or designated Roth account have already been taxed, but grow tax-free and future withdrawals are not taxed, provided the funds are not withdrawn prematurely (until age 59½ and five years from the date of conversion; however, tax-free distributions may also be made under other circumstances such as disability). For more information, see the section on *Roth IRAs* in chapter 17, *Individual retirement arrangements (IRAs)*.

TAXSAVER

If you want to roll over the taxable portion of a distribution to a traditional IRA (so it is not currently taxed), and your basis to a Roth IRA so the earnings on the basis won't be taxed when eventually distributed, the safest way to do it is to have the plan distribute the full amount to you (withholding the necessary 20%). Within 60 days of the distribution, (in this order) roll over the taxable amount plus other funds equal to the amount withheld to a traditional IRA, and then on the next day (or after the first rollover and before 60 days from the date of the distribution), roll the remaining amount (all basis) to the Roth IRA. In this way, you will pay no tax on the distribution now, and the earnings on the basis will not be taxed on eventual distribution. If you are considering rolling over only your basis amount to a Roth IRA, you should consult with your tax advisor, as this is a complicated area.

Example

Example 1—401(k) Plan. You have $100,000 in the company's 401(k) plan and you will be retiring shortly at age 65. You may have the following options, depending on the plan's distribution and other provisions:

Option 1—*Leave the $100,000 in the Plan.* Some plans require terminated participants to begin benefit payments at normal retirement age. However, many plans have the option of not requiring payments until April 1 of the year following the year the participant attains age 70½. Leaving amounts in the 401(k) plan as long as possible has some advantages, especially if you can direct the investments and are happy with the investment choices. A significant advantage is that you do not have to pay IRA administrative fees. It is also quite possible that the 401(k) plan allows investing in "wholesale" funds, which have lower fees than the "retail" funds you would have available for an IRA.

Option 2–*Take the $100,000 in the Form of a Lump-Sum Payment*. Taking the lump-sum payment is only the first of your decisions. Remember, other than social security, this money may be the only money you have to live on for a long retirement. Consider other sources of income, such as savings, other plans, benefits from a prior employer, existing IRAs, and continued employment. All of these factors go into what decisions you make.

Option 3–*Roll the $100,000 into an IRA*. Assuming you do not intend to spend the money immediately, another option is to directly roll it over to an IRA. (If you receive the distribution yourself and then roll it, the plan must withhold 20%–$20,000–for federal withholding, and to roll the entire distribution you will need to find that $20,000 from other resources.) Since you are older than 59½, you face no early distribution penalty, even if you take it all out the next day (if you've rolled it to a new Roth IRA, the rules are slightly different). Once you decide to directly roll it to an IRA, you will have to determine how to invest the money. Different IRAs may have different investment options and/or different fee structures. You should examine these before investing. Another alternative is to invest in an annuity through the IRA. An annuity pays a set monthly benefit for your life and the life of your spouse (if you elect). Individual annuities–even through an IRA–can be costly because only a select group of healthy people with good family health histories are inclined to purchase them.

Option 4–*If Available, Have the Plan Purchase an Annuity*. The example involves a 401(k) plan. Generally, such plans are not required to provide an annuity. However, some do. In that case the plan administrator would take your account balance and purchase an annuity from an insurance company. Such an annuity may be expensive because of the unique nature of persons wanting an annuity. The annuity must be in the form of a joint and at least 50% survivor benefit unless you and, where appropriate, your spouse waive that form for another form such as a single life annuity or a lump sum.

Example 2–Defined Benefit Plan. Assume you are a participant in a defined benefit plan and the plan would pay you a joint and 50% annuity of $12,000 per year while you are alive, and pay your spouse $6,000 a year after you die. Also assume the plan offers you the alternative of electing, with spousal consent, either an actuarially equivalent single life annuity of, say, $14,000 a year (not actuarially precise) or a one-time lump-sum payment of $100,000 (not actuarially precise).

Option 1–*Joint and 50% Annuity Starting Immediately*. All defined benefit pension plans and money purchase plans must offer you a joint and 50% survivor annuity (they generally also have to offer at least a joint and 75% survivor annuity; other offerings are possible). Typically, a defined benefit plan of any size will pay you the annuity directly from the plan. Employers maintaining such plans fund the plan on an aggregate employee basis over time and your benefit is determined in the form of an annuity then converted to other forms on an actuarial basis.

Option 2–*Single Life Annuity*. A joint and survivor annuity protects your spouse if you die before her/him. The greater the percentage, for example 75% vs. 50%, the greater the survivor benefit and generally the lower the joint benefit is (i.e., the benefit when you are alive). Whether a joint and survivor benefit is best and, if so, what size, depends on individual circumstances. Generally, if the other spouse has an annuity of his/her own of similar size, the joint and survivor benefit is unnecessary. Otherwise, it could be critical. There are downsides to an annuity. With an annuity, there is generally no money left if you die early and you cannot tap a larger monthly payment if you have needs for more money, for example because of medical costs. You also usually will not be able to leave any money for your heirs.

Option 3–*Lump Sum*. An annuity form avoids you running out of money if you live a long time (although inflation will cut into the value of those monthly payments). However, in many instances, an annuity results in your survivors not receiving the value of your unpaid benefits if you die early. You could have a lump sum transferred directly to an IRA, where you can manage the investments and the flow of funds. However, in such situations, you have to worry about not overspending early. You can try to take the money out over your life expectancy, but what "life expectancy" means is that half the people die before it and half live past it. If you are one of those fortunate to live beyond life expectancy (or your spouse is) you could find yourself with no money left in the IRA.

Example 3–Self-Employed or New Employer. If you will be self-employed during the year in which you retire, you can transfer your qualified pension plan account into a Keogh plan. The benefit of transferring your pension into a Keogh plan instead of an IRA is that, if you were born before January 2, 1936, you can be taxed using the 10-year averaging method (discussed earlier) if you withdraw the money from the Keogh in a lump-sum distribution. You cannot use the 10-year averaging method if you transfer your qualified pension plan account into an IRA. Many people find it easy to arrange to be self-employed in the year in which they retire. If the plan-to-plan transfer is done properly, you can preserve your pre-transfer service from the old plan for purposes of the 5-year minimum participation requirement. If you go to work for another employer immediately, you can directly transfer your balance to that employer's plan and preserve the 10-year averaging option. Remember, 10-year averaging is only available to those born before January 2, 1936.

The choices are tricky and require analysis under various assumptions of interest rates, life expectancy, medical expenses, current needs, and tax rates. Professional help is necessary; you should consult your tax advisor.

If you are a public safety officer (e.g., police, firefighters, and emergency medical technicians) who retires or becomes disabled, there is a special provision allowing you to withdraw up to $3,000 per year tax-free from your governmental retirement plan, if the distribution is used to purchase health, accident, or long-term insurance covering yourself, your spouse, or your dependents.

Special Additional Taxes

To discourage the use of pension funds for purposes other than normal retirement, the law imposes additional taxes on early distributions of those funds and on failures to withdraw the funds timely. Ordinarily, you will not be subject to these taxes if you roll over all early distributions you receive, as explained earlier, and begin drawing out the funds at a normal retirement age, in reasonable amounts over your life expectancy. These special additional taxes are the taxes on:

- Early distributions, and
- Excess accumulation (not receiving minimum distributions).

These taxes are discussed in the following sections.

If you must pay either of these taxes, report them on Form 5329. However, you do not have to file Form 5329 if you owe only the tax on early distributions and your Form 1099-R correctly shows a "1" in box 7. Instead, enter 10% of the taxable part of the distribution on Form 1040, line 58 and write "No" under the heading "Other Taxes" to the left of line 58.

Even if you do not owe any of these taxes, you may have to complete Form 5329 and attach it to your Form 1040. This applies if you meet an exception to the tax on early distributions but box 7 of your Form 1099-R does not indicate an exception.

Tax on Early Distributions

Most distributions (both periodic and nonperiodic) from qualified retirement plans and nonqualified annuity contracts made to you before you reach age 59½ are subject to an additional tax of 10%. This tax applies to the part of the distribution that you must include in gross income.

For this purpose, a qualified retirement plan is:

- A qualified employee plan,
- A qualified employee annuity plan,
- A tax-sheltered annuity plan, or
- An eligible state or local government section 457 deferred compensation plan (to the extent that any distribution is attributable to amounts the plan received in a direct transfer or rollover from one of the other plans listed here or an IRA).

5% rate on certain early distributions from deferred annuity contracts. If an early withdrawal from a deferred annuity is otherwise subject to the 10% additional tax, a 5% rate may apply instead. A 5% rate applies to distributions under a written election providing a specific schedule for the distribution of your interest in the contract if, as of March 1, 1986, you had begun receiving payments under the election. On line 4 of Form 5329, multiply the line 3 amount by 5% instead of 10%. Attach an explanation to your return.

Distributions from Roth IRAs allocable to a rollover from an eligible retirement plan within the 5-year period. If, within the 5-year period starting with the first day of your tax year in which you rolled over an amount from an eligible retirement plan to a Roth IRA, you take a distribution from the Roth IRA, you may have to pay the additional 10% tax on early distributions. You generally must pay the 10% additional tax on any amount attributable to the part of the rollover that you had to include in income. The additional tax is figured on Form 5329. For more information, see Form 5329 and its instructions. For information on qualified distributions from Roth IRAs, see *Additional Tax on Early Distributions* in chapter 2 of Publication 590.

Distributions from designated Roth accounts allocable to in-plan Roth rollovers within the 5-year period. If, within the 5-year period starting with the first day of your tax year in which you rolled over an amount from a 401(k), 403(b), or 457(b) plan to a designated Roth account, you take a distribution from the designated Roth account, you may have to pay the additional 10% tax on early distributions. You generally must pay the 10% additional tax on any amount attributable to the part of the in-plan rollover that you had to include in income. The additional tax is figured on Form 5329. For more information, see Form 5329 and its instructions. For information on qualified distributions from designated Roth accounts, see *Designated Roth accounts* under *Taxation of Periodic Payments* in Publication 575.

Exceptions to tax. Certain early distributions are excepted from the early distribution tax. If the payer knows that an exception applies to your early distribution, distribution code "2," "3," or "4" should be shown in box 7 of your Form 1099-R and you do not have to report the distribution on Form 5329. If an exception applies but distribution code "1" (early distribution, no known exception) is shown in box 7, you must file Form 5329. Enter the taxable amount of the distribution shown in box 2a of your Form 1099-R on line 1 of Form 5329. On line 2, enter the amount that can be excluded and the exception number shown in the Form 5329 instructions.

General exceptions. The tax does not apply to distributions that are:
- Made as part of a series of substantially equal periodic payments (made at least annually) for your life (or life expectancy) or the joint lives (or joint life expectancies) of you and your designated beneficiary (if from a qualified retirement plan, the payments must begin after your separation from service),
- Made because you are totally and permanently disabled, or
- Made on or after the death of the plan participant or contract holder.

TAXPLANNER

You should carefully consider whether substantially equal periodic distributions commencing before you attain age 59½ would be sufficient to satisfy your income needs. Although these distributions are not subject to the 10% early distribution tax, they will be subject to this tax if the amount of the distribution is modified (other than by reason of death, disability, or a change in method described later) either before you attain age 59½ or before the end of the calendar 5-year period beginning with the date of the first distribution and after you attain age 59½. In the year the distributions are modified, you will have to pay the 10% penalty tax on all of the distributions you have received to date, plus interest. For example, if you start receiving substantially equal periodic payments over your life expectancy in 2014 when you are age 58, and when you are age 62 in 2018 you take a larger distribution, you will have to pay the 10% penalty tax on all distributions received to date, plus interest. However, if you wait until the 5-year period ends, that is until 2019, there is no penalty if you modify the life expectancy distributions.

Payments are considered to be substantially equal periodic payments if they are made in accordance with one of three calculations: (1) the required minimum distribution method, (2) the fixed amortization method, or (3) the fixed annuitization method. Because of the rule against modification of substantially equal periodic payments, described earlier, individuals who chose annuitization or amortization (which require a fixed amount to be withdrawn each year) would have to pay a retroactive penalty on all of the distributions made, if they wanted to reduce the amount of money they received in order to keep their account from being dissipated. The IRS allows individuals who started distributions using the fixed amortization method or the fixed annuitization method to change to the required minimum distribution method once without incurring that penalty.

Additional exceptions for qualified retirement plans. The tax does not apply to distributions that are:
- From a qualified retirement plan (other than an IRA) after your separation from service in or after the year you reached age 55 (age 50 for qualified public safety employees),
- From a qualified retirement plan (other than an IRA) to an alternate payee under a qualified domestic relations order,
- From a qualified retirement plan to the extent you have deductible medical expenses that exceed 10% (or 7.5% if you or your spouse are age 65 or older) of your adjusted gross income, whether or not you itemize your deductions for the year,

- From an employer plan under a written election that provides a specific schedule for distribution of your entire interest if, as of March 1, 1986, you had separated from service and had begun receiving payments under the election,
- From an employee stock ownership plan for dividends on employer securities held by the plan,
- From a qualified retirement plan due to an IRS levy of the plan,
- From elective deferral accounts under 401(k) or 403(b) plans or similar arrangements that are qualified reservist distributions, or
- Phased retirement annuity payments made to federal employees. See Pub. 721 for more information on the phased retirement program.

Qualified public safety employees. If you are a qualified public safety employee, distributions made from a governmental defined benefit pension plan are not subject to the additional tax on early distributions. You are a qualified public safety employee if you provide police protection, firefighting services, or emergency medical services for a state or municipality, and you separated from service in or after the year you attained age 50.

Qualified reservist distributions. A qualified reservist distribution is not subject to the additional tax on early distributions. A qualified reservist distribution is a distribution (a) from elective deferrals under a section 401(k) or 403(b) plan, or a similar arrangement, (b) to an individual ordered or called to active duty (because he or she is a member of a reserve component) for a period of more than 179 days or for an indefinite period, and (c) made during the period beginning on the date of the order or call and ending at the close of the active duty period. You must have been ordered or called to active duty after September 11, 2001. For more information, see *Qualified reservist distributions* under *Special Additional Taxes* in Publication 575.

TAXPLANNER

Withdrawals from a 401(k), 403(b), or similar plan by members of the National Guard or Reserves while on active duty for at least 179 days after September 11, 2001, are not subject to the 10% additional tax on early withdrawals. (This exception to the 10% additional penalty tax is also available for similar distributions from an IRA. See *Exemption from Additional 10% Tax for Distributions Received by National Guard or Reservists Called to Active Duty* in chapter 17, *Individual retirement arrangements (IRAs)*.) A refund or credit of the 10% early withdrawal tax previously paid on distributions that qualify for exemption from this penalty tax may be obtained.

The distribution received may otherwise be subject to ordinary income tax in the year received. See *Taxation of Nonperiodic Payments*, earlier.

The law also permits any portion of such distributions to be contributed back into an IRA anytime within the 2-year period following the end of the period of active duty. Although amounts contributed are not eligible for an IRA deduction, you may obtain a refund of the regular income tax you previously paid on the distribution by filing an amended return. Distributions that are contributed into an IRA do not reduce the maximum amount that you can otherwise contribute to an IRA based on compensation you earned during the year.

Additional exceptions for nonqualified annuity contracts. The tax does not apply to distributions from:
- A deferred annuity contract to the extent allocable to investment in the contract before August 14, 1982,
- A deferred annuity contract under a qualified personal injury settlement,
- A deferred annuity contract purchased by your employer upon termination of a qualified employee plan or qualified employee annuity plan and held by your employer until your separation from service, or
- An immediate annuity contract (a single premium contract providing substantially equal annuity payments that start within 1 year from the date of purchase and are paid at least annually).

TAXPLANNER

Early distributions from IRAs are also subject to the 10% excise tax. The earlier list for qualified plans indicates those that do not apply to IRAs. IRAs also have some additional exceptions if they are:
- Made after separation from employment if, among other requirements, the individual received unemployment compensation for 12 consecutive weeks by reason of the separation, but only to the extent the distributions do not exceed the amount paid for medical insurance or qualified long-term care insurance during the year,
- Distributions to pay for certain higher education expenses, or

TAXSAVER

Note that the 10% excise tax also does not apply in the year of distribution if you roll over a qualifying distribution (including a direct rollover of an eligible rollover distribution). This is because the tax is applied only to taxable distributions. This helps to make rollovers an even more attractive alternative.

TAXORGANIZER

On Form 1099-R, distributions should be coded by the payer without regard to whether a rollover is made or anticipated (except for a direct rollover). Thus, for purposes of Form 1099-R reporting, a rollover that is planned or has already occurred should not be considered an exception to the early distribution penalty.

Example
If Ben Jones withdraws the total balance in his qualified plan, informs the plan administrator that the funds will be rolled over, is under age 59½, and meets no other exception under the early distribution rules, the Form 1099-R should contain a code "1" in box 7, "Early distribution, no known exception." If Mr. Jones then rolls over his distribution, he should properly report the rollover on his federal income tax return to avoid the early distribution penalty.

Tax on Excess Accumulation

To make sure that most of your retirement benefits are paid to you during your lifetime, rather than to your beneficiaries after your death, the payments that you receive from qualified retirement plans must begin no later than your required beginning date (defined later). The payments each year cannot be less than the required minimum distribution.

Required distributions not made. If the actual distributions to you in any year are less than the minimum required distribution for that year, you are subject to an additional tax. The tax equals 50% of the part of the required minimum distribution that was not distributed.

For this purpose, a qualified retirement plan includes:
- A qualified employee plan,
- A qualified employee annuity plan,
- An eligible section 457 deferred compensation plan, or
- A tax-sheltered annuity plan (403(b) plan) (for benefits accruing after 1986).

Waiver. The tax may be waived if you establish that the shortfall in distributions was due to reasonable error and that reasonable steps are being taken to remedy the shortfall. See the Instructions for Form 5329 for the procedure to follow if you believe you qualify for a waiver of this tax.

State insurer delinquency proceedings. You might not receive the minimum distribution because assets are invested in a contract issued by an insurance company in state insurer delinquency proceedings. If your payments are reduced below the minimum due to these proceedings, you should contact your plan administrator. Under certain conditions, you will not have to pay the 50% excise tax.

Required beginning date. Unless the rule for 5% owners applies, you generally must begin to receive distributions from your qualified retirement plan by April 1 of the year that follows the later of:
- The calendar year in which you reach age 70½, or
- The calendar year in which you retire from employment with the employer maintaining the plan.

However, your plan may require you to begin to receive distributions by April 1 of the year that follows the year in which you reach age 70½, even if you have not retired.

If you reached age 70½ in 2014, you may be required to receive your first distribution by April 1, 2015. Your required distribution then must be made for 2015 by December 31, 2015.

5% owners. If you are a 5% owner, you must begin to receive distributions by April 1 of the year that follows the calendar year in which you reach age 70½.

You are a 5% owner if, for the plan year ending in the calendar year in which you reach age 70½, you own (or are considered to own under section 318 of the Internal Revenue Code) more than 5% of the outstanding stock (or more than 5% of the total voting power of all stock) of the employer, or more than 5% of the capital or profits interest in the employer.

Age 70½. You reach age 70½ on the date that is 6 calendar months after the date of your 70th birthday.

For example, if you are retired and your 70th birthday was on June 30, 2014, you were age 70½ on December 30, 2014. If your 70th birthday was on July 1, 2014, you reached age 70½ on January 1, 2015.

Required distributions. By the required beginning date, as explained earlier, you must either:

- Receive your entire interest in the plan (for a tax-sheltered annuity, your entire benefit accruing after 1986), or
- Begin receiving periodic distributions in annual amounts calculated to distribute your entire interest (for a tax-sheltered annuity, your entire benefit accruing after 1986) over your life or life expectancy or over the joint lives or joint life expectancies of you and a designated beneficiary (or over a shorter period).

TAXALERT

The IRS has issued final regulations that provide the life expectancy and distribution period tables to be used for determining required minimum distributions (see Table 10-1).

Table 10-1. **Uniform Lifetime Table**

The following table is used for determining the distribution period for lifetime distributions to an employee (or IRA owner) in situations in which the employee's (or IRA owner's) spouse is either not the sole designated beneficiary or is the sole designated beneficiary but is not more than 10 years younger than the employee (or IRA owner).

Age	Distribution Period	Age	Distribution Period
70	27.4	93	9.6
71	26.5	94	9.1
72	25.6	95	8.6
73	24.7	96	8.1
74	23.8	97	7.6
75	22.9	98	7.1
76	22.0	99	6.7
77	21.2	100	6.3
78	20.3	101	5.9
79	19.5	102	5.5
80	18.7	103	5.2
81	17.9	104	4.9
82	17.1	105	4.5
83	16.3	106	4.2
84	15.5	107	3.9
85	14.8	108	3.7
86	14.1	109	3.4
87	13.4	110	3.1
88	12.7	111	2.9
89	12.0	112	2.6
90	11.4	113	2.4
91	10.2	114	2.1
92	10.2	115 and older	1.9

Explanation

Retirement plans must begin to make minimum distributions to you no later than April 1 of the calendar year following the later of:

1. The calendar year in which you reach age 70½, or
2. The calendar year in which you retire (not applicable to 5% owners or to any employee with respect to an IRA).

Roth IRAs do not have to satisfy any minimum distribution requirement while the participant is alive.

Explanation

Although plans must begin making minimum distributions by the later of the calendar year after you retire or the year after you turn 70½, they are not required to wait until you actually retire. They may begin making minimum distributions in the year after you reach retirement age under the plan. Your plan administrator can provide details on the provisions of your plan.

TAXPLANNER

If you work beyond age 70½ and are not a 5% owner, it may be advantageous to delay the minimum distributions (if your plan allows) and allow the amounts in the retirement plan to grow on a tax-deferred basis. You may also be able to defer the minimum distributions from your IRA, if you are still working, by transferring your IRA balance to an employer plan sponsored by the employer for whom you are working as long as you're not a 5% or more owner of that employer. Consult your plan administrator or tax advisor for more information on the decision to delay minimum distributions.

TAXPLANNER

Because the penalty for failure to receive required minimum distributions is severe, you must take steps to ensure that you receive these amounts on a timely basis. The minimum distribution rules are particularly onerous for IRA owners who are required to determine their minimum distributions on their own. The IRS has issued final regulations and guidance that will make it easier for IRA owners to meet the minimum required distribution requirements. If a minimum distribution is required with respect to an IRA for a calendar year and the IRA owner is alive at the beginning of the year, the IRA trustee must provide a statement to the IRA owner by January 31 of the calendar year regarding the required minimum distribution in accordance with two alternatives.

Under the first alternative, the IRA trustee must furnish the IRA owner with a statement of the amount of the required minimum distribution with respect to the IRA for the calendar year and the date by which such amount must be distributed. Under the second alternative, the IRA trustee must provide a statement to the IRA owner that: (1) informs the IRA owner that a minimum distribution with respect to the IRA is required for the calendar year and the date by which such amount must be distributed and (2) includes an offer to furnish the IRA owner, upon request, with a calculation of the amount of the required minimum distribution with respect to the IRA for that calendar year. If the IRA owner requests such a calculation, the IRA trustee must calculate the required minimum distribution for the IRA owner and report that amount to the IRA owner. IRA trustees may provide some IRA owners with statements that satisfy the first alternative and other IRA owners with statements that satisfy the second alternative.

TAXPLANNER

If you have made after-tax contributions to your employer's retirement plan (e.g., contributions other than pre-tax salary deferrals to a 401(k) plan or 403(b) tax-sheltered annuity), you may be able to satisfy the minimum distribution rules without being taxed for the first year (or possibly the first 2 years) the minimum distributions are required. This may be accomplished by: (1) electing to receive a lump-sum distribution from your retirement plan or IRA by April 1 of the year the minimum distributions are required to begin, (2) retaining the portion of the distribution that represents the tax-free return of your after-tax employee contributions, and (3) electing to roll over the remaining amount of the lump-sum distribution to another qualified retirement plan or IRA.

Example

Assume Dawn reaches age 70½ in 2014 and elects to retire in 2014. Also assume that Dawn has made a total of $40,000 in after-tax employee contributions to her employer's retirement plan over the years and has a balance of $100,000 in the plan as of the end of 2014. Dawn must receive the required minimum distribution (RMD) for 2014 by April 1, 2015. In addition, she must receive the RMD for 2015 by December 31, 2015. Assume the RMD amounts are $15,000 and $20,000 for 2014 and 2015, respectively.

Dawn elects to receive a lump-sum distribution of her entire $100,000 account balance by April 1, 2015; retains $35,000 of this amount attributable to her after-tax employee contributions; and rolls over $65,000 to an IRA within 60 days of the distribution. As a result, she will not be taxed on the $35,000 she did not roll over since this is a nontaxable return of her after-tax contributions. More importantly, such nontaxable amounts may be used to satisfy the minimum distribution requirements. In this example, the $35,000 distributed to Dawn by April 1, 2015, equaled the sum of the $15,000 that was required to be distributed by April 1, 2015, and the $20,000 that was required to be distributed to her by December 31, 2015. After the rollover, Dawn would have basis of $5,000 (the balance of her after-tax contributions rolled into the IRA) in her new IRA.

Additional information. For more information on this rule, see *Tax on Excess Accumulation* in Publication 575.

Form 5329. You must file Form 5329 if you owe tax because you did not receive a minimum required distribution from your qualified retirement plan.

Survivors and Beneficiaries

Generally, a survivor or beneficiary reports pension or annuity income in the same way the plan participant would have. However, some special rules apply. See Publication 575 for more information.

Survivors of employees. If you are entitled to receive a survivor annuity on the death of an employee who died, you can exclude part of each annuity payment as a tax-free recovery of the employee's investment in the contract. You must figure the taxable and tax-free parts of your annuity payments using the method that applies as if you were the employee.

Survivors of retirees. If you receive benefits as a survivor under a joint and survivor annuity, include those benefits in income in the same way the retiree would have included them in income. If you receive a survivor annuity because of the death of a retiree who had reported the annuity under the Three-Year Rule and recovered all of the cost tax free, your survivor payments are fully taxable.

If the retiree was reporting the annuity payments under the General Rule, you must apply the same exclusion percentage to your initial survivor annuity payment called for in the contract. The resulting tax-free amount will then remain fixed. Any increases in the survivor annuity are fully taxable.

If the retiree was reporting the annuity payments under the Simplified Method, the part of each payment that is tax free is the same as the tax-free amount figured by the retiree at the annuity starting date. This amount remains fixed even if the annuity payments are increased or decreased. See *Simplified Method*, earlier.

In any case, if the annuity starting date is after 1986, the total exclusion over the years cannot be more than the cost.

Estate tax deduction. If your annuity was a joint and survivor annuity that was included in the decedent's estate, an estate tax may have been paid on it. You can deduct the part of the total estate tax that was based on the annuity. The deceased annuitant must have died after the annuity starting date. (For details, see section 1.691(d)-1 of the regulations.) Deduct it in equal amounts over your remaining life expectancy.

If the decedent died before the annuity starting date of a deferred annuity contract and you receive a death benefit under that contract, the amount you receive (either in a lump sum or as periodic payments) in excess of the decedent's cost is included in your gross income as income in respect of a decedent for which you may be able to claim an estate tax deduction.

You can take the estate tax deduction as an itemized deduction on Schedule A, Form 1040. This deduction is not subject to the 2%-of-adjusted-gross-income limit on miscellaneous deductions. See Publication 559, Survivors, Executors, and Administrators, for more information on the estate tax deduction.

EXPLANATION

Example

Alexander dies while receiving an annuity worth $10,000. Alexander's beneficiary will receive $1,000 per year for the next 15 years. The estate tax figured with the annuity included is $4,500 more than when figured without the annuity.

The recipient may claim an itemized deduction (not subject to the 2%-of-adjusted-gross-income limitation) each year of $300 ($1,000/$15,000 × $4,500). In this computation, the $15,000 represents the total dollars that will be received over the 15-year period.

Chapter 11

Social security and equivalent railroad retirement benefits

ey.com/EYTaxGuide

Note

IRS Publication 17 (*Your Federal Income Tax*) has been updated by Ernst & Young LLP for 2014. Dates and dollar amounts shown are for 2014. Underlined type is used to indicate where IRS text has been updated. Places where text has been removed are indicated by the sentence: *Text intentionally omitted.*

ey.com/EYTaxGuide
Ernst & Young LLP will update the *EY Tax Guide 2015* website with relevant taxpayer information as it becomes available. You can also sign up for email alerts to let you know when changes have been made.

Introduction

Social security income and equivalent railroad retirement benefits were once tax-free. But that hasn't been the case since 1984. Potentially, up to 85% of the benefits you receive may be subject to income tax, depending on your filing status and total income for the year. Figuring out whether the benefits you receive are taxable is not an easy task. It requires navigating through complicated rules and numerous computations. This chapter will aid in simplifying your task. Among other things, it includes worksheets to help you make the necessary calculations.

This chapter explains the federal income tax rules for social security benefits and equivalent tier 1 railroad retirement benefits. It explains the following topics.
- How to figure whether your benefits are taxable.
- How to use the social security benefits worksheet (with examples).
- How to report your taxable benefits.
- How to treat repayments that are more than the benefits you received during the year.

Social security benefits include monthly retirement, survivor, and disability benefits. They do not include supplemental security income (SSI) payments, which are not taxable.

Equivalent tier 1 railroad retirement benefits are the part of tier 1 benefits that a railroad employee or beneficiary would have been entitled to receive under the social security system. They are commonly called the social security equivalent benefit (SSEB) portion of tier 1 benefits.

If you received these benefits during 2014, you should have received a Form SSA-1099, Social Security Benefit Statement, or Form RRB-1099, Payments by the Railroad Retirement Board. These forms show the amounts received and repaid, and taxes withheld for the year. You may receive more than one of these forms for the same year. You should add the amounts shown on all the Forms SSA-1099 and Forms RRB-1099 you receive for the year to determine the total amounts received and repaid, and taxes withheld for that year. See the *Appendix* at the end of Publication 915 for more information.

Note. When the term "benefits" is used in this chapter, it applies to both social security benefits and the SSEB portion of tier 1 railroad retirement benefits.

What is not covered in this chapter. This chapter does not cover the tax rules for the following railroad retirement benefits.
- Non-social security equivalent benefit (NSSEB) portion of tier 1 benefits.
- Tier 2 benefits.
- Vested dual benefits.
- Supplemental annuity benefits.

For information on these benefits, see Publication 575, Pension and Annuity Income.

This chapter does not cover the tax rules for social security benefits reported on Form SSA-1042S, Social Security Benefit Statement, or Form RRB-1042S, Statement for Nonresident Alien Recipients of: Payments by the Railroad Retirement Board. For information about these benefits, see Publication 519, U.S. Tax Guide for Aliens, and Publication 915, Social Security and Equivalent Railroad Retirement Benefits.

This chapter also does not cover the tax rules for foreign social security benefits. These benefits are taxable as annuities, unless they are exempt from U.S. tax or treated as a U.S. social security benefit under a tax treaty.

Useful Items

You may want to see:

Publication

☐ **505** Tax Withholding and Estimated Tax
☐ **575** Pension and Annuity Income
☐ **590** Individual Retirement Arrangements (IRAs)
☐ **915** Social Security and Equivalent Railroad Retirement Benefits

Forms (and Instructions)

☐ **1040-ES** Estimated Tax for Individuals
☐ **SSA-1099** Social Security Benefit Statement
☐ **RRB-1099** Payments by the Railroad Retirement Board
☐ **W-4V** Voluntary Withholding Request

TAXPLANNER

For additional social security and retirement information, you may want to consult the following websites: *www.ssa.gov*, *www.rrb.gov*, and *www.seniors.gov*.

Are Any of Your Benefits Taxable?

To find out whether any of your benefits may be taxable, compare the base amount for your filing status with the total of:

1. One-half of your benefits, plus
2. All your other income, including tax-exempt interest.

When making this comparison, do not reduce your other income by any exclusions for:

- Interest from qualified U.S. savings bonds,
- Employer-provided adoption benefits,
- Foreign earned income or foreign housing, or
- Income earned by bona fide residents of American Samoa or Puerto Rico.

Children's benefits. The rules in this chapter apply to benefits received by children. See *Who is taxed*, later.

TAXPLANNER

If you want to plan ahead, you can request an estimate of your social security benefits by filing Form SSA-7004, Your Social Security Statement. Copies of the form can be obtained from your local social security office, by calling (800) 772-1213, or by visiting *www.ssa.gov*. You can also receive a copy of your statement online at *www.socialsecurity.gov/mystatement*.

Explanation

Taxation of benefits. In figuring if any of your benefits are taxable, use the amount shown in box 5 of the Form SSA-1099 or Form RRB-1099 you received. If you received more than one form, add together the amount in box 5 of each form.

SSI payments. If you received any SSI payments during the year, do not include these payments in your social security benefits received. SSI payments are made under Title XVI of the Social Security Act. They are not taxable for federal income tax purposes.

Form SSA-1099. If you received or repaid social security benefits during 2014, you will receive Form SSA-1099, Social Security Benefit Statement. An IRS Notice 703 will be enclosed with your Form SSA-1099. This notice includes a worksheet you can use to determine if any of your benefits may be taxable. Keep this notice for your own records. Do not mail it to either the Internal Revenue Service or the SSA.

Every person who received social security benefits will receive a Form SSA-1099, even if the benefit is combined with another person's in a single check. If you receive benefits on more than one social security record, you may get more than one Form SSA-1099.

Figuring total income. To figure the total of one-half of your benefits plus your other income, use Worksheet 11-1 later in this discussion. If the total is more than your base amount, part of your benefits may be taxable.

If you are married and file a joint return for 2014, you and your spouse must combine your incomes and your benefits to figure whether any of your combined benefits are taxable. Even if your spouse did not receive any benefits, you must add your spouse's income to yours to figure whether any of your benefits are taxable.

Base amount. Your base amount is:

- $25,000 if you are single, head of household, or qualifying widow(er),
- $25,000 if you are married filing separately and lived apart from your spouse for all of 2014,
- $32,000 if you are married filing jointly, or
- $-0- if you are married filing separately and lived with your spouse at any time during 2014.

EXPLANATION

The filing requirements for individuals are based on income, age, and filing status (e.g., married filing jointly, single). See chapter 1, *Filing information.*

EXPLANATION

Social security and railroad retirement benefits are partially taxable if your *total income* (defined later in this paragraph) is more than $32,000 for married taxpayers filing jointly and $25,000 for single filers. If you are married filing separately and you lived with your spouse at any time during the year, your base amount is $0, which means that your social security retirement benefits are partially taxable regardless of your income level. Your *total income* is the sum of your adjusted gross income, tax-exempt income, excluded employer-provided adoption benefits, excluded foreign source income, excluded interest from U.S. savings bonds (interest excluded in connection with the payment of qualified education expenses), and one-half of your social security retirement benefits.

Tax-exempt income is *not taxable* for federal purposes, even if you receive social security benefits. However, it is one of the items taken into consideration in determining whether or not your income exceeds the threshold amount so that your social security benefits are taxable.

TAXSAVER

If you expect your total income (defined in the preceding explanation) to exceed the base amount ($32,000 if you are filing a joint return, $25,000 if you are filing single), you may wish to consider the following strategies:

- Defer the recognition of income by investing in U.S. savings bonds. Generally, the increase in value of the bonds issued at a discount (Series E and EE) is not taxable until you surrender the bonds. Additionally, if you hold the bonds until death, your heirs will recognize the income (assuming you did not elect to include in income the annual increase in the value of the bond).
- Purchase a certificate of deposit that matures in 2015 or later. None of the interest earned will be subject to tax in 2014, as long as any interest received this year would be penalized by the issuer of the CD upon withdrawal by the purchaser.
- Offset capital gains in 2014 by selling property in which you have unrealized capital losses.
- Stagger the recognition of income so that you have alternating years of higher income. Depending on your income level, you could structure income so that your social security benefits are taxed every other year. For example, when considering sources of cash flow, you could surrender U.S. savings bonds and sell appreciated property in alternate years. You could also schedule the maturity dates of U.S. Treasury notes and bills to ensure that your income is under the base amount in certain years.
- If you have earned income, consider contributing to your company's 401(k) plan, your not-for-profit 403(b) plan, or a deductible Individual Retirement Arrangement (IRA) account (see chapter 17, *Individual retirement arrangements (IRAs),* to determine if you qualify) to decrease your adjusted gross income and also reduce the taxable portion of your social security benefits.

TAXPLANNER

Tax-exempt income is added to your adjusted gross income for purposes of calculating how much, if any, of your social security benefits will be subject to tax. Keep this in mind when evaluating the after-tax rate of return of tax-exempt investments vs. taxable investments.

Worksheet 11-1. You can use Worksheet 11-1 to figure the amount of income to compare with your base amount. This is a quick way to check whether some of your benefits may be taxable.

Worksheet 11-1.   **A Quick Way To Check if Your Benefits May Be Taxable**

A.	Enter the amount from **box 5** of all your Forms SSA-1099 and RRB-1099. Include the full amount of any lump-sum benefit payments received in 2014, for 2014 and earlier years. (If you received more than one form, combine the amounts from box 5 and enter the total.) .... A._____

Note. If the amount on line A is zero or less, stop here; none of your benefits are taxable this year.

B.	Enter one-half of the amount on line A .... B._____
C.	Enter your taxable pensions, wages, interest, dividends, and other taxable income .... C._____
D.	Enter any tax-exempt interest income (such as interest on municipal bonds) plus any exclusions from income (<u>listed earlier</u>) .... D._____
E.	Add lines B, C, and D.. E._____

Note. Compare the amount on line E to your **base amount** for your filing status. If the amount on line E equals or is less than the **base amount** for your filing status, none of your benefits are taxable this year. If the amount on line E is more than your **base amount**, some of your benefits may be taxable. You need to complete Worksheet 1 in Publication 915 (or the Social Security Benefits Worksheet in your tax form instructions). If none of your benefits are taxable, but you otherwise must file a tax return, see <u>Benefits not taxable</u>, later, under *How To Report Your Benefits*.

Example. You and your spouse (both over 65) are filing a joint return for 2014 and you both received social security benefits during the year. In January 2015, you received a Form SSA-1099 showing net benefits of $7,500 in box 5. Your spouse received a Form SSA-1099 showing net benefits of $3,500 in box 5. You also received a taxable pension of $22,800 and interest income of $500. You did not have any tax-exempt interest income. Your benefits are not taxable for 2014 because your income, as figured in Worksheet 11-1, is not more than your base amount ($32,000) for married filing jointly.

Even though none of your benefits are taxable, you must file a return for 2014 because your taxable gross income ($23,300) exceeds the minimum filing requirement amount for your filing status.

Filled-in Worksheet 11-1.   **A Quick Way To Check if Your Benefits May Be Taxable**

A.	Enter the amount from *box 5* of all your Forms SSA-1099 and RRB-1099. Include the full amount of any lump-sum benefit payments received in 2014, for 2014 and earlier years. (If you received more than one form, combine the amounts from box 5 and enter the total.)... A. $11,000

Note. If the amount on line A is zero or less, stop here; none of your benefits are taxable this year.

B.	Enter one-half of the amount on line A .... B. 5,500
C.	Enter your taxable pensions, wages, interest, dividends, and other taxable income .... C. 23,300
D.	Enter any tax-exempt interest income (such as interest on municipal bonds) plus any exclusions from income (<u>listed earlier</u>)... D. -0-
E.	Add lines B, C, and D.. E. $28,800

(continued)

Filled-in Worksheet 11-1. *(Continued)*

> **Note.** Compare the amount on line E to your **base amount** for your filing status. If the amount on line E equals or is less than the **base amount** for your filing status, none of your benefits are taxable this year. If the amount on line E is more than your **base amount**, some of your benefits may be taxable. You need to complete Worksheet 1 in Publication 915 (or the Social Security Benefits Worksheet in your tax form instructions). If none of your benefits are taxable, but you otherwise must file a tax return, see *Benefits not taxable*, later, under *How To Report Your Benefits*.

Who is taxed. Benefits are included in the taxable income (to the extent they are taxable) of the person who has the legal right to receive the benefits. For example, if you and your child receive benefits, but the check for your child is made out in your name, you must use only your part of the benefits to see whether any benefits are taxable to you. One-half of the part that belongs to your child must be added to your child's other income to see whether any of those benefits are taxable to your child.

Repayment of benefits. Any repayment of benefits you made during 2014 must be subtracted from the gross benefits you received in 2014. It does not matter whether the repayment was for a benefit you received in 2014 or in an earlier year. If you repaid more than the gross benefits you received in 2014, see *Repayments More Than Gross Benefits*, later.

Your gross benefits are shown in box 3 of Form SSA-1099 or RRB-1099. Your repayments are shown in box 4. The amount in box 5 shows your net benefits for 2014 (box 3 minus box 4). Use the amount in box 5 to figure whether any of your benefits are taxable.

EXAMPLE

Assume that in 2013 you received $13,000 in social security benefits, and in 2014 you received $12,700. In March 2014, SSA notified you that you should have received only $12,500 in benefits in 2013. During 2014, you repaid $500 to SSA. The Form SSA-1099 you will receive for 2014 will show $12,700 in box 3 (gross amount) and $500 in box 4 (repayment). The amount in box 5 will show your net benefits of $12,200 ($12,700 minus $500). The amount in box 5 (the $12,200) will be the amount you will use to figure whether any of your benefits are taxable.

Tax withholding and estimated tax. You can choose to have federal income tax withheld from your social security benefits and/or the SSEB portion of your tier 1 railroad retirement benefits. If you choose to do this, you must complete a Form W-4V.

If you do not choose to have income tax withheld, you may have to request additional withholding from other income or pay estimated tax during the year. For details, see Publication 505 or the instructions for Form 1040-ES.

How To Report Your Benefits

If part of your benefits are taxable, you must use Form 1040 or Form 1040A. You cannot use Form 1040EZ.

Reporting on Form 1040. Report your net benefits (the total amount from box 5 of all your Forms SSA-1099 and Forms RRB-1099) on line 20a and the taxable part on line 20b. If you are married filing separately and you lived apart from your spouse for all of 2014, also enter "D" to the right of the word "benefits" on line 20a.

Reporting on Form 1040A. Report your net benefits (the total amount from box 5 of all your Forms SSA-1099 and Forms RRB-1099) on line 14a and the taxable part on line 14b. If you are married filing separately and you lived apart from your spouse for all of 2014, also enter "D" to the right of the word "benefits" on line 14a.

Benefits not taxable. If you are filing Form 1040EZ, do not report any benefits on your tax return. If you are filing Form 1040 or Form 1040A, report your net benefits (the total amount from box 5 of all your Forms SSA-1099 and Forms RRB-1099) on Form 1040, line 20a, or Form 1040A, line 14a. Enter -0- on Form 1040, line 20b, or Form 1040A, line 14b. If you are married filing separately and you lived apart from your spouse for all of 2014, also enter "D" to the right of the word "benefits" on Form 1040, line 20a, or Form 1040A, line 14a.

How Much Is Taxable?

If part of your benefits are taxable, how much is taxable depends on the total amount of your benefits and other income. Generally, the higher that total amount, the greater the taxable part of your benefits.

Maximum taxable part. Generally, up to 50% of your benefits will be taxable. However, up to 85% of your benefits can be taxable if either of the following situations applies to you.

- The total of one-half of your benefits and all your other income is more than $34,000 ($44,000 if you are married filing jointly).
- You are married filing separately and lived with your spouse at any time during 2014.

EXPLANATION

After determining whether or not your social security retirement benefits are taxable, you must then determine what percentage (either 50% or 85%) of the total benefit is taxable. If you are filing a joint return and your *total income* (adjusted gross income + tax-exempt income + excluded foreign source income + excluded interest income from U.S. savings bonds + one-half of your social security retirement benefits) is less than $44,000 but greater than $32,000, a maximum of 50% of your social security retirement benefits is subject to federal tax. If, however, your total income exceeds $44,000, up to 85% of your social security retirement benefits will be included in income and taxed accordingly.

TAXSAVER

Many states allow a deduction or exclusion for the amount of social security retirement benefits taxed at the federal level. Consult your tax advisor or state income tax authority for details.

Which worksheet to use. A worksheet you can use to figure your taxable benefits is in the instructions for your Form 1040 or Form 1040A. You can use either that worksheet or Worksheet 1 in Publication 915, unless any of the following situations applies to you.

1. You contributed to a traditional individual retirement arrangement (IRA) and you or your spouse is covered by a retirement plan at work. In this situation, you must use the special worksheets in *Appendix B* of Publication 590 to figure both your IRA deduction and your taxable benefits.
2. Situation (1) does not apply and you take an exclusion for interest from qualified U.S. savings bonds (Form 8815), for adoption benefits (Form 8839), for foreign earned income or housing (Form 2555 or Form 2555-EZ), or for income earned in American Samoa (Form 4563) or Puerto Rico by bona fide residents. In this situation, you must use Worksheet 1 in Publication 915 to figure your taxable benefits.
3. You received a lump-sum payment for an earlier year. In this situation, also complete Worksheet 2 or 3 and Worksheet 4 in Publication 915. See *Lump-sum election* next.

Lump-sum election. You must include the taxable part of a lump-sum (retroactive) payment of benefits received in 2014 in your 2014 income, even if the payment includes benefits for an earlier year.

Generally, you use your 2014 income to figure the taxable part of the total benefits received in 2014. However, you may be able to figure the taxable part of a lump-sum payment for an earlier year separately, using your income for the earlier year. You can elect this method if it lowers your taxable benefits.

Tip

This type of lump-sum benefit payment should not be confused with the lump-sum death benefit that both the SSA and RRB pay to many of their beneficiaries. No part of the lump-sum death benefit is subject to tax.

Making the election. If you received a lump-sum benefit payment in 2014 that includes benefits for one or more earlier years, follow the instructions in Publication 915 under *Lump-Sum Election* to see whether making the election will lower your taxable benefits. That discussion also explains how to make the election.

TAXPLANNER

Estimated tax. Generally, tax is not withheld on social security benefits. This means that you may have to pay estimated tax during the year if these benefits are taxable and you do not have enough taxes withheld from other income. However, you may request to have federal income tax withheld from your benefits at 7%, 10%, 15%, or 25%, but no other percentage or amount is allowed. This request is made by completing Form W-4V, Voluntary Withholding Request, and giving it to the agency making the payments. See chapter 4, *Tax withholding and estimated tax*, for more information on estimated tax.

Examples

The following are a few examples you can use as a guide to figure the taxable part of your benefits.

Example 1. George White is single and files Form 1040 for 2014. He received the following income in 2014:

Fully taxable pension	$18,600
Wages from part-time job...................................	9,400
Taxable interest income	990
Total	$28,990

George also received social security benefits during 2014. The Form SSA-1099 he received in January 2015 shows $5,980 in box 5. To figure his taxable benefits, George completes the worksheet shown here.

Filled-in Worksheet 1. **Figuring Your Taxable Benefits**

1.	Enter the total amount from box 5 of ALL your Forms SSA-1099 and RRB-1099. Also enter this amount on Form 1040, line 20a, or Form 1040A, line 14a............................	$5,980
2.	Enter one-half of line 1	2,990
3.	Combine the amounts from:	
	Form 1040: Lines 7, 8a, 9a, 10 through 14, 15b, 16b, 17 through 19, and 21.	
	Form 1040A: Lines 7, 8a, 9a, 10, 11b, 12b, and 13.................................	28,990
4.	Enter the amount, if any, from Form 1040 or 1040A, line 8b......................................	-0-
5.	Enter the total of any exclusions/adjustments for:	
	• Adoption benefits (Form 8839, line 28),	
	• Foreign earned income or housing (Form 2555, lines 45 and 50, or Form 2555-EZ, line 18), and	
	• Certain income of bona fide residents of American Samoa (Form 4563, line 15) or Puerto Rico...	-0-
6.	Combine lines 2, 3, 4, and 5..	31,980
7.	*Form 1040 filers:* Enter the amount from Form 1040, lines 23 through 32, and any write-in adjustments you entered on the dotted line next to line 36.	
	Form 1040A filers: Enter the amount from Form 1040A, lines 16 and 17....................	-0-
8.	Is the amount on line 7 less than the amount on line 6?	
	No. None of your social security benefits are taxable. Enter -0- on Form 1040, line 20b, or Form 1040A, line 14b.	
	Yes. Subtract line 7 from line 6	31,980

9. If you are:

- Married filing jointly, enter $32,000 _____

- Single, head of household, qualifying widow(er), or married filing separately and you **lived apart** from your spouse for all of 2014, enter $25,000 25,000

   Note. If you are married filing separately and you lived with your spouse at any time in 2014, skip lines 9 through 16; multiply line 8 by 85% (.85) and enter the result on line 17. Then go to line 18.

10. Is the amount on line 9 less than the amount on line 8?

   No. None of your benefits are taxable. Enter -0- on Form 1040, line 20b, or on Form 1040A, line 14b. If you are married filing separately and you **lived apart** from your spouse for all of 2014, be sure you entered "D" to the right of the word "benefits" on Form 1040, line 20a, or on Form 1040A, line 14a.

   Yes. Subtract line 9 from line 8 6,980

11. Enter $12,000 if married filing jointly; $9,000 if single, head of household, qualifying widow(er), or married filing separately and you **lived apart** from your spouse for all of 2014... 9,000

12. Subtract line 11 from line 10. If zero or less, enter -0-... -0-

13. Enter the **smaller** of line 10 or line 11 6,980

14. Enter one-half of line 13 3,490

15. Enter the **smaller** of line 2 or line 14 2,990

16. Multiply line 12 by 85% (.85). If line 12 is zero, enter -0- .... -0-

17. Add lines 15 and 16 2,990

18. Multiply line 1 by 85% (.85)... 5,083

19. **Taxable benefits.** Enter the **smaller** of line 17 or line 18. Also enter this amount on Form 1040, line 20b, or Form 1040A, line 14b... $2,990

The amount on line 19 of George's worksheet shows that $2,990 of his social security benefits is taxable. On line 20a of his Form 1040, George enters his net benefits of $5,980. On line 20b, he enters his taxable benefits of $2,990.

Example 2. Ray and Alice Hopkins file a joint return on Form 1040A for 2014. Ray is retired and received a fully taxable pension of $15,500. He also received social security benefits, and his Form SSA-1099 for 2014 shows net benefits of $5,600 in box 5. Alice worked during the year and had wages of $14,000. She made a deductible payment to her IRA account of $1,000. Ray and Alice have two savings accounts with a total of $250 in taxable interest income. They complete Worksheet 1, entering $29,750 ($15,500 + $14,000 + $250) on line 3. They find none of Ray's social security benefits are taxable. On Form 1040A, they enter $5,600 on line 14a and -0- on line 14b.

Filled-in Worksheet 1. **Figuring Your Taxable Benefits**

1. Enter the total amount from box 5 of ALL your Forms SSA-1099 and RRB-1099. Also enter this amount on Form 1040, line 20a, or Form 1040A, line 14a............................. $5,600

2. Enter one-half of line 1 2,800

3. Combine the amounts from:

   Form 1040: Lines 7, 8a, 9a, 10 through 14, 15b, 16b, 17 through 19, and 21.

   Form 1040A: Lines 7, 8a, 9a, 10, 11b, 12b, and 13................................. 29,750

4. Enter the amount, if any, from Form 1040 or 1040A, line 8b..................................... -0-

5. Enter the total of any exclusions/adjustments for:

   - Adoption benefits (Form 8839, line 28),

   - Foreign earned income or housing (Form 2555, lines 45 and 50, or Form 2555-EZ, line 18), and

(continued)

Filled-in Worksheet 1. *(Continued)*

	• Certain income of bona fide residents of American Samoa (Form 4563, line 15) or Puerto Rico	-0-
6.	Combine lines 2, 3, 4, and 5..	32,550
7.	**Form 1040 filers:** Enter the amount from Form 1040, lines 23 through 32, and any write-in adjustments you entered on the dotted line next to line 36.	
	Form 1040A filers: Enter the amount from Form 1040A, lines 16 and 17	1,000
8.	Is the amount on line 7 less than the amount on line 6?	
	No. None of your social security benefits are taxable. Enter -0- on Form 1040, line 20b, or Form 1040A, line 14b.	
	Yes. Subtract line 7 from line 6	31,550
9.	If you are:	
	• Married filing jointly, enter $32,000	
	• Single, head of household, qualifying widow(er), or married filing separately and you **lived apart** from your spouse for all of 2014, enter $25,000	32,000
	Note. If you are married filing separately and you lived with your spouse at any time in 2014, skip lines 9 through 16; multiply line 8 by 85% (.85) and enter the result on line 17. Then go to line 18.	
10.	Is the amount on line 9 less than the amount on line 8?	
	No. None of your benefits are taxable. Enter -0- on Form 1040, line 20b, or on Form 1040A, line 14b. If you are married filing separately and you **lived apart** from your spouse for all of 2014, be sure you entered "D" to the right of the word "benefits" on Form 1040, line 20a, or on Form 1040A, line 14a.	
	Yes. Subtract line 9 from line 8	_____
11.	Enter $12,000 if married filing jointly; $9,000 if single, head of household, qualifying widow(er), or married filing separately and you **lived apart** from your spouse for all of 2014..	_____
12.	Subtract line 11 from line 10. If zero or less, enter -0-.................................	_____
13.	Enter the **smaller** of line 10 or line 11	_____
14.	Enter one-half of line 13	_____
15.	Enter the **smaller** of line 2 or line 14	_____
16.	Multiply line 12 by 85% (.85). If line 12 is zero, enter -0-	_____
17.	Add lines 15 and 16	_____
18.	Multiply line 1 by 85% (.85)...	_____
19.	**Taxable benefits.** Enter the **smaller** of line 17 or line 18. Also enter this amount on Form 1040, line 20b, or Form 1040A, line 14b...	_____

Example 3. Joe and Betty Johnson file a joint return on Form 1040 for 2014. Joe is a retired railroad worker and in 2014 received the social security equivalent benefit (SSEB) portion of tier 1 railroad retirement benefits. Joe's Form RRB-1099 shows $10,000 in box 5. Betty is a retired government worker and receives a fully taxable pension of $38,000. They had $2,300 in taxable interest income plus interest of $200 on a qualified U.S. savings bond. The savings bond interest qualified for the exclusion. They figure their taxable benefits by completing Worksheet 1. Because they have qualified U.S. savings bond interest, they follow the note at the beginning of the worksheet and use the amount from line 2 of their Schedule B (Form 1040A or 1040) on line 3 of the worksheet instead of the amount from line 8a of their Form 1040. On line 3 of the worksheet, they enter $40,500 ($38,000 + $2,500).

Filled-in Worksheet 1. **Figuring Your Taxable Benefits**

Before you begin:

- If you are married filing separately and you lived apart from your spouse for all of 2014, enter "D" to the right of the word "benefits" on Form 1040, line 20a, or Form 1040A, line 14a.

- Do not use this worksheet if you repaid benefits in 2014 and your total repayments (box 4 of Forms SSA-1099 and RRB-1099) were more than your gross benefits for 2014 (box 3 of Forms SSA-1099 and RRB-1099). None of your benefits are taxable for 2014. For more information, see <u>Repayments More Than Gross Benefits</u>.

- If you are filing Form 8815, Exclusion of Interest From Series EE and I U.S. Savings Bonds Issued After 1989, do not include the amount from line 8a of Form 1040 or Form 1040A on line 3 of this worksheet. Instead, include the amount from Schedule B (Form 1040A or 1040), line 2.

1. Enter the total amount from box 5 of ALL your Forms SSA-1099 and RRB-1099. Also enter this amount on Form 1040, line 20a, or Form 1040A, line 14a............................ $10,000

2. Enter one-half of line 1 5,000

3. Combine the amounts from:

    Form 1040: Lines 7, 8a, 9a, 10 through 14, 15b, 16b, 17 through 19, and 21.

    Form 1040A: Lines 7, 8a, 9a, 10, 11b, 12b, and 13 40,500

4. Enter the amount, if any, from Form 1040 or 1040A, line 8b.................................... -0-

5. Enter the total of any exclusions/adjustments for:

    - Adoption benefits (Form 8839, line 28),

    - Foreign earned income or housing (Form 2555, lines 45 and 50, or Form 2555-EZ, line 18), and

    - Certain income of bona fide residents of American Samoa (Form 4563, line 15) or Puerto Rico .... -0-

6. Combine lines 2, 3, 4, and 5.. 45,500

7. **Form 1040 filers:** Enter the amount from Form 1040, lines 23 through 32, and any write-in adjustments you entered on the dotted line next to line 36,

    Form 1040A filers: Enter the amount from Form 1040A, lines 16 and 17.................. -0-

8. Is the amount on line 7 less than the amount on line 6?

    No. None of your social security benefits are taxable. Enter -0- on Form 1040, line 20b, or Form 1040A, line 14b.

    Yes. Subtract line 7 from line 6 45,500

9. If you are:

    - Married filing jointly, enter $32,000

    - Single, head of household, qualifying widow(er), or married filing separately and you **lived apart** from your spouse for all of 2014, enter $25,000 32,000

    Note. If you are married filing separately and you lived with your spouse at any time in 2014, skip lines 9 through 16; multiply line 8 by 85% (.85) and enter the result on line 17. Then go to line 18.

10. Is the amount on line 9 less than the amount on line 8?

    No. None of your benefits are taxable. Enter -0- on Form 1040, line 20b, or on Form 1040A, line 14b. If you are married filing separately and you **lived apart** from your spouse for all of 2014, be sure you entered "D" to the right of the word "benefits" on Form 1040, line 20a, or on Form 1040A, line 14a.

    Yes. Subtract line 9 from line 8 13,500

11. Enter $12,000 if married filing jointly; $9,000 if single, head of household, qualifying widow(er), or married filing separately and you **lived apart** from your spouse for all of 2014... 12,000

(continued)

Filled-in Worksheet 1. *(Continued)*

12.	Subtract line 11 from line 10. If zero or less, enter -0-	1,500
13.	Enter the **smaller** of line 10 or line 11	12,000
14.	Enter one-half of line 13	6,000
15.	Enter the **smaller** of line 2 or line 14	5,000
16.	Multiply line 12 by 85% (.85). If line 12 is zero, enter -0-	1,275
17.	Add lines 15 and 16	6,275
18.	Multiply line 1 by 85% (.85)	8,500
19.	**Taxable benefits.** Enter the **smaller** of line 17 or line 18. Also enter this amount on Form 1040, line 20b, or Form 1040A, line 14b	$6,275

More than 50% of Joe's net benefits are taxable because the income on line 8 of the worksheet ($45,500) is more than $44,000. Joe and Betty enter $10,000 on Form 1040, line 20a, and $6,275 on Form 1040, line 20b.

Deductions Related to Your Benefits

You may be entitled to deduct certain amounts related to the benefits you receive.

Disability payments. You may have received disability payments from your employer or an insurance company that you included as income on your tax return in an earlier year. If you received a lump-sum payment from SSA or RRB, and you had to repay the employer or insurance company for the disability payments, you can take an itemized deduction for the part of the payments you included in gross income in the earlier year. If the amount you repay is more than $3,000, you may be able to claim a tax credit instead. Claim the deduction or credit in the same way explained under *Repayments More Than Gross Benefits*, later.

Legal expenses. You can usually deduct legal expenses that you pay or incur to produce or collect taxable income or in connection with the determination, collection, or refund of any tax.

Legal expenses for collecting the taxable part of your benefits are deductible as a miscellaneous itemized deduction on Schedule A (Form 1040), line 23.

Repayments More Than Gross Benefits

In some situations, your Form SSA-1099 or Form RRB-1099 will show that the total benefits you repaid (box 4) are more than the gross benefits (box 3) you received. If this occurred, your net benefits in box 5 will be a negative figure (a figure in parentheses) and none of your benefits will be taxable. Do not use a worksheet in this case. If you receive more than one form, a negative figure in box 5 of one form is used to offset a positive figure in box 5 of another form for that same year.

If you have any questions about this negative figure, contact your local SSA office or your local RRB field office.

Joint return. If you and your spouse file a joint return, and your Form SSA-1099 or RRB-1099 has a negative figure in box 5, but your spouse's does not, subtract the amount in box 5 of your form from the amount in box 5 of your spouse's form. You do this to get your net benefits when figuring if your combined benefits are taxable.

Example. John and Mary file a joint return for 2014. John received Form SSA-1099 showing $3,000 in box 5. Mary also received Form SSA-1099 and the amount in box 5 was ($500). John and Mary will use $2,500 ($3,000 minus $500) as the amount of their net benefits when figuring if any of their combined benefits are taxable.

> ### EXPLANATION
> Social security benefits are determined on a cash basis, just like most other income of individuals. Accordingly, repayments of prior-year amounts reduce current-year benefits.

Repayment of benefits received in an earlier year. If the total amount shown in box 5 of all of your Forms SSA-1099 and RRB-1099 is a negative figure, you can take an itemized deduction for the part of this negative figure that represents benefits you included in gross income in an earlier year.

Deduction $3,000 or less. If this deduction is $3,000 or less, it is subject to the 2%-of-adjusted-gross-income limit that applies to certain miscellaneous itemized deductions. Claim it on Schedule A (Form 1040), line 23.

Deduction more than $3,000. If this deduction is more than $3,000, you should figure your tax two ways:

1. Figure your tax for 2014 with the itemized deduction included on Schedule A, line 28.
2. Figure your tax for 2014 in the following steps.
   a. Figure the tax without the itemized deduction included on Schedule A, line 28.
   b. For each year after 1983 for which part of the negative figure represents a repayment of benefits, refigure your taxable benefits as if your total benefits for the year were reduced by that part of the negative figure. Then refigure the tax for that year.
   c. Subtract the total of the refigured tax amounts in (b) from the total of your actual tax amounts.
   d. Subtract the result in (c) from the result in (a).

Compare the tax figured in methods (1) and (2). Your tax for 2014 is the smaller of the two amounts. If method (1) results in less tax, take the itemized deduction on Schedule A (Form 1040), line 28. If method (2) results in less tax, claim a credit for the amount from step 2(c) above on Form 1040, line 71. Check box d and enter "I.R.C. 1341" in the space next to that box. If both methods produce the same tax, deduct the repayment on Schedule A (Form 1040), line 28.

EXPLANATION

This confusing computation allows you to reduce your current tax by the greater of two amounts: (1) the amount of tax you would save by taking the deduction this year; or (2) the net increase in tax in the prior year(s) as a result of including the amount in income.

TAXSAVER

The Social Security Administration (SSA) can reduce your monthly benefits if you have earned income in excess of the threshold amounts and are under full retirement age. The retirement earnings test has been eliminated for individuals attaining full retirement. However, a test remains in effect for individuals ages 62 through full retirement age. For individuals between the ages of 62 and the year their full retirement age is reached, each $2 of income earned in 2014 over $15,480 will reduce their social security benefits by $1. For the year in which an individual reaches full retirement age, each $3 of income earned in 2014 over $41,400 will reduce social security benefits by $1. The $41,400 threshold applies only for the year in which you reach full retirement age, up to the actual month you attain full retirement age. There is no limit on earnings beginning the month you attain full retirement age. Other exceptions apply during the initial year you receive social security retirement benefits. Consult the SSA for further explanation.

Earned Income Threshold for Early Recipients of Social Security Benefits

	Self-Employed	Not Self-Employed
Included as income	Net earnings	Wages
Excluded as income	Government benefits	Government benefits
	Investment earnings	Investment earnings
	Interest	Interest
	Pensions	Pensions
	Annuities	Annuities
	Capital gains	Capital gains
	IRA distributions	IRA distributions
	Inheritance payments	Inheritance payments

TAXALERT

If you were born after 1937, your "full retirement age" occurs later than age 65. Full retirement age is the age at which full (100%) social security retirement benefits are available. Beginning with individuals who attained age 62 in the year 2000 (born in 1938), the full retirement age increases over the next 22 years, leveling off at age 67 for individuals who were born in 1960 or later. In other words, the full retirement age for individuals born between 1955 and 1969 will be age 66, plus 2 months for every year after 1954. Refer to the chart below entitled *"Scheduled Increases in Social Security Normal Retirement Age"* for the scheduled increases in the normal retirement age for those born in 1945 and thereafter.

Scheduled Increases in Social Security Normal Retirement Age

Birth Year	Year Worker Attains Age 62	Normal Retirement Age
1945	2007	66
1946	2008	66
1947	2009	66
1948	2010	66
1949	2011	66
1950	2012	66
1951	2013	66
1952	2014	66
1953	2015	66
1954	2016	66
1955	2017	66 + 2 months
1956	2018	66 + 4 months
1957	2019	66 + 6 months
1958	2020	66 + 8 months
1959	2021	66 + 10 months
1960	2022	67
1961 and subsequent years	2023 and later	67

TAXORGANIZER
Records you should keep:
- Copy of Forms SSA-1099, RRB-1099, and 1042S for 3 years following the due date (including extensions) of your income tax return
- Copies of all worksheets used to determine taxability of benefits

Chapter 12
Other income

Note

IRS Publication 17 (*Your Federal Income Tax*) has been updated by Ernst & Young LLP for 2014. Dates and dollar amounts shown are for 2014. Underlined type is used to indicate where IRS text has been updated. Places where text has been removed are indicated by the sentence: *Text intentionally omitted*.

ey.com/EYTaxGuide

Ernst & Young LLP will update the *EY Tax Guide 2015* website with relevant taxpayer information as it becomes available. You can also sign up for email alerts to let you know when changes have been made.

ey.com/EYTaxGuide

Introduction

Your salary, interest you earn, dividends received, a gain from the sale of securities—all of these, of course, are taxable income.

Unfortunately, so are a lot of other things: a debt forgiven by a friend, jury pay, a free trip you receive from a travel agency for organizing a group of tourists, lottery and gambling winnings, and royalties you earn on a book.

The general rule is that anything that enriches you should be included in your gross income, unless it is specifically excluded by the tax law.

Indeed, some things are excluded from taxation. Generally, you don't have to pay income tax on life insurance proceeds that you receive because of the death of the insured. Most gifts and inheritances are excluded from income tax. The value of the vegetables you grow in your garden and eat yourself is not taxable. This chapter tells you what kind of income is not taxable, and how you can tell the difference.

This chapter includes a discussion on passive activity losses. Passive investments include all rental activities, investments in limited partnerships, and those other businesses in which the taxpayer is not involved in the operations on a regular, continuous, and substantial basis.

You must include on your return all items of income you receive in the form of money, property, and services unless the tax law states that you do not include them. Some items, however, are only partly excluded from income. This chapter discusses many kinds of income and explains whether they are taxable or nontaxable.

- Income that is taxable must be reported on your tax return and is subject to tax.
- Income that is nontaxable may have to be shown on your tax return but is not taxable.

This chapter begins with discussions of the following income items.

- Bartering.
- Canceled debts.
- Sales parties at which you are the host or hostess.
- Life insurance proceeds.
- Partnership income.

Tax Breaks and Deductions You Can Use Checklist

Canceled debts. Generally, you must include in income the portion of any debt that is canceled or forgiven. However, amounts forgiven as a gift or bequest are exempt from your income. For more information, see *Canceled Debts*, later.

Disaster relief grants. You can exclude from your gross income a grant you receive under the Disaster Relief and Emergency Assistance Act if the grant payments are received to help you meet certain serious needs, such as housing, transportation, and medical expenses. For more information, see *Welfare and Other Public Assistance Benefits: Disaster Relief Grants*, later.

Disaster relief payments. Qualified disaster relief payments you receive are not subject to income tax, social security, or Medicare taxes. Qualified payments include amounts paid as a result of a qualified disaster to reimburse or pay reasonable and necessary personal, family, living, or funeral expenses that result from a qualified disaster; to repair or rehabilitate your personal residence; or to repair or replace damaged personal contents. For more information, see *Welfare and Other Public Assistance Benefits: Disaster Relief Payments*, later.

Disaster mitigation payments. You can exclude from your gross income a qualified disaster mitigation payment grant that you receive from a state or local government if you use the grant to reduce

- S Corporation income.
- Recoveries (including state income tax refunds).
- Rents from personal property.
- Repayments.
- Royalties.
- Unemployment benefits.
- Welfare and other public assistance benefits.

These discussions are followed by brief discussions of other income items.

Useful Items

You may want to see:

Publication

- ☐ **525** Taxable and Nontaxable Income
- ☐ **544** Sales and Other Dispositions of Assets
- ☐ **4681** Canceled Debts, Foreclosures, Repossessions, and Abandonments

Bartering

Bartering is an exchange of property or services. You must include in your income, at the time received, the fair market value of property or services you receive in bartering. If you exchange services with another person and you both have agreed ahead of time on the value of the services, that value will be accepted as fair market value unless the value can be shown to be otherwise.

Generally, you report this income on Schedule C (Form 1040), Profit or Loss From Business, or Schedule C-EZ (Form 1040), Net Profit From Business. However, if the barter involves an exchange of something other than services, such as in *Example 3* below, you may have to use another form or schedule instead.

EXPLANATION

The IRS explanation is correct in stating that if you exchange your property and/or services for the property and/or services of another, you have taxable income. However, when you exchange property for property, you generally recognize income only to the extent that the fair market value of the property you receive exceeds your adjusted basis in the property you give up (note that an exception to this general rule is for like-kind exchanges). The proper way of determining gain on exchanges of property and your basis in the property you receive are discussed in chapter 13, *Basis of property*, and chapter 14, *Sale of property*.

Example 1. You are a self-employed attorney who performs legal services for a client, a small corporation. The corporation gives you shares of its stock as payment for your services. You must include the fair market value of the shares in your income on Schedule C (Form 1040) or Schedule C-EZ (Form 1040) in the year you receive them.

Example 2. You are self-employed and a member of a barter club. The club uses "credit units" as a means of exchange. It adds credit units to your account for goods or services you provide to members, which you can use to purchase goods or services offered by other members of the barter club. The club subtracts credit units from your account when you receive goods or services from other members. You must include in your income the value of the credit units that are added to your account, even though you may not actually receive goods or services from other members until a later tax year.

Example 3. You own a small apartment building. In return for 6 months rent-free use of an apartment, an artist gives you a work of art she created. You must report as rental income on Schedule E (Form 1040), Supplemental Income and Loss, the fair market value of the artwork, and the artist must report as income on Schedule C (Form 1040) or Schedule C-EZ (Form 1040) the fair rental value of the apartment.

Form 1099-B from barter exchange. If you exchanged property or services through a barter exchange, Form 1099-B, Proceeds From Broker and Barter Exchange Transactions, or a similar statement from the barter exchange should be sent to you by February 17, 2015. It should show the value of cash, property, services, credits, or scrip you received from exchanges during 2014. The IRS also will receive a copy of Form 1099-B.

Canceled Debts

In most cases, if a debt you owe is canceled or forgiven, other than as a gift or bequest, you must include the canceled amount in your income. You have no income from the canceled debt if it is intended as a gift to you. A debt includes any indebtedness for which you are liable or which attaches to property you hold.

If the debt is a nonbusiness debt, report the canceled amount on Form 1040, line 21. If it is a business debt, report the amount on Schedule C (Form 1040) or Schedule C-EZ (Form 1040) (or on Schedule F (Form 1040), Profit or Loss From Farming, if the debt is farm debt and you are a farmer).

TAXALERT

In 2009 and 2010 an election was available to recognize canceled business debt in income over a 5-tax-year period if the income was realized in a reacquisition that occurred in either of those years. Although this election is no longer available after 2010, you may have income to recognize in 2014 from a prior year election made to report the income over the 5-year period. For information on this election, see Revenue Procedure 2009-37 available at _www.irs.gov/ irb/2009-36_IRB/ar07.html_.

TAXPLANNER

Family members often make interest-free or below-market interest rate loans to one another. The IRS may re-characterize these loans as arm's-length transactions and impute interest income to the lender and interest expense to the borrower, which are then reported on their respective tax returns, although the interest expense may not be deductible if it is considered nondeductible personal interest (discussed in chapter 24, _Interest expense_). See chapter 7, _Interest income_, for further discussion of below-market loans. You should consult your tax advisor about how to report any below-market loan transactions.

Form 1099-C. If a Federal Government agency, financial institution, or credit union cancels or forgives a debt you owe of $600 or more, you will receive a Form 1099-C, Cancellation of Debt. The amount of the canceled debt is shown in box 2.

**Interest included in canceled debt.** If any interest is forgiven and included in the amount of canceled debt in box 2, the amount of interest also will be shown in box 3. Whether or not you must include the interest portion of the canceled debt in your income depends on whether the interest would be deductible when you paid it. See _Deductible debt_ under _Exceptions_, later.

If the interest would not be deductible (such as interest on a personal loan), include in your income the amount from Form 1099-C, box 2. If the interest would be deductible (such as on a business loan), include in your income the net amount of the canceled debt (the amount shown in box 2 less the interest amount shown in box 3).

Discounted mortgage loan. If your financial institution offers a discount for the early payment of your mortgage loan, the amount of the discount is canceled debt. You must include the canceled amount in your income.

TAXSAVER

Proceed cautiously if the financial institution that holds your mortgage offers you a substantial discount on your loan balance in exchange for a prepayment on it. Although this might at first appear very attractive, remember that you will have to pay ordinary income tax on the amount of the discount offered, which may considerably reduce any advantage to you. Your money might be put to better use in investments with a high after-tax yield or in paying off expensive consumer credit debt.

Mortgage relief upon sale or other disposition. If you are personally liable for a mortgage (recourse debt), and you are relieved of the mortgage when you dispose of the property, you may realize gain or loss up to the fair market value of the property. To the extent the mortgage discharge exceeds the fair market value of the property, it is income from discharge of indebtedness unless it qualifies for exclusion under _Excluded debt_, later. Report any income from discharge of indebtedness on nonbusiness debt that does not qualify for exclusion as other income on Form 1040, line 21.

If you are not personally liable for a mortgage (nonrecourse debt), and you are relieved of the mortgage when you dispose of the property (such as through foreclosure), that relief is included

the severity of potential damage from a future natural disaster. For more information, see _Welfare and Other Public Assistance Benefits: Disaster Mitigation Payments_, later.

Unlawful discrimination claims. If you receive damages from a settlement or judgment in a lawsuit for unlawful discrimination that was settled or decided after October 22, 2004, you may be able to deduct attorney fees and court costs paid after that date. Your deduction is limited to the amount of the settlement or judgment you included in income. For more information, see _Court awards and damages_ and _Deduction for costs involved in unlawful discrimination suits_, later, and Publication 525.

Life insurance proceeds. Life insurance proceeds paid to you because of the death of the insured person are not taxable unless the policy was turned over to you for a price. For more information, see _Life Insurance Proceeds_, later.

Tip

You may be able to exclude part of the mortgage relief on your principal residence. See Excluded debt, _later._

in the amount you realize. You may have a taxable gain if the amount you realize exceeds your adjusted basis in the property. Report any gain on nonbusiness property as a capital gain.

See Publication 4681 for more information.

> ### ◤ TAXALERT
> *Exclusion from Gross Income of Certain Discharged Mortgage Debt expired in 2013.* Under prior law, you could exclude from gross income, income realized from the discharge after 2006 and before 2014 of up to $2 million ($1 million if married filing separately) of qualified principal residence indebtedness. (However, your basis in your principal residence would be reduced by the amount excluded from income.) This exclusion is not available for discharges of mortgage debt occurring after 2013. However, as of the time this book was published in October 2014, Congress had been considering legislation that would extend the availability of this exclusion through at least 2014, but no such extension had yet been passed. For updated information on this and any other tax law changes that occur after this book was published, see our website, *ey.com/EYTaxGuide*.

> ### ◤ TAXSAVER
> If you have gross income from the discharge of mortgage indebtedness and you are insolvent, you may be able to exclude the amount of the canceled debt in your gross income. IRS Publication 908, Bankrupcty Tax Guide, explains that a debtor is insolvent when, and to the extent, the debtor's liabilities exceed the fair market value of his or her assets. Whether or not the debtor is insolvent is tested immediately before the cancellation of the debtor's debt. So if the debtor is insolvent, the debtor can exclude from gross income the canceled debt, but only up the amount by which the debtor is insolvent.
>
> If your mortgage indebtedness is discharged, it is key to establish whether and to what extent you are insolvent. It is important to keep appropriate records establishing the amount of the insolvency. The downside of claiming insolvency and choosing not to include the amount of the canceled debt in your income is that certain tax attributes are reduced by the amount the cancelled debt is not included in gross income. IRS Form 982, Reduction of Tax Attributes Due to Discharge of Indebtedness, will need to be completed. Tax attributes that can be reduced include net operating losses, minimum tax credit, capital losses, basis in the debtor's property, and passive activity losses and carryovers.

Stockholder debt. If you are a stockholder in a corporation and the corporation cancels or forgives your debt to it, the canceled debt is a constructive distribution that is generally dividend income to you. For more information, see Publication 542, Corporations.

If you are a stockholder in a corporation and you cancel a debt owed to you by the corporation, you generally do not realize income. This is because the canceled debt is considered as a contribution to the capital of the corporation equal to the amount of debt principal that you canceled.

Repayment of canceled debt. If you included a canceled amount in your income and later pay the debt, you may be able to file a claim for refund for the year the amount was included in income. You can file a claim on Form 1040X if the statute of limitations for filing a claim is still open. The statute of limitations generally does not end until 3 years after the due date of your original return.

Exceptions
There are several exceptions to the inclusion of canceled debt in income. These are explained next.

Student loans. Certain student loans contain a provision that all or part of the debt incurred to attend the qualified educational institution will be canceled if you work for a certain period of time in certain professions for any of a broad class of employers.

You do not have income if your student loan is canceled after you agreed to this provision and then performed the services required. To qualify, the loan must have been made by:
1. The Federal Government, a state or local government, or an instrumentality, agency, or subdivision thereof,
2. A tax-exempt public benefit corporation that has assumed control of a state, county, or municipal hospital, and whose employees are considered public employees under state law, or
3. An educational institution:
   a. Under an agreement with an entity described in (1) or (2) that provided the funds to the institution to make the loan, or
   b. As part of a program of the institution designed to encourage its students to serve in occupations with unmet needs or in areas with unmet needs and under which the

services provided by the students (or former students) are for or under the direction of a governmental unit or a tax-exempt organization described in Section 501(c)(3).

A loan to refinance a qualified student loan also will qualify if it was made by an educational institution or a qualified tax-exempt organization under its program designed as described in (3) (b) above.

Education loan repayment assistance. Education loan repayments made to you by the National Health Service Corps Loan Repayment Program (NHSC Loan Repayment Program), a state education loan repayment program eligible for funds under the Public Health Service Act, or any other state loan repayment or loan forgiveness program that is intended to provide for the increased availability of health services in underserved or health professional shortage areas are not taxable.

Deductible debt. You do not have income from the cancellation of a debt if your payment of the debt would be deductible. This exception applies only if you use the cash method of accounting. For more information, see chapter 5 of Publication 334, Tax Guide for Small Business.

Price reduced after purchase. In most cases, if the seller reduces the amount of debt you owe for property you purchased, you do not have income from the reduction. The reduction of the debt is treated as a purchase price adjustment and reduces your basis in the property.

Excluded debt. Do not include a canceled debt in your gross income in the following situations.

- The debt is canceled in a bankruptcy case under title 11 of the U.S. Code. See Publication 908, Bankruptcy Tax Guide.
- The debt is canceled when you are insolvent. However, you cannot exclude any amount of canceled debt that is more than the amount by which you are insolvent. See Publication 908.
- The debt is qualified farm debt and is canceled by a qualified person. See chapter 3 of Publication 225, Farmer's Tax Guide.
- The debt is qualified real property business debt. See chapter 5 of Publication 334.
- The cancellation is intended as a gift.
- The debt is qualified principal residence indebtedness. See Publication 525 for additional information.

> **TAXPLANNER**
> To claim the exclusions listed above, Form 982 should be completed and attached to your federal income tax return. Also see the worksheet in Publication 4681 to determine the extent of your insolvency immediately prior to the debt forgiveness.

> **TAXALERT**
> You cannot exclude from your gross income debt you owe to your employer that is forgiven even if it was incurred for purchasing stock.

Host or Hostess

If you host a party or event at which sales are made, any gift or gratuity you receive for giving the event is a payment for helping a direct seller make sales. You must report this item as income at its fair market value.

Your out-of-pocket party expenses are subject to the 50% limit for meal and entertainment expenses. These expenses are deductible as miscellaneous itemized deductions subject to the 2%-of-AGI limit on Schedule A (Form 1040), but only up to the amount of income you receive for giving the party.

For more information about the 50% limit for meal and entertainment expenses, see chapter 27.

Life Insurance Proceeds

Life insurance proceeds paid to you because of the death of the insured person are not taxable unless the policy was turned over to you for a price. This is true even if the proceeds were paid under an accident or health insurance policy or an endowment contract. However, interest income received as a result of life insurance proceeds may be taxable.

> **TAXALERT**
> Nontaxable life insurance proceeds are also not subject to the 3.8% Net Investment Income Tax (NIIT) that was imposed by the Affordable Care Act starting in 2013. However, interest income received that is taxable for regular income tax purposes is subject to the 3.8% NIIT.

Tip

The provision relating to the "other state loan repayment or loan forgiveness program" was added to this exclusion for amounts received in tax years beginning after December 31, 2008. If you included these amounts in income in 2011, 2012, or 2013, you should file an amended tax return to exclude this income. See Form 1040X and its instructions for details on filing.

Proceeds not received in installments. If death benefits are paid to you in a lump sum or other than at regular intervals, include in your income only the benefits that are more than the amount payable to you at the time of the insured person's death. If the benefit payable at death is not specified, you include in your income the benefit payments that are more than the present value of the payments at the time of death.

Proceeds received in installments. If you receive life insurance proceeds in installments, you can exclude part of each installment from your income.

To determine the excluded part, divide the amount held by the insurance company (generally the total lump sum payable at the death of the insured person) by the number of installments to be paid. Include anything over this excluded part in your income as interest.

> ### EXAMPLE
> Suppose you receive a $100,000 life insurance death benefit that you elect to receive over 10 annual installments. Any amount that you receive in excess of $10,000 each year will be considered taxable interest income to you.

Surviving spouse. If your spouse died before October 23, 1986, and insurance proceeds paid to you because of the death of your spouse are received in installments, you can exclude up to $1,000 a year of the interest included in the installments. If you remarry, you can continue to take the exclusion.

> ### TAXSAVER
> **Interest option on insurance.** If an insurance company pays you only interest on proceeds from life insurance left on deposit with them, the interest you are paid is taxable.
>
> *Example*
> Assume you are a beneficiary of a life insurance death benefit. If under the payment structure of the benefit, you are only receiving the interest, then your entire payment would be considered taxable. The individual (or successor beneficiary) who will be receiving the principal of the benefit would receive it income tax-free. Special exclusion ratio rules apply to individuals receiving annuity death benefits in the form of principal and interest.

Surrender of policy for cash. If you surrender a life insurance policy for cash, you must include in income any proceeds that are more than the cost of the life insurance policy. In most cases, your cost (or investment in the contract) is the total of premiums that you paid for the life insurance policy, less any refunded premiums, rebates, dividends, or unpaid loans that were not included in your income.

You should receive a Form 1099-R showing the total proceeds and the taxable part. Report these amounts on lines 16a and 16b of Form 1040 or lines 12a and 12b of Form 1040A.

> ### EXAMPLE
> Assuming you terminated a life insurance policy with a cash value of $50,000 and of that amount you only paid $40,000 in net premiums, $10,000 would be considered taxable income to you at that time.
>
> However, if you exchange one life insurance policy for another policy, it is possible that you may not have a taxable transaction. See your tax advisor.

More information. For more information, see *Life Insurance Proceeds* in Publication 525.

Endowment Contract Proceeds

An endowment contract is a policy under which you are paid a specified amount of money on a certain date unless you die before that date, in which case, the money is paid to your designated beneficiary. Endowment proceeds paid in a lump sum to you at maturity are taxable only if the proceeds are more than the cost of the policy. To determine your cost, subtract any amount that you previously received under the contract and excluded from your income from the total premiums (or other consideration) paid for the contract. Include the part of the lump sum payment that is more than your cost in your income.

EXPLANATION

Endowment contracts, much like whole life insurance contracts, require you, as the owner, to pay annual premiums in return for a certain sum of cash that is paid when you reach a specified age or upon death. Unless you choose to receive the endowment proceeds in installments, the excess of the proceeds over the cost of the policy is taxable in the year of maturity, even *if the proceeds are not received until a later year*. The excess of the proceeds over the cost of the policy is taxed as ordinary income, not as capital gain. The cost of the endowment contract is the total amount of the premiums you paid for it, not its cash value at the time of maturity or when you surrender it.

However, if you agree to take the proceeds as an annuity within 60 days after the lump-sum payment becomes available and before you receive any cash, you are not considered to have received the lump sum for tax purposes. The lump sum is taxed as an annuity; that is, you are taxed on the amounts as you receive them each year.

For certain contracts entered into or materially changed after June 21, 1988, you may be required to treat distributions first as income and then as recovery of investment. Distributions are defined for this purpose to include a loan. In certain circumstances, an additional 10% tax will be imposed on the amount that is includible in gross income. Consult your tax advisor to determine if you are subject to this provision.

Accelerated Death Benefits

Certain amounts paid as accelerated death benefits under a life insurance contract or viatical settlement before the insured's death are excluded from income if the insured is terminally or chronically ill.

Viatical settlement. This is the sale or assignment of any part of the death benefit under a life insurance contract to a viatical settlement provider. A viatical settlement provider is a person who regularly engages in the business of buying or taking assignment of life insurance contracts on the lives of insured individuals who are terminally or chronically ill and who meets the requirements of Section 101(g)(2)(B) of the Internal Revenue Code.

Exclusion for terminal illness. Accelerated death benefits are fully excludable if the insured is a terminally ill individual. This is a person who has been certified by a physician as having an illness or physical condition that can reasonably be expected to result in death within 24 months from the date of the certification.

Exclusion for chronic illness. If the insured is a chronically ill individual who is not terminally ill, accelerated death benefits paid on the basis of costs incurred for qualified long-term care services are fully excludable. Accelerated death benefits paid on a *per diem* or other periodic basis are excludable up to a limit. This limit applies to the total of the accelerated death benefits and any periodic payments received from long-term care insurance contracts. For information on the limit and the definitions of chronically ill individual, qualified long-term care services, and long-term care insurance contracts, see *Long-Term Care Insurance Contracts* under *Sickness and Injury Benefits* in Publication 525.

Exception. The exclusion does not apply to any amount paid to a person (other than the insured) who has an insurable interest in the life of the insured because the insured:
- Is a director, officer, or employee of the person, or
- Has a financial interest in the person's business.

Form 8853. To claim an exclusion for accelerated death benefits made on a *per diem* or other periodic basis, you must file Form 8853, Archer MSAs and Long-Term Care Insurance Contracts, with your return. You do not have to file Form 8853 to exclude accelerated death benefits paid on the basis of actual expenses incurred.

Public Safety Officer Killed in the Line of Duty

If you are a survivor of a public safety officer who was killed in the line of duty, you may be able to exclude from income certain amounts you receive.

For this purpose, the term public safety officer includes law enforcement officers, firefighters, chaplains, and rescue squad and ambulance crew members. For more information, see Publication 559, Survivors, Executors, and Administrators.

Partnership Income

A partnership generally is not a taxable entity. The income, gains, losses, deductions, and credits of a partnership are passed through to the partners based on each partner's distributive share of these items.

Schedule K-1 (Form 1065). Although a partnership generally pays no tax, it must file an information return on Form 1065, U.S. Return of Partnership Income, and send Schedule K-1 (Form 1065) to each partner. In addition, the partnership will send each partner a copy of the Partner's Instructions for Schedule K-1 (Form 1065) to help each partner report his or her share of the partnership's income, deductions, credits, and tax preference items.

For more information on partnerships, see Publication 541, Partnerships.

Records

Keep Schedule K-1 (Form 1065) for your records. Do not attach it to your Form 1040, unless you are specifically required to do so.

EXPLANATION

General. A partnership includes a group, pool, joint venture, or other unincorporated organization that carries on a business or financial operation. Most entities that qualify for partnership treatment can elect out of partnership treatment under the "check-the-box" regulations. See your tax advisor for more information.

Limited liability companies. All states permit the formation of limited liability companies (LLCs). In an LLC, members and designated managers are not personally liable for any debts of the company. Absent an election to the contrary the entity will generally be treated as a partnership and, as a result, enjoy the same federal income tax benefits that apply to partnerships. If the entity is appropriately established, LLCs combine the benefits of corporate limited liability with the advantages of partnership taxation. In addition to LLCs, one may consider the formation of a limited liability partnership (LLP). Consult your tax advisor or attorney to find out if these are options for your business in the state you live in.

Reporting income. Because a partnership is not a taxable entity, all tax items are passed through to the partners. A partnership is required to give you a Schedule K-1, Partner's Share of Income, Credits, Deductions, etc. A Schedule K-1 will list your distributive share of income, gains, losses, deductions, and credits that is required to be included in your individual tax return. If, for example, the Schedule K-1 indicates interest income of $100, you will need to include $100 as interest income on your Schedule B, Form 1040 or 1040A. (See chapter 7, *Interest income.*)

Basis. Because the partnership's income and losses flow directly through to you, that income or loss will affect your tax basis in the partnership. It is important that you maintain and update this tax-basis calculation every year for two reasons. First, your distributive share of the partnership losses is limited to the adjusted basis of your interest in the partnership at the end of the partnership year in which the losses took place. Second, in the year you sell your partnership interest, you will need to know your tax basis in order to calculate your gain or loss. To determine the adjusted basis of your interest in the partnership, begin with your initial investment and your initial share of the partnership's liabilities and make the following adjustments.

Additions to basis
1. Your distributive share of the partnership's taxable income
2. Your share of any tax-exempt income earned by the partnership
3. Your share of the excess of partnership deductions for depletion over the basis of partnership property subject to depletion
4. Any additional capital you contribute
5. Your share of any increase in partnership liabilities

Subtractions from basis
1. Any cash distributions you receive
2. The basis that you take in any property distributed to you by the partnership
3. Your share of oil and gas depletion claimed by the partnership
4. Your distributive share of partnership deductions, losses, and certain credits
5. Your share of nondeductible, noncapital expenditures made by the partnership
6. Your share of any decrease in partnership liabilities

The partnership agreement usually covers the distribution of profits, losses, and other items. However, if there is no agreement for sharing a specific item of gain or loss, generally, each partner's distributive share is figured according to the partner's interest in the partnership.

In addition, special "at-risk" rules apply to a partnership engaged in any activity.

You may deduct your share of a partnership loss from any activity only up to the total amount that you are at risk in the activity at the end of the partnership's tax year.

The amount you are at risk in an activity is the cash and the adjusted basis of other property you contributed to the activity. Also, you are at risk for any amounts borrowed for use in the activity for which you either are personally liable or have pledged property, except property used in the activity, as security.

Generally, you are not at risk for:

1. Any nonrecourse loans used to finance the activity, to acquire property used in the activity, or to acquire your interest in the activity, unless they are secured by property not used in the activity;
2. Amounts for which you are protected against loss by guarantees, stop-loss agreements, or other similar arrangements; or
3. Amounts borrowed from interested or related parties if your partnership is engaged in certain activities.

For more information on the at-risk rules, see Publication 925, *Passive Activity and At-Risk Rules*.

In addition to the factors discussed above, your amount at risk is affected by the operating results of the activity itself. Income from the activity increases the amount you are at risk. Losses from the activity decrease the amount you are at risk. The at-risk amount is determined at the end of each tax year. Any loss in excess of that amount is disallowed for that year. It may, however, be carried over to future years, and to the extent that you subsequently have amounts at risk, it may be deducted in those years.

Under prior law, a partnership engaged in real estate activity was not subject to the at-risk rules. The Tax Reform Act of 1986 extended the at-risk rules to include real estate activities placed in service after December 31, 1986, but made exceptions for third-party nonrecourse debt from commercial lenders and certain other parties.

In addition to the at-risk rules, the income from real estate partnerships is also subject to the passive activity rules. See *Passive Activity Limitations and At-Risk Limitations*, at the end of this chapter. Also, consult your tax advisor for further information.

When to report partnership income. Generally, you must include your distributive share of partnership items on your return for the tax year in which the last day of the partnership year falls. (See chapter 43, *Decedents: Dealing with the death of a family member*, for exceptions relating to partnership interests held by a decedent.) If you receive income from a partnership other than in your capacity as a partner, however, you must report the income in the year in which it was received. For instance, if you sell property to your partnership at a gain, the gain is generally included in income when you receive the sales proceeds, regardless of when your partnership's tax year ends.

Estimated tax payments. A partner must take into account his or her share of the partnership's income or deductions to date at each estimated tax payment date. Often, this information is not readily available. If you are a member of a partnership you may protect yourself from underpayment penalties by basing your payments on one of the exceptions described in chapter 4, *Tax withholding and estimated tax*.

However, additional issues arise if an individual's residence changes during the year. An individual's resident state income tax return generally must include all the income the individual recognized during the year. A part-year resident would include all income recognized during the period of residency, as well as income sourced to that state during the period of nonresidency. The state tax treatment of flow-through entity income for a part-year resident varies from state to state. You should review the rules for the state(s) in which you reside for guidance.

Sale of partnership interest. If you have a gain or a loss from the sale or exchange of a partnership interest, it is treated as a gain or a loss from the sale of a capital asset. The gain or loss is the difference between the amount you receive and the adjusted basis of your interest in the partnership. If you are relieved of any debts of the partnership, you must include these debts in the amount you receive.

However, you may have ordinary income as well as capital gain or loss on the sale of your partnership interest if the sale involves uncollected accounts receivable or inventory items that have increased in value. Consult your tax advisor for further help.

Qualified joint venture. If you and your spouse each materially participate as the only members of a jointly owned and operated business, and you file a joint return for the tax year, you can make a joint election to be treated as a qualified joint venture instead of a partnership. To make this election, you must divide all items of income, gain, loss, deduction, and credit attributable to the business between you and your spouse in accordance with your respective interests in the venture. For further information on how to make the election and which schedule(s) to file, see the instructions for your individual tax return.

S Corporation Income

In most cases, an S corporation does not pay tax on its income. Instead, the income, losses, deductions, and credits of the corporation are passed through to the shareholders based on each shareholder's *pro rata* share.

Schedule K-1 (Form 1120S). An S corporation must file a return on Form 1120S, U.S. Income Tax Return for an S Corporation, and send Schedule K-1 (Form 1120S) to each shareholder. In addition, the S corporation will send each shareholder a copy of the Shareholder's Instructions for Schedule K-1 (Form 1120S) to help each shareholder report his or her share of the S corporation's income, losses, credits, and deductions.

For more information on S corporations and their shareholders, see the Instructions for Form 1120S.

EXPLANATION

Shareholder's return. Generally, S corporation distributions are considered a nontaxable return of your basis in the corporation's stock. However, in certain cases, part of the distributions may be taxable as a dividend or as a long-term or short-term capital gain, or as both. The corporation's distributions may be in the form of cash or property.

All current-year income or loss and other tax items are taxed to you at the corporation's year-end. Generally, the items that are passed through to you as a shareholder will increase or decrease the basis of your S corporation stock as appropriate. Dividends are paid only from prior-year earnings (generally retained earnings from years prior to becoming an S corporation). Generally, property (including cash) distributions, except dividend distributions, are considered a return of capital to the extent of your basis in the stock of the corporation. Distributions in excess of basis are treated as a gain from the sale or exchange of property.

You should receive from the S corporation in which you are a shareholder a copy of the Shareholder's Instructions for Schedule K-1 (Form 1120S), together with a copy of Schedule K-1 (Form 1120S), showing your share of the income, credits, and deductions of the S corporation for the tax year. Your distributive share of the items of income, gain, loss, deduction, or credit of the S corporation must be shown separately on your Form 1040 or 1040A. The tax treatment of these items generally is the same as if you had realized or incurred them personally.

Individuals form an S corporation to get the legal benefits of a corporation, such as limited liability, while retaining the tax benefits of an individual. Usually, an S corporation does not pay federal income tax. One exception is a tax on net passive investment income that is paid by the S corporation, but normally, the individual owners of the corporation pay tax or accrue tax benefits on their personal returns based on the corporation's profits and losses. Income from an S corporation is included in an individual's return as if the S corporation did not exist. Dividends that the S corporation receives are included as dividends on your return on Schedule B (Form 1040). Capital gains are included on Schedule D (Form 1040). Items of income from an S corporation that are not separately stated on an individual's return, such as interest, dividends, and capital gains/losses, are combined and included on Schedule E (Form 1040). If you have losses from an S corporation when you are not an active participant in the corporation's business activities, your losses will be subject to the passive activity loss limitations. See the section on *Passive Activity Losses* at the end of this chapter.

Estimated tax payments. A shareholder must take into account his or her share of the S corporation's income or deductions to date at each estimated tax payment date. Often, this information is not readily available. If you are a member of an S corporation, you may protect yourself from underpayment penalties by basing your payments on one of the exceptions described in chapter 4, *Tax withholding and estimated tax*.

Generally, an S corporation must have its tax year-end on December 31. However, under certain circumstances, an S corporation may operate on a fiscal year; that is, its tax year may end on a date other than December 31. Your return should include all S corporation income for its operating year that ends within your tax year.

Example

If your S corporation's year ends on October 31, your return for 2014 will include the income items for the corporation's entire year that ended October 31, 2014, even though that means including 2 months of 2013.

Deducting losses. You may deduct any losses of the S corporation for the year up to the amount of your basis.

Basis in an S corporation. Your basis in an S corporation at the end of a year is your investment (basis of stock owned plus loans made directly by you to the S corporation), with the following adjustments:

Additions to basis

1. Your distributive share of the S corporation's separately and non-separately stated taxable income
2. Your share of tax-exempt income earned by the S corporation
3. Any additional capital that you contribute
4. Deductions for depletion in excess of the basis of the property
5. A loan to the corporation directly from the shareholder; however, a guarantee of a third-party loan by a shareholder does not qualify as an addition to basis

Subtractions from basis

1. Generally, any cash distributed and the fair market value of property distributed (other than taxable dividends), but not below zero
2. Your distributive share of the S corporation's separately and non-separately stated items of loss, deductions, and certain credits.
3. Your share of nondeductible, noncapital expenditures made by the S corporation
4. Your share of the deductions for depletion for any oil and gas property held by the S corporation to the extent that the deduction does not exceed the proportionate share of the property's adjusted basis allocated to you

Example 1

Your basis in an S corporation is $20,000. The corporation makes a distribution to you of $30,000 in cash or property. You would have to recognize income of $10,000 due to a distribution in excess of basis.

Example 2

Your basis in an S corporation is $20,000. If it reports losses of $30,000, you may deduct only $20,000 for the year. The other $10,000 of losses is carried over to subsequent tax years and deducted in the year you have more basis.

All you need to prepare your individual tax return is the Form K-1 provided by the S corporation. It tells you what the numbers are and where to put them on your Form 1040.

TAXPLANNER

An S corporation is just one of several alternatives to consider as a vehicle to conduct business activities, but it does offer some of the best features of a regular corporation, a partnership, and a sole proprietorship.

1. As in a regular corporation, the stockholders of an S corporation are normally immune from liabilities in excess of their investment.
2. Like a regular corporation, the S corporation structure is convenient for transferring equity to heirs as part of your estate planning and the gradual transition of management and control to your heirs or successors (see chapter 44, *Estate and gift tax planning*, for further information). As shareholders, the heirs then report their proportionate share of S corporation income and losses on their respective tax returns.
3. Like a partnership or sole proprietorship, the S corporation permits the investors to deduct operating losses. Just as important, profits are not taxed twice, as they are in a regular corporation. A regular corporation itself pays taxes, and so do the individuals who receive a share of those profits when dividends are paid. An S corporation is, except in certain circumstances, exempt from taxes—at least at the federal level.

Recoveries

A recovery is a return of an amount you deducted or took a credit for in an earlier year. The most common recoveries are refunds, reimbursements, and rebates of deductions itemized on Schedule A (Form 1040). You also may have recoveries of non-itemized deductions (such as payments on previously deducted bad debts) and recoveries of items for which you previously claimed a tax credit.

Tax benefit rule. You must include a recovery in your income in the year you receive it up to the amount by which the deduction or credit you took for the recovered amount reduced your tax in the earlier year. For this purpose, any increase to an amount carried over to the current year that resulted from the deduction or credit is considered to have reduced your tax in the earlier year. For more information, see Publication 525.

Federal income tax refund. Refunds of federal income taxes are not included in your income because they are never allowed as a deduction from income.

State tax refund. If you received a state or local income tax refund (or credit or offset) in 2014, you generally must include it in income if you deducted the tax in an earlier year. The payer should send Form 1099-G, Certain Government Payments, to you by January 31, 2015. The IRS also will receive a copy of the Form 1099-G. If you file Form 1040, use the State and Local Income Tax Refund Worksheet in the 2014 Form 1040 instructions for line 10 to figure the amount (if any) to include in your income. See Publication 525 for when you must use another worksheet.

> ### TAXORGANIZER
> Many states are no longer sending the Form 1099-G in paper form to taxpayers. To receive a copy of the 1099-G, which reports state tax refunds, the taxpayer in these states must go to their state tax department or department of revenue website to print a copy of the form for their records.

If you could choose to deduct for a tax year either:
- State and local income taxes, or
- State and local general sales taxes, then

the maximum refund that you may have to include in income is limited to the excess of the tax you chose to deduct for that year over the tax you did not choose to deduct for that year. For examples, see Publication 525.

Mortgage interest refund. If you received a refund or credit in 2014 of mortgage interest paid in an earlier year, the amount should be shown in box 3 of your Form 1098, Mortgage Interest Statement. Do not subtract the refund amount from the interest you paid in 2014. You may have to include it in your income under the rules explained in the following discussions.

Interest on recovery. Interest on any of the amounts you recover must be reported as interest income in the year received. For example, report any interest you received on state or local income tax refunds on Form 1040, line 8a.

> ### EXPLANATION
> Although the amount of a state tax refund may not be included in gross income, any interest you receive on federal or state tax refunds is taxable.

Recovery and expense in same year. If the refund or other recovery and the expense occur in the same year, the recovery reduces the deduction or credit and is not reported as income.

Recovery for 2 or more years. If you receive a refund or other recovery that is for amounts you paid in 2 or more separate years, you must allocate, on a *pro rata* basis, the recovered amount between the years in which you paid it. This allocation is necessary to determine the amount of recovery from any earlier years and to determine the amount, if any, of your allowable deduction for this item for the current year. For information on how to compute the allocation, see *Recoveries* in Publication 525.

Itemized Deduction Recoveries

If you recover any amount that you deducted in an earlier year on Schedule A (Form 1040), you generally must include the full amount of the recovery in your income in the year you receive it.

Where to report. Enter your state or local income tax refund on Form 1040, line 10, and the total of all other recoveries as other income on Form 1040, line 21. You cannot use Form 1040A or Form 1040EZ.

Standard deduction limit. You generally are allowed to claim the standard deduction if you do not itemize your deductions. Only your itemized deductions that are more than your standard deduction are subject to the recovery rule (unless you are required to itemize your deductions). If your total deductions on the earlier year return were not more than your income for that year, include in your income this year the lesser of:
- Your recoveries, or
- The amount by which your itemized deductions exceeded the standard deduction.

Example. For 2013, you filed a joint return. Your taxable income was $60,000 and you were not entitled to any tax credits. Your standard deduction was $12,200, and you had itemized deductions of $14,300. In 2014, you received the following recoveries for amounts deducted on your 2013 return:

Medical expenses	$200
State and local income tax refund	400
Refund of mortgage interest	325
Total recoveries	$925

None of the recoveries were more than the deductions taken for 2013. The difference between the state and local income tax you deducted and your local general sales tax was more than $400.

Your total recoveries are less than the amount by which your itemized deductions exceeded the standard deduction ($14,300 − 12,200 = $2,100), so you must include your total recoveries in your income for 2014. Report the state and local income tax refund of $400 on Form 1040, line 10, and the balance of your recoveries, $525, on Form 1040, line 21.

TAXPLANNER

The IRS correctly points out that the recovery of certain amounts you deducted is not income if you did not itemize your deductions in the year in which you paid these expenses. However, if the payer of the refund submits a Form 1099 or Form 1099-G to the IRS, we suggest that you attach a statement to your return including the item in income and then subtracting it out explaining why the item does not represent taxable income. This may prevent an inquiry from the IRS.

If you were subject to the alternative minimum tax in 2013, you may not have obtained any benefit for all or part of your state income tax deduction. This is because state income taxes are not deductible for purposes of computing the alternative minimum tax. (The alternative minimum tax is explained in chapter 31, *How to figure your tax*.) You will want to compute carefully the amount of the refund you received in 2014 that did not give you any tax benefit in 2013. Attach a statement in your return explaining why the item does not represent taxable income.

This will require a "with-and-without" computation. If your prior-year tax was not lower with the deduction, you did not receive a benefit, and, therefore, the refund is not taxable income when received.

Standard deduction for earlier years. To determine if amounts recovered in 2014 must be included in your income, you must know the standard deduction for your filing status for the year the deduction was claimed. Look in the instructions for your tax return from prior years to locate the standard deduction for the filing status for that prior year.

EXPLANATION

The following table can be used as a reference to determine the amount of standard deduction allowed in previous years.

	2013	2012	2011	2010	2009	2008	2007
Single	6,100	5,950	5,800	5,700	5,700	5,450	5,350
Married filing jointly/ qualifying widower	12,200	11,900	11,600	11,400	11,400	10,900	10,700
Married filing separately	6,100	5,950	5,800	5,700	5,700	5,450	5,350
Head of household	8,950	8,700	8,500	8,400	8,350	8,000	7,850

Example. You filed a joint return on Form 1040 for 2013 with taxable income of $45,000. Your itemized deductions were $12,650. The standard deduction that you could have claimed was $12,200. In 2014, you recovered $2,100 of your 2013 itemized deductions. None of the recoveries were more than the actual deductions for 2013. Include $450 of the recoveries in your 2013 income. This is the smaller of your recoveries ($2,100) or the amount by which your itemized deductions were more than the standard deduction ($12,650 − $12,200 = $450).

EXPLANATION

Sometimes you get some money back in a year after you paid and deducted it (e.g., a refund of state income tax or real estate tax). To the extent that you got a tax benefit in the earlier year, and only to that extent, you must include the refund in income.

Example

In 2014, Stan and Lori received a refund of $1,000 for real estate taxes they paid in 2013. In 2013, they reported $12,350 in itemized deductions, all of which was from their real estate taxes. The standard deduction for 2013 was $12,200. Because they only have to report the amount of the refund to the extent they received a tax benefit in 2013, they would include $150 ($12,350 − $12,200) of the refund in income in 2013.

Recovery limited to deduction. You do not include in your income any amount of your recovery that is more than the amount you deducted in the earlier year. The amount you include in your income is limited to the smaller of:
- The amount deducted on Schedule A (Form 1040), or
- The amount recovered.

Example. During 2013 you paid $1,700 for medical expenses. From this amount you subtracted $1,500, which was 10% of your adjusted gross income. Your actual medical expense deduction was $200. In 2014, you received a $500 reimbursement from your medical insurance for your 2013 expenses. The only amount of the $500 reimbursement that must be included in your income for 2014 is $200—the amount actually deducted.

Other recoveries. See *Recoveries* in Publication 525 if:
- You have recoveries of items other than itemized deductions, or
- You received a recovery for an item for which you claimed a tax credit (other than investment credit or foreign tax credit) in a prior year.

Rents from Personal Property

If you rent out personal property, such as equipment or vehicles, how you report your income and expenses is in most cases determined by:
- Whether or not the rental activity is a business, and
- Whether or not the rental activity is conducted for profit.

In most cases, if your primary purpose is income or profit and you are involved in the rental activity with continuity and regularity, your rental activity is a business. See Publication 535, Business Expenses, for details on deducting expenses for both business and not-for-profit activities.

Reporting business income and expenses. If you are in the business of renting personal property, report your income and expenses on Schedule C or Schedule C-EZ (Form 1040). The form instructions have information on how to complete them.

Reporting nonbusiness income. If you are not in the business of renting personal property, report your rental income on Form 1040, line 21. List the type and amount of the income on the dotted line next to line 21.

Reporting nonbusiness expenses. If you rent personal property for profit, include your rental expenses in the total amount you enter on Form 1040, line 36. Also enter the amount and "PPR" on the dotted line next to line 36.

If you do not rent personal property for profit, your deductions are limited and you cannot report a loss to offset other income. See *Activity not for profit*, under *Other Income*, later.

Repayments

If you had to repay an amount that you included in your income in an earlier year, you may be able to deduct the amount repaid from your income for the year in which you repaid it. Or, if the amount you repaid is more than $3,000, you may be able to take a credit against your tax for the year in which you repaid it. Generally, you can claim a deduction or credit only if the repayment qualifies as an expense or loss incurred in your trade or business or in a for-profit transaction.

Type of deduction. The type of deduction you are allowed in the year of repayment depends on the type of income you included in the earlier year. You generally deduct the repayment on the same form or schedule on which you previously reported it as income. For example, if you reported it as self-employment income, deduct it as a business expense on Schedule C or Schedule C-EZ (Form 1040) or Schedule F (Form 1040). If you reported it as a capital gain, deduct it as a capital loss as explained in the Instructions for Schedule D (Form 1040). If you reported it as wages, unemployment compensation, or other nonbusiness income, deduct it as a miscellaneous itemized deduction on Schedule A (Form 1040).

Repaid social security benefits. If you repaid social security benefits or equivalent railroad retirement benefits, see *Repayment of benefits* in chapter 11.

Repayment of $3,000 or less. If the amount you repaid was $3,000 or less, deduct it from your income in the year you repaid it. If you must deduct it as a miscellaneous itemized deduction, enter it on Schedule A (Form 1040), line 23.

Repayment over $3,000. If the amount you repaid was more than $3,000, you can deduct the repayment (as explained under *Type of deduction*, earlier). However, you can choose instead to take a tax credit for the year of repayment if you included the income under a claim of right. This means that at the time you included the income, it appeared that you had an unrestricted right to it. If you qualify for this choice, figure your tax under both methods and compare the results. Use the method (deduction or credit) that results in less tax.

Method 1. Figure your tax for 2014 claiming a deduction for the repaid amount. If you must deduct it as a miscellaneous itemized deduction, enter it on Schedule A (Form 1040), line 28.

Method 2. Figure your tax for 2014 claiming a credit for the repaid amount. Follow these steps.

1. Figure your tax for 2014 without deducting the repaid amount.
2. Refigure your tax from the earlier year without including in income the amount you repaid in 2014.
3. Subtract the tax in (2) from the tax shown on your return for the earlier year. This is the credit.
4. Subtract the answer in (3) from the tax for 2014 figured without the deduction (Step 1).

If method 1 results in less tax, deduct the amount repaid. If method 2 results in less tax, claim the credit figured in (3) above on Form 1040, line 71, by adding the amount of the credit to any other credits on this line, and entering "I.R.C. 1341" in the column to the right of line 71.

An example of this computation can be found in Publication 525.

> ### Caution
> *When determining whether the amount you repaid was more or less than $3,000, consider the total amount being repaid on the return. Each instance of repayment is not considered separately.*

EXAMPLE

For tax year 2013, you were married with no dependents. You filed a joint return with your spouse and reported taxable income of $90,000 (after all deductions and exemptions). Your return showed a tax liability of $14,566, which you paid. In 2014, you had to return $5,000 that you had received and had included in your 2013 gross income. Your marital and filing statuses were the same in 2014 as in 2013, and your taxable income for 2014 is $140,000 (after all deductions and exemptions and assuming all income is taxed at ordinary tax rates).

To determine how to treat the repayment on your 2013 return, the following calculations must be performed.

Method 1

2014 taxable income	$160,000
Less: Deduction for repayment	−5,000
Revised 2014 taxable income	$155,000
Tax using method 1	$30,865.50

Method 2

2014 taxable income	$160,000
Recomputed 2014 tax liability	$32,265.50
(a) 2013 taxable income as previously reported	$90,000
Less: Deduction for repayment	−5,000
2013 taxable income w/out repayment	$85,000
Recomputed 2013 tax liability	$13,316
(b) 2013 tax as reported	$14,566
Recomputed 2013 tax liability (w/out repayment)	−13,316
Difference	$1,250
(c) Recomputed 2014 tax liability	$32,265.50
Difference from (b)	−1,250
Tax using method 2	**$31,015.50**

To determine which method should be used to account for your repayment in 2014, you must now compare the two methods and choose the one that generates the lower tax liability. In the example, method 1 generates the lesser tax liability; therefore, you would deduct the amount repaid by you in 2014 on your 2014 tax return.

Note that these two methods will only result in different tax liabilities if you fall into different marginal tax brackets in each year (e.g., in 2013, you are in the 25% marginal tax bracket, and in 2014, you are in the 28% marginal tax bracket).

Repaid wages subject to social security and Medicare taxes. If you had to repay an amount that you included in your wages or compensation in an earlier year on which social security, Medicare, or tier 1 RRTA taxes were paid, ask your employer to refund the excess amount to you. If the employer refuses to refund the taxes, ask for a statement indicating the amount of the overcollection to support your claim. File a claim for refund using Form 843, Claim for Refund and Request for Abatement.

Repaid wages subject to Additional Medicare Tax. Employers cannot make an adjustment or file a claim for refund for Additional Medicare Tax withholding when there is a repayment of wages received by an employee in a prior year because the employee determines liability for Additional Medicare Tax on the employee's income tax return for the prior year. If you had to repay an amount that you included in your wages or compensation in an earlier year, and on which Additional Medicare Tax was paid, you may be able to recover the Additional Medicare Tax paid on the amount. To recover Additional Medicare Tax on the repaid wages or compensation, you must file Form 1040X, Amended U.S. Individual Income Tax Return, for the prior year in which the wages or compensation were originally received. See the Instructions for Form 1040X.

Royalties

Royalties from copyrights, patents, and oil, gas, and mineral properties are taxable as ordinary income.

In most cases you report royalties in Part I of Schedule E (Form 1040). However, if you hold an operating oil, gas, or mineral interest or are in business as a self-employed writer, inventor, artist, etc., report your income and expenses on Schedule C or Schedule C-EZ (Form 1040).

Copyrights and patents. Royalties from copyrights on literary, musical, or artistic works, and similar property, or from patents on inventions, are amounts paid to you for the right to use your work over a specified period of time. Royalties generally are based on the number of units sold, such as the number of books, tickets to a performance, or machines sold.

TAXSAVER

Musical compositions and copyrights. Beginning in 2007, if a musical composition or copyright is sold by the creator of that work, that seller can elect to treat any gain as a capital gain. If the gain qualifies as a long-term capital gain, it will be eligible for the 0%, 15%, or 20% preferential tax rates. See chapter 16, *Reporting gains and losses*, for more information.

Oil, gas, and minerals. Royalty income from oil, gas, and mineral properties is the amount you receive when natural resources are extracted from your property. The royalties are based on units, such as barrels, tons, etc., and are paid to you by a person or company who leases the property from you.

EXPLANATION

Income derived by an individual from a working interest in an oil or gas property is reported on Schedule C and is generally subject to self-employment tax, even though you may not actively participate in the operations that produce the income. Such income, however, is not eligible for individual retirement arrangement (IRA) or Keogh plan contributions, because it is not earned by personal services you performed.

Depletion. If you are the owner of an economic interest in mineral deposits or oil and gas wells, you can recover your investment through the depletion allowance. For information on this subject, see chapter 9 of Publication 535.

Coal and iron ore. Under certain circumstances, you can treat amounts you receive from the disposal of coal and iron ore as payments from the sale of a capital asset, rather than as royalty income. For information about gain or loss from the sale of coal and iron ore, see Publication 544.

Sale of property interest. If you sell your complete interest in oil, gas, or mineral rights, the amount you receive is considered payment for the sale of property used in a trade or business under section 1231, not royalty income. Under certain circumstances, the sale is subject to capital gain or loss treatment as explained in the Instructions for Schedule D (Form 1040). For more information on selling section 1231 property, see chapter 3 of Publication 544.

If you retain a royalty, an overriding royalty, or a net profit interest in a mineral property for the life of the property, you have made a lease or a sublease, and any cash you receive for the assignment of other interests in the property is ordinary income subject to a depletion allowance.

> **EXPLANATION**
> The sale of most items producing royalty income is treated as a capital transaction. However, this is not true for copyrights and other property created by your personal efforts. The sole purpose of this exception is to prevent people such as authors from receiving capital gain treatment for their literary efforts. For more information, see chapter 14, *Sale of property*.

Part of future production sold. If you own mineral property but sell part of the future production, in most cases you treat the money you receive from the buyer at the time of the sale as a loan from the buyer. Do not include it in your income or take depletion based on it.

When production begins, you include all the proceeds in your income, deduct all the production expenses, and deduct depletion from that amount to arrive at your taxable income from the property.

> **EXPLANATION**
> If you are paid royalties or bonuses for the production of oil before production actually begins, you may qualify for a depletion allowance in the year in which the advance royalty or bonus is included in your income. You should consult your tax advisor for further clarification of this point.

Unemployment Benefits

The tax treatment of unemployment benefits you receive depends on the type of program paying the benefits.

Unemployment compensation. You must include in income all unemployment compensation you receive. You should receive a Form 1099-G showing in box 1 the total unemployment compensation paid to you. In most cases, you enter unemployment compensation on line 19 of Form 1040, line 13 of Form 1040A, or line 3 of Form 1040EZ.

Types of unemployment compensation. Unemployment compensation generally includes any amount received under an unemployment compensation law of the United States or of a state. It includes the following benefits.

- Benefits paid by a state or the District of Columbia from the Federal Unemployment Trust Fund.
- State unemployment insurance benefits.
- Railroad unemployment compensation benefits.
- Disability payments from a government program paid as a substitute for unemployment compensation. (Amounts received as workers' compensation for injuries or illness are not unemployment compensation. See chapter 5 for more information.)
- Trade readjustment allowances under the Trade Act of 1974.
- Unemployment assistance under the Disaster Relief and Emergency Assistance Act.
- Unemployment assistance under the Airline Deregulation Act of 1974 Program.

Governmental program. If you contribute to a governmental unemployment compensation program and your contributions are not deductible, amounts you receive under the program are not included as unemployment compensation until you recover your contributions. If you deducted all of your contributions to the program, the entire amount you receive under the program is included in your income.

Repayment of unemployment compensation. If you repaid in 2014 unemployment compensation you received in 2014, subtract the amount you repaid from the total amount you received and enter the difference on line 19 of Form 1040, line 13 of Form 1040A, or line 3 of Form 1040EZ. On the dotted line next to your entry enter "Repaid" and the amount you repaid. If you repaid unemployment compensation in 2014 that you included in income in an earlier year, you can deduct the amount repaid on Schedule A (Form 1040), line 23, if you itemize deductions. If the amount is more than $3,000, see *Repayments*, earlier.

Tax withholding. You can choose to have federal income tax withheld from your unemployment compensation. To make this choice, complete Form W-4V, Voluntary Withholding Request, and give it to the paying office. Tax will be withheld at 10% of your payment.

> **Caution**
> *If you do not choose to have tax withheld from your unemployment compensation, you may be liable for estimated tax. If you do not pay enough tax, either through withholding or estimated tax, or a combination of both, you may have to pay a penalty. For more information on estimated tax, see chapter 4.*

Supplemental unemployment benefits. Benefits received from an employer-financed fund (to which the employees did not contribute) are not unemployment compensation. They are taxable as wages and are subject to withholding for income tax. They may be subject to social security and Medicare taxes. For more information, see *Supplemental Unemployment Benefits* in section 5 of Publication 15-A, Employer's Supplemental Tax Guide. Report these payments on line 7 of Form 1040 or Form 1040A or on line 1 of Form 1040EZ.

Repayment of benefits. You may have to repay some of your supplemental unemployment benefits to qualify for trade readjustment allowances under the Trade Act of 1974. If you repay supplemental unemployment benefits in the same year you receive them, reduce the total benefits by the amount you repay. If you repay the benefits in a later year, you must include the full amount of the benefits received in your income for the year you received them.

Deduct the repayment in the later year as an adjustment to gross income on Form 1040. (You cannot use Form 1040A or Form 1040EZ.) Include the repayment on Form 1040, line 36, and enter "Sub-Pay TRA" and the amount on the dotted line next to line 36. If the amount you repay in a later year is more than $3,000, you may be able to take a credit against your tax for the later year instead of deducting the amount repaid. For more information on this, see *Repayments*, earlier.

Private unemployment fund. Unemployment benefit payments from a private (nonunion) fund to which you voluntarily contribute are taxable only if the amounts you receive are more than your total payments into the fund. Report the taxable amount on Form 1040, line 21.

Payments by a union. Benefits paid to you as an unemployed member of a union from regular union dues are included in your income on Form 1040, line 21. However, if you contribute to a special union fund and your payments to the fund are not deductible, the unemployment benefits you receive from the fund are includible in your income only to the extent they are more than your contributions.

Guaranteed annual wage. Payments you receive from your employer during periods of unemployment, under a union agreement that guarantees you full pay during the year, are taxable as wages. Include them on line 7 of Form 1040 or Form 1040A or on line 1 of Form 1040EZ.

State employees. Payments similar to a state's unemployment compensation may be made by the state to its employees who are not covered by the state's unemployment compensation law. Although the payments are fully taxable, do not report them as unemployment compensation. Report these payments on Form 1040, line 21.

Welfare and Other Public Assistance Benefits

Do not include in your income governmental benefit payments from a public welfare fund based upon need, such as payments to blind individuals under a state public assistance law. Payments from a state fund for the victims of crime should not be included in the victims' incomes if they are in the nature of welfare payments. Do not deduct medical expenses that are reimbursed by such a fund. You must include in your income any welfare payments that are compensation for services or that are obtained fraudulently.

Reemployment Trade Adjustment Assistance (RTAA) payments. RTAA payments received from a state must be included in your income. The state must send you Form 1099-G to advise you of the amount you should include in income. The amount should be reported on Form 1040, line 21.

Persons with disabilities. If you have a disability, you must include in income compensation you receive for services you perform unless the compensation is otherwise excluded. However, you do not include in income the value of goods, services, and cash that you receive, not in return for your services, but for your training and rehabilitation because you have a disability. Excludable amounts include payments for transportation and attendant care, such as interpreter services for the deaf, reader services for the blind, and services to help individuals with an intellectual disability do their work.

Disaster relief grants. Do not include post-disaster grants received under the Robert T. Stafford Disaster Relief and Emergency Assistance Act in your income if the grant payments are made to help you meet necessary expenses or serious needs for medical, dental, housing, personal property, transportation, child care, or funeral expenses. Do not deduct casualty losses or medical expenses that are specifically reimbursed by these disaster relief grants. If you have deducted a casualty loss for the loss of your personal residence and you later receive a disaster relief grant for the loss of the same residence, you may have to include part or all of the grant in your taxable income. See *Recoveries*, earlier. Unemployment assistance payments under the Act are taxable unemployment compensation. See *Unemployment compensation* under *Unemployment Benefits*, earlier.

Disaster relief payments. You can exclude from income any amount you receive that is a qualified disaster relief payment. A qualified disaster relief payment is an amount paid to you:

1. To reimburse or pay reasonable and necessary personal, family, living, or funeral expenses that result from a qualified disaster;
2. To reimburse or pay reasonable and necessary expenses incurred for the repair or rehabilitation of your home or repair or replacement of its contents to the extent it is due to a qualified disaster;
3. By a person engaged in the furnishing or sale of transportation as a common carrier because of the death or personal physical injuries incurred as a result of a qualified disaster; or
4. By a federal, state, or local government, or agency, or instrumentality in connection with a qualified disaster in order to promote the general welfare.

You can exclude this amount only to the extent any expense it pays for is not paid for by insurance or otherwise. The exclusion does not apply if you were a participant or conspirator in a terrorist action or a representative of one. A qualified disaster is:

-   A disaster which results from a terrorist or military action;
-   A federally declared disaster; or
-   A disaster which results from an accident involving a common carrier, or from any other event, which is determined to be catastrophic by the Secretary of the Treasury or his or her delegate.

For amounts paid under item (4), a disaster is qualified if it is determined by an applicable federal, state, or local authority to warrant assistance from the federal, state, or local government, agency, or instrumentality.

TAXALERT

If you received payments for lost wages or income due to a disaster, such as the federal disasters declared during 2014 because of severe storms, flooding, and tornadoes, such payments are taxable to you in the same way the wages or business income these payments are replacing would have been. Payments received for property damage are taxable to the extent the payments exceed your basis in the property. Payments received for physical injury are generally not taxable income.

Disaster mitigation payments. You also can exclude from income any amount you receive that is a qualified disaster mitigation payment. Qualified disaster mitigation payments are also most commonly paid to you in the period immediately following damage to property as a result of a natural disaster. However, disaster mitigation payments are used to mitigate (reduce the severity of) potential damage from future natural disasters. They are paid to you through state and local governments based on the provisions of the Robert T. Stafford Disaster Relief and Emergency Assistance Act or the National Flood Insurance Act.

You cannot increase the basis or adjusted basis of your property for improvements made with nontaxable disaster mitigation payments.

Home Affordable Modification Program (HAMP). If you benefit from Pay-for-Performance Success Payments under HAMP, the payments are not taxable.

TAXSAVER

Hardest Hit Fund and Emergency Homeowners' Loan Program. If you receive or benefit from payments made under:

-   A State Housing Finance agency (State HFA) Hardest Hit Fund program in which program payments can be used to pay mortgage interest, or
-   An Emergency Homeowners' Loan Program (EHLP) administered by the Department of Housing and Urban Development (HUD) or a state,

the payments are not included in gross income and are not taxable.

Mortgage assistance payments under section 235 of the National Housing Act. Payments made under section 235 of the National Housing Act for mortgage assistance are not included in the homeowner's income. Interest paid for the homeowner under the mortgage assistance program cannot be deducted.

Medicare. Medicare benefits received under title XVIII of the Social Security Act are not includible in the gross income of the individuals for whom they are paid. This includes basic (part A (Hospital Insurance Benefits for the Aged)) and supplementary (part B (Supplementary Medical Insurance Benefits for the Aged)).

Old-age, survivors, and disability insurance benefits (OASDI). Generally, OASDI payments under section 202 of title II of the Social Security Act are not includible in the gross income of the individuals to whom they are paid. This applies to old-age insurance benefits, and insurance benefits for wives, husbands, children, widows, widowers, mothers and fathers, and parents, as well as the lump-sum death payment.

Nutrition Program for the Elderly. Food benefits you receive under the Nutrition Program for the Elderly are not taxable. If you prepare and serve free meals for the program, include in your income as wages the cash pay you receive, even if you are also eligible for food benefits.

Other Sickness and Injury Benefits

In addition to welfare or insurance benefits, you may receive other payments for sickness or injury.

Workers' compensation. Amounts you receive as workers' compensation for an occupational sickness or injury are fully exempt from tax if they are paid under a workers' compensation act or a statute in the nature of a workers' compensation act. The exemption also applies to your survivor(s). The exemption from tax, however, does not apply to retirement benefits you receive based on your age, length of service, or prior contributions to the plan, even if you retired because of occupational sickness or injury.

Note: If part of your workers' compensation reduces your social security or equivalent railroad retirement benefits received, that part is considered social security (or equivalent railroad retirement) benefits and may be taxable. For more information, see Publication 915, *Social Security and Equivalent Railroad Retirement Benefits*.

Return to work. If you return to work after qualifying for workers' compensation, payments you continue to receive while assigned to light duties are taxable. Report these payments as wages on line 7 of Form 1040 or Form 1040A or on line 1 of Form 1040EZ.

Federal Employees' Compensation Act (FECA). Payments received under this Act for personal injury or sickness, including payments to beneficiaries in case of death, are not taxable. However, you are taxed on amounts you receive under this Act as "continuation of pay" for up to 45 days while a claim is being decided. Report this income on line 7 of Form 1040 or Form 1040A or on line 1 of Form 1040EZ. Also, pay for sick leave while a claim is being processed is taxable and must be included in your income as wages.

The IRS has ruled that the subsidized portion of health benefits provided by an employer to an employee's domestic partner, who does not qualify as a spouse or a dependent, will be taxable as wages to the employee.

You can deduct the amount you spend to "buy back" sick leave for an earlier year to be eligible for nontaxable FECA benefits for that period. It is a miscellaneous deduction subject to the 2% limit on Schedule A (Form 1040). If you buy back sick leave in the same year you use it, the amount reduces your taxable sick leave pay. Do not deduct it separately.

Other compensation. Many other amounts you receive as compensation for injury or illness are not taxable. These include:

- **Compensatory damages** you receive for physical injury or physical illness, whether paid in a lump sum or in periodic payments,
- **Benefits you receive under an accident or health insurance policy** on which either you paid the premiums or your employer paid the premiums but you had to include them in your gross income,
- **Disability benefits** you receive for loss of income or earning capacity as a result of injuries under a "no-fault" car insurance policy, and
- **Compensation you receive for permanent loss or loss of use** of a part or function of your body, or for your permanent disfigurement. This compensation must be based only on the injury and not on the period of your absence from work. These benefits are exempt from tax even if your employer pays for the accident and health plan that provides these benefits.

Only damages received on account of personal physical injury or sickness are nontaxable. Punitive damages will be taxable except those received in a wrongful death action where state law stipulates that they are nontaxable. This law is effective for amounts received after August 20, 1996, unless there was a binding settlement in effect on September 13, 1995.

Reimbursement for medical care. A reimbursement for medical care is generally not taxable. However, this reimbursement may reduce your medical expense deduction. For more information, see Table 22-1 in chapter 22, *Medical and dental expenses*.

Payments to reduce cost of winter energy. Payments made by a state to qualified people to reduce their cost of winter energy use are not taxable.

Other Income

The following brief discussions are arranged in alphabetical order. Other income items briefly discussed below are referenced to publications which provide more topical information.

Activity not for profit. You must include on your return income from an activity from which you do not expect to make a profit. An example of this type of activity is a hobby or a farm you operate mostly for recreation and pleasure. Enter this income on Form 1040, line 21. Deductions for expenses related to the activity are limited. They cannot total more than the income you report and can be taken only if you itemize deductions on Schedule A (Form 1040). See *Not-for-Profit Activities* in chapter 1 of Publication 535 for information on whether an activity is considered carried on for a profit.

EXPLANATION

An activity will be presumed to have been for profit if it results in a profit in at least 3 out of 5 consecutive tax years whether the activity is held individually, in trust, as a partnership, or as an S corporation. However, for the breeding, training, showing, or racing of horses, the activity must result in a profit in at least 2 out of 7 consecutive tax years. If the activity meets this test, it is presumed to be carried on for profit and the limits will not apply.

If you have engaged in an activity for less than 3 years, you can postpone the determination that the activity is not for profit by filing Form 5213, Election to Postpone Determination. Get Publication 535, *Business Expenses*, for more information.

It is possible that the IRS may treat you as engaged in a profit-making activity, even if you do not have a profit for 3 or more years during a period of 5 consecutive tax years. The IRS determines the activity's status—for profit or as a hobby—by considering the facts and circumstances surrounding the case. Some factors that will be considered include the following:

1. The manner in which you carry on the activity. For example, do you conduct your actions in a business-like manner (records, activity details, separate bank accounts, etc.)?
2. The level of expertise possessed by you and your advisors
3. The time and effort you expend in carrying on the activity
4. Any expectations you have that assets used in the activity may appreciate in value
5. Prior success in similar or dissimilar activities
6. Your history of income or loss with respect to the activity
7. The amount of occasional profits, if any, that you earn through the activity
8. Your financial status. For example, the fact that you do not have substantial income from other sources may indicate that you are engaging in the activity for profit
9. Elements of personal pleasure or recreation

These factors are not exclusive, and no one factor or number of factors is determinative.

Alaska Permanent Fund dividend. If you received a payment from Alaska's mineral income fund (Alaska Permanent Fund dividend), report it as income on line 21 of Form 1040, line 13 of Form 1040A, or line 3 of Form 1040EZ. The state of Alaska sends each recipient a document that shows the amount of the payment with the check. The amount also is reported to IRS.

Alimony. Include in your income on Form 1040, line 11, any alimony payments you receive. Amounts you receive for child support are not income to you. Alimony and child support payments are discussed in chapter 18.

Bribes. If you receive a bribe, include it in your income.

Campaign contributions. These contributions are not income to a candidate unless they are diverted to his or her personal use. To be exempt from tax, the contributions must be spent for campaign purposes or kept in a fund for use in future campaigns. However, interest earned on bank deposits, dividends received on contributed securities, and net gains realized on sales of contributed securities are taxable and must be reported on Form 1120-POL, U.S. Income Tax Return for Certain Political Organizations. Excess campaign funds transferred to an office account must be included in the office-holder's income on Form 1040, line 21, in the year transferred.

Car pools. Do not include in your income amounts you receive from the passengers for driving a car in a car pool to and from work. These amounts are considered reimbursement for your expenses. However, this rule does not apply if you have developed car pool arrangements into a profit-making business of transporting workers for hire.

Cash rebates. A cash rebate you receive from a dealer or manufacturer of an item you buy is not income, but you must reduce your basis by the amount of the rebate.

Example. You buy a new car for $24,000 cash and receive a $2,000 rebate check from the manufacturer. The $2,000 is not income to you. Your basis in the car is $22,000. This is the basis on which you figure gain or loss if you sell the car and depreciation if you use it for business.

Casualty insurance and other reimbursements. You generally should not report these reimbursements on your return unless you are figuring gain or loss from the casualty or theft. See chapter 26 for more information.

Child support payments. You should not report these payments on your return. See chapter 18 for more information.

Court awards and damages. To determine if settlement amounts you receive by compromise or judgment must be included in your income, you must consider the item that the settlement replaces. The character of the income as ordinary income or capital gain depends on the nature of the underlying claim. Include the following as ordinary income.

1. Interest on any award.
2. Compensation for lost wages or lost profits in most cases.
3. Punitive damages, in most cases. It does not matter if they relate to a physical injury or physical sickness.
4. Amounts received in settlement of pension rights (if you did not contribute to the plan).
5. Damages for:
   a. Patent or copyright infringement,
   b. Breach of contract, or
   c. Interference with business operations.
6. Back pay and damages for emotional distress received to satisfy a claim under title VII of the Civil Rights Act of 1964.
7. Attorney fees and costs (including contingent fees) where the underlying recovery is included in gross income.

Do not include in your income compensatory damages for personal physical injury or physical sickness (whether received in a lump sum or installments).

Emotional distress. Emotional distress itself is not a physical injury or physical sickness, but damages you receive for emotional distress due to a physical injury or sickness are treated as received for the physical injury or sickness. Do not include them in your income.

If the emotional distress is due to a personal injury that is not due to a physical injury or sickness (for example, employment discrimination or injury to reputation), you must include the damages in your income, except for any damages you receive for medical care due to that emotional distress. Emotional distress includes physical symptoms that result from emotional distress, such as headaches, insomnia, and stomach disorders.

EXPLANATION
The tax law states that only damages received on account of personal injury or sickness are nontaxable. Punitive damages will be taxable, unless they are received in a wrongful death action for which state law stipulates as of September 13, 1995, that only punitive damages may be awarded. This law is effective for amounts received after August 20, 1996, unless there was a binding settlement in effect on September 13, 1995. If you have a question about whether the award is taxable, you should consult your tax advisor.

TAXSAVER
The legal expense that you incur in the process of getting a damage award may be claimed as an itemized deduction (subject to the 2%-of-AGI floor) only if the award is included in your gross income. The same holds true for the deduction in calculating your adjusted gross income for legal fees for "civil rights" type cases created under a 2004 tax act. A "civil rights" type case is one involving claims of discrimination of any sort. If the award is only partially included in your gross income, you may deduct only a proportional amount in legal fees. Thus, if the entire award is excluded from your gross income, none of your legal fees are deductible.

TAXSAVER
A technique now being used in large personal injury cases is the structured settlement, in which the defendant's insurance company offers an annuity to the injured party instead of a lump-sum distribution. The IRS has ruled that the entire amount of the annuity payments may be excluded from the recipient's gross income, even though the recipient is, in effect, receiving interest.

Deduction for costs involved in unlawful discrimination suits. You may be able to deduct attorney fees and court costs paid to recover a judgment or settlement for a claim of unlawful discrimination under various provisions of federal, state, and local law listed in Internal Revenue Code Section 62(e), a claim against the United States government, or a claim under Section 1862(b)(3)(A) of the Social Security Act. For more information, see Publication 525.

Credit card insurance. In most cases, if you receive benefits under a credit card disability or unemployment insurance plan, the benefits are taxable to you. These plans make the minimum monthly payment on your credit card account if you cannot make the payment due to injury, illness, disability, or unemployment. Report on Form 1040, line 21, the amount of benefits you received during the year that is more than the amount of the premiums you paid during the year.

Down payment assistance. If you purchase a home and receive assistance from a nonprofit corporation to make the down payment, that assistance is not included in your income. If the corporation qualifies as a tax-exempt charitable organization, the assistance is treated as a gift and is included in your basis of the house. If the corporation does not qualify, the assistance is treated as a rebate or reduction of the purchase price and is not included in your basis.

Employment agency fees. If you get a job through an employment agency, and the fee is paid by your employer, the fee is not includible in your income if you are not liable for it. However, if you pay it and your employer reimburses you for it, it is includible in your income.

Energy conservation subsidies. You can exclude from gross income any subsidy provided, either directly or indirectly, by public utilities for the purchase or installation of an energy conservation measure for a dwelling unit.

Energy conservation measure. This includes installations or modifications that are primarily designed to reduce consumption of electricity or natural gas, or improve the management of energy demand.

Dwelling unit. This includes a house, apartment, condominium, mobile home, boat, or similar property. If a building or structure contains both dwelling and other units, any subsidy must be properly allocated.

Estate and trust income. An estate or trust, unlike a partnership, may have to pay federal income tax. If you are a beneficiary of an estate or trust, you may be taxed on your share of its income distributed or required to be distributed to you. However, there is never a double tax. Estates and trusts file their returns on Form 1041, U.S. Income Tax Return for Estates and Trusts, and your share of the income is reported to you on Schedule K-1 (Form 1041).

EXPLANATION

Generally speaking, there are three types of trusts: (1) a trust that is required to distribute all the income it earns during the year (simple trust), (2) a trust that has the choice of whether to distribute all, part, or none of the income (complex trust), and (3) a trust where the person creating the trust is treated as the owner of the trust's assets (grantor trust). The taxability of these trusts varies. A beneficiary of a simple trust must report all the income (though generally not capital gains), whether actually distributed or not, on his or her income tax return (Form 1040). A beneficiary of a complex trust will only report the income of the trust to the extent of distributions actually made by the trust to the beneficiary. The grantor of a grantor trust must report all income, gains, and deductions on his or her individual income tax return, as they are not taxed on the grantor trust return.

Current income required to be distributed. If you are the beneficiary of an estate or trust that must distribute all of its current income, you must report your share of the distributable net income, whether or not you actually received it.

EXAMPLE

A beneficiary of a trust that is required to distribute all of its current income receives a Schedule K-1 reporting $100 of interest income. However, the beneficiary has not received any distributions from the trust. The beneficiary must report the $100 of interest income on Schedule B of Form 1040 even though the beneficiary has not received any distributions.

Current income not required to be distributed. If you are the beneficiary of an estate or trust and the fiduciary has the choice of whether to distribute all or part of the current income, you must report:

- All income that is required to be distributed to you, whether or not it is actually distributed, plus
- All other amounts actually paid or credited to you,

up to the amount of your share of distributable net income.

EXPLANATION

When an estate earns income before the assets have all been distributed, it is taxed like a complex trust. Many people find this area of estate taxation very confusing, and for good reason. Gifts and inheritances are not gross income to the recipient. However, money or property that you inherit may earn some interest, dividends, or rent while the estate is being settled. It is that income that must be reported either by you or by the estate. Ordinarily, the executor of the estate files an income tax return for the estate, reporting the income, but he or she may shift the tax burden of that income to the beneficiaries if the property has already been distributed to them. See chapter 43, *Decedents: Dealing with the death of a family member*, for more detail.

TAXALERT

In some instances, adjustments for the alternative minimum tax could flow through a trust to the beneficiary. See chapter 31, *How to figure your tax*, for more detail.

TAXPLANNER

The Affordable Care Act imposes a 3.8% Net Investment Income Tax (NIIT) on unearned income of individuals effective for tax years beginning after December 31, 2012. This 3.8% tax also applies to estates and trusts on the lesser of: (1) undistributed net investment income or (2) the excess of adjusted gross income (AGI) over $11,950. If the trust or estate has Net Investment Income that can be carried out to the beneficiary, trustees of discretionary trusts and estates may wish to consider an individual beneficiary's threshold for triggering the NIIT since the modified AGI threshold levels at which liability for the NIIT arises for individuals are much higher; i.e., over $200,000 ($250,000 if married filing jointly or qualifying widow(er) with dependent child; $125,000 if married filing separately). There are many other considerations for the trustee to evaluate in determining how much to distribute to beneficiaries. We suggest that you and your trustee should consult with tax advisors who specialize in these matters.

How to report. Treat each item of income the same way that the estate or trust would treat it. For example, if a trust's dividend income is distributed to you, you report the distribution as dividend income on your return. The same rule applies to distributions of tax-exempt interest and capital gains.

The fiduciary of the estate or trust must tell you the type of items making up your share of the estate or trust income and any credits you are allowed on your individual income tax return.

Losses. Losses of estates and trusts generally are not deductible by the beneficiaries.

EXCEPTION

There are significant exceptions to the rule that losses of estates and trusts are not deductible by the beneficiaries. When an estate or a trust terminates, the beneficiaries are frequently allowed a deduction for certain expenses that the estate or trust had but was unable to use as a deduction. These items are (1) net operating loss carryovers, (2) certain excess deductions in the year of termination, and (3) capital loss carryovers.

When an estate is terminated, it is not unusual for the attorney's and executor's fees to be paid in the year in which the estate is closed. If these expenses and the net operating loss carryover exceed the estate's income for that year, the excess is deductible by the beneficiaries. This deduction may be claimed only by itemizing deductions on Schedule A (Form 1040). These deductions are subject to the 2% rule on miscellaneous itemized deductions. This means that they are only deductible to the extent that total miscellaneous itemized deductions exceed 2% of AGI.

A capital loss carryover from an estate or a trust may be used in the beneficiaries' current or subsequent returns to reduce capital gains and/or to generate a deduction subject to the limitation that only $3,000 ($1,500 if your filing status is married filing separately) of capital losses in excess of capital gains may be deducted each year.

When to report estate and trust income. You must include your share of the estate or trust income on your return for your tax year in which the last day of the estate or trust tax year falls.

The trustee of the trust or estate will provide you with a Schedule K-1 (Form 1041) that tells you each item of income and deductions, and where they are to be reported on your personal tax return.

TAXSAVER

It may be a good idea if you are the beneficiary of a trust to inform the trustee of your tax situation so that all possible tax-saving alternatives can be explored. Amounts that are not required to be distributed currently, according to the terms of the trust, may sometimes be distributed at the discretion of the trustee. There may be substantial tax planning opportunities relating to the timing, amounts, and methods of such distributions. You and the trustee should consult with a tax professional specializing in this area.

TAXPLANNER

If you are receiving trust income, you should consider whether it is necessary for you to make estimated tax payments or increase your withholding taxes as a result of this additional income. See chapter 4, *Tax withholding and estimated tax*.

Grantor trust. Income earned by a grantor trust is taxable to the grantor, not the beneficiary, if the grantor keeps certain control over the trust. (The grantor is the one who transferred property to the trust.) This rule applies if the property (or income from the property) put into the trust will or may revert (be returned) to the grantor or the grantor's spouse.

Generally, a trust is a grantor trust if the grantor has a reversionary interest valued (at the date of transfer) at more than 5% of the value of the transferred property.

TAXALERT

Even though the grantor is taxed on the trust income, the trustee of a grantor trust may need to file Form 1041 if the trust income reaches a level that requires a return or if a separate federal identification number has been established by the trust. The items of income, deduction, and credit are treated as owned by the grantor or another person, and are reported on a separate statement (Tax Information Letter) that is attached to Form 1041.

The IRS issued regulations that provide guidance for optional methods of reporting trust income by a grantor trust. For example, alternative methods of reporting include the issuance of a Form 1099 directly from the payer of income to the grantor for inclusion on the grantor's individual income tax return; the issuance of a Form 1099 by the trust to the grantor; or the filing of a Form 1041 by the trustee of the grantor trust.

The rules can get complicated, especially if there is more than one grantor. You should consult with your tax advisor for more information.

Expenses paid by another. If your personal expenses are paid for by another person, such as a corporation, the payment may be taxable to you depending upon your relationship with that person and the nature of the payment. But if the payment makes up for a loss caused by that person, and only restores you to the position you were in before the loss, the payment is not includible in your income.

Fees for services. Include all fees for your services in your income. Examples of these fees are amounts you receive for services you perform as:
- A corporate director,
- An executor, administrator, or personal representative of an estate,

- A manager of a trade or business you operated before declaring Chapter 11 bankruptcy,
- A notary public, or
- An election precinct official.

Nonemployee compensation. If you are not an employee and the fees for your services from the same payer total $600 or more for the year, you may receive a Form 1099-MISC. You may need to report your fees as self-employment income. See *Self-Employed Persons*, in chapter 1, for a discussion of when you are considered self-employed.

Corporate director. Corporate director fees are self-employment income. Report these payments on Schedule C or Schedule C-EZ (Form 1040).

Personal representatives. All personal representatives must include in their gross income fees paid to them from an estate. If you are not in the trade or business of being an executor (for instance, you are the executor of a friend's or relative's estate), report these fees on Form 1040, line 21. If you are in the trade or business of being an executor, report these fees as self-employment income on Schedule C or Schedule C-EZ (Form 1040). The fee is not includible in income if it is waived.

Manager of trade or business for bankruptcy estate. Include in your income all payments received from your bankruptcy estate for managing or operating a trade or business that you operated before you filed for bankruptcy. Report this income on Form 1040, line 21.

Notary public. Report payments for these services on Schedule C or Schedule C-EZ (Form 1040). These payments are not subject to self-employment tax. See the separate instructions for Schedule SE (Form 1040) for details.

Election precinct official. You should receive a Form W-2 showing payments for services performed as an election official or election worker. Report these payments on line 7 of Form 1040 or Form 1040A or on line 1 of Form 1040EZ.

EXPLANATION

Self-employment income. Chapter 38, *Self-employment income: How to file Schedule C*, includes a more comprehensive discussion of self-employment income.

Corporate director fees and executor fees (if you are in the trade or business of being an executor) are considered self-employment income, and are subject to self-employment tax. For both employees and self-employed individuals, the 2014 wage base is $117,000 for Old Age, Survivor, and Disability Insurance (OASDI) and is unlimited for Medicare. The OASDI rate is 12.4%

The Medicare tax rate is 2.9%. However, under the Affordable Care Act (the comprehensive health care law that was passed in 2010 and upheld as constitutional by the U.S. Supreme Court in June 2012), beginning in 2013, an Additional Medicare Tax of 0.9% is assessed on top of the current 2.9% rate—for a total rate of 3.8%—on self-employment income (as well as wages) received in excess of specified threshold amounts ($250,000 for a joint return; $125,000 for a married individual filing a separate return; and $200,000 for all other taxpayers. (For joint filers, the additional 0.9% tax applies to the couple's combined wages in excess of $250,000.)

The combined 12.4% OASDI, 2.9% Medicare, and, if applicable, 0.9% additional Medicare tax rates are applied to 92.35% of your self-employment income. However, if your net earnings from self-employment are less than $400, no self-employment tax is payable. Thus, for example, if a person on earns self-employment income of $130,000 in 2014, he or she will pay self-employment tax of $17,990—i.e., ($117,000 × 15.3%) plus [($130,000 × 92.35%) − $117,000] × 2.9%. For a single filer who has self-employment income of $230,000 in 2014, he or she will pay self-employment tax of $20,779—i.e., ($117,000 × 15.3%) plus [($230,000 × 92.35%) − $117,000] × 2.9% plus [($230,000 × 92.35%) − $200,000] × 0.9%. See Schedule SE.

Fees are self-employment income only if you present yourself as being in the trade or business that produces the fees. Therefore, unless you regularly appear as a witness, act as an executor or trustee, or judge elections, the fees earned will not be self-employment income subject to self-employment tax.

Clergy fees. Fees received by clergy for performing funerals, marriages, baptisms, or other services must be included in gross income.

TAXSAVER

A member of the clergy, however, can request to be exempt from the self-employment tax on such income by filing Form 4361, Application for Exemption from Self-Employment Tax for Use by Ministers, Members of Religious Orders, and Christian Science Practitioners.

Foster care providers. Payments you receive from a state, political subdivision, or a qualified foster care placement agency for providing care to qualified foster individuals in your home generally are not included in your income. However, you must include in your income payments received for the care of more than 5 individuals age 19 or older and certain difficulty-of-care payments.

A qualified foster individual is a person who:
1. Is living in a foster family home, and
2. Was placed there by:
   a. An agency of a state or one of its political subdivisions, or
   b. A qualified foster care placement agency.

Difficulty-of-care payments. These are additional payments that are designated by the payer as compensation for providing the additional care that is required for physically, mentally, or emotionally handicapped qualified foster individuals. A state must determine that the additional compensation is needed, and the care for which the payments are made must be provided in your home.

You must include in your income difficulty-of-care payments received for more than:
- 10 qualified foster individuals under age 19, or
- 5 qualified foster individuals age 19 or older.

Maintaining space in home. If you are paid to maintain space in your home for emergency foster care, you must include the payment in your income.

Reporting taxable payments. If you receive payments that you must include in your income, you are in business as a foster care provider and you are self-employed. Report the payments on Schedule C or Schedule C-EZ (Form 1040). See Publication 587, Business Use of Your Home, to help you determine the amount you can deduct for the use of your home.

Found property. If you find and keep property that does not belong to you that has been lost or abandoned (treasure-trove), it is taxable to you at its fair market value in the first year it is your undisputed possession.

Free tour. If you received a free tour from a travel agency for organizing a group of tourists, you must include its value in your income. Report the fair market value of the tour on Form 1040, line 21, if you are not in the trade or business of organizing tours. You cannot deduct your expenses in serving as the voluntary leader of the group at the group's request. If you organize tours as a trade or business, report the tour's value on Schedule C or Schedule C-EZ (Form 1040).

Gambling winnings. You must include your gambling winnings in income on Form 1040, line 21. If you itemize your deductions on Schedule A (Form 1040), you can deduct gambling losses you had during the year, but only up to the amount of your winnings.

Lotteries and raffles. Winnings from lotteries and raffles are gambling winnings. In addition to cash winnings, you must include in your income the fair market value of bonds, cars, houses, and other noncash prizes.

TAXPLANNER
If you win a large lottery, proper financial planning can help you minimize the tax bite. You should consult with a financial planner and/or your tax advisor.

Form W-2G. You may have received a Form W-2G, Certain Gambling Winnings, showing the amount of your gambling winnings and any tax taken out of them. Include the amount from box 1 on Form 1040, line 21. Include the amount shown in box 4 on Form 1040, line 62, as federal income tax withheld.

Reporting winnings and recordkeeping. For more information on reporting gambling winnings and recordkeeping, see *Gambling Losses Up to the Amount of Gambling Winnings* in chapter 29.

> **Tip**
> *If you win a state lottery prize payable in installments, see Publication 525 for more information.*

EXPLANATION
While a winner of the Canadian government lottery does not have to pay Canadian tax on the winnings, a U.S. citizen or resident who wins does have to pay U.S. tax on the amount. Citizens and residents of the United States have to report all income, including foreign income. See chapter 41, *U.S. citizens working abroad: Tax treatment of foreign earned income*, and chapter 42, *Foreign citizens living in the United States*, for more information about worldwide income.

TAXPLANNER
Because you may not win money gambling until late in the year and gambling losses are deductible only up to the amount of your winnings, you should plan ahead by keeping losing racetrack, lottery, and other gambling tickets. In that way, if you do win, you will be able to itemize your gambling losses. It's also a good idea to keep a diary of gambling losses incurred during the entire year. Note that losses from one kind of gambling are deductible against gains from another kind. These losses are claimed as miscellaneous itemized deductions but are not subject to the 2%-of-AGI floor and are reported on Schedule A, line 28. These losses are also allowed for purposes of the alternative minimum tax (AMT).

Gifts and inheritances. In most cases, property you receive as a gift, bequest, or inheritance is not included in your income. However, if property you receive this way later produces income such as interest, dividends, or rents, that income is taxable to you. If property is given to a trust and the income from it is paid, credited, or distributed to you, that income is also taxable to you. If the gift, bequest, or inheritance is the income from the property, that income is taxable to you.

> ### *EXPLANATION*
> Items given to you as an incentive to enter into a business transaction are not tax-free gifts. For example, incentive items such as small appliances or dinnerware given to you by a bank as an incentive to open an account are treated as taxable interest income to you and must be reported at their fair market value.

Inherited pension or IRA. If you inherited a pension or an individual retirement arrangement (IRA), you may have to include part of the inherited amount in your income. See chapter 10 if you inherited a pension. See chapter 17 if you inherited an IRA.

> ### *TAXALERT*
> Distributions from qualified retirement plans and IRAs are not subject to the 3.8% Net Investment Income Tax (NIIT) that is imposed by the Affordable Care Act. On the other hand, these distributions are taken into account in determining a taxpayer's modified adjusted gross income threshold for purposes of figuring the amount subject to the 3.8% NIIT.

Hobby losses. Losses from a hobby are not deductible from other income. A hobby is an activity from which you do not expect to make a profit. See *Activity not for profit*, earlier.

> ### *EXPLANATION*
> While a net loss from the sale of stamps, coins, or other items that you collect for a hobby may not be deducted, a loss from the sale of these items may be offset against a gain from the sale of similar items occurring in the same year.
>
> #### *Example*
> You sell several stamps at a gain of $1,000. You may offset this gain by up to $1,000 in losses from the sale of other stamps. The result is that there is no net taxable gain to report on your income tax return. Each sale should be listed separately on Form 8949 and reported on Schedule D.

> ### *TAXSAVER*
> If you are planning to sell an item in your collection that has appreciated in value and your collection also contains an item that has decreased in value, you may want to sell both in the same year to incur the least amount of tax. In short, clean out the junk to establish losses in a year when you have gains.

Illegal activities. Income from illegal activities, such as money from dealing illegal drugs, must be included in your income on Form 1040, line 21, or on Schedule C or Schedule C-EZ (Form 1040) if from your self-employment activity.

Tip

If you collect stamps, coins, or other items as a hobby for recreation and pleasure, and you sell any of the items, your gain is taxable as a capital gain. (See chapter 16.) However, if you sell items from your collection at a loss, you cannot deduct the loss.

> ### *EXPLANATION*
> It is not necessary for the activity that produces income to be legal for the income to be taxable. Income from illegal activities, such as embezzlement, drug dealing, bookmaking, and bootlegging, is taxable. Al Capone, the notorious Chicago bootlegger during Prohibition, was convicted of income tax evasion because he did not report his illegal income.
> Embezzlement income is taxable in the year in which the funds are stolen. If the embezzler pays back the stolen funds in a later year, he or she can claim a deduction in the year of repayment.

Indian fishing rights. If you are a member of a qualified Indian tribe that has fishing rights secured by treaty, executive order, or an Act of Congress as of March 17, 1988, do not include in your income amounts you receive from activities related to those fishing rights. The income is not subject to income tax, self-employment tax, or employment taxes.

TAXALERT

Investment clubs. An investment club is a group of friends, neighbors, business associates, or others who pool limited or stated amounts of funds to invest in stock or other securities. The club may or may not have a written agreement, charter, or bylaws. Usually, the group operates informally with members pledging a regular amount to be paid into the club monthly. Some clubs have a committee that gathers information on securities, selects the most promising, and recommends that the club invest in them. Other clubs rotate the investigatory responsibilities among all their members. Most require all members to vote for or against all investments, sales, exchanges, or other transactions.

How the income from an investment club is reported on your tax return depends on how the club operates. Most clubs operate as partnerships and are treated as such for federal tax purposes. Others operate as corporations, trusts, or associations taxed as corporations.

Members of an investment club organized as a partnership should include their share of each type of the club's income on their returns. For example, dividends are reported on Schedule B, Part II, line 5, and capital gains are reported on Form 8949 and Schedule D.

The expenses incurred by the club to produce or to collect income, to manage investment property, or to determine any tax due are also reported separately. You may deduct your share of these items on Schedule A as a miscellaneous deduction if you itemize your deductions.

Note: These expenses—along with some others—must exceed 2% of your AGI to be deductible as miscellaneous itemized deductions.

Depending on how your investment club is organized, it may be required to file a separate partnership, corporation, or trust tax return. More details are explained in IRS Publication 550, *Investment Income and Expenses*, some of which follow.

Tax returns and identifying numbers. Investment clubs must file either Form 1065, U.S. Partnership Return of Income; Form 1041, U.S. Income Tax Return for Estates and Trusts; or Form 1120, U.S. Corporation Income Tax Return. Certain small corporations may be able to file Form 1120-A, U.S. Corporation Short-Form Income Tax Return. See the instructions for Forms 1120 and 1120-A.

Form SS-4. Each club must have an employer identification number (EIN) to use when filing its return. The club's EIN also may have to be given to the payer of dividends. If your club does not have an EIN, use Form SS-4, Application for Employer Identification Number. Mail the completed Form SS-4 to the IRS Center where you file the club's tax return. Form SS-4 can be found on the IRS website at *www.irs.gov*.

Stock in name of club. When stock is recorded in the name of the investment club, the club must give its own EIN to the payer of dividends.

If the club is a partnership or a trust, the dividends distributed to the partners or beneficiaries must be shown on Form 1065 or Form 1041, respectively. The partners' or the beneficiaries' identifying numbers also must be shown on the return.

If the club is an association taxed as a corporation, any distribution it makes that qualifies as a dividend must be reported on Forms 1096 and 1099-DIV if total distributions to the shareholder are $10 or more for the year.

Stock in name of member. When stock is recorded in the name of one club member, this member must give his or her social security number to the payer of dividends. (When stock is held in the names of two or more club members, the social security number of only one member must be given to the payer.) This member is considered as the record owner for the actual owner of the stock, the investment club. This member is a "nominee" and must file Form 1099-DIV showing the club to be the owner of the dividend, his or her social security number, and the EIN of the club.

Example
In order to avoid any matching notices from the IRS, the nominee should report the dividend income on his or her tax return on line 5, Part II, of Form 1040, Schedule B and then subtract out the nominee distribution.

ABC company	$100
Less: Nominee distribution	($100)

Interest on frozen deposits. In general, you exclude from your income the amount of interest earned on a frozen deposit. See *Interest income on frozen deposits* in chapter 7.

Interest on qualified savings bonds. You may be able to exclude from income the interest from qualified U.S. savings bonds you redeem if you pay qualified higher educational expenses in the same year. For more information on this exclusion, see *Education Savings Bond Program* under *U.S. Savings Bonds* in chapter 7.

Job interview expenses. If a prospective employer asks you to appear for an interview and either pays you an allowance or reimburses you for your transportation and other travel expenses, the amount you receive is generally not taxable. You include in income only the amount you receive that is more than your actual expenses.

Jury duty. Jury duty pay you receive must be included in your income on Form 1040, line 21. If you must give the pay to your employer because your employer continues to pay your salary while you serve on the jury, you can deduct the amount turned over to your employer as an adjustment to your income. Enter the amount you repay your employer on Form 1040, line 36. Enter "Jury Pay" and the amount on the dotted line next to line 36.

EXPLANATION

Jury fees. This item is often overlooked. Just because a fee is paid by a government body does not mean that it is not subject to tax. However, the Tax Court has ruled that the mileage allowance received by a juror to cover the cost of transportation between the court and his or her home is not included in income. In addition, if you are required to give your jury pay to your employer, you can claim a deduction for the amount paid over. You can claim this deduction whether or not you itemize your deductions. You would report the income on line 21 of Form 1040 and, if you give your jury pay to your employer, report it as an adjustment on line 36 and write "Jury Pay" next to the amount.

Kickbacks. You must include kickbacks, side commissions, push money, or similar payments you receive in your income on Form 1040, line 21, or on Schedule C or Schedule C-EZ (Form 1040), if from your self-employment activity.

Example. You sell cars and help arrange car insurance for buyers. Insurance brokers pay back part of their commissions to you for referring customers to them. You must include the kickbacks in your income.

Medical savings accounts (MSAs). In most cases, you do not include in income amounts you withdraw from your Archer MSA or Medicare Advantage MSA if you use the money to pay for qualified medical expenses. Generally, qualified medical expenses are those you can deduct on Schedule A (Form 1040), Itemized Deductions. For more information about qualified medical expenses, see chapter 22. For more information about Archer MSAs or Medicare Advantage MSAs, see Publication 969, Health Savings Accounts and Other Tax-Favored Health Plans.

TAXSAVER

Contributions to an MSA or HSA can also be deductible. See chapter 22, *Medical and dental expenses*, for details.

Prizes and awards. If you win a prize in a lucky number drawing, television or radio quiz program, beauty contest, or other event, you must include it in your income. For example, if you win a $50 prize in a photography contest, you must report this income on Form 1040, line 21. If you refuse to accept a prize, do not include its value in your income.

Prizes and awards in goods or services must be included in your income at their fair market value.

Employee awards or bonuses. Cash awards or bonuses given to you by your employer for good work or suggestions generally must be included in your income as wages. However, certain noncash employee achievement awards can be excluded from income. See *Bonuses and awards* in chapter 5.

Pulitzer, Nobel, and similar prizes. If you were awarded a prize in recognition of accomplishments in religious, charitable, scientific, artistic, educational, literary, or civic fields, you generally must include the value of the prize in your income. However, you do not include this prize in your income if you meet all of the following requirements.

- You were selected without any action on your part to enter the contest or proceeding.
- You are not required to perform substantial future services as a condition to receiving the prize or award.
- The prize or award is transferred by the payer directly to a governmental unit or tax-exempt charitable organization as designated by you.

See Publication 525 for more information about the conditions that apply to the transfer.

Qualified tuition programs (QTPs). A qualified tuition program (also known as a 529 program) is a program set up to allow you to either prepay or contribute to an account established for paying a student's qualified higher education expenses at an eligible educational institution. A program can be established and maintained by a state, an agency or instrumentality of a state, or an eligible educational institution.

The part of a distribution representing the amount paid or contributed to a QTP is not included in income. This is a return of the investment in the program.

In most cases, the beneficiary does not include in income any earnings distributed from a QTP if the total distribution is less than or equal to adjusted qualified higher education expenses. See Publication 970 for more information.

EXPLANATION

See chapter 36, *Education credits and other education tax benefits,* for further information on qualified tuition programs (QTPs) and qualified education expenses.

Railroad retirement annuities. The following types of payments are treated as pension or annuity income and are taxable under the rules explained in Publication 575, Pension and Annuity Income.

- Tier 1 railroad retirement benefits that are more than the social security equivalent benefit.
- Tier 2 benefits.
- Vested dual benefits.

Rewards. If you receive a reward for providing information, include it in your income.

Sale of home. You may be able to exclude from income all or part of any gain from the sale or exchange of your main home. See chapter 15.

Sale of personal items. If you sold an item you owned for personal use, such as a car, refrigerator, furniture, stereo, jewelry, or silverware, your gain is taxable as a capital gain. Report it as explained in the Instructions for Schedule D (Form 1040). You cannot deduct a loss.

However, if you sold an item you held for investment, such as gold or silver bullion, coins, or gems, any gain is taxable as a capital gain and any loss is deductible as a capital loss.

Example. You sold a painting on an online auction website for $100. You bought the painting for $20 at a garage sale years ago. Report your gain as a capital gain as explained in the Instructions for Schedule D (Form 1040).

Scholarships and fellowships. A candidate for a degree can exclude amounts received as a qualified scholarship or fellowship. A qualified scholarship or fellowship is any amount you receive that is for:

- Tuition and fees to enroll at or attend an educational institution, or
- Fees, books, supplies, and equipment required for courses at the educational institution.

Amounts used for room and board do not qualify for the exclusion. See Publication 970 for more information on qualified scholarships and fellowship grants.

Payment for services. In most cases, you must include in income the part of any scholarship or fellowship that represents payment for past, present, or future teaching, research, or other services. This applies even if all candidates for a degree must perform the services to receive the degree.

For information about the rules that apply to a tax-free qualified tuition reduction provided to employees and their families by an educational institution, see Publication 970.

VA payments. Allowances paid by the Department of Veterans Affairs are not included in your income. These allowances are not considered scholarship or fellowship grants.

Prizes. Scholarship prizes won in a contest are not scholarships or fellowships if you do not have to use the prizes for educational purposes. You must include these amounts in your income on Form 1040, line 21, whether or not you use the amounts for educational purposes.

Stolen property. If you steal property, you must report its fair market value in your income in the year you steal it unless in the same year, you return it to its rightful owner.

Transporting school children. Do not include in your income a school board mileage allowance for taking children to and from school if you are not in the business of taking children to school. You cannot deduct expenses for providing this transportation.

Union benefits and dues. Amounts deducted from your pay for union dues, assessments, contributions, or other payments to a union cannot be excluded from your income.

You may be able to deduct some of these payments as a miscellaneous deduction subject to the 2%-of-AGI limit if they are related to your job and if you itemize deductions on Schedule A (Form 1040). For more information, see *Union Dues and Expenses* in chapter 29.

Strike and lockout benefits. Benefits paid to you by a union as strike or lockout benefits, including both cash and the fair market value of other property, are usually included in your income as compensation. You can exclude these benefits from your income only when the facts clearly show that the union intended them as gifts to you.

Utility rebates. If you are a customer of an electric utility company and you participate in the utility's energy conservation program, you may receive on your monthly electric bill either:
- A reduction in the purchase price of electricity furnished to you (rate reduction), or
- A nonrefundable credit against the purchase price of the electricity.

The amount of the rate reduction or nonrefundable credit is not included in your income.

Passive Activity Limitations and At-Risk Limitations

Explanation

Individuals, estates, trusts, closely held corporations, and personal service corporations are generally prohibited from deducting net losses generated by passive activities. In addition, tax credits from passive activities are generally limited to the tax liability attributable to those activities. Disallowed passive activity losses are suspended and carried forward indefinitely to offset passive activity income generated in future years. Similar carryforward treatment applies to suspended credits.

Note that these rules relate to passive income/losses and do not apply to portfolio income/losses. Portfolio income/losses include interest, dividends, annuities, and royalties, as well as gain or loss from the disposition of income-producing or investment property that is not derived in the ordinary course of a trade or business.

TAXALERT

The Affordable Care Act (the comprehensive health care law that was enacted in 2010 and upheld by the U.S. Supreme Court in 2012) imposes a Net Investment Income Tax (NIIT) on unearned income of individuals effective for tax years beginning after December 31, 2012. For individuals, the NIIT is 3.8% of the lesser of: (1) "Net Investment Income" or (2) the excess of modified adjusted gross income (MAGI) over $200,000 ($250,000 if married filing jointly or qualifying widow(er) with dependent child; $125,000 if married filing separately).

Net investment income subject to the tax is defined as investment income reduced by allocable deductions. Investment income includes income from businesses that are passive activities to the taxpayer (as well as other unearned income from interest, dividends, rents, and annuities not derived in the ordinary course of a trade or business, trade or business income from trading in financial instruments or commodities, and net gains from the disposition of property not used in a trade or business). On the other hand, income from an activity in which a taxpayer materially participates is not included in net investment income.

The NIIT is payable regardless of whether you otherwise pay any regular income tax or are subject to alternative minimum tax on your income.

For more information about these new taxes, see *Changes in the tax law you should know about* in the front section of this book.

Defining passive activities. A passive activity involves the conduct of any trade or business in which you do not materially participate. You are treated as a material participant only if you are involved in the operations of the activity on a regular, continuous, and substantial basis. If you are not a material participant in an activity but your spouse is, you are treated as being a material participant and the activity is not considered passive.

Seven tests. The IRS has seven tests you can meet to be considered a material participant. If you satisfy one of these tests, you will be considered a material participant in any activity. These tests are:

1. You participate more than 500 hours per taxable year.
2. Your participation during the taxable year constitutes substantially all of the participation of all individuals involved.
3. You participate for more than 100 hours during the taxable year and no one else participates more than you participated.
4. The activity is a significant participation activity (SPA) for the taxable year, and your participation in all SPAs during the taxable year exceeds 500 hours. An SPA is an activity in which an individual participates for more than 100 hours but does not otherwise meet a material participation test.
5. You materially participated in any 5 of the 10 preceding taxable years.
6. The activity is a personal service activity, and you materially participated for any 3 preceding taxable years. A personal service activity involves performance of personal services in the fields of health, law, engineering, architecture, accounting, actuarial sciences, performing arts, consulting, or any other business in which capital is not a material income-producing factor.
7. Based on all the facts and circumstances, your participation is regular, continuous, and substantial during the taxable year.

Defining an activity. The proper grouping of business operations into one or more activities is important in determining the allocation of suspended losses, measuring material participation, separating rental and nonrental activities, and determining when a disposition of an activity has occurred. IRS regulations define an activity as any "appropriate economic unit for measuring gain or loss." What constitutes an "appropriate economic unit" is determined by looking at all facts and circumstances. The regulations list five factors that are to be given the greatest weight. They are:

1. Similarities and differences in types of business
2. The extent of common control
3. The extent of common ownership
4. Geographical location
5. Interdependence between the activities

Generally, taxpayers must be consistent from year to year in determining the business operations that constitute an activity. Consult your tax advisor for more information.

TAXPLANNER

IRS regulations regarding the 3.8% Net Investment Income Tax (NIIT) allow taxpayers to review their activity groupings beginning in the tax year in which they are first subject to this tax. Formerly, a taxpayer may have chosen groupings in order to maximize passive income (to offset passive losses). With the additional 3.8% tax imposed on passive trade or business income, taxpayers may desire a different grouping choice going forward. Consult your tax advisor for more information.

"At-Risk" Limitation Provisions

The deduction for business losses is generally limited to the amount by which you are considered to be "at-risk" in the activity. You are considered at risk for the amount of cash you have invested in the venture and the basis of property invested plus certain amounts borrowed for use in the activity.

Borrowed amounts that are considered at risk are (1) loans for which you are personally liable for repayment or (2) loans secured by property, other than that used in the activity. Generally, liabilities that are secured by property within the activity for which you are not otherwise personally liable are not considered to be at risk. An exception: If nonrecourse financing—financing for which you are not personally liable—is secured against real property used in the activity, you may be considered at risk for the amount of financing.

The law provides a broad list of activities (including the holding of real estate acquired after 1986) that are subject to the "at-risk" provisions. If the "at-risk" provisions apply to you, you should consult with your tax advisor.

Passive Activity Losses

The passive activity rules limit losses and credits from passive trade or business activities. Deductions attributable to passive activities, to the extent they exceed income from passive activities, generally may not be deducted against other income, such as wages, portfolio income, or business income that is not derived from a passive activity. Losses that are suspended under these rules are carried forward indefinitely and are treated as losses from passive activities in succeeding years. Suspended losses from a particular activity are allowed in full when a taxpayer disposes of his or her entire interest in that particular passive activity to an unrelated person. For dispositions made after January 1, 1995, you must dispose of "substantially all" of a passive activity in order to deduct that same portion. You may also be able to deduct suspended losses in a passive activity if your interest is disposed of in other ways, including abandonment and death of the taxpayer. See *Disposition of Passive Activity*, discussed later. Special rules may apply; you should consult your tax advisor.

Rental Real Estate

As previously discussed, generally, a trade or business activity is passive unless the taxpayer materially participates in that activity. Rental real estate activities, however, are passive regardless of the level of the taxpayer's participation. A special rule permits the deduction of up to $25,000 of losses from certain rental real estate activities (even though they are considered passive) if the taxpayer actively participates in them. This special rule is available in full to taxpayers with a modified AGI of $100,000 or less and phases out for taxpayers with a modified AGI between $100,000 and $150,000. For further information about rental real estate passive rules, see chapter 9, *Rental income and expenses*.

Real Estate Professionals

Passive activity limitations for certain real estate professionals are more liberal than they used to be. Taxpayers who satisfy certain eligibility thresholds and materially participate in rental real estate activities may treat any losses as losses from a nonpassive activity and may use these losses against all sources of taxable income.

Eligibility. Only individuals and closely held C corporations can qualify for this special rule. An individual taxpayer will qualify for any tax year if more than one-half of the personal services (with more than 750 hours) performed in trades or businesses by the taxpayer during such a tax year are performed in real property trades or businesses in which the taxpayer materially participates. A real property trade or business includes any real property development, redevelopment, construction, reconstruction, acquisition, conversion, rental, operation, management, leasing, or brokerage trade or business. Personal services performed as an employee are not considered in determining material participation unless the employee has more than a 5% ownership in the business during any part of the tax year. However, independent contractor realtor services would qualify for this purpose. For closely held C corporations, the eligibility requirements are met if more than 50% of the corporation's gross receipts for the tax year are derived from real property trades or businesses in which the corporation materially participates.

Example 1

During 2014, a self-employed real estate developer earned $100,000 in development fees from projects the developer spent 1,200 hours developing. In addition, the developer incurred rental real estate losses of $200,000 from properties that the developer spent over 800 hours managing during 2014. The developer performs no other personal services during the year and has no other items of income or deduction. Because the developer (1) materially participated in the rental real estate activity, (2) performed more than 750 hours in real property trades or businesses, and (3) performed more than 50% of the developer's total personal service hours in real estate trades or businesses in which the developer materially participated, the developer will have a net operating loss of $100,000 to carry back (and the excess to carry forward) to offset any source of income.

This rule for real estate professionals' passive loss relief is a two-step process. First, you must demonstrate eligibility for the relief provision by achieving the required levels of personal services in real estate trades or businesses. Thereafter, you get relief from the passive loss limitations only for your rental real estate activities for which you satisfy the material participation standards.

For spouses filing joint returns, each spouse's personal services are taken into account separately. However, in determining material participation, the participation of the other spouse is taken into account as required under current law.

Example 2

A husband and wife filing a joint return meet the eligibility requirements if, during the tax year, one spouse performs more than 750 hours representing at least half of his or her personal services in a real estate trade or business in which either spouse materially participates.

Aggregation of Activities

Whether a taxpayer *materially participates* in his or her rental real estate activities is determined generally as if each interest of the taxpayer in rental real estate is a separate activity. However, the taxpayer may elect to treat all interest in rental real estate as one activity.

The election permitting a taxpayer to aggregate his or her rental real estate activities for testing for material participation is not intended to alter the rules with respect to material participation through limited partnership interest. Generally, no interest as a limited partner is treated as an interest with respect to which a taxpayer materially participates. However, Treasury regulations provide that a limited partner is considered to materially participate in the activities conducted through the partnership in certain situations where (1) the limited partner is also a general partner at all times during the partnership's tax year, (2) the limited partner materially participates in the activity during any 5 of the preceding 10 years, or (3) the activity is a personal service activity in which the limited partner materially participated for any 3 preceding years.

Losses attributable to limited partnership interests are considered passive, except where regulations provide otherwise. In general, working interests in any oil or gas property held directly or through an entity that does not limit the taxpayer's liability are not considered passive, whether or not the taxpayer is a material participant.

The IRS has issued regulations with regard to the aggregation of activities in order to satisfy the material participation tests for real estate professionals. These rules are very complex and hold potential tax traps for the unwary. We recommend that you consult with your tax advisor if you believe that electing to aggregate activities may be beneficial to you.

Example 1
Three brothers own a hardware store as partners. Two of them consider it their full-time job, because it is their only source of income. The third brother lives 200 miles away and is consulted only on major issues. The two brothers who work at the store meet the material participation test. The third brother has a passive investment.

Example 2
Bonnie owns a one-sixteenth interest in four different racehorses. She does not own the stables where the horses are trained and fed. She is not involved in the daily care of the horses. She pays her fair share of the costs and offers advice regarding when and where the horses are to run. Bonnie has significant salary income from a full-time job and from managing her portfolio. Bonnie is probably not a material participant.

Example 3
Chris owns rental property. He has a passive investment.

Exception
An exception to the general rule that does not allow grouping rental activities with business activity is that, in certain instances, passive rental losses can offset income from business activities. For this exception to apply, you must hold the same proportionate ownership interest in each activity.

Example
Jack and Jill are married and file a joint return. Jack owns and operates a grocery store that generates net income for the current year. Jill owns the building, of which 25% is rented to Jack's grocery store activity (grocery store rental). The building rental activities generate a net loss in the current year.

Because they file a joint return, Jack and Jill are treated as one taxpayer. Therefore, the sole owner of the grocery store activity is also the sole owner of the rental activity. Consequently, each owner of the business activity has the same proportionate ownership interest in the rental activity. Accordingly, both activities may be grouped together; thus, the net income from Jack's grocery store can be offset by the amount of net loss from Jill's building rental activities. See your tax advisor for more information if you think this exception applies to your situation.

TAXPLANNER
You should try to realign your personal finances so that you maximize your interest expense deductions. If you borrowed money to purchase a passive investment, any interest on the loan will be considered part of your passive investment loss. If you are in a real estate limited partnership, you may be able to have all the partners contribute additional capital so that the entity's passive loss is reduced or limited because the entity no longer has interest expense on the entity's loan. Your capital contribution could come from your other investments or from a mortgage on a personal residence. If you have untapped appreciation in your personal residence, you can borrow against it and deduct the interest cost subject to certain limitations. Make sure, however, that any mortgage does not exceed the limits applicable to your situation, because such disallowed interest would be considered nondeductible personal interest.

Disposition of Passive Activity

Previously disallowed losses (but not credits if you are in an overall loss position in the year of disposition) are recognized in full when the taxpayer disposes of his or her entire interest in the passive activity in a fully taxable transaction. However, suspended losses are not deductible when the taxpayer sells the interest to a related party. Rather, the losses remain with the individual (and may offset passive income) until the related purchaser disposes of the interest in a taxable transaction to an unrelated person. Various other types of dispositions trigger suspended losses, including abandonment, death of the taxpayer, gifts, and installment sales of entire interests, although special rules apply.

A sale in a taxable year beginning before January 1, 1987, reported on the installment method and included in income after December 31, 1986, would be considered income from a passive activity.

Example

Bob disposes of rental property in 1986 under the installment sale method and properly reports $2,000 of taxable gain in his 1987 through 2014 tax returns. Bob may treat the 1987 through 2014 gains as income from a passive activity and may offset other passive losses in these years.

Tax Relief for Victims of Terrorism

The following section discusses the tax treatment of certain amounts received by victims injured in a terrorist attack or survivors of victims killed as a result of a terrorist attack.

Qualified disaster relief payments. Qualified disaster relief payments are not included in income. These payments are not subject to income tax, self-employment tax, or employment taxes (social security, Medicare, and federal unemployment taxes). No withholding applies to these payments.

Qualified disaster relief payments include payments you receive (regardless of the source) for the following reasons:

- Reasonable and necessary personal, family, living, or funeral expenses incurred as a result of a terrorist attack.
- Reasonable and necessary expenses incurred for the repair or rehabilitation of a personal residence due to a terrorist attack. (A personal residence can be a rented residence or one you own.)
- Reasonable and necessary expenses incurred for the repair or replacement of the contents of a personal residence due to a terrorist attack.
  Qualified disaster relief payments also include the following:
- Payments made by common carriers (for example, American Airlines and United Airlines regarding the September 11 attacks) because of death or physical injury incurred as a result of a terrorist attack.
- Amounts received from a federal, state, or local government in connection with a terrorist attack by those affected by the attack.

Disability payments. Disability payments received for injuries incurred as a direct result of a terrorist attack directed against the United States (or its allies), whether inside or outside of the United States, are not included in income.

Payments to survivors of public safety officers. If you are the survivor of a public safety officer who died in the line of duty, the following types of payments are not included in your income:

Bureau of Justice Assistance payments. If you are a surviving dependent of a public safety officer (law enforcement officer or firefighter) who died in the line of duty, do not include in your income the death benefit paid to you by the Bureau of Justice Assistance.

Government plan annuity. If you receive a survivor annuity as the child or spouse (or former spouse) of a public safety officer who was killed in the line of duty, you generally do not have to include it in income. This exclusion applies to the amount of the annuity based upon the officer's service as a public safety officer.

Public safety officer defined. A public safety officer, for the purpose of these exclusions, includes police and law enforcement officers, firefighters, and rescue squads and ambulance crews.

More information. For more information, see Publication 559, *Survivors, Executors, and Administrators*, and Publication 3920, *Tax Relief for Victims of Terrorist Attacks*.

Part 3
Gains and losses

ey.com/EYTaxGuide

The four chapters in this part discuss investment gains and losses, including how to figure your basis in property. A gain from selling or trading stocks, bonds, or other investment property may be taxed or it may be tax free, at least in part. A loss may or may not be deductible. These chapters also discuss gains from selling property you personally use—including the special rules for selling your home. Nonbusiness casualty and theft losses are discussed in chapter 26 in Part 5.

Chapter 13   Basis of property
Chapter 14   Sale of property
Chapter 15   Selling your home
Chapter 16   Reporting gains and losses

Chapter 13
Basis of property

Note

IRS Publication 17 (*Your Federal Income Tax*) has been updated by Ernst & Young LLP for 2014. Dates and dollar amounts shown are for 2014. Underlined type is used to indicate where IRS text has been updated. Places where text has been removed are indicated by the sentence: *Text intentionally omitted.*

ey.com/EYTaxGuide

Ernst & Young LLP will update the *EY Tax Guide 2015* website with relevant taxpayer information as it becomes available. You can also sign up for email alerts to let you know when changes have been made.

Introduction

The gain or loss you realize on the disposition of property—whether through a sale or exchange—is measured by the difference between the selling price and your basis. In many cases, the basis of an asset is no more than your cost. However, if you acquire property in exchange for services, by inheritance or in exchange for other property, different factors besides cost are likely to have a crucial impact when determining your tax basis.

This chapter tells you how to calculate the basis of property. Particular attention is given to some of the more complicated situations that may arise. You'll learn, for instance, how to calculate your basis in a particular piece of property by referring to other assets you already hold. To help you determine which expenditures increase your basis in a piece of property and which do not, comprehensive lists of allowable—but often overlooked—expenditures are provided.

This chapter discusses how to figure your basis in property. It is divided into the following sections.
- Cost basis.
- Adjusted basis.
- Basis other than cost.

Your basis is the amount of your investment in property for tax purposes. Use the basis to figure gain or loss on the sale, exchange, or other disposition of property. Also use it to figure deductions for depreciation, amortization, depletion, and casualty losses.

If you use property for both business or investment purposes and for personal purposes, you must allocate the basis based on the use. Only the basis allocated to the business or investment use of the property can be depreciated.

Your original basis in property is adjusted (increased or decreased) by certain events. For example, if you make improvements to the property, increase your basis. If you take deductions for depreciation or casualty losses, or claim certain credits, reduce your basis.

Useful Items

You may want to see:

Publication
☐ **15-B** Employer's Tax Guide to Fringe Benefits
☐ **525** Taxable and Nontaxable Income

Cost Basis

The basis of property you buy is usually its cost. The cost is the amount you pay in cash, debt obligations, other property, or services. Your cost also includes amounts you pay for the following items:

- Sales tax,
- Freight,
- Installation and testing,
- Excise taxes,
- Legal and accounting fees (when they must be capitalized),
- Revenue stamps,
- Recording fees, and
- Real estate taxes (if you assume liability for the seller).

In addition, the basis of real estate and business assets may include other items.

TAXALERT

Individuals do not derive any tax benefit from realizing a loss related to the disposition of personal-use property, unless the loss qualifies as a nonbusiness casualty or theft loss (see chapter 26, *Nonbusiness casualty and theft losses*). Personal-use property is generally considered a capital asset and includes any property that is: (1) not considered an investment (such as a refrigerator) or (2) not property used in a trade or business. On the other hand, gain realized from a sale or exchange of personal-use property is a taxable capital gain.

Loans with low or no interest. If you buy property on a time-payment plan that charges little or no interest, the basis of your property is your stated purchase price minus any amount considered to be unstated interest. You generally have unstated interest if your interest rate is less than the applicable federal rate.

For more information, see *Unstated Interest and Original Issue Discount (OID)* in Publication 537.

EXPLANATION

If you buy tangible personal property under a contract that you will use in connection with a trade or business or an investment activity and the carrying charges are separately stated, but you cannot determine the interest you paid, the IRS assumes that interest is being charged at the applicable federal rate (AFR) and applied to the average unpaid balance of the contract during the tax year. Your tax basis is determined by subtracting the interest from the total contract cost of the property. You may deduct the interest in the year in which it is (in effect) being paid. But see chapter 24, *Interest expense*, for possible limitations on your deductions. These rules do not apply to personal-use property.

Real Property

Real property, also called real estate, is land and generally anything built on, growing on, or attached to land.

If you buy real property, certain fees and other expenses you pay are part of your cost basis in the property.

Lump sum purchase. If you buy buildings and the land on which they stand for a lump sum, allocate the cost basis among the land and the buildings. Allocate the cost basis according to the respec-

---

Tax Breaks and Deductions You Can Use Checklist

Like-kind exchanges. In general, any gain realized from selling your property must be included in your taxable income. However, if you trade or exchange business or investment property for "like-kind" property–i.e., property of a similar nature or character–you defer any gain in the property you exchanged. Your newly acquired property is considered to be a continuation of the investment in the original property. Therefore, your basis in the new property is generally the same as the basis in the property you traded. For more information, see *Nontaxable Exchanges and Like-Kind Exchanges*, later.

Identifying specific shares of stock or bonds sold. Keep accurate, detailed records of your tax basis in specific lots of stocks or bonds you purchase. By doing so, you can identify those shares with the highest basis when you sell in order to minimize the amount of gain you will need to recognize. Alternatively, since it is generally to your advantage to make charitable contributions of shares with the lowest basis, your ability to specifically identify such shares will enable you to optimize your tax benefit from donating shares.

Records

Keep accurate records of all items that affect the basis of your property. For more information on keeping records, see chapter 1.

---

tive fair market values (FMVs) of the land and buildings at the time of purchase. Figure the basis of each asset by multiplying the lump sum by a fraction. The numerator is the FMV of that asset and the denominator is the FMV of the whole property at the time of purchase.

Fair market value (FMV). FMV is the price at which the property would change hands between a willing buyer and a willing seller, neither having to buy or sell, and both having reasonable knowledge of all the necessary facts. Sales of similar property on or about the same date may be helpful in figuring the FMV of the property.

Assumption of mortgage. If you buy property and assume (or buy the property subject to) an existing mortgage on the property, your basis includes the amount you pay for the property plus the amount to be paid on the mortgage.

Settlement costs. Your basis includes the settlement fees and closing costs you paid for buying the property. (A fee for buying property is a cost that must be paid even if you buy the property for cash.) Do not include fees and costs for getting a loan on the property in your basis.

The following are some of the settlement fees or closing costs you can include in the basis of your property.
- Abstract fees (abstract of title fees).
- Charges for installing utility services.
- Legal fees (including fees for the title search and preparation of the sales contract and deed).
- Recording fees.
- Survey fees.
- Transfer taxes.
- Owner's title insurance.
- Any amounts the seller owes that you agree to pay, such as back taxes or interest, recording or mortgage fees, charges for improvements or repairs, and sales commissions.

> **Tip**
>
> *If you are not certain of the FMVs of the land and buildings, you can allocate the basis according to their assessed values for real estate tax purposes.*

> **EXPLANATION**
> If you use the real property in your trade or business or as a rental property, you cannot elect to deduct transfer taxes in lieu of adding them to your basis.

Settlement costs do not include amounts placed in escrow for the future payment of items such as taxes and insurance.

The following are some of the settlement fees and closing costs you cannot include in the basis of property.
- Casualty insurance premiums.
- Rent for occupancy of the property before closing.
- Charges for utilities or other services related to occupancy of the property before closing.
- Charges connected with getting a loan, such as points (discount points, loan origination fees), mortgage insurance premiums, loan assumption fees, cost of a credit report, and fees for an appraisal required by a lender.
- Fees for refinancing a mortgage.

Real estate taxes. If you pay real estate taxes the seller owed on real property you bought, and the seller did not reimburse you, treat those taxes as part of your basis. You cannot deduct them as an expense.

If you reimburse the seller for taxes the seller paid for you, you can usually deduct that amount as an expense in the year of purchase. Do not include that amount in the basis of your property. If you did not reimburse the seller, you must reduce your basis by the amount of those taxes.

Points. If you pay points to get a loan (including a mortgage, second mortgage, line of credit, or a home equity loan), do not add the points to the basis of the related property. Generally, you deduct the points over the term of the loan. For more information on how to deduct points, see chapter 24.

Points on home mortgage. Special rules may apply to points you and the seller pay when you get a mortgage to buy your main home. If certain requirements are met, you can deduct the points in full for the year in which they are paid. Reduce the basis of your home by any seller-paid points.

Adjusted Basis

Before figuring gain or loss on a sale, exchange, or other disposition of property or figuring allowable depreciation, depletion, or amortization, you must usually make certain adjustments (increases and decreases) to the cost basis or basis other than cost (discussed later) of the property. The result is the adjusted basis.

Increases to Basis

Increase the basis of any property by all items properly added to a capital account. Examples of items that increase basis are shown in Table 13-1. These include the items discussed below.

Improvements. Add to your basis in property the cost of improvements having a useful life of more than 1 year, that increase the value of the property, lengthen its life, or adapt it to a different use. For example, improvements include putting a recreation room in your unfinished basement, adding another bathroom or bedroom, putting up a fence, putting in new plumbing or wiring, installing a new roof, or paving your driveway.

3. Installing new plumbing
4. Installing a new heating or air-conditioning system
5. Installing a new furnace
6. Restoring a rundown house
7. Landscaping: adding new trees, shrubs, or lawn
8. Building a swimming pool, tennis court, or sauna
9. Constructing or improving a driveway
10. Constructing walks
11. Constructing patios and decks
12. Constructing walls
13. Kitchen or bathroom remodeling, including cost of new appliances
14. Payment of legal fees stemming from improvements, zoning, and so on
15. Payment of real estate commissions
16. Other selling expenses, such as advertising or paying professional fees related to staging your property
17. Payment of closing costs

It is important to distinguish between expenditures that constitute additions to basis and those that constitute repairs. If the asset is used in a trade or a business, repairs are deductible, but do not increase its basis. If the asset is personal, the costs of repairs are not deductible and do not increase the asset's basis. For a more complete discussion of this matter, see chapter 9, *Rental income and expenses*.

As noted by the IRS, your basis in property is reduced by money you receive as a return of capital. See chapter 8, *Dividends and other corporate distributions*, for further details.

Example

You buy land and a building for $25,000 for use as a parking lot. You pay $3,000 to have the building torn down, and you sell some of the materials you salvage from it for $5,000. You figure your adjusted basis in the property by taking your $25,000 initial cost, adding the $3,000 you spent for tearing down the building, and subtracting the $5,000 you received for the materials you salvaged. Your adjusted basis for the lot is $23,000. The money you received from the sale of the salvaged materials is not income, and the cost of tearing down the building is not deductible.

TAXORGANIZER

You should keep a copy of all invoices you receive and pay for improvements that increase your basis in real property.

EXPLANATION

The following costs increase your tax basis:

1. Interest on debt incurred to finance the construction or production of real property, long-lived personal property with a useful life of 20 years or more, and other tangible property requiring more than 2 years (1 year in the case of property costing more than $1 million) to produce, construct, or reach a productive stage. Additionally, interest incurred to finance property produced under a long-term contract increases your tax basis to the extent that income is not reported under the percentage of completion method. These rules do not apply to interest incurred during the construction of real property to be used as your principal residence or a second home. For a definition of principal residence, see chapter 15, *Selling your home*. See chapter 24, *Interest expense*, for other rules affecting how much interest you may be able to deduct on a residence.
2. The costs of defending or perfecting a title, architect's fees, and financing and finder's fees. (Loan origination fees—commonly called "points"—incurred while financing the purchase of a principal residence may be currently deducted in certain circumstances. See chapter 24, *Interest expense*, for further information.)
3. Certain start-up and organizational costs for a business. These include costs of investigating the creation or acquisition of an active trade or business, legal fees for the drafting of documents, accounting fees, and other similar expenses directly associated with the organization of a business. The costs of organizing a partnership, such as the expenses incurred in raising capital, putting together a prospectus and paying commissions on the sale of investment units, also increase your basis. See chapter 38, *Self-employment income: How to file Schedule C*, and Publication 535, *Business Expenses*, for further information.

Table 13-1. **Examples of Adjustments to Basis**

Increases to Basis	Decreases to Basis

• Capital improvements:
  Putting an addition on your home
  Replacing an entire roof
  Paving your driveway
  Installing central air conditioning
  Rewiring your home
• Assessments for local improvements:
  Water connections
  Extending utility service lines to the property
  Sidewalks
  Roads
• Casualty losses:
  Restoring damaged property
• Legal fees:
  Cost of defending and perfecting a title
  Fees for getting a reduction of an assessment
• Zoning costs
	• Exclusion from income of subsidies for energy conservation measures
	• Casualty or theft loss deductions and insurance reimbursements
	• Postponed gain from the sale of a home
	• Alternative motor vehicle credit (Form 8910)
	• Alternative fuel vehicle refueling property credit (Form 8911)
	• Residential energy credits (Form 5695)
	• Depreciation and Section 179 deduction
	• Nontaxable corporate distributions
	• Certain canceled debt excluded from income
	• Easements
	• Adoption tax benefits

TAXPLANNER

Taxpayers who are starting a new business may be able to deduct expenses incurred before the business actually begins. If you started your new business in 2014, you can elect a current deduction of up to $10,000 for start-up expenditures. However, this $10,000 amount is reduced (but not below zero) by the amount by which the cumulative cost of start-up expenditures exceeds $60,000. The remainder of the start-up expenditures can be claimed as a deduction ratably over a 15-year period. If you currently neither deduct nor amortize a start-up, the tax benefit from adding such expenses to basis is obtained when the entity is eventually sold or ceases operation.

Unlike the costs of organizing a partnership or starting up its business, the costs of selling partnership interests (syndication costs) may not be amortized or deducted. For further discussion, see Adjusted Basis, later.

Assessments for local improvements. Add to the basis of property assessments for improvements such as streets and sidewalks if they increase the value of the property assessed. Do not deduct them as taxes. However, you can deduct as taxes assessments for maintenance or repairs, or for meeting interest charges related to the improvements.

Example. Your city changes the street in front of your store into an enclosed pedestrian mall and assesses you and other affected property owners for the cost of the conversion. Add the assessment to your property's basis. In this example, the assessment is a depreciable asset.

EXPLANATION

For further discussion of assessments and how to treat them, see <u>chapter 23</u>, *Taxes you may deduct*.

Decreases to Basis

Decrease the basis of any property by all items that represent a return of capital for the period during which you held the property. Examples of items that decrease basis are shown in Table 13-1. These include the items discussed below.

Casualty and theft losses. If you have a casualty or theft loss, decrease the basis in your property by any insurance proceeds or other reimbursement and by any deductible loss not covered by insurance.

You must increase your basis in the property by the amount you spend on repairs that restore the property to its pre-casualty condition.

For more information on casualty and theft losses, see <u>chapter 26</u>.

Depreciation and Section 179 deduction. Decrease the basis of your qualifying business property by any Section 179 deduction you take and the depreciation you deducted, or could have deducted (including any special depreciation allowance), on your tax returns under the method of depreciation you selected.

For more information about depreciation and the Section 179 deduction, see Publication 946 and the Instructions for Form 4562.

Example. You owned a duplex used as rental property that cost you $40,000, of which $35,000 was allocated to the building and $5,000 to the land. You added an improvement to the duplex that cost $10,000. In February last year, the duplex was damaged by fire. Up to that time, you had been allowed depreciation of $23,000. You sold some salvaged material for $1,300 and collected $19,700 from your insurance company. You deducted a casualty loss of $1,000 on your income tax return for last year.

You spent $19,000 of the insurance proceeds for restoration of the duplex, which was completed this year. You must use the duplex's adjusted basis after the restoration to determine depreciation for the rest of the property's recovery period. Figure the adjusted basis of the duplex as follows:

Original cost of duplex		$35,000
Addition to duplex		10,000
Total cost of duplex		$45,000
Minus: Depreciation		23,000
Adjusted basis before casualty		$22,000
Minus: Insurance proceeds	$19,700	
Deducted casualty loss	1,000	
Salvage proceeds	1,300	22,000
Adjusted basis after casualty		$–0–
Add: Cost of restoring duplex		19,000
Adjusted basis after restoration		**$19,000**

Note. Your basis in the land is its original cost of $5,000.

Easements. The amount you receive for granting an easement is generally considered to be proceeds from the sale of an interest in real property. It reduces the basis of the affected part of the property. If the amount received is more than the basis of the part of the property affected by the easement, reduce your basis in that part to zero and treat the excess as a recognized gain.

If the gain is on a capital asset, see <u>chapter 16</u> for information about how to report it. If the gain is on property used in a trade or business, see Publication 544 for information about how to report it.

Exclusion of subsidies for energy conservation measures. You can exclude from gross income any subsidy you received from a public utility company for the purchase or installation of an energy conservation measure for a dwelling unit. Reduce the basis of the property for which you received the subsidy by the excluded amount. For more information about this subsidy, see <u>chapter 12</u>.

Postponed gain from sale of home. If you postponed gain from the sale of your main home under rules in effect before May 7, 1997, you must reduce the basis of the home you acquired as a replacement by the amount of the postponed gain. For more information on the rules for the sale of a home, see <u>chapter 15</u>.

Basis Other Than Cost

There are many times when you cannot use cost as basis. In these cases, the fair market value or the adjusted basis of the property can be used. Fair market value (FMV) and adjusted basis were discussed earlier.

Property Received for Services

If you receive property for your services, include the FMV of the property in income. The amount you include in income becomes your basis. If the services were performed for a price agreed on beforehand, it will be accepted as the FMV of the property if there is no evidence to the contrary.

TAXPLANNER

If you perform services for an entity, and in exchange receive stock or a partnership capital interest, the fair market value (FMV) of what you receive is treated as compensation. Your basis in the stock or partnership interest is equal to the amount of compensation you report, increased by the amount, if any, you paid for the stock or partnership interest.

TAXSAVER

If you receive an equity interest in a business in exchange for services rendered, you may be able to discount the value of the equity interest received. You may do this if the shares are restricted, not readily marketable, or if they represent only a minority holding. If you receive stock compensation of this kind, you should consider employing a professional appraiser to value the equity interest received to ensure the valuation discount is properly applied so that you do not have an underpayment of tax and accompanying interest and penalties.

Restricted property. If you receive property for your services and the property is subject to certain restrictions, your basis in the property is its FMV when it becomes substantially vested. However, this rule does not apply if you make an election to include in income the FMV of the property at the time it is transferred to you, less any amount you paid for it. Property is substantially vested when it is transferable or when it is not subject to a substantial risk of forfeiture (you do not have a good chance of losing it). For more information, see *Restricted Property* in Publication 525.

TAXPLANNER

Although a general rule of tax planning is that it is best to defer income and accelerate deductions, under certain circumstances it may be to your benefit to recognize income sooner rather than later. One such situation in which it may be beneficial to accelerate income is when the tax rate at which the income would be taxed would be lower in that earlier year. Accelerating income may also be beneficial if you receive restricted property as compensation for your services, you anticipate the property will appreciate in value by the time the restriction lapses, and you have the opportunity to elect to recognize the property's value as compensation income at the time of receipt (minus the amount, if any, you paid for the property). Making the election may produce tax savings if the value of the property has indeed appreciated by the time the restriction lapses. For a discussion about this potential planning opportunity, see *Restricted Property* in chapter 5, *Wages, salaries, and other earnings*.

Bargain purchases. A bargain purchase is a purchase of an item for less than its FMV. If, as compensation for services, you buy goods or other property at less than FMV, include the difference between the purchase price and the property's FMV in your income. Your basis in the property is its FMV (your purchase price plus the amount you include in income).

If the difference between your purchase price and the FMV is a qualified employee discount, do not include the difference in income. However, your basis in the property is still its FMV. See *Employee Discounts* in Publication 15-B.

EXAMPLES

Airline, railroad, and subway employees are not required to include free travel provided by their employer in their income if the employer does not incur any substantial additional cost in providing such travel. Employee clothing discounts, discount brokerage fees, and lodging and meal discounts can also qualify as nontaxable compensation. Employees are eligible for such tax-free benefits only if the merchandise or services are also offered to customers in the ordinary course of the employer's business. The amount of the tax-free discount is subject to specific dollar limitations.

Business use of a company car, parking at or near your business premises, business periodicals and any other property or service provided by your employer can be excluded from your taxable income if you would be allowed to take a business deduction had you paid for the benefit yourself.

Other nontaxable fringe benefits from employers include medical savings account (MSA) or health savings account (HSA) contributions, free medical services, reimbursement of medical expenses, payments of premiums for up to $50,000 of group-term life insurance coverage, tuition given to children of university employees, and meals furnished to employees on the employer's business premises for the convenience of the employer.

Taxable Exchanges

A taxable exchange is one in which the gain is taxable or the loss is deductible. A taxable gain or deductible loss also is known as a recognized gain or loss. If you receive property in exchange for other property in a taxable exchange, the basis of the property you receive is usually its FMV at the time of the exchange.

Involuntary Conversions

If you receive replacement property as a result of an involuntary conversion, such as a casualty, theft, or condemnation, figure the basis of the replacement property using the basis of the converted property.

Similar or related property. If you receive replacement property similar or related in service or use to the converted property, the replacement property's basis is the same as the converted property's basis on the date of the conversion, with the following adjustments.

1. Decrease the basis by the following.
   a. Any loss you recognize on the involuntary conversion.
   b. Any money you receive that you do not spend on similar property.
2. Increase the basis by the following.
   a. Any gain you recognize on the involuntary conversion.
   b. Any cost of acquiring the replacement property.

Money or property not similar or related. If you receive money or property not similar or related in service or use to the converted property, and you buy replacement property similar or related in service or use to the converted property, the basis of the replacement property is its cost decreased by the gain not recognized on the conversion.

Example. The state condemned your property. The adjusted basis of the property was $26,000 and the state paid you $31,000 for it. You realized a gain of $5,000 ($31,000 –$26,000). You bought replacement property similar in use to the converted property for $29,000. You recognize a gain of $2,000 ($31,000 – $29,000), the unspent part of the payment from the state. Your unrecognized gain is $3,000, the difference between the $5,000 realized gain and the $2,000 recognized gain. The basis of the replacement property is figured as follows:

Cost of replacement property	$29,000
Minus: Gain not recognized	3,000
Basis of replacement property	**$26,000**

Allocating the basis. If you buy more than one piece of replacement property, allocate your basis among the properties based on their respective costs.

For information about asset allocations, see chapter 38, *Self-employment income: How to file Schedule C.*

The residual method must be used to allocate the purchase price of acquired assets. Under the residual method, the amount allocated to the value of goodwill and going concern value is the excess of the purchase price over the FMV of the tangible assets and the other identifiable intangible assets.

For certain types of acquisitions of assets used in a trade or a business, the buyer and seller must file Form 8594 with the IRS, showing how the purchase price was allocated among various classes of assets. For more information, consult your tax advisor.

Basis for depreciation. Special rules apply in determining and depreciating the basis of MACRS property acquired in an involuntary conversion. For information, see *What Is the Basis of Your Depreciable Property?* in chapter 1 of Publication 946.

Nontaxable Exchanges

A nontaxable exchange is an exchange in which you are not taxed on any gain and you cannot deduct any loss. If you receive property in a nontaxable exchange, its basis is generally the same as the basis of the property you transferred. See *Nontaxable Trades* in chapter 14.

Like-Kind Exchanges

The exchange of property for the same kind of property is the most common type of nontaxable exchange. To qualify as a like-kind exchange, the property traded and the property received must be both of the following.

- Qualifying property.
- Like-kind property.

The basis of the property you receive is generally the same as the adjusted basis of the property you gave up. If you trade property in a like-kind exchange and also pay money, the basis of the property received is the adjusted basis of the property you gave up increased by the money you paid.

Qualifying property. In a like-kind exchange, you must hold for investment or for productive use in your trade or business both the property you give up and the property you receive.

Like-kind property. There must be an exchange of like-kind property. Like-kind properties are properties of the same nature or character, even if they differ in grade or quality. The exchange of real estate for real estate and personal property for similar personal property are exchanges of like-kind property.

Example. You trade in an old truck used in your business with an adjusted basis of $1,700 for a new one costing $6,800. The dealer allows you $2,000 on the old truck, and you pay $4,800. This is a like-kind exchange. The basis of the new truck is $6,500 (the adjusted basis of the old one, $1,700, plus the amount you paid, $4,800).

If you sell your old truck to a third party for $2,000 instead of trading it in and then buy a new one from the dealer, you have a taxable gain of $300 on the sale (the $2,000 sale price minus the $1,700 adjusted basis). The basis of the new truck is the price you pay the dealer.

EXPLANATION

In general, all gains realized on sales and other dispositions of property are taxable, but an exception exists for situations where business or investment property is traded or exchanged for "like-kind" property. In this case, the newly acquired property is viewed as a continuation of the investment in the original property, so the tax basis does not change. The reason to make tax-free exchanges is not to avoid taxes but to defer them while realizing some other investment aims. (For more details on nontaxable exchanges, see chapter 14, *Sale of property.*)

Partially nontaxable exchanges. A partially nontaxable exchange is an exchange in which you receive unlike property or money in addition to like-kind property. The basis of the property you receive is the same as the adjusted basis of the property you gave up, with the following adjustments.

1. Decrease the basis by the following amounts.
   a. Any money you receive.
   b. Any loss you recognize on the exchange.

2. Increase the basis by the following amounts.
   a. Any additional costs you incur.
   b. Any gain you recognize on the exchange.

If the other party to the exchange assumes your liabilities, treat the debt assumption as money you received in the exchange.

Allocation of basis. If you receive like-kind and unlike properties in the exchange, allocate the basis first to the unlike property, other than money, up to its FMV on the date of the exchange. The rest is the basis of the like-kind property.

More information. See *Like-Kind Exchanges* in chapter 1 of Publication 544 for more information.

Basis for depreciation. Special rules apply in determining and depreciating the basis of MACRS property acquired in a like-kind exchange. For information, see *What Is the Basis of Your Depreciable Property?* in chapter 1 of Publication 946.

Property Transferred From a Spouse

The basis of property transferred to you or transferred in trust for your benefit by your spouse is the same as your spouse's adjusted basis. The same rule applies to a transfer by your former spouse that is incident to divorce. However, for property transferred in trust, adjust your basis for any gain recognized by your spouse or former spouse if the liabilities assumed, plus the liabilities to which the property is subject, are more than the adjusted basis of the property transferred.

If the property transferred to you is a series E, series EE, or series I U.S. savings bond, the transferor must include in income the interest accrued to the date of transfer. Your basis in the bond immediately after the transfer is equal to the transferor's basis increased by the interest income includible in the transferor's income. For more information on these bonds, see chapter 7.

At the time of the transfer, the transferor must give you the records needed to determine the adjusted basis and holding period of the property as of the date of the transfer.

For more information about the transfer of property from a spouse, see chapter 14.

Property Received as a Gift

To figure the basis of property you receive as a gift, you must know its adjusted basis to the donor just before it was given to you, its FMV at the time it was given to you, and any gift tax paid on it.

> **EXPLANATION**
> If a gift tax return was filed, you should examine it for information on the donor's tax basis.

FMV less than donor's adjusted basis. If the FMV of the property at the time of the gift is less than the donor's adjusted basis, your basis depends on whether you have a gain or a loss when you dispose of the property. Your basis for figuring gain is the same as the donor's adjusted basis plus or minus any required adjustments to basis while you held the property. Your basis for figuring loss is its FMV when you received the gift plus or minus any required adjustments to basis while you held the property. See *Adjusted Basis*, earlier.

Example. You received an acre of land as a gift. At the time of the gift, the land had an FMV of $8,000. The donor's adjusted basis was $10,000. After you received the property, no events occurred to increase or decrease your basis. If you later sell the property for $12,000, you will have a $2,000 gain because you must use the donor's adjusted basis at the time of the gift ($10,000) as your basis to figure gain. If you sell the property for $7,000, you will have a $1,000 loss because you must use the FMV at the time of the gift ($8,000) as your basis to figure loss.

If the sales price is between $8,000 and $10,000, you have neither gain nor loss.

> **EXAMPLE**
> Owen owns a building in which his adjusted basis is $40,000. The fair market value (FMV) of the building, however, is only $30,000. Owen gives the building to Jim. Jim's basis is $40,000—Owen's adjusted basis—for determining depreciation and for computing a gain on the sale of the building. Jim's basis is $30,000—the FMV at the time of the gift—for computing a loss on the sale of the building.
> *Note:* If the FMV of the building increases to $35,000, Jim may sell the property without recognizing a gain or a loss. His proceeds of $35,000 would be greater than the basis used for computing a loss on the sale and less than the basis used for computing a gain on the sale.

Business property. If you hold the gift as business property, your basis for figuring any depreciation, depletion, or amortization deductions is the same as the donor's adjusted basis plus or minus any required adjustments to basis while you hold the property.

FMV equal to or greater than donor's adjusted basis. If the FMV of the property is equal to or greater than the donor's adjusted basis, your basis is the donor's adjusted basis at the time you received the gift. Increase your basis by all or part of any gift tax paid, depending on the date of the gift, explained later.

Also, for figuring gain or loss from a sale or other disposition or for figuring depreciation, depletion, or amortization deductions on business property, you must increase or decrease your basis (the donor's adjusted basis) by any required adjustments to basis while you held the property. See *Adjusted Basis*, earlier.

If you received a gift during the tax year, increase your basis in the gift (the donor's adjusted basis) by the part of the gift tax paid on it due to the net increase in value of the gift. Figure the increase by multiplying the gift tax paid by a fraction. The numerator of the fraction is the net increase in value of the gift and the denominator is the amount of the gift.

The net increase in value of the gift is the FMV of the gift minus the donor's adjusted basis. The amount of the gift is its value for gift tax purposes after reduction by any annual exclusion and marital or charitable deduction that applies to the gift.

Example. In 2014, you received a gift of property from your mother that had an FMV of $50,000. Her adjusted basis was $20,000. The amount of the gift for gift tax purposes was $36,000 ($50,000 minus the $14,000 annual exclusion). She paid a gift tax of $7,320 on the property. Your basis is $26,076, figured as follows:

Fair market value	$50,000
Minus: Adjusted basis	−20,000
Net increase in value	$30,000
Gift tax paid	$7,320
Multiplied by ($30,000 ÷ $36,000)	× .83
Gift tax due to net increase in value	$6,076
Adjusted basis of property to your mother	+20,000
Your basis in the property	**$26,076**

Note. If you received a gift before 1977, your basis in the gift (the donor's adjusted basis) includes any gift tax paid on it. However, your basis cannot exceed the FMV of the gift at the time it was given to you.

Inherited Property

Your basis in property you inherited from a decedent, who died before January 1, 2010, or after December 31, 2010, is generally one of the following:

- The FMV of the property at the date of the decedent's death.
- The FMV on the alternate valuation date if the personal representative for the estate elects to use alternate valuation.

EXPLANATION

The above rules for "stepped up" basis do not apply to appreciated property you receive from a decedent if you or your spouse originally gave the property to the decedent within 1 year before the decedent's death. In such a case, your basis in this property is the same as the decedent's adjusted basis in the property immediately before his or her death, rather than its FMV. Appreciated property is any property whose FMV on the day it was given to the decedent is more than its adjusted basis.

An executor or administrator of an estate can elect an alternate valuation, which values all property included in the estate as of the date 6 months after death. Property disposed of during that 6 month period receives the value as of the date it is distributed, sold, exchanged, or otherwise disposed of. The alternate valuation election is made on the estate tax return (which must be filed no later than 1 year past the time prescribed by law for filing the return). Furthermore, application of the alternate valuation date must result in a decrease in both: (1) the gross estate and (2) federal estate taxes due.

TAXSAVER

Choosing an alternate valuation date may be helpful in reducing estate tax if the market value of the assets in the estate is declining. However, if this is the case, the tax basis of those assets must also be reduced; this means increased income taxes to the recipient in the future if the market value of the assets rises and they are then sold. Thus, the decision to elect the alternate valuation date to reduce estate tax should be balanced against a possible increase in future income taxes.

- The value under the special-use valuation method for real property used in farming or a closely held business if elected for estate tax purposes.

EXPLANATION

If a decedent used property that he or she owned for farming, trade, or business purposes at the date of death, the executor of the decedent's estate may, under most conditions, choose the special-use valuation method for that property. This means that the property is included in the decedent's estate at the value based on its *current* use and not at the value based on what its most lucrative—i.e., its "highest and best" use might be. For example, if the land is being used for farming, its value is figured on its worth as farmland and not on what it might be worth if used for industrial purposes.

Certain conditions must be met before you use the special-use valuation method; consult your tax advisor.

The maximum amount that the special-use method can decrease the value of the estate is $1,090,000 in 2014. This amount is increased each year for cost-of-living adjustments.

TAXALERT

In a recent Tax Court case, the beneficiaries who received property from their father's estate for which the special-use valuation election had been made ignored the basis based upon the special use valuation that was elected when they subsequently sold the property. Instead, they used the value of the property based on its highest and best use as the amount of basis. The court agreed with the IRS's position that the special-use value should have been used for purposes of determining the tax basis of the beneficiaries. To rule otherwise would have allowed the beneficiaries to benefit both from the position taken on the estate tax return (receiving a substantially larger bequest because the value of the property and associated estate taxes were reduced), as well as from the position taken on their income tax returns (realizing substantially less income because basis was increased), effectively benefiting twice from inconsistent positions relating to the same property. There are other cases in which beneficiaries of property have taken the position that for basis purposes they are not bound by the estate tax value of property received from a decedent. That position has had limited success. The president has included a provision in his proposed budgets that would bind beneficiaries who receive property from a decedent to basis as determined by the value of the property listed on the decedent's estate tax return. For more information, see your tax advisor.

- The decedent's adjusted basis in land to the extent of the value excluded from the decedent's taxable estate as a qualified conservation easement.

If a federal estate tax return does not have to be filed, your basis in the inherited property is its appraised value at the date of death for state inheritance or transmission taxes.

For more information, see the instructions to Form 706, United States Estate (and Generation-Skipping Transfer) Tax Return.

Property inherited from a decedent who died in 2010. If you inherited property from a decedent who died in 2010, special rules may apply. For more information, see Publication 4895, Tax Treatment of Property Acquired From a Decedent Dying in 2010.

TAXALERT

For most of 2010, the estate tax was repealed. However, a December 2010 tax law retroactively reinstated the estate tax for 2010. This law also allowed the executor of an estate of a decedent who died during 2010 to opt out of having the estate tax apply. If the estate tax applied to a decedent who died during 2010, then your basis in property you inherited from such decedent is generally the fair market value (FMV) of property at the date of the decedent's death (or alternate valuation date if the executor chose to use the alternate valuation). On the other hand, if the executor chose not to have the estate tax apply to the estate of a decedent who died during 2010, then "modified carryover basis" rules applied to determine your basis in inherited property. If you received a distribution from an estate to which the modified carryover basis rules apply, the executor should have provided you with a written statement that describes the tax basis of the property you received.

Modified carryover basis rules. Under these rules, you will generally receive a basis equal to the lesser of the fair market value of the property on the decedent's date of death or the decedent's adjusted basis in the property.

Exception. There is one key exception to this 2010 carryover basis rule: A decedent's executor was able to increase (often referred to as "step up") the basis of assets transferred by a total of $1.3 million plus any unused capital losses, net operating losses, and certain "built-in" losses of the decedent. An additional $3 million basis increase was allowed for property transferred to a surviving spouse, which means that property transferred to a spouse will be allowed a basis increase of up to $4.3 million. However, certain types of assets are not eligible for this increase in basis and further, nonresident aliens were only allowed an increase in basis of $60,000 under the 2010 modified carryover basis regime.

The executor was able to choose to allocate the step up in basis on an asset-by-asset basis. For example, the basis increase could have been allocated to a share of stock or a block of stock. However, in no case could the basis of an asset be adjusted above its fair market value. If the amount of basis increase is less than the fair market value of assets whose bases are eligible to be increased under these rules, the executor was able to determine which assets and to what extent each asset received a basis increase. This could put the executor in an awkward spot: deciding which family members or other heirs would get tax-free assets and which ones get assets with built-in capital gain.

If you report the sale of inherited property on your income tax return and calculate gain using an incorrect basis amount, you risk underpaying tax on the transaction and being subject to additional tax, interest, and penalties.

For more information about the estate tax, see chapter 44, *Estate and gift tax planning*.

TAXORGANIZER

If you sold property in 2014 that you originally inherited from a decedent who died during 2010, you should contact the executor of the decedent's estate to confirm the basis in the property you received.

TAXPLANNER

If you receive a distribution from an estate of a decedent who died either before or after 2010, the tax basis of the property you inherit is generally the FMV of the property at the date of the decedent's death (or alternate valuation date). See chapter 44, *Estate and gift tax planning*, for more information.

Community property. In community property states (Arizona, California, Idaho, Louisiana, Nevada, New Mexico, Texas, Washington, and Wisconsin), husband and wife are each usually considered to own half the community property. When either spouse dies, the total value of the community property, even the part belonging to the surviving spouse, generally becomes the basis of the entire property. For this rule to apply, at least half the value of the community property interest must be includible in the decedent's gross estate, whether or not the estate must file a return.

Example. You and your spouse owned community property that had a basis of $80,000. When your spouse died, half the FMV of the community interest was includible in your spouse's estate. The FMV of the community interest was $100,000. The basis of your half of the property after the death of your spouse is $50,000 (half of the $100,000 FMV). The basis of the other half to your spouse's heirs is also $50,000.

For more information about community property, see Publication 555, Community Property.

> ### TAXSAVER
> The inclusion of community property in a decedent's estate is not determined under federal law. Instead, state law determines federal estate tax treatment. In community property states, the basis of the surviving spouse's one-half share of community property assets will also receive a step-up in basis, normally to its FMV, at the date of the decedent spouse's death, even though only one-half of the property is actually includible in the gross estate. Assets held jointly by spouses and not as community property will only receive a step up for the decedent spouse's one-half share of the asset, because only one-half of the property is includible in the deceased spouse's estate. There are advantages and disadvantages for the various forms of holding title to assets. You should consult your tax advisor for recommendations on how to hold title to property in your state.

Property Changed From Personal to Business or Rental Use
If you hold property for personal use and then change it to business use or use it to produce rent, you can begin to depreciate the property at the time of the change. To do so, you must figure its basis for depreciation at the time of the change. An example of changing property held for personal use to business or rental use would be renting out your former personal residence.

Basis for depreciation. The basis for depreciation is the lesser of the following amounts.
- The FMV of the property on the date of the change.
- Your adjusted basis on the date of the change.

Example. Several years ago, you paid $160,000 to have your house built on a lot that cost $25,000. You paid $20,000 for permanent improvements to the house and claimed a $2,000 casualty loss deduction for damage to the house before changing the property to rental use last year. Because land is not depreciable, you include only the cost of the house when figuring the basis for depreciation.

Your adjusted basis in the house when you changed its use was $178,000 ($160,000 + $20,000 − $2,000). On the same date, your property had an FMV of $180,000, of which $15,000 was for the land and $165,000 was for the house. The basis for figuring depreciation on the house is its FMV on the date of the change ($165,000) because it is less than your adjusted basis ($178,000).

Sale of property. If you later sell or dispose of property changed to business or rental use, the basis you use will depend on whether you are figuring gain or loss.

Gain. The basis for figuring a gain is your adjusted basis in the property when you sell the property.

Example. Assume the same facts as in the previous example except that you sell the property at a gain after being allowed depreciation deductions of $37,500. Your adjusted basis for figuring gain is $165,500 ($178,000 + $25,000 (land) − $37,500).

Loss. Figure the basis for a loss starting with the smaller of your adjusted basis or the FMV of the property at the time of the change to business or rental use. Then make adjustments (increases and decreases) for the period after the change in the property's use, as discussed earlier under *Adjusted Basis*.

Example. Assume the same facts as in the previous example, except that you sell the property at a loss after being allowed depreciation deductions of $37,500. In this case, you would start with the FMV on the date of the change to rental use ($180,000), because it is less than the adjusted basis of $203,000 ($178,000 + $25,000 (land)) on that date. Reduce that amount ($180,000) by the depreciation deductions ($37,500). The basis for loss is $142,500 ($180,000 − $37,500).

Stocks and Bonds

The basis of stocks or bonds you buy generally is the purchase price plus any costs of purchase, such as commissions and recording or transfer fees. If you get stocks or bonds other than by purchase, your basis is usually determined by the FMV or the previous owner's adjusted basis, as discussed earlier.

You must adjust the basis of stocks for certain events that occur after purchase. For example, if you receive additional stock from nontaxable stock dividends or stock splits, reduce your basis for each share of stock by dividing the adjusted basis of the old stock by the number of shares of old and new stock. This rule applies only when the additional stock received is identical to the stock held. Also reduce your basis when you receive nontaxable distributions. They are a return of capital.

Example. In 2012 you bought 100 shares of XYZ stock for $1,000 or $10 a share. In 2013 you bought 100 shares of XYZ stock for $1,600 or $16 a share. In 2014 XYZ declared a 2-for-1 stock split. You now have 200 shares of stock with a basis of $5 a share and 200 shares with a basis of $8 a share.

Other basis. There are other ways to figure the basis of stocks or bonds depending on how you acquired them. For detailed information, see *Stocks and Bonds* under *Basis of Investment Property* in chapter 4 of Publication 550.

Identifying stocks or bonds sold. If you can adequately identify the shares of stock or the bonds you sold, their basis is the cost or other basis of the particular shares of stocks or bonds. If you buy and sell securities at various times in varying quantities and you cannot adequately identify the shares you sell, the basis of the securities you sell is the basis of the securities you acquired first. For more information about identifying securities you sell, see *Stocks and Bonds under Basis of Investment Property* in chapter 4 of Publication 550.

TAXALERT

If you sold property such as stocks, bonds, mutual funds or certain commodities through a broker during 2014, for each sale your broker should send you a Form 1099-B (Proceeds From Broker and Barter Exchange Transactions) or an equivalent statement that will show the gross proceeds from the particular sale. The broker will also file a copy of Form 1099-B with the IRS.

If you sold stock during 2014 that you acquired after 2010, your broker is also generally required to report your basis in the shares sold and whether any capital gain or loss was short-term or long-term on Form 1099-B. For example, stock purchased and sold during 2014 will be classified as short-term since the securities have been held for less than a year. On the other hand, brokers are not required to report basis or holding period for any securities acquired before 2011.

TAXPLANNER

If you made multiple purchases of a particular stock during 2014 and sold only a portion of the total shares you acquired, then your broker is required to report your basis in the shares sold on Form 1099-B using the first-in, first-out (FIFO) method; that is, the broker must consider the oldest shares you acquired as the ones sold first. However, your broker does not need to use the FIFO method if you provide him or her with an adequate and timely identification of the specific shares that you want to sell. You must identify the stock to be sold by the earlier of the settlement date or the time for settlement under SEC regulations. You may also issue a standing order to specify a lot selection method.

TAXALERT

There is an exception for mutual fund shares that allows you to use the average method for computing cost basis. The average method is allowed if you acquired identical mutual fund shares at various times and prices, or you acquired the shares after December 31, 2010, in connection with a dividend reinvestment plan (DRP), which requires at least 10% of every dividend to be reinvested in identical stock, and left the shares on deposit in an account kept by a custodian or agent. A DRP may also average the basis of shares acquired through non-dividend distributions such as capital gain distributions, nontaxable returns of capital, and cash in lieu.

TAXPLANNER

If your portfolio consists of various lots of the same stock acquired at different times and at different costs, you should exercise some care when contemplating a sale of a portion of these shares. For example, assume that you own five different lots of ABC Motors stock acquired at different times and ranging in cost basis between $40 and $80 per share. If the stock is currently selling for $60 per share and you sell a lot with a basis of $40 per share, you recognize a gain; on the other hand, if you sell a lot having a basis of $80 per share, you sustain a loss. The situation may be far more complicated if the company has paid stock dividends or has split its stock one or more times.

It may be advisable to take any shares that you receive as the result of a stock dividend or a stock split and combine them with the shares that gave rise to the dividend or split. Have your broker convert all such related stock certificates into one certificate. Thus, each block of stock having a distinguishable cost basis is separately maintained. Although you are certainly not required to do this, it simplifies your recordkeeping task and makes it much easier to compute gain or loss when you sell the shares.

TAXORGANIZER

You should keep a copy of your broker confirmation statement as a record for your cost basis in the shares of stock you have purchased during the year. When you are not selling your entire position in the stock, this information will be useful in determining whether there is a benefit to identifying a specific lot of shares to sell.

EXPLANATION

For tax purposes, the selling instructions given to your broker or fund representative must be in writing. Even if stock certificates from a different lot are actually delivered to the transfer agent, you may consider the stock sold as you specified, provided that you identified the shares to be sold and received written confirmation of your orders.

TAXPLANNER

Incentive stock options. If the shares you are selling were acquired by exercising an incentive stock option (ISO) with previously owned employer shares, special rules will apply in determining the basis of the ISO shares.

The sale or transfer of stock acquired through the exercise of an ISO within 2 years of the option's grant date and within 1 year of the option's exercise date is known as a "disqualifying disposition." If the sale constitutes a disqualifying disposition of the ISO shares, the lowest basis shares are considered to be sold first, regardless of your effort to identify and sell specific shares. For more information, see _Stock Options_ in chapter 5, _Wages, salaries, and other earnings_, and Publication 525, _Taxable and Nontaxable Income_.

TAXPLANNER

Charitable contributions. If you own several blocks of appreciated shares, it is generally to your advantage to give away those shares with the lowest tax basis. When you make a contribution of the stock, you should be especially careful to designate which shares are being contributed. Let your stockbroker or transfer agent and the charity know the date you purchased the shares that you are now donating. It's important to take these steps at the time you are making the gift. For more information, see chapter 25, _Contributions_.

Mutual fund shares. If you sell mutual fund shares you acquired at various times and prices and left on deposit in an account kept by a custodian or agent, you can elect to use an average basis. For more information, see Publication 550.

EXPLANATION

For further discussion, see chapter 16, _Reporting gains and losses_. Also, mutual funds are discussed in chapter 39, _Mutual funds_.

Bond premium. If you buy a taxable bond at a premium and elect to amortize the premium, reduce the basis of the bond by the amortized premium you deduct each year. See *Bond Premium Amortization* in chapter 3 of Publication 550 for more information. Although you cannot deduct the premium on a tax-exempt bond, you must amortize the premium each year and reduce your basis in the bond by the amortized amount.

> ### EXAMPLE
> On February 18, 2013, Tamera purchases a tax-exempt obligation maturing on February 18, 2017, for $120,000. The bond has a stated principal amount of $100,000, payable at maturity. The obligation provides for unconditional payments of interest of $9,000, payable on February 18 of each year. The interest payments on the obligation are qualified stated interest. The amount of bond premium is $20,000 ($120,000 - $100,000).
>
> Based on the remaining payment schedule of the bond and Tamera's basis in the bond, Tamera's yield is 3.55%, compounded annually (per her broker, who looked up the yield rate). The bond premium amortized annually is equal to the qualified stated interest payment ($9,000) less the adjusted acquisition price at the beginning of the period ($120,000 for 2014) multiplied by Tamera's yield (3.55%, compounded annually) ($120,000 × 3.55%, or $4,260).
>
> Thus, the bond premium that must be amortized on February 18, 2014, is $4,740 ($9,000 - $4,260). Since the bond is a tax-exempt obligation, Tamera may not claim the amortization as a deduction on her tax return.

Original issue discount (OID) on debt instruments. You must increase your basis in an OID debt instrument by the OID you include in income for that instrument. See *Original Issue Discount (OID)* in chapter 7 and Publication 1212, Guide To Original Issue Discount (OID) Instruments.

Tax-exempt obligations. OID on tax-exempt obligations is generally not taxable. However, when you dispose of a tax-exempt obligation issued after September 3, 1982, and acquired after March 1, 1984, you must accrue OID on the obligation to determine its adjusted basis. The accrued OID is added to the basis of the obligation to determine your gain or loss. See chapter 4 of Publication 550.

> ### TAXSAVER
> **Automatic investment service and dividend reinvestment plans.** If you take part in an automatic investment service, your cost basis per share of stock, including fractional shares, bought by the bank or other agent is your proportionate share of the agent's cost of all shares purchased at the same time plus the same share of the brokerage commission paid by the agent. If you take part in a dividend reinvestment plan and you receive stock from the corporation at a discount, your cost is the full FMV of the stock on the dividend payment date. You must include the amount of the discount in your income as an additional dividend.
>
> Beginning in 2011, all shares acquired on or after January 1 through a dividend reinvestment plan (DRP) are permitted to use the average method for tracking basis provided that the DRP shares are held in plans for which a written document requires at least 10% of every dividend paid is reinvested in identical stock.
>
> **Stock dividends.** Special rules apply in determining the basis of stock you acquired through a stock dividend or a stock right. Stock dividends are distributions by a corporation of its own stock. Usually, stock dividends are not taxable to the shareholder. However, for exceptions to this rule, see chapter 8, *Dividends and other corporate distributions*. If stock dividends are not taxable, you must allocate your basis for the stock between the old and the new stock in proportion to the FMV of each on the date of the distribution of the new stock. If your stock dividend is taxable on receipt, the original basis of your new stock is its FMV on the date of distribution. Your holding period begins on the date of distribution.
>
> **New and old stock identical.** If the new stock you received as a nontaxable dividend is the same as the old stock on which the dividend is declared, both new and old shares probably have equal FMVs and you can divide the adjusted basis of the old stock by the number of shares of old and new stock. The result is your basis for each share of stock.
>
> *Example*
> You owned one share of common stock that you bought for $45. The corporation distributed two new shares of common stock for each share you held. You then had three shares of common stock, each with a basis of $15 ($45 ÷ 3). If you owned two shares before the distribution, one

bought for $30 and the other for $45, you would have six shares after the distribution: three with a basis of $10 each and three with a basis of $15 each.

New and old stock not identical. If the new stock you received as a nontaxable dividend is not the same as the old stock on which the dividend was declared, the FMVs of the old stock and the new stock will probably be different, so you should allocate the adjusted basis of your old stock between the old stock and the new stock in proportion to the FMVs of each on the date of the distribution of the new stock.

Example 1
This example shows how to account for stock splits and stock dividends.

	Block 1		
	Shares	Total Cost	Cost per Share
March 14, 2012	100	$3,000	$30
Nov. 29, 2013			
2 for 1 stock split	100	-0-	
	200	$3,000	$15
Nov. 3, 2014			
10% stock dividend	20		
Dec. 30, 2014	220	$3,000	$13.636

	Block 2		
	Shares	Total Cost	Cost per Share
Oct. 28, 2014	100	$2,000	$20
10% stock dividend	10		
Dec. 30, 2014	110	$2,000	$18.182

The original cost of each block of stock must be divided by the number of shares on hand at any given date to arrive at basis per share.

Example 2
This example shows how to account for nontaxable stock dividends with an FMV that is different from the value of the original stock held.

	Shares	Total Cost	Cost per Share	Total FMV	FMV per Share
Feb. 5, 2014 Purchased common stock	1,000	$14,000	$14	$14,000	$14
Sept. 1, 2014 10% stock dividend of preferred stock	100			$1,000	$10
FMV of original stock is $22 per share.					
1,000 shares × $14 = $14,000	Cost of originating stock				
1,000 shares × $22 = $22,000	Market value of original stock				
100 shares × $10 = $1,000	Market value of preferred stock				
$22,000/$23,000 × $14,000 = $13,391	Cost of original stock apportioned to such stock				
$1,000/$23,000 × $14,000 = $609	Cost of original stock apportioned to the preferred stock				

Example 3

This example shows how to calculate the basis of shares in a DRP using the average basis method election.

For shares purchased after December 31, 2011, the average basis method applies on an account-by-account basis. If Betty wishes to continue to use the average basis method with identical shares held across all of her accounts, she must contact her broker to make this election.

On June 3, 2014, Betty acquires 100 shares of stock at $25 per share and enrolls them in the company's DRP plan. On August 15, 2014, the company pays a dividend of $3.00 per share while the shares are trading at $30 per share, and on November 10, 2014, the company pays a dividend of $4.73 per share while the shares are trading at $32.50 per share. Since Betty elects to use the average basis method upon her initial purchase, this election will be effective for identical shares held across all of Betty's accounts through December 31, 2014. Assuming she makes the election, for share sales after January 1, 2014, the average basis will be computed as follows:

Date	Action	Share Price	No. of Shares	Total Shares Owned
Original shares				
June 3, 2014	Invest $2,500	$25.00	100	100
DRP shares Aug. 15, 2014	Reinvest $300 Dividend	$30.00	10	110
Nov. 10, 2014	Reinvest $520	$32.50	16	126
AVERAGE BASIS	To figure the basis of the shares, use the basis of all shares acquired in 2014.			
	cost of 126 shares	$3,320.00		
	number of shares ÷	126		
	average basis per share	$26.35		

If Betty does not notify her broker of her average basis election, the basis on the first 100 shares sold will be calculated using the FIFO method ($25/share).

EXPLANATION

Stock rights. A stock right is rarely taxable when you receive it. For more information, see chapter 8, *Dividends and other corporate distributions*.

If you receive stock rights that are taxable, the basis of the rights is their FMV at the time of distribution.

If you receive stock rights that are not taxable and you allow them to expire, they have no basis.

If you exercise or sell the nontaxable stock rights and if, at the time of distribution, the rights had an FMV of 15% or more of the FMV of the old stock, you must divide the adjusted basis of the stock between the stock and the stock rights. Use a ratio of the FMV of each to the FMV of both at the time of distribution of the rights. If the FMV of the stock rights is less than 15%, their basis is zero unless you choose to allocate a part of the basis of the old stock to the rights. You make this allocation on your return for the tax year in which the rights are received.

Basis of new stock. If you exercise the stock rights, the basis of the new stock is its cost plus the basis of the stock rights exercised. The holding period of the new stock begins on the date on which you exercised the stock rights.

Example

You own 100 shares of Tan Company stock, which cost you $22 per share. Tan Company gave you 10 nontaxable stock rights that would allow you to buy 10 additional shares of stock at $26 per share. At the time the rights were distributed, the stock had a market value of $30, without the rights, and each right had a market value of $3. The market value of the stock rights is less than 15% of the market value of the stock, but you choose to divide the basis of your stock between the stock and the rights. You figure the basis of the rights and the basis of the old stock as follows:

100 shares × $22 = $2,200, basis of old stock
100 shares × $30 = $3,000, market value of old stock
10 rights × $3 = $30, market value of rights
30/3,030 × $2,200 = $21.78, basis of rights
3,000/3,030 × $2,200 = $2,178.22, new basis of old stock

If you sell the stock rights, the basis for figuring gain or loss is $2.178 per right. If you exercise the stock rights, the basis of the new stock you receive is $28.178 per share, the subscription price paid ($26) plus the basis of the stock rights exercised ($2.178 each). The remaining basis of the 100 shares of old stock for figuring gain or loss on a later sale is $2,178.22, or $21.7822 per share.

Explanation

Other basis rules. There are many other special rules you must follow in determining your basis in certain types of property. Here are some examples.

If you receive stock of one corporation solely in exchange for stock of another corporation in certain types of corporate reorganizations, your basis in the stock received will be equal to the basis of the stock you exchanged.

Certain types of tax credits may reduce basis in whole or in part. For example, if you claim rehabilitation credits on a building, the basis of the property is reduced by the amount of the credit.

If you lease real property on which the lessee makes improvements and the value of such improvements is excluded from income, your basis in the improvements is zero.

If you sell property to charity in a bargain sale, your basis for determining the gain from the sale is reduced by the ratio of the total basis of the property to its FMV.

For more information, you should consult your tax advisor.

Chapter 14
Sale of property

Note

IRS Publication 17 (*Your Federal Income Tax*) has been updated by Ernst & Young LLP for 2014. Dates and dollar amounts shown are for 2014. Underlined type is used to indicate where IRS text has been updated. Places where text has been removed are indicated by the sentence: *Text intentionally omitted*.

ey.com/EYTaxGuide

Ernst & Young LLP will update the *EY Tax Guide 2015* website with relevant taxpayer information as it becomes available. You can also sign up for email alerts to let you know when changes have been made.

Introduction

Anytime you sell or exchange a piece of property at a gain—whether it be your house, a stock you own, or something you use in your trade or business—you usually have to pay taxes on the transaction. That, of course, doesn't mean that sales and exchanges should be avoided, but the manner in which you choose to dispose of an asset may determine how much you will have to pay in taxes. This chapter describes the various options available to you and the tax consequences of each.

Because the amounts involved in sales and exchanges of property are often quite large relative to other items that make up your income, this chapter merits careful attention. It not only spells out how you determine the way in which various transactions are taxed but also offers suggestions about how to minimize or defer the tax burdens that you may incur.

In addition, this chapter discusses bad debts. When a borrower cannot repay a loan, it is known as a bad debt. Some loans are made in connection with a trade or a business, some are made for purely personal reasons, and still others are made to make a profit. All sorts of rules have to be followed, and not every bad debt qualifies for a deduction. This chapter spells out what kind of documentation you need to prove that the money you lost was a bona fide debt and that there is no chance of repayment—the two conditions that must be met for you to take a deduction.

What's New

50% Exclusion of Qualified Small Business Stock Capital Gains. 50% (60% for certain empowerment zone businesses) of the gain from the sale of certain qualified small business stock acquired at original issue after December 31, 2013 or before February 18, 2009, and held for more than five years is excluded from income.

EXPLANATION

The portion of the gain includible in taxable income is taxed at a maximum rate of 28 percent under the regular tax. For alternative minimum tax (AMT) purposes (see chapter 31, *How to figure your tax*), 7% of the amount excluded from gross income is an AMT preference item and is added back to taxable income to arrive at alternative minimum taxable income. See *Gain on qualified small business stock* later in this chapter for more information.

The exclusion is available only to taxpayers that are not corporations. See the **TAXSAVER** *Gain on sale of qualified small business stock* later in this chapter for a description of the rules for determining whether stock is qualified small business stock.

TAXALERT

For qualified small business stock acquired after February 17, 2009, and before September 28, 2010, the exclusion is increased to 75%. For such stock acquired after September 27, 2010, and before January 1, 2014, 100% of the gain is excluded and there is no AMT preference item attributable for that sale.

As of the date this book was published in October 2014, Congress had been considering legislation that would extend the availability of the 100% exclusion and eliminate the AMT preference to qualified stock acquired at least during 2014 and 2015; however, no extension had yet been passed. For updated information on this and any other tax law changes that occur after this book was published, see our website, *ey.com/EYTaxGuide*.

S Corporation Built-In Gains Tax. For tax years beginning in 2014, no tax is imposed on the net recognized built-in gain of an S corporation after the 10th year in the recognition period.

EXPLANATION

When a C corporation elects to become an S corporation, the conversion is not a taxable event. However, following such a conversion, an S corporation must hold on to its assets for a certain period of time. If the S corporation sells an asset sooner (i.e., within 10 calendar years beginning with the first day of the first taxable year for which the S election is in effect), then any built-in gain in such assets that existed at the time of the conversion is taxed to the S corporation at the existing highest marginal tax rate applicable to corporations; currently, 35%.

Under prior law, no tax was imposed on the net recognized built-in gain of an S corporation after the 7th year in the recognition period for taxable years beginning in 2009 and 2010 nor after the 5th year for taxable years beginning in 2011. For tax years beginning in either 2012 or 2013, the recognition period for purposes of determining a net recognized built-in gain was reduced to 5 years.

As of the date this book was published in October 2014, Congress had been considering legislation that would extend the reduced 5-year built-in gains tax holding period that applied for 2012 and 2013 to at least 2014 and 2015 (the U.S. House of Representatives passed legislation that would permanently extend the 5-year recognition period); however, no extension had yet been enacted. For updated information on this and any other tax law changes that occur after this book was published, see our website, *ey.com/EYTaxGuide*.

Reminder

Foreign income. If you are a U.S. citizen who sells property located outside the United States, you must report all gains and losses from the sale of that property on your tax return unless it is exempt by U.S. law. This is true whether you reside inside or outside the United States and whether or not you receive a Form 1099 from the payer.

TAXALERT

U.S. citizens are subject to U.S. income tax on their worldwide income, regardless of whether they live in the United States. The IRS has significantly increased its scrutiny of offshore income and investments of U.S. citizens. In addition to reporting income from the sale of property located outside of the United States, virtually any kind of income that a U.S. citizen receives or has the right to receive is generally taxable and must be reported on a U.S. tax return. U.S. citizens are also generally required to disclose investments and financial accounts held outside of the United States, even if those assets do not generate current income. If you have overseas income or investments you may be eligible to take a credit on your U.S. return for the related foreign income taxes paid. Furthermore, you may be eligible for benefits under a U.S. tax treaty with the country in which your foreign income arises. Substantial penalties may apply if foreign income and financial interests are not properly reported. If you have foreign income, you should consult your tax advisor to confirm that your foreign interests are reported completely and timely. For more information, see chapter 37, *Other credits including the earned income credit*, and chapter 41, *U.S. citizens working abroad: Tax treatment of foreign earned income*.

This chapter discusses the tax consequences of selling or trading investment property. It explains the following.

- What a sale or trade is.
- Figuring gain or loss.
- Nontaxable trades.
- Related party transactions.
- Capital gains or losses.
- Capital assets and noncapital assets.
- Holding period.
- Rollover of gain from publicly traded securities.

Other property transactions. Certain transfers of property are not discussed here. They are discussed in other IRS publications. These include the following.

- Sales of a main home, covered in chapter 15.
- Installment sales, covered in Publication 537, Installment Sales.
- Transactions involving business property, covered in Publication 544, Sales and Other Dispositions of Assets.
- Dispositions of an interest in a passive activity, covered in Publication 925, Passive Activity and At-Risk Rules.

Publication 550, Investment Income and Expenses (Including Capital Gains and Losses), provides a more detailed discussion about sales and trades of investment property. Publication 550 includes information about the rules covering nonbusiness bad debts, straddles, Section 1256 contracts, puts and calls, commodity futures, short sales, and wash sales. It also discusses investment-related expenses.

Useful Items

You may want to see:

Publication

- ☐ **550** Investment Income and Expenses

Form (and Instructions)

- ☐ **Schedule D (Form 1040)** Capital Gains and Losses
- ☐ **4797** Sales of Business Property
- ☐ **8949** Sales and Other Dispositions of Capital Assets
- ☐ **8824** Like-Kind Exchanges

Sales and Trades

If you sold property such as stocks, bonds, or certain commodities through a broker during the year, you should receive, for each sale, a Form 1099-B, Proceeds From Broker and Barter Exchange Transactions, or substitute statement, from the broker. Generally, you should receive the statement by February 15 of the next year. It will show the gross proceeds from the sale. If you sold a covered security in 2014, your 1099-B (or substitute statement) will show your basis. Generally, a covered security is a security you acquired after 2010, with certain exceptions. See the Instructions for Form 8949. The IRS will also get a copy of Form 1099-B from the broker.

Use Form 1099-B (or substitute statement received from your broker) to complete Form 8949.

What Is a Sale or Trade?

This section explains what is a sale or trade. It also explains certain transactions and events that are treated as sales or trades.

A sale is generally a transfer of property for money or a mortgage, note, or other promise to pay money.

A trade is a transfer of property for other property or services and may be taxed in the same way as a sale.

Sale and purchase. Ordinarily, a transaction is not a trade when you voluntarily sell property for cash and immediately buy similar property to replace it. The sale and purchase are two separate transactions. But see *Like-kind exchanges* under *Nontaxable Trades*, later.

Redemption of stock. A redemption of stock is treated as a sale or trade and is subject to the capital gain or loss provisions unless the redemption is a dividend or other distribution on stock.

Dividend versus sale or trade. Whether a redemption is treated as a sale, trade, dividend, or other distribution depends on the circumstances in each case. Both direct and indirect ownership of stock will be considered. The redemption is treated as a sale or trade of stock if:

- The redemption is not essentially equivalent to a dividend (see chapter 8),
- There is a substantially disproportionate redemption of stock,
- There is a complete redemption of all the stock of the corporation owned by the shareholder, or
- The redemption is a distribution in partial liquidation of a corporation.

Redemption or retirement of bonds. A redemption or retirement of bonds or notes at their maturity is generally treated as a sale or trade.

In addition, a significant modification of a bond is treated as a trade of the original bond for a new bond. For details, see Regulations section 1.1001-3.

Surrender of stock. A surrender of stock by a dominant shareholder who retains ownership of more than half of the corporation's voting shares is treated as a contribution to capital rather than as an immediate loss deductible from taxable income. The surrendering shareholder must reallocate his or her basis in the surrendered shares to the shares he or she retains.

Worthless securities. Stocks, stock rights, and bonds (other than those held for sale by a securities dealer) that became completely worthless during the tax year are treated as though they were sold on the last day of the tax year. This affects whether your capital loss is long term or short term. See *Holding Period*, later.

Worthless securities also include securities that you abandon after March 12, 2008. To abandon a security, you must permanently surrender and relinquish all rights in the security and receive no consideration in exchange for it. All the facts and circumstances determine whether the transaction is properly characterized as an abandonment or other type of transaction, such as an actual sale or exchange, contribution to capital, dividend, or gift.

If you are a cash basis taxpayer and make payments on a negotiable promissory note that you issued for stock that became worthless, you can deduct these payments as losses in the years you actually make the payments. Do not deduct them in the year the stock became worthless.

EXPLANATION

A security is considered worthless when it has no recognizable value. You should be able to establish that the worthless security had value in the year preceding the year in which you take the deduction, and that an identifiable event reduced the value to zero, causing the loss in the year in which you deduct it. A drop in the value of a stock, even though substantial, does not constitute worthlessness. The courts have held that if stock is sold for a very nominal sum to an unrelated third party (e.g., less than 1 cent per share), that is proof of worthlessness.

TAXPLANNER

The deduction for a worthless security must be taken in the year the security becomes worthless, even if it is sold for a nominal sum in the following year. If you do not learn that a security has become worthless until a later year, you should file an amended return for the year in which it became worthless. Because it may be difficult to determine exactly when a stock becomes worthless, the capital loss deduction should be claimed in the earliest year a claim may be reasonably made.

If you hold securities that seem to be on the verge of worthlessness, it may be easier to sell them now and take your capital loss without waiting for proof of worthlessness. Make sure you sell the securities to an unrelated buyer—otherwise your loss may be disallowed. If you hold shares that are delisted—stock that is removed from a national exchange such as the New York Stock Exchange or NASDAQ (this sometimes happens because the share trading price drops below the minimum price required to continue trading)—you may want to consider abandoning your ownership of the shares, as they may be very difficult to sell. To abandon shares, you must give up your legal right to the shares and receive no remuneration in exchange for giving up that right. You should retain documentation of the shares being removed from your account, as the transaction generates no proceeds and therefore may not be reported on your year-end statements.

When securities are bought on credit, the timing of the deduction for worthlessness depends on the type of debt you have incurred. If the stock is purchased by giving the seller a note and the stock becomes worthless before the note is paid off, you may deduct the loss only as you make the payments on the note. However, if you borrow the funds from a third party, you may deduct the loss in the year in which the stock becomes worthless. In either case, an accrual basis taxpayer takes the deduction in the year the security becomes worthless.

TAXORGANIZER

You should keep any documents indicating the date on which the security becomes worthless. Examples of sufficient documentation are bankruptcy documents and financial statements.

How to report loss. Report worthless securities in Part I or Part II, whichever applies, of Form 8949. In column (a), enter "Worthless."

Filing a claim for refund. If you do not claim a loss for a worthless security on your original return for the year it becomes worthless, you can file a claim for a credit or refund due to the loss. You must use Form 1040X, Amended U.S. Individual Income Tax Return, to amend your return for the year the security became worthless. You must file it within 7 years from the date your original return for that year had to be filed, or 2 years from the date you paid the tax, whichever is later. For more information about filing a claim, see *Amended Returns and Claims for Refund* in chapter 1.

Tax Breaks and Deductions You Can Use Checklist

Worthless securities. You can claim a capital loss on a security, such as stocks, stock rights, and bonds that become worthless during the year. The security is treated as if it had been sold on the last day of the year for purposes of determining whether your loss is short-term or long-term. You are permitted to claim the loss only in the year the security actually becomes worthless. That can be tricky to determine. As an alternative, if you hold securities that are on the verge of becoming worthless, consider selling them now and take your capital loss in the year you sell, rather than having to discover proof that the securities have, in fact, become worthless. Make sure you sell the securities to an unrelated buyer—otherwise your loss may be disallowed. Tax regulations adopted in 2008 allow you to treat securities abandoned after March 12, 2008, as

Caution

Report your worthless securities transactions on Form 8949 with the correct box checked for these transactions. See Form 8949 and the Instructions for Form 8949.

Tip

For more information on Form 8949 and Schedule D (Form 1040), see Reporting Capital Gains and Losses *in chapter 16. See also Schedule D (Form 1040), Form 8949, and their separate instructions.*

worthless securities. For more information, see _Worthless securities_, in _What Is a Sale or Trade_, later.

Like-Kind Exchanges. In general, any gain realized from selling your property must be included in your taxable income. However, if you trade or exchange business or investment property for "like-kind" property–that is, property of a similar nature or character–the gain on the property you traded is deferred until you ultimately sell the new property received in the trade. Your newly acquired property is considered to be a continuation of the investment in the original property. Therefore, your basis in the new property is generally the same as it was in the property you traded. For more information, see _Nontaxable Exchanges and Like-Kind Exchanges_ in chapter 13, _Basis of property_.

Installment Sales. Selling property through an installment sale can enable you to spread out the recognition of the tax gain on the sale over a period of years. This may result in a lower overall tax on your realized gain. With an installment sale, you receive part or all of the sales proceeds in one or more years after the year in which you sold the property. You report your gain only as you actually receive the payment, and are taxed only on the portion of each payment that represents your profit from the sale. For more information, see _Installment sales_, later.

Nontaxable Trades: You usually have to pay tax on any gains you realize when you sell or exchange a piece of property. However, the tax

EXCEPTIONS
While an exchange is generally taxable, the following "exchanges" are not:
- The extension of the maturity date of promissory notes
- The exercise of an option to convert a bond into stock of the issuing corporation, if the conversion privilege is provided for in the bond
- The conversion of security interests to stock in the same corporation subsequent to certain reorganizations (one example: the exchange of common stock for preferred stock)

TAXPLANNER
You may save taxes by carefully planning major sales and exchanges. It may be better to wait until after the end of the year before finalizing a sale so that a gain may be deferred until the next year. Alternatively, you may want to finalize the sale before the end of the year to take advantage of any losses in the current year. Professional advice should be obtained before a major transaction, not after.

Explanation
Estates. The transfer of property of a decedent to the executor or administrator of the estate, or to the heirs or beneficiaries, generally is not a sale or exchange. No taxable gain or deductible loss results from the transfer.

Easements. Granting or selling an easement may not be a taxable sale of property. Instead, the amount received for the easement is subtracted from the basis of the property. If only a part of an entire tract of property is permanently affected by the easement, only the basis of that part is reduced by the amount received. Any amount received that is more than the basis of the property to be reduced is a taxable gain. The transaction is reported as if it were a sale of the property.

If you transfer a perpetual easement for consideration, the transaction will be treated as a sale of property.

Life estate, etc. The entire amount you realize from disposing of a life interest in property, an interest in property for a set number of years, or an income interest in a trust is a taxable gain if you first got the interest as a gift, inheritance, or transfer in trust. Your basis in the property is considered to be zero. This rule does not apply if all interests in the property are disposed of at the same time.

Example 1
Your father dies, leaving his farm to you for life, with a remainder interest to your younger brother. You decide to sell your life interest in the farm. The entire amount you receive is a taxable gain, and your basis in the farm is disregarded.

Example 2
The facts are the same as in Example 1, except that your younger brother joins you in selling the farm. Because the entire interest in the property is conveyed, your taxable gain is the amount by which your share of the proceeds exceeds your adjusted basis in the farm.

Note: In Example 2, each brother's gain is computed by allocating the tax basis between them. The basis for the entire property–the fair market value at the date of the decedent's death–is adjusted for depreciation and improvements. Then, using actuarial tables, you compute the value of the life interest and of the remainder interest at the date of sale.

The younger brother could sell his remainder interest in the property independently of his brother, using his separate basis in computing his gain or loss on the sale. However, the older brother may not get the benefit of his basis in the property if he sells his life interest separately. The moral of the story is: Sometimes you save on taxes if you get along with your brother.

Sale versus lease. Just because a document says that it is a lease does not necessarily make it a lease for tax purposes. The rules are very complicated and not completely clear. Professional help is advisable. See Publication 544, _Sales and Other Dispositions of Assets_.

Installment sales. Some sales are made under a plan that provides for part or the entire sales price to be paid in a later year. These are called installment sales. If you finance the buyer's purchase of your property instead of the buyer getting a loan or mortgage from a bank, you probably have an installment sale.

You report your gain on an installment sale only as you actually receive payment. You are taxed only on the part of each payment that represents your profit on the sale. In this way, the installment method of reporting income relieves you of paying tax on income that you have not yet collected.

The first step in using the installment method is to find what portion of each installment payment represents a gain. This is determined by calculating the gross profit percentage, which is your gross profit divided by the contract price. Apply this percentage to all payments you receive in a year.

Gross profit is the selling price less the adjusted basis of the property sold. The selling price includes any cash you receive, the fair market value of any property received from the buyer, plus the amount of any existing mortgage on the property that the buyer became subject to or assumed.

Contract price is the selling price less any mortgage encumbrance on the property. However, if the amount of the mortgage is more than the adjusted basis of the property, then the selling price is reduced only by the adjusted basis, so the gross profit percentage is 100%.

Example

In 1994, Martha bought commercial real estate for $100,000. She put $20,000 down and took out a mortgage for $80,000. By 2014, Martha had reduced the mortgage to $40,000 and had an adjusted basis in the real estate of $85,000 (original cost, less depreciation, plus improvements). Martha sold the real estate to Benjamin for $190,000. To pay Martha, Benjamin assumed the rest of the mortgage and made three installment payments of $50,000 each.

Martha figures her gross profit as follows:

Selling price	$190,000
Less: Adjusted tax basis	(85,000)
Gross profit	$105,000
Martha figures her contract price as follows:	
Selling price	$190,000
Less: Mortgage assumed	(40,000)
Contract price	$150,000

Martha's gross profit percentage is 70% (gross profit divided by contract price). Martha must report 70% of all contract-price collections as a taxable gain in the year they are received.

TAXSAVER

Using the installment sale method may spread out your gain over several years and may result in a lower total tax on your gain.

By taking only a portion of the gain into income each year, you may avoid reaching a higher tax bracket. Even if you are already in the highest bracket, use of the installment sale method may still be beneficial, because taxes may be deferred to later years.

A disadvantage of the installment sale method is that if you are the seller, you do not obtain the sale proceeds immediately and therefore cannot reinvest them elsewhere. Also, a special rule applies to installment obligations arising from a sale of real or personal property if you're a non-dealer where the sales price exceeds $150,000. To the extent the total face amount of these obligations arising during any tax year and outstanding at the end of that tax year exceed $5,000,000, interest is payable to the IRS annually on a certain percentage of the deferred tax liability.

TAXSAVER

Installment sale treatment is not obligatory. You may elect not to follow the installment sale rules, in which case your total gain is recognized in the year of the sale.

While it is generally advantageous to defer recognition of a gain or part of a gain by using the installment sale method, under certain circumstances, accelerating recognition may result in overall tax savings. For example, if you expect your income in future years to be much higher than it is now or if you currently have a capital loss that may be offset by a gain, you may want to recognize your gain immediately.

The law limits the ability to defer tax by restricting use of the installment sale method to certain kinds of property. For example, the installment sale method may not be used for sales of publicly traded stocks or securities. However, you may sell other types of property, such as real property used in your business or for rental, under an installment sale and still defer the tax on the gain.

law provides a number of specific exceptions to this general rule. Following is a list of exchanges or trades that do not result in a taxable gain (nor trigger a deductible loss):

- *Like-kind exchanges:* an exchange of business or investment property for other business or investment property of a similar nature;
- *Corporate reorganizations:* an exchange of common stock for preferred stock or vice versa, or stock in one corporation for stock in another company as a result of a reorganization of a corporation, such as through a merger, recapitalization, or corporate division or acquisition;
- *Stock for stock of the same corporation:* an exchange of common stock for other common stock or preferred stock for other preferred stock in the same corporation;
- *Convertible stocks and bonds:* a conversion of bonds into stock or preferred stock into common stock of the same corporation in accordance with a conversion privilege that was included in the terms of the bond or the preferred stock certificate; and
- *Property for stock of a controlled corporation:* an exchange of property with a corporation in return for stock in the company, and you control the corporation immediately after the trade.

For more information, see *Nontaxable Trades*, later.

Nontaxable exchanges of insurance policies and annuities. You will not have to recognize a gain or loss on the exchange of a life insurance contract for another life insurance contract, endowment, or annuity contract, or an annuity contract for another annuity contract, if the insured or annuitant are the same under both contracts. However, starting in 2011, restrictions have changed for certain annuity contract exchanges. For more information, see *Nontaxable Trades: Insurance policies and annuities*, later.

Nonbusiness bad debts. If you are owed money, and you can no longer collect on that debt, you may be able to deduct the amount still owed to you as a bad debt. If the debt came about from operating your trade or business, the bad debt deduction is an ordinary loss. A non-business bad debt, on the other hand, can only be deducted as a short-term capital loss. You are entitled to claim a bad debt deduction only in the year the debt becomes totally worthless. That can be tricky to determine. As a result, you should claim the bad debt deduction at the earliest time you believe the debt to be worthless. For more information, see *Nonbusiness Bad Debts*, later.

If you decide not to use the installment sale reporting method, indicate this decision by reporting the full transaction sales price on either Form 8949 and Schedule D (Form 1040) or Form 4797 by the date your tax return for the year of the sale is due. (Form 8949 and Schedule D are used to report sales of capital assets. Form 4797 is used to report sales of trade or business property and other noncapital assets.) Once you decide not to use the installment sale method, you may change your decision only with the consent of the IRS.

TAXALERT

Sales at a loss do not qualify for installment sale reporting. Also, sales by dealers or by persons who regularly sell personal property on the installment basis no longer qualify for the installment method.

Explanation

The gain you have from an installment sale will be treated as capital gain if the property you sold was a capital asset (discussed later). However, if you took depreciation deductions on the assets, including the Section 179 deduction, part of your gain may be treated as ordinary income.

Example

On January 31, 2014, Susan sells property for $4,000 on which she has a $1,000 gain. Half of the gain is taxable at ordinary rates.

If Susan receives the initial $2,000 payment in 2014, she is receiving one-half the proceeds and must report one-half of the gain, or $500. Because the ordinary income portion must be reported first, the entire $500 is treated as an ordinary gain. When Susan receives the second $2,000 payment, she reports the second half of the gain, $500, as a capital gain.

Explanation

Any depreciation claimed on personal property must be recaptured as ordinary income in the year of sale, even if there are no payments received in the year of sale. The depreciation recapture for real property is generally limited to the amount by which the depreciation claimed exceeds the amount available under the straight-line method of depreciation. The adjusted basis of the property being sold is increased by the amount of recaptured income that you include in your gross income in the year of sale so that the gain recognized in future years is decreased.

Example

Sam sells tangible personal property to Betty in 2014 for $100,000 to be paid in installments over 5 years, beginning in 2014. Interest is payable at market rates. The property was originally purchased for $30,000. Because of depreciation, it has an adjusted basis of $20,000. There is a gain of $80,000 ($100,000 − $20,000), of which $10,000 is recaptured income to be reported on Sam's 2014 return.

The $10,000 that is included in Sam's income in the year of sale is added to the $20,000 adjusted basis to figure how much income Sam must report using the installment method. Therefore, Sam's gross profit is $70,000 ($100,000 − $30,000). Sam's gross profit percentage is 70%.

On each of the $20,000 payments that Sam receives from 2014 through 2018, $14,000 would be included in his income ($20,000 × 70%).

Explanation

The installment sale rules contain a number of very important limitations.

Sales to a spouse or an 80% controlled entity. If you sell depreciable property to your spouse or to a partnership or corporation of which you own 80% or more, you must report all of the gain in the year of the sale, despite any installment payment schedules set up under the sale agreement. The same rule may also apply to the sale of property to a trust of which you (or your spouse) are a beneficiary.

Sales to other relatives. If you sell property, other than marketable securities, to a related person on an installment basis and that person resells (or makes a gift of) the property within 2 years, you have to recognize any additional gain in the year of the resale.

A related person includes your spouse, children, grandchildren, brothers and sisters, and parents. A related person is also any partnership in which you are a partner, any estates and trusts of which you are a beneficiary, any grantor trusts of which you are treated as an owner, and any corporation in which you own at least half of the total value of the stock.

The normal 3-year statute of limitations for tax assessments by the IRS is extended for resales of installment property by a related person. In these cases, the statute of limitations will not expire until 2 years after you report to the IRS that a resale took place.

Nontaxable trades. Special rules apply to the exchange of like-kind property, which is tax-free. However, property that is not like-kind included in the exchange is taxable. The installment method may be used for the property that is not like-kind.

Like-kind exchanges. For like-kind exchanges involving related parties, both parties must hold the property for more than 2 years for the original exchange to qualify as tax-free. This rule is applicable to both parties to the transaction, even though only one party avails himself or herself of like-kind treatment. Also, real property located in the United States and real property located outside the United States does not qualify as property of a like kind.

Disposing of installment obligations. If you sell property on an installment basis and then later dispose of the installment note, you may have to report a gain or a loss. Generally, the amount of your gain or loss is equal to the difference between your basis in the installment note and the amount you receive when you dispose of the note.

Example

Toni sells real estate on an installment basis for a $200,000 note receivable and has a $120,000 gross profit from the sale. After she collects $100,000 (and reports a profit of $60,000, half her gross profit), she sells the remaining $100,000 note receivable to a bank for $95,000. Toni reports a $55,000 profit in the year of the sale of the note (the remaining $60,000 of gross profit less the $5,000 loss on the sale of the note).

Explanation

A disposition for this purpose is not limited to a sale of the installment note. For example, if you make a sale of property after December 31, 1988, for more than $150,000, and you assign the installment obligation as collateral security for a loan, the IRS will treat this as a disposition. This is because you would have deferred the gain on the sale while obtaining the use of the money through a loan.

Publicly traded property. The installment method cannot be used for sales of publicly traded property, including stock or securities that are traded on an established securities market.

Repossessing property sold under the installment method. If you sell property on an installment plan, you may have to repossess it if, for example, the buyer defaults on his or her obligation. When repossession takes place, you may have to report a gain or a loss. You follow different rules for determining your gain or loss, depending on whether the property being repossessed is personal property or real property.

Personal property. If you repossess personal property sold under an installment plan, you must compare the fair market value of the property recovered with your basis in the installment notes plus any expenses you had in connection with repossession. Under the installment method, your basis is the face value of the note still outstanding less the amount of unreported profit on the original sale. (If you did not use the installment reporting method, your basis is the value of the property at the time of the original sale less payments of principal received to date.)

Your gain or loss is of the same character (short term or long term) as the gain or loss realized on the original sale if you used the installment method. If you did not, any gain resulting from repossession is treated as **ordinary income**. Any loss is an ordinary loss if the property is business property. If it is nonbusiness property, any loss resulting from repossession is treated as a short term capital loss.

Real property. If you have to repossess your former residence because the buyer defaults and you excluded the gain (see chapter 15, *Selling your home*, for details), no gain or loss is recognized if you resell the house within 1 year of repossession. If the property is not resold within 1 year, you may have to recognize the gain. The amount of tax you may have to pay on the gain will depend on whether the house you repossessed was originally sold before, on, or after May 6, 1997. For houses sold before May 7, 1997, $125,000 of the gain could have been excluded or the gain could have been deferred by acquiring a replacement home. For houses sold after May 6, 1997, up to $250,000 or $500,000 of the gain may be excluded (see chapter 15, *Selling your home*, for more information). You may never deduct a loss on repossession because you may not deduct losses on property used primarily for personal purposes.

Computing your gain or loss on repossessed real property. Generally, your gain or loss on property that you have repossessed equals (1) the total amount of payments you have received under the installment sale minus (2) the amount of taxable gain you have already reported on the installment sale.

The gain you report on the repossessed property is limited, however, to the gross profit you expected on the installment sale less repossession costs and the amount of taxable gain you have already reported on the installment sale. Your basis in the repossessed property is your adjusted basis at the time of the original sale less deferred gain on repossession.

Example

Linda Smith sold a building that was not her personal residence to Ann Carter in 2009 for $100,000, payable in 10 annual installments. Linda's basis in the building was $70,000, and no mortgage was outstanding. The expected gross profit in the sale was $30,000, and the gross profit percentage was 30%.

In 2014, Ann failed to pay the sixth installment. By then, Linda had recognized $15,000 of gain from the $50,000 in payments received. She repossessed the building, incurring legal fees of $1,000 in the process. Linda's gain is computed as follows:

Gain

Payments received	$50,000
Less: Taxable gain already reported on sale	(15,000)
Gain subject to limitation	$35,000

Limitation on gain

Gross profit expected on installment sale	$30,000
Less: Repossession costs	(1,000)
Less: Taxable gain already reported on sale	(15,000)
Limitation	$14,000

Linda must report a $14,000 gain on repossession. Her basis in the reacquired building is $49,000, figured by taking $70,000 (her original adjusted basis) and subtracting $21,000 ($35,000 − $14,000), the amount of gain on repossession unrecognized because of the limitation on gain.

TAXPLANNER

Computing interest on installment sales. Special rules may apply regarding the amount of interest to be recognized on installment sales of more than $3,000.

If the amount of interest is not specifically stated in the sales agreement or if the stated interest is at an unrealistically low rate, you must calculate unstated or imputed interest. In general, you have unstated interest if (1) the sum of all payments due more than 6 months after the date of sale exceeds (2) the present value of such payments and the present value of any interest payment provided for in the contract. Present value is determined by using a so-called testing rate compounded semiannually. If there is unstated interest, you are required to impute interest using the testing rate.

The testing rate is calculated by using the applicable federal rate (AFR). The AFR is based on average market yields of U.S. obligations. The AFR may be the short-, medium-, or long-term rate that U.S. obligations are yielding, depending on the length of the contract. If unstated interest results using the testing rate, then interest must be computed using the testing rate, compounded semiannually.

Example

On June 1, 2014, Nicholas and Alexandra sell their limousine for $45,000, to be paid in three annual installments of $15,000 each on June 1, 2014, June 1, 2015, and June 1, 2016. No interest is stated in the sales contract. Their basis in the car is $35,000.

The imputed interest over the 2 years is $108 (0.18% compounded semiannually). This amount must be subtracted from the selling price when the gain on the sale is computed:

Stated selling price	$45,000
Less: Unstated interest	(108)
Adjusted selling price	$44,892
Less: Basis	(35,000)
Gain on sale	$ 9,892
Gross profit percentage: ($9,892 ÷ $44,892)	22.04%

Imputed interest is important to consider for two reasons: (1) It alters the amount of gain on a sale, and (2) it is deductible as an interest expense by the buyer, subject to limitations (see chapter 24, *Interest expense*), and must be reported as interest income by the seller.

Note: If all of the installment payments are due within 1 year after the date of sale, it is not necessary to figure your imputed interest. Additionally, payments received within the first 6 months of a sale have no imputed interest. The AFR will be determined by the IRS every month.

How To Figure Gain or Loss

You figure gain or loss on a sale or trade of property by comparing the amount you realize with the adjusted basis of the property.

Gain. If the amount you realize from a sale or trade is more than the adjusted basis of the property you transfer, the difference is a gain.

Loss. If the adjusted basis of the property you transfer is more than the amount you realize, the difference is a loss.

Adjusted basis. The adjusted basis of property is your original cost or other original basis properly adjusted (increased or decreased) for certain items. See chapter 13 for more information about determining the adjusted basis of property.

Amount realized. The amount you realize from a sale or trade of property is everything you receive for the property minus your expenses of sale (such as redemption fees, sales commissions, sales charges, or exit fees). Amount realized includes the money you receive plus the fair market value of any property or services you receive. If you received a note or other debt instrument for the property, see *How To Figure Gain or Loss* in chapter 4 of Publication 550 to figure the amount realized.

If you finance the buyer's purchase of your property and the debt instrument does not provide for adequate stated interest, the unstated interest that you must report as ordinary income will reduce the amount realized from the sale. For more information, see Publication 537.

Fair market value. Fair market value is the price at which the property would change hands between a buyer and a seller, neither being forced to buy or sell and both having reasonable knowledge of all the relevant facts.

Example. You trade A Company stock with an adjusted basis of $7,000 for B Company stock with a fair market value of $10,000, which is your amount realized. Your gain is $3,000 ($10,000 – $7,000).

Debt paid off. A debt against the property, or against you, that is paid off as a part of the transaction, or that is assumed by the buyer, must be included in the amount realized. This is true even if neither you nor the buyer is personally liable for the debt. For example, if you sell or trade property that is subject to a nonrecourse loan, the amount you realize generally includes the full amount of the note assumed by the buyer even if the amount of the note is more than the fair market value of the property.

Example. You sell stock that you had pledged as security for a bank loan of $8,000. Your basis in the stock is $6,000. The buyer pays off your bank loan and pays you $20,000 in cash. The amount realized is $28,000 ($20,000 + $8,000). Your gain is $22,000 ($28,000 – $6,000).

EXAMPLE
You sell property and the buyer pays you $20,000 cash and assumes an existing mortgage on the property of $8,000. You bought the property for $6,000 and added improvements costing $10,000. Your selling expenses were $1,400. Your gain on the sale is computed:

Amount realized		
Cash	$20,000	
Mortgage assumed by buyer	8,000	$28,000
Minus: Adjusted basis		
Cost	$6,000	
Improvements	10,000	
Total	$16,000	
Plus: Selling expenses	1,400	($17,400)
Gain		$10,600

Payment of cash. If you trade property and cash for other property, the amount you realize is the fair market value of the property you receive. Determine your gain or loss by subtracting the cash you pay plus the adjusted basis of the property you trade in from the amount you realize. If the result is a positive number, it is a gain. If the result is a negative number, it is a loss.

EXPLANATION
If you receive a mortgage or a trust note, payments include some interest income in addition to principal.

Example
Assume that a $10,000 installment note with a discounted value of $8,000 is given by an individual to a cash basis taxpayer in payment for a capital asset with a basis of $7,000. The taxpayer recognizes $1,000 ($8,000 – $7,000) as a capital gain. As each installment is paid, eight-tenths ($8,000 ÷ $10,000) of the payment is a return of principal and two-tenths is interest income.

Explanation
If you are an accrual basis taxpayer—and most people are not—use the full face value of the note in computing your gain or loss on the sale. Consequently, payments on the note are returns of principal.

If you are a cash basis taxpayer, and if the installment note is given by a corporation and the discounted value of the note is used to compute your gain on the sale of a capital asset, the income to be recognized is a capital gain. If the note is given by an individual, the income is taxable as ordinary income.

Example
A cash basis taxpayer sells a capital asset to a corporation in exchange for a $10,000 note with an interest rate of 5%. Because current interest rates are more than 5% or because of the corporation's low credit status, the note has a discounted value of $8,000, 80% of its face value. The taxpayer uses the $8,000 value to compute gain or loss on the sale. When the corporation later pays the note, the $2,000 difference, which must be reported as income, is treated as a capital gain. If an individual had issued the note, the $2,000 gain to the taxpayer realized on payment of the note would be taxed as ordinary income.

No gain or loss. You may have to use a basis for figuring gain that is different from the basis used for figuring loss. In this case, you may have neither a gain nor a loss. See *Basis Other Than Cost* in chapter 13.

Nontaxable Trades

This section discusses trades that generally do not result in a taxable gain or deductible loss. For more information on nontaxable trades, see chapter 1 of Publication 544.

Like-kind exchanges. If you trade business or investment property for other business or investment property of a like kind, you do not pay tax on any gain or deduct any loss until you sell or dispose of the property you receive. To be nontaxable, a trade must meet all six of the following conditions.

1. The property must be business or investment property. You must hold both the property you trade and the property you receive for productive use in your trade or business or for investment. Neither property may be property used for personal purposes, such as your home or family car.
2. The property must not be held primarily for sale. The property you trade and the property you receive must not be property you sell to customers, such as merchandise.
3. The property must not be stocks, bonds, notes, choses in action, certificates of trust or beneficial interest, or other securities or evidences of indebtedness or interest, including partnership interests. However, see *Special rules for mutual ditch, reservoir, or irrigation company stock*, in chapter 4 of Publication 550 for an exception. Also, you can have a nontaxable trade of corporate stocks under a different rule, as discussed later.
4. There must be a trade of like property. The trade of real estate for real estate, or personal property for similar personal property, is a trade of like property. The trade of an apartment house for a store building, or a panel truck for a pickup truck, is a trade of like property. The trade of a piece of machinery for a store building is not a trade of like property. Real property located in the United States and real property located outside the United States are not like property. Also, personal property used predominantly within the United States and personal property used predominantly outside the United States are not like property.
5. The property to be received must be identified in writing within 45 days after the date you transfer the property given up in the trade.
6. The property to be received must be received by the earlier of:
    a. The 180th day after the date on which you transfer the property given up in the trade, or
    b. The due date, including extensions, for your tax return for the year in which the transfer of the property given up occurs.

Like-kind exchanges include the following:
- Improved for unimproved real estate when exchanged by a person who does not deal in real estate
- A used car for a new one to be used for the same purpose.

The following are *not* considered like-kind exchanges:
- Personal property (such as a boat) for real property
- Gold numismatic coins for gold bullion (the IRS ruled that an investment in gold coins was an investment in the coins themselves, while the investment in bullion was an investment in the world gold market)
- Gold bullion for silver bullion
- Male livestock for female livestock

TAXALERT

Depreciable, tangible personal property may be exchanged for either like-kind or like-class property and may qualify for like-kind exchange treatment. Like-class properties are depreciable, tangible personal properties within the same "general asset classes" as defined in the Standard Industrial Classification Manual (see Publication 544, *Sales and Other Dispositions of Assets*).

You are not required to make a property-by-property comparison if you:
1. Separate the properties into two or more exchange groups, or
2. Transfer or receive more than one property within a single exchange group.

If you trade property with a related party in a like-kind exchange, a special rule may apply. See *Related Party Transactions*, later in this chapter. Also, see chapter 1 of Publication 544 for more information on exchanges of business property and special rules for exchanges using qualified intermediaries or involving multiple properties.

Partly nontaxable exchange. If you receive money or unlike property in addition to like property, and the above six conditions are met, you have a partly nontaxable trade. You are taxed on any gain you realize, but only up to the amount of the money and the fair market value of the unlike property you receive. You cannot deduct a loss.

EXAMPLE

You exchange real estate held for investment that has an adjusted basis of $8,000 for other real estate that you want to hold for investment. The real estate you receive has a fair market value of $10,000, and you also receive $1,000 in cash. Although the total gain realized on the transaction is $3,000, only $1,000 (cash received) is included in your income.

TAXSAVER

Assume that you are to receive property that is worth less than the property you are to give up and you expect to make improvements on the new property. Rather than receive money or unlike property from the other owner to make up the difference in value, you might ask her to make the improvements on her property before the transfer. In that way, you reduce the amount of unlike property included in the exchange and therefore reduce the amount of tax you have to pay on the transfer. What is the incentive for the other owner? Making the improvement might induce you to make the deal.

TAXSAVER

If the amount of liabilities you assume in an exchange is less than the amount of liabilities you give up, the difference is treated as cash received. Consequently, if you assume a mortgage that is less than the mortgage you had been carrying on the exchanged property, you recognize gain as if you had received cash for the difference.

If you receive cash but assume more debt than you were relieved of, you cannot offset the cash received with the debt assumed. In this case, you should have the buyer pay down some of the debt you are assuming rather than paying you the cash directly. You may be able to borrow the difference against the property at a later date.

Like property and unlike property transferred. If you give up unlike property in addition to the like property, you must recognize gain or loss on the unlike property you give up. The gain or loss is the difference between the adjusted basis of the unlike property and its fair market value.

Like property and money transferred. If all of the above conditions (1) – (6) are met, you have a nontaxable trade even if you pay money in addition to the like property.

Basis of property received. To figure the basis of the property received, see *Nontaxable Exchanges* in chapter 13.

How to report. You must report the trade of like property on Form 8824. If you figure a recognized gain or loss on Form 8824, report it on Schedule D (Form 1040), or on Form 4797, Sales of Business Property, whichever applies. See the instructions for Line 22 in the Instructions for Form 8824.

For information on using Form 4797, see chapter 4 of Publication 544.

TAXSAVER

A like-kind exchange is a useful planning tool in deferring tax on appreciated property if you intend to reinvest in a similar property within a relatively short period. No gain or loss is recognized in a deferred like-kind exchange if you meet the following requirements:

1. You must follow specific procedures to identify replacement property within 45 days after relinquishing the old property.
2. You must receive the replacement property within 180 days after relinquishing the old property.
3. You must structure the exchange to comply with one or more of the guidelines described below. The reason for this step is that if the exchange does not fall within one of the guidelines, then the exchange could be subject to scrutiny by the IRS.

Taxpayers should design their transactions to comply with one of the following IRS guidelines:

1. You cannot have an immediate ability or unrestricted right to receive money or other property pursuant to the security or guarantee arrangement. However, the replacement property may be secured or guaranteed before you actually receive like-kind replacement property by one or more of the following:
   a. Mortgage, deed of trust, or other security interest in property
   b. Standby letter of credit meeting certain specifications and a guarantee of a third party
2. You may not have an immediate ability or unrestricted right to receive, pledge, borrow, or otherwise obtain the benefits of the cash or cash equivalent held in an escrow account or qualified trust. However, the replacement property may be secured by cash or a cash equivalent if the cash or cash equivalent is held in a qualified escrow account or in a qualified trust.
3. You may not have an immediate ability or unrestricted right to receive, pledge, borrow, or otherwise obtain the benefits of money or other property held by a qualified intermediary. However, you may use a qualified intermediary in a deferred exchange if the qualified intermediary is unrelated to you (see the IRS final regulations for details). A qualified intermediary may be an escrow or title company.

More than one IRS guideline can be used in the same deferred exchange, but the terms and conditions of each must be separately satisfied. You should consult your tax advisor if you are contemplating a like-kind exchange.

Corporate stocks. The following trades of corporate stocks generally do not result in a taxable gain or a deductible loss.

Corporate reorganizations. In some instances, a company will give you common stock for preferred stock, preferred stock for common stock, or stock in one corporation for stock in another corporation. If this is a result of a merger, recapitalization, transfer to a controlled corporation, bankruptcy, corporate division, corporate acquisition, or other corporate reorganization, you do not recognize gain or loss.

Stock for stock of the same corporation. You can exchange common stock for common stock or preferred stock for preferred stock in the same corporation without having a recognized gain or loss. This is true for a trade between two stockholders as well as a trade between a stockholder and the corporation.

Convertible stocks and bonds. You generally will not have a recognized gain or loss if you convert bonds into stock or preferred stock into common stock of the same corporation according to a conversion privilege in the terms of the bond or the preferred stock certificate.

Property for stock of a controlled corporation. If you transfer property to a corporation solely in exchange for stock in that corporation, and immediately after the trade you are in control of the corporation, you ordinarily will not recognize a gain or loss. This rule applies both to individuals and to groups who transfer property to a corporation. It does not apply if the corporation is an investment company.

For this purpose, to be in control of a corporation, you or your group of transferors must own, immediately after the exchange, at least 80% of the total combined voting power of all classes of stock entitled to vote and at least 80% of the outstanding shares of each class of nonvoting stock of the corporation.

If this provision applies to you, you may have to attach to your return a complete statement of all facts pertinent to the exchange. For details, see Regulations section 1.351-3.

Additional information. For more information on trades of stock, see *Nontaxable Trades* in chapter 4 of Publication 550.

EXPLANATION

The statement must include the following information:
- A description of the property transferred, with its cost or other basis
- The kind of stock received, including the number of shares and fair market value
- The principal amount and fair market value of any securities received
- The amount of money received, if any
- A description of any liabilities assumed by the corporation in the transaction, including the corporate business reason for the assumption

Generally, when you transfer property to a corporation that you alone will control in exchange for its stock, no gain or loss is recognized. "Control" means that you or your group of investors owns at least 80% of the outstanding voting stock and at least 80% of the shares of all other classes of outstanding stock. However, if you receive property other than stock, then you may have to recognize a gain equal to that additional property's value. Moreover, if the property you transfer to the corporation has been depreciated, all or a portion of your gain may be ordinary income rather than a capital gain.

Example

You transfer machinery that has an adjusted basis of $10,000 and a fair market value of $25,000 to a corporation that you and your associates will control in exchange for stock worth $20,000 and $5,000 in cash. You realize a $15,000 gain on the transfer of the machinery.

The transfer would have been tax-free if all you had received in return was stock. However, you have to report a gain of $5,000 for the cash received. Furthermore, if you previously claimed $5,000 or more in depreciation on the machinery, all of the $5,000 you received is treated as ordinary income under the depreciation recapture rules. For a complete discussion of depreciation, see chapter 9, *Rental income and expenses*.

Explanation

There has been much litigation over the issue of momentary control—a situation that arises when investors hold the required 80% of stock only briefly and then dispose of a portion of it. Generally, momentary control is not sufficient to ensure preferential tax treatment if there was an agreement or prearranged plan for subsequent disposition of the stock acquired in the exchange. Preferential tax treatment may also be disallowed if the transaction lacks economic substance or a business purpose, that is, it doesn't change the taxpayer's economic position in a meaningful way.

Condemnations and involuntary exchanges. Condemnation is the process by which private property is legally taken by governments or certain entities, such as public utilities, in exchange for money or property.

If the condemnation award you receive is more than your adjusted basis in the condemned property, you have a gain. This gain may be postponed if you receive similar property instead of cash or if replacement property is purchased with the cash you receive. If you purchase replacement property, it must be put to a use similar to that of the original property. It also must be purchased within 2 years from the close of the first year in which any part of the gain on condemnation is realized. For business real property, the purchase must be made within 3 years.

If the condemnation award you receive is less than your basis in the property, you have a loss. This loss is not deductible if the property was your residence. Your loss, however, may be deducted if the property was used in a trade or a business or for the production of income.

Insurance policies and annuities. You will not have a recognized gain or loss if the insured or annuitant is the same under both contracts and you trade:

- A life insurance contract for another life insurance contract or for an endowment or annuity contract or for a qualified long-term care insurance contract,
- An endowment contract for another endowment contract that provides for regular payments beginning at a date no later than the beginning date under the old contract or for an annuity contract or for a qualified long-term insurance contract,
- An annuity contract for annuity contract or for a qualified long-term care insurance contract, or
- A qualified long-term care insurance contract for a qualified long-term care insurance contract.

You also may not have to recognize gain or loss on an exchange of a portion of an annuity contract for another annuity contract. For transfers completed before October 24, 2011, see Revenue Ruling 2003-76 in Internal Revenue Bulletin 2003-33 and Revenue Procedure 2008-24 in Internal Revenue Bulletin 2008-13. Revenue Ruling 2003-76 is available at *www.irs.gov/irb/2003-33_IRB/ar11.html*. Revenue Procedure 2008-24 is available at *www.irs.gov/irb/2008-13_IRB/ar13.html*. For transfers completed on or after October 24, 2011, see Revenue Ruling 2003-76, above, and Revenue Procedure 2011-38, in Internal Revenue Bulletin 2011-30. Revenue Procedure 2011-38 is available at *www.irs.gov/irb/2011-30_IRB/ar09.html*.

For tax years beginning after December 31, 2010, amounts received as an annuity for a period of 10 years or more, or for the lives of one or more individuals, under any portion of an annuity, endowment, or life insurance contract, are treated as a separate contract and are considered partial annuities. A portion of an annuity, endowment, or life insurance contract may be annuitized, provided that the annuitization period is for 10 years or more or for the lives of one or more individuals. The investment in the contract is allocated between the part of the contract from which amounts are received as an annuity and the part of the contract from which amounts are not received as an annuity.

Exchanges of contracts not included in this list, such as an annuity contract for an endowment contract, or an annuity or endowment contract for a life insurance contract, are taxable.

Demutualization of life insurance companies. If you received stock in exchange for your equity interest as a policyholder or an annuitant, you generally will not have a recognized gain or loss. See *Demutualization of Life Insurance Companies* in Publication 550.

U.S. Treasury notes or bonds. You can trade certain issues of U.S. Treasury obligations for other issues designated by the Secretary of the Treasury, with no gain or loss recognized on the trade. See *Savings bonds traded* in chapter 1 of Publication 550 for more information.

Transfers Between Spouses

Generally, no gain or loss is recognized on a transfer of property from an individual to (or in trust for the benefit of) a spouse, or if incident to a divorce, a former spouse. This nonrecognition rule does not apply in the following situations.

- The recipient spouse or former spouse is a nonresident alien.
- Property is transferred in trust and liability exceeds basis. Gain must be recognized to the extent the amount of the liabilities assumed by the trust, plus any liabilities on the property, exceed the adjusted basis of the property.

For other situations, see *Transfers Between Spouses* in chapter 4 of Publication 550.

Any transfer of property to a spouse or former spouse on which gain or loss is not recognized is treated by the recipient as a gift and is not considered a sale or exchange. The recipient's basis in the property will be the same as the adjusted basis of the giver immediately before the transfer. This carryover basis rule applies whether the adjusted basis of the transferred property is less than, equal to, or greater than either its fair market value at the time of transfer or any consideration paid by the recipient. This rule applies for purposes of determining loss as well as gain. Any gain recognized on a transfer in trust increases the basis.

A transfer of property is incident to a divorce if the transfer occurs within 1 year after the date on which the marriage ends, or if the transfer is related to the ending of the marriage.

EXPLANATION

For transfers of property incident to divorce to a former spouse who is a nonresident alien, gain or loss may be recognized to the spouse who transferred the property based on the fair market value of the property transferred.

Related Party Transactions

Special rules apply to the sale or trade of property between related parties.

Gain on sale or trade of depreciable property. Your gain from the sale or trade of property to a related party may be ordinary income, rather than capital gain, if the property can be depreciated by the party receiving it. See chapter 3 of Publication 544 for more information.

Like-kind exchanges. Generally, if you trade business or investment property for other business or investment property of a like kind, no gain or loss is recognized. See *Like-kind exchanges*, earlier, under *Nontaxable Trades*.

This rule also applies to trades of property between related parties, defined next under *Losses on sales or trades of property*. However, if either you or the related party disposes of the like property within 2 years after the trade, you both must report any gain or loss not recognized on the original trade on your return filed for the year in which the later disposition occurs. See *Related Party Transactions* in chapter 4 of Publication 550 for exceptions.

Losses on sales or trades of property. You cannot deduct a loss on the sale or trade of property, other than a distribution in complete liquidation of a corporation, if the transaction is directly or indirectly between you and the following related parties.

- Members of your family. This includes only your brothers and sisters, half-brothers and half-sisters, spouse, ancestors (parents, grandparents, etc.), and lineal descendants (children, grandchildren, etc.).
- A partnership in which you directly or indirectly own more than 50% of the capital interest or the profits interest.
- A corporation in which you directly or indirectly own more than 50% in value of the outstanding stock. (See *Constructive ownership of stock*, later.)
- A tax-exempt charitable or educational organization directly or indirectly controlled, in any manner or by any method, by you or by a member of your family, whether or not this control is legally enforceable.

In addition, a loss on the sale or trade of property is not deductible if the transaction is directly or indirectly between the following related parties.

- A grantor and fiduciary, or the fiduciary and beneficiary, of any trust.
- Fiduciaries of two different trusts, or the fiduciary and beneficiary of two different trusts, if the same person is the grantor of both trusts.
- A trust fiduciary and a corporation of which more than 50% in value of the outstanding stock is directly or indirectly owned by or for the trust, or by or for the grantor of the trust.

- A corporation and a partnership if the same persons own more than 50% in value of the outstanding stock of the corporation and more than 50% of the capital interest, or the profits interest, in the partnership.
- Two S corporations if the same persons own more than 50% in value of the outstanding stock of each corporation.
- Two corporations, one of which is an S corporation, if the same persons own more than 50% in value of the outstanding stock of each corporation.
- An executor and a beneficiary of an estate (except in the case of a sale or trade to satisfy a pecuniary bequest).
- Two corporations that are members of the same controlled group. (Under certain conditions, however, these losses are not disallowed but must be deferred.)
- Two partnerships if the same persons own, directly or indirectly, more than 50% of the capital interests or the profit interests in both partnerships.

Multiple property sales or trades. If you sell or trade to a related party a number of blocks of stock or pieces of property in a lump sum, you must figure the gain or loss separately for each block of stock or piece of property. The gain on each item may be taxable. However, you cannot deduct the loss on any item. Also, you cannot reduce gains from the sales of any of these items by losses on the sales of any of the other items.

Indirect transactions. You cannot deduct your loss on the sale of stock through your broker if, under a prearranged plan, a related party buys the same stock you had owned. This does not apply to a trade between related parties through an exchange that is purely coincidental and is not prearranged.

Constructive ownership of stock. In determining whether a person directly or indirectly owns any of the outstanding stock of a corporation, the following rules apply.

Rule 1. Stock directly or indirectly owned by or for a corporation, partnership, estate, or trust is considered owned proportionately by or for its shareholders, partners, or beneficiaries.

Rule 2. An individual is considered to own the stock directly or indirectly owned by or for his or her family. Family includes only brothers and sisters, half-brothers and half-sisters, spouse, ancestors, and lineal descendants.

Rule 3. An individual owning, other than by applying rule 2, any stock in a corporation is considered to own the stock directly or indirectly owned by or for his or her partner.

Rule 4. When applying rule 1, 2, or 3, stock constructively owned by a person under rule 1 is treated as actually owned by that person. But stock constructively owned by an individual under rule 2 or rule 3 is not treated as owned by that individual for again applying either rule 2 or rule 3 to make another person the constructive owner of the stock.

Property received from a related party. If you sell or trade at a gain property you acquired from a related party, you recognize the gain only to the extent it is more than the loss previously disallowed to the related party. This rule applies only if you are the original transferee and you acquired the property by purchase or exchange. This rule does not apply if the related party's loss was disallowed because of the wash sale rules described in chapter 4 of Publication 550 under *Wash Sales.*

If you sell or trade at a loss property you acquired from a related party, you cannot recognize the loss that was not allowed to the related party.

Example 1. Your brother sells you stock for $7,600. His cost basis is $10,000. Your brother cannot deduct the loss of $2,400. Later, you sell the same stock to an unrelated party for $10,500, realizing a gain of $2,900. Your reportable gain is $500 (the $2,900 gain minus the $2,400 loss not allowed to your brother).

Example 2. If, in *Example 1*, you sold the stock for $6,900 instead of $10,500, your recognized loss is only $700 (your $7,600 basis minus $6,900). You cannot deduct the loss that was not allowed to your brother.

EXPLANATION
Transactions between a trust and the relative of a trust beneficiary may be indirect related-party transactions. Similarly, the sale of stock by one spouse followed by the purchase by the other spouse of an equal number of the same corporation's shares is an indirect sale between related parties, even though both spouses deal through brokers on the New York Stock Exchange. However, if there is a significant time lapse between the two transactions—a month or more—the transactions are not considered linked.

Capital Gains and Losses

This section discusses the tax treatment of gains and losses from different types of investment transactions.

Character of gain or loss. You need to classify your gains and losses as either ordinary or capital gains or losses. You then need to classify your capital gains and losses as either short term or long term. If you have long-term gains and losses, you must identify your 28% rate gains and losses. If you have a net capital gain, you must also identify any unrecaptured Section 1250 gain.

The correct classification and identification helps you figure the limit on capital losses and the correct tax on capital gains. Reporting capital gains and losses is explained in chapter 16.

Capital or Ordinary Gain or Loss

If you have a taxable gain or a deductible loss from a transaction, it may be either a capital gain or loss or an ordinary gain or loss, depending on the circumstances. Generally, a sale or trade of a capital asset (defined next) results in a capital gain or loss. A sale or trade of a noncapital asset generally results in ordinary gain or loss. Depending on the circumstances, a gain or loss on a sale or trade of property used in a trade or business may be treated as either capital or ordinary, as explained in Publication 544. In some situations, part of your gain or loss may be a capital gain or loss and part may be an ordinary gain or loss.

Capital Assets and Noncapital Assets

For the most part, everything you own and use for personal purposes, pleasure, or investment is a capital asset. Some examples are:
- Stocks or bonds held in your personal account,
- A house owned and used by you and your family,
- Household furnishings,
- A car used for pleasure or commuting,
- Coin or stamp collections,
- Gems and jewelry, and
- Gold, silver, or any other metal.

EXAMPLE

You bought a car for personal use and later sold it for less than you paid for it. The loss is not deductible. However, if you had sold it for more than you paid for it, the gain would be taxable. A loss would be deductible only if, or to the extent that, the car was used for business. If the car had been stolen, you would have had a theft loss.

Note: In determining the amount of the loss, what you paid for the car would have to be reduced by any depreciation allowed as a deduction. This would reduce the amount of the loss you could claim.

Explanation

While losses on personal property generally are not deductible, losses associated with a trade or a business may be. However, property originally held for personal use may be converted to business use under certain circumstances (and vice versa). There are very few court cases in this area, and those that exist do not provide much guidance about how long property must be rented before it is considered converted to business use. Each case depends on the specific facts and circumstances. In general, if a residence has been rented for a period of years, there is strong evidence that it has been converted to rental property.

Examples

In one case, a residence was rented out for several months under a bona fide lease. The property could not be re-occupied by the owner during the term of the lease. The owner's motive for leasing the house was to make money. The court held that the property had been converted to rental use.

In another case, a building was remodeled to make it fit for business purposes. This was considered to be strong evidence that the property was being converted to rental use.

Note: There are no clear-cut guidelines for what constitutes conversion to business use. However, simply listing the property with a rental agent is not sufficient. The guidelines in chapter 15, *Selling your home,* may be helpful.

Any property you own is a capital asset, except the following noncapital assets.
1. Property held mainly for sale to customers or property that will physically become a part of the merchandise for sale to customers. For an exception, see *Capital Asset Treatment for Self-Created Musical Works*, later.
2. Depreciable property used in your trade or business, even if fully depreciated.

3. Real property used in your trade or business.
4. A copyright, a literary, musical, or artistic composition, a letter or memorandum, or similar property that is:
   a. Created by your personal efforts,
   b. Prepared or produced for you (in the case of a letter, memorandum, or similar property), or
   c. Acquired under circumstances (for example, by gift) entitling you to the basis of the person who created the property or for whom it was prepared or produced.
      For an exception to this rule, see *Capital Asset Treatment for Self-Created Musical Works*, later.
5. Accounts or notes receivable acquired in the ordinary course of a trade or business for services rendered or from the sale of property described in (1).
6. U.S. Government publications that you received from the government free or for less than the normal sales price, or that you acquired under circumstances entitling you to the basis of someone who received the publications free or for less than the normal sales price.
7. Certain commodities derivative financial instruments held by commodities derivatives dealers.
8. Hedging transactions, but only if the transaction is clearly identified as a hedging transaction before the close of the day on which it was acquired, originated, or entered into.
9. Supplies of a type you regularly use or consume in the ordinary course of your trade or business.

Investment Property
Investment property is a capital asset. Any gain or loss from its sale or trade is generally a capital gain or loss.

Gold, silver, stamps, coins, gems, etc. These are capital assets except when they are held for sale by a dealer. Any gain or loss you have from their sale or trade generally is a capital gain or loss.

TAXPLANNER
If you collect gold, silver, stamps, antiques, and the like, you should be aware that losses from the sale or trade of such property generally are not deductible. In order to claim a loss, you must be able to show that your primary purpose in collecting the property was to make a profit. Furthermore, you must show that you were not collecting the items purely as a hobby or for personal enjoyment. Obviously, there may be a very fine line between a hobby and a profit-making activity.

Example
The Tax Court did not allow a taxpayer to deduct a loss on the sale of antiques he used to furnish his home. The taxpayer argued that he was speculating on large increases in the value of the antiques. The Tax Court emphasized his personal use of the antiques and noted that most of the taxpayer's sales of antiques were merely a means of financing the acquisition of more antiques.

Stocks, stock rights, and bonds. All of these (including stock received as a dividend) are capital assets except when held for sale by a securities dealer. However, if you own small business stock, see *Losses on Section 1244 (Small Business) Stock*, later, and *Losses on Small Business Investment Company Stock*, in chapter 4 of Publication 550.

TAXALERT
For covered securities acquired on or after January 1, 2011, brokers are required to report basis and holding period information upon sale. For more information on the definition of covered securities, see chapter 16, *Reporting gains and loss*. For more information on the reporting of basis, see chapter 13, *Basis of property*.

Personal Use Property
Property held for personal use only, rather than for investment, is a capital asset, and you must report a gain from its sale as a capital gain. However, you cannot deduct a loss from selling personal use property.

Capital Asset Treatment for Self-Created Musical Works
You can elect to treat musical compositions and copyrights in musical works as capital assets when you sell or exchange them if:
• Your personal efforts created the property, or
• You acquired the property under circumstances (for example, by gift) entitling you to the basis of the person who created the property or for whom it was prepared or produced.

Tip

For more information on Form 8949 and Schedule D (Form 1040), see Reporting Capital Gains and Losses *in chapter 16. See also Schedule D (Form 1040), Form 8949, and their separate instructions.*

You must make a separate election for each musical composition (or copyright in a musical work) sold or exchanged during the tax year. You must make the election on or before the due date (including extensions) of the income tax return for the tax year of the sale or exchange. You must make the election on Form 8949 by treating the sale or exchange as the sale or exchange of a capital asset, according to Form 8949, Schedule D (Form 1040), and their separate instructions.

TAXPLANNER

Since 2007, the creator of a musical work is able to treat a gain on the sale of the musical work as a capital gain. However, if you get such property, or a copyright to it, in any other way, the amounts you got for granting the exclusive use or right to exploit the work throughout the life of the copyright are treated as being received from the sale of property. It does not matter if the payment is a fixed amount or a percentage of receipts from the sale, performance, exhibition, or publication of the copyright work, on an amount based on the number of copies sold, performances given, or exhibitions made. It also does not matter if the payment is made over the same period as that covering the grantee's use of the copyrighted work.

You can revoke the election if you have IRS approval. To get IRS approval, you must submit a request for a letter ruling under the appropriate IRS revenue procedure. See, for example, Rev. Proc. 2013-1, corrected by Announcement 2013-9, and amplified and modified by Rev. Proc. 2013-32, available at *www.irs.gov/irb/2013-01_IRB/ar06.html*. Alternatively, you are granted an automatic 6-month extension from the due date of your income tax return (excluding extensions) to revoke the election, provided you timely file your income tax return, and within this 6-month extension period, you file Form 1040X that treats the sale or exchange as the sale or exchange of property that is not a capital asset.

Discounted Debt Instruments

Treat your gain or loss on the sale, redemption, or retirement of a bond or other debt instrument originally issued at a discount or bought at a discount as capital gain or loss, except as explained in the following discussions.

Short-term government obligations. Treat gains on short-term federal, state, or local government obligations (other than tax-exempt obligations) as ordinary income up to your ratable share of the acquisition discount. This treatment applies to obligations with a fixed maturity date not more than 1 year from the date of issue. Acquisition discount is the stated redemption price at maturity minus your basis in the obligation.

However, do not treat these gains as income to the extent you previously included the discount in income. See *Discount on Short-Term Obligations* in chapter 1 of Publication 550.

Short-term nongovernment obligations. Treat gains on short-term nongovernment obligations as ordinary income up to your ratable share of original issue discount (OID). This treatment applies to obligations with a fixed maturity date of not more than 1 year from the date of issue.

However, to the extent you previously included the discount in income, you do not have to include it in income again. See *Discount on Short-Term Obligations* in chapter 1 of Publication 550.

Tax-exempt state and local government bonds. If these bonds were originally issued at a discount before September 4, 1982, or you acquired them before March 2, 1984, treat your part of OID as tax-exempt interest. To figure your gain or loss on the sale or trade of these bonds, reduce the amount realized by your part of OID.

If the bonds were issued after September 3, 1982, and acquired after March 1, 1984, increase the adjusted basis by your part of OID to figure gain or loss. For more information on the basis of these bonds, see *Discounted Debt Instruments* in chapter 4 of Publication 550.

EXAMPLE

On March 1, 2000, Kathy bought a $10,000 tax-exempt state government bond for $9,000 that was originally issued at $8,500 on September 1, 1998. Kathy must treat her part of the original issue discount (OID) as tax-exempt interest. The accumulated OID from the date of issue to the date Kathy purchased the bond was $600. On August 16, 2014, Kathy sold the bond for $9,800. Kathy must report a $100 capital gain on the sale. The market discount in the bond is the original issue price ($8,500) plus the accumulated OID from the date of issue that represented interest to any earlier holders ($600) and minus the price Kathy paid for the bond ($9,000). As a result, the market discount is $100 ($9,100 − $9,000). The remaining difference of $700 ($9,800 − $9,100) is treated as tax-exempt interest.

Any gain from market discount is usually taxable on disposition or redemption of tax-exempt bonds. If you bought the bonds before May 1, 1993, the gain from market discount is capital gain. If you bought the bonds after April 30, 1993, the gain is ordinary income.

You figure the market discount by subtracting the price you paid for the bond from the sum of the original issue price of the bond and the amount of accumulated OID from the date of issue that represented interest to any earlier holders. For more information, see *Market Discount Bonds* in chapter 1 of Publication 550.

A loss on the sale or other disposition of a tax-exempt state or local government bond is deductible as a capital loss.

> ### *EXPLANATION*
> You must accrue OID on tax-exempt state and local government bonds issued after September 3, 1982, and acquired after March 1, 1984. Your adjusted basis at the time of disposition is figured by adding accrued OID to your basis. You must accrue OID on tax-exempt obligations under the same method used for OID on corporate obligations issued after July 1, 1982.
>
> #### *Example*
> On March 1, 2000, Julie bought a $10,000 tax-exempt state government bond for $9,100 that was originally issued at $8,500 on September 1, 1997. On August 16, 2014, Julie sold the bond for $9,800. Julie previously accrued $500 of OID tax-exempt interest over the period she held the bond. Julie must report a $200 capital gain on the sale of the bond [$9,800 − ($9,100 + $500)].

Redeemed before maturity. If a state or local bond issued before June 9, 1980, is redeemed before it matures, the OID is not taxable to you.

If a state or local bond issued after June 8, 1980, is redeemed before it matures, the part of OID earned while you hold the bond is not taxable to you. However, you must report the unearned part of OID as a capital gain.

Example. On July 2, 2003, the date of issue, you bought a 20-year, 6% municipal bond for $800. The face amount of the bond was $1,000. The $200 discount was OID. At the time the bond was issued, the issuer had no intention of redeeming it before it matured. The bond was callable at its face amount beginning 10 years after the issue date.

The issuer redeemed the bond at the end of 11 years (July 2, 2014) for its face amount of $1,000 plus accrued annual interest of $60. The OID earned during the time you held the bond, $73, is not taxable. The $60 accrued annual interest also is not taxable. However, you must report the unearned part of OID ($127) as a capital gain.

Long-term debt instruments issued after 1954 and before May 28, 1969 (or before July 2, 1982, if a government instrument). If you sell, trade, or redeem for a gain one of these debt instruments, the part of your gain that is not more than your ratable share of the OID at the time of the sale or redemption is ordinary income. The rest of the gain is capital gain. If, however, there was an intention to call the debt instrument before maturity, all of your gain that is not more than the entire OID is treated as ordinary income at the time of the sale. This treatment of taxable gain also applies to corporate instruments issued after May 27, 1969, under a written commitment that was binding on May 27, 1969, and at all times thereafter.

Long-term debt instruments issued after May 27, 1969 (or after July 1, 1982, if a government instrument). If you hold one of these debt instruments, you must include a part of OID in your gross income each year you own the instrument. Your basis in that debt instrument is increased by the amount of OID that you have included in your gross income. See *Original Issue Discount (OID)* in chapter 7 for information about OID that you must report on your tax return.

If you sell or trade the debt instrument before maturity, your gain is a capital gain. However, if at the time the instrument was originally issued there was an intention to call it before its maturity, your gain generally is ordinary income to the extent of the entire OID reduced by any amounts of OID previously includible in your income. In this case, the rest of the gain is capital gain.

Market discount bonds. If the debt instrument has market discount and you chose to include the discount in income as it accrued, increase your basis in the debt instrument by the accrued discount to figure capital gain or loss on its disposition. If you did not choose to include the discount in income as it accrued, you must report gain as ordinary interest income up to the instrument's accrued market discount. The rest of the gain is capital gain. See *Market Discount Bonds* in chapter 1 of Publication 550.

A different rule applies to market discount bonds issued before July 19, 1984, and purchased by you before May 1, 1993. See *Market discount bonds* under *Discounted Debt Instruments* in chapter 4 of Publication 550.

Retirement of debt instrument. Any amount you receive on the retirement of a debt instrument is treated in the same way as if you had sold or traded that instrument.

Notes of individuals. If you hold an obligation of an individual issued with OID after March 1, 1984, you generally must include the OID in your income currently, and your gain or loss on its sale or retirement is generally capital gain or loss. An exception to this treatment applies if the obligation is a loan between individuals and all the following requirements are met.

- The lender is not in the business of lending money.
- The amount of the loan, plus the amount of any outstanding prior loans, is $10,000 or less.
- Avoiding federal tax is not one of the principal purposes of the loan.

If the exception applies, or the obligation was issued before March 2, 1984, you do not include the OID in your income currently. When you sell or redeem the obligation, the part of your gain that is not more than your accrued share of OID at that time is ordinary income. The rest of the gain, if any, is capital gain. Any loss on the sale or redemption is capital loss.

EXPLANATION
Short Sales, Put Options, Other Kinds of Options, Wash Sales, and Other Types of Sales
There are other kinds of sales or trades that many individuals enter into. Some of these transactions—short sales, put options, and wash sales—are discussed below. The tax rules are very complicated. Professional advice should be obtained if you plan to invest in any of these transactions.

Short sales. A short sale occurs when the seller borrows the property delivered to the buyer and, at a later date, either buys substantially identical property and delivers it to the lender or makes delivery out of such property held by the seller at the time of the sale. The holding period on a short sale is usually determined by the length of time the seller actually holds the property that is eventually delivered to the lender to close the short sale.

Example
Even though you do not own any stock in the Ace Corporation, you contract to sell 100 shares of it, which you borrow from your broker. After 13 months, when the price of the stock has fallen, you buy 100 shares of Ace Corporation stock and immediately deliver them to your broker to close out the short sale. Your gain is treated as a short-term capital gain because your holding period for the delivered property is less than 1 day.

Explanation
Long and short positions. If you have held substantially identical property to the property sold short for 1 year or less on the date of the short sale, the following two rules apply:

1. Any gain on closing a short sale is a short-term gain.
2. The holding period of the substantially identical property begins on the date of the closing of the short sale or on the date of the sale, gift, or other disposition of this property, whichever comes first.

These two rules also apply if you acquire substantially identical property after the originating short sale and before the closing of the short sale.

Example
On February 6, 2013, you bought 100 shares of Able Corporation stock for $1,000. On June 4, 2013, you sold short 100 shares of similar Able stock for $1,600. On November 5, 2013, you purchased 100 more shares of Able stock for $1,800 and used them to close the short sale. On this short sale, you realized a $200 short-term capital loss.

On February 7, 2014, you sold for $1,800 the stock originally bought on February 6, 2013. Although you have actually held this stock for more than 1 year, by using rule 2, the holding period is treated as having begun on November 5, 2013, the date of the closing of the short sale. The $800 gain realized on the sale is therefore a short-term capital gain.

TAXALERT
Short sales take away the tax benefits of long-term holding periods with respect to any substantially identical stock held in a long position, unless you have already met the long-term holding requirement at the time you make the short sale.

TAXALERT

The basis reporting rules that went into effect in 2011 require basis and holding period reporting of short sale transactions on Form 1099-B. Previously, brokers were required to report short sales for the year in which the sale opened. Under the new reporting rules, for all short sales opened on or after January 1, 2011, brokers must report gross proceeds for the year in which the short sale closed. For more information, see chapter 13, *Basis of property*.

Treatment of losses. If, on the date of a short sale of a capital asset, you have held substantially identical property for more than 1 year, any loss you have on the short sale is treated as a long-term capital loss, even though the property used to close the sale was held for 1 year or less.

TAXORGANIZER

You should keep a copy of your broker confirmation statement for the purchase of any securities or options. Also, keep a copy of the Form 1099-B provided by your broker for any sales of securities or options. Remember that the information shown on your Form 1099-B is also provided to the IRS. It is important to ensure that the amounts you report on your tax return match the amounts shown on the Form 1099-B received from your broker. If you are issued an incorrect Form 1099-B, request a corrected form from your broker.

TAXPLANNER

Short sales against the box. Selling short against the box means that you are selling borrowed securities while owning substantially identical securities that you later deliver to close the short sale.

You will generally be required to recognize gain (but not loss) of any appreciated position in stock, a partnership interest, or certain debt instruments that has the effect of eliminating your risk of loss and upside gain potential. You will be treated as making a constructive sale of an appreciated position when you do one of the following: (1) enter into a short sale of the same or substantially identical property; (2) enter into an offsetting contract with respect to the same or substantially identical property (an equity swap, for example); or (3) enter into a futures or forward contract to deliver the same or substantially identical property. In addition, future Treasury regulations are expected to expand these rules to other transactions that have substantially the same effects as the ones described in the Internal Revenue Code.

Exceptions

Certain exceptions apply to these rules. One of the most important is that short sales against the box are effective for tax purposes, so long as the following requirements are met:

1. The transaction is closed within 30 days of the close of the taxable year; and
2. You hold the appreciated financial position throughout the 60-day period beginning on the date such transaction is closed, and you do not enter into certain positions that would diminish the risk of loss during that time.

TAXPLANNER

Purchasing put options. Acquiring a put option means that you are buying an option contract to sell 100 shares of stock at a set price during a specific time period. Investors who own appreciated securities that they are not yet ready to sell because of tax reasons often buy put options as a way of protecting their securities against possible price declines.

If the stock price subsequently increases, you obtain the benefit of the price increase less the cost of the put, which expires as worthless. If the stock price declines, however, you may either sell your shares at the put option price or sell the put option separately.

Example

Jim Smith purchased 100 shares of XYZ stock in July 2013 at $25 per share. The selling price in November 2013 was $55. Jim could have sold his shares in November and realized a $30 per-share gain, but it would have been taxed in 2013. Since Jim believed that the stock still had some upward potential and also wanted to postpone recognizing the gain, he bought a put option with an expiration date in March 2014, giving him the right to sell his stock at $55 per share. He locked in his gain and limited his loss to the cost of the put option.

Tax Treatment of Put Options

1. If you sell the put—in lieu of exercising it—the gain or loss is a short-term or long-term capital gain or loss, depending on how long the put has been held.
2. If you neither sell nor exercise the put, the expiration is treated as a sale or an exchange of the put on the expiration date. Whether the loss you incur is a short-term or long-term capital loss depends on how long the put has been held.
3. If you exercise the put, its cost increases your basis in the underlying securities and thus is included in computing your gain or loss at the time of the securities' sale. Whether the gain or loss is short-term or long-term usually depends on the holding period of the underlying stock at the time the put option was acquired.

TAXPLANNER

Stock index options. Unlike a put option, which is based on shares in a specific company, a stock index option represents a group of stocks. For example, an index option is available that is keyed to Standard & Poor's 500 stock averages. Investors use stock index options to reduce portfolio exposure to general market or industry fluctuations and to improve their return on investment. Stock index options may also be used to protect current paper gains (gains you have on paper but have not yet realized) and to save taxes when a taxpayer owns appreciated stock that has not been held long enough to qualify for long-term capital gain treatment.

If you expect the stock market to go down, you might purchase stock index put options. If the market does go down, the put options gain in value, perhaps offsetting the loss in any appreciated stock you might hold.

TAXPLANNER

Writing covered call options. If you have stock that has appreciated in value but want to (1) defer the gain until the following year and (2) provide yourself with protection from market declines, consider writing a covered call option with an expiration date next year. A covered call is the selling of an option to purchase shares that you own at a specified price within a set time frame. If the purchaser of the call doesn't exercise it until next year (or lets it lapse), both the amount you receive from selling the call and the proceeds from disposition of the stock are not reported until the following year.

One disadvantage is that you give up the opportunity to benefit from a price increase in the stock you own above the option exercise price.

Example

Bill purchased 100 shares of XYZ stock for $20 per share on December 20, 2012. On December 21, 2013, the stock was selling for $50 per share, but Bill wanted to defer the gain until 2014 and protect himself against a market decline. Bill wrote a covered call option, agreeing to sell his 100 shares for $50 per share at any time within the next 3 months. He received $3 per share for selling this call option. Bill has acquired protection against a market decline because he now has $3 per share in the bank. If the person who bought the option does not exercise it, Bill reports the $3 per share as a short-term capital gain in 2014. If the option is exercised, the $3 per share is added to the $50 per-share exercise price.

If the stock had continued to appreciate, Bill could have bought other shares of the stock in the open market to deliver against the call, or he could have chosen to purchase, or buy back, the option. A short-term loss would have been realized when the option position was closed in either of these two ways.

Explanation

Wash sales. A wash sale occurs when you sell stock or securities, and, within 30 days before or after the sale, you buy, acquire in a taxable exchange, or acquire a contract or option to buy substantially identical stock. The substantially identical stock may be acquired by subscription for newly issued stock as well as by buying old stock. However, the unallowable loss is added to the basis of the newly acquired stock or security. For additional information about wash sales, see the section on *Wash Sales* later in this chapter.

Losses from wash sales or exchanges of stocks or securities are not deductible. However, the gain from these sales is taxable. Commodity futures contracts are not stock or securities and are not covered by the wash sale rule. Any position of a straddle acquired after June 23, 1981, however, is covered by the wash sale rule. This includes futures contracts. See Publication 550, *Investment Income and Expenses*.

Explanation
Options. Gain or loss from the sale or exchange of a purchased option to buy or sell property that is a capital asset in your hands, or would be if you acquired it, is a capital gain or loss.

If you do not exercise an option to buy or sell, and you have a loss, the option is treated as having been sold or exchanged on the date that it expired.

The Capital Asset Treatment Does Not Apply
1. To a gain from the sale or exchange of an option, if the gain from the sale of the property underlying the option would be ordinary income, or
2. To a dealer in options, if the option is part of inventory, or
3. To a loss from failure to exercise a fixed-price option acquired on same day the property identified in the option was acquired; such loss is not deductible.

If you grant an option on stocks, securities, commodities, or commodity futures and it is not exercised, the amount you receive (if you are not in the business of granting options) is treated as a short-term capital gain reportable on Schedule D (Form 1040), regardless of the classification of the property in your hands. If the option is exercised, you add the option payment to other amounts you receive to figure the amount you realize on the sale of the property. The classification of your gain or loss is then determined by the type of property you sold.

Your holding period for property acquired under an option to purchase begins on the day after the property was acquired, not the day after the option was acquired.

Commodity futures. A commodity future is a contract for the sale or purchase of some fixed amount of a commodity at a future date for a fixed price. The contracts are treated as either (1) hedges to ensure against unfavorable price changes in a commodity bought or sold in the course of business or (2) capital investments.

Gains and losses on hedging contracts for a commodity purchased in the ordinary course of a trade or a business to ensure the price of, and an adequate supply of, the commodity for use in the business are treated as ordinary business gains and losses.

Straddles. A straddle is a position that offsets an interest an investor has in personal property other than stock. It may take the form of a futures contract, an option, or cash. The purpose of a straddle is to reduce an individual's risk of property loss.

Example
Karen bought an option to have 5,000 bushels of wheat delivered to her in June 2014. At the same time, she bought an option to deliver 5,000 bushels of wheat in July 2014. Karen has a straddle.

Explanation
The treatment of straddles is designed to prevent the deferral of income and the conversion of ordinary income to capital gains.

Example 1
ABC stock is selling at $30. Peter purchases two options on ABC. He purchases a call to buy 100 shares of the stock for $25 per share and a put to sell 100 shares of the stock for $35 per share. As long as the stock does not stay at $30, one of the options will produce a gain and the other one will produce a loss.

Assume that by the end of the year the price of ABC is $34. The value of the call should have increased by $400, and the value of the put should have declined by $400.

Peter cannot recognize the loss on the put until he recognizes the offsetting gain on the call.

Example 2
James purchases 100 shares of BCD stock on September 3, 2013, at $40 per share. On November 1, BCD sells at $46 per share. James sells a call due in February 2014 for $100. In December, the stock is selling for $50, and James repurchases the call for $400. James has a $300 short-term loss, which he cannot yet deduct. When he sells BCD in the following year, he could have a long-term gain. The loss cannot be deducted until the year in which the call is closed. The holding period of BCD stock is also changed. If James sells BCD in February 2014 for $50 per share, he would have a short-term gain of $700 to report (the $1,000 gain on the stock minus the $300 loss on the call).

Note: There are many special terms, rules, and exceptions to learn if you want to try your luck on these investment strategies. You should study the markets and the tax law very carefully.

TAXPLANNER

Specific types of capital gains can be treated as ordinary income for certain gains from the sale of a conversion transaction and for certain other financial transactions.

Conversion transaction. A conversion transaction occurs when substantially all of the expected return from an investment is attributable to the time value of the net investment. In addition, if the transaction falls within one of the following classifications, it will be considered a conversion transaction:

1. Acquiring property and, on a contemporaneous basis, contracting to sell the same property for a determined price
2. Certain straddles
3. Any other transaction that is marketed and sold as producing capital gains from a transaction in which substantially all of your expected return is due to the time value of your net investment
4. Other transactions that the U.S. Treasury Department will describe in future regulations

A special rule exempts options dealers and commodities traders from these provisions, but anti-abuse rules prevent limited partners or entrepreneurs from unduly profiting by this exception.

The amount of gain that can be considered ordinary income will not exceed the amount of interest that would have accrued on your net investment in the property at a rate equal to 120% of the applicable federal rate for the period of time you held the investment. This amount is then reduced by the amount of ordinary income that was recognized from the conversion transaction and any interest expense in connection with purchasing the property.

Example

Celine acquires stock for $10,000 on April 1, 2012, and on that same day agrees to sell it to Ricardo for $11,500 on April 1, 2014. Assume that the applicable federal rate is 5%. On April 1, 2014, Celine delivers the stock to Ricardo in exchange for $11,500.

This arrangement is a conversion transaction. Thus, $1,236 of Celine's gain is ordinary income (120% of 5% compounded for 2 years, applied to an investment of $10,000).

Computation of ordinary gain	
Investment	$10,000
Applicable rate (120% × 5%)	6%
	$600
Amount after first year ($10,000 + $600)	$10,600
Applicable rate (120% × 5%)	6%
	$636
Amount after second year ($10,600 + $636)	$11,236
Investment	($10,000)
Ordinary income	$1,236

The difference between the ordinary income and the appreciation, $264 ($1,500 - $1,236), is classified as a long-term capital gain.

Additional requirements are imposed on conversion transactions with respect to built-in losses, options dealers, commodities traders, and limited partners and limited entrepreneurs in an entity that deals in options or trades in commodities.

See chapter 4 of IRS Publication 550 for more details. Because the application of these rules is complex, you should consult your tax advisor when considering a potential conversion transaction.

Sale of business. The sale of a business is not usually the sale of one asset. If you sell your business or your interest in a business and need more information, see Publication 544, *Sales and Other Dispositions of Assets*.

Canceling a sale of real property. If you sell real property to an individual and the sales contract gives the buyer the right to return the property to you for the amount paid, you may not have to recognize gain or loss on the sale. You will not recognize gain or loss if the property is returned to you within the same tax year as the sale. However, if the property is returned to you in a future tax year, you must recognize gain or loss in the year of the sale. In the year in which the property is returned to you, your new basis in the property will be equal to the amount of cash, notes, or other property you give back to the buyer.

Lease canceled or sold. If a tenant receives payments for the cancellation of a lease on property used as the tenant's home, a gain is taxed as a capital gain, but any loss is not deductible. If the lease was used in the tenant's trade or business, gain or loss may be capital or ordinary, as explained in Publication 544, *Sales and Other Dispositions of Assets*.

Payments received by a landlord. If a landlord receives payments for cancellation of a lease, they are ordinary income and not capital gains.

Subleases. When you transfer leased property under an arrangement in which the new occupant takes over your monthly lease payments and also pays you an amount each month for relinquishing use of the property, a sublease has been entered into and payments you receive are ordinary income.

Repossession of real property. If real property that is a capital asset in your hands is repossessed by the seller under the terms of the sales contract or by foreclosure of a mortgage, you may have a capital gain or loss. The gain or loss is the difference between your adjusted basis in the property (purchase price with adjustments) and the full amount of your obligation canceled, plus any money received in exchange for the property. Losses on repossessions of property held for personal use, however, are not deductible. See Publication 537, *Installment Sales*. Also see the discussion of installment sales in this chapter.

Subdivision of land. If you own a tract of land, and, in order to sell or exchange it, you subdivide it into individual lots or parcels, you may receive capital gains treatment on at least a part of the proceeds if you meet the following four conditions:

1. You are not a dealer in real estate.
2. As the owner, you have not made any major improvement on the tract that substantially enhances the value of the lot or parcel sold, and no such improvement will be made as part of the contract of sale with the buyer. A substantial improvement is generally one that increases the value of the property by more than 10%. Some improvements that are considered substantial are: structural work on commercial and residential buildings, laying down hard-surface roads, and installing utility services.
3. You have held the land for at least 5 years, unless you got it by inheritance or devise.
4. You did not previously hold the tract or any lot or parcel on such tract mainly for sale to customers in the ordinary course of your trade or business (unless the tract previously would have qualified for this treatment), and, during the same tax year in which the sale occurred, you were not holding any other land for sale to customers in the ordinary course of trade or business. This treatment also applies to S corporations.

Gain on sale of lots. If your land meets these tests, the gain realized on the sale or exchange will be treated in the following manner:

If you sell less than six lots or parcels from the same tract, the entire gain is a capital gain. In figuring the number of lots or parcels sold, two or more adjoining lots sold to a single buyer in a single sale are counted as only one parcel.

When you sell or exchange the sixth lot or parcel from the same tract, the amount by which 5% of the selling price is more than the expenses of the sale is treated as ordinary income, and the rest of any gain will be a capital gain. Additionally, 5% of the selling price of all lots sold or exchanged from the tract in the tax year in which the sixth lot is sold or exchanged, as well as in later years, is treated as ordinary income.

If you sell the first six lots of a single tract in 1 year, to the extent of gain, the lesser of 5% of the selling price of each lot sold, or the gain is treated as ordinary income. On the other hand, if you sold the first three lots in a single tract in 1 year and the next three lots in the following year, the 5% rule would apply only to the gains realized in the second year.

The selling expenses of the sale must first be deducted from the part of the gain treated as ordinary income, and any remaining expenses must be deducted from the part treated as a capital gain. You may not deduct the selling expenses from other income as ordinary business expenses.

Example 1

You sold five lots from a single tract last year. This year, you sell the sixth lot for $20,000. Your basis for this lot is $10,000, and your selling expenses are $1,500. Your gain is $8,500, all of which is capital gain, figured as follows:

Selling price		$20,000
Less:		
Basis	$10,000	
Expense of sale	1,500	(11,500)
Gain from sale of lot		$8,500
5% of selling price	$1,000	
Less: Expense of sale	1,500	
Gain reported as ordinary income		-0-
Gain reported as capital gain		$8,500

Because the selling expenses are more than 5% of the selling price, none of the gain is treated as ordinary income.

Example 2

Assume in Example 1 that the selling expenses are $800. The amount of gain is $9,200, of which $200 is ordinary income and $9,000 is capital gain, figured as follows:

Selling price		$20,000
Less:		
Basis	$10,000	
Expense of sale	800	(10,800)
Gain from sale of lot		$9,200
5% of selling price	$1,000	
Less: Expense of sale	800	
Gain reported as ordinary income		(200)
Gain reported as capital gain		$9,000

Explanation

Loss on sale of lots. The 5% rule does not apply to losses. If you sell a lot at a loss, it will be treated as a capital loss if you held it for investment.

For more information on subdivision of land, see Publication 544, Sales and Other Dispositions of Assets.

Inventions. An invention is usually a capital asset in the hands of the inventor, whether or not a patent has been applied for or has been obtained. The inventor is the individual whose efforts created the property, and who qualifies as the original and first inventor or joint inventor.

If you are an inventor and transfer all substantial rights to patent property, you may get special tax treatment, as described below, if the transfer is not to your employer or to a related person.

If, for a consideration paid to the inventor, you acquire all the substantial rights to patent property before the invention is reduced to practice (tested and operated successfully under operating conditions), you may, when you dispose of your interest, get special tax treatment if you are not the employer of the inventor or related to the inventor. However, if you buy patent property after it is reduced to practice, it may be treated as either a capital or a noncapital asset, depending on the circumstances.

Special tax treatment. If you are the inventor or an individual who acquired all the substantial rights to the patent property before the invention was reduced to practice, and you transfer all the substantial rights or an undivided interest in all such rights, the transfer will be treated as a sale or an exchange of a long-term capital asset. This rule applies even if you have not held the patent property for more than 1 year and whether or not the payments received are made periodically during the transferee's use of the patent or are contingent on the productivity, use, or disposition of the property transferred.

Courts have enforced the substantial rights requirement very strictly. Generally, a patent seller must be able to show that any rights he or she retains are insubstantial in order to treat the sale of rights in the patent property as a long-term capital gain.

The U.S. Courts of Appeals for the Sixth, Seventh, and Ninth Circuits have overturned lower court rulings that allowed patent owners transferring exclusive rights to impose geographical limitations within the United States on the person purchasing the patent. However, the official IRS position is that a transfer of all substantial rights may be limited to one or more countries.

Payment for the patent may be received by the seller in a lump sum, as an installment sale, as a fixed percentage of all future profits from the patent, or as a fee per item produced. All these methods qualify for capital gains treatment, even if the total amount of payment is uncertain.

Transfers between related parties. The special tax treatment does not apply if the transfer is either directly or indirectly between you and certain related parties. The rules defining related parties are very specific. You should consult your tax advisor for assistance with the interpretation.

Copyrights. Literary, musical, or artistic compositions, or similar property, are not treated as capital assets if your personal efforts created them or if you got the property in such a way that all or part of your basis in the property is determined by reference to a person whose personal efforts created the property (e.g., if you got the property as a gift). The sale of such property, whether or not it is copyrighted, results in ordinary income.

Deposit in Insolvent or Bankrupt Financial Institution

If you lose money you have on deposit in a bank, credit union, or other financial institution that becomes insolvent or bankrupt, you may be able to deduct your loss in one of three ways.

- Ordinary loss.
- Casualty loss.
- Nonbusiness bad debt (short-term capital loss).

For more information, see *Deposit in Insolvent or Bankrupt Financial Institution*, in chapter 4 of Publication 550.

Sale of Annuity

The part of any gain on the sale of an annuity contract before its maturity date that is based on interest accumulated on the contract is ordinary income.

Losses on Section 1244 (Small Business) Stock

You can deduct as an ordinary loss, rather than as a capital loss, your loss on the sale, trade, or worthlessness of Section 1244 stock. Report the loss on Form 4797, line 10.

Any gain on Section 1244 stock is a capital gain if the stock is a capital asset in your hands. Report the gain on Form 8949. See *Losses on Section 1244 (Small Business) Stock* in chapter 4 of Publication 550.

> **Tip**
>
> *For more information on Form 8949 and Schedule D (Form 1040), see* <u>Reporting Capital Gains and Losses</u> *in chapter 16. See also Schedule D (Form 1040), Form 8949, and their separate instructions.*

EXPLANATION

While individuals who own certain stock in a small business investment company may be allowed to deduct an ordinary loss on the sale, exchange, or worthlessness of their stock, the amount that may be claimed is subject to an annual limit of $50,000 per taxpayer ($100,000 for a married couple filing a joint return).

Ordinary loss treatment is generally available only to the original owner. If you obtain stock in a small business corporation or investment company through purchase, gift, inheritance, or the like, you may not claim ordinary losses. Similarly, if small business stock is owned through a partnership, to claim a loss, you must have been a partner when the stock was issued. If you were not a partner at such time and the partnership later distributed the stock to the partners, you may not take an ordinary loss deduction.

To qualify for ordinary loss treatment, you must own Section 1244 stock. This is the stock of a small business corporation or investment company with total capital of under $1 million that meets a *passive income test*. To meet this test, the aggregate of any gross receipts generated over the last 5 years by royalties, rents, dividends, interest, annuities, and sales of stock or securities must be less than 50% of total gross receipts taken in by the corporation in the 5-year period. In addition, the corporation's stock must have been issued for money or property other than securities. Stock that is convertible into other securities of the corporation is not treated as Section 1244 stock.

TAXPLANNER

The loss limitation of $50,000 per taxpayer is an annual limitation. Therefore, if you are considering a sale of Section 1244 stock that is expected to produce a loss of over $50,000, you should consider structuring the transaction so that stock sales will take place in more than 1 year.

Example

Craig, a bachelor, has owned 10,000 shares of qualified small business stock for several years. The stock has a basis of $150,000. He plans to dispose of the stock but expects to realize only $50,000 on the sale. If he sells all 10,000 shares in 2014, he will recognize a $100,000 loss in 1 year. Only $50,000 will be deductible as an ordinary loss. The other $50,000 will be treated as a long-term capital loss. The long-term capital loss can be offset against other capital gains, but the excess can be deducted at the rate of only $3,000 per year.

If Craig sells 5,000 shares in 2014 and 5,000 shares in 2015 for the same price, he will still have a total loss of $100,000. Yet, because $50,000 of the loss will be recognized in 2014 and the other $50,000 in 2015, Craig may treat both losses as ordinary losses, which makes the total $100,000 loss fully deductible without regard to capital gains from other sources.

Craig should use Form 4797 to report the Section 1244 loss as a sale of a noncapital asset.

TAXSAVER

Gain on sale of qualified small business stock.

Generally, a taxpayer other than a corporation may exclude 50% of the gain from the sale of qualified small business stock (QSBS) acquired at original issue after December 31, 2013, or before February 18, 2009, and held for at least five years. (The exclusion can be up to 60% for certain empowerment zone business stock and the stock was acquired after December 21, 2000.) For QSBS acquired after February 17, 2009, and before September 28, 2010, the exclusion is increased to 75%. For such stock acquired after September 27, 2010, and before January 1, 2014, 100% of the gain is excluded. (The respective 75% and 100% exclusions also apply to QSBS of empowerment zone businesses.)

As of the date this book was published in October 2014, Congress had been considering legislation that would extend the availability of the 100% exclusion and eliminate the AMT preference to QSBS acquired at least during 2014 and 2015; however, no extension had yet been passed. For updated information on this and any other tax law changes that occur after this book was published, see our website, *ey.com/EYTaxGuide*.

The portion of the gain includible in taxable income is taxed at a maximum rate of 28% under the regular tax. (This is an exception to the general maximum capital gain rate of 20% that is applicable to taxpayers who are otherwise in the 39.6% regular tax bracket, 0% for those in the 10% and 15% brackets, and 15% for all other taxpayers.) For alternative minimum tax (AMT) purposes (see chapter 31, *How to figure your tax*), 7% of the amount excluded from gross income is an AMT preference item and is added back to taxable income to arrive at alternative minimum taxable income.

For QSBS eligible for the 50% exclusion, the effective tax rate on gains realized is 14% for regular tax (as half of the gain is excluded and the other half is taxed at a 28% rate; i.e., 28% tax rate x 50%). The amount of the AMT tax preference item is 3.5% of the total gain realized (50% x 7%). For a taxpayer subject to the highest AMT tax rate of 28%, the effective maximum rate on the gain realized is 14.98%. The additional 0.98% results from the 7% add back of the excluded gain taxed at a 28% rate.

Although the 28% tax rate applicable to a sale of qualified small business stock ("QSBS") remains the same for QSBS eligible for the 75% exclusion, the higher exclusion lowers the effective tax rate on gains realized for regular tax purposes to 7% (28% tax rate × 25%). The amount of the AMT tax preference item is 5.25% of the total gain realized (75% × 7%). For a taxpayer subject to the highest AMT tax rate of 28%, the effective maximum rate on the gain realized is 8.47%. The additional 1.47% results from the 7% add back of the excluded gain taxed at a 28% rate.

For QSBS acquired after September 27, 2010, and before January 1, 2014, 100% of the gain is excluded and there is no AMT preference item attributable for that sale.

You should consider the after-tax benefit of owning QSBS as compared to other long-term investments taxed at the general rate applicable to net long-term capital gains of 20%, 15%, or 0%—depending on your tax bracket—before purchasing the stock.

Note: Gain from the sale of QSBS can be rolled over into other QSBS. Under the rollover rules, a taxpayer other than a corporation may elect to roll over capital gains from the sale of QSBS held for more than 6 months if other small business stock is purchased by the individual during the 60-day period beginning on the date of sale.

This exclusion is limited to the greater of:

1. 10 times the taxpayer's basis in the stock; or
2. $10 million in gain from all of the taxpayer's transactions in stock of that corporation (held for more than 5 years); $5 million if married filing separately

The rules for determining whether stock is qualified small business stock can be summarized as follows:

- The stock must be newly issued stock and issued after August 10, 1993.
- The stock cannot be acquired in exchange for other stock.
- The issuing corporation must be a C corporation but may not be a cooperative, domestic international sales corporation (DISC), former DISC, real estate investment trust (REIT), regulated investment company (RIC), real estate mortgage investment conduit (REMIC), or a corporation having a possessions tax credit election in effect or owning a subsidiary that has a possessions tax credit election in effect.
- At least 80% of the corporation's assets must be used in the active conduct of a qualified trade or business or in the start-up of a future qualified trade or business.
- A qualified trade or business is any business other than one involving the performance of services in the fields of health, law, engineering, architecture, accounting, actuarial science, performing arts, consulting, athletics, financial services, brokerage services, or any other trade or business where the principal asset of the business is the reputation or skill of one or more employees. A qualified trade or business also cannot involve the businesses of banking, insurance, financing, leasing, investing or similar businesses, farming or certain businesses involving natural resource extraction or production, or businesses operating a hotel, motel, restaurant, or similar business.
- The corporation may not have greater than $50 million in gross assets (i.e., the sum of cash plus the aggregate fair market value of other corporate property) at the time the qualified small business stock is issued. If the corporation meets this test at the time of issuance of the stock, a subsequent event that violates this rule will not disqualify stock that previously qualified.
- The following stock redemption or "buy back" tests must be met:
  i. Within the period beginning 2 years before and ending 2 years after the stock was issued, the corporation cannot have bought more than a minimal amount of its stock from you or a related party.
  ii. Within the period beginning 1 year before and ending 1 year after the stock was issued, the corporation cannot have bought more than a de minimis amount of its stock from anyone, unless the total value of the stock it bought is 5% or less of the total value of all its stock.

Note: Under certain circumstances, the gain on the sale of publicly traded securities will not be taxed if the proceeds from the sale are used to acquire common stock in a specialized small business investment company (SSBIC) within a 60-day period. See chapter 4 of Publication 550, *Investment Income and Expenses,* for a detailed description of these additional requirements. Because of the complexity of the rules related to QSBS transactions, you should consult your tax advisor prior to completing any sale transaction to which these rules may apply.

Holding Period

If you sold or traded investment property, you must determine your holding period for the property. Your holding period determines whether any capital gain or loss was a short-term or long-term capital gain or loss.

Long-term or short-term. If you hold investment property more than 1 year, any capital gain or loss is a long-term capital gain or loss. If you hold the property 1 year or less, any capital gain or loss is a short-term capital gain or loss.

To determine how long you held the investment property, begin counting on the date after the day you acquired the property. The day you disposed of the property is part of your holding period.

Example. If you bought investment property on February 6, 2013, and sold it on February 6, 2014, your holding period is not more than 1 year and you have a short-term capital gain or loss. If you sold it on February 7, 2014, your holding period is more than 1 year and you will have a long-term capital gain or loss.

Securities traded on established market. For securities traded on an established securities market, your holding period begins the day after the trade date you bought the securities, and ends on the trade date you sold them.

Example. You are a cash method, calendar year taxpayer. You sold stock at a gain on December 30, 2014. According to the rules of the stock exchange, the sale was closed by delivery of the stock 4 trading days after the sale, on January 6, 2015. You received payment of the sales price on that same day. Report your gain on your 2014 return, even though you received the payment in 2015. The gain is long term or short term depending on whether you held the stock more than 1 year. Your holding period ended on December 30. If you had sold the stock at a loss, you would also report it on your 2014 return.

U.S. Treasury notes and bonds. The holding period of U.S. Treasury notes and bonds sold at auction on the basis of yield starts the day after the Secretary of the Treasury, through news releases, gives notification of acceptance to successful bidders. The holding period of U.S. Treasury notes and bonds sold through an offering on a subscription basis at a specified yield starts the day after the subscription is submitted.

Automatic investment service. In determining your holding period for shares bought by the bank or other agent, full shares are considered bought first and any fractional shares are considered bought last. Your holding period starts on the day after the bank's purchase date. If a share was bought over more than one purchase date, your holding period for that share is a split holding period. A part of the share is considered to have been bought on each date that stock was bought by the bank with the proceeds of available funds.

Nontaxable trades. If you acquire investment property in a trade for other investment property and your basis for the new property is determined, in whole or in part, by your basis in the old property, your holding period for the new property begins on the day following the date you acquired the old property.

Caution

Do not confuse the trade date with the settlement date, which is the date by which the stock must be delivered and payment must be made.

Property received as a gift. If you receive a gift of property and your basis is determined by the donor's adjusted basis, your holding period is considered to have started on the same day the donor's holding period started.

If your basis is determined by the fair market value of the property, your holding period starts on the day after the date of the gift.

Inherited property. Generally, if you inherited investment property, your capital gain or loss on any later disposition of that property is long-term capital gain or loss. This is true regardless of how long you actually held the property. However, if you inherited property from someone who died in 2010, see the information below.

Inherited property from someone who died in 2010. If you inherit investment property from a decedent who died in 2010, and the executor of the decedent's estate made the election to file Form 8939, refer to the information provided by the executor or see Publication 4895, Tax Treatment of Property Acquired From a Decedent Dying in 2010, to determine your holding period.

EXPLANATION

For most of 2010, the estate tax was repealed. However, the December 2010 tax law that extended the so-called Bush tax cuts retroactively reinstated the estate tax for 2010. This law also allowed the executor of an estate of a decedent who died during 2010 a choice of having the estate tax apply. If the estate tax is applied to a decedent who died during 2010, then your capital gain or loss on any later disposition of that property is long-term capital gain or loss. On the other hand, if the executor chose not to have the estate tax apply, then your holding period (and basis) are determined under special rules.

If you sell property that you originally inherited from a decedent who died in 2010, you should contact the executor of the decedent's estate to confirm the holding period—and basis—in any property received. You should also request a copy of Form 8939, Allocation of Increase in Basis for Property Acquired From a Decedent, if it was filed by the executor.

For additional information, see chapter 44, *Estate and gift tax planning*, and Publication 4895, *Tax Treatment of Property Acquired From a Decedent Dying in 2010.*

Real property bought. To figure how long you have held real property bought under an unconditional contract, begin counting on the day after you received title to it or on the day after you took possession of it and assumed the burdens and privileges of ownership, whichever happened first. However, taking delivery or possession of real property under an option agreement is not enough to start the holding period. The holding period cannot start until there is an actual contract of sale. The holding period of the seller cannot end before that time.

Real property repossessed. If you sell real property but keep a security interest in it, and then later repossess the property under the terms of the sales contract, your holding period for a later sale includes the period you held the property before the original sale and the period after the repossession. Your holding period does not include the time between the original sale and the repossession. That is, it does not include the period during which the first buyer held the property.

Stock dividends. The holding period for stock you received as a taxable stock dividend begins on the date of distribution.

The holding period for new stock you received as a nontaxable stock dividend begins on the same day as the holding period of the old stock. This rule also applies to stock acquired in a "spin-off," which is a distribution of stock or securities in a controlled corporation.

Nontaxable stock rights. Your holding period for nontaxable stock rights begins on the same day as the holding period of the underlying stock. The holding period for stock acquired through the exercise of stock rights begins on the date the right was exercised.

Nonbusiness Bad Debts

If someone owes you money that you cannot collect, you have a bad debt. You may be able to deduct the amount owed to you when you figure your tax for the year the debt becomes worthless.

Generally, nonbusiness bad debts are bad debts that did not come from operating your trade or business, and are deductible as short-term capital losses. To be deductible, nonbusiness bad debts must be totally worthless. You cannot deduct a partly worthless nonbusiness debt.

Caution

Make sure you report your bad debt(s) (and any other short-term transactions for which you did not receive a Form 1099-B) on Form 8949, Part I, with box C checked.

Tip

For more information on Form 8949 and Schedule D (Form 1040), see Reporting Capital Gains and Losses in chapter 16. See also Schedule D (Form 1040), Form 8949, and their separate instructions.

Genuine debt required. A debt must be genuine for you to deduct a loss. A debt is genuine if it arises from a debtor-creditor relationship based on a valid and enforceable obligation to repay a fixed or determinable sum of money.

Basis in bad debt required. To deduct a bad debt, you must have a basis in it—that is, you must have already included the amount in your income or loaned out your cash. For example, you cannot claim a bad debt deduction for court-ordered child support not paid to you by your former spouse. If you are a cash method taxpayer (as most individuals are), you generally cannot take a bad debt deduction for unpaid salaries, wages, rents, fees, interest, dividends, and similar items.

EXPLANATION

The distinction between business and nonbusiness bad debts is generally clear. Business bad debts usually occur because of credit transactions with customers, employees, and others closely related to a trade or a business. The dominant motive in these transactions is to support the business activity. Nonbusiness bad debts frequently arise from casual loans, such as those made to friends or acquaintances. But there is often confusion between business and nonbusiness bad debts in the following areas:

1. **You make loans frequently, but making loans is not a full-time business.** The IRS's position is that business bad debt treatment is limited to those situations in which the taxpayer derives his or her main source of income from credit transactions. Whether or not you are in a trade or business is a question of fact. However, the greater the regularity of the activity, the more likely that a trade or business exists.

Example

You occasionally lend money to individuals starting new businesses. That is an investment activity, not a trade or a business.

2. **You make a loan to a corporation in which you are an employee and a stockholder.** You are allowed a business bad debt deduction if the loan was made primarily to protect your salary. If the loan was made primarily to protect your investment, it is considered a nonbusiness loan. The larger your investment is in a company and the smaller your salary is from it, the greater the chance that a court will determine that a loan you make to the company is for nonbusiness purposes.

TAXPLANNER

If you make advances to a corporation you own, the IRS may attempt to recharacterize the advances as equity capital rather than bona fide loans. This might postpone a deduction for a bad debt until the year in which your stock is wholly worthless. Therefore, it is important that you properly document advances you make to the corporation as bona fide loans. Generally, written, interest-bearing instruments with fixed repayment terms will qualify as bona fide debt.

TAXPLANNER

If you want a loan to a family member to be considered a bona fide debt, you should document the transaction so that it is clear that both parties expect and intend repayment of the loan.

A child may borrow money from his or her parents for a business venture. To indicate that the borrowed money is not intended as a gift, the parents should draft a note saying who owes whom money. (The parties might check with a lawyer about the exact form the note should take.) If the note calls for partial payments of the debt, each payment should be made on time. This provides evidence that a legitimate creditor-debtor relationship exists. To further support their status as creditors, parents may consider investigating the business in which the child is investing the borrowed money. An arm's-length lender typically makes such an investigation.

It's also a good idea for the note from the parents to provide that the money be repaid with interest. Charging interest provides another bit of evidence that the loan between parents and child is a valid arm's-length transaction. Failure to charge adequate interest can also have important gift and income tax consequences. For details, see chapter 7, *Interest income*.

Example 1

Gail lends her son $20,000, which the son then invests in a new business venture. Gail draws up a note that provides for a specific repayment schedule and a stated rate of interest. Collateral is also established on the note to provide Gail with some security. Later, before any payments on the note have been made, the son's business venture fails. Despite repeated efforts to collect the debt, Gail is able to recover only a small amount based on the collateral established at the time of the loan.

Gail may take a bad debt deduction of $20,000, less the amount of collateral she recovered. Gail's son may deduct his loss as a business loss.

Example 2

Assume the same facts as in Example 1 except that Gail does not document the loan. No note is drawn up, and no specific provisions are made about when her son will repay the loan. If the son's business venture fails, he may deduct his loss. The mother, however, may not take a bad debt deduction.

Explanation

Loans in your business. If you are in a business or a profession, you may have bad debts that come from loans you make to your clients. If you are not in the business of lending money and the loans have no close relationship to your business or profession, these bad debts are nonbusiness bad debts.

Mechanics' and suppliers' liens. Workers and material suppliers sometimes file liens against property because of debts owed by a builder or a contractor. If you pay off such a lien to avoid foreclosure and loss of your property, you are entitled to repayment from the builder or contractor. If the debt is uncollectible, you may take a deduction for a bad debt.

Insolvency of contractor. You can take a bad debt deduction for the amount you deposit with a contractor if the contractor becomes insolvent and you are unable to recover (collect) your deposit. If the deposit is for work that is not related to your trade or business, it is a nonbusiness bad debt deduction.

Secondary liability on home mortgage. If you sell your home and the purchaser assumes your mortgage, you may remain secondarily liable for repayment of the mortgage loan. If the purchaser defaults on the loan, you may have to make up the difference if the house is then sold for less than the amount outstanding on the mortgage. You can take a bad debt deduction for the amount you pay to satisfy the mortgage if you cannot collect it from the purchaser.

Corporate securities that become worthless are generally deductible as capital losses. This includes shares of stock, stock rights, bonds, debentures, notes, or certificates, as explained in chapter 16, *Reporting gains and losses*.

TAXPLANNER

Frequently, it is difficult to establish the year in which a corporate security becomes worthless. One guide is a publication called *Capital Changes Reporter*, published by Commerce Clearing House. The section called *Worthless Securities* provides a current list of companies whose securities have lost their value.

It is even more difficult to determine when a closely held business becomes worthless. It is not necessary for the company to declare bankruptcy. If you are aware that a company is insolvent, you may be able to take a loss. If the business continues to operate and has more than nominal assets, however, it may be only temporarily insolvent. If that is the case, you may not be able to take a loss.

Explanation

Recovery of a bad debt. Any amount recovered for a bad debt deducted in a previous year generally must be included in your income in the year in which the amount was recovered. However, you may exclude the amount recovered up to the amount of the deduction that did not reduce your income subject to tax in the year deducted. Recovery of amounts deducted in previous years is discussed in chapter 12, *Other income*.

Example

In 2009, Bill had a $25,000 long-term capital gain and a $25,000 bad debt loss. Bill had no taxable income for 2009.

In 2014, Bill recovered the entire $25,000 debt. To figure how much he should include in his 2014 income, see the calculations below.

	2009 with bad debt	2009 without bad debt
Income:		
Net long-term capital gain	$25,000	$25,000
Bad debt loss	(25,000)	
Adjusted gross income	–0–	$25,000
Less:		
Standard deductions	–0–	($5,700)
Personal exemption	–0–	($3,650)
Taxable income	–0–	$15,650

The calculations show that Bill's 2009 taxable income was reduced by $15,650 by including the bad debt. Therefore, $15,650 is included in Bill's taxable income for 2014, the year in which he collected the $25,000 debt.

Explanation

Business bad debts. There are two crucial differences in the treatment of business bad debts and nonbusiness bad debts:

1. Business bad debts are treated as **ordinary losses**, which may be deducted directly from gross income. Nonbusiness bad debts are short-term capital losses and should be shown on Schedule D, along with your short-term and long-term gains and losses from other sources. The maximum capital loss that you may use to offset your other income each year is $3,000. see chapter 16, *Reporting gains and losses*, for further information.
2. A business bad debt may be just *partially* worthless and still give rise to a tax deduction. A nonbusiness bad debt has to be totally worthless.

Example

Janet Jones, an accrual basis taxpayer, performs some plumbing work for XYZ Corporation and sends them an invoice for $20,000 in 2013. In 2014, Janet learns that XYZ Corporation will not be able to pay the entire amount of the bill. She may claim a bad debt deduction for the amount of the invoice that is worthless.

Explanation

Some businesses use the reserve method of computing bad debt expense in keeping their books. Under this method, an estimate of accounts for services expected to be uncollectible is computed, based on prior years' experience, and the amount is placed in reserve as bad debt expense.

The reserve method is no longer allowed for tax purposes, except for certain financial institutions. A business bad debt will be allowed only if it is specifically charged off the taxpayer's books during the year. Therefore, if you own a business with a large number of accounts receivable, to maximize your allowable tax deduction, you should carefully review old accounts at year-end to make sure all worthless accounts are written off.

A special rule applies to taxpayers using the accrual method of accounting for amounts to be received for the performance of services: You are not required to include in income any portion of accrued income for services performed that, on the basis of experience, will not be collected. This rule does not apply if interest is required to be paid on a receivable amount or if there is any penalty for failure to pay such amount on time.

The IRS guidelines that spell out how a taxpayer estimates uncollectible amounts for services are somewhat complex. You should consult your tax advisor if these special rules apply to your situation.

Guarantees. If you guarantee payment of another person's debt and then have to pay it off, you may be able to take a bad debt deduction for your loss. It does not matter in what capacity you make the guarantee, whether as guarantor, endorser, or indemnitor.

To qualify for a bad debt deduction, the guarantee must either be entered into with a profit motive or be related to your trade or business or employment.

A worthless debt qualifies as a nonbusiness bad debt if you can show that your reason for making the guarantee was to protect your investment or to make a profit. If you make the guarantee as a favor to friends and are not given anything in return, it is considered a gift and you may not take a deduction.

You are justified in taking the deduction if you can show that you expected to receive something in return at a future time. The expectation must be reasonable.

Example 1

A taxpayer who ran a successful car rental operation loaned money to her brother-in-law to assist him in starting his own car rental business. The taxpayer received a promissory note due 1 year after the date of the loan, with a stated rate of interest. The brother-in-law's business venture was a flop, and the taxpayer eventually took a bad debt deduction. The court allowed the deduction, pointing out that at the time the loan was made, the brother-in-law was solvent and there was a reasonable expectation that the rental business would serve as a source of repayment.

Example 2

A taxpayer loaned his brother-in-law about $2,000 over a 2-year period to help him support the taxpayer's sister and her children. During the entire period, the brother-in-law was low on cash and his business was failing. There was no record of the loan or any understanding about how it would be repaid. The court ruled that the taxpayer could not take a bad debt deduction because there was no reasonable expectation that the loan would be repaid. Instead, the court said that the $2,000 "loan" should be considered a gift.

When deductible. You can take a bad debt deduction only in the year the debt becomes worthless. You do not have to wait until a debt is due to determine whether it is worthless. A debt becomes worthless when there is no longer any chance that the amount owed will be paid.

It is not necessary to go to court if you can show that a judgment from the court would be uncollectible. You must only show that you have taken reasonable steps to collect the debt. Bankruptcy of your debtor is generally good evidence of the worthlessness of at least a part of an unsecured and unpreferred debt.

EXPLANATION

Determining when a debt becomes worthless. It's not always easy to tell when a debt has become worthless, but the following factors are some indications to look for: (1) bankruptcy of the debtor, (2) termination of the debtor's business, (3) debtor's disappearance or departure from the country, (4) debtor's death, (5) receivership of the debtor, (6) a monetary judgment against the debtor that cannot be collected, and (7) drop in value of property securing the debt.

A sharp decline in the debtor's business may support a finding of worthlessness. In one case, a court allowed a taxpayer to take a bad debt deduction when the small, closely held company that had borrowed the money had to cancel some of its business contracts, had severe cash flow problems, and was unable to obtain bank loans to carry on. However, in other cases, the courts have stressed that a debt is not worthless if the borrower remains a viable going concern engaged in business, even if it is suffering a business decline and losing a lot of money.

If a foreclosure sale of pledged or mortgaged property yields less than the principal amount of the defaulted debt, worthlessness may exist. If the creditor shows that the remaining unpaid debt is uncollectible, he or she may take a bad debt deduction in the year of the foreclosure sale.

If a seller of real property reacquires the property to satisfy a debt that is secured by the property, no debt is considered to become worthless.

If an amount is owed by two or more debtors jointly, inability to collect from one of the debtors does not justify a deduction for a proportionate amount of the debt.

TAXPLANNER

It is important to know when a debt becomes worthless because you may not take a loss in a subsequent year. Because, in many cases, it may be difficult to determine when a debt loses its value, you should claim a deduction at the earliest time you reasonably believe the debt to be worthless. If you discover you have overlooked a bad debt deduction that you should have taken, amend your return for that year. The statute of limitations for bad debts generally runs 7 years from the due date of the tax return filed for the year in which the debt became worthless.

TAXPLANNER

A debt becomes worthless when a prudent person would abandon the effort to collect the debt. This may mean that you expended a lot of effort trying to collect or that you didn't try at all. You have the burden of proving that the debt is worthless.

TAXORGANIZER

You should document any steps you have taken to recover the amount owed to you. Also, you should get a copy of the debtor's financial statements to substantiate the inability to pay back the loan.

How to report bad debts. Deduct nonbusiness bad debts as short-term capital losses on Form 8949. For each bad debt, attach a statement to your return that contains:

- A description of the debt, including the amount, and the date it became due,
- The name of the debtor, and any business or family relationship between you and the debtor,
- The efforts you made to collect the debt, and
- Why you decided the debt was worthless. For example, you could show that the borrower has declared bankruptcy, or that legal action to collect would probably not result in payment of any part of the debt.

Filing a claim for refund. If you do not deduct a bad debt on your original return for the year it becomes worthless, you can file a claim for a credit or refund due to the bad debt. To do this, use Form 1040X to amend your return for the year the debt became worthless. You must file it within 7 years from the date your original return for that year had to be filed, or 2 years from the date you paid the tax, whichever is later. For more information about filing a claim, see *Amended Returns and Claims for Refund* in chapter 1.

Additional information. For more information, see *Nonbusiness Bad Debts* in Publication 550. For information on business bad debts, see chapter 10 of Publication 535, Business Expenses.

Wash Sales

You cannot deduct losses from sales or trades of stock or securities in a wash sale.

A wash sale occurs when you sell or trade stock or securities at a loss and within 30 days before or after the sale you:

1. Buy substantially identical stock or securities,
2. Acquire substantially identical stock or securities in a fully taxable trade,
3. Acquire a contract or option to buy substantially identical stock or securities, or
4. Acquire substantially identical stock for your individual retirement arrangement (IRA) or Roth IRA.

If your loss was disallowed because of the wash sale rules, add the disallowed loss to the cost of the new stock or securities (except in (4) above). The result is your basis in the new stock or securities. This adjustment postpones the loss deduction until the disposition of the new stock or securities. Your holding period for the new stock or securities includes the holding period of the stock or securities sold.

EXAMPLE

You buy 100 shares of X stock for $1,000. At a later date, you sell these shares for $750. Then, within 30 days of the sale, you acquire 100 shares of the same stock for $800. Your loss of $250 on the sale is not deductible. However, the disallowed loss ($250) is added to the cost of the new stock ($800) to get the basis of the new stock ($1,050).

Explanation

For purposes of the wash sale rule, a short sale is considered complete on the date the short sale is entered into if on that date:

1. You own (or, on or before that date, you enter into a contract or option to acquire) stock or securities identical to those sold short, and
2. You later deliver such stock or securities to close the short sale.

Otherwise, a short sale is not considered complete until the property is delivered to close the sale.

TAXALERT

As previously discussed in this chapter, for securities acquired on or after January 1, 2011, the basis and holding period of short sales and wash sales will be reported by your broker on Form 1099-B. For any securities acquired prior to January 1, 2011, it will remain your responsibility to calculate cost basis and holding period upon the sale or transfer. It is important that you evaluate the information reported on the Form 1099-B and notify your broker immediately if you do not agree with the reported amounts. If you receive an incorrect Form 1099-B, request a corrected copy from your broker prior to filing your income tax return. Because the IRS matches documents filed with the Service to the related income tax returns, it is important that your broker-reported transactions match those on your tax return.

For more information, see *Wash Sales*, in chapter 4 of Publication 550.

Rollover of Gain From Publicly Traded Securities

You may qualify for a tax-free rollover of certain gains from the sale of publicly traded securities. This means that if you buy certain replacement property and make the choice described in this section, you postpone part or all of your gain.

You postpone the gain by adjusting the basis of the replacement property as described in *Basis of replacement property*, later. This postpones your gain until the year you dispose of the replacement property.

You qualify to make this choice if you meet all the following tests.

- You sell publicly traded securities at a gain. Publicly traded securities are securities traded on an established securities market.
- Your gain from the sale is a capital gain.
- During the 60-day period beginning on the date of the sale, you buy replacement property. This replacement property must be either common stock of, or a partnership interest in a specialized small business investment company (SSBIC). This is any partnership or corporation licensed by the Small Business Administration under section 301(d) of the Small Business Investment Act of 1958, as in effect on May 13, 1993.

Amount of gain recognized. If you make the choice described in this section, you must recognize gain only up to the following amount.

- The amount realized on the sale, minus
- The cost of any common stock or partnership interest in an SSBIC that you bought during the 60-day period beginning on the date of sale (and did not previously take into account on an earlier sale of publicly traded securities).

If this amount is less than the amount of your gain, you can postpone the rest of your gain, subject to the limit described next. If this amount is equal to or more than the amount of your gain, you must recognize the full amount of your gain.

Limit on gain postponed. The amount of gain you can postpone each year is limited to the smaller of:

- $50,000 ($25,000 if you are married and file a separate return), or
- $500,000 ($250,000 if you are married and file a separate return), minus the amount of gain you postponed for all earlier years.

Basis of replacement property. You must subtract the amount of postponed gain from the basis of your replacement property.

How to report and postpone gain. See *How to report and postpone gain* under *Rollover of Gain From Publicly Traded Securities* in chapter 4 of Publication 550 for details.

Chapter 15

Selling your home

ey.com/EYTaxGuide

Note

IRS Publication 17 (*Your Federal Income Tax*) has been updated by Ernst & Young LLP for 2014. Dates and dollar amounts shown are for 2014. Underlined type is used to indicate where IRS text has been updated. Places where text has been removed are indicated by the sentence: *Text intentionally omitted*.

ey.com/EYTaxGuide

Ernst & Young LLP will update the *EY Tax Guide 2015* website with relevant taxpayer information as it becomes available. You can also sign up for email alerts to let you know when changes have been made.

Introduction

Your home is likely to be the most valuable asset you own and may increase in value as the housing recovery continues. If you've owned your home for a number of years or live in an area where home values have rebounded, you may have a significant gain—and lots of taxes to pay—when you sell it. On the other hand, the value of your home may still be much less than you paid for it. As a result, you may find yourself selling your home at a loss. Unfortunately, a loss on the sale of your personal home is generally not deductible. This chapter tells you what you should and shouldn't do when you're considering selling your home.

Your home is probably your best tax shelter. Homeowners are eligible for a number of tax breaks. You may deduct the cost of real estate taxes and, subject to certain limitations, the cost of interest paid on your mortgage. (See chapter 24, *Interest expense*, for an explanation of the limitations on deducting home mortgage interest.) You may also be able to completely exclude up to $250,000 of gain ($500,000 if you're married filing jointly) on the sale of your home if you meet certain conditions. In addition, you may qualify for the residential energy efficient property credit for making energy-efficient improvements to your home. (See chapter 37, *Other credits including the earned income credit*, for more information.) In addition to federal tax benefits, some states continue to allow local residential energy conservation and solar energy tax credits against your state income tax liability. Refer to your state's tax return instruction guide to determine if state tax credits are available.

Any gain you are required to recognize on the sale of a home will be treated as long-term capital gain if the home was held for more than one year. The tax rate applied to long-term capital gains depends on your marginal tax bracket. In 2014, net long-term capital gains are taxed at a maximum rate of 20% for high income taxpayers who are otherwise in the 39.6% ordinary income tax bracket (i.e., taxable incomes over $406,750 for individual filers, $432,200 for heads of households, $457,600 married filing jointly, and $228,800 if married filing separately). Net long-term capital gains received by taxpayers in the 10% and 15% ordinary income tax brackets are taxed at a zero rate. For all others, (i.e., taxpayers in the 25%, 28%, 33%, or 35% ordinary income tax brackets) net long-term capital gains are taxed at 15%. These lower rates apply to both the regular tax and the alternative minimum tax.

In addition to paying regular income tax or alternative minimum tax on capital gains, the 3.8% Net Investment Income Tax (NIIT) is assessed on unearned Net Investment Income (NII). For individuals, the NIIT is 3.8% of the lesser of: (1) NII or (2) the excess of modified adjusted gross income (MAGI) over $200,000 ($250,000 if married filing jointly; $125,000 if married filing separately). Generally, NII includes both short- and long-term capital gains, including taxable gains from the sale of residential and investment real estate. To the extent any gain you realize from the sale of your main home is eligible to be excluded from your gross income—see *Excluding the Gain*, later in this chapter—the excluded gain is also not subject to the 3.8% NIIT.

Reminder

Home sold with undeducted points. If you have not deducted all the points you paid to secure a mortgage on your old home, you may be able to deduct the remaining points in the year of the sale. See *Mortgage ending early* under *Points* in chapter 24.

TAXPLANNER

Nonqualified use. If you plan to convert a rental property into your principal residence, the amount of gain you may be able to exclude from a future sale of that home will be limited as a result of tax legislation enacted in 2008. Generally, you are allowed to exclude up to $250,000 ($500,000 if married filing a joint return) of gain realized on the sale or exchange of a principal residence. The sale of a home will qualify for this exclusion if the home is a taxpayer's principal residence for at least 2 of the 5 years ending on the date of the sale or exchange. However, the period of time you rented the residence after 2008 and before you converted it into your principal residence will figure into a formula that reduces the amount of gain that qualifies for the exclusion (maximum of $250,000 or $500,000 if married filing a joint return) when you ultimately sell that home.

This chapter explains the tax rules that apply when you sell your main home. In most cases, your main home is the one in which you live most of the time.

If you sold your main home in 2014, you may be able to exclude from income any gain up to a limit of $250,000 ($500,000 on a joint return in most cases). See *Excluding the Gain*, later. Generally, if you can exclude all the gain, you do not need to report the sale on your tax return.

If you have gain that cannot be excluded, it is taxable. Report it on Form 8949, Sales and Other Dispositions of Capital Assets, and Schedule D (Form 1040). You may also have to complete Form 4797, Sales of Business Property. See *Reporting the Sale*, later.

If you have a loss on the sale, you generally cannot deduct it on your return. However, you may need to report it. See *Reporting the Sale*, later.

The following are main topics in this chapter.
- Figuring gain or loss.
- Basis.
- Excluding the gain.
- Ownership and use tests.
- Reporting the sale.

Other topics include the following.
- Business use or rental of home.
- Recapturing a federal mortgage subsidy.

Useful Items

You may want to see:

Publication
- ☐ **523** Selling Your Home
- ☐ **530** Tax Information for Homeowners
- ☐ **547** Casualties, Disasters, and Thefts

Form (and Instructions)
- ☐ **Schedule D (Form 1040)** Capital Gains and Losses
- ☐ **982** Reduction of Tax Attributes Due to Discharge of Indebtedness
- ☐ **8828** Recapture of Federal Mortgage Subsidy
- ☐ **8949** Sales and Other Dispositions of Capital Assets

Tax Breaks and Deductions You Can Use Checklist

Excluding gain realized from selling your home. You may be able to exclude from your gross income up to $250,000 ($500,000, if you file jointly with your spouse) of the gain from the sale of your main home. For more information, see *Excluding the Gain*, later.

Reduced exclusion available if you do not meet the ownership and use requirements for the sale of your main home. Generally, in order to qualify to exclude gain realized from the sale of your main home, you must have owned and occupied the property as your main home for at least 2 years within the 5-year period that preceded the sale. However, you may be able to claim a reduced, prorated exclusion even if you do not meet the ownership or use tests or sold more than one main home during a 2-year period if you sold the home due to:
- A change in your place of employment, and the new place of employment is at least 50 miles farther from the home you sold than was your former place of employment; or
- Health reasons; or
- An unforeseen circumstance

For more information on what constitutes a sale for health reasons or an unforeseen circumstance, and how to calculate the reduced exclusion, see *Reduced Maximum Exclusion*, later.

Exclusion reduced to extent gain relates to nonqualified use. You will not be able to exclude the gain realized from the sale or exchange of a principal residence to the extent that the gain is associated with a period of nonqualified use after December 31, 2008. For this purpose, a period of nonqualified use means any period after December 31, 2008, where the home is not used as a principal residence by you, your spouse, or your former spouse. See *Periods of nonqualified use*, later.

Loss on the sale of a home. You cannot deduct any loss realized from the sale of your home. However, if you own a house as an investment—and do not use it for personal purposes—you may be able to deduct the loss. For more information, see *Amount of Gain or Loss: Loss on sale*, later.

Mortgage debt forgiveness. From 2007 through 2013, you may have been able to exclude from your gross income the income realized from the forgiveness or cancellation of up to $2 million ($1 million if married filing separately) of "Qualified principal residence indebtedness." (Note, however, that the amount of any canceled debt you can exclude from your income reduces your basis in your principal residence. That will increase the amount of gain (or decrease any loss) you realize when you ultimately sell your home.)

As of the date this book was published, this exclusion is not available after 2013. While Congress had been considering legislation that would extend its availability at least through 2015, no such extension had yet been passed. The discussion of mortgage debt forgiveness is included in this

Main Home

This section explains the term "main home." Usually, the home you live in most of the time is your main home and can be a:

- House,
- Houseboat,
- Mobile home,
- Cooperative apartment, or
- Condominium.

To exclude gain under the rules of this chapter, you in most cases must have owned and lived in the property as your main home for at least 2 years during the 5-year period ending on the date of sale.

Land. If you sell the land on which your main home is located, but not the house itself, you cannot exclude any gain you have from the sale of the land. However, if you sell vacant land used as part of your main home and that is adjacent to it, you may be able to exclude the gain from the sale under certain circumstances. See *Vacant land* under *Main Home* in Publication 523 for more information.

Example. You buy a piece of land and move your main home to it. Then you sell the land on which your main home was located. This sale is not considered a sale of your main home, and you cannot exclude any gain on the sale of the land.

More than one home. If you have more than one home, you can exclude gain only from the sale of your main home. You must include in income gain from the sale of any other home. If you have two homes and live in both of them, your main home is ordinarily the one you live in most of the time during the year.

Example 1. You own two homes, one in New York and one in Florida. From 2010 through 2014, you live in the New York home for 7 months and in the Florida residence for 5 months of each year. In the absence of facts and circumstances indicating otherwise, the New York home is your main home. You would be eligible to exclude the gain from the sale of the New York home but not of the Florida home in 2014.

Example 2. You own a house, but you live in another house that you rent. The rented house is your main home.

EXPLANATION

If you own more than one property, it is important to determine which is your principal, or main, residence. The IRS will not issue a ruling on whether or not a home qualifies as a principal residence. The gain on the sale of your principal residence may be excluded, but the gain on the sale of your nonprincipal residence or rental property is taxed in the year of the sale.

If you use more than one property as a residence, the determination of which property is your principal residence will be based on all the facts and circumstances. The IRS has said that if you alternate between two properties, the one you use for a majority of time during the year will ordinarily be considered your principal residence. However, regulations indicate that other factors are also relevant in determining which property is your principal residence. Those factors include:

- Where you vote,
- The address you use on your tax returns,
- The address you claim to be your residence in other financial dealings,
- Where your children go to school,
- Where you work,
- Where your car is registered,
- Where you belong to social and religious groups.

That the property is currently rented or has been rented in the past does not mean that you may not consider it to be your principal residence. For example, a property that is rented out for a brief period while you are away or while you are trying to sell it should not affect the property's status as your principal residence. In order to exclude the gain, the home's status as your principal residence at the time of sale is no longer relevant as long as it was your principal residence for 2 of the 5 years prior to the date of sale.

Example 3. You own two homes, one in Virginia and one in New Hampshire. In 2010 and 2011, you lived in the Virginia home. In 2012 and 2013, you lived in the New Hampshire home. In 2014, you lived again in the Virginia home. Your main home in 2010, 2011, and 2014 is the Virginia home. Your main home in 2012 and 2013 is the New Hampshire home. You would be eligible to exclude gain from the sale of either home (but not both) in 2014.

Property used partly as your main home. If you use only part of the property as your main home, the rules discussed in this publication apply only to the gain or loss on the sale of that part of the property. For details, see *Business Use or Rental of Home*, later.

Figuring Gain or Loss

To figure the gain or loss on the sale of your main home, you must know the selling price, the amount realized, and the adjusted basis. Subtract the adjusted basis from the amount realized to get your gain or loss.

$$\frac{\text{Selling price} - \text{Selling expenses}}{\text{Amount realized}}$$

$$\frac{\text{Amount realized} - \text{Adjusted basis}}{\text{Gain or loss}}$$

Selling Price

The selling price is the total amount you receive for your home. It includes money and the fair market value of any other property or any other services you receive and all notes, mortgages or other debts assumed by the buyer as part of the sale.

Payment by employer. You may have to sell your home because of a job transfer. If your employer pays you for a loss on the sale or for your selling expenses, do not include the payment as part of the selling price. Your employer will include it as wages in box 1 of your Form W-2, and you will include it in your income on Form 1040, line 7.

> ### TAXSAVER
> **Selling your home to your employer.** If during 2014 you sold your home directly to your employer at **fair market value**, no portion of the proceeds is treated as additional compensation. Any gain is subject to the regular rules for home sales. However, if your home was sold to your employer at an amount above fair market value, part of the proceeds would be treated as compensation or ordinary income.

Option to buy. If you grant an option to buy your home and the option is exercised, add the amount you receive for the option to the selling price of your home. If the option is not exercised, you must report the amount as ordinary income in the year the option expires. Report this amount on Form 1040, line 21.

Form 1099-S. If you received Form 1099-S, Proceeds From Real Estate Transactions, box 2 (Gross proceeds) should show the total amount you received for your home.

However, box 2 will not include the fair market value of any services or property other than cash or notes you received or will receive. Instead, box 4 will be checked to indicate your receipt or expected receipt of these items.

Amount Realized

The amount realized is the selling price minus selling expenses.

Selling expenses. Selling expenses include:
- Commissions,
- Advertising fees,
- Legal fees, and
- Loan charges paid by the seller, such as loan placement fees or "points."

> ### EXPLANATION
> **Other selling expenses.** The following items are also considered selling expenses: (1) broker's fees, (2) fees for drafting a contract of sale, (3) fees for drafting the deed, (4) escrow fees, (5) geological surveys, (6) maps, (7) title insurance, (8) recording fees, (9) abstracts of title, (10) title certificate, (11) title opinion, and (12) title registration.

chapter in case Congress acts to extend it. For updated information on this and any other tax law changes that occur after this book was published, see our website, *ey.com/EYTaxGuide*.

Repayment of first-time homebuyer credit claimed in 2008. If you claimed the first-time homebuyer credit for a principal residence you purchased in 2008, you should have begun repaying the credit in 2010, and must continue repaying the credit in equal installments through 2024.

Adjusted Basis

While you owned your home, you may have made adjustments (increases or decreases) to the basis. This adjusted basis must be determined before you can figure gain or loss on the sale of your home. For information on how to figure your home's adjusted basis, see *Determining Basis*, later.

Amount of Gain or Loss

To figure the amount of gain or loss, compare the amount realized to the adjusted basis.

Gain on sale. If the amount realized is more than the adjusted basis, the difference is a gain and, except for any part you can exclude, in most cases is taxable.

Loss on sale. If the amount realized is less than the adjusted basis, the difference is a loss. A loss on the sale of your main home cannot be deducted.

TAXSAVER

Loss on sale of a house held for investment. While you cannot deduct a loss on the sale of your personal home, you may be able to deduct a loss realized on the sale of a house you own as an investment (and do not use for personal purposes).

Explanation

If you convert your residence to rental property, your basis for purposes of calculating depreciation and a loss on the sale is limited to the lower of your adjusted basis or the value of the residence on the date of conversion. Your basis, however, for calculating a gain is your adjusted basis less allowable depreciation.

Example

Assume you have a residence with a basis of $150,000, which you convert to business use when its fair market value is $125,000. You would use $125,000 as your basis for calculating depreciation (i.e., the lesser of the adjusted basis or the fair market value on the date of conversion). If you subsequently sold the residence for $130,000 after having deducted $4,000 for depreciation, your adjusted basis for determining whether you realized a loss would be $121,000 ($125,000 − $4,000), and your adjusted basis for determining whether you realized a gain would be $146,000 ($150,000 − $4,000). In this situation, you would not recognize a gain or loss because a loss results on the gain calculation and a gain results on the loss calculation.

	Gain Calculation	Loss Calculation
Selling price	$130,000	$130,000
Less:		
Adjusted basis	146,000	121,000
Gain/(loss)	($16,000)	$9,000

Jointly owned home. If you and your spouse sell your jointly owned home and file a joint return, you figure your gain or loss as one taxpayer.

Separate returns. If you file separate returns, each of you must figure your own gain or loss according to your ownership interest in the home. Your ownership interest is generally determined by state law.

Joint owners not married. If you and a joint owner other than your spouse sell your jointly owned home, each of you must figure your own gain or loss according to your ownership interest in the home. Each of you applies the rules discussed in this chapter on an individual basis.

Dispositions Other Than Sales

Some special rules apply to other dispositions of your main home.

Foreclosure or repossession. If your home was foreclosed on or repossessed, you have a disposition. See Publication 4681, Canceled Debts, Foreclosures, Repossessions, and Abandonments, to determine if you have ordinary income, gain, or loss.

Abandonment. If you abandon your home, see Publication 4681 to determine if you have ordinary income, gain, or loss.

Trading (exchanging) homes. If you trade your old home for another home, treat the trade as a sale and a purchase.

Example. You owned and lived in a home with an adjusted basis of $41,000. A real estate dealer accepted your old home as a trade-in and allowed you $50,000 toward a new home priced at $80,000. This is treated as a sale of your old home for $50,000 with a gain of $9,000 ($50,000 − $41,000).

If the dealer had allowed you $27,000 and assumed your unpaid mortgage of $23,000 on your old home, your sales price would still be $50,000 (the $27,000 trade-in allowed plus the $23,000 mortgage assumed).

Transfer to spouse. If you transfer your home to your spouse or you transfer it to your former spouse incident to your divorce, you in most cases have no gain or loss. This is true even if you receive cash or other consideration for the home. As a result, the rules in this chapter do not apply.

More information. If you need more information, see *Transfer to spouse* in Publication 523 and *Property Settlements* in Publication 504, Divorced or Separated Individuals.

Involuntary conversion. You have a disposition when your home is destroyed or condemned and you receive other property or money in payment, such as insurance or a condemnation award. This is treated as a sale and you may be able to exclude all or part of any gain from the destruction or condemnation of your home, as explained later under *Special Situations*.

Determining Basis

You need to know your basis in your home to figure any gain or loss when you sell it. Your basis in your home is determined by how you got the home. Generally, your basis is its cost if you bought it or built it. If you got it in some other way (inheritance, gift, etc.), your basis is generally either its fair market value when you received it or the adjusted basis of the previous owner.

While you owned your home, you may have made adjustments (increases or decreases) to your home's basis. The result of these adjustments is your home's adjusted basis, which is used to figure gain or loss on the sale of your home. See *Adjusted Basis*, later.

You can find more information on basis and adjusted basis in chapter 13 of this publication and in Publication 523.

Cost As Basis

The cost of property is the amount you paid for it in cash, debt obligations, other property, or services.

Purchase. If you bought your home, your basis is its cost to you. This includes the purchase price and certain settlement or closing costs. In most cases, your purchase price includes your down payment and any debt, such as a first or second mortgage or notes you gave the seller in payment for the home. If you build, or contract to build, a new home, your purchase price can include costs of construction, as discussed in Publication 523.

Settlement fees or closing costs. When you bought your home, you may have paid settlement fees or closing costs in addition to the contract price of the property. You can include in your basis some of the settlement fees and closing costs you paid for buying the home, but not the fees and costs for getting a mortgage loan. A fee paid for buying the home is any fee you would have had to pay even if you paid cash for the home (that is, without the need for financing).

Chapter 13 lists some of the settlement fees and closing costs that you can include in the basis of property, including your home. It also lists some settlement costs that cannot be included in basis.

Also see Publication 523 for additional items and a discussion of basis other than cost.

Adjusted Basis

Adjusted basis is your cost or other basis increased or decreased by certain amounts. To figure your adjusted basis, you can use Worksheet 1 in Publication 523.

Increases to basis. These include the following.
- Additions and other improvements that have a useful life of more than 1 year.
- Special assessments for local improvements.
- Amounts you spent after a casualty to restore damaged property.

Improvements. These add to the value of your home, prolong its useful life, or adapt it to new uses. You add the cost of additions and other improvements to the basis of your property.

For example, putting a recreation room or another bathroom in your unfinished basement, putting up a new fence, putting in new plumbing or wiring, putting on a new roof, or paving your unpaved driveway are improvements. An addition to your house, such as a new deck, a sun-room, or a new garage, is also an improvement.

TAXSAVER
Shrubs and trees. The Tax Court has held that shrubbery and trees may qualify as improvements to be added to the basis of your property.

Repairs. These maintain your home in good condition but do not add to its value or prolong its life. You do not add their cost to the basis of your property.

Examples of repairs include repainting your house inside or outside, fixing your gutters or floors, repairing leaks or plastering, and replacing broken window panes.

Decreases to basis. These include the following.
- Discharge of qualified principal residence indebtedness that was excluded from income.
- Some or all of the cancellation of debt income that was excluded due to your bankruptcy or insolvency. For details, see Publication 4681.
- Gain you postponed from the sale of a previous home before May 7, 1997.
- Deductible casualty losses.
- Insurance payments you received or expect to receive for casualty losses.
- Payments you received for granting an easement or right-of-way.
- Depreciation allowed or allowable if you used your home for business or rental purposes.

Caution

Do not use Worksheet 1 if you acquired an interest in your home from a decedent who died in 2010 and whose executor filed Form 8939, Allocation of Increase in Basis for Property Acquired From a Decedent.

- Energy-related credits allowed for expenditures made on the residence. (Reduce the increase in basis otherwise allowable for expenditures on the residence by the amount of credit allowed for those expenditures.)
- Adoption credit you claimed for improvements added to the basis of your home.
- Nontaxable payments from an adoption assistance program of your employer you used for improvements you added to the basis of your home.
- Energy conservation subsidy excluded from your gross income because you received it (directly or indirectly) from a public utility after 1992 to buy or install any energy conservation measure. An energy conservation measure is an installation or modification primarily designed either to reduce consumption of electricity or natural gas or to improve the management of energy demand for a home.
- District of Columbia first-time homebuyer credit (allowed on the purchase of a principal residence in the District of Columbia beginning on August 5, 1997, and before January 1, 2012).
- General sales taxes (allowed beginning 2004 and ending before 2014) claimed as an itemized deduction on Schedule A (Form 1040) that were imposed on the purchase of personal property, such as a houseboat used as your home or a mobile home.

Discharges of qualified principal residence indebtedness. You may be able to exclude from gross income a discharge of qualified principal residence indebtedness. This exclusion applies to discharges made after 2006 and before 2014. If you choose to exclude this income, you must reduce (but not below zero) the basis of the principal residence by the amount excluded from your gross income.

File Form 982 with your tax return. See the form's instructions for detailed information.

TAXALERT

As of the date this book was published, this exclusion is not available after 2013. While Congress had been considering legislation that would extend its availability at least through 2015, no such extension had yet been passed. The discussion of mortgage debt forgiveness is included in this chapter in case Congress acts to extend it. For updated information on this and any other tax law changes that occur after this book was published, see our website, ey.com/EYTaxGuide.

TAXALERT

The amount of any discharged debt you can exclude from your income reduces the basis in your principal residence. That will increase the amount of gain (or decrease any loss) you realize when you ultimately sell your home.

The records you should keep include:
- Proof of the home's purchase price and purchase expenses,
- Receipts and other records for all improvements, additions, and other items that affect the home's adjusted basis,
- Any worksheets or other computations you used to figure the adjusted basis of the home you sold, the gain or loss on the sale, the exclusion, and the taxable gain,
- Any Form 982 you filed to report any discharge of qualified principal residence indebtedness,
- Any Form 2119, Sale of Your Home, you filed to postpone gain from the sale of a previous home before May 7, 1997, and
- Any worksheets you used to prepare Form 2119, such as the Adjusted Basis of Home Sold Worksheet or the Capital Improvements Worksheet from the Form 2119 instructions, or other source of computations.

Excluding the Gain

You may qualify to exclude from your income all or part of any gain from the sale of your main home. This means that, if you qualify, you will not have to pay tax on the gain up to the limit described under *Maximum Exclusion*, next. To qualify, you must meet the ownership and use tests described later.

Records

Recordkeeping. You should keep records to prove your home's adjusted basis. Ordinarily, you must keep records for 3 years after the due date for filing your return for the tax year in which you sold your home. But if you sold a home before May 7, 1997, and postponed tax on any gain, the basis of that home affects the basis of the new home you bought. Keep records proving the basis of both homes as long as they are needed for tax purposes.

You can choose not to take the exclusion by including the gain from the sale in your gross income on your tax return for the year of the sale.

You can use Worksheet 2 in Publication 523 to figure the amount of your exclusion and your taxable gain, if any.

TAXALERT

In addition to paying regular income tax or alternative minimum tax on capital gains, the 3.8% Net Investment Income Tax (NIIT) is assessed on unearned Net Investment Income (NII). NII includes both short- and long-term capital gains, including gains from the sale of residential and investment real estate. The tax will apply to you only if your modified adjusted gross income is in excess of $200,000 (individuals), $250,000 (married filing jointly), or $125,000 (married filing separately). The tax is applied on the gain from the sale of real estate after the exclusion of gain on your main home; i.e., you do not owe the NIIT on any excluded gain. The calculation can be complex and you should consult your tax advisor to determine the application of the NIIT to you.

Maximum Exclusion

You can exclude up to $250,000 of the gain (other than gain allocated to periods of nonqualified use) on the sale of your main home if all of the following are true.

- You meet the ownership test.
- You meet the use test.
- During the 2-year period ending on the date of the sale, you did not exclude gain from the sale of another home.

For details on gain allocated to periods of nonqualified use, see *Periods of nonqualified use*, later.

You may be able to exclude up to $500,000 of the gain (other than gain allocated to periods of nonqualified use) on the sale of your main home if you are married and file a joint return and meet the requirements listed in the discussion of the special rules for joint returns, later, under *Married Persons*.

Ownership and Use Tests

To claim the exclusion, you must meet the ownership and use tests. This means that during the 5-year period ending on the date of the sale, you must have:

- Owned the home for at least 2 years (the ownership test), and
- Lived in the home as your main home for at least 2 years (the use test).

Exception. If you owned and lived in the property as your main home for less than 2 years, you can still claim an exclusion in some cases. However, the maximum amount you may be able to exclude will be reduced. See *Reduced Maximum Exclusion*, later.

Example 1—home owned and occupied for at least 2 years. Mya bought and moved into her main home in September 2012. She sold the home at a gain in October 2014. During the 5-year period ending on the date of sale in October 2014, she owned and lived in the home for more than 2 years. She meets the ownership and use tests.

Example 2—ownership test met but use test not met. Ayden bought a home, lived in it for 6 months, moved out, and never occupied the home again. He later sold the home for a gain. He owned the home during the entire 5-year period ending on the date of sale. He meets the ownership test but not the use test. He cannot exclude any part of his gain on the sale unless he qualified for a reduced maximum exclusion (explained later).

Period of Ownership and Use

The required 2 years of ownership and use during the 5-year period ending on the date of the sale do not have to be continuous nor do they both have to occur at the same time.

You meet the tests if you can show that you owned and lived in the property as your main home for either 24 full months or 730 days (365 × 2) during the 5-year period ending on the date of sale.

EXPLANATION

The home you sold must have been owned and lived in as a principal residence by you for 2 of the 5 years prior to its sale. The key terms to remember are "owned" and "lived in" for 2 years.

Temporary absence. Short temporary absences for vacations or other seasonal absences, even if you rent out the property during the absences, are counted as periods of use. The following examples assume that the reduced maximum exclusion (discussed later) does not apply to the sales.

Example 1. David Johnson, who is single, bought and moved into his home on February 1, 2012. Each year during 2012 and 2013, David left his home for a 2-month summer vacation. David sold the house on March 1, 2014. Although the total time David used his home is less than 2 years (21 months), he meets the requirement and may exclude gain. The 2-month vacations are short temporary absences and are counted as periods of use in determining whether David used the home for the required 2 years.

Example 2. Professor Paul Beard, who is single, bought and moved into a house on August 18, 2011. He lived in it as his main home continuously until January 5, 2013, when he went abroad for a 1-year sabbatical leave. On February 6, 2014, 1 month after returning from the leave, Paul sold the house at a gain. Because his leave was not a short temporary absence, he cannot include the period of leave to meet the 2-year use test. He cannot exclude any part of his gain, because he did not use the residence for the required 2 years.

EXAMPLE

Maurice and Mavis purchased a home in 2008. In 2009, Maurice was transferred overseas for 5 years, during which time the house was rented. When Maurice and Mavis returned in 2014, Maurice's employer sent Maurice to another city in the United States, instead of back to the city where the home was located. Maurice and Mavis sold the original house in 2014 without ever reoccupying it. They are generally not eligible for any exclusion as they did not live in the house at any time during the last 5 years prior to sale.

TAXSAVER

Status of your home. The occupancy status of the home when you sell it is irrelevant. Even if you haven't lived in it for 3 years at the time of sale, the exclusion is still available if you meet the 2-year rule.

Ownership and use tests met at different times. You can meet the ownership and use tests during different 2-year periods. However, you must meet both tests during the 5-year period ending on the date of the sale.

Example. Beginning in 2003, Helen Jones lived in a rented apartment. The apartment building was later converted to condominiums, and she bought her same apartment on December 3, 2011. In 2012, Helen became ill and on April 14 of that year she moved to her daughter's home. On July 12, 2014, while still living in her daughter's home, she sold her condominium.

Helen can exclude gain on the sale of her condominium because she met the ownership and use tests during the 5-year period from July 13, 2009, to July 12, 2014, the date she sold the condominium. She owned her condominium from December 3, 2011, to July 12, 2014 (more than 2 years). She lived in the property from July 13, 2009 (the beginning of the 5-year period), to April 14, 2012 (more than 2 years).

The time Helen lived in her daughter's home during the 5-year period can be counted toward her period of ownership, and the time she lived in her rented apartment during the 5-year period can be counted toward her period of use.

Cooperative apartment. If you sold stock as a tenant-stockholder in a cooperative housing corporation, the ownership and use tests are met if, during the 5-year period ending on the date of sale, you:

- Owned the stock for at least 2 years, and
- Lived in the house or apartment that the stock entitles you to occupy as your main home for at least 2 years.

Exceptions to Ownership and Use Tests
The following sections contain exceptions to the ownership and use tests for certain taxpayers.

Exception for individuals with a disability. There is an exception to the use test if:

- You become physically or mentally unable to care for yourself, and
- You owned and lived in your home as your main home for a total of at least 1 year during the 5-year period before the sale of your home.

Under this exception, you are considered to live in your home during any time within the 5-year period that you own the home and live in a facility (including a nursing home) licensed by a state or political subdivision to care for persons in your condition.

If you meet this exception to the use test, you still have to meet the 2-out-of-5-year ownership test to claim the exclusion.

Previous home destroyed or condemned. For the ownership and use tests, you add the time you owned and lived in a previous home that was destroyed or condemned to the time you owned and lived in the replacement home on whose sale you wish to exclude gain. This rule applies if any part of the basis of the home you sold depended on the basis of the destroyed or condemned home. Otherwise, you must have owned and lived in the same home for 2 of the 5 years before the sale to qualify for the exclusion.

Members of the uniformed services or Foreign Service, employees of the intelligence community, or employees or volunteers of the Peace Corps. You can choose to have the 5-year test period for ownership and use suspended during any period you or your spouse serve on "qualified official extended duty" as a member of the uniformed services or Foreign Service of the United States, or as an employee of the intelligence community. You can choose to have the 5-year test period for ownership and use suspended during any period you or your spouse serve outside the United States either as an employee of the Peace Corps on "qualified official extended duty" or as an enrolled volunteer or volunteer leader of the Peace Corps. This means that you may be able to meet the 2-year use test even if, because of your service, you did not actually live in your home for at least the required 2 years during the 5-year period ending on the date of sale.

If this helps you qualify to exclude gain, you can choose to have the 5-year test period suspended by filing a return for the year of sale that does not include the gain.

For more information about the suspension of the 5-year test period, see *Members of the uniformed services or Foreign Service, employees of the intelligence community, or employees or volunteers of the Peace Corps* in Publication 523.

Married Persons

If you and your spouse file a joint return for the year of sale and one spouse meets the ownership and use tests, you can exclude up to $250,000 of the gain. (But see *Special rules for joint returns*, next.)

Special rules for joint returns. You can exclude up to $500,000 of the gain on the sale of your main home if all of the following are true.
- You are married and file a joint return for the year.
- Either you or your spouse meets the ownership test.
- Both you and your spouse meet the use test.
- During the 2-year period ending on the date of the sale, neither you nor your spouse excluded gain from the sale of another home.

If either spouse does not satisfy all these requirements, the maximum exclusion that can be claimed by the couple is the total of the maximum exclusions that each spouse would qualify for if not married and the amounts were figured separately. For this purpose, each spouse is treated as owning the property during the period that either spouse owned the property.

> **EXAMPLE**
>
> In December 2013, Karen, who is single, sells the home she has been living in as a principal residence for the past 4 years and has a gain of $75,000 on the sale. The entire $75,000 qualifies for the exclusion. On December 31, 2013, Karen marries Ray. On January 2, 2014, Ray sells the home he has owned and been living in as a principal residence for over 2 years and has a gain of $350,000 on the sale. Ray can only exclude $250,000 of the gain even if he and Karen file a joint tax return. The $500,000 exclusion does not apply for two reasons: First, Karen sold her home within the 2-year period ending on the date Ray sold his home; second, Karen did not use Ray's home as her principal residence for at least 2 of the 5 years before the sale.

Example 1—one spouse sells a home. Emily sells her home in June 2014 for a gain of $300,000. She marries Jamie later in the year. She meets the ownership and use tests, but Jamie does not. Emily can exclude up to $250,000 of gain on a separate or joint return for 2014. The $500,000 maximum exclusion for certain joint returns does not apply because Jamie does not meet the use test.

Example 2—each spouse sells a home. The facts are the same as in *Example 1* except that Jamie also sells a home in 2014 for a gain of $200,000 before he marries Emily. He meets the ownership and use tests on his home, but Emily does not. Emily can exclude $250,000 of gain and Jamie can exclude $200,000 of gain on the respective sales of their individual homes. However, Emily cannot use Jamie's unused exclusion to exclude more than $250,000 of gain. Therefore, Emily and Jamie must recognize $50,000 of gain on the sale of Emily's home. The $500,000 maximum exclusion for certain joint returns does not apply because Emily and Jamie do not both meet the use test for the same home.

Sale of main home by surviving spouse. If your spouse died and you did not remarry before the date of sale, you are considered to have owned and lived in the property as your main home during any period of time when your spouse owned and lived in it as a main home.

If you meet all of the following requirements, you may qualify to exclude up to $500,000 of any gain from the sale or exchange of your main home.

- The sale or exchange took place after 2008.
- The sale or exchange took place no more than 2 years after the date of death of your spouse.
- You have not remarried.
- You and your spouse met the use test at the time of your spouse's death.
- You or your spouse met the ownership test at the time of your spouse's death.
- Neither you nor your spouse excluded gain from the sale of another home during the last 2 years.

Example. Harry owned and used a house as his main home since 2010. Harry and Wilma married on July 1, 2014, and from that date they use Harry's house as their main home. Harry died on August 15, 2014, and Wilma inherited the property. Wilma sold the property on September 3, 2014, at which time she had not remarried. Although Wilma owned and used the house for less than 2 years, Wilma is considered to have satisfied the ownership and use tests because her period of ownership and use includes the period that Harry owned and used the property before death.

TAXALERT

If you acquired property from a decedent who died in 2010, special rules may apply in determining tax items including basis, gain, loss, holding period, and character for the property. The 2010 Tax Relief Act allows the executor of the estate of any decedent who died in 2010 to elect not to have the estate tax rules apply and instead to have a modified basis carryover regime apply. This election could impact the amount of tax you owe upon the sale of inherited property. For more information on these rules, see *Property inherited from a decedent who died in 2010*, in chapter 13, *Basis of property*, and Publication 4895, *Tax Treatment of Property Acquired From a Decedent Dying in 2010*.

TAXORGANIZER

If you sold property in 2014 that you originally inherited from a decedent who died during 2010, you should contact the executor of the decedent's estate to confirm the basis in the property you received.

Home transferred from spouse. If your home was transferred to you by your spouse (or former spouse if the transfer was incident to divorce), you are considered to have owned it during any period of time when your spouse owned it.

Use of home after divorce. You are considered to have used property as your main home during any period when:

- You owned it, and
- Your spouse or former spouse is allowed to live in it under a divorce or separation instrument and uses it as his or her main home.

EXPLANATION

The divorce provision removes the old requirement that the home be your residence at the time of sale.

Reduced Maximum Exclusion

If you fail to meet the requirements to qualify for the $250,000 or $500,000 exclusion, you may still qualify for a reduced exclusion. This applies to those who:

- Fail to meet the ownership and use tests, or
- Have used the exclusion within 2 years of selling their current home.

In both cases, to qualify for a reduced exclusion, the sale of your main home must be due to one of the following reasons.

- A change in place of employment.
- Health.
- Unforeseen circumstances.

TAXALERT

In certain cases, you may be able to claim an exclusion from income even though you have not met the ownership and use tests, or if you have sold more than one home during a 2-year period. A reduced maximum exclusion may apply if the sale or exchange is made by reason of a change of place of employment, health, or unforeseen circumstances. The IRS has issued regulations defining when these special exceptions may apply.

The reduced maximum exclusion is computed by multiplying the maximum dollar limitation of $250,000 (or $500,000 in the case of married filing jointly filers) by a fraction. The numerator of the fraction is the shortest of: (1) the period of time that you owned the property during the 5-year period ending on the date of sale; (2) the period of time that you used the property as your principal residence during the 5-year period ending on the date of sale; or (3) the period of time between the date of a prior sale for which you excluded gain and the date of the current sale. The numerator of the fraction may be expressed in days or months. The denominator of the fraction is 730 days or 24 months (depending on the measure of time used in the numerator).

Explanation

If a new place of employment is at least 50 miles farther from the residence sold or exchanged than was the former place of employment, the change of place of employment exception will apply. If this test is not met, you may still qualify for a reduced maximum exclusion under this exception if the facts and circumstances indicate that a change of place of employment was the primary reason for the sale or exchange.

Example

Steve and Tina purchase a home in Boston in 2013. In 2014, Steve's employer transfers him to Chicago. At the time of the transfer, Steve and Tina owned the home as their principal residence for 13 months. They can exclude up to $270,833 of gain ($500,000 times the ratio of 13 months / 24 months).

Explanation

A sale or exchange is due to health reasons if the taxpayer's primary motivation for the sale or exchange is:

- To obtain, provide, or facilitate the diagnosis, cure, mitigation, or treatment of disease, illness, or injury, or
- To obtain or provide medical or personal care for a qualified individual suffering from a disease, illness, or injury.

A sale or exchange is not due to health reasons if it is merely beneficial to the individual's general health or well-being. However, if a doctor recommends a change of residence for health reasons, the primary reason will be deemed to be for health reasons.

Example

Steve and Cheryl live in an upstate community where it snows or is overcast for most of the year. They have owned their current home for less than 2 years. Steve believes that moving to Hawaii will permit them to exercise more and will make them both much happier. Although the move may be beneficial to the couple's general well-being, a sale of their residence will not qualify for an exception to the 2-year ownership and use requirement for health reasons.

Unforeseen circumstances. The sale of your main home is because of an unforeseen circumstance if your primary reason for the sale is the occurrence of an event that you could not reasonably have anticipated before buying and occupying your main home.

See Publication 523 for more information and to use Worksheet 3 to figure your reduced maximum exclusion.

Business Use or Rental of Home

You may be able to exclude gain from the sale of a home you have used for business or to produce rental income. But you must meet the ownership and use tests.

Periods of nonqualified use. In most cases, gain from the sale or exchange of your main home will not qualify for the exclusion to the extent that the gains are allocated to periods of nonqualified use. Nonqualified use is any period after 2008 during which neither you nor your spouse (or your former spouse) used the property as a main home with the following exceptions.

Exceptions. A period of nonqualified use does not include:
1. Any portion of the 5-year period ending on the date of the sale or exchange after the last date you (or your spouse) use the property as a main home;
2. Any period (not to exceed an aggregate period of 10 years) during which you (or your spouse) are serving on qualified official extended duty:
   a. As a member of the uniformed services;
   b. As a member of the Foreign Service of the United States; or
   c. As an employee of the intelligence community; and
3. Any other period of temporary absence (not to exceed an aggregate period of 2 years) due to change of employment, health conditions, or such other unforeseen circumstances as may be specified by the IRS.

The gain resulting from the sale of the property is allocated between qualified and nonqualified use periods based on the amount of time the property was held for qualified and nonqualified use. Gain from the sale or exchange of a main home allocable to periods of qualified use will continue to qualify for the exclusion for the sale of your main home. Gain from the sale or exchange of property allocable to nonqualified use will not qualify for the exclusion.

Calculation. To figure the portion of the gain allocated to the period of nonqualified use, multiply the gain by the following fraction:

$$\frac{\text{Total nonqualified use during the period of ownership after 2008}}{\text{Total period of ownership}}$$

This calculation can be found in Worksheet 2, line 10, in Publication 523.

Example 1. On May 23, 2008, Amy, who is unmarried for all years in this example, bought a house. She moved in on that date and lived in it until May 31, 2010, when she moved out of the house and put it up for rent. The house was rented from June 1, 2010, to March 31, 2012. Amy claimed depreciation deductions in 2010 through 2012 totaling $10,000. Amy moved back into the house on April 1, 2012, and lived there until she sold it on January 31, 2014, for a gain of $200,000. During the 5-year period ending on the date of the sale (January 31, 2009–January 31, 2014), Amy owned and lived in the house for more than 2 years as shown in the following table.

Five Year Period	Used as Home	Used as Rental
1/31/09 – 5/31/10	16 months	
6/1/10 – 3/31/12		22 months
4/1/12 – 1/31/14	22 months	
	38 months	22 months

During the period Amy owned the house (2,080 days), her period of nonqualified use was 670 days. Amy divides 670 by 2,080 and obtains a decimal (rounded to at least three decimal places) of 0.322. To figure her gain attributable to the period of nonqualified use, she multiplies $190,000 (the gain not attributable to the $10,000 depreciation deduction) by 0.322. Because the gain attributable to periods of nonqualified use is $61,180, Amy can exclude $128,820 of her gain.

Example 2. William owned and used a house as his main home from 2008 through 2011. On January 1, 2012, he moved to another state. He rented his house from that date until April 30, 2014, when he sold it. During the 5-year period ending on the date of sale (May 1, 2009–April 30, 2014), William owned and lived in the house for more than 2 years. He must report the sale on Form 4797 because it was rental property at the time of sale. Because the period of nonqualified use does not include any part of the 5-year period after the last date William lived in the house, he has no period of nonqualified use. Because he met the ownership and use tests, he can exclude gain up to $250,000. However, he cannot exclude the part of the gain equal to the depreciation he claimed or could have claimed for renting the house, as explained next.

Depreciation after May 6, 1997. If you were entitled to take depreciation deductions because you used your home for business purposes or as rental property, you cannot exclude the part of your gain equal to any depreciation allowed or allowable as a deduction for periods after May 6, 1997. If you can show by adequate records or other evidence that the depreciation allowed was less than the amount allowable, then you may limit the amount of gain recognized to the depreciation allowed. See Publication 544 for more information.

Property used partly for business or rental. If you used property partly as a home and partly for business or to produce rental income, see Publication 523.

Example

You own a four-unit apartment house. You live in one unit and rent three units. You sell the apartment house for cash. Your records show the following:

Apartment house

Cost...	$80,000
Capital improvements...	20,000
Subtotal..	$100,000
Minus: Depreciation (on three rented units only)...................................	(40,000)
Adjusted basis...	$60,000
Selling price..	$120,000
Selling expense..	$8,000

Because one-fourth of the apartment building is your home, you figure the gain on each portion of the property as follows:

		Personal (1/4)	Rental (3/4)
1)	Selling price...	$30,000	$90,000
2)	Selling expense	(2,000)	(6,000)
3)	Amount realized (adjusted sales price) .... [(1) minus (2)]	$28,000	$84,000
4)	Basis (including improvements)	$25,000	$75,000
5)	Depreciation	-0-	40,000
6)	Adjusted basis [(4) minus (5)].....................................	$25,000	$35,000
7)	Gain [(3) minus (6)]	$3,000	$49,000
Next you figure out your taxable gain:			
8)	Depreciation allowed/allowable....................................	-0-	$40,000
9)	Gain less depreciation [(7) minus (8)]...........................	$3,000	$9,000
10)	Maximum exclusion (prorated).....................................	$62,500	$187,500
11)	Gain excluded (lesser of 9, 10)	$3,000	$9,000
12)	Taxable gain [(7) minus (11)].......................................	-0-	$40,000

$40,000 of the $49,000 total gain ($9,000 is eligible for exclusion) on the three-fourths of the building that was rental property is subject to tax in the year of sale. This gain is reported on Form 4797, *Gains and Losses from Sales or Exchanges of Assets Used in a Trade or Business and Involuntary Conversions.* The gain on the one-fourth that was your home is excluded.

TAXSAVER

Improvements to rental property. If improvements have been made solely to rental units, their cost should be specifically allocated to the rental part of the property. This allocation will decrease the gain on the business portion of the property, which is taxable in the year of sale.

Keep detailed records of improvements. Be careful to specify whether the improvements were made exclusively to either the business or the personal portion of the residence, or whether they improved the residence as a whole.

Example

Jane Smith purchased a two-family house. The two units in the house are identical. Jane rents out one unit and uses the other as her personal residence. The house cost $80,000—$20,000 for the land and $60,000 ($30,000 per unit) for the building. Jane remodeled the kitchen in the rental unit. The remodeling cost $10,000, which is added to the basis of the rental unit, increasing it to $40,000. Because the one unit is rented, depreciation may be calculated based on this $40,000 basis.

When the property is sold, the selling price must be apportioned between the business and personal portions of the residence. If, at the time of sale, the adjusted basis of the rental unit, including the amount allocated to land, is $28,000, and if $60,000 of the selling price is allocated to the rental unit, there would be a taxable gain of $32,000. Without the $10,000 capital expense to remodel the kitchen, the adjusted basis would be only $18,000, increasing the currently taxable gain to $42,000.

Explanation

The apportionment of the selling price between the business and personal portions of a house should be based on the relative fair market value of each portion. Substantial improvements made to each portion of the property should be considered in determining the amount of the selling price that is allocated to each part.

Consequently, the allocation of the sales price, as well as the allocation of the cost of the improvements, may affect the amount of gain to be excluded or taxed on the sale of property used partly as your principal home. Evidence to support a particular allocation of the sales price can include a real estate broker's appraisal or the negotiated terms of the sales contract.

Reporting the Sale

Do not report the 2014 sale of your main home on your tax return unless:

- You have a gain and do not qualify to exclude all of it,
- You have a gain and choose not to exclude it, or
- You received Form 1099-S.

If any of these conditions apply, report the entire gain or loss. For details on how to report the gain or loss, see the Instructions for Schedule D (Form 1040) and the Instructions for Form 8949.

If you used the home for business or to produce rental income, you may have to use Form 4797 to report the sale of the business or rental part (or the sale of the entire property if used entirely for business or rental). See *Business Use or Rental of Home* in Publication 523 and the Instructions for Form 4797.

Installment sale. Some sales are made under arrangements that provide for part or all of the selling price to be paid in a later year. These sales are called "installment sales." If you finance the buyer's purchase of your home yourself instead of having the buyer get a loan or mortgage from a bank, you probably have an installment sale. You may be able to report the part of the gain you cannot exclude on the installment basis.

Use Form 6252, Installment Sale Income, to report the sale. Enter your exclusion on line 15 of Form 6252.

EXPLANATION

If the buyer defaults on an installment sale and the seller repossesses the property, the seller will be required to recognize all of the previously excluded gain on the installment sales received prior to the repossession unless the home is resold within one year.

Example

On January 1, 2000, JR purchased a home for $250,000. He lived in it until January 1, 2012, when he sold the home to Annette for $500,000. Annette agreed to pay $100,000 down and $100,000 on January 1 for the next 4 years. She made the $100,000 downpayment and paid $100,000 on January 1, 2013. JR would have been required to report $50,000 of gain on each payment received; however, the entire gain of $250,000 on the sale of his primary home was excluded and he reported no income as a result of the sale in 2012 or 2013. Annette didn't make a payment on January 1, 2014, and on June 1, 2014, JR repossessed the home. If JR can't sell the home by June 1, 2015, he would be required to report the $100,000 of previously excluded gain as income in 2014.

Seller-financed mortgage. If you sell your home and hold a note, mortgage, or other financial agreement, the payments you receive in most cases consist of both interest and principal. You must separately report as interest income the interest you receive as part of each payment. If the buyer of your home uses the property as a main or second home, you must also report the name, address, and social security number (SSN) of the buyer on line 1 of Schedule B (Form 1040A or 1040). The buyer must give you his or her SSN, and you must give the buyer your SSN. Failure to meet these requirements may result in a $50 penalty for each failure. If either you or the buyer does not have and is not eligible to get an SSN, see *Social Security Number* in chapter 1.

More information. For more information on installment sales, see Publication 537, Installment Sales.

Special Situations
The situations that follow may affect your exclusion.

Sale of home acquired in a like-kind exchange. You cannot claim the exclusion if:
- You acquired your home in a like-kind exchange (also known as a Section 1031 exchange), or your basis in your home is determined by reference to the basis of the home in the hands of the person who acquired the property in a like-kind exchange (for example, you received the home from that person as a gift), and
- You sold the home during the 5-year period beginning with the date your home was acquired in the like-kind exchange.

Gain from a like-kind exchange is not taxable at the time of the exchange. This means that gain will not be taxed until you sell or otherwise dispose of the property you receive. To defer gain from a like-kind exchange, you must have exchanged business or investment property for business or investment property of a like kind. For more information about like-kind exchanges, see Publication 544, Sales and Other Dispositions of Assets.

Home relinquished in a like-kind exchange. If you use your main home partly for business or rental purposes and then exchange the home for another property, see Publication 523.

> ### TAXSAVER
> Under an IRS ruling you can take advantage of both the principal residence gain exclusion and the deferral of gain in a like-kind exchange. For example, assume that you convert your home into rental property after you owned and lived in it for 3 years. Two years after the conversion, you exchange your home in a like-kind exchange. At that time, the cost basis of your home is $400,000 but its fair market value is $1 million. (We won't consider depreciation in this example.) You exchange it for another rental property worth $1 million. Your total gain on the exchange is $600,000 ($1 million less $400,000). You can exclude $250,000 of that gain since you meet the ownership and use tests at the date of sale. The balance of the gain ($600,000 – $250,000, or $350,000) is not currently taxable if the like-kind exchange meets the requirements of the tax law. Your adjusted basis in the new home is the carryover basis from the first residence ($400,000), plus the excluded amount of the gain ($250,000). As a result, your cost basis in the new property will be $650,000 ($400,000 plus $250,000).

Expatriates. You cannot claim the exclusion if the expatriation tax applies to you. The expatriation tax applies to certain U.S. citizens who have renounced their citizenship (and to certain long-term residents who have ended their residency). For more information about the expatriation tax, see *Expatriation Tax* in chapter 4 of Publication 519, U.S. Tax Guide for Aliens.

Home destroyed or condemned. If your home was destroyed or condemned, any gain (for example, because of insurance proceeds you received) qualifies for the exclusion.

Any part of the gain that cannot be excluded (because it is more than the maximum exclusion) can be postponed under the rules explained in:
- Publication 547, in the case of a home that was destroyed, or
- Publication 544, chapter 1, in the case of a home that was condemned.

Sale of remainder interest. Subject to the other rules in this chapter, you can choose to exclude gain from the sale of a remainder interest in your home. If you make this choice, you cannot choose to exclude gain from your sale of any other interest in the home that you sell separately.

Exception for sales to related persons. You cannot exclude gain from the sale of a remainder interest in your home to a related person. Related persons include your brothers, sisters, half-brothers, half-sisters, spouse, ancestors (parents, grandparents, etc.), and lineal descendants (children, grandchildren, etc.). Related persons also include certain corporations, partnerships, trusts, and exempt organizations.

Recapturing (Paying Back) a Federal Mortgage Subsidy
If you financed your home under a federally subsidized program (loans from tax-exempt qualified mortgage bonds or loans with mortgage credit certificates), you may have to recapture all or part of the benefit you received from that program when you sell or otherwise dispose of your home. You

recapture the benefit by increasing your federal income tax for the year of the sale. You may have to pay this recapture tax even if you can exclude your gain from income under the rules discussed earlier; that exclusion does not affect the recapture tax.

Loans subject to recapture rules. The recapture applies to loans that:
1. Came from the proceeds of qualified mortgage bonds, or
2. Were based on mortgage credit certificates.

The recapture also applies to assumptions of these loans.

When recapture applies. Recapture of the federal mortgage subsidy applies only if you meet both of the following conditions.
- You sell or otherwise dispose of your home at a gain within the first 9 years after the date you close your mortgage loan.
- Your income for the year of disposition is more than that year's adjusted qualifying income for your family size for that year (related to the income requirements a person must meet to qualify for the federally subsidized program).

When recapture does not apply. Recapture does not apply in any of the following situations.
- Your mortgage loan was a qualified home improvement loan (QHIL) of not more than $15,000 used for alterations, repairs, and improvements that protect or improve the basic livability or energy efficiency of your home.
- Your mortgage loan was a QHIL of not more than $150,000 in the case of a QHIL used to repair damage from Hurricane Katrina to homes in the hurricane disaster area; a QHIL funded by a qualified mortgage bond that is a qualified Gulf Opportunity Zone Bond; or a QHIL for an owner-occupied home in the Gulf Opportunity Zone (GO Zone), Rita GO Zone, or Wilma GO Zone. For more information, see Publication 4492, Information for Taxpayers Affected by Hurricanes Katrina, Rita, and Wilma. Also see Publication 4492-B, Information for Affected Taxpayers in the Midwestern Disaster Areas.
- The home is disposed of as a result of your death.
- You dispose of the home more than 9 years after the date you closed your mortgage loan.
- You transfer the home to your spouse, or to your former spouse incident to a divorce, where no gain is included in your income.
- You dispose of the home at a loss.
- Your home is destroyed by a casualty, and you replace it on its original site within 2 years after the end of the tax year when the destruction happened. The replacement period is extended for main homes destroyed in a federally declared disaster area, a Midwestern disaster area, the Kansas disaster area, and the Hurricane Katrina disaster area. For more information, see *Replacement Period* in Publication 547.
- You refinance your mortgage loan (unless you later meet the conditions listed previously under *When recapture applies*).

Notice of amounts. At or near the time of settlement of your mortgage loan, you should receive a notice that provides the federally subsidized amount and other information you will need to figure your recapture tax.

How to figure and report the recapture. The recapture tax is figured on Form 8828. If you sell your home and your mortgage is subject to recapture rules, you must file Form 8828 even if you do not owe a recapture tax. Attach Form 8828 to your Form 1040. For more information, see Form 8828 and its instructions.

Chapter 16

Reporting gains and losses

ey.com/EYTaxGuide

Note

IRS Publication 17 (*Your Federal Income Tax*) has been updated by Ernst & Young LLP for 2014. Dates and dollar amounts shown are for 2014. Underlined type is used to indicate where IRS text has been updated. Places where text has been removed are indicated by the sentence: *Text intentionally omitted.*

ey.com/EYTaxGuide

Ernst & Young LLP will update the *Ernst & Young Tax Guide 2015* website with relevant taxpayer information as it becomes available. You can also sign up for email alerts to let you know when changes have been made.

Introduction

One of the best ways to save tax dollars is to generate long-term capital gains, i.e., profits you make from the sale of assets such as stocks, bonds, and real estate. While short-term capital gains are taxed at the same ordinary income tax rates as wages, self-employment income, interest, and nonqualified dividends, special lower tax rates are assessed on long-term capital gains. To qualify for long-term capital gains treatment, you must hold a capital asset for more than 1 year.

The tax benefit of generating long-term capital gains is substantial. The tax rate applied to long-term capital gains depends on your marginal tax bracket. Net long-term capital gains are taxed at a maximum rate of 20% for high income taxpayers who are otherwise in the 39.6% regular income tax bracket (i.e., taxable incomes over $406,750 for individual filers, $432,200 for heads of households, $457,600 married filing jointly, and $228,800 if married filing separately). Net long-term capital gains received by taxpayers in the 10% and 15% tax brackets are taxed at a zero rate. For all others (i.e., taxpayers in the 25%, 28%, 33%, or 35% tax brackets), net long-term capital gains are taxed at 15%. These lower rates apply to both the regular tax and the alternative minimum tax.

Your net capital gain equals net long-term capital gains less net short-term capital losses. On top of the above rates that apply to most long-term capital gains, higher rates apply for certain assets. A 28% rate applies to collectibles held for more than 12 months and to the portion of the gain from the sale of qualified small business stock that is includable in taxable income; a 25% rate applies to real estate gains to the extent of depreciation taken in prior years.

In addition to paying regular income tax or alternative minimum tax on capital gains, the 3.8% Net Investment Income Tax (NIIT) is assessed on unearned Net Investment Income (NII). NII includes both short- and long-term capital gains, other than gains attributable to an active trade or business conducted by a sole proprietor, partnership, or S corporation. For individuals, the NIIT is 3.8% of the lesser of: (1) "net investment income" or (2) the excess of modified adjusted gross income (MAGI) over $200,000 ($250,000 if married filing jointly or a qualifying widow(er) with dependent child; $125,000 if married filing separately).

The tax rate differences between ordinary income and long-term capital gains have a profound effect on tax planning and investment allocation. This chapter will provide you with examples of how the rules work. It also provides advice on year-end planning such as capital gain harvesting.

TAXALERT

For higher income taxpayers, the combination of the 20% maximum tax rate on long-term capital gains and the 3.8% NIIT effectively raises the top tax rate on long-term capital gains to 23.8%. For short-term capital gains, as well as other ordinary income subject to regular income tax rates, the combination of the higher 39.6% marginal tax rate plus the 3.8% NIIT raises the top tax rate on income subject to both taxes to 43.4%.

What's New

50% Exclusion of Qualified Small Business Stock Capital Gains. 50% (60 percent for certain empowerment zone businesses) of the gain from the sale of certain qualified small business stock acquired at original issue after December 31, 2013, or before February 18, 2009, and held for more than five years is excluded from income.

EXPLANATION

The portion of the gain includible in taxable income is taxed at a maximum rate of 28 percent under the regular tax. For alternative minimum tax (AMT) purposes (see chapter 31, *How to figure your tax*), 7% of the amount excluded from gross income is an AMT preference item and is added back to taxable income to arrive at alternative minimum taxable income. See *Gain on qualified small business stock* later in this chapter for more information.

The exclusion is available only to taxpayers that are not corporations. See the **TAXSAVER** *Gain on sale of qualified small business stock* in chapter 14, *Sale of property*, for the rules for determining whether stock is qualified small business stock.

TAXALERT

For qualified small business stock acquired after February 17, 2009, and before September 28, 2010, the exclusion is increased to 75%. For such stock acquired after September 27, 2010, and before January 1, 2014, 100% of the gain is excluded and there is no AMT preference item attributable for that sale.

As of the date this book was published in October 2014, Congress had been considering legislation that would extend the availability of the 100% exclusion and eliminate the AMT preference to qualified stock acquired at least during 2014 and 2015; however, no extension had yet been passed. For updated information on this and any other tax law changes that occur after this book was published, see our website, *ey.com/EYTaxGuide*.

S Corporation Built-In Gains Tax. For tax years beginning in 2014, no tax is imposed on the net recognized built-in gain of an S corporation after the 10th year in the recognition period.

EXPLANATION

When a C corporation elects to become an S corporation, the conversion is not a taxable event. However, following such a conversion, an S corporation must hold on to its assets for a certain period of time. If the S corporation sells an asset sooner (i.e., within 10 calendar years beginning with the first day of the first taxable year for which the S election is in effect), then any built-in gain in such assets that existed at the time of the conversion is taxed to the S corporation at the existing highest marginal tax rate applicable to corporations; currently, 35%.

Under prior law, no tax was imposed on the net recognized built-in gain of an S corporation after the 7th year in the recognition period for taxable years beginning in 2009 and 2010 nor after the 5th year for taxable years beginning in 2011. For tax years beginning in either 2012 or 2013, the recognition period for purposes of determining a net recognized built-in gain was reduced to 5 years.

As of the date this book was published in October 2015, Congress had been considering legislation that would extend the reduced 5-year built-in gains tax holding period that applied for 2012 and 2013 to at least 2014 and 2015 (the U.S. House of Representatives passed legislation that would permanently extend the 5-year recognition period); however, no extension had yet been enacted. For updated information on this and any other tax law changes that occur after this book was published, see our website, *ey.com/EYTaxGuide*.

Text intentionally omitted.

This chapter discusses how to report capital gains and losses from sales, exchanges, and other dispositions of investment property on Form 8949 and Schedule D (Form 1040). The discussion includes the following topics.

- How to report short-term gains and losses.
- How to report long-term gains and losses.
- How to figure capital loss carryovers.
- How to figure your tax on a net capital gain.

If you sell or otherwise dispose of property used in a trade or business or for the production of income, see Publication 544, Sales and Other Dispositions of Assets, before completing Schedule D (Form 1040).

Tax Breaks and Deductions You Can Use Checklist

Lower tax rate on long-term capital gains. Generally, the gain realized from the sale of a capital asset is treated as a long-term capital gain if the property has been held more than one year (i.e., at least one year and a day) as of the date it is sold. The top tax rate on long-term capital gains is 20%, while the top rate on short-term capital gains and ordinary income is 39.6%. Therefore, if compatible with your investment goals, you should try to generate long-term capital gains, rather than short-term capital gains or ordinary income. For more information, see *Reporting Capital Gains and Losses*, later.

Family Tax Planning Opportunity. Given the 0% capital gains rate for low bracket taxpayers, if you have appreciated stock or other capital assets that you plan to sell, consider gifting the asset to your children who are over age 18. (Unearned income of younger children is generally taxed at the marginal rate of the child's parents, as if the parents had received the income, rather than at the child's lower rate. See chapter 32, *Tax on investment income of certain children*, for more information about the so-called "kiddie tax.") To the extent their other taxable income would be taxed at a regular tax rate of less than 25% (i.e., for 2014, taxable income of no more than $36,900 for single returns), they can take advantage of the 0% rate for net capital gains. (For children under age 19, and children age

19-23 who are full-time students, the "kiddie tax" rules can cause the child's income to be taxed at the parent's higher tax rates.) Depending on the value of the asset gifted, there may be gift tax implications. The gift tax exemption is $14,000 per individual in 2014. See chapter 44, *Estate and gift tax planning*, for further information.

Specific identification of share lots or bonds sold. Being able to specifically identify share lots and/or bonds sold provides you with the greatest opportunity to manage the amount of a gain or loss generated, as well as whether that gain or loss is treated as long term or short term. For more information, see *Determination of cost basis and holding period*, later.

Sale of qualified small business stock (QSBS). If you hold qualified small business stock, it is important that you keep track of your holding period to ensure you meet the minimum five-year holding period before you sell the stock to generate the potential tax savings associated with the sale of QSBS as discussed in this chapter and in chapter 14, *Sale of property*.

Useful Items

You may want to see:

Publication
- ☐ **537** Installment Sales
- ☐ **544** Sales and Other Dispositions of Assets
- ☐ **550** Investment Income and Expenses

Form (and Instructions)
- ☐ **4797** Sales of Business Property
- ☐ **6252** Installment Sale Income
- ☐ **8582** Passive Activity Loss Limitations
- ☐ **8949** Sales and Other Dispositions of Capital Assets
- ☐ **Schedule D (Form 1040)** Capital Gains and Losses

TAXALERT

Beginning in 2011, the IRS required brokers to report the adjusted cost basis in addition to the gross proceeds on the sale of "covered securities" and also to report whether the realized gain or loss is long term or short term. "Covered securities" are securities that are purchased or acquired on or after the following effective dates:

Equities. Equity securities are covered securities if they are purchased or acquired on or after January 1, 2011.

Mutual funds and dividend reinvestment plan (DRP) shares. These types of investments are covered if they are purchased or acquired on or after January 1, 2012.

Other specified securities. Basis reporting is required for sales of options and sales of what might be called "simple" debt securities acquired after 2013, and sales of more complex debt securities acquired after 2015. Sales of debt securities with an original term to maturity of one year or less are exempt from basis reporting. Simple debt instruments include:
- Debt instruments with a single fixed rate of interest payable at least annually in cash
- Debt instruments with two or more alternative payment schedules (such as would arise from put and call features) but no other contingencies
- Demand debt instruments with a fixed yield to maturity.

Noncovered securities are those purchased or acquired before the effective dates.

EXPLANATION

In connection with the new basis reporting requirements that took effect in 2011, the IRS replaced Schedule D-1 with Form 8949 for reporting each sale and exchange of capital assets not reported on another form or schedule, gains from involuntary conversions (other than from casualty or theft) of capital assets not held for business or profit, and nonbusiness bad debts. When completing your tax returns, use a separate Form 8949 (Part I for short-term capital gains and losses and Part II for long-term capital gains and losses) for each of the following types of transactions:
1. Form 8949, Box A or Box D – Basis was reported on Form 1099-B and reported to the IRS (Form 1099-B box 3 is completed and box 6b is checked);
2. Form 8949, Box B or Box E – Basis was NOT reported to the IRS (Form 1099-B box 3 may or may not be blank and box 6a is checked);
3. Form 8949, Box C or Box F – Transaction was not reported on Form 1099-B.

You may use as many Forms 8949 as you need to report your transactions. The combined totals from all of your Forms 8949 flow to Schedule D and then to Form 1040.

Exception to reporting each transaction on a separate line. Instead of reporting each of your transactions on a separate line of Form 8949, you can report them on an attached statement containing all the same information as Form 8949 and in a similar format. Use as many attached statements as you need. Enter the combined totals from all of your attached statements on a Form 8949 with the appropriate box checked. For example, report on line 1 of Form 8949 with box D checked all long-term gains and losses from transactions your broker reported to you on a statement showing that the basis of the property sold was reported to the IRS. If you have statements from more than one broker, report the totals from each broker on a separate line.

> Do not enter "available upon request" and summary totals in lieu of reporting the details of each transaction on Form(s) 8949 or attached statements.
>
> **E-file.** If you e-file your return, but choose not to include your transactions on the electronic short-term capital gain (or loss) or long-term capital gain (or loss) records, you must attach Form 8949 (or a statement with the same information) to Form 8453, *U.S. Individual Income Tax Transmittal for an IRS e-file Return,* and mail the forms to the IRS. See chapter 45, *Everything you need to know about e-filing,* for additional information.

Reporting Capital Gains and Losses

Generally, report capital gains and losses on Form 8949. Complete Form 8949 before you complete line 1b, 2, 3, 8b, 9, or 10 of Schedule D (Form 1040).

Use Form 8949 to report:

- The sale or exchange of a capital asset not reported on another form or schedule;
- Gains from involuntary conversions (other than from casualty or theft) of capital assets not held for business or profit; and
- Nonbusiness bad debts.

Use Schedule D (Form 1040):

- To figure the overall gain or loss from transactions reported on Form 8949;
- To report a gain from Form 6252 or Part I of Form 4797;
- To report a gain or loss from Form 4684, 6781, or 8824;
- To report capital gain distributions not reported directly on Form 1040 or Form 1040A;
- To report a capital loss carryover from the previous tax year to the current tax year;
- To report your share of a gain or (loss) from a partnership, S corporation, estate, or trust;
- To report transactions reported to you on a Form 1099-B (or substitute statement) showing basis was reported to the IRS and to which none of the Form 8949 adjustments or codes apply; and
- To report undistributed long-term capital gains from Form 2439.

On Form 8949, enter all sales and exchanges of capital assets, including stocks, bonds, etc., and real estate (if not reported on Form 4684, 4797, 6252, 6781, 8824, or line 1a or 8a of Schedule D). Include these transactions even if you did not receive a Form 1099-B or 1099-S (or substitute statement) for the transaction. Report short-term gains or losses in Part I. Report long-term gains or losses in Part II. Use as many Forms 8949 as you need.

Exceptions to filing Form 8949 and Schedule D (Form 1040). There are certain situations where you may not have to file Form 8949 and/or Schedule D (Form 1040).

Exception 1. You do not have to file Form 8949 or Schedule D (Form 1040) if you have no capital losses and your only capital gains are capital gain distributions from Form(s) 1099-DIV, box 2a (or substitute statements). (If any Form(s) 1099-DIV (or substitute statements) you receive have an amount in box 2b (unrecaptured Section 1250 gain), box 2c (Section 1202 gain), or box 2d (collectibles (28%) gain), you do not qualify for this exception.) If you qualify for this exception, report your capital gain distributions directly on line 13 of Form 1040 (and check the box on line 13). Also use the Qualified Dividends and Capital Gain Tax Worksheet in the Form 1040 instructions to figure your tax. You can report your capital gain distributions on line 10 of Form 1040A, instead of on Form 1040, if none of the Forms 1099-DIV (or substitute statements) you received have an amount in box 2b, 2c, or 2d, and you do not have to file Form 1040.

Exception 2. You must file Schedule D (Form 1040), but generally do not have to file Form 8949, if *Exception 1* does not apply and your only capital gains and losses are:

- Capital gain distributions;
- A capital loss carryover;
- A gain from Form 2439 or 6252 or Part I of Form 4797;
- A gain or loss from Form 4684, 6781, or 8824;
- A gain or loss from a partnership, S corporation, estate, or trust; or
- Gains and losses from transactions for which you received a Form 1099-B (or substitute statement) that shows the basis was reported to the IRS and for which you do not need to make any adjustments in column (g) of Form 8949 or enter any codes in column (f) of Form 8949.

EXPLANATION

Use Part I, Line 1a, or Part II, Line 8a for gains and losses from transactions for which you received a Form 1099-B (or substitute statement) that shows that basis was reported to the IRS and for which you do not need to make any adjustments in column (g) of Form 8949 and do not need to enter any codes in column (f) of Form 8949.

EXPLANATION

Characterizing your gain or loss. When you sell or dispose of property, you must determine whether your gain or loss is capital or ordinary. Only capital gains and capital losses are reported on Form 8949 and Schedule D, while ordinary gains and losses are reported elsewhere. This distinction is significant because (1) you can use capital losses to offset gains only to the extent of capital gains plus $3,000 and (2) net capital gains may be subject to a lower tax rate than ordinary income. Any unused capital losses can be carried over to the next year.

Example

Assume that Alan is married filing a joint return and has $12,000 of capital losses and $4,000 of capital gains in 2014. Alan can deduct only $7,000 of his capital losses in 2014, which is equal to his $4,000 of capital gains plus $3,000. The remaining $5,000 of losses ($12,000 gross losses minus $7,000 of losses used) may be carried over and used in later years, subject to the $3,000 limitation. If Alan's filing status was married filing separately, his capital loss limitation would be $1,500 instead of $3,000. If Alan's losses were ordinary, he could have used all of them in 2014 unless subject to other limitations by special provisions of the Internal Revenue Code.

EXPLANATION

Determining your capital gains rate. The capital gains rate depends on the type of property sold, the holding period prior to sale, and your overall income level. Short-term capital gains are subject to ordinary income rates. Net capital gains are the excess of: (1) net long-term capital gains, over (2) net short-term capital losses.

For 2014, the top marginal ordinary income tax rate—which applies to short-term capital gains—is 39.6%. This rate applies to taxpayers with taxable incomes over $406,750 for individual filers, $432,200 for heads of households, $457,600 married filing jointly, and $228,800 for married filing separately. The top rate on net capital gains (defined as the excess of net long-term capital gains over net short-term capital losses) is 20% for high income taxpayers who are otherwise in the 39.6% regular income tax bracket. Net capital gains received by taxpayers in the 10% and 15% tax brackets are not subject to federal income tax; i.e., they are taxed at a 0% rate. For taxpayers in the 25%, 28%, 33%, or 35% tax brackets, net capital gains are taxed at 15%. These lower rates on net capital gains apply to both the regular tax and the alternative minimum tax.

You can achieve substantial tax savings by generating long-term capital gains in lieu of short-term capital gains or ordinary income, to which applicable ordinary tax rates are generally greater.

(In addition to paying regular income tax or alternative minimum tax on capital gains, the 3.8% Net Investment Income Tax (NIIT) is assessed on unearned Net Investment Income (NII). NII includes both short- and long-term capital gains, other than gains attributable to an active trade or business conducted by a sole proprietor, partnership, or S corporation. For individuals, the NIIT is 3.8% of the lesser of: (1) "net investment income" or (2) the excess of modified adjusted gross income (MAGI) over $200,000 ($250,000 if married filing jointly or a qualifying widow(er) with dependent child; $125,000 if married filing separately). These threshold dollar amounts are not be indexed each year for inflation. For more information, see *Net Investment Income Tax*, later.)

Example

Erik bought 3,000 shares of ABC Company on April 1, 2013, when the price of the stock was $20 per share. On May 1, 2014, he sold all of his ABC holdings for $25 per share, realizing a profit of $15,000. Erik files a joint return with his wife showing a combined taxable income that places him in the 39.6% tax bracket. Because he held the ABC stock for more than 12 months, Erik is eligible for the favorable capital gain tax rates. As a 39.6% taxpayer, his long-term capital gain on ABC stock would be taxed at 20%. (This example does not consider the calculation of the 3.8% Net Investment Income Tax that applies to higher income taxpayers.)

TAXPLANNER

Long-term capital gains vs. ordinary income. The difference between the top marginal rate on ordinary taxable income including short-term capital gains of 39.6% and the top rate on net capital gains of 20% is significant—a 19.6% difference. Since the long-term capital gain rate is much lower than ordinary rates, you should try to generate long-term capital gains whenever possible. It should be noted, however, that the tax law recharacterizes gains from certain conversion transactions into ordinary income. See later in this chapter for an explanation of conversion transactions.

Example

Nancy is in the 39.6% marginal tax bracket for 2014 and has the following unrealized capital gains and losses:

Stock A: Unrealized short-term capital gain	$10,000
Stock B: Unrealized long-term capital loss	($13,000)
Stock C: Unrealized long-term capital gain	$15,000

Assume that Nancy sells all three stocks in 2014. Nancy will compute her net capital gain for the year as follows:

Net long-term capital gain	$2,000
Net short-term capital gain	$10,000
Total gains	$12,000

Nancy has a net capital gain of $12,000. Nancy will pay $400 of tax on her net long-term capital gain ($2,000 × 20%) and $3,960 on her short-term capital gains, which are taxed at her regular 39.6% rate ($10,000 × 39.6%). Thus, Nancy will pay a total tax of $4,360 ($400 + $3,960) on her capital gains. Additionally, assuming the 3.8% Net Investment Income Tax (NIIT) tax applies, Nancy will be subject to an additional tax of $456 ($12,000 × 3.8%).

Assume instead that Nancy sells stocks A and B in 2014, but waits until 2015 to sell stock C.

Nancy will have a net long-term capital loss of $3,000 for 2014 ($10,000 gain on stock A, less $13,000 loss on stock B). Nancy will be allowed to offset the $3,000 capital loss against her ordinary income, giving her a $1,188 tax saving for 2014.

Nancy will also have a $15,000 net long-term capital gain in 2015 from the sale of stock C. This will represent a net capital gain subject to the maximum 20% rate on net capital gains. Nancy will pay $3,000 of tax in 2015 on her net capital gain ($15,000 × 20%).

By using tax planning, Nancy's total liability on her capital gains would be $1,812 ($3,000 for 2015, less $1,188 of tax savings in 2014). As compared to the $4,360 of tax liability without tax planning, Nancy has saved $2,548. Additionally, assuming the 3.8% NIIT applies to Nancy's $15,000 net capital gain in 2015, she will be subject to an additional tax of $570 ($15,000 × 3.8%) in 2015. Nancy delayed the payment of the tax by waiting until 2015 to trigger some of her gains.

The tax savings to Nancy may be small relative to the investment ramifications of holding stock C for a longer period. Nancy must therefore balance the potential tax savings against her overall investment strategy.

EXPLANATION

A capital gain or loss results from (1) the sale or exchange of a capital asset or (2) net Section 1231 gains being treated as a capital gain.

Almost everything you own and use for personal or investment purposes is a capital asset. For example, stocks, bonds, artwork, jewelry, and household furnishings generally are all capital assets. Most properties held in a business (e.g., inventory, accounts receivable, machinery) are not capital assets. See chapter 14, *Sale of property*, for a further explanation on what constitutes a capital asset.

A net Section 1231 gain is also treated as a capital gain, while a net Section 1231 loss is treated as an ordinary loss. A Section 1231 gain or loss is any gain or loss from the sale or exchange of real property or depreciable personal property used in your trade or business and held by you for more than 1 year. Any depreciation recapture must be separately computed on the sale of depreciable property and reported as ordinary income. Thus, the portion of the gain that is considered depreciation recapture is ordinary income, rather than a Section 1231 gain. The computation of depreciation recapture is discussed in more detail at the end of this chapter.

Section 1231 gains also include recognized gains on the involuntary conversion of (1) property used in a trade or a business and held for more than 1 year, and (2) any capital asset held for more than 1 year and held in connection with a trade or a business or a transaction entered into for profit. Net involuntary conversion losses on these properties are not Section 1231 losses, and instead are deductible as ordinary losses. An involuntary conversion is the loss of property resulting from destruction (complete or partial), theft, seizure, requisition, or condemnation. An involuntary conversion also includes the sale or exchange of property under the threat or imminence of seizure, requisition, or condemnation.

For more information, see Publication 544, *Sales and Other Dispositions of Assets*.

Tax treatment of gains and losses. Once the disposition is properly classified, you can determine whether your gains and losses will be considered ordinary, capital, or, in the case of losses, nondeductible.

Losses on the sale of personal-use property (e.g., a family car, jewelry) cannot be used to offset capital gains and are not reported on your income tax return. Capital gains on the sale of personal-use property are taxable and should be reported on Form 8949.

You must aggregate all of your Section 1231 gains and losses during the year to determine the tax treatment of these items. Net Section 1231 gains are treated as capital, while net Section 1231 losses are treated as ordinary. Under a special look-back rule, if you have a net Section 1231 gain in 2014, the gain will be treated as ordinary income to the extent of any Section 1231 losses in the preceding 5 years (which were not previously used to recharacterize gains). Remember, any gain resulting in depreciation recapture is ordinary income and as a result is not considered in these computations. You should fill out Form 4797 to report these items. Ordinary gains and losses are generally reported separately on Form 1040 when arriving at adjusted gross income, while capital gains are reported on Schedule D.

Capital gains and losses reported on Schedule D and Form 8949 are further classified under long term and short term. Net Section 1231 gains are long term. For other classifications, see the discussion in chapter 14, *Sale of property*. For the limitation of Section 1231 losses that are classified as passive losses, see Passive activity gains and losses, later.

TAXALERT
Recharacterizing capital gains. The Internal Revenue Code contains a provision that recharacterizes capital gains from certain conversion transactions as ordinary income. The purpose of this provision is to prohibit taxpayers from taking advantage of the favorable tax rate on capital gains by entering into transactions that are in effect loans, but because of their form generate capital gains. In a conversion transaction, the taxpayer is in the economic position of a lender and substantially all of the taxpayer's return is attributable to the amount of time the investment is held. A transaction will be treated as a conversion transaction, if it contains at least one of the following four elements: (1) the transaction consists of the acquisition of property by the taxpayer and a substantially contemporaneous agreement to sell the same or substantially identical property in the future; (2) the transaction is a straddle (see chapter 14, *Sale of property*); (3) the transaction is one that is marketed or sold to the taxpayer on the basis that it would have the economic characteristics of a loan, but the interest-like return would be taxed as capital gain; or (4) the transaction is described in regulations promulgated by the Secretary of the Treasury.

Installment sales. You cannot use the installment method to report a gain from the sale of stock or securities traded on an established securities market. You must report the entire gain in the year of sale (the year in which the trade date occurs).

TAXALERT
Date of installment payments. For purposes of the dates that determine when capital gains are taxed, the date you receive an installment payment governs, not the actual date of sale.

Passive activity gains and losses. If you have gains or losses from a passive activity, you may also have to report them on Form 8582. In some cases, the loss may be limited under the passive activity rules. Refer to Form 8582 and its instructions for more information about reporting capital gains and losses from a passive activity.

EXPLANATION
The gain or loss realized upon the sale or disposition of an interest in a passive activity must be combined with other items of income, expense, gain, or loss from investments in passive activities in order to determine the amount of passive activity losses that will be deductible on Form 1040. See chapter 12, *Other income*, for more information.

Form 1099-B transactions. If you sold property, such as stocks, bonds, or certain commodities, through a broker, you should receive Form 1099-B or substitute statement from the broker. Use the Form 1099-B or the substitute statement to complete Form 8949. If you sold a covered security in 2014, your broker should send you a Form 1099-B (or substitute statement) that shows your basis. This will help you complete Form 8949. Generally, a covered security is a security you acquired after 2010.

Report the gross proceeds shown in box <u>1d</u> of Form 1099-B as the sales price in column (d) of either Part I or Part II of Form 8949, whichever applies. *Text intentionally omitted.*

Include in column (g) any expense of sale, such as broker's fees, commissions, state and local transfer taxes, and option premiums, unless you reported the net sales price in column (d). If you include an expense of sale in column (g), enter "E" in column (f).

Form 1099-CAP transactions. If a corporation in which you own stock has had a change in control or a substantial change in capital structure, you should receive Form 1099-CAP or a substitute statement from the corporation. Use the Form 1099-CAP or substitute statement to fill in Form 8949. If your computations show that you would have a loss because of the change, do not enter any amounts on Form 8949 or Schedule D (Form 1040). You cannot claim a loss on Schedule D (Form 1040) as a result of this transaction.

Report the aggregate amount received shown in box 2 of Form 1099-CAP as the sales price in column (d) of either Part I or Part II of Form 8949, whichever applies.

Form 1099-S transactions. If you sold or traded reportable real estate, you generally should receive from the real estate reporting person a Form 1099-S showing the gross proceeds.

"Reportable real estate" is defined as any present or future ownership interest in any of the following:

- Improved or unimproved land, including air space;
- Inherently permanent structures, including any residential, commercial, or industrial building;
- A condominium unit and its accessory fixtures and common elements, including land; and
- Stock in a cooperative housing corporation (as defined in Section 216 of the Internal Revenue Code).

A "real estate reporting person" could include the buyer's attorney, your attorney, the title or escrow company, a mortgage lender, your broker, the buyer's broker, or the person acquiring the biggest interest in the property.

Your Form 1099-S will show the gross proceeds from the sale or exchange in box 2. See the Instructions for Form 8949 and the Instructions for Schedule D (Form 1040) for how to report these transactions and include them in Part I or Part II of Form 8949 as appropriate. However, report like-kind exchanges on Form 8824 instead.

It is unlawful for any real estate reporting person to separately charge you for complying with the requirement to file Form 1099-S.

EXPLANATION

See chapter 15, *Selling your home*, for further instructions on Form 1099-S received for the sale of your home and when to report the sale on Form 8949.

EXPLANATION

Amounts reported to you on Form 1099-B are also reported to the IRS. The IRS matches the amounts reported on Forms 1099-B to your return to ensure you reported all of your security sales. The amounts reported on Forms 1099-B should equal the sum of the amounts on Form(s) 8949, all line(s) 2, columns (d) and (e), if applicable. There may be up to 6 Line 2's, Part I, Box A, B, C and Part II Box D, E, F. If not, you will probably receive a letter from the IRS asking you to explain the difference. If the amounts are different, you should attach a schedule to your return explaining the reason for the inconsistency.

TAXORGANIZER

Documents you need to complete Form(s) 8949 and Schedule D. Taxpayers who sell stocks, bonds, or other property through a broker should maintain the following documentation in order to facilitate the completion of Form(s) 8949 and Schedule D:

- **Confirmations received from the broker documenting all sales transactions executed.** You can use these to ensure the accuracy of any Forms 1099-B received.
- **Confirmations received from the broker documenting all purchase transactions executed.** You may need these to calculate any gains or losses realized upon the sale of the property and to determine if you have long-term or short-term gains and losses to the extent the broker is not yet required to report the cost basis on Form 1099-B for the particular property you sold. Alternatively, if your broker reports the cost basis on your Form 1099-B, the purchase confirmation ensures the accuracy of the purchase price and date of acquisition.

TAXPLANNER

Real property tax. A person reporting a real estate transaction is also responsible for including the portion of any real property tax that is properly allocable to the purchaser on Form 1099-S. A person reports any property tax allocable from the date of sale to year-end on Form 1099-S. Note though, that if the purchaser agrees to pay the taxes the seller owed on the new home (up to the date of sale), these taxes are not treated as taxes paid by the purchaser, but are instead treated as part of the purchaser's cost. Accordingly, these amounts are not included on Form 1099-S as real property tax allocable to the purchaser. Instead, these amounts are included on Form 1099-S as part of the seller's proceeds.

Nominees. If you receive gross proceeds as a nominee (that is, the gross proceeds are in your name but actually belong to someone else), see the Instructions for Form 8949 for how to report these amounts on Form 8949.

File Form 1099-B or Form 1099-S with the IRS. If you received gross proceeds as a nominee in 2014, you must file a Form 1099-B or Form 1099-S for those proceeds with the IRS. Send the Form 1099-B or Form 1099-S with a Form 1096, Annual Summary and Transmittal of U.S. Information Returns, to your Internal Revenue Service Center by March 2, 2015 (March 31, 2015, if you file Form 1099-B or Form 1099-S electronically). Give the actual owner of the proceeds Copy B of the Form 1099-B or Form 1099-S by February 17, 2015. On Form 1099-B, you should be listed as the "Payer." The other owner should be listed as the "Recipient." On Form 1099-S, you should be listed as the "Filer." The other owner should be listed as the "Transferor." You do not have to file a Form 1099-B or Form 1099-S to show proceeds for your spouse. For more information about the reporting requirements and the penalties for failure to file (or furnish) certain information returns, see the General Instructions for Certain Information Returns. If you are filing electronically see Publication 1220.

Sale of property bought at various times. If you sell a block of stock or other property that you bought at various times, report the short-term gain or loss from the sale on one row in Part I of Form 8949, and the long-term gain or loss on one row in Part II of Form 8949. Write "Various" in column (b) for the "Date acquired."

Sale expenses. On Form 8949, include in column (g) any expense of sale, such as broker's fees, commissions, state and local transfer taxes, and option premiums, unless you reported the net sales price in column (d). If you include an expense of sale in column (g), enter "E" in column (f).

For more information about adjustments to basis, see chapter 13.

EXPLANATION

Most property you own and use for personal purposes or for pleasure, such as your house, furniture, and car, falls under the category of capital assets. Any gain you recognize on the sale of this kind of property is treated as a capital gain, but you are not permitted to recognize a capital loss for income tax purposes unless the property was used for business or investment purposes. If you realize a loss on property used both for business and personal purposes, the portion of the loss that is allocated to the business portion of the property may be recognized, but you are precluded from recognizing the portion attributable to personal use.

Short-term gains and losses. Capital gain or loss on the sale or trade of investment property held 1 year or less is a short-term capital gain or loss. You report it in Part I of Form 8949.

You combine your share of short-term capital gain or loss from partnerships, S corporations, estates, and trusts, and any short-term capital loss carryover, with your other short-term capital gains and losses to figure your net short-term capital gain or loss on line 7 of Schedule D (Form 1040).

Long-term gains and losses. A capital gain or loss on the sale or trade of investment property held more than 1 year is a long-term capital gain or loss. You report it in Part II of Form 8949.

EXPLANATION

The shortest length of time that qualifies for long-term status is 1 year plus 1 day. To calculate this period, your holding period begins on the day after you buy the property and includes the day you sell it.

Example

Donald pays $1,000 for Corporation X stock on August 1, 2013. His holding period begins on August 2, 2013. Donald sells the stock on August 1, 2014, for $1,500. His holding period runs from August 2, 2013 (the day after he purchased the stock), through August 1, 2014 (the day he sold the stock). Donald has a short-term capital gain of $500 because he has held the stock for exactly 1 year.

Assume instead that Donald sells the stock on August 2, 2014. His holding period runs from August 2, 2013, through August 2, 2014. His holding period is now in excess of 1 year (1 year and 1 day), so Donald's gain will be long term.

You report the following in Part II of Schedule D (Form 1040):
- Undistributed long-term capital gains from a mutual fund (or other regulated investment company) or real estate investment trust (REIT);
- Your share of long-term capital gains or losses from partnerships, S corporations, estates, and trusts;
- All capital gain distributions from mutual funds and REITs not reported directly on line 10 of Form 1040A or line 13 of Form 1040; and
- Long-term capital loss carryovers.

The result after combining these items with your other long-term capital gains and losses is your net long-term capital gain or loss (Schedule D (Form 1040), line 15).

EXPLANATION

Dividends from mutual funds, which are technically known as regulated investment companies, are frequently composed of a combination of long-term capital gains and ordinary income. The nature of the gain is determined by how long the mutual fund has held the underlying property that generates the income, not how long you have held the mutual fund shares. Consequently, you may realize a long-term capital gain, although you have held the mutual fund shares for less than the required long-term holding period.

Determination of cost basis and holding period. Mutual fund shares may be acquired on various dates, in various quantities, and at various prices. Some individuals may purchase shares through participation in a dividend reinvestment plan or a payroll deduction plan. Shares may also be sold on a periodic basis. As a result, individuals often encounter difficulty in determining their cost basis and gain or loss on the sale of their mutual fund shares. Mutual fund shareholders have three options for determining the cost basis of their shares. They are as follows:

1. The specific identification method.
2. The FIFO (first in, first out) method.
3. The single-category method using the average approach.

   Effective April 1, 2011, the IRS eliminated a fourth category, which was the double-category method. If you used the double-category method for shares you acquired before and sold after April 1, 2011, the average basis of your shares is calculated by averaging together all identical shares in the account on April 1, 2011.

The specific identification method. In order to specifically identify the shares sold, the following requirements must be met:

1. Specific instructions to the broker or agent must be given by the customer, indicating the particular shares to be sold. These instructions must be given at the time of sale or transfer.
2. Written *confirmation* of this request must be received from the broker or agent within a reasonable time after the sale.

   The individual shareholder bears the burden of proof that he or she owned and chose to sell the specific shares at the time of sale.

TAXPLANNER

Managing gains and losses. The specific identification method provides an investor with the greatest opportunity to manage his or her reported gain or loss. For example, if a shareholder has other capital losses during the year and wishes to generate capital gains, he or she can specifically identify those shares acquired at the *lowest prices* as the shares being sold. One problem with this method, particularly with mutual funds, is the inability of transfer agents to confirm specific shares sold to the shareholder in writing.

EXPLANATION

The FIFO method. Under the FIFO (first in, first out) method, the basis of shares acquired first represents the cost of the shares sold. In other words, the oldest shares held by the taxpayer are considered to be the first sold. The FIFO method is also a default method for the sales of securities other than the sale of mutual funds or dividend reinvestment plan (DRP) stock. If specific identification procedures are not or cannot be followed and the average basis approach (discussed below) is not elected, then the FIFO method will apply. Brokers must report the adjusted basis of mutual fund or DRP stock (for which a customer may average the basis of stock) in accordance with the broker's default method unless the broker is notified in writing that a different permitted method is elected.

TAXSAVER

Trap for the unwary. In a rising market, the FIFO method generally produces the greatest gain (and least loss) and hence, generally, the most tax.

EXPLANATION

The single-category method using the average approach. The average basis method for non-covered securities (as defined earlier in this chapter) must be elected by the individual shareholder on his or her income tax return for the first taxable year for which the election applies and must indicate on such return that the average basis method was used to report the gain or loss on the sale or disposition of the securities. If you acquired the securities by gift and would like to elect the average basis method, you should consult your tax advisor regarding specific language that must be included in the statement you need to attach to your tax return to make this election. You must maintain adequate records to support the average cost basis reported on your return.

You can elect the average basis method for covered securities (as defined earlier in this chapter) by notifying your broker of the election in writing or you may make a written average basis election electronically. You may elect the average basis method at any time and the election takes effect for sales that occur after the election. To make the election for securities acquired by gift, you should consult your broker regarding specific language that must be included with your election. The election is made separately for each account holding or you may specify that it applies to all accounts with the particular broker including future accounts yet to be created.

You may revoke an average basis election by the earlier of one year from the date of making the election or the first sale or other disposition of the stock following the election. After a revocation, your stock basis is the basis before averaging. However, you may change from the average basis method to another permissible method prospectively. You are not limited to the number of times or the frequency at which you can change your basis determination method. Following a change, your stock basis remains the same as the basis immediately before the change.

The average method permits the taxpayer to calculate his or her gain or loss based on the average price paid for the shares. With the single-category method, all shares are included in a single category; that is, the basis of each share is the total adjusted basis of all shares at the time of disposition divided by the total shares. In determining the holding period (long- or short-term), the shares disposed of are considered to be those shares acquired *first* (using a FIFO-type method, discussed earlier).

TAXALERT

Prior to 2012, if an average basis election was made, it was required to apply to all shares of a particular mutual fund in all accounts in which you held shares of that fund. Starting in 2012, you may elect to use average basis for shares of a particular mutual fund held in one account but not apply average basis to shares of that particular fund held in another account. If you elect to average the basis of mutual fund shares, you will compute separate averages for fund shares held in different accounts. Further, unless the fund or broker holding the fund shares elects otherwise, you will compute a separate average for fund shares in an account that is covered securities and a separate average for fund shares in an account that is not covered securities.

Beginning in 2012, mutual funds and DRP stocks that are a noncovered security are treated as being held in a separate account from stock that is a covered security. Because stock is averaged on an account-by-account basis starting in 2012, the basis of shares that are covered securities will be the average basis of only the covered securities and the basis of the shares that are noncovered securities will be the average basis of only the noncovered securities. However, if a broker has accurate basis information for shares that are noncovered securities and makes a "single-account election" for some or all of the shares, the shares subject to the single-account election are treated as covered securities and their basis is averaged along with the shares that are covered securities.

TAXPLANNER

Since the IRS eliminated the double category method for all mutual fund sales occurring on or after April 1, 2011, taxpayers must calculate the average basis of all identical shares in the account regardless of holding period.

TAXPLANNER

Under the new basis reporting rules, brokers are required to track adjusted cost basis for mutual fund and DRP shares acquired on or after January 1, 2012. The basis of mutual fund stock purchased prior to January 1, 2012, could be reported using any acceptable method (i.e., FIFO, specific identification, or average cost); however, for stock acquired after December 31, 2011, brokers must track adjusted cost basis in accordance with their default method unless a taxpayer notifies the broker in writing to elect a different method. As the broker is not required to inform you of their default method, you can contact your broker to find out their elected default method and their procedures for you as the shareowner to utilize another method.

EXPLANATION

Mutual fund dividends. If an individual who purchases shares in a mutual fund receives a capital gain distribution and then sells the shares at a loss within 6 months after purchase, the loss is treated as a *long-term* capital loss to the extent of the capital gain distribution received. The rationale behind this rule is to prevent taxpayers from purchasing stock in a mutual fund to receive the capital gain distribution and then turn around and sell the stock at a loss when the fund's value decreases as a result of the distributions. Without the rule, the capital gain distribution would be taxed at the lower long-term capital gain rate and the short-term capital loss would be available to offset other short-term capital gains taxed at the higher ordinary income tax rate.

Example

You pay $10,000 for ABC Mutual Fund on June 30. On July 1, ABC Mutual Fund pays you a long-term capital gain distribution of $1,000. The same day, the value of your ABC shares drops to $9,000. The $1,000 capital gain distribution will be taxed at the lower long-term rate. If the stock is sold within six months at a $1,000 loss, the loss will offset the capital gain distribution at the same lower long-term rate. If the stock is sold after six months but less than one year, the loss will offset gains at the higher short-term rate.

TAXSAVER

When to generate losses. If at the end of the year you find that you only have short-term capital gains, you might consider generating capital losses by selling assets that have declined in value. Short-term gains are taxed as ordinary income, but you can avoid paying tax on them by offsetting them against both short-term and long-term losses. However, if you sell stock or securities at a loss and then acquire substantially identical securities within 30 days before or 30 days after the sale, your loss may be disallowed in the year of sale. The purpose of this "wash sale" rule is to prevent taxpayers from generating losses on securities when the taxpayers remain in the same economic position after the sale.

EXPLANATION

Sales or load charges. When a person invests in a mutual fund, he or she may be subject to a sales or load charge, which is similar to a commission. When shares are sold or redeemed, the sales or load charge is generally taken into account as part of the purchaser's basis for purposes of computing gain or loss on the sale.

If an investor exchanges shares in a mutual fund for shares in the same "family" of funds or "complex" of funds, an additional sales or load charge may be waived or reduced if the investor acquires a reinvestment right (i.e., the right to acquire stock of one or more mutual funds without the payment of all or part of the standard load charge) on the original purchase. If such an exchange occurs within 90 days of the original purchase of mutual fund shares, the original sales or load charge will not be included as basis in determining the gain or loss on the exchange. This rule only applies to the extent that the additional sales or load charge is waived or reduced on the exchange. To the extent that the sales charge or load charge is not treated as basis in computing gain or loss, such a charge will be taken into account when you subsequently sell the shares.

Example

On February 1, Kurt Norton purchased 100 shares of mutual fund A for $110, which included a $10 sales or load charge. On February 22, of the same year Kurt exchanged these shares for 50 shares of mutual fund B, worth $115. Mutual fund B is in the same family as mutual fund A. The sales or load charge of $10 on Kurt's purchase of mutual fund B was waived. Kurt's gain or loss on the exchange is computed as follows:

Sales price of mutual fund A	$115
Cost basis of mutual fund A	(100)
Gain (loss)	$15

The sales or load charge of $10 on the purchase of mutual fund A did not affect the taxable gain or loss on the exchange but will become part of the basis of mutual fund B.

For more about mutual funds see chapter 39, *Mutual funds*.

Total net gain or loss. To figure your total net gain or loss, combine your net short-term capital gain or loss (Schedule D (Form 1040), line 7) with your net long-term capital gain or loss (Schedule D (Form 1040), line 15). Enter the result on Schedule D (Form 1040), Part III, line 16. If your losses are more than your gains, see *Capital Losses*, next. If both lines 15 and 16 of your Schedule D (Form 1040) are gains and your taxable income on your Form 1040 is more than zero, see *Capital Gain Tax Rates*, later.

TAXPLANNER

S corporation built-in gains tax. When a C corporation elects to become an S corporation, the conversion is not a taxable event. However, following such a conversion, an S corporation must hold on to its assets for a certain period of time. If the S corporation sells an asset sooner (i.e., within 10 calendar years beginning with the first day of the first taxable year for which the S election is in effect), then any built-in gain in such assets that existed at the time of the conversion is taxed to the S corporation at the existing highest marginal tax rate applicable to corporations; currently, 35%.

Under prior law, no tax was imposed on the net recognized built-in gain of an S corporation after the 7th year in the recognition period for taxable years beginning in 2009 and 2010 nor after the 5th year for taxable years beginning in 2011. For tax years beginning in either 2012 or 2013, the recognition period for purposes of determining a net recognized built-in gain was reduced to 5 years.

As of the date this book was published in October 2014, Congress had been considering legislation that would extend the reduced 5-year built-in gains tax holding period that applied for 2012 and 2013 to at least 2014 and 2015 (the U.S. House of Representatives passed legislation that would permanently extend the 5-year recognition period); however, no extension had yet been enacted. For updated information on this and any other tax law changes that occur after this book was published, see our website, *ey.com/EYTaxGuide*.

Capital Losses

If your capital losses are more than your capital gains, you can claim a capital loss deduction. Report the amount of the deduction on line 13 of Form 1040, in parentheses.

EXAMPLES

Example 1

You have capital gains and losses for the year as follows:

	Short-term	Long-term
Gains	$700	$400
Losses	800	2,000

Your net deductible capital loss is $1,700, which you figure as follows:

Short-term capital losses	$800	
Less: Short-term capital gains	(700)	
Net short-term capital loss		$100
Long-term capital losses	$2,000	
Less: Long-term capital gains	(400)	
Net long-term capital loss		$1,600
Net deductible capital loss		$1,700

Your deduction is limited to the lesser of $3,000 ($1,500 if married filing separately) or your capital loss of $1,700.

Example 2

You have a net long-term capital loss of $1,600 and a net short-term capital gain of $450. Your deductible capital loss is $1,150 ($1,600 − $450).

Limit on deduction. Your allowable capital loss deduction, figured on Schedule D (Form 1040), is the lesser of:

- $3,000 ($1,500 if you are married and file a separate return); or
- Your total net loss as shown on line 16 of Schedule D (Form 1040).

You can use your total net loss to reduce your income dollar for dollar, up to the $3,000 limit.

Capital loss carryover. If you have a total net loss on line 16 of Schedule D (Form 1040) that is more than the yearly limit on capital loss deductions, you can carry over the unused part to the next year and treat it as if you had incurred it in that next year. If part of the loss is still unused, you can carry it over to later years until it is completely used up.

When you figure the amount of any capital loss carryover to the next year, you must take the current year's allowable deduction into account, whether or not you claimed it and whether or not you filed a return for the current year.

When you carry over a loss, it remains long term or short term. A long-term capital loss you carry over to the next tax year will reduce that year's long-term capital gains before it reduces that year's short-term capital gains.

Figuring your carryover. The amount of your capital loss carryover is the amount of your total net loss that is more than the lesser of:

1. Your allowable capital loss deduction for the year; or
2. Your taxable income increased by your allowable capital loss deduction for the year and your deduction for personal exemptions.

If your deductions are more than your gross income for the tax year, use your negative taxable income in computing the amount in item (2).

Complete the Capital Loss Carryover Worksheet in the Instructions for Schedule D or Publication 550 to determine the part of your capital loss that you can carry over.

Example. Bob and Gloria sold securities in 2014. The sales resulted in a capital loss of $7,000. They had no other capital transactions. Their taxable income was $26,000. On their joint 2014 return, they can deduct $3,000. The unused part of the loss, $4,000 ($7,000 – $3,000), can be carried over to 2015.

If their capital loss had been $2,000, their capital loss deduction would have been $2,000. They would have no carryover.

Use short-term losses first. When you figure your capital loss carryover, use your short-term capital losses first, even if you incurred them after a long-term capital loss. If you have not reached the limit on the capital loss deduction after using the short-term capital losses, use the long-term capital losses until you reach the limit.

EXPLANATION
A net loss may be carried forward until it is exhausted or until the taxpayer dies. This carryforward may be used to reduce your capital gain income generated in subsequent tax years. Even if you do not have future gains, the carryforward loss may be used to offset taxable ordinary income up to $3,000 per year (or $1,500 if married filing separately).

Decedent's capital loss. A capital loss sustained by a decedent during his or her last tax year (or carried over to that year from an earlier year) can be deducted only on the final income tax return filed for the decedent. The capital loss limits discussed earlier still apply in this situation. The decedent's estate cannot deduct any of the loss or carry it over to following years.

TAXPLANNER
If the decedent filed a joint return in the year of death, the surviving spouse may offset gains recognized after the decedent's death but before the end of the tax year against the decedent's capital loss carryforward. Therefore, if the surviving spouse has assets that have appreciated in value, he or she should consider selling them in the year of the decedent's death. For a further discussion of this point, see chapter 43, *Decedents: Dealing with the death of a family member*.

Joint and separate returns. If you and your spouse once filed separate returns and are now filing a joint return, combine your separate capital loss carryovers. However, if you and your spouse once filed a joint return and are now filing separate returns, any capital loss carryover from the joint return can be deducted only on the return of the spouse who actually had the loss.

Capital Gain Tax Rates
The tax rates that apply to a net capital gain are generally lower than the tax rates that apply to other income. These lower rates are called the maximum capital gain rates.

The term "net capital gain" means the amount by which your net long-term capital gain for the year is more than your net short-term capital loss.

For 2014, the maximum capital gain rates are 0%, 15%, 20%, 25%, and 28%. See Table 16-1 for details.

Table 16-1.   **What Is Your Maximum Capital Gain Rate?**

IF your net capital gain is from ...	THEN your maximum capital gain rate is ...
a collectibles gain	28%
an eligible gain on qualified small business stock minus the Section 1202 exclusion	28%
an unrecaptured Section 1250 gain	25%
other gain[1] and the regular tax rate that would apply is 39.6%	20%
other gain[1] and the regular tax rate that would apply is 25%, 28%, 33%, or 35%	15%
other gain[1] and the regular tax rate that would apply is 10% or 15%	0%

[1]Other gain means any gain that is not collectibles gain, gain on qualified small business stock, or unrecaptured Section 1250 gain.

TAXALERT

In addition to paying regular income tax or alternative minimum tax on capital gains, the 3.8% Net Investment Income Tax (NIIT) is assessed on unearned Net Investment Income (NII). NII includes both short- and long-term capital gains, other than gains attributable to an active trade or business conducted by a sole proprietor, partnership, or S corporation. For individuals, the NIIT is 3.8% of the lesser of: (1) "net investment income" or (2) the excess of modified adjusted gross income (MAGI) over $200,000 ($250,000 if married filing jointly or a qualifying widow(er) with dependent child; $125,000 if married filing separately). These threshold dollar amounts are not indexed each year for inflation. For more information, see *Net Investment Income Tax*, later.

TAXPLANNER

Long-term investment strategies. Investment strategies that emphasize capital appreciation over current income can significantly enhance your after-tax portfolio returns. For example, "buy-and-hold" investors may want to keep growth-oriented investments outside of tax-deferred accounts to benefit from the lower tax rates on long-term capital gains. Also, long-term gains in a tax-deferred account are taxed at ordinary income rates—currently as high as 39.6%—when withdrawn. Outside a tax-deferred account, those same long-term gains would be taxed at the more favorable capital gains rate. In addition, new investments in tax-deferred variable annuities will require much longer holding periods to outperform "comparable" investments held in a taxable account. Although mutual funds have not historically paid considerable attention to the impact of taxes on shareholder returns—with some notable exceptions—more fund families are developing "tax-managed" funds that seek to minimize taxable distributions to shareholders.

To take advantage of the 0%, 15%, and 20% rates, you should specifically identify shares of securities and/or mutual funds held more than 12 months prior to executing the sale. For tax purposes, you must provide your broker or fund representative with written selling instructions. You should also retain confirmation of these instructions in your personal files.

High-income taxpayers who have the option of deferring current compensation may be better off paying tax currently and reinvesting the after-tax proceeds in assets expected to appreciate over the long term. For example, this may apply in the case of a corporate executive with significant nonqualified stock option holdings where the current option spread and associated tax liability is small, but the outlook for the company's stock price is favorable.

Example. All of your net capital gain is from selling collectibles, so the capital gain rate would be 28%. If you are otherwise subject to a rate lower than 28%, the 28% rate does not apply.

Investment interest deducted. If you claim a deduction for investment interest, you may have to reduce the amount of your net capital gain that is eligible for the capital gain tax rates. Reduce it by the amount of the net capital gain you choose to include in investment income when figuring the limit on your investment interest deduction. This is done on the Schedule D Tax Worksheet or the Qualified Dividends and Capital Gain Tax Worksheet. For more information about the limit on investment interest, see *Interest Expenses* in chapter 3 of Publication 550.

Tip

If you figure your tax using the maximum capital gain rate and the regular tax computation results in a lower tax, the regular tax computation applies.

Collectibles gain or loss. This is gain or loss from the sale or trade of a work of art, rug, antique, metal (such as gold, silver, and platinum bullion), gem, stamp, coin, or alcoholic beverage held more than 1 year.

Collectibles gain includes gain from sale of an interest in a partnership, S corporation, or trust due to unrealized appreciation of collectibles.

Gain on qualified small business stock. If you realized a gain from qualified small business stock that you held more than 5 years, you generally can exclude some or all of your gain under Section 1202. The eligible gain minus your Section 1202 exclusion is a 28% rate gain. See *Gains on Qualified Small Business Stock* in chapter 4 of Publication 550.

Unrecaptured Section 1250 gain. Generally, this is any part of your capital gain from selling Section 1250 property (real property) that is due to depreciation (but not more than your net Section 1231 gain), reduced by any net loss in the 28% group. Use the Unrecaptured Section 1250 Gain

Worksheet in the Schedule D (Form 1040) instructions to figure your unrecaptured Section 1250 gain. For more information about Section 1250 property and Section 1231 gain, see chapter 3 of Publication 544.

EXPLANATION

Computing depreciation recapture. If you sell property at a gain, you must generally compute the portion of your gain that is depreciation recapture. Depreciation recapture is treated as ordinary income. The portion of the gain that is not depreciation recapture is treated as a Section 1231 gain. Unrecaptured Section 1250 gain on the sale of Section 1231 assets is subject to either the 20% maximum rate or, if the gain is attributable to adjustments in the basis of real estate, the 25% maximum rate. Complete Form 4797 to determine the amount of your gain that is depreciation recapture.

Sale of depreciable personal property. The depreciation recapture rules for depreciable personal property are relatively simple, compared to the rules for real property. Depreciation recapture is the lesser of: (1) the gain recognized and (2) depreciation taken on the property since 1962. Note that under these rules if depreciable personal property is sold at less than its original cost, the full gain will inevitably be depreciation recapture.

Example

In 2010, Alan bought personal property that he used in his trade for $5,000. Alan sold the property for $2,500 in 2014. He had already taken $3,885 in depreciation. Alan computes his gain or loss as follows:

Sales price	$2,500
Purchase price	5,000
Less: Depreciation taken	(3,885)
Adjusted basis	1,115
Gain on sale	$1,385

Alan's gain on the sale is $1,385, which is less than the $3,885 of depreciation he had taken on the property. Therefore, his depreciation recapture is $1,385. Because this represents the full gain on the sale, no portion of the gain is treated as a Section 1231 gain and all of it will be treated as ordinary income.

Assume instead that the property had appreciated and that Alan sold the property for $6,000:

Sales price	$6,000
Adjusted basis (computed above)	(1,115)
Gain on sale	$4,885

Because the depreciation Alan took on the property ($3,885) is less than the gain on the sale ($4,885), Alan reports the $3,885 depreciation taken as depreciation recapture. The remaining $1,000 of his gain ($4,885 - $3,885) is treated as a Section 1231 gain.

Explanation

Sale of depreciable real estate. The depreciation recapture rules relating to the sale of real estate are quite complex. These rules depend on: (1) when you placed the property in service, (2) what method of depreciation was used, and (3) whether the property was residential rental property or held for business use. It should be noted that no depreciation recapture should occur for real property acquired after 1986, because straight-line depreciation is the only method available for such property.

Residential real property acquired after 1980 and before 1987. Any gain on the sale of residential real property is ordinary income if the deductions taken under the Accelerated Cost Recovery System (ACRS) method of depreciation exceed the depreciation allowed under the 15-year straight-line method of depreciation. However, any gain you incur in excess of the amount you have to recapture is treated as a capital gain. For property acquired after March 15, 1984, the ACRS period is 18 years, and for property acquired after May 8, 1985, the ACRS period is 19 years.

Tax computation using maximum capital gain rates. Use the Qualified Dividends and Capital Gain Tax Worksheet or the Schedule D Tax Worksheet (whichever applies) to figure your tax if you have qualified dividends or net capital gain. You have net capital gain if Schedule D (Form 1040), lines 15 and 16, are both gains.

Schedule D Tax Worksheet. Use the Schedule D Tax Worksheet in the Schedule D (Form 1040) instructions to figure your tax if:

- You have to file Schedule D (Form 1040); and
- Schedule D (Form 1040), line 18 (28% rate gain) or line 19 (unrecaptured Section 1250 gain), is more than zero.

Qualified Dividends and Capital Gain Tax Worksheet. If you do not have to use the Schedule D Tax Worksheet (as explained above) and any of the following apply, use the Qualified Dividends and Capital Gain Tax Worksheet in the instructions for Form 1040 or Form 1040A (whichever you file) to figure your tax.

- You received qualified dividends. (See *Qualified Dividends* in chapter 8.)
- You do not have to file Schedule D (Form 1040) and you received capital gain distributions. (See *Exceptions to filing Form 8949 and Schedule D (Form 1040)*, earlier.)
- Schedule D (Form 1040), lines 15 and 16, are both more than zero.

Alternative minimum tax. These capital gain rates are also used in figuring alternative minimum tax.

TAXALERT

Net Investment Income Tax. Regardless of whether net capital gains (the excess of your net long-term capital gains over your net short-term capital losses) are taxed at the lower 0%, 15%, or 20% preferential tax rates or are short-term capital gains subject to the higher regular income tax rates that apply to ordinary income, both short- and long-term capital gains, along with certain other investment income including dividends and interest income, may be subject to the 3.8% Net Investment Income Tax (NIIT). For individuals, the tax is 3.8% of the lesser of: (1) "net investment income" or (2) the excess of modified adjusted gross income (MAGI) over $200,000 ($250,000 if married filing jointly or a qualifying widow(er) with dependent child; $125,000 if married filing separately). These threshold dollar amounts are not be indexed each year for inflation.

Net investment income subject to the NIIT is defined as investment income reduced by allocable deductions. NII includes the following types of short- and long-term capital gains—to the extent that such capital gains are not otherwise offset by capital losses:

1. Gains from the sale of stocks, bonds, and mutual funds.
2. Capital gain distributions from mutual funds.
3. Gain from the sale of investment real estate (including gain from the sale of a second home that is not a primary residence).
4. Gains from the sale of interests in partnerships and S corporations (to the extent you were a passive owner).

On the other hand NII does not include any gains that are otherwise excludable from income for regular tax purposes. This includes gain excluded from the sale of your principal residence as discussed in chapter 15, *Selling your home*. NII also does not include gains attributable to an active trade or business conducted by a sole proprietor, partnership, or S corporation.

The NIIT is payable regardless of whether you otherwise pay any regular income tax or are subject to alternative minimum tax on your income.

TAXALERT

For higher income taxpayers, the combination of the 20% maximum tax rate on long-term capital gains and the 3.8% NIIT effectively raises the top tax rate on long-term capital gains to 23.8%. For short-term capital gains, as well as other ordinary income subject to regular income tax rates, the combination of the higher 39.6% marginal tax rate plus the 3.8% NIIT raises the top tax rate on income subject to both taxes to 43.4%.

Part 4

Adjustments to income

ey.com/EYTaxGuide

The four chapters in this part discuss some of the adjustments to income that you can deduct in figuring your adjusted gross income. These chapters cover:
- Contributions you make to traditional individual retirement arrangements (IRAs)–chapter 17.
- Alimony you pay–chapter 18.
- Student loan interest you pay–chapter 19.
- Moving expenses–chapter 20.

Other adjustments to income are discussed elsewhere. See the table on the following page.

Chapter 17	Individual retirement arrangements (IRAs)
Chapter 18	Alimony
Chapter 19	Education-related adjustments
Chapter 20	Moving expenses

Other Adjustments to Income

Use this table to find information about other adjustments to income not covered in this part of the publication.

IF you are looking for more information about the deduction for . . .	THEN see . . .
Certain business expenses of reservists, performing artists, and fee-basis officials	chapter 27.
Contributions to a health savings account	Publication 969, Health Savings Accounts and Other Tax-Favored Health Plans.
Part of your self-employment tax	chapter 23.
Self-employed health insurance	chapter 22.
Payments to self-employed SEP, SIMPLE, and qualified plans	Publication 560, Retirement Plans for Small Business (SEP, SIMPLE, and Qualified Plans).
Penalty on the early withdrawal of savings	chapter 7.
Contributions to an Archer MSA	Publication 969.
Reforestation amortization or expense	chapters 7 and 8 of Publication 535, Business Expenses.
Contributions to Internal Revenue Code section 501(c)(18)(D) pension plans	Publication 525, Taxable and Nontaxable Income.
Expenses from the rental of personal property	chapter 12.
Certain required repayments of supplemental unemployment benefits (sub-pay)	chapter 12.
Foreign housing costs	chapter 4 of Publication 54, Tax Guide for U.S. Citizens and Resident Aliens Abroad.
Jury duty pay given to your employer	chapter 12.
Contributions by certain chaplains to Internal Revenue Code section 403(b) plans	Publication 517, Social Security and Other Information for Members of the Clergy and Religious Workers.
Attorney fees and certain costs for actions involving certain unlawful discrimination claims or awards to whistleblowers	Publication 525.
Domestic production activities deduction	Form 8903.

Chapter 17
Individual retirement arrangements (IRAs)

ey.com/EYTaxGuide

Note

IRS Publication 17 (*Your Federal Income Tax*) has been updated by Ernst & Young LLP for 2014. Dates and dollar amounts shown are for 2014. Underlined type is used to indicate where IRS text has been updated. Places where text has been removed are indicated by the sentence: *Text intentionally omitted.*

ey.com/EYTaxGuide

Ernst & Young LLP will update the *EY Tax Guide 2015* website with relevant taxpayer information as it becomes available. You can also sign up for email alerts to let you know when changes have been made.

Introduction

There are two basic types of individual retirement arrangements (IRAs) discussed in this chapter: traditional IRAs and Roth IRAs. Each has different eligibility requirements and characteristics.

- **Traditional IRAs:** If you are not eligible for your employer's qualified retirement plan(s), or you are eligible but your income does not exceed specified limits, your contributions to a traditional IRA are deductible. Otherwise, you can only make nondeductible contributions to an IRA. Your maximum annual contribution is the lesser of $5,500 ($6,500 if you're age 50 by the end of the year) or your taxable compensation. (This limit applies on a combined basis to your traditional [whether deductible or not deductible] and Roth contributions.) You defer paying taxes on the income earned by the funds held in your IRA until withdrawal. How distributions from traditional IRAs are taxed at the time of withdrawal depends on whether your contribution was deductible or nondeductible at the time it was made. Where all the contributions to the traditional IRA were deductible, all of the distribution is taxable. Where some or all of the contributions to the traditional IRA were nondeductible, the pro rata portion of the distribution that is attributable to your nondeductible contributions is not taxable.

- **Roth IRAs:** If your income is below specified levels, you can make nondeductible contributions to a Roth IRA. Although contributions are not deductible, distributions from your Roth IRA account, including income and any gains, are tax free if the distribution meets certain requirements. Like a traditional IRA, the maximum amount you can contribute to a Roth IRA in 2014 is limited to the lesser of $5,500 ($6,500 if you're age 50 by the end of the year) or the amount of your taxable compensation. Your maximum allowable contribution to the Roth IRA may be further reduced depending on the amount of your modified adjusted gross income and your filing status.

This chapter also discusses the simplified employee pension IRA (SEP IRA) and the Savings Incentive Match Plans for Employees (SIMPLE IRA). These are employer-sponsored plans that are established using IRAs. The SEP IRA and the SIMPLE IRA have different contribution limits, both from each other and from traditional and Roth IRAs.

Individual Retirement Arrangements (IRAs). IRAs come in several different "flavors"–traditional IRA, Roth IRA, SIMPLE IRA, and SEP IRA. Each type of IRA has different eligibility requirements and characteristics–all offer tax benefits of one variety or another.

- **Traditional IRA.** There are two types of contributions to traditional IRAs–deductible and nondeductible. If you meet the eligibility standards for the year, the amount you contribute is deductible when contributed. If you don't meet the eligibility standards for the year because of your income level and your employer provides a retirement plan, you can still contribute, but the amount is not deductible (nondeductible IRA). You may establish separate IRAs for deductible and nondeductible contributions or combine them into one IRA. The income you accumulate in a traditional IRA account is not taxed until you take a withdrawal. This is true whether the earnings are on deductible or nondeductible con-

What's New

Modified AGI limit for traditional IRA contributions increased. For 2014, if you were covered by a retirement plan at work, your deduction for contributions to a traditional IRA is reduced (phased out) if your modified AGI is:

- More than $96,000 but less than $116,000 for a married couple filing a joint return or a qualifying widow(er),
- More than $60,000 but less than $70,000 for a single individual or head of household, or
- Less than $10,000 for a married individual filing a separate return.

If you either lived with your spouse or file a joint return, and your spouse was covered by a retirement plan at work, but you were not, your deduction is phased out if your modified AGI is more than $181,000 but less than $191,000. If your modified AGI is $191,000 or more, you cannot take a deduction for contributions to a traditional IRA. See *How Much Can You Deduct?*, later.

Modified AGI limit for Roth IRA contributions increased. For 2014, your Roth IRA contribution limit is reduced (phased out) in the following situations.

- Your filing status is married filing jointly or qualifying widow(er) and your modified AGI is at least $181,000. You cannot make a Roth IRA contribution if your modified AGI is $191,000 or more.
- Your filing status is single, head of household, or married filing separately and you did not live with your spouse at any time in 2014 and your modified AGI is at least $114,000. You cannot make a Roth IRA contribution if your modified AGI is $129,000 or more.
- Your filing status is married filing separately, you lived with your spouse at any time during the year, and your modified AGI is more than -0-. You cannot make a Roth IRA contribution if your modified AGI is $10,000 or more.

See *Can You Contribute to a Roth IRA?*, later.

Qualified charitable distributions (QCDs). The provision for tax-free distributions from IRAs for charitable purposes does not apply for 2014 or later years.

TAXALERT

As of the time this book was published in October 2014, Congress had been considering legislation that would extend the availability of this exclusion from income through 2014, but no such extension had yet been passed. For updated information on this and any other tax law changes that occur after this book was published, see our website, *ey.com/EYTaxGuide*.

A QCD was generally a nontaxable distribution made directly by the trustee of an IRA to an organization eligible to receive tax-deductible contributions. Under prior law, a person who was 70½ or older could instruct the trustee of his or her IRA to directly contribute a distribution of up to $100,000 per year from the IRA to a charity.

The amount distributed as a QCD would not be taxable to the account holder and counted toward the minimum required distributions the IRA account holder had for the year and. Furthermore, the opportunity to exclude IRA distributions that satisfied the requirements for qualified charitable distributions reduced adjusted gross income (AGI), which, in turn reduced the percentage limitations based on AGI that apply to various deductions and credits. On the other hand, a charitable deduction could not be claimed for the QCD.

TAXALERT

The tax law provides that generally any amount you have distributed from an IRA will not be included in your gross income to the extent you contribute–i.e., roll over–the amount that had been distributed to you into an IRA for your benefit no later than 60 days after you received the distribution. The law further provides that an individual is permitted to make only one rollover described in the preceding sentence in any 1-year period. Proposed regulations issued years ago by the IRS provided that this 1-year limitation is applied on an IRA-by-IRA basis. However, in 2014, the U.S. Tax Court held that you cannot make a non-taxable rollover from one IRA to another if you have already made a rollover from **any** of your other IRAs in the preceding 1-year period. The IRS subsequently announced that it will follow the court decision and, beginning January 1, 2015, only one rollover from an IRA to another (or the same) IRA will be permitted

Tip

The term "50 or older" is used several times in this chapter. It refers to an IRA owner who is age 50 or older by the end of the tax year.

in any 12-month period, regardless of the number of IRAs you own. This change does not affect your ability to transfer funds from one IRA trustee directly to another since these types of transfers are not considered to be rollovers. Therefore, you may continue to make as many trustee-to-trustee transfers between IRAs as you would like. You may also continue to make as many conversions from traditional IRAs to Roth IRAs as you want.

Reminders

2014 limits. You can find information about the 2014 contribution and AGI limits in Publication 590.

Contributions to both traditional and Roth IRAs. For information on your combined contribution limit if you contribute to both traditional and Roth IRAs, see *Roth IRAs and traditional IRAs* under *How Much Can Be Contributed?* in *Roth IRAs*, later.

Statement of required minimum distribution. If a minimum distribution from your IRA is required, the trustee, custodian, or issuer that held the IRA at the end of the preceding year must either report the amount of the required minimum distribution to you, or offer to calculate it for you. The report or offer must include the date by which the amount must be distributed. The report is due January 31 of the year in which the minimum distribution is required. It can be provided with the year-end fair market value statement that you normally get each year. No report is required for IRAs of owners who have died.

IRA interest. Although interest earned from your IRA is generally not taxed in the year earned, it is not tax-exempt interest. Tax on your traditional IRA is generally deferred until you take a distribution. Do not report this interest on your tax return as tax-exempt interest.

Form 8606. To designate contributions as nondeductible, you must file Form 8606, Nondeductible IRAs.

Net Investment Income Tax. For purposes of the Net Investment Income Tax (NIIT), net investment income does not include distributions from a qualified retirement plan including IRAs (for example, 401(a), 403(a), 403(b), 408, 408A, or 457(b) plans). However, these distributions are taken into account when determining the modified adjusted gross income threshold. Distributions from a nonqualified retirement plan are included in net investment income. See Form 8960, Net Investment Income Tax—Individuals, Estates, and Trusts, and its instructions for more information.

TAXALERT

Same-sex married couples. For all federal tax purposes for which marriage is a factor, including the subject matter covered in this chapter, same-sex couples who legally married in a state (including the District of Columbia) or foreign jurisdiction that recognizes same-sex marriages are treated as married for U.S. federal tax purposes—even if they reside in a jurisdiction that does not recognize same-sex marriage. However, registered domestic partners and individuals who enter into a civil union or other similar formal relationship are not treated as a married couple for federal tax purposes.

TAXSAVER

Retirement savings through IRAs. Wealth can build up much faster in an IRA or other tax-deferred retirement plan than in a savings account or other non-tax-exempt investment. Because you do not have to pay income tax as your earnings accumulate within the IRA or plan, your investments compound in value more quickly. A person in the 28% tax bracket, for example, could end up with 1.7 times more money after tax on a $5,500 deductible IRA contribution held for 20

tributions. However, when you take a distribution, whether the original contribution was deductible or nondeductible, makes a difference. Where all the contributions to the traditional IRA were deductible, all of the distribution is taxable. Where some or all of the contributions to the traditional IRA were nondeductible, the pro rata portion of the distribution that is attributable to your nondeductible contributions is not taxable. In 2014, you can contribute up to the lesser of $5,500 ($6,500 if you're age 50 by the end of the year) or the amount of your taxable compensation to a traditional IRA. (This is a combined limit with the Roth IRA.) You may also be eligible to deduct all or a portion of the contribution. The deduction is allowed as an adjustment in arriving at your adjusted gross income. Therefore, deducting your IRA contributions reduces your income subject to tax regardless of whether you itemize deductions. Three factors determine the extent to which you may deduct your contribution: the amount of your modified adjusted gross income; your filing status; and whether you are covered by a retirement plan at work.

For more information on figuring the deductible portion of your contribution to a traditional IRA, see *How Much Can You Deduct?* later in this chapter.

- **Roth IRA.** You can receive income accumulated within a Roth IRA account completely tax-free and penalty-free if certain conditions are met. In comparison, the income built up inside a traditional IRA is eventually subject to income tax at ordinary income tax rates as distributions are received.

To qualify as a tax-free and penalty-free distribution, generally, the Roth IRA must have been established more than five years earlier and the distribution is received after you reach age 59½, made because you are disabled, made to a beneficiary following your death, or made to pay up to $10,000 (lifetime limit) of certain qualified first-time homebuyer amounts. Roth IRAs also have the advantage that there is no age at which minimum distributions must commence while you are alive.

Like with a traditional IRA, the maximum amount you can contribute to a Roth IRA in 2014 is limited to the lesser of $5,500 ($6,500 if you're age 50 by the end of the year) or the amount of your taxable compensation. Your maximum allowable contribution may be further reduced depending on the amount of your modified adjusted gross income and your filing status. No portion of your contribution to a Roth IRA is deductible.

See *Roth IRAs*, later in this chapter, for more information.

- **SIMPLE IRA.** If you work for a small employer, your employer may be eligible to establish a SIMPLE IRA account for you. This is a plan similar to a 401(k) plan, but with lower limits on both the amount of contributions the employer can make and the salary deferrals you can make, compared to a 401(k) plan. Your employer will also be

years than if he or she did not make the contribution. If the person's marginal tax rate drops to 15% in retirement, he or she could have 2 times more money after tax.

Example

If in 2014 you invested $5,500 in an IRA that earns 10% per year, it will be worth $26,640 in 2033 after all taxes are paid if you are in the 28% bracket. If in 2034 you retire and drop into the 15% tax bracket and take a distribution, your original $5,500 investment will be worth $31,451 after all taxes are paid.

However, if you do not have an IRA, the $5,500 you receive in 2014 is subject to tax immediately. If you are in the 28% bracket, you are left with only $3,960. Investing that $3,960 in 2014 in a non-IRA investment earning 10%, remaining in the 28% bracket until you retire, and being in the 15% bracket when you retire, will leave you with only $15,907 in 2034 after taxes.

Note: The highest tax bracket in 2014 is 39.6%. The savings resulting from an IRA may be different than indicated in this example for taxpayers in higher or lower tax brackets. Also, the results will be different for a contribution to a nondeductible IRA or to a Roth IRA.

An individual retirement arrangement (IRA) is a personal savings plan that gives you tax advantages for setting aside money for your retirement.

This chapter discusses the following topics.

- The rules for a traditional IRA (any IRA that is not a Roth or SIMPLE IRA).
- The Roth IRA, which features nondeductible contributions and tax-free distributions.

Simplified Employee Pensions (SEPs) and Savings Incentive Match Plans for Employees (SIMPLEs) are not discussed in this chapter. For more information on these plans and employees' SEP IRAs and SIMPLE IRAs that are part of these plans, see Publications 560 and 590.

For information about contributions, deductions, withdrawals, transfers, rollovers, and other transactions, see Publication 590.

Useful Items

You may want to see:

Publication

- ☐ **560** Retirement Plans for Small Business
- ☐ **590** Individual Retirement Arrangements (IRAs)

Form (and Instructions)

- ☐ **5329** Additional Taxes on Qualified Plans (including IRAs) and Other Tax-Favored Accounts
- ☐ **8606** Nondeductible IRAs

TAXPLANNER

Self-employed persons often overlook the benefits available to them from establishing an IRA. The only requirement for contributing to an IRA is that you have not reached age 70½ (note: this does not apply to Roth IRAs), and have earned income, which includes income from your business, provided that your personal efforts create a major portion of the business income. Therefore, a self-employed person could establish both a Keogh plan and an IRA. For more information on retirement plans for the self-employed, see chapter 10, *Retirement plans, pensions, and annuities*.

TAXSAVER

You are a sole proprietor and you hire your spouse or child to perform bona fide services, such as bookkeeping, as an employee. Assuming that the family member works in a genuine employment relationship, the salary paid is compensation for personal services and should be included in the family member's gross income. The family member's salary is a deductible expense to you. This gross income would entitle that family member to make a contribution to an IRA of up to $5,500 (or, if a non-spouse with less than $5,500 income, up to the non-spouse's actual income).

Your spouse's wages constitute wages subject to social security tax, so this strategy may not work to your advantage.

Be prepared to defend the genuine employment relationship of your spouse if the IRS should question it.

Traditional IRAs

In this chapter, the original IRA (sometimes called an ordinary or regular IRA) is referred to as a "traditional IRA." A traditional IRA is any IRA that is not a Roth IRA or a SIMPLE IRA. Two advantages of a traditional IRA are:

- You may be able to deduct some or all of your contributions to it, depending on your circumstances, and
- Generally, amounts in your IRA, including earnings and gains, are not taxed until they are distributed.

Who Can Open a Traditional IRA?

You can open and make contributions to a traditional IRA if:

- You (or, if you file a joint return, your spouse) received taxable compensation during the year, and
- You were not age 70½ by the end of the year.

What is compensation? Generally, compensation is what you earn from working. Compensation includes wages, salaries, tips, professional fees, bonuses, and other amounts you receive for providing personal services. The IRS treats as compensation any amount properly shown in box 1 (Wages, tips, other compensation) of Form W-2, Wage and Tax Statement, provided that amount is reduced by any amount properly shown in box 11 (Nonqualified plans).

Scholarship and fellowship payments are compensation for this purpose only if shown in box 1 of Form W-2.

Compensation also includes commissions and taxable alimony and separate maintenance payments.

Self-employment income. If you are self-employed (a sole proprietor or a partner), compensation is the net earnings from your trade or business (provided your personal services are a material income-producing factor) reduced by the total of:

- The deduction for contributions made on your behalf to retirement plans, and
- The deductible part of your self-employment tax.

Compensation includes earnings from self-employment even if they are not subject to self-employment tax because of your religious beliefs.

Nontaxable combat pay. For IRA purposes, if you were a member of the U.S. Armed Forces, your compensation includes any nontaxable combat pay you receive.

TAXSAVER

Taxpayers can now count tax-free combat pay when determining whether they qualify to contribute to either a traditional or Roth IRA. Before this change, part of the Heroes Earned Retirement Opportunities (HERO) Act enacted in 2006, members of the military whose earnings came entirely from tax-free combat pay were generally barred from using IRAs to save for retirement. This was because they had only combat pay, which did not count as "earnings" for purposes of establishing an IRA.

What is not compensation? Compensation does not include any of the following items.

- Earnings and profits from property, such as rental income, interest income, and dividend income.
- Pension or annuity income.
- Deferred compensation received (compensation payments postponed from a past year).
- Income from a partnership for which you do not provide services that are a material income-producing factor.
- Conservation Reserve Program (CRP) payments reported on Schedule SE (Form 1040), line 1b.
- Any amounts (other than combat pay) you exclude from income, such as foreign earned income and housing costs.

EXPLANATION

For purposes of figuring your contribution to your IRA, compensation includes sales commissions, net income from your business, and partnership income that is subject to self-employment tax. Business and partnership income must be reduced by any contributions to a Keogh or SEP

---

required to make a matching contribution of either 2% or 3% of your annual compensation to your SIMPLE account, depending on the terms of the plan adopted by your employer. Under a SIMPLE IRA, the contributions for you are made to your IRA rather than to an employer trust. You may also be able to establish a SIMPLE IRA if you are self-employed. Generally, the annual contributions and accumulated income are not taxable until you take distributions.

The maximum limits on annual contributions to a SIMPLE IRA are substantially greater than for either a traditional or Roth IRA. In 2014, the limit is $12,000 ($14,500 if you are over age 50 by the end of the year). This is less than if your employer had established a 401(k) plan, and is coordinated with any amounts deferred to a 401(k) plan or a salary reduction simplified employee pension (SARSEP) plan of another employer. (New SARSEPS were prohibited after December 31, 1996.)

For more information on SIMPLE plans, see *Savings Incentive Match Plans for Employees (SIMPLE),* later in this chapter.

- **SEP IRA.** Employers may also establish a SEP IRA. In this structure, like the SIMPLE IRA, your employer makes contributions for you to your IRA. In most cases, there are only employer contributions to the SEP; however, before 1997 small employers were able to establish SARSEPs to accept elective deferrals. Employers who established a SARSEP before 1997 can continue to use them for both old and new employees as long as they had 25 or fewer employees in the prior year. The SEP contribution is made to a traditional IRA. The salary deferral limits are the same as for 401(k) plans ($17,500 in 2014, plus $5,500 if you have attained age 50 by the end of the 2014 calendar year). The limit is coordinated with any amounts deferred to a 401(k) plan or SIMPLE IRA of another employer.

Rollovers to a traditional IRA. You can make a tax-free transfer of money or property you receive from a qualified retirement plan, including a traditional IRA, into a traditional IRA. This tax-free rollover must generally be accomplished by the 60th day after the day you first received the distribution. In addition, if the rollover is from one traditional IRA account into another traditional IRA account, you can only perform the rollover once per year. Through the end of 2014, the limitation of one rollover per 12-month period is applied with respect to each separate IRA account you own. After 2014, however, the 12-month limitation is applied to all of your IRA accounts on an aggregate basis, and you cannot make a non-taxable rollover from one IRA to another if you have already made a rollover from **any** of your other IRAs in the preceding 12-month period. This change does not affect the ability to transfer funds from one IRA trustee directly to another since such direct transfers

plan you make. Compensation does not include nontaxable amounts (other than combat pay), deferred compensation, severance pay, or pension distributions. If you have multiple sources of self-employment income and/or partnership income subject to self-employment tax, all gains and losses from these sources must be aggregated for purposes of computing compensation from self-employment. If the result is a gain, it is added to your wages, possibly permitting you to make a larger deductible contribution to your IRA. If the result of your self-employment activities is a loss, however, you need not account for it in determining your IRA contribution eligibility. Income earned outside the United States is compensation to the extent that it is taxable in the United States (other than combat pay). Your foreign earned income must be adjusted for any foreign income exclusion. For more information, see chapter 41, *U.S. citizens working abroad: Tax treatment of foreign earned income.*

When and How Can a Traditional IRA Be Opened?

You can open a traditional IRA at any time. However, the time for making contributions for any year is limited. See *When Can Contributions Be Made?*, later.

You can open different kinds of IRAs with a variety of organizations. You can open an IRA at a bank or other financial institution or with a mutual fund or life insurance company. You can also open an IRA through your stockbroker. Any IRA must meet Internal Revenue Code requirements.

Kinds of traditional IRAs. Your traditional IRA can be an individual retirement account or annuity. It can be part of either a simplified employee pension (SEP) or an employer or employee association trust account.

EXPLANATION

The basic difference between individual retirement arrangements and individual retirement annuities lies in the type of investment and the method of funding it. An individual retirement arrangement is generally a type of trust with varied investments, such as stocks, bonds, savings accounts, certificates of deposit, credit union accounts, common trust funds, and real estate, among other things. An individual retirement annuity is an investment in an insurance contract.

TAXPLANNER

Self-directed IRAs. If you want to actively manage your IRA investments, you may consider setting up a self-directed IRA. To do so, without having to obtain preapproval from the IRS, you may use Form 5305, a model trust form, and Form 5305-A, a model custodial account agreement. However, keep in mind that even if you use these model forms, you still will have to find a financial institution to administer your account.

TAXPLANNER

In deciding whether or not to create a self-directed IRA, keep in mind that an investment in the following collectibles is not allowed by an IRA:
- Artworks
- Coins (unless state issued, U.S. minted gold, and silver coins of 1 ounce or less)
- Stamps
- Gems
- Antiques
- Rugs
- Alcoholic beverages
- Metals (except for certain types of bullion traded on a contract market)

How Much Can Be Contributed?

There are limits and other rules that affect the amount that can be contributed to a traditional IRA. These limits and other rules are explained below.

Community property laws. Except as discussed later under *Kay Bailey Hutchison Spousal IRA limit*, each spouse figures his or her limit separately, using his or her own compensation. This is the rule even in states with community property laws.

Brokers' commissions. Brokers' commissions paid in connection with your traditional IRA are subject to the contribution limit.

Trustees' fees. Trustees' administrative fees are not subject to the contribution limit.

Qualified reservist repayments. If you are (or were) a member of a reserve component and you were ordered or called to active duty after September 11, 2001, you may be able to contribute (repay) to an IRA amounts equal to any qualified reservist distributions you received. You can make these repayment contributions even if they would cause your total contributions to the IRA to be more than the general limit on contributions. To be eligible to make these repayment contributions, you must have received a qualified reservist distribution from an IRA or from a Section 401(k) or 403(b) plan or similar arrangement.

For more information, see *Qualified reservist repayments* under *How Much Can Be Contributed?* in chapter 1 of Publication 590.

General limit. For 2014, the most that can be contributed to your traditional IRA generally is the smaller of the following amounts.
- $5,500 ($6,500 if you are 50 or older).
- Your taxable <u>compensation</u> (defined earlier) for the year.

This is the most that can be contributed regardless of whether the contributions are to one or more traditional IRAs or whether all or part of the contributions are nondeductible. (See <u>Nondeductible Contributions</u>, later.) Qualified reservist repayments do not affect this limit.

Example 1. Betty, who is 34 years old and single, earned $24,000 in 2014. Her IRA contributions for 2014 are limited to $5,500.

Example 2. John, an unmarried college student working part time, earned $3,500 in 2014. His IRA contributions for 2014 are limited to $3,500, the amount of his compensation.

Kay Bailey Hutchison Spousal IRA limit. For 2014, if you file a joint return and your taxable compensation is less than that of your spouse, the most that can be contributed for the year to your IRA is the smaller of the following amounts.
1. $5,500 ($6,500 if you are 50 or older).
2. The total compensation includible in the gross income of both you and your spouse for the year, reduced by the following two amounts.
   a. Your spouse's IRA contribution for the year to a traditional IRA.
   b. Any contribution for the year to a Roth IRA on behalf of your spouse.

This means that the total combined contributions that can be made for the year to your IRA and your spouse's IRA can be as much as $11,000 ($12,000 if only one of you is 50 or older, or $13,000 if both of you are 50 or older).

are not rollovers. You can also make a direct rollover from a qualified retirement plan to a traditional IRA. In this case, the one-time rule does not apply. For more information, see <u>Can You Move Retirement Plan Assets?</u> later.

Converting a traditional IRA to a Roth IRA. You can convert assets held in a traditional IRA account into a Roth IRA. If you make the conversion, you will have to pay income tax on any portion of the distribution of the traditional IRA that had not been previously taxed. Converting to a Roth IRA may be more beneficial than leaving the assets in a traditional IRA if you plan on leaving the money invested for a long period of time. For more information, see <u>Converting From Any Traditional IRA to a Roth IRA</u>, later.

Converting a qualified retirement plan to a Roth IRA. You can convert investments held in a qualified retirement plan (i.e., 401(k)), 403(b) tax-sheltered annuities, and government plans under Section 457 into a Roth. If you make the conversion, you will have to pay income tax on any portion of the distribution of the qualified plan that had not been previously taxed. However, the conversion from a qualified employer plan may take place only if there is a "distributable event," such as separation from your employer or, under some plans, attaining age 59½.

When Can Contributions Be Made?

As soon as you open your traditional IRA, contributions can be made to it through your chosen sponsor (trustee or other administrator). Contributions must be in the form of money (cash, check, or money order). Property cannot be contributed.

Contributions must be made by due date. Contributions can be made to your traditional IRA for a year at any time during the year or by the due date for filing your return for that year, not including extensions.

Age 70½ rule. Contributions cannot be made to your traditional IRA for the year in which you reach age 70½ or for any later year.

You attain age 70½ on the date that is 6 calendar months after the 70th anniversary of your birth. If you were born on or before June 30, 1944, you cannot contribute for 2014 or any later year.

Designating year for which contribution is made. If an amount is contributed to your traditional IRA between January 1 and April 15, you should tell the sponsor which year (the current year or the previous year) the contribution is for. If you do not tell the sponsor which year it is for, the sponsor can assume, and report to the IRS, that the contribution is for the current year (the year the sponsor received it).

Filing before a contribution is made. You can file your return claiming a traditional IRA contribution before the contribution is actually made. Generally, the contribution must be made by the due date of your return, not including extensions.

Contributions not required. You do not have to contribute to your traditional IRA for every tax year, even if you can.

TAXPLANNER

You can make your 2014 IRA contribution as late as April 15, 2015. However, funding your IRA as early as possible maximizes your ending balance (assuming positive earnings throughout the year). For example, assume you have 20 years until retirement, make the maximum $11,000 contribution for you and your spouse, and the account earns 8% each year. If you make your contributions at year end, your ending IRA balance will be $554,652. If you make your contributions at the beginning of the year, your ending account balance will be $594,923, an increase of $40,271.

If you don't have available funds to make an IRA contribution by December 31, 2014, you may be able to generate the cash by filing your tax return early in 2014, taking the deduction for the contribution, and using your tax refund (if any) to make the contribution when it's received prior to April 15, 2015, the latest date on which contributions may be made for 2014. Caution must be taken to ensure the contribution is made timely if a deduction is taken on the 2014 tax return.

If you do not have the cash available to make your 2014 IRA contribution by April 15, 2015, the deadline for 2014 contributions, you could "borrow" money by distributing part or all of an existing IRA (IRA 1) to yourself and use the money to make your 2014 IRA contribution to another IRA account (IRA 2). You would have to complete the rollover to IRA 2 within 60 days of the withdrawal from IRA 1. If you do not come up with the funds to complete the rollover to IRA 2, you would be subject to income tax and possibly the 10% penalty for early withdrawal. This approach only helps if you have a very short-term cash shortage and know you will have the needed cash within 60 days of the distribution.

Note: You may only roll over an IRA fund to a new IRA once in a 12-month period. Through the end of 2014, the limitation of one rollover per 12-month period is applied with respect to each separate IRA account you own. However, beginning January, 1, 2015, the 12-month limitation is applied to all of your IRA accounts on an aggregate basis. Therefore, you will not be able to make a non-taxable rollover from one IRA to another if you have already made a rollover from any of your other IRAs within the preceding 12-month period.

For more information about *Rollovers*, see the discussion later in this chapter.

TAXPLANNER

Direct deposit of tax refunds into an IRA account. You can choose to have the IRS directly deposit your tax refund into your IRA account(s) (and/or your spouse's IRA account(s)) if you file a joint tax return. Use Form 8888 to instruct the IRS to make a direct deposit to the IRA.

(You can also use Form 8888 to instruct the IRS to directly deposit your tax refund in up to three accounts. In addition to an IRA, an account can be a checking, savings, or health savings account (HSA), an Archer MSA, or Coverdell education savings account. You cannot have your refund deposited into more than one account if you file Form 8379, Injured Spouse Allocation.)

To have the IRS directly deposit your tax refund into your IRA account, you must establish the IRA at a bank or other financial institution before you request direct deposit. You must also notify the trustee of your account of the year to which the deposit is to be applied. If you do not, the trustee can assume the deposit is for the year during which you are filing the return. For example, if you file your 2014 return during 2015 and do not notify the trustee in advance, the trustee can assume the deposit into your IRA is for 2015. If you designate your deposit to be for 2014, you must verify that the deposit was actually made to the account by the original due date of the return, without regard to extensions. If the deposit was not made into your account by April 15, 2015, the deposit is not an IRA contribution for 2014 and you must file an amended return and reduce any IRA deduction and any retirement savings contribution credit you claimed.

How Much Can You Deduct?

Generally, you can deduct the lesser of:
- The contributions to your traditional IRA for the year, or
- The general limit (or the Kay Bailey Hutchison Spousal IRA limit, if it applies).

However, if you or your spouse was covered by an employer retirement plan, you may not be able to deduct this amount. See *Limit If Covered by Employer Plan*, later.

Trustees' fees. Trustees' administrative fees that are billed separately and paid in connection with your traditional IRA are not deductible as IRA contributions. However, they may be deductible as a miscellaneous itemized deduction on Schedule A (Form 1040). See chapter 28.

Brokers' commissions. Brokers' commissions are part of your IRA contribution and, as such, are deductible subject to the limits.

Full deduction. If neither you nor your spouse was covered for any part of the year by an employer retirement plan, you can take a deduction for total contributions to one or more traditional IRAs of up to the lesser of:
- $5,500 ($6,500 if you are age 50 or older in 2014).
- 100% of your compensation.

This limit is reduced by any contributions made to a 501(c)(18) plan on your behalf.

Kay Bailey Hutchison Spousal IRA. In the case of a married couple with unequal compensation who file a joint return, the deduction for contributions to the traditional IRA of the spouse with less compensation is limited to the lesser of the following amounts.

1. $5,500 ($6,500 if the spouse with the lower compensation is age 50 or older in 2014).
2. The total compensation includible in the gross income of both spouses for the year reduced by the following three amounts.
   a. The IRA deduction for the year of the spouse with the greater compensation.
   b. Any designated nondeductible contribution for the year made on behalf of the spouse with the greater compensation.
   c. Any contributions for the year to a Roth IRA on behalf of the spouse with the greater compensation.

This limit is reduced by any contributions to a 501(c)(18) plan on behalf of the spouse with the lesser compensation.

Note. If you were divorced or legally separated (and did not remarry) before the end of the year, you cannot deduct any contributions to your spouse's IRA. After a divorce or legal separation, you can deduct only contributions to your own IRA. Your deductions are subject to the rules for single individuals.

Covered by an employer retirement plan. If you or your spouse was covered by an employer retirement plan at any time during the year for which contributions were made, your deduction may be further limited. This is discussed later under *Limit If Covered by Employer Plan*. Limits on the amount you can deduct do not affect the amount that can be contributed. See *Nondeductible Contributions*, later.

Are You Covered by an Employer Plan?

The Form W-2 you receive from your employer has a box used to indicate whether you were covered for the year. The "Retirement plan" box should be checked if you were covered.

Reservists and volunteer firefighters should also see *Situations in Which You Are Not Covered by an Employer Plan*, later.

> **Tip**
>
> *You may be able to claim a credit for contributions to your traditional IRA. For more information, see chapter 37.*

If you are not certain whether you were covered by your employer's retirement plan, you should ask your employer.

TAXPLANNER

We recommend that you check your Form W-2 to ensure that the coverage status is accurate. The rules used to determine if you are covered by an employer's plan will depend on the type of plan maintained by your employer. If you are not sure what type of plan your employer maintains, you should ask your employer. The information may also be found in the Summary Plan Description, which can be obtained from your employer. You test eligibility to participate in your employer's plan based on the plan year ending with or within the tax year. Generally, you will be considered covered if:

1. Your employer maintains a defined benefit pension plan and you meet the plan's eligibility requirements.
2. Your employer maintains a defined contribution money purchase plan, you meet the plan's eligibility requirements, and your employer is required to make a contribution to your account.
3. Your employer maintains a profit-sharing plan and makes a contribution that is allocated to your account or allocates a forfeiture to your account, or you make any contribution with respect to a plan year ending with or within your tax year.
4. Your employer maintains a 401(k), a SEP, or a 403(b) plan, and for the plan year ending with or within your tax year, you elect to defer any compensation.

Example
Assume that you first became eligible to participate in your employer's profit-sharing plan on July 2, 2014. Your employer makes a contribution for the plan year ending on June 30, 2015. You will not be considered an active participant until 2015, since that is the first tax year during which an allocation was made to your account.

Federal judges. For purposes of the IRA deduction, federal judges are covered by an employer retirement plan.

For Which Year(s) Are You Covered by an Employer Plan?
Special rules apply to determine the tax years for which you are covered by an employer plan. These rules differ depending on whether the plan is a defined contribution plan or a defined benefit plan.

Tax year. Your tax year is the annual accounting period you use to keep records and report income and expenses on your income tax return. For almost all people, the tax year is the calendar year.

Defined contribution plan. Generally, you are covered by a defined contribution plan for a tax year if amounts are contributed or allocated to your account for the plan year that ends with or within that tax year.

A defined contribution plan is a plan that provides for a separate account for each person covered by the plan. Types of defined contribution plans include profit-sharing plans, stock bonus plans, and money purchase pension plans.

Defined benefit plan. If you are eligible to participate in your employer's defined benefit plan for the plan year that ends within your tax year, you are covered by the plan. This rule applies even if you:
• Declined to participate in the plan,
• Did not make a required contribution, or
• Did not perform the minimum service required to accrue a benefit for the year.

A defined benefit plan is any plan that is not a defined contribution plan. Defined benefit plans include pension plans and annuity plans.

No vested interest. If you accrue a benefit for a plan year, you are covered by that plan even if you have no vested interest in (legal right to) the accrual.

Situations in Which You Are Not Covered by an Employer Plan
Unless you are covered under another employer plan, you are not covered by an employer plan if you are in one of the situations described next.

Social security or railroad retirement. Coverage under social security or railroad retirement is not coverage under an employer retirement plan.

Benefits from a previous employer's plan. If you receive retirement benefits from a previous employer's plan, you are not covered by that plan.

Reservists. If the only reason you participate in a plan is because you are a member of a reserve unit of the armed forces, you may not be covered by the plan. You are not covered by the plan if both of the following conditions are met.
1. The plan you participate in is established for its employees by:
   a. The United States,
   b. A state or political subdivision of a state, or
   c. An instrumentality of either (a) or (b) above.
2. You did not serve more than 90 days on active duty during the year (not counting duty for training).

Volunteer firefighters. If the only reason you participate in a plan is because you are a volunteer firefighter, you may not be covered by the plan. You are not covered by the plan if both of the following conditions are met.
1. The plan you participate in is established for its employees by:
   a. The United States,
   b. A state or political subdivision of a state, or
   c. An instrumentality of either (a) or (b) above.
2. Your accrued retirement benefits at the beginning of the year will not provide more than $1,800 per year at retirement.

Limit If Covered by Employer Plan

If either you or your spouse was covered by an employer retirement plan, you may be entitled to only a partial (reduced) deduction or no deduction at all, depending on your income and your filing status.

Your deduction begins to decrease (phase out) when your income rises above a certain amount and is eliminated altogether when it reaches a higher amount. These amounts vary depending on your filing status.

To determine if your deduction is subject to phaseout, you must determine your modified adjusted gross income (AGI) and your filing status. See *Filing status* and *Modified adjusted gross income (AGI)*, later. Then use Table 17-1 or 17-2 to determine if the phaseout applies.

Table 17-1. **Effect of Modified AGI[1] on Deduction If You Are Covered by Retirement Plan at Work**

If you are covered by a retirement plan at work, use this table to determine if your modified AGI affects the amount of your deduction.

IF your filing status is...	AND your modified AGI is...	THEN you can take...
single or head of household	$60,000 or less	a full deduction.
	more than $60,000 but less than $70,000	a partial deduction.
	$70,000 or more	no deduction.
married filing jointly or qualifying widow(er)	$96,000 or less	a full deduction.
	more than $96,000 but less than $116,000	a partial deduction.
	$116,000 or more	no deduction.
married filing separately[2]	less than $10,000	a partial deduction.
	$10,000 or more	no deduction.

[1]Modified AGI (adjusted gross income). See *Modified adjusted gross income (AGI)*.
[2]If you did not live with your spouse at any time during the year, your filing status is considered Single for this purpose (therefore, your IRA deduction is determined under the "Single" column).

Table 17-2. Effect of Modified AGI[1] on Deduction If You Are NOT Covered by Retirement Plan at Work

If you are not covered by a retirement plan at work, use this table to determine if your modified AGI affects the amount of your deduction.

IF your filing status is...	AND your modified AGI is...	THEN you can take...
single, head of household, or **qualifying widow(er)**	any amount	a full deduction.
married filing jointly or **separately** with a spouse who **is not** covered by a plan at work	any amount	a full deduction.
married filing jointly with a spouse who *is* covered by a plan at work	$181,000 or less	a full deduction.
	more than $181,000 but less than $191,000	a partial deduction.
	$191,000 or more	no deduction.
married filing separately with a spouse who *is* covered by a plan at work[2]	less than $10,000	a partial deduction.
	$10,000 or more	no deduction.

[1]Modified AGI (adjusted gross income). See *Modified adjusted gross income (AGI)*.
[2]You are entitled to the full deduction if you did not live with your spouse at any time during the year.

Social security recipients. Instead of using Table 17-1 or Table 17-2, use the worksheets in Appendix B of Publication 590 if, for the year, all of the following apply.
- You received social security benefits.
- You received taxable compensation.
- Contributions were made to your traditional IRA.
- You or your spouse was covered by an employer retirement plan.

Use those worksheets to figure your IRA deduction, your nondeductible contribution, and the taxable portion, if any, of your social security benefits.

Deduction phaseout. If you were covered by an employer retirement plan and you did not receive any social security retirement benefits, your IRA deduction may be reduced or eliminated depending on your filing status and modified AGI as shown in Table 17-1.

If your spouse is covered. If you are not covered by an employer retirement plan, but your spouse is, and you did not receive any social security benefits, your IRA deduction may be reduced or eliminated entirely depending on your filing status and modified AGI as shown in Table 17-2.

Filing status. Your filing status depends primarily on your marital status. For this purpose, you need to know if your filing status is single or head of household, married filing jointly or qualifying widow(er), or married filing separately. If you need more information on filing status, see chapter 2.

Lived apart from spouse. If you did not live with your spouse at any time during the year and you file a separate return, your filing status, for this purpose, is single.

Caution

Do not assume that your modified AGI is the same as your compensation. Your modified AGI may include income in addition to your compensation *(discussed earlier), such as interest, dividends, and income from IRA distributions.*

EXAMPLE

Joe and Mary are both employed. During 2014, Mary's compensation was $80,000, and she was not covered by her employer's retirement plan. Joe's compensation was $36,000, and he was covered by his employer's plan. If Joe and Mary file a joint return, Mary can claim a deduction for an IRA contribution since she is not covered by her employer's retirement plan. However, Joe cannot claim an IRA contribution deduction. If Joe and Mary didn't live together at all during the year and file separate returns, Joe could deduct an IRA contribution of $5,500 (subject to the adjusted gross income limitation), while Mary could deduct $5,500, since she is not covered by her employer's plan.

If they lived together for part of the year and file separate returns, neither can make a deductible IRA contribution.

Worksheet 17-1. Figuring Your Modified AGI

Use this worksheet to figure your modified adjusted gross income for traditional IRA purposes.

Keep for Your Records

1. Enter your adjusted gross income (AGI) from Form 1040, line 38, or Form 1040A, line 22, figured without taking into account the amount from Form 1040, line 32, or Form 1040A, line 17..	1. _____
2. Enter any student loan interest deduction from Form 1040, line 33, or Form 1040A, line 18...............................	2. _____
3. Enter any tuition and fees deduction from Form 1040, line 34, or Form 1040A, line 19	3. _____
4. Enter any domestic production activities deduction from Form 1040, line 35	4. _____
5. Enter any foreign earned income and/or housing exclusion from Form 2555, line 45, or Form 2555-EZ, line 18	5. _____
6. Enter any foreign housing deduction from Form 2555, line 50	6. _____
7. Enter any excludable savings bond interest from Form 8815, line 14................................	7. _____
8. Enter any excluded employer-provided adoption benefits from Form 8839, line 28.............................	8. _____
9. Add lines 1 through 8. This is your **Modified AGI** for traditional IRA purposes	9. _____

Modified adjusted gross income (AGI). How you figure your modified AGI depends on whether you are filing Form 1040 or Form 1040A. If you made contributions to your IRA for 2014 and received a distribution from your IRA in 2014, see Publication 590. You may be able to use Worksheet 17-1 to figure your modified AGI.

Form 1040. If you file Form 1040, refigure the amount on the page 1 "adjusted gross income" line without taking into account any of the following eight amounts.

- IRA deduction.
- Student loan interest deduction.
- Tuition and fees deduction.
- Domestic production activities deduction.
- Foreign earned income exclusion.
- Foreign housing exclusion or deduction.
- Exclusion of qualified savings bond interest shown on Form 8815, Exclusion of Interest From Series EE and I U.S. Savings Bonds Issued After 1989.
- Exclusion of employer-provided adoption benefits shown on Form 8839, Qualified Adoption Expenses.

This is your modified AGI.

Form 1040A. If you file Form 1040A, refigure the amount on the page 1 "adjusted gross income" line without taking into account any of the following amounts.

- IRA deduction.
- Student loan interest deduction.
- Tuition and fees deduction.
- Exclusion of qualified savings bond interest shown on Form 8815.

This is your modified AGI.

Both contributions for 2014 and distributions in 2014. If all three of the following apply, any IRA distributions you received in 2014 may be partly tax free and partly taxable.

- You received distributions in 2014 from one or more traditional IRAs.
- You made contributions to a traditional IRA for 2014.
- Some of those contributions may be nondeductible contributions.

If this is your situation, you must figure the taxable part of the traditional IRA distribution before you can figure your modified AGI. To do this, you can use Worksheet 1-5, Figuring the Taxable Part of Your IRA Distribution, in Publication 590.

If at least one of the above does not apply, figure your modified AGI using Worksheet 17-1, later.

How to figure your reduced IRA deduction. You can figure your reduced IRA deduction for either Form 1040 or Form 1040A by using the worksheets in chapter 1 of Publication 590. Also, the instructions for Form 1040 and Form 1040A include similar worksheets that you may be able to use instead.

Reporting Deductible Contributions

If you file Form 1040, enter your IRA deduction on line 32 of that form. If you file Form 1040A, enter your IRA deduction on line 17. You cannot deduct IRA contributions on Form 1040EZ.

Nondeductible Contributions

Although your deduction for IRA contributions may be reduced or eliminated, contributions can be made to your IRA up to the general limit or, if it applies, the Kay Bailey Hutchison Spousal IRA limit. The difference between your total permitted contributions and your IRA deduction, if any, is your nondeductible contribution.

Example. Mike is 28 years old and single. In 2014, he was covered by a retirement plan at work. His salary was $57,312. His modified AGI was $71,000. Mike made a $5,500 IRA contribution for 2014. Because he was covered by a retirement plan and his modified AGI was over $70,000, he cannot deduct his $5,500 IRA contribution. He must designate this contribution as a nondeductible contribution by reporting it on Form 8606, as explained next.

Form 8606. To designate contributions as nondeductible, you must file Form 8606.

You do not have to designate a contribution as nondeductible until you file your tax return. When you file, you can even designate otherwise deductible contributions as nondeductible.

You must file Form 8606 to report nondeductible contributions even if you do not have to file a tax return for the year.

EXPLANATION

The chief advantage of nondeductible IRA contributions is that since the income compounds on a tax-deferred basis, the ending balance will be substantially larger under an IRA than in a taxable account. In deciding whether to make nondeductible contributions, you should compare the IRA's estimated rate of return over time against the estimated rate of return of other investments, such as tax-exempt municipal bonds and annuity contracts, and after-tax rates of return on taxable investments. You must also consider the expected tax effect when you begin taking distributions (i.e., whether you expect to be in a lower tax bracket when you receive distributions). In most cases, if you are eligible, you will be better off making a contribution to a Roth IRA than to a nondeductible IRA. The taxation of IRA distributions is discussed later.

Failure to report nondeductible contributions. If you do not report nondeductible contributions, all of the contributions to your traditional IRA will be treated as deductible contributions when withdrawn. All distributions from your IRA will be taxed unless you can show, with satisfactory evidence, that nondeductible contributions were made.

Penalty for overstatement. If you overstate the amount of nondeductible contributions on your Form 8606 for any tax year, you must pay a penalty of $100 for each overstatement, unless it was due to reasonable cause.

Penalty for failure to file Form 8606. You will have to pay a $50 penalty if you do not file a required Form 8606, unless you can prove that the failure was due to reasonable cause.

EXPLANATION

The law subjecting taxpayers to a $50 fine for failure to file Form 8606 applies retroactively to 1987. If you should have filed Form 8606 for a prior tax year but failed to do so, you should consider amending your return. See chapter 1, *Filing information*, for additional details regarding amending your return.

Tax on earnings on nondeductible contributions. As long as contributions are within the contribution limits, none of the earnings or gains on contributions (deductible or nondeductible) will be taxed until they are distributed. See *When Can You Withdraw or Use IRA Assets?*, later.

Cost basis. You will have a cost basis in your traditional IRA if you made any nondeductible contributions. Your cost basis is the sum of the nondeductible contributions to your IRA minus any withdrawals or distributions of nondeductible contributions.

Inherited IRAs

If you inherit a traditional IRA, you are called a beneficiary. A beneficiary can be any person or entity the owner chooses to receive the benefits of the IRA after he or she dies. Beneficiaries of a traditional IRA must include in their gross income any taxable distributions they receive.

Inherited from spouse. If you inherit a traditional IRA from your spouse, you generally have the following three choices. You can:

1. Treat it as your own IRA by designating yourself as the account owner.
2. Treat it as your own by rolling it over into your IRA, or to the extent it is taxable, into a:
   a. Qualified employer plan,
   b. Qualified employee annuity plan (Section 403(a) plan),
   c. Tax-sheltered annuity plan (Section 403(b) plan), or
   d. Deferred compensation plan of a state or local government (Section 457 plan).
3. Treat yourself as the beneficiary rather than treating the IRA as your own.

Treating it as your own. You will be considered to have chosen to treat the IRA as your own if:
- Contributions (including rollover contributions) are made to the inherited IRA, or
- You do not take the required minimum distribution for a year as a beneficiary of the IRA.

You will only be considered to have chosen to treat the IRA as your own if:
- You are the sole beneficiary of the IRA, and
- You have an unlimited right to withdraw amounts from it.

However, if you receive a distribution from your deceased spouse's IRA, you can roll that distribution over into your own IRA within the 60-day time limit, as long as the distribution is not a required distribution, even if you are not the sole beneficiary of your deceased spouse's IRA.

> ### TAXPLANNER
> If you are the beneficiary of a deceased employee's IRA or other eligible retirement plan (such as a qualified pension, profit-sharing, stock bonus, Section 403(b) or Section 457 plan), and are not the employee's surviving spouse (surviving spouses have additional options), you may be able to roll over a distribution from the plan tax free to an IRA you specifically set up to receive the distribution. To qualify as an eligible rollover distribution, the distribution must be a direct trustee-to-trustee transfer completed within 60 days of the distribution. The IRA receiving the distribution is treated as an inherited IRA. For more information, see *What if You Inherit an IRA?* in Publication 590, *Individual Retirement Arrangements (IRAs)*.

Inherited from someone other than spouse. If you inherit a traditional IRA from anyone other than your deceased spouse, you cannot treat the inherited IRA as your own. This means that you cannot make any contributions to the IRA. It also means you cannot roll over any amounts into or out of the inherited IRA. However, you can make a trustee-to-trustee transfer as long as the IRA into which amounts are being moved is set up and maintained in the name of the deceased IRA owner for the benefit of you as beneficiary.

For more information, see the discussion of inherited IRAs under *Rollover From One IRA Into Another*, later.

Can You Move Retirement Plan Assets?

You can transfer, tax free, assets (money or property) from other retirement plans (including traditional IRAs) to a traditional IRA. You can make the following kinds of transfers.
- Transfers from one trustee to another.
- Rollovers.
- Transfers incident to a divorce.

Transfers to Roth IRAs. Under certain conditions, you can move assets from a traditional IRA or from a designated Roth account to a Roth IRA. You can also move assets from a qualified retirement plan to a Roth IRA. See *Can You Move Amounts Into a Roth IRA?* under *Roth IRAs*, later.

Trustee-to-Trustee Transfer

A transfer of funds in your traditional IRA from one trustee directly to another, either at your request or at the trustee's request, is not a rollover. Because there is no distribution to you, the transfer is tax free. Because it is not a rollover, it is not affected by the 1-year waiting period required between rollovers, discussed later under *Rollover From One IRA Into Another*. For information about direct transfers to IRAs from retirement plans other than IRAs, see *Can You Move Retirement Plan Assets?* in chapter 1 and *Can You Move Amounts Into a Roth IRA?* in chapter 2 of Publication 590.

Rollovers

Generally, a rollover is a tax-free distribution to you of cash or other assets from one retirement plan that you contribute (roll over) to another retirement plan. The contribution to the second retirement plan is called a "rollover contribution."

Note. An amount rolled over tax free from one retirement plan to another is generally includible in income when it is distributed from the second plan.

Kinds of rollovers to a traditional IRA. You can roll over amounts from the following plans into a traditional IRA:

- A traditional IRA,
- An employer's qualified retirement plan for its employees,
- A deferred compensation plan of a state or local government (Section 457 plan), or
- A tax-sheltered annuity plan (Section 403(b) plan).

Treatment of rollovers. You cannot deduct a rollover contribution, but you must report the rollover distribution on your tax return as discussed later under *Reporting rollovers from IRAs* and under *Reporting rollovers from employer plans*.

Kinds of rollovers from a traditional IRA. You may be able to roll over, tax free, a distribution from your traditional IRA into a qualified plan. These plans include the federal Thrift Savings Fund (for federal employees), deferred compensation plans of state or local governments (Section 457 plans), and tax-sheltered annuity plans (Section 403(b) plans). The part of the distribution that you can roll over is the part that would otherwise be taxable (includible in your income). Qualified plans may, but are not required to, accept such rollovers.

Time limit for making a rollover contribution. You generally must make the rollover contribution by the 60th day after the day you receive the distribution from your traditional IRA or your employer's plan.

The IRS may waive the 60-day requirement where the failure to do so would be against equity or good conscience, such as in the event of a casualty, disaster, or other event beyond your reasonable control. For more information, see *Can You Move Retirement Plan Assets?* in chapter 1 of Publication 590.

Extension of rollover period. If an amount distributed to you from a traditional IRA or a qualified employer retirement plan is a frozen deposit at any time during the 60-day period allowed for a rollover, special rules extend the rollover period. For more information, see *Can You Move Retirement Plan Assets?* in chapter 1 of Publication 590.

More information. For more information on rollovers, see *Can You Move Retirement Plan Assets?* in chapter 1 of Publication 590.

Rollover From One IRA Into Another

You can withdraw, tax free, all or part of the assets from one traditional IRA if you reinvest them within 60 days in the same or another traditional IRA. Because this is a rollover, you cannot deduct the amount that you reinvest in an IRA.

Waiting period between rollovers through the end of 2014. Generally, if you make a tax-free rollover of any part of a distribution from a traditional IRA, you cannot, within a 1-year period, make a tax-free rollover of any later distribution from that same IRA. You also cannot make a tax-free rollover of any amount distributed, within the same 1-year period, from the IRA into which you made the tax-free rollover.

The 1-year period begins on the date you receive the IRA distribution, not on the date you roll it over into an IRA.

Example. You have two traditional IRAs, IRA-1 and IRA-2. You make a tax-free rollover of a distribution from IRA-1 into a new traditional IRA (IRA-3). You cannot, within 1 year of the distribution from IRA-1, make a tax-free rollover of any distribution from either IRA-1 or IRA-3 into another traditional IRA.

However, the rollover from IRA-1 into IRA-3 does not prevent you from making a tax-free rollover from IRA-2 into any other traditional IRA. This is because you have not, within the last year, rolled over, tax free, any distribution from IRA-2 or made a tax-free rollover into IRA-2.

Exception. For an exception for distributions from failed financial institutions, see *Rollover From One IRA Into Another* under *Can You Move Retirement Plan Assets?* in chapter 1 of Publication 590.

Partial rollovers. If you withdraw assets from a traditional IRA, you can roll over part of the withdrawal tax free and keep the rest of it. The amount you keep will generally be taxable (except for the part that is a return of nondeductible contributions). The amount you keep may be subject to the 10% additional tax on early distributions, discussed later under *What Acts Result in Penalties or Additional Taxes?*.

Required distributions. Amounts that must be distributed during a particular year under the required distribution rules (discussed later) are not eligible for rollover treatment.

Inherited IRAs. If you inherit a traditional IRA from your spouse, you generally can roll it over, or you can choose to make the inherited IRA your own. See *Treating it as your own*, earlier.

Not inherited from spouse. If you inherit a traditional IRA from someone other than your spouse, you cannot roll it over or allow it to receive a rollover contribution. You must withdraw the IRA assets within a certain period. For more information, see *When Must You Withdraw Assets?* in chapter 1 of Publication 590.

Reporting rollovers from IRAs. Report any rollover from one traditional IRA to the same or another traditional IRA on lines 15a and 15b, Form 1040, or lines 11a and 11b, Form 1040A, as follows.

Enter the total amount of the distribution on Form 1040, line 15a, or Form 1040A, line 11a. If the total amount on Form 1040, line 15a, or Form 1040A, line 11a, was rolled over, enter zero on Form 1040, line 15b, or Form 1040A, line 11b. If the total distribution was not rolled over, enter the taxable portion of the part that was not rolled over on Form 1040, line 15b, or Form 1040A, line 11b. Put "Rollover" next to Form 1040, line 15b, or Form 1040A, line 11b. See your tax return instructions.

If you rolled over the distribution into a qualified plan (other than an IRA) or you make the rollover in 2015, attach a statement explaining what you did.

Rollover From Employer's Plan Into an IRA

You can roll over into a traditional IRA all or part of an eligible rollover distribution you receive from your (or your deceased spouse's):

- Employer's qualified pension, profit-sharing, or stock bonus plan;
- Annuity plan;
- Tax-sheltered annuity plan (Section 403(b) plan); or
- Governmental deferred compensation plan (Section 457 plan).

A qualified plan is one that meets the requirements of the Internal Revenue Code.

TAXPLANNER

Income tax withholding may apply to distributions made from qualified employer plans. Withholding at a rate of 20% is required on a distribution unless it is transferred directly from your former employer's qualified plan to an IRA trustee or another employer's qualified plan.

The withholding rules do not apply to distributions from IRAs (or simplified employee pensions [SEPs]). However, if you wish to roll over a qualified plan distribution to an IRA, be sure to transfer the amount directly from your employer's plan to an IRA trustee or another employer plan. Otherwise, 20% of the distribution will be withheld while 100% of the taxable distribution must be rolled over within 60 days to avoid taxation on the taxable amount not rolled over (i.e., the 20% withheld is not exempt from tax unless an equal amount is rolled over timely). If you don't have the money to cover the 20% shortage, income taxes (and possibly a 10% penalty) will be due on the amount not rolled over.

For further information, see chapter 10, *Retirement plans, pensions, and annuities.*

Eligible rollover distribution. Generally, an eligible rollover distribution is any distribution of all or part of the balance to your credit in a qualified retirement plan except the following.

1. A required minimum distribution (explained later under *When Must You Withdraw IRA Assets? (Required Minimum Distributions)*).
2. A hardship distribution.
3. Any of a series of substantially equal periodic distributions paid at least once a year over:
   a. Your lifetime or life expectancy,
   b. The lifetimes or life expectancies of you and your beneficiary, or
   c. A period of 10 years or more.
4. Corrective distributions of excess contributions or excess deferrals, and any income allocable to the excess, or of excess annual additions and any allocable gains.
5. A loan treated as a distribution because it does not satisfy certain requirements either when made or later (such as upon default), unless the participant's accrued benefits are reduced (offset) to repay the loan.
6. Dividends on employer securities.
7. The cost of life insurance coverage.

Tip

Any nontaxable amounts that you roll over into your traditional IRA become part of your basis (cost) in your IRAs. To recover your basis when you take distributions from your IRA, you must complete Form 8606 for the year of the distribution. See Form 8606 under Distributions Fully or Partly Taxable, later.

EXPLANATION

You may withdraw the balance in your IRA and reinvest it in another IRA with no tax consequences if the money is reinvested within 60 days after the funds are received. This type of rollover may be done only once in a 1-year period. This rule applies to each separate IRA you own.

Example

You have two or more IRAs. You can roll over a single distribution from each or all of them to a new IRA or to another existing IRA within a 1-year period (i.e., only once for each IRA). For example, you can do one 60-day rollover from your first IRA and one 60-day rollover from your other IRA, but you cannot do two 60-day rollovers from your first IRA. Trustee-to-trustee transfers do not count as a rollover for this purpose and are unlimited.

TAXALERT

The 60-day rule described above applies to the day you receive the distribution, not the day the distribution is made. Therefore, if you receive the distribution in the mail, you have 60 days from the date you received it in the mail to roll the funds into a new account, regardless of the date the check was cut.

TAXPLANNER

If you transfer funds directly between trustees of your IRA and you never actually control or use the account assets, you may transfer your account as often as you like.

All or part of a lump-sum distribution from a qualified employer benefit plan may be transferred to an IRA. You may affect a partial rollover—and be taxed at ordinary income rates—only on the portion of the money not reinvested within 60 days. As mentioned earlier, withholding at a rate of 20% is required on a qualified employer plan distribution unless it is transferred directly from your employer to the trustee of an IRA.

TAXPLANNER

A partial distribution from a qualified plan is eligible for rollover treatment as long as it is not:
1. A required minimum distribution (e.g., for individuals who have attained age 70½);
2. A distribution that is part of a series of substantially equal payments that are received at least annually over life, life expectancy, or a period of at least 10 years;
3. A hardship distribution;
4. A return of excess contributions, excess aggregate contributions, or excess deferrals;
5. A loan treated as a distribution because it does not satisfy certain requirements either when made or later (such as upon default), unless the participant's accrued benefits are reduced (offset) to repay the loan;
6. Dividends on employer securities; or
7. Payment for life insurance coverage.

TAXPLANNER

Not all distributions from qualified employer benefit plans may be rolled over into an IRA. IRAs are specifically prohibited from investing in life insurance contracts. Therefore, if your employer plan distributes to you both cash and a life insurance policy, the value of the life insurance policy (except for your contributions) is currently taxable to you. If this is the case, you should consider rolling over the life insurance contract into another qualified pension, profit-sharing, or stock bonus plan that allows investments in life insurance contracts. You can also cash in the life insurance policy and roll over the proceeds.

TAXPLANNER

A court has held that a tax-free rollover can be made only if the employer's plan and trust are tax-exempt when the distribution is made. In this particular case, the IRS retroactively revoked the tax exempt status of the trust. This made the distribution retroactively ineligible for a rollover.

The IRS believes that once you have made a rollover, you cannot change your mind and report the distribution as taxable income. However, you could replicate this effect by taking a distribution from the IRA to which you rolled the prior distribution. You could also transfer it to a Roth IRA, which would mean you would pay tax upon the transfer to the Roth but not when the transferred amount (and earnings thereon) are distributed from the Roth IRA (as long as the requirements for a tax-free, qualified distribution are met).

You may roll over a lump-sum distribution from a former spouse's IRA or employee plan that was transferred to you by a divorce decree or written agreement incident to the divorce.

TAXALERT

The IRS has the ability to waive the 60-day rule where there are extenuating circumstances, such as a casualty, disaster, or an egregious error by a financial institution. In certain circumstances the waiver may be automatic; in others you may have to file a request with the IRS. The IRS has been relatively sympathetic to taxpayers and has issued a number of waiver rulings in recent years.

Rollover by nonspouse beneficiary. A direct transfer from a deceased employee's qualified pension, profit-sharing, or stock bonus plan; annuity plan; tax-sheltered annuity (Section 403(b)) plan; or governmental deferred compensation (Section 457) plan to an IRA set up to receive the distribution on your behalf can be treated as an eligible rollover distribution if you are the designated beneficiary of the plan and not the employee's spouse. The IRA is treated as an inherited IRA. For more information about inherited IRAs, see *Inherited IRAs*, earlier.

Reporting rollovers from employer plans. Enter the total distribution (before income tax or other deductions were withheld) on Form 1040, line 16a, or Form 1040A, line 12a. This amount should be shown in box 1 of Form 1099-R. From this amount, subtract any contributions (usually shown in box 5 of Form 1099-R) that were taxable to you when made. From that result, subtract the amount that was rolled over either directly or within 60 days of receiving the distribution. Enter the remaining amount, even if zero, on Form 1040, line 16b, or Form 1040A, line 12b. Also, enter "Rollover" next to Form 1040, line 16b, or Form 1040A, line 12b.

Transfers Incident to Divorce

If an interest in a traditional IRA is transferred from your spouse or former spouse to you by a divorce or separate maintenance decree or a written document related to such a decree, the interest in the IRA, starting from the date of the transfer, is treated as your IRA. The transfer is tax free. For detailed information, see *Can You Move Retirement Plan Assets?* in chapter 1 of Publication 590.

Converting From Any Traditional IRA to a Roth IRA

Allowable conversions. You can withdraw all or part of the assets from a traditional IRA and reinvest them (within 60 days) in a Roth IRA. The amount that you withdraw and timely contribute (convert) to the Roth IRA is called a conversion contribution. If properly (and timely) rolled over, the 10% additional tax on early distributions will not apply. However, a part or all of the conversion contribution from your traditional IRA is included in your gross income.

TAXALERT

Prior to 2010, only taxpayers with modified AGI of less than $100,000 and whose filing status was anything other than married filing separate were eligible to convert tax-deferred savings accounts, such as traditional IRAs, to Roth IRAs. Beginning with 2010, these restrictions were lifted, and now anyone can make the conversion to a Roth IRA.

TAXPLANNER

Although modified AGI limitations restrict contributions to a Roth IRA for taxpayers with income over certain thresholds, there is no income limitation prohibiting you from making a conversion from a traditional IRA to a Roth IRA. If you want to make a Roth IRA contribution but are restricted due to your modified AGI level, consider making a nondeductible contribution to a traditional IRA and then electing to convert that nontraditional IRA to a Roth IRA. This achieves the same result as a direct contribution to a Roth IRA account.

Required distributions. You cannot convert amounts that must be distributed from your traditional IRA for a particular year (including the calendar year in which you reach age 70½) under the required distribution rules (discussed later).

Income. You must include in your gross income distributions from a traditional IRA that you would have had to include in income if you had not converted them into a Roth IRA. These amounts are normally included in income on your return for the year that you converted them from a traditional IRA to a Roth IRA.

You do not include in gross income any part of a distribution from a traditional IRA that is a return of your basis, as discussed later.

You must file Form 8606 to report 2014 conversions from traditional, SEP, or SIMPLE IRAs to a Roth IRA in 2014 (unless you recharacterized the entire amount) and to figure the amount to include in income.

If you must include any amount in your gross income, you may have to increase your withholding or make estimated tax payments. See chapter 4.

Recharacterizations

You may be able to treat a contribution made to one type of IRA as having been made to a different type of IRA. This is called recharacterizing the contribution. See *Can You Move Retirement Plan Assets?* in chapter 1 of Publication 590 for more detailed information.

How to recharacterize a contribution. To recharacterize a contribution, you generally must have the contribution transferred from the first IRA (the one to which it was made) to the second IRA in a trustee-to-trustee transfer. If the transfer is made by the due date (including extensions) for your tax return for the year during which the contribution was made, you can elect to treat the contribution as having been originally made to the second IRA instead of to the first IRA. If you recharacterize your contribution, you must do all three of the following.

- Include in the transfer any net income allocable to the contribution. If there was a loss, the net income you must transfer may be a negative amount.
- Report the recharacterization on your tax return for the year during which the contribution was made.
- Treat the contribution as having been made to the second IRA on the date that it was actually made to the first IRA.

No deduction allowed. You cannot deduct the contribution to the first IRA. Any net income you transfer with the recharacterized contribution is treated as earned in the second IRA.

Required notifications. To recharacterize a contribution, you must notify both the trustee of the first IRA (the one to which the contribution was actually made) and the trustee of the second IRA (the one to which the contribution is being moved) that you have elected to treat the contribution as having been made to the second IRA rather than the first. You must make the notifications by the date of the transfer. Only one notification is required if both IRAs are maintained by the same trustee. The notification(s) must include all of the following information.

- The type and amount of the contribution to the first IRA that is to be recharacterized.
- The date on which the contribution was made to the first IRA and the year for which it was made.
- A direction to the trustee of the first IRA to transfer in a trustee-to-trustee transfer the amount of the contribution and any net income (or loss) allocable to the contribution to the trustee of the second IRA.
- The name of the trustee of the first IRA and the name of the trustee of the second IRA.
- Any additional information needed to make the transfer.

Reporting a recharacterization. If you elect to recharacterize a contribution to one IRA as a contribution to another IRA, you must report the recharacterization on your tax return as directed by Form 8606 and its instructions. You must treat the contribution as having been made to the second IRA.

When Can You Withdraw or Use IRA Assets?

There are rules limiting use of your IRA assets and distributions from it. Violation of the rules generally results in additional taxes in the year of violation. See *What Acts Result in Penalties or Additional Taxes?*, later.

Contributions returned before the due date of return. If you made IRA contributions in 2014, you can withdraw them tax free by the due date of your return. If you have an extension of time to file your return, you can withdraw them tax free by the extended due date. You can do this if, for each contribution you withdraw, both of the following conditions apply.

- You did not take a deduction for the contribution.
- You withdraw any interest or other income earned on the contribution. You can take into account any loss on the contribution while it was in the IRA when calculating the amount that must be withdrawn. If there was a loss, the net income earned on the contribution may be a negative amount.

Note. To calculate the amount you must withdraw, see *Worksheet 1-4* under *When Can You Withdraw or Use Assets?* in chapter 1 of Publication 590.

Earnings includible in income. You must include in income any earnings on the contributions you withdraw. Include the earnings in income for the year in which you made the contributions, not in the year in which you withdraw them.

Early distributions tax. The 10% additional tax on distributions made before you reach age 59½ does not apply to these tax-free withdrawals of your contributions. However, the distribution of

Caution

Generally, except for any part of a withdrawal that is a return of nondeductible contributions (basis), any withdrawal of your contributions after the due date (or extended due date) of your return will be treated as a taxable distribution. Excess contributions can also be recovered tax free as discussed under What Acts Result in Penalties or Additional Taxes?, *later.*

interest or other income must be reported on Form 5329 and, unless the distribution qualifies as an exception to the age 59½ rule, it will be subject to this tax.

TAXPLANNER

Withdrawals from IRAs before age 59½ to pay educational expenses. Withdrawals from an IRA are not subject to the 10% early distribution additional tax if, for the year of withdrawal, you have paid sufficient (i.e., in excess of the withdrawal) qualified higher education expenses for yourself, your spouse, or for your or your spouse's children or grandchildren. This exception does not apply if you use the money to pay for expenses you incurred in a different year.

Qualifications and income limits. There are no specific income limits restricting the use of this provision.

When Must You Withdraw IRA Assets? (Required Minimum Distributions)

You cannot keep funds in a traditional IRA indefinitely. Eventually they must be distributed. If there are no distributions, or if the distributions are not large enough, you may have to pay a 50% excise tax on the amount not distributed as required. See *Excess Accumulations (Insufficient Distributions)*, later. The requirements for distributing IRA funds differ depending on whether you are the IRA owner or the beneficiary of a decedent's IRA.

Required minimum distribution. The amount that must be distributed each year is referred to as the required minimum distribution.

Required distributions not eligible for rollover. Amounts that must be distributed (required minimum distributions) during a particular year are not eligible for rollover treatment.

IRA owners. If you are the owner of a traditional IRA, you must generally start receiving distributions from your IRA by April 1 of the year following the year in which you reach age 70½. April 1 of the year following the year in which you reach age 70½ is referred to as the required beginning date.

Distributions by the required beginning date. You must receive at least a minimum amount for each year starting with the year you reach age 70½ (your 70½ year). If you do not (or did not) receive that minimum amount in your 70½ year, then you must receive distributions for your 70½ year by April 1 of the next year.

If an IRA owner dies after reaching age 70½, but before April 1 of the next year, no minimum distribution is required because death occurred before the required beginning date.

Distributions after the required beginning date. The required minimum distribution for any year after the year you turn 70½ must be made by December 31 of that later year.

Caution

Even if you begin receiving distributions before you attain age 70½, you must begin calculating and receiving required minimum distributions by your required beginning date.

TAXPLANNER
Explanation

The purpose of an IRA is to provide retirement income. Therefore, when you reach age 70½, you are expected to begin withdrawing the proceeds in your IRA rather than continue to let the funds accumulate and use the IRA as a tool to build your estate. If you don't withdraw the minimum amounts yearly, a 50% nondeductible tax is levied on the amount of the minimum payment left in your IRA.

You must start receiving minimum payments from your IRA by April 1 of the year after the year in which you reach age 70½. Unlike the qualified plan rule for non-5% owners, there is no delay because you are still working.

It is only your first distribution (the distribution for the year you reach age 70½) that may be delayed until April 1 of the following year. The second distribution must be made by December 31 of the same year. The doubling of distributions will have an effect on your tax liability.

Generally, the minimum distribution is based on the joint life expectancy of both you and a survivor who is assumed to be no more than 10 years younger (see IRS Publication 590 or chapter 10 for the appropriate life expectancy table). Alternatively, if your spouse is more than 10 years younger than you, and your spouse is the sole beneficiary of your IRA, the minimum distribution is based on your and your spouse's actual joint life expectancy (see IRS Publication 590 for the appropriate life expectancy table). Using this alternate method will result in a lower minimum distribution than the general method due to using a longer life expectancy.

It's worth noting that your IRA fund may continue to grow, even if you are taking the required distributions. For example, if the table used indicates a life expectancy of 20 years, you must withdraw only one-twentieth (5%) of your IRA funds in that year. If the funds in your IRA are earning income at the rate of 10%, your account will continue to grow. You may not make additional annual contributions after you attain age 70½. However, this rule does not prevent you from making contributions to a new or existing Roth IRA if you meet the income standards. There are no minimum distribution requirements from a Roth IRA while you are alive. Because there are such requirements for qualified plans, including Roth 401(k) plans, and the income limit has been removed on Roth conversions, you should consult with your tax advisor about rolling over qualified plan accounts to a Roth IRA. Remember that if you roll over a qualified plan account to a Roth IRA, you may pay tax immediately.

TAXALERT

Once distributions are required, a minimum distribution must be made each year based on the age of the IRA owner and, where relevant, his or her spouse using the appropriate life expectancy or annuity table.

Example

Jack Jones, who is single, attains age 70½ years old on May 1, 2014. He has an IRA with a December 31, 2013, balance of $80,000. By looking at tables published by the IRS, he finds that his life expectancy for purposes of his IRA distributions is 26.5 years. This is the life expectancy for a person who is 71, which he will be during 2014. To figure his minimum distribution, he divides the amount in his IRA by 26.5. He must receive a distribution of $3,019 prior to April 1, 2015, to avoid a penalty. If Jack was married, he would use the same life expectancy table as long as his wife isn't 10 or more years younger than him. If she was, Jack would use a different table. For example, if Jack's wife is age 60 when he attains age 70½, he would use a life expectancy of 27.2 years, providing for a required minimum distribution of $2,941.

TAXPLANNER

You are always permitted to take more out of your IRA than the required minimum distribution. However, while the distribution will reduce the balance on which the following year's required minimum distribution is calculated, you cannot get "advance credit" to offset the minimum distribution requirement in that following year.

TAXPLANNER

The rules for determining required minimum distributions for beneficiaries depend on whether the beneficiary is the sole beneficiary of an individual. The rules for individuals are explained below. If the owner's beneficiary is not an individual (for example, the owner's estate), see IRS Publication 590.

Surviving spouse. If you are a surviving spouse who is the sole beneficiary of your deceased spouse's IRA, you may elect to be treated as the owner and not the beneficiary. If you elect to be treated as the owner, you determine the required minimum distribution (if any) as if you were the owner beginning with the year you elect or are deemed to be the owner. However, if you become the owner in the year your deceased spouse died, you are not required to determine the required minimum distribution for that year using your life; rather, you can take the deceased owner's required minimum distribution for that year (to the extent it was not already distributed to the owner before his or her death).

Taking balance within 5 years. A beneficiary who is an individual may be required to take the entire account by the end of the fifth year following the year of the owner's death. If this rule applies, no distribution is required for any year before that fifth year.

Owner died on or after required beginning date. If the owner died on or after his or her required beginning date, and you are the designated beneficiary, you generally must base required minimum distributions for years after the year of the owner's death on the longer of your single life expectancy, or the owner's life expectancy.

Owner died before required beginning date. If the owner died before the required beginning date, base required minimum distributions for years after the year of the owner's death generally on your single life expectancy.

Generally, the designated beneficiary is determined on September 30 of the calendar year following the calendar year of the IRA owner's death. In order to be a designated beneficiary, an individual must be a beneficiary as of the date of death. Any person who was a beneficiary on the date of the owner's death, but is not a beneficiary on September 30 of the calendar year following the calendar year of the owner's death (because, for example, he or she disclaimed entitlement or received his or her entire benefit), will not be taken into account in determining the designated beneficiary.

See IRS Publication 590 for further guidance and examples. However, these rules are quite complex and you should seek tax advice.

TAXPLANNER

There are no minimum required distributions for a Roth IRA during the life of the account owner (see _Roth IRAs_ for more details).

TAXPLANNER

Keogh plans. The same withdrawal techniques described earlier in the TaxPlanners may be used with a Keogh plan, a retirement arrangement that self-employed people may set up.

TAXPLANNER

Employer stock bonus plans and company profit-sharing plans. The main attraction of having your employer put some of your compensation into a stock bonus plan or a company profit-sharing plan is that you are not currently taxed on the contributions to or the earnings in the plan. In addition, these plans have certain advantages that IRAs do not:
1. Borrowing is permitted if the loan is repaid within 5 years.
2. A lump-sum distribution may qualify for 10-year averaging for those born before January 2, 1936.
3. Minimum distributions from the employer's plan can be deferred if you continue to work for that employer after age 70½.
4. The contribution limits are higher.

Caution

Although a conversion of a traditional IRA is considered a rollover for Roth IRA purposes, it is not an exception to the rule that distributions from a traditional IRA are taxable in the year you receive them. Conversion distributions are includible in your gross income subject to this rule and the special rules for conversions explained in Converting From Any Traditional IRA Into a Roth IRA under Can You Move Retirement Plan Assets? in chapter 1 of Publication 590.

Beneficiaries. If you are the beneficiary of a decedent's traditional IRA, the requirements for distributions from that IRA generally depend on whether the IRA owner died before or after the required beginning date for distributions.

More information. For more information, including how to figure your minimum required distribution each year and how to figure your required distribution if you are a beneficiary of a decedent's IRA, see _When Must You Withdraw Assets?_ in chapter 1 of Publication 590.

Are Distributions Taxable?

In general, distributions from a traditional IRA are taxable in the year you receive them.

Exceptions. Exceptions to distributions from traditional IRAs being taxable in the year you receive them are:
- Rollovers,
- _Text intentionally omitted._
- Tax-free withdrawals of contributions, discussed earlier, and
- The return of nondeductible contributions, discussed later under _Distributions Fully or Partly Taxable_.

IRA distributions are taxed in a manner similar to annuities. If you do not make nondeductible contributions, all distributions from a traditional IRA are taxed as ordinary income. You may not use special 10-year averaging on a lump-sum distribution from your IRA, even if the account is a rollover from a qualified plan. If you made nondeductible contributions, a portion of the distribution may be excludable from income. The excludable amount is computed as follows:

$$\frac{\text{Undistributed Nondeductible Contributions}}{\text{Total of All IRA Balances}} \times \text{Distribution Amount}$$

Example
Assume that Mary has one IRA to which she made a $2,000 nondeductible contribution and that her total account balance is $20,000. In 2014, she takes a $5,000 distribution. Her tax-free amount is:

$$\$2,000/\$20,000 \times \$5,000 = \$500$$

Undistributed nondeductible contributions are obtained from the last Form 8606 you filed. Therefore, make sure you always keep the most recent copy in your files.

Money that you withdraw from your IRA is treated as a distribution to you and may trigger the 10% penalty that is imposed on premature distributions. However, it is possible to "borrow" temporarily from your IRA by taking a distribution and rolling over the funds to the same or to a new IRA within 60 days. That money is not considered premature distributions. You may not contribute any money you earn on it during those 60 days to your IRA account, nor may you reduce the amount you must roll over by any losses during those 60 days.

Text intentionally omitted.

Ordinary income. Distributions from traditional IRAs that you include in income are taxed as ordinary income.

No special treatment. In figuring your tax, you cannot use the 10-year tax option or capital gain treatment that applies to lump-sum distributions from qualified retirement plans.

Distributions Fully or Partly Taxable

Distributions from your traditional IRA may be fully or partly taxable, depending on whether your IRA includes any nondeductible contributions.

Fully taxable. If only deductible contributions were made to your traditional IRA (or IRAs, if you have more than one), you have no basis in your IRA. Because you have no basis in your IRA, any distributions are fully taxable when received. See *Reporting taxable distributions on your return*, later.

Partly taxable. If you made nondeductible contributions or rolled over any after-tax amounts to any of your traditional IRAs, you have a cost basis (investment in the contract) equal to the amount of those contributions. These nondeductible contributions are not taxed when they are distributed to you. They are a return of your investment in your IRA.

1. The occurrence of a prohibited transaction causes the entire amount in your individual retirement account to be treated as distributed and therefore taxable to you. For instance, if you lend yourself the money in your IRA, the entire amount in the account is then currently taxable to you (see *Prohibited Transactions*, following).
2. The pledging of an IRA causes the portion pledged to be treated as distributed. For example, if you have an IRA with a value of $7,500 that you pledge as security for a $5,000 bank loan, you are taxed on the $5,000.
3. The pledging of an IRA annuity causes the entire account to be treated as distributed.

Only the part of the distribution that represents nondeductible contributions and rolled over after-tax amounts (your cost basis) is tax free. If nondeductible contributions have been made or after-tax amounts have been rolled over to your IRA, distributions consist partly of nondeductible contributions (basis) and partly of deductible contributions, earnings, and gains (if there are any). Until all of your basis has been distributed, each distribution is partly nontaxable and partly taxable.

Form 8606. You must complete Form 8606 and attach it to your return if you receive a distribution from a traditional IRA and have ever made nondeductible contributions or rolled over after-tax amounts to any of your traditional IRAs. Using the form, you will figure the nontaxable distributions for 2014 and your total IRA basis for 2014 and earlier years.

Note. If you are required to file Form 8606, but you are not required to file an income tax return, you still must file Form 8606. Send it to the IRS at the time and place you would otherwise file an income tax return.

Distributions reported on Form 1099-R. If you receive a distribution from your traditional IRA, you will receive Form 1099-R, Distributions From Pensions, Annuities, Retirement or Profit-Sharing Plans, IRAs, Insurance Contracts, etc., or a similar statement. IRA distributions are shown in boxes 1 and 2a of Form 1099-R. A number or letter code in box 7 tells you what type of distribution you received from your IRA.

TAXORGANIZER
Keep Form 1099-R with your records to substantiate IRA distributions and federal income tax withholding.

Withholding. Federal income tax is withheld from distributions from traditional IRAs unless you choose not to have tax withheld. See chapter 4.

EXPLANATION
You may elect at any time not to have taxes withheld on the distribution. Before electing not to withhold, however, you must review your withholdings from other sources and estimated payments. See chapter 4, *Tax withholding and estimated tax*, for the rules relating to underpayment penalties.

IRA distributions delivered outside the United States. In general, if you are a U.S. citizen or resident alien and your home address is outside the United States or its possessions, you cannot choose exemption from withholding on distributions from your traditional IRA.

Reporting taxable distributions on your return. Report fully taxable distributions, including early distributions on Form 1040, line 15b, or Form 1040A, line 11b (no entry is required on Form 1040, line 15a, or Form 1040A, line 11a). If only part of the distribution is taxable, enter the total amount on Form 1040, line 15a, or Form 1040A, line 11a, and the taxable part on Form 1040, line 15b, or Form 1040A, line 11b. You cannot report distributions on Form 1040EZ.

What Acts Result in Penalties or Additional Taxes?
The tax advantages of using traditional IRAs for retirement savings can be offset by additional taxes and penalties if you do not follow the rules.

There are additions to the regular tax for using your IRA funds in prohibited transactions. There are also additional taxes for the following activities.
- Investing in collectibles.
- Making excess contributions.
- Taking early distributions.
- Allowing excess amounts to accumulate (failing to take required distributions).

There are penalties for overstating the amount of nondeductible contributions and for failure to file a Form 8606, if required.

Prohibited Transactions
Generally, a prohibited transaction is any improper use of your traditional IRA by you, your beneficiary, or any disqualified person.

Disqualified persons include your fiduciary and members of your family (spouse, ancestor, lineal descendent, and any spouse of a lineal descendent).

The following are examples of prohibited transactions with a traditional IRA.
- Borrowing money from it.
- Selling property to it.
- Receiving unreasonable compensation for managing it.
- Using it as security for a loan.
- Buying property for personal use (present or future) with IRA funds.

Effect on an IRA account. Generally, if you or your beneficiary engages in a prohibited transaction in connection with your traditional IRA account at any time during the year, the account stops being an IRA as of the first day of that year.

Effect on you or your beneficiary. If your account stops being an IRA because you or your beneficiary engaged in a prohibited transaction, the account is treated as distributing all its assets to you at their fair market values on the first day of the year. If the total of those values is more than your basis in the IRA, you will have a taxable gain that is includible in your income. For information on figuring your gain and reporting it in income, see _Are Distributions Taxable?_, earlier. The distribution may be subject to additional taxes or penalties.

Taxes on prohibited transactions. If someone other than the owner or beneficiary of a traditional IRA engages in a prohibited transaction, that person may be liable for certain taxes. In general, there is a 15% tax on the amount of the prohibited transaction and a 100% additional tax if the transaction is not corrected.

More information. For more information on prohibited transactions, see _What Acts Result in Penalties or Additional Taxes?_ in chapter 1 of Publication 590.

EXPLANATION
The rules relating to prohibited transactions are designed to prevent the manipulation of IRA funds by the person who has set the funds aside for his or her retirement.

Investment in Collectibles
If your traditional IRA invests in collectibles, the amount invested is considered distributed to you in the year invested. You may have to pay the 10% additional tax on early distributions, discussed later.

Collectibles. These include:
- Artworks,
- Rugs,
- Antiques,
- Metals,
- Gems,
- Stamps,
- Coins,
- Alcoholic beverages, and
- Certain other tangible personal property.

Exception. Your IRA can invest in one, one-half, one-quarter, or one-tenth ounce U.S. gold coins, or one-ounce silver coins minted by the Treasury Department. It can also invest in certain platinum coins and certain gold, silver, palladium, and platinum bullion.

EXPLANATION
Although an investment in tangible property, such as artworks, precious metals or gems, antiques, or alcoholic beverages, is not technically a prohibited transaction, the cost of the item is treated as a distribution from your IRA. The amount is included in your income and may be subject to the 10% premature distribution penalty tax.

This rule is designed to prevent you from directing your IRA to invest in property that the trustee could conceivably allow you to keep in your home for your personal enjoyment (e.g., art for display on your home or office walls).

In order to help sell U.S. and state-issued gold and silver coins, Congress removed the penalty for such coins acquired after October 1, 1986.

Excess Contributions

Generally, an excess contribution is the amount contributed to your traditional IRA(s) for the year that is more than the smaller of:

- The maximum deductible amount for the year. For 2014, this is $5,500 ($6,500 if you are 50 or older), or
- Your taxable compensation for the year.

> ### EXAMPLE
> You contribute $11,000 to IRAs you have set up for you and your nonworking spouse. You put $6,050 into your account and $4,950 into your spouse's account. There is a $550 excess contribution to your account. Only $10,450 ($5,500 + $4,950) can be contributed and deducted on your joint income tax return. In order to obtain the full $11,000 contribution, you can withdraw the $550 excess contribution from your account and put it into your spouse's account. This must be done no later than April 15, 2015.

Tax on excess contributions. In general, if the excess contributions for a year are not withdrawn by the date your return for the year is due (including extensions), you are subject to a 6% tax. You must pay the 6% tax each year on excess amounts that remain in your traditional IRA at the end of your tax year. The tax cannot be more than 6% of the combined value of all your IRAs as of the end of your tax year.

Excess contributions withdrawn by due date of return. You will not have to pay the 6% tax if you withdraw an excess contribution made during a tax year and you also withdraw interest or other income earned on the excess contribution. You must complete your withdrawal by the date your tax return for that year is due, including extensions.

How to treat withdrawn contributions. Do not include in your gross income an excess contribution that you withdraw from your traditional IRA before your tax return is due if both the following conditions are met.

- No deduction was allowed for the excess contribution.
- You withdraw the interest or other income earned on the excess contribution.

You can take into account any loss on the contribution while it was in the IRA when calculating the amount that must be withdrawn. If there was a loss, the net income you must withdraw may be a negative amount.

How to treat withdrawn interest or other income. You must include in your gross income the interest or other income that was earned on the excess contribution. Report it on your return for the year in which the excess contribution was made. Your withdrawal of interest or other income may be subject to an additional 10% tax on early distributions, discussed later.

> ### EXPLANATION
> Excess contributions you withdraw before the due date of the return are not subject to the 6% excise tax, provided that the full amount of income attributable to the excess contribution is also distributed. The income portion of the distribution is then included in your income in the year in which the excess contribution was made. The withdrawn income may be subject to the 10% tax on premature distributions (see *Early Distributions*, following).

Excess contributions withdrawn after due date of return. In general, you must include all distributions (withdrawals) from your traditional IRA in your gross income. However, if the following conditions are met, you can withdraw excess contributions from your IRA and not include the amount withdrawn in your gross income.

- Total contributions (other than rollover contributions) for 2014 to your IRA were not more than $5,500 ($6,500 if you are 50 or older).
- You did not take a deduction for the excess contribution being withdrawn.

The withdrawal can take place at any time, even after the due date, including extensions, for filing your tax return for the year.

> ### EXPLANATION
> Excess payments may also be adjusted by deducting the correct amount in the current year and applying the excess to the following year's contribution.
>
> #### Example
> If you mistakenly contributed $5,500 to your IRA in 2013, when you were entitled to only a $5,000 contribution, you may reduce your 2014 contribution by the excess $500. If you are

entitled to a $5,500 contribution in 2014, you should then contribute no more than $5,000 that year. To make this application work, you must deduct only $5,000 for 2013—not the actual $5,500 you contributed. Although you are still subject to the 6% tax on the $500 excess contribution in 2014, if you reduce the following year's contribution to $5,000, there is no excess contribution remaining in your IRA and no tax would be imposed for 2014.

You would receive a $5,500 deduction for 2014 consisting of the $5,000 you actually contributed in 2014 plus the excess contribution from 2013.

Excess contribution deducted in an earlier year. If you deducted an excess contribution in an earlier year for which the total contributions were not more than the maximum deductible amount for that year (see the following table), you can still remove the excess from your traditional IRA and not include it in your gross income. To do this, file Form 1040X for that year and do not deduct the excess contribution on the amended return. Generally, you can file an amended return within 3 years after you filed your return, or 2 years from the time the tax was paid, whichever is later.

Year(s)	Contribution limit	Contribution limit if age 50 or older at the end of the year
2013 or 2014	$5,500	$6,500
2008 through 2012	$5,000	$6,000
2006 or 2007	$4,000	$5,000
2005	$4,000	$4,500
2002 through 2004	$3,000	$3,500
1997 through 2001	$2,000	–
before 1997	$2,250	–

Excess due to incorrect rollover information. If an excess contribution in your traditional IRA is the result of a rollover and the excess occurred because the information the plan was required to give you was incorrect, you can withdraw the excess contribution. The limits mentioned above are increased by the amount of the excess that is due to the incorrect information. You will have to amend your return for the year in which the excess occurred to correct the reporting of the rollover amounts in that year. Do not include in your gross income the part of the excess contribution caused by the incorrect information.

Early Distributions

You must include early distributions of taxable amounts from your traditional IRA in your gross income. Early distributions are also subject to an additional 10% tax. See the discussion of Form 5329 under *Reporting Additional Taxes*, later, to figure and report the tax.

Early distributions defined. Early distributions generally are amounts distributed from your traditional IRA account or annuity before you are age 59½.

TAXPLANNER

If you are fortunate enough to have sufficient income without taking any distributions from your IRA, you may wish to postpone withdrawing money from your IRA as long as possible. Distributions do not have to begin until April 1 of the calendar year following the year in which you reach age 70½. See *Required Distributions*, earlier.

Age 59½ rule. Generally, if you are under age 59½, you must pay a 10% additional tax on the distribution of any assets (money or other property) from your traditional IRA. Distributions before you are age 59½ are called early distributions.

The 10% additional tax applies to the part of the distribution that you have to include in gross income. It is in addition to any regular income tax on that amount.

Exceptions. There are several exceptions to the age 59½ rule. Even if you receive a distribution before you are age 59½, you may not have to pay the 10% additional tax if you are in one of the following situations.

- You have unreimbursed medical expenses that are more than 10% (or 7.5% if you or your spouse are age 65 or older) of your adjusted gross income.
- The distributions are not more than the cost of your medical insurance due to a period of unemployment.

- You are totally and permanently disabled.
- You are the beneficiary of a deceased IRA owner.
- You are receiving distributions in the form of an annuity.
- The distributions are not more than your qualified higher education expenses.
- You use the distributions to buy, build, or rebuild a first home.
- The distribution is due to an IRS levy of the qualified plan.
- The distribution is a qualified reservist distribution.

Most of these exceptions are explained under *Early Distributions* in *What Acts Result in Penalties or Additional Taxes?* in chapter 1 of Publication 590.

Note. Distributions that are timely and properly <u>rolled over</u>, as discussed earlier, are not subject to either regular income tax or the 10% additional tax. Certain withdrawals of excess contributions after the due date of your return are also tax free and therefore not subject to the 10% additional tax. (See *Excess contributions withdrawn after due date of return*, earlier.) This also applies to <u>transfers incident to divorce</u>, as discussed earlier.

TAXPLANNER

The life annuity exception may be beneficial if you retire before age 55, your employer's plan does not provide for a life annuity, and you don't want to pay the penalty and taxes on the distribution, but you need supplemental income. You will not be subject to the penalty if the plan distribution is rolled over into an IRA and then distributed as part of a series of substantially equal periodic payments (made no less frequently than annually) over your life expectancy or the joint life expectancies of you and a beneficiary.

Note that using the life annuity exception, you would not be making a single withdrawal. Rather, you would effectively be receiving an annuity in which the payments will be substantially equal. Modifying the payments before you reach age 59½, or, in any event, within 5 years of the date of the first payment, will result in the imposition of the 10% penalty tax that would have applied absent the exception, plus interest. The only exception is if you switch once from the amortization or the annuity factor method to the straight life expectancy method.

The IRS has identified three methods available for determining whether distributions from an IRA are considered to be "substantially equal periodic payments."
1. The "straight life expectancy" method: To use this method, you divide the balance in the individual retirement account at the end of each year by the owner's life expectancy or joint and survivor life expectancy, as determined from tables published by the IRS. Under this method, distributions may vary from year to year due to:
   a. account balance changes resulting from earnings and distributions during the year, and
   b. changes in the owner's life expectancy as the owner gets older.
2. The amortization method: This method involves determining an annuity payment based on the balance in the individual retirement account, the beneficiary's life expectancy, and an assumed interest rate. Under this method, you would essentially be able to choose among various distribution amounts: IRS rules allow you to select from several interest rate assumptions and between two published life expectancy tables. However, once the annuity amount has been determined, it will not change from year to year.
3. The annuity factor method: This method involves determining an annuity payment by dividing the balance in the individual retirement account by an annuity factor derived from a reasonable mortality table using a reasonable rate of interest. As under the amortization method, once determined, the annuity amount will not change.

TAXALERT

Note that the substantially equal periodic payment exception (described previously) is applied on an IRA-by-IRA basis. Therefore, an IRA owner who wants the flexibility in the future to increase the annual withdrawal amounts can divide an existing IRA into several IRAs before distributions begin. Substantially equal periodic distributions could be taken prior to age 59½ from only one of the IRAs. In the future, if additional payments are needed, distributions could be taken from one or more of the other IRAs.

Taxpayers have the ability to make a one-time switch from either the amortization method or annuity factor method to the straight life expectancy method. The one-time switch may be beneficial if you are locked into a fixed payment under either the amortization or annuity factor methods and your account has dropped in value. By using the one-time switch to the straight life expectancy method, a new lower payment can be calculated based on the lower account balance. You should consult your tax advisor for additional details.

The straight life expectancy method (method 1, described earlier) is the easiest to use but will result in the smallest annual distribution. The amortization and annuity factor methods result in larger distributions and are more difficult to compute, respectively, than the straight life expectancy method.

Since the rules regarding substantially equal periodic payments are complex and substantial penalties apply for failure to comply, you should consult your tax advisor when planning to take early distributions from your IRA(s).

Receivership distributions. Early distributions (with or without your consent) from savings institutions placed in receivership are subject to this tax unless one of the exceptions listed earlier applies. This is true even if the distribution is from a receiver that is a state agency.

Additional 10% tax. The additional tax on early distributions is 10% of the amount of the early distribution that you must include in your gross income. This tax is in addition to any regular income tax resulting from including the distribution in income.

Nondeductible contributions. The tax on early distributions does not apply to the part of a distribution that represents a return of your nondeductible contributions (basis).

TAXALERT

Distributions received from an IRA by members of the National Guard and Reserves, called to active duty for a period in excess of 179 days or for an indefinite period after September 11, 2001, are not subject to the 10% additional tax. (This exemption from the 10% additional tax also applies to distributions received from 401(k), 403(b), and similar plans. See chapter 10, *Retirement plans, pensions, and annuities*.) The distribution received may otherwise be subject to ordinary income tax in the year received. See *Distributions Fully or Partly Taxable,* earlier.

A refund or credit of the 10% early withdrawal tax previously paid on distributions that qualify for exemption from this penalty tax may be obtained.

Any portion of such distributions may be contributed into an IRA account anytime within the 2-year period following the end of the period of active duty. The dollar limitations otherwise applicable to contributions to IRAs do not apply to any contribution made pursuant to the provision. No deduction is allowed for any contribution made under the provision.

TAXALERT

Although amounts contributed back into an IRA cannot be deducted, such amounts do not reduce the maximum amount that you can otherwise contribute during the year to your IRA based on your earnings.

TAXPLANNER

If you are eligible for this provision, consider rolling over a prior distribution and filing an amended return for a refund of tax or any penalty you paid.

More information. For more information on early distributions, see *What Acts Result in Penalties or Additional Taxes?* in chapter 1 of Publication 590.

Excess Accumulations (Insufficient Distributions)

You cannot keep amounts in your traditional IRA indefinitely. Generally, you must begin receiving distributions by April 1 of the year following the year in which you reach age 70½. The required minimum distribution for any year after the year in which you reach age 70½ must be made by December 31 of that later year.

Tax on excess. If distributions are less than the required minimum distribution for the year, you may have to pay a 50% excise tax for that year on the amount not distributed as required.

Request to waive the tax. If the excess accumulation is due to reasonable error, and you have taken, or are taking, steps to remedy the insufficient distribution, you can request that the tax be waived. If you believe you qualify for this relief, attach a statement of explanation and complete Form 5329 as instructed under *Waiver of tax* in the Instructions for Form 5329.

Exemption from tax. If you are unable to take required distributions because you have a traditional IRA invested in a contract issued by an insurance company that is in state insurer delinquency proceedings, the 50% excise tax does not apply if the conditions and requirements of Revenue Procedure 92-10 are satisfied.

TAXALERT

If you cannot receive required distributions from your IRA because your insurance company is in state insurer delinquency proceedings, consult a tax advisor to see if you can avoid the 50% excise tax.

More information. For more information on excess accumulations, see *What Acts Result in Penalties or Additional Taxes?* in chapter 1 of Publication 590.

Reporting Additional Taxes

Generally, you must use Form 5329 to report the tax on excess contributions, early distributions, and excess accumulations. If you must file Form 5329, you cannot use Form 1040A or Form 1040EZ.

Filing a tax return. If you must file an individual income tax return, complete Form 5329 and attach it to your Form 1040. Enter the total additional taxes due on Form 1040, line 58.

Not filing a tax return. If you do not have to file a tax return but do have to pay one of the additional taxes mentioned earlier, file the completed Form 5329 with the IRS at the time and place you would have filed your Form 1040. Be sure to include your address on page 1 and your signature and date on page 2. Enclose, but do not attach, a check or money order payable to the United States Treasury for the tax you owe, as shown on Form 5329. Enter your social security number and "2014 Form 5329" on your check or money order.

Form 5329 not required. You do not have to use Form 5329 if either of the following situations exists.

- Distribution code 1 (early distribution) is correctly shown in box 7 of Form 1099-R. If you do not owe any other additional tax on a distribution, multiply the taxable part of the early distribution by 10% and enter the result on Form 1040, line 58. Put "No" to the left of the line to indicate that you do not have to file Form 5329. However, if you owe this tax and also owe any other additional tax on a distribution, do not enter this 10% additional tax directly on your Form 1040. You must file Form 5329 to report your additional taxes.
- If you rolled over part or all of a distribution from a qualified retirement plan, the part rolled over is not subject to the tax on early distributions.

Roth IRAs

Regardless of your age, you may be able to establish and make nondeductible contributions to a retirement plan called a Roth IRA.

Contributions not reported. You do not report Roth IRA contributions on your return.

What Is a Roth IRA?

A Roth IRA is an individual retirement plan that, except as explained in this chapter, is subject to the rules that apply to a traditional IRA (defined earlier). It can be either an account or an annuity. Individual retirement accounts and annuities are described under *How Can a Traditional IRA Be Opened?* in chapter 1 of Publication 590.

To be a Roth IRA, the account or annuity must be designated as a Roth IRA when it is opened. A deemed IRA can be a Roth IRA, but neither a SEP IRA nor a SIMPLE IRA can be designated as a Roth IRA.

Unlike a traditional IRA, you cannot deduct contributions to a Roth IRA. But, if you satisfy the requirements, qualified distributions (discussed later) are tax free. Contributions can be made to your Roth IRA after you reach age 70½ and you can leave amounts in your Roth IRA as long as you live.

When Can a Roth IRA Be Opened?

You can open a Roth IRA at any time. However, the time for making contributions for any year is limited. See _When Can You Make Contributions?_, later, under _Can You Contribute to a Roth IRA?_

Can You Contribute to a Roth IRA?

Generally, you can contribute to a Roth IRA if you have taxable compensation (defined later) and your modified AGI (defined later) is less than:

- $191,000 for married filing jointly or qualifying widow(er),
- $129,000 for single, head of household, or married filing separately and you did not live with your spouse at any time during the year, or
- $10,000 for married filing separately and you lived with your spouse at any time during the year.

Is there an age limit for contributions? Contributions can be made to your Roth IRA regardless of your age.

Can you contribute to a Roth IRA for your spouse? You can contribute to a Roth IRA for your spouse provided the contributions satisfy the Kay Bailey Hutchison Spousal IRA limit (discussed in _How Much Can Be Contributed?_ under _Traditional IRAs_), you file jointly, and your modified AGI is less than$191,000.

Compensation. Compensation includes wages, salaries, tips, professional fees, bonuses, and other amounts received for providing personal services. It also includes commissions, self-employment income, nontaxable combat pay, military differential pay, and taxable alimony and separate maintenance payments.

Modified AGI. Your modified AGI for Roth IRA purposes is your adjusted gross income (AGI) as shown on your return with some adjustments. Use Worksheet 17-2 below to determine your modified AGI.

How Much Can Be Contributed?

The contribution limit for Roth IRAs generally depends on whether contributions are made only to Roth IRAs or to both traditional IRAs and Roth IRAs.

Roth IRAs only. If contributions are made only to Roth IRAs, your contribution limit generally is the lesser of the following amounts.

- $5,500 ($6,500 if you are 50 or older in 2014).
- Your taxable compensation.

However, if your modified AGI is above a certain amount, your contribution limit may be reduced, as explained later under _Contribution limit reduced_.

Roth IRAs and traditional IRAs. If contributions are made to both Roth IRAs and traditional IRAs established for your benefit, your contribution limit for Roth IRAs generally is the same as your limit would be if contributions were made only to Roth IRAs, but then reduced by all contributions for the year to all IRAs other than Roth IRAs. Employer contributions under a SEP or SIMPLE IRA plan do not affect this limit.

This means that your contribution limit is generally the lesser of the following amounts.

- $5,500 ($6,500 if you are 50 or older in 2014) minus all contributions (other than employer contributions under a SEP or SIMPLE IRA plan) for the year to all IRAs other than Roth IRAs.
- Your taxable compensation minus all contributions (other than employer contributions under a SEP or SIMPLE IRA plan) for the year to all IRAs other than Roth IRAs.

However, if your modified AGI is above a certain amount, your contribution limit may be reduced, as explained next under _Contribution limit reduced_.

Contribution limit reduced. If your modified AGI is above a certain amount, your contribution limit is gradually reduced. Use Table 17-3 to determine if this reduction applies to you.

Tip

You may be eligible to claim a credit for contributions to your Roth IRA. For more information, see chapter 37.

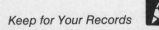

Use this worksheet to figure your modified adjusted gross income for Roth IRA purposes.   *Keep for Your Records*

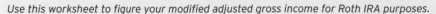

1.	Enter your adjusted gross income from Form 1040, line 38, or Form 1040A, line 22..	1. _____
2.	Enter any income resulting from the conversion of an IRA (other than a Roth IRA) to a Roth IRA (included on Form 1040, line 15b, or Form 1040A, line 11b) and a rollover from a qualified retirement plan to a Roth IRA (included on Form 1040, line 16b, or Form 1040A, line 12b)...	2. _____
3.	Subtract line 2 from line 1	3. _____
4.	Enter any traditional IRA deduction from Form 1040, line 32, or Form 1040A, line 17	4. _____
5.	Enter any student loan interest deduction from Form 1040, line 33, or Form 1040A, line 18	5. _____
6.	Enter any tuition and fees deduction from Form 1040, line 34, or Form 1040A, line 19................................	6. _____
7.	Enter any domestic production activities deduction from Form 1040, line 35......................................	7. _____
8.	Enter any foreign earned income and/or housing exclusion from Form 2555, line 45, or Form 2555-EZ, line 18	8. _____
9.	Enter any foreign housing deduction from Form 2555, line 50...	9. _____
10.	Enter any excludable savings bond interest from Form 8815, line 14..	10. _____
11.	Enter any excluded employer-provided adoption benefits from Form 8839, line 28..	11. _____
12.	Add the amounts on lines 3 through 11	12. _____

13. Enter:
   • $191,000 if married filing jointly or qualifying widow(er)
   • $10,000 if married filing separately and you lived with your spouse at any time during the year
   • $129,000 for all others

13. _____

   Is the amount on line 12 more than the amount on line 13?
   If yes, then see the **Note** below.
   If no, then the amount on line 12 is your ***modified AGI*** for Roth IRA purposes.

Note. If the amount on line 12 is more than the amount on line 13 and you have other income or loss items, such as social security income or passive activity losses, that are subject to AGI-based phaseouts, you can refigure your AGI solely for the purpose of figuring your modified AGI for Roth IRA purposes. (If you receive social security benefits, use *Worksheet 1* in *Appendix B* of Publication 590 to refigure your AGI.) Then go to line 3 above in this *Worksheet 17-2* to refigure your modified AGI. If you do not have other income or loss items subject to AGI-based phaseouts, your modified AGI for Roth IRA purposes is the amount on line 12.

Table 17-3.   **Effect of Modified AGI on Roth IRA Contribution**

This table shows whether your contribution to a Roth IRA is affected by the amount of your modified adjusted gross income (modified AGI).

IF you have taxable compensation and your filing status is...	AND your modified AGI is...	THEN...
married filing jointly, or **qualifying widow(er)**	less than $181,000	you can contribute up to $5,500 ($6,500 if you are 50 or older in 2014).
	at least $181,000 but less than $191,000	the amount you can contribute is reduced as explained under *Contribution limit reduced* in chapter 2 of Publication 590.
	$191,000 or more	you cannot contribute to a Roth IRA.
married filing separately and you lived with your spouse at any time during the year	zero (-0-)	you can contribute up to $5,500 ($6,500 if you are 50 or older in 2014).
	more than zero (-0-) but less than $10,000	the amount you can contribute is reduced as explained under *Contribution limit reduced* in chapter 2 of Publication 590.
	$10,000 or more	you cannot contribute to a Roth IRA.
single, head of household, or **married filing separately** and you did not live with your spouse at any time during the year	less than $114,000	you can contribute up to $5,500 ($6,500 if you are 50 or older in 2014).
	at least $114,000 but less than $129,000	the amount you can contribute is reduced as explained under *Contribution limit reduced* in chapter 2 of Publication 590.
	$129,000 or more	you cannot contribute to a Roth IRA.

Figuring the reduction. If the amount you can contribute to your Roth IRA is reduced, see *Worksheet 2-2* under *Can You Contribute to a Roth IRA?* in chapter 2 of Publication 590 for how to figure the reduction.

When Can You Make Contributions?

You can make contributions to a Roth IRA for a year at any time during the year or by the due date of your return for that year (not including extensions).

Tip

You can make contributions for 2014 by the due date (not including extensions) for filing your 2014 tax return.

EXPLANATION
Roth IRAs

Roth IRAs are tax-free retirement savings vehicles. By permitting tax-free withdrawals, contributions made early in your working life receive the greatest tax benefit.

Example 1

John is 25 years old on January 1, 2014. On January 1 of each year, he contributes $5,500 to a Roth IRA. The account earns 8% per year. John retires on January 1, 2054, at age 65 (immediately after he makes his last Roth IRA contribution). He will have accumulated $1,664,131 toward retirement—all available tax free.

Example 2

Jim is also 25 years old on January 1, 2014. Rather than make his $5,500 Roth contribution on January 1 of each year, he waits until April 15 of the next year to make his contribution. His account also earns 8% per year. In order to retire with the same amount as John, he must wait until April 15, 2054, to retire. Alternatively, if he retires on January 1, 2054, he will only have accumulated $1,496,550 toward retirement—$167,581 less than John.

Example 3

Mary is 16 years old and earns wages of $5,500 in 2014. Her father gifts her $5,500, which she uses to open a Roth IRA on December 31, 2014. If the account earns 8% per year, it will be worth approximately $258,000 (tax free) if she retires at age 66.

What If You Contribute Too Much?

A 6% excise tax applies to any excess contribution to a Roth IRA.

Excess contributions. These are the contributions to your Roth IRAs for a year that equal the total of:

1. Amounts contributed for the tax year to your Roth IRAs (other than amounts properly and timely rolled over from a Roth IRA or properly converted from a traditional IRA or rolled over from a qualified retirement plan, as described later) that are more than your contribution limit for the year, plus
2. Any excess contributions for the preceding year, reduced by the total of:
   a. Any distributions out of your Roth IRAs for the year, plus
   b. Your contribution limit for the year minus your contributions to all your IRAs for the year.

Withdrawal of excess contributions. For purposes of determining excess contributions, any contribution that is withdrawn on or before the due date (including extensions) for filing your tax return for the year is treated as an amount not contributed. This treatment applies only if any earnings on the contributions are also withdrawn. The earnings are considered to have been earned and received in the year the excess contribution was made.

Applying excess contributions. If contributions to your Roth IRA for a year were more than the limit, you can apply the excess contribution in one year to a later year if the contributions for that later year are less than the maximum allowed for that year.

Can You Move Amounts Into a Roth IRA?

You may be able to convert amounts from either a traditional, SEP, or SIMPLE IRA into a Roth IRA. You may be able to roll amounts over from a qualified retirement plan to a Roth IRA. You may be able to recharacterize contributions made to one IRA as having been made directly to a different IRA. You can roll amounts over from a designated Roth account or from one Roth IRA to another Roth IRA.

Conversions

You can convert a traditional IRA to a Roth IRA. The conversion is treated as a rollover, regardless of the conversion method used. Most of the rules for rollovers, described earlier under *Rollover From One IRA Into Another* under *Traditional IRAs*, apply to these rollovers. However, the 1-year waiting period does not apply.

Conversion methods. You can convert amounts from a traditional IRA to a Roth IRA in any of the following ways.

- *Rollover.* You can receive a distribution from a traditional IRA and roll it over (contribute it) to a Roth IRA within 60 days after the distribution.
- *Trustee-to-trustee transfer.* You can direct the trustee of the traditional IRA to transfer an amount from the traditional IRA to the trustee of the Roth IRA.
- *Same trustee transfer.* If the trustee of the traditional IRA also maintains the Roth IRA, you can direct the trustee to transfer an amount from the traditional IRA to the Roth IRA.

Same trustee. Conversions made with the same trustee can be made by redesignating the traditional IRA as a Roth IRA, rather than opening a new account or issuing a new contract.

Rollover from a qualified retirement plan into a Roth IRA. You can roll over into a Roth IRA all or part of an eligible rollover distribution you receive from your (or your deceased spouse's):

- Employer's qualified pension, profit-sharing, or stock bonus plan;
- Annuity plan;
- Tax-sheltered annuity plan (Section 403(b) plan); or
- Governmental deferred compensation plan (Section 457 plan).

Any amount rolled over is subject to the same rules as those for converting a traditional IRA into a Roth IRA. Also, the rollover contribution must meet the rollover requirements that apply to the specific type of retirement plan.

Income. You must include in your gross income distributions from a qualified retirement plan that you would have had to include in income if you had not rolled them over into a Roth IRA. You do not include in gross income any part of a distribution from a qualified retirement plan that is a return of contributions (after-tax contributions) to the plan that was taxable to you when paid. These amounts are normally included in income on your return for the year you rolled them over from the employer plan to a Roth IRA.

For more information, see *Rollover From Employer's Plan Into a Roth IRA* in chapter 2 of Publication 590.

Converting from a SIMPLE IRA. Generally, you can convert an amount in your SIMPLE IRA to a Roth IRA under the same rules explained earlier under <u>Converting From Any Traditional IRA to a Roth IRA</u> under *Traditional IRAs*.

> **Caution**
>
> *If you must include any amount in your gross income, you may have to increase your withholding or make estimated tax payments. See Publication 505, Tax Withholding and Estimated Tax.*

However, you cannot convert any amount distributed from the SIMPLE IRA during the 2-year period beginning on the date you first participated in any SIMPLE IRA plan maintained by your employer.

More information. For more detailed information on conversions, see *Can You Move Amounts Into a Roth IRA?* under chapter 2 in Publication 590.

Rollover From a Roth IRA

You can withdraw, tax free, all or part of the assets from one Roth IRA if you contribute them within 60 days to another Roth IRA. Most of the rules for rollovers, explained earlier under *Rollover From One IRA Into Another* under *Traditional IRAs*, apply to these rollovers.

Rollover from designated Roth account. A rollover from a designated Roth account can only be made to another designated Roth account or to a Roth IRA. For more information about designated Roth accounts, see chapter 10.

Are Distributions Taxable?

You do not include in your gross income qualified distributions or distributions that are a return of your regular contributions from your Roth IRA(s). You also do not include distributions from your Roth IRA that you roll over tax free into another Roth IRA. You may have to include part of other distributions in your income. See *Ordering rules for distributions*, later.

What are qualified distributions? A qualified distribution is any payment or distribution from your Roth IRA that meets the following requirements.

1. It is made after the 5-year period beginning with the first taxable year for which a contribution was made to a Roth IRA set up for your benefit, and
2. The payment or distribution is:
    a. Made on or after the date you reach age 59½,
    b. Made because you are disabled,
    c. Made to a beneficiary or to your estate after your death, or
    d. To pay up to $10,000 (lifetime limit) of certain qualified first-time homebuyer amounts. See *First home* under *What Acts Result in Penalties or Additional Taxes?* in chapter 1 of Publication 590 for more information.

Additional tax on distributions of conversion and certain rollover contributions within 5-year period. If, within the 5-year period starting with the first day of your tax year in which you convert an amount from a traditional IRA or rollover an amount from a qualified retirement plan to a Roth IRA, you take a distribution from a Roth IRA, you may have to pay the 10% additional tax on early distributions. You generally must pay the 10% additional tax on any amount attributable to the part of the amount converted or rolled over (the conversion or rollover contribution) that you had to include in income. A separate 5-year period applies to each conversion and rollover. See *Ordering rules for distributions*, later, to determine the amount, if any, of the distribution that is attributable to the part of the conversion or rollover contribution that you had to include in income.

Additional tax on other early distributions. Unless an exception applies, you must pay the 10% additional tax on the taxable part of any distributions that are not qualified distributions. See Publication 590 for more information.

Ordering rules for distributions. If you receive a distribution from your Roth IRA that is not a qualified distribution, part of it may be taxable. There is a set order in which contributions (including conversion contributions and rollover contributions from qualified retirement plans) and earnings are considered to be distributed from your Roth IRA. Regular contributions are distributed first. See *Ordering Rules for Distributions* under *Are Distributions Taxable?* in chapter 2 of Publication 590 for more information.

Must you withdraw or use Roth IRA assets? You are not required to take distributions from your Roth IRA at any age. The minimum distribution rules that apply to traditional IRAs do not apply to Roth IRAs while the owner is alive. However, after the death of a Roth IRA owner, certain minimum distribution rules that apply to traditional IRAs also apply to Roth IRAs.

TAXPLANNER

There are no required minimum distributions (RMDs) for a Roth IRA during the life of the account owner. This means that your account can stay intact for as long as you live, allowing investment earnings to grow on a tax-free basis. In addition, if you're married, your spouse—if named the beneficiary of the account—can "step into your shoes" (e.g., by establishing a Roth IRA rollover account) and continue to defer distributions during the remainder of his or her lifetime.

Following your death (or the death of your surviving spouse if he or she were named the account beneficiary and rolled over the account after your death), the normal postmortem RMD rules would apply (see *Required Distributions*, earlier). Since there is technically no required beginning date for making RMDs from a Roth IRA during your life, the schedule of required distributions after your death would be determined by your designated beneficiary, who can receive distributions over his or her remaining life expectancy, so long as the first RMD is made by December 31 in the year following the year of your death. The ability to delay distributions until after your death, and then have the account gradually distributed tax free to heirs over their lifetimes, creates a valuable way to transfer wealth from one generation to another.

More information. For more detailed information on Roth IRAs, see chapter 2 of Publication 590.

Simplified Employee Pensions (SEPs)

A simplified employee pension is a written plan that allows an employer to make contributions toward an employee's retirement without becoming involved in more complex retirement plans. If you are self-employed, you can contribute to your own SEP.

For 2014, the SEP rules permit an employer to contribute and deduct each year to each participating employee's SEP up to 25% of the employee's compensation, up to $260,000 or $52,000, whichever is less. If you are self-employed, special rules apply when figuring the maximum deduction for these contributions. In determining the percentage limit on contributions, compensation is net earnings from self-employment, taking into account the contributions to the SEP.

TAXSAVER

Even if your employer makes contributions to a SEP for your account, you can make contributions to your own IRA. The IRA deduction rules, previously discussed, apply to any amounts you contribute to your IRA.

TAXSAVER

A self-employed person can claim a deduction to a SEP as long as the contribution is made by the due date of the return, including extensions. Even if you failed to set up a plan by December 31, you can still establish a SEP after the end of the year and make a timely payment.

TAXALERT

SEPs permitting salary reduction contributions could not be established after 1996, although SEPs that allowed elective deferrals before 1997 (SARSEPs) can continue to do so.

Savings Incentive Match Plans for Employees (SIMPLE)

Your employer can establish a type of retirement plan called the savings incentive match plan for employees. In general, employers with 100 or fewer employees earning at least $5,500 and who do not maintain another employer-sponsored retirement plan are eligible to set up SIMPLE plans. SIMPLE plans, which are not subject to some of the complicated rules that apply to other types of retirement plans, can be adopted as an IRA or as part of a 401(k) plan. All employees who earn more than $5,500 a year must be eligible to participate, and self-employed individuals may also participate in SIMPLE plans. In general, contributions to a SIMPLE plan are not taxable until withdrawn.

The employer generally must either match elective employee contributions dollar for dollar up to 3% of compensation or make a "nonelective" contribution of 2% of compensation on behalf of each eligible employee. No other contributions may be made to a SIMPLE account. Contributions to a SIMPLE account generally are deductible by the employer; however, matching contributions are deductible only if made by the due date (including extensions) of the employer's tax return.

TAXALERT

The limit on maximum annual elective deferrals to a SIMPLE plan are:

Year	Regular Amount	"Catch-up"* Amount
2006	$10,000	$12,500
2007	10,500	13,000
2008	10,500	13,000
2009	11,500	14,000
2010	11,500	14,000
2011	11,500	14,000
2012	11,500	14,000
2013	12,000	14,500
2014	12,000**	14,500**

*For taxpayers who reach age 50 before the end of the plan year.

**Adjusted for inflation in $500 increments.

Employers are given a 2-year grace period to maintain a SIMPLE plan once they are no longer eligible to establish one.

Chapter 18
Alimony

Note

IRS Publication 17 (*Your Federal Income Tax*) has been updated by Ernst & Young LLP for 2014. Dates and dollar amounts shown are for 2014. Underlined type is used to indicate where IRS text has been updated. Places where text has been removed are indicated by the sentence: *Text intentionally omitted.*

ey.com/EYTaxGuide

Ernst & Young LLP will update the *EY Tax Guide 2015* website with relevant taxpayer information as it becomes available. You can also sign up for email alerts to let you know when changes have been made.

Introduction

This chapter discusses alimony and child support and the complicated tax rules and regulations that apply.

Designing a divorce decree, a separation agreement, or a support decree is rarely an easy task. Marital settlements are so diverse and so complex that no two situations are the same. One common element, however, is likely to be the payment of alimony. Alimony is an amount subject to one of these settlement agreements that is not considered child support or a property settlement, and that meets certain specific tests. If certain circumstances are met, alimony is a deduction from gross income for the spouse who pays it and included in the income of the spouse who receives it.

Alimony may take many different forms. The payment by one spouse of the other spouse's share of mortgage and other costs for jointly owned property may be considered alimony. The payment of life insurance premiums on policies irrevocably assigned to a spouse may also be considered alimony. Alimony may even include the payment of medical and dental expenses. This chapter discusses what should and should not be considered an alimony payment.

The Deficit Reduction Act of 1984 completely restructured the alimony rules. The old rules still apply to alimony payments made under pre-1985 divorce and separation agreements, unless those agreements have been specifically modified. For related information, refer to *Dependency exemption* (see chapter 3, *Personal exemptions and dependents*), the *Child and dependent care credit* (see chapter 33, *Child and dependent care credit*), *Head of household status* (see chapter 2, *Filing status*), the *Earned income credit*, and the *Retirement savings credit* (for both, see chapter 37, *Other credits including the earned income credit*).

This chapter discusses the rules that apply if you pay or receive alimony. It covers the following topics.

- What payments are alimony.
- What payments are not alimony, such as child support.
- How to deduct alimony you paid.
- How to report alimony you received as income.
- Whether you must recapture the tax benefits of alimony. Recapture means adding back in your income all or part of a deduction you took in a prior year.

TAXALERT

For all federal tax purposes for which marriage is a factor, including the subject matter covered in this chapter, same-sex couples who legally married in a state (including the District of Columbia) or foreign jurisdiction that recognizes same-sex marriages are treated as married for U.S. federal tax purposes—even if they reside in a jurisdiction that does not recognize same-sex marriage. However, registered domestic partners and individuals who enter into a civil union or other similar formal relationship are not treated as a married couple for federal tax purposes.

Alimony is a payment to or for a spouse or former spouse under a divorce or separation instrument. It does not include voluntary payments that are not made under a divorce or separation instrument.

Alimony is deductible by the payer and must be included in the spouse's or former spouse's income. Although this chapter is generally written for the payer of the alimony, the recipient can use the information to determine whether an amount received is alimony.

To be alimony, a payment must meet certain requirements. Different requirements generally apply to payments under instruments executed after 1984 and to payments under instruments executed before 1985. This chapter discusses the rules for payments under instruments executed after 1984. If you need the rules for payments under pre-1985 instruments, get and keep a copy of the 2004 version of Publication 504. That was the last year the information on pre-1985 instruments was included in Publication 504.

Use Table 18-1 in this chapter as a guide to determine whether certain payments are considered alimony.

Definitions. The following definitions apply throughout this chapter.

Spouse or former spouse. Unless otherwise stated, the term "spouse" includes former spouse.

Divorce or separation instrument. The term "divorce or separation instrument" means:

- A decree of divorce or separate maintenance or a written instrument incident to that decree,
- A written separation agreement, or
- A decree or any type of court order requiring a spouse to make payments for the support or maintenance of the other spouse. This includes a temporary decree, an interlocutory (not final) decree, and a decree of alimony pendente lite (while awaiting action on the final decree or agreement).

Useful Items

You may want to see:

Publication

☐ **504**   Divorced or Separated Individuals

General Rules

The following rules apply to alimony regardless of when the divorce or separation instrument was executed.

Payments not alimony. Not all payments under a divorce or separation instrument are alimony. Alimony does not include:

- Child support,
- Noncash property settlements,
- Payments that are your spouse's part of community income, as explained under *Community Property* in Publication 504,
- Payments to keep up the payer's property, or
- Use of the payer's property.

EXPLANATION
Other Payments Not Deductible as Alimony
Do not deduct as alimony the following:
1. Any payment not required by the decree or agreement
2. Any payment that does not arise out of the marital relationship but that is required by the decree or agreement, such as repayment of a loan to your spouse
3. Any payment you make before the decree or agreement
4. Any payment you agreed to make before the decree or agreement and paid later
5. Any payment you make after your former spouse's remarriage
6. Any payment you make after your divorced spouse's death, even though required by the decree or agreement
7. Any payment you make that is part of a property settlement

---

Payments to a third party. Cash payments, checks, or money orders to a third party on behalf of your spouse under the terms of your divorce or separation instrument can be alimony, if they otherwise qualify. These include payments for your spouse's medical expenses, housing costs (rent, utilities, etc.), taxes, tuition, etc. The payments are treated as received by your spouse and then paid to the third party.

Table 18-1. Alimony Requirements (Instruments Executed After 1984)

Payments ARE alimony if all of the following are true:	Payments are NOT alimony if any of the following are true:
Payments are required by a divorce or separation instrument.	Payments are not required by a divorce or separation instrument.
Payer and recipient spouse do not file a joint return with each other.	Payer and recipient spouse file a joint return with each other.
Payment is in cash (including checks or money orders).	Payment is: • Not in cash, • A noncash property settlement, • Spouse's part of community income, or • To keep up the payer's property.
Payment is not designated in the instrument as not alimony.	Payment is designated in the instrument as not alimony.
Spouses legally separated under a decree of divorce or separate maintenance are not members of the same household.	Spouses legally separated under a decree of divorce or separate maintenance are members of the same household.
Payments are not required after death of the recipient spouse.	Payments are required after death of the recipient spouse.
Payment is not treated as child support.	Payment is treated as child support.
These payments are deductible by the payer and includible in income by the recipient.	*These payments are neither deductible by the payer nor includible in income by the recipient.*

EXPLANATION

The ownership of a life insurance policy must be assigned to your former spouse before you may deduct the premiums you pay as alimony. In addition, your former spouse must be the irrevocable beneficiary of the policy. Your children may be irrevocable contingent beneficiaries.

If your children are the beneficiaries of a life insurance policy and your former spouse is a contingent beneficiary, you still control the policy. The premiums you pay are not considered alimony.

For the premiums to be considered alimony, your former spouse's benefit from the life insurance policy must be measurable in dollars. If your former spouse would benefit from the policy only under certain contingencies, the economic advantage cannot be measured and your premiums would not be considered alimony.

Life insurance premiums. Alimony includes premiums you must pay under your divorce or separation instrument for insurance on your life to the extent your spouse owns the policy.

Payments for jointly-owned home. If your divorce or separation instrument states that you must pay expenses for a home owned by you and your spouse, some of your payments may be alimony.

Mortgage payments. If you must pay all the mortgage payments (principal and interest) on a jointly-owned home, and they otherwise qualify as alimony, you can deduct one-half of the total payments as alimony. If you itemize deductions and the home is a qualified home, you can claim one-half of the interest in figuring your deductible interest. Your spouse must report one-half of the payments as alimony received. If your spouse itemizes deductions and the home is a qualified home, he or she can claim one-half of the interest on the mortgage in figuring deductible interest.

Taxes and insurance. If you must pay all the real estate taxes or insurance on a home held as tenants in common, you can deduct one-half of these payments as alimony. Your spouse must report one-half of these payments as alimony received. If you and your spouse itemize deductions, you can each claim one-half of the real estate taxes and none of the home insurance.

If your home is held as tenants by the entirety or joint tenants, none of your payments for taxes or insurance are alimony. But if you itemize deductions, you can claim all of the real estate taxes and none of the home insurance.

if you itemize deductions. For more information, see *Expenses of a home*, later.

Deducting mortgage payments and other housing costs paid on a home owned by your former spouse following divorce or separation. If the terms of a divorce or separation agreement require you to pay the mortgage payments and/or other housing expenses, such as real estate taxes, property insurance, and utilities, on the home owned by your former spouse, and the payments otherwise meet the tax law definition of alimony, you may be able to deduct these payments as alimony. Your former spouse will have to include these alimony payments in income. For more information, see *Expenses of a home*, later.

Deducting mortgage payments and other housing costs paid on a home you own and that is lived in rent-free by your former spouse following divorce or separation. Because you own the home and the debts are yours, you cannot deduct the mortgage or real estate tax payments you make as alimony. Nor are you allowed to claim the fair rental value of your former spouse's use of the home as alimony. However, you can deduct qualifying mortgage interest and real estate taxes paid if you itemize deductions.

While mortgage and real estate tax payments do not qualify as deductible alimony, payments you make for utilities on behalf of a former spouse who is entitled to occupy your home under the terms of a divorce or separation agreement can be deducted as alimony. Your former spouse will have to include these utility payments in income. For more information, see *Expenses of a home*, later.

Other payments to a third party. If you made other third-party payments, see Publication 504 to see whether any part of the payments qualifies as alimony.

Instruments Executed After 1984

The following rules for alimony apply to payments under divorce or separation instruments executed after 1984.

Exception for instruments executed before 1985. There are two situations where the rules for instruments executed after 1984 apply to instruments executed before 1985.

1. A divorce or separation instrument executed before 1985 and then modified after 1984 to specify that the after-1984 rules will apply.
2. A temporary divorce or separation instrument executed before 1985 and incorporated into, or adopted by, a final decree executed after 1984 that:
   a. Changes the amount or period of payment, or
   b. Adds or deletes any contingency or condition.

For the rules for alimony payments under pre-1985 instruments not meeting these exceptions, get the 2004 version of Publication 504 at *www.irs.gov/pub504*.

Example 1. In November 1984, you and your former spouse executed a written separation agreement. In February 1985, a decree of divorce was substituted for the written separation agreement. The decree of divorce did not change the terms for the alimony you pay your former spouse. The decree of divorce is treated as executed before 1985. Alimony payments under this decree are not subject to the rules for payments under instruments executed after 1984.

Example 2. Assume the same facts as in *Example 1* except that the decree of divorce changed the amount of the alimony. In this example, the decree of divorce is not treated as executed before 1985. The alimony payments are subject to the rules for payments under instruments executed after 1984.

EXPLANATION

For divorce decrees and separation agreements executed after 1984 (and, in certain cases, decrees or agreements executed before 1985 that have been modified), payments may not be deductible, even if there is a legal obligation to make them. Payments would be deductible only if all the other requirements were fulfilled. See *Alimony requirements*, later.

TAXPLANNER

Don't overlook the opportunity to use the new rules on an old divorce.

Example

Bob and Mary were divorced in 1982, with Mary agreeing to pay Bob $2,000 per month in qualifying alimony payments. Mary was a stockbroker earning top dollars in 1982. Bob had never had a full-time job. In 2014, Mary's fortunes are not so rosy, whereas Bob is a top Los Angeles real estate broker.

Bob and Mary could agree that, in 2014, Mary will pay less money to Bob but that it won't be considered alimony. If Mary's marginal tax bracket has dropped to 15% and Bob's tax bracket is 39.6%, Mary could pay Bob as little as 60.4% of what her normal payment is ($1,208), and both would win. If Mary were to pay Bob $2,000 in alimony, and take the associated deduction, her after-tax out-of-pocket expense would be $1,700. Bob would reflect $2,000 in income, which would equate to $1,208 after tax. Thus, if they would agree to a $1,208 payment, Bob would receive the same amount in after-tax dollars, but Mary would come out ahead.

Alimony requirements. A payment to or for a spouse under a divorce or separation instrument is alimony if the spouses do not file a joint return with each other and all the following requirements are met.

- The payment is in cash.
- The instrument does not designate the payment as not alimony.
- Spouses legally separated under a decree of divorce or separate maintenance are not members of the same household.
- There is no liability to make any payment (in cash or property) after the death of the recipient spouse.
- The payment is not treated as child support.

Each of these requirements is discussed below.

Cash payment requirement. Only cash payments, including checks and money orders, qualify as alimony. The following do not qualify as alimony.
- Transfers of services or property (including a debt instrument of a third party or an annuity contract).
- Execution of a debt instrument by the payer.
- The use of the payer's property.

Payments to a third party. Cash payments to a third party under the terms of your divorce or separation instrument can qualify as cash payments to your spouse. See *Payments to a third party* under *General Rules*, earlier.

Also, cash payments made to a third party at the written request of your spouse may qualify as alimony if all the following requirements are met.
- The payments are in lieu of payments of alimony directly to your spouse.
- The written request states that both spouses intend the payments to be treated as alimony.
- You receive the written request from your spouse before you file your return for the year you made the payments.

Payments designated as not alimony. You and your spouse can designate that otherwise qualifying payments are not alimony. You do this by including a provision in your divorce or separation instrument that states the payments are not deductible as alimony by you and are excludable from your spouse's income. For this purpose, any instrument (written statement) signed by both of you that makes this designation and that refers to a previous written separation agreement is treated as a written separation agreement (and therefore a divorce or separation instrument). If you are subject to temporary support orders, the designation must be made in the original or a later temporary support order.

Your spouse can exclude the payments from income only if he or she attaches a copy of the instrument designating them as not alimony to his or her return. The copy must be attached each year the designation applies.

Spouses cannot be members of the same household. Payments to your spouse while you are members of the same household are not alimony if you are legally separated under a decree of divorce or separate maintenance. A home you formerly shared is considered one household, even if you physically separate yourselves in the home.

You are not treated as members of the same household if one of you is preparing to leave the household and does leave no later than 1 month after the date of the payment.

Exception. If you are not legally separated under a decree of divorce or separate maintenance, a payment under a written separation agreement, support decree, or other court order may qualify as alimony even if you are members of the same household when the payment is made.

Liability for payments after death of recipient spouse. If any part of payments you make must continue to be made for any period after your spouse's death, that part of your payments is not alimony, whether made before or after the death. If all of the payments would continue, then none of the payments made before or after the death are alimony.

The divorce or separation instrument does not have to expressly state that the payments cease upon the death of your spouse if, for example, the liability for continued payments would end under state law.

Example. You must pay your former spouse $10,000 in cash each year for 10 years. Your divorce decree states that the payments will end upon your former spouse's death. You must also pay your former spouse or your former spouse's estate $20,000 in cash each year for 10 years. The death of your spouse would not terminate these payments under state law.

The $10,000 annual payments may qualify as alimony. The $20,000 annual payments that do not end upon your former spouse's death are not alimony.

Substitute payments. If you must make any payments in cash or property after your spouse's death as a substitute for continuing otherwise qualifying payments before the death, the otherwise qualifying payments are not alimony. To the extent that your payments begin, accelerate, or increase because of the death of your spouse, otherwise qualifying payments you made may be treated as payments that were not alimony. Whether or not such payments will be treated as not alimony depends on all the facts and circumstances.

Example 1. Under your divorce decree, you must pay your former spouse $30,000 annually. The payments will stop at the end of 6 years or upon your former spouse's death, if earlier.

Your former spouse has custody of your minor children. The decree provides that if any child is still a minor at your spouse's death, you must pay $10,000 annually to a trust until the youngest child reaches the age of majority. The trust income and corpus (principal) are to be used for your children's benefit.

These facts indicate that the payments to be made after your former spouse's death are a substitute for $10,000 of the $30,000 annual payments. Of each of the $30,000 annual payments, $10,000 is not alimony.

Example 2. Under your divorce decree, you must pay your former spouse $30,000 annually. The payments will stop at the end of 15 years or upon your former spouse's death, if earlier. The decree provides that if your former spouse dies before the end of the 15-year period, you must pay the estate the difference between $450,000 ($30,000 × 15) and the total amount paid up to that time. For example, if your spouse dies at the end of the tenth year, you must pay the estate $150,000 ($450,000 − $300,000).

These facts indicate that the lump-sum payment to be made after your former spouse's death is a substitute for the full amount of the $30,000 annual payments. None of the annual payments are alimony. The result would be the same if the payment required at death were to be discounted by an appropriate interest factor to account for the prepayment.

TAXALERT

A court decision denied an alimony deduction because the taxpayer was required to make payments to his children in the same amount as the alimony if his ex-wife died. The agreement stated that the alimony payments ended at death; however, the alimony was set up as installment payments and if the ex-wife died before all payments were made, the remaining payments were to be paid to the children. Although no post-death payments were actually made, the alimony deduction was still disallowed.

Child support. A payment that is specifically designated as child support or treated as specifically designated as child support under your divorce or separation instrument is not alimony. The amount of child support may vary over time. Child support payments are not deductible by the payer and are not taxable to the recipient.

Specifically designated as child support. A payment will be treated as specifically designated as child support to the extent that the payment is reduced either:

- On the happening of a contingency relating to your child, or
- At a time that can be clearly associated with the contingency.

A payment may be treated as specifically designated as child support even if other separate payments are specifically designated as child support.

TAXPLANNER

Since child support payments are considered fixed, any reductions in child support that are not part of the original decree or a subsequent court-approved modified divorce decree are considered reductions in alimony, not child support. Therefore, be sure to have the court approve any child support reductions so that you can continue to deduct the full alimony payments.

Example

After a taxpayer remarried, his son from his previous marriage began to live with him. The taxpayer and his former wife agreed that, as a result, his child support payments should be eliminated. Even though both former spouses agreed that the payment reductions applied to child support, the courts held that they applied to alimony because the taxpayer and his former spouse did not obtain a modification of their divorce decree in court.

Contingency relating to your child. A contingency relates to your child if it depends on any event relating to that child. It does not matter whether the event is certain or likely to occur. Events relating to your child include the child's:

- Becoming employed,
- Dying,
- Leaving the household,
- Leaving school,
- Marrying, or
- Reaching a specified age or income level.

Clearly associated with a contingency. Payments that would otherwise qualify as alimony are presumed to be reduced at a time clearly associated with the happening of a contingency relating to your child only in the following situations.

- The payments are to be reduced not more than 6 months before or after the date the child will reach 18, 21, or local age of majority.
- The payments are to be reduced on two or more occasions that occur not more than 1 year before or after a different one of your children reaches a certain age from 18 to 24. This certain age must be the same for each child, but need not be a whole number of years.

In all other situations, reductions in payments are not treated as clearly associated with the happening of a contingency relating to your child.

Either you or the IRS can overcome the presumption in the two situations above. This is done by showing that the time at which the payments are to be reduced was determined independently of any contingencies relating to your children. For example, if you can show that the period of alimony payments is customary in the local jurisdiction, such as a period equal to one-half of the duration of the marriage, you can overcome the presumption and may be able to treat the amount as alimony.

EXPLANATION

Child Support in Agreements Executed Before 1985

Child support amounts may not be inferred for payments made under agreements executed before 1985 and not revised. You may not assume that portions of the alimony payments are used by a former spouse for support of a child. The U.S. Supreme Court has held that payments are not treated as child support payments unless they are expressly designated as such in the governing document.

Child Support in Agreements Executed After 1984

Child support amounts may be inferred for payments made under agreements executed or revised after 1984, even if such payments are not specifically earmarked. However, such payments will be reduced upon certain contingencies related to the child. Such contingencies would include the child attaining a certain age or income level, dying, marrying, leaving school, leaving the spouse's household, or getting a job.

Payments that are reduced at a time that can clearly be associated with a contingency will be treated as child support. For example, if a payment was to stop at a certain calendar date that just happened to be the child's nineteenth birthday, that payment would be considered child support.

The parent who has custody of the child is entitled to take the dependency exemption for the child, as long as the parents themselves could have claimed the exemption had they filed a joint return. This will not apply if:

1. There is a multiple support agreement in effect specifying who gets the exemption.
2. The custodial parent relinquishes the exemption in writing (using language in IRS Form 8332).
3. There is an executed, pre-1985 divorce or separation agreement in effect that provides that the noncustodial parent who also furnishes at least $600 of child support can claim the exemption.

Note: The custodial parent is still entitled to claim the dependent care credit, even if he or she relinquishes the dependency exemption to the noncustodial parent.

A parent can deduct medical expenses that he or she paid directly for a child's benefit, even though the dependency exemption for the child is claimed by the other parent. This is the case as long as a multiple-support agreement is not in effect.

How To Deduct Alimony Paid

You can deduct alimony you paid, whether or not you itemize deductions on your return. You must file Form 1040. You cannot use Form 1040A or Form 1040EZ.

Enter the amount of alimony you paid on Form 1040, line 31a. In the space provided on line 31b, enter your spouse's social security number (SSN) or individual taxpayer identification number (ITIN).

If you paid alimony to more than one person, enter the SSN or ITIN of one of the recipients. Show the SSN or ITIN and amount paid to each other recipient on an attached statement. Enter your total payments on line 31a.

How To Report Alimony Received

Report alimony you received as income on Form 1040, line 11. You cannot use Form 1040A or Form 1040EZ.

Recapture Rule

If your alimony payments decrease or end during the first 3 calendar years, you may be subject to the recapture rule. If you are subject to this rule, you have to include in income in the third year part of the alimony payments you previously deducted. Your spouse can deduct in the third year part of the alimony payments he or she previously included in income.

The 3-year period starts with the first calendar year you make a payment qualifying as alimony under a decree of divorce or separate maintenance or a written separation agreement. Do not include any time in which payments were being made under temporary support orders. The second and third years are the next 2 calendar years, whether or not payments are made during those years.

The reasons for a reduction or end of alimony payments that can require a recapture include:
- A change in your divorce or separation instrument,
- A failure to make timely payments,
- A reduction in your ability to provide support, or
- A reduction in your spouse's support needs.

When to apply the recapture rule. You are subject to the recapture rule in the third year if the alimony you pay in the third year decreases by more than $15,000 from the second year or the alimony you pay in the second and third years decreases significantly from the alimony you pay in the first year.

TAXSAVER
If the payments are spread out equally over the 3 years, they are all deductible. Also, when determining the timing of making extraordinary payments, consider making them in year 3 rather than year 2. This will prevent the payments in year 3 from declining by more than $15,000 from the payments in year 2.

When you figure a decrease in alimony, do not include the following amounts.
- Payments made under a temporary support order.
- Payments required over a period of at least 3 calendar years that vary because they are a fixed part of your income from a business or property, or from compensation for employment or self-employment.
- Payments that decrease because of the death of either spouse or the remarriage of the spouse receiving the payments before the end of the third year.

TAXPLANNER
Determining the post-separation years is critical in order to apply the recapture rules properly. The first year is the first calendar year in which the taxpayer pays alimony or maintenance payments to the former spouse. This is not necessarily the year the spouses physically separate or even the year in which a final decree of divorce is entered. It may also not be the year payments are first made, if those payments do not qualify as alimony or separate maintenance payments. The second and third years are the next two succeeding calendar years.

Example
A divorce decree is entered in October 2014 and it calls for Henry to pay to Wilma alimony payments beginning in November 2014. However, Henry and Wilma occupy the same household until March 2015. Their cohabitation prevents the payments from being treated as deductible alimony, and so 2014 cannot be the first year.

Figuring the recapture. You can use Worksheet 1 in Publication 504 to figure recaptured alimony.

Including the recapture in income. If you must include a recapture amount in income, show it on Form 1040, line 11 ("Alimony received"). Cross out "received" and enter "recapture." On the dotted line next to the amount, enter your spouse's last name and SSN or ITIN.

Deducting the recapture. If you can deduct a recapture amount, show it on Form 1040, line 31a ("Alimony paid"). Cross out "paid" and enter "recapture." In the space provided, enter your spouse's SSN or ITIN.

TAXPLANNER

A spouse who is to receive property with a tax basis substantially less than its current value should carefully evaluate the tax consequences of disposing of it. The recipient may be subject to tax from recapture of investment tax credit and depreciation and should obtain the advice of competent counsel on such matters.

Example

As part of the divorce property settlement, Kyle gives Mary a computer that he used for 4 years in his sole proprietorship business. Kyle paid $5,000 for the computer, claimed investment credit on it, and claimed depreciation of $3,950. Since the computer ceased to be business property when it was given to Mary, she must recapture part of the investment credit claimed by Kyle. Further, Mary must pay ordinary income tax on her profit if she sells the computer for more than $1,050. See chapter 16, *Reporting gains and losses*, and chapter 37, *Other credits including the earned income credit*.

Explanation

Trust property. If income-producing property is placed in trust to pay alimony, the alimony payments are not included in or deducted from income. This rule applies whether the alimony payments are made out of the trust income or principal. Trust distributions must be reported as income by your spouse. If your obligation to pay alimony is stated in a divorce decree, other court order, or written separation agreement, your spouse reports the distributions as alimony on line 11 of Form 1040. If your obligation is not so stated, your spouse reports the income distributions as income received from a trust on Schedule E (Form 1040).

You may also set up a trust to pay both alimony and child support. If your former spouse remarries and you are no longer required to pay alimony, the trust may continue disbursing monies for child support.

TAXPLANNER

If a trust that is set up to disburse alimony payments holds municipal bonds, the distributions to the former spouse are nontaxable to the extent that they are attributable to the trust's municipal bond income. Also, if the distributions from the trust exceed the trust's income, the excess distribution of trust principal is not taxable.

Explanation

Insurance, endowment, or annuity. If an insurance or endowment policy or an annuity contract is purchased to discharge alimony or support called for in a divorce decree, the payer does not include in, or deduct from, income payments made under the contract. The recipient must include the payments in income.

Annulments. Generally, state laws blur the distinction between a divorce and an annulment. The rules on alimony often apply to an annulment decree as well as to a divorce decree. You should examine the law of the state in which you reside to determine if this is the case.

Example

In New York, a marriage was annulled due to the wife's insanity. The husband was required to provide for her care and maintenance. Since under the general rules of law the annulment would be considered a divorce, the husband's payments were treated as alimony.

TAXPLANNER

Expenses of a home. If part of an alimony award is used to pay such expenses as real estate taxes, insurance, mortgage payments, or utilities for a home owned by a divorced couple, the facts in each case determine the amount deductible by one spouse and includible by the other spouse. Two facts to consider are the type of ownership and the kinds of expenses that must be paid. The spouse making the payments will only be entitled to a deduction if he or she has an ownership interest in the home. However, in each case, the payments must cover a period of more than 10 years or otherwise qualify as periodic payments if made pursuant to a pre-1985 agreement.

Ownership

You should check your state law, ownership documents, and your divorce decree to determine what type of ownership you have.

1. **Joint tenants or tenants by the entirety.** You and your former spouse own a home jointly as tenants by the entirety or joint tenants with a right of survivorship. You are both jointly and individually responsible for the entire mortgage balance. If your divorce decree states that your former spouse is to pay the mortgage (principal and interest) on the property from money that he or she receives from you as support, then your former spouse must include one-half of each principal and interest payment as income from alimony, and you may deduct one-half of each principal and interest payment as alimony. Your former spouse may also deduct one-half of the interest if he or she itemizes deductions on Schedule A (Form 1040). If you itemize your deductions, it is not clear how your share of the interest should be handled. It may be deductible under the home mortgage rules if your children live there and you are not already deducting interest on two personal residences. Or it might be considered investment interest, since as far as you are concerned, the property is now just an investment. Lastly, it could be personal interest and therefore not deductible.

2. **Tenants in common.** If you and your former spouse own a home as tenants in common, your former spouse owns half of the property. Therefore, you may deduct as alimony amounts you pay on your former spouse's half of the property for principal, interest, insurance, and taxes. Your former spouse must include these amounts in income. If your former spouse itemizes deductions on Schedule A (Form 1040), he or she may deduct as taxes and interest the part you paid for real estate taxes and interest on your former spouse's half of the property. He or she may not deduct amounts for insurance. Insurance is a nondeductible personal expense. Amounts you paid on your half of the property are not deductible as alimony, nor are they includible in income by your former spouse. If you itemize your deductions on Schedule A (Form 1040), you may deduct the part you pay for real estate taxes and interest on your half of the property. You may not deduct insurance payments on your half of the property.

3. **Your former spouse owns the home.** If the home is owned by your former spouse, and under a decree or agreement you pay the real estate taxes, mortgage payments, and insurance premiums on it, you may deduct these payments as alimony. Your former spouse must include these payments in income. If your former spouse itemizes deductions on Schedule A (Form 1040), he or she may deduct the part of each payment that is for taxes and interest on the mortgage.

4. **You own the home.** If the home you own is lived in rent-free by your former spouse, you may not deduct your mortgage payments or the fair rental value of the home as alimony. However, if you itemize your deductions, you may deduct on Schedule A (Form 1040) any real estate taxes and interest you pay on the property.

Rent. If, under a divorce or separate maintenance decree or written separation agreement, you must pay rent to a third-party lessor to provide housing for your spouse or former spouse, you may deduct the rent payments as alimony. Your former spouse must include these payments in income.

Utilities. If your former spouse is the one who has the right to use the home, regardless of the type of ownership, you may deduct as alimony the amount you pay for utilities under a decree or agreement. Your former spouse must include these amounts in income.

Property ownership. There are many consequences of property ownership that must be considered in a divorce settlement. Any payments made pursuant to a divorce decree by you for the mortgage, property taxes, insurance, and so on are considered alimony only if the house belongs to your former spouse. If you transfer your interest in the property to your children, payments to cover their portion of the mortgage payments would be treated as child support, not alimony.

Sale of property. If you sell property that you and your spouse own jointly, you must report your share of the recognized gain or loss on your income tax return for the year of the sale. Your share of the gain or loss is determined by your state law governing ownership of property. For more information on how to report the gain or loss, see IRS Publication 544.

Example

John and Mary owned a home that cost them $150,000. In their divorce, the court decree holds that Mary can remain in the home until their son, who is 10 years old, reaches 18. Mary must pay rent to John for using his half of the house. In 2014, the house is sold and John and Mary together receive $250,000.

Upon sale of the home, Mary is subject to tax on the gain on the home sale. Assuming she meets the requirements, she can exclude up to $250,000 of her portion of the total gain. See chapter 15, *Selling your home*.

John was a landlord during the rental years and probably claimed related expenses and depreciation on his tax return. If the rent charged was reasonable, John could deduct any losses, subject to the restrictions on passive activities.

Upon sale, John is subject to tax on his entire portion of the gain.

TAXPLANNER

Other aspects of obtaining a divorce. IRS Publication 504, *Divorced or Separated Individuals*, examines more closely some of the tax aspects of obtaining a divorce, including the tax treatment of costs incurred in working out a settlement.

Court costs and legal fees related to the divorce are not deductible. However, the portion of these fees attributable to obtaining alimony is deductible as an itemized deduction, since it is an expense associated with the production of income. Any additional costs incurred to obtain alimony are also deductible, as are costs for tax advice.

Be sure to have itemized invoices for professional services. Deductible items should be specifically listed on any bill. You may claim only the deductible portion of your own legal expenses. You may not deduct the legal expenses of your spouse. Those expenses also may not be considered alimony payments.

A portion of your legal fees may give rise to a tax benefit, even though the fees are not paid for obtaining alimony or tax advice. For example, if a portion of your legal fees may be allocated to obtaining property, the tax basis of the property should be increased by the amount of the allocated fees. If the property is business property, you will have larger depreciation deductions and a smaller gain if the property is sold.

There are several additional aspects that you should consider in a year in which you become divorced:

1. **Revising Form W-4.** Form W-4 should be changed if you are no longer able to claim as many withholding allowances due to your change in marital status. This may occur because you no longer file a joint return with your former spouse. It also may occur if you are not entitled to a dependency exemption for one or more of your children. When you revise your Form W-4, your employer adjusts your tax withholding to reflect the changes in your marital status or number of dependents.

2. **Estimated taxes on alimony.** If you are receiving alimony, you may be required to make estimated tax payments, since alimony is not covered by withholding. (See chapter 4, *Tax withholding and estimated tax*.)

3. **Allocating joint estimated tax payments between you and your former spouse.** If you and your former spouse are divorced during the year and have been making joint estimated tax payments, the payments you have already made may be applied to either person's separate return or may be divided between you, as the two of you see fit. If no allocation can be agreed on, the estimated payments should be applied between the separate returns in proportion to the taxes due on each.

Example

Your return shows a tax liability of $5,100. Your former spouse's return shows a tax liability of $2,300. You would be entitled to apply 69% [$5,100 ÷ ($5,100 + $2,300)] of your total joint estimated payments against your tax liability.

4. **Retirement plans.** An employee's interest in a qualified retirement plan can be allocated between a current and a former spouse by a qualified domestic relations order. Benefits so allocated are taxed to the current and former spouses when the payments are actually received. If the benefits are received by anyone other than the employee or the current or former spouses, the benefits are taxed to the employee, not the recipient.

5. **Federal income taxes withheld.** Taxes withheld from your income are treated the same way as the income that generates them. If salary is split equally between you and your spouse because of community property rules, then the tax withholding is also divided evenly between the two of you.

6. **Alimony and your IRA.** All taxable alimony or separate maintenance payments received by an individual under a decree of divorce or separate maintenance are treated as eligible compensation for making IRA contributions. See chapter 17, *Individual retirement arrangements (IRAs)*, for details.

7. **Stock options.** If you transfer nonqualified stock options you received from your employer to your spouse in a divorce, there would be no tax at that time. When the options are exercised, your spouse will be taxed on the difference between the exercise price of the option and the value of the stock.

Chapter 19
Education-related adjustments

Note

IRS Publication 17 (*Your Federal Income Tax*) has been updated by Ernst & Young LLP for 2014. Dates and dollar amounts shown are for 2014. Underlined type is used to indicate where IRS text has been updated. Places where text has been removed are indicated by the sentence: *Text intentionally omitted*.

ey.com/EYTaxGuide

Ernst & Young LLP will update the *EY Tax Guide 2015* website with relevant taxpayer information as it becomes available. You can also sign up for email alerts to let you know when changes have been made.

Introduction

This chapter discusses the education-related adjustments you can deduct in figuring your adjusted gross income (AGI). As of the date this book was published, the only education-related adjustment available for 2014 was the student loan interest deduction. The adjustments to reduce AGI for certain amounts paid for tuition and fees as well as for up to $250 in eligible expenses paid by qualified educators expired at the end of 2013. On the other hand, Congress had been considering legislation that would extend these adjustments. A discussion of these expired adjustments is included in this chapter in case Congress acts to extend them. For updated information on this and any other tax law changes that occur after this book was published, see our website, *ey.com/EYTaxGuide*. In addition to education adjustments that can lower your AGI, and, ultimately, your tax bill, you may also be eligible for education credits to offset your tax. See chapter 36, *Education credits and other education tax benefits*.

What's New

<u>Expired tax benefits.</u> The following benefits expired at the end of 2013 and are not available for 2014:
- <u>Deduction for educator expenses in figuring AGI</u>
- <u>Tuition and fees deduction in figuring AGI</u>

<u>Student loan interest deduction.</u> <u>The amount of your student loan interest deduction for 2014 is gradually reduced (phased out) if your modified adjusted gross income (MAGI) is between $65,000 and $80,000 ($130,000 and $160,000 if you file a joint return). You cannot take a deduction if your MAGI is $80,000 or more ($160,000 or more if you file a joint return). This is an increase from the 2013 limits of $60,000 and $75,000 ($125,000 and $155,000 if filing a joint return).</u>

This chapter discusses the education-related adjustment you can deduct in figuring your adjusted gross income.

This chapter covers the student loan interest deduction, tuition and fees deduction, and the deduction for educator expenses.

TAXSAVER

Chapter 36, *Education credits and other education tax benefits*, discusses other education-related items that you may be able to claim.

Useful Items

You may want to see:

Publication
- **970** Tax Benefits for Education

Tax Breaks and Deductions You Can Use Checklist

Student loan interest deduction. You may be able to deduct up to $2,500 in interest you paid in 2014 on a qualified student loan used for higher education. This deduction reduces the amount of your income subject to tax, regardless of whether or not you itemize deductions. To qualify for the deduction, your modified adjusted gross income in 2014 must be less than $80,000 ($160,000 if you file a joint return) and you cannot file a return as married filing separately nor be claimed as a dependent on the tax return of another person. For more information, see *Student Loan Interest Deduction*.

Tuition and fees deduction. *(Note that this deduction expired at the end of 2013 and is not available for 2014 under current law. However, as of the date this book was published, Congress had been considering legislation to extend its availability for 2014. This discussion is included in the event the deduction is extended. For updated information on this and any other tax law changes that occur after this book was published, see our website, ey.com/EYTax-Guide.)* You may be able to deduct qualified education expenses you paid during the year for tuition and fees at a college, university, or other qualifying postsecondary education institution. This deduction for tuition and fees is allowed as an adjustment in figuring your AGI; therefore, it reduces your taxable income even if you do not itemize deductions. The maximum deduction is $4,000 if your modified adjusted gross income (MAGI) is less than $65,000 ($130,000

Student Loan Interest Deduction

Generally, personal interest you pay, other than certain mortgage interest, is not deductible on your tax return. However, if your modified adjusted gross income (MAGI) is less than $80,000 ($160,000 if filing a joint return) there is a special deduction allowed for paying interest on a student loan (also known as an education loan) used for higher education. For most taxpayers, MAGI is the adjusted gross income as figured on their federal income tax return before subtracting any deduction for student loan interest. This deduction can reduce the amount of your income subject to tax by up to $2,500 in 2014. Table 19-1 summarizes the features of the student loan interest deduction.

Student Loan Interest Defined

Student loan interest is interest you paid during the year on a qualified student loan. It includes both required and voluntary interest payments.

Qualified Student Loan

This is a loan you took out solely to pay qualified education expenses (defined later) that were:
- For you, your spouse, or a person who was your dependent (defined in chapter 3) when you took out the loan,
- Paid or incurred within a reasonable period of time before or after you took out the loan, and
- For education provided during an academic period when the student is an eligible student.

Loans from the following sources are not qualified student loans.
- A related person.
- A qualified employer plan.

Exceptions. For purposes of the student loan interest deduction, the following are exceptions to the general rules for dependents.
- An individual can be your dependent even if you are the dependent of another taxpayer.
- An individual can be your dependent even if the individual files a joint return with a spouse.
- An individual can be your dependent even if the individual had gross income for the year that was equal to or more than the exemption amount for the year ($3,950 for 2014).

Reasonable period of time. Qualified education expenses are treated as paid or incurred within a reasonable period of time before or after you take out the loan if they are paid with the proceeds of student loans that are part of a federal postsecondary education loan program.

Even if not paid with the proceeds of that type of loan, the expenses are treated as paid or incurred within a reasonable period of time if both of the following requirements are met.
- The expenses relate to a specific academic period.
- The loan proceeds are disbursed within a period that begins 90 days before the start of that academic period and ends 90 days after the end of that academic period.

If neither of the above situations applies, the reasonable period of time is determined based on all the relevant facts and circumstances.

Table 19-1. **Student Loan Interest Deduction at a Glance**

Do not rely on this table alone. Refer to the text for more details.

Feature	Description
Maximum benefit	You can reduce your income subject to tax by up to $2,500.
Loan qualifications	Your student loan: • must have been taken out solely to pay qualified education expenses, and • cannot be from a related person or made under a qualified employer plan.
Student qualifications	The student must be: • you, your spouse, or your dependent, and • enrolled at least half-time in a program leading to a degree, certificate, or other recognized educational credential at an eligible educational institution.
Time limit on deduction	You can deduct interest paid during the remaining period of your student loan.
Phaseout	The amount of your deduction depends on your income level.

Academic period. An academic period includes a semester, trimester, quarter, or other period of study (such as a summer school session) as reasonably determined by an educational institution. In the case of an educational institution that uses credit hours or clock hours and does not have academic terms, each payment period can be treated as an academic period.

Eligible student. This is a student who was enrolled at least half-time in a program leading to a degree, certificate, or other recognized educational credential.

Enrolled at least half-time. A student was enrolled at least half-time if the student was taking at least half the normal full-time work load for his or her course of study.

The standard for what is half of the normal full-time work load is determined by each eligible educational institution. However, the standard may not be lower than any of those established by the U.S. Department of Education under the Higher Education Act of 1965.

Related person. You cannot deduct interest on a loan you get from a related person. Related persons include:

- Your spouse,
- Your brothers and sisters,
- Your half brothers and half sisters,
- Your ancestors (parents, grandparents, etc.),
- Your lineal descendants (children, grandchildren, etc.), and
- Certain corporations, partnerships, trusts, and exempt organizations.

Qualified employer plan. You cannot deduct interest on a loan made under a qualified employer plan or under a contract purchased under such a plan.

Qualified Education Expenses

For purposes of the student loan interest deduction, these expenses are the total costs of attending an eligible educational institution, including graduate school. They include amounts paid for the following items.

- Tuition and fees.
- Room and board.
- Books, supplies, and equipment.
- Other necessary expenses (such as transportation).

The cost of room and board qualifies only to the extent that it is not more than:

- The allowance for room and board, as determined by the eligible educational institution, that was included in the cost of attendance (for federal financial aid purposes) for a particular academic period and living arrangement of the student, or
- If greater, the actual amount charged if the student is residing in housing owned or operated by the eligible educational institution.

Eligible educational institution. An eligible educational institution is any college, university, vocational school, or other postsecondary educational institution eligible to participate in a student aid program administered by the U.S. Department of Education. It includes virtually all accredited public, nonprofit, and proprietary (privately owned profit-making) postsecondary institutions.

Certain educational institutions located outside the United States also participate in the U.S. Department of Education's Federal Student Aid (FSA) programs.

For purposes of the student loan interest deduction, an eligible educational institution also includes an institution conducting an internship or residency program leading to a degree or certificate from an institution of higher education, a hospital, or a health care facility that offers post-graduate training.

An educational institution must meet the above criteria only during the academic period(s) for which the student loan was incurred. The deductibility of interest on the loan is not affected by the institution's subsequent loss of eligibility.

Adjustments to qualified education expenses. You must reduce your qualified education expenses by certain tax-free items (such as the tax-free part of scholarships and fellowships). See chapter 4 of Publication 970 for details.

Include as Interest

In addition to simple interest on the loan, certain loan origination fees, capitalized interest, interest on revolving lines of credit, and interest on refinanced student loans can be student loan interest if all other requirements are met.

if you are married filing jointly). The maximum available deduction shrinks to $2,000 if your MAGI is over $65,000 ($130,000 if filing jointly) and below $80,000 ($160,000 if filing jointly). No deduction is available if your MAGI exceeds $80,000 ($160,000 if filing jointly). The deduction is also unavailable—regardless of your MAGI—if your filing status for the year is married filing separately or you can be claimed as a dependent on the tax return of another person. In addition, deduction is disallowed if you or anyone else claims an American opportunity credit or lifetime learning credit with respect to the same student. See *Tuition and Fees Deduction.*

Educator expenses deduction. *(Note that this deduction expired at the end of 2013 and is not available for 2014 under current law. However, as of the date this book was published, Congress had been considering legislation to extend its availability for 2014. This discussion is included in the event the deduction is extended. For updated information on this and any other tax law changes that occur after this book was published, see our website, ey.com/EYTaxGuide.)* If you were a teacher, instructor, counselor, principal, or aide for any grade(s) between kindergarten and 12th grade during the year, you can deduct up to $250 of qualified expenses you paid for books, supplies, equipment (including computer equipment, software, and other related services), and other materials used in the classroom. This deduction is allowed as an adjustment in figuring your adjusted gross income; therefore, it reduces your taxable income even if you do not itemize deductions. For more information, see *Educator Expenses*.

The educational institution should be able to tell you if it is an eligible educational institution.

Caution

If you refinance a qualified student loan for more than your original loan and you use the additional amount for any purpose other than qualified education expenses, you cannot deduct any interest paid on the refinanced loan.

Loan origination fee. In general, this is a one-time fee charged by the lender when a loan is made. To be deductible as interest, the fee must be for the use of money rather than for property or services (such as commitment fees or processing costs) provided by the lender. A loan origination fee treated as interest accrues over the life of the loan.

Capitalized interest. This is unpaid interest on a student loan that is added by the lender to the outstanding principal balance of the loan.

Interest on revolving lines of credit. This interest, which includes interest on credit card debt, is student loan interest if the borrower uses the line of credit (credit card) only to pay qualified education expenses. See *Qualified Education Expenses*, earlier.

Interest on refinanced student loans. This includes interest on both:
- Consolidated loans—loans used to refinance more than one student loan of the same borrower, and
- Collapsed loans—two or more loans of the same borrower that are treated by both the lender and the borrower as one loan.

Voluntary interest payments. These are payments made on a qualified student loan during a period when interest payments are not required, such as when the borrower has been granted a deferment or the loan has not yet entered repayment status.

Do Not Include as Interest
You cannot claim a student loan interest deduction for any of the following items.
- Interest you paid on a loan if, under the terms of the loan, you are not legally obligated to make interest payments.
- Loan origination fees that are payments for property or services provided by the lender, such as commitment fees or processing costs.
- Interest you paid on a loan to the extent payments were made through your participation in the National Health Service Corps Loan Repayment Program (the "NHSC Loan Repayment Program") or certain other loan repayment assistance programs. For more information, see *Student Loan Repayment Assistance* in chapter 5 of Publication 970.

Can You Claim the Deduction
Generally, you can claim the deduction if all of the following requirements are met.
- Your filing status is any filing status except married filing separately.
- No one else is claiming an exemption for you on his or her tax return.
- You are legally obligated to pay interest on a qualified student loan.
- You paid interest on a qualified student loan.

Interest paid by others. If you are the person legally obligated to make interest payments and someone else makes a payment of interest on your behalf, you are treated as receiving the payments from the other person and, in turn, paying the interest. See chapter 4 of Publication 970 for more information.

No Double Benefit Allowed
You cannot deduct as interest on a student loan any amount that is an allowable deduction under any other provision of the tax law (for example, home mortgage interest).

TAXPLANNER
You can deduct interest paid on a student loan for your dependent only if:
- The person for whom you took the loan was a dependent when you took out the loan,
- You are legally obligated to make the interest payments, and
- You actually made the payments during the tax year. You are not considered to have made student loan interest payments actually made by your dependent, regardless of whether your dependent is legally liable for the loan.

How Much Can You Deduct
Your student loan interest deduction for 2014 is generally the smaller of:
- $2,500, or
- The interest you paid in 2014.

However, the amount determined above is phased out (gradually reduced) if your MAGI is between $65,000 and $80,000 ($130,000 and $160,000 if you file a joint return). You cannot take a student loan interest deduction if your MAGI is $80,000 or more ($160,000 or more if you file a joint return). For details on figuring your MAGI, see chapter 4 of Publication 970.

How Do You Figure the Deduction

Generally, you figure the deduction using the Student Loan Interest Deduction Worksheet in the Form 1040 or Form 1040A instructions. However, if you are filing Form 2555, 2555-EZ, or 4563, or you are excluding income from sources within Puerto Rico, you must complete Worksheet 4-1 in chapter 4 of Publication 970.

To help you figure your student loan interest deduction, you should receive Form 1098-E, Student Loan Interest Statement. Generally, an institution (such as a bank or governmental agency) that received interest payments of $600 or more during 2014 on one or more qualified student loans must send Form 1098-E (or acceptable substitute) to each borrower by February 2, 2015.

For qualified student loans taken out before September 1, 2004, the institution is required to include on Form 1098-E only payments of stated interest. Other interest payments, such as certain loan origination fees and capitalized interest, may not appear on the form you receive. However, if you pay qualifying interest that is not included on Form 1098-E, you can also deduct those amounts. For information on allocating payments between interest and principal, see chapter 4 of Publication 970.

To claim the deduction, enter the allowable amount on Form 1040, line 33, or Form 1040A, line 18.

Tuition and Fees Deduction

TAXALERT
The availability of the Tuition and Fees deduction expired at the end of 2013. As of the date this book was published, Congress had been considering legislation that would extend its availability through 2014, but no such extension had yet been passed. The discussion of this adjustment is included in this chapter in case Congress acts to extend it. For updated information on this and any other tax law changes that occur after this book was published, see our website, ey.com/EYTaxGuide.

You may be able to deduct qualified education expenses paid during the year for yourself, your spouse, or your dependent(s). You cannot claim this deduction if your filing status is married filing separately or if another person can claim an exemption for you as a dependent on his or her tax return. The qualified expenses must be for higher education, as explained later under *What Expenses Qualify*.

The tuition and fees deduction can reduce the amount of your income subject to tax by up to $4,000.

Table 19-2 summarizes the features of the tuition and fees deduction.

Table 19-2.   **Tuition and Fees Deduction at a Glance**

Do not rely on this table alone. Refer to the text for more details.

Question	Answer
What is the maximum benefit?	You can reduce your income subject to tax by up to $4,000.
Where is the deduction taken?	As an adjustment to income on Form 1040, line 34, or Form 1040A, line 19.
For whom must the expenses be paid?	A student enrolled in an eligible educational institution who is either: you, your spouse, or your dependent for whom you claim an exemption.
What tuition and fees are deductible?	Tuition and fees required for enrollment or attendance at an eligible postsecondary educational institution, but not including personal, living, or family expenses, such as room and board.

Tip

You may be able to take a credit for your education expenses instead of a deduction. You can choose the one that will give you the lower tax. See chapter 36, Education Credits, for details about the credits.

Can You Claim the Deduction

The following rules will help you determine if you can claim the tuition and fees deduction.

Who Can Claim the Deduction

Generally, you can claim the tuition and fees deduction if all three of the following requirements are met.

1. You paid qualified education expenses of higher education in 2014 for academic periods beginning in 2014 and those beginning in the first three months of 2015.
2. You paid the education expenses for an eligible student.
3. The eligible student is yourself, your spouse, or your dependent for whom you claim an exemption (defined in chapter 3) on your tax return.

Qualified education expenses are defined under *What Expenses Qualify*. Eligible students are defined later under *Who Is an Eligible Student.*

Who Cannot Claim the Deduction

You cannot claim the tuition and fees deduction if any of the following apply.

- Your filing status is married filing separately.
- Another person can claim an exemption for you as a dependent on his or her tax return. You cannot take the deduction even if the other person does not actually claim that exemption.
- Your modified adjusted gross income (MAGI) is more than $80,000 ($160,000 if filing a joint return).
- You (or your spouse) were a nonresident alien for any part of 2014 and the nonresident alien did not elect to be treated as a resident alien for tax purposes. More information on nonresident aliens can be found in Publication 519, U.S. Tax Guide for Aliens.
- You or anyone else claims an American opportunity or lifetime learning credit in 2014 with respect to expenses of the student for whom the qualified education expenses were paid. However, a state tax credit will not disqualify you from claiming a tuition and fees deduction.

What Expenses Qualify

The tuition and fees deduction is based on qualified education expenses you pay for yourself, your spouse, or a dependent for whom you claim an exemption on your tax return. Generally, the deduction is allowed for qualified education expenses paid in 2014 in connection with enrollment at an institution of higher education during 2014 or for an academic period (defined earlier under *Student Loan Interest Deduction*) beginning in 2014 or in the first 3 months of 2015.

Payments with borrowed funds. You can claim a tuition and fees deduction for qualified education expenses paid with the proceeds of a loan. Use the expenses to figure the deduction for the year in which the expenses are paid, not the year in which the loan is repaid. Treat loan payments sent directly to the educational institution as paid on the date the institution credits the student's account.

Student withdraws from class(es). You can claim a tuition and fees deduction for qualified education expenses not refunded when a student withdraws.

Qualified Education Expenses

For purposes of the tuition and fees deduction, qualified education expenses are tuition and certain related expenses required for enrollment or attendance at an eligible educational institution.

Eligible educational institution. An eligible educational institution is any college, university, vocational school, or other postsecondary educational institution eligible to participate in a student aid program administered by the U.S. Department of Education. It includes virtually all accredited public, nonprofit, and proprietary (privately owned profit-making) postsecondary institutions. The educational institution should be able to tell you if it is an eligible educational institution.

Certain educational institutions located outside the United States also participate in the U.S. Department of Education's Federal Student Aid (FSA) programs.

Academic period. An academic period is any quarter, semester, trimester, or any other period of study as reasonably determined by an eligible educational institution. If an eligible educational institution uses credit hours and does not have academic terms, each payment period may be treated as an academic period.

Related expenses. Student-activity fees and expenses for course-related books, supplies, and equipment are included in qualified education expenses for the tuition and fees deduction **only** if the fees and expenses must be paid to the institution as a condition of enrollment or attendance.

Prepaid expenses. Qualified education expenses paid in 2014 for an academic period that begins in the first three months of 2015 can be used in figuring the tuition and fees deduction. See *Academic period*, earlier. For example, if you pay $2,000 in December 2014 for qualified tuition for the 2015 winter quarter that begins in January 2015, you can use that $2,000 in figuring the tuition and fees deduction for 2014 only if you meet all the other requirements.

No Double Benefit Allowed

You cannot do any of the following.

- Deduct qualified education expenses you deduct under any other provision of the law, for example, as a business expense.
- Deduct qualified education expenses for a student on your income tax return if you or anyone else claims an American opportunity or lifetime learning credit for that same student in the same year.
- Deduct qualified education expenses that have been used to figure the tax-free portion of a distribution from a Coverdell education savings account (ESA) or a qualified tuition program (QTP). For a QTP, this applies only to the amount of tax-free earnings that were distributed, not to the recovery of contributions to the program. See *Figuring the Taxable Portion of a Distribution* in chapter 7 (Coverdell ESA) and chapter 8 (QTP) of Publication 970.
- Deduct qualified education expenses that have been paid with tax-free interest on U.S. savings bonds (Form 8815). See *Figuring the Tax-Free Amount* in chapter 10 of Publication 970.
- Deduct qualified education expenses that have been paid with tax-free educational assistance such as a scholarship, grant, or employer-provided educational assistance. See *Adjustments to qualified education expenses*, later.

Adjustments to qualified education expenses. For each student, reduce the qualified education expenses paid by or on behalf of that student under the following rules. The result is the amount of adjusted qualified education expenses for each student.

Tax-free educational assistance. For tax-free educational assistance you received in 2014, reduce the qualified educational expenses for each academic period by the amount of tax-free educational assistance to that academic period. See *Academic period*, earlier. This includes:

- The tax-free part of scholarships and fellowships, including Pell grants (see chapter 1 of Publication 970),
- The tax-free part of any employer-provided educational assistance (see chapter 11 of Publication 970),
- Veterans' educational assistance (see chapter 1 of Publication 970), and
- Any other nontaxable (tax-free) payments (other than gifts or inheritances) received as educational assistance.

Generally, any scholarship or fellowship you receive is treated as tax-free educational assistance. However, a scholarship or fellowship is not treated as tax-free educational assistance to the extent you include it in gross income (if you are required to file a tax return) for the year the scholarship or fellowship is received and either:

- The scholarship or fellowship (or any part of it) **must** be applied (by its terms) to expenses (such as room and board) other than qualified education expenses as defined in *Qualified education expenses* in Pub. 970, chapter 1.
- The scholarship or fellowship (or any part of it) may be applied (by its terms) to expenses (such as room and board) other than qualified education expenses as defined in *Qualified education expenses* in Pub. 970, chapter 1.

Some tax-free educational assistance received in 2014 may be treated as a refund of qualified education expenses paid in 2014. This tax-free educational assistance is any tax-free educational assistance received by you or anyone else after 2014 for qualified education expenses paid on behalf of a student in 2014 (or attributable to enrollment at an eligible educational institution during 2014).

If this tax-free educational assistance is received after 2014 but before you file your 2014 income tax return, see *Refunds received after 2014 but before your income tax return is filed*, later. If this tax-free educational assistance is received after 2014 and after you file your 2014 income tax return, see *Refunds received after 2014 and after your income tax return is filed*, later.

Refunds. A refund of qualified education expenses may reduce adjusted qualified education expenses for the tax year or may require you to include some or all of the refund in your gross income for the year the refund is received. See chapter 6 of Pub. 970 for more information. Some tax-free educational assistance received after 2014 may be treated as a refund. See *Tax-free educational assistance*, earlier.

Refunds received in 2014. For each student, figure the adjusted qualified education expenses for 2014 by adding all the qualified education expenses paid in 2014 and subtracting any refunds of those expenses received from the eligible educational institution during 2014.

Refunds received after 2014 but before your income tax return is filed. If you receive a refund after 2014 of qualified education expenses you paid in 2014 and the refund is received before you file your 2014 income tax return, reduce the amount of qualified education expenses for 2014 by the amount of the refund.

Refunds received after 2014 and after your income tax return is filed. If you receive a refund after 2014 of qualified education expenses you paid in 2014 and the refund is received after you file your 2014 income tax return, you may need to include some or all of the refund in your gross income for the year the refund is received. See chapter 6 of Pub. 970 for more information.

Coordination with Coverdell education savings accounts and qualified tuition programs. Reduce your qualified education expenses by any qualified education expenses used to figure the exclusion from gross income of (a) interest received under an education savings bond program, or (b) any distribution from a Coverdell education savings account or qualified tuition program (QTP). For a QTP, this applies only to the amount of tax-free earnings that were distributed, not to the recovery of contributions to the program.

Amounts that do not reduce qualified education expenses. Do not reduce qualified education expenses by amounts paid with funds the student receives as:
- Payment for services, such as wages,
- A loan,
- A gift,
- An inheritance, or
- A withdrawal from the student's personal savings.

Do not reduce the qualified education expenses by any scholarship or fellowship reported as income on the student's tax return in the following situations.
- The use of the money is restricted, by the terms of the scholarship or fellowship, to costs of attendance (such as room and board) other than qualified education expenses.
- The use of the money is not restricted.

Expenses That Do Not Qualify

Qualified education expenses do not include amounts paid for:
- Insurance,
- Medical expenses (including student health fees),
- Room and board,
- Transportation, or
- Similar personal, living, or family expenses.

This is true even if the amount must be paid to the institution as a condition of enrollment or attendance.

Sports, games, hobbies, and noncredit courses. Qualified education expenses generally do not include expenses that relate to any course of instruction or other education that involves sports, games or hobbies, or any noncredit course. However, if the course of instruction or other education is part of the student's degree program, these expenses can qualify.

Comprehensive or bundled fees. Some eligible educational institutions combine all of their fees for an academic period into one amount. If you do not receive, or do not have access to, an allocation showing how much you paid for qualified education expenses and how much you paid for personal expenses, such as those listed above, contact the institution. The institution is required to make this allocation and provide you with the amount you paid (or were billed) for qualified education expenses on Form 1098-T, Tuition Statement. *See How Do You Figure the Deduction*, later, for more information about Form 1098-T.

Who Is an Eligible Student

For purposes of the tuition and fees deduction, an eligible student is a student who is enrolled in one or more courses at an eligible educational institution (defined earlier).

Who Can Claim a Dependent's Expenses

Generally, in order to claim the tuition and fees deduction for qualified education expenses for a dependent, you must:
- Have paid the expenses, and
- Claim an exemption for the student as a dependent.

Table 19-3 summarizes who can claim the deduction.

Table 19-3. **Who Can Claim a Dependent's Expenses**

Do not rely on this table alone. See Who Can Claim a Dependent's Expenses in chapter 6 of Publication 970.

IF your dependent is an eligible student and you...	AND...	THEN...
claim an exemption for your dependent	**you** paid all qualified education expenses for your dependent	only **you** can deduct the qualified education expenses that you paid. Your dependent cannot take a deduction.
claim an exemption for your dependent	**your dependent** paid all qualified education expenses	**no one** is allowed to take a deduction.
do not claim an exemption for your dependent	**you** paid all qualified education expenses	**no one** is allowed to take a deduction.
do not claim an exemption for your dependent	**your dependent** paid all qualified education expenses	**no one** is allowed to take a deduction.

How Much Can You Deduct
The maximum tuition and fees deduction in 2014 is $4,000, $2,000, or $0, depending on the amount of your MAGI. For details on figuring your MAGI, see chapter 6 of Publication 970.

How Do You Figure the Deduction
Figure the deduction using Form 8917.

To help you figure your tuition and fees deduction, you should receive Form 1098-T, Tuition Statement. Generally, an eligible educational institution (such as a college or university) must send Form 1098-T (or acceptable substitute) to each enrolled student by February 2, 2015.

To claim the deduction, enter the allowable amount on Form 1040, line 34, or Form 1040A, line 19, and attach your completed Form 8917.

TAXPLANNER

If availability of the tuition and fees deduction is extended through at least 2014 and, as a result, eligible taxpayers are allowed to claim a deduction in 2014 for up to $4,000 of qualified higher education expenses, qualified expenses must be incurred in connection with an academic term which began in 2014 or which will begin during the first 3 months of 2015. To be an eligible taxpayer in 2014, you must meet a number of requirements and must not have adjusted gross income in excess of $65,000 if single or $130,000 if married filing jointly to claim the $4,000 deduction. You may claim a deduction for up to $2,000 of qualified expenses if your adjusted gross income is more than $65,000 but not more than $80,000 if single, or more than $130,000 but not more than $160,000 if married filing jointly.

Educator Expenses

TAXALERT

The availability of the adjustment for Educator Expenses expired at the end of 2013. As of the date this book was published, Congress had been considering legislation that would extend its availability to tax year 2014, but no such extension had yet been passed. The discussion of this adjustment is included in this chapter in case Congress acts to extend it. For updated information on this and any other tax law changes that occur after this book was published, see our website, *ey.com/EYTaxGuide.*

If you were an eligible educator in 2014, you can deduct on Form 1040, line 23, or Form 1040A, line 16, up to $250 of qualified expenses you paid in 20143. If you and your spouse are filing jointly and both of you were eligible educators, the maximum deduction is $500. However, neither spouse can deduct more than $250 of his or her qualified expenses on Form 1040, line 23, or Form 1040A, line 16. You may be able to deduct expenses that are more than the $250 (or $500) limit on Schedule A (Form 1040), line 21.

Eligible educator. An eligible educator is a kindergarten through grade 12 teacher, instructor, counselor, principal, or aide who worked in a school for at least 900 hours during a school year.

Qualified expenses. Qualified expenses include ordinary and necessary expenses paid in connection with books, supplies, equipment (including computer equipment, software, and services), and other materials used in the classroom. An ordinary expense is one that is common and accepted in your educational field. A necessary expense is one that is helpful and appropriate for your profession as an educator. An expense does not have to be required to be considered necessary.

Qualified expenses do not include expenses for home schooling or for nonathletic supplies for courses in health or physical education.

You must reduce your qualified expenses by the following amounts.

- Excludable U.S. series EE and I savings bond interest from Form 8815. See *Figuring the Tax-Free Amount* in chapter 10 of Publication 970.
- Nontaxable qualified tuition program earnings or distributions. See *Figuring the Taxable Portion of a Distribution* in chapter 8 of Publication 970.
- Nontaxable distribution of earnings from a Coverdell education savings account. See *Figuring the Taxable Portion of a Distribution* in chapter 7 of Publication 970.
- Any reimbursements you received for these expenses that were not reported to you in box 1 of your Form W-2.

> ### TAXALERT
> Ordinary and necessary educator expenses that do not qualify for the $250 adjustment may be deductible as a miscellaneous itemized deduction subject to the 2% limitation. For more information on this itemized deduction, see *Educator Expenses* in chapter 29, *Miscellaneous deductions*.

Chapter 20
Moving expenses

Note

ey.com/EYTaxGuide

Ernst & Young LLP will update the *EY Guide 2015* website with relevant taxpayer information as it becomes available. You can also sign up for email alerts to let you know when changes have been made.

Introduction

Moving expenses are deducted from your gross income in arriving at your adjusted gross income (AGI). This can be advantageous, since you do not have to complete Schedule A, *Itemized Deductions*, in order to receive the benefit of this deduction.

But, in general, most expenses connected with a move are not deductible. For example, meals bought in connection with a move, expenses related to searching for a residence or living in temporary quarters, and expenses incurred in selling, purchasing, or leasing a residence in connection with a move are not deductible expenses.

The good news about moving expenses is that you usually may deduct them if you move because you change jobs. The not-so-good news is that, because no two moves are alike, there are several tests you must meet in order to claim the deductions. Disagreements with the IRS over moving expenses are frequent.

If you are interested in deducting as much of your move as possible, the first rule you should follow is to keep adequate records of all your moving-related expenditures. Receipts, plus a log of your activities, will generally suffice. Additional ins and outs related to moving expenses are detailed in this chapter.

What's New

Standard mileage rate. For 2014, the standard mileage rate for the cost of operating your car as part of a deductible move was 23½ cents per mile.

Reminder

Change of address. If you change your mailing address, be sure to notify the IRS using Form 8822, Change of Address. Mail it to the Internal Revenue Service Center for your old address. Addresses for the Service Centers are on the back of the form.

This chapter explains the deduction of certain expenses of moving to a new home because you changed job locations or started a new job. It includes the following topics.
- Who can deduct moving expenses.
- What moving expenses are deductible.
- What moving expenses are not deductible.
- How a reimbursement affects your moving expense deduction.
- How and when to report moving expenses.
- Special rules for members of the Armed Forces.

You may be able to deduct moving expenses whether you are self-employed or an employee. Your expenses generally must be related to starting work at your new job location. However, certain retirees and survivors may qualify to claim the deduction even though they are not starting work at a new job location. See *Who Can Deduct Moving Expenses*.

Moves to locations outside the United States. This chapter does not discuss moves outside the United States. If you are a United States citizen or resident alien who moved outside the United States or its possessions because of your job or business, see Publication 521, *Moving Expenses*, for special rules that apply to your move.

Useful Items

You may want to see:

Publication
☐ **521** Moving Expenses

Form (and Instructions)
☐ **3903** Moving Expenses
☐ **8822** Change of Address

Who Can Deduct Moving Expenses

You can deduct your moving expenses if you meet all three of the following requirements.
1. Your move is closely related to the start of work.
2. You meet the distance test.
3. You meet the time test.

After you have read these rules, see Figure 20-B to help you determine if you can deduct your moving expenses.

Different rules may apply if you are a member of the Armed Forces or a retiree or survivor moving to the United States. These rules are discussed later in this chapter.

Related to Start of Work

Your move must be closely related, both in time and in place, to the start of work at your new job location.

Closely related in time. You can generally consider moving expenses incurred within 1 year from the date you first reported to work at the new location as closely related in time to the start of work. It is not necessary that you arrange to work before moving to a new location, as long as you actually do go to work.

If you do not move within 1 year of the date you begin work, you ordinarily cannot deduct the expenses unless you can show that circumstances existed that prevented the move within that time frame.

Example. Your family moved more than a year after you started work at a new location. You delayed the move for 18 months to allow your child to complete high school. You can deduct your moving expenses. This is an exception to the rule listed above.

EXPLANATION
You must make the actual move within a year of starting a new job, unless circumstances prevent you from doing so. Not moving your family so that your child may complete high school in the same school is an acceptable reason, but not moving because you haven't been able to sell your home is not. Good intentions are not enough.

Closely related in place. You can generally consider your move closely related in place to the start of work if the distance from your new home to the new job location is not more than the distance from your former home to the new job location. If your move does not meet this requirement, you may still be able to deduct moving expenses if you can show that:
1. You are required to live at your new home as a condition of your employment, or
2. You will spend less time or money commuting from your new home to your new job location.

Home defined. Your home means your main home (residence). It can be a house, apartment, condominium, houseboat, house trailer, or similar dwelling. It does not include other homes owned or kept up by you or members of your family. It also does not include a seasonal home, such as a summer beach cottage. Your former home means your home before you left for your new job location. Your new home means your home within the area of your new job location.

Retirees or survivors. You may be able to deduct the expenses of moving to the United States or its possessions even though the move is not related to the start of work at a new job location. You must have worked outside the United States or be a survivor of someone who did. See *Retirees or Survivors Who Move to the United States*, later.

Distance Test

Your move will meet the distance test if your new main job location is at least 50 miles farther from your former home than your old main job location was from your former home. For example, if your old main job location was 3 miles from your former home, your new main job location must be at least 53 miles from that former home. See Worksheet 20-1 to determine if you meet this test.

The distance between a job location and your home is the shortest of the more commonly traveled routes between the two. The distance test considers only the location of your former home. It does not take into account the location of your new home. See Figure 20-A.

Example. You moved to a new home less than 50 miles from your former home because you changed main job locations. Your old main job location was 3 miles from your former home. Your new main job location is 60 miles from that home. Because your new main job location is 57 miles farther from your former home than the distance from your former home to your old main job location, you meet the distance test.

Worksheet 20-1. **Distance Test**

Note. Members of the armed forces may not have to meet this test. See *Members of the Armed Forces*.
1. Enter the number of miles from your old home to your new workplace..........................   1. _____ miles
2. Enter the number of miles from your old home to your old workplace..........................   2. _____ miles
3. Subtract line 2 from line 1. If zero or less, enter -0-..   3. _____ miles
4. Is line 3 at least 50 miles?
• Yes. You meet this test.
• No. You do not meet this test. You cannot deduct your moving expenses.

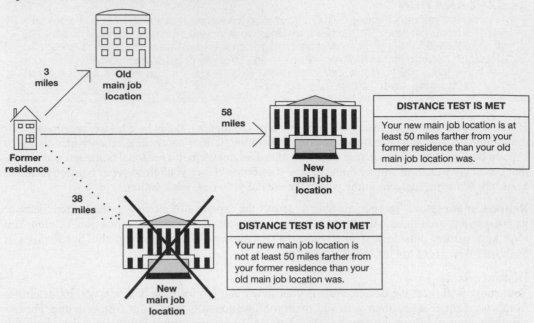

Figure 20-A. **Illustration of Distance Test**

DISTANCE TEST IS MET

Your new main job location is at least 50 miles farther from your former residence than your old main job location was.

DISTANCE TEST IS NOT MET

Your new main job location is not at least 50 miles farther from your former residence than your old main job location was.

> **Example**
> Even though you may now live 55 miles from your office, the fact that your office is only 45 miles further from your old home than it used to be means that you will not be able to deduct your moving expenses.
>
> You can tell whether you meet the distance test simply by subtracting the total miles from your old home to the old job from the total miles from the old home to the new job. The difference must be 50 miles or greater.

First job or return to full-time work. If you go to work full time for the first time, your place of work must be at least 50 miles from your former home to meet the distance test.

If you go back to full-time work after a substantial period of part-time work or unemployment, your place of work must also be at least 50 miles from your former home.

> **TAXSAVER**
> First-time job seekers, such as high school and college graduates, and people reentering the labor force after a substantial period of unemployment may deduct moving expenses.
>
> You must move from a former principal home to a new principal home, which means that you must have a principal home from which to move. According to one court, a college graduate could not deduct his expenses to move to his new job location because his student residence was not his principal home.
>
> **Explanation**
> Two months of unemployment is not long enough to qualify as a substantial period of unemployment. If you had only a brief break in employment, you must meet the same distance requirement that you would if you had been working continuously.

Armed Forces. If you are in the Armed Forces and you moved because of a permanent change of station, you are not required to meet the distance test. See *Members of the Armed Forces*, later.

Main job location. Your main job location is usually the place where you spend most of your working time. If there is no one place where you spend most of your working time, your main job location is the place where your work is centered, such as where you report for work or are otherwise required to "base" your work.

Union members. If you work for several employers on a short-term basis and you get work under a union hall system (such as a construction or building trades worker), your main job location is the union hall.

More than one job. If you have more than one job at any time, your main job location depends on the facts in each case. The more important factors to be considered are:

- The total time you spend at each place,
- The amount of work you do at each place, and
- How much money you earn at each place.

Time Test

To deduct your moving expenses, you also must meet one of the following two time tests.

1. The time test for employees.
2. The time test for self-employed persons.

Both of these tests are explained below. See Table 20-1 for a summary of these tests.

Time Test for Employees

If you are an employee, you must work full time for at least 39 weeks during the first 12 months (39-week test) after you arrive in the general area of your new job location. Full-time employment depends on what is usual for the type of work you perform in your area.

For purposes of this test, the following four rules apply.

1. You count only your full-time work as an employee, not any work you do as a self-employed person.
2. You do not have to work for the same employer for all 39 weeks.
3. You do not have to work 39 weeks in a row.
4. You must work full time within the same general commuting area for all 39 weeks.

Table 20-1. **Satisfying the Time Test for Employees and Self-Employed Persons**

IF you are...	THEN you satisfy the time test by meeting the...
an employee	39-week test for employees.
both self-employed and an employee, but unable to satisfy the 39-week test for employees	78-week test for self-employed persons.
both self-employed and an employee at the same time	78-week test for self-employed persons or the 39-week test for an employee. Your principal place of work determines which test applies.
self-employed	78-week test for self-employed persons.

Temporary absence from work. You are considered to have worked full time during any week you are temporarily absent from work because of illness, strikes, lockouts, layoffs, natural disasters, or similar causes. You are also considered to have worked full time during any week you are absent from work for leave or vacation provided for in your work contract or agreement.

Seasonal work. If your work is seasonal, you are considered to be working full time during the off-season only if your work contract or agreement covers an off-season period of less than 6 months. For example, a school teacher on a 12-month contract who teaches on a full-time basis for more than 6 months is considered to have worked full time for the entire 12 months.

Time Test for Self-Employed Persons

If you are self-employed, you must work full time for at least 39 weeks during the first 12 months and for a total of at least 78 weeks during the first 24 months (78-week test) after you arrive in the general area of your new job location.

For purposes of the time test for self-employed persons, the following three rules apply.

1. You count any full-time work you do either as an employee or as a self-employed person.
2. You do not have to work for the same employer or be self-employed in the same trade or business for the 78 weeks.
3. You must work within the same general commuting area for all 78 weeks.

EXAMPLE

You are a self-employed accountant who moves from Atlanta to New York City, and begin to work there on December 1, 2014. You pay moving expenses in 2014 and 2015 in connection with this move. On April 15, 2015, when you file your income tax return for the year 2014, you have been performing services as a self-employed individual on a full-time basis in New York City for approximately 20 weeks. Although you have not satisfied the 78-week employment condition at this time, you can deduct your 2014 moving expenses on your 2014 income tax return as there is still sufficient time remaining before December 1, 2016, to satisfy such condition. You can deduct any moving expenses you pay in 2015 on your 2015 income tax return even if you have not met the 78-week test. You have until December 1, 2016, to satisfy this requirement.

Self-employment. You are self-employed if you work as the sole owner of an unincorporated business or as a partner in a partnership carrying on a business. You are not considered self-employed if you are semiretired, are a part-time student, or work only a few hours each week.

Full-time work. You can count only those weeks during which you work full time as a week of work. Whether you work full time during any week depends on what is usual for your type of work in your area.

For example, you are a self-employed dentist and maintain office hours 4 days a week. You are considered to perform services full time if maintaining office hours 4 days a week is not unusual for other self-employed dentists in your area.

If you were both an employee and self-employed, see Table 20-1 for the requirements.

Joint Return

If you are married, file a joint return, and both you and your spouse work full time, either of you can satisfy the full-time work test. However, you cannot add the weeks your spouse worked to the weeks you worked to satisfy that test.

TAXSAVER

If you file separate returns, each person must meet the time test individually and deduct only his or her own expenses.

The time test may be met by either spouse if a joint return is filed. However, weeks worked by both husband and wife cannot be added together to meet the time test.

If you and your spouse are living together, and if both of you have been working full-time but one of you loses your job, you obtain the maximum tax benefits by filing a joint return. This is the case even if you reside in a **community property** state. Moving expenses paid by both husband and wife may be aggregated and are deductible in full.

Time test not yet met. You can deduct your moving expenses on your 2014 tax return even though you have not yet met the time test by the date your 2014 return is due. You can do this if you expect to meet the 39-week test in 2015, or the 78-week test in 2015 or 2016. If you deduct moving expenses but do not meet the time test in 2015 or 2016, you must either:

1. Report your moving expense deduction as other income on your Form 1040 for the year you cannot meet the test, or
2. Amend your 2014 return.

If you do not deduct your moving expenses on your 2014 return and you later meet the time test, you can file an amended return for 2014 to take the deduction.

Example. You arrive in the general area of your new job location September 10, 2014. You deduct moving expenses on your 2014 return, the year of the move, even though you have not met the time test by the date your return is due. If you do not meet the 39-week test during the 12-month period following your arrival in the general area of your new job location, you must either:

1. Report your moving expense deduction as other income on your Form 1040 for 2015, or
2. Amend your 2014 return.

Exceptions to the Time Test

You do not have to meet the time test if one of the following applies.

1. You are in the Armed Forces and you moved because of a permanent change of station. See *Members of the Armed Forces*, later.
2. Your main job location was outside the United States and you moved to the United States because you retired. See *Retirees or Survivors Who Move to the United States*, later.
3. You are the survivor of a person whose main job location at the time of death was outside the United States. See *Retirees or Survivors Who Move to the United States*, later.
4. Your job at the new location ends because of death or disability.
5. You are transferred for your employer's benefit or laid off for a reason other than willful misconduct. For this exception, you must have obtained full-time employment and you must have expected to meet the test at the time you started the job.

EXPLANATION

The courts have held and the IRS agrees that if, after moving for job-related purposes, you are fired or laid off, involuntarily lose your job (for other than willful misconduct), or are required to move again by your employer before the 39 weeks are up, you are still able to deduct your moving expenses. Death and disability also exempt a taxpayer from the 39-week requirement. However, if you voluntarily take a leave of absence—even if employment benefits continue—you may not count the leave period toward the 39 weeks.

Example

A taxpayer who terminated his employment voluntarily after working in his new location only 37 weeks (even though he did so in order to start a different job elsewhere) was not allowed the deduction for his original moving costs.

TAXSAVER

Since you have 2 years to fulfill the time requirement, you should assume that you will meet it and deduct moving expenses in the year in which you incur them. Even if you expect to incur more moving expenses later, do not wait to deduct those that you already have incurred. Any later expenses that qualify may be deducted in a subsequent year.

If you fail to meet the time test later, you may either file an amended return and repay any tax due along with interest or report as income the amount you previously deducted. In some cases, the 2-year period may be extended.

Example

A woman was allowed to deduct moving expenses incurred 30 months after her transfer because she waited until her child finished school before moving her family. The IRS rule is: You have to demonstrate that there is a good reason for the delay.

Members of the Armed Forces

If you are a member of the Armed Forces on active duty and you move because of a permanent change of station, you do not have to meet the distance and time tests, discussed earlier. You can deduct your unreimbursed moving expenses.

A permanent change of station includes:

- A move from your home to your first post of active duty,
- A move from one permanent post of duty to another, and
- A move from your last post of duty to your home or to a nearer point in the United States. The move must occur within 1 year of ending your active duty or within the period allowed under the Joint Travel Regulations.

Spouse and dependents. If a member of the Armed Forces dies, is imprisoned, or deserts, a permanent change of station for the spouse or dependent includes a move to:
- The place of enlistment,
- The member's, spouse's, or dependent's home of record, or
- A nearer point in the United States.

If the military moves you and your spouse and dependents to or from separate locations, the moves are treated as a single move to your new main job location.

More information. For more information on moving expenses for members of the Armed Forces, and instructions for completing Form 3903, see *Members of the Armed Forces* in Publication 521.

EXPLANATION
If an Armed Forces member's family can't move to his or her new permanent location, the cost of moving the family to a new location is still deductible.

An Armed Forces member's family may deduct expenses for a move to the foreign country to which the service member is transferred, even if the family obtains only 90-day tourist visas. The IRS recognizes the family as being part of the Armed Forces member's household, residing with him or her before and after the move.

In general, a dislocation allowance received by Armed Forces personnel is excludable from wages.

Retirees or Survivors Who Move to the United States
If you are a retiree who was working abroad or a survivor of a decedent who was working abroad and you move to the United States or one of its possessions, you do not have to meet the time test, discussed earlier. However, you must meet the requirements discussed below under *Retirees who were working abroad* or *Survivors of decedents who were working abroad*.

United States defined. For this section of this chapter, the term "United States" includes the possessions of the United States.

Retirees who were working abroad. You can deduct moving expenses for a move to a new home in the United States when you permanently retire. However, both your former main job location and your former home must have been outside the United States.

Permanently retired. You are considered permanently retired when you cease gainful full-time employment or self-employment. If, at the time you retire, you intend your retirement to be permanent, you will be considered retired though you later return to work. Your intention to retire permanently may be determined by:
1. Your age and health,
2. The customary retirement age for people who do similar work,
3. Whether you receive retirement payments from a pension or retirement fund, and
4. The length of time before you return to full-time work.

> **Caution**
>
> *If you are living in the United States, retire, and then move and remain retired, you cannot claim a moving expense deduction for that move.*

EXPLANATION
A retiree may deduct the cost of moving back to a residence in the United States without having to be employed on returning. Although there is no timetable for the move specified in the law, it must be "in connection with the bona fide retirement of an individual." Moving expenses incurred after a lengthy delay following retirement may not be deductible.

Survivors of decedents who were working abroad. If you are the spouse or the dependent of a person whose main job location at the time of death was outside the United States, you can deduct moving expenses if the following five requirements are met.
1. The move is to a home in the United States.
2. The move begins within 6 months after the decedent's death. (When a move begins is described later.)
3. The move is from the decedent's former home.
4. The decedent's former home was outside the United States.
5. The decedent's former home was also your home.

When a move begins. A move begins when one of the following events occurs.
1. You contract for your household goods and personal effects to be moved to your home in the United States, but only if the move is completed within a reasonable time.
2. Your household goods and personal effects are packed and on the way to your home in the United States.
3. You leave your former home to travel to your new home in the United States.

Deductible Moving Expenses

If you meet the requirements discussed earlier under <u>*Who Can Deduct Moving Expenses*</u>, you can deduct the reasonable expenses of:
1. Moving your household goods and personal effects (including in-transit or foreign-move storage expenses), and
2. Traveling (including lodging but not meals) to your new home.

Caution

You cannot deduct any expenses for meals.

Reasonable expenses. You can deduct only those expenses that are reasonable for the circumstances of your move. For example, the cost of traveling from your former home to your new one should be by the shortest, most direct route available by conventional transportation. If, during your trip to your new home, you stop over, or make side trips for sightseeing or visiting relatives, the additional expenses for your stopover or side trips are not deductible as moving expenses.

TAXPLANNER
Qualified moving expenses not paid or reimbursed by your employer will be allowed as a deduction in calculating your adjusted gross income. Moving expenses paid for by your employer directly or through reimbursement will be excludable from your gross income and wages for income and employment tax purposes, unless you actually deducted the expenses in a prior taxable year.

Travel by car. If you use your car to take yourself, members of your household, or your personal effects to your new home, you can figure your expenses by deducting either:
1. Your actual expenses, such as gas and oil for your car, if you keep an accurate record of each expense, or
2. The standard mileage rate of 23½ cents per mile for 2014

Whether you use actual expenses or the standard mileage rate to figure your expenses, you can deduct parking fees and tolls you paid in moving. You cannot deduct any part of general repairs, general maintenance, insurance, or depreciation for your car.

EXPLANATION
For 2014, the standard mileage rate for moving expenses is 23½ cents per mile, while the mileage rate for business expenses is 56 cents per mile.
The IRS has resisted any attempt to include depreciation of an automobile as a moving expense, maintaining that depreciation does not apply to a personal automobile.

Member of household. You can deduct moving expenses you pay for yourself and members of your household. A member of your household is anyone who has both your former and new home as his or her home. It does not include a tenant or employee, unless that person is your dependent.

EXPLANATION
The costs of moving dependent children who do not reside with the parents before the move are not deductible, even if the parents and children move to the new location simultaneously. The reason is that the children were not members of the former household.

Location of move. There are different rules for moving within or to the United States than for moving outside the United States. This chapter only discusses moves within or to the United States. The rules for moves outside the United States can be found in Publication 521.

Household Goods and Personal Effects

You can deduct the cost of packing, crating, and transporting your household goods and personal effects and those of the members of your household from your former home to your new home. For purposes of moving expenses, the term "personal effects" includes, but is not limited to, movable personal property that the taxpayer owns and frequently uses.

If you use your own car to move your things, see *Travel by car*, earlier.

You can deduct any costs of connecting or disconnecting utilities required because you are moving your household goods, appliances, or personal effects.

You can deduct the cost of shipping your car and household pets to your new home.

You can deduct the cost of moving your household goods and personal effects from a place other than your former home. Your deduction is limited to the amount it would have cost to move them from your former home.

Caution

You cannot deduct the cost of moving furniture you buy on the way to your new home.

EXPLANATION

Moving furniture that was in storage at the time of the move is deductible as long as the actual cost of moving it does not exceed what the cost of moving it would have been had the furniture been located at your former home.

Example

You are a resident of North Carolina and have been in college pursuing a degree for the past 4 years. Because of the small size of your apartment, you stored some of your furniture with your parents in Georgia.

You get a job in Washington, D.C. It costs you $1,100 to move the furniture from Georgia to Washington, D.C. If the furniture in Georgia had been shipped from North Carolina, your former home, it would have cost only $600. You may deduct only $600 of the $1,100 charge.

Note: If you lived in a dormitory or other rented quarters in North Carolina but you went home to Georgia for the summers, were considered an out-of-state or nonresident student in North Carolina, and otherwise maintained most of the major elements of residency (voting, automobile registration, charge accounts, etc.) in Georgia, you could argue that Georgia was your former home. In that case, all moving expenses would be deductible.

EXPLANATION

A Tax Court decision ruled that a rarely used yacht was not considered to be a part of personal effects. The rationale given was that Congress intended moving expenses to cover only items that you must move from your old home to a new location. To be deductible as a moving expense, an item must be, according to the courts, "intimately associated" with your home or your lifestyle. In this particular instance, the yacht was not.

However, the courts have upheld the deductibility of costs associated with moving a sailboat that the taxpayer owned for 4 years, frequently used, and even lived on for weeks at a time. The taxpayer proved that his lifestyle was "intimately associated" with the boat. This "intimate association" enabled the boat to be characterized as a "personal effect," thereby making all expenses associated with moving it deductible.

Storage expenses. You can include the cost of storing and insuring household goods and personal effects within any period of 30 consecutive days after the day your things are moved from your former home and before they are delivered to your new home.

Travel Expenses

You can deduct the cost of transportation and lodging for yourself and members of your household while traveling from your former home to your new home. This includes expenses for the day you arrive.

You can include any lodging expenses you had in the area of your former home within one day after you could no longer live in your former home because your furniture had been moved.

You can deduct expenses for only one trip to your new home for yourself and members of your household. However, all of you do not have to travel together or at the same time. If you use your own car, see *Travel by car*, earlier.

EXPLANATION
The courts allowed the cost of an escort as a moving expense when a taxpayer's mobile home broke down en route—the breakdown was attributable solely to the move. Generally, the charge for moving a mobile home by a professional mover is deductible. However, the replacement cost of tires for the mobile home would not qualify as a deductible moving expense. The reason is that new tires are essentially capital improvements.

TAXALERT
Travel expenses from your former home to your new home are only deductible as moving expenses when incurred after obtaining employment in the area to which you are moving. However, some travel expenses related to your job search, prior to obtaining employment, may be deductible. See *Job Search Expenses* in chapter 29, *Miscellaneous deductions*, for additional details.

Nondeductible Expenses
You cannot deduct the following items as moving expenses.
- Any part of the purchase price of your new home.

EXPLANATION
No deduction is allowed for the costs of selling your former home (or settling an unexpired lease) and purchasing your new home (or the acquisition of a new lease).

- Car tags.
- Driver's license.
- Expenses of buying or selling a home.
- Expenses of getting or breaking a lease.
- Home improvements to help sell your home.
- Loss on the sale of your home.

EXPLANATION
Under no circumstances is a loss on the sale of your personal residence deductible as a moving expense, or as any other kind of expense even if the move forced you to sell at a loss. However, if any portion of your home was used for income-producing purposes, then the portion of the loss allocable to such use may be deductible. For more information see chapter 15, *Selling your home*.

Although you may not deduct property taxes and interest as moving expenses, you may claim them as itemized deductions.
- Losses from disposing of memberships in clubs.
- Meal expenses.
- Mortgage penalties.
- Pre-move house-hunting expenses.
- Real estate taxes.
- Refitting of carpets and draperies.
- Return trips to your former residence.
- Security deposits (including any given up due to the move).
- Storage charges except those incurred in transit and for foreign moves.
- Temporary living expenses.

No double deduction. You cannot take a moving expense deduction and a business expense deduction for the same expenses. You must decide if your expenses are deductible as moving expenses or as business expenses. For example, expenses you have for travel, meals, and lodging while temporarily working at a place away from your regular place of work may be deductible as business expenses if you are considered away from home on business. Generally, your work at a single location is considered temporary if it is realistically expected to last (and does in fact last) for 1 year or less. See _Temporary Assignment or Job_ in chapter 27 for information on deducting your expenses.

How and When To Report

This section explains how and when to report your moving expenses and any reimbursements or allowances you received for your move.

Form 3903. Use Form 3903 to figure your moving expense deduction.

Where to deduct. Deduct your moving expenses on line 26 of Form 1040. The amount of moving expenses you can deduct is shown on line 5 of Form 3903.

Reimbursements. If you receive a reimbursement for your moving expenses, how you report this amount and your expenses depends on whether the reimbursement is paid to you under an accountable plan or a nonaccountable plan.

For more information on reimbursements, see Publication 521.

TAXSAVER

When your employer buys your home. If your employer purchases your former residence, the real estate commission that is avoided is not income to you, although the gain on the sale of the residence is taxed as a capital gain, subject to the special rule for excluding capital gain realized from the sale of your main home, discussed in <u>chapter 15</u>, *Selling your home.*

Any reimbursement by your employer for a loss on the sale of your home must be included in your income. You may not deduct the loss on your home, though you may deduct the amount attributable to the real estate commission, if any, as a selling expense.

If your employer purchases your former home from you at fair market value and there is a subsequent decline in its worth, the loss is sustained by your employer. The home's drop in value does not affect you.

If your employer purchases your former home from you at more than fair market value, the excess is ordinary taxable income to you and not capital gain. You cannot exclude that excess from your income, even if you purchased a new home for more than you got in total for the old one.

Explanation

Some employers use third-party relocation service companies to buy your home from you. If the third party pays any direct home-selling costs that are normally imposed on the seller by local law and/or custom, then you will be treated as having received taxable income.

Example

An employer agreed to pay home-selling costs but required that the employee repay them if he terminated employment within a stipulated period of time. The IRS held that an enforceable debt was created and that the employee had taxable income to report when the debt was canceled (or not paid). The employer must report the income on Form W-2.

When To Deduct Expenses

You may have a choice of when to deduct your moving expenses and report any reimbursement.

Expenses not reimbursed. If you were not reimbursed, deduct your allowable moving expenses either in the year you incurred them or in the year you paid them.

Example. In December 2013, your employer transferred you to another city in the United States, where you still work. You are single and were not reimbursed for your moving expenses. In 2013, you paid for moving your furniture and you deducted these expenses on your 2013 tax return. In January 2014, you paid for travel to the new city. You can deduct these additional expenses on your 2014 tax return.

Expenses reimbursed. If you are reimbursed for your expenses, you may be able to deduct your expenses either in the year you incurred them or in the year you paid them. If you use the cash method of accounting, you can choose to deduct the expenses in the year you are reimbursed even though you paid the expenses in a different year.

If you are reimbursed for your expenses in a year after you paid the expenses, you may want to delay taking the deduction until the year you receive the reimbursement. If you do not choose to delay your deduction until the year you are reimbursed and you deduct moving expenses that will be reimbursed, you must include the reimbursement in your income.

EXPLANATION

Your employer may give you a flat amount of money to cover all your moving expenses, some of which may not be deductible. The IRS says that the employer must apply the reimbursement first to the deductible moving expenses that are not subject to withholding and then deduct withholding and social security tax from the remainder.

Figure 20-B. **Can You Deduct Expenses for a Non-Military Move Within the United States?**[1]

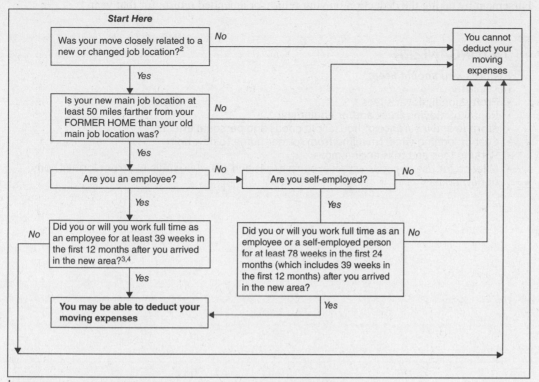

[1] Military persons should see *Members of the Armed Forces* for special rules that apply to them.
[2] Your move must be closely related to the start of work at your new job location. See *Related to Start of Work.*
[3] If you deduct expenses and do not meet this test later, you must either file an amended tax return or report your moving expense deduction as other income. See *Time test not yet met.*
[4] If you become self-employed during the first 12 months, answer YES if your time as a full-time employee added to your time as a self-employed person equals or will equal at least 78 weeks in the first 24 months (including 39 weeks in the first twelve months) after you arrived in the new area.

Choosing when to deduct. If you use the cash method of accounting, which is used by most individuals, you can choose to deduct moving expenses in the year your employer reimburses you if:
1. You paid the expenses in a year before the year of reimbursement, or
2. You paid the expenses in the year immediately after the year of reimbursement but by the due date, including extensions, for filing your return for the reimbursement year.

How to make the choice. You choose to deduct moving expenses in the year you received reimbursement by taking the deduction on your return, or amended return, for that year.

TAXORGANIZER

Records you should keep:
Receipts for:
- Professional mover's fees
- Rental of moving truck and/or equipment
- Storage and insurance of household goods and personal effects
- Cost of lodging while traveling from former home to new home
- Parking fees and tolls during move
- Mileage for use of car or actual expenses (gas and oil) while traveling from former home to new home

Part 5

Standard deduction and itemized deductions

ey.com/EYTaxGuide

After you have figured your adjusted gross income, you are ready to subtract the deductions used to figure taxable income. You can subtract either the standard deduction or itemized deductions. Itemized deductions are deductions for certain expenses that are listed on Schedule A (Form 1040). The ten chapters in this part discuss the standard deduction and each itemized deduction. See chapter 21 for the factors to consider when deciding whether to subtract the standard deduction or itemized deductions.

GENERALLY TAKE THE STANDARD DEDUCTION IF:

- Your standard deduction (chapter 21) is more than the total Itemized deductions you can claim (see chapters 22 through 29).

YOU GENERALLY CANNOT TAKE THE STANDARD DEDUCTION IF:

- You are filing a tax return with a short tax year,
- You were a nonresident or a dual-status alien during the year (chapter 21, *Standard deduction*), or
- You are married filing separately, and your spouse itemizes deductions.

ITEMIZE YOUR DEDUCTIONS IF:

- You cannot take the standard deduction (chapter 21, *Standard deduction*),
- You had large uninsured medical and dental expenses (chapter 22, *Medical and dental expenses*),
- You paid taxes and interest on your home (chapter 23, *Taxes you may deduct*, and chapter 24, *Interest expense*),
- You made large charitable contributions (chapter 25, *Contributions*),
- You had large uninsured casualty or theft losses (chapter 26, *Casualty and theft losses*),
- You had employee business expenses (chapter 27, *Car expenses and other employee business expenses*),
- You had employee educational expenses (chapter 28, *Tax benefits for work-related education*), or
- You had various miscellaneous expenses (chapter 29, *Miscellaneous deductions*), and
- Your total itemized deductions are more than the standard deduction you can claim (chapter 21 *Standard deduction*).

Chapter 21
Standard deduction

Introduction

Taxpayers who do not itemize their deductions are eligible for the standard deduction. However, you should determine whether itemizing deductions or taking the applicable standard deduction produces greater tax savings. In determining the amount of your standard deduction, you must consider many factors, including filing status, age, blindness, unearned income, and whether or not someone is claiming you as an exemption. Higher deductions are allowed if you or your spouse is over age 65 or is totally or partially blind. On the other hand, if another taxpayer can claim you as a dependent, your standard deduction may be limited. This chapter includes a useful worksheet that will help you figure out what your standard deduction is.

What's New

Standard deduction increased. The standard deduction for some taxpayers who do not itemize their deductions on Schedule A (Form 1040) is higher for 2014 than it was for 2013. The amount depends on your filing status. You can use the 2014 Standard Deduction Tables in this chapter to figure your standard deduction.

TAXALERT

The basic standard deduction amount for married couples filing joint returns is twice the basic standard deduction for single returns. This mitigates the so-called marriage penalty, where a married couple filing a joint return pays more in taxes than two single individuals with the same income.

This chapter discusses the following topics.
- How to figure the amount of your standard deduction.
- The standard deduction for dependents.
- Who should itemize deductions.

Most taxpayers have a choice of either taking a standard deduction or itemizing their deductions. If you have a choice, you can use the method that gives you the lower tax.

The standard deduction is a dollar amount that reduces your taxable income. It is a benefit that eliminates the need for many taxpayers to itemize actual deductions, such as medical expenses, charitable contributions, and taxes, on Schedule A (Form 1040). The standard deduction is higher for taxpayers who:
- Are 65 or older, or
- Are blind.

Persons not eligible for the standard deduction. Your standard deduction is zero and you should itemize any deductions you have if:
- Your filing status is married filing separately, and your spouse itemizes deductions on his or her return,
- You are filing a tax return for a short tax year because of a change in your annual accounting period, or

---

Note

IRS Publication 17 (*Your Federal Income Tax*) has been updated by Ernst & Young LLP for 2014. Dates and dollar amounts shown are for 2014. Underlined type is used to indicate where IRS text has been updated. Places where text has been removed are indicated by the sentence: *Text intentionally omitted.*

ey.com/EYTaxGuide
Ernst & Young LLP will update the *EY Tax Guide 2015* website with relevant taxpayer information as it becomes available. You can also sign up for email alerts to let you know when changes have been made.

Tip

You benefit from the standard deduction if your standard deduction is more than the total of your allowable itemized deductions.

Standard deduction. A standard deduction is allowed for every taxpayer who does not itemize deductions. An additional standard deduction is allowed for taxpayers who are blind or age 65 or older. Generally, you would use the standard deduction only if it's more than the total of the deductions you would otherwise itemize.

Itemizing even when the standard deduction is higher. Sometimes it may make sense to elect to itemize your deductions even when your standard deduction is higher. That may be the case if you're subject to the alternative minimum tax (AMT) (see chapter 31, *How to figure your tax*) since the standard deduction must be added back in full when calculating the AMT. You might have a lower overall tax if your itemized deductions consist of amounts that are allowed for AMT purposes, such as charitable contributions and mortgage interest. Another reason to itemize might be for state tax purposes. To make this election you check the box at the bottom of Schedule A (Form 1040).

- You are a nonresident or dual-status alien during the year. You are considered a dual-status alien if you were both a nonresident and resident alien during the year.

Note. If you are a nonresident alien who is married to a U.S. citizen or resident alien at the end of the year, you can choose to be treated as a U.S. resident. (See Publication 519, U.S. Tax Guide for Aliens.) If you make this choice, you can take the standard deduction.

EXPLANATION

Married persons who file separate returns must be consistent in claiming the standard deduction or itemizing deductions. If one spouse itemizes deductions, the other spouse must also itemize deductions and cannot claim the standard deduction.

Example

Mike and Denise are married. Each of them has a very successful business, and this year they plan to file separate income tax returns. Denise is very detail-oriented and keeps accurate records of all her itemized deductions. Mike has never cared much for what he considers tedious accounting, and would be happy to avoid this chore by claiming the standard deduction on his return ($6,200 in 2014 for a married taxpayer filing separately). If Denise itemizes deductions on her 2014 return, however, Mike will not be eligible to claim the standard deduction.

TAXPLANNER

You cannot forgo an otherwise allowable dependent exemption in order to increase that dependent's standard deduction.

Standard Deduction Amount

The standard deduction amount depends on your filing status, whether you are 65 or older or blind, and whether an exemption can be claimed for you by another taxpayer. Generally, the standard deduction amounts are adjusted each year for inflation. The standard deduction amounts for most people are shown in Table 21-1.

Decedent's final return. The standard deduction for a decedent's final tax return is the same as it would have been had the decedent continued to live. However, if the decedent was not 65 or older at the time of death, the higher standard deduction for age cannot be claimed.

EXPLANATION

A tax return filed for a decedent through the date of death is not considered a short tax year, so the decedent is entitled to the full standard deduction.

Example

John dies on June 15, 2014. John's final tax return will cover the period from January 1 through June 15.

The full amount of the standard deduction may be claimed on John's final return.

Caution

If an exemption for you can be claimed on another person's return (such as your parents' return), your standard deduction may be limited. See Standard Deduction for Dependents, later.

Higher Standard Deduction for Age (65 or Older)

If you are age 65 or older on the last day of the year and do not itemize deductions, you are entitled to a higher standard deduction. You are considered 65 on the day before your 65th birthday. Therefore, you can take a higher standard deduction for 2014 if you were born before January 2, 1950.

Use Table 21-2 to figure the standard deduction amount.

Higher Standard Deduction for Blindness

If you are blind on the last day of the year and you do not itemize deductions, you are entitled to a higher standard deduction.

Not totally blind. If you are not totally blind, you must get a certified statement from an eye doctor (ophthalmologist or optometrist) that:

- You cannot see better than 20/200 in the better eye with glasses or contact lenses, or
- Your field of vision is 20 degrees or less.

If your eye condition is not likely to improve beyond these limits, the statement should include this fact. You must keep the statement in your records.

If your vision can be corrected beyond these limits only by contact lenses that you can wear only briefly because of pain, infection, or ulcers, you can take the higher standard deduction for blindness if you otherwise qualify.

Caution

You cannot claim the higher standard deduction for an individual other than yourself and your spouse.

Spouse 65 or Older or Blind

You can take the higher standard deduction if your spouse is age 65 or older or blind and:

- You file a joint return, or
- You file a separate return and can claim an exemption for your spouse because your spouse had no gross income and cannot be claimed as a dependent by another taxpayer.

TAXSAVER

Itemizing vs. standard deduction. In calculating your taxable income, you generally should use the larger of your itemized deductions or your standard deduction. By doing some planning, it may be possible to use the standard deduction in some years and to itemize deductions in others.

Example

In December 2014, Bill and Barbara Chapman add up their itemized deductions for 2014 and find that the total is only $8,400. At that time, they receive an annual real estate tax bill for $1,550, which can be paid any time before January 31, 2015. A religious organization that the Chapmans are affiliated with is also requesting a $2,450 contribution for its building fund. If the Chapmans make both expenditures in 2014, they will receive no tax benefit from these tax-deductible expenditures because their itemized deductions would total $12,400, the same as their standard deduction. If they make the expenditures in 2015, they might generate more than the standard deduction for that year. Postponing would be a better strategy.

TAXALERT

Be cautious when determining whether to make expenditures in one year or another since they may be added back to your income when calculating alternative minimum taxable (AMT) income. Expenditures such as state income taxes, real estate taxes, and personal property taxes are not allowed in determining your alternative minimum taxable income and could subject you to AMT. See *Alternative Minimum Tax* in chapter 31, *How to figure your tax*.

TAXPLANNER

If you would not obtain a benefit from claiming an itemized deduction this year (because your total itemized deductions will be less than the standard deduction available for the year), you may be able to obtain a benefit from claiming that item in the following year. Review this carefully or speak with your tax advisor before proceeding because only certain itemized deductions may be deferred.

Examples

The following examples illustrate how to determine your standard deduction using Tables 21-1 and 21-2.

Example 1. Larry, 46, and Donna, 33, are filing a joint return for 2014. Neither is blind, and neither can be claimed as a dependent. They decide not to itemize their deductions. They use Table 21-1. Their standard deduction is $12,400.

Example 2. The facts are the same as in *Example 1* except that Larry is blind at the end of 2014. Larry and Donna use Table 21-2. Their standard deduction is $13,600.

Example 3. Bill and Lisa are filing a joint return for 2014. Both are over age 65. Neither is blind, and neither can be claimed as a dependent. If they do not itemize deductions, they use Table 21-2. Their standard deduction is $14,800.

Standard Deduction for Dependents

The standard deduction for an individual who can be claimed as a dependent on another person's tax return is generally limited to the greater of:

- $1,000, or
- The individual's earned income for the year plus $350 (but not more than the regular standard deduction amount, generally $6,200).

However, if the individual is 65 or older or blind, the standard deduction may be higher.

If you (or your spouse, if filing jointly) can be claimed as a dependent on someone else's return, use Table 21-3 to determine your standard deduction.

EXPLANATION

Although many taxpayers are aware that the standard deduction that can be claimed by your dependent children has been reduced, far fewer taxpayers know the standard deduction available to parents who are claimed as dependents on their child's tax return is similarly reduced.

Example

Assume that your 61-year-old widowed mother has $6,850 of interest income. If she is not your dependent, she has no tax liability. Her $6,200 standard deduction plus her $3,950 personal exemption eliminate her taxable income.

If you claim her as your dependent, however, her standard deduction drops to $1,000 and she loses her personal exemption entirely. Her taxable income would be $5,850 and she would pay $585 in tax. You might pay less tax because you could claim a $3,950 dependent exemption on your return. However, neither of you will benefit from the remaining unused standard deduction of $5,200 ($6,200 − $1,000).

Earned income defined. Earned income is salaries, wages, tips, professional fees, and other amounts received as pay for work you actually perform.

For purposes of the standard deduction, earned income also includes any part of a scholarship or fellowship grant that you must include in your gross income. See *Scholarships and fellowships* in chapter 12 for more information on what qualifies as a scholarship or fellowship grant.

Example 1. Michael is single. His parents can claim an exemption for him on their 2014 tax return. He has interest income of $780 and wages of $150. He has no itemized deductions. Michael uses Table 21-3 to find his standard deduction. He enters $150 (his earned income) on line 1, $500 ($150 + $350) on line 3, $1,000 (the larger of $500 and $1,000) on line 5, and $6,200 on line 6. His standard deduction, on line 7a, is $1,000 (the smaller of $1,000 and $6,200).

Example 2. Joe, a 22-year-old full-time college student, can be claimed as a dependent on his parents' 2014 tax return. Joe is married and files a separate return. His wife does not itemize deductions on her separate return. Joe has $1,500 in interest income and wages of $3,800. He has no itemized deductions. Joe finds his standard deduction by using Table 21-3. He enters his earned income, $3,800 on line 1. He adds lines 1 and 2 and enters $4,150 on line 3. On line 5, he enters $4,150, the larger of lines 3 and 4. Because Joe is married filing a separate return, he enters $6,200 on line 6. On line 7a he enters $4,150 as his standard deduction because it is smaller than $6,200, the amount on line 6.

Example 3. Amy, who is single, can be claimed as a dependent on her parents' 2014 tax return. She is 18 years old and blind. She has interest income of $1,300 and wages of $2,900. She has no itemized deductions. Amy uses Table 21-3 to find her standard deduction. She enters her wages of $2,900 on line 1. She adds lines 1 and 2 and enters $3,250 on line 3. On line 5, she enters $3,250, the larger of lines 3 and 4. Because she is single, Amy enters $6,200 on line 6. She enters $3,250 on line 7a. This is the smaller of the amounts on lines 5 and 6. Because she checked one box in the top part of the worksheet, she enters $1,550 on line 7b. She then adds the amounts on lines 7a and 7b and enters her standard deduction of $4,800 on line 7c.

Example 4. Ed is single. His parents can claim an exemption for him on their 2014 tax return. He has wages of $7,000, interest income of $500, and a business loss of $3,000. He has no itemized deductions. Ed uses Table 21-3 to figure his standard deduction. He enters $4,000 ($7,000 - $3,000) on line 1. He adds lines 1 and 2 and enters $4,350 on line 3. On line 5 he enters $4,350, the larger of lines 3 and 4. Because he is single, Ed enters $6,200 on line 6. On line 7a he enters $4,350 as his standard deduction because it is smaller than $6,200, the amount on line 6.

Who Should Itemize

You should itemize deductions if your total deductions are more than the standard deduction amount. Also, you should itemize if you do not qualify for the standard deduction, as discussed earlier under _Persons not eligible for the standard deduction_.

You should first figure your itemized deductions and compare that amount to your standard deduction to make sure you are using the method that gives you the greater benefit.

When to itemize. You may benefit from itemizing your deductions on Schedule A (Form 1040) if you:

- Do not qualify for the standard deduction, or the amount you can claim is limited,
- Had large uninsured medical and dental expenses during the year,
- Paid interest and taxes on your home,
- Had large unreimbursed employee business expenses or other miscellaneous deductions,
- Had large uninsured casualty or theft losses,
- Made large contributions to qualified charities, or
- Have total itemized deductions that are more than the standard deduction to which you otherwise are entitled.

These deductions are explained in chapters 22–29.

If you decide to itemize your deductions, complete Schedule A and attach it to your Form 1040. Enter the amount from Schedule A, line 29, on Form 1040, line 40.

Electing to itemize for state tax or other purposes. Even if your itemized deductions are less than your standard deduction, you can elect to itemize deductions on your federal return rather than take the standard deduction. You may want to do this if, for example, the tax benefit of itemizing your deductions on your state tax return is greater than the tax benefit you lose on your federal return by not taking the standard deduction. To make this election, you must check the box on line 30 of Schedule A.

> ### TAXPLANNER
> Another reason to itemize even when your deductions are less than the standard deduction may apply if you are subject to the alternative minimum tax (AMT). The entire standard deduction is disallowed for AMT purposes. If you instead itemize your deductions, some of those deductions, such as charitable contributions or mortgage interest, may reduce your AMT and therefore your tax bill. You make the election to itemize by checking the box on line 30 of Schedule A. For more information about the AMT, see the special section in chapter 31, _How to figure your tax_.

Changing your mind. If you do not itemize your deductions and later find that you should have itemized — or if you itemize your deductions and later find you should not have — you can change your return by filing Form 1040X, Amended U.S. Individual Income Tax Return. See _Amended Returns and Claims for Refund_ in chapter 1 for more information on amended returns.

Married persons who filed separate returns. You can change methods of taking deductions only if you and your spouse both make the same changes. Both of you must file a consent to assessment for any additional tax either one may owe as a result of the change.

You and your spouse can use the method that gives you the lower total tax, even though one of you may pay more tax than you would have paid by using the other method. You both must use the same method of claiming deductions. If one itemizes deductions, the other should itemize because he or she will not qualify for the standard deduction. See _Persons not eligible for the standard deduction_, earlier.

Caution

You may be subject to a limit on some of your itemized deductions if your adjusted gross income is more than: $254,200 if single ($279,650 if head of household, $305,050 if married filing jointly or qualifying widow(er); or $152,525 if married filing separately). See chapter 30 or the instructions for Schedule A (Form 1040) for more information on figuring the correct amount of your itemized deductions.

Caution

If you are married filing a separate return and your spouse itemizes deductions, or if you are a dual-status alien, you cannot take the standard deduction even if you were born before January 2, 1950, or are blind.

2014 Standard Deduction Tables

Table 21-1. Standard Deduction Chart for Most People*

If your filing status is...	Your standard deduction is:
Single or Married filing separately	$6,200
Married filing jointly or Qualifying widow(er) with dependent child	12,400
Head of household	9,100

Do not use this chart if you were born before January 2, 1950, are blind, or if someone else can claim you (or your spouse if filing jointly) as a dependent. Use Table 21-2 or 21-3 instead.

Table 21-2. Standard Deduction Chart for People Born Before January 2, 1950, or Who are Blind

Check the correct number of boxes below. Then go to the chart.		
You: Born before January 2, 1950 ☐		Blind ☐
Your spouse, if claiming spouse's exemption: Born before January 2, 1950 ☐		Blind ☐
Total number of boxes checked ☐		

IF your standard deduction is...	AND the number in the box above is...	THEN your filing status is...
Single	1	$7,750
	2	9,300
Married filing jointly or Qualifying widow(er) with dependent child	1	$13,600
	2	14,800
	3	16,000
	4	17,200
Married filing separately	1	$7,400
	2	8,600
	3	9,800
	4	11,000
Head of household	1	$10,650
	2	12,200

*If someone else can claim you (or your spouse if filing jointly) as a dependent, use Table 21-3 instead.

Table 21-3. Standard Deduction Worksheet for Dependents

Use this worksheet only if someone else can claim you (or your spouse if filing jointly) as a dependent.

Check the correct number of boxes below. Then go to the worksheet.		
You: Born before January 2, 1950 ☐ Blind ☐		
Your spouse, if claiming spouse's exemption: ☐ Born before January 2, 1950 ☐ Blind ☐		
Total number of boxes checked ☐		
1. Enter your earned income (defined below). If none, enter -0-.	**1.**	_____
2. Additional amount.	**2.**	$350
3. Add lines 1 and 2.	**3.**	_____
4. Minimum standard deduction.	**4.**	$1,000
5. Enter the larger of line 3 or line 4.	**5.**	_____
6. Enter the amount shown below for your filing status.		
• Single or Married filing separately–$6,200		
• Married filing jointly–$12,400	**6.**	_____
• Head of household–$9,100		
7. Standard deduction.		
a. Enter the smaller of line 5 or line 6. If born after January 1, 1950, and not blind, stop here. This is your standard deduction. Otherwise, go on to line 7b.	**7a.**	_____
b. If born before January 2, 1950, or blind, multiply $1,550 ($1,200 if married) by the number in the box above.	**7b.**	_____
c. Add lines 7a and 7b. This is your standard deduction for 2014.	**7c.**	_____
Earned income includes wages, salaries, tips, professional fees, and other compensation received for personal services you performed. It also includes any amount received as a scholarship that you must include in your income.		

Chapter 22
Medical and dental expenses

ey.com/EYTaxGuide

Note

IRS Publication 17 (*Your Federal Income Tax*) has been updated by Ernst & Young LLP for 2014. Dates and dollar amounts shown are for 2014. Underlined type is used to indicate where IRS text has been updated. Places where text has been removed are indicated by the sentence: *Text intentionally omitted*.

ey.com/EYTaxGuide
Ernst & Young LLP will update the *EY Tax Guide 2015* website with relevant taxpayer information as it becomes available. You can also sign up for email alerts to let you know when changes have been made.

Introduction

You can deduct most medical or dental costs that you paid for yourself, your spouse, and your dependents. However, most taxpayers can only claim medical and dental expenses if they itemize deductions on their federal income tax return; these expenses cannot be deducted if the standard deduction is claimed. On the other hand, if you were self-employed and had a net profit for the year, you may be able to deduct, as an adjustment to gross income, amounts paid for medical and qualified long-term care insurance on behalf of yourself and other qualifying individuals—see Health Insurance Costs for Self-Employed Persons later in this chapter.

Deductible medical expenses include payments for the diagnosis, cure, mitigation, treatment, and prevention of disease. Payments with respect to any part or function of the body are allowed, as are payments for the prevention or alleviation of mental illness. You may include even your cab or bus fare to the doctor's office. But you may not include expenditures that are merely beneficial to your general health or purely cosmetic medical procedures—like vacation costs or hair transplants, for example.

While almost any medical expense qualifies for the deduction, your medical expenses must total more than 10% of your adjusted gross income (AGI) before you can take any deduction. In other words, someone with an AGI of $30,000 in 2014 has to have more than $3,000 of medical expenses before he or she may deduct any of them. But, if you or your spouse were age 65 or older before the end of the year, the excess of medical expenses over 7.5% of your AGI is deductible. For alternative minimum tax (AMT) purposes, however, medical expenses are deductible only to the extent that they exceed 10% of AGI, regardless of your age.

For 2014, if the individual (or spouse, if applicable) in this example was born before January 2, 1950, then he or she could deduct medical expenses incurred during the year to the extent the total amounts paid exceed $2,250 ($30,000 × 7.5%). However, for purposes of calculating taxable income subject to the AMT, medical expenses are deductible only to the extent they exceed $3,000 ($30,000 × 10%), even though the individual (or spouse, if applicable) is at least age 65.

What's New

Standard mileage rate. The standard mileage rate allowed for operating expenses for a car when you use it for medical reasons is 23½ cents per mile. See _Transportation_ under _What Medical Expenses Are Includible._

> **TAXALERT**
>
> For purposes of the alternative minimum tax (AMT), medical expenses are deductible only to the extent that they exceed 10% of AGI, regardless of your age.

> **TAXALERT**
>
> You cannot claim a medical or dental expense tax deduction for expenses you paid with funds from your Health Savings Accounts or Flexible Spending Arrangements because funds from these plans are usually tax free. Therefore, you cannot claim a double tax benefit.

This chapter will help you determine the following.
- What medical expenses are.
- What expenses you can include this year.
- How much of the expenses you can deduct.
- Whose medical expenses you can include.
- What medical expenses are includible.
- How to treat reimbursements.
- How to report the deduction on your tax return.
- How to report impairment-related work expenses.
- How to report health insurance costs if you are self-employed.

Useful Items

You may want to see:

Publications
- ☐ **502** Medical and Dental Expenses
- ☐ **969** Health Savings Accounts and Other Tax-Favored Health Plans

Form (and Instructions)
- ☐ **Schedule A (Form 1040)** Itemized Deductions

What Are Medical Expenses?

Medical expenses are the costs of diagnosis, cure, mitigation, treatment, or prevention of disease, and the costs for treatments affecting any part or function of the body. These expenses include payments for legal medical services rendered by physicians, surgeons, dentists, and other medical practitioners. They include the costs of equipment, supplies, and diagnostic devices needed for these purposes.

Medical care expenses must be primarily to alleviate or prevent a physical or mental defect or illness. They do not include expenses that are merely beneficial to general health, such as vitamins or a vacation.

Medical expenses include the premiums you pay for insurance that covers the expenses of medical care, and the amounts you pay for transportation to get medical care. Medical expenses also include amounts paid for qualified long-term care services and limited amounts paid for any qualified long-term care insurance contract.

> **TAXALERT**
>
> **Marijuana and other controlled substances.** The IRS has ruled that the cost of marijuana or any other federally controlled substance, even if recommended by a physician in a state whose laws permit such purchase and use, is not deductible. The U.S. Supreme Court has upheld this ruling.

Tax Breaks and Deductions You Can Use Checklist

Medical and dental expenses. The tax law allows you to deduct the medical and dental expenses you incurred, but only to the extent the total is more than 10% of your adjusted gross income (AGI). However, if you or your spouse are age 65 or older, then you are able to deduct medical and dental expenses in excess of 7.5% of your AGI. (For alternative minimum tax (AMT) purposes, however, the threshold is 10% of AGI, regardless of your age.) Because of this limit, it's important to make sure that you've taken into account all the amounts you paid. Table 22-1, _Medical and Dental Expenses Checklist_, shows many common (and not so common) expenses which qualify for this deduction.

Smoking-Cessation programs. Amounts that you pay to participate in a smoking-cessation program and for prescribed drugs designed to alleviate nicotine withdrawal are deductible expenses for medical care. However, nonprescription nicotine gum and certain nicotine patches aren't deductible.

Weight-Loss programs. The amount you pay for a weight-loss program is a deductible medical expense if the program is undertaken as treatment for a disease diagnosed by a physician. The disease can be obesity itself or another disease, such as hypertension or heart disease, for which the doctor directs you to lose weight. You should get a written diagnosis before starting the program. Deductible expenses include fees paid to join the program and to attend periodic meetings. However, the cost of low-calorie food that you eat in place of your regular diet isn't deductible.

Laser eye surgery. Laser surgery to correct your vision is deductible as a medical expense, even though it may not be covered by your medical insurance. It is not considered to be cosmetic surgery, the cost of which is not deductible.

Cosmetic surgery. Cosmetic surgery, such as plastic surgery (not resulting from an accident or birth defect), and other treatments, such as tooth whitening, is not deductible as a medical expense.

Sex Change Operations. The IRS previously ruled that costs for gender reassignment surgery (and related medications, treatments, and transportation) may not be deducted as medical expenses. However, in February 2010, the U.S. Tax Court held that hormone therapy and sex reassignment surgery were not merely cosmetic, but instead deductible medical expenses, thereby permitting a taxpayer's deductions for those costs. On the other hand, the U.S. Tax Court disallowed a deduction for a taxpayer's breast augmentation surgery, because it was cosmetic surgery directed at improving appearance, not correcting a medical problem. The ruling was a partial victory for both the taxpayer and the IRS.

Breast-Feeding Supplies. Breast pumps and other lactation supplies are now tax deductible as medical expenses. In February 2011, the IRS reversed its long-held position prohibiting a medical expense deduction for such supplies. Amounts reimbursed for these expenses under flexible spending arrangements, Archer medical savings accounts, health reimbursement arrangements, or health savings accounts are not income to the taxpayer.

What Expenses Can You Include This Year?

You can include only the medical and dental expenses you paid this year, regardless of when the services were provided. If you pay medical expenses by check, the day you mail or deliver the check generally is the date of payment. If you use a "pay-by-phone" or "online" account to pay your medical expenses, the date reported on the statement of the financial institution showing when payment was made is the date of payment. If you use a credit card, include medical expenses you charge to your credit card in the year the charge is made, not when you actually pay the amount charged.

TAXPLANNER

Timing your medical expenses. Medical expenses don't usually lend themselves to tax planning. However, because a medical deduction is available only in the year of payment, you may be able to maximize your deduction if you can control the timing of your payment.

To determine the most beneficial year of payment, you need to assess your situation prior to the end of the year. If it is clear that your current-year medical expenses will not exceed the nondeductible floor—10% of your adjusted gross income (AGI) (or 7.5% if you or your spouse are age 65 or older by the end of the taxable year; however, for alternative minimum tax purposes, this limitation is 10% regardless of age)—try to defer payment of any medical bills until after year-end (i.e., pushing payment into the next year). You may be able to salvage a deduction next year.

If you can schedule major or minor surgery in nonemergency cases, you should compare this year's medical deductions with what they are likely to be next year to choose the more beneficial time. It is the date of payment—not the date of surgery—that determines the year in which you may deduct the expense. Remember, putting the charge on a credit card counts as payment at that time.

If you suspect that your adjusted gross income is going to drop substantially next year, defer the payment of medical bills. However, if you think your AGI is going to skyrocket next year, pay those bills now and try to salvage a deduction.

Exception
Prepaid medical expenses generally are not deductible until the year of treatment.

Separate returns. If you and your spouse live in a noncommunity property state and file separate returns, each of you can include only the medical expenses each actually paid. Any medical expenses paid out of a joint checking account in which you and your spouse have the same interest are considered to have been paid equally by each of you, unless you can show otherwise.

Community property states. If you and your spouse live in a community property state and file separate returns, or are registered domestic partners in Nevada, Washington, or California, any medical expenses paid out of community funds are divided equally. Each of you should include half the expenses. If medical expenses are paid out of the separate funds of one individual, only the individual who paid the medical expenses can include them. If you live in a community property state, and are not filing a joint return, see Publication 555, Community Property.

How Much of the Expenses Can You Deduct?

Generally, you can deduct on Schedule A (Form 1040) only the amount of your medical and dental expenses that is more than 10% of your AGI Form 1040, line 38).

Example. You are unmarried and under age 65 and your AGI is $40,000, 10% of which is $4,000. You paid medical expenses of $2,500. You cannot deduct any of your medical expenses because they are not more than 10% of your AGI.

TAXALERT

For 2014 through 2016, taxpayers under age 65 are only allowed to deduct medical and dental expenses that are more than 10% of adjusted gross income (AGI). The 7.5% limit will continue to apply for taxpayers age 65 and over. (For alternative minimum tax (AMT) purposes, however, medical expenses are deductible only to the extent that they exceed 10% of AGI, regardless of your age.) Beginning in 2017, the medical and dental expenses for all taxpayers is scheduled to be increased to a 10% limit.

Example 1. In 2014, you are 35 years old and your AGI is $40,000; 10% of which is $4,000. You paid medical expenses of $3,500. You cannot deduct any of your medical expenses because they are not more than 10% of your AGI.

Example 2. In 2014, you are 70 years old and your AGI is $40,000; 7.5% of which is $3,000. You paid medical expenses of $3,500. You can deduct $500 of medical expenses.

Example 3. You were born December 1, 1950. Since you will be under age 65 during all of 2014, you will be subject to the 10% of AGI limit. If your AGI is $40,000–10% of which is $4,000–and you paid $3,500 in medical expenses, you cannot deduct any of your medical expenses. Since you will reach age 65 during 2015, you in turn will be subject to the lower 7.5% limit on AGI for 2015 and 2016. If your AGI is $40,000–7.5% of which is $3,000–and you paid $3,500 in medical expenses, you can deduct $500 for medical expenses in 2015. Beginning in 2017, the 10% limit on AGI applies to you, regardless of age.

Example 4. You were born December 1, 1950, your spouse was born July 1, 1949, and you file a joint return. Since your spouse will turn age 65 during 2014, your combined medical and dental expenses are subject to the 7.5% of AGI limit through the end of 2016. Beginning in 2017, the 10% of AGI limit applies to you both regardless of your ages.

TAXPLANNER

If you are approaching age 65, you may consider scheduling nonemergency procedures and paying other medical bills in the year you turn 65 to take advantage of the lower nondeductible floor of 7.5% of your AGI, rather than the 10% of AGI floor if you are _under 65_. (For alternative minimum tax purposes, however, the threshold is 10% of AGI, regardless of your age.)

TAXPLANNER

If your spouse's medical expenses exceed yours. You should consider filing separate returns whenever the medical expenses of either spouse substantially exceed those of the other spouse. Compute and compare your tax liability if you and your spouse were to file jointly with the potential tax liability if you were to file separately before deciding which filing status to choose.

Whose Medical Expenses Can You Include?

You can generally include medical expenses you pay for yourself, as well as those you pay for someone who was your spouse or your dependent either when the services were provided or when you paid for them. There are different rules for decedents and for individuals who are the subject of multiple support agreements. See _Support claimed under a multiple support agreement_, later.

Yourself

You can include medical expenses you paid for yourself.

Spouse

You can include medical expenses you paid for your spouse. To include these expenses, you must have been married either at the time your spouse received the medical services or at the time you paid the medical expenses.

Example 1. Mary received medical treatment before she married Bill. Bill paid for the treatment after they married. Bill can include these expenses in figuring his medical expense deduction even if Bill and Mary file separate returns.

If Mary had paid the expenses, Bill could not include Mary's expenses in his separate return. Mary would include the amounts she paid during the year in her separate return. If they filed a joint return, the medical expenses both paid during the year would be used to figure their medical expense deduction.

Example 2. This year, John paid medical expenses for his wife Louise, who died last year. John married Belle this year and they file a joint return. Because John was married to Louise when she received the medical services, he can include those expenses in figuring his medical expense deduction for this year.

Dependent

You can include medical expenses you paid for your dependent. For you to include these expenses, the person must have been your dependent either at the time the medical services were provided or at the time you paid the expenses. A person generally qualifies as your dependent for purposes of the medical expense deduction if both of the following requirements are met.

1. The person was a *qualifying child* (defined later) or a *qualifying relative* (defined later), and
2. The person was a U.S. citizen or national, or a resident of the United States, Canada, or Mexico. If your qualifying child was adopted, see *Exception for adopted child*, next.

You can include medical expenses you paid for an individual that would have been your dependent except that:

1. He or she received gross income of $3,950 or more in 2014,
2. He or she filed a joint return for 2014, or
3. You, or your spouse if filing jointly, could be claimed as a dependent on someone else's 2014 return.

Exception for adopted child. If you are a U.S. citizen or U.S. national and your adopted child lived with you as a member of your household for 2014, that child does not have to be a U.S. citizen or national or a resident of the United States, Canada, or Mexico.

Qualifying Child

A qualifying child is a child who:

1. Is your son, daughter, stepchild, foster child, brother, sister, stepbrother, stepsister, half brother, half sister, or a descendant of any of them (for example, your grandchild, niece, or nephew),
2. Was:
   a. Under age 19 at the end of 2014 and younger than you (or your spouse, if filing jointly),
   b. Under age 24 at the end of 2014, a full-time student, and younger than you (or your spouse, if filing jointly), or
   c. Any age and permanently and totally disabled,
3. Lived with you for more than half of 2014,
4. Did not provide over half of his or her own support for 2014, and
5. Did not file a joint return, or, if he or she did, it was only to claim a refund.

TAXPLANNER

If you pay medical expenses for others. If you pay medical expenses on behalf of someone other than yourself, your spouse, or your dependent and your payment is made directly to the provider of the medical service, the payment is not deductible for income tax purposes. However, your payment will not be considered a gift to the individual for federal gift tax purposes, either. An unlimited gift tax exclusion is available for qualifying medical expenses paid on any individual's behalf directly to the provider of the medical service. This exclusion is also available for transfers that would otherwise be subject to the generation-skipping transfer (GST) tax; i.e., paid on behalf of a person two generations younger, such as a grandchild. For more information about gift tax and the GST tax, see chapter 44, *Estate and gift tax planning*.

Example

A grandparent pays medical expenses directly to the hospital on a grandchild's behalf. The payments will reduce the grandparent's taxable estate and will not be subject to gift tax or GST tax. This could result in significant tax savings. You should consult your tax advisor if you are interested in pursuing this type of tax planning.

Tip

You may be able to take an adoption credit for other expenses related to an adoption. See the Instructions for Form 8839, Qualified Adoption Expenses, for more information.

Adopted child. A legally adopted child is treated as your own child. This includes a child lawfully placed with you for legal adoption.

You can include medical expenses that you paid for a child before adoption if the child qualified as your dependent when the medical services were provided or when the expenses were paid.

If you pay back an adoption agency or other persons for medical expenses they paid under an agreement with you, you are treated as having paid those expenses provided you clearly substantiate that the payment is directly attributable to the medical care of the child.

But if you pay the agency or other person for medical care that was provided and paid for before adoption negotiations began, you cannot include them as medical expenses.

Child of divorced or separated parents. For purposes of the medical and dental expenses deduction, a child of divorced or separated parents can be treated as a dependent of both parents. Each parent can include the medical expenses he or she pays for the child, even if the other parent claims the child's dependency exemption, if:

1. The child is in the custody of one or both parents for more than half the year,
2. The child receives over half of his or her support during the year from his or her parents, and
3. The child's parents:
    a. Are divorced or legally separated under a decree of divorce or separate maintenance,
    b. Are separated under a written separation agreement, or
    c. Live apart at all times during the last 6 months of the year.

This does not apply if the child's exemption is being claimed under a <u>multiple support agreement</u> (discussed later).

Qualifying Relative

A qualifying relative is a person:

1. Who is your:
    a. Son, daughter, stepchild, foster child, or a descendant of any of them (for example, your grandchild),
    b. Brother, sister, half brother, half sister, or a son or daughter of either of them,
    c. Father, mother, or an ancestor or sibling of either of them (for example, your grandmother, grandfather, aunt, or uncle),
    d. Stepbrother, stepsister, stepfather, stepmother, son-in-law, daughter-in-law, father-in-law, mother-in-law, brother-in-law, or sister-in-law, or
    e. Any other person (other than your spouse) who lived with you all year as a member of your household if your relationship did not violate local law,
2. Who was not a qualifying child (see *Qualifying Child* earlier) of any other person for 2014, and
3. For whom you provided over half of the support in 2014. But see *Child of divorced or separated parents*, earlier, and *Support claimed under a multiple support agreement*, next.

Support claimed under a multiple support agreement. If you are considered to have provided more than half of a qualifying relative's support under a multiple support agreement, you can include medical expenses you pay for that person. A multiple support agreement is used when two or more people provide more than half of a person's support, but no one alone provides more than half.

Any medical expenses paid by others who joined you in the agreement cannot be included as medical expenses by anyone. However, you can include the entire unreimbursed amount you paid for medical expenses.

Example. You and your three brothers each provide one-fourth of your mother's total support. Under a multiple support agreement, you treat your mother as your dependent. You paid all of her medical expenses. Your brothers reimbursed you for three-fourths of these expenses. In figuring your medical expense deduction, you can include only one-fourth of your mother's medical expenses. Your brothers cannot include any part of the expenses. However, if you and your brothers share the nonmedical support items and you separately pay all of your mother's medical expenses, you can include the unreimbursed amount you paid for her medical expenses in your medical expenses.

Decedent

Medical expenses paid before death by the decedent are included in figuring any deduction for medical and dental expenses on the decedent's final income tax return. This includes expenses for the decedent's spouse and dependents as well as for the decedent.

The survivor or personal representative of a decedent can choose to treat certain expenses paid by the decedent's estate for the decedent's medical care as paid by the decedent at the time the medical services were provided. The expenses must be paid within the 1-year period beginning with the day after the date of death. If you are the survivor or personal representative making this choice, you must attach a statement to the decedent's Form 1040 (or the decedent's amended return, Form 1040X) saying that the expenses have not been and will not be claimed on the estate tax return.

Amended returns and claims for refund are discussed in chapter 1.

What if you pay medical expenses of a deceased spouse or dependent? If you paid medical expenses for your deceased spouse or dependent, include them as medical expenses on your Form 1040 in the year paid, whether they are paid before or after the decedent's death. The expenses can be included if the person was your spouse or dependent either at the time the medical services were provided or at the time you paid the expenses.

What Medical Expenses Are Includible?

Use Table 22-1, later, as a guide to determine which medical and dental expenses you can include on Schedule A (Form 1040).

This table does not include all possible medical expenses. To determine if an expense not listed can be included in figuring your medical expense deduction, see *What Are Medical Expenses*, earlier.

Table 22-1. **Medical and Dental Expenses Checklist**

See Publication 502 for more information about these and other expenses.

You can include:		You cannot include:	
• Bandages • Birth control pills prescribed by your doctor • Body scan • Braille books • Breast pump and supplies • Capital expenses for equipment or improvements to your home needed for medical care (see the worksheet in Publication 502) • Diagnostic devices • Expenses of an organ donor • Eye surgery—to promote the correct function of the eye • Fertility enhancement, certain procedures • Guide dogs or other animals aiding the blind, deaf, and disabled • Hospital services fees (lab work, therapy, nursing services, surgery, etc.) • Lead-based paint removal • Legal abortion • Legal operation to prevent having children such as a vasectomy or tubal ligation • Long-term care contracts, qualified • Meals and lodging provided by a hospital during medical treatment • Medical services fees (from doctors, dentists, surgeons, specialists, and other medical practitioners)	• Medicare Part D premiums • Medical and hospital insurance premiums • Nursing services • Oxygen equipment and oxygen • Part of life-care fee paid to retirement home designated for medical care • Physical examination • Pregnancy test kit • Prescription medicines (prescribed by a doctor) and insulin • Psychiatric and psychological treatment • Social security tax, Medicare tax, FUTA, and state employment tax for worker providing medical care (see Wages for nursing services, below) • Special items (artificial limbs, false teeth, eye-glasses, contact lenses, hearing aids, crutches, wheelchair, etc.) • Special education for mentally or physically disabled persons • Stop-smoking programs • Transportation for needed medical care • Treatment at a drug or alcohol center (includes meals and lodging provided by the center) • Wages for nursing services • Weight-loss, certain expenses for obesity	• Baby sitting and childcare • Bottled water • Contributions to Archer MSAs (see Publication 969) • Diaper service • Expenses for your general health (even if following your doctor's advice) such as— • Health club dues • Household help (even if recommended by a doctor) • Social activities, such as dancing or swimming lessons • Trip for general health improvement • Flexible spending account reimbursements for medical expenses (if contributions were on a pre-tax basis) • Funeral, burial, or cremation expenses • Health savings account payments for medical expenses • Illegal operation, treatment, or medicine • Life insurance or income protection policies, or policies providing payment for loss of life, limb, sight, etc. • Maternity clothes • Medical insurance included in a car insurance policy covering all persons injured in or by your car • Medicine you buy without a prescription • Nursing care for a healthy baby	• Prescription drugs you brought in (or ordered shipped) from another country, in most cases • Nutritional supplements, vitamins, herbal supplements, "natural medicines," etc., unless recommended by a medical practitioner as a treatment for a specific medical condition diagnosed by a physician • Surgery for purely cosmetic reasons • Toothpaste, toiletries, cosmetics, etc. • Teeth whitening • Weight-loss expenses not for the treatment of obesity or other disease

TAXPLANNER

If the IRS challenges your deduction. In case the IRS challenges your deduction of medical expenses, you should keep the following information in order to support your claim for medical expenses incurred:

- Receipts and canceled checks evidencing payment of medical expenses
- A permanent record of the name and address of the provider of medical care, the amount of the expenses, and the date paid
- Documentation that the expense was to obtain medical treatment, that medicine was prescribed, and that the expense was incurred on a doctor's recommendation

  After reviewing the checklist, you may still be wondering whether a particular expense is deductible or not. The most comprehensive listing of items that you may and may not include when figuring your medical expenses appears in Publication 502, *Medical and Dental Expenses*.

Examples

Here are more examples of items that have been held to be deductible:

- An annual physical examination and diagnostic testing. You do not have to be ill for these expenses to be deductible.
- A full-body electronic scan
- A pregnancy test kit
- A wig, if it is essential to your mental health and not just for enhancing your personal appearance
- Cosmetic surgery that is medically necessary (meaningfully promotes the proper function of the body or prevents or treats illness or disease) or needed to correct a deformity related to an injury, disease, or congenital abnormality and not just for enhancing personal appearance
- Special diet food that is necessary and prescribed by a doctor to the extent that the cost exceeds the amount spent for normal nutritional needs
- Orthopedic shoes in excess of the cost of normal shoes
- Fees paid to someone to accompany and guide a blind person
- Costs attributable to a dog or other animal that assists individuals with physical disabilities
- Fees paid for a note taker for a deaf person
- Legal fees to obtain guardianship over a mental patient who has refused to accept therapy voluntarily
- Fees paid for childbirth preparation classes if instruction relates to obstetrical care
- Costs of a weight loss program for treatment of a specific disease, such as hypertension or obesity
- Costs of a wheelchair lift and its installation in a van
- Reasonable costs for home modifications or improvements to accommodate a handicapped person's condition when incurred for the purpose of medical care or directly related to medical care
- Legal fees necessary to authorize medical treatment for mental illness
- Expenses incurred for radial keratotomy (i.e., eye surgery to correct nearsightedness)

TAXSAVER

Weight loss programs. The IRS has ruled that individuals who suffer from specific physician-diagnosed diseases, such as obesity and hypertension, may deduct, as a medical expense, uncompensated costs of participation in weight loss programs. Costs associated with weight loss programs to improve general health and appearance are not deductible. Whether the cost of the program is deductible or not, the costs of low-calorie foods purchased while in the program are not deductible.

TAXSAVER

Physical and dental exams. The cost of periodic physical and dental exams can be included as a deductible medical expense. Usually, these expenses are too small to be deductible, because only expenses over 10% of your adjusted gross income (AGI) can be deducted (or 7.5% if you or your spouse are age 65 or older in 2014). (For alternative minimum tax (AMT) purposes, however, the threshold is 10% of AGI, regardless of your age.) However, in years where other sufficient medical expenses have been incurred, the inclusion of these expenses in calculating your medical expense deduction can lead to tax savings.

TAXSAVER

Appraisals. The cost of an appraisal obtained to determine the increase in value of your home is deductible, but not as a medical expense. The appraisal cost is an expense associated with the determination of your tax liability and can be included as a miscellaneous itemized deduction. See chapter 29, *Miscellaneous deductions*.

Explanation

Operating and upkeep expenses. If a capital expense qualifies as a medical expense, amounts paid for operation or upkeep also qualify as medical expenses, as long as the medical reason for the capital expense still exists. These expenses are medical expenses even if none or only part of the original expense was deductible.

Example

Assume the same facts as in the previous example, except that the elevator increased the value of your home by $2,000. In this case, you are not entitled to a medical deduction for the cost of the elevator. However, the costs of electricity to operate the elevator and repairs to maintain it are deductible, as long as the medical reason for the elevator exists.

Exception

An exception to the general rule exists for expenditures incurred to accommodate the condition of a physically handicapped person that generally do not increase the value of a personal residence. These expenses are deductible in full as a medical expense. Examples of expenses made for the primary purpose of accommodating a personal residence to the handicapped condition of a taxpayer, the taxpayer's spouse, or dependents who reside there include:
- Construction of entrance or exit ramps to the residence
- Widening doorways at entrances or exits to the residence
- Widening or otherwise modifying hallways and interior doorways
- Installing railings, support bars, or other modifications to bathrooms
- Lowering or making other modifications to kitchen cabinets and equipment
- Altering the location or otherwise modifying electrical outlets and fixtures
- Installing porch lifts and other forms of lifts (an elevator, however, may also add to the fair market value of the residence, and any deduction would have to be decreased to that extent)
- Modifying fire alarms, smoke detectors, and other warning systems
- Modifying stairs
- Adding handrails or grab bars, whether or not in bathrooms
- Modifying hardware on doors
- Modifying areas in front entrance and exit doorways
- Grading of ground to provide access to the residence

According to the IRS, other similar expenditures may also be incurred in accommodating a personal residence to the handicapped condition of a taxpayer or a dependent. However, only reasonable costs for accommodating a handicapped person's condition will be considered incurred for the purpose of medical care. Additional costs attributable to personal desires are not deductible.

Example

You are physically handicapped and confined to a wheelchair. You incur expenses to widen doorways and lower kitchen cabinets in your residence to permit access by you. These expenses are deductible, subject to the 10% threshold discussed earlier (or 7.5% threshold if you or your spouse are age 65 or older). (For AMT purposes, the threshold is 10% of AGI, regardless of your age.)

TAXPLANNER

Medically related capital improvements. If you have to make a medically related capital improvement, you should request a written recommendation from your doctor. In addition, obtain a reliable written appraisal from a real estate appraiser or a valuation expert. Be prepared to prove to what extent the value of your property was or was not increased.

TAXPLANNER

Swimming pools. It is often difficult to obtain a medical deduction for the installation of a swimming pool. The IRS has held that swimming pools generally fall within the category of

recreational or luxury items and will look at various facts when it is determining the deduction for the cost of a swimming pool, including:
- Whether the primary purpose of the pool is for medical care
- Whether the expenditure is related to medical care
- Whether the pool does more than serve the convenience and/or comfort of the taxpayer
  You should contact your tax advisor if you intend to install a swimming pool for medical reasons.

TAXALERT
Limitation on itemized deductions. For 2014, overall itemized deductions may be limited for taxpayers with adjusted gross income (AGI) above $305,050 if married filing jointly or qualifying widow(er), $279,650 if head of household, $254,200 if single, and $152,525 if married filing separately.

Insurance Premiums

You can include in medical expenses insurance premiums you pay for policies that cover medical care. Medical care policies can provide payment for treatment that includes:
- Hospitalization, surgical services, X-rays,
- Prescription drugs and insulin,
- Dental care,
- Replacement of lost or damaged contact lenses, and
- Long-term care (subject to additional limitations). See *Qualified Long-Term Care Insurance Contracts* in Publication 502.

If you have a policy that provides payments for other than medical care, you can include the premiums for the medical care part of the policy if the charge for the medical part is reasonable. The cost of the medical part must be separately stated in the insurance contract or given to you in a separate statement.

Note. When figuring the amount of insurance premiums you can include in medical expenses on Schedule A, do not include any health coverage tax credit advance payments shown in box 1 of Form 1099-H, Health Coverage Tax Credit (HCTC) Advance Payments. Also, do not include insurance premiums attributable to a nondependent child under age 27 if your premiums increased as a result of adding this child to your policy.

TAXALERT
You can treat premiums paid for qualified long-term care insurance as a deductible medical expense subject to dollar limits based on your age at the close of the taxable year.

Age	Annual deductible limit
40 or less	$370
Over 40 but not more than 50	$700
Over 50 but not more than 60	$1,400
Over 60 but not more than 70	$3,720
Over 70	$4,660

Explanation
Amounts you pay to receive medical care from a health maintenance organization (HMO) are treated as medical insurance premiums.

TAXSAVER
Cafeteria plans. Employees who pay all or part of their medical insurance premiums via employer plans should ask their employer to investigate a flexible spending arrangement, which is sometimes referred to as a cafeteria plan.

Employer-sponsored health insurance plan. Do not include in your medical and dental expenses any insurance premiums paid by an employer-sponsored health insurance plan unless the premiums are included in box 1 of your Form W-2. Also, do not include any other medical and dental expenses paid by the plan unless the amount paid is included in box 1 of your Form W-2.

Example. You are a federal employee participating in the premium conversion plan of the Federal Employee Health Benefits (FEHB) program. Your share of the FEHB premium is paid by making a pre-tax reduction in your salary. Because you are an employee whose insurance premiums are paid with money that is never included in your gross income, you cannot deduct the premiums paid with that money.

Long-term care services. Contributions made by your employer to provide coverage for qualified long-term care services under a flexible spending or similar arrangement must be included in your income. This amount will be reported as wages in box 1 of your Form W-2.

Health reimbursement arrangement (HRA). If you have medical expenses that are reimbursed by a health reimbursement arrangement, you cannot include those expenses in your medical expenses. This is because an HRA is funded solely by the employer.

Retired public safety officers. If you are a retired public safety officer, do not include as medical expenses any health or long term care premiums that you elected to have paid with tax free distributions from your retirement plan. This applies only to distributions that would otherwise be included in income.

Medicare A. If you are covered under social security (or if you are a government employee who paid Medicare tax), you are enrolled in Medicare A. The payroll tax paid for Medicare A is not a medical expense.

If you are not covered under social security (or were not a government employee who paid Medicare tax), you can voluntarily enroll in Medicare A. In this situation you can include the premiums you paid for Medicare A as a medical expense.

Medicare B. Medicare B is supplemental medical insurance. Premiums you pay for Medicare B are a medical expense. Check the information you received from the Social Security Administration to find out your premium.

Medicare D. Medicare D is a voluntary prescription drug insurance program for persons with Medicare A or B. You can include as a medical expense premiums you pay for Medicare D.

Prepaid insurance premiums. Premiums you pay before you are age 65 for insurance for medical care for yourself, your spouse, or your dependents after you reach age 65 are medical care expenses in the year paid if they are:
- Payable in equal yearly installments, or more often, and
- Payable for at least 10 years, or until you reach age 65 (but not for less than 5 years).

Unused sick leave used to pay premiums. You must include in gross income cash payments you receive at the time of retirement for unused sick leave. You also must include in gross income the value of unused sick leave that, at your option, your employer applies to the cost of your continuing participation in your employer's health plan after you retire. You can include this cost of continuing participation in the health plan as a medical expense.

If you participate in a health plan where your employer automatically applies the value of unused sick leave to the cost of your continuing participation in the health plan (and you do not have the option to receive cash), do not include the value of the unused sick leave in gross income. You cannot include this cost of continuing participation in that health plan as a medical expense.

Meals and Lodging

You can include in medical expenses the cost of meals and lodging at a hospital or similar institution if a principal reason for being there is to get medical care. See *Nursing home*, later.

You may be able to include in medical expenses the cost of lodging not provided in a hospital or similar institution. You can include the cost of such lodging while away from home if all of the following requirements are met.

- The lodging is primarily for and essential to medical care.
- The medical care is provided by a doctor in a licensed hospital or in a medical care facility related to, or the equivalent of, a licensed hospital.
- The lodging is not lavish or extravagant under the circumstances.
- There is no significant element of personal pleasure, recreation, or vacation in the travel away from home.

The amount you include in medical expenses for lodging cannot be more than $50 for each night for each person. You can include lodging for a person traveling with the person receiving the medical care. For example, if a parent is traveling with a sick child, up to $100 per night can be included as a medical expense for lodging. Meals are not included.

EXAMPLES

Example 1
A businessman who became ill while out of town was allowed to deduct the costs of his meals and hotel room when, due to a shortage of hospital rooms, he was required to move into a hotel. He had not recovered sufficiently to return home. The courts found that the test of deductibility was not the nature of the institution (i.e., whether it was a hospital or a similar institution), but the condition of the individual and the nature of the services.

Example 2
The parents of a mentally ill son rented an apartment to be close to the son's clinic. They were not allowed to deduct its costs because no care was received in the apartment, and the apartment had not been altered in any way to facilitate their son's treatment. Therefore, the court held that the parents had not incurred any expenses for their son's care in the apartment.

Nursing home. You can include in medical expenses the cost of medical care in a nursing home, home for the aged, or similar institution, for yourself, your spouse, or your dependents. This includes the cost of meals and lodging in the home if a principal reason for being there is to get medical care.

Do not include the cost of meals and lodging if the reason for being in the home is personal. You can, however, include in medical expenses the part of the cost that is for medical or nursing care.

Transportation

Include in medical expenses amounts paid for transportation primarily for, and essential to, medical care. You can include:

- Bus, taxi, train, or plane fares, or ambulance service,
- Transportation expenses of a parent who must go with a child who needs medical care,
- Transportation expenses of a nurse or other person who can give injections, medications, or other treatment required by a patient who is traveling to get medical care and is unable to travel alone, and
- Transportation expenses for regular visits to see a mentally ill dependent, if these visits are recommended as a part of treatment.

TAXALERT
The IRS has ruled that transportation costs and registration fees for attending a medical conference on a chronic disease suffered by a dependent are deductible medical expenses. The cost of meals and lodging cannot be deducted.

Car expenses. You can include out-of-pocket expenses, such as the cost of gas and oil, when you use your car for medical reasons. You cannot include depreciation, insurance, general repair, or maintenance expenses.

If you do not want to use your actual expenses for 2014, you can use the standard medical mileage rate of 23½ cents per mile.

You can also include parking fees and tolls. You can add these fees and tolls to your medical expenses whether you use actual expenses or use the standard mileage rate.

Example. In 2014, Bill Jones drove 2,800 miles for medical reasons. He spent $500 for gas, $30 for oil, and $100 for tolls and parking. He wants to figure the amount he can include in medical expenses both ways to see which gives him the greater deduction.

He figures the actual expenses first. He adds the $500 for gas, the $30 for oil, and the $100 for tolls and parking for a total of $630.

He then figures the standard mileage amount. He multiplies 2,800 miles by 23½ cents a mile for a total of $658. He then adds the $100 tolls and parking for a total of $758.

Bill includes the $758 of car expenses with his other medical expenses for the year because the $758 is more than the $630 he figured using actual expenses.

Transportation expenses you cannot include. You cannot include in medical expenses the cost of transportation in the following situations.

- Going to and from work, even if your condition requires an unusual means of transportation.
- Travel for purely personal reasons to another city for an operation or other medical care.
- Travel that is merely for the general improvement of one's health.
- The costs of operating a specially equipped car for other than medical reasons.

Disabled Dependent Care Expenses

Some disabled dependent care expenses may qualify as either:

- Medical expenses, or
- Work-related expenses for purposes of taking a credit for dependent care. (See chapter 33 and Publication 503, Child and Dependent Care Expenses.)

You can choose to apply them either way as long as you do not use the same expenses to claim both a credit and a medical expense deduction.

How Do You Treat Reimbursements?

You can include in medical expenses only those amounts paid during the taxable year for which you received no insurance or other reimbursement.

Insurance Reimbursement

You must reduce your total medical expenses for the year by all reimbursements for medical expenses that you receive from insurance or other sources during the year. This includes payments from Medicare.

Even if a policy provides reimbursement for only certain specific medical expenses, you must use amounts you receive from that policy to reduce your total medical expenses, including those it does not reimburse.

Example. You have insurance policies that cover your hospital and doctors' bills but not your nursing bills. The insurance you receive for the hospital and doctors' bills is more than their charges. In figuring your medical deduction, you must reduce the total amount you spent for medical care by the total amount of insurance you received, even if the policies do not cover some of your medical expenses.

Health reimbursement arrangement (HRA). A health reimbursement arrangement is an employer-funded plan that reimburses employees for medical care expenses and allows unused amounts to be carried forward. An HRA is funded solely by the employer and the reimbursements for medical expenses, up to a maximum dollar amount for a coverage period, are not included in your income.

Other reimbursements. Generally, you do not reduce medical expenses by payments you receive for:
- Permanent loss or loss of use of a member or function of the body (loss of limb, sight, hearing, etc.) or disfigurement to the extent the payment is based on the nature of the injury without regard to the amount of time lost from work, or
- Loss of earnings.

Figure 22-A. **Is Your Excess Medical Reimbursement Taxable?**

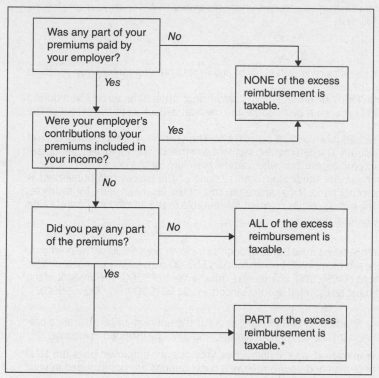

*See Premiums paid by you and your employer in this chapter.

You must, however, reduce your medical expenses by any part of these payments that is designated for medical costs. See *How Do You Figure and Report the Deduction on Your Tax Return*, later.

For how to treat damages received for personal injury or sickness, see *Damages for Personal Injuries*, later.

You do not have a medical deduction if you are reimbursed for all of your medical expenses for the year.

Excess reimbursement. If you are reimbursed more than your medical expenses, you may have to include the excess in income. You may want to use Figure 22-A to help you decide if any of your reimbursement is taxable.

Premiums paid by you. If you pay either the entire premium for your medical insurance or all of the costs of a plan similar to medical insurance and your insurance payments or other reimbursements are more than your total medical expenses for the year, you have an excess reimbursement. Generally, you do not include the excess reimbursement in your gross income.

Premiums paid by you and your employer. If both you and your employer contribute to your medical insurance plan and your employer's contributions are not included in your gross income, you must include in your gross income the part of your excess reimbursement that is from your employer's contribution.

See Publication 502 to figure the amount of the excess reimbursement you must include in gross income.

EXPLANATION
You can figure the percentage of the excess reimbursement you must include in gross income using the following formula.

$$\frac{\text{Amount paid by employer}}{\text{total annual cost of policy}} = \text{percent of excess reimbursement that is taxable}$$

Example
You are covered by your employer's medical insurance policy. The annual premium is $2,000. Your employer pays $600 of that amount and the balance of $1,400 is taken out of your wages.

The part of any excess reimbursement you receive under the policy that is from your employer's contributions is figured as follows:

$$\frac{\$600}{\$2,000} = 30\%$$

You must include in your gross income 30% (.30) of any excess reimbursement you received for medical expenses under the policy.

Insurance reimbursements. Reimbursements from insurance or other sources received during the year in which the medical expense is paid reduce the medical deduction to the extent of the reimbursement.

If total reimbursements exceed total medical expenses for the year, the excess reimbursement may have to be included in income. The determining factor of whether or not the excess reimbursement has to be included in income depends on who paid the premium for the insurance policy.

If you pay the entire premium for medical insurance, none of the excess reimbursement is includible in income. On the other hand, if you share the cost of the premium with, for example, your employer, the part of the excess reimbursement attributable to the employer's contribution to the premium must be included in income.

Example 1
John's annual medical insurance premium is $3,000. John's employer pays $900 of the premium, and John pays $2,100 of the premium. In 2014, John incurs $5,000 of medical expenses, and his insurance company reimburses him $5,500, an excess reimbursement of $500. The amount of the excess reimbursement that must be included in John's income is $150 ($900/$3,000 × $500).

Example 2
Assume the same facts as in Example 1, except John pays for the entire medical insurance premium himself. The $500 excess insurance reimbursement would not be included in income.

Premiums paid by your employer. If your employer or your former employer pays the total cost of your medical insurance plan and your employer's contributions are not included in your income, you must report all of your excess reimbursement as other income.

More than one policy. If you are covered under more than one policy, the costs of which are paid by both you and your employer, you must first divide the medical expense among the policies to figure the excess reimbursement from each policy. Then divide the policy costs to figure the part of any excess reimbursement that is from your employer's contribution.

Example
You are covered by your employer's health insurance policy. The annual premium is $1,200.

Your employer pays $300, and the balance of $900 is deducted from your wages. You also paid the entire premium ($250) for a personal health insurance policy.

During the year, you paid medical expenses of $3,600. In the same year, you were reimbursed $2,400 under your employer's policy and $1,600 under your personal policy.

You figure the part of any excess reimbursement you receive that is from your employer's contribution as follows:

Step 1.

Reimbursement from employer's policy	$2,400
Reimbursement from your policy	1,600
Total reimbursement	**$4,000**
Amount of reimbursed medical expenses from your policy [($1,600 ÷ $4,000) × $3,600 total medical expenses]	$1,440
Amount of reimbursed medical expenses from your employer's policy [($2,400 ÷ $4,000) x $3,600 total medical expenses]	2,160
Total medical expenses	**$3,600**
Excess reimbursement from your employer's policy ($2,400 – $2,160)	$240

Step 2.

Because both you and your employer contributed to the cost of this policy, you must divide the cost to determine the excess reimbursement from your employer's contribution.

Employer's contribution in relation to the annual cost of the policy ($300 ÷ $1,200)	25%
Amount to report as other income on line 21, Form 1040 (25% × $240)	**$60**

Reimbursement in a later year. If you are reimbursed in a later year for medical expenses you deducted in an earlier year, you generally must report the reimbursement as income up to the amount you previously deducted as medical expenses.

However, do not report as income the amount of reimbursement you received up to the amount of your medical deductions that did not reduce your tax for the earlier year. For more information about the recovery of an amount that you claimed as an itemized deduction in an earlier year, see *Itemized Deduction Recoveries* in chapter 12.

EXAMPLE

John pays $1,800 and his employer pays $600 toward the $2,400 annual premium for health insurance policy No. 1. Additionally, John pays the entire premium, $500, for health insurance policy No. 2. During 2014, John paid $7,200 of medical expenses and in the same year was reimbursed $5,000 under the first policy and $3,000 under the second policy.

The portion of excess reimbursement attributable to the employer's contribution is computed as follows:

Reimbursement from policy No. 1	$5,000
Reimbursement from policy No. 2	3,000
Total reimbursement	**$8,000**
Amount of reimbursed medical expenses from policy No. 1 ($5,000/$8,000 × $7,200 total medical expenses)	$4,500
Amount of reimbursed medical expenses from policy No. 2 ($3,000/$8,000 × $7,200 total medical expenses)	2,700
Total medical expenses	**$7,200**
Excess reimbursement from policy No. 1 ($5,000 – $4,500)	**$500**

The employer's contribution to the annual cost of policy No. 1 is 25% ($600/$2,400). Consequently, John must include $125 in income for 2014 ($500 × 25%).

None of the excess reimbursement from policy No. 2, $300 ($3,000 – $2,700), must be included in income, because John paid the entire premium of the policy.

Medical expenses not deducted. If you did not deduct a medical expense in the year you paid it because your medical expenses were not more than 10% of your AGI (7.5% of your AGI if either you or your spouse was age 65 or older), or because you did not itemize deductions, do not include the reimbursement up to the amount of the expense in income. However, if the reimbursement is more than the expense, see *Excess reimbursement*, earlier.

TAXALERT

For purposes of the alternative minimum tax (AMT), however, medical expenses are deductible only to the extent that they exceed 10% of AGI, regardless of your age.

Example. For 2014, you were unmarried and under age 65 and you had medical expenses of $500. You cannot deduct the $500 because it is less than 10% of your AGI. If, in a later year, you are reimbursed for any of the $500 in medical expenses, you do not include the amount reimbursed in your gross income.

Damages for Personal Injuries

If you receive an amount in settlement of a personal injury suit, part of that award may be for medical expenses that you deducted in an earlier year. If it is, you must include that part in your income in the year you receive it to the extent it reduced your taxable income in the earlier year. See *Reimbursement in a Later Year*, discussed under *How Do You Treat Reimbursements*, earlier.

Future medical expenses. If you receive an amount in settlement of a damage suit for personal injuries, part of that award may be for future medical expenses. If it is, you must reduce any future medical expenses for these injuries until the amount you received has been completely used.

How Do You Figure and Report the Deduction on Your Tax Return?

Once you have determined which medical expenses you can include, you figure and report the deduction on your tax return.

What Tax Form Do You Use?

You figure your medical expense deduction on Schedule A (Form 1040). You cannot claim medical expenses on Form 1040A or Form 1040EZ. If you need more information on itemized deductions or you are not sure if you can itemize, see chapter 21.

Enter the amount you paid for medical and dental expenses on Schedule A (Form 1040). This should be your expenses that were not reimbursed by insurance or any other sources.

Generally, you can deduct only the amount of your medical and dental expenses that is more than 10% of your AGI (7.5% if either you or your spouse was age 65 or older) shown on line 38, Form 1040.

TAXALERT

For purposes of the alternative minimum tax (AMT), however, medical expenses are deductible only to the extent that they exceed 10% of AGI, regardless of your age.

Impairment-Related Work Expenses

If you are a person with a disability, you can take a business deduction for expenses that are necessary for you to be able to work. If you take a business deduction for impairment-related work expenses, do not take a medical deduction for the same expenses.

You have a disability if you have:

- A physical or mental disability (for example, blindness or deafness) that functionally limits your being employed, or
- A physical or mental impairment (for example, a sight or hearing impairment) that substantially limits one or more of your major life activities, such as performing manual tasks, walking, speaking, breathing, learning, or working.

Impairment-related expenses defined. Impairment-related expenses are those ordinary and necessary business expenses that are:

- Necessary for you to do your work satisfactorily,
- For goods and services not required or used, other than incidentally, in your personal activities, and
- Not specifically covered under other income tax laws.

Where to report. If you are self-employed, deduct the business expenses on the appropriate form (Schedule C, C-EZ, E, or F) used to report your business income and expenses.

If you are an employee, complete Form 2106, Employee Business Expenses, or Form 2106-EZ, Unreimbursed Employee Business Expenses. Enter on Schedule A (Form 1040), that part of the amount on Form 2106, or Form 2106-EZ, that is related to your impairment. Enter the amount that is unrelated to your impairment also on Schedule A (Form 1040). Your impairment-related work expenses are not subject to the 2%-of-adjusted-gross-income limit that applies to other employee business expenses.

Example. You are blind. You must use a reader to do your work. You use the reader both during your regular working hours at your place of work and outside your regular working hours away from your place of work. The reader's services are only for your work. You can deduct your expenses for the reader as business expenses.

SCHEDULE A (Form 1040)	Itemized Deductions	OMB No. 1545-0074
Department of the Treasury Internal Revenue Service (99)	▶ Information about Schedule A and its separate instructions is at *www.irs.gov/schedulea*. ▶ Attach to Form 1040.	2014 Attachment Sequence No. 07

Name(s) shown on Form 1040	Your social security number
Bill and Helen Jones	000-00-0000

Medical and Dental Expenses	**Caution.** Do not include expenses reimbursed or paid by others.			
	1 Medical and dental expenses (see instructions)	**1**	4,434	
	2 Enter amount from Form 1040, line 38 **2** 33,000			
	3 Multiply line 2 by 10% (.10). But if either you or your spouse was born before January 2, 1950, multiply line 2 by 7.5% (.075) instead	**3**	3,300	
	4 Subtract line 3 from line 1. If line 3 is more than line 1, enter -0-		**4**	1,134

While most miscellaneous itemized deductions are only allowed to the extent that the aggregate of such deductions exceeds 2% of your adjusted gross income, "impairment-related work expenses" are not subject to this limitation.

Example 1

You are confined to a wheelchair. Sometimes you must go out of town on business. Your friend or spouse goes with you to help with such things as carrying your luggage or getting up steps. You do not pay your helper a salary, but you do pay for your helper's travel, meals, and lodging while on such trips. You have learned how to take care of yourself and to do your job in your hometown without a helper. Because the expenses for the transportation, meals, and lodging of your helper are directly related to doing your job, you may deduct them as miscellaneous deductions on Form 1040.

Example 2

Assume the same facts as in Example 1, except you are dependent on your friend's help at home as well as while traveling on business. The expenses of the friend are medical expenses, not business expenses.

If, in Example 2, your spouse goes with you on the out-of-town business trips, you may deduct as medical expenses only the out-of-pocket costs for your spouse's transportation. Expenses for your spouse's meals and lodging are not deductible.

Health Insurance Costs for Self-Employed Persons

If you were self-employed and had a net profit for the year, you may be able to deduct, as an adjustment to income, amounts paid for medical and qualified long-term care insurance on behalf of yourself, your spouse, your dependents, and, your children who were under age 27 at the end of 2014. For this purpose, you were self-employed if you were a general partner (or a limited partner receiving guaranteed payments) or you received wages from an S corporation in which you were more than a 2% shareholder. The insurance plan must be established under your trade or business and the deduction cannot be more than your earned income from that trade or business.

You cannot deduct payments for medical insurance for any month in which you were eligible to participate in a health plan subsidized by your employer, your spouse's employer, or an employer of your dependent or your child under age 27 at the end of 2014. You cannot deduct payments for a qualified long-term care insurance contract for any month in which you were eligible to participate in a long-term care insurance plan subsidized by your employer or your spouse's employer.

If you are self-employed and have a net profit for the year, you can deduct up to 100% of the amount you pay for health insurance on behalf of yourself, your spouse, and children under the age of 27 as of the end of 2014, even if they are not dependents. A child includes your son, daughter, stepchild, adopted child, or foster child. A foster child is any child placed with you by an authorized placement agency or by judgment, decree, or other order of any court of competent jurisdiction. This deduction cannot be greater than your net earnings from your trade or business.

You may also be able to deduct premiums if you received wages from an S corporation in which you were more than a 2% shareholder. Eligible premiums will be shown in box 14 of your W-2.

If you qualify to take the deduction, use the Self-Employed Health Insurance Deduction Worksheet in the Form 1040 instructions to figure the amount you can deduct. But if any of the following applies, do not use that worksheet.

- You had more than one source of income subject to self-employment tax.
- You file Form 2555, Foreign Earned Income, or Form 2555-EZ, Foreign Earned Income Exclusion.
- You are using amounts paid for qualified long-term care insurance to figure the deduction.

If you cannot use the worksheet in the Form 1040 instructions, use the worksheet in Publication 535, Business Expenses, to figure your deduction.

Note. When figuring the amount you can deduct for insurance premiums, do not include any advance payments shown on Form 1099-H, Health Coverage Tax Credit (HCTC) Advance Payments.

If you are claiming the health coverage tax credit, subtract the amount shown on Form 8885, from the total insurance premiums you paid.

Do not include amounts paid for health insurance coverage with retirement plan distributions that were tax-free because you are a retired public safety officer.

Where to report. You take this deduction on Form 1040. If you itemize your deductions and do not claim 100% of your self-employed health insurance on Form 1040, you can generally include any remaining premiums with all other medical expenses on Schedule A (Form 1040), subject to the 10% limit (7.5% if either you or your spouse was age 65 or older). See *Self-Employed Health Insurance Deduction* in chapter 6 of Publication 535, Business Expenses, and *Medical and Dental Expenses* in the Instructions for Schedule A (Form 1040), for more information.

TAXORGANIZER

Records you should keep:

- Receipts and canceled checks evidencing payment of medical expenses
- Statements or itemized invoices showing the following:
  - A description of the medical care received
  - Who received the care
  - The nature and purpose of the medical expenses.
- A permanent record of the name and address of the provider of medical care, the amount of the expenses, and the date paid
- Documentation that the expense was to obtain medical treatment, that medicine was prescribed, and that the expense was incurred on a doctor's recommendation
- Support for medically related capital improvements to your home, including written recommendations from your doctor, qualified appraisal, etc.
- Schedule of insurance reimbursements received and related supporting documentation

Do not send these documents with your tax return, but keep them for your own records.

Chapter 23
Taxes you may deduct

Note

IRS Publication 17 (*Your Federal Income Tax*) has been updated by Ernst & Young LLP for 2014. Dates and dollar amounts shown are for 2014. Underlined type is used to indicate where IRS text has been updated. Places where text has been removed are indicated by the sentence: *Text intentionally omitted.*

ey.com/EYTaxGuide
Ernst & Young LLP will update the *EY Tax Guide 2015* website with relevant taxpayer information as it becomes available. You can also sign up for email alerts to let you know when changes have been made.

Introduction

You have been allowed to deduct taxes you pay—other than your federal income tax—ever since the nation's income tax was first enacted. The underlying theory is that taxes are an involuntary expenditure and therefore should be deducted from an individual's gross income. But there is a practical consideration as well: The payment of state and local taxes makes it more difficult for an individual to meet the federal tax bill.

Taxpayers used to have a choice about which state and local taxes you could deduct: you could deduct your state and local income taxes or the amount of general sales taxes you paid during the year instead. But the option to deduct the amount of state and local *sales* tax you paid expired at the end of 2013 and is unavailable for 2014. As of the date this book was published in October 2014, Congress had been considering legislation to extend the availability of the deduction for general sales taxes paid at least through 2014. For updated information on this and any other tax law changes that occur after this book was published, see our website, *ey.com/EYTaxGuide.*

Taxes you pay to a foreign government may also be deducted. These and other taxes that you may deduct from your federal income tax are described in this chapter.

TAXALERT

Your 2014 itemized deductions may be subject to certain limitations if your adjusted gross income (AGI) exceeds certain thresholds based upon your filing status. These AGI thresholds are $305,050 for married persons filing jointly or qualifying widow(er)s; $254,200 for single individuals; $279,650 for heads of household; and $152,525 for married persons filing separately. See chapter 30, *Limit on Itemized Deductions*, for more information on how the deduction limitations are calculated.

What's New

Deduction for State and local general sales taxes. The itemized deduction for State and local general sales taxes expired at the end of 2013 and is not available for 2014.

TAXALERT

The provision allowing a taxpayer to elect to take an itemized deduction for state and local general sales taxes instead of the itemized deduction for state and local income taxes expired at the end of 2013. As of the date this book was published in October 2014, Congress had been considering legislation to extend the availability of the deduction for general sales taxes paid at least through 2014. For updated information on this and any other tax law changes that occur after this book was published, see our website, *ey.com/EYTaxGuide.*

This expired option to deduct state and local general sales taxes instead of deducting state and local income taxes particularly benefited residents of states with no state income tax such as Alaska, Florida, Nevada, South Dakota, Texas, Washington, and Wyoming. (New Hampshire and Tennessee tax interest and dividend income but otherwise do not tax income.) But, because it had been available to all taxpayers as an option, other taxpayers whose sales tax bill for the year exceeded their state income tax; e.g., in low-tax jurisdictions or in years when large taxable expenditures were incurred, might have also benefited from choosing the option to deduct general sales taxes.

On the other hand, the sales tax deduction was a preference item for Alternative Minimum Tax (AMT) purposes, and therefore may have provided little or no reduction in federal income taxes to taxpayers exposed to the AMT. But, if that taxpayer itemized deductions for state tax purposes, and could claim the sales tax deduction, the taxpayer might have still been better off deducting sales tax on the federal return in order to reduce state taxes, despite the fact that the deduction resulted in no federal tax savings.

This chapter discusses which taxes you can deduct if you itemize deductions on Schedule A (Form 1040). It also explains which taxes you can deduct on other schedules or forms and which taxes you cannot deduct.

This chapter covers the following topics.
- Income taxes (federal, state, local, and foreign).
- *Text intentionally omitted*.
- Real estate taxes (state, local, and foreign).
- Personal property taxes (state and local).
- Taxes and fees you cannot deduct.

Use Table 23-1 as a guide to determine which taxes you can deduct.

Table 23-1.   **Which Taxes Can You Deduct?**

Type of Tax	You Can Deduct	You Cannot Deduct
Fees and Charges	Fees and charges that are expenses of your trade or business or of producing income.	Fees and charges that are not expenses of your trade or business or of producing income, such as fees for driver's licenses, car inspections, parking, or charges for water bills (see *Taxes and Fees You Cannot Deduct*). Fines and penalties.
Income Taxes	State and local income taxes. Foreign income taxes. Employee contributions to state funds listed under *Contributions to state benefit funds*.	Federal income taxes. Employee contributions to private or voluntary disability plans.
General Sales Taxes—This deduction expired at the end of 2013 and is not allowed for 2014 unless Congress acts to extend it. *Text intentionally omitted*.		
Other Taxes	Taxes that are expenses of your trade or business. Taxes on property producing rent or royalty income. Occupational taxes. See chapter 29. One-half of self-employment tax paid.	Federal excise taxes, such as tax on gasoline, that are not expenses of your trade or business or of producing income. Per capita taxes.
Personal Property Taxes	State and local personal property taxes.	Customs duties that are not expenses of your trade or business or of producing income.
Real Estate Taxes	State and local real estate taxes. Foreign real estate taxes. Tenant's share of real estate taxes paid by cooperative housing corporation.	Real estate taxes that are treated as imposed on someone else (see *Division of real estate taxes between buyers and sellers*). Taxes for local benefits (with exceptions). See *Real Estate-Related Items You Cannot Deduct*. Trash and garbage pickup fees (with exceptions). See *Real Estate-Related Items You Cannot Deduct*. Rent increase due to higher real estate taxes. Homeowners' association charges.

The end of the chapter contains a section that explains which forms you use to deduct different types of taxes.

Business taxes. You can deduct certain taxes only if they are ordinary and necessary expenses of your trade or business or of producing income. For information on these taxes, see Publication 535, Business Expenses.

State or local taxes. These are taxes imposed by the 50 states, U.S. possessions, or any of their political subdivisions (such as a county or city), or by the District of Columbia.

Indian tribal government. An Indian tribal government recognized by the Secretary of the Treasury as performing substantial government functions will be treated as a state for purposes of claiming a deduction for taxes. Income taxes, real estate taxes, and personal property taxes imposed by that Indian tribal government (or by any of its subdivisions that are treated as political subdivisions of a state) are deductible.

Text intentionally omitted.

Foreign taxes. These are taxes imposed by a foreign country or any of its political subdivisions.

Useful Items
You may want to see:

Publication
☐ **514** Foreign Tax Credit for Individuals
☐ **530** Tax Information for Homeowners

Form (and instructions)
☐ **Schedule A (Form 1040)** Itemized Deductions
☐ **Schedule E (Form 1040)** Supplemental Income and Loss
☐ **1116** Foreign Tax Credit

Tests to Deduct Any Tax
The following two tests must be met for you to deduct any tax.
- The tax must be imposed on you.
- You must pay the tax during your tax year.

The tax must be imposed on you. In general, you can deduct only taxes imposed on you.

Generally, you can deduct property taxes only if you are an owner of the property. If your spouse owns the property and pays the real estate taxes, the taxes are deductible on your spouse's separate return or on your joint return.

You must pay the tax during your tax year. If you are a cash basis taxpayer, you can deduct only those taxes you actually paid during your tax year. If you pay your taxes by check, the day you mail or deliver the check is the date of payment, provided the check is honored by the financial institution. If you use a pay-by-phone account (such as a credit card or electronic funds withdrawal), the date reported on the statement of the financial institution showing when payment was made is the date of payment. If you contest a tax liability and are a cash basis taxpayer, you can deduct the tax only in the year you actually pay it (or transfer money or other property to provide for satisfaction of the contested liability). See Publication 538, Accounting Periods and Methods, for details.

If you use an accrual method of accounting, see Publication 538 for more information.

Income Taxes
This section discusses the deductibility of state and local income taxes (including employee contributions to state benefit funds) and foreign income taxes.

State and Local Income Taxes
You can deduct state and local income taxes. *Text intentionally omitted.*

Exception. You cannot deduct state and local income taxes you pay on income that is exempt from federal income tax, unless the exempt income is interest income. For example, you cannot deduct the part of a state's income tax that is on a cost-of-living allowance exempt from federal income tax.

What To Deduct

Your deduction may be for withheld taxes, estimated tax payments, or other tax payments as follows.

Withheld taxes. You can deduct state and local income taxes withheld from your salary in the year they are withheld. Your Form(s) W-2 will show these amounts. Forms W-2G, 1099-G, 1099-R, and 1099-MISC may also show state and local income taxes withheld.

Estimated tax payments. You can deduct estimated tax payments you made during the year to a state or local government. However, you must have a reasonable basis for making the estimated tax payments. Any estimated state or local tax payments that are not made in good faith at the time of payment are not deductible. For example, you made an estimated state income tax payment. However, the estimate of your state tax liability shows that you will get a refund of the full amount of your estimated payment. You had no reasonable basis to believe you had any additional liability for state income taxes and you cannot deduct the estimated tax payment.

EXPLANATION

Generally, all state, county, city, and municipal income taxes are deductible in the year in which you pay them—including the state and local taxes applicable to interest income that is not taxable at the federal level.

Example

You have the following income:

Salary	$18,000
Municipal bond income (exempt from federal tax but taxable by your state)	$2,000
Total income	$20,000

If your state income tax is $1,000, then 10%, or $100, is attributable to the federally exempt income. Nevertheless, you may deduct the entire $1,000 on your federal return.

TAXALERT

Municipal bonds. Municipal bonds issued by your state frequently are not subject to your state's income tax, whereas obligations for other states usually are subject to the state tax. Municipal bonds issued by Puerto Rico, Guam, Virgin Islands, Northern Mariana Islands, and American Samoa are exempt from state income tax for all investors regardless of their state of residence.

Be sure to use your effective state rate after the federal tax benefit when you are deciding between investing in a state tax-exempt municipal bond or an obligation that is subject to your state's tax.

TAXPLANNER

Deducting expenses. If you deduct an expense when you pay it rather than when the expense is incurred, as most people do, you may deduct the following:

1. State income tax withheld from salary in 2014
2. State estimated tax payments made in 2014 for 2014
3. Fourth-quarter state estimated tax payment for 2013 made in January 2014. In most states, the fourth-quarter estimated tax payment is due in January of the following year. A January 2015 payment for the last quarter of 2014 is deductible on your 2015 return. If, however, the payment is made by December 31, 2014, it is deductible on

your 2014 return. If you can accelerate your payment by a few weeks, you can accelerate your deduction for state income taxes by a full year. However, before accelerating the payment, prepare an income tax projection for 2014 to determine whether you expect to be subject to the alternative minimum tax (AMT). State income taxes are not deductible for AMT purposes and accelerating the payment into 2014 will not result in a tax benefit for you if you will be subject to AMT in 2014. See chapter 31, *How to figure your tax*, for more information about the AMT.

4. State income tax paid with your 2013 state income tax return filed in 2014
5. State income tax paid in 2014 with a request for a filing extension for your 2013 state income tax return
6. Additional state income tax paid in 2014 as a result of an audit, notice, or an amended return.

TAXALERT
Taxpayers have been denied deductions when state estimated tax payments made on December 31 were substantially in excess of their actual tax liability. To be assured of a deduction, you must be able to prove that the tax payment was based on a reasonable estimate of your actual tax bill. Also, be sure not to prepay your state taxes if you're in an alternative minimum tax position. See chapter 31, *How to figure your tax*.

TAXORGANIZER
You should keep canceled checks for payments of state estimated income tax (or any deductible tax) in order to support your claim for deductible taxes. Since estimated tax payments are deducted in the year the payments are made, it may be beneficial to retain proof of when the payment was made (e.g., canceled checks, certified mail receipts, etc.).

Refund applied to taxes. You can deduct any part of a refund of prior-year state or local income taxes that you chose to have credited to your 2014 estimated state or local income taxes.

Do not reduce your deduction by either of the following items.

• Any state or local income tax refund (or credit) you expect to receive for 2014.
• Any refund of (or credit for) prior-year state and local income taxes you actually received in 2014.

However, part or all of this refund (or credit) may be taxable. See *Refund (or credit) of state or local income taxes*, later.

Separate federal returns. If you and your spouse file separate state, local, and federal income tax returns, you each can deduct on your federal return only the amount of your own state and local income tax that you paid during the tax year.

Joint state and local returns. If you and your spouse file joint state and local returns and separate federal returns, each of you can deduct on your separate federal return a part of the total state and local income taxes paid during the tax year. You can deduct only the amount of the total taxes that is proportionate to your gross income compared to the combined gross income of you and your spouse. However, you cannot deduct more than the amount you actually paid during the year. You can avoid this calculation if you and your spouse are jointly and individually liable for the full amount of the state and local income taxes. If so, you and your spouse can deduct on your separate federal returns the amount you each actually paid.

Joint federal return. If you file a joint federal return, you can deduct the total of the state and local income taxes both of you paid.

TAXPLANNER
If you plan on filing a joint state return with your spouse and separate federal returns, and if you are both jointly and individually liable for the full amount of the state tax, the state tax should be paid, to the extent possible, by the person in the higher separate federal income tax bracket. (For advice on filing jointly or separately, see chapter 2, *Filing status*.)

Contributions to state benefit funds. As an employee, you can deduct mandatory contributions to state benefit funds withheld from your wages that provide protection against loss of wages. For example, certain states require employees to make contributions to state funds providing disability or unemployment insurance benefits. Mandatory payments made to the following state benefit funds are deductible as state income taxes on Schedule A (Form 1040), line 5.

- Alaska Unemployment Compensation Fund.
- California Nonoccupational Disability Benefit Fund.
- New Jersey Nonoccupational Disability Benefit Fund.
- New Jersey Unemployment Compensation Fund.
- New York Nonoccupational Disability Benefit Fund.
- Pennsylvania Unemployment Compensation Fund.
- Rhode Island Temporary Disability Benefit Fund.
- Washington State Supplemental Workmen's Compensation Fund.

Refund (or credit) of state or local income taxes. If you receive a refund of (or credit for) state or local income taxes in a year after the year in which you paid them, you may have to include the refund in income on Form 1040, line 10, in the year you receive it. This includes refunds resulting from taxes that were overwithheld, applied from a prior year return, not figured correctly, or figured again because of an amended return. If you did not itemize your deductions in the previous year, do not include the refund in income. If you deducted the taxes in the previous year, include all or part of the refund on Form 1040, line 10, in the year you receive the refund. For a discussion of how much to include, see *Recoveries* in chapter 12.

EXPLANATION

If you received a refund of taxes that you paid in an earlier year, such as 2012 or 2013, do not use that refund to reduce your deduction for taxes that you paid during 2014.

However, if you receive a refund of taxes in the same year in which you paid the taxes, you would use the refund to reduce your deduction for taxes.

Example

You paid $4,000 of estimated state income taxes for 2013 in four equal payments. You made your fourth payment in January 2014. You were not subject to state income tax withholding in 2013. In 2014, you received a $400 tax refund based on your 2013 state income tax return. One hundred dollars (25% of $400) of the refund is attributable to your 2014 payment. Your deduction for state and local income taxes paid in 2014 includes $900 ($1,000 − $100) plus any other payments you made during 2014 and any amount withheld during 2014. The amount of your state tax refund to be reported as income in 2014 would be $300 ($400 − $100).

TAXSAVER

Reducing the amount of the reported refund will reduce your adjusted gross income. If your adjusted gross income is lower, you may benefit from greater itemized deductions.

TAXPLANNER

If you subtract part of the refund from your other tax payments, the income reported by you will not match the amount reported to the IRS by the state on Form 1099-G. You may then receive a notice proposing an additional assessment of tax. You may avoid the notice by attaching an explanation to your return.

EXPLANATION

An overpayment of state income tax that is to be credited against the estimated state tax for the following year is treated as though it were refunded to you. The overpayment may then be deducted as an estimated tax payment.

Example

Your 2013 state return showed an overpayment of $500, which you indicated was to be credited against your 2014 state estimated tax declaration. In addition, you made three quarterly state estimated tax payments of $500 each during 2014. On your 2014 Form 1040, you report a tax refund of $500 on line 10 and a deduction on Schedule A of $2,000.

Foreign Income Taxes

Generally, you can take either a deduction or a credit for income taxes imposed on you by a foreign country or a U.S. possession. However, you cannot take a deduction or credit for foreign income taxes paid on income that is exempt from U.S. tax under the foreign earned income exclusion or the foreign housing exclusion. For information on these exclusions, see Publication 54, Tax Guide for U.S. Citizens and Resident Aliens Abroad. For information on the foreign tax credit, see Publication 514.

Text intentionally omitted.

Real Estate Taxes

Deductible real estate taxes are any state, local, or foreign taxes on real property levied for the general public welfare. You can deduct these taxes only if they are based on the assessed value of the real property and charged uniformly against all property under the jurisdiction of the taxing authority.

Deductible real estate taxes generally do not include taxes charged for local benefits and improvements that increase the value of the property. They also do not include itemized charges for services (such as trash collection) assessed against specific property or certain people, even if the charge is paid to the taxing authority. For more information about taxes and charges that are not deductible, see *Real Estate-Related Items You Cannot Deduct*, later.

Tenant-shareholders in a cooperative housing corporation. Generally, if you are a tenant-stockholder in a cooperative housing corporation, you can deduct the amount paid to the corporation that represents your share of the real estate taxes the corporation paid or incurred for your dwelling unit. The corporation should provide you with a statement showing your share of the taxes. For more information, see *Special Rules for Cooperatives* in Publication 530.

Division of real estate taxes between buyers and sellers. If you bought or sold real estate during the year, the real estate taxes must be divided between the buyer and the seller.

The buyer and the seller must divide the real estate taxes according to the number of days in the real property tax year (the period to which the tax is imposed relates) that each owned the property. The seller is treated as paying the taxes up to, but not including, the date of sale. The buyer is treated as paying the taxes beginning with the date of sale. This applies regardless of the lien dates under local law. Generally, this information is included on the settlement statement provided at the closing.

If you (the seller) cannot deduct taxes until they are paid because you use the cash method of accounting, and the buyer of your property is personally liable for the tax, you are considered to have paid your part of the tax at the time of the sale. This lets you deduct the part of the tax to the date of sale even though you did not actually pay it. However, you must also include the amount of that tax in the selling price of the property. The buyer must include the same amount in his or her cost of the property.

You figure your deduction for taxes on each property bought or sold during the real property tax year as follows.

Worksheet 23-1. **Figuring Your Real Estate Tax Deduction**   *Keep for Your Records*

1. Enter the total real estate taxes for the real property tax year	_____
2. Enter the number of days in the real property tax year that you owned the property.	_____
3. Divide line 2 by 365 (for leap years, divide line 2 by 366).	_____
4. Multiply line 1 by line 3. This is your deduction. Enter it on Schedule A (Form 1040), line 6	_____

Note. Repeat steps 1 through 4 for each property you bought or sold during the real property tax year. Your total deduction is the sum of the line 4 amounts for all of the properties.

Real estate taxes for prior years. Do not divide delinquent taxes between the buyer and seller if the taxes are for any real property tax year before the one in which the property is sold. Even if the buyer agrees to pay the delinquent taxes, the buyer cannot deduct them. The buyer must add them to the cost of the property. The seller can deduct these taxes paid by the buyer. However, the seller must include them in the selling price.

Examples. The following examples illustrate how real estate taxes are divided between buyer and seller.

Example 1. Dennis and Beth White's real property tax year for both their old home and their new home is the calendar year, with payment due August 1. The tax on their old home, sold on May 7, was $620. The tax on their new home, bought on May 3, was $732. Dennis and Beth are considered to have paid a proportionate share of the real estate taxes on the old home even though they did not actually pay them to the taxing authority. On the other hand, they can claim only a proportionate share of the taxes they paid on their new property even though they paid the entire amount.

Dennis and Beth owned their old home during the real property tax year for 126 days (January 1 to May 6, the day before the sale). They figure their deduction for taxes on their old home as follows.

Worksheet 23-1.   **Figuring Your Real Estate Tax Deduction—Taxes on Old Home**

1. Enter the total real estate taxes for the real property tax year	$620
2. Enter the number of days in the real property tax year that you owned the property	126
3. Divide line 2 by 365 (for leap years, divide line 2 by 366).	.3452
4. Multiply line 1 by line 3. This is your deduction. Enter it on Schedule A (Form 1040), line 6	$214

Since the buyers of their old home paid all of the taxes, Dennis and Beth also include the $214 in the selling price of the old home. (The buyers add the $214 to their cost of the home.)

Dennis and Beth owned their new home during the real property tax year for 243 days (May 3 to December 31, including their date of purchase). They figure their deduction for taxes on their new home as follows.

Worksheet 23-1. **Figuring Your Real Estate Tax Deduction—Taxes on New Home**

1.	Enter the total real estate taxes for the real property tax year	$732
2.	Enter the number of days in the real property tax year that you owned the property	243
3.	Divide line 2 by 365 (for leap years, divide line 2 by 366).	.6658
4.	Multiply line 1 by line 3. This is your deduction. Enter it on Schedule A (Form 1040), line 6	$487

Since Dennis and Beth paid all of the taxes on the new home, they add $245 ($732 paid less $487 deduction) to their cost of the new home. (The sellers add this $245 to their selling price and deduct the $245 as a real estate tax.)

Dennis and Beth's real estate tax deduction for their old and new homes is the sum of $214 and $487, or $701. They will enter this amount on Schedule A (Form 1040), line 6.

Example 2. George and Helen Brown bought a new home on May 2, 2014. Their real property tax year for the new home is the calendar year. Real estate taxes for 2013 were assessed in their state on January 1, 2014. The taxes became due on May 31, 2014, and October 31, 2014.

The Browns agreed to pay all taxes due after the date of purchase. Real estate taxes for 2013 were $680. They paid $340 on May 31, 2014, and $340 on October 31, 2014. These taxes were for the 2013 real property tax year. The Browns cannot deduct them since they did not own the property until 2014. Instead, they must add $680 to the cost of their new home.

In January 2015, the Browns receive their 2014 property tax statement for $752, which they will pay in 2015. The Browns owned their new home during the 2014 real property tax year for 243 days (May 3 to December 31). They will figure their 2015 deduction for taxes as follows.

Worksheet 23-1. **Figuring Your Real Estate Tax Deduction—Taxes on New Home**

1.	Enter the total real estate taxes for the real property tax year	$752
2.	Enter the number of days in the real property tax year that you owned the property	244
3.	Divide line 2 by 365 (for leap years, divide line 2 by 366).	.6685
4.	Multiply line 1 by line 3. This is your deduction. Claim it on Schedule A (Form 1040), line 6	$503

The remaining $249 ($752 paid less $503 deduction) of taxes paid in 2015, along with the $680 paid in 2014, is added to the cost of their new home.

Because the taxes up to the date of sale are considered paid by the seller on the date of sale, the seller is entitled to a 2014 tax deduction of $929. This is the sum of the $680 for 2013 and the $249 for the 121 days the seller owned the home in 2014. The seller must also include the $929 in the selling price when he or she figures the gain or loss on the sale. The seller should contact the Browns in January 2015 to find out how much real estate tax is due for 2014.

Form 1099-S. For certain sales or exchanges of real estate, the person responsible for closing the sale (generally the settlement agent) prepares Form 1099-S, Proceeds From Real Estate Transactions, to report certain information to the IRS and to the seller of the property. Box 2 of Form 1099-S is for the gross proceeds from the sale and should include the portion of the seller's real estate tax liability that the buyer will pay after the date of sale. The buyer includes these taxes in the cost basis of the property, and the seller both deducts this amount as a tax paid and includes it in the sales price of the property.

For a real estate transaction that involves a home, any real estate tax the seller paid in advance but that is the liability of the buyer appears on Form 1099-S, box 5. The buyer deducts this amount as a real estate tax, and the seller reduces his or her real estate tax deduction (or includes it in income) by the same amount. See *Refund (or rebate)*, later.

Taxes placed in escrow. If your monthly mortgage payment includes an amount placed in escrow (put in the care of a third party) for real estate taxes, you may not be able to deduct the total amount placed in escrow. You can deduct only the real estate tax that the third party actually paid to the taxing authority. If the third party does not notify you of the amount of real estate tax that was paid for you, contact the third party or the taxing authority to find the proper amount to show on your return.

Tenants by the entirety. If you and your spouse held property as tenants by the entirety and you file separate federal returns, each of you can deduct only the taxes each of you paid on the property.

Divorced individuals. If your divorce or separation agreement states that you must pay the real estate taxes for a home owned by you and your spouse, part of your payments may be deductible as alimony and part as real estate taxes. See *Taxes and insurance* in chapter 18 for more information.

Ministers' and military housing allowances. If you are a minister or a member of the uniformed services and receive a housing allowance that you can exclude from income, you still can deduct all of the real estate taxes you pay on your home.

Refund (or rebate). If you received a refund or rebate in 2014 of real estate taxes you paid in 2014, you must reduce your deduction by the amount refunded to you. If you received a refund or rebate in 2014 of real estate taxes you deducted in an earlier year (either as an itemized deduction or an increase to your standard deduction), you generally must include the refund or rebate in income in the year you receive it. However, the amount you include in income is limited to the amount of the deduction that reduced your tax in the earlier year. For more information, see *Recoveries* in chapter 12.

Real Estate-Related Items You Cannot Deduct
Payments for the following items generally are not deductible as real estate taxes.
- Taxes for local benefits.
- Itemized charges for services (such as trash and garbage pickup fees).
- Transfer taxes (or stamp taxes).
- Rent increases due to higher real estate taxes.
- Homeowners' association charges.

Taxes for local benefits. Deductible real estate taxes generally do not include taxes charged for local benefits and improvements tending to increase the value of your property. These include assessments for streets, sidewalks, water mains, sewer lines, public parking facilities, and similar improvements. You should increase the basis of your property by the amount of the assessment.

Local benefit taxes are deductible only if they are for maintenance, repair, or interest charges related to those benefits. If only a part of the taxes is for maintenance, repair, or interest, you must be able to show the amount of that part to claim the deduction. If you cannot determine what part of the tax is for maintenance, repair, or interest, none of it is deductible.

EXPLANATION
Real property taxes are deductible if they are levied for the welfare of the general public and are levied at a proportionate rate against all property within the taxing jurisdiction. Real property taxes should be distinguished from assessments paid for local benefits, such as repair of streets, sidewalks, sewers, curbs, gutters, and other improvements that tend to benefit specific properties. Assessments of this type generally are not deductible.

A property owner often has the option of paying a special assessment in one payment or spreading the assessment over a period of years. In either case, the assessment itself is not deductible. However, payment of certain special assessments may increase the tax basis of your home. (See chapter 13, *Basis of property*, for a full discussion of this matter.) If an assessment on business or investment property is paid in installments, any interest charged is deductible. If the property is personal rather than business property, the interest would not be deductible. See chapter 24, *Interest expense*.

The IRS and the courts have held that the following are deductible as real property taxes:
- Assessments for the repair and resurfacing of streets, but not the lengthening or widening of them
- Wheeling, West Virginia, police and fire department charges imposed on owners of buildings and tangible personal property

If you pay real estate taxes this year but you are not itemizing your deductions, see chapter 13, *Basis of property*.

Different rules apply to real estate taxes paid during the period in which you are making improvements intended for business use. These rules are discussed in chapter 24, *Interest expense*.

Itemized charges for services. An itemized charge for services assessed against specific property or certain people is not a tax, even if the charge is paid to the taxing authority. For example, you cannot deduct the charge as a real estate tax if it is:
- A unit fee for the delivery of a service (such as a $5 fee charged for every 1,000 gallons of water you use),
- A periodic charge for a residential service (such as a $20 per month or $240 annual fee charged to each homeowner for trash collection), or
- A flat fee charged for a single service provided by your government (such as a $30 charge for mowing your lawn because it was allowed to grow higher than permitted under your local ordinance).

Exception. Service charges used to maintain or improve services (such as trash collection or police and fire protection) are deductible as real estate taxes if:
- The fees or charges are imposed at a like rate against all property in the taxing jurisdiction,
- The funds collected are not earmarked; instead, they are commingled with general revenue funds, and
- Funds used to maintain or improve services are not limited to or determined by the amount of these fees or charges collected.

Transfer taxes (or stamp taxes). Transfer taxes and similar taxes and charges on the sale of a personal home are not deductible. If they are paid by the seller, they are expenses of the sale and reduce the amount realized on the sale. If paid by the buyer, they are included in the cost basis of the property.

Rent increase due to higher real estate taxes. If your landlord increases your rent in the form of a tax surcharge because of increased real estate taxes, you cannot deduct the increase as taxes.

Homeowners' association charges. These charges are not deductible because they are imposed by the homeowners' association, rather than the state or local government.

Personal Property Taxes

Personal property tax is deductible if it is a state or local tax that is:
- Charged on personal property,
- Based only on the value of the personal property, and
- Charged on a yearly basis, even if it is collected more or less than once a year.

A tax that meets the above requirements can be considered charged on personal property even if it is for the exercise of a privilege. For example, a yearly tax based on value qualifies as a personal property tax even if it is called a registration fee and is for the privilege of registering motor vehicles or using them on the highways.

If the tax is partly based on value and partly based on other criteria, it may qualify in part.

Example. Your state charges a yearly motor vehicle registration tax of 1% of value plus 50 cents per hundredweight. You paid $32 based on the value ($1,500) and weight (3,400 lbs.) of your car. You can deduct $15 (1% × $1,500) as a personal property tax because it is based on the value. The remaining $17 ($.50 × 34), based on the weight, is not deductible.

Taxes and Fees You Cannot Deduct

Many federal, state, and local government taxes are not deductible because they do not fall within the categories discussed earlier. Other taxes and fees, such as federal income taxes, are not deductible because the tax law specifically prohibits a deduction for them. See Table 23-1.

Taxes and fees that are generally not deductible include the following items.
- *Employment taxes.* This includes social security, Medicare, and railroad retirement taxes withheld from your pay. However, one-half of self-employment tax you pay is deductible. In addition, the social security and other employment taxes you pay on the wages of a household worker may be included in medical expenses that you can deduct or child care expenses that allow you to claim the child and dependent care credit. For more information, see chapters 22 and 33.
- *Estate, inheritance, legacy, or succession taxes.* However, you can deduct the estate tax attributable to income in respect of a decedent if you, as a beneficiary, must include that income in your gross income. In that case, deduct the estate tax as a miscellaneous deduction that is not subject to the 2%-of-adjusted-gross-income limit. For more information, see Publication 559, Survivors, Executors, and Administrators.
- *Federal income taxes.* This includes income taxes withheld from your pay.
- *Fines and penalties.* You cannot deduct fines and penalties paid to a government for violation of any law, including related amounts forfeited as collateral deposits.
- *Gift taxes.*

- *License fees.* You cannot deduct license fees for personal purposes (such as marriage, driver's, and dog license fees).
- *Per capita taxes.* You cannot deduct state or local per capita taxes.

Many taxes and fees other than those listed above are also nondeductible, unless they are ordinary and necessary expenses of a business or income producing activity. For other nondeductible items, see <u>Real Estate-Related Items You Cannot Deduct</u>, earlier.

Where To Deduct

You deduct taxes on the following schedules.

State and local income taxes. These taxes are deducted on Schedule A (Form 1040), line 5, even if your only source of income is from business, rents, or royalties. Check **box a** on line 5.

Text intentionally omitted.

Foreign income taxes. Generally, income taxes you pay to a foreign country or U.S. possession can be claimed as an itemized deduction on Schedule A (Form 1040), line 8, or as a credit against your U.S. income tax on Form 1040, line 48. To claim the credit, you may have to complete and attach Form 1116. For more information, see <u>chapter 37</u>, the Form 1040 instructions, or Publication 514.

Real estate taxes and personal property taxes. Real estate and personal property taxes are deducted on Schedule A (Form 1040), lines 6 and 7, respectively, unless they are paid on property used in your business, in which case they are deducted on Schedule C, Schedule C-EZ, or Schedule F (Form 1040). Taxes on property that produces rent or royalty income are deducted on Schedule E (Form 1040).

Self-employment tax. Deduct one-half of your self-employment tax on Form 1040, line 27.

Other taxes. All other deductible taxes are deducted on Schedule A (Form 1040), line 8.

Chapter 24
Interest expense

Note
IRS Publication 17 (*Your Federal Income Tax*) has been updated by Ernst & Young LLP for 2014. Dates and dollar amounts shown are for 2014. Underlined type is used to indicate where IRS text has been updated. Places where text has been removed are indicated by the sentence: *Text intentionally omitted*.

ey.com/EYTaxGuide
Ernst & Young LLP will update the *EY Tax Guide 2015* website with relevant taxpayer information as it becomes available. You can also sign up for email alerts to let you know when changes have been made.

Introduction
Interest expense is the amount of money you pay for the use of borrowed money. Depending on the use of the borrowed funds, certain types of interest expense may be deducted from your income.

To calculate your deduction, you must first separate your borrowings into five categories: (1) amounts used for investments generating portfolio income (interest, dividends, etc.), (2) amounts used for investment in passive activities (see chapter 12, *Other income*), (3) amounts used to purchase or improve a personal residence, (4) amounts used in an active trade or business, and (5) amounts used for personal reasons. Remember that no portion of your personal interest expense is deductible.

The interest paid on the other four categories of borrowings is subject to different rules regarding deductibility. This chapter will explain those rules and how to account for the use of your borrowings.

Your 2014 itemized deductions may be subject to certain limitations if your adjusted gross income (AGI) exceeds certain thresholds based on your filing status. These AGI thresholds are $305,050 for married persons filing jointly and or qualifying widow(er)s; $254,200 for single individuals; $279,650 for heads of household; and $152,525 for married persons filing separately. See chapter 30, *Limit on Itemized Deductions*, for more information.

What's New
Mortgage Insurance Premiums. The deduction for qualified mortgage insurance as home mortgage interest expired and is not available for 2014.

TAXALERT
The itemized deduction for mortgage insurance premiums paid on a qualified personal residence expired at the end of 2013 and is therefore not available for 2014. As of the date this book was published, Congress had been considering legislation to extend the availability of this deduction at least through 2014. For updated information on this and any other tax law changes that occur after this book was published, see our website, *ey.com/EYTaxGuide*.

In 2013, eligible taxpayers were able to take an itemized deduction for the cost of mortgage insurance premiums paid on a qualified personal residence. The insurance must have been in connection with home acquisition debt and the insurance contract must have been issued after 2006. The deduction was phased out by 10% for each $1,000 by which adjusted gross income (AGI) exceeded $100,000 ($50,000 if you were married filing separately). Therefore, the deduction was unavailable for a taxpayer with AGI over $109,000 ($54,500 if married filing separately).

This chapter discusses what interest expenses you can deduct. Interest is the amount you pay for the use of borrowed money.

The following are types of interest you can deduct as itemized deductions on Schedule A (Form 1040).
- Home mortgage interest, including certain points and mortgage insurance premiums.
- Investment interest.

This chapter explains these deductions. It also explains where to deduct other types of interest and lists some types of interest you cannot deduct.

Use Table 24-1 to find out where to get more information on various types of interest, including investment interest.

EXPLANATION

Loan payments generally are divided between principal and interest. In the absence of any specific division, partial payments are presumed to apply first to interest and then to principal. However, if a single payment is made in full settlement of an outstanding debt, the payment is first applied to the remaining principal balance and then to interest.

Interest paid to a related person is deductible, as long as it is paid for a bona fide debt. For example, parents may deduct interest paid on amounts borrowed from their minor children if the interest is otherwise deductible. If the borrower is not legally liable for the debt, or if there is no intent for the loan to be repaid, it is not a bona fide debt and interest payments are not deductible.

To deduct interest that you pay, the interest must be your liability. When two or more persons are jointly liable for the payment of interest, the person actually making the interest payment is entitled to the entire deduction.

It is not necessary to have a fixed percentage interest rate applied to the money that you have borrowed for the interest to be deducted. What is necessary is that the amount of interest paid can be definitely determined. It is usually based on a written agreement between the lender and the borrower. Low-interest and interest-free loans, which were once popular between family members, now have severe limitations applied to them. See chapter 7, *Interest income*.

Useful Items

You may want to see:

Publication
- ☐ **936** Home Mortgage Interest Deduction
- ☐ **550** Investment Income and Expenses

Home Mortgage Interest

Generally, home mortgage interest is any interest you pay on a loan secured by your home (main home or a second home). The loan may be a mortgage to buy your home, a second mortgage, a line of credit, or a home equity loan.

You can deduct home mortgage interest if all the following conditions are met.
- You file Form 1040 and itemize deductions on Schedule A (Form 1040).
- The mortgage is a secured debt on a qualified home in which you have an ownership interest. (Generally, your mortgage is a secured debt if you put your home up as collateral to protect the interest of the lender. The term "qualified home" means your main home or second home. For details, see Publication 936.)

Both you and the lender must intend that the loan be repaid.

EXPLANATION

To be fully deductible as home mortgage interest, the interest must be on a debt that is secured by property that is a qualified residence. A qualified residence is property that is owned by you and used as a principal or second residence. A residence may, among other things, be a house, a cooperative apartment, a condominium, a house trailer, or a houseboat. To be considered a qualified residence, a houseboat must include basic living accommodations, including sleeping space, a toilet, and cooking facilities.

TAXPLANNER

You may treat a home currently under construction as a qualified home for a period of up to 24 months if it becomes a qualifying residence as of the time that it is ready for occupancy.

Amount Deductible

In most cases, you can deduct all of your home mortgage interest. How much you can deduct depends on the date of the mortgage, the amount of the mortgage, and how you use the mortgage proceeds.

Fully deductible interest. If all of your mortgages fit into one or more of the following three categories at all times during the year, you can deduct all of the interest on those mortgages. (If any one mortgage fits into more than one category, add the debt that fits in each category to your other debt in the same category.)

The three categories are as follows:

1. Mortgages you took out on or before October 13, 1987 (called grandfathered debt).

EXPLANATION

All mortgage indebtedness existing on October 13, 1987 (grandfathered debt), is treated as acquisition indebtedness, regardless of the amount. The interest on this indebtedness is fully deductible.

Individuals who refinanced and increased their mortgage indebtedness before October 14, 1987, may have greater interest deductions than those individuals who waited until later, because new or refinanced indebtedness is limited in amount, as explained in this chapter.

When refinancing pre-October 14, 1987, mortgage debt, the amount that exceeds the existing debt, does not qualify as grandfathered debt. The excess may be treated as home acquisition or home equity indebtedness, but the total qualifying indebtedness cannot exceed the fair market value of the residence. Grandfathered debt refinanced after October 13, 1987, generally retains its status as grandfathered debt only for the remaining term of the original debt.

Example 1

An original mortgage note incurred prior to October 14, 1987, to purchase a qualified residence had been reduced to $100,000 in 2014, when the value of the residence was $175,000. If this mortgage is refinanced, $100,000 of the new mortgage note is treated as grandfathered debt. Up to $75,000 may be treated as home acquisition or home equity indebtedness. If the indebtedness exceeds the value of the residence ($175,000), the excess must be allocated in accordance with the use of the excess amount.

2. Mortgages you took out after October 13, 1987, to buy, build, or improve your home (called home acquisition debt), but only if throughout 2014 these mortgages plus any grandfathered debt totaled $1 million or less ($500,000 or less if married filing separately).

EXPLANATION

This limitation applies only to loans incurred to purchase, construct, or improve a home.

TAXPLANNER

Is your loan large enough? When purchasing or constructing a home, consider your future financial needs carefully. The original loan can never be refinanced to increase the amount available for this limitation.

If you believe that you will need money for personal uses in the near future, you may want to increase the original mortgage at the time of acquisition or improvement to meet those future needs. Otherwise, if you later obtain a home equity loan, the interest on only $100,000 of the loan ($50,000 if married filing separately) is deductible as mortgage interest.

Additionally, interest paid on a home equity loan where the loan proceeds were used for personal use, and not for home improvements, is not deductible under the alternative minimum tax rules (see chapter 31, *How to figure your tax*).

3. Mortgages you took out after October 13, 1987, other than to buy, build, or improve your home (called home equity debt), but only if throughout 2014 these mortgages totaled $100,000 or less ($50,000 or less if married filing separately) and totaled no more than the fair market value of your home reduced by (1) and (2).

The dollar limits for the second and third categories apply to the combined mortgages on your main home and second home.

See *Part II* of Publication 936 for more detailed definitions of grandfathered, home acquisition, and home equity debt.

You can use Figure 24-A to check whether your home mortgage interest is fully deductible.

Figure 24-A. **Is My Home Mortgage Interest Fully Deductible?**
(Instructions: Include balances of ALL mortgages secured by your main home and second home.)

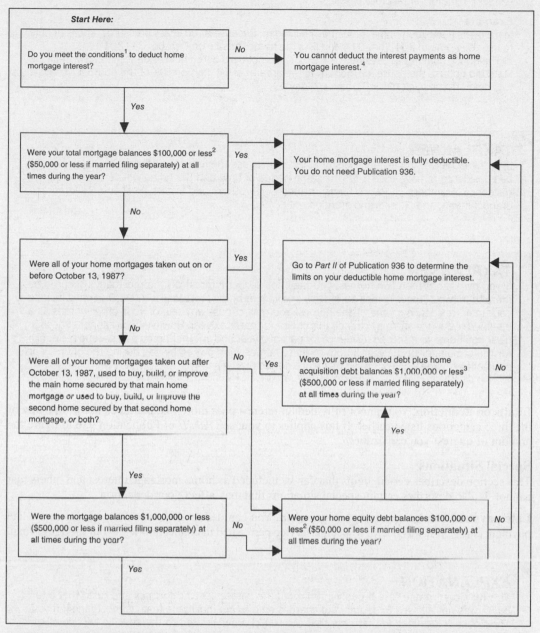

[1] You must itemize deductions on Schedule A (Form 1040). The loan must be a secured debt on a qualified home. See *Home Mortgage Interest.*

[2] If all mortgages on your main or second home exceed the home's fair market value, a lower limit may apply. See *Home equity debt limit* under *Home Equity Debt* in *Part II* of Publication 936.

[3] Amounts over the $1,000,000 limit ($500,000 if married filing separately) qualify as home equity debt if they are not more than the total home equity debt limit. See Publication 936 for more information about grandfathered debt, home acquisition debt, and home equity debt.

[4] See Table 24-1 for where to deduct other types of interest payments.

EXPLANATION

A second home also may be a qualified residence. A second home may be one that you do not occupy, a home that you occupy part of the year, or a home that you rent out. If the home is rented out, it is subject to the use requirements relating to vacation homes. It qualifies as your home only if you used it more than the greater of:

1. 4 days, or
2. 10% of the number of days during the year that it was rented at a fair rental or held out for sale.

If a dwelling is not rented at any time during the year, it may be treated as a qualified residence, even if it is not used by you. For this purpose, the IRS states that "rented" includes holding the residence out for rental or for resale.

Example
Mary owns a vacation home in northern Michigan. Because of business pressures, she is unable to use the home in 2013 or 2014 and lists the home for sale on October 31, 2014.

The house qualifies as a residence in 2013. It is not considered her residence in 2014, because Mary did not use the house for more than the greater of 14 days or 10% of the number of days it was held out for sale ($10\% \times 61$ days $= 6$ days).

TAXPLANNER

If, in the earlier example, members of Mary's family use the home for 15 days in 2014, she will be considered to have used it for the same period of time and the home will be considered her residence. Members of Mary's family include her brothers and sisters, husband, children and grandchildren, and parents and grandparents.

TAXPLANNER

If you own more than two homes, you may not deduct interest on the mortgages secured by more than two of these homes during any one year as home mortgage interest. You must include your main residence as one of the homes. You may choose any one of your other homes as a qualified residence and may change this choice for each tax year. However, you cannot choose to treat one home as a second residence for part of a year and another home as a second residence for the remainder of the year if both of these homes were owned by you during the entire year and neither home was your main residence during that year.

Limits on deduction. You cannot fully deduct interest on a mortgage that does not fit into any of the three categories listed earlier. If this applies to you, see *Part II* of Publication 936 to figure the amount of interest you can deduct.

Special Situations

This section describes certain items that can be included as home mortgage interest and others that cannot. It also describes certain special situations that may affect your deduction.

Late payment charge on mortgage payment. You can deduct as home mortgage interest a late payment charge if it was not for a specific service performed in connection with your mortgage loan.

EXPLANATION

The Tax Court in one case broadly interpreted the phrase *specific services* and ruled that a taxpayer was not allowed to deduct late charges on a home mortgage loan as mortgage interest. The Court determined in that case that the late charges related to the specific service of collecting the late payment. Furthermore, the formula used in calculating the late charge did not resemble standard interest computations, because the late charge was the same whether the payment was 1 day or 1 year late.

Mortgage prepayment penalty. If you pay off your home mortgage early, you may have to pay a penalty. You can deduct that penalty as home mortgage interest provided the penalty is not for a specific service performed or cost incurred in connection with your mortgage loan.

Sale of home. If you sell your home, you can deduct your home mortgage interest (subject to any limits that apply) paid up to, but not including, the date of sale.

Example. John and Peggy Harris sold their home on May 7. Through April 30, they made home mortgage interest payments of $1,220. The settlement sheet for the sale of the home showed $50 interest for the 6-day period in May up to, but not including, the date of sale. Their mortgage interest deduction is $1,270 ($1,220 + $50).

Prepaid interest. If you pay interest in advance for a period that goes beyond the end of the tax year, you must spread this interest over the tax years to which it applies. You can deduct in each year only the interest that qualifies as home mortgage interest for that year. However, there is an exception that applies to points, discussed later.

EXAMPLE

Example 1

When Dan borrowed $10,000 on a mortgage on November 1, 2014, he prepaid 16 months of interest ($1,600). The $1,600 of prepaid interest is considered to be paid, and therefore deductible, equally over the 16-month period ($100 per month). Dan should deduct $200 in 2014, $1,200 in 2015, and $200 in 2016.

Example 2

On March 26, Eric signed a mortgage note for $12,000 and agreed to repay it in 12 equal installments, beginning on April 1. Interest of $960 was subtracted from the face value of the note, and Eric received $11,040. If Eric uses the cash method of accounting, as most people do, interest is considered to be paid in 12 installments of $80 each ($960 ÷ 12). Eric may deduct $720 ($80 × 9 months) for the first year and $240 ($80 × 3 months) in the following year.

No deduction is permitted for the interest if payment for an installment period is not made. Therefore, if Eric were to miss two installment payments in the first year, he could deduct only $560 ($80 × 7 months).

Mortgage interest credit. You may be able to claim a mortgage interest credit if you were issued a mortgage credit certificate (MCC) by a state or local government. Figure the credit on Form 8396, Mortgage Interest Credit. If you take this credit, you must reduce your mortgage interest deduction by the amount of the credit.

For more information on the credit, see chapter 37.

Ministers' and military housing allowance. If you are a minister or a member of the uniformed services and receive a housing allowance that is not taxable, you can still deduct your home mortgage interest.

Hardest Hit Fund and Emergency Homeowners' Loan Programs. You can use a special method to compute your deduction for mortgage interest and real estate taxes on your main home if you meet the following two conditions.

1. You received assistance under:
   a. A State Housing Finance Agency (State HFA) Hardest Hit Fund program in which program payments could be used to pay mortgage interest, or
   b. An Emergency Homeowners' Loan Program administered by the Department of Housing and Urban Development (HUD) or a state.
2. You meet the rules to deduct all of the mortgage interest on your loan and all of the real estate taxes on your main home.

If you meet these tests, then you can deduct all of the payments you actually made during the year to your mortgage servicer, the State HFA, or HUD on the home mortgage (including the amount shown on box 3 of Form 1098-MA, Mortgage Assistance Payments), but not more than the sum of the amounts shown on Form 1098, Mortgage Interest Statement, in box 1 (mortgage interest received from payer(s) / borrower(s)), box 4 (mortgage insurance premiums), and box 5 (real property taxes). However, you are not required to use this special method to compute your deduction for mortgage interest and real estate taxes on your main home.

Mortgage assistance payments under section 235 of the National Housing Act. If you qualify for mortgage assistance payments for lower-income families under section 235 of the National Housing Act, part or all of the interest on your mortgage may be paid for you. You cannot deduct the interest that is paid for you.

No other effect on taxes. Do not include these mortgage assistance payments in your income. Also, do not use these payments to reduce other deductions, such as real estate taxes.

Divorced or separated individuals. If a divorce or separation agreement requires you or your spouse or former spouse to pay home mortgage interest on a home owned by both of you, the payment of interest may be alimony. See the discussion of *Payments for jointly-owned home* in chapter 18.

Redeemable ground rents. If you make annual or periodic rental payments on a redeemable ground rent, you can deduct them as mortgage interest.

Payments made to end the lease and to buy the lessor's entire interest in the land are not deductible as mortgage interest. For more information, see Publication 936.

Nonredeemable ground rents. Payments on a nonredeemable ground rent are not mortgage interest. You can deduct them as rent if they are a business expense or if they are for rental property.

Reverse mortgages. A reverse mortgage is a loan where the lender pays you (in a lump sum, a monthly advance, a line of credit, or a combination of all three) while you continue to live in your home. With a reverse mortgage, you retain title to your home. Depending on the plan, your reverse mortgage becomes due with interest when you move, sell your home, reach the end of a pre-selected loan period, or die. Because reverse mortgages are considered loan advances and not income, the amount you receive is not taxable. Any interest (including original issue discount) accrued on a reverse mortgage is not deductible until the loan is paid in full. Your deduction may be limited because a reverse mortgage loan generally is subject to the limit on *Home Equity Debt* discussed in Publication 936.

Rental payments. If you live in a house before final settlement on the purchase, any payments you make for that period are rent and not interest. This is true even if the settlement papers call them interest. You cannot deduct these payments as home mortgage interest.

Mortgage proceeds invested in tax-exempt securities. You cannot deduct the home mortgage interest on grandfathered debt or home equity debt if you used the proceeds of the mortgage to buy securities or certificates that produce tax-free income. "Grandfathered debt" and "home equity debt" are defined earlier under *Amount Deductible*.

Refunds of interest. If you receive a refund of interest in the same tax year you paid it, you must reduce your interest expense by the amount refunded to you. If you receive a refund of interest you deducted in an earlier year, you generally must include the refund in income in the year you receive it. However, you need to include it only up to the amount of the deduction that reduced your tax in the earlier year. This is true whether the interest overcharge was refunded to you or was used to reduce the outstanding principal on your mortgage.

If you received a refund of interest you overpaid in an earlier year, you generally will receive a Form 1098, Mortgage Interest Statement, showing the refund in box 3. For information about Form 1098, see *Form 1098, Mortgage Interest Statement*, later.

For more information on how to treat refunds of interest deducted in earlier years, see *Recoveries* in chapter 12.

EXAMPLE

During 2014, Andrea paid $2,000 in interest on her adjustable rate mortgage. On December 31, 2014, a $200 interest refund for 2014 was credited to her account. Andrea's net deduction for interest on her loans is $1,800 ($2,000 paid minus $200 refunded).

Refunds of interest paid must be included in income if they represent a return of interest deducted in a prior year. If you receive a refund in 2014 for interest paid in 2013 and *did not itemize* your deductions in 2013, the refund *should not be included* in your 2014 income. If you receive the refund in 2014 and *you did itemize* your deductions in 2013, the refund is generally included in your 2014 income to the extent the deduction reduced your tax in 2013.

Points

The term "points" is used to describe certain charges paid, or treated as paid, by a borrower to obtain a home mortgage. Points may also be called loan origination fees, maximum loan charges, loan discount, or discount points.

A borrower is treated as paying any points that a home seller pays for the borrower's mortgage. See *Points paid by the seller*, later.

EXPLANATION

Usually, for federally regulated mortgage loans, points will be designated on the Uniform Settlement Statement (also known as Form HUD-1) as "loan origination fee," "loan discount," "discount points," or simply "points."

General Rule

You generally cannot deduct the full amount of points in the year paid. Because they are prepaid interest, you generally deduct them ratably over the life (term) of the mortgage. See _Deduction Allowed Ratably_, next.

For exceptions to the general rule, see _Deduction Allowed in Year Paid_, later.

> ## EXPLANATION
>
> **Deducting points.** Generally, taxpayers are prohibited from deducting prepaid interest in the year of payment. Rather, they must capitalize the prepaid interest and deduct it ratably over the life of the loan.
>
> However, as discussed later, an exception exists for taxpayers who buy, build, or improve their principal residences and pay "points" in order to obtain a lower interest rate on their loans. The term "points" is a fee paid by the borrower that is like prepaid interest. To be deductible, the charge must represent interest paid for the use of money and must be paid before the time for which it represents a charge for the use of the money. Furthermore, the home must be the taxpayer's principal residence. You should note that the IRS has ruled that you can elect not to currently deduct points and to amortize them over the life of a loan. Such an election may be advantageous if the deduction does not benefit you in the year of purchase (e.g., you're not itemizing your deductions).

Deduction Allowed Ratably

If you do not meet the tests listed under _Deduction Allowed in Year Paid_, later, the loan is not a home improvement loan, or you choose not to deduct your points in full in the year paid, you can deduct the points ratably (equally) over the life of the loan if you meet all the following tests.

1. You use the cash method of accounting. This means you report income in the year you receive it and deduct expenses in the year you pay them. Most individuals use this method.
2. Your loan is secured by a home. (The home does not need to be your main home.)
3. Your loan period is not more than 30 years.
4. If your loan period is more than 10 years, the terms of your loan are the same as other loans offered in your area for the same or longer period.
5. Either your loan amount is $250,000 or less, or the number of points is not more than:
   a. 4, if your loan period is 15 years or less, or
   b. 6, if your loan period is more than 15 years.

Deduction Allowed in Year Paid

You can fully deduct points in the year paid if you meet all the following tests. (You can use Figure 24-B as a quick guide to see whether your points are fully deductible in the year paid.)

1. Your loan is secured by your main home. (Your main home is the one you ordinarily live in most of the time.)
2. Paying points is an established business practice in the area where the loan was made.
3. The points paid were not more than the points generally charged in that area.
4. You use the cash method of accounting. This means you report income in the year you receive it and deduct expenses in the year you pay them. (If you want more information about this method, see _Accounting Methods_ in chapter 1.)
5. The points were not paid in place of amounts that ordinarily are stated separately on the settlement statement, such as appraisal fees, inspection fees, title fees, attorney fees, and property taxes.
6. The funds you provided at or before closing, plus any points the seller paid, were at least as much as the points charged. The funds you provided are not required to have been applied to the points. They can include a down payment, an escrow deposit, earnest money, and other funds you paid at or before closing for any purpose. You cannot have borrowed these funds from your lender or mortgage broker.
7. You use your loan to buy or build your main home.
8. The points were computed as a percentage of the principal amount of the mortgage.
9. The amount is clearly shown on the settlement statement (such as the Settlement Statement, Form HUD-1) as points charged for the mortgage. The points may be shown as paid from either your funds or the seller's.

Note. If you meet all of these tests, you can choose to either fully deduct the points in the year paid, or deduct them over the life of the loan.

Figure 24-B. **Are My Points Fully Deductible This Year?**

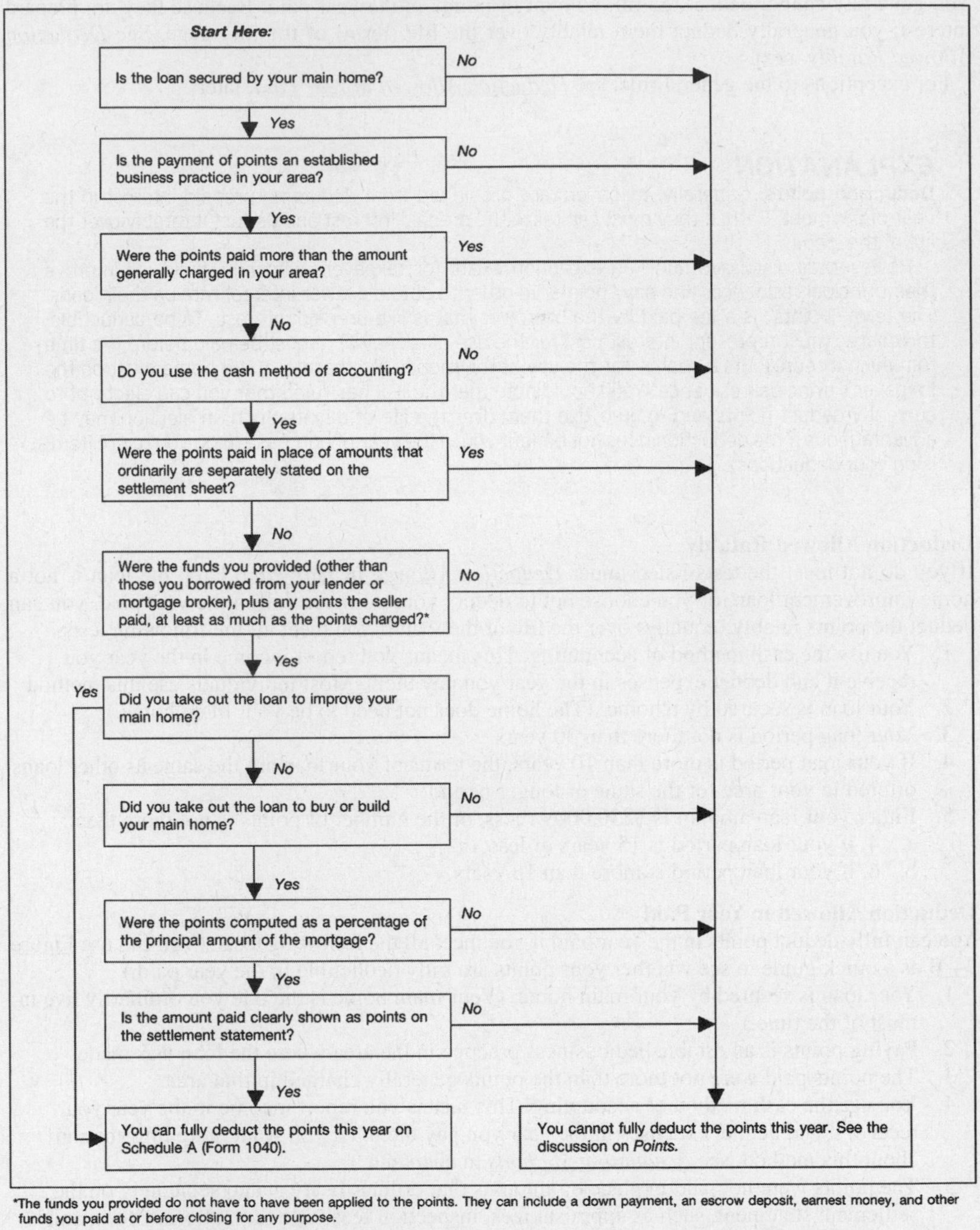

Start Here:
Is the loan secured by your main home?
No
Yes
Is the payment of points an established business practice in your area?
No
Yes
Were the points paid more than the amount generally charged in your area?
Yes
No
Do you use the cash method of accounting?
No
Yes
Were the points paid in place of amounts that ordinarily are separately stated on the settlement sheet?
Yes
No
Were the funds you provided (other than those you borrowed from your lender or mortgage broker), plus any points the seller paid, at least as much as the points charged?*
No
Yes
Did you take out the loan to improve your main home?
Yes
No
Did you take out the loan to buy or build your main home?
No
Yes
Were the points computed as a percentage of the principal amount of the mortgage?
No
Yes
Is the amount paid clearly shown as points on the settlement statement?
No
Yes
You can fully deduct the points this year on Schedule A (Form 1040).
You cannot fully deduct the points this year. See the discussion on Points.

*The funds you provided do not have to have been applied to the points. They can include a down payment, an escrow deposit, earnest money, and other funds you paid at or before closing for any purpose.

Caution

Second home. *You cannot fully deduct in the year paid points you pay on loans secured by your second home. You can deduct these points only over the life of the loan.*

Home improvement loan. You can also fully deduct in the year paid points paid on a loan to improve your main home, if tests (1) through (6) are met.

Refinancing. Generally, points you pay to refinance a mortgage are not deductible in full in the year you pay them. This is true even if the new mortgage is secured by your main home.

However, if you use part of the refinanced mortgage proceeds to improve your main home and you meet the first 6 tests listed under <u>*Deduction Allowed in Year Paid*</u>, earlier, you can fully deduct the part of the points related to the improvement in the year you paid them with your own funds. You can deduct the rest of the points over the life of the loan.

Example 1. In 1998, Bill Fields got a mortgage to buy a home. In 2014, Bill refinanced that mortgage with a 15-year $100,000 mortgage loan. The mortgage is secured by his home. To get the new loan, he had to pay three points ($3,000). Two points ($2,000) were for prepaid interest, and one point ($1,000) was charged for services, in place of amounts that ordinarily are stated separately on the settlement statement. Bill paid the points out of his private funds, rather than out of the proceeds of the new loan. The payment of points is an established practice in the area, and the points charged are not more than the amount generally charged there. Bill's first payment on the new loan was due July 1. He made six payments on the loan in 2014 and is a cash basis taxpayer.

Bill used the funds from the new mortgage to repay his existing mortgage. Although the new mortgage loan was for Bill's continued ownership of his main home, it was not for the purchase or improvement of that home. He cannot deduct all of the points in 2014. He can deduct two points ($2,000) ratably over the life of the loan. He deducts $67 [($2,000 ÷ 180 months) × 6 payments] of the points in 2014. The other point ($1,000) was a fee for services and is not deductible.

Example 2. The facts are the same as in *Example 1*, except that Bill used $25,000 of the loan proceeds to improve his home and $75,000 to repay his existing mortgage. Bill deducts 25% ($25,000 ÷ $100,000) of the points ($2,000) in 2014. His deduction is $500 ($2,000 × 25%).

Bill also deducts the ratable part of the remaining $1,500 ($2,000 − $500) that must be spread over the life of the loan. This is $50 [($1,500 ÷ 180 months) × 6 payments] in 2014. The total amount Bill deducts in 2014 is $550 ($500 + $50).

EXPLANATION

According to the IRS, points paid when you refinance an existing mortgage must be deducted ratably over the life of the new loan. They are not fully deductible in the year in which they were paid because they were not paid in connection with the improvement or purchase of a home, even though the original loan met the requirements for deductibility. However, points paid on a refinanced mortgage are fully deductible in the year paid to the extent the additional loan proceeds are used for home improvement and the points are paid with funds you provide. If only a portion of the loan proceeds is used for home improvement, then only a corresponding portion of the points is fully deductible in the year paid. The balance of the points is deducted ratably over the life of the loan.

However, an Eighth Circuit Court decision allowed a full immediate deduction for points paid by taxpayers in obtaining a permanent mortgage on their home, the proceeds of which were used to pay off a short-term, 3-year mortgage with a balloon payment and a recently obtained home improvement loan secured by a second mortgage. That court indicated that the permanent mortgage obtained was sufficiently "in connection with" the original purchase of the home.

TAXALERT

The IRS has disagreed with this court decision and still argues that points paid for a loan to refinance a mortgage on a taxpayer's principal residence are not deductible. Therefore, the IRS will not follow the decision outside of the Eighth Circuit (Arkansas, Iowa, Minnesota, Missouri, Nebraska, North Dakota, and South Dakota).

TAXPLANNER

Before you refinance. Before you refinance your home mortgage, you should consider both tax and financial factors.

For the interest to remain fully deductible, the following tax-related factors should be considered:

- Whether the term of the mortgage should be extended beyond the original term.
- In general, the total of all mortgage balances should not exceed the lesser of the fair market value of the house or $1.1 million ($1 million acquisition debt and $100,000 home equity debt) or, if married filing separately, $550,000. However, see previous discussion of refinanced grandfathered debt if you have a pre-October 14, 1987, mortgage. Other limitations may also apply. See limits on the deduction of mortgage interest, discussed previously in this chapter.
- When a loan is either refinanced or paid off, the remaining balance points being amortized on the old loan (the one being refinanced) can be taken as an itemized deduction.

Special Situations

This section describes certain special situations that may affect your deduction of points.

Original issue discount. If you do not qualify to either deduct the points in the year paid or deduct them ratably over the life of the loan, or if you choose not to use either of these methods, the points reduce the issue price of the loan. This reduction results in original issue discount, which is discussed in chapter 4 of Publication 535.

Amounts charged for services. Amounts charged by the lender for specific services connected to the loan are not interest. Examples of these charges are:

- Appraisal fees,
- Notary fees, and
- Preparation costs for the mortgage note or deed of trust.

You cannot deduct these amounts as points either in the year paid or over the life of the mortgage.

Points paid by the seller. The term "points" includes loan placement fees that the seller pays to the lender to arrange financing for the buyer.

Treatment by seller. The seller cannot deduct these fees as interest. But they are a selling expense that reduces the amount realized by the seller. See chapter 15 for information on selling your home.

Treatment by buyer. The buyer reduces the basis of the home by the amount of the seller-paid points and treats the points as if he or she had paid them. If all the tests under *Deduction Allowed in Year Paid*, earlier, are met, the buyer can deduct the points in the year paid. If any of those tests are not met, the buyer deducts the points over the life of the loan. For information about basis, see chapter 13.

Funds provided are less than points. If you meet all the tests in *Deduction Allowed in Year Paid*, earlier, except that the funds you provided were less than the points charged to you (test (6)), you can deduct the points in the year paid, up to the amount of funds you provided. In addition, you can deduct any points paid by the seller.

Example 1. When you took out a $100,000 mortgage loan to buy your home in December, you were charged one point ($1,000). You meet all the tests for deducting points in the year paid, except the only funds you provided were a $750 down payment. Of the $1,000 charged for points, you can deduct $750 in the year paid. You spread the remaining $250 over the life of the mortgage.

Example 2. The facts are the same as in *Example 1*, except that the person who sold you your home also paid one point ($1,000) to help you get your mortgage. In the year paid, you can deduct $1,750 ($750 of the amount you were charged plus the $1,000 paid by the seller). You spread the remaining $250 over the life of the mortgage. You must reduce the basis of your home by the $1,000 paid by the seller.

Excess points. If you meet all the tests in *Deduction Allowed in Year Paid*, earlier, except that the points paid were more than generally paid in your area (test (3)), you deduct in the year paid only the points that are generally charged. You must spread any additional points over the life of the mortgage.

Mortgage ending early. If you spread your deduction for points over the life of the mortgage, you can deduct any remaining balance in the year the mortgage ends. However, if you refinance the mortgage with the same lender, you cannot deduct any remaining balance of spread points. Instead, deduct the remaining balance over the term of the new loan.

A mortgage may end early due to a prepayment, refinancing, foreclosure, or similar event.

Example. Dan paid $3,000 in points in 2003 that he had to spread out over the 15-year life of the mortgage. He deducts $200 points per year. Through 2013, Dan has deducted $2,200 of the points.

Dan prepaid his mortgage in full in 2014. He can deduct the remaining $800 of points in 2014.

Limits on deduction. You cannot fully deduct points paid on a mortgage unless the mortgage fits into one of the categories listed earlier under *Fully deductible interest*. See Publication 936 for details.

Mortgage Insurance Premiums

Form 1098, Mortgage Interest Statement

If you paid $600 or more of mortgage interest (including certain points and mortgage insurance premiums) during the year on any one mortgage, you generally will receive a Form 1098 or a similar statement from the mortgage holder. You will receive the statement if you pay interest to a person (including a financial institution or a cooperative housing corporation) in the course of that person's trade or business. A governmental unit is a person for purposes of furnishing the statement.

The statement for each year should be sent to you by January 31 of the following year. A copy of this form will also be sent to the IRS.

The statement will show the total interest you paid during the year, any mortgage insurance premiums you paid, and if you purchased a main home during the year, it also will show the deductible points paid during the year, including seller-paid points. However, it should not show any interest that was paid for you by a government agency.

As a general rule, Form 1098 will include only points that you can fully deduct in the year paid. However, certain points not included on Form 1098 also may be deductible, either in the year paid or over the life of the loan. See *Points*, earlier, to determine whether you can deduct points not shown on Form 1098.

Prepaid interest on Form 1098. If you prepaid interest in 2014 that accrued in full by January 15, 2015, this prepaid interest may be included in box 1 of Form 1098. However, you cannot deduct the prepaid amount for January 2015 in 2014. (See *Prepaid interest*, earlier.) You will have to figure the interest that accrued for 2015 and subtract it from the amount in box 1. You will include the interest for January 2015 with the other interest you pay for 2015. See *How To Report*, later.

Refunded interest. If you received a refund of mortgage interest you overpaid in an earlier year, you generally will receive a Form 1098 showing the refund in box 3. See *Refunds of interest*, earlier.

Mortgage insurance premiums. The amount of mortgage insurance premiums you paid during 2014 may be shown in box 4 of Form 1098. See *Mortgage Insurance Premiums*, earlier.

Investment Interest

This section discusses interest expenses you may be able to deduct as an investor.

If you borrow money to buy property you hold for investment, the interest you pay is investment interest. You can deduct investment interest subject to the limit discussed later. However, you cannot deduct interest you incurred to produce tax-exempt income. Nor can you deduct interest expenses on straddles.

Investment interest does not include any qualified home mortgage interest or any interest taken into account in computing income or loss from a passive activity.

Investment Property

Property held for investment includes property that produces interest, dividends, annuities, or royalties not derived in the ordinary course of a trade or business. It also includes property that produces gain or loss (not derived in the ordinary course of a trade or business) from the sale or trade of property producing these types of income or held for investment (other than an interest in a passive activity). Investment property also includes an interest in a trade or business activity in which you did not materially participate (other than a passive activity).

Partners, shareholders, and beneficiaries. To determine your investment interest, combine your share of investment interest from a partnership, S corporation, estate, or trust with your other investment interest.

Allocation of Interest Expense

If you borrow money for business or personal purposes as well as for investment, you must allocate the debt among those purposes. Only the interest expense on the part of the debt used for investment purposes is treated as investment interest. The allocation is not affected by the use of property that secures the debt.

Limit on Deduction

Generally, your deduction for investment interest expense is limited to the amount of your net investment income.

You can carry over the amount of investment interest that you could not deduct because of this limit to the next tax year. The interest carried over is treated as investment interest paid or accrued in that next year.

You can carry over disallowed investment interest to the next tax year even if it is more than your taxable income in the year the interest was paid or accrued.

Net Investment Income

Determine the amount of your net investment income by subtracting your investment expenses (other than interest expense) from your investment income.

Investment income. This generally includes your gross income from property held for investment (such as interest, dividends, annuities, and royalties). Investment income does not include Alaska Permanent Fund dividends. It also does not include qualified dividends or net capital gain unless you choose to include them.

Choosing to include qualified dividends. Investment income generally does not include qualified dividends, discussed in chapter 8. However, you can choose to include all or part of your qualified dividends in investment income.

You make this choice by completing Form 4952, line 4g, according to its instructions.

If you choose to include any amount of your qualified dividends in investment income, you must reduce your qualified dividends that are eligible for the lower capital gains tax rates by the same amount.

Choosing to include net capital gain. Investment income generally does not include net capital gain from disposing of investment property (including capital gain distributions from mutual funds). However, you can choose to include all or part of your net capital gain in investment income.

You make this choice by completing Form 4952, line 4g, according to its instructions.

If you choose to include any amount of your net capital gain in investment income, you must reduce your net capital gain that is eligible for the lower capital gains tax rates by the same amount.

> **Tip**
>
> *Before making either choice, consider the overall effect on your tax liability. Compare your tax if you make one or both of these choices with your tax if you do not.*

EXPLANATION

Qualified dividends and long-term capital gains are not treated as "investment income" for purposes of determining the limitation on the deductibility of investment interest expense, unless you elect to treat the dividends or long-term capital gains as not eligible for the favorable capital gains rates.

TAXPLANNER

While it may be possible to borrow in order to acquire dividend-paying stocks, it will be necessary to analyze your entire portfolio to determine if the interest expense deduction will be limited due to insufficient investment income from other sources.

Explanation

A deduction is allowed for interest paid on indebtedness incurred to purchase or hold investment property. Investment property includes any property producing interest, dividends, annuities, royalties, or certain gains.

Example

Suppose you borrow money to purchase both taxable securities and tax-free investments (such as state municipal bonds). The interest income from the tax-free bonds is not taxable. Accordingly, the interest expense paid on the loan allocable to the tax-free bonds is not deductible. And the interest income from the tax-free bonds, since it is not taxable, does not count as investment income for purposes of calculating the limitation.

Explanation

The amount of investment interest that may be deducted is limited to the amount of investment income less allowable expenses, other than interest, that are directly connected with the production of investment income. Investment income does not include qualified dividends or long-term capital gains unless you make an election to treat them as not eligible for the favorable capital gains rates. The allowable expenses include those expenses that are deducted on your tax return, after the 2% of adjusted gross income limitation on miscellaneous deductions. (For more information, see chapter 29, *Miscellaneous deductions*.)

If the investment interest paid exceeds investment income, the excess may be carried forward to offset investment income in future years.

No deduction is allowed for interest paid on indebtedness incurred to hold obligations that are exempt from federal taxation.

Example 1

In 2014, Lorraine borrows $83,000 to purchase White Company securities. During the same year, she earns $30,000 of net investment income and incurs $10,000 of interest expense on her loan. Lorraine can deduct the $10,000 interest expense as investment interest on Schedule A (Form 1040).

Example 2

George and Lisa Salazar, who file a joint return, have the following income and deductions in 2014:

Salary	$30,000
Interest income from a state municipal bond	500
Interest income	20,000
Short-term capital gain	5,000
Adjusted gross income	$55,000
Investment advisory fees	$2,000
Investment interest expense	$31,000

Their deduction for investment interest is figured as follows:

Investment income	$25,000
Direct investment expense ($2,000 – 2% of $55,000)	(900)
Net investment income ($25,000 – $900)	$24,100
Investment interest deduction	$24,100

The $6,900 ($31,000 – $24,100) of investment interest expense that is not allowed as a deduction in 2014 may be carried forward to 2015.

TAXALERT

Net long-term capital gains from the disposition of investment property and qualified dividends are not treated as investment income for purposes of computing the limitation on investment interest deductions. You may, however, elect to include net long-term capital gain and qualified dividend amounts in investment income for this purpose if you also reduce by the same amount the net long-term capital gain and qualified dividends that are eligible for the special maximum capital gains rates. Short-term capital gains may still be included in the computation of investment income because they are taxable at ordinary income tax rates. For an additional discussion of reporting gains and losses, see chapter 16, *Reporting gains and losses*.

Explanation

The 2% limitation on miscellaneous deductions applies first to deductions other than investment expenses.

Example

In Example 2, if George and Lisa Salazar also had tax preparation fees of $500, the $1,100 (2% limitation) would reduce this amount first. The remainder, $600, would then reduce the investment expense, leaving $1,400 to be subtracted from investment income.

Explanation

Deduct interest on margin accounts on Schedule A (Form 1040) for the year in which you paid it. Interest on these accounts is considered paid when the broker is paid or when the interest becomes available to the broker through your account.

Deduct interest on money borrowed to buy a money market certificate on Schedule A (Form 1040). You must include the total interest you earn on the certificate in your income.

Investment income of child reported on parent's return. Investment income includes the part of your child's interest and dividend income that you choose to report on your return. If the child does not have qualified dividends, Alaska Permanent Fund dividends, or capital gain distributions, this is the amount on line 6 of Form 8814, Parents' Election To Report Child's Interest and Dividends.

Child's qualified dividends. If part of the amount you report is your child's qualified dividends, that part (which is reported on Form 1040, line 9b) generally does not count as investment income. However, you can choose to include all or part of it in investment income, as explained under *Choosing to include qualified dividends*, earlier.

Your investment income also includes the amount on Form 8814, line 12 (or, if applicable, the reduced amount figured next under *Child's Alaska Permanent Fund dividends*).

Child's Alaska Permanent Fund dividends. If part of the amount you report is your child's Alaska Permanent Fund dividends, that part does not count as investment income. To figure the amount of your child's income that you can consider your investment income, start with the amount on Form 8814, line 6. Multiply that amount by a percentage that is equal to the Alaska Permanent Fund dividends divided by the total amount on Form 8814, line 4. Subtract the result from the amount on Form 8814, line 12.

Child's capital gain distributions. If part of the amount you report is your child's capital gain distributions, that part (which is reported on Schedule D, line 13, or Form 1040, line 13) generally does not count as investment income. However, you can choose to include all or part of it in investment income, as explained in *Choosing to include net capital gain*, earlier.

Your investment income also includes the amount on Form 8814, line 12 (or, if applicable, the reduced amount figured under *Child's Alaska Permanent Fund dividends*, earlier).

Investment expenses. Investment expenses are your allowed deductions (other than interest expense) directly connected with the production of investment income. Investment expenses that are included as a miscellaneous itemized deduction on Schedule A (Form 1040) are allowable deductions after applying the 2% limit that applies to miscellaneous itemized deductions. Use the smaller of:

- The investment expenses included on Schedule A (Form 1040), line 23, or
- The amount on Schedule A, line 27.

Losses from passive activities. Income or expenses that you used in computing income or loss from a passive activity are not included in determining your investment income or investment expenses (including investment interest expense). See Publication 925, Passive Activity and At-Risk Rules, for information about passive activities.

Form 4952
Use Form 4952, Investment Interest Expense Deduction, to figure your deduction for investment interest.

Table 24-1. **Where To Deduct Your Interest Expense**

IF you have ...	THEN deduct it on ...	AND for more information go to ...
deductible student loan interest	Form 1040, line 33, or Form 1040A, line 18	Publication 970.
deductible home mortgage interest and points reported on Form 1098	Schedule A (Form 1040), line 10	Publication 936.
deductible home mortgage interest not reported on Form 1098	Schedule A (Form 1040), line 11	Publication 936.
deductible points not reported on Form 1098	Schedule A (Form 1040), line 12	Publication 936.
Text intentionally omitted.	*Text intentionally omitted.*	*Text intentionally omitted.*
deductible investment interest (other than incurred to produce rents or royalties)	Schedule A (Form 1040), line 14	Publication 550.
deductible business interest (non-farm)	Schedule C or C-EZ (Form 1040)	Publication 535.
deductible farm business interest	Schedule F (Form 1040)	Publications 225 and 535.
deductible interest incurred to produce rents or royalties	Schedule E (Form 1040)	Publications 527 and 535.
personal interest	not deductible.	

Exception to use of Form 4952. You do not have to complete Form 4952 or attach it to your return if you meet all of the following tests.

- Your investment interest expense is not more than your investment income from interest and ordinary dividends minus any qualified dividends.
- You do not have any other deductible investment expenses.
- You have no carryover of investment interest expense from 2013.

If you meet all of these tests, you can deduct all of your investment interest.

More Information

For more information on investment interest, see *Interest Expenses* in chapter 3 of Publication 550.

Items You Cannot Deduct

Some interest payments are not deductible. Certain expenses similar to interest also are not deductible. Nondeductible expenses include the following items.

- Personal interest (discussed later).
- Service charges (however, see *Other Expenses (Line 23)* in chapter 29).
- Annual fees for credit cards.
- Loan fees.
- Credit investigation fees.
- Interest to purchase or carry tax-exempt securities.

Tip

You may be able to deduct interest you pay on a qualified student loan. For details, see Publication 970, Tax Benefits for Education.

EXPLANATION

While the general rule is that interest paid on a debt incurred to purchase or carry tax-exempt obligations is not deductible, this does not mean that if you hold tax-exempt obligations, all interest expense deductions are disallowed. The courts have consistently held that there must be a sufficiently direct relationship between incurring the debt and the carrying of the tax-exempt obligation before the interest is disallowed. However, if you have significant interest expense and municipal bond income, you may lose your investment interest deductions.

The IRS has ruled that a direct relationship between debt and the purchase of tax-exempt obligations exists when the debt proceeds are used for, and are directly traceable to, the purchase of tax-exempts. Additionally, a direct relationship between debt and carrying tax-exempt obligations exists when tax-exempt obligations are used as collateral for a loan.

If only part of a debt you have is related to holding tax-exempt obligations, only that part of the interest paid is disallowed.

Example

Barry and Tricia borrow $10,000 from a bank and invest $2,500 of the proceeds in tax-exempt obligations. In this case, 25% ($2,500 × $10,000) of the interest they pay on the loan is directly related to their ownership of the tax-exempt investment and is not deductible as investment interest.

ey.com/EYTaxGuide

Penalties. You cannot deduct fines and penalties paid to a government for violations of law, regardless of their nature.

Personal Interest

Personal interest is not deductible. Personal interest is any interest that is not home mortgage interest, investment interest, business interest, or other deductible interest. It includes the following items.

- Interest on car loans (unless you use the car for business).
- Interest on federal, state, or local income tax.
- Finance charges on credit cards, retail installment contracts, and revolving charge accounts incurred for personal expenses.
- Late payment charges by a public utility.

Example 2
You are considering purchasing a new house and a new car within a relatively short time period. You may want to decrease your down payment on the house so that there will be extra cash available for a down payment on the car. By making a larger down payment on the car, your nondeductible interest, the interest paid on the car loan, will be less. Conversely, by decreasing your down payment on the house, you gain a tax benefit in the form of higher mortgage interest deductions.

EXPLANATION

Student loan interest deduction. You can claim a deduction for interest paid on qualified education loans that include indebtedness incurred for your benefit or the benefit of your spouse, or any dependent at the time the indebtedness is incurred. Qualified loans also include refinancings or consolidations of the original loans. You can claim this deduction whether or not you itemize your deductions.

The deduction is allowed only for interest paid on a qualified education loan. No deduction is allowed for individuals claimed as dependents on another taxpayer's return for the tax year. The maximum deduction is $2,500 in 2014.

The deduction is phased out for individual single taxpayers with modified adjusted gross income (AGI) in 2014 of $65,000–$80,000 and for couples filing jointly with modified AGI of $130,000–$160,000.

TAXSAVER

What loans cannot include in order to qualify. Education loans include loans covering both tuition and room and board. However, loans cannot include educational expenses that are paid through amounts from an employer educational assistance program or from amounts withdrawn from a Coverdell education savings account or qualified tuition programs. It is unclear how students or the IRS will be able to separate these expenses from the total loans received and payments made on those loans.

The U.S. Treasury is authorized to require lenders to report to borrowers the amount that constitutes deductible student loan interest. The government has also devised a method for borrowers to certify to lenders that loan proceeds are being used to pay for qualified educational expenses.

As with the education tax credits, this deduction is another factor to consider in determining whether or not a working student should be claimed as a dependent. Parents with income above the income thresholds cannot claim this deduction.

For further information about claiming the student loan interest deduction, see student loan interest deduction in chapter 19, *Education-related adjustments*.

Explanation
Interest you pay on loans acquired to purchase life insurance is also personal interest and generally is not deductible under current law. In addition, when a taxpayer borrows against his or her 401(k) plan account, the interest paid back to the plan is also generally not deductible.

TAXPLANNER

If you have loans outstanding for personal purposes, consider paying off these loans and substituting a different form of indebtedness.

Example
You have $5,000 of indebtedness on your credit card account. The funds were used for various personal purposes, and the interest is not deductible. You also have a $5,000 certificate of deposit (CD) that matures in 2014. Use the $5,000 from the maturity of the CD to pay off the credit card indebtedness. If you wish, you may borrow new funds to invest in a new CD. The interest on the new loan will be investment interest. The rules for deducting investment interest expense are more lenient than those for personal interest. Be sure to calculate the amount you would earn after taxes on the investment.

Allocation of Interest

If you use the proceeds of a loan for more than one purpose (for example, personal and business), you must allocate the interest on the loan to each use. However, you do not have to allocate home mortgage interest if it is fully deductible, regardless of how the funds are used.

You allocate interest (other than fully deductible home mortgage interest) on a loan in the same way as the loan itself is allocated. You do this by tracing disbursements of the debt proceeds to specific uses. For details on how to do this, see chapter 4 of Publication 535.

EXPLANATION

There are five types of interest expense, each of which has different limitations on deductibility:

1. Personal interest is not deductible (except for a limited amount of student loan interest described earlier in this chapter). Personal interest generally includes interest on credit card debts and on automobile loans. If you have to incur debt, try to make the debt related to either trade or business interest, investment interest, passive activity interest, or qualified residence interest.
2. Trade or business interest is fully deductible. Generally, it is interest on debt that relates to your trade or business. However, trade or business interest is not deductible if it is in connection with the trade or business of performing services as an employee.
3. Investment interest deductions may be limited because the deduction cannot exceed your net investment income for the taxable year. Any excess investment interest that is not deductible in the taxable year may be deducted in following years.
4. Passive activity interest is interest that is used to offset passive activity income. Generally, a passive activity is any interest in a real estate or other activity in which you do not materially participate. For tax purposes, you are considered a material participant if you are involved in the operations of the activity on a regular, continuous, and substantial basis. For additional discussion, see chapter 12, *Other income*.
5. Interest on a debt secured by a qualified residence is deductible within the limitations discussed earlier in this chapter.

TAXSAVER

When interest on debt used for investment exceeds investment income, the remaining investment interest may be deducted if it is qualified residence interest.

Example

In 2014, you purchase corporate bonds for $200,000, using a 6% home equity loan. Your investment income is $5,000.

Interest on your home equity loan	$12,000
Interest on portion of loan up to $100,000	(6,000)
Balance investment interest expense	$6,000
Deductible investment interest equal to investment income	(5,000)
Investment interest expense carried over to 2015	$1,000

TAXSAVER

Interest on debt used for a passive activity is subject to the same deduction rules as other passive activity expenses.

Example 1

Phil borrowed money to purchase a one-fourth interest in a partnership that manages an apartment building. In 2014, Phil paid $16,000 interest on the loan. His share of income and expenses was $60,000 and $40,000, respectively. Phil's passive income is $4,000 ($60,000 – $40,000 – $16,000). If his share of the partnership's expenses had been $50,000 instead of $40,000, Phil's $16,000 in interest expense would have resulted in a passive loss of $6,000 ($60,000 – $50,000 – $16,000). This loss can be carried over to future years and deducted in the year in which there is additional passive income or when the investment is sold.

Example 2

Karen Pan has the following income and expenses in 2014:

Wages	$79,000
Interest	18,000
Short-term capital gain from sale of stock	2,000
Long-term capital gain taxed at 15%	1,000
Adjusted gross income (AGI)	$100,000
Investment interest expense	$21,000
Investment fees	$2,500
Unreimbursed employee expenses	$1,000

Karen's total miscellaneous itemized deductions are $3,500 ($2,500 + $1,000). After considering the 2% floor limitation, her allowable miscellaneous itemized deductions are $1,500 [$3,500 − (2% × $100,000 AGI)]. Therefore, Karen's net investment income is $18,500 [($18,000 + $2,000) − $1,500]. Because the long-term capital gain is taxed at 15%, it is not considered investment income. Karen could elect to treat the gain as ordinary income and would then be allowed to treat the $1,000 as investment income. Note that, in computing the allowable deductions, the noninvestment expenses were disallowed before the investment expenses.

EXPLANATION

The proceeds of loans, other than qualified mortgage loans, which were used for mixed purposes must be allocated to each applicable category.

Example

Joan borrows $100,000 on September 1, 2014, at an interest rate of 12% and deposits the funds in one checking account. Joan uses the money to purchase investment securities ($30,000 on September 1), a personal automobile ($30,000 on October 1), and equipment for her business ($40,000 on November 1). Joan pays interest of $1,000 at the end of each month.

Under the allocation rules, the interest on the loan is considered investment interest unless the proceeds are traceable to other purposes. The allocation is made as follows:

	Investment interest		Personal interest		Business interest	
September	100%	$1,000	–		–	
October	70%	700	30%	$300	–	
November	30%	300	30%	300	40%	$400
December	30%	300	30%	300	40%	400
Total		$2,300		$900		$800

When repayments of the debt are made, the repayment amounts are allocated first to nondeductible personal expenditures, then to investment and passive activity expenditures, and then to business expenditures.

TAXSAVER

The accounting for interest expense on loans used for mixed purposes is extremely complex.

To simplify your tax records, establish separate loan and bank accounts for each category of expenditure.

How To Report

You must file Form 1040 to deduct any home mortgage interest expense on your tax return. Where you deduct your interest expense generally depends on how you use the loan proceeds. See Table 24-1 for a summary of where to deduct your interest expense.

Home mortgage interest and points. Deduct the home mortgage interest and points reported to you on Form 1098 on Schedule A (Form 1040), line 10. If you paid more deductible interest to the financial institution than the amount shown on Form 1098, show the larger deductible amount on line 10. Attach a statement explaining the difference and print "See attached" next to line 10.

Deduct home mortgage interest that was not reported to you on Form 1098 on Schedule A (Form 1040), line 11. If you paid home mortgage interest to the person from whom you bought your home, show that person's name, address, and taxpayer identification number (TIN) on the dotted lines next to line 11. The seller must give you this number and you must give the seller your TIN. A Form W-9, Request for Taxpayer Identification Number and Certification, can be used for this purpose. Failure to meet any of these requirements may result in a $50 penalty for each failure. The TIN can be either a social security number, an individual taxpayer identification number (issued by the Internal Revenue Service), or an employer identification number. See *Social Security Number (SSN)* in chapter 1 for more information about TINs.

If you can take a deduction for points that were not reported to you on Form 1098, deduct those points on Schedule A (Form 1040), line 12.

Deduct mortgage insurance premiums on Schedule A (Form 1040), line 13.

More than one borrower. If you and at least one other person (other than your spouse if you file a joint return) were liable for and paid interest on a mortgage that was for your home, and the other person received a Form 1098 showing the interest that was paid during the year, attach a statement to your return explaining this. Show how much of the interest each of you paid, and give the name and address of the person who received the form. Deduct your share of the interest on Schedule A (Form 1040), line 11, and print "See attached" next to the line. Also, deduct your share of any qualified mortgage insurance premiums on Schedule A (Form 1040), line 13.

Similarly, if you are the payer of record on a mortgage on which there are other borrowers entitled to a deduction for the interest shown on the Form 1098 you received, deduct only your share of the interest on Schedule A (Form 1040), line 10. You should let each of the other borrowers know what his or her share is.

Mortgage proceeds used for business or investment. If your home mortgage interest deduction is limited, but all or part of the mortgage proceeds were used for business, investment, or other deductible activities, see Table 24-1. It shows where to deduct the part of your excess interest that is for those activities.

Investment interest. Deduct investment interest, subject to certain limits discussed in Publication 550, on Schedule A (Form 1040), line 14.

Amortization of bond premium. There are various ways to treat the premium you pay to buy taxable bonds. See *Bond Premium Amortization* in Publication 550.

Income-producing rental or royalty interest. Deduct interest on a loan for income-producing rental or royalty property that is not used in your business in Part I of Schedule E (Form 1040).

Example. You rent out part of your home and borrow money to make repairs. You can deduct only the interest payment for the rented part in Part I of Schedule E (Form 1040). Deduct the rest of the interest payment on Schedule A (Form 1040) if it is deductible home mortgage interest.

Chapter 25
Contributions

ey.com/EYTaxGuide

Introduction

Americans give billions of dollars to charity each year. One explanation for that generosity may be that the federal government encourages charitable giving. It has long been the policy of the government to allow individuals tax deductions for charitable contributions they make. In effect, by allowing a deduction that reduces your taxable income (and therefore your tax), Uncle Sam is contributing part of every dollar you give to charity.

Even so, there are lots of rules governing charitable contributions, and it's important that you know them. This chapter tells you how to maximize your allowable charitable deductions and minimize your taxes. You'll learn why, for example, you might want to consider giving shares of stock instead of cash to your favorite charity. Just as important, the chapter tells you how to document your contributions.

In general, the amount you can deduct for charitable contributions cannot be more than 50% of your adjusted gross income (AGI). Your deduction may be further limited to 30% or even 20% of your AGI, depending on the type of property you give and the type of organization you give it to. If your total contributions for the year are 20% or less of your AGI, these limits do not apply to you. This chapter discusses these limits.

After applying the specific limitations on charitable contributions described in the paragraph above, your deductible contributions may be further reduced by additional "overall" limitation on a specific group of itemized deductions that include charitable contributions. The total of this group of itemized deductions must be reduced by 3% of the amount of your AGI in excess of $254,200 for individual filers, $279,650 for heads of households, $305,050 if married filing jointly or a surviving spouse, and $152,520 if married filing separately. (The threshold amounts are indexed annually for inflation.) However, no more than 80% of the otherwise allowable deductions are phased out. See chapter 30, *Limit on Itemized Deductions*, for more information.

Tax Breaks and Deductions You Can Use Checklist

Contributions of property. If you have capital gain property that you've held for more than a year, and you want to make a charitable contribution, you're usually better off donating that property rather than cash. That's because you get a market value deduction for capital gain property and you don't have to recognize any gain as income. You can always use the cash to buy back the property with a higher basis. See *Giving Property That Has Increased in Value,* later in this chapter.

Donating a used car to charity. If you donate a used car to charity, you should remember that the amount of the deduction you will be allowed to claim may be subject to special limitations. For cars worth over $500, the deduction will be the amount for which the charity actually sells the car, if it sells the car without materially improving it or using it in its operations. So in many cases, you won't know the amount of your deduction until the charity has sold the car and reported the sale proceeds to you.

Contributions of time. You can't deduct the value of the time you contribute to charity but you can deduct any out-of-pocket expenses you incurred as a result of your volunteering, such as mileage or the cost of uniforms. See *Out-of-Pocket Expenses in Giving Services,* later in this chapter.

Substantiating your charitable contributions. Properly substantiating charitable contributions is critical–the IRS can, and will, disallow your

What's New

<u>**Expired provisions.**</u> <u>The following provisions have expired and will not apply for 2014:</u>
- <u>The special 50% contribution limit for qualified conservation contributions.</u>
- <u>The special 100% contribution limit for qualified conservation contributions made by a qualified farmer or rancher.</u>
- <u>The adjustment to an S corporation shareholder's stock basis for charitable contributions of property.</u>
- <u>The exclusion from income of qualified charitable distributions made from IRA accounts.</u>

TAXALERT

The following tax breaks expired at the end of 2013 and are not available for 2014. However, as of the time this book was published in October 2014, Congress had been considering legislation that would extend these provision limits at least through 2014, but no such extension had yet been passed. For updated information on this and any other tax law changes that occur after this book was published, see our website, *ey.com/EYTaxGuide*.

Contributions of real property made for conservation purposes. Through the end of 2013, the charitable deduction limit for qualified conservation contributions (including partial interests in real estate) was 50% (100% for qualified farmers or ranchers) of the excess of the taxpayer's adjusted gross income (AGI) over the amount of all other allowable charitable contributions. Taxpayers could also carry over any qualified conservation contributions that exceeded the applicable limitation for up to 15 years, rather than the 5-year carryover period that generally applies to other types of charitable contributions.

These higher deduction limits and longer carryover periods expired at the end of 2013. Beginning in 2014, the limit for qualified conservation contributions dropped to 30% and the carryover period was reduced to 5 years. See the section on *Qualified Conservation Contribution*, later in this chapter, for more information.

<u>**Adjustment to S corporation shareholder's stock basis for contributions of property.**</u> If an S corporation contributes money or other property to a charity, each shareholder takes into account their pro rata share of the contribution for figuring their own income tax liability. Through the end of 2013, an S corporation shareholder's stock basis was reduced by a pro rata share of the adjusted basis of appreciated property donated by the corporation to charity. This provision expired at the end of 2013. Beginning in 2014, when an S corporation makes a charitable contribution of appreciated property that qualifies for a fair market value deduction, the shareholder's basis in the S corporation stock will be reduced by the full fair market value of the deduction. Consequently, when the S corporation shareholder ultimately sells shares, the shareholder will effectively pay tax on the appreciated value of the property that had been previously contributed to charity. This result differs from what the shareholder would have realized had he or she personally donated that appreciated property. In that case, the shareholder would not recognize the gain attributable to the appreciation.

Tax-free distributions from IRAs for charity. Through the end of 2013, an IRA owner age 70½ or older could take up to $100,000 in distributions from his or her IRA accounts (other than an SEP or SIMPLE IRA), contribute them to charity through a direct transfer received from the IRA trustee, and not recognize any income. Therefore, if all the requirements were met, a "Qualified Charitable Distribution" was nontaxable; however, one could not also claim a charitable contribution deduction for it. This exclusion expired at the end of 2013 and is not available for 2014. See *Qualified charitable distributions (QCDs)* in chapter 17, *Individual retirement arrangements (IRAs)*.

This chapter explains how to claim a deduction for your charitable contributions. It discusses the following topics.
- The types of organizations to which you can make deductible charitable contributions.
- The types of contributions you can deduct.
- How much you can deduct.
- What records you must keep.
- How to report your charitable contributions.

A charitable contribution is a donation or gift to, or for the use of, a qualified organization. It is voluntary and is made without getting, or expecting to get, anything of equal value.

Form 1040 required. To deduct a charitable contribution, you must file Form 1040 and itemize deductions on Schedule A. The amount of your deduction may be limited if certain rules and limits explained in this chapter apply to you. The limits are explained in detail in Publication 526.

Useful Items

You may want to see:

Publication
- □ **526** Charitable Contributions
- □ **561** Determining the Value of Donated Property

Form (and Instructions)
- □ **Schedule A** (Form 1040) Itemized Deductions
- □ **8283** Noncash Charitable Contributions

Organizations That Qualify To Receive Deductible Contributions

You can deduct your contributions only if you make them to a qualified organization. Most organizations other than churches and governments must apply to the IRS to become a qualified organization.

How to check whether an organization can receive deductible charitable contributions. You can ask any organization whether it is a qualified organization, and most will be able to tell you. Or go to IRS.gov. Click on "Tools" and then on "Exempt Organizations Select Check" (*www.irs.gov/Charities-&-Non-Profits/Exempt-Organizations-Select-Check*). This online tool will enable you to search for qualified organizations. You can also call the IRS to find out if an organization is qualified. Call 1-877-829-5500. People who are deaf, hard of hearing, or have a speech disability and who have access to TTY/TDD equipment can call 1-800-829-4059. Deaf or hard of hearing individuals can also contact the IRS through relay services such as the Federal Relay Service at *www.gsa.gov/fedrelay*.

Types of Qualified Organizations

Generally, only the following types of organizations can be qualified organizations.

1. A community chest, corporation, trust, fund, or foundation organized or created in or under the laws of the United States, any state, the District of Columbia, or any possession of the United States (including Puerto Rico). It must, however, be organized and operated only for charitable, religious, scientific, literary, or educational purposes, or for the prevention of cruelty to children or animals. Certain organizations that foster national or international amateur sports competition also qualify.

2. War veterans' organizations, including posts, auxiliaries, trusts, or foundations, organized in the United States or any of its possessions (including Puerto Rico).

3. Domestic fraternal societies, orders, and associations operating under the lodge system. (Your contribution to this type of organization is deductible only if it is to be used solely for charitable, religious, scientific, literary, or educational purposes, or for the prevention of cruelty to children or animals.)

4. Certain nonprofit cemetery companies or corporations. (Your contribution to this type of organization is not deductible if it can be used for the care of a specific lot or mausoleum crypt.)

5. The United States or any state, the District of Columbia, a U.S. possession (including Puerto Rico), a political subdivision of a state or U.S. possession, or an Indian tribal government or any of its subdivisions that perform substantial government functions. (Your contribution to this type of organization is only deductible if it is to be used solely for public purposes.)

EXAMPLE

Contributions to the following U.S. and political subdivisions have been allowed:
- Contributions to the National Park Foundation
- Money donated to a state by an individual to defray expenses of hosting a governor's conference
- Contributions to a state for a parade incidental to a presidential inauguration

The IRS has ruled that the following are *not deductible* as contributions:
- Payments made to a state hospital for the purpose of reimbursing the state for the care of a person confined in the hospital do not constitute contributions made to a state for exclusively public purposes.
- The amount spent by a tenant for additions or improvements to government-owned housing is not deductible as a charitable contribution. Such amounts represent a nondeductible personal, living, or family expense.

---

deduction if you don't have the necessary documentation. All contributions must be substantiated, but contributions of $250 or more require a written receipt from the charity that meets specific requirements. A deduction for a cash contribution of any amount to charity will not be allowed unless the donor has a bank record or a receipt or a written communication from the charitable organization that shows the name of the charity, as well as the date and the amount of the contribution. Maintaining your own written log of cash contributions will no longer be sufficient substantiation. If you donate property valued at more than $500, you must file Form 8283.

Examples. The following list gives some examples of qualified organizations.

- Churches, a convention or association of churches, temples, synagogues, mosques, and other religious organizations.
- Most nonprofit charitable organizations such as the American Red Cross and the United Way.
- Most nonprofit educational organizations, including the Boy Scouts of America, Girl Scouts of America, colleges, and museums. This also includes nonprofit daycare centers that provide childcare to the general public if substantially all the childcare is provided to enable parents and guardians to be gainfully employed. However, if your contribution is a substitute for tuition or other enrollment fee, it is not deductible as a charitable contribution, as explained later under *Contributions You Cannot Deduct*.
- Nonprofit hospitals and medical research organizations.
- Utility company emergency energy programs, if the utility company is an agent for a charitable organization that assists individuals with emergency energy needs.
- Nonprofit volunteer fire companies.
- Nonprofit organizations that develop and maintain public parks and recreation facilities.
- Civil defense organizations.

Certain foreign charitable organizations. Under income tax treaties with Canada, Israel, and Mexico, you may be able to deduct contributions to certain Canadian, Israeli, or Mexican charitable organizations. Generally, you must have income from sources in that country. For additional information on the deduction of contributions to Canadian charities, see Publication 597, Information on the United States–Canada Income Tax Treaty. If you need more information on how to figure your contribution to Mexican and Israeli charities, see Publication 526.

EXPLANATION

Any organization can tell you if it is a qualified organization.

Generally, charitable contributions must be made to organizations to be deductible. However, the courts have upheld contributions made to certain individuals on the grounds that the contribution was made to him or her as an agent for the organization. Consider the following cases in which deductions were allowed:

- An individual established a scholarship fund consisting of a personal checking account. Recipients were picked by school principals on the basis of need and scholastic merit. Each check was signed by the donor and made payable jointly to the scholar and the school. The donor was not involved in the selection process.
- A host family acting as a caretaker for an individual under a Department of Public Welfare/Medical Assistance Program is entitled to deduct as a charitable contribution any unreimbursed out-of-pocket expenses incurred in supporting a participant.
- A taxpayer directed his bank to send a check to a specifically named missionary. He instructed the bank to inform the missionary that the check was for Presbyterian mission work. The Tax Court held that this was really a contribution to the church through the missionary as an agent for the church.

Exception

The Supreme Court ruled that funds transferred by parents directly to their sons while they served as unpaid missionaries were not charitable contributions "for the use of" the church, even though the funds were requested by the church.

Contributions You Can Deduct

Generally, you can deduct contributions of money or property you make to, or for the use of, a qualified organization. A contribution is "for the use of" a qualified organization when it is held in a legally enforceable trust for the qualified organization or in a similar legal arrangement. The contributions must be made to a qualified organization and not set aside for use by a specific person.

If you give property to a qualified organization, you generally can deduct the fair market value of the property at the time of the contribution. See *Contributions of Property*, later in this chapter.

Your deduction for charitable contributions generally cannot be more than 50% of your adjusted gross income (AGI), but in some cases 20% and 30% limits may apply. See *Limits on Deductions*, later.

In addition, the total of your charitable contribution deduction and certain other itemized deductions may be limited. See chapter 30.

Table 25-1 gives examples of contributions you can and cannot deduct.

Table 25-1. Examples of Charitable Contributions—A Quick Check

Use the following lists for a quick check of whether you can deduct a contribution. See the rest of this chapter for more information and additional rules and limits that may apply.

Deductible As Charitable Contributions	Not Deductible As Charitable Contributions
Money or property you give to:	Money or property you give to:
• Churches, synagogues, temples, mosques, and other religious organizations • Federal, state, and local governments, if your contribution is solely for public purposes (for example, a gift to reduce the public debt or maintain a public park) • Nonprofit schools and hospitals • The Salvation Army, American Red Cross, CARE, Goodwill Industries, United Way, Boy Scouts of America, Girl Scouts of America, Boys and Girls Clubs of America, etc. • War veterans groups • Expenses paid for a student living with you, sponsored by a qualified organization • Out-of-pocket expenses when you serve a qualified organization as a volunteer	• Civic leagues, social and sports clubs, labor unions, and chambers of commerce • Foreign organizations (except certain Canadian, Israeli, and Mexican charities) • Groups that are run for personal profit • Groups whose purpose is to lobby for law changes • Homeowners' associations • Individuals • Political groups or candidates for public office • Cost of raffle, bingo, or lottery tickets • Dues, fees, or bills paid to country clubs, lodges, fraternal orders, or similar groups • Tuition • Value of your time or services • Value of blood given to a blood bank

EXPLANATION

Fair market value generally is the price that property would sell for on the open market. It takes into account many factors that affect the value of property on the date of the contribution.

Example

If you give used clothing to the Salvation Army, the fair market value is the price that typical buyers actually pay for clothing of this age, condition, style, and use. Usually, such items are worth far less than what you paid for them.

TAXPLANNER

Determining fair market value. A valuable tool for determining fair market value is IRS Publication 561, *Determining the Value of Donated Property*. The publication helps donors and appraisers determine the value of property given to qualified organizations and includes the kind of information you must have to support the charitable deduction you claim on your return.

A sale or purchase of similar property reasonably close to the date of your contribution is usually the best indication of fair market value. Replacement cost and opinions of experts are also valid methods for determining value.

IRS Publication 561 discusses pitfalls to be avoided in determining the value of donated property. Some pitfalls and how to avoid them are the following:

1. The best evidence of fair market value depends on actual transactions, not on some artificial estimate.
2. Do not consider unexpected events occurring after your donation of property in making the valuation. Generally, you should only consider facts known at the time of the gift.
3. Past events are not necessarily reliable in predicting future earnings and fair market value. For example, a taxpayer contributes all rights in a patent to a charitable organization. The patent has a history of high earnings, but the current trend reflects declining earnings. In this case, more emphasis should be placed on the earnings trend rather than on the earnings history.

The cost of an appraisal is not deductible as a charitable contribution, but it may be claimed as a miscellaneous itemized deduction.

A description of property for which a deduction of more than $500 is claimed must be attached to your return along with Form 8283. Additionally, you are required to obtain a qualified appraisal for certain noncash donations. A qualified appraisal must be made by an independent party. The charity or any person or entity related to the charity cannot render the appraisal. Appraisals are required for the donation of property with a claimed value in excess of $5,000. If you make gifts of two or more items of similar property during the year, the claimed value of all of those items will be added together in determining whether the $5,000 limit is exceeded. For contributions of property in excess of $500,000 the appraisal must be attached to your return.

The appraisal may not be made by the organization receiving the gift, the party from whom the taxpayer acquired the property, the taxpayer, or certain persons related to any of these persons. The appraisal fee cannot be based on a percentage of the appraised value of the gift.

Form 8283, containing an acknowledgment of receipt of the property by the receiving organization and a certification by the appraiser, must be filed with the tax return on which the deduction is taken.

Special Rules and Limitations: **The appraisal rules may be different for certain types of property.** In general, the above appraisal rules do not apply to contributions of intellectual property (e.g., patents, copyrights, trademarks, etc.), certain stock in trade or inventory held for sale in the normal course of business, publicly traded securities, and certain "qualified vehicles" (i.e., motor vehicles, boats, and airplanes).

TAXALERT
Donations of Vehicles—SPECIAL RULES

Under the American Jobs Creation Act of 2004 and under guidance issued by the IRS in 2005, donations of vehicles are subject to additional requirements and limitations. In general, to be fully deductible, the charity must either (1) use the vehicle in a significant way in performing its regularly conducted activities (known as "significant intervening use"), (2) materially improve the vehicle's condition (e.g., through major repairs that significantly increase the vehicle's value–minor repairs, routine maintenance, and cleaning are not considered material improvements), or (3) give or sell the vehicle to a needy individual for a price significantly below its fair market value (FMV) in furtherance of the organization's charitable purpose of relieving the poor, distressed, or underprivileged who are in need of transportation. If the charity sells the vehicle without any significant intervening use or material improvement, the deduction cannot exceed the gross proceeds received by the charity from the sale. In other words, if the charity sells the vehicle, your deduction will be limited to its sales proceeds.

You can't take a deduction of more than $500 for a contribution of a motor vehicle, boat, or airplane unless it is substantiated by a contemporaneous (i.e., within 30 days of the contribution, or sale if the vehicle is sold) written acknowledgment by the charity receiving the gift which contains:

1. The name and taxpayer identification number of the donor,
2. The vehicle identification number or similar number, and
3. Certification of use in one of the following forms:
   i. If the vehicle is to be used or improved by the charity: a certification of the intended use or material improvement of the vehicle and the intended duration of the use, and a certification that the vehicle will not be sold before the completion of such use or improvement.
   ii. If the vehicle is sold without intervening use or improvement: a certification that the vehicle was sold in an arm's-length transaction between unrelated parties, the gross proceeds from the sale, and a statement that the deductible amount may not exceed the amount of such gross proceeds.
   iii. If the vehicle is given or sold to a needy individual for a price significantly below its FMV: a certification that the vehicle was given or sold to a needy individual at a price significantly below its FMV in furtherance of the organization's charitable purpose of relieving the poor, distressed, or underprivileged who are in need of transportation.

The charity will use Form 1098-C for this purpose.

Examples

Example 1. As part of its regularly conducted activities, an organization delivers meals to needy individuals. The use requirement would be met if the organization actually used a donated qualified vehicle to deliver food to the needy. Use of the vehicle to deliver meals substantially furthers a regularly conducted activity of the organization. However, the use also must be significant, which depends on the nature, extent, and frequency of the use. If the organization used the vehicle only once or a few times to deliver meals, the use would not be considered significant. If the organization used the vehicle to deliver meals every day for one year, the use would be considered significant. If the organization drove the vehicle 10,000 miles while delivering meals, such use likely would be considered significant. However, use of a vehicle in such an activity for one week or for several hundreds of miles generally would not be considered a significant use.

Example 2. An organization uses a donated qualified vehicle to transport its volunteers. The use would not be significant merely because a volunteer used the vehicle over a brief period of time to drive to or from the organization's premises. On the other hand, if at the time the organization accepts the contribution of a qualified vehicle, the organization intends to use the vehicle as a regular and ongoing means of transport for volunteers of the organization, and such vehicle is so used, then the significant use test likely would be met.

Example 3. The following example is a general illustration of the provision. A taxpayer makes a charitable contribution of a used automobile in good running condition and that needs no immediate repairs to a charitable organization that operates an elder care facility. The charitable organization accepts the vehicle and immediately provides the donor a written acknowledgment containing the name and TIN of the donor, the vehicle identification number, a certification that it intends to retain the vehicle for a year or longer to transport the facility's residents to community and social events and deliver meals to the needy, and a certification that the vehicle will not be transferred in exchange for money, other property, or services before completion of such use by the organization. A few days after receiving the vehicle, the charitable organization commences to use the vehicle three times a week to transport some of its residents to various community events, and twice a week to deliver food to needy individuals. The organization continues to regularly use the vehicle for these purposes for approximately one year and then sells the vehicle. Under the provision, the charity's use of the vehicle constitutes a significant intervening use prior to the sale by the organization, and the donor's deduction is not limited to the gross proceeds received by the organization.

Intellectual Property
Due to the inherent difficulties in valuing intellectual property, such as patents, copyrights, trademarks, trade names, trade secrets, know-how, software, similar property, or applications or registrations of such property, the American Jobs Creation Act of 2004 contained significant revisions to the rules for deducting contributions of intellectual property, effective for contributions made after June 3, 2004. Under these rules, the deduction for a contribution of intellectual property is generally limited to the lesser of the taxpayer's basis in the property or the fair market value of the property.

Further, you would be allowed to deduct additional amounts in the year of contribution or in subsequent tax years based on a specified percentage of the "qualified donee income" received or accrued by the charitable recipient for the contributed property. Qualified donee income is only the income properly allocable to the intellectual property itself, rather than to the activity in which such property is used.

If you make a qualified intellectual property contribution, the deduction allowed for each tax year ending on or after the date of the contribution is increased by the applicable percentage of qualified income for the contribution that is properly allocable to that year. The amount of the additional deduction allowed per year phases out over the 12 years following the contribution.

The calculation of the charitable contribution deduction is very complex. You should consult your tax advisor if you're considering donating intellectual property to charity.

TAXALERT
Accurate assessments. It is very important to get an accurate assessment of donated property because you may be liable for a special penalty if you overstate its value. You may be liable for the penalty if the value claimed on your return is more than 150% (200% for tax returns filed before August 18, 2006) of the correct amount.

The penalty is 20% of the tax underpayment attributable to the overvaluation and may increase to 40% if the value claimed is 200% (400% for tax returns filed before August 18, 2006) or more of the correct amount.

Contributions From Which You Benefit
If you receive a benefit as a result of making a contribution to a qualified organization, you can deduct only the amount of your contribution that is more than the value of the benefit you receive. Also see *Contributions From Which You Benefit* under *Contributions You Cannot Deduct*, later.

If you pay more than fair market value to a qualified organization for goods or services, the excess may be a charitable contribution. For the excess amount to qualify, you must pay it with the intent to make a charitable contribution.

Example 1. You pay $65 for a ticket to a dinner-dance at a church. Your entire $65 payment goes to the church. The ticket to the dinner-dance has a fair market value of $25. When you buy your ticket, you know that its value is less than your payment. To figure the amount of your charitable contribution, subtract the value of the benefit you receive ($25) from your total payment ($65). You can deduct $40 as a contribution to the church.

Example 2. At a fundraising auction conducted by a charity, you pay $600 for a week's stay at a beach house. The amount you pay is no more than the fair rental value. You have not made a deductible charitable contribution.

Athletic events. If you make a payment to, or for the benefit of, a college or university and, as a result, you receive the right to buy tickets to an athletic event in the athletic stadium of the college or university, you can deduct 80% of the payment as a charitable contribution.

If any part of your payment is for tickets (rather than the right to buy tickets), that part is not deductible. Subtract the price of the tickets from your payment. You can deduct 80% of the remaining amount as a charitable contribution.

Example 1. You pay $300 a year for membership in a university's athletic scholarship program. The only benefit of membership is that you have the right to buy one season ticket for a seat in a designated area of the stadium at the university's home football games. You can deduct $240 (80% of $300) as a charitable contribution.

Example 2. The facts are the same as in Example 1 except your $300 payment includes the purchase of one season ticket for the stated ticket price of $120. You must subtract the usual price of a ticket ($120) from your $300 payment. The result is $180. Your deductible charitable contribution is $144 (80% of $180).

EXCEPTIONS
A deduction for a charitable contribution was not permitted in the following instances:
- A person contributed a computer to a university, and the donor reserved the right to use the computer for 12 weeks per year.
- A person released frontage to a county for widening a road in order to obtain the required approval by the county planning commission of the development plan for certain lots prior to their sale. (However, the cost of the frontage is part of the total cost basis of the remaining property for determining the gain or loss on the sale of the property.)
- The amount paid by a taxpayer to purchase building bonds issued by a church was not a gift made to the church. However, if the taxpayer had subsequently given the bonds to the church, he would have been entitled to a charitable deduction for their fair market value at the time of the gift.
- A person made contributions to a nonprofit organization formed by parents of pupils attending a private school. The organization provided school bus transportation for members' children. The contributions served a private rather than a public interest.
- A taxpayer paid a fee to a nonprofit corporation for the privilege of taking up residence in a home operated by the corporation. This fee, along with a required entrance fee, entitled the taxpayer to lifetime care in the home. The fee represented a personal expense.

Caution

Even if the ticket or other evidence of payment indicates that the payment is a "contribution," this does not mean you can deduct the entire amount. If the ticket shows the price of admission and the amount of the contribution, you can deduct the contribution amount.

Charity benefit events. If you pay a qualified organization more than fair market value for the right to attend a charity ball, banquet, show, sporting event, or other benefit event, you can deduct only the amount that is more than the value of the privileges or other benefits you receive.

If there is an established charge for the event, that charge is the value of your benefit. If there is no established charge, the reasonable value of the right to attend the event is the value of your benefit. Whether you use the tickets or other privileges has no effect on the amount you can deduct. However, if you return the ticket to the qualified organization for resale, you can deduct the entire amount you paid for the ticket.

Example. You pay $40 to see a special showing of a movie for the benefit of a qualified organization. Printed on the ticket is "Contribution—$40." If the regular price for the movie is $8, your contribution is $32 ($40 payment - $8 regular price).

EXPLANATION
The IRS requires that charities determine the fair market value of benefits offered in exchange for contributions in advance of the solicitation and state in the solicitation, as well as in the receipt, tickets, or other documents, what portion of the contribution is deductible. The charity may advise donors that the full amount of a contribution is deductible if any of the following applies:
- The fair market value of all the benefits received in conjunction with the contribution is not more than the lesser of 2% of the payment or $102 in 2014.
- The contribution is at least $51 in 2014, and the only benefits received in connection with the payment are token items, such as bookmarks, calendars, key chains, mugs, posters, and T-shirts bearing the organization's name or logo (i.e., low-cost articles with a cost not in excess of $10.20 in 2014).
- The charity distributes unordered items to patrons. The distributed item must be accompanied by a request for a contribution and by a statement that the item can be retained whether or not a contribution is made. The aggregate cost per patron of these items cannot exceed $10.20 in 2014.

Membership fees or dues. You may be able to deduct membership fees or dues you pay to a qualified organization. However, you can deduct only the amount that is more than the value of the benefits you receive.

You cannot deduct dues, fees, or assessments paid to country clubs and other social organizations. They are not qualified organizations.

Certain membership benefits can be disregarded. Both you and the organization can disregard the following membership benefits if you receive them in return for an annual payment of $75 or less.

1. Any rights or privileges, other than those discussed under *Athletic events*, earlier, that you can use frequently while you are a member, such as:
    a. Free or discounted admission to the organization's facilities or events,
    b. Free or discounted parking,
    c. Preferred access to goods or services, and
    d. Discounts on the purchase of goods and services.
2. Admission, while you are a member, to events open only to members of the organization, if the organization reasonably projects that the cost per person (excluding any allocated overhead) is not more than $10.20.

Token items. You do not have to reduce your contribution by the value of any benefit you receive if both of the following are true.

1. You receive only a small item or other benefit of token value.
2. The qualified organization correctly determines that the value of the item or benefit you received is not substantial and informs you that you can deduct your payment in full.

Written statement. A qualified organization must give you a written statement if you make a payment of more than $75 that is partly a contribution and partly for goods or services. The statement must say that you can deduct only the amount of your payment that is more than the value of the goods or services you received. It must also give you a good faith estimate of the value of those goods or services.

The organization can give you the statement either when it solicits or when it receives the payment from you.

Exception. An organization will not have to give you this statement if one of the following is true.

1. The organization is:
    a. A governmental organization described in (5) under *Types of Qualified Organizations*, earlier, or
    b. An organization formed only for religious purposes, and the only benefit you receive is an intangible religious benefit (such as admission to a religious ceremony) that generally is not sold in commercial transactions outside the donative context.
2. You receive only items whose value is not substantial as described under *Token items*, earlier.
3. You receive only membership benefits that can be disregarded, as described earlier.

Expenses Paid for Student Living With You

You may be able to deduct some expenses of having a student live with you. You can deduct qualifying expenses for a foreign or American student who:

1. Lives in your home under a written agreement between you and a qualified organization as part of a program of the organization to provide educational opportunities for the student,
2. Is not your relative or dependent, and
3. Is a full-time student in the twelfth or any lower grade at a school in the United States.

For additional information, see *Expenses Paid for Student Living With You* in Publication 526.

Tip

You can deduct up to $50 a month for each full calendar month the student lives with you. Any month when conditions (1) through (3) are met for 15 days or more counts as a full month.

Mutual exchange program. You cannot deduct the costs of a foreign student living in your home under a mutual exchange program through which your child will live with a family in a foreign country.

> ### EXPLANATION
> The deduction is limited to amounts that you actually spend for the well-being of the student during the taxable year while the student is a member of the household and a full-time student. Amounts you pay for the student's books, tuition, food, clothing, transportation, medical and dental care, and entertainment qualify for the deduction. Depreciation on your home, the fair market value of lodging at your home, or similar items are not considered an amount spent by you and are not deductible.
>
> If you are compensated or reimbursed for the costs of having a student live with you, you may not take a deduction for any part of these costs.

Out-of-Pocket Expenses in Giving Services

Although you cannot deduct the value of your services given to a qualified organization, you may be able to deduct some amounts you pay in giving services to a qualified organization. The amounts must be:

- Unreimbursed,
- Directly connected with the services,
- Expenses you had only because of the services you gave, and
- Not personal, living, or family expenses.

> ### EXPLANATION
> Unreimbursed out-of-pocket expenses incurred in rendering services to qualified charities are considered contributions made "to" the charitable entities rather than "for the use of" the charitable entities, and, as such, the deduction may be subject to the 50% limit rather than the 30% limit. See *Limits on Deductions*, later, to determine if further limitations apply.

Table 25-2 contains questions and answers that apply to some individuals who volunteer their services.

Table 25-2.   **Volunteers' Questions and Answers**

If you volunteer for a qualified organization, the following questions and answers may apply to you. All of the rules explained in this chapter also apply. See, in particular, Out-of-Pocket Expenses in Giving Services.	
Question	**Answer**
I volunteer 6 hours a week in the office of a qualified organization. The receptionist is paid $10 an hour for the same work. Can I deduct $60 a week for my time?	No, you cannot deduct the value of your time or services.
The office is 30 miles from my home. Can I deduct any of my car expenses for these trips?	Yes, you can deduct the costs of gas and oil that are directly related to getting to and from the place where you volunteer. If you don't want to figure your actual costs, you can deduct 14 cents for each mile.
I volunteer as a Red Cross nurse's aide at a hospital. Can I deduct the cost of the uniforms I must wear?	Yes, you can deduct the cost of buying and cleaning your uniforms if the hospital is a qualified organization, the uniforms are not suitable for everyday use, and you must wear them when volunteering.
I pay a babysitter to watch my children while I volunteer for a qualified organization. Can I deduct these costs?	No, you cannot deduct payments for childcare expenses as a charitable contribution, even if you would be unable to volunteer without childcare. (If you have childcare expenses so you can work for pay, see chapter 32.)

Conventions. If a qualified organization selects you to attend a convention as its representative, you can deduct unreimbursed expenses for travel, including reasonable amounts for meals and lodging, while away from home overnight in connection with the convention. However, see *Travel*, later.

You cannot deduct personal expenses for sightseeing, fishing parties, theater tickets, or nightclubs. You also cannot deduct transportation, meals and lodging, and other expenses for your spouse or children.

You cannot deduct your travel expenses in attending a church convention if you go only as a member of your church rather than as a chosen representative. You can, however, deduct unreimbursed expenses that are directly connected with giving services for your church during the convention.

Uniforms. You can deduct the cost and upkeep of uniforms that are not suitable for everyday use and that you must wear while performing donated services for a charitable organization.

Foster parents. You may be able to deduct as a charitable contribution some of the costs of being a foster parent (foster care provider) if you have no profit motive in providing the foster care and are not, in fact, making a profit. A qualified organization must select the individuals you take into your home for foster care.

You can deduct expenses that meet both of the following requirements.
1. They are unreimbursed out-of-pocket expenses to feed, clothe, and care for the foster child.
2. They are incurred primarily to benefit the qualified organization.

EXPLANATION
You may deduct reasonable, unreimbursed out-of-pocket expenses you spend for underprivileged children to attend athletic events, movies, or dinners. It must be part of an event sponsored on behalf of a qualifying organization. Expenses for yourself are not deductible.

Unreimbursed expenses that you cannot deduct as charitable contributions may be considered support provided by you in determining whether you can claim the foster child as a dependent. For details, see chapter 3.

Example. You cared for a foster child because you wanted to adopt her, not to benefit the agency that placed her in your home. Your unreimbursed expenses are not deductible as charitable contributions.

TAXALERT
Although you cannot claim a charitable deduction for your unreimbursed expenses, you may be entitled to a tax credit for certain qualified adoption expenses (see Form 8839).

Car expenses. You can deduct as a charitable contribution any unreimbursed out-of-pocket expenses, such as the cost of gas and oil, that are directly related to the use of your car in giving services to a charitable organization. You cannot deduct general repair and maintenance expenses, depreciation, registration fees, or the costs of tires or insurance.

If you do not want to deduct your actual expenses, you can use a standard mileage rate of 14 cents a mile to figure your contribution.

You can deduct parking fees and tolls whether you use your actual expenses or the standard mileage rate.

You must keep reliable written records of your car expenses. For more information, see *Car expenses* under *Records To Keep*, later.

Travel. Generally, you can claim a charitable contribution deduction for travel expenses necessarily incurred while you are away from home performing services for a charitable organization only if there is no significant element of personal pleasure, recreation, or vacation in the travel. This applies whether you pay the expenses directly or indirectly. You are paying the expenses indirectly if you make a payment to the charitable organization and the organization pays for your travel expenses.

The deduction for travel expenses will not be denied simply because you enjoy providing services to the charitable organization. Even if you enjoy the trip, you can take a charitable contribution deduction for your travel expenses if you are on duty in a genuine and substantial sense throughout the trip. However, if you have only nominal duties, or if for significant parts of the trip you do not have any duties, you cannot deduct your travel expenses.

Example 1. You are a troop leader for a tax-exempt youth group and you take the group on a camping trip. You are responsible for overseeing the setup of the camp and for providing adult supervision for other activities during the entire trip. You participate in the activities of the group and enjoy your time with them. You oversee the breaking of camp and you transport the group home. You can deduct your travel expenses.

Example 2. You sail from one island to another and spend 8 hours a day counting whales and other forms of marine life. The project is sponsored by a charitable organization. In most circumstances, you cannot deduct your expenses.

Example 3. You work for several hours each morning on an archaeological dig sponsored by a charitable organization. The rest of the day is free for recreation and sightseeing. You cannot take a charitable contribution deduction even though you work very hard during those few hours.

Example 4. You spend the entire day attending a charitable organization's regional meeting as a chosen representative. In the evening you go to the theater. You can claim your travel expenses as charitable contributions, but you cannot claim the cost of your evening at the theater.

Daily allowance (per diem). If you provide services for a charitable organization and receive a daily allowance to cover reasonable travel expenses, including meals and lodging while away from home overnight, you must include in income any part of the allowance that is more than your deductible travel expenses. You may be able to deduct any necessary travel expenses that are more than the allowance.

Deductible travel expenses. These include:
- Air, rail, and bus transportation,
- Out-of-pocket expenses for your car,
- Taxi fares or other costs of transportation between the airport or station and your hotel,
- Lodging costs, and
- The cost of meals.

Because these travel expenses are not business-related, they are not subject to the same limits as business-related expenses. For information on business travel expenses, see *Travel Expenses* in chapter 27.

Contributions You Cannot Deduct

There are some contributions you cannot deduct, such as those made to specific individuals and those made to nonqualified organizations. (See *Contributions to Individuals* and *Contributions to Nonqualified Organizations*, next.) There are others you can deduct only part of, as discussed later under *Contributions From Which You Benefit*.

Contributions to Individuals

You cannot deduct contributions to specific individuals, including the following.
- Contributions to fraternal societies made for the purpose of paying medical or burial expenses of deceased members.
- Contributions to individuals who are needy or worthy. You cannot deduct these contributions even if you make them to a qualified organization for the benefit of a specific person. But you can deduct a contribution to a qualified organization that helps needy or worthy individuals if you do not indicate that your contribution is for a specific person.

Example. You can deduct contributions to a qualified organization for flood relief, hurricane relief, or other disaster relief. However, you cannot deduct contributions earmarked for relief of a particular individual or family.
- Payments to a member of the clergy that can be spent as he or she wishes, such as for personal expenses.
- Expenses you paid for another person who provided services to a qualified organization.

Example. Your son does missionary work. You pay his expenses. You cannot claim a deduction for your son's unreimbursed expenses related to his contribution of services.
- Payments to a hospital that are for a specific patient's care or for services for a specific patient. You cannot deduct these payments even if the hospital is operated by a city, a state, or other qualified organization.

Contributions to Nonqualified Organizations

You cannot deduct contributions to organizations that are not qualified to receive tax-deductible contributions, including the following.

1. Certain state bar associations if:
   a. The bar is not a political subdivision of a state,
   b. The bar has private, as well as public, purposes, such as promoting the professional interests of members, and
   c. Your contribution is unrestricted and can be used for private purposes.
2. Chambers of commerce and other business leagues or organizations (but see chapter 29).
3. Civic leagues and associations.
4. Communist organizations.
5. Country clubs and other social clubs.
6. Most foreign organizations (other than certain Canadian, Israeli, or Mexican charitable organizations). For details, see Publication 526.
7. Homeowners' associations.
8. Labor unions (but see chapter 29).
9. Political organizations and candidates.

Contributions From Which You Benefit

If you receive or expect to receive a financial or economic benefit as a result of making a contribution to a qualified organization, you cannot deduct the part of the contribution that represents the value of the benefit you receive. See *Contributions From Which You Benefit* under *Contributions You Can Deduct*, earlier. These contributions include the following.

- Contributions for lobbying. This includes amounts that you earmark for use in, or in connection with, influencing specific legislation.
- Contributions to a retirement home for room, board, maintenance, or admittance. Also, if the amount of your contribution depends on the type or size of apartment you will occupy, it is not a charitable contribution.

- Costs of raffles, bingo, lottery, etc. You cannot deduct as a charitable contribution amounts you pay to buy raffle or lottery tickets or to play bingo or other games of chance. For information on how to report gambling winnings and losses, see *Gambling winnings* in chapter 12 and *Gambling Losses Up to the Amount of Gambling Winnings* in chapter 29.
- Dues to fraternal orders and similar groups. However, see *Membership fees or dues*, earlier, under *Contributions You Can Deduct.*
- Tuition, or amounts you pay instead of tuition. You cannot deduct as a charitable contribution amounts you pay as tuition even if you pay them for children to attend parochial schools or qualifying nonprofit daycare centers. You also cannot deduct any fixed amount you must pay in addition to, or instead of, tuition to enroll in a private school, even if it is designated as a "donation."

EXPLANATION

Tuition-type payments disguised as a charitable contribution are not deductible. Certain rules have been established by the IRS to determine whether an item is a tuition payment or a charitable contribution.

No deduction for a charitable contribution is allowed if at least one of the following conditions exists:
1. A contract under which a taxpayer agrees to make a "contribution," and that contract contains provisions ensuring the admission of the taxpayer's child;
2. A plan allowing taxpayers either to pay tuition or to make "contributions" in exchange for schooling;
3. The designation of a contribution for the direct benefit of a particular child;
4. The otherwise unexplained denial of admission or readmission to a school of children of taxpayers who are financially able but who do not contribute.

Other factors that are considered in deciding if a contribution is deductible include the following:
1. The absence of a significant tuition charge;
2. Substantial or unusual pressure to contribute applied to parents of students;
3. Contribution appeals made as part of the admissions or enrollment process;
4. The absence of significant potential sources of revenue for operating the school other than contributions by parents of students;
5. The contribution amounts are the same for all families or are paid pursuant to published guidelines for donations.

Value of Time or Services

You cannot deduct the value of your time or services, including:
- Blood donations to the American Red Cross or to blood banks, and
- The value of income lost while you work as an unpaid volunteer for a qualified organization.

TAXPLANNER

Services to a charitable organization. If you contribute your services to a charitable organization, you are not permitted to take a charitable deduction for the value of your time or services. However, you are entitled to take a charitable deduction if you acquire the right to services to be performed by another and then gratuitously transfer that right to the charity.

Example

You purchase a series of six golf lessons from a local golf professional. Because you are unable to use the lessons, you donate them to your church for use in their raffle. The cost of the six lessons is deductible as a charitable contribution.

Personal Expenses

You cannot deduct personal, living, or family expenses, such as the following items.
- The cost of meals you eat while you perform services for a qualified organization unless it is necessary for you to be away from home overnight while performing the services.
- Adoption expenses, including fees paid to an adoption agency and the costs of keeping a child in your home before adoption is final (but see *Adoption Credit* in chapter 37, and the instructions for Form 8839, Qualified Adoption Expenses). You also may be able to claim an exemption for the child. See *Adopted child* in chapter 3.

Appraisal Fees

You cannot deduct as a charitable contribution any fees you pay to find the fair market value of donated property (but see chapter 29).

Contributions of Property

If you contribute property to a qualified organization, the amount of your charitable contribution is generally the fair market value of the property at the time of the contribution. However, if the property has increased in value, you may have to make some adjustments to the amount of your deduction. See *Giving Property That Has Increased in Value*, later.

> ### EXPLANATION
>
> If you permit a charitable organization to use your property without charge (or at a minimal rate), no charitable deduction is allowed.

> ### TAXSAVER
>
> The IRS, however, will allow charitable deductions for the cost of operation, maintenance, and repair of property directly related to the charitable organization's use of the property.
>
> If you donate the use of your yacht to the church for use in their raffle, no income tax deduction is allowed for the rental value or other value of the donated use. Direct operating costs, such as fuel, used in connection with the donated use are allowable as a charitable contribution.

For information about the records you must keep and the information you must furnish with your return if you donate property, see *Records To Keep* and *How To Report*, later.

> ### TAXPLANNER
>
> Some of the rules for reporting contributions of certain noncash property were changed by 2004 tax legislation. The 2004 law extends to all C corporations the requirement previously and currently applicable to an individual, closely held corporation, personal service corporation, partnership, or S corporation, that the donor must obtain a qualified appraisal of the property if the deduction claimed exceeds $5,000. (A C corporation is generally a business entity owned by shareholders and treated as a separate tax entity.) In addition, the law provides that if the amount of the contribution of property exceeds $500,000, the donor (whether an individual, partnership, or corporation) must attach a qualified appraisal to the tax return. These rules apply to contributions made after June 3, 2004.

Clothing and household items. You cannot take a deduction for clothing or household items you donate unless the clothing or household items are in good used condition or better.

Exception. You can take a deduction for a contribution of an item of clothing or household item that is not in good used condition or better if you deduct more than $500 for it and include a qualified appraisal of it with your return.

Household items. Household items include:
- Furniture and furnishings,
- Electronics,
- Appliances,
- Linens, and
- Other similar items.

Household items do not include:
- Food,
- Paintings, antiques, and other objects of art,
- Jewelry and gems, and
- Collections.

Cars, boats, and airplanes. The following rules apply to any donation of a qualified vehicle.

A qualified vehicle is:
- A car or any motor vehicle manufactured mainly for use on public streets, roads, and highways,
- A boat, or
- An airplane.

Deduction more than $500. If you donate a qualified vehicle with a claimed fair market value of more than $500, you can deduct the smaller of:

- The gross proceeds from the sale of the vehicle by the organization, or
- The vehicle's fair market value on the date of the contribution. If the vehicle's fair market value was more than your cost or other basis, you may have to reduce the fair market value to figure the deductible amount, as described under *Giving Property That Has Increased in Value*, later.

Form 1098-C. You must attach to your return Copy B of the Form 1098-C, Contributions of Motor Vehicles, Boats, and Airplanes, (or other statement containing the same information as Form 1098-C) you received from the organization. The Form 1098-C (or other statement) will show the gross proceeds from the sale of the vehicle.

If you e-file your return, you must:

- Attach Copy B of Form 1098-C to Form 8453 and mail the forms to the IRS, or
- Include Copy B of Form 1098-C as a pdf attachment if your software program allows it.

If you do not attach Form 1098-C (or other statement), you cannot deduct your contribution.

You must get Form 1098-C (or other statement) within 30 days of the sale of the vehicle. But if exception 1 or 2 (described later) applies, you must get Form 1098-C (or other statement) within 30 days of your donation.

Filing deadline approaching and still no Form 1098-C. If the filing deadline is approaching and you still do not have a Form 1098-C, you have two choices.

- Request an automatic 6-month extension of time to file your return. You can get this extension by filing Form 4868, Application for Automatic Extension of Time to File U.S. Individual Income Tax Return. For more information, see *Automatic Extension* in chapter 1.
- File the return on time without claiming the deduction for the qualified vehicle. After receiving the Form 1098-C, file an amended return, Form 1040X, claiming the deduction. Attach Copy B of Form 1098-C (or other statement) to the amended return. For more information about amended returns, see *Amended Returns and Claims for Refund* in chapter 1.

Exceptions. There are two exceptions to the rules just described for deductions of more than $500.

Exception 1—vehicle used or improved by organization. If the qualified organization makes a significant intervening use of or material improvement to the vehicle before transferring it, you generally can deduct the vehicle's fair market value at the time of the contribution. But if the vehicle's fair market value was more than your cost or other basis, you may have to reduce the fair market value to get the deductible amount, as described under *Giving Property That Has Increased in Value*, later. The Form 1098-C (or other statement) will show whether this exception applies.

Exception 2—vehicle given or sold to needy individual. If the qualified organization will give the vehicle, or sell it for a price well below fair market value, to a needy individual to further the organization's charitable purpose, you generally can deduct the vehicle's fair market value at the time of the contribution. But if the vehicle's fair market value was more than your cost or other basis, you may have to reduce the fair market value to get the deductible amount, as described under *Giving Property That Has Increased in Value*, later. The Form 1098-C (or other statement) will show whether this exception applies.

This exception does not apply if the organization sells the vehicle at auction. In that case, you cannot deduct the vehicle's fair market value.

Example. Anita donates a used car to a qualified organization. She bought it 3 years ago for $9,000. A used car guide shows the fair market value for this type of car is $6,000. However, Anita gets a Form 1098-C from the organization showing the car was sold for $2,900. Neither exception 1 nor exception 2 applies. If Anita itemizes her deductions, she can deduct $2,900 for her donation. She must attach Form 1098-C and Form 8283 to her return.

Deduction $500 or less. If the qualified organization sells the vehicle for $500 or less and exceptions 1 and 2 do not apply, you can deduct the smaller of:

- $500, or
- The vehicle's fair market value on the date of the contribution. But if the vehicle's fair market value was more than your cost or other basis, you may have to reduce the fair market value to get the deductible amount, as described under *Giving Property That Has Increased in Value*, later.

If the vehicle's fair market value is at least $250 but not more than $500, you must have a written statement from the qualified organization acknowledging your donation. The statement must contain the information and meet the tests for an acknowledgment described under *Deductions of At Least $250 But Not More Than $500* under *Records To Keep*, later.

Partial interest in property. Generally, you cannot deduct a charitable contribution of less than your entire interest in property.

   Right to use property. A contribution of the right to use property is a contribution of less than your entire interest in that property and is not deductible. For exceptions and more information, see *Partial Interest in Property Not in Trust* in Publication 561.

EXPLANATION

This rule does not apply to a contribution of a partial interest in property if that interest is your entire interest in the property, such as an income interest.

   Nevertheless, there are some situations in which you may claim a deduction for a charitable contribution that is less than your entire interest in the property.

1. **Undivided part of your entire interest.** A contribution of an undivided part of your entire interest in property must consist of a part of each and every substantial interest or right you own in the property and must extend over the entire term of your interest in the property.

Example 1

If you own 100 acres of land and give 50 acres to a qualified organization, you may deduct the charitable contribution.

2. **Remainder interest in a personal home or farm.** You may take a charitable deduction for a gift to a qualified organization of a remainder interest in a personal home or a farm if the gift is irrevocable.

Example 2

If you transfer a remainder interest in your home to your church but keep the right to live there for life, you may take a deduction for the value of the remainder interest transferred.

3. **Valuation of a partial interest in property.** The amount of the deduction for a charitable contribution of a partial interest in property is the fair market value of the partial interest at the time of the contribution. If the contribution is a remainder interest in real property, depreciation (figured on the straight-line method) and depletion of the property must be taken into account in determining its value. This future value must be further discounted at a rate set by the government. The rate is published each month, and you may use the rate for the month in which the contribution is made or, if you elect, the rate in either of the preceding 2 months. You should use the rate that produces the largest charitable deduction.

TAXPLANNER

If a fractional interest in an item of tangible personal property (e.g., a painting or other artwork) is donated after August 17, 2006, the tax law requires that charities receiving property must take complete ownership of the item within 10 years of when the contribution was made or the date of death of the donor, whichever is first. In addition, the charity must have (1) taken possession of the item at least once during the 10-year period as long as the donor remains alive, and (2) used the item for the organization's exempt purpose. Failure to comply with these requirements results in the recapture of all tax benefits the donor previously recognized plus interest and the imposition of a 10% penalty.

TAXPLANNER

No deduction is allowed for the value of an interest in property transferred in trust unless the donor's entire interest is contributed to a qualified organization or unless the interest is an income interest or a remainder interest. A deduction for a charitable contribution of an income interest in property made by a transfer in trust is allowed if the income interest is either a guaranteed annuity interest or a unitrust interest. A unitrust interest is the irrevocable right to receive payment of a fixed percentage of the net fair market value of the trust assets determined on a yearly basis, while an annuity interest is a right to receive a fixed percentage of the initial fair market value of the transferred assets.

   A deduction for a charitable contribution of a remainder interest in trust is allowed if the trust is (1) a pooled income fund, (2) a charitable remainder annuity trust, or (3) a charitable remainder unitrust.

   The use of these trusts may be very beneficial both to the individual and to the individual's favorite charity. Individuals with substantial wealth should consult their tax and legal advisors about using these mechanisms.

Future interests in tangible personal property. You cannot deduct the value of a charitable contribution of a future interest in tangible personal property until all intervening interests in and rights to the actual possession or enjoyment of the property have either expired or been turned over to someone other than yourself, a related person, or a related organization.

Tangible personal property. This is any property, other than land or buildings, that can be seen or touched. It includes furniture, books, jewelry, paintings, and cars.

Future interest. This is any interest that is to begin at some future time, regardless of whether it is designated as a future interest under state law.

Determining Fair Market Value

This section discusses general guidelines for determining the fair market value of various types of donated property. Publication 561 contains a more complete discussion.

Fair market value is the price at which property would change hands between a willing buyer and a willing seller, neither having to buy or sell, and both having reasonable knowledge of all the relevant facts.

Used clothing and household items. The fair market value of used clothing and household goods is usually far less than what you paid for them when they were new.

For used clothing, you should claim as the value the price that buyers of used items actually pay in used clothing stores, such as consignment or thrift shops. See *Household Goods* in Publication 561 for information on the valuation of household goods, such as furniture, appliances, and linens.

Example. Dawn Greene donated a coat to a thrift store operated by her church. She paid $300 for the coat 3 years ago. Similar coats in the thrift store sell for $50. The fair market value of the coat is $50. Dawn's donation is limited to $50.

Cars, boats, and airplanes. If you contribute a car, boat, or airplane to a charitable organization, you must determine its fair market value. Certain commercial firms and trade organizations publish used car pricing guides, commonly called "blue books," containing complete dealer sale prices or dealer average prices for recent model years. The guides may be published monthly or seasonally and for different regions of the country. These guides also provide estimates for adjusting for unusual equipment, unusual mileage, and physical condition. The prices are not "official" and these publications are not considered an appraisal of any specific donated property. But they do provide clues for making an appraisal and suggest relative prices for comparison with current sales and offerings in your area.

You can also find used car pricing information on the Internet.

Example. You donate a used car in poor condition to a local high school for use by students studying car repair. A used car guide shows the dealer retail value for this type of car in poor condition is $1,600. However, the guide shows the price for a private party sale of the car is only $750. The fair market value of the car is considered to be $750.

Large quantities. If you contribute a large number of the same item, fair market value is the price at which comparable numbers of the item are being sold.

Giving Property That Has Decreased in Value

If you contribute property with a fair market value that is less than your basis in it, your deduction is limited to its fair market value. You cannot claim a deduction for the difference between the property's basis and its fair market value.

TAXPLANNER

If investment property that you are planning to donate has declined in value, you may wish to consider selling it and giving the proceeds to the charitable organization. By following this strategy, you get the deduction (subject to limitations) for the capital loss, as well as the deduction for the charitable cash gift.

Giving Property That Has Increased in Value

If you contribute property with a fair market value that is more than your basis in it, you may have to reduce the fair market value by the amount of appreciation (increase in value) when you figure your deduction.

Your basis in property is generally what you paid for it. See chapter 13 if you need more information about basis.

Different rules apply to figuring your deduction, depending on whether the property is:
- Ordinary income property, or
- Capital gain property.

Ordinary income property. Property is ordinary income property if you would have recognized ordinary income or short-term capital gain had you sold it at fair market value on the date it was contributed. Examples of ordinary income property are inventory, works of art created by the donor, manuscripts prepared by the donor, and capital assets (defined in chapter 14) held 1 year or less.

Amount of deduction. The amount you can deduct for a contribution of ordinary income property is its fair market value minus the amount that would be ordinary income or short-term capital gain if you sold the property for its fair market value. Generally, this rule limits the deduction to your basis in the property.

Example. You donate stock you held for 5 months to your church. The fair market value of the stock on the day you donate it is $1,000, but you paid only $800 (your basis). Because the $200 of appreciation would be short-term capital gain if you sold the stock, your deduction is limited to $800 (fair market value minus the appreciation).

EXPLANATION

Ordinary income property. If, on the date it was contributed, the sale of the property would have resulted in ordinary income or a short-term capital gain to the donor, it is ordinary income property. Examples of ordinary income property include inventory, letters, and memoranda given by the person who prepared them (or the person for whom they were prepared) and any property that was acquired and held for 1 year or less.

Example

You contribute inventory to your church with a fair market value of $20,000 and a cost of $8,000. Because the inventory is property that had previously been held for sale in the ordinary course of business, you would have recognized ordinary income of $12,000 had the property been sold. Therefore, your contribution of $20,000 is reduced by $12,000. Your deduction is limited to $8,000.

Capital gain property. Property is capital gain property if you would have recognized long-term capital gain had you sold it at fair market value on the date of the contribution. It includes capital assets held more than 1 year, as well as certain real property and depreciable property used in your trade or business and, generally, held more than 1 year.

Amount of deduction—general rule. When figuring your deduction for a contribution of capital gain property, you generally can use the fair market value of the property.

Exceptions. In certain situations, you must reduce the fair market value by any amount that would have been long-term capital gain if you had sold the property for its fair market value. Generally, this means reducing the fair market value to the property's cost or other basis.

EXAMPLE

An individual purchased stock in 1985 for $1,000. He contributed it to his church in 2014, at which time it was worth $20,000. His charitable contribution deduction is $20,000, the fair market value at the date of the contribution.

EXPLANATION

You usually may deduct a gift of capital gain property at its fair market value. However, your deduction is limited to your adjusted basis in the property in the following instances:

1. If the capital gain property (other than qualified appreciated stock) is contributed to certain private foundations. (A private foundation generally receives only small or no contributions from the general public.) **Contributions to private foundations.** Contributions of qualified appreciated stock to private foundations are deductible at full market value subject to the 20% limitation, discussed later. If, on the date of contribution, market quotes are readily available and the sale of the stock would result in a long-term capital gain, it is qualified appreciated stock. An example would be shares of Microsoft that qualify for long-term capital gain treatment.
2. If you choose the 50% limit instead of the special 30% limit, discussed later (see _Limit on Deductions_, later).
3. If the property contributed is tangible personal property that is put to an unrelated use by the charity, that is, a use that is unrelated to the purpose or function of the charitable organization for which it was granted its tax-exempt status.

Example

If a painting you contribute to an educational institution is placed in the organization's library for display and study by art students, the use is not an unrelated use. But, if the painting is sold and the proceeds are used by the organization for educational purposes, the use is unrelated and your deduction is limited to the painting's cost.

TAXPLANNER

Before you donate a gift of tangible personal property, attempt to determine whether the use will be related to the charitable organization's exempt function. In such circumstances, ask the charitable organization to prepare a statement of intended use and retain it in your tax return file.

TAXSAVER

If you donate appreciated securities that you have held for more than a year, not only can you take a deduction based on the fair market value of the securities, but you will also avoid paying tax on the appreciation. Consequently, the cost of your contribution is reduced by the tax deduction you claim and the tax you avoided by not selling the property. In most cases, the charity does not incur any tax when it sells the property. Be careful, though, if the securities are the subject of a tender offer or other purchase agreement. The Tax Court has ruled that a gift of securities subject to such an agreement will result in income to the donor for the gain.

Example

You own stock worth $1,000. When you bought the stock more than a year ago, it cost you $100. If you sell the stock and donate the $1,000 to your favorite charity, you incur capital gains tax—possibly as much as $180, depending on what tax bracket you're in. If you contribute the stock directly to the charity, the $900 gain is not subject to tax.

TAXSAVER

To get the maximum tax benefit from a contribution of appreciated property, be sure that the property qualifies for long-term capital gain treatment if it is sold.

Example

You purchased stock for $1,000 on January 7, 2013. The stock was donated to your church on January 5, 2014, at which time it was worth $3,000. Because the $2,000 of appreciation would have been a short-term capital gain if you had sold the stock, your deduction is limited to $1,000. If, however, you had waited to make your donation to the church until January 8, 2014, and the stock was still worth $3,000, you would have been able to deduct $3,000.

Bargain sales. A bargain sale of property is a sale or exchange for less than the property's fair market value. A bargain sale to a qualified organization is partly a charitable contribution and partly a sale or exchange. A bargain sale may result in a taxable gain.

More information. For more information on donating appreciated property, see *Giving Property That Has Increased in Value* in Publication 526.

When To Deduct

You can deduct your contributions only in the year you actually make them in cash or other property (or in a later carryover year, as explained later under *Carryovers*). This applies whether you use the cash or an accrual method of accounting.

Time of making contribution. Usually, you make a contribution at the time of its unconditional delivery.

Checks. A check you mail to a charity is considered delivered on the date you mail it.

Text message. Contributions made by text message are deductible in the year you send the text message if the contribution is charged to your telephone or wireless account.

Credit card. Contributions charged on your credit card are deductible in the year you make the charge.

Pay-by-phone account. Contributions made through a pay-by-phone account are considered delivered on the date the financial institution pays the amount.

Stock certificate. A properly endorsed stock certificate is considered delivered on the date of mailing or other delivery to the charity or to the charity's agent. However, if you give a stock certificate to your agent or to the issuing corporation for transfer to the name of the charity, your contribution is not delivered until the date the stock is transferred on the books of the corporation.

Promissory note. If you issue and deliver a promissory note to a charity as a contribution, it is not a contribution until you make the note payments.

Option. If you grant a charity an option to buy real property at a bargain price, it is not a contribution until the organization exercises the option.

Borrowed funds. If you contribute borrowed funds, you can deduct the contribution in the year you deliver the funds to the charity, regardless of when you repay the loan.

Limits on Deductions

The amount you can deduct for charitable contributions cannot be more than 50% of your adjusted gross income (AGI). Your deduction may be further limited to 30% or 20% of your AGI, depending on the type of property you give and the type of organization you give it to. If your total contributions for the year are 20% or less of your AGI, these limits do not apply to you. The limits are discussed in detail under *Limits on Deductions* in Publication 526.

Text intentionally omitted.

EXPLANATION

50% Limit
This limit applies to the total of all charitable contributions you make during the year. This means that your deduction for charitable contributions cannot be more than 50% of your adjusted gross income for the year.

Generally, the 50% limit is the only limit that applies to gifts to organizations listed under *50% limit organizations*. But there is one exception. A special 30% limit also applies to these gifts if they are gifts of capital gain property for which you figure your deduction using fair market value without reduction for appreciation. (See *Special 30% Limit for Capital Gain Property*, later.)

50% limit organizations. You can ask any organization whether it is a 50% limit organization and most will be able to tell you. Or you may check IRS Publication 78 or call the IRS at 1-877-829-5500 (TTY/TDD 1-800-829-4059). The following is a partial list of the types of organizations that are 50% limit organizations.
- Churches and conventions or associations of churches.
- Educational organizations with a regular faculty and curriculum that normally have a regularly enrolled student body attending classes on site.
- Hospitals and certain medical research organizations associated with these hospitals.
- Publicly supported charities.

30% Limit
A 30% limit applies to the following gifts.
- Gifts to all qualified organizations other than 50% limit organizations. This includes gifts to veterans' organizations, fraternal societies, nonprofit cemeteries, and certain private nonoperating foundations.
- Gifts for the use of any organization.
  However, if these gifts are of capital gain property, they are subject to the 20% limit, described later, rather than the 30% limit.

Student living with you. Amounts you spend on behalf of a student living with you are subject to the 30% limit. These amounts are considered a contribution for the use of a qualified organization. See *Expenses Paid for Student Living With You*, earlier.

Special 30% Limit for Capital Gain Property. A special 30% limit applies to gifts of capital gain property to 50% limit organizations. (For gifts of capital gain property to other organizations, see *20% Limit*, later.) However, the special 30% limit does not apply when you choose to reduce the fair market value of the property by the amount that would have been long-term capital gain if you had sold the property. Instead, only the 50% limit applies.

Two separate 30% limits. This special 30% limit for capital gain property is separate from the other 30% limit. Therefore, the deduction of a contribution subject to one 30% limit does not reduce the amount you can deduct for contributions subject to the other 30% limit. However, the total you deduct cannot be more than 50% of your adjusted gross income.

    Example. Your adjusted gross income is $50,000. During the year, you gave capital gain property with a fair market value of $15,000 to a 50% limit organization. You do not choose to reduce the property's fair market value by its appreciation in value. You also gave $10,000 cash to a qualified organization that is not a 50% limit organization. The $15,000 gift of property is subject to the special 30% limit. The $10,000 cash gift is subject to the other 30% limit. Both gifts are fully deductible because neither is more than the 30% limit that applies ($15,000 in each case) and together they are not more than the 50% limit ($25,000).

    For more information, see the rules for electing the 50% limit for capital gain property under *How To Figure Your Deduction When Limits Apply* in Publication 526.

20% Limit
This limit applies to all gifts of capital gain property to or for the use of qualified organizations (other than gifts of capital gain property to 50% limit organizations).

EXPLANATION
An organization can tell you whether contributions to it qualify for the 50%, 30%, or 20% limit. Contributions to any charitable organization are limited to 50% of your adjusted gross income. This includes a gift of an income interest in trust to a charitable organization.

How to figure your deduction. To figure your deduction, first you consider gifts to charitable organizations that qualify for the 50% limit. Second, you consider gifts to which the 20% and 30% limits apply. Third, you consider gifts of capital gain property to which the special 30% limit for capital gain property applies.

Example 1
Your adjusted gross income is $50,000 for 2014. On July 1, 2014, you gave your church $2,000 cash plus land with a fair market value of $30,000 and a basis to you of $10,000. You had held the land for investment for more than 1 year. You also gave $5,000 cash to a private foundation to which the 30% limit applies. Because your allowable contributions–$32,000 ($2,000 + $30,000)– to an organization to which the 50% limit applies are more than $25,000 (50% of $50,000), your deductions subject to the 30% limit are not allowable. The $2,000 cash donated to the church is considered first. The deduction for the gift of land does not have to be reduced by the appreciation in value and is limited to $15,000 (30% × $50,000). The unused part ($15,000) may be carried over for 5 years. Therefore, in 2014, your deduction is limited to $17,000 ($2,000 + $15,000). The $5,000 contribution to the private foundation may also be carried over for 5 years.

Example 2
Your 2014 adjusted gross income was $50,000. During the year, you gave $5,000 cash to a private foundation, to which the 30% limit applies. You made no other charitable contributions. The entire $5,000 is deductible, because 30% of $50,000 is greater than $5,000.

TAXPLANNER
Contributions of inventory property that was acquired during the taxable year in which the gift was made are not subject to the percentage limitation rules. The cost of these items is claimed as part of the cost of goods sold.

TAXPLANNER
To ease the restrictions on charitable contribution limitations, you may consider making a series of smaller gifts over several years rather than one or two large gifts per year.

Carryovers

You can carry over any contributions you cannot deduct in the current year because they exceed your adjusted-gross-income limits. You can deduct the excess in each of the next 5 years until it is used up, but not beyond that time. For more information, see *Carryovers* in Publication 526.

Your adjusted gross income for 2013 and 2014 is $50,000 and $20,000, respectively. During 2013, you contributed long-term capital gain property valued at $25,000 to your church. In 2013, you deducted $15,000 (30% of $50,000) and carried over $10,000. In 2014, however, your carryover deduction is limited to 30% of $20,000, or $6,000; the remaining $4,000 will have to be carried over to 2015.

EXPLANATION

If a gift of long-term capital gain property subject to the 30% limitation is made and, for some unforeseen reasons, cannot be utilized entirely in the current year or in carryover years, you may elect to reduce its value by 100% of the gain and deduct the lower net value of the gift under the 50% limitation.

Example
Julia Walsh makes a contribution of long-term capital gain property that cost her $40,000 and now has a fair market value of $50,000. Julia dies during the taxable year. Her adjusted gross income on her final return is $80,000.

Without the election mentioned above, Julia's deduction would be limited to $24,000 (30% × $80,000). However, if the value of the property is reduced by $10,000 to Julia's cost, the deduction is increased to $40,000 (50% × $80,000).

TAXPLANNER

For qualified conservation contributions made prior to January 1, 2014, the charitable contribution carryover period is 15 years.

Records To Keep
You must keep records to prove the amount of the contributions you make during the year. The kind of records you must keep depends on the amount of your contributions and whether they are:
- Cash contributions,
- Noncash contributions, or
- Out-of-pocket expenses when donating your services.

EXPLANATION

In order for you to be entitled to a charitable contribution deduction, your donation must meet the following requirements: (1) be a transfer (2) of money or property (3) to a qualified organization (4) that is voluntary and without receipt of any financial or other economic value and (5) made in proper form (with careful attention to the requirements, evidence, and records that must be kept).

The first requirements are relatively straightforward to satisfy as all it requires is that you make a gratuitous donation to an entity that the IRS allows to operate as a qualified organization. The failure to make sure the charitable contribution is in proper form is the requirement that trips up most taxpayers and leads to the disallowance of a deduction. The IRS and the courts require strict adherence to the substantiation (evidence) requirements in order for a taxpayer to be entitled to a charitable deduction.

TAXORGANIZER

If the IRS raises questions. In case the IRS questions your charitable contribution deductions, you should keep the following information to support your claim for charitable contribution deductions:
- Canceled checks evidencing payments of charitable contributions.
- Receipts (letters or other written communication) from the charitable organization showing the name of the organization, the date of the contribution, and the amount of the contribution. The IRS allows the use of e-mail receipts.
- Other reliable written records that include the information described above (records may be considered reliable if they were made at or near the time of the contribution, were regularly kept by you, or in the case of small donations, you have emblems, buttons, or other tokens that are regularly given to persons making small cash contributions).
- Copies of appraisals (if you are claiming a deduction in excess of $5,000) or other determinations of the market value of the contribution.

Note. An organization generally must give you a written statement if it receives a payment from you that is more than $75 and is partly a contribution and partly for goods or services. (See *Contributions From Which You Benefit* under *Contributions You Can Deduct*, earlier.) Keep the statement for your records. It may satisfy all or part of the recordkeeping requirements explained in the following discussions.

Cash Contributions

Cash contributions include those paid by cash, check, electronic funds transfer, debit card, credit card, or payroll deduction.

You cannot deduct a cash contribution, regardless of the amount, unless you keep one of the following.

1. A bank record that shows the name of the qualified organization, the date of the contribution, and the amount of the contribution. Bank records may include:
   a. A canceled check,
   b. A bank or credit union statement, or
   c. A credit card statement.
2. A receipt (or a letter or other written communication) from the qualified organization showing the name of the organization, the date of the contribution, and the amount of the contribution.
3. The payroll deduction records described next.

TAXALERT

A deduction for a cash contribution of any amount will not be allowed unless you have a bank record, such as a canceled check, a receipt, or a written communication from the charitable organization that shows the name of the charity, as well as the date and amount of the contribution. This means that cash contributions to a church collection plate, for example, will not be deductible unless you get a receipt from the church with date and amount details.

Payroll deductions. If you make a contribution by payroll deduction, you must keep:
1. A pay stub, Form W-2, or other document furnished by your employer that shows the date and amount of the contribution, and
2. A pledge card or other document prepared by or for the qualified organization that shows the name of the organization.

If your employer withheld $250 or more from a single paycheck, see *Contributions of $250 or More*, next.

Contributions of $250 or More

You can claim a deduction for a contribution of $250 or more only if you have an acknowledgment of your contribution from the qualified organization or certain payroll deduction records.

If you made more than one contribution of $250 or more, you must have either a separate acknowledgment for each or one acknowledgment that lists each contribution and the date of each contribution and shows your total contributions.

TAXALERT

Written acknowledgments. You are required to obtain a contemporaneous written acknowledgment from any charitable organization to which a contribution of $250 or more is made in order to deduct that contribution. Contemporaneous for this purpose means that you must obtain the written acknowledgment on or before the earlier of (1) the date on which your 2014 return is actually filed or (2) the due date for the return, including extensions. An e-mail receipt qualifies as a written acknowledgment.

A canceled check does not constitute adequate substantiation for a cash contribution of the amount. The written acknowledgment will have to state the amount of cash and a description (but not the value) of any property other than cash contributed. It must also state whether the charitable organization provided any goods or services in consideration for the contribution, and, if so, a description and good faith estimate of the value of goods or services provided. If the goods or services provided as consideration for the contribution consist solely of intangible religious benefits, a statement to that effect will have to be included in the written acknowledgment.

Note that the primary responsibility lies with you, not the charitable organization, to request and maintain the required substantiation in your records.

For any contribution over $75 for which the charity provides goods or services, such as a dinner, the charity must provide a statement to the donor that reports the estimated value of the goods or services received by the donor in exchange for the contribution. A payment to a charity is deductible only to the extent that it exceeds the value of any goods or services received in return.

TAXALERT

A 2012 tax court ruling denied a charitable deduction to a couple who made cash donations totaling over $25,000 to their church. Although the church sent a timely letter to the couple that acknowledged their donations, the letter lacked the required statement regarding the value, if any, of goods or services received by the taxpayers in exchange for their contributions. The church provided a second acknowledgment 18 months later that expressly included the proper statement. Nevertheless, the court agreed with the IRS that the contribution should be disallowed because the first acknowledgment letter did not include the required statement, while the second was not a "contemporaneous" receipt because it was not received by the taxpayers by the due date for filing their original return for the year.

TAXPLANNER

Separate payments. In general, separate payments are not combined for purposes of the substantiation requirement. Therefore, you could deduct separate contributions of less than $250 from each paycheck or make monthly payments to a charity without running afoul of the requirement. However, you could not, for example, simply write multiple checks on the same day in order to avoid substantiation. Similarly, separate payments made at different times with respect to different fund-raising events are not totaled in order to determine whether the charity must inform the donor of the value of any benefit received in return for a donation in excess of $75.

Amount of contribution. In figuring whether your contribution is $250 or more, do not combine separate contributions. For example, if you gave your church $25 each week, your weekly payments do not have to be combined. Each payment is a separate contribution.

If contributions are made by payroll deduction, the deduction from each paycheck is treated as a separate contribution.

If you made a payment that is partly for goods and services, as described earlier under *Contributions From Which You Benefit*, your contribution is the amount of the payment that is more than the value of the goods and services.

Acknowledgment. The acknowledgment must meet these tests.
1. It must be written.
2. It must include:
   a. The amount of cash you contributed,
   b. Whether the qualified organization gave you any goods or services as a result of your contribution (other than certain token items and membership benefits),
   c. A description and good faith estimate of the value of any goods or services described in (b) (other than intangible religious benefits), and
   d. A statement that the only benefit you received was an intangible religious benefit, if that was the case. The acknowledgment does not need to describe or estimate the value of an intangible religious benefit. An intangible religious benefit is a benefit that generally is not sold in commercial transactions outside a donative (gift) context. An example is admission to a religious ceremony.
3. You must get it on or before the earlier of:
   a. The date you file your return for the year you make the contribution, or
   b. The due date, including extensions, for filing the return.

If the acknowledgment does not show the date of the contribution, you must also have a bank record or receipt, as described earlier, that does show the date of the contribution. If the acknowledgment shows the date of the contribution and meets the other tests just described, you do not need any other records.

Payroll deductions. If you make a contribution by payroll deduction and your employer withholds $250 or more from a single paycheck, you must keep:

1. A pay stub, Form W-2, or other document furnished by your employer that shows the amount withheld as a contribution, and
2. A pledge card or other document prepared by or for the qualified organization that shows the name of the organization and states the organization does not provide goods or services in return for any contribution made to it by payroll deduction.

A single pledge card may be kept for all contributions made by payroll deduction regardless of amount as long as it contains all the required information.

If the pay stub, Form W-2, pledge card, or other document does not show the date of the contribution, you must have another document that does show the date of the contribution. If the pay stub, Form W-2, pledge card, or other document shows the date of the contribution, you do not need any other records except those just described in (1) and (2).

Noncash Contributions

For a contribution not made in cash, the records you must keep depend on whether your deduction for the contribution is:

1. Less than $250,
2. At least $250 but not more than $500,
3. Over $500 but not more than $5,000, or
4. Over $5,000.

Amount of deduction. In figuring whether your deduction is $500 or more, combine your claimed deductions for all similar items of property donated to any charitable organization during the year.

If you received goods or services in return, as described earlier in *Contributions From Which You Benefit*, reduce your contribution by the value of those goods or services. If you figure your deduction by reducing the fair market value of the donated property by its appreciation, as described earlier in *Giving Property That Has Increased in Value*, your contribution is the reduced amount.

Deductions of Less Than $250

If you make any noncash contribution, you must get and keep a receipt from the charitable organization showing:

1. The name of the charitable organization,
2. The date and location of the charitable contribution, and
3. A reasonably detailed description of the property.

A letter or other written communication from the charitable organization acknowledging receipt of the contribution and containing the information in (1), (2), and (3) will serve as a receipt.

You are not required to have a receipt where it is impractical to get one (for example, if you leave property at a charity's unattended drop site).

Additional records. You must also keep reliable written records for each item of contributed property. Your written records must include the following information.

- The name and address of the organization to which you contributed.
- The date and location of the contribution.
- A description of the property in detail reasonable under the circumstances. For a security, keep the name of the issuer, the type of security, and whether it is regularly traded on a stock exchange or in an over-the-counter market.
- The fair market value of the property at the time of the contribution and how you figured the fair market value. If it was determined by appraisal, keep a signed copy of the appraisal.
- The cost or other basis of the property, if you must reduce its fair market value by appreciation. Your records should also include the amount of the reduction and how you figured it.
- The amount you claim as a deduction for the tax year as a result of the contribution, if you contribute less than your entire interest in the property during the tax year. Your records must include the amount you claimed as a deduction in any earlier years for contributions of other interests in this property. They must also include the name and address of each organization to which you contributed the other interests, the place where any such tangible property is located or kept, and the name of any person in possession of the property, other than the organization to which you contributed it.
- The terms of any conditions attached to the contribution of property.

Deductions of At Least $250 But Not More Than $500

If you claim a deduction of at least $250 but not more than $500 for a noncash charitable contribution, you must get and keep an acknowledgment of your contribution from the qualified organization. If you made more than one contribution of $250 or more, you must have either a separate acknowledgment for each or one acknowledgment that shows your total contributions.

The acknowledgment must contain the information in items (1) through (3) under *Deductions of Less Than $250*, earlier, and your written records must include the information listed in that discussion under *Additional records*.

The acknowledgment must also meet these tests.

1. It must be written.
2. It must include:
   a. A description (but not necessarily the value) of any property you contributed,
   b. Whether the qualified organization gave you any goods or services as a result of your contribution (other than certain token items and membership benefits), and
   c. A description and good faith estimate of the value of any goods or services described in (b). If the only benefit you received was an intangible religious benefit (such as admission to a religious ceremony) that generally is not sold in a commercial transaction outside the donative context, the acknowledgment must say so and does not need to describe or estimate the value of the benefit.
3. You must get it on or before the earlier of:
   a. The date you file your return for the year you make the contribution, or
   b. The due date, including extensions, for filing the return.

Deductions Over $500

You are required to give additional information if you claim a deduction over $500 for noncash charitable contributions. See *Records To Keep* in Publication 526 for more information.

> ## EXPLANATION
> A receipt is not required if you deposit property at a charity's unattended drop site unless you claim that the property is worth more than $250. However, you must maintain a written record of the contribution, listing the items contributed and the date and location of the contribution.
>
> You are required to file Form 8283, Noncash Charitable Contributions, if you claim a deduction of over $500 for noncash contributions. Additionally, there are special rules for noncash contributions in excess of $5,000 and $500,000, as well as donations of vehicles, discussed previously in this chapter.
>
> For contributions having a fair market value of more than $500 but not more than $5,000, the donor must provide the following information:
> - The name and address of the charitable organization
> - The description of the donated property
> - The date of the contribution
> - The date it was acquired by the donor
> - How it was acquired by the donor
> - The donor's cost or adjusted basis (except for publicly traded securities or property held for more than 12 months)
> - The fair market value of the contribution
> - The method used to determine the fair market value (e.g., appraisal, thrift shop value, catalog, market quote, or comparable sales)
>   Form 8283 must be filed with the tax return on which the deduction is taken.
>
> For contributions in excess of $500,000 you must attach a copy of the qualified appraisal to your return.

Out-of-Pocket Expenses

If you give services to a qualified organization and have unreimbursed out-of-pocket expenses related to those services, the following two rules apply.

1. You must have adequate records to prove the amount of the expenses.
2. If any of your unreimbursed out-of-pocket expenses, considered separately, are $250 or more (for example, you pay $250 or more for an airline ticket to attend a convention of a qualified organization as a chosen representative), you must get an acknowledgment from the qualified organization that contains:
   a. A description of the services you provided,
   b. A statement of whether or not the organization provided you any goods or services to reimburse you for the expenses you incurred,

c. A description and a good faith estimate of the value of any goods or services (other than intangible religious benefits) provided to reimburse you, and

d. A statement that the only benefit you received was an intangible religious benefit, if that was the case. The acknowledgment does not need to describe or estimate the value of an intangible religious benefit (defined earlier under *Acknowledgment*).

You must get the acknowledgment on or before the earlier of:

1. The date you file your return for the year you make the contribution, or
2. The due date, including extensions, for filing the return.

Car expenses. If you claim expenses directly related to use of your car in giving services to a qualified organization, you must keep reliable written records of your expenses. Whether your records are considered reliable depends on all the facts and circumstances. Generally, they may be considered reliable if you made them regularly and at or near the time you had the expenses.

For example, your records might show the name of the organization you were serving and the dates you used your car for a charitable purpose. If you use the standard mileage rate of 14 cents a mile, your records must show the miles you drove your car for the charitable purpose. If you deduct your actual expenses, your records must show the costs of operating the car that are directly related to a charitable purpose.

See *Car expenses* under *Out-of-Pocket Expenses in Giving Services*, earlier, for the expenses you can deduct.

How To Report

Report your charitable contributions on Schedule A (Form 1040).

If your total deduction for all noncash contributions for the year is over $500, you must also file Form 8283. See *How To Report* in Publication 526 for more information.

Chapter 26
Nonbusiness casualty and theft losses

Note

IRS Publication 17 (*Your Federal Income Tax*) has been updated by Ernst & Young LLP for 2014. Dates and dollar amounts shown are for 2014. Underlined type is used to indicate where IRS text has been updated. Places where text has been removed are indicated by the sentence: *Text intentionally omitted.*

ey.com/EYTaxGuide

Ernst & Young LLP will update the *EY Tax Guide 2015* website with relevant taxpayer information as it becomes available. You can also sign up for email alerts to let you know when changes have been made.

Introduction

Almost any time something you own is stolen, damaged, or destroyed in an accident or by an act of nature, and you are not compensated by insurance, you are eligible for a tax deduction. The loss need not be connected in any way to your trade or business, and it may include such personal items as jewelry, furs, and antiques. That's small comfort if everything you own has been demolished in a terrible earthquake or a devastating hurricane, but it's something.

In order to claim a casualty loss deduction, you must first prove that the casualty occurred. The most difficult task is substantiating the value of the property you have lost. That gorgeous necklace that your grandmother gave you may be worth a substantial amount, but, unless you can prove it, you're going to have a difficult time claiming a tax deduction if it is stolen. (Of course, even if you can prove the value, your deduction is generally limited to your cost basis.) Recordkeeping and documentation are extremely important.

No matter how good your records are, you must itemize your deductions and pass two general limitations on the amount of your casualty and theft loss. First, for personal use losses that occurred in 2014 you may not deduct the first $100 of any loss. Second and more significant, you are able to deduct personal casualty and theft losses only when the total amount you lost in any year—reduced by $100 per casualty—exceeds 10% of your adjusted gross income (AGI).

This chapter spells out which casualty losses are deductible. You'll also learn about the details that should be considered in deciding when to take your deduction. The rules for deducting business losses are different. They are also discussed in this chapter. Most importantly, this chapter discusses the records and other evidence you need to support any claim that you make.

TAXPLANNER

You may be eligible for some tax relief if you were the victim of various storms that occurred during 2014. The IRS website, irs.gov, contains links to related news releases for the victims of the affected areas. A list of the 2014 Federal Disaster Declarations is available on the FEMA website at fema.gov/news/disasters.fema.

This chapter explains the tax treatment of personal (not business or investment related) casualty losses, theft losses, and losses on deposits.

The chapter also explains the following topics.
- How to figure the amount of your loss.
- How to treat insurance and other reimbursements you receive.
- The deduction limits.
- When and how to report a casualty or theft.

> **EXPLANATION**
>
> This chapter includes a discussion on what to do if a loss is partly business and partly personal. For example, if your basement flooded and damage occurred to both personal property and business property located in your home office located in the basement, the loss would be partly business and partly personal. See *Property Used Partly for Business and Partly for Personal Purposes*, later in this chapter.
>
> This chapter also discusses the special rules for disaster area losses.

Forms to file. When you have a casualty or theft, you have to file Form 4684. You will also have to file one or more of the following forms.
- Schedule A (Form 1040), Itemized Deductions
- Schedule D (Form 1040), Capital Gains and Losses

> **EXPLANATION**
>
> For details on which forms to use, see *How to Report Gains and Losses*, later in this chapter.

Condemnations. For information on condemnations of property, see *Involuntary Conversions* in chapter 1 of Publication 544, Sales and Other Disposition of Assets.

Workbook for casualties and thefts. Publication 584 is available to help you make a list of your stolen or damaged personal-use property and figure your loss. It includes schedules to help you figure the loss on your home, its contents, and your motor vehicles.

Business or investment-related losses. For information on a casualty or theft loss of business or income-producing property, see Publication 547, Casualties, Disasters, and Thefts.

> **TAXPLANNER**
>
> Publication 584-B, *Business Casualty, Disaster, and Theft Loss Workbook*, is available to help you make a list of your stolen or damaged business or income-producing property and figure your loss.

Useful Items

You may want to see:

Publication
- ☐ **544** Sales and Other Dispositions of Assets
- ☐ **547** Casualties, Disasters, and Thefts
- ☐ **584** Casualty, Disaster, and Theft Loss Workbook (Personal-Use Property)

Form (and Instructions)
- ☐ **Schedule A (Form 1040)** Itemized Deductions
- ☐ **Schedule D (Form 1040)** Capital Gains and Losses
- ☐ **4684** Casualties and Thefts

> **EXPLANATION**
>
> Other useful publications and references include:
>
> **Publication**
> - **584-B** Business Casualty, Disaster, and Theft Loss Workbook
> - **2194** Resource Guide for Individuals and Businesses
>
> **Form**
> - **4506** Request for Copy of Tax Return

Casualty

A casualty is the damage, destruction, or loss of property resulting from an identifiable event that is sudden, unexpected, or unusual.

- A sudden event is one that is swift, not gradual or progressive.
- An unexpected event is one that is ordinarily unanticipated and unintended.
- An unusual event is one that is not a day-to-day occurrence and that is not typical of the activity in which you were engaged.

Deductible losses. Deductible casualty losses can result from a number of different causes, including the following.

- Car accidents (but see *Nondeductible losses*, next, for exceptions).

> ### EXPLANATION
> Damage resulting from faulty but not intentionally reckless driving is a casualty loss. Damage incurred while an automobile was operated by an unauthorized person is also a casualty loss.
> The following are examples of casualty losses involving automobiles:
> - The loss of an automobile that fell through the ice while the taxpayer was ice fishing
> - Damage to an automobile starter caused by a child who pressed the starter button while the automobile's engine was operating

- Earthquakes.
- Fires (but see *Nondeductible losses*, next, for exceptions).
- Floods.
- Government-ordered demolition or relocation of a home that is unsafe to use because of a disaster as discussed under *Disaster Area Losses* in Publication 547.

> ### EXPLANATION
> Your state or local government must issue the order within 120 days after the area has been declared a disaster area.

- Mine cave-ins.
- Shipwrecks.
- Sonic booms.
- Storms, including hurricanes and tornadoes.
- Terrorist attacks.
- Vandalism.
- Volcanic eruptions.

> ### EXPLANATION
> Losses caused by a person's own negligence are deductible, as are losses that occur even though they could have been foreseen or prevented. The courts have also allowed casualty loss deductions in the following cases:
>
> **Animals and insects**
> - Damage caused by a mass attack of southern pine beetles capable of destroying a tree in 5 to 10 days
> - Death of a horse by swallowing the lining of a hat
>
> **Drought**
> - Cracking of foundation walls due to soil shrinkage
> - Death of trees and plants within 3 to 4 months as a result of extraordinary drought
>
> **Earthquakes and landslides**
> - Collapse of a garage wall due to subsoil hydraulic action
> - Damage caused by a mine cave-in even though the landslide was reasonably foreseeable

Tax Breaks and Deductions You Can Use Checklist

Casualty and theft losses. You can claim an itemized deduction for personal losses from fires, storms, car accidents, and similar "sudden, unexpected, or unusual" events, as well as losses from theft. These losses are deductible only to the extent they exceed $100 per occurrence in 2014 and 10% of your adjusted gross income.

Victims of federally declared disasters. Special tax law provisions may help taxpayers and businesses recover from the impact of a disaster, especially when the federal government declares their location to be a major disaster area. Depending on the circumstances, the IRS may grant additional time to file returns and pay taxes. Both individuals and businesses in a federally declared disaster area can get a faster refund by claiming losses related to the disaster on the tax return for the previous year, usually by filing an amended return. Search "Disaster Assistance" on irs.gov for the latest information regarding tax law provisions related to disaster relief. Generally, you must deduct a casualty loss in the year it occurred. However, if you incurred a casualty loss in a federally declared disaster area during 2014, the tax law allows you to claim that loss on your 2013 tax return or an amended return for 2013, instead of claiming the loss on your 2014 return. If you do so, the loss is treated as having occurred in 2013. Claiming a federally declared disaster loss incurred in

2014 on your 2013 return or amended return may result in a lower tax or produce or increase a cash refund. You should compare the tax savings you may recognize from claiming such a disaster loss on your 2014 return versus 2013.

Household
- Damage from corrosive drywall
- Bursting of hot water boiler caused by air obstruction in water pipes
- Damage to furniture dropped 16 floors by movers
- Damage caused by a flood due to faulty construction (however, the cost of repairing the defect was not deductible)
- Septic tank damage caused by plowing in preparation for planting shrubs

Lightning
- Any damage caused by lightning

Personal belongings
- Damage to a diamond ring inadvertently dropped in a kitchen garbage disposal
- Damage to a ring caused by a husband slamming a car door on his wife's finger

Storms
- Damage to an artificial beach due to abnormal rains
- Damage to a home by ice and snow
- Damage to a beach house that was caused by a hurricane but was not discovered until 2 years later, when the floorboards and porch buckled (the loss was deductible in the year in which the damage was discovered)
- Property damage due to unusually high water levels caused by storms

Trees, shrubs, and landscaping
- Damage caused by accidental application of chemical weed killer to a lawn
- Damage to trees caused by blizzards and snowstorms
- Loss of trees, shrubs, and grass due to fire
- Damage by a tractor plowing the ground

Vandalism
- Damage to household appliances caused by vandals who broke into a house under construction
- Damage and destruction of art objects by vandals

Nondeductible losses. A casualty loss is not deductible if the damage or destruction is caused by the following.
- Accidentally breaking articles such as glassware or china under normal conditions.
- A family pet (explained below).
- A fire if you willfully set it or pay someone else to set it.
- A car accident if your willful negligence or willful act caused it. The same is true if the willful act or willful negligence of someone acting for you caused the accident.
- Progressive deterioration (explained later).

Family pet. Loss of property due to damage by a family pet is not deductible as a casualty loss unless the requirements discussed earlier under *Casualty* are met.

Example. Your antique oriental rug was damaged by your new puppy before it was housebroken. Because the damage was not unexpected and unusual, the loss is not deductible as a casualty loss.

Progressive deterioration. Loss of property due to progressive deterioration is not deductible as a casualty loss. This is because the damage results from a steadily operating cause or a normal process, rather than from a sudden event. The following are examples of damage due to progressive deterioration.
- The steady weakening of a building due to normal wind and weather conditions.

EXPLANATION
The following also do *not* qualify as casualty losses: damage from faulty construction that caused walls and floors to settle, dry rot to a wooden sloop, and the decline in value of a piece of land affected by gradual deterioration. However, the breaking up of a driveway caused by weather conditions over a 4-month period has been allowed as a casualty loss.

- The deterioration and damage to a water heater that bursts. However, the rust and water damage to rugs and drapes caused by the bursting of a water heater does qualify as a casualty.

- Most losses of property caused by droughts. To be deductible, a drought-related loss generally must be incurred in a trade or business or in a transaction entered into for profit.
- Termite or moth damage.
- The damage or destruction of trees, shrubs, or other plants by a fungus, disease, insects, worms, or similar pests. However, a sudden destruction due to an unexpected or unusual infestation of beetles or other insects may result in a casualty loss.

Damage from corrosive drywall. Under a special procedure, you may be able to claim a casualty loss deduction for amounts you paid to repair damage to your home and household appliances that resulted from corrosive drywall. For details, see Publication 547.

Urban Development (HUD) in interim guidance dated January 28, 2010, as revised by the CPSC and HUD. Revised identification guidance and remediation guidelines are available at *www.cpsc.gov/info/drywall/InterimIDGuidance012810.pdf*. Incidents of corrosive drywall largely involve homes built in 2006 and 2007. A record number of new homes were built during this time period, largely as a result of the hurricanes in 2004 and 2005 that destroyed or damaged many homes.

The amount of the loss allowed under the special procedure for corrosive drywall is as follows:

- If a claim for reimbursement is not pending and is not intended to be filed, you can claim a loss for all unreimbursed amounts paid during the year to repair the damage from corrosive drywall to your personal residence and household appliances (otherwise if a reimbursement claim is pending or intended to be filed, the loss is limited to 75% of the unreimbursed amounts paid in the tax year).
- If you have been fully reimbursed before filing a return for the year the loss was sustained, you cannot claim a loss.

Refer to Publication 547 and Revenue Procedure 2010-36, 2010-42 IRB 439, for additional details related to reporting such claim.

Theft

A theft is the taking and removing of money or property with the intent to deprive the owner of it. The taking of property must be illegal under the laws of the state where it occurred and it must have been done with criminal intent. You do not need to show a conviction for theft.

EXPLANATION

A theft loss is deducted in the year of discovery, not the year of the theft, unless they both occur in the same year. If, in the year of discovery, an insurance claim exists and there is a reasonable expectation of recovering the cost of the asset from the insurance company, no deduction is permitted. Losses on securities which resulted from malfeasance of officers or directors—such as in the case of Enron—are not considered theft losses. Instead the loss is treated as a capital loss.

Theft includes the taking of money or property by the following means.

- Blackmail.
- Burglary.
- Embezzlement.
- Extortion.
- Kidnapping for ransom.
- Larceny.
- Robbery.

The taking of money or property through fraud or misrepresentation is theft if it is illegal under state or local law.

EXAMPLES

- A taxpayer from New York was allowed a deduction for a theft loss for money given to fortune-tellers. Under New York law, fortune-telling is a crime. The taxpayer's testimony and receipts were sufficient proof of the amounts paid to the fortune-tellers.
- A moving company placed an individual's belongings in storage until a price dispute could be resolved. A court ruled that because there was a reasonable likelihood that the individual would recover his property, no theft loss was allowed.
- In a recent case, the Tax Court concluded that a construction company misused funds an Illinois couple paid for an addition on their home and made misrepresentations to them, entitling the couple to a theft loss deduction.

Decline in market value of stock. You cannot deduct as a theft loss the decline in market value of stock acquired on the open market for investment if the decline is caused by disclosure of accounting fraud or other illegal misconduct by the officers or directors of the corporation that issued the stock. However, you can deduct as a capital loss the loss you sustain when you sell or exchange the stock or the stock becomes completely worthless. You report a capital loss on Schedule D (Form 1040). For more information about stock sales, worthless stock, and capital losses, see chapter 4 of Publication 550.

Mislaid or lost property. The simple disappearance of money or property is not a theft. However, an accidental loss or disappearance of property can qualify as a casualty if it results from an identifiable event that is sudden, unexpected, or unusual. Sudden, unexpected, and unusual events are defined earlier.

   Example. A car door is accidentally slammed on your hand, breaking the setting of your diamond ring. The diamond falls from the ring and is never found. The loss of the diamond is a casualty.

> ### EXPLANATION
> Another type of loss you may experience is seizure, requisition, or condemnation. For example, the government might seize your home in order to build a new highway. For further discussion, see chapter 13, *Basis of property*, and chapter 14, *Sale of property*.

Losses from Ponzi-type investment schemes. If you had a loss from a Ponzi-type investment scheme, see:
- Revenue Ruling 2009-9, 2009-14 I.R.B. 735 (available at *www.irs.gov/irb/2009-14 IRB/ar07.html*).
- Revenue Procedure 2009-20, 2009-14 I.R.B. 749 (available at *www.irs.gov/irb/2009-14 IRB/ar11.html*).
- Revenue Procedure 2011-58, 2011-50 I.R.B. 849 (available at *www.irs.gov/irb/2011-50 IRB/ar11.html*).

   If you qualify to use Revenue Procedure 2009-20, as modified by Revenue Procedure 2011-58, and you choose to follow the procedures in the guidance, first fill out Section C of Form 4684 to determine the amount to enter on Section B, line 28. Skip lines 19 to 27. Section C of Form 4684 replaces Appendix A in Revenue Procedure 2009-20. You do not need to complete Appendix A. For more information, see the above revenue ruling and revenue procedures, and the Instructions for Form 4684.

   If you choose not to use the procedures in Revenue Procedure 2009-20, you may claim your theft loss by filling out Section B, lines 19 to 39, as appropriate.

> ### EXPLANATION
> In a change to its long-standing position, the IRS ruled (Revenue Ruling 2009-9) that losses suffered in a Ponzi scheme (for example, the multibillion-dollar fraud perpetrated by Bernard Madoff and his investment company) are not subject to the restrictions generally applicable to personal theft losses. Therefore, losses from a Ponzi scheme are not reduced by 10% of adjusted gross income (AGI) plus $100. (Like personal theft losses generally, Ponzi scheme losses are also not subject to the 2%-of-AGI limitation on miscellaneous itemized deductions—see chapter 29, *Miscellaneous deductions*.)
>
> The IRS has also offered victims of Ponzi schemes an option to claim a significant portion of their potential theft loss deduction (the deduction can range from 75% up to 95% of the total potential loss, depending upon the taxpayer's recovery efforts) in the year of discovery. This is available for losses discovered after 2007. Under existing regulations and case law, a claim for reimbursement of a theft loss typically bars a current deduction if there is a reasonable prospect for recovery for any portion of the claim.
>
> In 2011, the IRS issued Revenue Procedure 2011-58, which modifies certain definitions relating to qualified losses from Ponzi-type investment schemes. In particular, this revenue procedure modifies the definitions of "qualified loss" in Section 4.02 and "discovery year" in Section 4.04 of Revenue Procedure 2009-20. The revenue procedure is available at *irs.gov/pub/irs-irbs/irb11-50.pdf*.
>
> The rules are very complex. Consult your tax advisor if you have suffered losses from a Ponzi scheme.

Loss on Deposits

A loss on deposits can occur when a bank, credit union, or other financial institution becomes insolvent or bankrupt. If you incurred this type of loss, you can choose one of the following ways to deduct the loss.
- As a casualty loss.
- As an ordinary loss.
- As a nonbusiness bad debt.

Casualty loss or ordinary loss. You can choose to deduct a loss on deposits as a casualty loss or as an ordinary loss for any year in which you can reasonably estimate how much of your deposits you have lost in an insolvent or bankrupt financial institution. The choice is generally made on the return you file for that year and applies to all your losses on deposits for the year in that particular financial institution. If you treat the loss as a casualty or ordinary loss, you cannot treat the same amount of the loss as a nonbusiness bad debt when it actually becomes worthless. However, you can take a nonbusiness bad debt deduction for any amount of loss that is more than the estimated amount you deducted as a casualty or ordinary loss. Once you make this choice, you cannot change it without permission from the Internal Revenue Service.

If you claim an ordinary loss, report it as a miscellaneous itemized deduction on Schedule A (Form 1040), line 23. The maximum amount you can claim is $20,000 ($10,000 if you are married filing separately) reduced by any expected state insurance proceeds. Your loss is subject to the 2%-of-adjusted-gross-income limit. You cannot choose to claim an ordinary loss if any part of the deposit is federally insured.

Nonbusiness bad debt. If you do not choose to deduct the loss as a casualty loss or as an ordinary loss, you must wait until the year the actual loss is determined and deduct the loss as a nonbusiness bad debt in that year.

How to report. The kind of deduction you choose for your loss on deposits determines how you report your loss. If you choose:
- Casualty loss — report it on Form 4684 first and then on Schedule A (Form 1040).
- Ordinary loss — report it on Schedule A (Form 1040) as a miscellaneous itemized deduction.
- Nonbusiness bad debt — report it on Form 8949 first and then on Schedule D (Form 1040).

More information. For more information, see *Special Treatment for Losses on Deposits in Insolvent or Bankrupt Financial Institutions* in the Instructions for Form 4684 or *Deposit in Insolvent or Bankrupt Financial Institution* in Publication 550.

EXPLANATION

Deducted loss recovered. If you recover an amount you deducted as a loss in an earlier year, you may have to include the amount recovered in your income for the year of recovery. If any part of the original deduction did not reduce your tax in the earlier year, you do not have to include that part of the recovery in your income. For more information, see *Recoveries* in Publication 525.

Proof of Loss

To deduct a casualty or theft loss, you must be able to prove that you had a casualty or theft. You also must be able to support the amount you take as a deduction.

Casualty loss proof. For a casualty loss, your records should show all the following.
- The type of casualty (car accident, fire, storm, etc.) and when it occurred.
- That the loss was a direct result of the casualty.
- That you were the owner of the property or, if you leased the property from someone else, that you were contractually liable to the owner for the damage.
- Whether a claim for reimbursement exists for which there is a reasonable expectation of recovery.

Theft loss proof. For a theft loss, your records should show all the following.
- When you discovered that your property was missing.
- That your property was stolen.
- That you were the owner of the property.
- Whether a claim for reimbursement exists for which there is a reasonable expectation of recovery.

Records

It is important that you have records that will prove your deduction. If you do not have the actual records to support your deduction, you can use other satisfactory evidence to support it.

TAXPLANNER

Proving a theft took place. For a loss from theft to be deductible, you must be able to prove that a theft has taken place. Therefore, if you think a theft may have occurred, you should file a report with the police and attach a copy of the police report to your return. The report should describe any evidence of breaking and entering and of any witness to the removal of the property. It is not necessary that the police investigate the alleged incident.

Supporting evidence. If you are going to claim a deduction for a casualty or theft loss, it is important that you gather as much supporting evidence as possible. Newspaper clippings about a storm, police reports, and insurance reports may all be helpful in proving the nature of the casualty or theft and when it occurred. You have the burden of proof to establish that a casualty occurred and that your loss was a direct result of the casualty.

Examples
- The Tax Court disallowed a casualty loss deduction for flood damage because the taxpayer failed to corroborate his testimony or provide reliable substantiation of the amount of loss, such as an inventory of damaged personal items and receipts for repairs to his residence.
- The Tax Court denied the amount of a casualty loss deduction that exceeded the insurance estimate for hurricane damage because the handwritten receipt for repairs appeared suspect to the IRS and insufficient to support the taxpayer's claim.
- A taxpayer was disallowed a casualty loss deduction relating to the alleged theft of rental equipment from the taxpayer's van. The rental invoices submitted for proof were considered inadmissible by the Court since they were provided on the day of the trial and were not for the same year the taxpayer claimed the deduction.

Explanation
- If there is no positive proof that a theft occurred, all details and evidence should be presented. If evidence points to a theft, the Tax Court has allowed a deduction. However, if the evidence points to a mysterious (unexplained) disappearance, deductions may be disallowed.
- If the property is leased. Losses are deductible only by the owner of the property, unless the property is leased and the lessee is obligated to repair casualty damage to the property.

Figuring a Loss

Figure the amount of your loss using the following steps.

1. Determine your adjusted basis in the property before the casualty or theft.
2. Determine the decrease in fair market value of the property as a result of the casualty or theft.
3. From the smaller of the amounts you determined in (1) and (2), subtract any insurance or other reimbursement you received or expect to receive.

EXPLANATION

Calculate your loss, taking into consideration any reimbursements you may receive. Your loss is limited to the lesser of your cost basis or the reduction in fair market value.

Proof of the amount of a casualty loss is as important as proving the existence of the casualty. There are numerous court cases in which the taxpayers have shown the existence of a casualty but failed to establish the amount of the loss and were, therefore, denied a casualty loss deduction.

Example 1

A ruby ring valued at $5,000 is stolen from your house. The ring was purchased by your grandfather in 1950 for $500 and was handed down through two generations by means of nontaxable gifts. The amount of the loss is limited to $500, the cost of the ring to your grandfather.

Example 2

A homeowner was not entitled to a casualty loss deduction resulting from hurricane damage to trees located on his property because a real estate agent's appraisal was not accepted as adequate proof of decline in the fair market value of the property. Thus, the decrease in the fair market value of the property as a result of the casualty was zero.

TAXPLANNER

Establishing the amount of your loss may be difficult, but the time you spend documenting the loss may be of great value in reducing your tax. In one court opinion, a taxpayer was denied a casualty loss deduction because she failed to establish either her basis in or the fair market value of the property.

You should make a list of all stolen, lost, damaged, or destroyed items as soon after the theft, disaster, or casualty as possible. IRS Publication 584, *Casualty, Disaster, and Theft Loss Workbook*, may be useful. It has schedules for each room in a typical house to help you calculate a loss on your home and its contents and on your automobile, van, truck, or motorcycle.

It is equally important to retain records that help you establish the adjusted basis of valuable property. In other words, you should keep receipts and documents establishing the original purchase price, costs of improvements, portions sold, or earlier losses in the value of the property.

Photographs or video of your home and contents before the casualty may provide evidence of value and may assist you in determining which items are missing or were destroyed in a casualty or theft. If you do not have photographs, drawing a sketch of each room may be helpful in identifying lost items.

Determining the decrease in market value of household items and personal belongings is often difficult. A certain percentage of the original cost of an item has often been used both by the IRS and by the courts to determine the fair market value of a particular item. Therefore, if you can produce evidence of the original cost of the items that were lost or damaged, you may help your case.

The IRS has provided methods that may be used to figure the deduction for a casualty loss of personal-use residential real property and personal belongings damaged, destroyed, or stolen as a result of storms and other federally declared disasters. See Publication 547, *Casualties, Disasters, and Thefts*, for more information.

For personal-use property and property used in performing services as an employee, apply the deduction limits, discussed later, to determine the amount of your deductible loss.

Gain from reimbursement. If your reimbursement is more than your adjusted basis in the property, you have a gain. This is true even if the decrease in the FMV of the property is smaller than your adjusted basis. If you have a gain, you may have to pay tax on it, or you may be able to postpone reporting the gain. See Publication 547 for more information on how to treat a gain from a reimbursement for a casualty or theft.

> ### EXPLANATION
> In addition to Publication 547, see _Insurance and Other Reimbursements_, later.

Leased property. If you are liable for casualty damage to property you lease, your loss is the amount you must pay to repair the property minus any insurance or other reimbursement you receive or expect to receive.

> ### EXPLANATION
> **Business or income-producing property.** If you have business or income-producing property, such as rental property, and it is stolen or completely destroyed, the decrease in fair market value is not considered. Your loss is figured as follows: your adjusted basis in the property minus any salvage value minus any insurance or other reimbursement you receive or expect to receive.

Decrease in Fair Market Value
Fair market value (FMV) is the price for which you could sell your property to a willing buyer when neither of you has to sell or buy and both of you know all the relevant facts.

The decrease in FMV used to figure the amount of a casualty or theft loss is the difference between the property's fair market value immediately before and immediately after the casualty or theft.

FMV of stolen property. The FMV of property immediately after a theft is considered to be zero, since you no longer have the property.

Example. Several years ago, you purchased silver dollars at face value for $150. This is your adjusted basis in the property. Your silver dollars were stolen this year. The FMV of the coins was $1,000 just before they were stolen, and insurance did not cover them. Your theft loss is $150.

> ### EXPLANATION
> Your theft loss is $150, the lesser of the adjusted basis in the property ($150) or the decrease in fair market value of the property ($1,000).

Recovered stolen property. Recovered stolen property is your property that was stolen and later returned to you. If you recovered property after you had already taken a theft loss deduction, you must refigure your loss using the smaller of the property's adjusted basis (explained later) or the decrease in FMV from the time just before it was stolen until the time it was recovered. Use this amount to refigure your total loss for the year in which the loss was deducted.

If your refigured loss is less than the loss you deducted, you generally have to report the difference as income in the recovery year. But report the difference only up to the amount of the loss that reduced your tax. For more information on the amount to report, see _Recoveries_ in chapter 12.

> ### EXAMPLE
> Your personal automobile is stolen. You paid $27,000 for it, and, on the day it was stolen, it had a fair market value of $15,500. Several days later, your automobile is found damaged and abandoned. The fair market value is reduced to $13,000 because of the damage. Your loss is $2,500. The decrease in market value ($15,500 – $13,000) is less than your cost of $27,000. Therefore, your deduction is limited to $2,500.

Figuring Decrease in FMV—Items To Consider

To figure the decrease in FMV because of a casualty or theft, you generally need a competent appraisal. However, other measures can also be used to establish certain decreases.

Appraisal. An appraisal to determine the difference between the FMV of the property immediately before a casualty or theft and immediately afterward should be made by a competent appraiser. The appraiser must recognize the effects of any general market decline that may occur along with the casualty. This information is needed to limit any deduction to the actual loss resulting from damage to the property.

Several factors are important in evaluating the accuracy of an appraisal, including the following.
- The appraiser's familiarity with your property before and after the casualty or theft.
- The appraiser's knowledge of sales of comparable property in the area.
- The appraiser's knowledge of conditions in the area of the casualty.
- The appraiser's method of appraisal.

EXPLANATION
Appraisal fee. The appraisal fee is not a part of the casualty or theft loss. It is an expense in determining your tax liability. You can deduct it as a miscellaneous deduction subject to the 2%-of-adjusted-gross-income limit on Schedule A (Form 1040). See *Costs of photographs and appraisals*, later. For information about miscellaneous deductions, see chapter 29, Miscellaneous deductions.

TAXSAVER
If you have property appraised because you have a casualty loss and the loss is not deductible because it does not exceed 10% of your adjusted gross income (see *10% Rule*, under *Deduction Limits*, later), the cost of the appraisal is still deductible as a miscellaneous deduction subject to the 2%-of-adjusted-gross-income limit on Schedule A (Form 1040).

Cost of cleaning up or making repairs. The cost of repairing damaged property is not part of a casualty loss. Neither is the cost of cleaning up after a casualty. But you can use the cost of cleaning up or making repairs after a casualty as a measure of the decrease in FMV if you meet all the following conditions.
- The repairs are actually made.
- The repairs are necessary to bring the property back to its condition before the casualty.
- The amount spent for repairs is not excessive.
- The repairs take care of the damage only.
- The value of the property after the repairs is not, due to the repairs, more than the value of the property before the casualty.

EXPLANATION
Courts have held that clean-up expenses are deductible in the following circumstances:
- Replanting of damaged trees necessary to restore the property to its approximate value before the casualty
- Removing destroyed or damaged trees and shrubs, less any salvage value received
- Replacing a windstorm-damaged carport

Note: Losses must be reduced by the $100 deductible limit and any money paid by an insurance company (see *$100 Rule*, under Deduction Limits, later).

TAXSAVER
Damaged trees. If a casualty occurs that damages or destroys trees or shrubs on your residential property and you do not plan to repair or replace them, make sure that the appraiser's valuation documenting the decrease in the value of the property considers the estimated clean-up costs.

Landscaping. The cost of restoring landscaping to its original condition after a casualty may indicate the decrease in FMV. You may be able to measure your loss by what you spend on the following.
- Removing destroyed or damaged trees and shrubs minus any salvage you receive.
- Pruning and other measures taken to preserve damaged trees and shrubs.
- Replanting necessary to restore the property to its approximate value before the casualty.

Car value. Books issued by various automobile organizations that list your car may be useful in figuring the value of your car. You can use the book's retail values and modify them by such factors as mileage and the condition of your car to figure its value. The prices are not official, but they may be useful in determining value and suggesting relative prices for comparison with current sales and offerings in your area. If your car is not listed in the books, determine its value from other sources. A dealer's offer for your car as a trade-in on a new car is not usually a measure of its true value.

Figuring Decrease in FMV—Items Not To Consider

You generally should not consider the following items when attempting to establish the decrease in FMV of your property.

Cost of protection. The cost of protecting your property against a casualty or theft is not part of a casualty or theft loss. The amount you spend on insurance or to board up your house against a storm is not part of your loss.

If you make permanent improvements to your property to protect it against a casualty or theft, add the cost of these improvements to your basis in the property. An example would be the cost of a dike to prevent flooding.

Exception. You cannot increase your basis in the property by, or deduct as a business expense, any expenditures you made with respect to qualified disaster mitigation payments. See *Disaster Area Losses* in Publication 547.

Incidental expenses. Any incidental expenses you have due to a casualty or theft, such as expenses for the treatment of personal injuries, for temporary housing, or for a rental car, are not part of your casualty or theft loss.

Replacement cost. The cost of replacing stolen or destroyed property is not part of a casualty or theft loss.

Sentimental value. Do not consider sentimental value when determining your loss. If a family portrait, heirloom, or keepsake is damaged, destroyed, or stolen, you must base your loss on its FMV, as limited by your adjusted basis in the property.

Decline in market value of property in or near casualty area. A decrease in the value of your property because it is in or near an area that suffered a casualty, or that might again suffer a casualty, is not to be taken into consideration. You have a loss only for actual casualty damage to your property. However, if your home is in a federally declared disaster area, see *Disaster Area Losses* in Publication 547.

Costs of photographs and appraisals. Photographs taken after a casualty will be helpful in establishing the condition and value of the property after it was damaged. Photographs showing the condition of the property after it was repaired, restored, or replaced may also be helpful.

Appraisals are used to figure the decrease in FMV because of a casualty or theft. See *Appraisal*, earlier, under *Figuring Decrease in FMV—Items To Consider*, for information about appraisals.

The costs of photographs and appraisals used as evidence of the value and condition of property damaged as a result of a casualty are not a part of the loss. You can claim these costs as a miscellaneous itemized deduction subject to the 2%-of-adjusted-gross-income limit on Schedule A (Form 1040). For information about miscellaneous deductions, see chapter 28.

TAXORGANIZER

Photographs or videotapes of your home and its contents may be useful in other ways as well. First, they may provide evidence of value before the casualty. Recent photos, or tapes, for example, may be used to prove that the property was in good condition prior to the casualty. Second, they may assist you in determining what items are missing or were destroyed in a fire or theft. People often do not have an accurate inventory of household items. Photos or tapes serve as useful reminders.

The photographs or videotapes should be updated annually and kept outside your house, preferably in a safe-deposit box. They may be even more important in dealing with your insurance claim than they are in helping you with the IRS.

Adjusted Basis

Adjusted basis is your basis in the property (usually cost) increased or decreased by various events, such as improvements and casualty losses. For more information, see chapter 13.

EXPLANATION

Restoring damaged property increases your basis in property, while casualty theft losses and insurance reimbursements decrease your basis in property. See Table 13-1, *Examples of Adjustments to Basis*, for more information.

Insurance and Other Reimbursements

If you receive an insurance payment or other type of reimbursement, you must subtract the reimbursement when you figure your loss. You do not have a casualty or theft loss to the extent you are reimbursed.

If you expect to be reimbursed for part or all of your loss, you must subtract the expected reimbursement when you figure your loss. You must reduce your loss even if you do not receive payment until a later tax year. See *Reimbursement Received After Deducting Loss*, later.

Failure to file a claim for reimbursement. If your property is covered by insurance, you must file a timely insurance claim for reimbursement of your loss. Otherwise, you cannot deduct this loss as a casualty or theft loss. However, this rule does not apply to the portion of the loss not covered by insurance (for example, a deductible).

Example. You have a car insurance policy with a $1,000 deductible. Because your insurance did not cover the first $1,000 of an auto collision, the $1,000 would be deductible (subject to the deduction limits discussed later). This is true even if you do not file an insurance claim, because your insurance policy would never have reimbursed you for the deductible.

EXPLANATION

You do not have to report a gain that results from a reimbursement that exceeds your basis in the lost, damaged, or destroyed property if you use the entire reimbursement to purchase property that is either similar or related in use to the original property. Instead, the recognition of the gain is postponed until the replacement property is sold. Your basis in the replacement property is its cost minus any postponed gain. With a home, the gain may not be taxable under the rules for exclusion of gain on home sales (see the rules discussed in chapter 15, *Selling your home*).

You are allowed a certain amount of time to select and purchase the replacement property. This time period begins on the day of the casualty or theft and ends 2 years after the close of the tax year in which the reimbursement is received (4 years for a federally declared disaster area. However, this period may have been extended to 5 years if your main home is located in certain federal disaster areas. See Instructions to Form 4684). Thus, if your house was robbed on August 1, 2011, and your insurance company reimbursed you for your loss on June 1, 2012, you would have until December 31, 2014, to repair or replace the damaged goods. If the cost of the replacement property is less than the reimbursement received, the unspent part of the reimbursement must be recognized as a gain.

Types of Reimbursements

The most common type of reimbursement is an insurance payment for your stolen or damaged property. Other types of reimbursements are discussed next. Also see the Instructions for Form 4684.

Employer's emergency disaster fund. If you receive money from your employer's emergency disaster fund and you must use that money to rehabilitate or replace property on which you are claiming a casualty loss deduction, you must take that money into consideration in computing the casualty loss deduction. Take into consideration only the amount you used to replace your destroyed or damaged property.

Example. Your home was extensively damaged by a tornado. Your loss after reimbursement from your insurance company was $10,000. Your employer set up a disaster relief fund for its employees. Employees receiving money from the fund had to use it to rehabilitate or replace their damaged or destroyed property. You received $4,000 from the fund and spent the entire amount on repairs to your home. In figuring your casualty loss, you must reduce your unreimbursed loss ($10,000) by the $4,000 you received from your employer's fund. Your casualty loss before applying the deduction limits discussed later is $6,000.

EXPLANATION

If you have use and occupancy insurance for your business and are reimbursed for loss of business income, it does not reduce your casualty or theft loss. However, the reimbursement is considered income and is taxed in the same way as your other business income.

Cash gifts. If you receive excludable cash gifts as a disaster victim and there are no limits on how you can use the money, you do not reduce your casualty loss by these excludable cash gifts. This applies even if you use the money to pay for repairs to property damaged in the disaster.

Example. Your home was damaged by a hurricane. Relatives and neighbors made cash gifts to you that were excludable from your income. You used part of the cash gifts to pay for repairs to your home. There were no limits or restrictions on how you could use the cash gifts. Because it was an excludable gift, the money you received and used to pay for repairs to your home does not reduce your casualty loss on the damaged home.

Insurance payments for living expenses. You do not reduce your casualty loss by insurance payments you receive to cover living expenses in either of the following situations.

- You lose the use of your main home because of a casualty.
- Government authorities do not allow you access to your main home because of a casualty or threat of one.

Inclusion in income. If these insurance payments are more than the temporary increase in your living expenses, you must include the excess in your income. Report this amount on Form 1040, line 21. However, if the casualty occurs in a federally declared disaster area, none of the insurance payments are taxable. See *Qualified disaster relief payments*, under *Disaster Area Losses* in Publication 547.

A temporary increase in your living expenses is the difference between the actual living expenses you and your family incurred during the period you could not use your home and your normal living expenses for that period. Actual living expenses are the reasonable and necessary expenses incurred because of the loss of your main home. Generally, these expenses include the amounts you pay for the following.

- Rent for suitable housing.
- Transportation.
- Food.
- Utilities.
- Miscellaneous services.

Normal living expenses consist of these same expenses that you would have incurred but did not because of the casualty or the threat of one.

Example. As a result of a fire, you vacated your apartment for a month and moved to a motel. You normally pay $525 a month for rent. None was charged for the month the apartment was vacated. Your motel rent for this month was $1,200. You normally pay $200 a month for food. Your food expenses for the month you lived in the motel were $400. You received $1,100 from your insurance company to cover your living expenses. You determine the payment you must include in income as follows.

1)	Insurance payment for living expenses	$1,100
2)	Actual expenses during the month you are unable to use your home because of fire	1,600
3)	Normal living expenses	725
4)	Temporary increase in living expenses: Subtract line 3 from line 2	875
5)	Amount of payment includible in income: Subtract line 4 from line 1	$225

Tax year of inclusion. You include the taxable part of the insurance payment in income for the year you regain the use of your main home or, if later, for the year you receive the taxable part of the insurance payment.

Example. Your main home was destroyed by a tornado in August 2012. You regained use of your home in November 2013. The insurance payments you received in 2012 and 2013 were $1,500 more than the temporary increase in your living expenses during those years. You include this amount in income on your 2013 Form 1040. If, in 2014, you receive further payments to cover the living expenses you had in 2012 and 2013, you must include those payments in income on your 2014 Form 1040.

Disaster relief. Food, medical supplies, and other forms of assistance you receive do not reduce your casualty loss unless they are replacements for lost or destroyed property.

Disaster unemployment assistance payments are unemployment benefits that are taxable.

Generally, disaster relief grants and qualified disaster mitigation payments made under the Robert T. Stafford Disaster Relief and Emergency Assistance Act or the National Flood Insurance Act (as in effect on April 15, 2005) are not includible in your income. See *Disaster Area Losses* in Publication 547.

Reimbursement Received After Deducting Loss
If you figured your casualty or theft loss using your expected reimbursement, you may have to adjust your tax return for the tax year in which you receive your actual reimbursement. This section explains the adjustment you may have to make.

Actual reimbursement less than expected. If you later receive less reimbursement than you expected, include that difference as a loss with your other losses (if any) on your return for the year in which you can reasonably expect no more reimbursement.

Example. Your personal car had an FMV of $2,000 when it was destroyed in a collision with another car in 2013. The accident was due to the negligence of the other driver. At the end of 2013, there was a reasonable prospect that the owner of the other car would reimburse you in full. You did not have a deductible loss in 2013.

In January 2014, the court awarded you a judgment of $2,000. However, in July it became apparent that you will be unable to collect any amount from the other driver. You can deduct the loss in 2014 subject to the limits discussed later.

Tip

Qualified disaster relief payments you receive for expenses you incurred as a result of a federally declared disaster are not taxable income to you. For more information, see Disaster Area Losses in Publication 547.

TAXPLANNER
Even though there is no formal IRS ruling, many IRS auditors tend to disallow any deduction for the unreimbursed amount if you are fully insured and settle your claim with the insurance carrier for less than the amount of the loss by signing a proof of loss statement. The proof of loss statement sets the value of the loss between you and the insurance company. Generally, the IRS auditor will only allow a deduction of the unreimbursed loss if he or she is convinced that you have attempted all reasonable remedies against the insurer.

Actual reimbursement more than expected. If you later receive more reimbursement than you expected after you claimed a deduction for the loss, you may have to include the extra reimbursement in your income for the year you receive it. However, if any part of the original deduction did not reduce your tax for the earlier year, do not include that part of the reimbursement in your income. You do not refigure your tax for the year you claimed the deduction. For more information, see *Recoveries* in chapter 12.

EXAMPLE

Last year, a hurricane destroyed your motorboat. Your loss was $3,000, and you estimated that your insurance would cover $2,500 of it. Because you did not itemize deductions on your return last year, you could not deduct the loss. When the insurance company reimburses you for the loss, you do not report any of the reimbursement as income. This is true even if it is for the full $3,000 because you did not deduct the loss on your return. The loss did not reduce your tax.

Actual reimbursement same as expected. If you receive exactly the reimbursement you expected to receive, you do not have to include any of the reimbursement in your income and you cannot deduct any additional loss.

Example. In December 2014, you had a collision while driving your personal car. Repairs to the car cost $950. You had $100 deductible collision insurance. Your insurance company agreed to reimburse you for the rest of the damage. Because you expected a reimbursement from the insurance company, you did not have a casualty loss deduction in 2014.

Due to the $100 rule (discussed later under *Deduction Limits*), you cannot deduct the $100 you paid as the deductible. When you receive the $850 from the insurance company in 2015, do not report it as income.

Single Casualty on Multiple Properties

Personal property. Personal property is any property that is not real property. If your personal property is stolen or is damaged or destroyed by a casualty, you must figure your loss separately for each item of property. Then combine these separate losses to figure the total loss from that casualty or theft.

Example. A fire in your home destroyed an upholstered chair, an oriental rug, and an antique table. You did not have fire insurance to cover your loss. (This was the only casualty or theft you had during the year.) You paid $750 for the chair and you established that it had an FMV of $500 just before the fire. The rug cost $3,000 and had an FMV of $2,500 just before the fire. You bought the table at an auction for $100 before discovering it was an antique. It had been appraised at $900 before the fire. You figure your loss on each of these items as follows:

		Chair	Rug	Table
1)	Basis (cost)	$750	$3,000	$100
2)	FMV before fire	$500	$2,500	$900
3)	FMV after fire	–0–	–0–	–0–
4)	Decrease in FMV	$500	$2,500	$900
5)	Loss (smaller of (1) or (4))	$500	$2,500	$100
6)	**Total loss**			**$3,100**

Real property. In figuring a casualty loss on personal-use real property, treat the entire property (including any improvements, such as buildings, trees, and shrubs) as one item. Figure the loss using the smaller of the adjusted basis or the decrease in FMV of the entire property.

Example. You bought your home a few years ago. You paid $160,000 ($20,000 for the land and $140,000 for the house). You also spent $2,000 for landscaping. This year a fire destroyed your home. The fire also damaged the shrubbery and trees in your yard. The fire was your only casualty or theft loss this year. Competent appraisers valued the property as a whole at $200,000 before the fire, but only $30,000 after the fire. (The loss to your household furnishings is not shown in this example. It would be figured separately on each item, as explained earlier under *Personal property*.)

Shortly after the fire, the insurance company paid you $155,000 for the loss. You figure your casualty loss as follows:

1)	Adjusted basis of the entire property (land, building, and landscaping)	$162,000
2)	FMV of entire property before fire	$200,000
3)	FMV of entire property after fire	30,000
4)	Decrease in FMV of entire property	$170,000
5)	Loss (smaller of (1) or (4))	$162,000
6)	Subtract insurance	155,000
7)	**Amount of loss after reimbursement**	**$7,000**

EXPLANATION

Separate computations. Generally, if a single casualty or theft involves more than one item of property, you must figure the loss on each item separately; then combine the losses to determine the total loss from that casualty or theft.

Exception for personal-use real property. In figuring a casualty loss on personal-use real property, the entire property (including any improvements, such as buildings, trees, and shrubs) is treated as one item.

Figure the loss using the smaller of the following:
- The decrease in fair market value of the entire property
- The adjusted basis of the entire property

Deduction Limits

After you have figured your casualty or theft loss, you must figure how much of the loss you can deduct. If the loss was to property for your personal use or your family's use, there are two limits on the amount you can deduct for your casualty or theft loss.

1. You must reduce each casualty or theft loss by $100 ($100 rule).
2. You must further reduce the total of all your casualty or theft losses by 10% of your adjusted gross income (10% rule).

You make these reductions on Form 4684.

These rules are explained next and *Table 26-1* summarizes how to apply the $100 rule and the 10% rule in various situations. For more detailed explanations and examples, see Publication 547.

Table 26-1. **How To Apply the Deduction Limits for Personal-Use Property**

		$100 Rule	10% Rule
General Application		You must reduce each casualty or theft loss by $100 when figuring your deduction. Apply this rule after you have figured the amount of your loss.	You must reduce your total casualty or theft loss by 10% of your adjusted gross income. Apply this rule after you reduce each loss by $100 (the $100 rule).
Single Event		Apply this rule only once, even if many pieces of property are affected.	Apply this rule only once, even if many pieces of property are affected.
More Than One Event		Apply to the loss from each event.	Apply to the total of all your losses from all events.
More Than One Person—With Loss From the Same Event (other than a married couple filing jointly)		Apply separately to each person.	Apply separately to each person.
Married Couple—With Loss From the Same Event	Filing Jointly	Apply as if you were one person.	Apply as if you were one person.
	Filing Separately	Apply separately to each spouse.	Apply separately to each spouse.
More Than One Owner (other than a married couple filing jointly)		Apply separately to each owner of jointly owned property.	Apply separately to each owner of jointly owned property.

Property used partly for business and partly for personal purposes. When property is used partly for personal purposes and partly for business or income-producing purposes, the casualty or theft loss deduction must be figured separately for the personal-use part and for the business or income-producing part. You must figure each loss separately because the $100 rule and the 10% rule apply only to the loss on the personal-use part of the property.

EXPLANATION

Business or income-producing property. A loss on business property, property that earns you rent or royalty income, or other income-producing property is not subject to either the $100 rule or the 10% rule. For business or income-producing property, you must figure your loss separately for each item that is stolen, damaged, or destroyed. If casualty damage occurs both to a building and to trees on the same piece of property, the loss is measured separately for each.

Total loss of business or income-producing property. If you have business or income-producing property that is completely lost because of a casualty or theft, your deductible loss is your basis in the property minus any salvage value and minus any insurance or other reimbursement you receive or expect to receive. It does not matter what the decrease in fair market value is.

Example
You owned machinery that you used in your business. The machinery had an adjusted basis of $25,000 when it was completely destroyed by fire. Its fair market value just before the fire was $20,000. Because this was business property, and because it was completely destroyed, your deductible loss is your adjusted basis in the machinery, $25,000, decreased by salvage value and by any insurance or other reimbursement. Fair market value is not considered when you are figuring your loss, even though it is less than your basis in the machinery.

Explanation
Partial loss of business or income-producing property. If business or income-producing property is damaged but not completely destroyed in a casualty, the loss is the decrease in value because of the casualty or your adjusted basis in the property, whichever is less. From this amount (the lesser of your adjusted basis or the decrease in value), you must subtract any insurance or other reimbursement you receive or expect to receive.

TAXSAVER

If your car is stolen. If your automobile is stolen or destroyed, you may be able to deduct more than the value listed in one of the various books issued or websites sponsored by automobile organizations. If you use the automobile for business, you must make a separate calculation of the business and personal portions of the loss. This may produce a larger loss.

Example
Blair Hunt's automobile, which cost $8,000, is stolen. The "blue book"—one of the books published by automobile organizations—values his automobile at $5,000. Blair used the automobile for business 40% of the time and deducted $800 of depreciation expense.

	Business portion	Personal portion
Value before theft	$2,000	$3,000
Value after theft	–0–	–0–
Decrease in value	$2,000	$3,000
Adjusted basis:		
Original cost	$3,200	$4,800
Depreciation	(800)	–0–
Adjusted basis	$2,400	$4,800

Blair's casualty loss before the $100 limitation is $5,400, computed as follows:

Business portion—adjusted basis	$2,400
Personal portion—the lower of the decrease in value or the adjusted basis	3,000
Total	$5,400

$100 Rule

After you have figured your casualty or theft loss on personal-use property, you must reduce that loss by $100. This reduction applies to each total casualty or theft loss. It does not matter how many pieces of property are involved in an event. Only a single $100 reduction applies.

Example. A hailstorm damages your home and your car. Determine the amount of loss, as discussed earlier, for each of these items. Since the losses are due to a single event, you combine the losses and reduce the combined amount by $100.

Single event. Generally, events closely related in origin cause a single casualty. It is a single casualty when the damage is from two or more closely related causes, such as wind and flood damage caused by the same storm.

10% Rule

You must reduce the total of all your casualty or theft losses on personal-use property by 10% of your adjusted gross income. Apply this rule after you reduce each loss by $100. For more information, see the Form 4684 instructions. If you have both gains and losses from casualties or thefts, see *Gains and losses*, later in this discussion.

Example 1. In June, you discovered that your house had been burglarized. Your loss after insurance reimbursement was $2,000. Your adjusted gross income for the year you discovered the theft is $29,500. You first apply the $100 rule and then the 10% rule. Figure your theft loss deduction as follows.

1)	Loss after insurance	$2,000
2)	Subtract $100	100
3)	Loss after $100 rule	$1,900
4)	Subtract 10% × $29,500 AGI	2,950
5)	Theft loss deduction	–0–

You do not have a theft loss deduction because your loss after you apply the $100 rule ($1,900) is less than 10% of your adjusted gross income ($2,950).

Example 2. In March, you had a car accident that totally destroyed your car. You did not have collision insurance on your car, so you did not receive any insurance reimbursement. Your loss on the car was $1,800. In November, a fire damaged your basement and totally destroyed the furniture, washer, dryer, and other items stored there. Your loss on the basement items after reimbursement was $2,100. Your adjusted gross income for the year that the accident and fire occurred is $25,000. You figure your casualty loss deduction as follows.

		Car	Basement
1)	Loss	$1,800	$2,100
2)	Subtract $100 per incident	100	100
3)	Loss after $100 rule	$1,700	$2,000
4)	Total loss		$3,700
5)	Subtract 10% × $25,000 AGI		2,500
6)	**Casualty loss deduction**		$1,200

Caution

Casualty or theft gains do not include gains you choose to postpone. See Publication 547 for information on the postponement of gain.

Gains and losses. If you had both gains and losses from casualties or thefts to personal-use property, you must compare your total gains to your total losses. Do this after you have reduced each loss by any reimbursements and by $100, but before you have reduced the losses by 10% of your adjusted gross income.

Losses more than gains. If your losses are more than your recognized gains, subtract your gains from your losses and reduce the result by 10% of your adjusted gross income. The rest, if any, is your deductible loss from personal-use property.

EXAMPLE

Your theft loss after reducing it by reimbursements and by $100 is $2,700. Your casualty gain is $700. Because your loss is more than your gain, you must reduce your net loss of $2,000 ($2,700 - $700) by 10% of your adjusted gross income.

Gains more than losses. If your recognized gains are more than your losses, subtract your losses from your gains. The difference is treated as capital gain and must be reported on Schedule D (Form 1040). The 10% rule does not apply to your gains.

EXAMPLE

Example 1
Your theft loss after reducing it by reimbursements and by $100 is $600. Your casualty gain is $1,600. Because your gain is more than your loss, you must report a net gain of $1,000 ($1,600 - $600) on Schedule D.

Example 2
During 2014, a storm completely destroyed your summer cottage, resulting in a casualty gain of $5,000 after you were reimbursed by your insurance company. Later in the year, your home was broken into on two separate occasions. Jewelry, silverware, and other items of personal property were stolen each time. The loss (after applying the $100 rule) on the first theft was $900 and on the second theft was $4,000. Your 2014 adjusted gross income is $25,000.

1)	Loss on first theft	$ 900
2)	Plus loss on second theft	4,000
3)	Total losses	$4,900
4)	Gain on cottage	5,000
5)	**Net gain for 2014 and Schedule D**	**$100**

The $100 gain will be reported on Form 4684 and Schedule D. See *Insurance and Other Reimbursements*, regarding recognition of gains, discussed earlier.

Table 26-2. **When To Deduct a Loss**

IF you have a loss...	THEN deduct it in the year...
from a casualty,	the loss occurred.
in a federally declared disaster area,	the disaster occurred or the year immediately before the disaster.
from a theft,	the theft was discovered.
on a deposit treated as a:	
• casualty or any ordinary loss,	• a reasonable estimate can be made.
• bad debt,	• deposits are totally worthless.

When To Report Gains and Losses

Gains. If you receive an insurance or other reimbursement that is more than your adjusted basis in the destroyed or stolen property, you have a gain from the casualty or theft. You must include this gain in your income in the year you receive the reimbursement, unless you choose to postpone reporting the gain as explained in Publication 547.

If you have a loss, see *Table 26-2*.

Losses. Generally, you can deduct a casualty loss that is not reimbursable only in the tax year in which the casualty occurred. This is true even if you do not repair or replace the damaged property until a later year.

You can deduct theft losses that are not reimbursable only in the year you discover your property was stolen.

If you are not sure whether part of your casualty or theft loss will be reimbursed, do not deduct that part until the tax year when you become reasonably certain that it will not be reimbursed.

> ### EXPLANATION
> The Tax Court denied a casualty loss deduction for a car that was totaled while stalled on the highway because the taxpayer admitted to an unresolved claim for damages with the insurance company and she was also not able to support the car's adjusted tax basis. The Court held that the taxpayer must establish the amount of the loss before a casualty loss deduction can be claimed.

> ### EXAMPLE
> A taxpayer suffered a casualty loss from vandalism and filed a claim with her insurance company in the year of the loss. The insurance company denied any liability for the damage. Consequently, the taxpayer filed suit against the insurance company. A court held that the taxpayer could not deduct the loss in the year in which it was incurred because a reasonable possibility of recovery still existed. No deduction was allowed while the suit against the insurance company was still pending.

Loss on deposits. If your loss is a loss on deposits in an insolvent or bankrupt financial institution, see *Loss on Deposits*, earlier.

Disaster Area Loss

You generally must deduct a casualty loss in the year it occurred. However, if you have a casualty loss from a federally declared disaster that occurred in an area warranting public or individual assistance (or both), you can choose to deduct the loss on your tax return or amended return for either of the following years.
- The year the disaster occurred.
- The year immediately preceding the year the disaster occurred.

Gains. Special rules apply if you choose to postpone reporting gain on property damaged or destroyed in a federally declared disaster area. For those special rules, see Publication 547.

Postponed tax deadlines. The IRS may postpone for up to 1 year certain tax deadlines of taxpayers who are affected by a federally declared disaster. The tax deadlines the IRS may postpone include those for filing income and employment tax returns, paying income and employment taxes, and making contributions to a traditional IRA or Roth IRA.

If any tax deadline is postponed, the IRS will publicize the postponement in your area by publishing a news release, revenue ruling, revenue procedure, notice, announcement, or other guidance in the Internal Revenue Bulletin (IRB). Go to *www.irs.gov/uac/Tax-Relief-in-Disaster-Situations* to find out if a tax deadline has been postponed for your area.

Who is eligible. If the IRS postpones a tax deadline, the following taxpayers are eligible for the postponement.

- Any individual whose main home is located in a <u>covered disaster area</u> (defined next).
- Any business entity or sole proprietor whose principal place of business is located in a covered disaster area.
- Any individual who is a relief worker affiliated with a recognized government or philanthropic organization who is assisting in a covered disaster area.
- Any individual, business entity, or sole proprietorship whose records are needed to meet a postponed tax deadline, provided those records are maintained in a covered disaster area. The main home or principal place of business does not have to be located in the covered disaster area.
- Any estate or trust that has tax records necessary to meet a postponed tax deadline, provided those records are maintained in a covered disaster area.
- The spouse on a joint return with a taxpayer who is eligible for postponements.
- Any individual, business entity, or sole proprietorship not located in a covered disaster area, but whose records necessary to meet a postponed tax deadline are located in the covered disaster area.
- Any individual visiting the covered disaster area who was killed or injured as a result of the disaster.
- Any other person determined by the IRS to be affected by a federally declared disaster.

Covered disaster area. This is an area of a federally declared disaster in which the IRS has decided to postpone tax deadlines for up to 1 year.

Abatement of interest and penalties. The IRS may abate the interest and penalties on underpaid income tax for the length of any postponement of tax deadlines.

More information. For more information, see *Disaster Area Losses* in Publication 547.

How To Report Gains and Losses

Use Form 4684 to report a gain or a deductible loss from a casualty or theft. If you have more than one casualty or theft, use a separate Form 4684 to determine your gain or loss for each event. Combine the gains and losses on one Form 4684. Follow the form instructions as to which lines to fill out. In addition, you must use the appropriate schedule to report a gain or loss. The schedule you use depends on whether you have a gain or loss.

If you have a:	Report it on:
Gain	Schedule D (Form 1040)
Loss	Schedule A (Form 1040)

Adjustments to basis. If you have a casualty or theft loss, you must decrease your basis in the property by any insurance or other reimbursement you receive, and by any deductible loss. Amounts you spend to restore your property after a casualty increase your adjusted basis. See _Adjusted Basis_ in chapter 13 for more information.

Net operating loss (NOL). If your casualty or theft loss deduction causes your deductions for the year to be more than your income for the year, you may have an NOL. You can use an NOL to lower your tax in an earlier year, allowing you to get a refund for tax you have already paid. Or, you can use it to lower your tax in a later year. You do not have to be in business to have an NOL from a casualty or theft loss. For more information, see Publication 536, Net Operating Losses (NOLs) for Individuals, Estates, and Trusts.

TAXPLANNER

If your loss exceeds your income. If your casualty loss exceeds your income, you should fill out Form 1045, Application for Tentative Refund, to see whether you have a net operating loss. When filling out this form, treat your casualty losses as business deductions rather than nonbusiness deductions. If your casualty loss results in a net operating loss, then your net operating loss can be carried back to prior years to offset your taxable income, and you may get a refund of prior-year taxes.

For example, a 2014 net operating loss caused by a casualty loss can be carried back first to 2011, any remaining loss should be carried back to 2012, and into 2013. If any loss still remains, it can be carried forward for the next 20 years. Alternatively, you may elect on your 2014 tax return not to carry back your net operating loss but carry it forward only. You should compare the refund available from a carryback to the expected tax benefits in the future in order to determine whether you should make the election. This is a very complex area. Affected taxpayers should consult a professional tax advisor.

TAXORGANIZER

Records you should keep:

- Documentation of date, time, and place of occurrence of the casualty or theft
- Police reports
- Insurance reports including evidence of amount of reimbursement, if any
- Original receipts (if applicable)
- Repair bills
- Form 1099 (if applicable)
- Any appraisals or valuations supporting property value immediately before and after the casualty or theft
- An inventory and/or supporting pictures or video of all household items before casualty or theft
- An inventory of stolen, lost, damaged, or destroyed items
- Pictures or video of damaged items (if any)
- Any type of supporting evidence such as newspaper clippings about a storm
- Electronic backup set of records (bank statements, tax returns, insurance policies, etc.) kept in a safe place away from the original set

Chapter 27

Car expenses and other employee business expenses

ey.com/EYTaxGuide

Note

IRS Publication 17 (*Your Federal Income Tax*) has been updated by Ernst & Young LLP for 2014. Dates and dollar amounts shown are for 2014. Underlined type is used to indicate where IRS text has been updated. Places where text has been removed are indicated by the sentence: *Text intentionally omitted*.

ey.com/EYTaxGuide

Ernst & Young LLP will update the *EY Tax Guide 2015* website with relevant taxpayer information as it becomes available. You can also sign up for email alerts to let you know when changes have been made.

Introduction

If you are traveling on business and your employer does not reimburse your expenses, you may deduct many of them on your income tax return. If you use your automobile partly for business purposes, you may be able to deduct some of your operating expenses. If you entertain a business associate at a restaurant or sporting event, you may be able to deduct that expense, too. Within strict limits, business gifts are also deductible.

You must be able to prove the business purpose, as well as the amount of the expense, to claim a deduction for employee expenses. All expenses should be substantiated with receipts and records indicating the time, place, and business nature of the expense. This chapter explains business-related expenses for travel, transportation, entertainment, and gifts that you may deduct on your income tax return. It also discusses the reporting and recordkeeping requirements for these expenses.

What's New

Standard mileage rate. For 2014, the standard mileage rate for the cost of operating your car for business use is 56 cents per mile.

TAXPLANNER

The business standard mileage rate can be used for vehicles used for hire, such as taxicabs, but cannot be used for more than four vehicles simultaneously.

Car expenses and use of the standard mileage rate are explained under *Transportation Expenses*, later.

Depreciation limits on cars, trucks, and vans. For 2014, the first-year limit on the total Section 179 deduction and depreciation deduction for cars is $3,160. *Text intentionally omitted*. For trucks and vans the first-year limit in 2014 is $3,460. For more information, see *Depreciation limits* in Publication 463.

Special depreciation allowance expired. The special ("bonus") depreciation allowance on qualified property (including cars, trucks, and vans) expired at the end of 2013 and is not available for 2014.

Section 179 deduction. For 2014, the Section 179 deduction limit on qualifying property purchases (including cars, trucks, and vans) is a total of $25,000 and the limit on those purchases at which the deduction begins to be phased out is $200,000.

You may be able to deduct the ordinary and necessary business-related expenses you have for:
- Travel,
- Entertainment,
- Gifts, or
- Transportation.

An ordinary expense is one that is common and accepted in your trade or business. A necessary expense is one that is helpful and appropriate for your business. An expense does not have to be required to be considered necessary.

This chapter explains the following.
- What expenses are deductible.
- How to report your expenses on your return.
- What records you need to prove your expenses.
- How to treat any expense reimbursements you may receive.

Who does not need to use this chapter. If you are an employee, you will not need to read this chapter if all of the following are true.
- You fully accounted to your employer for your work-related expenses.
- You received full reimbursement for your expenses.
- Your employer required you to return any excess reimbursement and you did so.
- There is no amount shown with a code "L" in box 12 of your Form W-2, Wage and Tax Statement.

If you meet all of these conditions, there is no need to show the expenses or the reimbursements on your return. See *Reimbursements*, later, if you would like more information on reimbursements and accounting to your employer.

Tip

If you meet these conditions and your employer included reimbursements on your Form W-2 in error, ask your employer for a corrected Form W-2.

Useful Items

You may want to see:

Publication
- ☐ **463** Travel, Entertainment, Gift, and Car Expenses
- ☐ **535** Business Expenses

Form (and Instructions)
- ☐ **Schedule A (Form 1040)** Itemized Deductions
- ☐ **Schedule C (Form 1040)** Profit or Loss From Business
- ☐ **Schedule C-EZ (Form 1040)** Net Profit From Business

□ **Schedule F (Form 1040)** Profit or Loss From Farming
□ **Form 2106** Employee Business Expenses
□ **Form 2106-EZ** Unreimbursed Employee Business Expenses

Travel Expenses

If you temporarily travel away from your tax home, you can use this section to determine if you have deductible travel expenses. This section discusses:

- Traveling away from home,
- Tax home,
- Temporary assignment or job, and
- What travel expenses are deductible.

It also discusses the standard meal allowance, rules for travel inside and outside the United States, and deductible convention expenses.

Travel expenses defined. For tax purposes, travel expenses are the ordinary and necessary expenses (defined earlier) of traveling away from home for your business, profession, or job.

You will find examples of deductible travel expenses in _Table 27-1_.

Table 27-1. **Travel Expenses You Can Deduct**

This chart summarizes expenses you can deduct when you travel away from home for business purposes.

IF you have expenses for...	THEN you can deduct the cost of...
transportation	travel by airplane, train, bus, or car between your home and your business destination. If you were provided with a ticket or you are riding free as a result of a frequent traveler or similar program, your cost is zero. If you travel by ship, see _Luxury Water Travel_ and _Cruise ships_ (under _Conventions_) in Publication 463 for additional rules and limits.
taxi, commuter bus, and airport limousine	fares for these and other types of transportation that take you between: • The airport or station and your hotel, and • The hotel and the work location of your customers or clients, your business meeting place, or your temporary work location.
baggage and shipping	sending baggage and sample or display material between your regular and temporary work locations.
car	operating and maintaining your car when traveling away from home on business. You can deduct actual expenses or the standard mileage rate as well as business-related tolls and parking. If you rent a car while away from home on business, you can deduct only the business-use portion of the expenses.
lodging and meals	your lodging and meals if your business trip is overnight or long enough that you need to stop for sleep or rest to properly perform your duties. Meals include amounts spent for food, beverages, taxes, and related tips. See _Meals and Incidental Expenses_ for additional rules and limits.
cleaning	dry cleaning and laundry.
telephone	business calls while on your business trip. This includes business communication by fax machine or other communication devices.
tips	tips you pay for any expenses in this chart.
other	other similar ordinary and necessary expenses related to your business travel. These expenses might include transportation to or from a business meal, public stenographer's fees, computer rental fees, and operating and maintaining a house trailer.

EXAMPLES

Example 1

The courts held that a stockholder of a corporation could not deduct the expense of operating his personal automobile while performing services for the corporation. The stockholder was not an employee or officer of the corporation. He was not reimbursed for his expenses. The courts held that the stockholder's interest in the corporation was too remote for the expense to be an ordinary business expense.

Tax Breaks and Deductions You Can Use Checklist

Employee business expenses. You can deduct any expenses you incur which are directly related to your employment. But these expenses are only deductible to the extent that, when combined with your other miscellaneous itemized deductions, they exceed 2% of your adjusted gross income (AGI). That's one of the reasons why you should try to get your employer to pay for these expenses on a pretax basis.

Qualified transportation fringe benefits. For 2014, you can exclude from your gross income certain qualified transportation fringe benefits received from your employer up to specified dollar amounts. Qualified transportation fringe benefits include: (1) transportation in a commuter highway vehicle (such as a van) between your home and workplace, (2) transit pass, (3) qualified parking, or (4) qualified bicycle commuting reimbursement. The exclusion for commuter vehicle transportation and transit pass fringe benefits cannot be more than $130 a month. The exclusion for qualified parking also cannot be more than $250 a month. The exclusion for qualified bicycle commuting is discussed immediately below. If the benefits have a value that is more than these limits, the excess must be included in your income. You are not entitled to these exclusions if the reimbursement is made under a compensation reduction agreement. See _Transportation_ in chapter 5, _Wages, salaries, and other earnings_, for more information.

Qualified bicycle commuting reimbursement. You may be able to exclude from your gross income reimbursements from your employer for reasonable expenses of qualified bicycle commuting. Reasonable expenses include the purchase of a bicycle and bicycle improvements, repair, and storage. These are considered reasonable expenses as long as the bicycle is regularly used for travel between the employee's residence and place of employment. The exclusion for a calendar year is $20 multiplied by the number of qualified bicycle commuting months during the year up to a maximum exclusion of $240. A qualified bicycle commuting month is any month you use the bicycle regularly for a substantial portion of the travel between your residence and place of employment and you do not receive any of the other qualified transportation fringe benefits.

Example 2
A government employee was allowed to deduct unreimbursed expenses incurred in the use of his private airplane for business purposes. He was also allowed to depreciate the business portion of the airplane's use.

TAXPLANNER
For you to deduct a business expense, a board resolution or a policy statement from the company that employs you should indicate that you may have to incur certain expenses for which you will not be reimbursed in order for you to fulfill your job.

TAXPLANNER
You are able to deduct only 50% of most business meal and entertainment costs. Other allowable unreimbursed entertainment expenses will be grouped with certain other of your miscellaneous itemized deductions. You will be allowed a tax deduction to the extent that all these deductions exceed 2% of your adjusted gross income.

Traveling Away From Home
You are traveling away from home if:
- Your duties require you to be away from the general area of your *tax home* (defined later) substantially longer than an ordinary day's work, and
- You need to sleep or rest to meet the demands of your work while away from home.

This rest requirement is not satisfied by merely napping in your car. You do not have to be away from your tax home for a whole day or from dusk to dawn as long as your relief from duty is long enough to get necessary sleep or rest.

Example 1. You are a railroad conductor. You leave your home terminal on a regularly scheduled round-trip run between two cities and return home 16 hours later. During the run, you have 6 hours off at your turnaround point where you eat two meals and rent a hotel room to get necessary sleep before starting the return trip. You are considered to be away from home.

Example 2. You are a truck driver. You leave your terminal and return to it later the same day. You get an hour off at your turnaround point to eat. Because you are not off to get necessary sleep and the brief time off is not an adequate rest period, you are not traveling away from home.

Members of the Armed Forces. If you are a member of the U.S. Armed Forces on a permanent duty assignment overseas, you are not traveling away from home. You cannot deduct your expenses for meals and lodging. You cannot deduct these expenses even if you have to maintain a home in the United States for your family members who are not allowed to accompany you overseas. If you are transferred from one permanent duty station to another, you may have deductible moving expenses, which are explained in Publication 521, Moving Expenses.

A naval officer assigned to permanent duty aboard a ship that has regular eating and living facilities has a tax home aboard ship for travel expense purposes.

Tax Home
To determine whether you are traveling away from home, you must first determine the location of your tax home.

Generally, your tax home is your regular place of business or post of duty, regardless of where you maintain your family home. It includes the entire city or general area in which your business or work is located.

If you have more than one regular place of business, your tax home is your main place of business. See *Main place of business or work*, later.

If you do not have a regular or a main place of business because of the nature of your work, then your tax home may be the place where you regularly live. See *No main place of business or work*, later.

If you do not have a regular or a main place of business or post of duty and there is no place where you regularly live, you are considered an itinerant (a transient) and your tax home is wherever you work. As an itinerant, you cannot claim a travel expense deduction because you are never considered to be traveling away from home.

Main place of business or work. If you have more than one place of business or work, consider the following when determining which one is your main place of business or work.

- The total time you ordinarily spend in each place.
- The level of your business activity in each place.
- Whether your income from each place is significant or insignificant.

Example. You live in Cincinnati where you have a seasonal job for 8 months each year and earn $40,000. You work the other 4 months in Miami, also at a seasonal job, and earn $15,000. Cincinnati is your main place of work because you spend most of your time there and earn most of your income there.

No main place of business or work. You may have a tax home even if you do not have a regular or main place of business or work. Your tax home may be the home where you regularly live.

Factors used to determine tax home. If you do not have a regular or main place of business or work, use the following three factors to determine where your tax home is.

1. You perform part of your business in the area of your main home and use that home for lodging while doing business in the area.
2. You have living expenses at your main home that you duplicate because your business requires you to be away from that home.
3. You have not abandoned the area in which both your historical place of lodging and your claimed main home are located; you have a member or members of your family living at your main home; or you often use that home for lodging.

If you satisfy all three factors, your tax home is the home where you regularly live. If you satisfy only two factors, you may have a tax home depending on all the facts and circumstances. If you satisfy only one factor, you are an itinerant; your tax home is wherever you work and you cannot deduct travel expenses.

EXAMPLES

After a taxpayer's employment in Cape Canaveral, Florida, was terminated, the taxpayer obtained temporary contract jobs in Virginia, Florida, North Carolina, Vermont, and Alabama. The Tax Court rejected the IRS assertion that the taxpayer had no tax home and allowed deductions for travel, meals, and lodging because he maintained a "tax home" in Cape Canaveral. The court noted that such deductions were allowed because the taxpayer returned to his Cape Canaveral home during periods of unemployment, and the taxpayer had a valid business purpose for maintaining his permanent address.

Example. You are single and live in Boston in an apartment you rent. You have worked for your employer in Boston for a number of years. Your employer enrolls you in a 12-month executive training program. You do not expect to return to work in Boston after you complete your training.

During your training, you do not do any work in Boston. Instead, you receive classroom and on-the-job training throughout the United States. You keep your apartment in Boston and return to it frequently. You use your apartment to conduct your personal business. You also keep up your community contacts in Boston. When you complete your training, you are transferred to Los Angeles.

You do not satisfy factor (1) because you did not work in Boston. You satisfy factor (2) because you had duplicate living expenses. You also satisfy factor (3) because you did not abandon your apartment in Boston as your main home, you kept your community contacts, and you frequently returned to live in your apartment. Therefore, you have a tax home in Boston.

EXPLANATION

According to the IRS, a home is a "regular place of abode in a real and substantial sense." The criteria are as follows:

1. You work in the same vicinity as your claimed abode and use it while doing business.
2. Your living expenses incurred at your claimed abode are duplicated when you're away on business.
3. You (a) have not abandoned the vicinity in which your place of lodging and claimed abode are both located; (b) have a family member or members (marital or lineal) currently residing at your claimed abode; or (c) use the claimed abode frequently.

If you maintain no fixed home, the burden of proof is on you to show the business portion of your daily expenses.

Tax home different from family home. If you (and your family) do not live at your _tax home_ (defined earlier), you cannot deduct the cost of traveling between your tax home and your family home. You also cannot deduct the cost of meals and lodging while at your tax home. See _Example 1_.

If you are working temporarily in the same city where you and your family live, you may be considered as traveling away from home. See _Example 2_.

Example 1. You are a truck driver and you and your family live in Tucson. You are employed by a trucking firm that has its terminal in Phoenix. At the end of your long runs, you return to your home terminal in Phoenix and spend one night there before returning home. You cannot deduct any expenses you have for meals and lodging in Phoenix or the cost of traveling from Phoenix to Tucson. This is because Phoenix is your tax home.

Example 2. Your family home is in Pittsburgh, where you work 12 weeks a year. The rest of the year you work for the same employer in Baltimore. In Baltimore, you eat in restaurants and sleep in a rooming house. Your salary is the same whether you are in Pittsburgh or Baltimore.

Because you spend most of your working time and earn most of your salary in Baltimore, that city is your tax home. You cannot deduct any expenses you have for meals and lodging there. However, when you return to work in Pittsburgh, you are away from your tax home even though you stay at your family home. You can deduct the cost of your round trip between Baltimore and Pittsburgh. You can also deduct your part of your family's living expenses for meals and lodging while you are living and working in Pittsburgh.

Temporary Assignment or Job

You may regularly work at your tax home and also work at another location. It may not be practical to return to your tax home from this other location at the end of each work day.

Temporary assignment vs. indefinite assignment. If your assignment or job away from your main place of work is temporary, your tax home does not change. You are considered to be away from home for the whole period you are away from your main place of work. You can deduct your travel expenses if they otherwise qualify for deduction. Generally, a temporary assignment in a single location is one that is realistically expected to last (and does in fact last) for 1 year or less.

However, if your assignment or job is indefinite, the location of the assignment or job becomes your new tax home and you cannot deduct your travel expenses while there. An assignment or job in a single location is considered indefinite if it is realistically expected to last for more than 1 year, whether or not it actually lasts for more than 1 year.

If your assignment is indefinite, you must include in your income any amounts you receive from your employer for living expenses, even if they are called travel allowances and you account to your employer for them. You may be able to deduct the cost of relocating to your new tax home as a moving expense. See Publication 521 for more information.

Exception for federal crime investigations or prosecutions. If you are a federal employee participating in a federal crime investigation or prosecution, you are not subject to the 1-year rule. This means you may be able to deduct travel expenses even if you are away from your tax home for more than 1 year, provided you meet the other requirements for deductibility.

For you to qualify, the Attorney General (or his or her designee) must certify that you are traveling:

- For the federal government,
- In a temporary duty status, and
- To investigate or prosecute, or provide support services for the investigation or prosecution of a federal crime.

Determining temporary or indefinite. You must determine whether your assignment is temporary or indefinite when you start work. If you expect an assignment or job to last for 1 year or less, it is temporary unless there are facts and circumstances that indicate otherwise. An assignment or job that is initially temporary may become indefinite due to changed circumstances. A series of assignments to the same location, all for short periods but that together cover a long period, may be considered an indefinite assignment.

Going home on days off. If you go back to your tax home from a temporary assignment on your days off, you are not considered away from home while you are in your hometown. You cannot deduct the cost of your meals and lodging there. However, you can deduct your travel expenses, including meals and lodging, while traveling between your temporary place of work and your tax home. You can claim these expenses up to the amount it would have cost you to stay at your temporary place of work.

If you keep your hotel room during your visit home, you can deduct the cost of your hotel room. In addition, you can deduct your expenses of returning home up to the amount you would have spent for meals had you stayed at your temporary place of work.

Probationary work period. If you take a job that requires you to move, with the understanding that you will keep the job if your work is satisfactory during a probationary period, the job is indefinite. You cannot deduct any of your expenses for meals and lodging during the probationary period.

What Travel Expenses Are Deductible?

Once you have determined that you are traveling away from your tax home, you can determine what travel expenses are deductible.

You can deduct ordinary and necessary expenses you have when you travel away from home on business. The type of expense you can deduct depends on the facts and your circumstances.

EXPLANATION

Ordinarily, you can deduct expenses that you incurred to produce or collect income, or to manage, conserve, or maintain property held for producing income, only on Schedule A (Form 1040). Therefore, you must itemize your deductions to claim these expenses. See chapter 29, *Miscellaneous deductions*.

To be deductible, an expense must be closely associated with an activity that is expected to produce income or must be incurred maintaining property that is held to produce income. Such expenses are deductible only if you itemize.

Travel and other costs of attending investment seminars are specifically disallowed.

Example 1
Transportation expenses to attend a stockholders' meeting are not deductible, unless you can demonstrate that you played a fairly substantial role in the meeting. Otherwise, it is not clear that the expenses were incurred to produce income.

Example 2
The courts held that an individual who spent his lunch hour at brokerage houses could not deduct his travel expenses because he could not establish the relationship between his visits and his investment activities.

Table 27-1 summarizes travel expenses you may be able to deduct. You may have other deductible travel expenses that are not covered there, depending on the facts and your circumstances.

Separating costs. If you have one expense that includes the costs of meals, entertainment, and other services (such as lodging or transportation), you must allocate that expense between the cost of meals and entertainment and the cost of other services. You must have a reasonable basis for making this allocation. For example, you must allocate your expenses if a hotel includes one or more meals in its room charge.

Travel expenses for another individual. If a spouse, dependent, or other individual goes with you (or your employee) on a business trip or to a business convention, you generally cannot deduct his or her travel expenses.

Employee. You can deduct the travel expenses of someone who goes with you if that person:
1. Is your employee,
2. Has a *bona fide* business purpose for the travel, and
3. Would otherwise be allowed to deduct the travel expenses.

Business associate. If a business associate travels with you and meets the conditions in (2) and (3) above, you can deduct the travel expenses you have for that person. A business associate is someone with whom you could reasonably expect to engage or deal in the active conduct of your business. A business associate can be a current or prospective (likely to become) customer, client, supplier, employee, agent, partner, or professional advisor.

Bona fide business purpose. A *bona fide* business purpose exists if you can prove a real business purpose for the individual's presence. Incidental services, such as typing notes or assisting in entertaining customers, are not enough to make the expenses deductible.

Example. Jerry drives to Chicago on business and takes his wife, Linda, with him. Linda is not Jerry's employee. Linda occasionally types notes, performs similar services, and accompanies Jerry to luncheons and dinners. The performance of these services does not establish that her presence on the trip is necessary to the conduct of Jerry's business. Her expenses are not deductible.

Jerry pays $199 a day for a double room. A single room costs $149 a day. He can deduct the total cost of driving his car to and from Chicago, but only $149 a day for his hotel room. If he uses public transportation, he can deduct only his fare.

> ### TAXALERT
> The tax law denies a deduction for travel expenses paid or incurred for a spouse, dependent, or other individual accompanying you on business travel, unless certain requirements are met. For the expenses to be deductible, your traveling companion must (1) be a bona fide employee of the person paying or reimbursing the expenses; (2) be traveling for a bona fide business purpose; and (3) have expenses that are otherwise deductible. The denial of the deduction does not apply to expenses that would otherwise qualify as deductible moving expenses.

Meals and Incidental Expenses

You can deduct the cost of meals in either of the following situations.
- It is necessary for you to stop for substantial sleep or rest to properly perform your duties while traveling away from home on business.
- The meal is business-related entertainment.

Business-related entertainment is discussed under *Entertainment Expenses*, later. The following discussion deals only with meals (and incidental expenses) that are not business-related entertainment.

Lavish or extravagant. You cannot deduct expenses for meals that are lavish or extravagant. An expense is not considered lavish or extravagant if it is reasonable based on the facts and circumstances. Expenses will not be disallowed merely because they are more than a fixed dollar amount or take place at deluxe restaurants, hotels, nightclubs, or resorts.

50% limit on meals. You can figure your meal expenses using either of the following methods.
- Actual cost.
- The standard meal allowance.

Both of these methods are explained below. But, regardless of the method you use, you generally can deduct only 50% of the unreimbursed cost of your meals.

> ### TAXALERT
> **Meal expenses when subject to hours of service limits.** Generally, you can deduct only 50% of your business-related meal expenses while traveling away from your tax home for business purposes. However, if you consume the meals during any period when you are subject to the Department of Transportation's hours of service limits, you can deduct 80%.
>
> Individuals subject to the Department of Transportation's hours of service limits include the following persons:
> 1. Certain air transportation workers (such as pilots, crew, dispatchers, mechanics, and control tower operators) who are under Federal Aviation Administration regulations.
> 2. Interstate truck operators and bus drivers who are under Department of Transportation regulations.
> 3. Certain railroad employees (such as engineers, conductors, train crews, dispatchers, and control operations personnel) who are under Federal Railroad Administration regulations.
> 4. Certain merchant mariners who are under Coast Guard regulations. For more information on business meal expenses, see Publication 463.

If you are reimbursed for the cost of your meals, how you apply the 50% limit depends on whether your employer's reimbursement plan was accountable or nonaccountable. If you are not reimbursed, the 50% limit applies whether the unreimbursed meal expense is for business travel or business entertainment. The 50% limit is explained later under *Entertainment Expenses*. Accountable and nonaccountable plans are discussed later under *Reimbursements*.

Actual cost. You can use the actual cost of your meals to figure the amount of your expense before reimbursement and application of the 50% deduction limit. If you use this method, you must keep records of your actual cost.

Standard meal allowance. Generally, you can use the "standard meal allowance" method as an alternative to the actual cost method. It allows you to use a set amount for your daily meals and incidental expenses (M&IE), instead of keeping records of your actual costs. The set amount varies depending on where and when you travel. In this chapter, "standard meal allowance" refers to the federal rate for M&IE, discussed later under *Amount of standard meal allowance*. If you use the standard meal allowance, you still must keep records to prove the time, place, and business purpose of your travel. See *Recordkeeping*, later.

    Incidental expenses. The term "incidental expenses" means fees and tips given to porters, baggage carriers, hotel staff, and staff on ships. Incidental expenses do not include expenses for laundry, cleaning and pressing of clothing, lodging taxes, costs of telegrams or telephone calls, transportation between places of lodging or business and places where meals are taken, or the mailing cost of filing travel vouchers and paying employer-sponsored charge card billings.

    Incidental expenses only method. You can use an optional method (instead of actual cost) for deducting incidental expenses only. The amount of the deduction is $5 a day. You can use this method only if you did not pay or incur any meal expenses. You cannot use this method on any day that you use the standard meal allowance.

    50% limit may apply. If you use the standard meal allowance method for meal expenses and you are not reimbursed or you are reimbursed under a nonaccountable plan, you can generally deduct only 50% of the standard meal allowance. If you are reimbursed under an accountable plan and you are deducting amounts that are more than your reimbursements, you can deduct only 50% of the excess amount. The 50% limit is explained later under *Entertainment Expenses*. Accountable and nonaccountable plans are discussed later under *Reimbursements*.

    Who can use the standard meal allowance. You can use the standard meal allowance whether you are an employee or self-employed, and whether or not you are reimbursed for your traveling expenses.

Use of the standard meal allowance for other travel. You can use the standard meal allowance to figure your meal expenses when you travel in connection with investment and other income-producing property. You can also use it to figure your meal expenses when you travel for qualifying educational purposes. You cannot use the standard meal allowance to figure the cost of your meals when you travel for medical or charitable purposes.

Amount of standard meal allowance. The standard meal allowance is the federal M&IE rate. For travel in 2014, the daily rate for most small localities in the United States is $46.

    Most major cities and many other localities in the United States are designated as high-cost areas, qualifying for higher standard meal allowances. You can find this information (organized by state) on the Internet at *www.gsa.gov*. Click on "Per Diem Rates," then select "2014" for the period January 1, 2014–September 30, 2014, and select "2015" for the period October 1, 2014–December 31, 2014. However, you can apply the rates in effect before October 1, 2014, for expenses of all travel within the United States for 2014 instead of the updated rates. You must consistently use either the rates for the first 9 months for all of 2014 or the updated rates for the period of October 1, 2014, through December 31, 2014.

    If you travel to more than one location in one day, use the rate in effect for the area where you stop for sleep or rest. If you work in the transportation industry, however, see *Special rate for transportation workers*, later.

> **TAXPLANNER**
> Whether or not you receive meal money from your employer, you may claim the standard meal allowance and therefore minimize your recordkeeping problems. If you are self-employed, you may also claim the standard meal allowance.

    Standard meal allowance for areas outside the continental United States. The standard meal allowance rates above do not apply to travel in Alaska, Hawaii, or any other location

---

Caution

Federal employees should refer to the Federal Travel Regulations at www.gsa.gov. Find "What GSA Offers" and click on "Regulations: FMR, FTR, & FAR" for Federal Travel Regulation (FTR) for changes affecting claims for reimbursement.

Caution

There is no optional standard lodging amount similar to the standard meal allowance. Your allowable lodging expense deduction is your actual cost.

Tip

You can access per diem rates for non-foreign areas outside the continental United States at: www.defensetravel.dod.mil/site/perdiemCalc.cfm. You can access all other foreign per diem rates at www.state.gov/travel/. Click on "Travel Per Diem Allowances for Foreign Areas" under "Foreign Per Diem Rates," to obtain the latest foreign per diem rates.

outside the continental United States. The Department of Defense establishes per diem rates for Alaska, Hawaii, Puerto Rico, American Samoa, Guam, Midway, the Northern Mariana Islands, the U.S. Virgin Islands, Wake Island, and other non-foreign areas outside the continental United States. The Department of State establishes per diem rates for all other foreign areas.

Special rate for transportation workers. You can use a special standard meal allowance if you work in the transportation industry. You are in the transportation industry if your work:
- Directly involves moving people or goods by airplane, barge, bus, ship, train, or truck, and
- Regularly requires you to travel away from home and, during any single trip, usually involves travel to areas eligible for different standard meal allowance rates.

If this applies to you, you can claim a standard daily meal allowance of $59 ($65 for travel outside the continental United States).

Using the special rate for transportation workers eliminates the need for you to determine the standard meal allowance for every area where you stop for sleep or rest. If you choose to use the special rate for any trip, you must use the special rate (and not use the regular standard meal allowance rates) for all trips you take that year.

Travel for days you depart and return. For both the day you depart for and the day you return from a business trip, you must prorate the standard meal allowance (figure a reduced amount for each day). You can do so by one of two methods.
- Method 1: You can claim ¾ of the standard meal allowance.
- Method 2: You can prorate using any method that you consistently apply and that is in accordance with reasonable business practice.

Example. Jen is employed in New Orleans as a convention planner. In March, her employer sent her on a 3-day trip to Washington, DC, to attend a planning seminar. She left her home in New Orleans at 10 a.m. on Wednesday and arrived in Washington, DC, at 5:30 p.m. After spending two nights there, she flew back to New Orleans on Friday and arrived back home at 8:00 p.m. Jen's employer gave her a flat amount to cover her expenses and included it with her wages.

Under Method 1, Jen can claim 2½ days of the standard meal allowance for Washington, DC: ¾ of the daily rate for Wednesday and Friday (the days she departed and returned), and the full daily rate for Thursday.

Under Method 2, Jen could also use any method that she applies consistently and that is in accordance with reasonable business practice. For example, she could claim 3 days of the standard meal allowance even though a federal employee would have to use Method 1 and be limited to only 2½ days.

Travel in the United States
The following discussion applies to travel in the United States. For this purpose, the United States includes only the 50 states and the District of Columbia. The treatment of your travel expenses depends on how much of your trip was business related and on how much of your trip occurred within the United States. See *Part of Trip Outside the United States*, later.

Trip Primarily for Business
You can deduct all your travel expenses if your trip was entirely business related. If your trip was primarily for business and, while at your business destination, you extended your stay for a vacation, made a personal side trip, or had other personal activities, you can deduct your business-related travel expenses. These expenses include the travel costs of getting to and from your business destination and any business-related expenses at your business destination.

Example. You work in Atlanta and take a business trip to New Orleans in May. On your way home, you stop in Mobile to visit your parents. You spend $1,996 for the 9 days you are away from home for travel, meals, lodging, and other travel expenses. If you had not stopped in Mobile, you would have been gone only 6 days, and your total cost would have been $1,696. You can deduct $1,696 for your trip, including the cost of round-trip transportation to and from New Orleans. The deduction for your meals is subject to the 50% limit on meals mentioned earlier.

Trip Primarily for Personal Reasons
If your trip was primarily for personal reasons, such as a vacation, the entire cost of the trip is a nondeductible personal expense. However, you can deduct any expenses you have while at your destination that are directly related to your business.

A trip to a resort or on a cruise ship may be a vacation even if the promoter advertises that it is primarily for business. The scheduling of incidental business activities during a trip, such as viewing videotapes or attending lectures dealing with general subjects, will not change what is really a vacation into a business trip.

> ## EXPLANATION
> The courts have not allowed expenses to be deducted for trips whose primary purpose is pleasure but whose secondary purpose is the investigation of business rental properties. If the primary purpose of the trip is to search for rental properties, all travel expenses can be deducted.

> ## TAXORGANIZER
> Careful records should be maintained when family members are along on business trips. If a spouse or other family member on a trip serves a business purpose, care should be taken to document that fact. Otherwise, the incremental travel expenses attributed to the additional person may not be deducted. Receipts and a diary of your activities will be of assistance in documenting the purpose of your trip.

Part of Trip Outside the United States
If part of your trip is outside the United States, use the rules described later under *Travel Outside the United States* for that part of the trip. For the part of your trip that is inside the United States, use the rules for travel in the United States. Travel outside the United States does not include travel from one point in the United States to another point in the United States. The following discussion can help you determine whether your trip was entirely within the United States.

Public transportation. If you travel by public transportation, any place in the United States where that vehicle makes a scheduled stop is a point in the United States. Once the vehicle leaves the last scheduled stop in the United States on its way to a point outside the United States, you apply the rules under *Travel Outside the United States*.

Example. You fly from New York to Puerto Rico with a scheduled stop in Miami. You return to New York nonstop. The flight from New York to Miami is in the United States, so only the flight from Miami to Puerto Rico is outside the United States. Because there are no scheduled stops between Puerto Rico and New York, all of the return trip is outside the United States.

Private car. Travel by private car in the United States is travel between points in the United States, even when you are on your way to a destination outside the United States.

Example. You travel by car from Denver to Mexico City and return. Your travel from Denver to the border and from the border back to Denver is travel in the United States, and the rules in this section apply. The rules under *Travel Outside the United States* apply to your trip from the border to Mexico City and back to the border.

Travel Outside the United States
If any part of your business travel is outside the United States, some of your deductions for the cost of getting to and from your destination may be limited. For this purpose, the United States includes only the 50 states and the District of Columbia.

How much of your travel expenses you can deduct depends in part upon how much of your trip outside the United States was business related.

See chapter 1 of Publication 463 for information on luxury water travel.

Travel Entirely for Business or Considered Entirely for Business
You can deduct all your travel expenses of getting to and from your business destination if your trip is entirely for business or considered entirely for business.

Travel entirely for business. If you travel outside the United States and you spend the entire time on business activities, you can deduct all of your travel expenses.

Travel considered entirely for business. Even if you did not spend your entire time on business activities, your trip is considered entirely for business if you meet at least one of the following four exceptions.

Exception 1 – No substantial control. Your trip is considered entirely for business if you did not have substantial control over arranging the trip. The fact that you control the timing of your trip does not, by itself, mean that you have substantial control over arranging your trip.

You do not have substantial control over your trip if you:
- Are an employee who was reimbursed or paid a travel expense allowance,
- Are not related to your employer, and
- Are not a managing executive.

"Related to your employer" is defined later in this chapter under *Per Diem and Car Allowances*.

A "managing executive" is an employee who has the authority and responsibility, without being subject to the veto of another, to decide on the need for the business travel.

A self-employed person generally has substantial control over arranging business trips.

Exception 2 – Outside United States no more than a week. Your trip is considered entirely for business if you were outside the United States for a week or less, combining business and nonbusiness activities. One week means 7 consecutive days. In counting the days, do not count the day you leave the United States, but do count the day you return to the United States.

Exception 3 – Less than 25% of time on personal activities. Your trip is considered entirely for business if:
- You were outside the United States for more than a week, and
- You spent less than 25% of the total time you were outside the United States on nonbusiness activities.

For this purpose, count both the day your trip began and the day it ended.

Exception 4 – Vacation not a major consideration. Your trip is considered entirely for business if you can establish that a personal vacation was not a major consideration, even if you have substantial control over arranging the trip.

Travel Primarily for Business

If you travel outside the United States primarily for business but spend some of your time on nonbusiness activities, you generally cannot deduct all of your travel expenses. You can only deduct the business portion of your cost of getting to and from your destination. You must allocate the costs between your business and nonbusiness activities to determine your deductible amount. These travel allocation rules are discussed in chapter 1 of Publication 463.

EXPLANATION

A business day is established if, during any part of the day, you are required to be present at a business-related event. Weekends falling between business days may be considered business days, but if they fall at the end of your business meetings and you remain for personal reasons, they are not business days. Transportation days are business days when you travel to your destination on a direct route.

TAXPLANNER

If, in order to take advantage of lower plane fares, your employer reimburses your travel expenses for staying overnight on Saturday at the end of a business trip, the meals and lodging costs for Saturday can be deducted by your employer and excluded from your income to the extent the costs do not exceed the cost savings. The IRS privately ruled that these travel expenses relating to the Saturday night away are deductible even though the day is spent sightseeing.

Travel Primarily for Personal Reasons

If you travel outside the United States primarily for vacation or for investment purposes, the entire cost of the trip is a nondeductible personal expense. If you spend some time attending brief professional seminars or a continuing education program, you can deduct your registration fees and other expenses you have that are directly related to your business.

Conventions

You can deduct your travel expenses when you attend a convention if you can show that your attendance benefits your trade or business. You cannot deduct the travel expenses for your family.

If the convention is for investment, political, social, or other purposes unrelated to your trade or business, you cannot deduct the expenses.

Convention agenda. The convention agenda or program generally shows the purpose of the convention. You can show your attendance at the convention benefits your trade or business by comparing the agenda with the official duties and responsibilities of your position. The agenda does not have to deal specifically with your official duties and responsibilities; it will be enough if the agenda is so related to your position that it shows your attendance was for business purposes.

Conventions held outside the North American area. See chapter 1 of Publication 463 for information on conventions held outside the North American area.

Entertainment Expenses

You may be able to deduct business-related entertainment expenses you have for entertaining a client, customer, or employee.

You can deduct entertainment expenses only if they are both ordinary and necessary (defined earlier in the _Introduction_) and meet one of the following tests.
- Directly related test.
- Associated test.

Both of these tests are explained in chapter 2 of Publication 463.

50% Limit

In general, you can deduct only 50% of your business-related meal and entertainment expenses. (If you are subject to the Department of Transportation's "hours of service" limits, you can deduct 80% of your business-related meal and entertainment expenses. See _Individuals subject to "hours of service" limits_, later.)

> **Caution**
>
> _The amount you can deduct for entertainment expenses may be limited. Generally, you can deduct only 50% of your unreimbursed entertainment expenses. This limit is discussed next._

Figure 27-A.   **Does the 50% Limit Apply to Your Expenses?**

There are exceptions to these rules. *See Exceptions to the 50% Limit*.

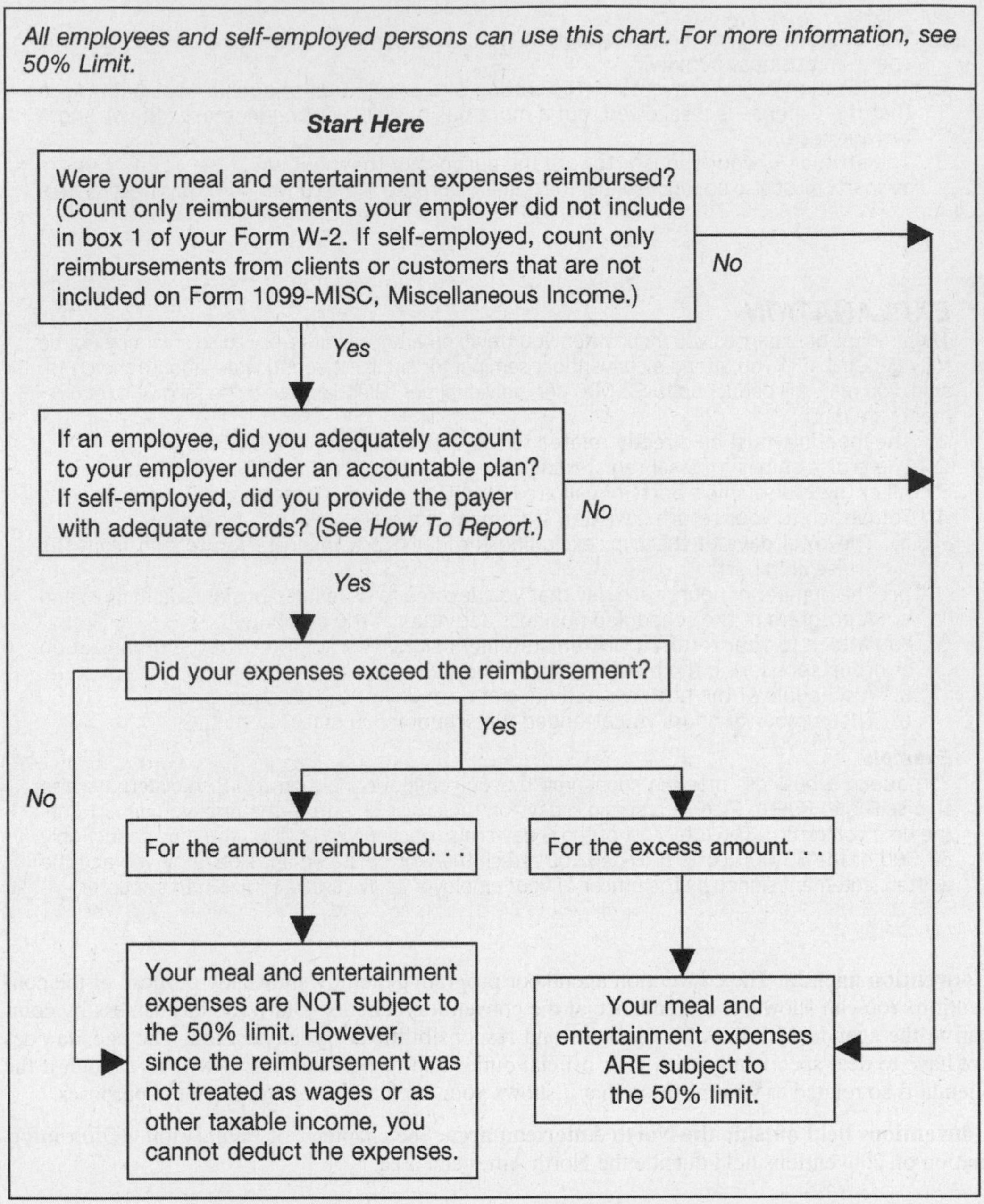

All employees and self-employed persons can use this chart. For more information, see 50% Limit.

Start Here

Were your meal and entertainment expenses reimbursed? (Count only reimbursements your employer did not include in box 1 of your Form W-2. If self-employed, count only reimbursements from clients or customers that are not included on Form 1099-MISC, Miscellaneous Income.) → **No**

↓ **Yes**

If an employee, did you adequately account to your employer under an accountable plan? If self-employed, did you provide the payer with adequate records? (See *How To Report*.) → **No**

↓ **Yes**

Did your expenses exceed the reimbursement?

No ←   **Yes** ↓

For the amount reimbursed. . .   For the excess amount. . .

↓   ↓

Your meal and entertainment expenses are NOT subject to the 50% limit. However, since the reimbursement was not treated as wages or as other taxable income, you cannot deduct the expenses.

Your meal and entertainment expenses ARE subject to the 50% limit.

The 50% limit applies to employees or their employers, and to self-employed persons (including independent contractors) or their clients, depending on whether the expenses are reimbursed. *Figure 27-A* summarizes the general rules explained in this section.

The 50% limit applies to business meals or entertainment expenses you have while:

- Traveling away from home (whether eating alone or with others) on business,
- Entertaining customers at your place of business, a restaurant, or other location, or
- Attending a business convention or reception, business meeting, or business luncheon at a club.

TAXPLANNER

The tax law denies a deduction for amounts paid or incurred for membership in any club organized for business, pleasure, recreation, or other social purpose. However, costs incurred to hold a business-related meeting at such club may be deductible if other conditions discussed earlier are met.

Included expenses. Expenses subject to the 50% limit include:
- Taxes and tips relating to a business meal or entertainment activity,
- Cover charges for admission to a nightclub,
- Rent paid for a room in which you hold a dinner or cocktail party, and
- Amounts paid for parking at a sports arena.

However, the cost of transportation to and from a business meal or a business-related entertainment activity is not subject to the 50% limit.

Application of 50% limit. The 50% limit on meal and entertainment expenses applies if the expense is otherwise deductible and is not covered by one of the exceptions discussed later in this section.

The 50% limit also applies to certain meal and entertainment expenses that are not business related. It applies to meal and entertainment expenses incurred for the production of income, including rental or royalty income. It also applies to the cost of meals included in deductible educational expenses.

When to apply the 50% limit. You apply the 50% limit after determining the amount that would otherwise qualify for a deduction. You first have to determine the amount of meal and entertainment expenses that would be deductible under the other rules discussed in this chapter.

Example 1. You spend $200 for a business-related meal. If $110 of that amount is not allowable because it is lavish and extravagant, the remaining $90 is subject to the 50% limit.

Your deduction cannot be more than $45 (.50 × $90).

Example 2. You purchase two tickets to a concert and give them to a client. You purchased the tickets through a ticket agent. You paid $200 for the two tickets, which had a face value of $80 each ($160 total). Your deduction cannot be more than $80 (.50 × $160).

Exceptions to the 50% Limit

Generally, business-related meal and entertainment expenses are subject to the 50% limit. *Figure 27-A* can help you determine if the 50% limit applies to you.

Your meal or entertainment expense is not subject to the 50% limit if the expense meets one of the following exceptions.

Employee's reimbursed expenses. If you are an employee, you are not subject to the 50% limit on expenses for which your employer reimburses you under an accountable plan. Accountable plans are discussed later under *Reimbursements*.

EXCEPTIONS

Entertainment test exceptions. Expenses incurred in the following situations generally are not subject to the directly related and associated with tests:
- Business meals in surroundings normally considered conducive to a business discussion.
- Recreational and social activities primarily benefiting employees (e.g., company picnics, office Christmas parties, and golf outings).
- Business meetings of employees, stockholders, agents, or directors.
- Attendance at a business meeting of a tax-exempt business league (e.g., a chamber of commerce, a board of trade, or a professional organization).
- Employee entertainment or recreation that is treated as compensation on the employee's income tax return and as wages for withholding purposes.
- Nonemployee entertainment or recreation that is treated as income on the nonemployee's tax return and reported to him or her on an informational return (Form 1099).

Exceptions to the 50% limit. Expenses incurred in the following situations are not subject to the 50% disallowance provision:
- Reimbursed meal or entertainment expenses.
- Employer-paid recreational expenses for employees (e.g., a holiday party).
- Entertainment taxable to the recipient.
- Entertainment expenses made available to the general public.
- Entertainment expenses related to charitable fund-raising sports events.

Individuals subject to "hours of service" limits. You can deduct a higher percentage of your meal expenses while traveling away from your tax home if the meals take place during or incident to any period subject to the Department of Transportation's "hours of service" limits. The percentage is 80%.

Individuals subject to the Department of Transportation's "hours of service" limits include the following persons.

- Certain air transportation workers (such as pilots, crew, dispatchers, mechanics, and control tower operators) who are under Federal Aviation Administration regulations.
- Interstate truck operators and bus drivers who are under Department of Transportation regulations.
- Certain railroad employees (such as engineers, conductors, train crews, dispatchers, and control operations personnel) who are under Federal Railroad Administration regulations.
- Certain merchant mariners who are under Coast Guard regulations.

Other exceptions. There are also exceptions for the self-employed, advertising expenses, selling meals or entertainment, and charitable sports events. These are discussed in Publication 463.

What Entertainment Expenses Are Deductible?
This section explains different types of entertainment expenses you may be able to deduct.

Entertainment. Entertainment includes any activity generally considered to provide entertainment, amusement, or recreation. Examples include entertaining guests at nightclubs; at social, athletic, and sporting clubs; at theaters; at sporting events; or on hunting, fishing, vacation, and similar trips.

A meal as a form of entertainment. Entertainment includes the cost of a meal you provide to a customer or client, whether the meal is a part of other entertainment or by itself. A meal expense includes the cost of food, beverages, taxes, and tips for the meal. To deduct an entertainment-related meal, you or your employee must be present when the food or beverages are provided.

Separating costs. If you have one expense that includes the costs of entertainment and other services (such as lodging or transportation), you must allocate that expense between the cost of entertainment and the cost of other services. You must have a reasonable basis for making this allocation. For example, you must allocate your expenses if a hotel includes entertainment in its lounge on the same bill with your room charge.

Taking turns paying for meals or entertainment. If a group of business acquaintances take turns picking up each others' meal or entertainment checks without regard to whether any business purposes are served, no member of the group can deduct any part of the expense.

Caution
You cannot claim the cost of your meal both as an entertainment expense and as a travel expense.

> ### EXPLANATION
> The courts have held that costs of entertaining fellow employees are not deductible, even though the entertaining may have contributed to high morale and increased productivity.

Lavish or extravagant expenses. You cannot deduct expenses for entertainment that is lavish or extravagant. An expense is not considered lavish or extravagant if it is reasonable considering the facts and circumstances. Expenses will not be disallowed just because they are more than a fixed dollar amount or take place at deluxe restaurants, hotels, nightclubs, or resorts.

Trade association meetings. You can deduct entertainment expenses that are directly related to, and necessary for, attending business meetings or conventions of certain exempt organizations if the expenses of your attendance are related to your active trade or business. These organizations include business leagues, chambers of commerce, real estate boards, trade associations, and professional associations.

Entertainment tickets. Generally, you cannot deduct more than the face value of an entertainment ticket, even if you paid a higher price. For example, you cannot deduct service fees you pay to ticket agencies or brokers or any amount over the face value of the tickets you pay to scalpers.

What Entertainment Expenses Are Not Deductible?
This section explains different types of entertainment expenses you generally may not be able to deduct.

Club dues and membership fees. You cannot deduct dues (including initiation fees) for membership in any club organized for:

- Business,
- Pleasure,

- Recreation, or
- Other social purpose.

This rule applies to any membership organization if one of its principal purposes is either:
- To conduct entertainment activities for members or their guests, or
- To provide members or their guests with access to entertainment facilities.

The purposes and activities of a club, not its name, will determine whether or not you can deduct the dues. You cannot deduct dues paid to:
- Country clubs,
- Golf and athletic clubs,
- Airline clubs,
- Hotel clubs, and
- Clubs operated to provide meals under circumstances generally considered to be conducive to business discussions.

Entertainment facilities. Generally, you cannot deduct any expense for the use of an entertainment facility. This includes expenses for depreciation and operating costs such as rent, utilities, maintenance, and protection.

An entertainment facility is any property you own, rent, or use for entertainment. Examples include a yacht, hunting lodge, fishing camp, swimming pool, tennis court, bowling alley, car, airplane, apartment, hotel suite, or home in a vacation resort.

Out-of-pocket expenses. You can deduct out-of-pocket expenses, such as for food and beverages, catering, gas, and fishing bait, that you provided during entertainment at a facility. These are not expenses for the use of an entertainment facility. However, these expenses are subject to the directly related and associated tests and to the *50% Limit* discussed earlier.

Additional information. For more information on entertainment expenses, including discussions of the directly-related and associated tests, see chapter 2 of Publication 463.

EXPLANATION

Although entertaining a client or a business associate often makes sound business sense, entertainment deductions have sometimes been abused. For this reason, Congress has imposed limitations on the deductibility of entertainment expenses. Only 50% of otherwise allowable entertainment expenses are deductible. The 50% disallowance generally applies to all taxpayers, regardless of the nature of the business. Even before the 50% disallowance, entertainment expenses are subject to stringent recordkeeping requirements and must pass one of two tests (see Publication 463 for the specific factors that should be considered):

1. **Directly related test.** The expenditure is directly related to the active conduct of your business.
2. **Associated test.** The expenditure is associated with the active conduct of your business, and the entertainment directly precedes or follows a substantial, bona fide business discussion.

Business meals—those that have a business purpose as opposed to a social and personal one—are not subject to these entertainment rules if they occur in surroundings conducive to business discussion, the taxpayer or an employee of the taxpayer is present when the food or beverages are served, and the expenses are properly substantiated.

Deductions for entertainment or business meals may not be taken if such expenses are considered lavish or extravagant.

Example

State police officers who are required to eat meals while on duty in public places were permitted to deduct expenses for these meals. The court found that the officers were significantly restricted by their employment regarding the time and place they were permitted to eat and that the meals were often subject to business-related interruptions.

EXPLANATION

Entertainment directly related to business. The directly related test is satisfied if all of the following are true:
- You expect to derive income or some other specific business benefit (other than mere goodwill) at some indefinite future time. However, it is not necessary to demonstrate that you actually receive the benefit.

- You actively engage in a business meeting, discussion, or other bona fide business transaction with the person being entertained.
- Your principal purpose of the combined business-entertainment activity is the active conduct of your business. It is not necessary to devote more time to business than to the entertainment to meet this requirement.

Certain entertainment activities generally do not meet the directly related test unless proven otherwise. If you are not present for the entertainment, if the group entertained includes persons other than business associates (such as spouses), or if there are substantial distractions (as may occur in nightclubs, theaters, sporting events, and vacation resorts), your activity may fail the directly related test.

The IRS gives taxpayers some relief from these strict rules when the activity is clearly in a business setting. For example, expenditures made to further your business by providing a hospitality room at a convention are treated as entertainment expenses directly related to business. Additionally, situations in which no meaningful personal or social relationship exists between you and the persons entertained are often considered to have occurred in a business setting. For example, entertaining business and civic leaders at the opening of a new hotel or theatrical production—for the purpose of obtaining business publicity rather than creating or maintaining goodwill—is a deductible entertainment expense directly related to business. Also, entertainment that represents a price rebate on the sale of your products (such as a restaurant owner occasionally providing a free meal to a loyal customer) is also considered a business setting by the IRS.

Example

An attorney paid for the costs of an annual fishing trip with three business associates who were sources of referrals to his law practice. He also used his cabin 75% of the time for entertaining business clients. The attorney could not prove that substantial and bona fide business discussions occurred during the fishing trip or on any of the occasions when business clients used the cabin. He showed that, at most, he had just a generalized expectation of deriving income or other business benefits at some indefinite future time from those entertained. As a result, he was denied deductions for these expenses because they did not meet the directly related test.

EXPLANATION

Entertainment associated with business. If an entertainment expenditure does not meet the directly related requirements, it may still be deductible if it passes the associated test. An entertainment activity passes the associated test only if it satisfies two conditions:
- The activity has a clear business purpose.
- The entertainment directly precedes or follows a substantial, bona fide business discussion.

The desire to obtain new business and the intent to maintain an existing business relationship—goodwill—are objectives that have a clear business purpose. A substantial, bona fide business discussion occurs when you actively engage in a business transaction to obtain some business benefit and the business meeting, negotiation, or discussion is substantial in relation to the entertainment. However, it is not necessary to spend more time on business than on entertainment.

Example

Bonnie McDonald, an independent consultant, spends 4 hours delivering a new management program to a group of executives in her client's New Orleans office. After the meeting, Bonnie takes the group to the French Quarter for dinner and a show. Dixieland jazz is played throughout dinner.

The entertainment passes the associated with test and is therefore deductible (subject to the 50% limitation) because Bonnie is maintaining a business relationship and the entertainment follows a substantial business meeting. The expense would not pass the directly related test because (1) goodwill generally does not qualify and (2) substantial distractions exist.

EXPLANATION

Entertainment directly precedes or follows a substantial business discussion if it occurs on the same day. If the entertainment and business discussion do not occur on the same day, the facts and circumstances of each case determine whether or not the entertainment and the business discussion occur close enough in time so that the expenses can be deducted.

EXPLANATION

Deducting goodwill entertainment. Generally, entertaining for goodwill alone is not deductible. However, you may deduct goodwill expenditures when:

- The goodwill occurs during a quiet business lunch or dinner.
- The goodwill precedes or follows a substantial business discussion (i.e., passes the associated with test).

Example 1

Liz Brown, a partner of a management consulting firm, plans a dinner party in a New York City hotel. She invites a number of current and prospective clients. Business is only casually discussed; her main goal is to cultivate goodwill. The expense for the dinner party is not deductible. The goodwill is a clear business purpose, but the dinner is not preceded or followed by a substantial business discussion.

Example 2

After considering the tax cost of the nondeductible goodwill expenses, Liz Brown holds a second dinner party, but she adds a formal presentation, which is substantial in relation to the time spent cultivating goodwill. The costs of the refreshments and dinner qualify as goodwill entertainment, since the entertainment is associated with business and the goodwill (the business purpose) is preceded by a substantial business discussion (the presentation). As a result, 50% of the qualifying expenses are deductible.

EXPLANATION

Out-of-pocket entertaining costs at clubs and lodges. Congress has made it clear that out-of-pocket entertainment costs—that otherwise qualify as "directly related to" or "associated with" business expenses—may still be partially deducted, even if they are incurred at an entertainment facility. Again, 50% of such costs may not be deducted.

An entertainment facility is usually real property, such as a fishing camp, a ski lodge, an apartment, or a hotel suite, but may also include personal property, such as a yacht, an airplane, or an automobile. You may own or rent the facility or just be a member of a club or organization, such as a country club or a sporting group, which provides use of a facility.

Example

Mike Franklin, a sports equipment manufacturer, takes a customer to a hunting lodge on an overnight trip. Immediately after the trip, the customer discusses products and market projections. The discussion ends with the customer placing his semiannual order.

In this instance, 50% of the costs of the meals, hunting rights, drinks in the nightclub, and transportation to and from the lodge are deductible. These costs qualify as entertainment associated with business and followed by a substantial business discussion (i.e., the expenses pass the associated test). Because 50% of the entertainment costs would have been deductible if not incurred at an entertainment facility, they are also deductible even though the hunting lodge is an entertainment facility. These costs are not directly associated with the operation and maintenance of the place. However, the cost of the lodging is associated with the operation and maintenance of the facility. Therefore, the lodging expense, though partially deductible if incurred at a nonentertainment facility (e.g., a hotel instead of the hunting lodge), is not deductible.

EXPLANATION

Deductions for the costs of tickets to cultural, theatrical, or sporting events are severely limited. In addition to meeting the directly related or associated with tests, the allowable portion of the ticket cost is limited to the face value of the ticket. The allowable portion of the ticket cost must be further reduced because only 50% of the allowable expense may be deducted.

Example

You pay a scalper $150 for three tickets to a sporting event. The face value of each ticket is $20. Your deduction is limited to $30 ($20 face value × three tickets × 50%).

Gift Expenses

If you give gifts in the course of your trade or business, you can deduct all or part of the cost. This section explains the limits and rules for deducting the costs of gifts.

$25 limit. You can deduct no more than $25 for business gifts you give directly or indirectly to each person during your tax year. A gift to a company that is intended for the eventual personal use or benefit of a particular person or a limited class of people will be considered an indirect gift to that particular person or to the individuals within that class of people who receive the gift.

If you give a gift to a member of a customer's family, the gift is generally considered to be an indirect gift to the customer. This rule does not apply if you have a *bona fide*, independent business connection with that family member and the gift is not intended for the customer's eventual use or benefit.

If you and your spouse both give gifts, both of you are treated as one taxpayer. It does not matter whether you have separate businesses, are separately employed, or whether each of you has an independent connection with the recipient. If a partnership gives gifts, the partnership and the partners are treated as one taxpayer.

Incidental costs. Incidental costs, such as engraving on jewelry, or packaging, insuring, and mailing, are generally not included in determining the cost of a gift for purposes of the $25 limit.

A cost is incidental only if it does not add substantial value to the gift. For example, the cost of customary gift wrapping is an incidental cost. However, the purchase of an ornamental basket for packaging fruit is not an incidental cost if the value of the basket is substantial compared to the value of the fruit.

Exceptions. The following items are not considered gifts for purposes of the $25 limit.
1. An item that costs $4 or less and:
   a. Has your name clearly and permanently imprinted on the gift, and
   b. Is one of a number of identical items you widely distribute. Examples include pens, desk sets, and plastic bags and cases.
2. Signs, display racks, or other promotional material to be used on the business premises of the recipient.

Gift or entertainment. Any item that might be considered either a gift or entertainment generally will be considered entertainment. However, if you give a customer packaged food or beverages you intend the customer to use at a later date, treat it as a gift.

If you give a customer tickets to a theater performance or sporting event and you do not go with the customer to the performance or event, you have a choice. You can treat the cost of the tickets as either a gift expense or an entertainment expense, whichever is to your advantage.

If you go with the customer to the event, you must treat the cost of the tickets as an entertainment expense. You cannot choose, in this case, to treat the cost of the tickets as a gift expense.

> **TAXPLANNER**
> It is usually to your advantage to define a particular item as an entertainment expense rather than as a gift. Although entertainment expenses are subject to the 50% limitation, there is no fixed dollar limitation on the deduction, though the expenses must be considered ordinary and necessary.

Transportation Expenses

This section discusses expenses you can deduct for business transportation when you are not traveling away from home as defined earlier under *Travel Expenses*. These expenses include the cost of transportation by air, rail, bus, taxi, etc., and the cost of driving and maintaining your car.

Transportation expenses include the ordinary and necessary costs of all of the following.
- Getting from one workplace to another in the course of your business or profession when you are traveling within the area of your tax home. (Tax home is defined earlier under *Travel Expenses*.)
- Visiting clients or customers.
- Going to a business meeting away from your regular workplace.
- Getting from your home to a temporary workplace when you have one or more regular places of work. These temporary workplaces can be either within the area of your tax home or outside that area.

Transportation expenses do not include expenses you have while traveling away from home overnight. Those expenses are travel expenses, discussed earlier. However, if you use your car while traveling away from home overnight, use the rules in this section to figure your car expense deduction. See *Car Expenses*, later.

Illustration of transportation expenses. *Figure 27-B* illustrates the rules for when you can deduct transportation expenses when you have a regular or main job away from your home. You may want to refer to it when deciding whether you can deduct your transportation expenses. Daily transportation expenses you incur while traveling from home to one or more regular places of business are generally nondeductible commuting expenses. However, there are many exceptions for deducting transportation expenses, like whether your work location is temporary (inside or outside the metropolitan area), traveling for same trade or business, or if you have a home office.

Temporary work location. If you have one or more regular work locations away from your home and you commute to a temporary work location in the same trade or business, you can deduct the expenses of the daily round-trip transportation between your home and the temporary location, regardless of distance.

If your employment at a work location is realistically expected to last (and does in fact last) for 1 year or less, the employment is temporary unless there are facts and circumstances that would indicate otherwise.

If your employment at a work location is realistically expected to last for more than 1 year or if there is no realistic expectation that the employment will last for 1 year or less, the employment is not temporary, regardless of whether it actually lasts for more than 1 year.

If employment at a work location initially is realistically expected to last for 1 year or less, but at some later date the employment is realistically expected to last more than 1 year, that employment will be treated as temporary (unless there are facts and circumstances that would indicate otherwise) until your expectation changes. It will not be treated as temporary after the date you determine it will last more than 1 year.

If the temporary work location is beyond the general area of your regular place of work and you stay overnight, you are traveling away from home. You may have deductible travel expenses as discussed earlier in this chapter.

Figure 27-B. **When Are Transportation Expenses Deductible?**

Most employees and self-employed persons can use this chart. (Do not use this chart if your home is your principal place of business. See *Office in the home*.)

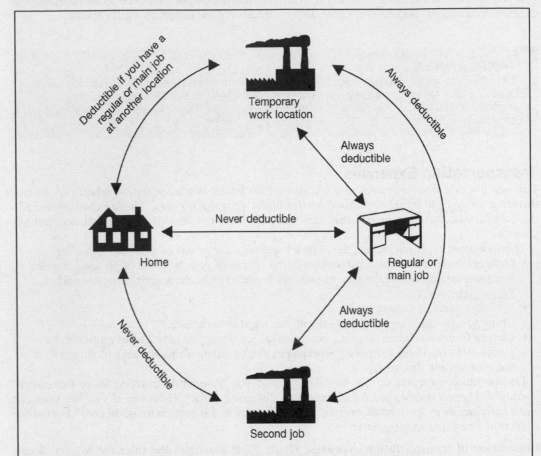

Home: The place where you reside. Transportation expenses between your home and your main or regular place of work are personal commuting expenses.

Regular or main job: Your principal place of business. If you have more than one job, you must determine which one is your regular or main job. Consider the time you spend at each, the activity you have at each, and the income you earn at each.

Temporary work location: A place where your work assignment is realistically expected to last (and does in fact last) one year or less. Unless you have a regular place of business, you can only deduct your transportation expenses to a temporary work location <u>outside</u> your metropolitan area.

Second job: If you regularly work at two or more places in one day, whether or not for the same employer, you can deduct your transportation expenses of getting from one workplace to another. If you do not go directly from your first job to your second job, you can only deduct the transportation expenses of going directly from your first job to your second job. You cannot deduct your transportation expenses between your home and a second job on a day off from your main job.

No regular place of work. If you have no regular place of work but ordinarily work in the metropolitan area where you live, you can deduct daily transportation costs between home and a temporary work site outside that metropolitan area.

Generally, a metropolitan area includes the area within the city limits and the suburbs that are considered part of that metropolitan area.

You cannot deduct daily transportation costs between your home and temporary work sites within your metropolitan area. These are nondeductible commuting expenses.

Two places of work. If you work at two places in one day, whether or not for the same employer, you can deduct the expense of getting from one workplace to the other. However, if for some personal reason you do not go directly from one location to the other, you cannot deduct more than the amount it would have cost you to go directly from the first location to the second.

Transportation expenses you have in going between home and a part-time job on a day off from your main job are commuting expenses. You cannot deduct them.

Armed Forces reservists. A meeting of an Armed Forces reserve unit is a second place of business if the meeting is held on a day on which you work at your regular job. You can deduct the expense of getting from one workplace to the other as just discussed under *Two places of work*, earlier.

You usually cannot deduct the expense if the reserve meeting is held on a day on which you do not work at your regular job. In this case, your transportation generally is a nondeductible commuting expense. However, you can deduct your transportation expenses if the location of the meeting is temporary and you have one or more regular places of work.

If you ordinarily work in a particular metropolitan area but not at any specific location and the reserve meeting is held at a temporary location outside that metropolitan area, you can deduct your transportation expenses.

If you travel away from home overnight to attend a guard or reserve meeting, you can deduct your travel expenses. These expenses are discussed earlier under *Travel Expenses*.

If you travel more than 100 miles away from home in connection with your performance of services as a member of the reserves, you may be able to deduct some of your reserve-related travel costs as an adjustment to income rather than as an itemized deduction. See *Armed Forces reservists traveling more than 100 miles from home* under *Special Rules*, later.

Commuting expenses. You cannot deduct the costs of taking a bus, trolley, subway, or taxi, or of driving a car between your home and your main or regular place of work. These costs are personal commuting expenses. You cannot deduct commuting expenses no matter how far your home is from your regular place of work. You cannot deduct commuting expenses even if you work during the commuting trip.

Example. You sometimes use your cell phone to make business calls while commuting to and from work. Sometimes business associates ride with you to and from work, and you have a business discussion in the car. These activities do not change the trip from personal to business. You cannot deduct your commuting expenses.

Parking fees. Fees you pay to park your car at your place of business are nondeductible commuting expenses. You can, however, deduct business-related parking fees when visiting a customer or client.

Advertising display on car. Putting display material that advertises your business on your car does not change the use of your car from personal use to business use. If you use this car for commuting or other personal uses, you still cannot deduct your expenses for those uses.

Car pools. You cannot deduct the cost of using your car in a nonprofit car pool. Do not include payments you receive from the passengers in your income. These payments are considered reimbursements of your expenses. However, if you operate a car pool for a profit, you must include payments from passengers in your income. You can then deduct your car expenses (using the rules in this chapter).

Hauling tools or instruments. Hauling tools or instruments in your car while commuting to and from work does not make your car expenses deductible. However, you can deduct any additional costs you have for hauling tools or instruments (such as for renting a trailer you tow with your car).

Union members' trips from a union hall. If you get your work assignments at a union hall and then go to your place of work, the costs of getting from the union hall to your place of work are nondeductible commuting expenses. Although you need the union to get your work assignments, you are employed where you work, not where the union hall is located.

Office in the home. If you have an office in your home that qualifies as a principal place of business, you can deduct your daily transportation costs between your home and another work location in the same trade or business. (See *chapter 29* for information on determining if your home office qualifies as a principal place of business.)

Examples of deductible transportation. The following examples show when you can deduct transportation expenses based on the location of your work and your home.

Example 1. You regularly work in an office in the city where you live. Your employer sends you to a 1-week training session at a different office in the same city. You travel directly from your home to the training location and return each day. You can deduct the cost of your daily round-trip transportation between your home and the training location.

Example 2. Your principal place of business is in your home. You can deduct the cost of round-trip transportation between your qualifying home office and your client's or customer's place of business.

Example 3. You have no regular office, and you do not have an office in your home. In this case, the location of your first business contact inside the metropolitan area is considered your office. Transportation expenses between your home and this first contact are nondeductible commuting expenses. Transportation expenses between your last business contact and your home are also nondeductible commuting expenses. While you cannot deduct the costs of these first and last trips, you can deduct the costs of going from one client or customer to another. With no regular or home office, the costs of travel between two or more business contacts in a metropolitan area are deductible while the costs of travel between the home to (and from) business contacts are not deductible.

Car Expenses

If you use your car for business purposes, you may be able to deduct car expenses. You generally can use one of the two following methods to figure your deductible expenses.

- Standard mileage rate.
- Actual car expenses.

If you use actual car expenses to figure your deduction for a car you lease, there are rules that affect the amount of your lease payments you can deduct. See *Leasing a car* under *Actual Car Expenses,* later.

In this chapter, "car" includes a van, pickup, or panel truck.

EXPLANATION

Fixed and variable rate. Under certain circumstances, employees' business expenses for car expenses will be deemed substantiated when their employer reimburses such expenses with a mileage allowance different from the standard mileage rates for 2014 (56 cents per mile).

TAXPLANNER

A court held that it was sufficient for a salesman to maintain records of personal miles driven only. The difference between his total mileage and his personal mileage represented his business mileage.

The courts have allowed a taxpayer a deduction for depreciation of a car used in business, even though his travel records were not very accurate or complete. Depreciation of a business asset is not subject to the strict record-keeping requirements that other types of travel expenses are. A deduction for depreciation is allowed if you can simply show that the car was used for business.

Rural mail carriers. If you are a rural mail carrier, you may be able to treat the amount of qualified reimbursement you received as the amount of your allowable expense. Because the qualified reimbursement is treated as paid under an accountable plan, your employer should not include the amount of reimbursement in your income.

If your vehicle expenses are more than the amount of your reimbursement, you can deduct the unreimbursed expenses as an itemized deduction on Schedule A (Form 1040). You must complete Form 2106 and attach it to your Form 1040.

A "qualified reimbursement" is the reimbursement you receive that meets both of the following conditions.
- It is given as an equipment maintenance allowance (EMA) to employees of the U.S. Postal Service.
- It is at the rate contained in the 1991 collective bargaining agreement. Any later agreement cannot increase the qualified reimbursement amount by more than the rate of inflation.

See your employer for information on your reimbursement.

Standard Mileage Rate

You may be able to use the standard mileage rate to figure the deductible costs of operating your car for business purposes. For 2014, the standard mileage rate for business use is 56 cents per mile.

TAXALERT

For 2014, the optional federal standard mileage rates for business, charitable, medical, and moving use of an automobile are:

Business	56¢
Charitable	14¢
Medical & Moving	23.5¢

You generally can use the standard mileage rate whether or not you are reimbursed and whether or not any reimbursement is more or less than the amount figured using the standard mileage rate. See *Reimbursements* under *How To Report,* later.

Choosing the standard mileage rate. If you want to use the standard mileage rate for a car you own, you must choose to use it in the first year the car is available for use in your business. Then in later years, you can choose to use either the standard mileage rate or actual expenses.

If you want to use the standard mileage rate for a car you lease, you must use it for the entire lease period.

You must make the choice to use the standard mileage rate by the due date (including extensions) of your return. You cannot revoke the choice. However, in a later year, you can switch from the standard mileage rate to the actual expenses method. If you change to the actual expenses method in a later year, but before your car is fully depreciated, you have to estimate the remaining useful life of the car and use straight line depreciation.

Example. Larry is an employee who occasionally uses his own car for business purposes. He purchased the car in 2012, but he did not claim any unreimbursed employee expenses on his 2012 tax return. Because Larry did not use the standard mileage rate the first year the car was available for business use, he cannot use the standard mileage rate in 2014 to claim unreimbursed employee business expenses.

For more information about depreciation included in the standard mileage rate, see the exception in *Methods of depreciation* under *Depreciation Deduction* in chapter 4 of Publication 463.

EXPLANATION

If you select the actual cost method (operating expenses and ACRS or MACRS depreciation expense method), the standard mileage rate may never be used for that automobile. However, if you use the standard mileage rate for the first year, you may switch to the actual cost method, but you then must use a straight-line depreciation rate for the remaining estimated life of the automobile. Generally, actual expenses exceed the amount you may claim by using the standard mileage rate. As long as you keep adequate records, you will probably be better off claiming actual expenses.

Standard mileage rate not allowed. You cannot use the standard mileage rate if you:
- Use five or more cars at the same time (as in fleet operations),
- Claimed a depreciation deduction for the car using any method other than straight line depreciation,
- Claimed a Section 179 deduction on the car,
- Claimed the special depreciation allowance on the car,

- Claimed actual car expenses after 1997 for a car you leased, or
- Are a rural mail carrier who received a qualified reimbursement. (See *Rural mail carriers*, earlier.)

Five or more cars. If you own or lease five or more cars that are used for business at the same time, you cannot use the standard mileage rate for the business use of any car. However, you may be able to deduct your actual expenses for operating each of the cars in your business. See *Actual Car Expenses* in chapter 4 of Publication 463 for information on how to figure your deduction.

You are not using five or more cars for business at the same time if you alternate using (use at different times) the cars for business.

Note. You can elect to use the standard mileage rate if you used a car for hire (such as a taxi).

Parking fees and tolls. In addition to using the standard mileage rate, you can deduct any business-related parking fees and tolls. (Parking fees you pay to park your car at your place of work are nondeductible commuting expenses.)

TAXALERT

Employer-provided parking. For 2014, you can exclude up to $250 per month of employer-provided parking, even if you choose it instead of cash or your employer reduces your compensation to provide the parking.

Actual Car Expenses

If you do not use the standard mileage rate, you may be able to deduct your actual car expenses. Actual car expenses include:

Depreciation	Tolls	Parking fees
Licenses	Lease payments	Registration fees
Gas	Insurance	Repairs
Oil	Garage rent	Tires

Tip

If you qualify to use both methods, you may want to figure your deduction both ways to see which gives you a larger deduction.

Business and personal use. If you use your car for both business and personal purposes, you must divide your expenses between business and personal use. You can divide your expenses based on the miles driven for each purpose.

Example. You are a contractor and drive your car 20,000 miles during the year: 12,000 miles for business use and 8,000 miles for personal use. You can claim only 60% (12,000 ÷ 20,000) of the cost of operating your car as a business expense.

EXPLANATION

To claim a deduction for car expenses properly, you must establish that you are entitled to the deduction because the car was used at least partially for business. The deduction will be allowed only to the extent of business use. If you can establish that you are entitled to the deduction but are unable to establish the precise amount of the deduction, the court will apply its own best judgment to make an approximation of the business portion of the expenses.

Example 1
A doctor who is constantly on emergency call may not deduct all of his automobile expenses and depreciation. He must calculate how much of the automobile's use is business and how much is personal. The business portion is deductible.

Example 2
A construction worker who kept a logbook of miles driven but failed to distinguish between business and personal mileage was not allowed to take any deduction.

Example 3
A salesman was able to prove that he used his automobile exclusively for business except for his round trip to and from work of 16 miles. However, he was unable to establish how many miles were dedicated to business use. The court concluded that his business use was 75% and his personal use was 25%.

Interest on car loans. If you are an employee, you cannot deduct any interest paid on a car loan. This interest is treated as personal interest and is not deductible. However, if you are self-employed and use your car in that business, see chapter 4 of Publication 535.

Tip

If you use a home equity loan to purchase your car, you may be able to deduct the interest. See chapter 24 for more information.

TAXPLANNER

If an employee who owns a home finances the purchase of an automobile through a loan secured by the home, the interest would be fully deductible as home mortgage interest if the employee is within the $100,000 home equity indebtedness rules.

Taxes paid on your car. If you are an employee, you can deduct personal property taxes paid on your car if you itemize deductions. Enter the amount paid on line 7 of Schedule A (Form 1040). (See *chapter 23* for more information on taxes.) If you are not an employee, see your form instructions for information on how to deduct personal property taxes paid on your car.

Sales taxes. Generally, sales taxes on your car are part of your car's basis and are recovered through depreciation, discussed later.

TAXALERT

To the extent the car is not used in your trade or business, you can choose to deduct the nonbusiness part of the sales tax deduction on Schedule A (Form 1040). You can only choose to deduct state and local sales taxes as an itemized deduction if you choose not to deduct state and local income taxes. For more information, see *General Sales Taxes* in chapter 23, *Taxes you may deduct*.

Fines and collateral. You cannot deduct fines you pay and collateral you forfeited for traffic violations.

Depreciation and Section 179 deductions. Generally, the cost of a car, plus sales tax and improvements, is a capital expense. Because the benefits last longer than 1 year, you generally cannot deduct a capital expense. However, you can recover this cost through the Section 179 deduction, special depreciation allowance, and depreciation deductions. Depreciation allows you to recover the cost over more than 1 year by deducting part of it each year. The Section 179 deduction, special depreciation allowance, and the depreciation deduction are discussed in more detail in chapter 4 of Publication 463.

Generally, there are limits on these deductions. Special rules apply if you use your car 50% or less in your work or business.

EXPLANATION

Severe limitations on deductions apply on luxury automobiles and automobiles used for both business and personal purposes.

Passenger automobile. The total initial-year depreciation deduction (including Section 179 expense) you can take for a passenger automobile (that is not a truck, van, or an electric vehicle) that you use in your business and first place in service in 2014 is $3,160.

Truck or van. The total initial-year depreciation deduction (including Section 179 expense) you can take for a truck or van (such as a minivan or a sports utility vehicle built on a truck chassis) that you use in your business and first place in service in 2014 is higher than for other passenger vehicles. The maximum amount allowable is $3,460.

Caution: The limits are reduced if the business use of the vehicle is less than 100%.

TAXALERT

Special depreciation allowance expired. The 50% special ("bonus") depreciation allowance on qualified property—including cars, trucks, and vans put into service for use in your trade or business—expired at the end of 2013 and is not available for 2014. However, as of the time this book was published in October 2014, Congress had been considering legislation that would extend 50% bonus depreciation at least through 2014; perhaps even permanently, but no such extension of this accelerated write-off had yet been passed. For updated information on this and any other tax law changes that occur after this book was published, see our website, *ey.com/EYTaxGuide*.

Leasing a car. If you lease a car, truck, or van that you use in your business, you can use the standard mileage rate or actual expenses to figure your deductible car expense.

Deductible payments. If you choose to use actual expenses, you can deduct the part of each lease payment that is for the use of the vehicle in your business. You cannot deduct any part of a lease payment that is for personal use of the vehicle, such as commuting.

You must spread any advance payments over the entire lease period. You cannot deduct any payments you make to buy a vehicle, even if the payments are called lease payments.

If you lease a car, truck, or van for 30 days or more, you may have to reduce your lease payment deduction by an "inclusion amount." For information on reporting lease inclusion amounts, see *Leasing a Car* in chapter 4 of Publication 463.

rather than buying it because you can deduct your lease payments subject to the business use rules discussed elsewhere in this chapter.

Leasing an automobile. Deducting employee business expenses for the cost of a leased automobile is similar to doing so for an automobile you own. You may deduct the portion of the total lease payments that is attributable to business use, using the ratio of business miles to total miles to make the calculation. This deduction represents the depreciation and financing costs. Normal operating costs and maintenance (if not included in the lease) and business parking may also be deducted.

The luxury automobile rules are intended to impose the same unfavorable treatment for leased automobiles as for purchased automobiles. If you lease an automobile for business use, you can deduct the lease payments and operating expenses for that business use. If you lease an automobile and the value exceeds certain levels, you are deemed to have received additional income.

Note: You must recapture a portion of your lease payment deductions and report them as income if your business use of the automobile falls below 50%.

See Publication 463, *Travel, Entertainment, Gift and Car Expenses*, for further details and the tables for computing the lease adjustments.

EXPLANATION

Unreimbursed automobile expenses are deductible only as miscellaneous itemized deductions. Employees formerly classified as "outside sales representatives" are also subject to this provision.

As a result, these expenses will be deductible only to the extent that, when aggregated with your other miscellaneous itemized deductions, they exceed 2% of your adjusted gross income.

TAXSAVER

In some cases, you may be able to deduct a greater mileage rate than the IRS customarily permits. For example, the courts have allowed truck drivers who were reimbursed at a greater rate than the standard rate to deduct the greater rate. The truck drivers had kept detailed weekly records of their trucks' operating costs.

TAXSAVER

If you own an expensive business automobile, the standard mileage rate is probably inadequate to cover your operating costs. You should keep detailed records of your total expenses so that you may claim a larger deduction than you would be able to claim by using the standard mileage rate.

Sale, Trade-In, or Other Disposition

If you sell, trade in, or otherwise dispose of your car, you may have a taxable gain or a deductible loss. This is true whether you used the standard mileage rate or actual car expenses to deduct the business use of your car. Publication 544 has information on sales of property used in a trade or business, and details on how to report the disposition.

Recordkeeping

If you deduct travel, entertainment, gift, or transportation expenses, you must be able to prove (substantiate) certain elements of the expense. This section discusses the records you need to keep to prove these expenses.

Records

If you keep timely and accurate records, you will have support to show the IRS if your tax return is ever examined. You will also have proof of expenses that your employer may require if you are reimbursed under an accountable plan. These plans are discussed later under <u>Reimbursements</u>.

TAXPLANNER

Good recordkeeping is a good business practice and a must for tax purposes. A clear and consistent set of records is the first step in justifying your expense deduction. Reasonable estimates of expenses are no longer acceptable, even if the estimate is moderate in relation to the income generated.

Form 4562, which is used to show your automobile depreciation, specifically asks whether you have evidence to support your business use percentage.

You must maintain adequate records or sufficient evidence, either written or oral, that will corroborate your own statement. Sufficient evidence includes account books, trip sheets, expense reports, appointment calendars, statements of witnesses, and certain accountings to an employer. Contemporaneous logs are no longer required, but a report made at the event would be more credible than records prepared at a later date.

If you are required to turn in the original copies of your receipts and logbooks to your employer, you should make copies for yourself. If the confidentiality of names is a consideration, special arrangements might have to be made with your employer to make necessary information available if and when it is needed.

When records are lost in circumstances beyond your control, such as destruction by fire, flood, earthquake, or other casualty, the IRS is more lenient in accepting reconstructed records and secondary evidence than it is when records are not available because of carelessness or mysterious disappearance.

Example
Travel expense records were lost during a change of residence resulting from marital problems. The court ruled that marital difficulties did not constitute a casualty warranting the use of reconstructed records.

How To Prove Expenses

Table 27-2 is a summary of records you need to prove each expense discussed in this chapter. You must be able to prove the elements listed across the top portion of the table. You prove them by having the information and receipts (where needed) for the expenses listed in the first column.

You should keep adequate records to prove your expenses or have sufficient evidence that will support your own statement. You must generally prepare a written record for it to be considered adequate. This is because written evidence is more reliable than oral evidence alone.

> **Caution**
>
> *You cannot deduct amounts that you approximate or estimate.*

TAXALERT
Generally, deductions are not allowed for any travel expenses without proper records. However, the IRS issued guidance in September 2009 that states if your employer provides a per diem allowance, your expenses can be "deemed" to be substantiated. The amount "deemed substantiated" is the lesser of the per diem allowance or the federal per diem rate for the locality on the day of travel.

> **Tip**
>
> *However, if you contemporaneously prepare a record on a computer it is considered an adequate record.*

TAXALERT
If you are self-employed or an employee who is not reimbursed for allowable meal and incidental expenses, you may use the lesser of the following to substantiate your deduction:
1. Actual expenses
2. The federal meals and incidental expenses rate for the locality of travel for that day

The amount will be deemed substantiated if you can substantiate the elements of time, place, and business purpose of travel for that day.

TAXALERT
In lieu of using actual expenses, the amount "deemed substantiated" for incidental expenses on a day you can document the time, place, and business purpose of travel will be $5 per day for any locality in the continental United States and localities outside the continental United States, after October 1, 2013.

As of the date this book was published, the amount deemed substantiated after October 1, 2014, had not yet been announced by the IRS. For updated information on this and any other tax law changes that occur after this book was published, see our website, *ey.com/EYTaxGuide*.

Table 27-2. How To Prove Certain Business Expenses

IF you have expenses for...	THEN you must keep records that show details of the following elements...			
	Amount	Time	Place or Description	Business Purpose and Business Relationship
Travel	Cost of each separate expense for travel, lodging, and meals. Incidental expenses may be totaled in reasonable categories such as taxis, fees and tips, etc.	Dates you left and returned for each trip and number of days spent on business.	Destination or area of your travel (name of city, town, or other designation).	Purpose: Business purpose for the expense or the business benefit gained or expected to be gained. Relationship: N/A
Entertainment	Cost of each separate expense. Incidental expenses such as taxis, telephones, etc., may be totaled on a daily basis.	Date of entertainment. (Also see *Business Purpose.*)	Name and address or location of place of entertainment. Type of entertainment if not otherwise apparent. (Also see *Business Purpose.*)	Purpose: Business purpose for the expense or the business benefit gained or expected to be gained. For entertainment, the nature of the business discussion or activity. If the entertainment was directly before or after a business discussion: the date, place, nature, and duration of the business discussion, and the identities of the persons who took part in both the business discussion and the entertainment activity. Relationship: Occupations or other information (such as names, titles, or other designations) about the recipients that shows their business relationship to you. For entertainment, you must also prove that you or your employee was present if the entertainment was a business meal.
Gifts	Cost of the gift.	Date of the gift.	Description of the gift.	
Transportation	Cost of each separate expense. For car expenses, the cost of the car and any improvements, the date you started using it for business, the mileage for each business use, and the total miles for the year.	Date of the expense. For car expenses, the date of the use of the car.	Your business destination.	Purpose: Business purpose for the expense. Relationship: N/A

What Are Adequate Records?

You should keep the proof you need in an account book, diary, statement of expense, or similar record. You should also keep documentary evidence that, together with your records, will support each element of an expense.

Documentary evidence. You generally must have documentary evidence, such as receipts, canceled checks, or bills, to support your expenses.

Exception. Documentary evidence is not needed if any of the following conditions apply.

- You have meals or lodging expenses while traveling away from home for which you account to your employer under an accountable plan and you use a per diem allowance method that includes meals and/or lodging. (Accountable plans and per diem allowances are discussed later under *Reimbursements*.)

- Your expense, other than lodging, is less than $75.
- You have a transportation expense for which a receipt is not readily available.

TAXALERT

The tax law disallows an otherwise allowable deduction for any expense for traveling, entertainment, gifts, or listed property, unless the expense is substantiated by adequate records. Taxpayers are required to maintain documentary evidence (such as receipts) for (1) any lodging expenditure and (2) any other expenditure of $75 or more.

Adequate evidence. Documentary evidence ordinarily will be considered adequate if it shows the amount, date, place, and essential character of the expense.

For example, a hotel receipt is enough to support expenses for business travel if it has all of the following information.
- The name and location of the hotel.
- The dates you stayed there.
- Separate amounts for charges such as lodging, meals, and telephone calls.

A restaurant receipt is enough to prove an expense for a business meal if it has all of the following information.
- The name and location of the restaurant.
- The number of people served.
- The date and amount of the expense.

If a charge is made for items other than food and beverages, the receipt must show that this is the case.

Canceled check. A canceled check, together with a bill from the payee, ordinarily establishes the cost. However, a canceled check by itself does not prove a business expense without other evidence to show that it was for a business purpose.

TAXPLANNER

You must maintain detailed records and report the required information on your tax return if you wish to claim a deduction for expenses that exceed reimbursements. You must keep these records, even though you do not have to give the completely detailed information to your employer because reimbursements by your employer meet the IRS per diem standards.

Duplicate information. You do not have to record information in your account book or other record that duplicates information shown on a receipt as long as your records and receipts complement each other in an orderly manner.

You do not have to record amounts your employer pays directly for any ticket or other travel item. However, if you charge these items to your employer, through a credit card or otherwise, you must keep a record of the amounts you spend.

Timely kept records. You should record the elements of an expense or of a business use at or near the time of the expense or use and support it with sufficient documentary evidence. A timely kept record has more value than a statement prepared later when generally there is a lack of accurate recall.

You do not need to write down the elements of every expense on the day of the expense. If you maintain a log on a weekly basis which accounts for use during the week, the log is considered a timely kept record.

If you give your employer, client, or customer an expense account statement, it can also be considered a timely kept record. This is true if you copy it from your account book, diary, statement of expense, or similar record.

Proving business purpose. You must generally provide a written statement of the business purpose of an expense. However, the degree of proof varies according to the circumstances in each case. If the business purpose of an expense is clear from the surrounding circumstances, then you do not need to give a written explanation.

Confidential information. You do not need to put confidential information relating to an element of a deductible expense (such as the place, business purpose, or business relationship) in your account book, diary, or other record. However, you do have to record the information elsewhere at or near the time of the expense and have it available to fully prove that element of the expense.

What if I Have Incomplete Records?

If you do not have complete records to prove an element of an expense, then you must prove the element with:

- Your own written or oral statement, containing specific information about the element, and
- Other supporting evidence that is sufficient to establish the element.

Destroyed records. If you cannot produce a receipt because of reasons beyond your control, you can prove a deduction by reconstructing your records or expenses. Reasons beyond your control include fire, flood, and other casualty.

Separating and Combining Expenses

This section explains when expenses must be kept separate and when expenses can be combined.

Separating expenses. Each separate payment is generally considered a separate expense. For example, if you entertain a customer or client at dinner and then go to the theater, the dinner expense and the cost of the theater tickets are two separate expenses. You must record them separately in your records.

Combining items. You can make one daily entry in your record for reasonable categories of expenses. Examples are taxi fares, telephone calls, or other incidental travel costs. Meals should be in a separate category. You can include tips for meal-related services with the costs of the meals.

Expenses of a similar nature occurring during the course of a single event are considered a single expense. For example, if during entertainment at a cocktail lounge, you pay separately for each serving of refreshments, the total expense for the refreshments is treated as a single expense.

Allocating total cost. If you can prove the total cost of travel or entertainment but you cannot prove how much it cost for each person who participated in the event, you may have to allocate the total cost among you and your guests on a pro rata basis. An allocation would be needed, for example, if you did not have a business relationship with all of your guests.

If your return is examined. If your return is examined, you may have to provide additional information to the IRS. This information could be needed to clarify or to establish the accuracy or reliability of information contained in your records, statements, testimony, or documentary evidence before a deduction is allowed.

How Long To Keep Records and Receipts

You must keep records as long as they may be needed for the administration of any provision of the Internal Revenue Code. Generally, this means you must keep your records that support your deduction (or an item of income) for 3 years from the date you file the income tax return on which the deduction is claimed. A return filed early is considered filed on the due date. For a more complete explanation, see Publication 583, Starting a Business and Keeping Records.

> ### EXPLANATION
> If you use your automobile less than 50% for business and claim actual expenses, you must keep those records for at least 6 years (i.e., more than the recovery period for straight-line depreciation).

Reimbursed for expenses. Employees who give their records and documentation to their employers and are reimbursed for their expenses generally do not have to keep copies of this information. However, you may have to prove your expenses if any of the following conditions apply.

- You claim deductions for expenses that are more than reimbursements.
- Your expenses are reimbursed under a nonaccountable plan.
- Your employer does not use adequate accounting procedures to verify expense accounts.
- You are related to your employer, as defined later under _Related to employer_.

See the next section, _How To Report_, for a discussion of reimbursements, adequate accounting, and nonaccountable plans.

Additional information. Chapter 5 of Publication 463 has more information on recordkeeping, including examples.

How To Report

This section explains where and how to report the expenses discussed in this chapter. It discusses reimbursements and how to treat them under accountable and nonaccountable plans. It also explains rules for independent contractors and clients, fee-basis officials, certain performing artists, Armed Forces reservists, and certain disabled employees. This section ends with an illustration of how to report travel, entertainment, gift, and car expenses on Form 2106-EZ.

Self-employed. You must report your income and expenses on Schedule C or C-EZ (Form 1040) if you are a sole proprietor, or on Schedule F (Form 1040) if you are a farmer. You do not use Form 2106 or 2106-EZ. See your form instructions for information on how to complete your tax return. You can also find information in Publication 535 if you are a sole proprietor, or in Publication 225, Farmer's Tax Guide, if you are a farmer.

Both self-employed and an employee. If you are both self-employed and an employee, you must keep separate records for each business activity. Report your business expenses for self-employment on Schedule C, C-EZ, or F (Form 1040), as discussed earlier. Report your business expenses for your work as an employee on Form 2106 or 2106-EZ, as discussed next.

Employees. If you are an employee, you generally must complete Form 2106 to deduct your travel, transportation, and entertainment expenses. However, you can use the shorter Form 2106-EZ instead of Form 2106 if you meet all of the following conditions.
- You are an employee deducting expenses attributable to your job.
- You were not reimbursed by your employer for your expenses (amounts included in box 1 of your Form W-2 are not considered reimbursements).
- If you claim car expenses, you use the standard mileage rate.

For more information on how to report your expenses on Forms 2106 and 2106-EZ, see _Completing Forms 2106 and 2106-EZ_, later.

Gifts. If you did not receive any reimbursements (or the reimbursements were all included in box 1 of your Form W-2), the only business expense you are claiming is for gifts, and the rules for certain individuals (such as performing artists) discussed later under _Special Rules_ do not apply to you, do not complete Form 2106 or 2106-EZ. Instead, claim the amount of your deductible gifts directly on line 21 of Schedule A (Form 1040).

Statutory employees. If you received a Form W-2 and the "Statutory employee" box in box 13 was checked, report your income and expenses related to that income on Schedule C or C-EZ (Form 1040). Do not complete Form 2106 or 2106-EZ.

Statutory employees include full-time life insurance salespersons, certain agent or commission drivers, traveling salespersons, and certain homeworkers.

EXAMPLES

Example 1
John Smith, a salesman working on behalf of a principal, solicits orders from wholesalers and restaurants for merchandise intended for resale. John reports his income and expenses on Schedule C as a statutory employee.

Example 2
An agent-driver engaged in distributing meat, vegetables, bakery goods, beverages (other than milk), or dry cleaning services is classified as a statutory employee.

EXPLANATION
While you may not claim a deduction for an expense that your employer would reimburse, you may be entitled to a deduction for a work-related expense that you feel was necessary to do your job but that your employer does not reimburse.

Example
You are a technician who works in a laboratory in which your employer requires you to wear a certain type of uniform while on the job. The uniform is unsuitable for street wear. Your employer refuses to reimburse you for the cost of the uniform. You are entitled to deduct the expense on your own income tax return.

Caution

If you are entitled to a reimbursement from your employer but you do not claim it, you cannot claim a deduction for the expenses to which that unclaimed reimbursement applies.

Reimbursement for personal expenses. If your employer reimburses you for nondeductible personal expenses, such as for vacation trips, your employer must report the reimbursement as wage income in box 1 of your Form W-2. You cannot deduct personal expenses.

Reimbursements
This section explains what to do when you receive an advance or are reimbursed for any of the employee business expenses discussed in this chapter.

TAXSAVER
If the various requirements discussed later are met, reimbursements are excluded from the employee's gross income for income tax as well as employment tax purposes. Amounts considered paid under a nonaccountable plan are subject to income tax as well as to employment taxes. A tax deduction is allowable as a miscellaneous itemized deduction, subject to applicable limitations, for employee business expenses reimbursed under a nonaccountable plan.

If you received an advance, allowance, or reimbursement for your expenses, how you report this amount and your expenses depends on whether your employer reimbursed you under an accountable plan or a nonaccountable plan.

This section explains the two types of plans, how per diem and car allowances simplify proving the amount of your expenses, and the tax treatment of your reimbursements and expenses.

No reimbursement. You are not reimbursed or given an allowance for your expenses if you are paid a salary or commission with the understanding that you will pay your own expenses. In this situation, you have no reimbursement or allowance arrangement, and you do not have to read this section on reimbursements. Instead, see *Completing Forms 2106 and 2106-EZ*, later, for information on completing your tax return.

Reimbursement, allowance, or advance. A reimbursement or other expense allowance arrangement is a system or plan that an employer uses to pay, substantiate, and recover the expenses, advances, reimbursements, and amounts charged to the employer for employee business expenses. Arrangements include per diem and car allowances.

A per diem allowance is a fixed amount of daily reimbursement your employer gives you for your lodging, meal, and incidental expenses when you are away from home on business. (The term "incidental expenses" is defined earlier under _Meals and Incidental Expenses._) A car allowance is an amount your employer gives you for the business use of your car.

Your employer should tell you what method of reimbursement is used and what records you must provide.

Accountable Plans

To be an accountable plan, your employer's reimbursement or allowance arrangement must include all of the following rules.

1. Your expenses must have a business connection—that is, you must have paid or incurred deductible expenses while performing services as an employee of your employer.
2. You must adequately account to your employer for these expenses within a reasonable period of time.
3. You must return any excess reimbursement or allowance within a reasonable period of time.

See _Adequate Accounting_ and _Returning Excess Reimbursements,_ later.

An excess reimbursement or allowance is any amount you are paid that is more than the business-related expenses that you adequately accounted for to your employer.

The definition of a reasonable period of time depends on the facts and circumstances of your situation. However, regardless of the facts and circumstances of your situation, actions that take place within the times specified in the following list will be treated as taking place within a reasonable period of time.

- You receive an advance within 30 days of the time you have an expense.
- You adequately account for your expenses within 60 days after they were paid or incurred.
- You return any excess reimbursement within 120 days after the expense was paid or incurred.
- You are given a periodic statement (at least quarterly) that asks you to either return or adequately account for outstanding advances and you comply within 120 days of the statement.

TAXALERT
It is imperative that the substantiation be done and that excess amounts are returned within a reasonable period of time. If the reasonable time requirement is not met, the unsubstantiated or excess amounts are treated as reimbursements under a nonaccountable plan.

Tip

If your employer included reimbursements in box 1 of your Form W-2 and you meet all the rules for accountable plans, ask your employer for a corrected Form W-2.

Employee meets accountable plan rules. If you meet the three rules for accountable plans, your employer should not include any reimbursements in your income in box 1 of your Form W-2. If your expenses equal your reimbursement, you do not complete Form 2106. You have no deduction since your expenses and reimbursement are equal.

Accountable plan rules not met. Even though you are reimbursed under an accountable plan, some of your expenses may not meet all the rules. Those expenses that fail to meet all three rules for accountable plans are treated as having been reimbursed under a *nonaccountable plan* (discussed later).

TAXPLANNER
A plan providing per diem allowances or mileage allowances that are reasonably calculated not to exceed the employee's expenses will satisfy the requirement for the return of excess reimbursement, even though the employee is not required to return the excess allowance. However, the employee must return the portion of the allowance attributable to unsubstantiated days or miles of travel.

Example
An employee receives a monthly mileage allowance of $224, based on anticipated business miles of 400 per month, reimbursed at the rate of 56 cents per mile. The 56-cent-per-mile rate is reasonably calculated not to exceed the employee's expenses. The employee travels and substantiates only 300 business miles. The requirement to return the excess is satisfied if the employee is required to return the $56.00 (100 miles x 56 cents) advance allowance that is attributable to the 100 unsubstantiated business miles.

Tip

The employer makes the decision whether to reimburse employees under an accountable plan or a nonaccountable plan. If you are an employee who receives payments under a nonaccountable plan, you cannot convert these amounts to payments under an accountable plan by voluntarily accounting to your employer for the expenses and voluntarily returning excess reimbursements to the employer.

Reimbursement of nondeductible expenses. You may be reimbursed under your employer's accountable plan for expenses related to that employer's business, some of which are deductible as employee business expenses and some of which are not deductible. The reimbursements you receive for the nondeductible expenses do not meet rule (1) for accountable plans, and they are treated as paid under a nonaccountable plan.

Example. Your employer's plan reimburses you for travel expenses while away from home on business and also for meals when you work late at the office, even though you are not away from home. The part of the arrangement that reimburses you for the nondeductible meals when you work late at the office is treated as paid under a nonaccountable plan.

Adequate Accounting
One of the rules for an accountable plan is that you must adequately account to your employer for your expenses. You adequately account by giving your employer a statement of expense, an account book, a diary, or a similar record in which you entered each expense at or near the time

you had it, along with documentary evidence (such as receipts) of your travel, mileage, and other employee business expenses. (See *Table 27-2*, earlier, for details you need to enter in your record and documents you need to prove certain expenses.) A per diem or car allowance satisfies the adequate accounting requirement under certain conditions. See *Per Diem and Car Allowances*, later.

You must account for all amounts you received from your employer during the year as advances, reimbursements, or allowances. This includes amounts you charged to your employer by credit card or other method. You must give your employer the same type of records and supporting information that you would have to give to the IRS if the IRS questioned a deduction on your return. You must pay back the amount of any reimbursement or other expense allowance for which you do not adequately account or that is more than the amount for which you accounted.

Per Diem and Car Allowances

If your employer reimburses you for your expenses using a per diem or car allowance, you can generally use the allowance as proof of the amount of your expenses. A per diem or car allowance satisfies the adequate accounting requirements for the amount of your expenses only if all the following conditions apply.

- Your employer reasonably limits payments of your expenses to those that are ordinary and necessary in the conduct of the trade or business.
- The allowance is similar in form to and not more than the <u>federal rate</u> (discussed later).
- You prove the time (dates), place, and business purpose of your expenses to your employer (as explained in *Table 27-2*) within a reasonable period of time.
- You are not related to your employer (as defined next). If you are related to your employer, you must be able to prove your expenses to the IRS even if you have already adequately accounted to your employer and returned any excess reimbursement.

If the IRS finds that an employer's travel allowance practices are not based on reasonably accurate estimates of travel costs (including recognition of cost differences in different areas for per diem amounts), you will not be considered to have accounted to your employer. In this case, you must be able to prove your expenses to the IRS.

Related to employer. You are related to your employer if:

1. Your employer is your brother or sister, half brother or half sister, spouse, ancestor, or lineal descendant,
2. Your employer is a corporation in which you own, directly or indirectly, more than 10% in value of the outstanding stock, or
3. Certain relationships (such as grantor, fiduciary, or beneficiary) exist between you, a trust, and your employer.

You may be considered to indirectly own stock, for purposes of (2), if you have an interest in a corporation, partnership, estate, or trust that owns the stock or if a member of your family or your partner owns the stock.

The federal rate. The federal rate can be figured using any one of the following methods.

1. For per diem amounts:
   a. The regular federal per diem rate.
   b. The standard meal allowance.
   c. The high-low rate.
2. For car expenses:
   a. The standard mileage rate.
   b. A fixed and variable rate (FAVR).

Regular federal per diem rate. The regular federal per diem rate is the highest amount that the federal government will pay to its employees for lodging, meal, and incidental expenses (or meal and incidental expenses only) while they are traveling away from home in a particular area. The rates are different for different locations. Your employer should have these rates available. (They are also available at *www.gsa.gov*.)

The standard meal allowance. The standard meal allowance (discussed earlier) is the federal rate for meals and incidental expenses (M&IE). The rate for most small localities in the United States is $46 a day. Most major cities and many other localities qualify for higher rates. You can find the rates for all localities within the continental United States on the Internet at *www.gsa.gov*.

You receive an allowance only for meals and incidental expenses when your employer does one of the following.

- Provides you with lodging (furnishes it in kind).
- Reimburses you, based on your receipts, for the actual cost of your lodging.

- Pays the hotel, motel, etc., directly for your lodging.
- Does not have a reasonable belief that you had (or will have) lodging expenses, such as when you stay with friends or relatives or sleep in the cab of your truck.
- Figures the allowance on a basis similar to that used in computing your compensation, such as number of hours worked or miles traveled.

High-low rate. This is a simplified method of computing the federal per diem rate for travel within the continental United States. It eliminates the need to keep a current list of the per diem rate for each city.

Under the high-low method, the per diem amount for travel during January through September 2014 is $251 (including $65 for M&IE) for certain high-cost locations. All other areas have a per diem amount of $170 (including $52 for M&IE). (You can find the areas eligible for the $251 per diem amount under the high-low method for all or part of this period at *www.gsa.gov*.)

> **TAXALERT**
>
> On September 7, 2011, the GSA published temporary regulations revising the definition of incidental expenses to include only fees and tips given to porters, baggage carriers, hotel staff, and staff on ships. Transportation between places of lodging or business and places where meals are taken, and the mailing cost of filing travel vouchers and paying employer-sponsored charge card billings, are no longer included in incidental expenses. Accordingly, taxpayers using per diem rates may separately deduct or be reimbursed for transportation and mailing expenses.

Prorating the standard meal allowance on partial days of travel. The standard meal allowance is for a full 24-hour day of travel. If you travel for part of a day, such as on the days you depart and return, you must prorate the full-day M&IE rate. This rule also applies if your employer uses the regular federal per diem rate or the high-low rate.

You can use either of the following methods to figure the federal M&IE for that day.

1. *Method 1:*
   a. For the day you depart, add ¾ of the standard meal allowance amount for that day.
   b. For the day you return, add ¾ of the standard meal allowance amount for the preceding day.
2. *Method 2:* Prorate the standard meal allowance using any method you consistently apply in accordance with reasonable business practice.

The standard mileage rate. This is a set rate per mile that you can use to compute your deductible car expenses. For 2014, the standard mileage rate for the cost of operating your car is 56 cents per mile.

Fixed and variable rate (FAVR). This is an allowance your employer may use to reimburse your car expenses. Under this method, your employer pays an allowance that includes a combination of payments covering fixed and variable costs, such as a cents-per-mile rate to cover your variable operating costs (such as gas, oil, etc.) plus a flat amount to cover your fixed costs (such as depreciation (or lease payments), insurance, etc.). If your employer chooses to use this method, your employer will request the necessary records from you.

Reporting your expenses with a per diem or car allowance. If your reimbursement is in the form of an allowance received under an accountable plan, the following facts affect your reporting.

- The federal rate.
- Whether the allowance or your actual expenses were more than the federal rate.

The following discussions explain where to report your expenses depending upon how the amount of your allowance compares to the federal rate.

Allowance less than or equal to the federal rate. If your allowance is less than or equal to the federal rate, the allowance will not be included in box 1 of your Form W-2. You do not need to report the related expenses or the allowance on your return if your expenses are equal to or less than the allowance.

However, if your actual expenses are more than your allowance, you can complete Form 2106 and deduct the excess amount on Schedule A (Form 1040). If you are using actual expenses, you must be able to prove to the IRS the total amount of your expenses and reimbursements for the entire year. If you are using the standard meal allowance or the standard mileage rate, you do not have to prove that amount.

Example. Nicole drives 10,000 miles in 2014 for business. Under her employer's accountable plan, she accounts for the time (dates), place, and business purpose of each trip. Her employer pays her a mileage allowance of 40 cents a mile.

Since Nicole's $5,600 expense computed under the standard mileage rate (10,000 miles × 56 cents) is more than her $4,000 reimbursement (10,000 miles × 40 cents), she itemizes her deductions to claim the excess expense. Nicole completes Form 2106 (showing all her expenses and reimbursements) and enters $1,600 ($5,600 − $4,000) as an itemized deduction.

Allowance more than the federal rate. If your allowance is more than the federal rate, your employer must include the allowance amount up to the federal rate in box 12 of your Form W-2. This amount is not taxable. However, the excess allowance will be included in box 1 of your Form W-2. You must report this part of your allowance as if it were wage income.

If your actual expenses are less than or equal to the federal rate, you do not complete Form 2106 or claim any of your expenses on your return.

However, if your actual expenses are more than the federal rate, you can complete Form 2106 and deduct those excess expenses. You must report on Form 2106 your reimbursements up to the federal rate (as shown in box 12 of your Form W-2) and all your expenses. You should be able to prove these amounts to the IRS.

Example. Joe lives and works in Austin. In May his employer sent him to San Diego for 4 days and paid the hotel directly for Joe's hotel bill. The employer reimbursed Joe $75 a day for his meals and incidental expenses. The federal rate for San Diego is $71 a day.

Joe can prove that his actual meal expenses totaled $380. His employer's accountable plan will not pay more than $75 a day for travel to San Diego, so Joe does not give his employer the records that prove that he actually spent $380. However, he does account for the time, place, and business purpose of the trip. This is Joe's only business trip this year.

Joe was reimbursed $300 ($75 × 4 days), which is $16 more than the federal rate of $284 ($71 × 4 days). His employer includes the $16 as income on Joe's Form W-2 in box 1. His employer also enters $284 in box 12 of Joe's Form W-2.

Joe completes Form 2106 to figure his deductible expenses. He enters the total of his actual expenses for the year ($380) on Form 2106. He also enters the reimbursements that were not included in his income ($284). His total deductible expense, before the 50% limit, is $96. After he figures the 50% limit on his unreimbursed meals and entertainment, he will include the balance, $48, as an itemized deduction on Schedule A (Form 1040).

Returning Excess Reimbursements

Under an accountable plan, you are required to return any excess reimbursement or other expense allowances for your business expenses to the person paying the reimbursement or allowance. Excess reimbursement means any amount for which you did not adequately account within a reasonable period of time. For example, if you received a travel advance and you did not spend all the money on business-related expenses or you do not have proof of all your expenses, you have an excess reimbursement.

"Adequate accounting" and "reasonable period of time" were discussed earlier in this chapter.

Travel advance. You receive a travel advance if your employer provides you with an expense allowance before you actually have the expense, and the allowance is reasonably expected to be no more than your expense. Under an accountable plan, you are required to adequately account to your employer for this advance and to return any excess within a reasonable period of time.

If you do not adequately account for or do not return any excess advance within a reasonable period of time, the amount you do not account for or return will be treated as having been paid under a nonaccountable plan (discussed later).

Unproven amounts. If you do not prove that you actually traveled on each day for which you received a per diem or car allowance (proving the elements described in *Table 27-2*), you must return this unproved amount of the travel advance within a reasonable period of time. If you do not do this, the unproved amount will be considered paid under a nonaccountable plan (discussed later).

Per diem allowance more than federal rate. If your employer's accountable plan pays you an allowance that is higher than the federal rate, you do not have to return the difference between the two rates for the period you can prove business-related travel expenses. However, the difference will be reported as wages on your Form W-2. This excess amount is considered paid under a nonaccountable plan (discussed later).

Example. Your employer sends you on a 5-day business trip to Phoenix in March 2014 and gives you a $400 ($80 × 5 days) advance to cover your meals and incidental expenses. The federal per diem for meals and incidental expenses for Phoenix is $71. Your trip lasts only 3 days. Under your employer's accountable plan, you must return the $160 ($80 × 2 days) advance for the 2 days you did not travel. For the 3 days you did travel you do not have to return the $27 difference between the allowance you received and the federal rate for Phoenix (($80 – $71) × 3 days). However, the $27 will be reported on your Form W-2 as wages.

Nonaccountable Plans
A nonaccountable plan is a reimbursement or expense allowance arrangement that does not meet one or more of the three rules listed earlier under *Accountable Plans*.

In addition, even if your employer has an accountable plan, the following payments will be treated as being paid under a nonaccountable plan.

- Excess reimbursements you fail to return to your employer.
- Reimbursement of nondeductible expenses related to your employer's business.

See *Reimbursement of nondeductible expenses* earlier under *Accountable Plans*.

If you are not sure if the reimbursement or expense allowance arrangement is an accountable or nonaccountable plan, ask your employer.

Reporting your expenses under a nonaccountable plan. Your employer will combine the amount of any reimbursement or other expense allowance paid to you under a nonaccountable plan with your wages, salary, or other pay. Your employer will report the total in box 1 of your Form W-2.

You must complete Form 2106 or 2106-EZ and itemize your deductions to deduct your expenses for travel, transportation, meals, or entertainment. Your meal and entertainment expenses will be subject to the 50% limit discussed earlier under *Entertainment Expenses*. Also, your total expenses will be subject to the 2%-of-adjusted-gross-income limit that applies to most miscellaneous itemized deductions on Schedule A (Form 1040).

Example. Kim's employer gives her $1,000 a month ($12,000 for the year) for her business expenses. Kim does not have to provide any proof of her expenses to her employer, and Kim can keep any funds that she does not spend.

Kim is being reimbursed under a nonaccountable plan. Her employer will include the $12,000 on Kim's Form W-2 as if it were wages. If Kim wants to deduct her business expenses, she must complete Form 2106 or 2106-EZ and itemize her deductions.

Completing Forms 2106 and 2106-EZ
This section briefly describes how employees complete Forms 2106 and 2106-EZ. *Table 27-3* explains what the employer reports on Form W-2 and what the employee reports on Form 2106. The instructions for the forms have more information on completing them.

Form 2106-EZ. You may be able to use the shorter Form 2106-EZ to claim your employee business expenses. You can use this form if you meet all the following conditions.

- You are an employee deducting expenses attributable to your job.
- You were not reimbursed by your employer for your expenses (amounts included in box 1 of your Form W-2 are not considered reimbursements).
- If you are claiming car expenses, you use the standard mileage rate.

Car expenses. If you used a car to perform your job as an employee, you may be able to deduct certain car expenses. These are generally figured on Form 2106, Part II, and then claimed on Form 2106, Part I, line 1, Column A. Car expenses using the standard mileage rate can also be figured on Form 2106-EZ by completing Part II and Part I, line 1.

Transportation expenses. Show your transportation expenses that did not involve overnight travel on Form 2106, line 2, Column A, or on Form 2106-EZ, Part I, line 2. Also include on this line business expenses you have for parking fees and tolls. Do not include expenses of operating your car or expenses of commuting between your home and work.

Employee business expenses other than meals and entertainment. Show your other employee business expenses on Form 2106, lines 3 and 4, Column A, or Form 2106-EZ, lines 3 and 4. Do not include expenses for meals and entertainment on those lines. Line 4 is for expenses such as gifts, educational expenses (tuition and books), office-in-the-home expenses, and trade and professional publications.

Meal and entertainment expenses. Show the full amount of your expenses for business-related meals and entertainment on Form 2106, line 5, Column B. Include meals while away from your tax home overnight and other business meals and entertainment. Enter 50% of the line 8, Column B, meal and entertainment expenses on line 9, Column B.

If you file Form 2106-EZ, enter the full amount of your meals and entertainment on the line to the left of line 5 and multiply the total by 50%. Enter the result on line 5.

Hours of service limits. If you are subject to the Department of Transportation's "hours of service" limits, use 80% instead of 50% for meals while away from your tax home.

Caution
If you are self-employed, do not file Form 2106 or 2106-EZ. Report your expenses on Schedule C, C-EZ, or F (Form 1040). See the instructions for the form that you must file.

Tip
If line 4 expenses are the only ones you are claiming, you received no reimbursements (or the reimbursements were all included in box 1 of your Form W-2), and the Special Rules *discussed later do not apply to you, do not complete Form 2106 or 2106-EZ. Claim these amounts directly on Schedule A (Form 1040), line 21. List the type and amount of each expense on the dotted lines and include the total on line 21.*

Table 27-3. **Reporting Travel, Entertainment, Gift, and Car Expenses and Reimbursements**

IF the type of reimbursement (or other expense allowance) arrangement is under:	THEN the employer reports on Form W-2:	AND the employee reports on Form 2106:*
An accountable plan with:		
Actual expense reimbursement: Adequate accounting made <u>and</u> excess returned.	No amount.	No amount.
Actual expense reimbursement: Adequate accounting and return of excess both required <u>but</u> excess not returned.	The excess amount as wages in box 1.	No amount.
Per diem or mileage allowance up to the federal rate: Adequate accounting made <u>and</u> excess returned.	No amount.	All expenses and reimbursements only if excess expenses are claimed. Otherwise, form is not filed.
Per diem or mileage allowance up to the federal rate: Adequate accounting and return of excess both required <u>but</u> excess not returned.	The excess amount as wages in box 1. The amount up to the federal rate is reported only in box 12—it is not reported in box 1.	No amount.
Per diem or mileage allowance exceeds the federal rate: Adequate accounting up to the federal rate only <u>and</u> excess not returned.	The excess amount as wages in box 1. The amount up to the federal rate is reported only in box 12—It Is not reported in box 1.	All expenses (and reimbursement reported on Form W-2, box 12) only if expenses in excess of the federal rate are claimed. Otherwise, form is not required.
A nonaccountable plan with:		
Either adequate accounting or return of excess, or both, not required by plan	The entire amount as wages in box 1.	All expenses.
No reimbursement plan:	The entire amount as wages in box 1.	All expenses.

* You may be able to use Form 2106-EZ. See <u>Completing Forms 2106 and 2106-EZ</u>.

Reimbursements. Enter on Form 2106, line 7, the amounts your employer (or third party) reimbursed you that were not included in box 1 of your Form W-2. (You cannot use Form 2106-EZ.) This includes any reimbursement reported under code L in box 12 of Form W-2.

Allocating your reimbursement. If you were reimbursed under an accountable plan and want to deduct excess expenses that were not reimbursed, you may have to allocate your reimbursement. This is necessary if your employer pays your reimbursement in the following manner:

- Pays you a single amount that covers meals and/or entertainment, as well as other business expenses, and
- Does not clearly identify how much is for deductible meals and/or entertainment.

You must allocate that single payment so that you know how much to enter on Form 2106, line 7, Column A and Column B.

Example. Rob's employer paid him an expense allowance of $12,000 this year under an accountable plan. The $12,000 payment consisted of $5,000 for airfare and $7,000 for entertainment and car expenses. Rob's employer did not clearly show how much of the $7,000 was for the cost of deductible entertainment. Rob actually spent $14,000 during the year ($5,500 for airfare, $4,500 for entertainment, and $4,000 for car expenses).

Since the airfare allowance was clearly identified, Rob knows that $5,000 of the payment goes in Column A, line 7 of Form 2106. To allocate the remaining $7,000, Rob uses the worksheet from the instructions for Form 2106. His completed worksheet follows.

Reimbursement Allocation Worksheet (keep for your records)	
1. Enter the total amount of reimbursements your employer gave you that were not reported to you in box 1 of Form W-2	$7,000
2. Enter the total amount of your expenses for the periods covered by this reimbursement..	8,500
3. Of the amount on line 2, enter your total expense for meals and entertainment	4,500
4. Divide line 3 by line 2. Enter the result as a decimal (rounded to at least three places)	.529
5. Multiply line 1 by line 4. Enter the result here and in Column B, line 7.................	3,703
6. Subtract line 5 from line 1. Enter the result here and in Column A, line 7..............	$3,297

On line 7 of Form 2106, Rob enters $8,297 ($5,000 airfare and $3,297 of the $7,000) in Column A and $3,703 (of the $7,000) in Column B.

After you complete the form. After you have completed your Form 2106 or 2106-EZ, follow the directions on that form to deduct your expenses on the appropriate line of your tax return. For most taxpayers, this is line 21 of Schedule A (Form 1040). However, if you are a government official paid on a fee basis, a performing artist, an Armed Forces reservist, or a disabled employee with impairment-related work expenses, see *Special Rules*, later.

Limits on employee business expenses. Your employee business expenses may be subject to either of the limits described next. These limits are figured in the following order on the specified form.

1. Limit on meals and entertainment. Certain meal and entertainment expenses are subject to a 50% limit. If you are an employee, you figure this limit on line 9 of Form 2106 or line 5 of Form 2106-EZ. See *50% Limit* under *Entertainment Expenses*, earlier.

2. Limit on miscellaneous itemized deductions. If you are an employee, deduct employee business expenses (as figured on Form 2106 or 2106-EZ) on line 21 of Schedule A (Form 1040). Most miscellaneous itemized deductions, including employee business expenses, are subject to a 2% limit. This limit is figured on line 26 of Schedule A (Form 1040).

3. Limit on total itemized deductions. Total itemized deductions may be limited if your adjusted gross income is over: $305,050 if filing as married filing jointly or qualifying widow(er); $279,650 if head of household; $254,200 if single; or $152,525 if married filing separately. This limit is figured on the Itemized Deductions Worksheet found in Instructions for Schedule A (Form 1040).

Special Rules

This section discusses special rules that apply to Armed Forces reservists, government officials who are paid on a fee basis, performing artists, and disabled employees with impairment-related work expenses.

Armed Forces reservists traveling more than 100 miles from home. If you are a member of a reserve component of the Armed Forces of the United States and you travel more than 100 miles away from home in connection with your performance of services as a member of the reserves, you can deduct your travel expenses as an adjustment to gross income rather than as a miscellaneous itemized deduction. The amount of expenses you can deduct as an adjustment to gross income is limited to the regular federal per diem rate (for lodging, meals, and incidental expenses) and the standard mileage rate (for car expenses) plus any parking fees, ferry fees, and tolls. The federal rate is explained earlier under *Per Diem and Car Allowances*. Any expenses in excess of these amounts can be claimed only as a miscellaneous itemized deduction subject to the 2% limit.

Member of a reserve component. You are a member of a reserve component of the Armed Forces of the United States if you are in the Army, Navy, Marine Corps, Air Force, or Coast Guard Reserve, the Army National Guard of the United States, the Air National Guard of the United States, or the Reserve Corps of the Public Health Service.

How to report. If you have reserve-related travel that takes you more than 100 miles from home, you should first complete Form 2106 or Form 2106-EZ. Then include your expenses for reserve travel over 100 miles from home, up to the federal rate, from Form 2106, line 10, or Form 2106-EZ, line 6, in the total on Form 1040, line 24. Subtract this amount from the total on Form 2106, line 10, or Form 2106-EZ, line 6, and deduct the balance as an itemized deduction on Schedule A (Form 1040), line 21.

You cannot deduct expenses of travel that does not take you more than 100 miles from home as an adjustment to gross income. Instead, you must complete Form 2106 or 2106-EZ and deduct those expenses as an itemized deduction on Schedule A (Form 1040), line 21.

Officials paid on a fee basis. Certain fee-basis officials can claim their employee business expenses whether or not they itemize their other deductions on Schedule A (Form 1040).

Fee-basis officials are persons who are employed by a state or local government and who are paid in whole or in part on a fee basis. They can deduct their business expenses in performing services in that job as an adjustment to gross income rather than as a miscellaneous itemized deduction.

If you are a fee-basis official, include your employee business expenses from Form 2106, line 10, or Form 2106-EZ, line 6, on Form 1040, line 24.

Expenses of certain performing artists. If you are a performing artist, you may qualify to deduct your employee business expenses as an adjustment to gross income rather than as a miscellaneous itemized deduction. To qualify, you must meet all of the following requirements.

1. During the tax year, you perform services in the performing arts as an employee for at least two employers.
2. You receive at least $200 each from any two of these employers.
3. Your related performing-arts business expenses are more than 10% of your gross income from the performance of those services.
4. Your adjusted gross income is not more than $16,000 before deducting these business expenses.

Special rules for married persons. If you are married, you must file a joint return unless you lived apart from your spouse at all times during the tax year.

If you file a joint return, you must figure requirements (1), (2), and (3) separately for both you and your spouse. However, requirement (4) applies to your and your spouse's combined adjusted gross income.

Where to report. If you meet all of the above requirements, you should first complete Form 2106 or 2106-EZ. Then you include your performing-arts-related expenses from line 10 of Form 2106 or line 6 of Form 2106-EZ in the total on line 24 of Form 1040.

If you do not meet all of the above requirements, you do not qualify to deduct your expenses as an adjustment to gross income. Instead, you must complete Form 2106 or 2106-EZ and deduct your employee business expenses as an itemized deduction on Schedule A (Form 1040), line 21.

Impairment-related work expenses of disabled employees. If you are an employee with a physical or mental disability, your impairment-related work expenses are not subject to the 2%-of-adjusted-gross-income limit that applies to most other employee business expenses. After you complete Form 2106 or 2106-EZ, enter your impairment-related work expenses from Form 2106, line 10, or Form 2106-EZ, line 6, on Schedule A (Form 1040), line 28, and identify the type and amount of this expense on the dotted line next to line 28. Enter your employee business expenses that are unrelated to your disability from Form 2106, line 10, or Form 2106-EZ, line 6, on Schedule A, line 21.

Impairment-related work expenses are your allowable expenses for attendant care at your workplace and other expenses you have in connection with your workplace that are necessary for you to be able to work. For more information, see *chapter 22*.

TAXORGANIZER

Records you should keep. If you deduct expenses for traveling away from home, you must be able to substantiate the expenses by keeping adequate evidence.

Adequate Evidence. Evidence is ordinarily considered adequate if it shows the amount, date, place, and essential character of the expense.

For example, a hotel receipt is sufficient to prove an expense for business travel if it has all of the following information:
1. The name and location of the hotel
2. The dates of your stay
3. Itemization of separate charges such as lodging, meals, and telephone calls

A restaurant receipt is enough to prove an expense for a business meal if it has all of the following:
1. The name and location of the restaurant
2. The number of people served
3. The date and amount of expense

Generally, you must have documentary evidence, such as receipts, canceled checks, or bills, to support your expenses. A canceled check, together with a bill from the payee, ordinarily establishes the cost. However, a canceled check alone does not prove a business expense without other evidence to show that it was for a business purpose.

Exceptions. Evidence is not needed if:
1. You have meals or lodging expenses while traveling away from home for which you account to your employer under an accountable plan and you use a per diem allowance method that includes meals and/or lodging.
2. Your expense, other than lodging, is less than $75.
3. You have transportation expense for which a receipt is not readily available.
  If a charge is made for an item other than food and beverage, the receipt must show that this is the case.

Incomplete Records. If you do not have complete records to prove an element of expense, then you must prove the element by:
1. Your own statement, whether written or oral, that contains specific information about the element, and
2. Other supporting evidence that is sufficient to establish the element.
  In addition, it is helpful to keep an account book, diary, or similar record that includes the following:
- Amount of each separate expense
- Time and place of travel or entertainment
- Number of days away from home spent on business
- Business purpose of the expense

Chapter 28

Tax benefits for work-related education

ey.com/EYTaxGuide

Note

IRS Publication 17 (*Your Federal Income Tax*) has been updated by Ernst & Young LLP for 2014. Dates and dollar amounts shown are for 2014. Underlined type is used to indicate where IRS text has been updated. Places where text has been removed are indicated by the sentence: *Text intentionally omitted.*

ey.com/EYTaxGuide

Ernst & Young LLP will update the *EY Tax Guide 2015* website with relevant taxpayer information as it becomes available. You can also sign up for email alerts to let you know when changes have been made.

Introduction

Educational expenses are generally considered to be personal in nature. The law, however, does recognize that certain educational expenses are necessary for you in your business or as an employee. Deductions may be allowed for these expenses as well as for reasonable expenses incurred in acquiring the education.

It's often difficult to determine if work-related educational expenses are deductible. You do not necessarily have to earn a new degree for such expenses to be claimed. On the other hand, earning a degree doesn't necessarily make the expenses deductible. The expenses do have to meet certain tests. For example, the expenses are deductible if the education either maintains or improves skills required in your trade or business or if the courses are required for you to retain your current job. The expenses are not deductible if they are spent on education that is required for you to meet the minimum educational requirements of your position. In addition, travel as a form of education is not deductible.

This chapter discusses work-related educational expenses. You'll learn that you may be able to deduct not only your fees for educational instruction but also a number of other expenses that you incur because you are simultaneously working and in school.

An employee's work-related educational expenses and other miscellaneous itemized deductions are deductible only to the extent that they exceed 2% of adjusted gross income. For more information, see chapter 29, *Miscellaneous deductions.*

After applying the 2% limitation on most types of miscellaneous itemized deductions, these, along with certain other itemized deductions, may be further reduced by an additional "overall" limitation. The total of this group of itemized deductions must be reduced by 3% of the amount of your adjusted gross income (AGI) in excess of specified thresholds. However, no more than 80% of the otherwise allowable deductions are phased out. See chapter 30, *Limit on Itemized Deductions,* for more information.

For a discussion of education credits and other education benefits—such as employer-provided educational programs and qualified tuition programs—see chapter 36, *Education credits and other education tax benefits.*

What's New

Standard mileage rate. Generally, if you claim a business deduction for work-related education and you drive your car to and from school, the amount you can deduct for miles driven from January 1, 2014, through December 31, 2014, is 56 cents per mile. For more information, see *Transportation Expenses* under *What Expenses Can Be Deducted*.

This chapter discusses work-related education expenses that you may be able to deduct as business expenses.

To claim such a deduction, you must:

- Itemize your deductions on Schedule A (Form 1040) if you are an employee,
- File Schedule C (Form 1040), Schedule C-EZ (Form 1040), or Schedule F (Form 1040) if you are self-employed, and
- Have expenses for education that meet the requirements discussed under *Qualifying Work-Related Education*.

If you are an employee and can itemize your deductions, you may be able to claim a deduction for the expenses you pay for your work-related education. Your deduction will be the amount by which your qualifying work-related education expenses plus other job and certain miscellaneous expenses (except for impairment-related work expenses of disabled individuals) is greater than 2% of your adjusted gross income. See chapter 29.

If you are self-employed, you deduct your expenses for qualifying work-related education directly from your self-employment income.

Your work-related education expenses may also qualify you for other tax benefits, such as the American opportunity and lifetime learning credits (see chapter 36). You may qualify for these other benefits even if you do not meet the requirements listed earlier.

Also, keep in mind that your work-related education expenses may qualify you to claim more than one tax benefit. Generally, you may claim any number of benefits as long as you use different expenses to figure each one.

TAXALERT

An employee's work-related educational expenses and other miscellaneous itemized deductions are deductible only to the extent that they exceed 2% of adjusted gross income. For more information, see chapter 29, *Miscellaneous deductions*.

After applying the 2% limitation on most types of miscellaneous itemized deductions, these, along with certain other itemized deductions, may be further reduced by an additional "overall" limitation. The total of this group of itemized deductions must be reduced by 3% of the amount of your adjusted gross income (AGI) in excess of specified thresholds. However, no more than 80% of the otherwise allowable deductions are phased out. See chapter 30, *Limit on Itemized Deductions*, for more information.

For more information about the overall limit on itemized deductions, see chapter 30, *Limit on itemized deductions*.

TAXALERT

Above-the-line deduction for qualified tuition and related expenses expired at the end of 2013. This chapter discusses when educational expenses may be deducted because they are work related. In 2013, eligible taxpayers could also claim an adjustment in figuring adjusted gross income (hence, the name "above the line") for up to $4,000 of qualified tuition and related expenses regardless of whether those expenses would be considered work related. (For more information, see *Tuition and Fees Deduction* in chapter 19, *Education-related adjustments.*) This deduction expired at the end of 2013. As of the time this book was published, Congress had been considering legislation that would extend its availability through at least 2014, but no such extension had yet been passed. For updated information on this and any other tax law changes that occur after this book was published, see our website, *ey.com/EYTaxGuide*.

TAXALERT

Exclusion for employer-provided educational assistance. In addition to work-related education expenses that you may be able to deduct or claim an education credit, an employee may be eligible to exclude from gross income up to $5,250 for income and employment tax purposes, per year, of employer-provided education assistance. This exclusion is available for qualifying undergraduate and graduate education. For more information, see Publication 970, *Tax Benefits for Education*.

Useful Items

You may want to see:

Publication

□ **463** Travel, Entertainment, Gift, and Car Expenses
□ **970** Tax Benefits for Education

Form (and Instructions)

□ **2106** Employee Business Expenses
□ **2106-EZ** Unreimbursed Employee Business Expenses
□ **Schedule A (Form 1040)** Itemized Deductions

Qualifying Work-Related Education

You can deduct the costs of qualifying work-related education as business expenses. This is education that meets at least one of the following two tests.

- The education is required by your employer or the law to keep your present salary, status, or job. The required education must serve a bona fide business purpose of your employer.
- The education maintains or improves skills needed in your present work.

However, even if the education meets one or both of the above tests, it is not qualifying work-related education if it:

- Is needed to meet the minimum educational requirements of your present trade or business, or
- Is part of a program of study that will qualify you for a new trade or business.

You can deduct the costs of qualifying work-related education as a business expense even if the education could lead to a degree.

Use Figure 28-A, later, as a quick check to see if your education qualifies.

EXPLANATION

In order to be deductible, work-related educational expenses must relate to your current occupation.

Example

A college student obtaining employment through his or her college cooperative program or work/study program is not engaged in a trade or a business. His or her college fees are not deductible as a work-related education expense, because they are incurred in preparation for an occupation.

A full-time student does not have a trade or a business and may not deduct the cost of courses toward a college degree, even though the student may be employed full-time during the summer months.

TAXPLANNER

The IRS does not explicitly allow or disallow work-related educational expenses for a semiretired person. Therefore, it appears that educational expenses to maintain skills are deductible, even though the individual has reduced the scope of his or her trade or business.

An individual who abandons a former profession for a period of years and acquires a new profession may not deduct courses related to resuming his or her original profession.

A fully retired individual is not considered to have a trade or a business and is not entitled to a deduction for work-related educational expenses.

Example

Gaby, an engineer, decides to teach math at a local high school. After teaching for a few years, she decides to resume her former career in engineering. Gaby takes refresher courses at a local college. The costs of these courses are not work-related educational expenses.

Education Required by Employer or by Law

Once you have met the minimum educational requirements for your job, your employer or the law may require you to get more education. This additional education is qualifying work-related education if all three of the following requirements are met.

- It is required for you to keep your present salary, status, or job,
- The requirement serves a bona fide business purpose of your employer, and
- The education is not part of a program that will qualify you for a new trade or business.

When you get more education than your employer or the law requires, the additional education can be qualifying work-related education only if it maintains or improves skills required in your present work. See *Education To Maintain or Improve Skills*, later.

Example. You are a teacher who has satisfied the minimum requirements for teaching. Your employer requires you to take an additional college course each year to keep your teaching job. If the courses will not qualify you for a new trade or business, they are qualifying work-related education even if you eventually receive a master's degree and an increase in salary because of this extra education.

Education To Maintain or Improve Skills

If your education is not required by your employer or the law, it can be qualifying work-related education only if it maintains or improves skills needed in your present work. This could include refresher courses, courses on current developments, and academic or vocational courses.

Example. You repair televisions, radios, and stereo systems for XYZ Store. To keep up with the latest changes, you take special courses in radio and stereo service. These courses maintain and improve skills required in your work.

Maintaining skills vs. qualifying for new job. Education to maintain or improve skills needed in your present work is not qualifying education if it will also qualify you for a new trade or business.

Education during temporary absence. If you stop working for a year or less in order to get education to maintain or improve skills needed in your present work and then return to the same general type of work, your absence is considered temporary. Education that you get during a temporary absence is qualifying work-related education if it maintains or improves skills needed in your present work.

Example. You quit your biology research job to become a full-time biology graduate student for one year. If you return to work in biology research after completing the courses, the education is related to your present work even if you do not go back to work with the same employer.

Education during indefinite absence. If you stop work for more than a year, your absence from your job is considered indefinite. Education during an indefinite absence, even if it maintains or improves skills needed in the work from which you are absent, is considered to qualify you for a new trade or business. Therefore, it is not qualifying work-related education.

Education To Meet Minimum Requirements

Education you need to meet the minimum educational requirements for your present trade or business is not qualifying work-related education. The minimum educational requirements are determined by:

- Laws and regulations,
- Standards of your profession, trade, or business, and
- Your employer.

Caution

You have not necessarily met the minimum educational requirements of your trade or business simply because you are already doing the work.

Once you have met the minimum educational requirements that were in effect when you were hired, you do not have to meet any new minimum educational requirements. This means that if the minimum requirements change after you were hired, any education you need to meet the new requirements can be qualifying education.

Example 1. You are a full-time engineering student. Although you have not received your degree or certification, you work part-time as an engineer for a firm that will employ you as a full-time engineer after you finish college. Although your college engineering courses improve your skills in your present job, they are also needed to meet the minimum job requirements for a full-time engineer. The education is not qualifying work-related education.

Example 2. You are an accountant and you have met the minimum educational requirements of your employer. Your employer later changes the minimum educational requirements and requires you to take college courses to keep your job. These additional courses can be qualifying work-related education because you have already satisfied the minimum requirements that were in effect when you were hired.

Requirements for Teachers

States or school districts usually set the minimum educational requirements for teachers. The requirement is the college degree or the minimum number of college hours usually required of a person hired for that position.

If there are no requirements, you will have met the minimum educational requirements when you become a faculty member. The determination of whether you are a faculty member of an educational institution must be made on the basis of the particular practices of the institution. You generally will be considered a faculty member when one or more of the following occurs.

- You have tenure.
- Your years of service count toward obtaining tenure.
- You have a vote in faculty decisions.
- Your school makes contributions for you to a retirement plan other than social security or a similar program.

Example 1. The law in your state requires beginning secondary school teachers to have a bachelor's degree, including 10 professional education courses. In addition, to keep the job a teacher must complete a fifth year of training within 10 years from the date of hire. If the employing school certifies to the state Department of Education that qualified teachers cannot be found, the school can hire persons with only 3 years of college. However, to keep their jobs, these teachers must get a bachelor's degree and the required professional education courses within 3 years.

Under these facts, the bachelor's degree, whether or not it includes the 10 professional education courses, is considered the minimum educational requirement for qualification as a teacher in your state.

If you have all the required education except the fifth year, you have met the minimum educational requirements. The fifth year of training is qualifying work-related education unless it is part of a program of study that will qualify you for a new trade or business.

Example 2. Assume the same facts as in *Example 1* except that you have a bachelor's degree and only six professional education courses. The additional four education courses can be qualifying work-related education. Although you do not have all the required courses, you have already met the minimum educational requirements.

Example 3. Assume the same facts as in *Example 1* except that you are hired with only 3 years of college. The courses you take that lead to a bachelor's degree (including those in education) are not qualifying work-related education. They are needed to meet the minimum educational requirements for employment as a teacher.

Example 4. You have a bachelor's degree and you work as a temporary instructor at a university. At the same time, you take graduate courses toward an advanced degree. The rules of the university state that you can become a faculty member only if you get a graduate degree. Also, you can keep your job as an instructor only as long as you show satisfactory progress toward getting this degree. You have not met the minimum educational requirements to qualify you as a faculty member. The graduate courses are not qualifying work-related education.

Certification in a new state. Once you have met the minimum educational requirements for teachers for your state, you are considered to have met the minimum educational requirements in all states. This is true even if you must get additional education to be certified in another state. Any additional education you need is qualifying work-related education. You have already met the minimum requirements for teaching. Teaching in another state is not a new trade or business.

Example. You hold a permanent teaching certificate in State A and are employed as a teacher in that state for several years. You move to State B and are promptly hired as a teacher. You are required, however, to complete certain prescribed courses to get a permanent teaching certificate in State B. These additional courses are qualifying work-related education because the teaching position in State B involves the same general kind of work for which you were qualified in State A.

Education That Qualifies You for a New Trade or Business

Education that is part of a program of study that will qualify you for a new trade or business is not qualifying work-related education. This is true even if you do not plan to enter that trade or business.

If you are an employee, a change of duties that involves the same general kind of work is not a new trade or business.

Example 1. You are an accountant. Your employer requires you to get a law degree at your own expense. You register at a law school for the regular curriculum that leads to a law degree. Even if you do not intend to become a lawyer, the education is not qualifying because the law degree will qualify you for a new trade or business.

Example 2. You are a general practitioner of medicine. You take a 2-week course to review developments in several specialized fields of medicine. The course does not qualify you for a new profession. It is qualifying work-related education because it maintains or improves skills required in your present profession.

TAXSAVER
You may be able to deduct expenses incurred in gaining a specialty within a trade or a business if the expenses are delayed until after you have established yourself in the trade or business.

Example 3. While working in the private practice of psychiatry, you enter a program to study and train at an accredited psychoanalytic institute. The program will lead to qualifying you to practice psychoanalysis. The psychoanalytic training does not qualify you for a new profession. It is qualifying work-related education because it maintains or improves skills required in your present profession.

EXPLANATION
Payment for psychoanalysis that is required as part of your training to be a psychoanalyst may be a deductible educational expense necessary for professional training. The law specifically permits an itemized deduction for the cost of psychoanalytic training undertaken by psychiatrists as education expenses, because the training maintains or improves skills required in their trade or business and does not qualify them for a new trade or business. The courts have also allowed deductions for expenses incurred by a clinical psychologist in studying to become a psychoanalyst and expenses incurred by a psychiatrist for psychoanalytic training as a condition to accepting the directorship of a child study center.

However, when a psychiatric residency was undertaken to qualify a taxpayer for a new profession, the expenses were not deductible.

Bar or CPA Review Course
Review courses to prepare for the bar examination or the certified public accountant (CPA) examination are not qualifying work-related education. They are part of a program of study that can qualify you for a new profession.

EXPLANATION
Bar review courses are not deductible, even if you are currently practicing in one state and are seeking admission to the bar in another state. However, you may be able to deduct the cost of graduate courses (LLM). See earlier examples under *Education To Maintain or Improve Skills* and *Education To Meet Minimum Requirements*.

Teaching and Related Duties
All teaching and related duties are considered the same general kind of work. A change in duties in any of the following ways is not considered a change to a new business.
- Elementary school teacher to secondary school teacher.
- Teacher of one subject, such as biology, to teacher of another subject, such as art.
- Classroom teacher to guidance counselor.
- Classroom teacher to school administrator.

What Expenses Can Be Deducted

If your education meets the requirements described earlier under _Qualifying Work-Related Education_, you can generally deduct your education expenses as business expenses. If you are not self-employed, you can deduct business expenses only if you itemize your deductions.

You cannot deduct expenses related to tax-exempt and excluded income.

Deductible expenses. The following education expenses can be deducted.
- Tuition, books, supplies, lab fees, and similar items.
- Certain transportation and travel costs.
- Other education expenses, such as costs of research and typing when writing a paper as part of an educational program.

Nondeductible expenses. You cannot deduct personal or capital expenses. For example, you cannot deduct the dollar value of vacation time or annual leave you take to attend classes. This amount is a personal expense.

Unclaimed reimbursement. If you do not claim reimbursement that you are entitled to receive from your employer, you cannot deduct the expenses that apply to that unclaimed reimbursement.

Example. Your employer agrees to pay your education expenses if you file a voucher showing your expenses. You do not file a voucher, and you do not get reimbursed. Because you did not file a voucher, you cannot deduct the expenses on your tax return.

Transportation Expenses

If your education qualifies, you can deduct local transportation costs of going directly from work to school. If you are regularly employed and go to school on a temporary basis, you can also deduct the costs of returning from school to home.

Temporary basis. You go to school on a temporary basis if either of the following situations applies to you.

1. Your attendance at school is realistically expected to last 1 year or less and does indeed last for 1 year or less.
2. Initially, your attendance at school is realistically expected to last 1 year or less, but at a later date your attendance is reasonably expected to last more than 1 year. Your attendance is temporary up to the date you determine it will last more than 1 year.

Note. If you are in either situation (1) or (2), your attendance is not temporary if facts and circumstances indicate otherwise.

Attendance not on a temporary basis. You do not go to school on a temporary basis if either of the following situations apply to you.

1. Your attendance at school is realistically expected to last more than 1 year. It does not matter how long you actually attend.
2. Initially, your attendance at school is realistically expected to last 1 year or less, but at a later date your attendance is reasonably expected to last more than 1 year. Your attendance is not temporary after the date you determine it will last more than 1 year.

Deductible Transportation Expenses

If you are regularly employed and go directly from home to school on a temporary basis, you can deduct the round-trip costs of transportation between your home and school. This is true regardless of the location of the school, the distance traveled, or whether you attend school on nonwork days.

Figure 28-A. **Does Your Work-Related Education Qualify?**

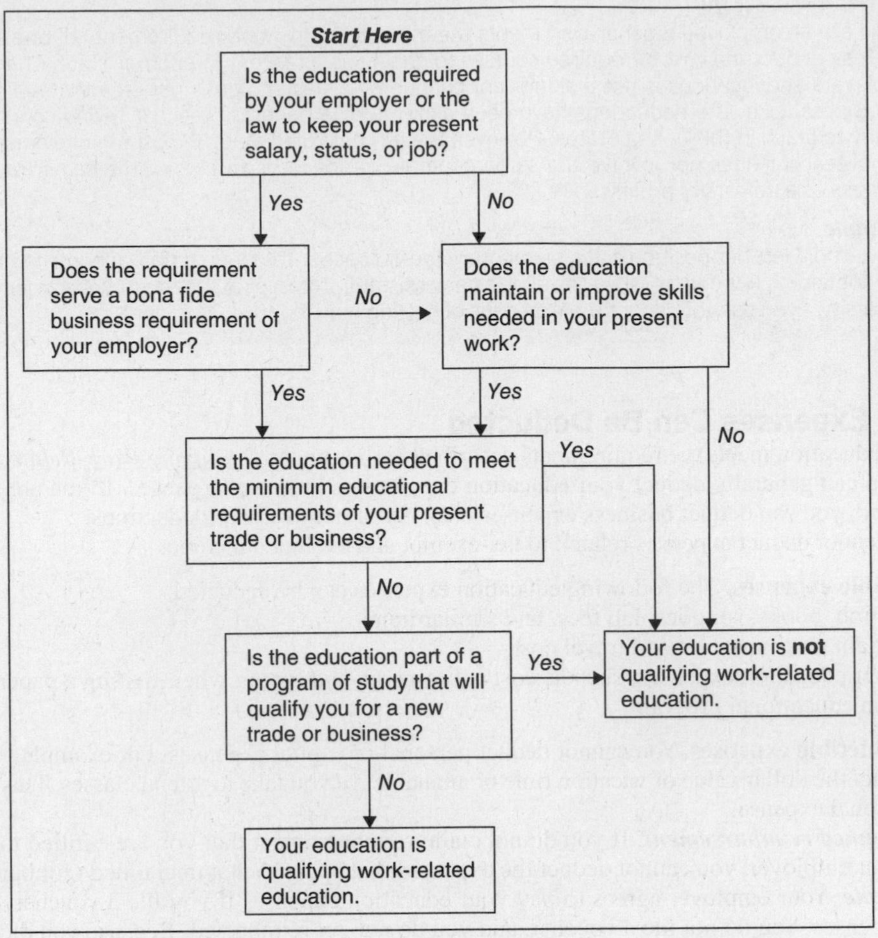

Start Here

Is the education required by your employer or the law to keep your present salary, status, or job?

— Yes → Does the requirement serve a bona fide business requirement of your employer?

— No → Does the education maintain or improve skills needed in your present work?

Does the requirement serve a bona fide business requirement of your employer? — No → Does the education maintain or improve skills needed in your present work?

Does the requirement serve a bona fide business requirement of your employer? — Yes → Is the education needed to meet the minimum educational requirements of your present trade or business?

Does the education maintain or improve skills needed in your present work? — Yes → Is the education needed to meet the minimum educational requirements of your present trade or business?

Does the education maintain or improve skills needed in your present work? — No → Your education is **not** qualifying work-related education.

Is the education needed to meet the minimum educational requirements of your present trade or business? — Yes → Your education is **not** qualifying work-related education.

Is the education needed to meet the minimum educational requirements of your present trade or business? — No → Is the education part of a program of study that will qualify you for a new trade or business?

Is the education part of a program of study that will qualify you for a new trade or business? — Yes → Your education is **not** qualifying work-related education.

Is the education part of a program of study that will qualify you for a new trade or business? — No → Your education is qualifying work-related education.

Transportation expenses include the actual costs of bus, subway, cab, or other fares, as well as the costs of using your car. Transportation expenses do not include amounts spent for travel, meals, or lodging while you are away from home overnight.

Example 1. You regularly work in a nearby town, and go directly from work to home. You also attend school every work night for 3 months to take a course that improves your job skills. Since you are attending school on a temporary basis, you can deduct your daily round-trip transportation expenses in going between home and school. This is true regardless of the distance traveled.

Example 2. Assume the same facts as in *Example 1* except that on certain nights you go directly from work to school and then home. You can deduct your transportation expenses from your regular work site to school and then home.

Example 3. Assume the same facts as in *Example 1* except that you attend the school for 9 months on Saturdays, nonwork days. Since you are attending school on a temporary basis, you can deduct your round-trip transportation expenses in going between home and school.

Example 4. Assume the same facts as in *Example 1* except that you attend classes twice a week for 15 months. Since your attendance in school is not considered temporary, you cannot deduct your transportation expenses in going between home and school. If you go directly from work to school, you can deduct the one-way transportation expenses of going from work to school. If you go from work to home to school and return home, your transportation expenses cannot be more than if you had gone directly from work to school.

Using your car. If you use your car (whether you own or lease it) for transportation to school, you can deduct your actual expenses or use the standard mileage rate to figure the amount you can deduct. The standard mileage rate for miles driven from January 1, 2014, through December 31, 2014, is 56 cents per mile. Whichever method you use, you can also deduct parking fees and tolls. See chapter 27 for information on deducting your actual expenses of using a car.

Travel Expenses

You can deduct expenses for travel, meals (see *50% limit on meals*, later), and lodging if you travel overnight mainly to obtain qualifying work-related education.

Travel expenses for qualifying work-related education are treated the same as travel expenses for other employee business purposes. For more information, see chapter 27.

Mainly personal travel. If your travel away from home is mainly personal, you cannot deduct all of your expenses for travel, meals, and lodging. You can deduct only your expenses for lodging and 50% of your expenses for meals during the time you attend the qualified educational activities.

Whether a trip's purpose is mainly personal or educational depends upon the facts and circumstances. An important factor is the comparison of time spent on personal activities with time spent on educational activities. If you spend more time on personal activities, the trip is considered mainly educational only if you can show a substantial nonpersonal reason for traveling to a particular location.

Example 1. John works in Newark, New Jersey. He traveled to Chicago to take a deductible 1-week course at the request of his employer. His main reason for going to Chicago was to take the course.

While there, he took a sight-seeing trip, entertained some friends, and took a side trip to Pleasantville for a day.

Since the trip was mainly for business, John can deduct his round-trip airfare to Chicago. He cannot deduct his transportation expenses of going to Pleasantville. He can deduct only the meals (subject to the 50% limit) and lodging connected with his educational activities.

Example 2. Sue works in Boston. She went to a university in Michigan to take a course for work. The course is qualifying work-related education.

She took one course, which is one-fourth of a full course load of study. She spent the rest of the time on personal activities. Her reasons for taking the course in Michigan were all personal.

Sue's trip is mainly personal because three-fourths of her time is considered personal time. She cannot deduct the cost of her round-trip train ticket to Michigan. She can deduct one-fourth of the meals (subject to the 50% limit) and lodging costs for the time she attended the university.

Example 3. Dave works in Nashville and recently traveled to California to take a 2-week seminar. The seminar is qualifying work-related education.

While there, he spent an extra 8 weeks on personal activities. The facts, including the extra 8-week stay, show that his main purpose was to take a vacation.

Dave cannot deduct his round-trip airfare or his meals and lodging for the 8 weeks. He can deduct only his expenses for meals (subject to the 50% limit) and lodging for the 2 weeks he attended the seminar.

TAXSAVER

Through careful planning and documentation, as well as recognition of the stringent tests applied by the courts, it's possible to mix business with pleasure and deduct some or all of your travel expenses. If you travel away from home primarily to obtain education, your expenditures for the education, as well as for travel, meals, and lodging while away from home, are deductible. It is helpful to be able to prove that the location you are visiting is unique and that, if education is involved, the education cannot be obtained elsewhere.

However, if you engage in some personal activity while on the trip, such as sightseeing, social visiting, entertaining, or other recreation, your expenses attributable to those personal activities are nondeductible personal expenses.

If your travel away from home is primarily personal, your expenditures for travel, meals, and lodging (other than meals and lodging during the time spent participating in deductible educational pursuits) are not deductible.

Whether a particular trip is primarily personal or primarily educational depends on all the facts and circumstances of each case, including the time devoted to personal activity as compared with the time devoted to educational pursuits. It is important to maintain good documentation regarding the types of expenses incurred and in what capacity they were incurred.

Example

Shannon, a hair stylist, decides to attend a 4-day workshop on the latest trends of hair coloring and styling that is offered in Tampa, Florida, 400 miles from her home. Her primary purpose in going to Tampa is to take the course, but she also takes a side trip to Orlando (a couple of hours away from Tampa) for 2 days. Shannon's transportation expenses to Tampa are deductible, but her transportation to Orlando is not. Additionally, her expenses for meals and lodging while away from home must be allocated between her educational pursuits and her personal activities. Those expenses that are entirely personal, such as sightseeing in Orlando, are not deductible. The cost of deductible meals must be reduced by 50%.

Cruises and conventions. Certain cruises and conventions offer seminars or courses as part of their itinerary. Even if the seminars or courses are work-related, your deduction for travel may be limited. This applies to:

- Travel by ocean liner, cruise ship, or other form of luxury water transportation, and
- Conventions outside the North American area.

For a discussion of the limits on travel expense deductions that apply to cruises and conventions, see *Luxury Water Travel and Conventions* in chapter 1 of Publication 463.

50% limit on meals. You can deduct only 50% of the cost of your meals while traveling away from home to obtain qualifying work-related education. You cannot have been reimbursed for the meals.

Employees must use Form 2106 or Form 2106-EZ to apply the 50% limit.

Travel as Education

You cannot deduct the cost of travel as a form of education even if it is directly related to your duties in your work or business.

Example. You are a French language teacher. While on sabbatical leave granted for travel, you traveled through France to improve your knowledge of the French language. You chose your itinerary and most of your activities to improve your French language skills. You cannot deduct your travel expenses as education expenses. This is true even if you spent most of your time learning French by visiting French schools and families, attending movies or plays, and engaging in similar activities.

EXPLANATION

The cost of travel is not a deductible educational expense when the educational aspect of a trip is the trip itself. However, if you establish an ordinary and necessary business need for the travel, such as research that can only be done in a specific location or a specific seminar, then a deduction may be allowed for travel expenses.

No Double Benefit Allowed

You cannot do either of the following.

- Deduct work-related education expenses as business expenses if you benefit from these expenses under any other provision of the law.
- Deduct work-related education expenses paid with tax-free scholarship, grant, or employer-provided educational assistance. See *Adjustments to Qualifying Work-Related Education Expenses*, next.

TAXSAVER

Student Loan Interest Expense. You may be able to claim a deduction for calculating your adjusted gross income (AGI)—typically called an "above-the-line" deduction—of up to $2,500 in interest you pay on a qualified student loan used for higher education. The amount of your student loan interest deduction is gradually reduced (phased out) if your modified adjusted gross income (MAGI) is between $65,000 and $80,000 ($130,000 and $160,000 if you file a joint return). You cannot take a deduction if your MAGI is $80,000 or more ($160,000 or more if you file a joint return). If you qualify, you can take this deduction whether or not the education is work related and even if you do not itemize deductions on Schedule A (Form 1040).

For more information on the deduction of student loan interest, see Publication 970 and the section on *Student Loan Interest Deduction* in chapter 19, *Education-related adjustments*.

Adjustments to Qualifying Work-Related Education Expenses

If you pay qualifying work-related education expenses with certain tax-free funds, you cannot claim a deduction for those amounts. You must reduce the qualifying expenses by the amount of such expenses allocable to the tax-free educational assistance. For more information, see chapter 12 of Publication 970.

Tax-free educational assistance includes:

- The tax-free part of scholarships and fellowships (see chapter 1 of Publication 970),
- The tax-free part of Pell grants (see chapter 1 of Publication 970),

- The tax-free part of employer-provided educational assistance (see chapter 11 of Publication 970),
- Veterans' educational assistance (see chapter 1 of Publication 970), and
- Any other nontaxable (tax-free) payments (other than gifts or inheritances) received for education assistance.

Amounts that do not reduce qualifying work-related education expenses. Do not reduce the qualifying work-related education expenses by amounts paid with funds the student receives as:
- Payment for services, such as wages,
- A loan,
- A gift,
- An inheritance, or
- A withdrawal from the student's personal savings.

Also, do not reduce the qualifying work-related education expenses by any scholarship or fellowship reported as income on the student's return or any scholarship which, by its terms, cannot be applied to qualifying work-related education expenses.

Reimbursements

How you treat reimbursements depends on the arrangement you have with your employer.

There are two basic types of reimbursement arrangements—accountable plans and nonaccountable plans. You can tell the type of plan you are reimbursed under by the way the reimbursement is reported on your Form W-2.

For information on how to treat reimbursements under both accountable and nonaccountable plans, see _Reimbursements_ in chapter 27.

Deducting Business Expenses

Self-employed persons and employees report business expenses differently.

The following information explains what forms you must use to deduct the cost of your qualifying work-related education as a business expense.

Self-Employed Persons

If you are self-employed, report the cost of your qualifying work-related education on the appropriate form used to report your business income and expenses (generally Schedule C, C-EZ, or F). If your educational expenses include expenses for a car or truck, travel, or meals, report those expenses the same way you report other business expenses for those items. See the instructions for the form you file for information on how to complete it.

> ### TAXSAVER
> From a tax perspective, it is more beneficial to report educational expenses on Schedules C, C-EZ, or F as appropriate. Reporting expenses on these forms will lower your adjusted gross income (AGI). As a result, the education expenses will not be subject to the 2%-of-AGI limitation on miscellaneous itemized deductions (see _Deductions Subject to the 2% Limit_, in chapter 29, _Miscellaneous deductions_). In addition, reporting the expenses on Schedules C, C-EZ, or F will reduce your self-employment tax.

Employees

If you are an employee, you can deduct the cost of qualifying work-related education only if you:
1. Did not receive (and were not entitled to receive) any reimbursement from your employer,
2. Were reimbursed under a nonaccountable plan (amount is included in box 1 of Form W-2), or
3. Received reimbursement under an accountable plan, but the amount received was less than your expenses for which you claimed reimbursement.

If either (1) or (2) applies, you can deduct the total qualifying cost. If (3) applies, you can deduct only the qualifying costs that were more than your reimbursement.

In order to deduct the cost of your qualifying work-related education as a business expense, include the amount with your deduction for any other employee business expenses on Schedule A

(Form 1040), line 21. (Special rules for expenses of certain performing artists and fee-basis officials and for impairment-related work expenses are explained later.)

This deduction (except for impairment-related work expenses of disabled individuals) is subject to the 2%-of-adjusted-gross-income limit that applies to most miscellaneous itemized deductions. See chapter 29.

Form 2106 or 2106-EZ. To figure your deduction for employee business expenses, including qualifying work-related education, you generally must complete Form 2106 or Form 2106-EZ.

Form not required. Do not complete either Form 2106 or Form 2106-EZ if:
- If amounts included in box 1 of your Form W-2, are not considered reimbursements, and
- You are not claiming travel, transportation, meal, or entertainment expenses.

If you meet both of these requirements, enter the expenses directly on Schedule A (Form 1040), line 21. (Special rules for expenses of certain performing artists and fee-basis officials and for impairment-related work expenses are explained later.)

Using Form 2106-EZ. This form is shorter and easier to use than Form 2106. Generally, you can use this form if:
- All reimbursements, if any, are included in box 1 of your Form W-2, and
- You are using the standard mileage rate if you are claiming vehicle expenses.

If you do not meet both of these requirements, use Form 2106.

Performing Artists and Fee-Basis Officials

If you are a qualified performing artist, or a state (or local) government official who is paid in whole or in part on a fee basis, you can deduct the cost of your qualifying work-related education as an adjustment to gross income rather than as an itemized deduction.

Include the cost of your qualifying work-related education with any other employee business expenses on Form 1040, line 24. You do not have to itemize your deductions on Schedule A (Form 1040), and, therefore, the deduction is not subject to the 2%-of-adjusted-gross-income limit. You must complete Form 2106 or 2106-EZ to figure your deduction, even if you meet the requirements described earlier under *Form not required.*

For more information on qualified performing artists, see chapter 6 of Publication 463.

Impairment-Related Work Expenses

If you are disabled and have impairment-related work expenses that are necessary for you to be able to get qualifying work-related education, you can deduct these expenses on Schedule A (Form 1040), line 28. They are not subject to the 2%-of-adjusted-gross-income limit. To deduct these expenses, you must complete Form 2106 or 2106-EZ even if you meet the requirements described earlier under *Form not required.*

For more information on impairment-related work expenses, see chapter 6 of Publication 463.

Recordkeeping

You must keep records as proof of any deduction claimed on your tax return. Generally, you should keep your records for 3 years from the date of filing the tax return and claiming the deduction.

For specific information about keeping records of business expenses, see *Recordkeeping* in chapter 27.

TAXORGANIZER
Records you should keep:
- Job descriptions and other employer-provided materials that would set forth the educational requirements of your job
- Descriptions of educational programs and courses taken
- Tuition statements and canceled checks
- Receipts for books, supplies, lab fees, and the like
- Records of travel, transportation, lodging, and meal expenses related to education and training activity

Chapter 29
Miscellaneous deductions

Note

IRS Publication 17 (*Your Federal Income Tax*) has been updated by Ernst & Young LLP for 2014. Dates and dollar amounts shown are for 2014. Underlined type is used to indicate where IRS text has been updated. Places where text has been removed are indicated by the sentence: *Text intentionally omitted.*

ey.com/EYTaxGuide

Ernst & Young LLP will update the *EY Tax Guide 2015* website with relevant taxpayer information as it becomes available. You can also sign up for email alerts to let you know when changes have been made.

Introduction

This chapter covers a variety of expenses, some of which are deductible on your tax return and some of which are not. Deductible expenses can be broadly broken down into three categories: (1) deductible employee expenses, (2) deductible expenses of producing or collecting income, and (3) other deductible expenses. The general rule is that you may deduct any "ordinary and necessary" expense related to your trade or business, connected with producing or collecting other taxable income, or paid to determine your tax. Note, however, that your deductions may be limited depending on the type of the expense and your income level. (See discussion later regarding *Deductions Subject to the 2% Limit*.)

Nondeductible expenses, by definition, are all expenses that are not deductible. These expenses are typically personal in nature. The nondeductible expenses discussed in this chapter are not all-inclusive, but rather reflect the more common expenses that people may think are (or should be) deductible.

With proper planning, you may be able to deduct more than you think. Be sure to take note of the special comments throughout this chapter with respect to documenting the appropriateness of your deductions. Also, check out the list at the front of the book for *50 of the Most Easily Overlooked Deductions* to be sure you haven't missed anything.

What's New

Standard mileage rate. The 2014 rate for business use of a vehicle is 56 cents per mile.

This chapter explains which expenses you can claim as miscellaneous itemized deductions on Schedule A (Form 1040). You must reduce the total of most miscellaneous itemized deductions by 2% of your adjusted gross income. This chapter covers the following topics.
- Deductions subject to the 2% limit.
- Deductions not subject to the 2% limit.
- Expenses you cannot deduct.

TAXALERT

Whether or not the miscellaneous itemized deductions you claim are subject to the 2% limit, miscellaneous itemized deductions—with the exception of casualty and theft losses and gambling losses—along with other specified itemized deductions (including home mortgage interest, state and local taxes, and charitable deductions), may be further reduced by an additional "overall" limitation. (Medical expense and investment interest expense deductions are not subject to this overall limitation.) The total of this group of itemized deductions must be reduced by 3% of the amount of your adjusted gross income (AGI) in excess of certain thresholds; i.e. $254,200 for individual filers, $279,650 for heads of households, $305,050 if married filing jointly or a surviving spouse, and $152,520 if married filing separately. (The threshold amounts are indexed annually for inflation.) However, no more than 80% of the otherwise allowable deductions are phased out. See chapter 30, *Limit on Itemized Deductions*, for more information.

You must keep records to verify your deductions. You should keep receipts, canceled checks, substitute checks, financial account statements, and other documentary evidence. For more information on recordkeeping, get Publication 552, Recordkeeping for Individuals.

Tax Breaks and Deductions You Can Use Checklist

Job-hunting expenses. Job-hunting expenses are deductible whether or not you find a new job. For job-search expenses to be deductible, you must be looking for employment in the same trade or business in which you are engaged. Accepting temporary employment in another line of work won't affect your deduction for expenses in searching for permanent employment in your regular line of work. But job-hunting costs aren't deductible if you are looking for a job in a new trade or business, even if you find employment as a result of the search.

IRA fees. Fees you pay to an IRA custodian are deductible as miscellaneous deductions as long as they are paid from an account other than your IRA account. If they are paid directly from your IRA, you get no deduction and your IRA account is reduced.

Deduction for estate tax on income in respect of a decedent. This deduction is missed by many taxpayers. If someone bequeaths taxable income (such as an IRA or nonqualified stock option) to an estate or beneficiary, the recipient

Useful Items

You may want to see:

Publication

- ☐ **463** Travel, Entertainment, Gift, and Car Expenses
- ☐ **525** Taxable and Nontaxable Income
- ☐ **529** Miscellaneous Deductions
- ☐ **535** Business Expenses
- ☐ **587** Business Use of Your Home (Including Use by Daycare Providers)
- ☐ **946** How To Depreciate Property

Form (and Instructions)

- ☐ **Schedule A (Form 1040)** Itemized Deductions
- ☐ **2106** Employee Business Expenses
- ☐ **2106-EZ** Unreimbursed Employee Business Expenses

Deductions Subject to the 2% Limit

You can deduct certain expenses as miscellaneous itemized deductions on Schedule A (Form 1040). You can claim the amount of expenses that is more than 2% of your adjusted gross income. You figure your deduction on Schedule A by subtracting 2% of your adjusted gross income from the total amount of these expenses. Your adjusted gross income is the amount on Form 1040, line 38.

Generally, you apply the 2% limit after you apply any other deduction limit. For example, you apply the 50% (or 80%) limit on business-related meals and entertainment (discussed in chapter 27) before you apply the 2% limit.

> ### EXPLANATION
> **2% limitation.** First, you must determine which expenses are deductible. Next, you must calculate the amount that is deductible, taking into account any limitation for certain types of expenses (e.g., 50% for meals and entertainment). The sum of all of your allowable miscellaneous deductions is then reduced by 2% of your adjusted gross income (AGI).
>
> #### Example
> Assume an individual's adjusted gross income is $45,000 in 2014. This person paid $1,500 in 2014 for the preparation of his 2013 income tax returns and also had $200 of unreimbursed business-related meal expenses for 2014. Both of these expenses are deductible. The $1,500 tax preparation fee is fully deductible, whereas only 50% of the $200 meal expense is deductible. Therefore, total miscellaneous deductions are $1,600 ($1,500 + [50% × $200]). However, 2% of the individual's AGI is $900 ($45,000 × 2%), so he is permitted a deduction of only $700 ($1,600 of total allowable deductions reduced by 2% of AGI, or $900).

Deductions subject to the 2% limit are discussed in the three categories in which you report them on Schedule A (Form 1040).

- Unreimbursed employee expenses (line 21).
- Tax preparation fees (line 22).
- Other expenses (line 23).

Unreimbursed Employee Expenses (Line 21)

Generally, you can deduct on Schedule A (Form 1040), line 21, unreimbursed employee expenses that are:

- Paid or incurred during your tax year,
- For carrying on your trade or business of being an employee, and
- Ordinary and necessary.

An expense is ordinary if it is common and accepted in your trade, business, or profession. An expense is necessary if it is appropriate and helpful to your business. An expense does not have to be required to be considered necessary.

> ### EXPLANATION
> **Unreimbursed employee business expenses.** If you are an employee and have business expenses that are either not reimbursed or are more than the amount reimbursed by your employer, you can generally deduct them only as a miscellaneous deduction (subject to the 2%-of-adjusted-gross-income limit) on Schedule A (Form 1040).

TAXPLANNER

If you can get your employer to reimburse you for what would otherwise be unreimbursed business expenses, in lieu of an equal amount of future salary, you should do so. The reimbursement for those expenses is not included on your Form W-2 as compensation, so your tax liability should be less. You benefit at no additional cost to your employer because reimbursed employee business expenses that you have adequately reported to your employer are deductible by your employer the same as wages. This only works, however, if you give up your right to receive payment in the event you don't incur any business expenses.

Examples of unreimbursed employee expenses are listed next. The list is followed by discussions of additional unreimbursed employee expenses.

- Business bad debt of an employee.
- Education that is work related. (See chapter 28.)
- Legal fees related to your job.
- Licenses and regulatory fees.
- Malpractice insurance premiums.
- Medical examinations required by an employer.
- Occupational taxes.
- Passport for a business trip.
- Subscriptions to professional journals and trade magazines related to your work.
- Travel, transportation, entertainment, and gifts related to your work. (See chapter 27.)

EXPLANATION

Business bad debt of an employee. A business bad debt is a loss from a debt created or acquired in your trade or business, or a loss when there is a very close relationship between the debt and your trade or business when the debt is created (e.g., as an employee, your main motive for creating the debt is a business reason). For example, if an employee makes a bona fide loan to his employer in order to keep his job, and the company fails to pay the debt, the employee has a business bad debt. See Publication 535 for more information on business bad debts.

EXPLANATION

Business travel and entertainment. Generally, only 50% of the amount spent for business meals (including meals away from home on overnight business) and entertainment will be deductible. This limit must be applied before arriving at the amount subject to the 2%-of-AGI limitation.

TAXALERT

You are not allowed to deduct the travel expenses of family members, even if there is a business purpose for their presence on the trip, unless the family member is also an employee. If your employer reimburses you for travel expenses, the portion of the expense attributable to family members who are not employees of the company may be included in your W-2 income. See chapter 27, *Car expenses and other employee business expenses*, for more information.

TAXALERT

The deduction percentage for meals consumed while away from home by individuals subject to hours of service limitations of the Department of Transportation, such as interstate truck and bus drivers, certain railroad employees, and certain merchant marines, is 80%. (See *Exceptions to the 50% Limit* under *50% Limit* in chapter 27, *Car expenses and other employee business expenses*.) Note that you must apply this percentage before applying the 2%-of-adjusted-gross-income (AGI) limitation.

is entitled to an income tax deduction for any federal estate tax paid which is allocable to that income. The deduction is not subject to the 2%-of-adjusted-gross-income (AGI) floor.

Gambling losses. Gambling losses can be claimed as a miscellaneous deduction not subject to the 2%-of-adjusted-gross-income (AGI) floor. But gambling losses are only deductible to the extent that you have gambling winnings during the same year. If your winnings are over certain specified amounts, they will be reported to you on Form W-2G, Certain Gambling Winnings. See *Gambling Losses Up to the Amount of Gambling Winnings* later in this chapter for more information.

Business Liability Insurance

You can deduct insurance premiums you paid for protection against personal liability for wrongful acts on the job.

Damages for Breach of Employment Contract

If you break an employment contract, you can deduct damages you pay your former employer that are attributable to the pay you received from that employer.

Depreciation on Computers

You can claim a depreciation deduction for a computer that you use in your work as an employee if its use is:

- For the convenience of your employer, and
- Required as a condition of your employment.

For more information about the rules and exceptions to the rules affecting the allowable deductions for a home computer, see Publication 529.

Dues to Chambers of Commerce and Professional Societies

You may be able to deduct dues paid to professional organizations (such as bar associations and medical associations) and to chambers of commerce and similar organizations, if membership helps you carry out the duties of your job. Similar organizations include:
- Boards of trade,
- Business leagues,
- Civic or public service organizations,
- Real estate boards, and
- Trade associations.

Lobbying and political activities. You may not be able to deduct that part of your dues that is for certain lobbying and political activities. See *Dues used for lobbying* under *Nondeductible Expenses*, later.

Educator Expenses

Text intentionally omitted. If you were an educator in 2014, you can deduct educator expenses as a miscellaneous itemized deduction subject to the 2% limit.

Home Office

If you use a part of your home regularly and exclusively for business purposes, you may be able to deduct a part of the operating expenses and depreciation of your home.

TAXALERT

Home office deduction. It is now easier for taxpayers to claim a home office deduction. Furthermore, the IRS has adopted an optional simplified method for calculating your deduction. (see *Simplified option for home office deduction*, later, in this section). Even if you were not able to claim a home office deduction in prior years and your business use of your home has not changed, you should check again to see if you are able to take this deduction.

Explanation

Individuals claiming home office deductions on Schedule C are required to figure those deductions on Form 8829, *Expenses for Business Use of Your Home*. However, if you are an employee claiming unreimbursed job-related expenses, use Form 2106, Employee Business Expenses, if applicable, or include the amount directly on Schedule A.

You can claim this deduction for the business use of a part of your home only if you use that part of your home regularly and exclusively:

- As your principal place of business for any trade or business,
- As a place to meet or deal with your patients, clients, or customers in the normal course of your trade or business, or
- In the case of a separate structure not attached to your home, in connection with your trade or business.

EXPLANATION

A home may be a house, an apartment, a condominium, a mobile home, or even a boat. It may also be other structures on the same property as the house you live in, such as a studio, a barn, a greenhouse, or an unattached garage.

The regular and exclusive business use must be for the convenience of your employer and not just appropriate and helpful in your job. See Publication 587 for more detailed information and a worksheet.

EXPLANATION

A home office deduction will only be allowed if you use your home in connection with a trade or business. All profit-seeking activities are not trades or businesses (e.g., if you invest from home and are not a broker or dealer investing on behalf of clients or are not a "trader," you are not in the business of investing). However, you may take a home office deduction for a trade or business that is not your full-time occupation, as long as all appropriate tests are met (an example would be an attorney who uses his home office for managing rental properties he owns).

TAXPLANNER

Principal place of business. Administrative and management activities for your trade or business that are performed exclusively and regularly in your home will qualify your home as your **principal place of business** if you have no other fixed location where you perform substantial administrative or management activities. Activities that are considered administrative or managerial include billing clients, customers, or patients; keeping books and records; ordering supplies; setting up appointments; and writing reports.

In addition, certain administrative and management activities may be performed in other locations and not disqualify your home office as your principal place of business for purposes of meeting the test described earlier. For example, you may hire another person or company to perform your administrative activities, such as computing employee payrolls, at locations other than your home. You may also conduct administrative and management activities at places that are not fixed locations, such as hotel rooms or airports, and you may occasionally conduct minimal administrative and managerial activities at a fixed location outside of your home. Also, performing substantial nonadministrative activities outside of your home, such as servicing clients or making sales calls, will not disqualify your home as your principal place of business. And, significantly, you may even have suitable space available to you outside your home for performing administrative and managerial tasks but choose to use your home instead. (Note, however, that if you are an employee, any use of your home must be for the convenience of your employer in order to qualify for the home office deduction.)

Example

Connor is a self-employed anesthesiologist, working for three different local hospitals. One of the hospitals provides him with a small shared office where he could perform administrative or management activities. However, Connor prefers to use a room in his home as an office. He regularly and exclusively uses this room to schedule patients, maintain patient logs, bill patients, and read medical journals.

Prior to 2001, Connor's home office did not qualify as his principal place of business because his most important activity, administering anesthetics, was performed in the hospitals. Under the current rules, Connor's office qualifies for the home office deduction in 2014 (i.e., his home office will qualify as his principal place of business) because he conducts administrative and managerial activities for his business there and has no other fixed location where these activities take place. Neither the fact that Connor has available space at the hospital for performing administrative tasks nor the fact that his most important task is performed outside of his home disqualifies his home office as his principal place of business.

Explanation

To qualify for the regular and exclusive use test, you must use a specific area of your home only for your trade or business and on a continuing basis. The specific area can be a separate room or any identifiable space (the space does not need to be marked off by a permanent enclosure). Any personal use of the space will cause you to fail the requirements of the exclusive use test. Occasional or incidental use will cause you to fail the regular use test, even if that area of your house is not used for any other purposes.

Exceptions

Note that there is an exception to the regular and exclusive use test if you use part of your home as a daycare facility for children, persons age 65 or older, or individuals who are physically or mentally incapable of caring for themselves. The daycare provider must be licensed or certified under applicable state law, or exempt from licensing, for the exception to apply. There is also an exception to the regular and exclusive use test if you use part of your home to store inventory or product samples. If your home is the principal place of your business, the space used for inventory and sample storage qualifies for the home office deduction as long as it is used regularly, but not necessarily exclusively, for business.

TAXPLANNER

Many home sales operations require a great deal of personal time and attention but produce a minimum of deductible expenses. You should note, however, that the use of space in your home to store inventory or product samples may produce valuable deductions for otherwise underutilized spaces, such as attics and basements. Remember, the storage space must be a specific area that is used as a part of your principal place of business.

TAXSAVER

Daycare providers. Daycare providers who operate businesses in their homes may benefit from a recent IRS ruling. The square footage of a room that is regularly used for daycare and is available throughout the business day will be considered used for daycare for the entire business day. Previously, taxpayers had to take partial days based on the hours of actual business use. The deduction for daycare providers is equal to the total costs of maintaining the home (e.g., electricity, gas, water, trash collection, general maintenance) to provide daycare, multiplied by the following two fractions:

$$\frac{\text{Total square feet available and used regularly each day}}{\text{total square feet of home}}$$

$$\frac{\text{Total hours each year home used for daycare business}}{\text{total hours each year (8,760 hours in 2014)}}$$

The resulting deduction is subject to the income limitation, discussed later. IRS Form 8829 will help you work through this calculation.

Example

A daycare provider uses a bedroom (available for child care throughout the business day) for the children's morning and afternoon naps every day. Although the bedroom is not used during every hour of the business day, the total square footage of that room is considered as daycare usage for the entire business day when the total area for business is calculated.

Explanation

If you are an employee and you meet the tests described earlier for the use of your home in your trade or business, you will only qualify for a home office deduction if your use of your home is for the **convenience of your employer** and you do not rent your home office to your employer. It is not sufficient that a home office is helpful to your job; it must be a requirement of your employer. Your home office must also be justified by the nature of your job, which depends on all the facts and circumstances.

How to figure the deduction. To figure the percentage of your home used for business, you may compare the square feet of space used for business to the total square feet in your home. Or, if the rooms in your home are approximately the same size, you may compare the number of rooms used for business to the total number of rooms in your home. You may also use any other reasonable method. Generally, you figure the business part of your expenses by applying the percentage to the total of each expense.

Example

The room in your home that you use for business measures 120 square feet. Your home measures 1,200 square feet. Therefore, you are using one-tenth, or 10%, of the total area for business.

If you use one room for business in a five-room house and the rooms in your home are about the same size, you are using one-fifth, or 20%, of the total area for business.

Basing the deduction on an approximation of the rental costs of comparable office space is not a proper method, according to one court ruling.

Explanation

The general rule is that the expenses you have for maintaining and running your entire home may be taken, in part, as deductions, because they benefit both the business and the personal parts of your home.

If you have purchased your home, you may deduct part of the interest you pay on your home mortgage as a business expense. To figure the business part of your mortgage interest, multiply the mortgage interest by the part of your home used for business. If you rent a home, you may deduct part of the rent you pay using a similar calculation.

If you have a casualty loss (see chapter 26, *Casualty and theft losses*) on your home or other property that you use in business, you may deduct the business part of the loss as a business expense. The amount of the loss that qualifies for a deduction depends on what property is affected. If the loss is sustained on property that you use only in your business, the entire loss is treated as a business deduction. If the loss affects property used for both business and personal purposes, only the business part is a business deduction.

If you use part of your home for business, you may also deduct part of the expenses for utilities and services, such as electricity, gas, trash removal, and cleaning services. Expenses that are related only to your business, such as business long-distance telephone calls and depreciation of office furniture and equipment, are fully deductible.

Likewise, if you use part of your home for business, you may deduct part of your insurance on your home. However, if your insurance premium gives you coverage for a period that extends past the end of your tax year, you may deduct for business only the part of the premium that covers you for the tax year.

Example

If you paid a 2-year premium of $240 on September 1, 2014, only 4 months of the policy are included in your 2014 tax year. Therefore, only four twenty-fourths (1/6) of the premium may be used to figure your deduction in 2014. In 2015, you may use twelve twenty-fourths (1/2), and in 2016 eight twenty-fourths (1/3) would be used to figure your deduction. The premium must then be allocated between business and nonbusiness uses of your home.

Explanation

When it comes to repairs, you may deduct the cost of labor and supplies for the business part of your home. Your own labor, however, is not a deductible expense.

You can deduct part of the cost of painting the outside of your home or repairing the roof based on the percentage of your home used for business. However, you cannot deduct expenses for lawn care and landscaping.

Example

A repair to your furnace benefits the entire home. If 10% of the area of your home is used for business, 10% of the cost of the furnace repair is deductible.

Depreciation. You can deduct depreciation on the part of your home used for business subject to the limit on the deduction previously discussed.

Home leased to employer. If you lease any part of your home to your employer, you cannot claim a home office deduction for that part for any period you use that part of your home to perform services for your employer. However, you may want to see chapter 9, *Rental income and expenses*, as well as Publication 527, *Residential Rental Property*, for information on deducting rental expenses.

Income limitation. Deductions for the business use of your home may not create or add to a business loss. Therefore, if the total gross income for your business exceeds all of your business expenses (both direct business expenses and the expenses you have allocated for the use of a home office), you may deduct all of your expenses. However, if your business expenses exceed your gross business income, your deduction of certain expenses may be limited. You can carry any excess business expenses that are not currently deductible over to the next tax year, assuming that you have income from the business in the next tax year. If you do not have income from the business in the next tax year, the deductions may be carried to any later year in which you have gross income from the business.

Explanation

Your business deductions for the business use of your home are deducted in the following order:

1. The business percentage of the expenses that would otherwise be allowable as deductions, that is, mortgage interest, real estate taxes, and deductible casualty losses.
2. The direct expenses for your business in your home, such as expenses for supplies and compensation, but not the other expenses of the office in your home (such as those listed later in item 3).
3. The other expenses for the business use of your home, such as maintenance, utilities, insurance, and depreciation. Deductions that adjust the basis in your home are taken last.

Example

Kaela is an employee who works in her home for the convenience of her employer. She uses 20% of her home regularly and exclusively for this business purpose. In 2014, her gross income, expenses for the business, and computation of the deduction for the business use of her home are as follows:

Gross income from business use of home		$7,500
Minus:		
Business percentage (20% of home use) of mortgage interest and real estate taxes	2,000	
Other business expenses (supplies, transportation, etc.)	5,000	(7,000)
Modified net income		$500
Business use of home expenses		
Maintenance, insurance, utilities (20%)		$800
Depreciation (20%)		700
Total		$1,500
Deduction limited to modified net income		500
Carryover expenses to 2014 (subject to income limitation in 2014)		$1,000

The deduction of $500 is considered to be maintenance, insurance, and utilities. Kaela will not reduce the basis in her home for the $700 of depreciation until that amount is deducted in a future year.

Job Search Expenses

You can deduct certain expenses you have in looking for a new job in your present occupation, even if you do not get a new job. You cannot deduct these expenses if:

- You are looking for a job in a new occupation,
- There was a substantial break between the ending of your last job and your looking for a new one, or
- You are looking for a job for the first time.

Employment and outplacement agency fees. You can deduct employment and outplacement agency fees you pay in looking for a new job in your present occupation.

Employer pays you back. If, in a later year, your employer pays you back for employment agency fees, you must include the amount you receive in your gross income up to the amount of your tax benefit in the earlier year. (See <u>Recoveries</u> in chapter 12.)

Employer pays the employment agency. If your employer pays the fees directly to the employment agency and you are not responsible for them, you do not include them in your gross income.

EXAMPLES
- A certified public accountant employed by a national accounting firm was permitted to deduct expenses incurred in investigating whether or not he could practice his profession as a self-employed person.
- A corporate executive could deduct expenses involved in seeking a position as a corporate executive with another corporation.
- An attorney for a state agency could deduct the costs of taking an examination for a position as an attorney in another city because the new position would be in the same trade or business.
- An unemployed electrician was allowed to deduct transportation costs for going to the union hall to check on potential job opportunities. He was considered to be in the electrical trade, even though he was unemployed at the time.

EXPLANATION
Job search expenses and fees are deductible, even if the agency does not find you a suitable job.
Expenses for career counseling are deductible if they are incurred in your effort to find other employment in the same trade or business.

Résumé. You can deduct amounts you spend for preparing and mailing copies of a résumé to prospective employers if you are looking for a new job in your present occupation.

Travel and transportation expenses. If you travel to an area and, while there, you look for a new job in your present occupation, you may be able to deduct travel expenses to and from the area. You can deduct the travel expenses if the trip is primarily to look for a new job. The amount of time you spend on personal activity compared to the amount of time you spend in looking for work is important in determining whether the trip is primarily personal or is primarily to look for a new job.

Even if you cannot deduct the travel expenses to and from an area, you can deduct the expenses of looking for a new job in your present occupation while in the area.

You can choose to use the standard mileage rate to figure your car expenses. The 2014 rate for business use of a vehicle is 56 cents per mile. See <u>chapter 27</u> for more information.

TAXORGANIZER
Records you should keep. In case the IRS challenges your deduction for job search expenses, you should keep the following information to support your claim for job search expense deductions:
- Evidence of your current occupation at the time the job search expenses were incurred
- Written records, such as a letter from a prospective employer or an employment agency contract, evidencing a search for employment and the nature of the job
- Receipts, canceled checks, credit card slips, plane tickets, and the like evidencing the amount and payment of job search expenses
- Detailed records and evidence of costs, such as automobile mileage, for which a direct payment is not made
- A log allocating the time spent while traveling on personal activities compared to the time spent looking for a job

Licenses and Regulatory Fees
You can deduct the amount you pay each year to state or local governments for licenses and regulatory fees for your trade, business, or profession.

Occupational Taxes
You can deduct an occupational tax charged at a flat rate by a locality for the privilege of working or conducting a business in the locality. If you are an employee, you can claim occupational taxes

only as a miscellaneous deduction subject to the 2% limit; you cannot claim them as a deduction for taxes elsewhere on your return.

Repayment of Income Aid Payment

An "income aid payment" is one that is received under an employer's plan to aid employees who lose their jobs because of lack of work. If you repay a lump-sum income aid payment that you received and included in income in an earlier year, you can deduct the repayment.

Research Expenses of a College Professor

If you are a college professor, you can deduct research expenses, including travel expenses, for teaching, lecturing, or writing and publishing on subjects that relate directly to your teaching duties. You must have undertaken the research as a means of carrying out the duties expected of a professor and without expectation of profit apart from salary. However, you cannot deduct the cost of travel as a form of education.

> ### EXPLANATION
> Travel as a form of education is never deductible. An example would be a French teacher who, in order to learn more about local customs in France, travels throughout the country. The travel in this case is not for research in writing or publishing and the person did not teach while traveling. Travel as a form of education tends to resemble travel for personal purposes, and the IRS will disallow a deduction for travel expenses as a form of educational expenses. See chapter 28, *Tax benefits for work-related education*, for more information on deductible expenses.

Tools Used in Your Work

Generally, you can deduct amounts you spend for tools used in your work if the tools wear out and are thrown away within 1 year from the date of purchase. You can depreciate the cost of tools that have a useful life substantially beyond the tax year. For more information about depreciation, see Publication 946.

Union Dues and Expenses

You can deduct dues and initiation fees you pay for union membership.

You can also deduct assessments for benefit payments to unemployed union members. However, you cannot deduct the part of the assessments or contributions that provides funds for the payment of sick, accident, or death benefits. Also, you cannot deduct contributions to a pension fund, even if the union requires you to make the contributions.

You may not be able to deduct amounts you pay to the union that are related to certain lobbying and political activities. See *Lobbying Expenses* under *Nondeductible Expenses*, later.

> ### EXPLANATION
> A fine paid by a union member is deductible if by not paying the fine the member would be dropped from the union.
> If a union contract provides that all employees, regardless of whether or not they are union members, must pay union dues, the nonmembers may also deduct the union dues.

Work Clothes and Uniforms

You can deduct the cost and upkeep of work clothes if the following two requirements are met.
- You must wear them as a condition of your employment.
- The clothes are not suitable for everyday wear.

Examples of workers who may be able to deduct the cost and upkeep of work clothes are: delivery workers, firefighters, health care workers, law enforcement officers, letter carriers, professional athletes, and transportation workers (air, rail, bus, etc.).

Musicians and entertainers can deduct the cost of theatrical clothing and accessories that are not suitable for everyday wear.

However, work clothing consisting of white cap, white shirt or white jacket, white bib overalls, and standard work shoes, which a painter is required by his union to wear on the job, is not distinctive in character or in the nature of a uniform. Similarly, the costs of buying and maintaining blue work clothes worn by a welder at the request of a foreman are not deductible.

Caution

It is not enough that you wear distinctive clothing. The clothing must be specifically required by your employer. Nor is it enough that you do not, in fact, wear your work clothes away from work. The clothing must not be suitable for taking the place of your regular clothing.

Protective clothing. You can deduct the cost of protective clothing required in your work, such as safety shoes or boots, safety glasses, hard hats, and work gloves.

Examples of workers who may be required to wear safety items are: carpenters, cement workers, chemical workers, electricians, fishing boat crew members, machinists, oil field workers, pipe fitters, steamfitters, and truck drivers.

Military uniforms. You generally cannot deduct the cost of your uniforms if you are on full-time active duty in the armed forces. However, if you are an armed forces reservist, you can deduct the unreimbursed cost of your uniform if military regulations restrict you from wearing it except while on duty as a reservist. In figuring the deduction, you must reduce the cost by any nontaxable allowance you receive for these expenses.

If local military rules do not allow you to wear fatigue uniforms when you are off duty, you can deduct the amount by which the cost of buying and keeping up these uniforms is more than the uniform allowance you receive.

You can deduct the cost of your uniforms if you are a civilian faculty or staff member of a military school.

EXPLANATION

The initial expense and the costs of maintaining work clothes and business uniforms are deductible, not only if they must be worn as a condition of employment and they are not suitable for general or personal use but also if they are in fact not used for personal purposes. Taxpayers have been allowed to deduct costs relating to uniforms in the following cases:

- An art teacher deducted the costs of protective smocks.
- An airline clerk deducted the cost of "unfeminine, businesslike" shoes that she was required to wear and, in fact, wore only at work.
- A hospital worker deducted work clothes he kept in a locker at the hospital. He was in frequent contact with contagious persons and never brought the clothing home.
- A private-duty nurse deducted a uniform that served as a mark of her profession and was necessary for patient care.
- A member of the National Ski Patrol was allowed to deduct the cost of the parkas and ski trousers patrol members are required to wear.
- Scoutmasters, Red Cross volunteers, and others who wear uniforms while performing charitable activities may deduct the cost of the uniforms as charitable donations.

Tax Preparation Fees (Line 22)

You can usually deduct tax preparation fees in the year you pay them. Thus, on your 2014 return, you can deduct fees paid in 2014 for preparing your 2013 return. These fees include the cost of tax preparation software programs and tax publications. They also include any fee you paid for electronic filing of your return.

EXPLANATION

You may deduct expenses paid for the determination, collection, or refund of any tax—income tax, estate tax, gift tax, sales tax, or property tax. Fees paid to a consultant to advise you on the tax consequences of a transaction are deductible. If you contest a tax assessment, any fees paid are deductible, even if the defense is unsuccessful. Professional fees incurred in obtaining federal tax rulings are deductible. However, the cost of filing a complaint in court relating to an IRS levy against property is considered a capital expenditure and therefore not deductible.

TAXPLANNER

Business related. Generally, most tax preparation fees are only deductible on Schedule A and are subject to the 2%-of-adjusted-gross-income floor. However, according to the IRS, business owners can deduct the portion of tax preparation fees relating to a business directly on Schedule C, E, or F (and related business schedules).

Other Expenses (Line 23)

You can deduct certain other expenses as miscellaneous itemized deductions subject to the 2% limit. On Schedule A (Form 1040), line 23, you can deduct expenses that you pay:

1. To produce or collect income that must be included in your gross income,
2. To manage, conserve, or maintain property held for producing such income, or
3. To determine, contest, pay, or claim a refund of any tax.

You can deduct expenses you pay for the purposes in (1) and (2) above only if they are reasonably and closely related to these purposes. Some of these other expenses are explained in the following discussions.

If the expenses you pay produce income that is only partially taxable, see *Tax-Exempt Income Expenses*, later, under *Nondeductible Expenses*.

Appraisal Fees

You can deduct appraisal fees if you pay them to figure a casualty loss or the fair market value of donated property.

Casualty and Theft Losses

You can deduct a casualty or theft loss as a miscellaneous itemized deduction subject to the 2% limit if you used the damaged or stolen property in performing services as an employee. First report the loss in Section B of Form 4684, Casualties and Thefts. You may also have to include the loss on Form 4797, Sales of Business Property, if you are otherwise required to file that form. To figure your deduction, add all casualty or theft losses from this type of property included on Form 4684, lines 32 and 38b, or Form 4797, line 18a. For other casualty and theft losses, see chapter 26.

Clerical Help and Office Rent

You can deduct office expenses, such as rent and clerical help, that you have in connection with your investments and collecting the taxable income on them.

Credit or Debit Card Convenience Fees

You can deduct the convenience fee charged by the card processor for paying your income tax (including estimated tax payments) by credit or debit card. The fees are deductible in the year paid.

Depreciation on Home Computer

You can deduct depreciation on your home computer if you use it to produce income (for example, to manage your investments that produce taxable income). You generally must depreciate the computer using the straight line method over the Alternative Depreciation System (ADS) recovery period. But if you work as an employee and also use the computer in that work, see Publication 946.

Excess Deductions of an Estate

If an estate's total deductions in its last tax year are more than its gross income for that year, the beneficiaries succeeding to the estate's property can deduct the excess. Do not include deductions for the estate's personal exemption and charitable contributions when figuring the estate's total deductions. The beneficiaries can claim the deduction only for the tax year in which, or with which, the estate terminates, whether the year of termination is a normal year or a short tax year. For more information, see *Termination of Estate* in Publication 559, Survivors, Executors, and Administrators.

Fees to Collect Interest and Dividends

You can deduct fees you pay to a broker, bank, trustee, or similar agent to collect your taxable bond interest or dividends on shares of stock. But you cannot deduct a fee you pay to a broker to buy investment property, such as stocks or bonds. You must add the fee to the cost of the property.

You cannot deduct the fee you pay to a broker to sell securities. You can use the fee only to figure gain or loss from the sale. See the Instructions for Form 8949 for information on how to report the fee.

Hobby Expenses

You can generally deduct hobby expenses, but only up to the amount of hobby income. A hobby is not a business because it is not carried on to make a profit. See *Activity not for profit* in chapter 12 under *Other Income*.

Indirect Deductions of Pass-Through Entities

Pass-through entities include partnerships, S corporations, and mutual funds that are not publicly offered. Deductions of pass-through entities are passed through to the partners or shareholders. The partners or shareholders can deduct their share of passed-through deductions for investment expenses as miscellaneous itemized deductions subject to the 2% limit.

Example. You are a member of an investment club that is formed solely to invest in securities. The club is treated as a partnership. The partnership's income is solely from taxable dividends, interest, and gains from sales of securities. In this case, you can deduct your share of the partnership's operating expenses as miscellaneous itemized deductions subject to the 2% limit. However, if the investment club partnership has investments that also produce nontaxable income, you cannot deduct your share of the partnership's expenses that produce the nontaxable income.

Publicly offered mutual funds. Publicly offered mutual funds do not pass deductions for investment expenses through to shareholders. A mutual fund is "publicly offered" if it is:

- Continuously offered pursuant to a public offering,
- Regularly traded on an established securities market, or
- Held by or for at least 500 persons at all times during the tax year.

A publicly offered mutual fund will send you a Form 1099-DIV, Dividends and Distributions, or a substitute form, showing the net amount of dividend income (gross dividends minus investment expenses). This net figure is the amount you report on your return as income. You cannot further deduct investment expenses related to publicly offered mutual funds because they are already included as part of the net income amount.

Information returns. You should receive information returns from pass-through entities.

Partnerships and S corporations. These entities issue Schedule K-1, which lists the items and amounts you must report and identifies the tax return schedules and lines to use.

Nonpublicly offered mutual funds. These funds will send you a Form 1099-DIV, Dividends and Distributions, or a substitute form, showing your share of gross income and investment expenses. You can claim the expenses only as a miscellaneous itemized deduction subject to the 2% limit.

Investment Fees and Expenses

You can deduct investment fees, custodial fees, trust administration fees, and other expenses you paid for managing your investments that produce taxable income.

Legal Expenses

You can usually deduct legal expenses that you incur in attempting to produce or collect taxable income or that you pay in connection with the determination, collection, or refund of any tax.

You can also deduct legal expenses that are:

- Related to either doing or keeping your job, such as those you paid to defend yourself against criminal charges arising out of your trade or business,
- For tax advice related to a divorce, if the bill specifies how much is for tax advice and it is determined in a reasonable way, or
- To collect taxable alimony.

You can deduct expenses of resolving tax issues relating to profit or loss from business (Schedule C or C-EZ), rentals or royalties (Schedule E), or farm income and expenses (Schedule F), on the appropriate schedule. You deduct expenses of resolving nonbusiness tax issues on Schedule A (Form 1040). See *Tax Preparation Fees*, earlier.

> ### EXPLANATION
> **Professional fees.** Legal, accounting, and professional fees often have deductible and nondeductible elements. Whether professional fees should be deducted, capitalized, or considered personal expenses depends on the reasons the fees were incurred. To be deductible as a miscellaneous expense on Schedule A, the expense must either be connected to producing income (advising you on your employment, collecting alimony, and the like) or be incurred for a tax-related matter.

> ### TAXSAVER
> The law now makes legal and other expenses deductible in calculating adjusted gross income for "civil rights" type lawsuits which are settled or paid after October 22, 2004.

> ### TAXORGANIZER
> **Records you should keep.** To minimize controversy with the IRS over what portion of a professional fee is deductible, it's best to have the professional give you a detailed breakdown of your bill, indicating which portions are tax-deductible.

Loss on Deposits

For information on whether, and if so, how, you may deduct a loss on your deposit in a qualified financial institution, see *Loss on Deposits* in chapter 26.

> ### TAXORGANIZER
> **Loss on IRA.** If you have a loss on your traditional IRA (or Roth IRA) investment, you can deduct the loss as a miscellaneous itemized deduction subject to the 2% limit, but only when all the amounts in all your traditional IRA (or Roth IRA) accounts have been distributed to you and the total distributions are less than your unrecovered basis. For more information, see Publication 590, *Individual Retirement Arrangements (IRAs)*.

Repayments of Income

If you had to repay an amount that you included in income in an earlier year, you may be able to deduct the amount you repaid. If the amount you had to repay was ordinary income of $3,000 or less, the deduction is subject to the 2% limit. If it was more than $3,000, see *Repayments Under Claim of Right* under *Deductions Not Subject to the 2% Limit*, later.

Repayments of Social Security Benefits

For information on how to deduct your repayments of certain social security benefits, see *Repayments More Than Gross Benefits* in chapter 11.

Safe Deposit Box Rent

You can deduct safe deposit box rent if you use the box to store taxable income-producing stocks, bonds, or investment-related papers and documents. You cannot deduct the rent if you use the box only for jewelry, other personal items, or tax-exempt securities.

Service Charges on Dividend Reinvestment Plans

You can deduct service charges you pay as a subscriber in a dividend reinvestment plan. These service charges include payments for:
- Holding shares acquired through a plan,
- Collecting and reinvesting cash dividends, and
- Keeping individual records and providing detailed statements of accounts.

Trustee's Administrative Fees for IRA

Trustee's administrative fees that are billed separately and paid by you in connection with your individual retirement arrangement (IRA) are deductible (if they are ordinary and necessary) as a miscellaneous itemized deduction subject to the 2% limit. For more information about IRAs, see chapter 17.

> **TAXSAVER**
>
> Administrative fees paid to IRA trustees are deductible if the fees are billed to, and paid by, the account owner separate from any IRA contribution. If the trustee takes the fee out of your $5,000 contribution, you then have less money remaining in the IRA account for investment. Because the income in the IRA account accumulates tax-free, the difference in these two amounts—the full $5,000 and the remainder of that sum after fees—compounded annually, becomes significant over the years. For example, if in 2014 you are under age 50, you can contribute up to $5,500 to your IRA. If the trustee's administration fee for the year is $500, and is not billed separately from the annual contribution, you will have an IRA contribution deduction of $5,500 but will not have any deduction for the fee charged and the IRA balance will only be increased by the net $5,000 that remains in the account. However, if the fee is billed and paid separately, your IRA contribution deduction will be $5,500 and your miscellaneous itemized deduction will be $500. The full $5,500 contribution will be added to your IRA account to accumulate tax free.

Deductions Not Subject to the 2% Limit

You can deduct the items listed below as miscellaneous itemized deductions. They are not subject to the 2% limit. Report these items on Schedule A (Form 1040), line 28.

List of Deductions

Each of the following items is discussed in detail after the list (except where indicated).
- Amortizable premium on taxable bonds.
- Casualty and theft losses from income-producing property.
- Federal estate tax on income in respect of a decedent.
- Gambling losses up to the amount of gambling winnings.
- Impairment-related work expenses of persons with disabilities.
- Loss from other activities from Schedule K-1 (Form 1065-B), box 2.
- Losses from Ponzi-type investment schemes. See *Losses from Ponzi-type investment schemes* under *Theft* in chapter 26.
- Repayments of more than $3,000 under a claim of right.
- Unrecovered investment in an annuity.

Amortizable Premium on Taxable Bonds

In general, if the amount you pay for a bond is greater than its stated principal amount, the excess is bond premium. You can elect to amortize the premium on taxable bonds. The amortization of the premium is generally an offset to interest income on the bond rather than a separate deduction item.

Part of the premium on some bonds may be a miscellaneous deduction not subject to the 2% limit. For more information, see *Amortizable Premium on Taxable Bonds* in Publication 529, and *Bond Premium Amortization* in chapter 3 of Publication 550, Investment Income and Expenses.

> **TAXORGANIZER**
>
> **Records You Should Keep.** You should keep documentation that shows the date of purchase, face value, and the purchase price of the bond. The types of documents you may want to keep include your broker's confirmation or monthly account statement.

Casualty and Theft Losses of Income-Producing Property

You can deduct a casualty or theft loss as a miscellaneous itemized deduction not subject to the 2% limit if the damaged or stolen property was income-producing property (property held for investment, such as stocks, notes, bonds, gold, silver, vacant lots, and works of art). First, report the loss in Form 4684, Section B. You may also have to include the loss on Form 4797, Sales of Business Property if you are otherwise required to file that form. To figure your deduction, add all casualty or theft losses from this type of property included on Form 4684, lines 32 and 38b, or Form 4797, line 18a. For more information on casualty and theft losses, see chapter 26.

> **TAXALERT**
>
> Some taxpayers had attempted to take the position that losses from stock, which resulted from corporate malfeasance, such as was the case with Enron or WorldCom, could be deducted as theft losses not subject to the 2%-of-AGI disallowance. The IRS has ruled that this position is incorrect. Because there was no direct relationship between shareholders and the executives of these companies there was no "theft." Instead, the losses would have to be claimed as capital losses subject to the $3,000 annual limit on such losses.

Federal Estate Tax on Income in Respect of a Decedent

You can deduct the federal estate tax attributable to income in respect of a decedent that you as a beneficiary include in your gross income. Income in respect of the decedent is gross income that the decedent would have received had death not occurred and that was not properly includible in the decedent's final income tax return. See Publication 559 for more information.

> **TAXALERT**
>
> Distributions to a beneficiary from an IRA or employer pension plan are common forms of income in respect of a decedent. If the decedent's estate owed federal estate tax on these amounts, the beneficiary may be entitled to claim this income tax deduction.

Gambling Losses Up to the Amount of Gambling Winnings

You must report the full amount of your gambling winnings for the year on Form 1040, line 21. You deduct your gambling losses for the year on Schedule A (Form 1040), line 28. You cannot deduct gambling losses that are more than your winnings.

> **TAXORGANIZER**
>
> **Records you should keep.** For specific wagering transactions, you can use the following items to support your winnings and losses:
> *Keno*: Copies of the keno tickets you purchased that were validated by the gambling establishment, copies of your casino credit records, and copies of your casino check-cashing records.
> *Slot machines*: A record of the machine number and all winnings by date and time the machine was played.

Caution

You cannot reduce your gambling winnings by your gambling losses and report the difference. You must report the full amount of your winnings as income and claim your losses (up to the amount of winnings) as an itemized deduction. Therefore, your records should show your winnings separately from your losses.

Records

Diary of winnings and losses. You must keep an accurate diary or similar record of your losses and winnings.

Your diary should contain at least the following information.

- *The date and type of your specific wager or wagering activity.*
- *The name and address or location of the gambling establishment.*
- *The names of other persons present with you at the gambling establishment.*
- *The amount(s) you won or lost.*

See Publication 529 for more information.

> *Table games* (twenty-one [blackjack], craps, poker, baccarat, roulette, wheel of fortune, etc.): The number of the table at which you were playing and casino credit card data indicating whether the credit was issued in the pit or at the cashier's cage.
>
> *Bingo*: A record of the number of games played, cost of tickets purchased, and amounts collected on winning tickets. Supplemental records include any receipts from the casino, parlor, etc.
>
> *Racing* (horse, harness, dog, etc.): A record of the races, amounts of wagers, amounts collected on winning tickets, and amounts lost on losing tickets. Supplemental records include unredeemed tickets and payment records from the racetrack.
>
> *Lotteries*: A record of ticket purchases, dates, winnings, and losses. Supplemental records include unredeemed tickets, payment slips, and winnings statements.

▶ **TAXPLANNER**
The cost of transportation, meals, and lodging related to gambling is not tax deductible.

Impairment-Related Work Expenses

If you have a physical or mental disability that limits your being employed, or substantially limits one or more of your major life activities, such as performing manual tasks, walking, speaking, breathing, learning, and working, you can deduct your impairment-related work expenses.

Impairment-related work expenses are ordinary and necessary business expenses for attendant care services at your place of work and for other expenses in connection with your place of work that are necessary for you to be able to work.

Self-employed. If you are self-employed, enter your impairment-related work expenses on the appropriate form (Schedule C, C-EZ, E, or F) used to report your business income and expenses.

Loss From Other Activities From Schedule K-1 (Form 1065-B), Box 2

If the amount reported in Schedule K-1 (Form 1065-B), box 2, is a loss, report it on Schedule A (Form 1040), line 28. It is not subject to the passive activity limitations.

Repayments Under Claim of Right

If you had to repay more than $3,000 that you included in your income in an earlier year because at the time you thought you had an unrestricted right to it, you may be able to deduct the amount you repaid or take a credit against your tax. See *Repayments* in chapter 12 for more information.

Unrecovered Investment in Annuity

A retiree who contributed to the cost of an annuity can exclude from income a part of each payment received as a tax-free return of the retiree's investment. If the retiree dies before the entire investment is recovered tax free, any unrecovered investment can be deducted on the retiree's final income tax return. See chapter 10 for more information about the tax treatment of pensions and annuities.

Nondeductible Expenses

Examples of nondeductible expenses are listed next. The list is followed by discussions of additional nondeductible expenses.

List of Nondeductible Expenses

- Broker's commissions that you paid in connection with your IRA or other investment property.
- Burial or funeral expenses, including the cost of a cemetery lot.
- Capital expenses.
- Fees and licenses, such as car licenses, marriage licenses, and dog tags.
- Hobby losses, but see *Hobby Expenses*, earlier.
- Home repairs, insurance, and rent.
- Illegal bribes and kickbacks. See *Bribes and kickbacks* in chapter 11 of Publication 535.
- Losses from the sale of your home, furniture, personal car, etc.
- Personal disability insurance premiums.
- Personal, living, or family expenses.
- The value of wages never received or lost vacation time.

Adoption Expenses

You cannot deduct the expenses of adopting a child, but you may be able to take a credit for those expenses. See chapter 37.

Campaign Expenses

You cannot deduct campaign expenses of a candidate for any office, even if the candidate is running for reelection to the office. These include qualification and registration fees for primary elections.

Legal fees. You cannot deduct legal fees paid to defend charges that arise from participation in a political campaign.

Check-Writing Fees on Personal Account

If you have a personal checking account, you cannot deduct fees charged by the bank for the privilege of writing checks, even if the account pays interest.

Club Dues

Generally, you cannot deduct the cost of membership in any club organized for business, pleasure, recreation, or other social purpose. This includes business, social, athletic, luncheon, sporting, airline, hotel, golf, and country clubs.

You cannot deduct dues paid to an organization if one of its main purposes is to:
• Conduct entertainment activities for members or their guests, or
• Provide members or their guests with access to entertainment facilities.
Dues paid to airline, hotel, and luncheon clubs are not deductible.

Commuting Expenses

You cannot deduct commuting expenses (the cost of transportation between your home and your main or regular place of work). If you haul tools, instruments, or other items, in your car to and from work, you can deduct only the additional cost of hauling the items such as the rent on a trailer to carry the items.

EXPLANATION

Commuting to a temporary work site can be a deductible expense. A work assignment is temporary if the individual has the expectation that it will last less than one year, and it actually does last for one year or less. If you have a regular place of business away from home, then travel expenses from home to a temporary work site are deductible, regardless of the distance.

An individual who has no regular place of business outside the home (or a home office), but who works at several locations within a metropolitan area, can deduct travel expenses to a temporary work site outside the metropolitan area. However, many people commute as many as 2 hours or more one way. Therefore, the IRS interpretation of a "metropolitan area" is expanding.

Another increasingly common scenario is an individual who loses his full-time job due to downsizing or outsourcing and subsequently works for several different employers on a part-time basis. This individual has no regular place of business. It is not clear whether his travel to a temporary work site outside the metropolitan area is deductible. A strict interpretation of the rules would indicate that such travel is deductible, because a regular business location is not a consideration. However, the IRS may argue that he has merely extended his personal commute, because he is working for a different employer in each location.

TAXSAVER

If you drive to a location close to home to perform a bona fide job function and then drive to your regular work location, the second leg of the trip is deductible. See chapter 27, *Car expenses and other employee business expenses*, for details.

Example

An accountant drives to the local IRS office to represent clients and then goes to his office downtown later that day. The second leg of his travel is deductible.

TAXORGANIZER

Records you should keep:
- Purchase price of car
- Monthly lease payments on car
- Gas receipts
- Toll receipts
- Receipts for repairs and maintenance
- Log showing the date of the trip, beginning mileage, ending mileage, and purpose of the trip
- Receipts for personal property tax and interest expense on car
  You should keep a written record of expenses and dates incurred to verify deductibility.

Fines or Penalties

You cannot deduct fines or penalties you pay to a governmental unit for violating a law. This includes an amount paid in settlement of your actual or potential liability for a fine or penalty (civil or criminal). Fines or penalties include parking tickets, tax penalties, and penalties deducted from teachers' paychecks after an illegal strike.

EXPLANATION

Although state taxes are deductible when itemizing your deductions, the penalties and interest related to the underpayment or late payment of taxes are not deductible.

Health Spa Expenses

You cannot deduct health spa expenses, even if there is a job requirement to stay in excellent physical condition, such as might be required of a law enforcement officer.

Home Security System

You cannot deduct the cost of a home security system as a miscellaneous deduction. However, you may be able to claim a deduction for a home security system as a business expense if you have a home office. See *Home Office* under *Unreimbursed Employee Expenses*, earlier, and *Security System* under *Deducting Expenses* in Publication 587.

Investment-Related Seminars

You cannot deduct any expenses for attending a convention, seminar, or similar meeting for investment purposes.

Life Insurance Premiums

You cannot deduct premiums you pay on your life insurance. You may be able to deduct, as alimony, premiums you pay on life insurance policies assigned to your former spouse. See chapter 18 for information on alimony.

Lobbying Expenses

You generally cannot deduct amounts paid or incurred for lobbying expenses. These include expenses to:

- Influence legislation,
- Participate or intervene in any political campaign for, or against, any candidate for public office,
- Attempt to influence the general public, or segments of the public, about elections, legislative matters, or referendums, or
- Communicate directly with covered executive branch officials in any attempt to influence the official actions or positions of those officials.

Lobbying expenses also include any amounts paid or incurred for research, preparation, planning, or coordination of any of these activities.

Dues used for lobbying. If a tax-exempt organization notifies you that part of the dues or other amounts you pay to the organization are used to pay nondeductible lobbying expenses, you cannot deduct that part. See *Lobbying Expenses* in Publication 529 for information on exceptions.

Lost or Mislaid Cash or Property

You cannot deduct a loss based on the mere disappearance of money or property. However, an accidental loss or disappearance of property can qualify as a casualty if it results from an identifiable event that is sudden, unexpected, or unusual. See chapter 26.

Example. A car door is accidentally slammed on your hand, breaking the setting of your diamond ring. The diamond falls from the ring and is never found. The loss of the diamond is a casualty.

Lunches with Co-workers

You cannot deduct the expenses of lunches with co-workers, except while traveling away from home on business. See chapter 27 for information on deductible expenses while traveling away from home.

Meals While Working Late

You cannot deduct the cost of meals while working late. However, you may be able to claim a deduction if the cost of meals is a deductible entertainment expense, or if you are traveling away from home. See chapter 27 for information on deductible entertainment expenses and expenses while traveling away from home.

Personal Legal Expenses

You cannot deduct personal legal expenses such as those for the following.

- Custody of children.
- Breach of promise to marry suit.
- Civil or criminal charges resulting from a personal relationship.
- Damages for personal injury, except for certain unlawful discrimination and whistle-blower claims.
- Preparation of a title (or defense or perfection of a title).
- Preparation of a will.
- Property claims or property settlement in a divorce.

You cannot deduct these expenses even if a result of the legal proceeding is the loss of income-producing property.

Political Contributions

You cannot deduct contributions made to a political candidate, a campaign committee, or a newsletter fund. Advertisements in convention bulletins and admissions to dinners or programs that benefit a political party or political candidate are not deductible.

Professional Accreditation Fees

You cannot deduct professional accreditation fees such as the following.

- Accounting certificate fees paid for the initial right to practice accounting.
- Bar exam fees and incidental expenses in securing initial admission to the bar.
- Medical and dental license fees paid to get initial licensing.

Professional Reputation

You cannot deduct expenses of radio and TV appearances to increase your personal prestige or establish your professional reputation.

Relief Fund Contributions

You cannot deduct contributions paid to a private plan that pays benefits to any covered employee who cannot work because of any injury or illness not related to the job.

Residential Telephone Service

You cannot deduct any charge (including taxes) for basic local telephone service for the first telephone line to your residence, even if it is used in a trade or business.

Stockholders' Meetings

You cannot deduct transportation and other expenses you pay to attend stockholders' meetings of companies in which you own stock but have no other interest. You cannot deduct these expenses even if you are attending the meeting to get information that would be useful in making further investments.

EXPLANATION

The courts have allowed deductions for stockholders' meetings when the shareholders' interests are more extensive. Consider the following:

- A shareholder who went to a meeting to present a resolution that management stop diluting shareholder equity was entitled to deduct his travel expenses. (See chapter 27, *Car expenses and other employee business expenses.*)
- A court held that an investor's travel expenses to an investment convention were deductible because (1) the trip was part of a rationally planned, systematic investigation of business operations; (2) the costs were reasonable in relation to the size of the investment and the value of the information expected; (3) there was no disguised personal motive for the trip; and (4) there was evidence of practical application of the information obtained on the trip.
- Nevertheless, if a person owns only a very small interest in a large corporation and cannot reasonably expect that his or her attendance at a stockholders' meeting would affect his or her income or investment, the deduction of travel expenses probably would not be allowed.

Tax-Exempt Income Expenses

You cannot deduct expenses to produce tax-exempt income. You cannot deduct interest on a debt incurred or continued to buy or carry tax-exempt securities.

If you have expenses to produce both taxable and tax-exempt income, but you cannot identify the expenses that produce each type of income, you must divide the expenses based on the amount of each type of income to determine the amount that you can deduct.

Example. During the year, you received taxable interest of $4,800 and tax-exempt interest of $1,200. In earning this income, you had total expenses of $500 during the year. You cannot identify the amount of each expense item that is for each income item. Therefore, 80% ($4,800/$6,000) of the expense is for the taxable interest and 20% ($1,200/$6,000) is for the tax-exempt interest. You can deduct, subject to the 2% limit, expenses of $400 (80% of $500).

Travel Expenses for Another Individual

You generally cannot deduct travel expenses you pay or incur for a spouse, dependent, or other individual who accompanies you (or your employee) on business or personal travel unless the spouse, dependent, or other individual is an employee of the taxpayer, the travel is for a bona fide business purpose, and such expenses would otherwise be deductible by the spouse, dependent, or other individual. See chapter 27 for more information on deductible travel expenses.

Voluntary Unemployment Benefit Fund Contributions

You cannot deduct voluntary unemployment benefit fund contributions you make to a union fund or a private fund. However, you can deduct contributions as taxes if state law requires you to make them to a state unemployment fund that covers you for the loss of wages from unemployment caused by business conditions.

Wristwatches

You cannot deduct the cost of a wristwatch, even if there is a job requirement that you know the correct time to properly perform your duties.

EXPLANATION

The courts have found the following to be nondeductible expenses:

- Amounts paid to guard a personal residence against burglary attempts
- The cost of a home security system installed to protect a collector's stamps and coins. (The IRS reasoned that the activity was an investment activity and not a regular trade or business; consequently, the expense did not meet the home office rules, discussed earlier in this chapter.)
- Payments for general advice pertaining to a family trust
- Legal fees for defending a libel suit arising from the purchase of the taxpayer's residence

TAXALERT

The cost of specific legal advice on the disposition of a stock is not deductible as a miscellaneous expense on Schedule A but must be treated as a selling expense and an increase to your basis.

TAXORGANIZER

Records you should keep:

- Legal fees itemizing services performed
- Tax preparation fees that allocate amounts between Schedules A, C, and E
- Financial account statements that indicate investment fees
- Logs substantiating the use of property (i.e., a home computer, an automobile) for both business and personal purposes
- Home office expenses and the calculation to allocate total expenses between business and personal use
- Evidence of job search expenses
- For miscellaneous deductions, taxpayers' records should demonstrate (1) why the expense is deductible due to its relationship to the production or collection of income or the determination of tax, and (2) that the expense is clearly incurred in support of that deductible purpose

Chapter 30
Limit on itemized deductions

ey.com/EYTaxGuide

Introduction
The tax law limits the amount of certain itemized deductions that individuals can use to reduce their taxable income. For example, the threshold for deducting medical and dental expenses is 10% of adjusted gross income (7.5% if you or your spouse are age 65 or older by the end of the taxable year) (AGI) (see chapter 22, *Medical and dental expenses*), certain miscellaneous deductions are limited to those in excess of 2% of adjusted gross income (see chapter 29, *Miscellaneous deductions*), and home mortgage interest expense is subject to various limitations (see chapter 24, *Interest expense*).

Congress has placed an additional "overall" limitation on the deductibility of a certain group of itemized deductions. Itemized deductions that are subject to this limitation include taxes, home mortgage interest, charitable contributions, and most miscellaneous itemized deductions. Medical expenses, casualty and theft losses, investment interest expense, and deductible gambling losses are not subject to this rule.

For 2014, the total of this group of deductions must be reduced by 3% of the amount of your adjusted gross income in excess of $254,200 for individual filers, $279,650 for heads of households, $305,050 if married filing jointly or a surviving spouse, and $152,525 if married filing separately. This limitation is applied after you have used any other limitations that exist in the law, such as the adjusted gross income limitation for charitable contributions and the mortgage interest expense limitations. No more than 80% of the otherwise allowable deductions are phased out. The threshold amounts are indexed annually for inflation.

This chapter discusses the overall limit on itemized deductions on Schedule A (Form 1040). The following topics are included.
- Who is subject to the limit.
- Which itemized deductions are limited.
- How to figure the limit.

Useful Items
You may want to see:

Forms (and Instructions)
□ **Schedule A (Form 1040)**   Itemized Deductions

Are You Subject to the Limit?
You are subject to the limit on certain itemized deductions if your adjusted gross income (AGI) is more than $305,050 if married filing jointly or qualifying widow(er), $279,650 if head of household, $254,200 if single, or $152,525 if married filing separately. Your AGI is the amount on Form 1040, line 38.

Which Itemized Deductions Are Limited?
The following Schedule A (Form 1040) deductions are subject to the overall limit on itemized deductions.
- Taxes paid—line 9
- Interest paid—lines 10, 11, 12, and 13
- Gifts to charity—line 19
- Job expenses and certain miscellaneous deductions—line 27
- Other miscellaneous deductions—line 28, excluding gambling and casualty or theft losses.

Which Itemized Deductions Are Not Limited?
The following Schedule A (Form 1040) deductions are not subject to the overall limit on itemized deductions. However, they are still subject to other applicable limits.
- Medical and dental expenses—line 4.
- Investment interest expense—line 14.

- Casualty and theft losses of personal use property—line 20.
- Casualty and theft losses of income-producing property—line 28.
- Gambling losses—line 28.

EXPLANATION

Whether a particular deduction will be limited or not depends on the character of the deduction.

Example 1

Martin and Judy Stone file a joint income tax return in 2014. They have an adjusted gross income of $450,000. The Stones' only itemized deductions are $20,000 of home mortgage interest and $8,000 of real estate taxes. Because both of these itemized deductions are subject to the limitation, their total deductions of $28,000 must be reduced by 3% of $144,950 (the amount by which AGI exceeds $305,050), or $4,349. They may reduce their taxable income by total itemized deductions of $23,651 ($28,000 – $4,349).

Example 2

Assume the same facts as above, except that the Stones live in a downtown apartment, and their only itemized deduction is $28,000 of otherwise allowable investment interest expense. Because investment interest expense is not subject to the 3% limitation, the entire $28,000 will be deductible.

How Do You Figure the Limit?

If your itemized deductions are subject to the limit, the total of all your itemized deductions is reduced by the smaller of:

- 80% of your itemized deductions that are affected by the limit. See *Which Itemized Deductions Are Limited*, earlier, or
- 3% of the amount by which your AGI exceeds $305,050 if married filing jointly or qualifying widow(er), $279,650 if head of household, $254,200 if single, or $152,525 if married filing separately.

Before you figure the overall limit on itemized deductions, you first must complete Schedule A (Form 1040), lines 1 through 28, including any related forms (such as Form 2106, Form 4684, etc.).

The overall limit on itemized deductions is figured after you have applied any other limit on the allowance of any itemized deduction. These other limits include charitable contribution limits (chapter 25), the limit on certain meal and entertainment expenses (chapter 27), and the 2%-of-adjusted-gross-income limit on certain miscellaneous deductions (chapter 29).

Itemized Deductions Worksheet. After you have completed Schedule A (Form 1040) through line 28, you can use the Itemized Deductions Worksheet in the Instructions for Schedule A (Form 1040) to figure your limit. Enter the result on Schedule A (Form 1040), line 29. Keep the worksheet for your records.

Example

For tax year 2014, Bill and Terry Willow are filing a joint return on Form 1040. Their adjusted gross income on line 38 is $325,500. Their Schedule A itemized deductions are as follows:

Taxes paid—line 9	$17,900
Interest paid—lines 10, 11, 12, and 13	45,000
Investment interest expense—line 14	41,000
Gifts to charity—line 19	21,000
Job expenses—line 27	17,240
Total	**$142,140**

The Willows' investment interest expense deduction ($41,000 from Schedule A (Form 1040), line 14) is not subject to the overall limit on itemized deductions. The Willows use the Itemized Deductions Worksheet in the Schedule A (Form 1040) instructions to figure their overall limit. Of their $142,140 total itemized deductions, the Willows can deduct only $141,526 ($142,140 – $614). They enter $141,526 on Schedule A (Form 1040), line 29.

TAXPLANNER
Calculating the 3% limitation. In certain situations, it is possible for the 3% limitation to reduce allowable itemized deductions below the standard deduction amount. You should consider this possibility when you are choosing whether to itemize your deductions or to use the standard deduction.

Example
Arthur and Karen White have adjusted gross income of $380,500. They have no mortgage on their home; however, they pay annual real estate taxes of $9,500. Each year they contribute $3,500 to their favorite charity. The Whites would compute their taxable income as follows:

Adjusted gross income	$380,500
Itemized deductions	
Real estate taxes	$9,500
Charitable contributions	3,500
Total	$13,000
Less 3% of AGI in excess of $305,050	2,264
Allowable itemized deductions $10,736	
Standard deduction if married, filing a joint return	$12,400
Greater of standard deduction or allowable itemized deductions	(12,400)
Personal Exemptions	(3,002)
Taxable Income	$365,098

Note: The personal exemptions have been reduced according to the phase-out rules discussed in chapter 3, *Personal exemptions and dependents.*

TAXALERT
You can elect to deduct state and local general sales taxes instead of state and local income taxes as an itemized deduction (see chapter 24, *Taxes you may deduct,* for details). Similar to state and local income taxes, state and local general sales taxes are also subject to the "overall itemized deduction limitation."

TAXPLANNER
Bunching. If your itemized deductions are subject to this 3% limitation, you may want to consider a technique called "bunching." Bunching is effective if you are able to accumulate deductions so that they are high in one year and low in the next. Bunching your itemized deductions so that they are higher in one year can help you take advantage of those itemized deductions if the limitation would normally cause the standard deduction to be higher.

Example
Assume the same facts as in the previous example. This time, however, the Whites are able to postpone payment of their 2014 real estate taxes until January 2015, and they can also pay $2,500 of their $3,500 charitable contributions in early 2015. Then next year, in December 2015, they will *accelerate* these payments to make sure that they fall in 2015 and not 2016. The Whites will end up with the following expenses for 2014 and 2015:

	2014	2015
2014 Real estate taxes	–	$9,500
2014 Charitable contributions	1,000	2,500
2015 Real estate taxes	–	$9,500
2015 Charitable contributions	–	3,500
Total	$1,000	$25,000

    By bunching the expenses, the Whites may use the $12,400 standard deduction in 2014 and itemized deductions of $22,736 ($25,000 less the 3% limit of $2,264) in 2015. Total deductions equal $35,136 for the two years ($12,400 + $22,736). In 2015, they will have reduced their taxable income by an additional $10,336 ($22,736 – $12,400). Without bunching, the Whites would have been limited to the standard deduction in each year. (These calculations assume that the standard deduction and the itemized deduction limit will not change in 2015.)

Part 6
Figuring your taxes and credits

ey.com/EYTaxGuide

The seven chapters in this part explain how to figure your tax and how to figure the tax of certain children who have more than $2,000 of investment income. They also discuss tax credits that, unlike deductions, are subtracted directly from your tax and reduce your tax, dollar for dollar. Chapter 37 discusses a wide variety of other credits, such as the adoption credit and the earned income credit.

Chapter 31
How to figure your tax

Note

IRS Publication 17 (*Your Federal Income Tax*) has been updated by Ernst & Young LLP for 2014. Dates and dollar amounts shown are for 2014. Underlined type is used to indicate where IRS text has been updated. Places where text has been removed are indicated by the sentence: *Text intentionally omitted*.

ey.com/EYTaxGuide

Ernst & Young LLP will update the *EY Tax Guide 2015* website with relevant taxpayer information as it becomes available. You can also sign up for email alerts to let you know when changes have been made.

Introduction

This chapter explains how to calculate your tax liability under all three available tax forms–Form 1040EZ, Form 1040A, and Form 1040. It will help you decide which of the forms to file.

In particular, you should review the section of this chapter on the alternative minimum tax to determine if that tax may apply to you.

What's New

Personal exemption amount increased for 2014. For tax years beginning in 2014, the personal exemption amount is increased to $3,950.

Standard deduction amount increased for 2014. The personal standard deduction amount for tax years beginning in 2014 is increased to $6,200 for unmarried taxpayers, $12,400 if married filing jointly or surviving spouse, $9,100 if head of household, and $6,200 if married filing separately.

Alternative Minimum Tax (AMT) exemption amount increased. For 2014, the exemption amounts for AMT are increased to $52,800 for unmarried taxpayers, $82,100 if married filing jointly or a surviving spouse, and $41,050 if married filing separately.

AMT exemption for a child with unearned income increased. The AMT exemption for a child whose unearned income is taxed at the parent's rate has increased to $7,250.

TAXALERT

In recent years, Congress has repeatedly enacted temporary measures (typically called an "AMT patch") that significantly raised the applicable exemption amounts above the level that last applied in 2000. The American Taxpayer Relief Act of 2012 enacted a permanent AMT patch and indexed it for inflation in future years. For 2014, the AMT exemption is:

- $82,100 (up from $80,800 in 2013) for married couples filing jointly and surviving spouses;
- $52,800 (up from $51,900 in 2013) for other unmarried individuals; and
- $41,050 (up from $40,400 in 2013) for married individuals filing separate returns.

The exemption phases out at higher levels of alternative minimum taxable income (AMTI). A taxpayer's exemption amount is reduced (but not below zero) by 25 percent of the amount by which AMTI exceeds the following:

1. For married taxpayers filing jointly or a surviving spouse, $156,500
2. For a taxpayer filing as single or as a head of household, $117,300
3. For a married taxpayer filing a separate return, $78,250

The exemptions fully phase out at: $484,900 of AMTI for married couples filing jointly and surviving spouses; $328,500 for other unmarried individuals; and $242,450 for married individuals filing separately. Those taxpayers with AMTI in the above phase-out income ranges can be subject to a marginal tax rate of as high as 27% (20% top statutory rate plus 7%, which is one-fourth of the 28 percent AMT rate) on capital gains and qualified dividends.

Individual Shared Responsibility Payment. When you file your 2014 federal income tax return in 2015, you will report minimum essential health care coverage, report exemptions, or make any individual shared responsibility payment. If you don't have coverage nor qualify for an exemption, you may have to make an individual shared responsibility payment when you file your 2014 income tax return. For 2014, generally, the payment amount is the greater of 1% of your household income above your filing threshold or $95 per adult ($47.50 per child) limited to a family maximum of $285. See Individual Shared Responsibility Provision—Calculating the Payment later in this chapter.

After you have figured your income and deductions as explained in *Parts One* through *Five*, your next step is to figure your tax. This chapter discusses:

- The general steps you take to figure your tax,
- An additional tax you may have to pay called the alternative minimum tax (AMT), and
- The conditions you must meet if you want the IRS to figure your tax.

TAXPLANNER

As described later in more detail in the Tax Alert on "*How the AMT works*," the AMT structure requires taxpayers to "add back" certain preference and adjustment items to arrive at AMT income, subject to tax at the 26% or 28% minimum tax rates. Under prior law, one of the preference items was tax-exempt interest on certain bonds issued for private activities.

Tax legislation enacted in 2009, however, provides that interest received on tax-exempt private activity bonds issued in 2009 and 2010 is not an AMT preference item. You should consult with your investment advisor to see how the new provision may have affected the interest rate on private activity bonds issued during this 2-year period (issuers may have been able to issue bonds with a somewhat lower interest rate than they otherwise would have had to do when interest paid was treated as a preference item), as well as the effect on market pricing for new and previously issued bonds. Interest received on private activity bonds issued prior to 2009 and after 2010 is counted as an AMT preference.

Figuring Your Tax

Your income tax is based on your taxable income. After you figure your income tax and AMT, if any, subtract your tax credits and add any other taxes you may owe. The result is your total tax. Compare your total tax with your total payments to determine whether you are entitled to a refund or if you must make a payment.

This section provides a general outline of how to figure your tax. You can find step-by-step directions in the Instructions for Forms 1040EZ, 1040A, and 1040. If you are unsure of which tax form you should file, see *Which Form Should I Use?* in chapter 1.

Tax. Most taxpayers use either the Tax Table or the Tax Computation Worksheet to figure their income tax. However, there are special methods if your income includes any of the following items.

- A net capital gain. (See chapter 16.)
- Qualified dividends taxed at the same rates as a net capital gain. (See chapters 8 and 16.)
- Lump-sum distributions. (See chapter 10.)
- Farming or fishing income. (See Schedule J (Form 1040), Income Averaging for Farmers and Fishermen.)
- Unearned income over $2,000 for certain children. (See chapter 32.)
- Parents' election to report child's interest and dividends. (See chapter 32.)
- Foreign earned income exclusion or the housing exclusion. (See Form 2555, Foreign Earned Income, or Form 2555-EZ, Foreign Earned Income Exclusion, and the Foreign Earned Income Tax Worksheet in the Form 1040 instructions.)

Credits. After you figure your income tax and any AMT (discussed later), determine if you are eligible for any tax credits. Eligibility information for these tax credits is discussed in chapters 33 through 37 and your form instructions. The following table lists the credits you may be able to subtract from your tax and shows where you can find more information on each credit.

CREDITS

For information on:	See chapter:
Adoption	37
	37
Child and dependent care	33
Child tax	35
Credit to holders of tax credit bonds	37
Education	36
Elderly or disabled	34
Foreign tax	37
Mortgage interest	37
Prior year minimum tax	37
Residential energy	37
Retirement savings contributions	37

TAXSAVER

The tax law provides for certain nonrefundable personal tax credits. Nonrefundable personal credits are allowed to the extent of the full amount of the individual's regular tax and alternative minimum tax. These credits include the dependent care credit, the credit for the elderly and disabled, the adoption credit, the child tax credit, the credit for interest on certain home mortgages, the Lifetime Learning and American Opportunity credits (except for the refundable portion of the American Opportunity credit), the savers credit for elective deferrals and IRA contributions by certain individuals, and the credit for residential energy efficient property and the credits for plug-in electric drive motor, alternative motor vehicles, and hydrogen refueling property. These credits are described in the section on *Nonrefundable Credits*, in chapter 37, *Other credits including the earned income credit*.

Some credits (such as the earned income credit) are not listed because they are treated as payments. See *Payments*, later.

There are other credits that are not discussed in this publication. These include the following credits.

- General business credit, which is made up of several separate business-related credits. These generally are reported on Form 3800, General Business Credit, and are discussed in chapter 4 of Publication 334, Tax Guide for Small Business.
- Renewable electricity, refined coal, and Indian coal production credit for electricity and refined coal produced at facilities placed in service after October 22, 2004 (after October 2, 2008, for electricity produced from marine and hydrokinetic renewables), and Indian coal produced at facilities placed in service after August 8, 2005. See Form 8835, Part II.
- *Text intentionally omitted.*
- Credit for employer social security and Medicare taxes paid on certain employee tips. See Form 8846.

Other taxes. After you subtract your tax credits, determine whether there are any other taxes you must pay. This chapter does not explain these other taxes. You can find that information in other chapters of this publication and your form instructions. See the following table for other taxes you may need to add to your income tax.

OTHER TAXES

For information on:	See chapter:
Additional taxes on qualified retirement plans and IRAs	10, 17
Household employment taxes	33
Recapture of an education credit	36
Social security and Medicare tax on wages	5
Social security and Medicare tax on tips	6
Uncollected social security and Medicare tax on tips	6

You also may have to pay AMT (discussed later in this chapter).

There are other taxes that are not discussed in this publication. These include the following items.

1. *Self-employment tax.* You must figure this tax if either of the following applies to you (or your spouse if you file a joint return).

   a. Your net earnings from self-employment from other than church employee income were $400 or more. The term "net earnings from self-employment" may include certain non-employee compensation and other amounts reported to you on Form 1099-MISC, Miscellaneous Income. If you received a Form 1099-MISC, see the *Instructions for Recipient* on the back. Also see the Instructions for Schedule SE (Form 1040), Self-Employment Tax; and Publication 334, Tax Guide for Small Business.

   b. You had church employee income of $108.28 or more.

   Text intentionally omitted.

2. *Recapture taxes.* You may have to pay these taxes if you previously claimed an investment credit, a low-income housing credit, a new markets credit, a qualified plug-in electric drive motor vehicle credit, an alternative motor vehicle credit, a credit for employer-provided child care facilities, an Indian employment credit, or other credits listed in the instructions for Form 1040, line 62. For more information, see the instructions for Form 1040, line 62.

3. *Section 72(m)(5) excess benefits tax.* If you are (or were) a 5% owner of a business and you received a distribution that exceeds the benefits provided for you under the qualified pension or annuity plan formula, you may have to pay this additional tax. See *Tax on Excess Benefits* in chapter 4 of Publication 560, Retirement Plans for Small Business.

4. *Uncollected social security and Medicare tax on group-term life insurance.* If your former employer provides you with more than $50,000 of group-term life insurance coverage, you must pay the employee part of social security and Medicare taxes on those premiums. The amount should be shown in box 12 of your Form W-2 with codes M and N.

5. *Tax on golden parachute payments.* This tax applies if you received an "excess parachute payment" (EPP) due to a change in a corporation's ownership or control. The amount should be shown in box 12 of your Form W-2 with code K. See the instructions for Form 1040, line 60.

6. *Tax on accumulation distribution of trusts.* This applies if you are the beneficiary of a trust that accumulated its income instead of distributing it currently. See Form 4970 and its instructions.

7. *Additional tax on HSAs or MSAs.* If amounts contributed to, or distributed from, your health savings account or medical savings account do not meet the rules for these accounts, you may have to pay additional taxes. See Publication 969, Health Savings Accounts and Other Tax-Favored Health Plans; Form 8853, Archer MSAs and Long-Term Care Insurance Contracts; Form 8889, Health Savings Accounts (HSAs); and Form 5329, Additional Taxes on Qualified Plans (Including IRAs) and Other Tax-Favored Accounts.

8. *Additional tax on Coverdell ESAs.* This applies if amounts contributed to, or distributed from, your Coverdell ESA do not meet the rules for these accounts. See Publication 970, Tax Benefits for Education, and Form 5329.

9. *Additional tax on qualified tuition programs.* This applies to amounts distributed from qualified tuition programs that do not meet the rules for these accounts. See Publication 970 and Form 5329.

10. *Excise tax on insider stock compensation from an expatriated corporation.* You may owe a 15% excise tax on the value of nonstatutory stock options and certain other stock-based compensation held by you or a member of your family from an expatriated corporation or its expanded affiliated group in which you were an officer, director, or more-than-10% owner. For more information, see the instructions for Form 1040, line 62.

11. *Additional tax on income you received from a nonqualified deferred compensation plan that fails to meet certain requirements.* This income should be shown in Form W-2, box 12, with code Z, or in Form 1099-MISC, box 15b. For more information, see the instructions for Form 1040, line 62.

12. *Interest on the tax due on installment income from the sale of certain residential lots and timeshares.* For more information, see the instructions for Form 1040, line 62.

13. *Interest on the deferred tax on gain from certain installment sales with a sales price over $150,000.* For more information, see the instructions for Form 1040, line 62 and Publication 537, *Installment Sales*.

14. *Excess advance premium tax credit repayment.* For more information, see the instructions for Form 8962.

Payments. After you determine your total tax, figure the total payments you have already made for the year. Include credits that are treated as payments. This chapter does not explain these payments and credits. You can find that information in other chapters of this publication and your form instructions. See the following table for amounts you can include in your total payments.

PAYMENTS

For information on:	See chapter:
Child tax credit (additional)	35
Earned income credit	37
Estimated tax paid	4
Excess social security and RRTA tax withheld	37
Federal income tax withheld	4
Health coverage tax credit	37
Credit for tax on undistributed capital gain	37
Refundable credit for prior year minimum tax	37
Tax paid with extension	1

Another credit that is treated as a payment is the credit for federal excise tax paid on fuels. This credit is for persons who have a nontaxable use of certain fuels, such as diesel fuel and kerosene. It is claimed on Form 1040, line 72. See Form 4136, Credit for Federal Tax Paid on Fuels.

Refund or balance due. To determine whether you are entitled to a refund or whether you must make a payment, compare your total payments with your total tax. If you are entitled to a refund, see your form instructions for information on having it directly deposited into one or more of your accounts, or to purchase U.S. savings bonds instead of receiving a paper check.

TAXPLANNER
You can elect to have your refund directly deposited into a traditional IRA, Roth IRA, or SEP-IRA, but not a SIMPLE IRA. You must establish the IRA at a bank or other financial institution before you request direct deposit.
- Caution: The amount of any refund you choose to deposit into your IRA cannot, in combination with any other IRA contributions you have made, exceed the applicable annual limit on your IRA contributions. See *How much can be contributed* in chapter 17, *Individual retirement arrangements (IRAs)*, for further details.
- Caution: Any deposits into your IRA made on or before April 15, 2015, may be attributed to calendar year 2014 or 2015. Deposits made after April 15, 2015, may only be attributed to calendar year 2015. If you chose to deposit your 2014 refund directly into an IRA and your refund is deposited in the IRA after April 15, 2015, it will be attributed to calendar year 2015 and may result in an underfunding in 2014 or an overfunding in 2015. The determination of when the contribution to the IRA is made is when the money is deposited in the IRA account, not the date when you file your return directing the refund into the IRA account.

EXPLANATION
For information on how to elect to pay your 2014 tax in installments, see *Amount You Owe* in chapter 1, *Filing information*.

Alternative Minimum Tax
This section briefly discusses an additional tax you may have to pay.

The tax law gives special treatment to some kinds of income and allows special deductions and credits for some kinds of expenses. Taxpayers who benefit from this special treatment may have to pay at least a minimum amount of tax through an additional tax called AMT.

TAXALERT

Begun in 1970, the AMT was originally intended to ensure the "rich" paid at least some minimum amount of tax. Until recently the vast majority of taxpayers were not subject to the AMT. But the reduction in regular income tax rates in 2001 and 2003 without a corresponding reduction in AMT rates caused more people to become subject to this tax.

How the AMT works: The simplest way to understand the AMT is to think of it as a separate tax system with its own allowable deductions and exclusions, many of which are different from those allowed for regular income tax purposes. Thus, although it is in many ways parallel to the "regular income tax" computation, some of the applicable rules are different. You first calculate your regular income tax as you always have, then you calculate your tax under the AMT system and pay the greater of the two amounts. The following are some of the more common items treated differently under the two tax systems that can affect your exposure to AMT:

- State and local income and sales taxes
- Real estate and personal property taxes
- Miscellaneous itemized deductions that exceed the 2% of AGI floor
- Interest expense from a mortgage or home equity loan that is not used for the purpose of acquiring, constructing, or improving a principal residence or "second home"
- The "spread" on the exercise of incentive stock options (ISOs)
- Deductions for personal exemptions
- The standard deduction

Most of these items consist of deductions that are allowed in computing your regular income tax liability but are not allowed when you figure your AMT. Take, for example, state and local income, sales, and real estate taxes that you pay. They are allowable as a deduction against your income for regular tax purposes but not for AMT. (You'll find a more detailed explanation of how to figure your AMT later in this section.)

TAXALERT

If your deduction for state taxes is unusually high—for example, perhaps you made a large payment with your 2013 state tax return when you filed in April 2014, or perhaps you have substantial state tax withholding during 2014 on your regular income—you should take a closer look at the possibility of being subject to the AMT.

Example

The Smiths have two children and gross wages totaling $250,000. Their itemized deductions consist of state and local income taxes and real estate taxes totaling $22,500 and mortgage interest of $20,000 (all related to the acquisition of their principal residence). Assume the Smiths have no interest, dividend, or capital gain income. Their regular tax will be $40,923. However, since their AMT tentative minimum tax is $43,232, the Smith's will pay the higher of the two taxes effectively denying them some of their deductions for taxes paid and personal exemptions. On the Smith's Form 1040, they will report $40,923 in regular tax and $2,309 in AMT.

TAXPLANNER

The AMT can not only affect the amount of tax you pay, but it can also potentially affect the most tax-efficient way to invest your money.

For example, if part of your investment portfolio consists of municipal bond holdings, beware. Interest paid on private activity bonds issued before 2009 and after 2010 is a preference item that can make it more likely that you will be subject to AMT. Generally, you earn a higher yield on such private activity bonds than other municipals. However, if you're subject to the AMT, your effective yield on these bonds will be slashed. If you're not sure what type of municipal bonds you have, ask your investment advisor. On the other hand, a tax law enacted in early 2009 provides that interest received on tax-exempt private activity bonds issued in 2009 and 2010 is not an AMT preference item. In 2014, long-term capital gains and qualifying dividends are subject to the same maximum rate, 20%, for AMT purposes as they are for regular tax purposes. But because these items of income are included in AMTI, which could reduce your allowable AMT exemption, the actual marginal AMT rate could be as high as 27%. Before deciding to invest in securities that generate these types of income, you should consider the effect of the AMT. In 2014 and beyond, tax and investment planning is further complicated for higher income taxpayers by the recent increases in the top tax rates on ordinary taxable income to 39.6% and on qualified dividends and net capital gains to 20%, as well as the additional 3.8% Net Investment Income Tax (NIIT) on certain Net Investment Income (NII) that was enacted as part of the Affordable Care Act.

Example

Consider the Smiths again in the earlier example. Assume that in addition to their other income ($250,000 in gross wages), the Smiths had a long-term capital gain from the sale of some stock investments in 2014 of $50,000. At first blush, you might expect that their federal tax bill would increase by about $7,500 (15% long-term capital gain rate on $50,000, given the Smith's taxable income and assuming no state income tax). However, because they are subject to AMT, the additional tax burden is actually $10,750. In addition, due to their income level, the 3.8% NIIT on NII applies, which increases their tax bill by $1,900 ($50,000 times 3.8%).

This estimate does not include any additional state income tax. Considering that most states do impose income taxes on capital gains, the Smiths would be liable for additional state tax. If, say, the Smiths lived in a state with an 8% tax rate, after taking into account the state tax itself, there would be a total of $16,650 of federal and state income taxes (or a combined effective tax rate of 33.3%) attributable to a long-term gain of $50,000!

You may have to pay the AMT if your taxable income for regular tax purposes, combined with certain adjustments and tax preference items, is more than a certain amount. See Form 6251, Alternative Minimum Tax—Individuals.

EXPLANATION

Individuals, trusts, and estates must pay the alternative minimum tax (AMT) if it exceeds their regular tax liability for the year. The amount subject to the AMT will be determined by adding a number of preference items to your taxable income and making various adjustments to your regular taxable income. This amount is reduced by the exemption amounts, and the balance is subject to the following AMT rates:

Rate	Married filing separately	All other filers
26%	Up to $91,250 over exemption amount	Up to $182,500 over exemption amount.
28%	Greater than $91,250 over exemption amount	Greater than $182,500 over exemption amount

		Exemption Amount	
Filing Status	Base amount	Less 25% of the amount by which AMTI* exceeds	
Single	$52,800	$117,300	
Married filing jointly & surviving spouses	$82,100	$156,500	
Married filing separately,	$41,050	$78,250	

*Alternative minimum taxable income.

TAXPLANNER

The chart below should provide you with a better understanding of whether you might be affected by the AMT. Look at where your taxable income falls—then see how much you would need to have in preferences and adjustments (state and local taxes, personal exemptions, miscellaneous itemized deductions, standard deduction, etc.) to see whether you'd be subject to the AMT. For example, say your taxable income is $300,000, claim four personal exemptions at $3,950 each ($15,800 in total), and take the standard deduction of $12,400. Your total preferences are $28,200 and you'd be subject to the AMT.

Regular taxable income	Adjustments & preferences needed to trigger AMT	Adjustments & preferences needed to trigger AMT
	Joint, 4 exemptions	Single, 1 exemption
$50,000	41,200	25,206
100,000	20,049	22,136
150,000	15,176	15,191
200,000	5,754	8,806
300,000	0*	4,714

*At this income level, no additional adjustments would be needed to trigger AMT.

Analysis assumes ordinary income, no capital gains or qualifying dividends.

Adjustments and tax preference items. The more common adjustments and tax preference items include:

- Addition of personal exemptions,
- Addition of the standard deduction (if claimed),
- Addition of itemized deductions claimed for state and local taxes, certain interest, most miscellaneous deductions, and part of medical expenses if age 65 or older,
- Subtraction of any refund of state and local taxes included in gross income,
- Changes to accelerated depreciation of certain property,
- Difference between gain or loss on the sale of property reported for regular tax purposes and AMT purposes,
- Addition of certain income from incentive stock options,
- Change in certain passive activity loss deductions,
- Addition of certain depletion that is more than the adjusted basis of the property,
- Addition of part of the deduction for certain intangible drilling costs, and
- Addition of tax-exempt interest on certain private activity bonds.

- Investment interest is deductible to the extent of net investment income that is adjusted for amounts relating to tax-exempt interest earned on certain private-activity bonds.
- Home mortgage interest is allowed as a deduction for AMT purposes. However, the definition of such interest is narrower than that of "qualified residence interest" for regular tax purposes. Refinanced home mortgage interest that is applicable to any mortgage in excess of the outstanding mortgage before refinancing is not deductible unless the excess was used for home improvements.
- No deduction is allowed for miscellaneous itemized deductions subject to the 2%-of-adjusted-gross-income limit.

6. No deduction is allowed for the standard deduction.
7. Circulation expenditures and research/experimental costs must be amortized over 3- and 10-year periods, respectively. (There would be no AMT adjustment if the circulation expenditures and research costs are amortized and the deduction is not taken in full for regular tax purposes.)
8. Deductions for passive losses from a tax shelter farm activity are denied, except to the extent that the taxpayer is insolvent or the activity is disposed of during the year.
9. Rules limiting passive loss deductions also apply to the AMT, except that (a) otherwise disallowed losses are reduced by the amount by which the taxpayer is insolvent, and (b) all AMT adjustments and preferences are taken into consideration in computing income and/or losses from passive activities.
10. Adjustments passed through to the beneficiary of an estate or trust (i.e., the difference between amounts included in income for regular tax purposes and the AMT income shown on Schedule K-1) must be taken into account in the calculation of AMT.
11. For property disposed of during the year, the gain or loss is refigured to take into consideration the impact that AMT adjustments, such as depreciation, have on the taxpayer's basis in the property.
12. For partners in partnerships and shareholders in S corporations, the income or loss is refigured to take into account AMT adjustments.
13. In exercising an incentive stock option (ISO), the taxpayer needs to adjust for the difference between the option price and the fair market value at the time the option is exercised. In calculating the AMT gain or loss on the subsequent sale of the ISO stock, the AMT basis in the stock is the sum of the option price paid and the AMT adjustment included in alternative minimum taxable income when the ISO was exercised.

TAXALERT

Adjustment for medical expenses. Beginning in 2013, taxpayers under age 65 are only allowed to deduct medical and dental expenses in calculating taxable income for both regular tax and AMT purposes that are more than 10% of their adjusted gross income (AGI). Before 2013, these expenses were deductible for regular tax purposes to the extent that they exceeded 7.5% of AGI.

Through 2016, the 7.5% limit for regular tax purposes continues to apply if you or your spouse are age 65 and over by the end of the year. On the other hand, for alternative minimum tax (AMT) purposes, medical expenses are deductible only to the extent that they exceed 10% of AGI, regardless of your age. Accordingly, taxpayers who were eligible for the 7.5%-of-AGI threshold for regular tax will need to adjust their taxable income subject to AMT for the higher 10%-of-AGI threshold that applies for AMT. In other words, the AMT preference is the lesser of (a) the amount of deductible medical expenses in excess of the 7.5% limit, or (b) 2.5% of your AGI.

Beginning in 2017, the medical and dental expenses for all taxpayers is scheduled to be increased to a 10% limit. When this occurs, there will no longer be an adjustment for AMT.

TAXALERT

Incentive stock options present a unique AMT trap. While the "spread"—the difference between the fair market value of the stock at the time the option is exercised and the exercise price—is not taxable for regular tax purposes, it is for the AMT. The larger the "spread," the more likely you will be liable for AMT.

In addition, you compute your "basis" (generally the amount you paid) for stock bought with incentive stock options one way for regular tax purposes and another way for figuring your AMT. Your basis for regular tax purposes will generally be the exercise price of the options. The basis for AMT will usually be the fair market value of the shares when exercised, assuming you held the shares more than one year from the date you exercised your option. Figuring your basis is more complicated if you sell the shares within a year of exercising your options. You should consult your tax advisor.

If matters weren't complicated enough, the amount of AMT attributable to an incentive stock option can be credited against your regular tax liability in a future year. So, should your regular tax liability exceed your AMT tax calculation in a subsequent year, you can apply the credit against the difference between the two.

Example

In 2014 Martin and Fern Burns have $125,000 of ordinary income and $18,000 of itemized deductions—$1,500 of state income taxes, $1,500 of real estate taxes, and $15,000 of mortgage interest. They have no dependents. Their regular tax would be $16,494. They would not be subject to the AMT since that amount ($7,254) would be less than their regular tax.

Now suppose that in 2014 Fern exercised 5,000 incentive stock options (ISOs) that had an exercise price of $10 a share and that the stock was worth $45 a share at the time of exercise. That results in a total spread of $175,000 (5,000 × $35) that has to be added back in calculating AMT. The Burns' gross AMT for 2014 would be $62,157, an additional tax of $45,663. But all is not lost. Since the additional $45,663 in AMT liability was a result of the ISO exercise, that amount can be carried forward to a future year and credited against their tax to the extent their regular tax exceeds their AMT in that future year.

Let's say that in 2016 Fern sells the stock she got from the ISO exercise for $50 a share. The basis of the stock for regular tax purposes is $10 a share, so she has a regular long-term capital gain of $200,000 (5,000 × $40). But her basis for AMT purposes is $45 a share—the value of the stock on the date of exercise—for an AMT long-term capital gain of $25,000 (5,000 × $5). So in calculating her AMT in 2016 she would reflect a negative adjustment on Form 6251 of $175,000.

Explanation

The law provides a credit against the regular tax for all or a portion of the AMT you paid in previous years. The credit is the AMT attributable to deferral, rather than exclusion, items. Deferral items, such as accelerated depreciation or the spread on incentive stock option (ISO), are those that have the effect of reducing your regular taxable income relative to alternative minimum taxable income in early years, but the situation reverses over time. Thus, the same total of deductions is eventually allowed under both tax systems.

When you pay AMT as a result of deferral preferences or adjustments, the law gives you a credit that can be used to reduce your regular tax liability in the future. This avoids double taxation on the same income. Exclusion preferences, such as certain private activity bond tax-exempt interest income, reduce your regular taxable income permanently. Because exclusion preferences never reverse in the future, you are not given a credit for AMT paid. The AMT credit is carried forward indefinitely from the year of payment and cannot be carried back.

In Fran's case above, assuming the same amount of income and deductions in 2016 as 2014 (with the exception of the stock sale), their AMT liability would be significantly less than their regular tax liability. As a result, the AMT credit generated in 2014 when Fern exercised the ISO can be applied to reduce their regular tax down to the amount of the AMT.

The AMT credit can be applied in any future year where your AMT liability is less than your regular tax liability. The availability of the AMT credit in a future year is not tied to the reversal of the same item (in Fern's case, the sale of the stock) that originally caused the credit to have been generated.

TAXALERT

Refundable AMT credit expired. This provision for claiming a refund of AMT credit that remained unused for at least three years is not available after 2012. However, you may be able to claim a nonrefundable credit for prior year minimum tax against your current year's regular tax. See _Nonrefundable Credit for Prior Year Minimum Tax_ in chapter 37, _Other credits including the earned income credit_ for more information.

TAXSAVER

To avoid treating excess intangible drilling costs as a tax preference item, you may elect to capitalize and amortize these expenses over a 10-year period in your regular tax calculation.

Example

The following example demonstrates how you would calculate your regular tax and your AMT for calendar year 2014 assuming your filing status is married filing jointly.

	Regular tax	Alternative minimum tax
Salary	$150,000	$150,000
Interest	11,000	11,000
Long-term capital gains (15%)	80,000	80,000
Net passive losses	(25,000)	(25,000)
Passive losses disallowed by Tax Reform Act of 1986	25,000	25,000
Adjusted gross income	$241,000	$241,000
State taxes	(30,000)	n/a
Charitable contributions	(50,000)	(50,000)
Interest expense–principal residence	(27,000)	(27,000)
Exemptions (4)	(15,800)	n/a
Tax Adjustment items:		
Incentive stock options	n/a	25,000
Alternative taxable income before exemption	n/a	$189,000
Exemption ($82,100 less 25% of alternative taxable income in excess of $156,500)	n/a	($73,975)
Taxable income	$118,200	$115,025
Tax due	$11,486	$15,767

*n/a means "not applicable"

Because your regular tax is less than your AMT, you must pay the AMT of $15,767.

The $30,000 you paid in state income tax was not allowed as a deduction from alternative minimum taxable income. Because deductions are based on actual payments made during the calendar year, good planning would require minimizing your state income taxes and your miscellaneous deductions to the extent that you are able in a year when it is possible you will be subject to the AMT.

Even if you have benefited from the tax preference items that generally subject you to the AMT, you may avoid the AMT by controlling the timing of certain transactions. The trick is not to exceed the amount exempt from the AMT for a given year. If you know that you will be subject to the AMT this year, and provided your current AMT situation is due to exclusion items, you should consider realizing income this year that otherwise would be realized next year so that it is taxed at 26% or 28% rather than at a higher rate next year. Likewise, consider deferring deductions, especially those that are not deductible for AMT purposes.

The $82,100 exemption for joint returns is phased out beginning at $156,500 of alternative minimum taxable income. For unmarried taxpayers, the exemption amount is $52,800, and it is phased out beginning at $117,300. You lose $1 of exemption for every $4 over the base amount. Consequently, the exemption amount is completely phased out at $484,900 for joint returns and $328,500 for unmarried taxpayers.

More information. For more information about the AMT, see the instructions for Form 6251.

Additional Medicare Tax

Additional Medicare Tax

Under the Affordable Care Act (the comprehensive health care law that was passed in 2010 and upheld as constitutional by the U.S. Supreme Court in June 2012), higher income individuals are subject to an additional 0.9% Medicare hospital insurance tax on wages and self-employment income received in excess of specified threshold amounts ($250,000 for a joint filers, $125,000 for a married individual filing a separate return; and $200,000 for all other taxpayers) starting in 2013. This tax is assessed in addition to the basic 1.45% Medicare tax employees already pay. There is no corresponding employer portion of the additional Medicare tax. As a result, the Medicare tax remains at 2.9% on all wages (with the worker and the employer each paying 1.45%) and self-employment income for income levels at or below these thresholds. However, beginning in 2013, the Medicare tax rate rises to 3.8% for wages and/or self-employment income over the applicable threshold levels.

Employers are required to withhold the 0.9% Additional Medicare Tax on wages paid to an employee in excess of $200,000 regardless of the tax filing status (married or single) indicated on the Form W-4 the employee submitted to the employer and without regard to other earned income on which the 0.9% Additional Medicare Tax may be owed. So, an employee may see this additional tax being withheld even though he or she may not even be liable for it because, for example, the employee's wages or other compensation together with that of his or her spouse (when filing a joint return) does not exceed the $250,000 liability threshold. In this case, however, any Additional Medicare Tax withheld can be credited against the total tax liability—including income taxes—shown on the couple's income tax return (Form 1040).

On the other hand, since an employer is only allowed to withhold the 0.9% Additional Medicare Tax on wages paid in excess of $200,000, married employees who file separately may have too little of this additional tax withheld since the threshold at which the 0.9% tax kicks in is only $125,000 for married taxpayers filing separately. To make up the difference, you can (a) increase your federal income tax withholding by submitting a new Form W-4 to your employer, or (b) make quarterly estimated tax payments in order to avoid a tax underpayment penalty.

If you are subject to the Additional Medicare Tax, you will report and pay this tax with your Form 1040. Use Form 8959, *Additional Medicare Tax*, to report your additional tax.

For more information on the Additional Medicare Tax, the IRS has Questions & Answer webpage dedicated to the Additional Medicare Tax. Go to *www.IRS.gov* and search for *"Additional Medicare Tax."*

Net Investment Income Tax (NIIT)

Net Investment Income Tax

Under Affordable Care Act (ACA), starting in 2013, a new 3.8% Net Investment Income Tax (NIIT) on certain unearned Net Investment Income (NII) takes effect for tax years beginning in 2013 and thereafter. For individuals, the tax is 3.8% of the lesser of: (1) "net investment income" or (2) the excess of modified adjusted gross income (MAGI) over $200,000 ($250,000 if married filing jointly or a surviving spouse with a dependent child; $125,000 if married filing separately). These threshold dollar amounts will not be indexed each year for inflation.

The NIIT is a surtax that is payable regardless of whether you otherwise pay any regular income tax or are subject to alternative minimum tax.

Net Investment Income is defined as investment income reduced by deductions that are properly allocable to such income. Investment income includes the following:

- Income not derived in the ordinary course of a trade or business, including interest, dividends, rents, royalties, and income from nonqualified annuities
- Trade or business income from passive activities or from trading in financial instruments or commodities
- Net capital and ordinary income gains from the disposition of property not used in a trade or business, such as
  - Gains from the sale of stocks, bonds, and mutual funds.
  - Capital gain distributions from mutual funds.
  - Gain from the sale of investment real estate (including gain from the sale of a second home that is not a primary residence).
  - Gains from the sale of interests in partnerships and S corporations (to the extent you were a passive owner).

Investment income does not include Social Security benefits, operating income and gains attributable to an active trade or business conducted by a sole proprietor, partnership, or S corporation, distributions from an IRA or qualified retirement plan, alimony, or Alaska Permanent Fund dividends. Nor does it include any wages, other compensation, and self-employment income.

Items that are otherwise excluded from your gross income for income tax purposes are also excluded from investment income subject to the 3.8% tax. Excluded items include: interest on tax-exempt bonds; income from tax-exempt trusts; life insurance proceeds paid out on death; inside build-up in life insurance and annuity contracts; and the portion of capital gains from the sale of a principal residence that is excluded from income tax.

Deductions that are properly allocable to reduce investment income for purposes of calculating Net Investment Income include, but are not limited to, investment interest expense, investment advisory and brokerage fees, expenses related to rental and royalty income, and state and local income taxes related to specific investment income.

Example. Abner is a single filer with wages of $175,000 and NII of $16,000. His MAGI is $191,000, which is less than the $200,000 NIIT threshold that applies to single filers. Therefore, Abner is not subject to the NIIT.

Example. Juanita is a single filer. She was paid $180,000 of wages and also received NII of $90,000. Since her MAGI is therefore $270,000, she exceeds the $200,000 NIIT threshold for single taxpayers by $70,000. Her NII is $90,000. Since the NIIT is applied to the lesser of $70,000 (the amount by which Juanita's MAGI exceeds the applicable $200,000 threshold) or $90,000 (her NII), her NIIT is calculated to be $2,660 ($70,000 x 3.8%).

Example. Ali's only income for 2014 is a pension of $500,000 and $30,000 of tax-exempt income. The NIIT surtax does not apply because Ali has no investment income.

Finally, nonresident aliens (NRAs) are also not subject to the NIIT. But, special rules apply if the NRA is married to a U.S. citizen or resident and has made, or is planning to make, an election to file a joint return with his/her spouse. See your tax advisor for assistance.

If you are subject to the NIIT, you will report and pay this tax with your Form 1040. Use Form 8960, *Net Investment Income Tax—Individuals, Estates, and Trusts*, to report NII and to calculate your NIIT. For more information on the Net Investment Income Tax, the IRS has Questions & Answer webpage dedicated to the NIIT. Go to *www.IRS.gov* and search for *"Net Investment Income Tax."*

TAXALERT

The NIIT is 3.8% of the lesser of: (1) "net investment income" or (2) the excess of modified adjusted gross income (MAGI). Although certain items, such as IRA distributions, are excluded from NII, they are still included in the calculation of your MAGI. In certain cases, an increase in these items may indirectly result in an NIIT liability.

Example. Fred, a retired engineer, turned 70 years old in March 2013. He received investment income from commercial annuities, and interest and dividends from his taxable brokerage account of $170,000, in addition to taxable social security income of $15,000. Fred's MAGI is $185,000 in 2013. Fred is not subject to the NIIT in 2013.

Beginning in 2014, Fred began taking required minimum distributions from his IRA of $30,000. Assuming his annuity, interest, dividend, and social security income is the same, Fred's MAGI is $215,000 for 2014. He will be liable for $570 of NIIT in 2014 ($15,000 x 3.8%). Although the IRA distribution is not included in Fred's NII, it caused his MAGI to exceed the threshold for the tax.

Individual Shared Responsibility Provision—Calculating the Payment

The individual shared responsibility provision requires you and each member of your family to either have basic health insurance coverage (also known as minimum essential coverage), qualify for an exemption, or make an individual shared responsibility payment when you file your federal income tax return. It is important to remember that choosing to make the individual shared responsibility payment instead of purchasing minimum essential coverage means you will also have to pay the entire cost of all your medical care. You won't be protected from the kind of very high medical bills that can sometimes lead to bankruptcy.

If you must make an individual shared responsibility payment with your return, the annual payment amount is the greater of a percentage of your household income or a flat dollar amount, but is capped at the national average premium for a bronze level health plan available through the Marketplace. You will owe 1/12th of the annual payment for each month you or your dependent(s) don't have either coverage or an exemption.

For 2014, the annual payment amount is:
- The greater of:
  - 1 percent of your household income that is above the tax return filing threshold for your filing status, or
  - Your family's flat dollar amount, which is $95 per adult and $47.50 per child, limited to a family maximum of $285,
- But capped at the cost of the national average premium for a bronze level health plan available through the Marketplace in 2014. For 2014, the annual national average premium for a bronze level health plan available through the Marketplace is $2,448 per individual ($204 per month per individual), but $12,240 for a family with five or more members ($1,020 per month for a family with five or more members). See Rev. Proc. 2014-46.

Calculating your payment requires you to know your household income and your tax return filing threshold.
- **Household income** is the adjusted gross income from your tax return plus any excludible foreign earned income and tax-exempt interest you receive during the taxable year. Household income also includes the incomes of all of your dependents who are required to file tax returns.
- **Tax return filing threshold** is the amount of gross income an individual of your age and with your filing status (e.g., single, married filing jointly, head of household) must make to be required to file a tax return.

2014 Federal Tax Filing Requirement Thresholds

Filing Status	Age	Must File a Return If Gross Income Exceeds
Single	Under 65	$10,150
	65 or older	$11,700
Head of Household	Under 65	$13,050
	65 or older	$14,600
Married Filing Jointly	Under 65 (both spouses)	$20,300
	65 or older (one spouse)	$21,500
	65 or older (both spouses)	$22,700
Married Filing Separately	Any age	$3,950
Qualifying Widow(er) with Dependent Children	Under 65	$16,350
	65 or older	$17,550

Examples

The examples below are used only to represent the mechanics of calculating the payment and are not estimates of current or future health insurance premium costs. For information on the cost of bronze level plans, visit HealthCare.gov.

Example 1: Single individual with $40,000 income

Jim, an unmarried individual with no dependents, does not have minimum essential coverage for any month during 2014 and does not qualify for an exemption. For 2014, Jim's household income is $40,000 and his filing threshold is $10,150.

- To determine his payment using the income formula, subtract $10,150 (filing threshold) from $40,000 (2014 household income). The result is $29,850. One percent of $29,850 equals $298.50.
- Jim's flat dollar amount is $95.

Jim's annual national average premium for bronze level coverage for 2014 is $2,448. Because $298.50 is greater than $95 and is less than $2,448, Jim's shared responsibility payment for 2014 is $298.50, or $24.87 for each month he is uninsured (1/12 of $298.50 equals $24.87).

Jim will make his shared responsibility payment for the months he was uninsured when he files his 2014 income tax return, which is due in April 2015.

Example 2: Married couple with 2 children, $70,000 income

Eduardo and Julia are married and have two children under 18. They do not have minimum essential coverage for any family member for any month during 2014 and no one in the family qualifies for an exemption. For 2014, their household income is $70,000 and their filing threshold is $20,300.

- To determine their payment using the income formula, subtract $20,300 (filing threshold) from $70,000 (2014 household income). The result is $49,700. One percent of $49,700 equals $497.
- Eduardo and Julia's flat dollar amount is $285, or $95 per adult and $47.50 per child. The total of $285 is the flat dollar amount in 2014.

The family's annual national average premium for bronze level coverage for 2014 is $9,792 ($2,448 × 4). Because $497 is greater than $285 and is less than $9,792, Eduardo and Julia's shared responsibility payment is $497 for 2014, or $41.41 per month for each month the family is uninsured (1/12 of $497 equals $41.41).

Eduardo and Julia will make their shared responsibility payment for the months they and their children were uninsured when they file their 2014 income tax return, which is due in April 2015.

TAXALERT

The annual flat-dollar amount used to determine the tax for each individual without coverage in 2015 is $325 per adult and $162.50 per child, but capped at $975 per household. The annual flat-dollar amount used to determine the tax for each individual without coverage in 2016 is $695 per adult and $347.50 per child, but capped at $2,085 per household. For purposes of the penalty, a child is an individual under the age of 18.

Tax Figured by IRS

If you file by April 15, 2015, you can have the IRS figure your tax for you on Form 1040EZ, Form 1040A, or Form 1040.

If the IRS figures your tax and you paid too much, you will receive a refund. If you did not pay enough, you will receive a bill for the balance. To avoid interest or the penalty for late payment, you must pay the bill within 30 days of the date of the bill or by the due date for your return, whichever is later.

The IRS can also figure the credit for the elderly or the disabled and the earned income credit for you.

TAXPLANNER

If you make a preliminary calculation and see that you owe money to the IRS, you might consider waiting until the April due date of April 15, 2015, to file your return and letting the IRS figure your tax. It will take the IRS some time to process your return and compute your tax. You will not have to come up with the money you owe until 30 days after the IRS sends you a bill. You will not have to pay any interest if you pay within 30 days of receiving your bill.

When the IRS cannot figure your tax. The IRS cannot figure your tax for you if any of the following apply.

1. You want your refund directly deposited into your accounts.
2. You want any part of your refund applied to your 2015 estimated tax.

3. You had income for the year from sources other than wages, salaries, tips, interest, dividends, taxable social security benefits, unemployment compensation, IRA distributions, pensions, and annuities.
4. Your taxable income is $100,000 or more.
5. You itemize deductions.
6. You file any of the following forms.
   a. Form 2555, Foreign Earned Income.
   b. Form 2555-EZ, Foreign Earned Income Exclusion.
   c. Form 4137, Social Security and Medicare Tax on Unreported Tip Income.
   d. Form 4970, Tax on Accumulation Distribution of Trusts.
   e. Form 4972, Tax on Lump-Sum Distributions.
   f. Form 6198, At-Risk Limitations.
   g. Form 6251, Alternative Minimum Tax—Individuals.
   h. Form 8606, Nondeductible IRAs.
   i. Form 8615, Tax for Certain Children Who Have Unearned Income.
   j. Form 8814, Parents' Election To Report Child's Interest and Dividends.
   k. Form 8839, Qualified Adoption Expenses.
   l. Form 8853, Archer MSAs and Long-Term Care Insurance Contracts.
   m. Form 8889, Health Savings Accounts (HSAs).
   n. Form 8919, Uncollected Social Security and Medicare Tax on Wages.

Filing the Return

After you complete the line entries for the tax form you are filing, fill in your name and address. Enter your social security number in the space provided. If you are married, enter the social security numbers of you and your spouse even if you file separately. Sign and date your return and enter your occupation(s). If you are filing a joint return, both you and your spouse must sign it. Enter your daytime phone number in the space provided. This may help speed the processing of your return if we have a question that can be answered over the phone. If you are filing a joint return, you may enter either your or your spouse's daytime phone number.

If you want to allow a friend, family member, or any other person you choose to discuss your 2014 tax return with the IRS, check the "Yes" box in the "Third party designee" area on your return. Also enter the designee's name, phone number, and any five digits the designee chooses as his or her personal identification number (PIN). If you check the "Yes" box, you, and your spouse if filing a joint return, are authorizing the IRS to call the designee to answer any questions that may arise during the processing of your return.

Fill in and attach any schedules and forms asked for on the lines you completed to your paper return. Attach a copy of each of your Forms W-2 to your paper return. Also attach to your paper return any Form 1099-R you received that has withholding tax in box 4.

Mail your return to the Internal Revenue Service Center for the area where you live. A list of Service Center addresses is in the instructions for your tax return.

TAXPLANNER
You may have an alternative to mailing your tax return to the IRS Service Center. See chapter 45, *Everything you need to know about e-filing,* for information on electronic filing.

Form 1040EZ Line Entries
Read lines 1 through 8b and fill in the lines that apply to you. Do not complete lines 9 through 12. If you are filing a joint return, use the space to the left of line 6 to separately show your taxable income and your spouse's taxable income.

Payments. Enter any federal income tax withheld on line 7. Federal income tax withheld is shown on Form W-2, box 2, or Form 1099, box 4.

Earned income credit. If you can take this credit, as discussed in chapter 37, the IRS can figure it for you. Enter "EIC" in the space to the left of line 8a. Enter the nontaxable combat pay you elect to include in earned income on line 8b.

If your credit for any year after 1996 was reduced or disallowed by the IRS, you may also have to file Form 8862, Information To Claim Earned Income Credit After Disallowance, with your return. For details, see the Form 1040EZ Instructions.

Form 1040A Line Entries

Read lines 1 through 27 and fill in the lines that apply to you. If you are filing a joint return, use the space to the left of the entry space for line 27 to separately show your taxable income and your spouse's taxable income. Do not complete line 28. Complete lines 29 and 31 through 35, 38 and 40 through 45 if they apply to you. However, do not fill in lines 32 and 42a if you want the IRS to figure the credits shown on those lines. Also, enter any write-in information that applies to you in the space to the left of line 46. Do not complete lines 36, 37, and 47 through 51.

Payments. Enter any federal income tax withheld that is shown on Form W-2, box 2, or Form 1099, box 4, on line 40. Enter any estimated tax payments you made on line 41.

Credit for child and dependent care expenses. If you can take this credit, as discussed in chapter 33, complete Form 2441, Child and Dependent Care Expenses, and attach it to your return. Enter the amount of the credit on line 31. The IRS will not figure this credit.

Credit for the elderly or the disabled. If you can take this credit, as discussed in chapter 34, the IRS can figure it for you. Enter "CFE" in the space to the left of line 30 and attach Schedule R (Form 1040A or 1040), Credit for the Elderly or the Disabled, to your paper return. On Schedule R (Form 1040A or 1040), check the box in Part I for your filing status and age. Complete Part II and Part III, lines 11 and 13, if they apply.

Earned income credit. If you can take this credit, as discussed in chapter 37, the IRS can figure it for you. Enter "EIC" to the left of the entry space for line 42a. Enter the nontaxable combat pay you elect to include in earned income on line 42b.

If you have a qualifying child, you must fill in Schedule EIC (Form 1040A or 1040), Earned Income Credit, and attach it to your paper return. If you do not provide the child's social security number on Schedule EIC, line 2, the credit will be reduced or disallowed unless the child was born and died in 2014.

If your credit for any year after 1996 was reduced or disallowed by the IRS, you may also have to file Form 8862 with your return. For details, see the Form 1040A Instructions.

Form 1040 Line Entries

Read lines 1 through 43 and fill in the lines that apply to you. Do not complete line 44.

If you are filing a joint return, use the space under the words "Adjusted Gross Income" on the front of your return to separately show your taxable income and your spouse's taxable income.

Read lines 45 through 73. Fill in the lines that apply to you, but do not fill in lines 55, 63, and 74. Also, do not complete line 56 and lines 75 through 79. Do not fill in line 54, box "c," if you are completing Schedule R (Form 1040A or 1040), or line 66a if you want the IRS to figure the credits shown on those lines.

Payments. Enter any federal income tax withheld that is shown on Form W-2, box 2, Form 1099, box 4, Form 1099-SSA, box 6, on line 64. Enter any estimated tax payments you made on line 65.

Credit for child and dependent care expenses. If you can take this credit, as discussed in chapter 33, complete Form 2441 and attach it to your paper return. Enter the amount of the credit on line 49. The IRS will not figure this credit.

Credit for the elderly or the disabled. If you can take this credit, as discussed in chapter 34, the IRS can figure it for you. Enter "CFE" on the line next to line 54, check box "c," and attach Schedule R (Form 1040A or 1040) to your paper return. On Schedule R (Form 1040A or 1040), check the box in Part I for your filing status and age. Complete Part II and Part III, lines 11 and 13, if they apply.

Earned income credit. If you can take this credit, as discussed in chapter 37, the IRS can figure it for you. Enter "EIC" on the dotted line next to Form 1040, line 66a. Enter the nontaxable combat pay you elect to include in earned income on line 66b.

If you have a qualifying child, you must fill in Schedule EIC (Form 1040A or 1040), Earned Income Credit, and attach it to your paper return. If you do not provide the child's social security number on Schedule EIC, line 2, the credit will be reduced or disallowed unless the child was born and died in 2014.

If your credit for any year after 1996 was reduced or disallowed by the IRS, you may also have to file Form 8862 with your return. For details, see the Form 1040 Instructions.

TAXORGANIZER

Records you should keep:

- **W-2** Wages, salaries, tips; allocated tips; advance EIC payments; dependent care benefits; adoption benefits; employer contributions to a medical savings account
- **W-2G** Gambling winnings
- **K-1** Partner's share of income, deductions, credits, etc.
- **1098** Mortgage interest; points; refund of overpaid interest
- **1098-E** Student loan interest
- **1099-A** Acquisition or abandonment of secured property
- **1099-B** Stocks and bonds; bartering; futures contracts
- **1099-C** Canceled debt
- **1099-DIV** Ordinary dividends; total capital gains distributions; nontaxable distributions; investment expenses; foreign tax paid
- **1099-G** Unemployment compensation; state or local income tax refund; taxable grants; agriculture payments
- **1099-INT** Interest income; early withdrawal penalty; interest on U.S. savings bonds and Treasury obligations
- **1099-LTC** Long-term care and accelerated death benefits
- **1099-MISC** Rents; royalties; other income (prizes, awards); nonemployee compensation
- **1099-MSA, 1099-HSA** Distributions from medical savings accounts and health savings accounts
- **1099-OID** Original issue discount; other periodic interest; early withdrawal penalty
- **1099-PATR** Patronage dividends and other distributions from a cooperative; credits; patron's AMT adjustment
- **1099-R** Distributions from IRAs; distributions from pensions, annuities; capital gain
- **1099-S** Gross proceeds from real estate transactions; buyer's part of real estate tax

In addition to the items listed above, you should retain any item that may be needed in a future year to calculate your tax. For example, you should retain in your permanent records items such as:

- HUD-1 from the purchase of real estate and invoices pertaining to significant improvements (such as a new roof or a kitchen remodel) to support your tax basis for a subsequent sale or for depreciation (if applicable)
- Confirmation of purchases of investments (stocks and bonds) or commercial annuities
- Records pertaining to nondeductible contributions to IRAs (generally, reported when made on Form 8606)

Chapter 32
Tax on investment income of certain children

ey.com/EYTaxGuide

Note

IRS Publication 17 (*Your Federal Income Tax*) has been updated by Ernst & Young LLP for 2014. Dates and dollar amounts shown are for 2014. Underlined type is used to indicate where IRS text has been updated. Places where text has been removed are indicated by the sentence: *Text intentionally omitted.*

ey.com/EYTaxGuide

Ernst & Young LLP will update the *EY Tax Guide 2015* website with relevant taxpayer information as it becomes available. You can also sign up for email alerts to let you know when changes have been made.

Introduction

There's nothing easy about raising a child these days, and that applies to the child's tax return as well. It is enormously complicated to fill out a proper tax return for a child under a certain age who has unearned (investment) income and determine the correct amount of income tax due.

Unearned income of a child under a certain age is taxed at the marginal rate of the child's parents, as if the parents had received the income, rather than at the child's lower rate. This is commonly referred to as the "kiddie tax." The affected ages are:

- Under age 18 by the end of 2014;
- Age 18 by the end of 2014 if the child's earned income is not over one-half of their support; or
- Over age 18 and under age 24 by the end of 2014 if the child was a full-time student and if the child's earned income is not over one-half of their support.

Because most parents have a higher marginal tax rate than their child, these rules generally eliminate the benefits of transferring income-producing assets, such as stocks or bonds, to your minor child in order for the income to be taxed at the child's lower marginal rate.

The following are additional complications:

1. A child may not claim a personal exemption for himself or herself if he or she is eligible to be claimed on a parent's return.
2. A child's unearned income falls under special rules. The child can use $1,000 of his or her standard deduction to offset unearned income. The next $1,000 of unearned income is taxed at the child's tax rate. The balance of a child's unearned income above $2,000 will be taxed at the parent's marginal tax rate. This is accomplished by either: (1) including the child's income on the parent's return and attaching Form 8814 to the parents' Form 1040 OR; (2) by filing a tax return for the child and attaching Form 8615 to the child's tax return.
3. If a child also has earned income, his or her tax return gets more complicated still. The earned income, while increasing gross income, can also increase his or her allowable standard deduction.

This chapter will help you sort through all the complications. Here's hoping that while you're muddling through it, your child will be out having fun.

TAXPLANNER

The rules for taxing a child's unearned (investment) income impact parents who are considering transferring money to their child. You should carefully evaluate the types of assets you want to transfer to your child.

Tax Breaks and Deductions You Can Use Checklist

The kiddie tax. The kiddie tax rules apply to a child who has more than a prescribed amount of unearned (investment) income for the tax year—$2,000 for 2014—and whose age is either:

- Under 18 years old by the end of 2014;
- 18 years old by the end of 2014 if the child's earned income is not greater than one-half of the support the child receives; or
- Between 19 and 23 by the end of 2014 if a full-time student and if the child's earned income is not greater than one-half of the support the child receives.

Basically, the rules take the investment income of the child above this amount (called "net unearned income") and tax it at the parent's (likely higher) tax rate. So while you can still save some tax by shifting unearned income (up to $2,000 in 2014) to a child who is subject to the kiddie tax, substantial tax savings aren't available.

You should consider investments for your child that generate little or no taxable income until your child "grows out" of the reach of the kiddie tax. For example, if the choice is between a growth-oriented mutual fund and an income-oriented mutual fund, it is clearly a better idea from an income tax perspective to transfer the growth-oriented fund to the child. No current income tax will be due since the fund is focused on capital appreciation, not income distribution.

In the future, any accumulated gain could be recognized after the child is no longer subject to the kiddie tax, and instead pays tax at his or her own tax rate.

Also, consider a 529 plan (qualified tuition programs) to build college savings. The investment income earned in the 529 plan accumulates tax-free and no tax is triggered for withdrawals if used to directly pay qualified higher education expenses. See the section on *Qualified Tuition Programs* in Publication 970, *Tax Benefits for Education*, for further information about 529 plans.

Reminder

Net Investment Income Tax. A child whose tax is figured on Form 8615 may be subject to the Net Investment Income Tax (NIIT). NIIT is a 3.8% tax on the lesser of the net investment income or the excess of the child's modified adjusted gross income (MAGI) over the threshold amount. Use Form 8960, Net Investment Income Tax, to figure this tax. For more information on NIIT, go to *www.irs.gov* and enter "Net Investment Income Tax" in the search box.

This chapter discusses the following two rules that may affect the tax on unearned income of certain children.

1. If the child's interest and dividend income (including capital gain distributions) total less than $10,000, the child's parent may be able to choose to include that income on the parent's return rather than file a return for the child. (See *Parent's Election To Report Child's Interest and Dividends*, later.)
2. If the child's interest, dividends, and other unearned income total more than $2,000, part of that income may be taxed at the parent's tax rate instead of the child's tax rate. (See *Tax for Certain Children Who Have Unearned Income*, later.)

For these rules, the term "child" includes a legally adopted child and a stepchild. These rules apply whether or not the child is a dependent.

Useful Items

You may want to see:

Publication
- ☐ **929**   Tax Rules for Children and Dependents

Form (and Instructions)
- ☐ **8615**   Tax for Certain Children Who Have Unearned Income
- ☐ **8814**   Parents' Election To Report Child's Interest and Dividends

TAXALERT
For 2014, the first $1,000 of income of a child subject to the kiddie tax will generally not be subject to tax, and the next $1,000 will be taxable at the child's own tax bracket. Unearned income in excess of $2,000 will be taxed to the child at the parent's tax rate.

EXPLANATION
For the 2014 tax year, "under age 19" means that the child has not reached age 19 by January 1, 2014. If your child reached age 19 at any time during 2014 (and they are not a full-time student), this chapter will not apply.

TAXSAVER
Although the tax benefit of transferring investment property to your child is likely limited, some advantages still exist. First, keep in mind that the first $2,000 of your child's investment income is taxed at a relatively low rate in 2014. Second, your child will eventually cease to be subject to the kiddie tax and will instead pay tax by applying his or her own tax bracket (which will probably be lower than yours). Third, if the transferred property appreciates in value while your child is subject to the kiddie tax, the appreciation will not complicate your own tax position.

Which Parent's Return To Use

If a child's parents are married to each other and file a joint return, use the joint return to figure the tax on the child's unearned income. The tax rate and other return information from that return are used to figure the child's tax as explained later under *Tax for Certain Children Who Have Unearned Income.*

Parents Who Do Not File a Joint Return

For parents who do not file a joint return, the following discussions explain which parent's tax return must be used to figure the tax.

Only the parent whose tax return is used can make the election described under *Parent's Election To Report Child's Interest and Dividends.*

Parents are married. If the child's parents file separate returns, use the return of the parent with the greater taxable income.

Parents not living together. If the child's parents are married to each other but not living together, and the parent with whom the child lives (the custodial parent) is considered unmarried, use the return of the custodial parent. If the custodial parent is not considered unmarried, use the return of the parent with the greater taxable income.

For an explanation of when a married person living apart from his or her spouse is considered unmarried, see *Head of Household* in chapter 2.

Parents are divorced. If the child's parents are divorced or legally separated, and the parent who had custody of the child for the greater part of the year (the custodial parent) has not remarried, use the return of the custodial parent.

Custodial parent remarried. If the custodial parent has remarried, the stepparent (rather than the noncustodial parent) is treated as the child's other parent. Therefore, if the custodial parent and the stepparent file a joint return, use that joint return. Do not use the return of the noncustodial parent.

If the custodial parent and the stepparent are married, but file separate returns, use the return of the one with the greater taxable income. If the custodial parent and the stepparent are married but not living together, the earlier discussion under *Parents not living together* applies.

Parents never married. If a child's parents have never been married to each other, but lived together all year, use the return of the parent with the greater taxable income. If the parents did not live together all year, the rules explained earlier under *Parents are divorced* apply.

Widowed parent remarried. If a widow or widower remarries, the new spouse is treated as the child's other parent. The rules explained earlier under *Custodial parent remarried* apply.

> ### EXPLANATION
> When both parents have custody of a child with unearned income, the custodial parent is the parent with custody for the greater portion of the calendar year.

Parent's Election To Report Child's Interest and Dividends

You may be able to elect to include your child's interest and dividend income (including capital gain distributions) on your tax return. If you do, your child will not have to file a return.

You can make this election only if all the following conditions are met.

- Your child was under age 19 (or under age 24 if a full-time student) at the end of the year.
- Your child had income only from interest and dividends (including capital gain distributions and Alaska Permanent Fund dividends).
- The child's gross income was less than $10,000.
- The child is required to file a return unless you make this election.
- The child does not file a joint return for the year.
- No estimated tax payment was made for the year, and no overpayment from the previous year (or from any amended return) was applied to this year under your child's name and social security number.
- No federal income tax was taken out of your child's income under the backup withholding rules.
- You are the parent whose return must be used when applying the special tax rules for children. (See *Which Parent's Return To Use*, earlier.)

These conditions are also shown in Figure 32-A.

Figure 32-A. **Can You Include Your Child's Income On Your Tax Return?**

Start Here

Yes ← Was your child under age 19 at the end of 2014?

↓ *No*

Was your child under age 24 at the end of 2014? → *No* →

↓ *Yes*

Was your child a full-time student in 2014? → *No* →

↓ *Yes*

Was the child's only income interest and dividends (including capital gain distributions and Alaska Permanent Fund dividends)? → *No* →

↓ *Yes*

Was the child's income less than $10,000? → *No* →

↓ *Yes*

Is your child required to file a tax return for 2014 if you do not make this election? → *No* →

↓ *Yes*

Is your child filing a joint return for 2014? → *Yes* →

↓ *No*

Did the child make any estimated tax payments for 2014? → *Yes* →

↓ *No*

Did the child have an overpayment of tax on his or her 2013 return (or on any amended return) applied to the 2014 estimated tax? → *Yes* →

↓ *No*

Was any federal income tax withheld from the child's income under backup withholding rules? → *Yes* →

↓ *No*

Are you the parent whose return must be used?* → *No* →

↓ *Yes*

You can include your child's income on your tax return by completing Form 8814 and attaching it to your return. If you do, your child is not required to file a return.

You cannot include your child's income on your return.

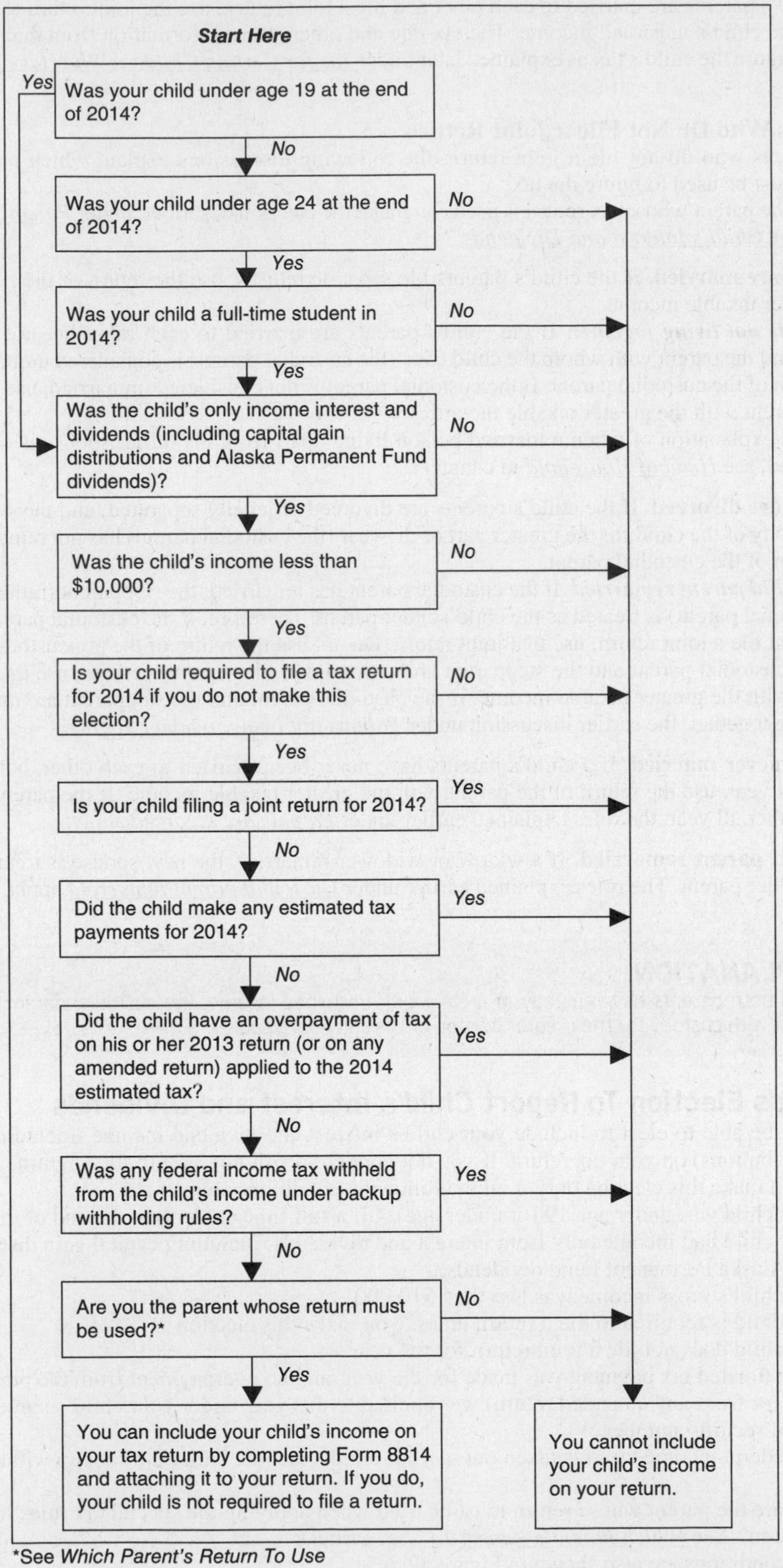

*See *Which Parent's Return To Use*

Certain January 1 birthdays. A child born on January 1, 1996, is considered to be age 19 at the end of 2014. You cannot make this election for such a child unless the child was a full-time student.

A child born on January 1, 1991, is considered to be age 24 at the end of 2014. You cannot make this election for such a child.

Full-time student. A full-time student is a child who during some part of each of any 5 calendar months of the year was enrolled as a full-time student at a school, or took a full-time on-farm training course given by a school or a state, county, or local government agency. A school includes a technical, trade, or mechanical school. It does not include an on-the-job training course, correspondence school, or school offering courses only through the Internet.

How to make the election. Make the election by attaching Form 8814 to your Form 1040. (If you make this election, you cannot file Form 1040A or Form 1040EZ.) Attach a separate Form 8814 for each child for whom you make the election. You can make the election for one or more children and not for others.

Effect of Making the Election
The federal income tax on your child's income may be more if you make the Form 8814 election.

Rate may be higher. If your child received qualified dividends or capital gain distributions, you may pay up to $100 more tax if you make this election instead of filing a separate tax return for the child. This is because the tax rate on the child's income between $1,000 and $2,000 is 10% if you make this election. However, if you file a separate return for the child, the tax rate may be as low as 0% (zero percent), because of the preferential tax rates for qualified dividends and capital gain distributions.

TAXSAVER
If you use Form 8814 to add your child's income to yours, the increased adjusted gross income may reduce the benefit of certain items on your return, such as any itemized deductions for medical expenses, casualty and theft losses, certain miscellaneous expenses, your deduction for IRA contributions (see chapter 17, *Individual retirement arrangements (IRAs)*), and your ability to claim the favorable $25,000 rental loss allowance under the passive activity rules (see chapter 12, *Other income*).

Also, the types of income added to your tax return by using Form 8814 are designated as Net Investment Income subject to the 3.8% Net Investment Income Tax (NIIT) that took effect starting in 2013. The amounts of Net Investment Income that are included on your own tax return by reason of Form 8814 are included in calculating the 3.8% NIIT that you may owe. (For individuals, the NIIT is 3.8% of the lesser of: (1) "net investment income"; or (2) the excess of modified adjusted gross income (MAGI) over $200,000 ($250,000 if married filing jointly or qualifying widow(er) with dependent child; $125,000 if married filing separately).) If you may be subject to the NIIT and have children subject to the "kiddie tax," you may consider having your children file their own tax returns to reduce the amount of income potentially subject to the NIIT.

Finally, adding your child's income to yours may also increase your state and local tax liability. Consider this election carefully before filing Form 8814.

Deductions you cannot take. By making the Form 8814 election, you cannot take any of the following deductions that the child would be entitled to on his or her return.
- The additional standard deduction if the child is blind.
- The deduction for a penalty on an early withdrawal of your child's savings.
- Itemized deductions (such as your child's investment expenses or charitable contributions).

Reduced deductions or credits. If you use Form 8814, your increased adjusted gross income may reduce certain deductions or credits on your return including the following.
- Deduction for contributions to a traditional individual retirement arrangement (IRA).
- Deduction for student loan interest.
- Itemized deductions for medical expenses, casualty and theft losses, and certain miscellaneous expenses.
- Credit for child and dependent care expenses.
- Child tax credit.
- Education tax credits.
- Earned income credit.

Penalty for underpayment of estimated tax. If you make this election for 2014 and did not have enough tax withheld or pay enough estimated tax to cover the tax you owe, you may be subject to a penalty. If you plan to make this election for 2015, you may need to increase your federal income tax withholding or your estimated tax payments to avoid the penalty. See chapter 4 for more information.

Figuring Child's Income

Use Form 8814, Part I, to figure your child's interest and dividend income to report on your return. Only the amount over $2,000 is added to your income. The amount over $2,000 is shown on Form 8814, line 6. Unless the child's income includes qualified dividends or capital gain distributions (discussed next), the same amount is shown on Form 8814, line 12. Include the amount from Form 8814, line 12, on Form 1040, line 21. Enter "Form 8814" on the dotted line next to line 21. If you file more than one Form 8814, include the total amounts from line 12 of all your Forms 8814 on Form 1040, line 21.

Capital gain distributions and qualified dividends. If your child's dividend income included any capital gain distributions, see *Capital gain distributions* under *Figuring Child's Income* in Publication 929, Part 2. If your child's dividend income included any qualified dividends, see *Qualified dividends* under *Figuring Child's Income* in Publication 929, Part 2.

Figuring Additional Tax

Use Form 8814, Part II, to figure the tax on the $2,000 of your child's interest and dividends that you do not include in your income. This tax is added to the tax figured on your income. This additional tax is the smaller of:

1. 10% × (your child's gross income – $1,000), or
2. $100.

Include the amount from line 15 of all your Forms 8814 in the total on Form 1040, line 44. Check box a on Form 1040, line 44.

Tax for Certain Children Who Have Unearned Income

If a child's interest, dividends, and other unearned income total more than $2,000, part of that income may be taxed at the parent's tax rate instead of the child's tax rate. If the parent does not or cannot choose to include the child's income on the parent's return, use Form 8615 to figure the child's tax. Attach the completed form to the child's Form 1040 or Form 1040A.

When Form 8615 must be filed. Form 8615 must be filed for a child if all of the following statements are true.

1. The child's investment income was more than $2,000.
2. The child is required to file a return for 2014.
3. The child either:
   a. Was under age 18 at the end of the year,
   b. Was age 18 at the end of the year and did not have earned income that was more than half of his or her support, or
   c. Was over age 18 and under age 24 at the end of the year, was a full-time student, and did not have earned income that was more than half of his or her support.
4. At least one of the child's parents was alive at the end of 2014.
5. The child does not file a joint return for 2014.

These conditions are also shown in Figure 32-B.

Earned income. Earned income includes salaries, wages, tips, and other payments received for personal services performed. It does not include unearned income as defined later in this chapter.

Support. Your child's support includes all amounts spent to provide the child with food, lodging, clothing, education, medical and dental care, recreation, transportation, and similar necessities. To figure your child's support, count support provided by you, your child, and others. However, a scholarship received by your child is not considered support if your child is a full-time student. See chapter 3 for details about support.

Certain January 1 birthdays. Use the following chart to determine whether certain children with January 1 birthdays meet condition 3 under *When Form 8615 must be filed.*

IF a child was born on...	THEN, at the end of 2014, the child is considered to be...
January 1, 1997	18*
January 1, 1996	19**
January 1, 1991	24***

*This child is not **under** age 18. The child meets condition 3 only if the child did not have earned income that was more than half of the child's support.
**This child meets condition 3 only if the child was a full-time student who did not have earned income that was more than half of the child's support.
***Do not use Form 8615 for this child.

Providing Parental Information (Form 8615, lines A–C)

On Form 8615, lines A and B, enter the parent's name and social security number. (If the parents filed a joint return, enter the name and social security number listed first on the joint return.) On line C, check the box for the parent's filing status.

See *Which Parent's Return To Use* at the beginning of this chapter for information on which parent's return information must be used on Form 8615.

Parent with different tax year. If the parent and the child do not have the same tax year, complete Form 8615 using the information on the parent's return for the tax year that ends in the child's tax year.

Parent's return information not known timely. If the information needed from the parent's return is not known by the time the child's return is due (usually April 15), you can file the return using estimates.

You can use any reasonable estimate. This includes using information from last year's return. If you use an estimated amount on Form 8615, enter "Estimated" on the line next to the amount.

When you get the correct information, file an amended return on Form 1040X, Amended U.S. Individual Income Tax Return.

Instead of using estimates, you can get an automatic 6-month extension of time to file if, by the date your return is due, you file Form 4868, Application for Automatic Extension of Time To File U.S. Individual Income Tax Return. Extensions are discussed in chapter 1.

Step 1. Figuring the Child's Net Investment Income (Form 8615, Part I)

The first step in figuring a child's tax using Form 8615 is to figure the child's net unearned income. To do that, use Form 8615, Part I.

Line 1 (unearned income). If the child had no earned income, enter on this line the adjusted gross income shown on the child's return. Adjusted gross income is shown on Form 1040, line 38, or Form 1040A, line 22. Form 1040EZ cannot be used if Form 8615 must be filed.

If the child had earned income, figure the amount to enter on Form 8615, line 1, by using the worksheet in the instructions for the form.

However, if the child has:
- excluded any foreign earned income,
- deducted either a loss from self-employment, or
- deducted a net operating loss from another year, then use the Alternate Worksheet for Form 8615, Line 1, in Publication 929 to figure the amount to enter on Form 8615, line 1.

Unearned income defined. Unearned income is generally all income other than salaries, wages, and other amounts received as pay for work actually done. It includes taxable interest, dividends (including capital gain distributions), capital gains, unemployment compensation, the taxable part of social security and pension payments, and certain distributions from trusts. Unearned income includes amounts produced by assets the child obtained with earned income (such as interest on a savings account into which the child deposited wages).

Nontaxable income. For this purpose, unearned income includes only amounts the child must include in total income. Nontaxable unearned income, such as tax-exempt interest and the nontaxable part of social security and pension payments, is not included.

Income from property received as a gift. A child's unearned income includes all income produced by property belonging to the child. This is true even if the property was transferred to the child, regardless of when the property was transferred or purchased or who transferred it.

A child's unearned income includes income produced by property given as a gift to the child. This includes gifts to the child from grandparents or any other person and gifts made under the Uniform Gift to Minors Act.

Figure 32-B.   Do You Have To Use Form 8615 To Figure Your Child's Tax?

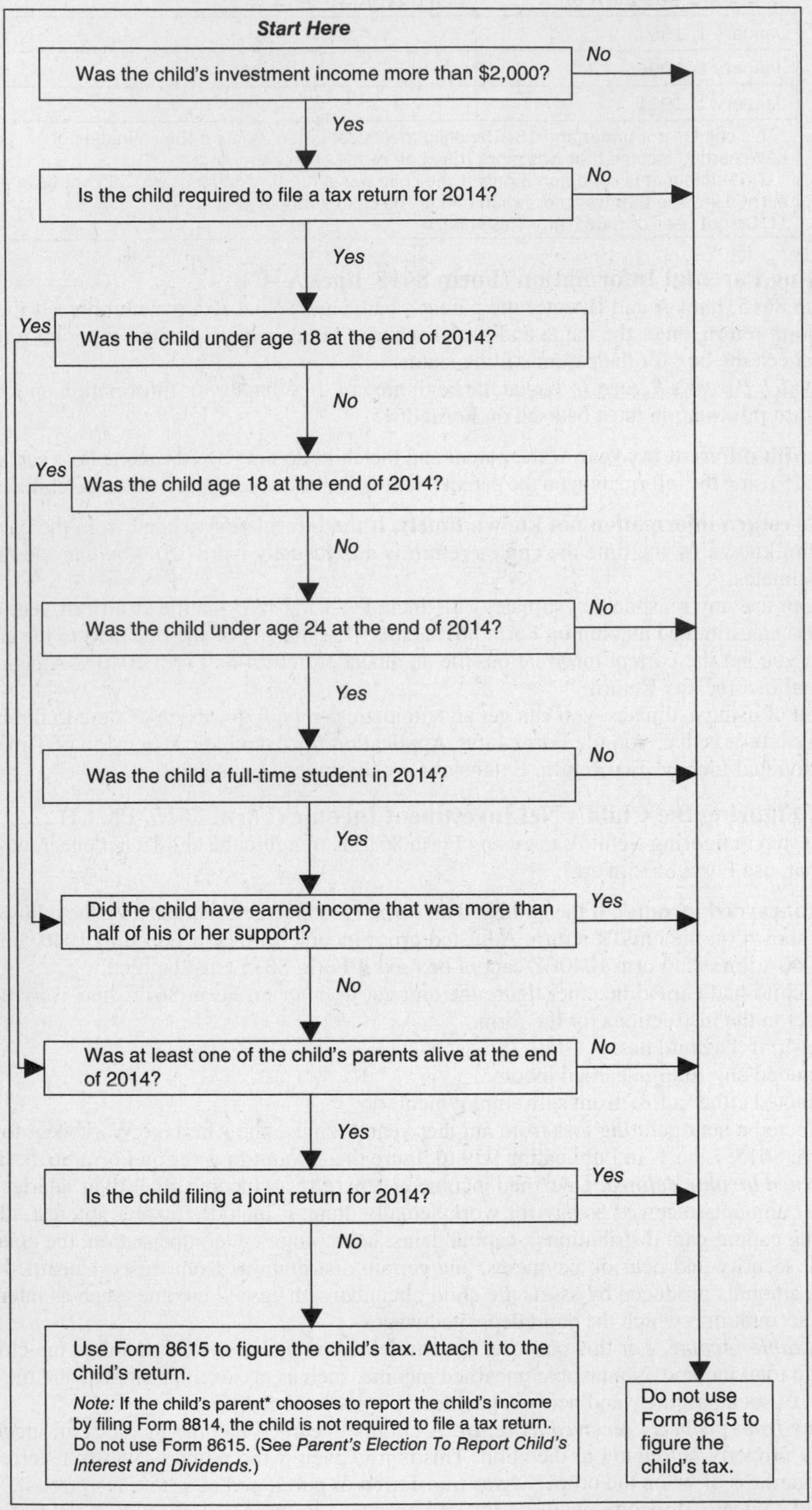

Start Here

Was the child's investment income more than $2,000? — **No** →

↓ **Yes**

Is the child required to file a tax return for 2014? — **No** →

↓ **Yes**

Yes ← Was the child under age 18 at the end of 2014?

↓ **No**

Yes ← Was the child age 18 at the end of 2014?

↓ **No**

Was the child under age 24 at the end of 2014? — **No** →

↓ **Yes**

Was the child a full-time student in 2014? — **No** →

↓ **Yes**

Did the child have earned income that was more than half of his or her support? — **Yes** →

↓ **No**

Was at least one of the child's parents alive at the end of 2014? — **No** →

↓ **Yes**

Is the child filing a joint return for 2014? — **Yes** →

↓ **No**

Use Form 8615 to figure the child's tax. Attach it to the child's return.

Note: If the child's parent* chooses to report the child's income by filing Form 8814, the child is not required to file a tax return. Do not use Form 8615. (See *Parent's Election To Report Child's Interest and Dividends.*)

Do not use Form 8615 to figure the child's tax.

*See *Which Parent's Return To Use*

Example. Amanda Black, age 13, received the following income.
- Dividends—$800
- Wages—$2,100
- Taxable interest—$1,200
- Tax-exempt interest—$100
- Net capital gains—$100

The dividends were qualified dividends on stock given to her by her grandparents.

Amanda's unearned income is $2,100. This is the total of the dividends ($800), taxable interest ($1,200), and net capital gains ($100). Her wages are earned (not unearned) income because they are received for work actually done. Her tax-exempt interest is not included because it is nontaxable.

Trust income. If a child is the beneficiary of a trust, distributions of taxable interest, dividends, capital gains, and other unearned income from the trust are unearned income to the child.

However, for purposes of completing Form 8615, a taxable distribution from a qualified disability trust is considered earned income, not unearned income.

Line 2 (deductions). If the child does not itemize deductions on Schedule A (Form 1040), enter $2,000 on line 2.

If the child does itemize deductions, enter on line 2 the larger of:
1. $1,000 plus the portion of the child's itemized deductions on Schedule A (Form 1040), line 29, that are directly connected with the production of unearned income entered on line 1, or
2. $2,000.

Directly connected. Itemized deductions are directly connected with the production of unearned income if they are for expenses paid to produce or collect taxable income or to manage, conserve, or maintain property held for producing income. These expenses include custodian fees and service charges, service fees to collect taxable interest and dividends, and certain investment counsel fees.

These expenses are added to certain other miscellaneous itemized deductions on Schedule A (Form 1040). Only the amount greater than 2% of the child's adjusted gross income can be deducted. See chapter 29 for more information.

EXPLANATION

Directly connected itemized deductions also include any investment interest expense deducted on the child's return that relates to debt incurred to finance the investments that produced the unearned income.

That said, an investment interest deduction can also be an itemized deduction subject to a deduction limitation. The amount allowed as a deduction for certain investment interest cannot exceed your net investment income for the year. Any amount captured by this limitation may be available to you in a future tax year. See *Investment Interest* in chapter 24, *Interest expense* for more information.

Example 1. Roger, age 12, has unearned income of $8,000, no other income, no adjustments to income, and itemized deductions of $300 (net of the 2% limit) that are directly connected with his unearned income. His adjusted gross income is $8,000, which is entered on Form 1040, line 38, and on Form 8615, line 1. Roger enters $2,000 on line 2 because that is more than the total of $1,000 plus his directly connected itemized deductions of $300.

Example 2. Eleanor, age 8, has unearned income of $16,000 and an early withdrawal penalty of $100. She has no other income. She has itemized deductions of $1,050 (net of the 2% limit) that are directly connected with the production of her unearned income. Her adjusted gross income, entered on line 1, is $15,900 ($16,000 − $100). The amount on line 2 is $2,050. This is the larger of:
1. $1,000 plus the $1,050 of directly connected itemized deductions, or
2. $2,000.

TAXSAVER

A child with investment income. If your child is subject to the kiddie tax, has investment income, and you are in the top income bracket, you may want to consider altering his or her investment strategy if it is financially appropriate. Because a child with over $2,000 in unearned income will be taxed at his or her parent's rate, it might be advisable to seek out deferred or tax-exempt income.

An example of deferred income might be generated by an investment in a growth-oriented stock or mutual fund. Such an investment may not pay high current dividends, and the realization of any appreciation in value may be deferred by holding the investment until the child is no longer subject to the kiddie tax. Tax-exempt income may be generated by municipal bonds.

Line 3. Subtract line 2 from line 1 and enter the result on this line. If zero or less, do not complete the rest of the form. However, you must still attach Form 8615 to the child's tax return. Figure the tax on the child's taxable income in the normal manner.

Line 4 (child's taxable income). Enter on line 4 the child's taxable income from Form 1040, line 43, or Form 1040A, line 27.

However, if the child files Form 2555 or 2555-EZ to claim the foreign earned income exclusion, housing exclusion, or housing deduction, see the Form 8615 instructions or Pub. 929.

Line 5 (net unearned income). A child's net unearned income cannot be more than his or her taxable income. Enter on Form 8615, line 5, the smaller of line 3 or line 4. This is the child's net unearned income.

If zero or less, do not complete the rest of the form. However, you must still attach Form 8615 to the child's tax return. Figure the tax on the child's taxable income in the normal manner.

Step 2. Figuring Tentative Tax at the Parent's Tax Rate (Form 8615, Part II)

The next step in completing Form 8615 is to figure a tentative tax on the child's net unearned income at the parent's tax rate. The tentative tax at the parent's tax rate is the difference between the tax on the parent's taxable income figured with the child's net unearned income (plus the net unearned income of any other child whose Form 8615 includes the tax return information of that parent) and the tax figured without it.

When figuring the tentative tax at the parent's tax rate on Form 8615, do not refigure any of the exclusions, deductions, or credits on the parent's return because of the child's net unearned income. For example, do not refigure the medical expense deduction.

Figure the tentative tax on Form 8615, lines 6 through 13.

Note. If the child or parent has any capital gains or losses, get Publication 929 for help in completing Form 8615, Part II.

Line 6 (parent's taxable income). Enter on line 6 the parent's taxable income from Form 1040, line 43, Form 1040A, line 27, or Form 1040EZ, line 6.

If the Foreign Earned Income Tax Worksheet (in the Form 1040 instructions) was used to figure the parent's tax, enter the amount from line 3 of that worksheet instead of the parent's taxable income.

Line 7 (net unearned income of other children). If the tax return information of the parent is also used on any other child's Form 8615, enter on line 7 the total of the amounts from line 5 of all the other children's Forms 8615. Do not include the amount from line 5 of the Form 8615 being completed.

Example. Paul and Jane Persimmon have three children, Sharon, Jerry, and Mike, who must attach Form 8615 to their tax returns. The children's net unearned income amounts on line 5 of their Forms 8615 are:

- Sharon—$800
- Jerry—$600
- Mike—$1,000

Line 7 of Sharon's Form 8615 will show $1,600, the total of the amounts on line 5 of Jerry's and Mike's Forms 8615.

Line 7 of Jerry's Form 8615 will show $1,800 ($800 + $1,000).

Line 7 of Mike's Form 8615 will show $1,400 ($800 + $600).

Other children's information not available. If the net unearned income of the other children is not available when the return is due, either file the return using estimates or get an extension of time to file. See *Parent's return information not known timely*, earlier.

Line 11 (tentative tax). Subtract line 10 from line 9 and enter the result on this line. This is the tentative tax.

If line 7 is blank, skip lines 12a and 12b and enter the amount from line 11 on line 13. Also skip the discussion for lines 12a and 12b that follows.

Lines 12a and 12b (dividing the tentative tax). If an amount is entered on line 7, divide the tentative tax shown on line 11 among the children according to each child's share of the total net unearned income. This is done on lines 12a, 12b, and 13. Add the amount on line 7 to the amount on line 5 and enter the total on line 12a. Divide the amount on line 5 by the amount on line 12a and enter the result, as a decimal, on line 12b.

Example. In the earlier example under *Line 7 (net unearned income of other children)*, Sharon's Form 8615 shows $1,600 on line 7. The amount entered on line 12a is $2,400, the total of the amounts on lines 5 and 7 ($800 + $1,600). The decimal on line 12b is .333, figured as follows and rounded to three places.

$$\frac{\$800}{2,400} = .333$$

Step 3. Figuring the Child's Tax (Form 8615, Part III)

The final step in figuring a child's tax using Form 8615 is to determine the larger of:
1. The total of:
   a. The child's share of the tentative tax based on the parent's tax rate, plus
   b. The tax on the child's taxable income in excess of net unearned income, figured at the child's tax rate, or
2. The tax on the child's taxable income, figured at the child's tax rate.

This is the child's tax. It is figured on Form 8615, lines 14 through 18.

Alternative minimum tax. A child may be subject to alternative minimum tax (AMT) if he or she has certain items given preferential treatment under the tax law. See *Alternative Minimum Tax (AMT)* in chapter 31.

For more information on who is liable for AMT and how to figure it, see Form 6251, Alternative Minimum Tax—Individuals. For information on special limits that apply to a child who files Form 6251, see *Certain Children Under Age 24* in the Instructions for Form 6251.

TAXORGANIZER
Records you should keep:
- 1099-INT or 1099-OID: Child's interest income.
- 1099-DIV: Child's dividend investment income; child's capital gain investment income.
- W-2: Child's earned income; child's estimated tax payments for the year (if any).

Chapter 33

Child and dependent care credit

Note

IRS Publication 17 (*Your Federal Income Tax*) has been updated by Ernst & Young LLP for 2014. Dates and dollar amounts shown are for 2014. Underlined type is used to indicate where IRS text has been updated. Places where text has been removed are indicated by the sentence: *Text intentionally omitted*.

ey.com/EYTaxGuide

Ernst & Young LLP will update the *Ernst & Young Tax Guide 2015* website with relevant taxpayer information as it becomes available. You can also sign up for email alerts to let you know when changes have been made.

Introduction

A credit that directly reduces your taxes is available for certain child and dependent care expenses that enable you to work. The credit may be as much as $1,050 if you have one qualifying individual or $2,100 if you have more than one qualifying individual. The credit is designed to help ease the tax burden of persons who must work and who also have the responsibility for the care of children or disabled dependents and spouses. The credit is nonrefundable; that is, although it may be used to bring your tax liability to zero, any credit in excess of your liability is not refunded to you.

   In general, to claim this credit, you must pay someone (other than a dependent) to care for a qualifying individual so that you can work or look for work. You must also have earned income from your work during the year and must have maintained a home for yourself and the qualifying individual for more than one-half of the year. This chapter spells out all the details.

Reminders

Taxpayer identification number needed for each qualifying person. You must include on line 2 of Form 2441 the name and taxpayer identification number (generally the social security number) of each qualifying person. See *Taxpayer identification number* under *Qualifying Person Test*, later.

You may have to pay employment taxes. If you pay someone to come to your home and care for your dependent or spouse, you may be a household employer who has to pay employment taxes. Usually, you are not a household employer if the person who cares for your dependent or spouse does so at his or her home or place of business. See *Employment Taxes for Household Employers*, later.

EXPLANATION

See chapter 40, *What to do if you employ domestic help*, for additional information.

   This chapter discusses the credit for child and dependent care expenses and covers the following topics.
- Tests you must meet to claim the credit.
- How to figure the credit.

- How to claim the credit.
- Employment taxes you may have to pay as a household employer.

You may be able to claim the credit if you pay someone to care for your dependent who is under age 13 or for your spouse or dependent who is not able to care for himself or herself. The credit can be up to 35% of your expenses. To qualify, you must pay these expenses so you can work or look for work.

Dependent care benefits. If you received any dependent care benefits from your employer during the year, you may be able to exclude from your income all or part of them. You must complete Form 2441, Part III, before you can figure the amount of your credit. See *Dependent Care Benefits* under *How To Figure the Credit*, later.

> **Caution**
>
> *This credit should not be confused with the child tax credit discussed in chapter 35.*

Useful Items
You may want to see:

Publication
- ☐ **501** Exemptions, Standard Deduction, and Filing Information
- ☐ **503** Child and Dependent Care Expenses
- ☐ **926** Household Employer's Tax Guide

Form (and Instructions)
- ☐ **2441** Child and Dependent Care Expenses
- ☐ **Schedule H (Form 1040)** Household Employment Taxes
- ☐ **W-7** Application for IRS Individual Taxpayer Identification Number
- ☐ **W-10** Dependent Care Provider's Identification and Certification

Tests To Claim the Credit
To be able to claim the credit for child and dependent care expenses, you must file Form 1040, Form 1040A, or Form 1040NR, not Form 1040EZ or Form 1040NR-EZ, and meet all the following tests.

1. The care must be for one or more qualifying persons who are identified on Form 2441. (See *Qualifying Person Test*.)
2. You (and your spouse if filing jointly) must have earned income during the year. (However, see *Rule for student-spouse or spouse not able to care for self* under *Earned Income Test*, later.)
3. You must pay child and dependent care expenses so you (and your spouse if filing jointly) can work or look for work. (See *Work-Related Expense Test*, later.)
4. You must make payments for child and dependent care to someone you (and your spouse) cannot claim as a dependent. If you make payments to your child, he or she cannot be your dependent and must be age 19 or older by the end of the year. You cannot make payments to:
   a. Your spouse, or
   b. The parent of your qualifying person if your qualifying person is your child and under age 13.
   (See *Payments to Relatives or Dependents* under *Work-Related Expense Test*, later.)
5. Your filing status may be single, head of household, or qualifying widow(er) with dependent child. If you are married, you must file a joint return, unless an exception applies to you. (See *Joint Return Test*, later.)
6. You must identify the care provider on your tax return. (See *Provider Identification Test*, later.)
7. If you exclude or deduct dependent care benefits provided by a dependent care benefits plan, the total amount you exclude or deduct must be less than the dollar limit for qualifying expenses (generally, $3,000 if one qualifying person was cared for or $6,000 if two or more qualifying persons were cared for). (If two or more qualifying persons were cared for, the amount you exclude or deduct will always be less than the dollar limit, since the total amount you can exclude or deduct is limited to $5,000. See *Reduced Dollar Limit* under *How To Figure the Credit*, later.)

These tests are presented in Figure 33-A and are also explained in detail in this chapter.

Figure 33-A. **Can You Claim the Credit?**

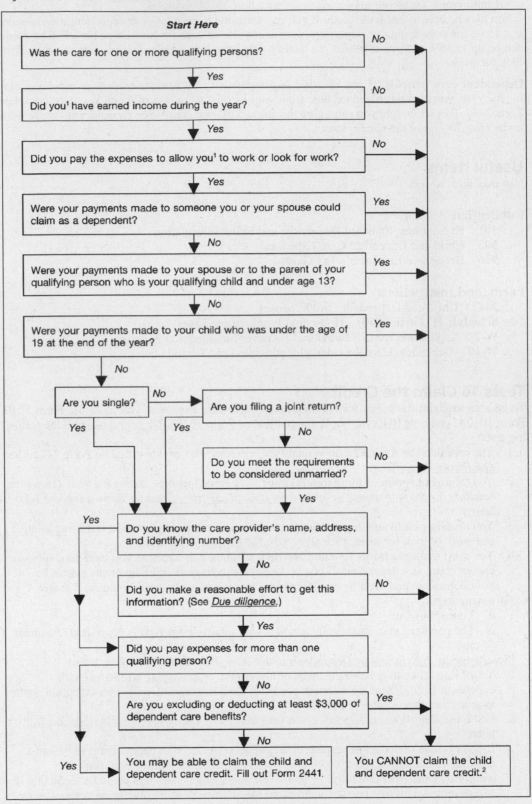

[1] This also applies to your spouse, unless your spouse was disabled or a full-time student.

[2] If you had expenses that met the requirements for 2013, except that you did not pay them until 2014, you may be able to claim those expenses in 2014.

See Expenses not paid until the following year under How To Figure the Credit.

Qualifying Person Test

Your child and dependent care expenses must be for the care of one or more qualifying persons. A qualifying person is:

1. Your qualifying child who is your dependent and who was under age 13 when the care was provided (but see *Child of divorced or separated parents or parents living apart*, later),
2. Your spouse who was not physically or mentally able to care for himself or herself and lived with you for more than half the year, or
3. A person who was not physically or mentally able to care for himself or herself, lived with you for more than half the year, and either:
   a. Was your dependent, or
   b. Would have been your dependent except that:
      i. He or she received gross income of $3,900 or more,
      ii. He or she filed a joint return, or
      iii. You, or your spouse if filing jointly, could be claimed as a dependent on someone else's 2014 return.

Dependent defined. A dependent is a person, other than you or your spouse, for whom you can claim an exemption. To be your dependent, a person must be your qualifying child (or your qualifying relative).

Qualifying child. To be your qualifying child, a child must live with you for more than half the year and meet other requirements.

More information. For more information about who is a dependent or a qualifying child, see chapter 3.

Physically or mentally not able to care for oneself. Persons who cannot dress, clean, or feed themselves because of physical or mental problems are considered not able to care for themselves. Also, persons who must have constant attention to prevent them from injuring themselves or others are considered not able to care for themselves.

Person qualifying for part of year. You determine a person's qualifying status each day.

For example, if the person for whom you pay child and dependent care expenses no longer qualifies on September 16, count only those expenses through September 15. Also see *Yearly limit* under *Dollar Limit*, later.

Birth or death of otherwise qualifying person. In determining whether a person is a qualifying person, a person who was born or died in 2014 is treated as having lived with you for more than half of 2014 if your home was the person's home for more than half the time he or she was alive in 2014.

Taxpayer identification number. You must include on your return the name and taxpayer identification number (generally the social security number) of the qualifying person(s). If the correct information is not shown, the credit may be reduced or disallowed.

Tax Breaks and Deductions You Can Use Checklist

Child and dependent care credit. The tax law allows you a credit against your tax if you pay child and dependent care expenses under certain circumstances. For an expense to qualify for the credit, it must be an "employment-related" expense, meaning that it must enable you and your spouse to work or look for work, and it must be for the care of your child, stepchild, or foster child, or your brother or sister or stepsibling (or a descendant of any of these) who is under 13, lives in your home for over half the year, and does not provide over half of his or her own support for the year. You may also be eligible for the credit if you pay for the care of your spouse or dependent who is physically or mentally incapable of caring for himself or herself and lives with you for over half the year. To claim the credit, you and your spouse must file a joint return. Further, you must include the social security number of the qualifying individual and the caregiver's name, address, and social security number (or ID number if it's a daycare center or nursery school) on the form for Child and Dependent Care expenses (Form 2441). A daycare center must be in compliance with state and local regulations.

Earned income test. If married, both you and your spouse must have earned income to be eligible to claim the child and dependent care credit. However, a nonworking spouse who cannot physically or mentally care for himself, or a spouse who is a full-time student for at least 5 months of the year is considered to have earned income.

> ### EXPLANATION
> For additional information, you can also visit the ITIN page at *http://www.irs.gov/Individuals/Individual-Taxpayer-Identification-Number-(ITIN)*.

An ITIN is for tax use only. It does not entitle the holder to social security benefits or change the holder's employment or immigration status under U.S. law.

Adoption taxpayer identification number (ATIN). If your qualifying person is a child who was placed in your home for adoption and for whom you do not have an SSN, you must get an ATIN for the child. File Form W-7A, Application for Taxpayer Identification Number for Pending U.S. Adoptions.

Child of divorced or separated parents or parents living apart. Even if you cannot claim your child as a dependent, he or she is treated as your qualifying person if:
- The child was under age 13 or was not physically or mentally able to care for himself or herself,
- The child received over half of his or her support during the calendar year from one or both parents who are divorced or legally separated under a decree of divorce or separate maintenance, are separated under a written separation agreement, or lived apart at all times during the last 6 months of the calendar year,
- The child was in the custody of one or both parents for more than half the year, and
- You were the child's custodial parent.

The custodial parent is the parent with whom the child lived for the greater number of nights in 2014. If the child was with each parent for an equal number of nights, the custodial parent is the parent with the higher adjusted gross income. For details and an exception for a parent who works at night, see Pub. 501.

The noncustodial parent cannot treat the child as a qualifying person even if that parent is entitled to claim the child as a dependent under the special rules for a child of divorced or separated parents.

> ### EXPLANATION
> To take the credit, you do not necessarily have to claim the child as a dependent. If you have custody of the child even though you have signed a statement that entitles your ex-spouse to the child's dependency exemption, you may still claim the credit. To receive the credit, however, you must write your child's name on line 2 of Form 2441. To avoid questions from the IRS, you may want to attach to your tax return a copy of the signed statement authorizing the release of your dependency claim.
>
> #### Example
> Charles and Katherine are divorced and share custody of their 3-year-old son, Dieter. Dieter lives 10 months a year with Katherine and attends a daycare center while his mother works. Charles and Katherine provide all of Dieter's support. Dieter is a qualifying person, since he is under age 13, is in the custody of his parents for more than half the year, and receives more than half his support from his parents. He is a qualifying person for Katherine and not Charles, because Katherine has custody of him for a longer period of time during the year than Charles. Under these circumstances, Dieter is a qualifying person only for Katherine, even if she has released her right to claim him as a dependent to Charles by providing a signed Form 8332, *Release/Revocation of Release of Claim to Exemption for Child by Custodial Parent,* to Charles.
>
> In no case may two taxpayers filing separate returns claim the same tax credit (whether the child and dependent care tax credit or the child tax credit discussed in chapter 35) or dependent exemption for the same qualifying individual.

Earned Income Test
To claim the credit, you (and your spouse if filing jointly) must have earned income during the year.

Earned income. Earned income includes wages, salaries, tips, other taxable employee compensation, and net earnings from self-employment. A net loss from self-employment reduces earned income. Earned income also includes strike benefits and any disability pay you report as wages.

Generally, only taxable compensation is included. However, you can elect to include nontaxable combat pay in earned income. If you are filing a joint return and both you and your spouse received nontaxable combat pay, you can each make your own election. (In other words, if one of you makes the election, the other one can also make it but does not have to.) You should figure your credit both ways and make the election if it gives you a greater tax benefit.

Members of certain religious faiths opposed to social security. Certain income earned by persons who are members of certain religious faiths that are opposed to participation in Social Security Act programs and have an IRS-approved form that exempts certain income from social security and Medicare taxes may not be considered earned income for this purpose. See *Earned Income Test* in Publication 503.

Not earned income. Earned income does not include:

- Pensions and annuities,
- Social security and railroad retirement benefits,
- Workers' compensation,
- Interest and dividends,
- Unemployment compensation,
- Scholarship or fellowship grants, except for those reported on a Form W-2 and paid to you for teaching or other services,
- Nontaxable workfare payments,
- Child support payments received by you,
- Income of nonresident aliens that is not effectively connected with a U.S. trade or business, or
- Any amount received for work while an inmate in a penal institution.

Rule for student-spouse or spouse not able to care for self. Your spouse is treated as having earned income for any month that he or she is:

1. A full-time student, or
2. Physically or mentally not able to care for himself or herself. (Your spouse also must live with you for more than half the year.)

If you are filing a joint return, this rule also applies to you. You can be treated as having earned income for any month you are a full-time student or not able to care for yourself.

Figure the earned income of the nonworking spouse described under (1) or (2) above as explained under *Earned Income Limit*, later.

This rule applies to only one spouse for any one month. If, in the same month, both you and your spouse do not work and are either full-time students or not physically or mentally able to care for yourselves, only one of you can be treated as having earned income in that month.

Full-time student. You are a full-time student if you are enrolled at a school for the number of hours or classes that the school considers full time. You must have been a full-time student for some part of each of 5 calendar months during the year. (The months need not be consecutive.)

School. The term "school" includes high schools, colleges, universities, and technical, trade, and mechanical schools. A school does not include an on-the-job training course, correspondence school, or school offering courses only through the Internet.

EXAMPLE

Ben and David are married and file a joint return. David works full-time. Ben was a full-time student from January through May and from September through December. Their 6-year-old son attends a daycare center while Ben is in school. Since Ben was a full-time student during at least 5 months of the year, the minimum required by the IRS, he is considered to have worked each of the 9 months he was a full-time student.

Assume the same facts, except that both Ben and David were full-time students for 9 months during the year. Only one of them may be considered as having worked during the months they were students. For this reason, they would not be able to claim a credit for child care expenses.

Assume instead that while Ben and David were full-time students, Ben also held a part-time job. Both may now be considered as having worked during the 9 months they were students—Ben because he was working and David because he was a full-time student. They may claim a credit for child care expenses.

Work-Related Expense Test

Child and dependent care expenses must be work-related to qualify for the credit. Expenses are considered work-related only if both of the following are true.

- They allow you (and your spouse if filing jointly) to work or look for work.
- They are for a qualifying person's care.

Working or Looking for Work

To be work-related, your expenses must allow you to work or look for work. If you are married, generally both you and your spouse must work or look for work. One spouse is treated as working during any month he or she is a full-time student or is not physically or mentally able to care for himself or herself.

Your work can be for others or in your own business or partnership. It can be either full time or part time.

Work also includes actively looking for work. However, if you do not find a job and have no earned income for the year, you cannot take this credit. See *Earned Income Test*, earlier.

An expense is not considered work-related merely because you had it while you were working. The purpose of the expense must be to allow you to work. Whether your expenses allow you to work or look for work depends on the facts.

Example 1. The cost of a babysitter while you and your spouse go out to eat is not normally a work-related expense.

Example 2. You work during the day. Your spouse works at night and sleeps during the day. You pay for care of your 5-year-old child during the hours when you are working and your spouse is sleeping. Your expenses are considered work-related.

Volunteer work. For this purpose, you are not considered to be working if you do unpaid volunteer work or volunteer work for a nominal salary.

EXAMPLES
Example 1
Susan is single. She began looking for a job in November 2014. Prior to this time, she had not worked. While looking for a job, she paid a sitter to watch her 2-year-old daughter. She finally found a job in February 2015. Her child care expenses during November and December 2014 were $125. Since Susan did not have income from work in 2014, she may not claim a credit for her child care expenses for that year.

Assume the same facts, except that Susan had worked until October 2014 when she was laid off and began looking for a new job. In this instance, she did have income from work during the year, so she may claim a credit for her child care expenses incurred while looking for work.

Example 2
Missy works 12 hours per week as an unpaid volunteer in the local library. She pays a sitter to watch her 3-year-old twins while she is working. Since she is not compensated for her work, she may not claim a credit for her child care expenses.

If Missy were paid $15 per week for her services in the library, she still could not claim a credit for her child care expenses because her work is for a nominal salary. What is considered a nominal salary is determined by the facts and circumstances of each situation. As a general rule, however, if you are working for less than the minimum wage, you would generally be considered to be working for a nominal salary.

Work for part of year. If you work or actively look for work during only part of the period covered by the expenses, then you must figure your expenses for each day. For example, if you work all year and pay care expenses of $250 a month ($3,000 for the year), all the expenses are work-related. However, if you work or look for work for only 2 months and 15 days during the year and pay expenses of $250 a month, your work-related expenses are limited to $625 (2½ months × $250).

Temporary absence from work. You do not have to figure your expenses for each day during a short, temporary absence from work, such as for vacation or a minor illness, if you have to pay for care anyway. Instead, you can figure your credit including the expenses you paid for the period of absence.

An absence of 2 weeks or less is a short, temporary absence. An absence of more than 2 weeks may be considered a short, temporary absence, depending on the circumstances.

Example. You pay a nanny to care for your 2-year-old son and 4-year-old daughter so you can work. You become ill and miss 4 months of work, but receive sick pay. You continue to pay the nanny to care for the children while you are ill. Your absence is not a short, temporary absence, and your expenses are not considered work-related.

Part-time work. If you work part-time, you generally must figure your expenses for each day. However, if you have to pay for care weekly, monthly, or in another way that includes both days worked and days not worked, you can figure your credit including the expenses you paid for days you did not work. Any day when you work at least 1 hour is a day of work.

Example 1. You work 3 days a week. While you work, your 6-year-old child attends a dependent care center, which complies with all state and local regulations. You can pay the center $150 for any 3 days a week or $250 for 5 days a week. Your child attends the center 5 days a week. Your work-related expenses are limited to $150 a week.

Example 2. The facts are the same as in *Example 1* except the center does not offer a 3-day option. The entire $250 weekly fee may be a work-related expense.

Care of a Qualifying Person

To be work-related, your expenses must be to provide care for a qualifying person.

You do not have to choose the least expensive way of providing care. The cost of a paid care provider may be an expense for the care of a qualifying person even if another care provider is available at no cost.

Expenses are for the care of a qualifying person only if their main purpose is the person's well-being and protection.

Expenses for household services qualify if part of the services is for the care of qualifying persons. See *Household services*, later.

Expenses not for care. Expenses for care do not include amounts you pay for food, lodging, clothing, education, and entertainment. However, you can include small amounts paid for these items if they are incidental to and cannot be separated from the cost of caring for the qualifying person.

Child support payments are not for care and do not qualify for the credit.

Education. Expenses for a child in nursery school, preschool, or similar programs for children below the level of kindergarten are expenses for care. Expenses to attend kindergarten or a higher grade are not expenses for care. Do not use these expenses to figure your credit.

However, expenses for before- or after-school care of a child in kindergarten or a higher grade may be expenses for care.

Summer school and tutoring programs are not for care.

Example 1. You take your 3-year-old child to a nursery school that provides lunch and educational activities as a part of its preschool childcare service. The lunch and educational activities are incidental to the childcare, and their cost cannot be separated from the cost of care. You can count the total cost when you figure the credit.

Example 2. You place your 10-year-old child in a boarding school so you can work full time. Only the part of the boarding school expense that is for the care of your child is a work-related expense.

You can count that part of the expense in figuring your credit if it can be separated from the cost of education. You cannot count any part of the amount you pay the school for your child's education.

Care outside your home. You can count the cost of care provided outside your home if the care is for your dependent under age 13 or any other qualifying person who regularly spends at least 8 hours each day in your home.

Dependent care center. You can count care provided outside your home by a dependent care center only if the center complies with all state and local regulations that apply to these centers.

A dependent care center is a place that provides care for more than six persons (other than persons who live there) and receives a fee, payment, or grant for providing services for any of those persons, even if the center is not run for profit.

Camp. The cost of sending your child to an overnight camp is not considered a work-related expense. The cost of sending your child to a day camp may be a work-related expense, even if the camp specializes in a particular activity, such as computers or soccer.

Transportation. If a care provider takes a qualifying person to or from a place where care is provided, that transportation is for the care of the qualifying person. This includes transportation by bus, subway, taxi, or private car. However, transportation not provided by a care provider is not for the care of a qualifying person. Also, if you pay the transportation cost for the care provider to come to your home, that expense is not for care of a qualifying person.

Fees and deposits. Fees you paid to an agency to get the services of a care provider, deposits you paid to an agency or preschool, application fees, and other indirect expenses are work-related expenses if you have to pay them to get care, even though they are not directly for care. However, a forfeited deposit is not for the care of a qualifying person if care is not provided.

Example 1. You paid a fee to an agency to get the services of the nanny who cares for your 2-year-old daughter while you work. The fee you paid is a work-related expense.

Example 2. You placed a deposit with a preschool to reserve a place for your 3-year-old child. You later sent your child to a different preschool and forfeited the deposit. The forfeited deposit is not for care and so is not a work-related expense.

Household services. Expenses you pay for household services meet the work-related expense test if they are at least partly for the well-being and protection of a qualifying person.

Household services are ordinary and usual services done in and around your home that are necessary to run your home. They include the services of a housekeeper, maid, or cook. However, they do not include the services of a chauffeur, bartender, or gardener. See *Household Services* in Publication 503 for more information.

In this chapter, the term housekeeper refers to any household employee whose services include the care of a qualifying person.

Taxes paid on wages. The taxes you pay on wages for qualifying child and dependent care services are work-related expenses. See *Employment Taxes for Household Employers*, later.

Payments to Relatives or Dependents

You can count work-related payments you make to relatives who are not your dependents, even if they live in your home. However, do not count any amounts you pay to:

1. A dependent for whom you (or your spouse if filing jointly) can claim an exemption,
2. Your child who was under age 19 at the end of the year, even if he or she is not your dependent,
3. A person who was your spouse any time during the year, or
4. The parent of your qualifying person if your qualifying person is your child and under age 13.

EXAMPLE

Edward lives with his daughter Stacy and cares for his granddaughter Melissa after school while Stacy is at work. Stacy pays her father $300 per month and cannot claim him as a dependent. These payments qualify as work-related expenses for Stacy.

Assume, instead, that Stacy pays her other daughter, Sarah, $150 per month to look after Melissa, Sarah's sister. Sarah turns 19 during the year and can be claimed as a dependent by Stacy. Stacy's payments to Sarah are not qualified work-related expenses.

Joint Return Test

Generally, married couples must file a joint return to take the credit. However, if you are legally separated or living apart from your spouse, you may be able to file a separate return and still take the credit.

Legally separated. You are not considered married if you are legally separated from your spouse under a decree of divorce or separate maintenance. You may be eligible to take the credit on your return using head of household filing status.

Married and living apart. You are not considered married and are eligible to take the credit if all the following apply.

1. You file a return apart from your spouse.
2. Your home is the home of a qualifying person for more than half the year.
3. You pay more than half the cost of keeping up your home for the year.
4. Your spouse does not live in your home for the last 6 months of the year.

EXAMPLE

Cole and Christine separated in April. They are not legally separated at the end of the year and plan to file separate returns. Their two children lived with Christine for the entire year, and she provided more than half the costs of maintaining her household for the year. Christine may claim a credit on her separate return.

Assume, instead, that Cole and Christine were separated in August. Since Cole lived in Christine's home during part of the last 6 months of the year, a joint return must be filed to claim the credit.

Costs of keeping up a home. The costs of keeping up a home normally include property taxes, mortgage interest, rent, utility charges, home repairs, insurance on the home, and food eaten at home.

The costs of keeping up a home do not include payments for clothing, education, medical treatment, vacations, life insurance, transportation, or mortgage principal.

They also do not include the purchase, permanent improvement, or replacement of property. For example, you cannot include the cost of replacing a water heater. However, you can include the cost of repairing a water heater.

Death of spouse. If your spouse died during the year and you do not remarry before the end of the year, you generally must file a joint return to take the credit. If you do remarry before the end of the year, the credit can be claimed on your deceased spouse's return.

Provider Identification Test

You must identify all persons or organizations that provide care for your child or dependent. Use Form 2441, Part I, to show the information.

If you do not have any care providers and you are filing Form 2441 only to report taxable income in Part III, enter "none" in line 1, column (a).

Information needed. To identify the care provider, you must give the provider's:
1. Name,
2. Address, and
3. Taxpayer identification number.

If the care provider is an individual, the taxpayer identification number is his or her social security number or individual taxpayer identification number. If the care provider is an organization, then it is the employer identification number (EIN).

You do not have to show the taxpayer identification number if the care provider is a tax-exempt organization (such as a church or school). In this case, enter "Tax-Exempt" in the space where Form 2441 asks for the number.

If you cannot provide all of the information or if the information is incorrect, you must be able to show that you used due diligence (discussed later) in trying to furnish the necessary information.

Getting the information. You can use Form W-10 to request the required information from the care provider. If you do not use Form W-10, you can get the information from one of the other sources listed in the instructions for Form W-10 including:
1. A copy of the provider's social security card,
2. A copy of the provider's completed Form W-4 if he or she is your household employee,
3. A copy of the statement furnished by your employer if the provider is your employer's dependent care plan, or
4. A letter or invoice from the provider if it shows the information.

EXPLANATION
Also see _Records You Need_ in chapter 40, _What to do if you employ domestic help_, if the care provider does not have a social security number.

TAXORGANIZER
Keep Form W-10 with your tax records to substantiate the name, address, and taxpayer identification number(s) of your daycare provider(s). If Form W-10 is not used, keep any other documents that substantiate the required information.

Records

You should keep this information with your tax records. Do not send Form W-10 (or other document containing this information) to the Internal Revenue Service.

Tip

If you had expenses in 2014 that you did not pay until 2015, you cannot count them when figuring your 2014 credit. You may be able to claim a credit for them on your 2015 return.

Due diligence. If the care provider information you give is incorrect or incomplete, your credit may not be allowed. However, if you can show that you used due diligence in trying to supply the information, you can still claim the credit.

You can show due diligence by getting and keeping the provider's completed Form W-10 or one of the other sources of information just listed. Care providers can be penalized if they do not provide this information to you or if they provide incorrect information.

Provider refusal. If the provider refuses to give you their identifying information, you should report on Form 2441 whatever information you have (such as the name and address). Enter "See Attached Statement" in the columns calling for the information you do not have. Then attach a statement explaining that you requested the information from the care provider, but the provider did not give you the information. Be sure to write your name and social security number on this statement. The statement will show that you used due diligence in trying to furnish the necessary information.

U.S. citizens and resident aliens living abroad. If you are living abroad, your care provider may not have, and may not be required to get, a U.S. taxpayer identification number (for example, an SSN or EIN). If so, enter "LAFCP" (Living Abroad Foreign Care Provider) in the space for the care provider's taxpayer identification number.

How To Figure the Credit

Your credit is a percentage of your work-related expenses. Your expenses are subject to the earned income limit and the dollar limit. The percentage is based on your adjusted gross income.

Figuring Total Work-Related Expenses

To figure the credit for 2014 work-related expenses, count only those you paid by December 31, 2014.

Expenses prepaid in an earlier year. If you pay for services before they are provided, you can count the prepaid expenses only in the year the care is received. Claim the expenses for the later year as if they were actually paid in that later year.

EXAMPLE

Martha paid $1,800 in November 2014 to the daycare center her son attends. The payment was for the 6-month period from November 201 through April 2015. She may use $600 (2/6 × $1,800) of this payment in calculating her credit for 2014. This amount represents payment for services rendered in November and December 2014. She may use $1,200 (4/6 × $1,800) of this payment in 2015. This amount represents payment for services rendered in January through April 2015.

TAXPLANNER

The general rule is that expenses used in computing your child care credit are included in figuring your tax for the year in which the expenses are paid or for the year in which the services are provided, whichever is later. However, regardless of when the expenses are paid, they are subject to a dollar limitation for the year in which the services are provided. You may not reap an additional tax benefit by paying your expenses in a year earlier than the year in which the services are provided. See *Amount of Credit* and *Worksheet A* in IRS Publication 503, *Child and Dependent Care Expenses*.

Example

Bernadette, who is divorced and files a separate return, paid $300 in January 2014 for care provided for her daughter in November and December 2013. Her adjusted gross income and earned income in 2013 was $25,000, and she paid $1,200 for work-related expenses in 2013. Bernadette may increase her 2014 child care credit by $90, as calculated in Column A, following:

	Column A	Column B
1. 2013 qualified expenses paid in 2012	$1,200	$3,000
2. 2013 qualified expenses paid in 2013	300	300
3. Total qualified 2013 expenses	$1,500	$3,300
4. Limitation for one qualifying person	$3,000	$3,000
5. Earned income limitation	25,000	25,000
6. Smallest of lines 3, 4, and 5	1,500	3,000
7. Child care expenses used in calculating 2013 credit	(1,200)	(3,000)
8. 2013 expenses carried over to 2014	$300	-0-
9. Credit percentage applicable for 2013 adjusted gross income	30%	30%
10. Increase in 2014 credit (line 8 x line 9)	$90	-0-

Bernadette should attach a statement to her 2014 return, showing the name and taxpayer identification number of her daughter (for whom she paid the prior year's expenses) and the calculation in Column A as support for her inclusion of $90 on line 9, Form 2441. She should write "CPYE" and the amount of the additional credit in the dotted line next to line 9 on Form 2441 and should increase line 9 by this amount.

Assume, instead, that Bernadette paid $3,000 in work-related expenses during 2013. No increase in her 2014 credit is available (see Column B, earlier), since the maximum amount of expenses for 2013 is already used in calculating the credit. She receives no benefit for the $300 paid in 2014, as she would have received no benefit if it had been paid in 2013.

Expenses reimbursed. If a state social services agency pays you a nontaxable amount to reimburse you for some of your child and dependent care expenses, you cannot count the expenses that are reimbursed as work-related expenses.

Example. You paid work-related expenses of $3,000. You are reimbursed $2,000 by a state social services agency. You can use only $1,000 to figure your credit.

Expenses not paid until the following year. Do not count 2013 expenses that you paid in 2014 as work-related expenses for 2014. You may be able to claim an additional credit for them on your 2014 return, but you must figure it separately. See *Payments for prior year's expenses* under *Amount of Credit* in Publication 503.

Medical expenses. Some expenses for the care of qualifying persons who are not able to care for themselves may qualify as work-related expenses and also as medical expenses. You can use them either way, but you cannot use the same expenses to claim both a credit and a medical expense deduction.

If you use these expenses to figure the credit and they are more than the earned income limit or the dollar limit, discussed later, you can add the excess to your medical expenses. However, if you use your total expenses to figure your medical expense deduction, you cannot use any part of them to figure your credit.

EXAMPLE
During the year, you pay $3,350 to a private-duty nurse for the care of your physically handicapped dependent daughter, who is not able to care for herself. These expenses are for work done in your home and qualify as medical expenses. Your earned income for the year is $25,000. Because your work-related expenses are for one qualifying person, you may take a maximum of $3,000 of these expenses into account in figuring your tax credit. You may treat the remaining $350 as a medical expense.

TAXORGANIZER
Keep copies of receipts and canceled checks to document the amount of dependent care expenses that you paid for the year. The fact that you have provided these to your employer's plan may not be sufficient without such records.

Dependent Care Benefits
If you receive dependent care benefits, your dollar limit for purposes of the credit may be reduced. See *Reduced Dollar Limit*, later. But, even if you cannot take the credit, you may be able to take an exclusion or deduction for the dependent care benefits.

Dependent care benefits. Dependent care benefits include:

1. Amounts your employer paid directly to either you or your care provider for the care of your qualifying person while you work,
2. The fair market value of care in a daycare facility provided or sponsored by your employer, and
3. Pre-tax contributions you made under a dependent care flexible spending arrangement.

Your salary may have been reduced to pay for these benefits. If you received benefits as an employee, they should be shown in box 10 of your Form W-2. See *Statement for employee*, later. Benefits you received as a partner should be shown in box 13 of your Schedule K-1 (Form 1065) with code O. Enter the amount of these benefits on Form 2441, Part III, line 12.

Exclusion or deduction. If your employer provides dependent care benefits under a qualified plan, you may be able to exclude these benefits from your income. Your employer can tell you whether your benefit plan qualifies. To claim the exclusion, you must complete Part III of Form 2441. You cannot use Form 1040EZ.

If you are self-employed and receive benefits from a qualified dependent care benefit plan, you are treated as both employer and employee. Therefore, you would not get an exclusion from wages. Instead, you would get a deduction on Form 1040, Schedule C, line 14; Schedule E, line 19 or 28; or Schedule F, line 15. To claim the deduction, you must use Form 2441.

The amount you can exclude or deduct is limited to the smallest of:

1. The total amount of dependent care benefits you received during the year,
2. The total amount of qualified expenses you incurred during the year,
3. Your earned income,
4. Your spouse's earned income, or
5. $5,000 ($2,500 if married filing separately).

The definition of earned income for the exclusion or deduction is the same as the definition used when figuring the credit except that earned income for the exclusion or deduction does not include any dependent care benefits you receive. See *Earned Income Limit*, later.

TAXSAVER

If your employer provides dependent care benefits, you will see them reported on your W-2 in Box 10. These benefits reduce your expenses available for the child care credit.

For example, if your employer excluded $1,000 from your income for dependent care, you would only be allowed to use $2,000 to claim the credit.

Child care expenses paid during 2014	$3,000
Less: Employer-provided benefits	(1,000)
Maximum expenses available for the credit	$2,000

To ensure that you get the greater tax savings, you should carefully consider the impact of a reduction in income as compared to the value of the credit. Generally, as long as the credit amount is not greater than the taxpayer's tax liability, those with lower levels of adjusted gross income will benefit more from the dependent care credit than from a dependent care benefit reduction to taxable income.

EXPLANATION

If you incur expenses for more than one qualifying person, you can still claim a credit if your employer has reduced your income by the full $5,000 and you have been reimbursed the full $5,000. See *Reduced Dollar Limit*, later. But your credit will be based on a maximum of $1,000 of expenses ($6,000 less $5,000) since your expenses must be reduced by the amount of any reimbursement.

Statement for employee. Your employer must give you a Form W-2 (or similar statement) showing in box 10 the total amount of dependent care benefits provided to you during the year under a qualified plan. Your employer will also include any dependent care benefits over $5,000 in your wages shown on your Form W-2 in box 1.

Effect of exclusion on credit. If you exclude dependent care benefits from your income, the amount of the excluded benefits:

1. Is not included in your work-related expenses, and
2. Reduces the dollar limit, discussed later.

Earned Income Limit

The amount of work-related expenses you use to figure your credit cannot be more than:

1. Your earned income for the year if you are single at the end of the year, or
2. The smaller of your or your spouse's earned income for the year if you are married at the end of the year.

Earned income is defined under *Earned Income Test*, earlier.

TAXPLANNER

At year-end, if you are self-employed, you should review your income and expenses for the year. To the extent it is possible, income and expenses for the remaining part of the year should be timed to take maximum advantage of the dependent care credit.

Separated spouse. If you are legally separated or married and living apart from your spouse (as described under *Joint Return Test*, earlier), you are not considered married for purposes of the earned income limit. Use only your income in figuring the earned income limit.

Surviving spouse. If your spouse died during the year and you file a joint return as a surviving spouse, you may, but are not required to, take into account the earned income of your spouse who died during the year.

Community property laws. You should disregard community property laws when you figure earned income for this credit.

> ### EXAMPLE
> Durwood and Sheila are married and live in a community property state. Durwood earns $52,000 as an engineer, while Sheila earns $15,000 as a teaching assistant. Under community property laws, each is considered to have earned half the other's compensation, and is considered to bring in $33,500 [(50% × $52,000) + (50% × $15,000)]. Community property laws are disregarded, however, for the purpose of calculating this tax credit. Under the Earned Income Limit test, Durwood has $52,000 of earned income and Sheila has $15,000.

You or your spouse is a student or not able to care for self. Your spouse who is either a full-time student or not able to care for himself or herself is treated as having earned income. His or her earned income for each month is considered to be at least $250 if there is one qualifying person in your home, or at least $500 if there are two or more.

Spouse works. If your spouse works during that month, use the higher of $250 (or $500) or his or her actual earned income for that month.

Spouse qualifies for part of month. If your spouse is a full-time student or not able to care for himself or herself for only part of a month, the full $250 (or $500) still applies for that month.

You are a student or not able to care for self. These rules also apply if you are a student or not able to care for yourself and you are filing a joint return. For each month or part of a month you are a student or not able to care for yourself, your earned income is considered to be at least $250 (or $500). If you also work during that month, use the higher of $250 (or $500) or your actual earned income for that month.

Both spouses qualify. If, in the same month, both you and your spouse are either full-time students or not able to care for yourselves, only one spouse can be considered to have this earned income of $250 (or $500) for that month.

> ### TAXALERT
> As stated under the *Qualifying Person Test*, if the dependent for whom you have work-related expenses is disabled for only part of a month, the total work-related expenses are limited to that part of the month.
>
> #### Example 1
> David and Donna are married and file a joint return. Because of an accident, David is incapable of self-care for the entire tax year. To keep working, Donna pays a neighbor $2,000 to take care of him. Donna's adjusted gross income is $29,000. The entire amount is earned income. They figure their credit on the smallest of the following amounts:
>
> | | |
> |---|---|
> | 1) Total work-related care expenses | $2,000 |
> | 2) Donna's earned income | $29,000 |
> | 3) Income considered earned by David (12 × $250) | $3,000 |
> | **Allowable credit (28% of $2,000)** | **$560** |
>
> #### Example 2
> Carlos works and keeps up a home for himself, his wife, Diana, and their two children (both under age 13). Carlos has adjusted gross income of $35,000. The entire amount is earned income.
>
>   Diana is a full-time student at State University from January 4 through June 10. She does not return to school after June 10.

They paid a neighbor $600 per month from January 4 to June 10 (total $3,600) to care for their two children in her home while the children were not in school.

They figure the credit on the smallest of the following amounts:

1) Total work-related care expenses	$3,600
2) Carlos' earned income	$35,000
3) Income considered earned by Diana (6 x $500)	$3,000
Allowable credit (25% of $3,000)	**$750**

Dollar Limit

There is a dollar limit on the amount of your work-related expenses you can use to figure the credit. This limit is $3,000 for one qualifying person, or $6,000 for two or more qualifying persons.

Yearly limit. The dollar limit is a yearly limit. The amount of the dollar limit remains the same no matter how long, during the year, you have a qualifying person in your household. Use the $3,000 limit if you paid work-related expenses for the care of one qualifying person at any time during the year. Use $6,000 if you paid work-related expenses for the care of more than one qualifying person at any time during the year.

EXAMPLE

Wendy employs a full-time housekeeper to care for her two children while she works. Her older child turned 13 years old during the year. The dollar limit on her work-related expenses is $6,000, since at some time during the year she had two qualifying persons.

Assume the same facts, except that Wendy has only one child, Paris, who turned 13 years old on August 31. The dollar limit on her work-related expenses is $3,000. Only her expenses through August 30 may be used. The limit is the maximum amount that may be used in calculating the credit. If her actual expenses through August 30 are less than $3,000, she must use that amount in calculating her tax credit.

Reduced Dollar Limit

If you received dependent care benefits that you exclude or deduct from your income, you must subtract that amount from the dollar limit that applies to you. Your reduced dollar limit is figured on Form 2441, Part III. See *Dependent Care Benefits*, earlier, for information on excluding or deducting these benefits.

Example 1. George is a widower with one child and earns $24,000 a year. He pays work-related expenses of $2,900 for the care of his 4-year-old child and qualifies to claim the credit for child and dependent care expenses. His employer pays an additional $1,000 under a dependent care benefit plan. This $1,000 is excluded from George's income.

Although the dollar limit for his work-related expenses is $3,000 (one qualifying person), George figures his credit on only $2,000 of the $2,900 work-related expenses he paid. This is because his dollar limit is reduced as shown next.

George's Reduced Dollar Limit

1) Maximum allowable expenses for one qualifying person	$3,000
2) Minus: Dependent care benefits George excludes from income	~1,000
3) Reduced dollar limit on expenses George can use for the credit.	$2,000

Example 2. Randall is married and both he and his wife are employed. Each has earned income in excess of $6,000. They have two children, Anne and Andy, ages 2 and 4, who attend a daycare facility licensed and regulated by the state. Randall's work-related expenses are $6,000 for the year.

Randall's employer has a dependent care assistance program as part of its cafeteria plan, which allows employees to make pre-tax contributions to a dependent care flexible spending arrangement. Randall has elected to take the maximum $5,000 exclusion from his salary to cover dependent care expenses through this program.

Although the dollar limit for his work- related expenses is $6,000 (two or more qualifying persons), Randall figures his credit on only $1,000 of the $6,000 work-related expense paid. This is because his dollar limit is reduced as shown next.

Randall's Reduced Dollar Limit

1) Maximum allowable expenses for two qualifying persons $6,000

2) Minus: Dependent care benefits Randall selects from employer's cafeteria plan and excludes from income .... ~5,000

3) Reduced dollar limit on expenses Randall can use for the credit $1,000

Amount of Credit

To determine the amount of your credit, multiply your work-related expenses (after applying the earned income and dollar limits) by a percentage. This percentage depends on your adjusted gross income shown on Form 1040, line 38; Form 1040A, line 22; or Form 1040NR, line 37. The following table shows the percentage to use based on adjusted gross income.

IF your adjusted gross income is:		THEN the percentage is:
Over	**But not over**	
$ 0	$15,000	35%
15,000	17,000	34%
17,000	19,000	33%
19,000	21,000	32%
21,000	23,000	31%
23,000	25,000	30%
25,000	27,000	29%
27,000	29,000	28%
29,000	31,000	27%
31,000	33,000	26%
33,000	35,000	25%
35,000	37,000	24%
37,000	39,000	23%
39,000	41,000	22%
41,000	43,000	21%
43,000	No limit	20%

EXAMPLES

Example 1

Karl is single, has adjusted gross income of $83,500, and has $1,800 in qualified expenses for 2014. The credit available to him is $540 (30% × $1,800).

Assume, instead, that Karl has adjusted gross income of $88,500. Now his available tax credit is $504 (28% × $1,800).

Example 2

Joni has a tax liability of $730 before credits and a potential child care credit of $1,050. She may use $730 of the child care credit to bring her tax liability to zero. The excess credit of $320 is effectively lost. It may not be refunded, carried forward to a future year, or carried back to a prior year.

How To Claim the Credit

To claim the credit, you can file Form 1040, Form 1040A or Form 1040NR. You cannot claim the credit on Form 1040EZ or Form 1040NR-EZ.

Form 1040, Form 1040A or Form 1040NR. You must complete Form 2441 and attach it to your Form 1040, Form 1040A or Form 1040NR. Enter the credit on Form 1040, line 49; Form 1040A, line 31; or Form 1040NR, line 47.

Limit on credit. The amount of credit you can claim is generally limited to the amount of your tax. For more information, see the Instructions for Form 2441.

Tax credit not refundable. You cannot get a refund for any part of the credit that is more than this limit.

EXPLANATION

The American Taxpayer Relief Act of 2012 included a provision that permanently extended the ability for individuals to offset their entire regular and AMT tax liabilities with personal nonrefundable tax credits (including the child and dependent care credit).

Recordkeeping. You should keep records of your work-related expenses. Also, if your dependent or spouse is not able to care for himself or herself, your records should show both the nature and the length of the disability. Other records you should keep to support your claim for the credit are described earlier under *Provider Identification Test*.

TAXORGANIZER

Your records of work-related expenses may be either canceled checks or cash receipt tickets. A note in your files recording the nature and length of a person's disability should be sufficient documentation in most cases.

Employment Taxes for Household Employers

If you pay someone to come to your home and care for your dependent or spouse, you may be a household employer. If you are a household employer, you will need an employer identification number (EIN) and you may have to pay employment taxes. If the individuals who work in your home are self-employed, you are not liable for any of the taxes discussed in this section. Self-employed persons who are in business for themselves are not household employees. Usually, you are not a household employer if the person who cares for your dependent or spouse does so at his or her home or place of business.

If you use a placement agency that exercises control over what work is done and how it will be done by a babysitter or companion who works in your home, the worker is not your employee. This control could include providing rules of conduct and appearance and requiring regular reports. In this case, you do not have to pay employment taxes. But, if an agency merely gives you a list of sitters and you hire one from that list, and pay the sitter directly, the sitter may be your employee.

If you have a household employee, you may be subject to:
1. Social security and Medicare taxes,
2. Federal unemployment tax, and
3. Federal income tax withholding.

Social security and Medicare taxes are generally withheld from the employee's pay and matched by the employer. Federal unemployment (FUTA) tax is paid by the employer only and provides for payments of unemployment compensation to workers who have lost their jobs. Federal income tax is withheld from the employee's total pay if the employee asks you to do so and you agree.

For more information on a household employer's tax responsibilities, see Publication 926 and Schedule H (Form 1040) and its instructions.

State employment tax. You may also have to pay state unemployment tax. Contact your state unemployment tax office for information. You should also find out whether you need to pay or collect other state employment taxes or carry workers' compensation insurance. For a list of state unemployment tax agencies, visit the U.S. Department of Labor's website. A link to that website is in Publication 926, or you can find it with an online search.

EXPLANATION

Also, see chapter 40, *What to do if you employ domestic help.*

EXAMPLES

The following example shows how to figure the credit for child and dependent care expenses for two children when employer-provided dependent care benefits are involved. The filled-in Form 2441 is shown at the end of this chapter.

Illustrated example. Joan Thomas is divorced and has two children, ages 3 and 9. She works at ACME Computers. Her adjusted gross income (AGI) is $29,000, and the entire amount is earned income.

Joan's younger child (Susan) stays at her employer's on-site childcare center while she works. The benefits from this childcare center qualify to be excluded from her income. Her employer reports the value of this service as $3,000 for the year. This $3,000 is shown on her Form W-2 in box 10, but is not included in taxable wages in box 1.

A neighbor, Pat Green, cares for Joan's older child (Seth) after school, on holidays, and during the summer. Joan pays her neighbor $2,400 for this care.

Joan figures her credit on Form 2441 as follows:

1)	Work-related expenses Joan paid	$2,400
2)	Dollar limit (2 or more qualified individuals)	$6,000
3)	Minus: Dependent care benefits excluded from Joan's income	−3,000
4)	Reduced dollar limit	$3,000
5)	Lesser of expenses paid ($2,400) or dollar limit ($3,000)	$2,400
6)	Percentage for AGI of $29,000 (28%).	.28
7)	Multiply the amount on line 5 by the percentage on line 6 ($2,400 × .28)	$672
8)	Enter the tax liability limit from Form 2441, line 10	$943
9)	Credit (Enter the smaller of line 7 or line 8)	$672

EXPLANATION

Note: The dollar limit for two or more qualifying persons ($6,000) is reduced by the amount of excluded benefits, as discussed earlier under *Reduced Dollar Limit.*

TAXORGANIZER

Records you should keep:

Keep copies of receipts and canceled checks to document the amount of dependent care expenses that you paid for the year.

Keep Form W-10 with your tax records to substantiate the name, address, and taxpayer identification number(s) of your daycare provider(s). If Form W-10 is not used, keep any other documents that substantiate the required daycare provider information.

If your dependent or spouse is disabled, your records should contain the description and the length of the disability.

Form **2441**

Department of the Treasury
Internal Revenue Service (99)

Child and Dependent Care Expenses

▶ Attach to Form 1040, Form 1040A, or Form 1040NR.

▶ Information about Form 2441 and its separate instructions is at *www.irs.gov/form2441.*

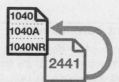

OMB No. 1545-0074

20**14**

Attachment
Sequence No. **21**

Name(s) shown on return

Joan Thomas

Your social security number

559-00-3436

Part I Persons or Organizations Who Provided the Care—You **must** complete this part.
(If you have more than two care providers, see the instructions.)

1	(a) Care provider's name	(b) Address (number, street, apt. no., city, state, and ZIP code)	(c) Identifying number (SSN or EIN)	(d) Amount paid (see instructions)
	Pat Green	12 Ash Avenue		
		Hometown, GA 30078	240-00-3811	2,400
	ACME Computers	(See W-2)		

Did you receive **dependent care benefits?**
No ▶ Complete only Part II below.
Yes ▶ Complete Part III on the back next.

Caution. If the care was provided in your home, you may owe employment taxes. If you do, you cannot file Form 1040A. For details, see the instructions for Form 1040, line 60a, or Form 1040NR, line 59a.

Part II Credit for Child and Dependent Care Expenses

2   Information about your **qualifying person(s).** If you have more than two qualifying persons, see the instructions.

(a) Qualifying person's name		(b) Qualifying person's social security number	(c) Qualified expenses you incurred and paid in 2014 for the person listed in column (a)
First	Last		
Seth	Thomas	559-00-1235	2,400
Susan	Thomas	559-00-5678	

3	Add the amounts in column (c) of line 2. **Do not** enter more than $3,000 for one qualifying person or $6,000 for two or more persons. If you completed Part III, enter the amount from line 31	**3**	2,400
4	Enter your **earned income.** See instructions	**4**	29,000
5	If married filing jointly, enter your spouse's earned income (if you or your spouse was a student or was disabled, see the instructions); **all others**, enter the amount from line 4 .	**5**	29,000
6	Enter the **smallest** of line 3, 4, or 5	**6**	2,400
7	Enter the amount from Form 1040, line 38; Form 1040A, line 22; or Form 1040NR, line 37 . . . . . [7	29,000]		
8	Enter on line 8 the decimal amount shown below that applies to the amount on line 7		

If line 7 is:			If line 7 is:		
Over	But not over	Decimal amount is	Over	But not over	Decimal amount is
$0—15,000		.35	$29,000—31,000		.27
15,000—17,000		.34	31,000—33,000		.26
17,000—19,000		.33	33,000—35,000		.25
19,000—21,000		.32	35,000—37,000		.24
21,000—23,000		.31	37,000—39,000		.23
23,000—25,000		.30	39,000—41,000		.22
25,000—27,000		.29	41,000—43,000		.21
27,000—29,000		.28	43,000—No limit		.20

8 | X . | 28

9	Multiply line 6 by the decimal amount on line 8. If you paid 2013 expenses in 2014, see the instructions	**9**	672
10	Tax liability limit. Enter the amount from the Credit Limit Worksheet in the instructions. . . . . . . [10	943]		
11	**Credit for child and dependent care expenses.** Enter the **smaller** of line 9 or line 10 here and on Form 1040, line 49; Form 1040A, line 31; or Form 1040NR, line 47	**11**	672

For Paperwork Reduction Act Notice, see your tax return instructions.

Cat. No. 11862M

Form **2441** (2014)

DRAFT AS OF July 2, 2014 DO NOT FILE

Part III   **Dependent Care Benefits**

12	Enter the total amount of **dependent care benefits** you received in 2014. Amounts you received as an employee should be shown in box 10 of your Form(s) W-2. **Do not** include amounts reported as wages in box 1 of Form(s) W-2. If you were self-employed or a partner, include amounts you received under a dependent care assistance program from your sole proprietorship or partnership	**12**	3,000
13	Enter the amount, if any, you carried over from 2013 and used in 2014 during the grace period. See instructions	**13**	
14	Enter the amount, if any, you forfeited or carried forward to 2015. See instructions . . .	**14**	( )
15	Combine lines 12 through 14. See instructions	**15**	3,000

16	Enter the total amount of **qualified expenses** incurred in 2014 for the care of the **qualifying person(s)** . . .	**16**	5,400		
17	Enter the **smaller** of line 15 or 16	**17**	3,000		
18	Enter your **earned income**. See instructions . . .	**18**	29,000		
19	Enter the amount shown below that applies to you. • If married filing jointly, enter your spouse's earned income (if you or your spouse was a student or was disabled, see the instructions for line 5). • If married filing separately, see instructions. • All others, enter the amount from line 18.	**19**	29,000		
20	Enter the **smallest** of line 17, 18, or 19	**20**	3,000		
21	Enter $5,000 ($2,500 if married filing separately **and** you were required to enter your spouse's earned income on line 19).	**21**	5,000		

22	Is any amount on line 12 from your sole proprietorship or partnership? (Form 1040A filers go to line 25.) ☐ **No.** Enter -0-. ☐ **Yes.** Enter the amount here	**22**	
23	Subtract line 22 from line 15 . . . . **23**		
24	**Deductible benefits.** Enter the **smallest** of line 20, 21, or 22. Also, include this amount on the appropriate line(s) of your return. See instructions	**24**	
25	**Excluded benefits. Form 1040 and 1040NR filers:** If you checked "No" on line 22, enter the smaller of line 20 or 21. Otherwise, subtract line 24 from the smaller of line 20 or line 21. If zero or less, enter -0-. **Form 1040A filers:** Enter the **smaller** of line 20 or line 21 . .	**25**	3,000
26	**Taxable benefits. Form 1040 and 1040NR filers:** Subtract line 25 from line 23. If zero or less, enter -0-. Also, include this amount on Form 1040, line 7, or Form 1040NR, line 8. On the dotted line next to Form 1040, line 7, or Form 1040NR, line 8, enter "DCB." **Form 1040A filers:** Subtract line 25 from line 15. Also, include this amount on Form 1040A, line 7. In the space to the left of line 7, enter "DCB".	**26**	-0-

To claim the child and dependent care
credit, complete lines 27 through 31 below.

27	Enter $3,000 ($6,000 if two or more qualifying persons)	**27**	6,000
28	**Form 1040 and 1040NR filers:** Add lines 24 and 25. **Form 1040A filers:** Enter the amount from line 25	**28**	3,000
29	Subtract line 28 from line 27. If zero or less, **stop.** You cannot take the credit. **Exception.** If you paid 2013 expenses in 2014, see the instructions for line 9	**29**	3,000
30	Complete line 2 on the front of this form. **Do not** include in column (c) any benefits shown on line 28 above. Then, add the amounts in column (c) and enter the total here.	**30**	2,400
31	Enter the **smaller** of line 29 or 30. Also, enter this amount on line 3 on the front of this form and complete lines 4 through 11	**31**	2,400

Form **2441** (2014)

Chapter 34

Credit for the elderly or the disabled

Note

IRS Publication 17 (*Your Federal Income Tax*) has been updated by Ernst & Young LLP for 2014. Dates and dollar amounts shown are for 2014. Underlined type is used to indicate where IRS text has been updated. Places where text has been removed are indicated by the sentence: *Text intentionally omitted.*

ey.com/EYTaxGuide

Ernst & Young LLP will update the *EY Tax Guide 2015* website with relevant taxpayer information as it becomes available. You can also sign up for email alerts to let you know when changes have been made.

Introduction

When Congress passed legislation giving the elderly a tax credit, the idea was to provide a measure of tax relief for older citizens who were not receiving adequate amounts of social security or other nontaxable *pensions*. Consequently, if you or your spouse is 65 years old or older, you may be entitled to a credit of as much as $1,125 against your tax.

Taxpayers under 65 years of age who are permanently and totally disabled may also be eligible for the credit.

In general, if you file as a *single* individual, you do not qualify for the tax credit if (1) you receive nontaxable social security or other nontaxable pensions of $5,000 or more, (2) your *adjusted gross income (AGI)* is $17,500 or more, or (3) your tax is zero. Different AGI limitations apply to taxpayers filing as married filing jointly or married filing separately.

This chapter tells you specifically if you are eligible for the credit for the elderly and, if so, how you may claim it—whether you are single or married.

If you qualify, you may be able to reduce the tax you owe by taking the credit for the elderly or the disabled which is figured on Schedule R (Form 1040A or 1040).

This chapter explains the following.
- Who qualifies for the credit for the elderly or the disabled.
- How to claim the credit.

You may be able to take the credit for the elderly or the disabled if:
- You are age 65 or older at the end of 2014, or
- You retired on permanent and total disability and have taxable disability income.

Useful Items

You may want to see:

Publication
- ☐ **524** Credit for the Elderly or the Disabled
- ☐ **554** Tax Guide for Seniors

Form (and Instruction)
- ☐ **Schedule R (Form 1040A or 1040)** Credit for the Elderly or the Disabled

EXPLANATION

See chapter 11, *Social security and equivalent railroad retirement benefits*, for a discussion of how social security and equivalent railroad retirement benefits are taxed.

Credit for the elderly or disabled. Someone who is 65 or older, or is under 65 and who retired with a permanent and total disability and receives taxable disability income, can claim a credit equal to 15% of a specific amount. That amount equals an initial (or base) amount—generally $3,750, $5,000, or $7,500, depending on age and filing status—reduced by nontaxable social security benefits and certain other nontaxable payments received. The base amount must also be reduced by half of adjusted gross income in excess of certain minimum levels. The maximum credit is $1,125, on a joint return where both spouses qualify and no reductions apply. Because of the low base amounts only people with very small amounts of income can claim the credit.

Tip

You can take the credit only if you file Form 1040 or Form 1040A. You cannot take the credit if you file Form 1040EZ or Form 1040NR.

Are You Eligible for the Credit?

You can take the credit for the elderly or the disabled if you meet both of the following requirements.

- You are a qualified individual.
- Your income is not more than certain limits.

You can use Figure 34-A and Table 34-1 as guides to see if you are eligible for the credit.

Use Figure 34-A first to see if you are a qualified individual. If you are, go to Table 34-1 to make sure your income is not too high to take the credit.

Qualified Individual

You are a qualified individual for this credit if you are a U.S. citizen or resident alien, and either of the following applies.

1. You were age 65 or older at the end of 2014.
2. You were under age 65 at the end of 2014 and all three of the following statements are true.
   a. You retired on permanent and total disability (explained later).
   b. You received taxable disability income for 2014.
   c. On January 1, 2014, you had not reached mandatory retirement age (defined later under *Disability income*).

EXPLANATION

To qualify for the credit, you cannot have reached your employer's mandatory retirement age before the beginning of the year. The reason for the requirement is that any amount received from your employer after you have reached mandatory retirement age is not disability income.

Age 65. You are considered to be age 65 on the day before your 65th birthday. Therefore, if you were born on January 1, 1950, you are considered to be age 65 at the end of 2014.

U.S. Citizen or Resident Alien

You must be a U.S. citizen or resident alien (or be treated as a resident alien) to take the credit. Generally, you cannot take the credit if you were a nonresident alien at any time during the tax year.

Exceptions. You may be able to take the credit if you are a nonresident alien who is married to a U.S. citizen or resident alien at the end of the tax year and you and your spouse choose to treat you as a U.S. resident alien. If you make that choice, both you and your spouse are taxed on your worldwide incomes.

If you were a nonresident alien at the beginning of the year and a resident alien at the end of the year, and you were married to a U.S. citizen or resident alien at the end of the year, you may be able to choose to be treated as a U.S. resident alien for the entire year. In that case, you may be allowed to take the credit.

For information on these choices, see chapter 1 of Publication 519, U.S. Tax Guide for Aliens.

EXPLANATION

For more information about resident and nonresident aliens, see chapter 42, *Foreign citizens living in the United States.*

Married Persons

Generally, if you are married at the end of the tax year, you and your spouse must file a joint return to take the credit. However, if you and your spouse did not live in the same household at any time during the tax year, you can file either a joint return or separate returns and still take the credit.

EXAMPLES

Example 1

Don and Sylvia Fitch are both past the age of 65 and are married at year's end, but they have been living apart since May. They must file a joint return to claim the credit. Next year, if they remain married and live apart for the entire year, they may file separate returns and claim the credit.

Example 2

Sam and Leah Wilkins are married at year's end and have lived apart for the entire year. Leah is 63 years old, is permanently and totally disabled, and receives a disability pension from her former employer. Sam is 69 years old. They may file separate returns, and each may claim a credit, since both meet the basic tests for eligibility.

Figure 34-A. **Are You a Qualified Individual?**

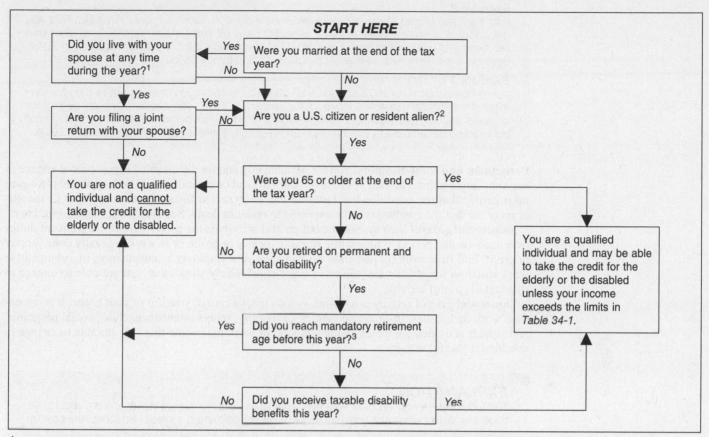

START HERE

Were you married at the end of the tax year? — Yes → Did you live with your spouse at any time during the year?[1]

Were you married at the end of the tax year? — No ↓ No

Did you live with your spouse at any time during the year?[1] — Yes ↓

Are you filing a joint return with your spouse? — Yes → Are you a U.S. citizen or resident alien?[2]

Are you filing a joint return with your spouse? — No ↓

Are you a U.S. citizen or resident alien?[2] — No →

Are you a U.S. citizen or resident alien?[2] — Yes ↓

You are not a qualified individual and <u>cannot</u> take the credit for the elderly or the disabled.

Were you 65 or older at the end of the tax year? — Yes → You are a qualified individual and may be able to take the credit for the elderly or the disabled unless your income exceeds the limits in *Table 34-1.*

Were you 65 or older at the end of the tax year? — No ↓

Are you retired on permanent and total disability? — No →

Are you retired on permanent and total disability? — Yes ↓

Did you reach mandatory retirement age before this year?[3] — Yes →

Did you reach mandatory retirement age before this year?[3] — No ↓

Did you receive taxable disability benefits this year? — No →

Did you receive taxable disability benefits this year? — Yes →

[1] However, you may be able to claim this credit if you lived with your spouse during the first 6 months of the year and you qualify to file as head of household. You qualify to file as head of household if you are considered unmarried and meet certain other conditions. See Publication 501 for more information.

[2] If you were a nonresident alien at any time during the tax year and were married to a U.S. citizen or resident alien at the end of the tax year, see *U.S. Citizen or Resident Alien* under *Qualified Individual.* If you and your spouse choose to treat you as a U.S. resident alien, answer "Yes" to this question.

[3] Mandatory retirement age is the age set by your employer at which you would have been required to retire, had you not become disabled.

Head of household. You can file as head of household and qualify to take the credit, even if your spouse lived with you during the first 6 months of the year, if you meet certain tests. See *Head of Household* in chapter 2 for the tests you must meet.

Under Age 65

If you are under age 65 at the end of 2014, you can qualify for the credit only if you are retired on permanent and total disability (discussed next) and have taxable disability income (discussed later under *Disability income*). You are retired on permanent and total disability if:

- You were permanently and totally disabled when you retired, and
- You retired on disability before the close of the tax year.

Even if you do not retire formally, you may be considered retired on disability when you have stopped working because of your disability.

If you retired on disability before 1977, and were not permanently and totally disabled at the time, you can qualify for the credit if you were permanently and totally disabled on January 1, 1976, or January 1, 1977.

Permanent and total disability. You are permanently and totally disabled if you cannot engage in any substantial gainful activity because of your physical or mental condition. A qualified physician must certify that the condition has lasted or can be expected to last continuously for 12 months or more, or that the condition can be expected to result in death. See *Physician's statement*, later.

Substantial gainful activity. Substantial gainful activity is the performance of significant duties over a reasonable period of time while working for pay or profit, or in work generally done for pay or profit. Full-time work (or part-time work done at your employer's convenience) in a competitive work situation for at least the minimum wage conclusively shows that you are able to engage in substantial gainful activity.

Substantial gainful activity is not work you do to take care of yourself or your home. It is not unpaid work on hobbies, institutional therapy or training, school attendance, clubs, social programs, and similar activities. However, doing this kind of work may show that you are able to engage in substantial gainful activity.

EXPLANATION

The facts and circumstances of your particular situation determine whether you are able to "engage in substantial gainful activity" for purposes of claiming the credit. No strict rule governs every case. The most important question to remember is "Did you hold a job that paid at least the minimum wage?" This can mean any job, not just the job you held before your disability.

The fact that you have not worked for some time is not, of itself, conclusive evidence that you cannot engage in substantial gainful activity.

Sheltered employment. Certain work offered at qualified locations to physically or mentally impaired persons is considered sheltered employment. These qualified locations are in sheltered workshops, hospitals, and similar institutions, homebound programs, and Department of Veterans Affairs (VA) sponsored homes.

Compared to commercial employment, pay is lower for sheltered employment. Therefore, one usually does not look for sheltered employment if he or she can get other employment. The fact that one has accepted sheltered employment is not proof of the person's ability to engage in substantial gainful activity.

Physician's statement. If you are under age 65, you must have your physician complete a statement certifying that you were permanently and totally disabled on the date you retired. You can use the statement in the Instructions for Schedule R.

You do not have to file this statement with your Form 1040 or Form 1040A, but you must keep it for your records.

Veterans. If the Department of Veterans Affairs (VA) certifies that you are permanently and totally disabled, you can substitute VA Form 21-0172, Certification of Permanent and Total Disability, for the physician's statement you are required to keep. VA Form 21-0172 must be signed by a person authorized by the VA to do so. You can get this form from your local VA regional office.

Physician's statement obtained in earlier year. If you got a physician's statement in an earlier year and, due to your continued disabled condition, you were unable to engage in any substantial gainful activity during 2014, you may not need to get another physician's statement for 2014. For a detailed explanation of the conditions you must meet, see the instructions for Schedule R, Part II. If you meet the required conditions, check the box on your Schedule R, Part II, line 2.

If you checked box 4, 5, or 6 in Part I of Schedule R, enter in the space above the box on line 2 in Part II the first name(s) of the spouse(s) for whom the box is checked.

Table 34-1. **Income Limits**

IF your filing status is...	THEN, even if you qualify (see *Figure 34-A*), you CANNOT take the credit if...	
	Your adjusted gross income (AGI)* is equal to or more than...	OR the total of your nontaxable social security and other nontaxable pension(s), annuities, or disability income is equal to or more than...
single, head of household, or qualifying widow(er) with dependent child	$17,500	$5,000
married filing jointly **and** only one spouse qualifies in <u>Figure 34-A</u>	$20,000	$5,000
married filing jointly **and** both spouses qualify in <u>Figure 34-A</u>	$25,000	$7,500
married filing separately **and** you lived apart from your spouse for all of 2014	$12,500	$3,750

* AGI is the amount on Form 1040A, line 22, or Form 1040, line 38.

Disability income. If you are under age 65, you must also have taxable disability income to qualify for the credit. Disability income must meet both of the following requirements.
1. It must be paid under your employer's accident or health plan or pension plan.
2. It must be included in your income as wages (or payments instead of wages) for the time you are absent from work because of permanent and total disability.

Payments that are not disability income. Any payment you receive from a plan that does not provide for disability retirement is not disability income. Any lump-sum payment for accrued annual leave that you receive when you retire on disability is a salary payment and is not disability income.

For purposes of the credit for the elderly or the disabled, disability income does not include amounts you receive after you reach mandatory retirement age. Mandatory retirement age is the age set by your employer at which you would have had to retire, had you not become disabled.

EXAMPLES

Example 1
Melissa Lee retired in June at age 55 with a total and permanent disability. At retirement, she received a $5,000 payment for accrued vacation and sick-leave days. The amount is not disability income, since it is not paid to her as wages or in lieu of wages because of her permanent and total disability.

Example 2
Adam LeBleu turned 62 years old on September 9, 2014. He had retired several years earlier as a result of a total and permanent disability. He has received disability payments from his employer since retirement. His former employer's mandatory retirement age is 62. As a result, any amount Adam receives after he reaches the age of 62 will not be disability income.

Income Limits
To determine if you can claim the credit, you must consider two income limits. The first limit is the amount of your adjusted gross income (AGI). The second limit is the amount of nontaxable social security and other nontaxable pensions, annuities, or disability income you received. The limits are shown in <u>Table 34-1</u>.

If your AGI and nontaxable pensions, annuities, or disability income are less than the income limits, you may be able to claim the credit. See *How to Claim the Credit*, later.

How to Claim the Credit
You can figure the credit yourself or the Internal Revenue Service will figure it for you.

Credit Figured for You
If you choose to have the IRS figure the credit for you, read the following discussion for the form you will file (Form 1040 or 1040A).

Caution

If either your AGI or your nontaxable pensions, annuities, or disability income are equal to or more than the income limits, you cannot take the credit.

If you want the IRS to figure your tax, see chapter 31.

Form 1040. If you want the IRS to figure your credit, see *Form 1040 Line Entries* under *Tax Figured by IRS* in chapter 31.

Form 1040A. If you want the IRS to figure your credit, see *Form 1040A Line Entries* under *Tax Figured by IRS* in chapter 31.

Credit Figured by You

If you choose to figure the credit yourself, fill out the front of Schedule R. Next, fill out Schedule R, Part III. If you file Form 1040A, enter the amount from Schedule R, line 22, on Form 1040A, line 32. If you file Form 1040, include the amount from Schedule R, line 22, on line 54; check box c, and enter "Sch R" on the line next to that box.

For a step-by-step discussion about filling out Part III of Schedule R, see *Figuring the Credit Yourself* in Publication 524.

Limit on credit. The amount of the credit you can claim is generally limited to the amount of your tax. Use the Credit Limit Worksheet in the Instructions for Schedule R to determine if your credit is limited.

Chapter 35
Child tax credit

ey.com/EYTaxGuide

Introduction

The child tax credit is a credit of up to $1,000 for each qualifying child under age 17. A qualifying child (defined in greater detail in chapter 3, *Personal exemptions and dependents*) is an individual for whom the taxpayer can claim a dependency exemption and who is the child, stepchild, or eligible foster child of the taxpayer or is a brother, sister, stepbrother, or stepsister of the taxpayer or a descendant of any of these relatives ("brother" and "sister" include a brother or sister by half-blood). That means a "qualifying child" doesn't necessarily have to be your child!

The child tax credit is phased out depending on your adjusted gross income and the number of qualifying children. While the child tax credit is nonrefundable, meaning the credit is limited to the amount of the tax liability on the return, there are certain cases in which you may be able to receive a refund when the child tax credit exceeds your tax liability. This refundable portion of the child tax credit is called the additional child tax credit.

The child tax credit is the largest tax code provision benefiting families with children. Be careful not to confuse the child tax credit with the credit for child and dependent care expenses, which is explained in chapter 33, *Child and dependent care credit*.

The child tax credit is a credit that may reduce your tax by as much as $1,000 for each of your qualifying children.

The additional child tax credit is a credit you may be able to take if you are not able to claim the full amount of the child tax credit.

This chapter explains the following.
- Who is a qualifying child.
- The amount of the credit.
- How to claim the credit.

Caution

The child tax credit and the additional child tax credit should not be confused with the child and dependent care credit discussed in chapter 33.

TAXSAVER

The child tax credit discussed in this chapter should not be confused with the child and dependent care credit discussed in chapter 33. They are completely different credits with different requirements. It may be possible, however, to qualify for both credits.

If you have no tax. Credits, such as the child tax credit or the credit for child and dependent care expenses, are used to reduce tax. If your tax on Form 1040, line 47, or Form 1040A, line 30, is zero, do not figure the child tax credit because there is no tax to reduce. However, you may qualify for the additional child tax credit on line 67 (Form 1040) or line 43 (Form 1040A).

Useful items

You may want to see:

Publication
- **972** Child Tax Credit

Form (and instructions)

- ☐ **Schedule 8812 (Form 1040A or 1040)**   Child Tax Credit
- ☐ **W-4**   Employee's Withholding Allowance Certificate

Qualifying Child

A qualifying child for purposes of the child tax credit is a child who:

1. Is your son, daughter, stepchild, foster child, brother, sister, stepbrother, stepsister, or a descendant of any of them (for example, your grandchild, niece, or nephew),
2. Was under age 17 at the end of 2014,
3. Did not provide over half of his or her own support for 2014,
4. Lived with you for more than half of 2014 (see *Exceptions to time lived with you*, later),
5. Is claimed as a dependent on your return,
6. Does not file a joint return for the year (or files it only as a claim for refund), and
7. Was a U.S. citizen, a U.S. national, or a resident of the United States. If the child was adopted, see *Adopted child*, later.

For each qualifying child you must check the box on Form 1040 or Form 1040A, line 6c, box (4).

Example 1. Your son turned 17 on December 30, 2014. He is a citizen of the United States and you claimed him as a dependent on your return. He is not a qualifying child for the child tax credit because he was not under age 17 at the end of 2014.

Example 2. Your daughter turned 8 years old in 2014. She is not a citizen of the United States, has an ITIN, and lived in Mexico all of 2014. She is not a qualifying child for the child tax credit because she was not a resident of the United States for 2014.

Filers who have certain child dependents with an individual Taxpayer identification Number (ITIN). If you are claiming a child tax credit or additional child tax credit for a child you identified on your tax return with an ITIN instead of an SSN, you must complete Part I of Schedule 8812 (Form 1040A or 1040).

Although a child may be your dependent, you may only claim a child tax credit or additional child tax credit for a dependent who is a citizen, national, or resident of the United States. To be treated as a resident of the United States, a child generally will need to meet the requirements of the substantial presence test. For more information about the substantial presence test, see Publication 519, U.S. Tax Guide for Aliens.

Adopted child. An adopted child is always treated as your own child. An adopted child includes a child lawfully placed with you for legal adoption.

If you are a U.S. citizen or U.S. national and your adopted child lived with you all year as a member of your household in 2014, that child meets condition (7) above to be a qualifying child for the child tax credit.

Exceptions to time lived with you. A child is considered to have lived with you for more than half of 2014 if the child was born or died in 2014 and your home was this child's home for more than half the time he or she was alive. Temporary absences by you or the child for special circumstances, such as for school, vacation, business, medical care, military service, or detention in a juvenile facility, count as time the child lived with you.

There are also exceptions for kidnapped children and children of divorced or separated parents. For details, see *Residency Test* in chapter 3.

Qualifying child of more than one person. A special rule applies if your qualifying child is the qualifying child of more than one person. For details, see *Special Rule for Qualifying Child of More Than One Person* in chapter 3.

Amount of Credit

The maximum amount you can claim for the credit is $1,000 for each qualifying child.

Limits on the Credit

You must reduce your child tax credit if either (1) or (2) applies.

1. The amount on Form 1040, line 47, or Form 1040A, line 30, is less than the credit. If this amount is zero, you cannot take this credit because there is no tax to reduce. But you may be able to take the additional child tax credit. See *Additional Child Tax Credit*, later.
2. Your modified adjusted gross income (AGI) is more than the amount shown below for your filing status.
    a. Married filing jointly – $110,000.
    b. Single, head of household, or qualifying widow(er) – $75,000.
    c. Married filing separately – $55,000.

Modified AGI. For purposes of the child tax credit, your modified AGI is your AGI plus the following amounts that may apply to you.

- Any amount excluded from income because of the exclusion of income from Puerto Rico. On the dotted line next to Form 1040, line 38, enter the amount excluded and identify it as "EPRI." Also attach a copy of any Form(s) 499R-2/W-2PR to your return.
- Any amount on line 45 or line 50 of Form 2555, Foreign Earned Income.
- Any amount on line 18 of Form 2555-EZ, Foreign Earned Income Exclusion.
- Any amount on line 15 of Form 4563, Exclusion of Income for Bona Fide Residents of American Samoa.

If you do not have any of the above, your modified AGI is the same as your AGI.

AGI. Your AGI is the amount on Form 1040, line 38, or Form 1040A, line 22.

Claiming the Credit

To claim the child tax credit, you must file Form 1040 or Form 1040A. You cannot claim the child tax credit on Form 1040EZ. You must provide the name and identification number (usually a social security number) on your tax return for each qualifying child.

To figure your credit, first review the Child Tax Credit Worksheet in your Form 1040 or 1040A instructions. If you are instructed to use Publication 972, you may not use the worksheet in your tax return instructions; instead, you must use Publication 972 to figure the credit. If you are not instructed to use Publication 972, you may use the Child Tax Credit Worksheet in your Form 1040 or 1040A instructions or Publication 972 to figure the credit.

> **Caution**
>
> *If you claim the child tax credit with a child identified by an ITIN, you must also file Schedule 8812.*

Additional Child Tax Credit

This credit is for certain individuals who get less than the full amount of the child tax credit. The additional child tax credit may give you a refund even if you do not owe any tax.

How to claim the additional child tax credit.

To claim the additional child tax credit, follow the steps below.

1. Make sure you figured the amount, if any, of your child tax credit. See *Claiming the Credit*, earlier.
2. If you answered "Yes" on line 9 or line 10 of the Child Tax Credit Worksheet in the Form 1040 or Form 1040A instructions, or line 13 of the Child Tax Credit Worksheet in Publication 972, use Parts II through IV of Schedule 8812 to see if you can take the additional child tax credit.
3. If you have an additional child tax credit on line 13 of Schedule 8812, carry it to Form 1040, line 67, or Form 1040A, line 43.

Completing Schedule 8812 (Form 1040A or 1040)

Schedule 8812 contains four parts, but can really be thought of as two sections. Part I is distinct and separate from Parts II–IV.

Part I

You only need to complete Part I if you are claiming the child tax credit for a child identified by an IRS individual taxpayer identification number (ITIN). When completing Part I, only answer the questions with regard to children identified by an ITIN; you do not need to complete Part I of Schedule 8812 for any child that is identified by a social security number (SSN) or an IRS adoption taxpayer identification number (ATIN). If all the children for whom you checked the box in column 4 of line 6c on your Form 1040 or Form 1040A are identified by an SSN or an ATIN, you do not need to complete Part I of Schedule 8812.

Parts II–IV

Parts II–IV help you figure your additional child tax credit. Generally, you should only complete Parts II–IV if you are instructed to do so after completing the Child Tax Credit Worksheet in your tax return instructions or Publication 972. See *How to claim the additional child tax credit*, earlier.

Chapter 36
Education credits and other education tax benefits

ey.com/EYTaxGuide

Note

IRS Publication 17 (*Your Federal Income Tax*) has been updated by Ernst & Young LLP for 2014. Dates and dollar amounts shown are for 2014. Underlined type is used to indicate where IRS text has been updated. Places where text has been removed are indicated by the sentence: *Text intentionally omitted*.

ey.com/EYTaxGuide

Ernst & Young LLP will update the *EY Tax Guide 2015* website with relevant taxpayer information as it becomes available. You can also sign up for email alerts to let you know when changes have been made.

Introduction

If you have eligible education expenses in 2014, you may be able to benefit from two education credits that can reduce your taxes. These are the American opportunity credit and the lifetime learning credit.

Here are some of the key details of the American opportunity credit:

1. The American Taxpayer Relief Act of 2012 extended this credit through 2017.
2. The maximum amount of the credit is $2,500 per student. The credit can be claimed for qualified tuition and related expenses for the first four years of a student's postsecondary degree or certificate program.
3. The credit phases out if your modified adjusted gross income (AGI) is between $80,000 and $90,000 ($160,000 and $180,000 if you file a joint return).
4. Generally, up to 40% of the American opportunity credit is refundable (provided the taxpayer claiming the credit is not a child to whom the "kiddie tax" rules apply—discussed later). This means that you can receive up to a $1,000 refund even if the total amount of the credit exceeds your federal income tax liability. The term "qualified tuition and related expenses" includes expenditures for "course materials." These include books, supplies, and equipment needed for a course of study whether or not the materials are purchased from the educational institution as a condition of enrollment or attendance.

You might also be able to claim a lifetime learning credit of up to $2,000 on your tax return for educational expenditures incurred in any year of postsecondary education. However, you cannot claim both the lifetime learning credit and the American opportunity credit for the same student in the same year. For 2014, the amount of your lifetime learning credit is phased out if your AGI is between $54,000 and $64,000 ($108,000 and $128,000 if you file a joint return). The lifetime learning credit is nonrefundable. Although the lifetime learning credit can reduce your tax liability to zero, any credit in excess of your tax liability is not refunded to you.

Amounts expended for education that are otherwise excludable from gross income or deductible as a business expense cannot be claimed as qualified tuition expenses for the American opportunity credit or the lifetime learning credit.

This chapter also discusses a variety of other education benefits that may be available to you—student loan deductions, Coverdell education savings accounts, deduction for qualified tuition expenses, and employer-provided educational assistance programs, among others.

For 2014, there are two tax credits available to persons who pay expenses for higher (postsecondary) education. They are:

- The American opportunity credit, and
- The lifetime learning credit.

The chapter will present an overview of these education credits. To get the detailed information you will need to claim either of the credits, and for examples illustrating that information, see chapters 2 and 3 of Publication 970.

Can you claim more than one education credit this year? For each student, you can choose for any year only one of the credits. For example, if you choose to take the American opportunity credit for a child on your 2014 tax return, you cannot, for that same child, also claim the lifetime learning credit for 2014.

If you are eligible to claim the American opportunity credit and you are also eligible to claim the lifetime learning credit for the same student in the same year, you can choose to claim either credit, but not both.

If you pay qualified education expenses for more than one student in the same year, you can choose to take the American opportunity and the lifetime learning credits on a per-student, per-year basis. This means that, for example, you can claim the American opportunity credit for one student and the lifetime learning credit for another student in the same year.

TAXPLANNER

For 2014, it may be more beneficial for you to claim the American opportunity credit than the lifetime learning credit. However, it is advisable to compute your tax liability using each credit, respectively, and choose the credit that produces the greatest tax savings.

Differences between the American opportunity and lifetime learning credits. There are several differences between these two credits. These differences are summarized in <u>Table 36-1</u>, later.

Useful Items

You may want to see:

Publication

☐ **970** Tax Benefits for Education

Form (and Instructions)

☐ **8863** Education Credits (American Opportunity and Lifetime Learning Credits)

TAXPLANNER

The IRS launched a section on its website, *www.irs.gov*, highlighting various education incentives designed to help parents and students pay for college. The *Tax Benefits for Education: Information Center* section includes tips for taking advantage of long-standing education deductions, credits, and savings plans. In addition, there is a special section, *Tax Incentives for Higher Education*, with a summary of the education incentives and a link to frequently asked questions regarding the lifetime learning credit.

Who Can Claim an Education Credit

You may be able to claim an education credit if you, your spouse, or a dependent you claim on your tax return was a student enrolled at or attending an eligible educational institution. The credits are based on the amount of qualified education expenses paid for the student in 2014 for academic periods beginning in 2014 and in the first 3 months of 2015.

For example, if you paid $1,500 in December 2014 for qualified tuition for the spring 2015 semester beginning in January 2015, you may be able to use that $1,500 in figuring your 2014 education credit(s).

Academic period. An academic period includes a semester, trimester, quarter, or other period of study (such as a summer school session) as reasonably determined by an educational institution. In the case of an educational institution that uses credit hours or clock hours and does not have academic terms, each payment period can be treated as an academic period.

Eligible educational institution. An eligible educational institution is any college, university, vocational school, or other postsecondary educational institution eligible to participate in a student aid program administered by the U.S. Department of Education. It includes virtually all accredited public, nonprofit, and proprietary (privately owned profit-making) postsecondary institutions. The educational institution should be able to tell you if it is an eligible educational institution.

Certain educational institutions located outside the United States also participate in the U.S. Department of Education's Federal Student Aid (FSA) programs.

Who can claim a dependent's expenses. If an exemption is allowed as a deduction for any person who claims the student as a dependent, all qualified education expenses of the student are treated as having been paid by that person. Therefore, only that person can claim an education credit for the student. If a student is not claimed as a dependent on another person's tax return, only the student can claim a credit.

> ### TAXPLANNER
> **Who should claim the education credit.** If you claim your child as a dependent, only you may claim the education credit for the child's qualified tuition and related expenses. If, however, you are eligible to claim your child as a dependent but choose not to do so, your child may claim the education credit for his or her qualified tuition and related expenses even if the tuition and expenses were paid by you, the parent. The American opportunity credit is not refundable to the child, however, if the kiddie tax rules apply to that child.
>
> It is important to note, however, that if a parent who is eligible to claim a dependency exemption for a student does not do so, the student is not allowed to take a personal exemption for himself or herself on his or her own return. As a result, the exemption for the student may be lost. If you are subject to the income phase-out limitation of the education credits, you should review the overall tax effect of not claiming an exemption for your child and allowing your child to claim the education credits.

Expenses paid by a third party. Qualified education expenses paid on behalf of the student by someone other than the student (such as a relative) are treated as paid by the student. However, qualified education expenses paid (or treated as paid) by a student who is claimed as a dependent on your tax return are treated as paid by you. Therefore, you are treated as having paid expenses that were paid by the third party. For more information and an example see *Who Can Claim a Dependent's Expenses* in Pub. 970, chapter 2 or 3.

Who cannot claim a credit. You cannot take an education credit if any of the following apply.
1. You are claimed as a dependent on another person's tax return, such as your parent's return.
2. Your filing status is married filing separately.
3. You (or your spouse) were a nonresident alien for any part of 2014 and did not elect to be treated as a resident alien for tax purposes.
4. Your MAGI is one of the following.
   a. American opportunity credit: $180,000 or more if married filing jointly, or $90,000 or more if single, head of household, or qualifying widow(er).
   b. Lifetime learning credit: $128,000 or more if married filing jointly, or $64,000 or more if single, head of household, or qualifying widow(er).

Generally, your MAGI is the amount on your Form 1040, line 38, or Form 1040A, line 22. However, if you are filing Form 2555, Form 2555-EZ, or Form 4563, or are excluding income from Puerto Rico, add to the amount on your Form 1040, line 38, or Form 1040A, line 22, the amount of income you excluded. For details, see Pub. 970.

Figure 36-A may be helpful in determining if you can claim an education credit on your tax return.

Qualified Education Expenses

Generally, qualified education expenses are amounts paid in 2014 for tuition and fees required for the student's enrollment or attendance at an eligible educational institution. It does not matter whether the expenses were paid in cash, by check, by credit or debit card, or with borrowed funds.

For course-related books, supplies, and equipment, only certain expenses qualify.
- American opportunity credit: Qualified education expenses include amounts spent on books, supplies, and equipment needed for a course of study, whether or not the materials are purchased from the educational institution as a condition of enrollment or attendance.
- Lifetime learning credit: Qualified education expenses include amounts for books, supplies, and equipment **only if** required to be paid to the institution as a condition of enrollment or attendance.

Qualified education expenses include nonacademic fees, such as student activity fees, athletic fees, or other expenses unrelated to the academic course of instruction, **only if** the fee must be paid to the institution as a condition of enrollment or attendance. However, fees for personal expenses (described below) are never qualified education expenses.

ernments or by private education institutions. Contributions to these programs are not deductible, but the earnings on the contributions accumulate tax-free until the college costs are paid from the funds. In addition, distributions from qualified tuition programs are tax-free to the extent the funds are used to pay qualified higher education expenses. Qualified expenses include tuition and fees, books, supplies, and equipment. However, expenses for computer technology and equipment, as well as Internet access, are not qualified expenses. Distributions of earnings that are not used for qualified higher education expenses will be subject to income tax plus a 10% penalty tax.

Coverdell Education Savings Account (ESA). You can establish Coverdell ESAs and make contributions of up to $2,000 annually for each child under age 18. The right to make these contributions begins to phase out once your adjusted gross income (AGI) is over $190,000 on a joint return ($95,000 for singles). A child can make a contribution to his or her own account. As with Section 529 plans, the contributions are not deductible but funds in the account are not taxed, and distributions are tax-free if spent on qualified education expenses, which include pre-college expenses like private elementary school tuition.

Table 36-1. **Comparison of Education Credits**

Caution. You can claim both the American opportunity credit and the lifetime learning credit on the same return—but not for the same student.

	American Opportunity Credit	Lifetime Learning Credit
Maximum credit	Up to $2,500 credit per **eligible student**	Up to $2,000 credit per **return**
Limit on modified adjusted gross income (MAGI)	$180,000 if married filing jointly; $90,000 if single, head of household, or qualifying widow(er)	$128,000 if married filing jointly; $64,000 if single, head of household, or qualifying widow(er)
Refundable or nonrefundable	40% of credit may be refundable	Credit limited to the amount of tax you must pay on your taxable income
Number of years of postsecondary education	Available **ONLY** if the student had not completed the first 4 years of postsecondary education before 2014	Available for all years of postsecondary education and for courses to acquire or improve job skills
Number of tax years credit available	Available **ONLY** for **4** tax years per eligible student (including any year(s) the Hope credit was claimed)	Available for an unlimited number of years
Type of program required	Student must be pursuing a program leading to a degree or other recognized education credential	Student does not need to be pursuing a program leading to a degree or other recognized education credential
Number of courses	Student must be enrolled at least half time for at least one academic period beginning during the tax year	Available for one or more courses
Felony drug conviction	At the end of 2014, the student had not been convicted of a felony for possessing or distributing a controlled substance	Felony drug convictions do not make the student ineligible
Qualified expenses	Tuition, required enrollment fees, and course materials that the student needs for a course of study whether or not the materials are bought at the educational institution as a condition of enrollment or attendance	Tuition and fees required for enrollment or attendance (including amounts required to be paid to the institution for course-related books, supplies, and equipment)
Payments for academic periods	Payments made in 2014 for academic periods beginning in 2014 or beginning in the first 3 months of 2015	

Tip

The American opportunity credit will always be greater than or equal to the lifetime learning credit for any student who is eligible for both credits. However, if any of the conditions for the American opportunity credit, listed in Table 36-1 earlier, are not met for any student, you cannot take the American opportunity credit for that student. You may be able to take the lifetime learning credit for part or all of that student's qualified education expenses instead. See Pub. 970 for information on other education benefits.

Qualified education expenses for either credit **do not** include amounts paid for:
• Personal expenses. This means room and board, insurance, medical expenses (including student health fees), transportation, and other similar personal, living, or family expenses.
• Any course or other education involving sports, games, or hobbies, or any noncredit course, unless such course or other education is part of the student's degree program or (for the lifetime learning credit only) helps the student acquire or improve job skills.

You should receive Form 1098–T, Tuition Statement, from the institution reporting either payments received in 2014 (box 1) or amounts billed in 2014 (box 2). However, the amount in box 1 or 2 of Form 1098-T may be different from the amount you paid (or are treated as having paid). In completing Form 8863, use only the amounts you actually paid (plus any amounts you are treated as having paid) in 2014, reduced as necessary, as described in *Adjustments to Qualified Education Expenses*, later.

EXPLANATION
Use Form 8863, *Education Credits (American Opportunity and Lifetime Learning Credits)*, to figure and claim your education credits. You must complete a separate Part III on page 2 for each individual for whom you are claiming either credit (American opportunity credit or lifetime learning credit) before you complete Parts I and II.

Qualified education expenses paid on behalf of the student by someone other than the student (such as a relative) are treated as paid by the student. Qualified education expenses paid (or treated as paid) by a student who is claimed as a dependent on your tax return are treated as paid by you.

If you or the student takes a deduction for higher education expenses, such as on Schedule A or C (Form 1040), you cannot use those expenses in your qualified education expenses when figuring your education credits.

Prepaid Expenses. Qualified education expenses paid in 2014 for an academic period that begins in the first 3 months of 2015 can be used in figuring an education credit for 2014 only. See *Academic period*, earlier. For example, if you pay $2,000 in December 2014 for qualified tuition for the 2015 winter quarter that begins in January 2015, you can use that $2,000 in figuring an education credit for 2014 only (if you meet all the other requirements).

Paid with borrowed funds. You can claim an education credit for qualified education expenses paid with the proceeds of a loan. Use the expenses to figure the credit for the year in which the expenses are paid, not the year in which the loan is repaid. Treat loan payments sent directly to the educational institution as paid on the date the institution credits the student's account.

Student withdraws from class(es). You can claim an education credit for qualified education expenses not refunded when a student withdraws.

No Double Benefit Allowed
You cannot do any of the following.
- Deduct higher education expenses on your income tax return (as, for example, a business expense) and also claim an education credit based on those same expenses.
- Claim more than one education credit based on the same qualified education expenses.
- Claim an education credit based on the same expenses used to figure the tax-free portion of a distribution from a Coverdell education savings account (ESA) or qualified tuition program (QTP).
- Claim an education credit based on qualified education expenses paid with educational assistance, such as a tax-free scholarship, grant, or employer-provided educational assistance. See *Adjustments to Qualified Education Expenses*, next.

> **TAXALERT**
> **One credit per customer.** The American opportunity credit and lifetime learning credit are mutually exclusive. For each eligible student in each tax year, you must elect either one of the tax credits. The American opportunity credit or the lifetime learning credit can be claimed in the same year that a distribution from a Coverdell education savings account or qualified tuition program is made, as long as the distribution is not used to cover the same expenses for which the education credits are claimed.
>
> The American opportunity credit is phased out for single taxpayers with modified adjusted gross income (MAGI) of $80,000 to $90,000 and for couples filing jointly with MAGI between $160,000 and $180,000. The lifetime learning credit is phased out for single taxpayers with modified adjusted gross income (MAGI) of $54,000 to $64,000 and, if married filing jointly, $108,000 to $128,000.

Adjustments to Qualified Education Expenses
For each student, reduce the qualified education expenses paid in 2014 by or on behalf of that student under the following rules. The result is the amount of adjusted qualified education expenses for each student.

Tax-free educational assistance. For tax-free educational assistance received in 2014, reduce the qualified educational expenses for each academic period by the amount of tax-free educational assistance allocable to that academic period. See *Academic period*, earlier.

Tax-free educational assistance includes:
- Tax-free parts of scholarships and fellowships (see chapter 12 of this publication and chapter 1 of Pub. 970),
- The tax-free part of Pell grants (see chapter 1 of Pub. 970),
- The tax-free part of employer-provided educational assistance (see Pub. 970),
- Veterans' educational assistance (see chapter 1 of Pub. 970), and
- Any other nontaxable (tax-free) payments (other than gifts or inheritances) received as educational assistance.

Caution

Qualified education expenses for any academic period must be reduced by any tax-free educational assistance allocable to that academic period. See Adjustments to Qualified Education Expenses, later.

Caution

You cannot use any amount you paid in 2013 or 2015 to figure the qualified education expenses you use to figure your 2014 education credit(s).

Tip

You may be able to increase the combined value of an education credit and certain educational assistance if the student includes some or all of the educational assistance in income in the year received. For details, see Adjustments of Qualified Education Expenses, in chapters 2 and 3 of Pub. 970.

Generally, any scholarship or fellowship is treated as tax-free educational assistance. However, a scholarship or fellowship is not treated as tax-free educational assistance to the extent the **student** includes it in gross income (if the **student** is required to file a tax return) for the year the scholarship or fellowship is received and either:

- The scholarship or fellowship (or any part of it) **must** be applied (by its terms) to expenses (such as room and board) other than qualified education expenses as defined in Qualified education expenses in Pub. 970, chapter 1; or
- The scholarship or fellowship (or any part of it) **may** be applied (by its terms) to expenses (such as room and board) other than qualified education expenses as defined in Qualified education expenses in Pub. 970, chapter 1.

Some tax-free educational assistance received after 2014 may be treated as a refund of qualified education expenses paid in 2014. This tax-free educational assistance is any tax-free educational assistance received by you or anyone else after 2014 for qualified education expenses paid on behalf of a student in 2014 (or attributable to enrollment at an eligible educational institution during 2014).

If this tax-free educational assistance is received after 2014 but before you file your 2014 income tax return, see *Refunds received after 2014 but before your income tax return is filed*, later. If this tax-free educational assistance is received after 2014 and after you file your 2014 income tax return, see *Refunds received after 2014 and after your income tax return is filed*, later.

Refunds. A refund of qualified education expenses may reduce qualified education expenses for the tax year or may require you to repay (recapture) the credit that you claimed in an earlier year. Some tax-free educational assistance received after 2014 may be treated as a refund. See Tax-free educational assistance, earlier.

Refunds received in 2014. For each student, figure the adjusted qualified education expenses for 2014 by adding all the qualified education expenses paid in 2014 and subtracting any refunds of those expenses received from the eligible educational institution during 2014.

Refunds received after 2014 but before your income tax return is filed. If anyone receives a refund after 2014 of qualified education expenses paid on behalf of a student in 2014 and the refund is received before you file your 2014 income tax return, reduce the amount of qualified education expenses for 2014 by the amount of the refund.

Refunds received after 2014 and after your income tax return is filed. If anyone receives a refund after 2014 of qualified education expenses paid on behalf of a student in 2014 and the refund is received after you file your 2014 income tax return, you may need to repay some or all of the credit that you claimed. See Credit recapture, next.

Caution

If you also pay qualified education expenses in 2015 for an academic period that begins in the first 3 months of 2015 and you receive tax-free educational assistance, or a refund, as described above, you may choose to reduce your qualified education expenses for 2015 instead of reducing your expenses for 2014.

Credit recapture. If any tax-free educational assistance for the qualified education expenses paid in 2014, or any refund of your qualified education expenses paid in 2014, is received after you file your 2014 income tax return, you must recapture (repay) any excess credit. You do this by refiguring the amount of your adjusted qualified education expenses for 2014 by reducing the expenses by the amount of the refund or tax-free educational assistance. You then refigure your education credit(s) for 2014 and figure the amount by which your 2014 tax liability would have increased if you had claimed the refigured credit(s). Include that amount as an additional tax for the year the refund or tax-free assistance was received.

Example. You paid $8,000 tuition and fees in December 2014 for your child's Spring semester beginning in January 2015. You filed your 2014 tax return on February 3, 2015, and claimed a lifetime learning credit of $1,600 ($8,000 qualified education expense paid × .20). You claimed no other tax credits. After you filed your return, your child withdrew from two courses and you received a refund of $1,400. You must refigure your 2014 lifetime learning credit using $6,600 ($8,000 qualified education expenses − $1,400 refund). The refigured credit is $1,320 and your tax liability increased by $280. You must include the difference of $280 ($1,600 credit originally claimed − $1,320 refigured credit) as additional tax on your 2015 income tax return. See the instructions for your 2015 income tax return to determine where to include this tax.

Amounts that do not reduce qualified education expenses. Do not reduce qualified education expenses by amounts paid with funds the student receives as:

- Payment for services, such as wages,
- A loan,
- A gift,
- An inheritance, or
- A withdrawal from the student's personal savings.

Figure 36-A. **Can You Claim an Education Credit for 2014?**

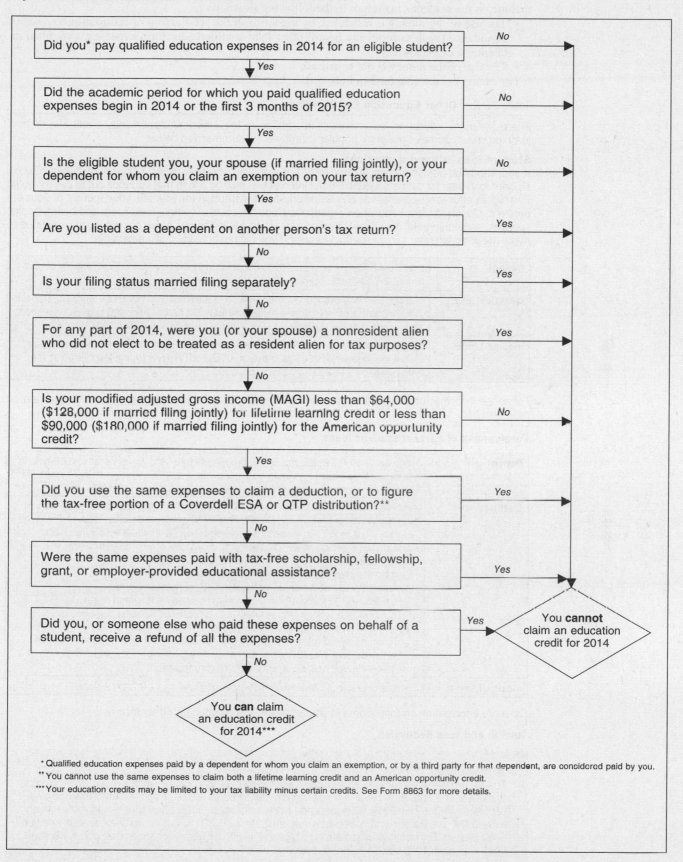

Figure 36-A. **Can You Claim an Education Credit for 2014?**

Did you* pay qualified education expenses in 2014 for an eligible student? — **No** →

Did the academic period for which you paid qualified education expenses begin in 2014 or the first 3 months of 2015? — **No** →

Is the eligible student you, your spouse (if married filing jointly), or your dependent for whom you claim an exemption on your tax return? — **No** →

Are you listed as a dependent on another person's tax return? — **Yes** →

Is your filing status married filing separately? — **Yes** →

For any part of 2014, were you (or your spouse) a nonresident alien who did not elect to be treated as a resident alien for tax purposes? — **Yes** →

Is your modified adjusted gross income (MAGI) less than $64,000 ($128,000 if married filing jointly) for lifetime learning credit or less than $90,000 ($180,000 if married filing jointly) for the American opportunity credit? — **No** →

Did you use the same expenses to claim a deduction, or to figure the tax-free portion of a Coverdell ESA or QTP distribution?** — **Yes** →

Were the same expenses paid with tax-free scholarship, fellowship, grant, or employer-provided educational assistance? — **Yes** →

Did you, or someone else who paid these expenses on behalf of a student, receive a refund of all the expenses? — **Yes** →

You cannot claim an education credit for 2014

You can claim an education credit for 2014***

* Qualified education expenses paid by a dependent for whom you claim an exemption, or by a third party for that dependent, are considered paid by you.

** You cannot use the same expenses to claim both a lifetime learning credit and an American opportunity credit.

*** Your education credits may be limited to your tax liability minus certain credits. See Form 8863 for more details.

Do not reduce the qualified education expenses by any scholarship or fellowship reported as income on the student's tax return in the following situations.

- The use of the money is restricted, by the terms of the scholarship or fellowship, to costs of attendance (such as room and board) other than qualified education expenses, as defined in chapter 1 of Pub. 970.
- The use of the money is not restricted.

For examples, see chapter 2 in Pub. 970.

Table 36-2. **Other Education Tax Benefits**

There are many education tax incentives in addition to the American opportunity credit and lifetime learning credit. Some of the more popular incentives are summarized below.

Student loan interest deductions

If your modified adjusted gross income (MAGI) is less than $80,000 ($160,000 if filing a joint return), student loan interest paid is deductible if the interest was paid on a loan that you took out to pay for qualified higher education expenses at an eligible education institution for yourself, your spouse, or your dependent. Qualified higher education expenses include the costs of tuition, fees, room and board, books, supplies, and equipment. You cannot deduct interest on a loan for which you are not legally obligated to make the payments nor can you deduct interest if you did not actually make payments.

Benefit	If you paid interest on a qualified education loan in 2014 you may be able to deduct up to $2,500 of the interest paid on your 2014 tax return.
Qualifications	You can claim the deduction if the following requirements are met: (1) Your filing status is any filing status except married filing separately, (2) No one else can claim an exemption for you on his or her tax return, (3) You paid interest on a qualified student loan.
Income Limits	For 2014, the phase-out range for taxpayers who are single, head of household, or qualifying widow(er) is $65,000 to $80,000. For taxpayers filing joint returns, the phase-out range is $130,000 to $160,000.

For more information on the student loan interest deduction, see chapter 19, *Education-related adjustments*.

Forgiveness of certain student loans

Benefit	When any loan for which you are responsible is forgiven, you generally must include the amount that was forgiven in your gross income. When certain student loans are forgiven, however, you may not have to include the amount in your income.
Qualifications	Your loan must provide that all or a portion of the debt will be canceled if you work for a certain period of time, in certain professions, and for a designated class of employers. The loan must have been made by a qualified lender. A qualified lender includes: • The United States, a state (or political subdivision), or any governmental agency or instrumentality. • Certain tax-exempt public benefit corporations. • An educational institution in connection with certain programs. If you refinanced a student loan with a loan from an educational or tax-exempt organization, the refinanced loan may also be considered as having been made by a qualified lender. In order to qualify, it must have been made in connection with a program designed to encourage students to serve in occupations or areas with unmet needs, and the services required must be performed under the direction of a governmental unit or tax-exempt 501(c)(3) organization.
Income Limits	There are no specific income limits restricting the use of this provision.

For more information on forgiveness of student loans, see chapter 12, *Other income*.

Tuition and fees deduction

TAXALERT

The deduction of up to $4,000 for higher education expenses paid by or for qualified taxpayers expired at the end of 2013, and is not currently allowed for 2014. As of the time this book was published in October 2014, Congress had been considering legislation that would retroactively extend the availability of this deduction at least through 2015, but no such extension had yet been passed. For updated information on this and any other tax law changes that occur after this book was published, see our website, ey.com/EYTaxGuide.

Tax-free scholarships and fellowships

In general, scholarships and fellowships received to assist an individual with payment of educational expenses are not considered taxable income. See the chart below for more details.

Benefit	A candidate for a degree at an education institution can exclude from income amounts received as a qualified scholarship or fellowship.

Qualifications	A candidate for a degree includes a student who:
	1. Attends a primary or secondary school or is pursuing a degree at a college or university, or
	2. Attends a qualifying accredited educational organization that is authorized to provide a program:
	   a. That is acceptable for full credit toward a bachelor's or higher degree, or
	   b. That trains students for employment in a recognized occupation.
	A scholarship or fellowship grant is generally an amount paid for the benefit of an individual to aid such individual in the pursuit of study or research. A scholarship or fellowship grant does not include any amount provided by an individual to aid a relative, friend, or other individual if the grantor is motivated by family or philanthropic considerations.
	
	Amounts received that are used for qualified tuition and related expenses can be excluded from income. These expenses include tuition and fees required to enroll in, or to attend, an educational institution, and fees, books, supplies, and equipment required of all students in your course of instruction. Incidental expenses including room and board and travel expenses do not qualify. Although scholarships are usually taxable if they carry a future service requirement, qualified amounts received under the National Health Service Corps Scholarship Program or the Armed Forces Health Professions Scholarship and Financial Assistance Program will not be taxed.

Income Limits	There are no specific income limits restricting the use of this provision.

For more information on scholarships and fellowships, see chapter 12, *Other income*, and IRS Publication 970.

Withdrawals from IRAs before age 59½ to pay qualified higher educational expenses

Benefit	Generally, withdrawals from a traditional or Roth IRA before age 59½ are subject to an additional 10% tax on the part of the distribution included in gross income. You will not be subject to the 10% additional tax, however, if for the year of withdrawal you have paid sufficient higher education expenses for yourself, your spouse, or for your or your spouse's children or grandchildren.
Qualifications	N/A
Income Limits	There are no specific income limits restricting the use of this provision.

Education savings bond program

Benefit	Interest earned on U.S. savings bonds is generally taxed either in the year the interest is earned or, more typically, in the year in which you cash in the bonds. Under the education savings bond program, when you cash in qualified U.S. savings bonds, you may be able to exclude from your income all or a portion of the interest earned.
Qualifications	Only Series EE bonds issued after 1989 and Series I savings bonds qualify. In addition, the owner of the bond must be at least 24 years old before the bond's issue date, and cannot have a filing status of married filing separately. To be able to exclude interest from your taxable income, you must pay "qualified higher education expenses" for yourself, your spouse, or a dependent for whom you claim an exemption on your return. If the total that you receive when you cash in the bonds is not more than the available qualified expenses, part of the interest may be tax-free.
Income Limits	The interest exclusion is phased out for higher income taxpayers. The phase out range for single taxpayers in 2014 is $76,000 to $91,000. For taxpayers filing joint returns, the phase-out range is $113,950 to $143,950.

For more information on the education savings bond programs, see chapter 7, *Interest income*.

Educational assistance as a working condition fringe benefit

Benefit	Certain educational expenses paid by your employer may be excludable from your income if the expenditures are considered a working condition fringe benefit.
Qualifications	Expenses qualify if the education you receive maintains or improves skills required in your employment or meets the express requirements of your employer or applicable law required as a condition of employment. Educational expenses that are incurred to meet minimum educational requirements or that qualify you for a new trade or business (such as a law or medical degree) do not qualify. Amounts paid by your employer will generally qualify as a working condition fringe benefit if the item would have been deductible as an employee business expense had you paid the expense. Treatment as a working condition fringe benefit is generally more beneficial than a deduction, however, since employee business expenses are deductible only if you itemize your deductions, and then only to the extent that they, in combination with other miscellaneous itemized deductions, exceed 2% of your adjusted gross income.
Income Limits	There are no specific income limits restricting the use of this provision.

For more information about working condition fringe benefits, see IRS Publication 15-B.

Employer-provided educational assistance programs

Your employer may assist you with educational payments, a portion of which may be excludable from your income (see chart below). Qualified payments include payments for tuition, fees, books, supplies, and equipment (not including meals and transportation). Courses in sports, games, or hobbies are not qualified expenses unless there is a reasonable relationship between the courses and the business of the employer or if the courses are required as part of a degree program.

Benefit	Up to $5,250 of employer-provided education assistance payments may be excluded from your income each calendar year when provided under an employer-sponsored educational assistance program. Qualifying payments are excludable from income whether or not the courses taken are job-related. This benefit covers educational assistance for undergraduate or graduate level courses.
Qualifications	Payments must be made under a qualifying written plan that does not discriminate in favor of highly compensated employees. Payments may be made for tuition, fees, books, supplies, and equipment. Payments made for meals, lodging, and transportation generally do not qualify.
Income Limits	There are no specific income limits restricting the use of this provision.

For more information on education as a working condition fringe benefit and on employer-provided educational assistance programs, see chapter 12, *Other income*, and chapter 28, *Tax benefits for work-related education*.

Coverdell education savings accounts

Benefit	There is no federal income tax on earnings in Coverdell education savings accounts when distributions are used to pay qualifying educational expenses.
Qualifications	Qualified educational expenses include tuition, fees, books, supplies, and equipment, and costs of room and board. Qualified expenses include elementary and secondary school expenses. The purchase of computer equipment, Internet access, and related technology, if used by the student or the student's family, also qualifies. There is no federal income tax deduction for contributions to Coverdell accounts. Except in the case of a special needs beneficiary, you cannot contribute to a Coverdell account after the beneficiary reaches age 18. To the extent that distributions are not used for qualifying educational expenses, an income and penalty tax may apply to the distributed earnings.
Income Limits	The maximum contribution to a Coverdell account is $2,000 per year. The amount that a taxpayer is allowed to contribute to a Coverdell account is phased out for higher income taxpayers. In 2014 for joint returns, the phase-out range is $190,000 to $220,000. For other taxpayers, the phase-out range is $95,000 to $110,000.

TAXSAVER

An individual who has received a military death gratuity or Servicemembers' Group Life Insurance (SGLI) payment may contribute all or a part of the amounts received to one or more Coverdell education savings accounts. The contribution is treated as a rollover, except that this type of rollover does not count when figuring the annual limit on the number of rollovers allowed.

Qualified tuition (Section 529) programs

A qualified tuition program allows you to prepay or contribute to an account that has been established to pay qualified higher education expenses. Unlike Coverdell education savings accounts, there are no income limits restricting the use of these accounts. Although contributions are not deductible for federal income tax purposes, many states permit you to deduct a portion or all of your contribution on your state income tax return.

Benefit	There is no federal income tax imposed when distributions from qualified tuition programs (popularly known as 529 plans) are used to pay qualifying higher education expenses.
Qualifications	There are two basic types of 529 plans. Under the prepaid educational service type plan, you purchase tuition credits today for use in the future. The other type of plan (often referred to as "college savings plan") permits you to contribute to a special higher education savings account for a designated beneficiary. In both types of plans, your initial investment is designed to grow over time and the value of that growth is not subject to federal income tax when distributions are made for qualifying higher education expenses. There is no federal income tax deduction for contributions to a 529 plan. Unlike distributions from Coverdell accounts, qualifying expenditures may only be made for higher education expenses. To the extent that distributions are not used for qualifying higher educational expenses, an income and penalty tax may apply. Higher educational expenses include tuition, required fees, books, and supplies. (Amounts paid for computer technology and equipment, as well as Internet access, are not qualified expenses.) For someone who is at least a half-time student, room and board are qualifying higher educational expenses.
Income Limits	529 plans are not subject to income limits and permit you to make contributions far in excess of the $2,000 annual contribution permitted for Coverdell accounts. The combination of benefits and flexibility offered by these plans make them the most widely used education tax incentive program. Be sure to discuss the investment options and limitations of the various programs with your financial advisor.

For more information on qualified tuition programs, Coverdell education savings accounts, and other education incentives, see Publication 970, *Tax Benefits for Education*.

Chapter 37

Other credits including the earned income credit

ey.com/EYTaxGuide

Note

IRS Publication 17 (*Your Federal Income Tax*) has been updated by Ernst & Young LLP for 2014. Dates and dollar amounts shown are for 2014. Underlined type is used to indicate where IRS text has been updated. Places where text has been removed are indicated by the sentence: *Text intentionally omitted.*

ey.com/EYTaxGuide

Ernst & Young LLP will update the *EY Tax Guide 2015* website with relevant taxpayer information as it becomes available. You can also sign up for email alerts to let you know when changes have been made.

Introduction

Unlike tax deductions, which reduce your taxable income, tax credits reduce your tax liability dollar-for-dollar, which makes them especially valuable. This chapter discusses fifteen credits you may use to reduce your tax liability. Ten of these credits are nonrefundable; that is, although they may be used to bring your tax liability to zero, any credit in excess of your liability is not refunded to you. Five of these credits are refundable. That means that any unused credit is refunded to you.

What's New

Adoption credit. The maximum adoption credit is $13,190 for 2014. See *Adoption Credit*.

Excess withholding of social security and railroad retirement tax. Social security tax and tier 1 railroad retirement (RRTA) tax were both withheld during 2014 at a rate of 6.2% of wages up to $117,000. If you worked for more than one employer and had too much social security or RRTA tax withheld during 2014, you may be entitled to a credit for the excess withholding. See *Credit for Excess Social Security Tax or Railroad Retirement Tax Withheld*.

Alternative fuel vehicle refueling property credit (non-hydrogen refueling property). Generally, this credit is not available for property placed in service after 2013, except for hydrogen refueling property. See *Alternative Fuel Vehicle Refueling Property Credit.*

Health Coverage Tax Credit. The legislation that authorized this credit has expired. The tax credit is not available for tax years after 2013.

Nonbusiness energy property credit. The credit is not available for property placed in service after December 31, 2013.

Plug-in electric drive motor vehicle credit. This credit is not available for electric motorcycles and three-wheeled vehicles placed in service after December 31, 2013.

Premium Tax Credit. If you purchased your health insurance through the Health Insurance Marketplace, you may be eligible for the Premium Tax Credit. Whether you chose to have some or all of the estimated credit paid in advance directly to your insurance company to lower what you paid out-of-pocket for your monthly premiums during 2014 or you decided to wait to get the credit when you file your 2014 income tax return in 2015, you must claim the credit you are actually allowed by filing a federal income tax return. See *Premium Tax Credit*, later.

Tax Breaks and Deductions You Can Use Checklist

Tax credits. There are two types of credits: nonrefundable and refundable. Nonrefundable credits are limited to the amount of your tax liability. Refundable credits can reduce your tax liability to zero and beyond—actually entitling you to a refund. The credits available to individuals (nonbusiness-related) are:

1. Social security and railroad retirement tax overpayments (discussed in this chapter)
2. Tax withheld on wages, pension annuities, and other deferred income (chapter 4)
3. Tax withheld on interest, dividends, and patronage dividends (chapter 4)
4. Credit for interest on certain home mortgages (discussed in this chapter)
5. Credit from a regulated investment company (discussed in this chapter)
6. Withheld gambling winnings (chapter 4)
7. Child tax credit (chapter 35)
8. Elderly and disabled credit (chapter 34)
9. Earned income credit (discussed in this chapter)
10. Credit for health insurance costs of individuals receiving a trade adjustment allowance or a benefit from the Pension Benefits Guaranty Corp. (PBGC) (discussed in this chapter)
11. Child and dependent care credit (chapter 33)

EXPLANATION

When you figure the actual amount of the credit, you will subtract the total of any advance payments you elected to receive during the year from the amount of the premium tax credit calculated on your tax return. This may reduce your tax refund or raise your tax balance due. If you are entitled to more credit than you have already received, this will either increase your refund or lower your balance due. For more information about the premium tax credit, see _irs.gov/aca._

This chapter discusses the following nonrefundable credits.
- Adoption credit.
- Alternative motor vehicle credit.
- Alternative fuel vehicle refueling property credit.
- Credit to holders of tax credit bonds.
- Foreign tax credit.
- Mortgage interest credit.
- Nonrefundable credit for prior year minimum tax.
- Plug-in electric drive motor vehicle credit.
- Residential energy credit.
- Retirement savings contributions credit.

This chapter also discusses the following refundable credits.
- Credit for tax on undistributed capital gain.
- Health coverage tax credit.
- Credit for excess social security tax or railroad retirement tax withheld.
- Earned income tax credit
- Premium Tax Credit

Several other credits are discussed in other chapters in this publication.
- Child and dependent care credit (chapter 33).
- Credit for the elderly or the disabled (chapter 34).
- Child tax credit (chapter 35).
- Education credits (chapter 36).

Nonrefundable credits. The first part of this chapter, _Nonrefundable Credits_, covers ten credits that you subtract from your tax. These credits may reduce your tax to zero. If these credits are more than your tax, the excess is not refunded to you.

Refundable credits. The second part of this chapter, _Refundable Credits_, covers five credits that are treated as payments and are refundable to you. These credits are added to the federal income tax withheld and any estimated tax payments you made. If this total is more than your total tax, the excess will be refunded to you.

Useful Items

You may want to see:

Publication
- ☐ **502** Medical and Dental Expenses
- ☐ **514** Foreign Tax Credit for Individuals
- ☐ **530** Tax Information for Homeowners
- ☐ **590** Individual Retirement Arrangements (IRAs)

Form (and Instructions)
- ☐ **1116** Foreign Tax Credit
- ☐ **2439** Notice to Shareholder of Undistributed Long-Term Capital Gains
- ☐ **5695** Residential Energy Credit
- ☐ **8396** Mortgage Interest Credit
- ☐ **8801** Credit For Prior Year Minimum Tax—Individuals, Estates, and Trusts
- ☐ **8828** Recapture of Federal Mortgage Subsidy
- ☐ **8839** Qualified Adoption Expenses
- ☐ **8880** Credit for Qualified Retirement Savings Contributions

Text intentionally omitted

- ☐ **8910** Alternative Motor Vehicle Credit
- ☐ **8911** Alternative Fuel Vehicle Refueling Property Credit
- ☐ **8912** Credit to Holders of Tax Credit Bonds
- ☐ **8936** Qualified Plug-in Electric Drive Motor Vehicle Credit
- ☐ **8962** Premium Tax Credit (PTC)

Nonrefundable Credits

The credits discussed in this part of the chapter can reduce your tax. However, if the total of these credits is more than your tax, the excess is not refunded to you.

Adoption Credit

You may be able to take a tax credit of up to $13,190 for qualified expenses paid to adopt an eligible child. The credit may be allowed for the adoption of a child with special needs even if you do not have any qualified expenses.

If your modified adjusted gross income (AGI) is more than $197,880, your credit is reduced. If your modified AGI is $237,880 or more, you cannot take the credit.

> **TAXALERT**
>
> During 2010 and 2011, the adoption credit was fully refundable, which allowed taxpayers to receive a refund for the full amount of the credit claimed, even when the credit exceeded their tax liability. After 2011, the credit is no longer refundable, but it can still be credited to offset any tax you have to pay. If you cannot utilize your full credit in the year your expenses are incurred, you may be able to carry the excess forward for up to five years.

Qualified adoption expenses. Qualified adoption expenses are reasonable and necessary expenses directly related to, and whose principal purpose is for, the legal adoption of an eligible child. These expenses include:

- Adoption fees,
- Court costs,
- Attorney fees,
- Travel expenses (including amounts spent for meals and lodging) while away from home, and
- Re-adoption expenses to adopt a foreign child.

Nonqualified expenses. Qualified adoption expenses do not include expenses:

- That violate state or federal law,
- For carrying out any surrogate parenting arrangement,
- For the adoption of your spouse's child,
- For which you received funds under any federal, state, or local program,
- Allowed as a credit or deduction under any other federal income tax rule, or
- Paid or reimbursed by your employer or any other person or organization.

Eligible child. The term "eligible child" means any individual:

- Under 18 years old, or
- Physically or mentally incapable of caring for himself or herself.

> **TAXALERT**
>
> Qualified adoption expenses eligible for the credit include expenses paid or incurred in an unsuccessful effort to adopt an otherwise eligible child who is a citizen or resident of the United States. In the case of a child who is not a citizen or resident of the United States, the credit is available only for adoptions that become final.

Child with special needs. An eligible child is a child with special needs if all three of the following apply.

1. The child was a citizen or resident of the United States (including U.S. possessions) at the time the adoption process began.
2. A state (including the District of Columbia) has determined that the child cannot or should not be returned to his or her parents' home.

3. The state has determined that the child will not be adopted unless assistance is provided to the adoptive parents. Factors used by states to make this determination include:
   a. The child's ethnic background,
   b. The child's age,
   c. Whether the child is a member of a minority or sibling group, and
   d. Whether the child has a medical condition or a physical, mental, or emotional handicap.

> ### TAXALERT
> In the case of the adoption of a child with special needs, you may claim a credit of $13,190 when the adoption becomes finalized, regardless of whether you have actually paid qualified adoption expenses.

When to take the credit. Generally, until the adoption becomes final, you take the credit in the year after your qualified expenses were paid or incurred. If the adoption becomes final, you take the credit in the year your expenses were paid or incurred. See the Instructions for Form 8839 for more specific information on when to take the credit.

Foreign child. If the child is not a U.S. citizen or resident at the time the adoption process began, you cannot take the credit unless the adoption becomes final. You treat all adoption expenses paid or incurred in years before the adoption becomes final as paid or incurred in the year it becomes final.

How to take the credit. Figure your 2014 nonrefundable credit and any carryforward to 2015 on Form 8839 and attach it to your Form 1040. Include the credit in your total for Form 1040, line 54. Check box c and enter "8839" on the line next to that box.

More information. For more information, see the Instructions for Form 8839.

> ### TAXALERT
> In addition to claiming the adoption credit, you may be able to exclude a maximum of $13,190 related to employer-provided adopted assistance (refer to chapter 5, *Wages, salaries, and other earnings,* for more information on the exclusion). You may claim both the credit and the exclusion in connection with the adoption of an eligible child, but not for the same expense. For example, Rick paid qualified adoption expenses in the amount of $13,000 during the year and the adoption was finalized in the same year. Rick's employer, under a qualified adoption assistance program, paid an additional $10,000 for other qualified adoption expenses on behalf of Rick to adopt the child. Assuming Rick is not subject to the phase-outs for either the credit or exclusion, he can claim a credit for the $13,000 of expenses he paid and may exclude $10,000 from gross because the credit and exclusion are not for the same expenses.
> Note that expenses paid or reimbursed by the employer do not qualify for the credit. If, in the example above, Rick only paid $1,000 in qualified adoption expenses and the employer paid $14,000, Rick may take a credit up to the $1,000 and may exclude $13,190 from his gross income. The remaining $810 ($14,000–$13,190) paid by his employer cannot be claimed as a credit (or excluded).
> The credit can offset both your regular tax and alternative minimum tax liability.

Alternative Motor Vehicle Credit

You may be able to take this credit if you place a qualified fuel cell vehicle in service in 2014.

Amount of credit. Generally, you can rely on the manufacturer's certification to the IRS that a specific make, model, and model year vehicle qualifies for the credit and the amount of the credit for which it qualifies. In the case of a foreign manufacturer, you generally can rely on its domestic distributor's certification to the IRS.

Ordinarily the amount of the credit is 100% of the manufacturer's (or domestic distributor's) certification to the IRS of the maximum credit allowable.

How to take the credit. To take the credit, you must complete Form 8910 and attach it to your Form 1040. Include the credit in your total for Form 1040, line 54. Check box c and enter "8910" on the line next to that box.

More information. For more information on the credit, see the Instructions for Form 8910.

Hydrogen Refueling Property Credit

You may be able to take a credit if you place qualified <u>hydrogen</u> refueling property in service in 2014.

Qualified <u>hydrogen</u> refueling property. Qualified <u>hydrogen</u> refueling property is any property (other than a building or its structural components) used for either of the following.

- To store or dispense <u>hydrogen</u> into the fuel tank of a motor vehicle propelled by the <u>hydrogen</u>, but only if the storage or dispensing is at the point where the fuel is delivered into that tank.
- To recharge an electric vehicle, but only if the recharging property is located at the point where the vehicle is recharged.

Text intentionally omitted.

Amount of the credit. For personal use property, the credit is generally the smaller of 30% of the property's cost or $1,000. For business use property, the credit is generally the smaller of 30% of the property's cost or $30,000.

How to take the credit. To take the credit, you must complete Form 8911 and attach it to your Form 1040. Include the credit in your total for Form 1040, line 54. Check box c and enter "8911" on the line next to that box.

More information. For more information on the credit, see the Form 8911 instructions.

Credit to Holders of Tax Credit Bonds

Tax credit bonds are bonds in which the holder receives a tax credit in lieu of some or all of the interest on the bond.

You may be able to take a credit if you are a holder of one of the following bonds.
- Clean renewable energy bonds (issued before 2010).
- Qualified forestry conservation bond
- New clean renewable energy bonds.
- Qualified energy conservation bonds.
- Qualified school construction bonds.

- Qualified zone academy bonds.
- Build America bonds.

In some instances, an issuer may elect to receive a credit for interest paid on the bond. If the issuer makes this election, you cannot also claim a credit.

Interest income. The amount of any tax credit allowed (figured before applying tax liability limits) must be included as interest income on your tax return.

How to take the credit. Complete Form 8912 and attach it to your Form 1040. Include the credit in your total for Form 1040, line 54. Check box c and enter "8912" on the line next to that box.

More information. For more information, see the Instructions for Form 8912.

TAXALERT

For 2014, if you are a holder of a tax credit bond, you may receive Form 1097-BTC, which will provide the amount of the credit you may be entitled to take against your tax liability.

Foreign Tax Credit

You generally can choose to take income taxes you paid or accrued during the year to a foreign country or U.S. possession as a credit against your U.S. income tax. Or, you can deduct them as an itemized deduction (see chapter 23).

You cannot take a credit (or deduction) for foreign income taxes paid on income that you exclude from U.S. tax under any of the following.
1. Foreign earned income exclusion.
2. Foreign housing exclusion.
3. Income from Puerto Rico exempt from U.S. tax.
4. Possession exclusion.

Limit on the credit. Unless you can elect not to file Form 1116 (see *Exception*, later), your foreign tax credit cannot be more than your U.S. tax liability (Form 1040, line 44), multiplied by a fraction. The numerator of the fraction is your taxable income from sources outside the United States. The denominator is your total taxable income from U.S. and foreign sources. See Publication 514 for more information.

EXPLANATION

To take the foreign tax credit, the foreign taxes must have been imposed on you, and you must have paid or accrued the taxes during your tax year. Furthermore, if you work overseas and elect to claim the foreign earned income exclusion or the foreign housing exclusion, the amount of foreign taxes eligible for credit and foreign sourced income is reduced. The foreign earned income exclusion allows U.S. citizens or residents, who meet one of the tests for living abroad, to exclude up to $99,200 in 2014 of foreign earned income from their gross income. The foreign housing exclusion allows U.S. citizens or residents to exclude excess foreign housing costs from their gross income. See chapter 41, *U.S. citizens working abroad: Tax treatment of foreign earned income*, for a more complete discussion of these subjects.

The amount you may claim as a foreign tax credit is limited. You can figure your maximum credit by performing the following calculation:

$$\frac{\text{Net taxable income from sources outside the U.S.}}{\text{Net taxable income from all sources}} \times \text{U.S. income tax} = \text{Maximum credit}$$

Separate foreign tax credit limitations must be calculated for passive income and several other categories.

However, while you are limited in the amount of credit for foreign taxes you may claim in any one year, you are able to carry back or carry forward the unused credits. See chapter 41, *U.S. citizens working abroad: Tax treatment of foreign earned income and* Form 1116 instructions for a further discussion of how to calculate your foreign tax credit.

TAXALERT

For tax years beginning on or after October 23, 2004, you may carry back the unused credits for 1 year and carry forward the unused credits for 10 years.

How to take the credit. Complete Form 1116 and attach it to your Form 1040. Enter the credit on Form 1040, line 48.

Exception. You do not have to complete Form 1116 to take the credit if all of the following apply.

1. All of your gross foreign source income was from interest and dividends and all of that income and the foreign tax paid on it were reported to you on Form 1099-INT, Form 1099-DIV, or Schedule K-1 (or substitute statement).
2. If you had dividend income from shares of stock, you held those shares for at least 16 days.
3. You are not filing Form 4563 or excluding income from sources within Puerto Rico.
4. The total of your foreign taxes was not more than $300 (not more than $600 if married filing jointly).
5. All of your foreign taxes were:
   a. Legally owed and not eligible for a refund, and
   b. Paid to countries that are recognized by the United States and do not support terrorism.

More information. For more information on the credit and these requirements, see the Instructions for Form 1116.

Mortgage Interest Credit

The mortgage interest credit is intended to help lower-income individuals own a home. If you qualify, you can take the credit each year for part of the home mortgage interest you pay.

Who qualifies. You may be eligible for the credit if you were issued a qualified mortgage credit certificate (MCC) from your state or local government. Generally, an MCC is issued only in connection with a new mortgage for the purchase of your main home.

Amount of credit. Figure your credit on Form 8396. If your mortgage loan amount is equal to (or smaller than) the certified indebtedness (loan) amount shown on your MCC, enter on Form 8396, line 1, all the interest you paid on your mortgage during the year.

If your mortgage loan amount is larger than the certified indebtedness amount shown on your MCC, you can figure the credit on only part of the interest you paid. To find the amount to enter on line 1, multiply the total interest you paid during the year on your mortgage by the following fraction.

Certified indebtedness amount on your MCC/Original amount of your mortgage

$$\frac{\text{Certified indebtedness amount on your MCC}}{\text{Original amount of your mortage}}$$

Limit based on credit rate. If the certificate credit rate is more than 20%, the credit you are allowed cannot be more than $2,000. If two or more persons (other than a married couple filing a joint return) hold an interest in the home to which the MCC relates, this $2,000 limit must be divided based on the interest held by each person. See Publication 530 for more information.

Carryforward. Your credit (after applying the limit based on the credit rate) is also subject to a limit based on your tax that is figured using Form 8396. If your allowable credit is reduced because of this tax liability limit, you can carry forward the unused portion of the credit to the next 3 years or until used, whichever comes first.

If you are subject to the $2,000 limit because your certificate credit rate is more than 20%, you cannot carry forward any amount more than $2,000 (or your share of the $2,000 if you must divide the credit).

How to take the credit. Figure your 2014 credit and any carryforward to 2015 on Form 8396, and attach it to your Form 1040. Be sure to include any credit carryforward from 2011, 2012, and 2013.

Include the credit in your total for Form 1040, line 54. Check box c and enter "8396" on the line next to that box.

Reduced home mortgage interest deduction. If you itemize your deductions on Schedule A (Form 1040), you must reduce your home mortgage interest deduction by the amount of the mortgage interest credit shown on Form 8396, line 3. You must do this even if part of that amount is to be carried forward to 2015. For more information about the home mortgage interest deduction, see chapter 24.

Recapture of federal mortgage subsidy. If you received an MCC with your mortgage loan, you may have to recapture (pay back) all or part of the benefit you received from that program. The recapture may be required if you sell or dispose of your home at a gain during the first 9 years after the date you closed your mortgage loan. See the Instructions for Form 8828 and chapter 15 for more information.

More information. For more information on the credit, see the Form 8396 instructions.

Nonrefundable Credit for Prior Year Minimum Tax

The tax laws give special treatment to some kinds of income and allow special deductions and credits for some kinds of expenses. If you benefit from these laws, you may have to pay at least a minimum amount of tax in addition to any other tax on these items. This is called the alternative minimum tax.

The special treatment of some items of income and expenses only allows you to postpone paying tax until a later year. If in prior years you paid alternative minimum tax because of these tax postponement items, you may be able to take a credit for prior year minimum tax against your current year's regular tax.

You may be able to take a credit against your regular tax if for 2013 you had:
- An alternative minimum tax liability and adjustments or preferences other than exclusion items,
- A minimum tax credit that you are carrying forward to 2014, or
- An unallowed qualified electric vehicle credit.

How to take the credit. Figure your 2014 nonrefundable credit (if any), and any carryforward to 2015 on Form 8801, and attach it to your Form 1040. Include the credit in your total for Form 1040, line 54, and check box b. You can carry forward any unused credit for prior year minimum tax to later years until it is completely used.

More information. For more information on the credit, see the Instructions for Form 8801.

TAXPLANNER

If you report varying income from year to year, you may find yourself in a regular tax position in one year and in an AMT position the next. By accelerating income into an AMT year and deferring expenses until a regular tax year, you may take advantage of the different tax rates between the regular tax and the AMT. The effect of such a strategy is reduced due to the AMT credit, which is designed to even out the effect of AMT over time. However, the AMT credit will be of no benefit for AMT arising from the exclusion of items such as certain itemized deductions, certain tax-exempt interest, depletion, and the exclusion for gains on the sale of certain small business stock. This should be considered if you undertake any plans to defer or accelerate income or expenses.

TAXPLANNER

Where possible, you should arrange income and deductions so that any AMT incurred will result in an AMT credit that is quickly usable.

Plug-in Electric Drive Motor Vehicle Credit

You may be able to take this credit if you placed in service for business or personal use a qualified plug-in electric drive motor vehicle in 2014 and you meet some other requirements.

Qualified plug-in electric drive motor vehicle. This is a new vehicle with at least four wheels that:
- Is propelled to a significant extent by an electric motor that draws electricity from a battery that has a capacity of not less than 4 kilowatt hours and is capable of being recharged from an external source of electricity, and
- Has a gross vehicle weight of less than 14,000 pounds.

> ### TAXALERT
> Qualified electric motorcycles and three-wheeled plug-in electric vehicles acquired in 2012 or 2013 were also eligible for the credit. Such qualified vehicles were:
> - capable of achieving a speed of 45 miles per hour or greater,
> - propelled to a significant extent by an electric motor that drew electricity from a battery that had a capacity of not less than 2.5 kilowatt hours and is capable of being recharged from an external source of electricity, and
> - Had a gross vehicle weight of less than 14,000 pounds.
>
> As of the time this book was published in October 2014, Congress had been considering legislation that would extend the availability of the credit to qualifying electric motorcycles acquired before 2016. It does not appear that the credit would be extended for three-wheeled vehicles, however. For updated information on this and any other tax law changes that occur after this book was published, see our website, *ey.com/EYTaxGuide*.

Text intentionally omitted.

Certification and other requirements. Generally, you can rely on the manufacturer's (or, in the case of a foreign manufacturer, its domestic distributor's) certification to the IRS that a specific make, model, and model year vehicle qualifies for the credit and, if applicable, the amount of the credit for which it qualifies. However, if the IRS publishes an announcement that the certification for any specific make, model, and model year vehicle has been withdrawn, you cannot rely on the certification for such a vehicle purchased after the date of publication of the withdrawal announcement.

The following requirements must also be met to qualify for the credit.
- You are the owner of the vehicle. If the vehicle is leased, only the lessor, and not the lessee, is entitled to the credit.
- You placed the vehicle in service during 2014.
- The vehicle is manufactured primarily for use on public streets, roads, and highways.
- The original use of the vehicle began with you.
- You acquired the vehicle for your use or to lease to others, and not for resale.
- *Text intentionally omitted.*
- You use the vehicle primarily in the United States.

How to take the credit. To take the credit, you must complete Form 8936 and attach it to your Form 1040. Include the credit in your total for Form 1040, line 54. Check box c and enter "8936" on the line next to that box.

More information. For more information on the credit, see the Form 8936 instructions.

> ### TAXPLANNER
> IRS Notice 2009-89 (available online at *www.irs.gov*) provides guidance for you to know when you can rely on the vehicle manufacturer's certification in determining whether a credit is allowable with respect to a vehicle.

Residential Energy Efficient Property Credit

Text intentionally omitted.

You may be able to take a credit of 30% of your costs of qualified solar electric property, solar water heating property, fuel cell property, small wind energy property, and geothermal heat pump property. The credit amount for costs paid for qualified fuel cell property is limited to $500 for each one-half kilowatt of capacity of the property.

If you are a member of a condominium management association for a condominium you own or a tenant-stockholder in a cooperative housing corporation, you are treated as having paid your proportionate share of any costs of the association or corporation for purposes of this credit.

Basis reduction. You must reduce the basis of your home by the amount of any credit allowed.

How to take the credit. Complete Form 5695 and attach it to your Form 1040. Enter the credit on Form 1040, line 52.

More information. For more information on these credits, see the Form 5695 instructions.

> ### TAXSAVER
> This credit applies to property placed in service after December 31, 2005, and before January 1, 2017.
> The credit is nonrefundable and may be used to offset AMT. If the amount of the credit you can claim is limited (due to an overall limit on the various nonrefundable personal credits that are allowed in a tax year), it may be carried forward to the next tax year.

> ### TAXALERT
> A credit for certain nonbusiness energy property expired at the end of 2013. It was limited to 10% of the cost of qualified energy efficiency improvements made to existing homes before January 1, 2014. The maximum credit for a taxpayer was $500, but no more than $200 of such credit could be attributable to expenditures on windows.

Retirement Savings Contributions Credit (Saver's Credit)

You may be able to take this credit if you, or your spouse if filing jointly, made:
- Contributions (other than rollover contributions) to a traditional or Roth IRA,
- Elective deferrals to a 401(k) or 403(b) plan (including designated Roth contributions) or to a governmental 457, SEP, or SIMPLE plan,
- Voluntary employee contributions to a qualified retirement plan (including the federal Thrift Savings Plan), or
- Contributions to a 501(c)(18)(D) plan.

However, you cannot take the credit if either of the following applies.
1. The amount on Form 1040, line 38, or Form 1040A, line 22, is more than $30,000 ($45,000 if head of household; $60,000 if married filing jointly).
2. The person(s) who made the qualified contribution or elective deferral (a) was born after January 1, 1997, (b) is claimed as a dependent on someone else's 2014 tax return, or (c) was a student (defined next).

Student. You were a student if during any part of 5 calendar months of 2014 you:
- Were enrolled as a full-time student at a school, or
- Took a full-time, on-farm training course given by a school or a state, county, or local government agency.

School. A school includes a technical, trade, or mechanical school. It does not include an on-the-job training course, correspondence school, or school offering courses only through the Internet.

How to take the credit. Figure the credit on Form 8880. Enter the credit on your Form 1040, line 51, or your Form 1040A, line 34, and attach Form 8880 to your return.

More information. For more information on the credit, see the Form 8880 instructions.

> ### TAXALERT
> The credit for savers is allowed to the full extent of your regular tax and alternative minimum tax. See *Alternative Minimum Tax* in chapter 31, *How to figure your tax*, for more information on the AMT.

> ### TAXSAVER
> If you are eligible to deduct your IRA contributions (see chapter 17, *Individual retirement accounts (IRAs)*, for more information) or to exclude qualified plan contributions from your gross income, you will be able to deduct or exclude those amounts and also claim the saver's credit.

Refundable Credits

The credits discussed in this part of the chapter are treated as payments of tax. If the total of these credits, withheld federal income tax, and estimated tax payments is more than your total tax, the excess can be refunded to you.

Premium Tax Credit

Premium Tax Credit. The premium tax credit is an advanceable, refundable tax credit designed to help eligible individuals and families with low or moderate income afford health insurance purchased through the Health Insurance Marketplace, also known as the Exchange, beginning in 2014. You can choose to have the credit paid in advance to your insurance company to lower what you pay for your monthly premiums, or you can claim all of the credit when you file your tax return for the year. If you choose to have the credit paid in advance, you will reconcile the amount paid in advance with the actual credit you compute when you file your tax return.

TAXALERT

In late July 2014, two Federal Appeals Courts issued conflicting decisions on the same day about the availability of premium assistance tax credits to individuals purchasing health insurance through federally-facilitated health insurance exchanges. One court ruled that the credit was available; the other ruled that it was not. Both decisions are being appealed and may eventually end up before the U.S. Supreme Court. These decisions do not impact insurance purchased through state-operated exchanges. In response to these opposing decisions, the IRS has posted the following message on its website:

"It's important for individuals receiving advance payments of the premium tax credit to know that at this time, nothing has changed and tax credits remain available. Whether enrolled in coverage through a federally-run or state-run Health Insurance Exchange, also known as a Marketplace, individuals do not need to take any additional action or make any changes in response to the court rulings. We will provide any updates on IRS.gov/aca."

EXPLANATION

Eligibility for the credit. Starting in 2014, you may be eligible for the premium tax credit if you meet the following criteria:

- buy health insurance through the Marketplace;
- are ineligible for coverage through an employer or government plan;
- are within certain income limits;
- do not file a married filing separate tax return (refer to exceptions below); and
- cannot be claimed as a dependent by another person.

Married filing separately is permitted in limited circumstances. A married individual may still qualify for the credit using married filing separately status if they are living apart from their spouse, unable to file jointly because they are a domestic abuse victim, and indicate such on their return.

Buying health insurance through the Marketplace. For the 2014 tax year, the period of time in which individuals were eligible to enroll in a Qualified Health Plan on the Marketplace—called the 2014 Open Enrollment Period—was from October 1, 2013, through March 31, 2014. The Open Enrollment Period for 2015 will be from November 15, 2014, through February 15, 2015. There are certain circumstances that permit an individual to qualify for Special Enrollment Periods outside of the Open Enrollment. Visit *healthcare.gov* for details to determine if you qualify for Special Enrollment.

Computing the credit. The premium tax credit is the lesser of:

- the premiums for the plan or plans in which the taxpayer or one or more member of the taxpayer's family enroll and
- the excess of the premiums for the applicable second lowest cost silver plan covering the taxpayer's family over the taxpayer's contribution amount

A taxpayer's contribution amount is computed by multiplying the taxpayer's household income by an applicable percentage. The percentages for 2014 are presented below. The Federal poverty line generally is the most recently published poverty line issued by The Department of Health and Human Services as of the 1st day of the regular enrollment period for coverage for that calendar year.

Household income generally includes the taxpayer's modified adjusted gross income (i.e., adjusted gross income increased by the earned income exclusion (if taken), tax-exempt interest received or accrued during the year, and social security benefits not included in gross income) plus any individual's adjusted modified adjusted gross income for whom the taxpayer is claiming a deduction for a personal exemption and is required to file a tax return.

In the case of household income (expressed as a percent of poverty line) within the following income tier:	The initial premium percentage is:	The final premium percentage is:
Up to 133%	2.0%	2.0%
133% up to 150%	3.0%	4.0%
150% up to 200%	4.0%	6.3%
200% up to 250%	6.3%	8.05%
250% up to 300%	8.05%	9.5%
300% up to 400%	9.5%	9.5%

Getting the credit. To qualify for the credit, you must obtain insurance through the Marketplace. If you are eligible for the credit, you can choose to:
• *Get It Now:* have some or all of the estimated credit paid in advance directly to your insurance company to lower what you pay out-of-pocket for your monthly premiums; or
• *Get It Later:* wait to get all of the credit when you file your tax return.

During enrollment through the Marketplace, using information you provide about your projected income and family composition for the year, the Marketplace will estimate the amount of the premium tax credit you will be able to claim on your tax return.

You will then decide whether you want to have all, some, or none of your estimated credit paid in advance directly to your insurance company.

If you chose to apply the estimated premium tax credit in advance to offset health insurance premiums, notify the Marketplace when changes occur during the year in your household income, family size (e.g., marriage, divorce, birth or adoption of a child, or death), or other family circumstances (e.g., gaining or losing eligibility for government-sponsored or employer-sponsored health care coverage) so that the expected amount of advance premium credit can be adjusted. This adjustment will decrease the likelihood of a significant difference between your advance credit payments and the actual premium tax credit figured on your tax return. If, for example, unreported changes cause the actual premium tax credit you report on your tax return to decrease, you may receive a smaller tax refund than you expected or face a larger balance due when you file your 2014 tax return.

Claiming the credit on your federal income tax return. For any tax year, if you receive advance credit payments in any amount or if you plan to claim the premium tax credit, you must file a federal income tax return for that year and include Form 8962 to calculate the actual credit allowed.
• *If you chose to get it now:* When you file your tax return, you will subtract the total advance payments you received during the year from the amount of the premium tax credit calculated on your tax return. If the premium tax credit computed on the return is more than the advance payments made on your behalf during the year, the difference will increase your refund or lower the amount of tax you owe. If the advance credit payments are more than the premium tax credit, the difference will increase the amount you owe and result in either a smaller refund or a balance due.
• *If you chose to get it later:* You will claim the full amount of the premium tax credit when you file your tax return. This will either increase your refund or lower your balance due. For more information about the premium tax credit, see *irs.gov/aca.*

Credit for Tax on Undistributed Capital Gain

You must include in your income any amounts that regulated investment companies (commonly called mutual funds) or real estate investment trusts (REITs) allocated to you as capital gain distributions, even if you did not actually receive them. If the mutual fund or REIT paid a tax on the capital gain, you are allowed a credit for the tax since it is considered paid by you. The mutual fund or REIT will send you Form 2439 showing your share of the undistributed capital gains and the tax paid, if any.

How to take the credit. To take the credit, attach Copy B of Form 2439 to your Form 1040. Include the amount from box 2 of your Form 2439 in the total for Form 1040, line 73, and check box a.

More information. See *Capital Gain Distributions* in chapter 8 for more information on undistributed capital gains.

Recapturing (Paying Back) the First-Time Homebuyer Credit
If you took this credit prior to 2012, you may be responsible for repayment.

TAXALERT

Recapture of 2008 first-time homebuyer credit. In 2008, Congress provided first-time home-buyers a refundable tax credit equal to 10% of the purchase of a home (up to a maximum credit of $7,500; $3,750 for a married person filing a separate return). This provision applies to homes purchased after April 8, 2008, and before January 1, 2009. This refundable tax credit is required to be repaid over a 15-year period in 15 equal installments. (The credit essentially functions as an interest-free loan to you from the Federal government.) The repayment period began in 2010.

Example

You bought a home on June, 10, 2008, and claimed the full credit of $7,500 on your 2008 tax return. One-fifteenth of $7,500, or $500, would be treated as additional tax on your tax return for 2010 and successive years, until it is fully paid back in 2024.

In addition, you generally must repay any credit you claimed for a home you bought in 2008 if you sold the home in 2014 or the home stopped being your main home in 2014. However, you do not have to repay the credit if one of the exceptions to the repayment rule applies.

If you claimed the first-time homebuyer credit in 2008, and you sold the home or the home stopped being your main home in 2014, you generally must repay the unrecaptured balance of the credit. You repay the credit by including it as additional tax on the return for the year your home stops being your main home.

The following are exceptions to the requirement to repay the credit for homes purchased in 2008:

- If you sell the home to someone who is not related to you, the repayment in the year of sale is limited to the amount of gain on the sale. When figuring the gain, reduce the adjusted basis of the home by the amount of the credit you did not repay.
- If the home is destroyed, condemned, or disposed of under threat of condemnation, and you acquire a new main home within 2 years of the event, you continue to pay the installments over the remainder of the 15-year repayment period.
- If, as part of a divorce settlement, the home is transferred to a spouse or former spouse, the spouse who receives the home is responsible for making all subsequent installment payments.
- If you die, any remaining annual installments are not due. If you filed a joint return and then you die, your surviving spouse would be required to repay his or her half of the remaining repayment amount.

Recapture of first time homebuyer credit for purchases in 2009 or 2010. If you claimed the 2009 or 2010 first-time homebuyer credit when you purchased your home, the credit is not required to be repaid unless your home ceases to be your main home within 36 months of the date of purchase.

Explanation

If you purchased the home after 2008, you generally must repay the credit if, during the 36-month period beginning on the purchase date, you dispose of the home or it ceases to be your main home. This includes situations where you sell the home, you convert the entire home to business or rental property, the home is destroyed, condemned, or disposed of under threat of condemnation, or the lender forecloses on the mortgage.

You repay the credit by including it as additional tax on the return for the year you dispose of the home or it ceases to be your main home. However, if the home is destroyed, condemned, or disposed of under threat of condemnation, and you do not acquire a new home within 2 years of the event, you must repay the entire repayment amount with the return for the year in which the 2-year period ends.

If you and your spouse claim the credit on a joint return, each spouse is treated as having been allowed half of the credit for purposes of repaying the credit.

The following are exceptions to the repayment rule:

- If you sell the home to someone who is not related to you (see the instructions to Form 5405 for the definition of related parties), the repayment in the year of sale is limited to the amount of gain on the sale. The amount of the credit in excess of the gain does not have to be repaid. When figuring the gain, reduce the adjusted basis of the home by the amount of the credit.
- If the home is destroyed, condemned, or disposed of under threat of condemnation, you do not have to repay the credit if you purchase a new main home within 2 years of the event and you own and use it as your new main home during the remainder of the 36-month period.

- If, as part of a divorce settlement, the home is transferred to a spouse or former spouse, the spouse who receives the home is responsible for repaying the credit if, during the 36-month period beginning on the purchase date, he or she disposes of the home or it ceases to be his or her main home and none of the other exceptions apply.
- Members of the uniformed services or Foreign Service and employees of the intelligence community do not have to repay the credit if, after 2008, they sell the home or the home ceases to be their main home because they received government orders to serve on qualified official extended duty (see the instructions for Form 5405, Part I, line 2 for more information).
- If you die, repayment of the credit is not required. If you claimed the credit on a joint return and then you die, your surviving spouse would be required to repay his or her half of the credit if, during the 36-month period beginning on the purchase date, he or she disposes of the home or it ceases to be his or her main home and none of the other exceptions apply.

How to repay the credit. If you are required to repay the credit, complete Part I of Form 5405. You may have to complete Parts II and III as well. Attach the form to your Form 1040. Include the repayment on Form 1040, line 60b.

If you bought the home in 2008 and owned and used it as your main home for all of 2014, you can enter your 2014 repayment directly on Form 1040, line 60b, without attaching Form 5405.

More information. For more information, see Form 5405 and its instructions.

Health Coverage Tax Credit—expired in 2013; not available for 2014

Health Coverage Tax Credit. The legislation that authorized this credit has expired. The tax credit is not available for tax years after 2013.

Text intentionally omitted.

> **TAXALERT**
>
> As of the time this book was published in October 2014, Congress had been considering legislation that would extend the HCTC related to Trade Adjustment Assistance (TAA) at least through 2014, but no such extension had yet been passed. For updated information on this and any other tax law changes that occur after this book was published, see our website, *ey.com/EYTaxGuide*.

Credit for Excess Social Security Tax or Railroad Retirement Tax Withheld

> **TAXALERT**
>
> Since 1994, there has not been a cap on wages subject to the 1.45% Medicare tax. However, there is still a cap for social security taxes. In 2014, employees are subject to 6.2% social security tax on the first $117,000 of wages. If you worked for two or more employers during the year, you may have had excess social security or railroad retirement taxes withheld on your wages, for which you can claim a credit.

Most employers must withhold social security tax from your wages. If you work for a railroad employer, that employer must withhold tier 1 railroad retirement (RRTA) tax and tier 2 RRTA tax.

If you worked for two or more employers in 2014, you may have had too much social security tax withheld from your pay. If one or more of those employers was a railroad employer, too much tier 1 RRTA tax may also have been withheld at the 6.2% rate. You can claim the excess social security or tier 1 RRTA tax as a credit against your income tax when you file your return. For the tier 1 RRTA tax, only use the portion of the tier 1 RRTA tax that was taxed at the 6.2% rate when figuring if excess tier 1 RRTA tax was withheld; do not include any portion of the tier 1 RRTA tax that was withheld at the Medicare tax rate (1.45%) or the Additional Medicare Tax rate (.9%). The following table shows the maximum amount of wages subject to tax and the maximum amount of tax that should have been withheld for 2014.

Type of tax	Maximum wages subject to tax	Maximum tax that should have been withheld
Social security or RRTA tier 1	$117,000	$7,254
RRTA tier 2	$87,000	$3,828

Caution

All wages are subject to Medicare tax withholding.

Employer's error. If any one employer withheld too much social security or tier 1 RRTA tax, you cannot take the excess as a credit against your income tax. The employer should adjust the tax for you. If the employer does not adjust the overcollection, you can file a claim for refund using Form 843.

Joint return. If you are filing a joint return, you cannot add the social security or tier 1 RRTA tax withheld from your spouse's wages to the amount withheld from your wages. Figure the withholding separately for you and your spouse to determine if either of you has excess withholding.

EXAMPLES

Example 1
Marie earned $120,000 during 2014. Her sole employer for the year inadvertently withheld $9,204.60 in social security and Medicare taxes from her salary. The amount that should have been withheld was $8,994 (6.2% × $117,000 plus 1.45% × $120,000). She may not claim the $210.60 overwithholding as a credit on her return. Instead, her employer should adjust her next check for this amount.

Example 2
Assume instead that Marie worked for two different employers during the year, and that her total withholding for social security and Medicare taxes was $9,204.60. She should now claim the $210.60 excess withholding as a credit.

How to figure the credit if you did not work for a railroad. If you did not work for a railroad during 2014, figure the credit as follows:

1. Add all social security tax withheld (but not more than $7,254 for each employer) Enter the total here...

2. Enter any uncollected social security tax on tips or group-term life insurance included in the total on Form 1040, line 62, identified by "UT" ....

3. Add lines 1 and 2. If $7,254 or less, stop here. You cannot take the credit...

4. Social security tax limit.. | 7,254

5. Credit. Subtract line 4 from line 3. Enter the result here and on Form 1040, line 71 (or Form 1040A, line 46) .... | $

Example. You are married and file a joint return with your spouse who had no gross income in 2014. During 2014, you worked for the Brown Technology Company and earned $63,300 in wages. Social security tax of $3,924.60 was withheld. You also worked for another employer in 2014 and earned $55,000 in wages. $3,410 of social security tax was withheld from these wages. Because you worked for more than one employer and your total wages were more than $117,000, you can take a credit of $80.60 for the excess social security tax withheld.

1. Add all social security tax withheld (but not more than $7,254 for each employer). Enter the total here.. | $7,334.60

2. Enter any uncollected social security tax on tips or group-term life insurance included in the total on Form 1040, line 60, identified by "UT" .... | -0-

3. Add lines 1 and 2. If $7,254 or less, stop here. You cannot take the credit... | 7,334.60

4. Social security tax limit.. | 7,254.00

5. Credit. Subtract line 4 from line 3. Enter the result here and on Form 1040, line 71 (or Form 1040A, line 46) .... | $80.60

How to figure the credit if you worked for a railroad. If you were a railroad employee at any time during 2014, figure the credit as follows:

1. Add all social security and tier 1 RRTA tax withheld at the 6.2% rate (but not more than $7,254 for each employer). Enter the total here..................

2. Enter any uncollected social security and tier 1 RRTA tax on tips or group-term life insurance included in the total on Form 1040, line 60, identified by "UT" ....

3. Add lines 1 and 2. If $7,254 or less, stop here. You cannot take the credit ....

4. Social security and tier 1 RRTA tax limit...   7,254

5. Credit. Subtract line 4 from line 3. Enter the result here and on Form 1040, line 71(or Form 1040A, line 46) .... $ _____

How to take the credit. Enter the credit on Form 1040, line 71, or include it in the total for Form 1040A, line 46.

More information. For more information on the credit, see Publication 505.

EXAMPLE

In 2014, Maurice worked for a railroad for 7 months and had $2,073.00 in tier 1 railroad retirement tax, $601.75 in Medicare tax, and $1,826.00 in tier 2 railroad retirement tax withheld. He worked the remaining 5 months for a nonrailroad employer and had $5,705.00 in social security tax and $1,100.36 in Medicare tax withheld. He had no income from tips or group-term life insurance on either job. His credit is calculated as follows:

1. Total social security and tier 1 RRTA tax withheld (do not include more than $7,254 for each employer) $7,778.00

2. Total social security and tier 1 RRTA tax on tips or group-term life insurance included on line 61, Form 1040 0

3. Total: Add lines 1 and 2 .... $7,778.00

4. Limit $7,254.00

5. Credit: Subtract line 4 from line 3 .... $524.00

Earned Income Credit (EIC)

The earned income credit (EIC) is a tax credit for certain people who work and have less than $52,427 of earned income. A tax credit usually means more money in your pocket. It reduces the amount of tax you owe. The EIC may also give you a refund.

What's New

Earned income amount is more. The maximum amount of income you can earn and still get the credit has increased. You may be able to take the credit if:

- You have three or more qualifying children and you earned less than $46,997($52,427 if married filing jointly),
- You have two qualifying children and you earned less than $43,756 ($49,186 if married filing jointly),
- You have one qualifying child and you earned less than $38,511 ($43,941 if married filing jointly), or
- You do not have a qualifying child and you earned less than $14,590 ($20,020 if married filing jointly).

Your adjusted gross income also must be less than the amount in the above list that applies to you. For details, see _Rules 1_ and _15_.

Investment income amount is more. The maximum amount of investment income you can have and still get the credit has increased to $3,350. See _Rule 6_.

Reminders

Increased EIC on certain joint returns. A married person filing a joint return may get more EIC than someone with the same income but a different filing status. As a result, the EIC table has different columns for married persons filing jointly than for everyone else. When you look up your EIC in the EIC Table, be sure to use the correct column for your filing status and the number of children you have.

Online help. You can use the EITC Assistant at *www.irs.gov/eitc* to find out if you are eligible for the credit. The EITC Assistant is available in English and Spanish.

EIC questioned by IRS. The IRS may ask you to provide documents to prove you are entitled to claim the EIC. We will tell you what documents to send us. These may include: birth certificates, school records, medical records, etc. The process of establishing your eligibility will delay your refund.

How do you get the earned income credit? To claim the EIC, you must:
1. Qualify by meeting certain rules, and
2. File a tax return, even if you:
   a. Do not owe any tax,
   b. Did not earn enough money to file a return, or
   c. Did not have income taxes withheld from your pay.

When you complete your return, you can figure your EIC by using a worksheet in the instructions for Form 1040, Form 1040A, or Form 1040EZ. Or, if you prefer, you can let the IRS figure the credit for you.

> **TAXALERT**
>
> The EIC is a credit available to certain low-income taxpayers. For 2014, a taxpayer without any qualifying children (see later) may be eligible for a maximum credit of $496.
>
> A taxpayer with one child may be eligible for a maximum credit of $3,305 for 2014, while a taxpayer with two qualifying children may be eligible for a maximum credit of $5,460, and a taxpayer with three or more qualifying children may be eligible for a maximum credit of $6,143.

> **TAXALERT**
>
> You are not eligible to claim the EIC if your investment income exceeds $3,350 in 2014. Investment income includes dividends, interest, tax-exempt interest, net capital gain, net passive income, and net rental and royalty income not derived in the ordinary course of a trade or business.

> **TAXALERT**
>
> Taxpayers claiming the EIC must include a taxpayer identification number for themselves, their spouses (if married), and any qualifying children on the return. For this purpose only, a taxpayer identification number is a social security number issued by the Social Security Administration, rather than one issued to an individual for the purpose of applying for federally funded benefits.

How will this chapter help you? This chapter will explain the following.
- The rules you must meet to qualify for the EIC.
- How to figure the EIC.

Useful Items
You may want to see:

Publication
- ☐ **596** Earned Income Credit (EIC)

Form (and Instructions)
- ☐ **Schedule EIC** Earned Income Credit (Qualifying Child Information)
- ☐ **8862** Information To Claim Earned Income Credit After Disallowance

> **TAXSAVER**
>
> You must file a tax return to receive the EIC. If the tax you owe is less than the amount of the EIC, you will receive a refund from the government. Therefore, even if you are not required to file a tax return because your income is less than the income required to file, you still must do so in order to receive the credit. While the IRS estimates that four out of five eligible workers qualify for the EIC, millions miss taking it because they don't claim it on their return or they don't file a tax return at all.

Do You Qualify for the Credit?

To qualify to claim the EIC, you must first meet all of the rules explained in *Part A, Rules for Everyone*. Then you must meet the rules in *Part B, Rules If You Have a Qualifying Child*, or *Part C, Rules If You Do Not Have a Qualifying Child*. There is one final rule you must meet in *Part D, Figuring and Claiming the EIC*. You qualify for the credit if you meet all the rules in each part that applies to you.

- If you have a qualifying child, the rules in *Parts A*, *B*, and *D* apply to you.
- If you do not have a qualifying child, the rules in *Parts A*, *C*, and *D* apply to you.

Table 37-1, Earned Income Credit in a Nutshell. Use Table 37-1 as a guide to *Parts A*, *B*, *C*, and *D*. The table is a summary of all the rules in each part.

Do you have a qualifying child? You have a qualifying child only if you have a child who meets the four tests described in *Rule 8* and illustrated in Figure 37-1.

If Improper Claim Made in Prior Year

If your EIC for any year after 1996 was denied or reduced for any reason other than a math or clerical error, you must attach a completed Form 8862 to your next tax return to claim the EIC. You must also qualify to claim the EIC by meeting all the rules described in this chapter.

However, if your EIC was denied or reduced as a result of a math or clerical error, do not attach Form 8862 to your next tax return. For example, if your arithmetic is incorrect, the IRS can correct it. If you do not provide a correct social security number, the IRS can deny the EIC. These kinds of errors are called math or clerical errors.

If your EIC for any year after 1996 was denied and it was determined that your error was due to reckless or intentional disregard of the EIC rules, then you cannot claim the EIC for the next 2 years. If your error was due to fraud, then you cannot claim the EIC for the next 10 years.

More information. See chapter 5 in Publication 596 for more detailed information about the disallowance period and Form 8862.

Table 37-1. Earned Income Credit in a Nutshell

First, you must meet all the rules in this column.		Second, you must meet all the rules in *one of* these columns, whichever applies.		Third, you must meet the rule in this column.
Part A. **Rules for Everyone**		**Part B.** **Rules If You Have a Qualifying Child**	**Part C.** **Rules If You Do Not Have a Qualifying Child**	**Part D.** **Figuring and Claiming the EIC**
1. Your adjusted gross income (AGI) must be less than: • $46,997 ($52,427 for married filing jointly) if you have three or more qualifying children, • $43,756 ($49,186 for married filing jointly) if you have two qualifying children, • $38,511 ($43,941 for married filing jointly) if you have one qualifying child, or • $14,590 ($20,020 for married filing jointly) if you do not have a qualifying child.	2. You must have a valid social security number. 3. Your filing status cannot be "Married filing separately." 4. You must be a U.S. citizen or resident alien all year. 5. You cannot file Form 2555 or Form 2555-EZ (relating to foreign earned income). 6. Your investment income must be $3,350 or less. 7. You must have earned income.	8. Your child must meet the relationship, age, residency, and joint return tests. 9. Your qualifying child cannot be used by more than one person to claim the EIC. 10. You cannot be a qualifying child of another person.	11. You must be at least age 25 but under age 65. 12. You cannot be the dependent of another person. 13. You cannot be a qualifying child of another person. 14. You must have lived in the United States more than half of the year.	15. Your earned income must be less than: • $46,997($52,427 for married filing jointly) if you have three or more qualifying children, • $43,756 ($49,186 for married filing jointly) if you have two qualifying children, • $38,511 ($43,941 for married filing jointly) if you have one qualifying child, or • $14,590 ($20,020 for married filing jointly) if you do not have a qualifying child.

Figure 37-1. **Tests for Qualifying Child**

Relationship

A qualifying child is a child who is your . . .

Son, daughter, stepchild, foster child, or a descendant of any of them (for example, your grandchild)

OR

Brother, sister, half brother, half sister, stepbrother, stepsister, or a descendant of any of them (for example, your niece or nephew)

Age

AND

was . . .

Under age 19 at the end of 2014 and younger than you (or your spouse, if filing jointly)

OR

Under age 24 at the end of 2014, a student, and younger than you (or your spouse, if filing jointly)

OR

Permanently and totally disabled at any time during the year, regardless of age

Joint Return

AND

Who is not filing a joint return for 2014 (or is filing a joint return for 2014 only as a claim for refund)

Residency

AND

Who lived with you in the United States for more than half of 2014.

Part A. Rules for Everyone

This part of the chapter discusses *Rules 1 through 7*. You must meet all seven rules to qualify for the earned income credit. If you do not meet all seven rules, you cannot get the credit and you do not need to read the rest of the chapter.

If you meet all seven rules in this part, then read either *Part B* or *Part C* (whichever applies) for more rules you must meet.

Rule 1. Your AGI Must Be Less Than:

- $46,997 ($52,427 for married filing jointly) if you have three or more qualifying children,
- $43,756 ($49,186 for married filing jointly) if you have two qualifying children,
- $38,511 ($43,941 for married filing jointly) if you have one qualifying child, or
- $14,590 ($20,020 for married filing jointly) if you do not have a qualifying child.

Adjusted gross income (AGI). AGI is the amount on line 38 (Form 1040), line 22 (Form 1040A), or line 4 (Form 1040EZ). If your AGI is equal to or more than the applicable limit listed above, you cannot claim the EIC.

Example. Your AGI is $38,550, you are single, and you have one qualifying child. You cannot claim the EIC because your AGI is not less than $38,511. However, if your filing status was married filing jointly, you might be able to claim the EIC because your AGI is less than $43,941.

Community property. If you are married, but qualify to file as head of household under special rules for married taxpayers living apart (see *Rule 3*), and live in a state that has community property laws, your AGI includes that portion of both your and your spouse's wages that you are required to include in gross income. This is different from the community property rules that apply under *Rule 7*.

Rule 2. You Must Have a Valid Social Security Number (SSN)

To claim the EIC, you (and your spouse, if filing a joint return) must have a valid SSN issued by the Social Security Administration (SSA). Any qualifying child listed on Schedule EIC also must have a valid SSN. (See *Rule 8* if you have a qualifying child.)

If your social security card (or your spouse's, if filing a joint return) says "Not valid for employment" and your SSN was issued so that you (or your spouse) could get a federally funded benefit, you cannot get the EIC. An example of a federally funded benefit is Medicaid.

If you have a card with the legend "Not valid for employment" and your immigration status has changed so that you are now a U.S. citizen or permanent resident, ask the SSA for a new social security card without the legend.

U. S. citizen. If you were a U. S. citizen when you received your SSN, you have a valid SSN.

Valid for work only with INS or DHS authorization. If your social security card reads "Valid for work only with INS authorization" or "Valid for work only with DHS authorization," you have a valid SSN, but only if that authorization is still valid.

SSN missing or incorrect. If an SSN for you or your spouse is missing from your tax return or is incorrect, you may not get the EIC.

Other taxpayer identification number. You cannot get the EIC if, instead of an SSN, you (or your spouse, if filing a joint return) have an individual taxpayer identification number (ITIN). ITINs are issued by the Internal Revenue Service to noncitizens who cannot get an SSN.

No SSN. If you do not have a valid SSN, put "No" next to line 66a (Form 1040), line 42a (Form 1040A), or line 8a (Form 1040EZ). You cannot claim the EIC.

Getting an SSN. If you (or your spouse, if filing a joint return) do not have an SSN, you can apply for one by filing Form SS-5, Application for a Social Security Card, with the SSA. You can get Form SS-5 online at *www.socialsecurity.gov*, from your local SSA office, or by calling the SSA at 1-800-772-1213.

Filing deadline approaching and still no SSN. If the filing deadline is approaching and you still do not have an SSN, you have two choices.

1. Request an automatic 6-month extension of time to file your return. You can get this extension by filing Form 4868, Application for Automatic Extension of Time to File U.S. Individual Income Tax Return. For more information, see *chapter 1*.
2. File the return on time without claiming the EIC. After receiving the SSN, file an amended return (Form 1040X, Amended U.S. Individual Income Tax Return) claiming the EIC. Attach a filled-in Schedule EIC if you have a qualifying child.

Rule 3. Your Filing Status Cannot Be Married Filing Separately

If you are married, you usually must file a joint return to claim the EIC. Your filing status cannot be "Married filing separately."

Spouse did not live with you. If you are married and your spouse did not live in your home at any time during the last 6 months of the year, you may be able to file as head of household, instead of married filing separately. In that case, you may be able to claim the EIC. For detailed information about filing as head of household, see *chapter 2*.

Rule 4. You Must Be a U.S. Citizen or Resident Alien All Year

If you (or your spouse, if married) were a nonresident alien for any part of the year, you cannot claim the earned income credit unless your filing status is married filing jointly. You can use that filing status only if one spouse is a U.S. citizen or resident alien and you choose to treat the nonresident spouse as a U.S. resident. If you make this choice, you and your spouse are taxed on your worldwide income. If you (or your spouse, if married) were a nonresident alien for any part of the year and your filing status is not married filing jointly, enter "No" on the dotted line next to line 66a (Form 1040) or in the space to the left of line 42a (Form 1040A). If you need more information on making this choice, get Publication 519, U.S. Tax Guide for Aliens.

Rule 5. You Cannot File Form 2555 or Form 2555-EZ

You cannot claim the earned income credit if you file Form 2555, Foreign Earned Income, or Form 2555-EZ, Foreign Earned Income Exclusion. You file these forms to exclude income earned in foreign countries from your gross income, or to deduct or exclude a foreign housing amount. U.S. possessions are not foreign countries. See Publication 54, Tax Guide for U.S. Citizens and Resident Aliens Abroad, for more detailed information.

Rule 6. Your Investment Income Must Be $3,350 or Less

You cannot claim the earned income credit unless your investment income is $3,350 or less. If your investment income is more than $3,350, you cannot claim the credit. For most people, investment income is the total of the following amounts.

- Taxable interest (line 8a of Form 1040 or 1040A).
- Tax-exempt interest (line 8b of Form 1040 or 1040A).
- Dividend income (line 9a of Form 1040 or 1040A).
- Capital gain net income (line 13 of Form 1040, if more than zero, or line 10 of Form 1040A).

If you file Form 1040EZ, your investment income is the total of the amount of line 2 and the amount of any tax-exempt interest you wrote to the right of the words "Form 1040EZ" on line 2.

However, see Rule 6 in chapter 1 of Publication 596 if:

- You are filing Schedule E (Form 1040), Form 4797, or Form 8814, or
- You are reporting income from the rental of personal property on Form 1040, line 21.

Rule 7. You Must Have Earned Income

This credit is called the "earned income" credit because, to qualify, you must work and have earned income. If you are married and file a joint return, you meet this rule if at least one spouse works and has earned income. If you are an employee, earned income includes all the taxable income you get from your employer. If you are self-employed or a statutory employee, you will figure your earned income on EIC Worksheet B in the instructions for Form 1040.

Earned Income

Earned income includes all of the following types of income.

1. Wages, salaries, tips, and other taxable employee pay. Employee pay is earned income only if it is taxable. Nontaxable employee pay, such as certain dependent care benefits and adoption benefits, is not earned income. But there is an exception for nontaxable combat pay, which you can choose to include in earned income, as explained below.
2. Net earnings from self-employment.
3. Gross income received as a statutory employee.

Wages, salaries, and tips. Wages, salaries, and tips you receive for working are reported to you on Form W-2, in box 1. You should report these on line 1 (Form 1040EZ) or line 7 (Forms 1040A and 1040).

Nontaxable combat pay election. You can elect to include your nontaxable combat pay in earned income for the earned income credit. Electing to include nontaxable combat pay in earned income may increase or decrease your EIC. Figure the credit with and without your nontaxable combat pay before making the election.

If you make the election, you must include in earned income all nontaxable combat pay you received. If you are filing a joint return and both you and your spouse received nontaxable combat pay, you can each make your own election. In other words, if one of you makes the election, the other one can also make it but does not have to.

The amount of your nontaxable combat pay should be shown in box 12 of your Form W-2 with code "Q."

Self-employed persons and statutory employees. If you are self-employed or received income as a statutory employee, you must use the Form 1040 instructions to see if you qualify to get the EIC.

Approved Form 4361 or Form 4029

This section is for persons who have an approved:

- Form 4361, Application for Exemption From Self-Employment Tax for Use by Ministers, Members of Religious Orders and Christian Science Practitioners, or
- Form 4029, Application for Exemption From Social Security and Medicare Taxes and Waiver of Benefits.

Each approved form exempts certain income from social security taxes. Each form is discussed here in terms of what is or is not earned income for the EIC.

Form 4361. Whether or not you have an approved Form 4361, amounts you received for performing ministerial duties as an employee count as earned income. This includes wages, salaries, tips, and other taxable employee compensation. A nontaxable housing allowance or the nontaxable rental value of a home is not earned income. Also, amounts you received for performing ministerial duties, but not as an employee, do not count as earned income. Examples include fees for performing marriages and honoraria for delivering speeches.

Form 4029. Whether or not you have an approved Form 4029, all wages, salaries, tips, and other taxable employee compensation count as earned income. However, amounts you received as a self-employed individual do not count as earned income. Also, in figuring earned income, do not subtract losses on Schedule C, C-EZ, or F from wages on line 7 of Form 1040.

Disability Benefits

If you retired on disability, taxable benefits you receive under your employer's disability retirement plan are considered earned income until you reach minimum retirement age. Minimum retirement age generally is the earliest age at which you could have received a pension or annuity if you were not disabled. You must report your taxable disability payments on line 7 of either Form 1040 or Form 1040A until you reach minimum retirement age.

Beginning on the day after you reach minimum retirement age, payments you receive are taxable as a pension and are not considered earned income. Report taxable pension payments on Form 1040, lines 16a and 16b (or Form 1040A, lines 12a and 12b).

Disability insurance payments. Payments you received from a disability insurance policy that you paid the premiums for are not earned income. It does not matter whether you have reached minimum retirement age. If this policy is through your employer, the amount may be shown in box 12 of your Form W-2 with code "J."

Income That Is Not Earned Income

Examples of items that are **not** earned income include interest and dividends, pensions and annuities, social security and railroad retirement benefits (including disability benefits), alimony and child support, welfare benefits, workers' compensation benefits, unemployment compensation (insurance), nontaxable foster care payments, and veterans' benefits, including VA rehabilitation payments. Do not include any of these items in your earned income.

Earnings while an inmate. Amounts received for work performed while an inmate in a penal institution are not earned income when figuring the earned income credit. This includes amounts for work performed while in a work release program or while in a halfway house.

Workfare payments. Nontaxable workfare payments are not earned income for the EIC. These are cash payments certain people receive from a state or local agency that administers public assistance programs funded under the federal Temporary Assistance for Needy Families (TANF) program in return for certain work activities such as (1) work experience activities (including remodeling or repairing public housing) if private sector employment is not available, or (2) community service program activities.

Community property. If you are married, but qualify to file as head of household under special rules for married taxpayers living apart (see *Rule 3*), and live in a state that has community property laws, your earned income for the EIC does not include any amount earned by your spouse that is treated as belonging to you under those laws. That amount is not earned income for the EIC, even though you must include it in your gross income on your income tax return. Your earned income includes the entire amount you earned, even if part of it is treated as belonging to your spouse under your state's community property laws.

Nevada, Washington, and California domestic partners. If you are a registered domestic partner in Nevada, Washington, or California, the same rules apply. Your earned income for the EIC does not include any amount earned by your partner. Your earned income includes the entire amount you earned. For details, see Publication 555.

Conservation Reserve Program (CRP) payments. If you were receiving social security retirement benefits or social security disability benefits at the time you received any CRP payments, your CRP payments are not earned income for the EIC.

Nontaxable military pay. Nontaxable pay for members of the Armed Forces is not considered earned income for the EIC. Examples of nontaxable military pay are combat pay, the Basic Allowance for Housing (BAH), and the Basic Allowance for Subsistence (BAS). See Publication 3, Armed Forces' Tax Guide, for more information.

Part B. Rules If You Have a Qualifying Child

If you have met all of the rules in *Part A*, read *Part B* to see if you have a qualifying child.

Part B discusses *Rules 8* through *10*. You must meet all three of these rules, in addition to the rules in *Parts A* and *D*, to qualify for the earned income credit with a qualifying child.

You must file Form 1040 or Form 1040A to claim the EIC with a qualifying child. (You cannot file Form 1040EZ.) You also must complete Schedule EIC and attach it to your return. If you meet all the rules in *Part A* and this part, read *Part D* to find out what to do next.

Rule 8. Your Child Must Meet the Relationship, Age, Residency, and Joint Return Tests

Your child is a qualifying child if your child meets four tests. The four tests are:
1. Relationship,
2. Age,
3. Residency, and
4. Joint return.

The four tests are illustrated in Figure 37-1. The paragraphs that follow contain more information about each test.

Relationship Test

To be your qualifying child, a child must be your:
- Son, daughter, stepchild, foster child, or a descendant of any of them (for example, your grandchild), or
- Brother, sister, half brother, half sister, stepbrother, stepsister, or a descendant of any of them (for example, your niece or nephew).

The following definitions clarify the relationship test.

Adopted child. An adopted child is always treated as your own child. The term "adopted child" includes a child who was lawfully placed with you for legal adoption.

Foster child. For the EIC, a person is your foster child if the child is placed with you by an authorized placement agency or by judgement, decree, or other order of any court of competent jurisdiction. An authorized placement agency includes a state or local government agency. It also includes a tax-exempt organization licensed by a state. In addition, it includes an Indian tribal government or an organization authorized by an Indian tribal government to place Indian children.

Example. Debbie, who is 12 years old, was placed in your care 2 years ago by an authorized agency responsible for placing children in foster homes. Debbie is your foster child.

Age Test

Your child must be:
1. Under age 19 at the end of 2014 and younger than you (or your spouse, if filing jointly),
2. Under age 24 at the end of 2014, a student, and younger than you (or your spouse, if filing jointly), or
3. Permanently and totally disabled at any time during 2014, regardless of age.

The following examples and definitions clarify the age test.

Example 1—child not under age 19. Your son turned 19 on December 10. Unless he was permanently and totally disabled or a student, he is not a qualifying child because, at the end of the year, he was not **under** age 19.

Example 2—child not younger than you or your spouse. Your 23-year-old brother, who is a full-time student and unmarried, lives with you and your spouse. He is not disabled. Both you and your spouse are 21 years old and you file a joint return. Your brother is not your qualifying child because he is not younger than you or your spouse.

Example 3—child younger than your spouse but not younger than you. The facts are the same as in *Example 2* except that your spouse is 25 years old. Because your brother is younger than your spouse, he is your qualifying child even though he is not younger than you.

Combat pay. You can elect to include your nontaxable combat pay in earned income for the EIC. See Nontaxable combat pay election, earlier.

Caution

If you do not meet Rule 8, you do not have a qualifying child. Read Part C to find out if you can get the earned income credit without a qualifying child.

Student defined. To qualify as a student, your child must be, during some part of each of any 5 calendar months during the calendar year:

1. A full-time student at a school that has a regular teaching staff, course of study, and regular student body at the school, or
2. A student taking a full-time, on-farm training course given by a school described in (1), or a state, county, or local government.

The 5 calendar months need not be consecutive.

A full-time student is a student who is enrolled for the number of hours or courses the school considers to be full-time attendance.

School defined. A school can be an elementary school, junior or senior high school, college, university, or technical, trade, or mechanical school. However, on-the-job training courses, correspondence schools, and schools offering courses only through the Internet do not count as schools for the EIC.

Vocational high school students. Students who work in co-op jobs in private industry as a part of a school's regular course of classroom and practical training are considered full-time students.

Permanently and totally disabled. Your child is permanently and totally disabled if both of the following apply.

1. He or she cannot engage in any substantial gainful activity because of a physical or mental condition.
2. A doctor determines the condition has lasted or can be expected to last continuously for at least a year or can lead to death.

Residency Test
Your child must have lived with you in the United States for more than half of 2014. The following definitions clarify the residency test.

United States. This means the 50 states and the District of Columbia. It does not include Puerto Rico or U.S. possessions such as Guam.

Homeless shelter. Your home can be any location where you regularly live. You do not need a traditional home. For example, if your child lived with you for more than half the year in one or more homeless shelters, your child meets the residency test.

Military personnel stationed outside the United States. U.S. military personnel stationed outside the United States on extended active duty are considered to live in the United States during that duty period for purposes of the EIC.

Extended active duty. Extended active duty means you are called or ordered to duty for an indefinite period or for a period of more than 90 days. Once you begin serving your extended active duty, you are still considered to have been on extended active duty even if you do not serve more than 90 days.

Birth or death of a child. A child who was born or died in 2014 is treated as having lived with you for more than half of 2014 if your home was the child's home for more than half the time he or she was alive in 2014.

Temporary absences. Count time that you or your child is away from home on a temporary absence due to a special circumstance as time the child lived with you. Examples of a special circumstance include illness, school attendance, business, vacation, military service, and detention in a juvenile facility.

Kidnapped child. A kidnapped child is treated as living with you for more than half of the year if the child lived with you for more than half the part of the year before the date of the kidnapping. The child must be presumed by law enforcement authorities to have been kidnapped by someone who is not a member of your family or your child's family. This treatment applies for all years until the child is returned. However, the last year this treatment can apply is the earlier of:

1. The year there is a determination that the child is dead, or
2. The year the child would have reached age 18.

If your qualifying child has been kidnapped and meets these requirements, enter "KC," instead of a number, on line 6 of Schedule EIC.

Joint Return Test
To meet this test, the child cannot file a joint return for the year.

Exception. An exception to the joint return test applies if your child and his or her spouse file a joint return only to claim a refund of income tax withheld or estimated tax paid.

Example 1—child files joint return. You supported your 18-year-old daughter, and she lived with you all year while her husband was in the Armed Forces. He earned $25,000 for the year. The couple files a joint return. Because your daughter and her husband filed a joint return, she is not your qualifying child.

Example 2—child files joint return only to claim a refund of withheld tax. Your 18-year-old son and his 17-year-old wife had $800 of wages from part-time jobs and no other income. They do not have a child. Neither is required to file a tax return. Taxes were taken out of their pay, so they filed a joint return only to get a refund of the withheld taxes. The exception to the joint return test applies, so your son may be your qualifying child if all the other tests are met.

Example 3—child files joint return to claim American opportunity credit. The facts are the same as in *Example 2* except no taxes were taken out of your son's pay. He and his wife are not required to file a tax return, but they file a joint return to claim an American opportunity credit of $124 and get a refund of that amount. Because claiming the American opportunity credit is their reason for filing the return, they are not filing it only to get a refund of income tax withheld or estimated tax paid. The exception to the joint return test does not apply, so your son is not your qualifying child.

Married child. Even if your child does not file a joint return, if your child was married at the end of the year, he or she cannot be your qualifying child unless:

1. You can claim an exemption for the child, or
2. The reason you cannot claim an exemption for the child is that you let the child's other parent claim the exemption under the *Special rule for divorced or separated parents (or parents who live apart)*, described later.

Social security number. The qualifying child must have a valid social security number (SSN) unless the child was born and died in 2014 and you attach to your return a copy of the child's birth certificate, death certificate, or hospital records showing a live birth. You cannot claim the EIC on the basis of a qualifying child if:

1. The qualifying child's SSN is missing from your tax return or is incorrect,
2. The qualifying child's social security card says "Not valid for employment" and was issued for use in getting a federally funded benefit, or
3. Instead of an SSN, the qualifying child has:
   a. An individual taxpayer identification number (ITIN), which is issued to a noncitizen who cannot get an SSN, or
   b. An adoption taxpayer identification number (ATIN), which is issued to adopting parents who cannot get an SSN for the child being adopted until the adoption is final.

If you have more than one qualifying child and only one has a valid SSN, you can use only that child to claim the EIC. For more information about SSNs, see *Rule 2*.

Rule 9. Your Qualifying Child Cannot Be Used By More Than One Person To Claim the EIC

Sometimes a child meets the tests to be a qualifying child of more than one person. However, only one of these persons can actually treat the child as a qualifying child. Only that person can use the child as a qualifying child to take all of the following tax benefits (provided the person is eligible for each benefit).

1. The exemption for the child.
2. The child tax credit.
3. Head of household filing status.
4. The credit for child and dependent care expenses.
5. The exclusion for dependent care benefits.
6. The EIC.

The other person cannot take any of these benefits based on this qualifying child. In other words, you and the other person cannot agree to divide these tax benefits between you. The other person cannot take any of these tax benefits unless he or she has a different qualifying child.

The tiebreaker rules explained next explain who, if anyone, can claim the EIC when more than one person has the same qualifying child. However, the tiebreaker rules do not apply if the other person is your spouse and you file a joint return.

Tiebreaker rules. To determine which person can treat the child as a qualifying child to claim the six tax benefits just listed, the following tiebreaker rules apply.

- If only one of the persons is the child's parent, the child is treated as the qualifying child of the parent.
- If the parents file a joint return together and can claim the child as a qualifying child, the child is treated as the qualifying child of the parents.

- If the parents do not file a joint return together but both parents claim the child as a qualifying child, the IRS will treat the child as the qualifying child of the parent with whom the child lived for the longer period of time during the year. If the child lived with each parent for the same amount of time, the IRS will treat the child as the qualifying child of the parent who had the higher adjusted gross income (AGI) for the year.
- If no parent can claim the child as a qualifying child, the child is treated as the qualifying child of the person who had the highest AGI for the year.
- If a parent can claim the child as a qualifying child but no parent does so claim the child, the child is treated as the qualifying child of the person who had the highest AGI for the year, but only if that person's AGI is higher than the highest AGI of any of the child's parents who can claim the child. If the child's parents file a joint return with each other, this rule can be applied by treating the parents' total AGI as divided evenly between them. See *Example 8*.

Subject to these tiebreaker rules, you and the other person may be able to choose which of you claims the child as a qualifying child. See *Examples 1* through *13*.

If you cannot claim the EIC because your qualifying child is treated under the tiebreaker rules as the qualifying child of another person for 2014, you may be able to take the EIC using a different qualifying child, but you cannot take the EIC using the rules in *Part C* for people who do not have a qualifying child.

If the other person cannot claim the EIC. If you and someone else have the same qualifying child but the other person cannot claim the EIC because he or she is not eligible or his or her earned income or AGI is too high, you may be able to treat the child as a qualifying child. See *Examples 6* and *7*. But you cannot treat the child as a qualifying child to claim the EIC if the other person uses the child to claim any of the other six tax benefits listed earlier.

Examples. The following examples may help you in determining whether you can claim the EIC when you and someone else have the same qualifying child.

Example 1. You and your 2-year-old son Jimmy lived with your mother all year. You are 25 years old, unmarried, and your AGI is $9,000. Your only income was $9,000 from a part-time job. Your mother's only income was $20,000 from her job, and her AGI is $20,000. Jimmy's father did not live with you or Jimmy. The special rule explained later for divorced or separated parents (or parents who live apart) does not apply. Jimmy is a qualifying child of both you and your mother because he meets the relationship, age, residency, and joint return tests for both you and your mother. However, only one of you can treat him as a qualifying child to claim the EIC (and the other tax benefits listed earlier for which that person qualifies). He is not a qualifying child of anyone else, including his father. If you do not claim Jimmy as a qualifying child for the EIC or any of the other tax benefits listed earlier, your mother can treat him as a qualifying child to claim the EIC (and any of the other tax benefits listed earlier for which she qualifies).

Example 2. The facts are the same as in *Example 1* except your AGI is $25,000. Because your mother's AGI is not higher than yours, she cannot claim Jimmy as a qualifying child. Only you can claim him.

Example 3. The facts are the same as in *Example 1* except that you and your mother both claim Jimmy as a qualifying child. In this case, you as the child's parent will be the only one allowed to claim Jimmy as a qualifying child for the EIC and the other tax benefits listed earlier for which you qualify. The IRS will disallow your mother's claim to the EIC and any of the other tax benefits listed earlier unless she has another qualifying child.

Example 4. The facts are the same as in *Example 1* except that you also have two other young children who are qualifying children of both you and your mother. Only one of you can claim each child. However, if your mother's AGI is higher than yours, you can allow your mother to claim one or more of the children. For example, if you claim one child, your mother can claim the other two.

Example 5. The facts are the same as in *Example 1* except that you are only 18 years old. This means you are a qualifying child of your mother. Because of *Rule 10*, discussed next, you cannot claim the EIC and cannot claim Jimmy as a qualifying child. Only your mother may be able to treat Jimmy as a qualifying child to claim the EIC. If your mother meets all the other requirements for claiming the EIC and you do not claim Jimmy as a qualifying child for any of the other tax benefits listed earlier, your mother can claim both you and Jimmy as qualifying children for the EIC.

Example 6. The facts are the same as in *Example 1* except that your mother earned $50,000 from her job. Because your mother's earned income is too high for her to claim the EIC, only you can claim the EIC using your son.

Example 7. The facts are the same as in *Example 1* except that you earned $50,000 from your job and your AGI is $50,500. Your earned income is too high for you to claim the EIC. But your mother cannot claim the EIC either, because her AGI is not higher than yours.

Example 8. The facts are the same as in *Example 1* except that you and Jimmy's father are married to each other, live with Jimmy and your mother, and have an AGI of $30,000 on a joint return. If you and your husband do not claim Jimmy as a qualifying child for the EIC or any of the other tax benefits listed earlier, your mother can claim him instead. Even though the AGI on your joint return, $30,000, is more than your mother's AGI of $20,000, for this purpose half of the joint AGI can be treated as yours and half as your husband's. In other words, each parent's AGI can be treated as $15,000.

Example 9. You, your husband, and your 10-year-old son Joey lived together until August 1, 2013, when your husband moved out of the household. In August and September, Joey lived with you. For the rest of the year, Joey lived with your husband, who is Joey's father. Joey is a qualifying child of both you and your husband because he lived with each of you for more than half the year and because he met the relationship, age, and joint return tests for both of you. At the end of the year, you and your husband still were not divorced, legally separated, or separated under a written separation agreement, so the special rule for divorced or separated parents (or parents who live apart) does not apply.

You and your husband will file separate returns. Your husband agrees to let you treat Joey as a qualifying child. This means, if your husband does not claim Joey as a qualifying child for any of the tax benefits listed earlier, you can claim him as a qualifying child for any tax benefit listed earlier for which you qualify. However, your filing status is married filing separately, so you cannot claim the EIC or the credit for child and dependent care expenses. See *Rule 3*.

Example 10. The facts are the same as in *Example 9* except that you and your husband both claim Joey as a qualifying child. In this case, only your husband will be allowed to treat Joey as a qualifying child. This is because, during 2014, the boy lived with him longer than with you. You cannot claim the EIC (either with or without a qualifying child). However, your husband's filing status is married filing separately, so he cannot claim the EIC or the credit for child and dependent care expenses. See *Rule 3*.

Example 11. You, your 5-year-old son, and your son's father lived together all year. You and your son's father are not married. Your son is a qualifying child of both you and his father because he meets the relationship, age, residency, and joint return tests for both you and his father. Your earned income and AGI are $12,000, and your son's father's earned income and AGI are $14,000. Neither of you had any other income. Your son's father agrees to let you treat the child as a qualifying child. This means, if your son's father does not claim your son as a qualifying child for the EIC or any of the other tax benefits listed earlier, you can claim him as a qualifying child for the EIC and any of the other tax benefits listed earlier for which you qualify.

Example 12. The facts are the same as in *Example 11* except that you and your son's father both claim your son as a qualifying child. In this case, only your son's father will be allowed to treat your son as a qualifying child. This is because his AGI, $14,000, is more than your AGI, $12,000. You cannot claim the EIC (either with or without a qualifying child).

Example 13. You and your 7-year-old niece, your sister's child, lived with your mother all year. You are 25 years old, and your AGI is $9,300. Your only income was from a part-time job. Your mother's AGI is $15,000. Her only income was from her job. Your niece's parents file jointly, have an AGI of less than $9,000, and do not live with you or their child. Your niece is a qualifying child of both you and your mother because she meets the relationship, age, residency, and joint return tests for both you and your mother. However, only your mother can treat her as a qualifying child. This is because your mother's AGI, $15,000, is more than your AGI, $9,300.

Special rule for divorced or separated parents (or parents who live apart). A child will be treated as the qualifying child of his or her noncustodial parent (for purposes of claiming an exemption and the child tax credit, but not for the EIC) if all of the following statements are true.
1. The parents:
    a. Are divorced or legally separated under a decree of divorce or separate maintenance,
    b. Are separated under a written separation agreement, or
    c. Lived apart at all times during the last 6 months of 2014, whether or not they are or were married.
2. The child received over half of his or her support for the year from the parents.
3. The child is in the custody of one or both parents for more than half of 2014.

4. Either of the following statements is true.
    a. The custodial parent signs Form 8332 or a substantially similar statement that he or she will not claim the child as a dependent for the year, and the noncustodial parent attaches the form or statement to his or her return. If the divorce decree or separation agreement went into effect after 1984 and before 2009, the noncustodial parent may be able to attach certain pages from the decree or agreement instead of Form 8332.
    b. A pre-1985 decree of divorce or separate maintenance or written separation agreement that applies to 2014 provides that the noncustodial parent can claim the child as a dependent, and the noncustodial parent provides at least $600 for support of the child during 2014.

For details, see chapter 3. Also see *Applying Rule 9 to divorced or separated parents (or parents who live apart)*, next.

Applying Rule 9 to divorced or separated parents (or parents who live apart). If a child is treated as the qualifying child of the noncustodial parent under the special rule just described for children of divorced or separated parents (or parents who live apart), only the noncustodial parent can claim an exemption and the child tax credit for the child. However, the custodial parent, if eligible, or another eligible taxpayer can claim the child as a qualifying child for the EIC and other tax benefits listed earlier in this chapter. If the child is the qualifying child of more than one person for these benefits, then the tiebreaker rules determine which person can treat the child as a qualifying child.

Example 1. You and your 5-year-old son lived all year with your mother, who paid the entire cost of keeping up the home. Your AGI is $10,000. Your mother's AGI is $25,000. Your son's father did not live with you or your son. Under the special rule for children of divorced or separated parents (or parents who live apart), your son is treated as the qualifying child of his father, who can claim an exemption and the child tax credit for the child. However, your son's father cannot claim your son as a qualifying child for head of household filing status, the credit for child and dependent care expenses, the exclusion for dependent care benefits, or the EIC. You and your mother did not have any child care expenses or dependent care benefits. If you do not claim your son as a qualifying child, your mother can claim him as a qualifying child for the EIC and head of household filing status, if she qualifies for these tax benefits.

Example 2. The facts are the same as in *Example 1* except that your AGI is $25,000 and your mother's AGI is $21,000. Your mother cannot claim your son as a qualifying child for any purpose because her AGI is not higher than yours.

Example 3. The facts are the same as in *Example 1* except that you and your mother both claim your son as a qualifying child for the EIC. Your mother also claims him as a qualifying child for head of household filing status. You as the child's parent will be the only one allowed to claim your son as a qualifying child for the EIC. The IRS will disallow your mother's claim to the EIC and head of household filing status unless she has another qualifying child.

Rule 10. You Cannot Be a Qualifying Child of Another Taxpayer

You are a qualifying child of another taxpayer (your parent, guardian, foster parent, etc.) if all of the following statements are true.

1. You are that person's son, daughter, stepchild, foster child, or a descendant of any of them. Or, you are that person's brother, sister, half brother, half sister, stepbrother, or stepsister (or a descendant of any of them).
2. You were:
    a. Under age 19 at the end of the year and younger than that person (or that person's spouse, if the person files jointly),
    b. Under age 24 at the end of the year, a student, and younger than that person (or that person's spouse, if the person files jointly), or
    c. Permanently and totally disabled, regardless of age.
3. You lived with that person in the United States for more than half of the year.
4. You are not filing a joint return for the year (or are filing a joint return only to claim a refund of withheld income tax or estimated tax paid).

For more details about the tests to be a qualifying child, see *Rule 8*.

If you are a qualifying child of another taxpayer, you cannot claim the EIC. This is true even if the person for whom you are a qualifying child does not claim the EIC or meet all of the rules to claim the EIC. Put "No" beside line 66a (Form 1040) or line 42a (Form 1040A).

Example. You and your daughter lived with your mother all year. You are 22 years old, unmarried, and attended a trade school full time. You had a part-time job and earned $5,700. You had no other income. Because you meet the relationship, age, residency, and joint return tests, you are a qualifying child of your mother. She can claim the EIC if she meets all the other requirements. Because you are your mother's qualifying child, you cannot claim the EIC. This is so even if your mother cannot or does not claim the EIC.

Child of person not required to file a return. You are not the qualifying child of another taxpayer (and so may qualify to claim the EIC) if the person for whom you meet the relationship, age, residency, and joint return tests is not required to file an income tax return and either:

- Does not file an income tax return, or
- Files a return only to get a refund of income tax withheld or estimated tax paid.

Example. The facts are the same as in the last example except your mother had no gross income, is not required to file a 2014 tax return, and does not file a 2014 tax return. As a result, you are not your mother's qualifying child. You can claim the EIC if you meet all the other requirements to do so.

See *Rule 10* in Publication 596 for additional examples.

Part C. Rules If You Do Not Have a Qualifying Child

Read this part if you:

1. Do not have a qualifying child, and
2. Have met all the rules in *Part A*.

Part C discusses *Rules 11* through *14*. You must meet all four of these rules, in addition to the rules in *Parts A* and *D*, to qualify for the earned income credit without a qualifying child.

Rule 11. You Must Be at Least Age 25 but Under Age 65

You must be at least age 25 but under age 65 at the end of 2014. If you are married filing a joint return, either you or your spouse must be at least age 25 but under age 65 at the end of 2014. It does not matter which spouse meets the age test, as long as one of the spouses does.

You meet the age test if you were born after December 31, 1949, and before January 2, 1990. If you are married filing a joint return, you meet the age test if either you or your spouse was born after December 31, 1949, and before January 2, 1990.

If neither you nor your spouse meets the age test, you cannot claim the EIC. Put "No" next to line 66a (Form 1040), line 42a (Form 1040A), or line 8a (Form 1040EZ).

Death of spouse. If you are filing a joint return with your spouse who died in 2014, you meet the age test if your spouse was at least age 25 but under age 65 at the time of death.

Example 1. You are age 28 and unmarried. You meet the age test.

Example 2—spouse meets age test. You are married and filing a joint return. You are age 23 and your spouse is age 27. You meet the age test because your spouse is at least age 25 but under age 65.

Example 3—spouse dies in 2014. You are married and filing a joint return with your spouse who died in August 2014. You are age 67. Your spouse would have become age 65 in November 2014. Because your spouse was under age 65 when she died, you meet the age test.

Rule 12. You Cannot Be the Dependent of Another Person

If you are **not** filing a joint return, you meet this rule if:

- You checked box 6a on Form 1040 or 1040A, or
- You did not check the "You" box on line 5 of Form 1040EZ, and you entered $10,150 on that line.

If you are filing a joint return, you meet this rule if:

- You checked both box 6a and box 6b on Form 1040 or 1040A, or
- You and your spouse did not check either the "You" box or the "Spouse" box on line 5 of Form 1040EZ, and you entered $20,300 on that line.

If you are not sure whether someone else can claim you (or your spouse, if filing a joint return) as a dependent, read the rules for claiming a dependent in chapter 3.

If someone else can claim you (or your spouse, if filing a joint return) as a dependent on his or her return, but does not, you still cannot claim the credit.

Example 1. In 2014, you were age 25, single, and living at home with your parents. You worked and were not a student. You earned $7,500. Your parents cannot claim you as a dependent. When you file your return, you claim an exemption for yourself by not checking the "You" box on line 5 of your Form 1040EZ and by entering $10,150 on that line. You meet this rule. You can claim the EIC if you meet all the other requirements.

Example 2. The facts are the same as in *Example 1*, except that you earned $2,000. Your parents can claim you as a dependent but decide not to. You do not meet this rule. You cannot claim the credit because your parents could have claimed you as a dependent.

Joint returns. You generally cannot be claimed as a dependent by another person if you are married and file a joint return.

However, another person may be able to claim you as a dependent if you and your spouse file a joint return only to get a refund of income tax withheld or estimated tax paid. But neither you nor your spouse can be claimed as a dependent by another person if you claim the EIC on your joint return.

Example 1. You are 26 years old. You and your wife live with your parents and had $800 of wages from part-time jobs and no other income. Neither you nor your wife is required to file a tax return. You do not have a child. Taxes were taken out of your pay, so you file a joint return only to get a refund of the withheld taxes. Your parents are not disqualified from claiming an exemption for you just because you filed a joint return. They can claim exemptions for you and your wife if all the other tests to do so are met.

Example 2. The facts are the same as in <u>Example 1</u> except no taxes were taken out of your pay. Also, you and your wife are not required to file a tax return, but you file a joint return to claim an EIC of $63 and get a refund of that amount. Because claiming the EIC is your reason for filing the return, you are not filing it only to get a refund of income tax withheld or estimated tax paid. Your parents cannot claim an exemption for either you or your wife.

Rule 13. You Cannot Be a Qualifying Child of Another Taxpayer

You are a qualifying child of another taxpayer (your parent, guardian, foster parent, etc.) if all of the following statements are true.

1. You are that person's son, daughter, stepchild, foster child, or a descendant of any of them. Or, you are that person's brother, sister, half brother, half sister, stepbrother, or stepsister (or a descendant of any of them).
2. You were:
   a. Under age 19 at the end of the year and younger than that person (or that person's spouse, if the person files jointly),
   b. Under age 24 at the end of the year, a student (as defined in *Rule 8*), and younger than that person (or that person's spouse, if the person files jointly), or
   c. Permanently and totally disabled, regardless of age.
3. You lived with that person in the United States for more than half of the year.
4. You are not filing a joint return for the year (or are filing a joint return only to claim a refund of withheld income tax or estimated tax paid).

For more details about the tests to be a qualifying child, see *Rule 8*.

If you are a qualifying child of another taxpayer, you cannot claim the EIC. This is true even if the person for whom you are a qualifying child does not claim the EIC or meet all of the rules to claim the EIC. Put "No" next to line 66a (Form 1040), line 42a (Form 1040A), or line 8a (Form 1040EZ).

Example. You lived with your mother all year. You are age 26, unmarried, and permanently and totally disabled. Your only income was from a community center where you went three days a week to answer telephones. You earned $5,000 for the year and provided more than half of your own support. Because you meet the relationship, age, residency, and joint return tests, you are a qualifying child of your mother for the EIC. She can claim the EIC if she meets all the other requirements. Because you are a qualifying child of your mother, you cannot claim the EIC. This is so even if your mother cannot or does not claim the EIC.

Joint returns. You generally cannot be a qualifying child of another taxpayer if you are married and file a joint return.

However, you may be a qualifying child of another taxpayer if you and your spouse file a joint return for the year only to get a refund of income tax withheld or estimated tax paid. But neither you nor your spouse can be a qualifying child of another taxpayer if you claim the EIC on your joint return.

Child of person not required to file a return. You are not the qualifying child of another taxpayer (and so may qualify to claim the EIC) if the person for whom you meet the relationship, age, residency, and joint return tests is not required to file an income tax return and either:

- Does not file an income tax return, or
- Files a return only to get a refund of income tax withheld or estimated tax paid.

Example. You lived all year with your father. You are 27 years old, unmarried, permanently and totally disabled, and earned $13,000. You have no other income, no children, and provided more than half of your own support. Your father had no gross income, is not required to file a 2014 tax return, and does not file a 2014 tax return. As a result, you are not your father's qualifying child. You can claim the EIC if you meet all the other requirements to do so.

See *Rule 13* in Publication 596 for additional examples.

Rule 14. You Must Have Lived in the United States More Than Half of the Year

Your home (and your spouse's, if filing a joint return) must have been in the United States for more than half the year.

If it was not, put "No" next to line 66a (Form 1040), line 42a (Form 1040A), or line 8a (Form 1040EZ).

United States. This means the 50 states and the District of Columbia. It does not include Puerto Rico or U.S. possessions such as Guam.

Homeless shelter. Your home can be any location where you regularly live. You do not need a traditional home. If you lived in one or more homeless shelters in the United States for more than half the year, you meet this rule.

Military personnel stationed outside the United States. U.S. military personnel stationed outside the United States on extended active duty (defined in *Rule 8*) are considered to live in the United States during that duty period for purposes of the EIC.

Part D. Figuring and Claiming the EIC

Read this part if you have met all the rules in *Parts A* and *B*, or all the rules in *Parts A* and *C*.

Part D discusses *Rule 15*. You must meet this rule, in addition to the rules in *Parts A* and *B*, or *Parts A* and *C*, to qualify for the earned income credit.

This part of the chapter also explains how to figure the amount of your credit. You have two choices.

1. Have the IRS figure the EIC for you. If you want to do this, see *IRS Will Figure the EIC for You*.
2. Figure the EIC yourself. If you want to do this, see *How To Figure the EIC Yourself*.

Rule 15. Your Earned Income Must Be Less Than:

- $46,997 ($52,427 for married filing jointly) if you have three or more qualifying children,
- $43,756 ($49,186 for married filing jointly) if you have two qualifying children,
- $38,511 ($43,941 for married filing jointly) if you have one qualifying child, or
- $14,590 ($20,020 for married filing jointly) if you do not have a qualifying child.

Earned income generally means wages, salaries, tips, other taxable employee pay, and net earnings from self-employment. Employee pay is earned income only if it is taxable. Nontaxable employee pay, such as certain dependent care benefits and adoption benefits, is not earned income. But there is an exception for nontaxable combat pay, which you can choose to include in earned income. Earned income is explained in detail in *Rule 7*.

Figuring earned income. If you are self-employed, a statutory employee, or a member of the clergy or a church employee who files Schedule SE (Form 1040), you will figure your earned income when you fill out Part 4 of EIC Worksheet B in the Form 1040 instructions.

Otherwise, figure your earned income by using the worksheet in *Step 5* of the Form 1040 instructions for lines 66a and 66b or the Form 1040A instructions for lines 42a and 42b, or the worksheet in *Step 2* of the Form 1040EZ instructions for lines 8a and 8b.

When using one of those worksheets to figure your earned income, you will start with the amount on line 7 (Form 1040 or Form 1040A) or line 1 (Form 1040EZ). You will then reduce that amount by any amount included on that line and described in the following list:

- Scholarship or fellowship grants not reported on a Form W-2,
- Inmate's income, and
- Pension or annuity from deferred compensation plans.

Scholarship or fellowship grants not reported on a Form W-2. A scholarship or fellowship grant that was not reported to you on a Form W-2 is not considered earned income for the earned income credit.

Inmate's income. Amounts received for work performed while an inmate in a penal institution are not earned income for the earned income credit. This includes amounts received for work performed while in a work release program or while in a halfway house. If you received any amount for work done while an inmate in a penal institution and that amount is included in the total on line 7 (Form 1040 or Form 1040A) or line 1 (Form 1040EZ), put "PRI" and the amount on the dotted line next to line 7 (Form 1040), in the space to the left of the entry space for line 7 (Form 1040A), or in the space to the left of line 1 (Form 1040EZ).

Pension or annuity from deferred compensation plans. A pension or annuity from a nonqualified deferred compensation plan or a nongovernmental Section 457 plan is not considered earned income for the earned income credit. If you received such an amount and it was included in the total on line 7 (Form 1040 or Form 1040A) or line 1 (Form 1040EZ), put "DFC" and the amount on the dotted line next to line 7 (Form 1040), in the space to the left of the entry space for line 7 (Form 1040A), or in the space to the left of line 1 (Form 1040EZ). This amount may be reported in box 11 of your Form W-2. If you received such an amount but box 11 is blank, contact your employer for the amount received as a pension or annuity.

Clergy. If you are a member of the clergy who files Schedule SE and the amount on line 2 of that schedule includes an amount that was also reported on line 7 (Form 1040), subtract that amount from the amount on line 7 (Form 1040) and enter the result in the first space of the worksheet in *Step 5* of the Form 1040 instructions for lines 66a and 66b. Put "Clergy" on the dotted line next to line 66a (Form 1040).

Church employees. A church employee means an employee (other than a minister or member of a religious order) of a church or qualified church-controlled organization that is exempt from employer social security and Medicare taxes. If you received wages as a church employee and included any amount on both line 5a of Schedule SE and line 7 (Form 1040), subtract that amount from the amount on line 7 (Form 1040) and enter the result in the first space of the worksheet in *Step 5* of the Form 1040 instructions for lines 66a and 66b.

Tip

If you want the IRS to figure the amount of your EIC, see chapter 31

IRS Will Figure the EIC for You
How To Figure the EIC Yourself
To figure the EIC yourself, use the EIC Worksheet in the instructions for the form you are using (Form 1040, Form 1040A, or Form 1040EZ). If you have a qualifying child, complete Schedule EIC and attach it to your return.

Special Instructions for Form 1040 Filers
If you file Form 1040, you will need to decide whether to use EIC Worksheet A or EIC Worksheet B to figure the amount of your EIC. This section explains how to use these worksheets and how to report the EIC on your return.

EIC Worksheet A. Use EIC Worksheet A if you were not self-employed at any time in 2014 and are not a member of the clergy, a church employee who files Schedule SE, or a statutory employee filing Schedule C or C-EZ.

EIC Worksheet B. Use EIC Worksheet B if you were self-employed at any time in 2014 or are a member of the clergy, a church employee who files Schedule SE, or a statutory employee filing Schedule C or C-EZ. If any of the following situations apply to you, read the paragraph and then complete EIC Worksheet B.

Caution

When figuring your net earnings from self-employment, you must claim all your allowable business expenses.

Net earnings from self-employment $400 or more. If your net earnings from self-employment are $400 or more, be sure to correctly fill out Schedule SE (Form 1040) and pay the proper amount of self-employment tax. If you do not, you may not get all the EIC you are entitled to.

When to use the optional methods of figuring net earnings. Using the optional methods on Schedule SE to figure your net earnings from self-employment may qualify you for the EIC or give you a larger credit. If your net earnings (without using the optional methods) are less than $4,800, see the instructions for Schedule SE for details about the optional methods.

More information. If you and your spouse both have self-employment income or either of you is a statutory employee, see *How To Figure the EIC Yourself* in Publication 596.

Examples
The following two comprehensive examples (complete with filled-in forms) may be helpful.
1. John and Janet Smith, a married couple with one qualifying child and using Form 1040A.
2. Kelly Green, age 30, a student, with no qualifying child and using Form 1040EZ.

Example 1. John and Janet Smith (Form 1040A)

John and Janet Smith are married and will file a joint return. They have one child, Amy, who is 3 years old. Amy lived with John and Janet for all of 2014. John worked and earned $9,500. Janet worked part of the year and earned $1,500. Their earned income and AGI are $11,000. John and Janet qualify for the earned income credit and fill out the EIC Worksheet and Schedule EIC. The Smiths will attach Schedule EIC to Form 1040A when they send their completed return to the IRS.

They took the following steps to complete Schedule EIC and the EIC Worksheet.

Completing Schedule EIC

The Smiths complete Schedule EIC because they have a qualifying child.

Completing the EIC Worksheet

Next, the Smiths will complete the EIC Worksheet to figure their earned income credit.

Line 1. The Smiths enter $11,000 (their earned income).

Line 2. The Smiths go to the Earned Income Credit Table in the Form 1040A instructions. The Smiths find their income of $11,000 within the range of $11,000 to $11,050. They follow this line across to the column that describes their filing status and number of children and find $3,305. They enter $3,305 on line 2.

Line 3. The Smiths enter their AGI of $11,000.

Line 4. The Smiths check the "Yes" box because lines 1 and 3 are the same ($11,000). They skip line 5 and enter the amount from line 2 ($3,305) on line 6.

Line 6. The Smiths' EIC is $3,305.

Example 2. Kelly Green (Form 1040EZ)

Kelly Green is age 30 and a full-time student. She lived with her parents in the United States for all of 2014. She had a part-time job and earned $6,240. She earned $20 interest on a savings account. She is not eligible to be claimed as a dependent on her parents' return. Although she lived with her parents, she is not their qualifying child because she does not meet the age test. She does not have any children.

Kelly qualifies for the earned income credit. Kelly will file Form 1040EZ and complete the EIC Worksheet.

Completing the EIC Worksheet

Kelly figures the amount of her earned income credit on the EIC Worksheet as follows.

Line 1. She enters $6,240 (her earned income).

Line 2. Kelly goes to the Earned Income Credit Table in the Form 1040EZ instructions. She finds her earned income of $6,240 in the range of $6,200 to $6,250. Kelly follows this line across to the column that describes her filing status and finds $476. She enters $476 on line 2.

Line 3. Kelly enters $6,260 (her AGI).

Line 4. Kelly checks the "No" box because lines 1 and 3 are not the same.

Line 5. Kelly checks the "Yes" box because the amount on line 3 ($6,260) is less than $7,800. She leaves line 5 blank and enters the amount from line 2, $476, on line 6.

Line 6. She enters $476 here and on Form 1040EZ, line 9a. Kelly's earned income credit is $476.

> **Caution**
>
> *If your EIC for a year after 1996 was reduced or disallowed, see Form 8862, who must file, earlier to find out if you must file Form 8862 to take the credit for 2014.*

SCHEDULE EIC
(Form 1040A or 1040)

Department of the Treasury
Internal Revenue Service (99)

Earned Income Credit
Qualifying Child Information

▶ Complete and attach to Form 1040A or 1040 only if you have a qualifying child.

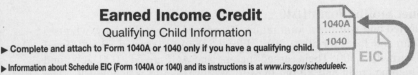

▶ Information about Schedule EIC (Form 1040A or 1040) and its instructions is at www.irs.gov/scheduleeic.

OMB No. 1545-0074

20**14**

Attachment
Sequence No. **43**

Name(s) shown on return

John and Janet Smith

Your social security number

222-22-2222

Before you begin:
- See the instructions for Form 1040A, lines 42a and 42b, or Form 1040, lines 66a and 66b, to make sure that (**a**) you can take the EIC, and (**b**) you have a qualifying child.
- Be sure the child's name on line 1 and social security number (SSN) on line 2 agree with the child's social security card. Otherwise, at the time we process your return, we may reduce or disallow your EIC. If the name or SSN on the child's social security card is not correct, call the Social Security Administration at 1-800-772-1213.

⚠ CAUTION
- If you take the EIC even though you are not eligible, you may not be allowed to take the credit for up to 10 years. See the instructions for details.
- It will take us longer to process your return and issue your refund if you do not fill in all lines that apply for each qualifying child.

DRAFT AS OF June 3, 2014 DO NOT FILE

Qualifying Child Information	Child 1	Child 2	Child 3
1 Child's name If you have more than three qualifying children, you have to list only three to get the maximum credit.	First name / Last name **Amy Smith**	First name / Last name	First name / Last name
2 Child's SSN The child must have an SSN as defined in the instructions for Form 1040A, lines 42a and 42b, or Form 1040, lines 66a and 66b, unless the child was born and died in 2014. If your child was born and died in 2014 and did not have an SSN, enter "Died" on this line and attach a copy of the child's birth certificate, death certificate, or hospital medical records.	**000-00-2223**		
3 Child's year of birth	Year **2 0 1 1** *If born after 1995 and the child is younger than you (or your spouse, if filing jointly), skip lines 4a and 4b; go to line 5.*	Year ___ ___ ___ ___ *If born after 1995 and the child is younger than you (or your spouse, if filing jointly), skip lines 4a and 4b; go to line 5.*	Year ___ ___ ___ ___ *If born after 1995 and the child is younger than you (or your spouse, if filing jointly), skip lines 4a and 4b; go to line 5.*
4 a Was the child under age 24 at the end of 2014, a student, and younger than you (or your spouse, if filing jointly)?	☐ **Yes.** *Go to line 5.* ☐ **No.** *Go to line 4b.*	☐ **Yes.** *Go to line 5.* ☐ **No.** *Go to line 4b.*	☐ **Yes.** *Go to line 5.* ☐ **No.** *Go to line 4b.*
b Was the child permanently and totally disabled during any part of 2014?	☐ **Yes.** *Go to line 5.* ☐ **No.** The child is not a qualifying child.	☐ **Yes.** *Go to line 5.* ☐ **No.** The child is not a qualifying child.	☐ **Yes.** *Go to line 5.* ☐ **No.** The child is not a qualifying child.
5 Child's relationship to you (for example, son, daughter, grandchild, niece, nephew, foster child, etc.)	**Daughter**		
6 Number of months child lived with you in the United States during 2014 • If the child lived with you for more than half of 2014 but less than 7 months, enter "7." • If the child was born or died in 2014 and your home was the child's home for more than half the time he or she was alive during 2014, enter "12."	**12** ____ months *Do not enter more than 12 months.*	____ months *Do not enter more than 12 months.*	____ months *Do not enter more than 12 months.*

For Paperwork Reduction Act Notice, see your tax return instructions.

Cat. No. 13339M

Schedule EIC (Form 1040A or 1040) 2014

Purpose of Schedule

After you have figured your earned income credit (EIC), use Schedule EIC to give the IRS information about your qualifying child(ren).

To figure the amount of your credit or to have the IRS figure it for you, see the instructions for Form 1040A, lines 42a and 42b, or Form 1040, lines 66a and 66b.

Taking the EIC when not eligible. If you take the EIC even though you are not eligible and it is determined that your error is due to reckless or intentional disregard of the

EIC rules, you will not be allowed to take the credit for 2 years even if you are otherwise eligible to do so. If you fraudulently take the EIC, you will not be allowed to take the credit for 10 years. You may also have to pay penalties.

Future developments. For the latest information about developments related to Schedule EIC (Form 1040A or 1040) and its instructions, such as legislation enacted after they were published, go to *www.irs.gov/scheduleeic*.

 TIP — *You may also be able to take the additional child tax credit if your child was your dependent and under age 17 at the end of 2014. For more details, see the instructions for line 43 of Form 1040A or line 67 of Form 1040.*

Qualifying Child

A qualifying child for the EIC is a child who is your . . .

Son, daughter, stepchild, foster child, brother, sister, stepbrother, stepsister, half brother, half sister, or a descendant of any of them (for example, your grandchild, niece, or nephew)

 AND

was . . .

Under age 19 at the end of 2014 and younger than you (or your spouse, if filing jointly)
or
Under age 24 at the end of 2014, a student, and younger than you (or your spouse, if filing jointly)
or
Any age and permanently and totally disabled

 AND

Who is not filing a joint return for 2014
or is filing a joint return for 2014 only to claim
a refund of withheld income tax or estimated tax paid

 AND

Who lived with you in the United States for more than half of 2014. If the child did not live with you for the required time, see *Exception to time lived with you* in the instructions for Form 1040A, lines 42a and 42b, or Form 1040, lines 66a and 66b.

 CAUTION — *If the child was married or meets the conditions to be a qualifying child of another person (other than your spouse if filing a joint return), special rules apply. For details, see* Married child *or* Qualifying child of more than one person *in the instructions for Form 1040A, lines 42a and 42b, or Form 1040, lines 66a and 66b.*

Part 1

All Filers

1. Enter your earned income from Step 5.

   | 1 | 11,000 |

2. Look up the amount on line 1 in the EIC Table to find the credit. Be sure you use the correct column for your filing status and the number of children you have. Enter the credit here.

   | 2 | 3,305 |

   If line 2 is zero, (STOP) You cannot take the credit. Enter "No" to the left of the entry space for line 38a.

3. Enter the amount from Form 1040A, line 22.

   | 3 | 11,000 |

4. Are the amounts on lines 3 and 1 the same?

   ☒ **Yes.** Skip line 5; enter the amount from line 2 on line 6.

   ☐ **No.** Go to line 5.

Part 2

Filers Who Answered "No" on Line 4

5. If you have:
   - No qualifying children, is the amount on line 3 less than $7,800 ($13,000 if married filing jointly)?
   - 1 or more qualifying children, is the amount on line 3 less than $17,100 ($22,300 if married filing jointly)?

   ☐ **Yes.** Leave line 5 blank; enter the amount from line 2 on line 6.

   ☐ **No.** Look up the amount on line 3 in the EIC Table to find the credit. Be sure you use the correct column for your filing status and the number of children you have. Enter the credit here.

   | 5 | |

   Look at the amounts on lines 5 and 2.
   Then, enter the smaller amount on line 6.

Part 3

Your Earned Income Credit

6. This is your earned income credit.

   | 6 | 3,305 |

   Enter this amount on Form 1040A, line 38a.

Reminder—

✓ If you have a qualifying child, complete and attach Schedule EIC.

⚠ **CAUTION**
If your EIC for a year after 1996 was reduced or disallowed, see Form 8862, Who Must File, earlier to find out if you must file Form 8862 to take the credit for 2014.

Earned Income Credit (EIC) Worksheet— Lines 8a and 8b

1. Enter your earned income from Step 2 on page 14 . . . . **1.** _____6,240_____

2. Look up the amount on line 1 above in the EIC Table on page 16 to find the credit. Be sure you use the correct column for your filing status (Single or Married filing jointly).

   Enter the credit here . . . . **2.** _____476_____

   If line 2 is zero, (STOP) You cannot take the credit. Enter "No" in the space to the left of line 8a.

3. Enter the amount from Form 1040EZ, line 4 . . . . **3.** _____6,260_____

4. Are the amounts on lines 3 and 1 the same?

   ☐ **Yes.** Skip line 5; enter the amount from line 2 on line 6.

   ☑ **No.** Go to line 5.

5. Is the amount on line 3 less than $7,800 ($13,000 if married filing jointly)?

   ☑ **Yes.** Leave line 5 blank; enter the amount from line 2 on line 6.

   ☐ **No.** Look up the amount on line 3 in the EIC Table on page 16 to find the credit. Be sure you use the correct column for your filing status (Single or Married filing jointly).

   Enter the credit here . . . . **5.** _____

   Look at the amounts on lines 5 and 2. Then, enter the **smaller** amount on line 6.

6. **Earned income credit.** Enter this amount on Form 1040EZ, line 8a . . . . **6.** | 476 |

> ⚠️ **CAUTION**
> If your EIC for a year after 1996 was reduced or disallowed, see above to find out if you **must file Form 8862** to take the credit for 2012.

EIC Eligibility Checklist

	Yes	**No**
You may claim the EIC if you answer "Yes" to all the following questions.*		

You may claim the EIC if you answer "Yes" to all the following questions.*

1. Is your AGI less than:
   - $14,590 ($20,020 for married filing jointly) if you do not have a qualifying child,
   - $38,511 ($43,941 for married filing jointly) if you have one qualifying child,
   - $43,756 ($49,186 for married filing jointly) if you have two qualifying children, or
   - $46,997 ($52,427 for married filing jointly) if you have more than two qualifying children?
   (See *Rule 1*.)   ☐ ☐

2. Do you, your spouse, and your qualifying child each have a valid SSN? (See *Rule 2*.)   ☐ ☐

3. Is your filing status married filing jointly, head of household, qualifying widow(er), or single? (See *Rule 3*.)
   Caution: If you or your spouse is a nonresident alien, answer **"Yes"** only if your filing status is married filing jointly.
   (See *Rule 4*.)   ☐ ☐

4. Answer **"Yes"** if you are not filing Form 2555 or Form 2555-EZ. Otherwise, answer **"No."** (See *Rule 5*.)   ☐ ☐

5. Is your investment income $3,350 or less? (See *Rule 6*.)   ☐ ☐

6. Is your total earned income at least $1 but less than:
   - $14,590 ($20,020 for married filing jointly) if you do not have a qualifying child,
   - $38,511 ($43,941 for married filing jointly) if you have one qualifying child,
   - $43,756 ($49,186 for married filing jointly) if you have two qualifying children, or
   - $46,997 ($52,427 for married filing jointly) if you have more than two qualifying children?
   (See *Rules 7* and *15*.)   ☐ ☐

7. Answer **"Yes"** if you (and your spouse if filing a joint return) are not a qualifying child of another person. Otherwise, answer **"No."** (See *Rules 10* and *13*.)   ☐ ☐

   STOP: If you have a qualifying child, answer questions 8 and 9 and skip 10 – 12. If you do not have a qualifying child, skip questions 8 and 9 and answer 10 – 12.*

8. Does your child meet the age, residency, and relationship tests for a qualifying child? (See *Rule 8*.)   ☐ ☐

9. Is your child a qualifying child only for you? Answer **"Yes"** if your qualifying child also meets the tests to be a qualifying child of another person, but the other person is not claiming any child-related tax benefits using that child. Answer **"No"** if you do not know whether the other person is claiming any child-related tax benefits using that child.   ☐ ☐

10. Were you (or your spouse if filing a joint return) at least age 25 but under 65 at the end of 2014? (See *Rule 11*.)   ☐ ☐

11. Answer **"Yes"** if you (and your spouse if filing a joint return) cannot be claimed as a dependent on anyone else's return. Answer **"No"** if you (or your spouse if filing a joint return) can be claimed as a dependent on someone else's return. (See *Rule 12*.)   ☐ ☐

12. Was your main home (and your spouse's if filing a joint return) in the United States for more than half the year? (See *Rule 14*.)   ☐ ☐

***PERSONS WITH A QUALIFYING CHILD:** If you answered **"Yes"** to questions 1 through 9, you can claim the EIC. Remember to fill out Schedule EIC and attach it to your Form 1040 or Form 1040A. You cannot use Form 1040EZ. If you answered **"Yes"** to questions 1 through 8 and **"No"** to question 9, see *Rule 9* to help you determine whether you can claim the EIC. If you answered **"Yes"** to questions 1 through 7 and **"No"** to question 8, answer questions 10 through 12 to see if you can claim the EIC without a qualifying child.*

***PERSONS WITHOUT A QUALIFYING CHILD:** If you answered **"Yes"** to questions 1 through 7, and 10 through 12, you can claim the EIC.*

***If you answered "No" to any question that applies to you:** You cannot claim the EIC.*

Part 7
Special situations and tax planning

ey.com/EYTaxGuide

The first seven chapters in this part discuss some special situations. Chapter 38, *Self-employment income: How to file Schedule C*, is essential reading for anyone who is self-employed: freelancers, artists, and small business owners. Mutual fund investors will want to pay special attention to chapter 39, *Mutual funds*. It discusses what you need to know about the tax treatment of gains, losses, dividends, and distributions from a mutual fund. Chapter 40, *What to do if you employ domestic help*, will be of interest to taxpayers who employ domestic help, whether it is to care for their children or a disabled or elderly dependent. Chapter 41, *U.S. citizens working abroad: Tax treatment of foreign earned income*, discusses how U.S. citizens working abroad should handle their taxes. Among other matters, it explains how you can get a credit against your U.S. taxes for taxes you have paid to a foreign government. Chapter 42, *Foreign citizens living in the United States*, discusses the tax rules applicable to foreign citizens living in the United States. Chapter 43, *Decedents: Dealing with the death of a family member*, discusses a broad range of special issues that survivors face in handling the final tax matters of a deceased family member. Generous-spirited readers will want to peruse chapter 44, *Estate and gift tax planning*. It explains the tax intricacies of giving assets to others while you are alive and also discusses the estate tax and various strategies you can use.

Following these chapters on special situations, the next chapters offer a further helping hand. Chapter 45, *Everything you need to know about e-filing*, leads you through the electronic filing process. With luck, you won't need to refer to chapter 46, *If your return is examined*, but in case your tax return is examined and you are subject to an audit, you will find it useful. Chapter 47, *Planning ahead for 2015 and beyond*, can help you save money on your taxes next year and beyond. It discusses tax developments in 2015 and after.

Chapter 48, *2014 Tax rate schedules*, is the final chapter. It provides the 2014 tax rate schedules that you need to complete your tax return. The 2014 Tax Tables can be easily viewed and printed out at www.irs.gov. The tax tables must be used by taxpayers with taxable income of less than $100,000. Taxpayers with taxable income of $100,000 or more should use the tax rate schedules.

Chapter 38
Self-employment income: How to file Schedule C

Note

ey.com/EYTaxGuide

Ernst & Young LLP will update the *EY Tax Guide 2015* website with relevant taxpayer information as it becomes available. You can also sign up for email alerts to let you know when changes have been made.

Introduction

More and more people work for themselves. Whether your business is your sole source of income, it supplements other income, or is new or existing, you will face a number of perplexing tax questions that ordinary wage earners do not face. What income do you report? What expenses can you deduct? What forms do you need to file?

Unlike a partnership or a regular corporation, a sole proprietorship is not a separate entity for tax purposes. (A limited liability company [LLC] which has only one member, is treated as a sole proprietorship for tax purposes.) In a sole proprietorship, you and your business are one and the same. You report net profit or loss for the year from a sole proprietorship on Form 1040, Schedule C (or Schedule C-EZ), and it becomes part of your adjusted gross income. In addition to owing income tax on such income, you, as the sole proprietor, usually will be liable for self-employment tax, and will also be required to make payments of estimated taxes. A net loss from the business generally can be deducted when you compute your adjusted gross income (see *Hobby loss rules*, later in this chapter).

This chapter concentrates on how a sole proprietorship recognizes business profit and losses on Form 1040, Schedule C, and Schedule SE. Examples of completed forms are included at the end of this chapter.

Useful Items

You may want to see:

Publication

- □ **15**   Circular E, Employer's Tax Guide
- □ **15-A**   Employer's Supplemental Tax Guide
- □ **225**   Farmer's Tax Guide
- □ **334**   Tax Guide for Small Business
- □ **463**   Travel, Entertainment, Gift and Car Expenses
- □ **535**   Business Expenses
- □ **541**   Partnerships
- □ **587**   Business Use of Your Home (Including Use by Day-Care Providers)

Who Must File Schedule C

If you are a sole proprietor, an independent contractor, a statutory employee, a statutory nonemployee, or a single member LLC, you may be required to report business income and expenses on Schedule C.

Sole proprietor. If you operate a business as a sole proprietor, you must file Schedule C to report your income and expenses from your business. If you operate more than one business, or if you and your spouse had separate businesses, you must prepare a separate Schedule C for each business.

TAXPLANNER

Husband-wife businesses. If spouses carry on a business together and share in the profits and losses, they may be partners whether or not they have a formal partnership agreement. If so, they should report income or loss from the business on Form 1065, U.S. Return of Partnership Income. They should not report the income on Schedule C (Form 1040) in the name of one spouse as a sole proprietor. However, a husband and wife can elect not to treat the joint venture as a partnership if they meet each of the following requirements:

1. The only members of the joint venture are the husband and wife.
2. The husband and wife file a joint return.
3. Both spouses materially participate in the business.
4. Both spouses elect this treatment.
   Note: The election not to treat the joint venture as a partnership is not revocable without IRS consent.

Independent contractor. A person whose work hours and procedures are not controlled by another and who is therefore deemed to be self-employed for tax purposes must also file a Schedule C.

Statutory employee. If you are a statutory employee, you should file Schedule C. If you file Schedule C, you can deduct certain business expenses when computing your adjusted gross income. A statutory employee's business expenses will not be subject to the reduction by 2% of his or her adjusted gross income that applies to "regular" employee business expenses reported as a part of Schedule A, Itemized Deductions. A statutory employee includes the following occupations:

1. Certain agent and commission drivers
2. Full-time life insurance sales representatives
3. Certain home workers performing work, according to specifications furnished by the person for whom the services are performed
4. Certain traveling or city salespeople who work full-time (except for sideline sales activities) for one firm or person, soliciting orders from customers

   If you meet the definition of a statutory employee, your employer will indicate this classification by checking box 13, "Statutory employee," on your Form W-2. This indicates to the IRS that you have the right to report your income and expenses on Schedule C.

   As a statutory employee, you are considered an employee for social security and Medicare purposes. However, if you and your employer agree, federal income tax withholding is optional, rather than mandatory.

   A statutory employee reports his or her wages from box 1 of Form W-2 on line 1 of Schedule C. He or she then deducts allowable expenses on Part II of Schedule C to arrive at reportable income.

Statutory nonemployee. If you are a statutory nonemployee, you must file Schedule C to report your income and expenses.

Explanation

There are two categories of statutory nonemployees. The two categories are a direct seller of consumer products and a licensed real estate agent. They are treated as self-employed for federal income tax and employment tax purposes if:

1. Substantially all payments for their services as direct sellers or real estate agents are directly related to sales or other output, rather than to the number of hours worked; and
2. Their services are performed under a written contract providing that they will not be treated as employees for federal tax purposes.

Direct sellers. Direct sellers are persons:

1. Engaged in selling (or soliciting the sale of) consumer products in the home or at a place of business other than a permanent retail establishment; or
2. Engaged in selling (or soliciting the sale of) consumer products to any buyer on a buy-sell basis, a deposit-commission basis, or any similar basis prescribed by regulations for resale in the home or at a place of business other than a permanent retail establishment.

Direct selling also includes activities of individuals who attempt to increase direct sales activities of their direct sellers and who earn income based on the productivity of their direct sellers. Such activities include providing motivation and encouragement; imparting skills, knowledge, or experience; and recruiting.

Licensed real estate agents. This category includes real estate agents as well as individuals engaged in appraisal activities for real estate sales, if they earn income based on sales or other output.

TAXALERT

Unlike a statutory employee, a statutory nonemployee is not subject to social security and Medicare withholding. Therefore, he or she is required to pay self-employment tax on net earnings. Additionally, federal income tax withholding is not required; therefore, estimated taxes must be paid.

Single Member LLC (limited liability company). If you operate your business through a single member LLC (this is generally done for liability purposes), you should report your income and expenses with respect to the LLC activity on Schedule C.

What's Included on Schedule C

Schedule C is used to report income and related expenses applicable to the above activities. Income includes cash, property, and services received from all sources, unless specifically excluded under the tax code. Expenses include all ordinary and necessary expenses incurred in connection with the activity.

For sole proprietorships in the business of selling goods or inventory, the primary expense will be the cost of goods sold. The cost of goods sold represents the cost of materials, labor, and overhead included in the inventory sold during the year. Other expenses you may deduct on Schedule C include salaries and wages, interest on loans used in the activity, rent, depreciation, bad debts, travel, 50% of entertainment expenses, insurance, real estate taxes, state and local taxes, and an allocable portion of your tax return preparation fee.

TAXPLANNER

Schedule C-EZ. You may use Schedule C-EZ instead of Schedule C if you operated a business or practiced a profession as a sole proprietorship and you have met all of the requirements listed below:

• Had business expenses of $5,000 or less
• Used the cash method of accounting
• Did not have an inventory at any time during the year
• Did not have a net loss from your business
• Had only one business as a sole proprietor, qualified joint venture, or statutory employee and you:
• Had no employees during the year
• Are not required to file Form 4562, Depreciation and Amortization, for this business
• Do not deduct expenses for business use of your home
• Do not have prior year, disallowed passive activity losses from this business

Where to Report on Your Return

The net income or net loss calculated on Schedule C is reported on page 1 of Form 1040. The net income or net loss (subject to certain limitations) generated on your Schedule C will cause either an increase or a decrease to adjusted gross income (AGI).

Losses. If Schedule C expenses exceed Schedule C income, a loss will result. There is a possibility the amount of Schedule C loss that can be deducted on your current year's income tax return may be limited. The amount of the loss that can be deducted on your return depends on whether you materially participate in the operation of the business (defined below), and/or whether you have enough investment at risk to cover the loss.

Defining material participation. You are treated as a material participant only if you are involved in the operations of the activity on a regular, continuous, and substantial basis. If you are not a material participant in an activity, but your spouse is, you are treated as being a material participant, and the activity is not considered passive. A passive activity involves the conduct of any trade or business in which you do not materially participate.

For more information about passive activities and the at-risk limitation, see chapter 12, *Other income*, and IRS Publication 925, *Passive Activity and At-Risk Rules*.

What is a hobby loss? The IRS presumes that an activity which produces net income in 3 or more taxable years within a period of 5 consecutive years is engaged in for profit. Therefore, if an activity produces a loss for 3 or more years in a consecutive 5-year period, the IRS may infer that the activity is not engaged in for profit and disallow the loss.

Carrybacks and carryforwards. If you have incurred a Schedule C loss, it is possible that the loss may be large enough to offset all taxable income reported on your Form 1040. If this is the case, you may have generated a net operating loss (NOL).

TAXSAVER

If you have more than one trade or business, you must combine the net earnings from each business to determine your net self-employment income. A loss that you incur in one business will offset your income in another business.

When an individual's self-employment earnings multiplied by 0.9235 are less than $400, he or she is not required to file Form 1040, Schedule SE, or to pay self-employment tax.

Joint returns. Show the name of the spouse with self-employment income on Schedule SE. If both spouses have self-employment income, each must file a separate Schedule SE. If one spouse qualifies to use Short Schedule SE and the other has to use Long Schedule SE, both can use one Schedule SE. One spouse should complete the front (short form) and the other the back (long form).

Include the total profits or losses from all businesses on Form 1040, as appropriate. Enter the combined Schedule SE tax on Form 1040.

TAXSAVER

Self-employment tax deduction. You can deduct one-half of your self-employment tax in figuring your adjusted gross income. This is an income tax adjustment only. It does not affect either your net earnings from self-employment or your self-employment tax. To deduct the tax, enter on Form 1040, line 27, the amount shown on line 6 of Short Schedule SE or line 13 of Long Schedule SE and include Schedule SE with your 1040.

What Is Included in Net Self-Employment Earnings?

In most cases, net earnings include your net profit from a farm or nonfarm business, plus the following items:

- Rental income from a farm if, as landlord, you materially participated in the production or management of the production of farm products on this land.
- Cash or a payment in kind from the Department of Agriculture for participating in a land diversion program.
- Payments for the use of rooms or other space when you also provided substantial services for the convenience of your tenants. Examples are hotel rooms, boarding houses, tourist camps or homes, trailer parks, parking lots, warehouses, and storage garages.
- Income from the retail sale of newspapers and magazines if you were age 18 or older and kept the profits.
- Income you receive as a direct seller.
- Amounts received by current or former self-employed insurance agents and salespersons that are:
  1. Paid after retirement but figured as a percentage of commissions received from the paying company before retirement;
  2. Renewal commissions; or
  3. Deferred commissions paid after retirement for sales made before retirement.
- Fees as a state or local government employee if you were paid only on a fee basis and the job was not covered under a federal-state social security coverage agreement.
- Interest received in the course of any trade or business, such as interest on notes or accounts receivable.
- Fees and other payments received by you for services as a director of a corporation.
- Fees you received as a professional fiduciary.
- Recapture amounts under Sections 179 and 280F that you included in gross income because the business use of the property dropped to 50% or less.
- Gain or loss from Section 1256 contracts or related property by an options or commodities dealer in the normal course of dealing in or trading Section 1256 contracts.

Income and Losses Not Included in Net Earnings from Self-Employment

- Salaries, fees, and so on, subject to social security or Medicare tax that you received for performing services as an employee.
- Fees received for services performed as a notary public
- Income you received as a retired partner under a written partnership plan that provides for lifelong periodic retirement payments if you had no other interest in the partnership and did not perform services for it during the year.
- Income from real estate rentals, if you did not receive the income in the course of a trade or business as a real estate dealer. This includes cash and crop shares received from a tenant or sharefarmer.

- Dividends on shares of stock and interest on bonds, notes, and so on, if you did not receive the income in the course of your trade or business as a dealer in stocks or securities.
- Gain or loss from:
  1. The sale or exchange of a capital asset;
  2. The sale, exchange, involuntary conversion, or other disposition of property unless the property is stock in trade or other property that would be includible in inventory, or held primarily for sale to customers in the ordinary course of the business; or
  3. Certain transactions in timber, coal, or domestic iron ore.
- Net operating losses from other years.

Statutory employee income. If you were a statutory employee, do not include the net profit or loss from that Schedule C (or the net profit from Schedule C-EZ) on Schedule SE. A statutory employee is defined above.

Self-Employment Tax Calculation

Self-employment tax can be calculated using one of the following methods: the regular method, the farm optional method, and the nonfarm optional method.

Regular Method. Under the regular method, your self-employment tax should be calculated as follows:

1. Figure your net self-employment income. The net profit from your business or profession is generally your net self-employment income.
2. After you figure your net self-employment income, determine how much is subject to self-employment tax. The amount subject to self-employment tax is called net earnings from self-employment. It is figured on Short Schedule SE, line 4, or Long Schedule SE, line 4a. It is generally 92.35% of net self-employment income.
3. Figure your self-employment tax as follows:
   - If, for 2014, your net earnings from self-employment plus any wages and tips are not more than $117,000 and you do not have to use Long Schedule SE, use Short Schedule SE. On line 5, multiply your net earnings by 15.3% (0.153). The result is the amount of your self-employment tax.
   - If you had no wages or tips in 2014, your net earnings from self-employment are more than $117,000, and you are not required to complete Long Schedule SE (see guidelines at the top of Short Schedule SE), use Short Schedule SE. On line 5, multiply the line 4 net earnings by 2.9% (0.029) Medicare tax and add the result to $14,508 (12.4% of $117,000). The total is the amount of your self-employment tax.
   - If you received wages or tips in 2014 and your net earnings from self-employment plus any wages and tips are more than $117,000, you must use Long Schedule SE. Subtract your total wages and tips from $117,000 to find the maximum amount of earnings subject to social security tax. If more than zero, multiply the amount by 12.4% (0.124). The result is the social security tax due. Next, multiply your net earnings from self-employment by 2.9% (0.029). Multiply the amount of self-employment income (as well as wages) received in excess of the specified threshold amounts ($250,000 for a joint return; $125,000 for a married individual filing a separate return; and $200,000 for all other filers) by 3.8% (0.038). The result is the Medicare tax due. The total of the social security tax and the Medicare tax is your self-employment tax.

Optional Methods. Generally, you can use the optional methods when you have a loss or small amount of net income from self-employment and:

1. You want to receive credit for social security benefit coverage (in 2014, the maximum social security coverage under the optional methods is four credits, the equivalent of $4,800 of net earnings from self-employment);
2. You incurred child or dependent care expenses for which you could claim a credit (this method will increase your earned income, which could increase your credit); or
3. You are entitled to the earned income credit (this method will increase your earned income, which could increase your credit).

TAXALERT

The ability to use an optional method of calculating self-employment tax allows you to maintain the benefits of contributing to social security and eligibility for credits based on income even in a down year in your business. In a year where your self-employment earnings are lower, you can use the following optional methods to achieve the result of contributing the maximum amount to social security. Also, an optional method would permit you to take the earned income or child and dependent

care credit (depending on eligibility). This benefit is allowed only five times during your lifetime. To be eligible for these methods, net earnings from self-employment must have been $400 or more in 2 out of the previous 3 years and your net nonfarm profits were less than $5,198 and also less than 72.189% of your gross nonfarm income. The optional methods are as follows:
- If gross nonfarm income from self-employment is $6,960 or less, report 2/3 of gross income; or
- If gross income is greater than $6,960, then your net earnings are equal to $4,800.

For tax years after 2008, the maximum amount reportable using this method will be equal to the amount needed to get four work credits for a given year. For example, for tax year 2014, the maximum amount reportable using the optional method would be $1,200 × 4, or $4,800.

How to Determine Items of Income and Expenses

Start-Up and Pre-Operating Expenses

Start-up expenditures are the costs of getting started in business before you actually begin doing business. Start-up costs may include expenses for advertising, travel, utilities, repairs, or employees' wages. These are often the same kinds of costs that can be deducted when they occur after you open for business.

Pre-operating costs include what you pay for both investigating a prospective business and getting the business started. For example, they may include costs for the following items:
- A survey of potential markets
- An analysis of available facilities, labor, supplies, etc.
- Advertisements for the opening of the business
- Salaries and wages for employees who are being trained and their instructors
- Travel and other necessary costs for securing prospective distributors, suppliers, or customers
- Salaries and fees for executives and consultants or for other professional services.

Start-up costs do not include deductible interest, taxes, or research and experimental costs. Therefore, subject to other limitations, these items are currently deductible.

The deductibility of your start-up expenditures depends on whether you actually begin the active trade or business.

If you go into business, start-up expenses of a trade or business are not deductible unless you elect to deduct them.

TAXALERT

For tax year 2014, the deductible amount of start-up expenditures is the lesser of:
1. The amount of the start-up expenditures for the active trade or business; or
2. $5,000, reduced (but not below zero) by the amount by which the start-up expenditures exceed $50,000.

Any remaining start-up expenditures are to be claimed as a deduction spread over a 15-year period.

All start-up expenditures related to a particular trade or business are considered in determining whether the cumulative cost of start-up expenditures exceeds $50,000. For more information on start-up expenditures, see Publication 535, *Business Expenses*.

TAXPLANNER

If you have start-up costs in 2014 for a new business exceeding the $5,000 limited amount, you should attach a statement to your tax return electing to amortize the portion exceeding $5,000 ratably over a period of 15 years. Complete and attach Form 4562, Depreciation and Amortization, for start-up expenses you are beginning to amortize in 2014.

Example. Tony's repair shop started business on June 4, 2014. Prior to starting business, Tony incurred various expenses totaling $11,000 to set up shop. Tony can deduct $5,000 of these expenses in 2014 and deduct the balance of $6,000 ratably over 15 years.

Although the IRS has been instructed to do so, no guidance has been issued as to when a trade or a business begins. When it does so, the IRS is likely to take a conservative stance. In the meantime, there has been substantial litigation about this issue. The generally accepted rule seems to be that even though a taxpayer has made a firm decision to enter into a business, and over a considerable period of time has spent money in preparation for entering that business, he or she still has not engaged in carrying on any trade or business until such time as the business has begun to function as a going concern and has performed those activities for which it was organized.

Failure to go into business. If an attempt to go into business is not successful, your ability to deduct the expenses incurred trying to establish your business depends on the type of expenses incurred.

Investigatory expenses. The costs incurred before making a decision to acquire or to begin a specific business are classified as personal and therefore are not deductible. Investigatory expenses include costs incurred in the course of a general search for, or preliminary investigation of, a business prior to reaching a decision to acquire or enter any business. Examples include: expenses incurred for the analysis or survey of potential markets, products, labor supply, transportation facilities, and so on.

Start-up expenses. The costs incurred after making a decision to acquire or to establish a particular business, and prior to its actual operation, are classified as capital expenditures and may be deductible in the year in which the attempt to go into business fails, if prior to the end of the amortization period.

Business sold. If you completely dispose of a trade or a business before the end of the amortization period you have selected, any deferred start-up costs for the trade or business that have not yet been deducted may be deducted to the extent that they qualify as a loss from a trade or a business.

TAXYEAR

Every taxpayer must determine taxable income and file a tax return on the basis of an annual accounting period. The term "tax year" is the annual accounting period you use for keeping your records and for reporting your income and expenses. The accounting periods you can use are as follows:
1. A calendar year
2. A fiscal year

A tax year is adopted when you file your first income tax return. It cannot be longer than 12 months.

Calendar tax year. If you adopt the calendar year for your annual accounting period, you must maintain your books and records, and report your income and expenses for the period from January 1 through December 31 of each year.

Fiscal tax year. A regular fiscal tax year is 12 consecutive months, ending on the last day of any month except December.

If you adopt a fiscal tax year, you must maintain your books and records, and report your income and expenses using the same tax year.

TAXALERT

If you filed your first return using the calendar tax year and you later begin business as a sole proprietor, you must continue to use the calendar tax year, unless you get permission from the IRS to change. You must report your income from all sources, including your sole proprietorship, using the same tax year.

Accounting Methods

Accounting methods are described in chapter 1, *Filing information*. The discussion that follows relates mainly to self-employed entrepreneurs, sole proprietors, and others who file Schedule C.

No single accounting method is required for all taxpayers. Generally, you may figure your taxable income under any one of the following accounting methods:

1. Cash method
2. Accrual method
3. Special methods of accounting for certain items of income and expenses
4. Combination (hybrid) method using elements of (1), (2), or (3)

Cash method. The cash method of accounting is used by most individuals and many small businesses with no inventories. However, if inventories are necessary in accounting for your income, you must use the accrual method for your sales and purchases of merchandise. If you are not required to maintain inventories, it is often more advantageous to use the cash method, because it allows more flexibility and control over your income.

Income. All items of income are generally included in gross income when actually or constructively received. Income is constructively received when an amount is credited to your account or made available to you without restriction. This does not mean you need to have possession of it. Your agent is also allowed to receive income for you (if you authorize them).

Expenses. Usually, you must deduct expenses in the tax year in which you actually pay them. However, you may be required to postpone the deduction for expenses you pay in advance. In addition, you may have to capitalize certain costs.

Accrual method. Under an accrual method of accounting, income generally is reported in the year in which it is earned, regardless of when the income is actually collected, and expenses generally are deducted in the year in which they are incurred, regardless of when the expenses are paid. The purpose of an accrual method of accounting is to match your income and your expenses. If inventories are necessary in your business, only the accrual method of accounting can be used for purchases and sales.

Income. All items of income are generally included in your gross income when you earn them, even though you may receive payment in another tax year. All events that fix your right to receive the income must have happened, and you must be able to determine the amount with reasonable accuracy.

Example. You are a calendar year taxpayer. You sold a radio on November 26, 2014. You billed the customer 3 days later but did not receive payment until February 2015. You must include the amount of the sale in your income for 2014 because you earned the income in 2014.

Income received in advance. Prepaid income is generally included in gross income in the year you receive it. Your method of accounting does not matter as long as the income is available to you. Prepaid income includes rents or interest received in advance and compensation for services to be performed later.

If, under an agreement, you receive advance payment for services to be performed by the end of the next tax year, you can defer the inclusion in income of the payments received until you earn them by performing the service. You **must** be an accrual method taxpayer to defer recognition of income on advance payments for services. You cannot defer the income beyond the year after the year you receive the payment.

Example 1. You are in the television repair business. In 2014, you received payment for 1-year contracts under which you agree to repair or replace certain parts that fail to function properly in television sets that were sold by an unrelated party. You include the payments in gross income as you earn them (which is when you perform the contracted services).

If for any reason you do not perform part of the services by the end of the following tax year, 2015, you must include in gross income for 2015 the amount of the advance payments that are for services yet to be performed.

Example 2. You own a dance studio. On November 7, 2014, you received payment for a 1-year contract, beginning on that date and providing for 48 1-hour lessons. You gave 8 lessons in 2014. If you recognize income under the accrual method of including advance payments, you must include one-sixth (8/48) of the payment in income for 2014 and five-sixths (40/48) of the payment in 2015.

Expenses. You deduct expenses when you become liable for them, whether or not they are paid in the same year. Before you can deduct expenses, all of the events that set the amount of the liability must have happened, you must be able to determine the amount of the liability with reasonable accuracy, and economic performance (see below) must occur.

Economic performance rule. Even if all of the events that determine the amount of your expenses have occurred, you still cannot deduct business expenses until economic performance occurs. If your expense is for property or services provided to you, or for use of property by you, economic performance occurs as the property or services are provided or as the property is used. If your expense is for property or services that you provide to others, economic performance occurs as the property or services are provided, or as the property is used.

Special rules for related persons. An accrual basis taxpayer cannot deduct business expenses and interest owed to a related cash basis taxpayer until the amount is actually paid. For purposes of applying this rule, related persons include, but are not limited to:

1. Members of the immediate family, including only brothers and sisters, husband and wife, ancestors, and lineal descendants
2. An individual and a corporation, if more than 50% in value of the outstanding stock is owned, directly or indirectly, by or for such individual
3. An S corporation and any individual who owns any of the stock of such S corporation
4. A partnership and any person who owns any capital interest or profits interest of such partnership

Special methods. In addition to the cash or accrual methods, certain items of income or expenses are accounted for under special methods. They include:
• Depreciation
• Amortization and depletion
• Bad debts
• Installment sales

The method of accounting for depreciation and bad debts is discussed later in this chapter. Methods for deducting amortization and depletion are discussed in Publication 535, *Business Expenses*. Methods for reporting installment sales are discussed in Publication 537, *Installment Sales*.

Combination (hybrid) method. Any combination of cash, accrual, and special methods of accounting can be used if the combination clearly reflects income and is consistently used. As an example, if you maintain inventory, the accrual method of accounting for purchases and sales must be used; however, you may use the cash method for all other items of income and expenses.

Two or more businesses. If you operate more than one business, you generally may use a different accounting method for each separate and distinct business if the method you use for each clearly reflects your income. For example, if you operate a personal-service business and a manufacturing business, you may use the cash method for the personal-service business, but you must use the accrual method for the manufacturing business.

How to Complete Schedule C

Schedule C is divided into five parts:

Part I: Income
Part II: Expenses
Part III: Cost of Goods Sold
Part IV: Information on Your Vehicle
Part V: Other Expenses

In addition, Schedule C requires that you answer a number of general questions about the activity.

Completing the General Information Sections

Line A asks for the principal business or profession, including the product or service that provided your principal source of income.

Line B asks for the six-digit code that identifies your principal business or professional activity. The instructions to Schedule C contain a list of the principal business or professional activity codes that you should use.

Line C asks for your business name. If none, leave this line blank.

Line D asks for your employer identification number (EIN). An EIN is needed only if you had a Keogh plan, a SIMPLE, or a SEP (discussed later in this chapter and in chapter 17, *Individual retirement arrangements (IRAs)*), or if you were required to file an employment or excise tax return. If you do not have an EIN, do not enter your social security number. To apply for an EIN, you may either file Form SS-4 with the IRS where you file your individual tax return or apply online at *www.irs.gov*.

Line E requests your business address. If you conducted business out of your home, you do not have to complete this line.

Line F asks for your accounting method, as discussed earlier in this chapter and in chapter 1, *Filing information*.

Line G asks whether or not you "materially participated" in the business. If you did not, your losses from the business that you can deduct currently may be limited. See chapter 12, *Other income*.

Line H must be checked if this is the initial Schedule C filed for this particular business.

Line I must be checked if you are required to file any Form 1099s. You may have to file information returns for wages paid to employees, interest, rents, royalties, etc. You may also need to file Form 1099 if you sold $5,000 or more worth of goods to someone for resale.

In addition, Part III of the form asks two additional questions. Line 33 asks for the method used to value closing inventory, if your business maintains inventory. The inventory can be valued under any one of the following three methods: (1) cost, (2) lower of cost or market, or (3) any other method approved by the IRS. Methods of valuing inventory will be discussed later in this chapter.

Line 34 does not need to be answered if your business does not have inventory. If the business does maintain inventory and there was a change in determining quantities, costs, or valuations between opening and closing inventories, answer the question "yes" and attach an explanation for the change.

Income

Part I of Schedule C is used to report the gross income from the business. Do not combine receipts from two separate businesses on this line. Remember that you must file a separate Schedule C for each business. Statutory employees enter the amount from box 1 of Form W-2 on line 1 and check the box indicated as—Form W-2 and the "Statutory employee" box on that form was checked.

On line 2, report such items as sales returns, rebates, and allowances. For example, if an item you previously sold is returned for a cash refund, the cash refund should be reported here and not included as a reduction of the gross receipts or sales reported on line 1.

Subtract line 2 from line 1, and enter the difference on line 3. From this amount, deduct the cost of goods sold. After deducting the cost of goods sold, you arrive at the gross profit from the business.

Expenses

Part II of Schedule C is used to report expenses associated with your business. To be deductible, a business expense must be both ordinary and necessary. An ordinary expense is one that is common and accepted in your field of business, trade, or profession. A necessary expense is one that is helpful and appropriate for your trade, business, or profession. An expense does not have to be indispensable to be considered necessary. Examples of deductible business expenses include (1) reasonable allowance for salaries and other compensation, (2) traveling expenses while away from home, and (3) rentals or other payments for property used in a trade or a business.

You must keep business expenses separate from personal expenses. If you have any expense that is partly business and partly personal, a reasonable allocation should be made to separate the personal part from the business part.

Capital expenditures. A capital expenditure is defined as an expense that must be capitalized rather than deducted. These costs are considered a part of your investment in your business. There are, in general, three types of costs that must be capitalized: (1) costs of going into business, (2) costs to purchase business assets, and (3) cost of improvements.

Although you generally cannot directly deduct a capital expenditure, you may be able to take deductions for the amount you spend through a method of depreciation, amortization, or depletion.

A discussion of some of the more common expenses you will encounter in your business follows.

Bad debts. If someone owes you money that you cannot collect, you have a bad debt. You may be able to deduct the amount owed to you when you figure your business income in the year in which the debt becomes worthless. There are two kinds of bad debts: business bad debts and nonbusiness bad debts. A business bad debt generally is one that comes from your trade or business. All other bad debts are nonbusiness bad debts. For a discussion of nonbusiness bad debts and when a debt becomes worthless, see chapter 14, *Sale of property*.

Business bad debts usually occur because of credit sales to customers. They can also be loans to suppliers, employees, and others associated with your trade or business. These debts are usually shown on your books as either accounts receivable or notes receivable. If you are unable to collect any part of these accounts or notes receivable, the uncollectible part is a business bad debt.

You may take a bad debt deduction on your accounts and notes receivable only if you have basis in the debt; that is, you already included the amount you are owed in your current or earlier gross income (i.e., accounts receivable), or you actually loaned the money (i.e., notes receivable). Only individuals filing a Schedule C using either the accrual or hybrid (cash accrual) accounting method will be able to deduct bad debts relating to accounts receivable. Cash method taxpayers do not report income that is due them until they actually receive payment. Therefore, they cannot take a bad debt deduction on payments they cannot collect.

Example 1. Paul, who uses the accrual method on his Schedule C, reported income in 2013 of $1,000 related to an account receivable from a customer. In 2014, that account receivable became worthless. Because Paul is on the accrual method and has already included the $1,000 in income, he is permitted to recognize a bad debt deduction in 2014.

Example 2. Assume the same facts as in Example 1, except that Paul is on the cash method. Because Paul has not recognized the $1,000 income in 2013, he cannot take a bad debt deduction when the debt becomes worthless in 2014.

The net effect on Paul's income in either situation is the same.

	Accrual	Cash
Income recognized in 2013	$1,000	-0-
Less bad debt deduction in 2014	1,000	-0-
Net effect	-0-	-0-

Methods of treating bad debts. The method of accounting for bad debts is referred to as the "specific charge-off method," because it requires the specific identification of the debt that has become worthless. Using the specific charge-off method, you can deduct specific business bad debts that become either partly or totally worthless during the tax year.

Partially worthless debts. You may deduct specific bad debts that are partially uncollectible. To take the deduction, however, the amount must be written off on your books; that is, you must eliminate the worthless portion of the debt from your books as an asset. You do not have to write off and deduct your partially worthless debts annually. Instead, you may delay the write-off until a later year. Also, you may wait until more of the debt has become worthless or until you have collected all you can on the debt and it is totally worthless. You may not, however, deduct any part of the bad debt in a year after the year in which the debt becomes totally worthless. This rule affords you the opportunity to select the year in which to claim the partial bad debt deduction.

Totally worthless debts. A totally worthless debt is deducted only in the tax year in which it becomes totally worthless. The deduction for the debt must not include any amount deducted in an earlier tax year when the debt was only partially worthless. You are not required to make an actual write-off on your books to claim a bad debt deduction for a totally worthless debt. However, you may want to do so. If a debt you claim to be totally worthless is not written off on your books and the IRS later rules that the debt is only partially worthless, you will not be allowed a deduction until the amount is actually written off your books.

Recovery of bad debt. If you deducted a bad debt and in a later tax year recover (collect) all or part of it, you may have to include the amount you recover in your gross income. However, you may exclude from gross income the amount recovered, up to the amount of the deduction that did not reduce your tax in the year in which it was deducted.

Example. In 2013, Beatriz had a $25,000 bad debt loss relating to her Schedule C. She also had $25,000 of income from the activity. Beatriz had no taxable income for 2013.

In 2014, Beatriz recovered the entire $25,000 debt. To figure how much she should include in her 2014 income, see the following calculation.

	2013 with bad debt	2013 without bad debt
Income:		
Schedule C	$25,000	$25,000
Bad debt loss	(25,000)	-0-
Adjusted gross income	-0-	25,000
Less:		
Standard deductions	-0-	6,100
Personal exemption	-0-	3,900
Taxable income	-0-	15,000

The calculations show that Beatriz's 2013 taxable income was reduced by $15,000 by including the bad debt. Therefore, $15,000 is included in Beatriz's taxable income for 2014, the year in which she collected the $25,000 debt.

Automobile and truck expenses. If you use your automobile for business purposes, you may be able to deduct expenses associated with the business use of the automobile. You generally can use one of two methods to figure your expense: actual expenses or the standard mileage rate. Refer to chapter 27, *Car expenses and other employee business expenses*, for more information on expenses for business use of your automobile.

TAXALERT

You can report business vehicle information on Part IV of Schedule C rather than Form 4562 if you are claiming the standard mileage rate (56 cents per mile for 2014), you lease your vehicle, or your vehicle is fully depreciated. However, if you wish to deduct actual automobile expenses, or if you must file Form 4562 for any other reason, you must continue to use Part V of Form 4562 to report the vehicle information.

Depreciating and Expensing Certain Assets

When you use property in your business, you are permitted to recover your investment in the property through tax deductions. You do this by "depreciating" the property—that is, deducting some of your cost on your income tax return each year. You depreciate "tangible" property, such as a car, a building, or machinery. You amortize "intangible" property, such as a copyright or a patent. Your depreciation deduction is generally based on the cost of the qualifying property. However, the total amount you can elect to deduct is subject to a dollar limit and a business income limit. These limits apply to each taxpayer, not to each business. Depreciation is reported on Part II or Part III of Form 4562, whereas amortization is reported on Part VI of Form 4562. You cannot depreciate land, property you rent from a third party, or inventory.

Property is depreciable if it meets the following requirements:
1. It must be used in business or held for the production of income.
2. It must have a determinable life, and that life must be longer than 1 year.
3. It must be something that wears out, decays, gets used up, becomes obsolete, or loses value from natural causes.

In general, if property does not meet all three of these conditions, it is not depreciable.

The amount of depreciation you can deduct depends on (1) how much the property costs, (2) when you began using it, (3) how long it will take to recover your cost, and (4) which one of the several depreciation methods you use.

You begin to claim depreciation on property when you place it in service in your trade or business or for the production of income. You continue to depreciate the property until you recover your basis (generally the cost) in it, dispose of it, or stop using it for business or investment purposes.

Form 4562, Depreciation and Amortization, is used to report your depreciation. Additional information can be found in Publication 946, *How to Depreciate Property*.

TAXALERT

Expensing certain assets (Section 179 deduction). You can elect to deduct all or part of the cost, up to specified limits, of certain qualifying property in the year in which the property is purchased, rather than capitalizing the cost and depreciating it over its life. This means that you can deduct all or part of the cost up front in one year rather than take depreciation deductions spread out over many years. You must decide for each item of qualifying property whether to deduct, subject to the yearly limit, or capitalize and depreciate its cost.

Qualifying property is property purchased for use in your trade or business and property that would have qualified for the investment tax credit.

Specified limits. The maximum Section 179 deduction available for qualifying property placed into service during 2014 is $25,000 (down from $500,000 in 2013). The allowable deduction is reduced dollar for dollar once the cost of qualifying property placed into service during 2014 exceeds $200,000 (down from $2 million in 2013). Unlike 2013, in 2014, the definition of Section 179 property does not include certain qualified real qualified leasehold improvement property, qualified restaurant property, or qualified retail improvement property. As of the time this book was published in October 2014, Congress had been considering legislation that would extend the higher limits that expired at the end of 2013 at least through 2014; perhaps even permanently, but no such extension had yet been passed. For updated information on this and any other tax law changes that occur after this book was published, see our website, *ey.com/EYTaxGuide*.

Basis of qualifying property. The amount you elect to deduct is subtracted from the basis of the qualifying property. If you elect the Section 179 deduction, the amount of your allowable ACRS or MACRS deduction for this property will be reduced. If you and your spouse file separate returns in 2014, you can each deduct only $12,500, unless you and your spouse agree on a different split of the $25,000.

Other restrictions. The amount of the Section 179 deduction cannot be greater than the income derived from the active conduct by the taxpayer of any business during such taxable year (computed without regard to the property to be expensed). This rule prevents you from generating or adding to a net operating loss due to the Section 179 expense. Any Section 179 deductions disallowed under this income limitation are carried forward to the succeeding taxable year and added to the allowable amount for such year. Therefore, in the following year, you are eligible to receive the deduction ($25,000 in 2015) plus the carryover from the preceding year, limited to the amount of income.

Cost. The cost of property for the Section 179 deduction does not include any part of the basis of the property that is determined by reference to the basis of other property held at any time by the person acquiring this property. For example, if you buy a new truck to use in your business, your cost for purposes of the Section 179 deduction does not include the adjusted basis of the truck you trade in on the new vehicle.

Example. You buy a new piece of equipment, paying $2,500 cash and trading in your old equipment, which had an undepreciated cost to you of $4,000. Even though the new equipment has a tax basis to you of $6,500, you may claim the Section 179 deduction only on the $2,500 you paid out.

When to elect. You must make an election to take the Section 179 deduction, which can only be made in the first tax year in which the property is placed in service.

If you elect to deduct the cost of qualifying property, you must specify the items to which the election applies and the part of the cost of each you elect to deduct. If in 2014 you purchase and place in service two items of qualifying property costing $15,000 and $20,000, and you want to elect the $25,000 deduction, you must specify what part of the $15,000 property and the $20,000 property you want to deduct. You may arbitrarily allocate the maximum $25,000 between the two properties. Your remaining basis of $10,000 ($35,000 total cost of property placed in service, less $25,000 maximum Section 179 expense) may be depreciated.

Use Form 4562 to make the election and report the Section 179 deduction. The election is made by taking the deduction on Form 4562, filed with your original tax return. The election can be made on an amended tax return filed after the due date (including extensions), and can be revoked as long as the statute of limitations for the return is still open. Consult your tax advisor regarding the Section 179 rules.

TAXALERT

50% bonus depreciation expired at the end of 2013. Except for certain aircraft and long-production period property placed into service before 2015, 50% first-year bonus depreciation is no longer available for qualified property placed in service during 2014. (Qualified property included MACRS—Modified Accelerated Cost Recovery System—property with a recovery period of 20 years or less, computer software not covered under Section 179, and qualified leasehold improvement property.) However, as of the time this book was published in October 2014, Congress had been considering legislation that would extend 50% bonus depreciation at least through 2014; perhaps even permanently, but no such extension of this accelerated write-off had yet been passed. For updated information on this and any other tax law changes that occur after this book was published, see our website, *ey.com/EYTaxGuide*.

The rules for claiming depreciation are complex. See Publication 946, *How to Depreciate Property*, for more information.

Computers. If you use a computer for both business and personal use, there are special rules that may limit the amount of depreciation that can be deducted.

The amount of depreciation you are allowed to deduct depends on what percentage of use was business and what percentage was personal. The allocation is made on the basis of the most appropriate unit of time. For example, determine the percentage of use in a trade or a business for a tax year by dividing the number of hours the computer is used for business purposes by the total number of hours the computer is used for any purpose for that tax year.

Luxury automobiles. See chapter 27, *Car expenses and other employee business expenses*, for a discussion of luxury cars and depreciation.

Amortization. Capitalized costs of certain intangible property acquired and held in connection with the conduct of a trade or business, or an activity engaged in for the production of income, may be amortized. The amount of the deduction is determined by amortizing the adjusted basis (generally the cost) of the intangible property ratably over a 15-year period. The amortization period begins with the month the intangible property is acquired.

These amortization rules apply to "Section 197 intangible" property. "Section 197 intangible" property is defined as any property that is included in any one or more of the following categories:
1. Goodwill and going concern value
2. Certain specified types of intangible property that generally relate to workforce, information base, know-how, customers, suppliers, or other similar items

3. Any license, permit, or other right granted by a governmental unit or agency, or instrumentality thereof
4. Any covenant not to compete (or other arrangement to the extent that the arrangement has substantially the same effect as a covenant not to compete) entered into in connection with the direct or indirect acquisition of an interest in a trade or business (or substantial portion thereof)
5. Any franchise, trademark, or trade name

Special rules apply if a taxpayer disposes of some, but not all, "Section 197 intangible" property that was acquired in a transaction. No loss is to be recognized by reason of such a disposition. Instead, the adjusted bases of the retained "Section 197 intangible" properties acquired in connection with such transaction are increased by the amount of any loss not recognized.

Leasing Business Assets

Many sole proprietors decide to lease a business asset, rather than purchase it. This is ideal if the asset is only needed for a limited period of time. For example, a tax practitioner may only need a computer for the months of February through April. Instead of incurring the large capital outlay required to purchase the asset, he or she can free up cash by leasing a computer.

Generally, the entire expense for leasing a business asset is deductible. This assumes the asset is used 100% of the time for business purposes. If, however, the asset is for both business and personal use, only the portion attributable to business use is allowed as a deduction. The most common business asset leased by a sole proprietor or a statutory employee is an automobile.

If you lease an automobile, you can deduct the portion of each lease payment related to the use of the automobile in your business or work. You cannot deduct any part of a lease payment that is for commuting to or from your regular job, or other personal use of the automobile. You must amortize any advance payments made on the lease over the entire lease period.

Autos leased after December 31, 1986, and used in a business, for a lease term of 30 days or more, may require an "inclusion amount" in income each year. If the fair market value of the automobile when the lease began exceeds the amounts depicted in the chart below, you must include in your gross income an inclusion amount each tax year during which you lease the automobile. For more about leasing, see chapter 27, *Car expenses and other employee business expenses*.

Year Lease Began	Base Value
2009	$18,500
2010	$18,500
2011	$18,500
2012	$18,500
2013	$19,000
2014	$18,500

Health Insurance

Self-employed individuals, including those filing Schedule C, may deduct the amount paid for health insurance premiums on behalf of themselves, their spouses, and–beginning March 30, 2010–their child who was under age 27 at the end of 2014, even if the child was not their dependent.

A child includes your son, daughter, stepchild, adopted child, or foster child. A foster child is any child placed with you by an authorized placement agency or by judgment, decree, or other order of any court of competent jurisdiction.

This deduction is only available if you had net profits from self-employment for the year and were not eligible to participate in a subsidized health plan maintained by you or your spouse's employer. The determination of whether a self-employed individual or his or her spouse may be eligible for employer-provided health benefits is made on a monthly basis.

Medicare premiums you voluntarily pay to obtain insurance that is similar to qualifying private health insurance can be used to figure the deduction. If you previously filed a return without using Medicare premiums to figure the deduction, you can file an amended return to refigure the deduction. For more information, see Form 1040X, Amended U.S. Individual Income Tax Return.

The allowable deduction is limited to the lesser of (1) 100% of the amount paid for health insurance premiums during 2014 for the self-employed individual, spouse, and children under age 27 as of the end of 2014, or (2) the net profit from the trade or business less the amount claimed for a Keogh plan, SIMPLE, or a SEP deduction on Form 1040, line 28.

The deduction is not claimed on Schedule C but is instead claimed on Form 1040, line 29, as an adjustment to income. Any medical insurance expenses in excess of the allowable deduction may be claimed as an itemized deduction on Schedule A (Form 1040), subject to the 10% (7.5% if you or your spouse are age 65 and older at the end of the taxable year) of adjusted gross income floor for medical expenses.

Employees

Who are employees? Before you can know how to treat payments that you make for services rendered to you, you must first know the business relationship that exists between you and the person performing those services. The person performing the services may be: (1) an independent contractor, (2) a common-law employee, (3) a statutory employee, or (4) a statutory independent contractor.

The determination of a worker's classification can have significant tax consequences to an employer. When workers are not treated as employees, the employer can avoid employment tax and wage withholding responsibilities, as well as costs related to pension plans, health insurance, and other fringe benefits.

Independent contractors. People, such as lawyers, contractors, subcontractors, public stenographers, auctioneers, and so on, who follow an independent trade, business, or profession in which they offer their services to the general public, are generally not employees. However, whether such people are employees or independent contractors depends on the facts in each case. The general rule is that an individual is an independent contractor if you, the employer, have the right to control or direct only the result of the work and not the means and methods of accomplishing the result.

You do not have to withhold or pay taxes on payments made to independent contractors.

Common-law employees. Under common-law rules, every individual who performs services subject to the will and control of an employer, as to both what must be done and how it must be done, is an employee. It does not matter that the employer allows the employee discretion and freedom of action, so long as the employer has the legal right to control both the method and the result of the services.

Two usual characteristics of an employer-employee relationship are that the employer has the right to discharge the employee, and that the employer supplies the employee with tools and a place to work.

No distinction is made between classes of employees. Superintendents, managers, and other supervisory personnel are all employees. An officer of a corporation is generally an employee, but a director is not. An officer who performs no services or only minor services, and neither receives nor is entitled to receive any pay, is not considered an employee.

You generally must withhold and pay federal, social security, and Medicare taxes on wages you pay to common-law employees.

Statutory employees and statutory independent contractors are discussed at the beginning of this chapter.

Salaries, wages, and other forms of pay that you make to employees are generally deductible business expenses. However, a deduction for salaries and wages must be reduced by any work opportunity credit determined for the tax year. This will be discussed later in this chapter.

Tests for deductibility. To be deductible, employees' pay must meet all of the following four tests:

Test 1-Ordinary and necessary. You must be able to show that salaries, wages, and other payments for employees' services are ordinary and necessary expenses directly connected with your trade or business.

Test 2-Reasonable. What is reasonable pay is determined by the facts. Generally, it is the amount that would ordinarily be paid for these services by like enterprises under similar circumstances.

Test 3-For services performed. You must be able to prove that the payments were made for services actually performed.

Test 4-Paid or incurred. You must have actually made the payments or incurred the expense during the tax year.

If you use the cash method of accounting, the expense for salaries and wages can be deducted only in the year in which the salaries and wages were paid. If you use the accrual method of accounting, the expense for salaries and wages is deducted when your obligation to make the payments is established and economic performance occurs (generally, when an employee performs his or her services for you). In addition, the expense must be paid within 2½ months after the end of the tax year. However, the deduction of an accrual of salary to an owner may be limited. (See the previous discussion on the deduction of an accrual to a related party.)

Payroll taxes—general rules for withholding. As an employer, you must generally withhold income taxes, social security, and Medicare taxes from wages that you pay employees. In addition, the amounts withheld with respect to social security and Medicare taxes will have to be matched by you, the employer. Also, unemployment tax payments may be required.

For information about the payroll tax deposit rules, see Publication 15 as well as IRS Circular E, *Employer's Tax Guide*.

You may find it helpful to remember the following general rules for withholding:

1. **Independent contractors.** Do not withhold income tax or social security and Medicare taxes from amounts you paid to an independent contractor.
2. **Common-law employees.** You generally have to withhold income tax, social security tax, and Medicare tax from the wages paid to common-law employees. Employers pay federal unemployment tax and their share of social security and Medicare taxes on these wages.
3. **Statutory employees.** You are not required to withhold income tax from the wages of statutory employees. You must withhold and pay social security and Medicare taxes. Unless they are full-time life insurance sales agents or work at home, you must also pay federal unemployment tax on their wages.
4. **Statutory nonemployees.** You do not withhold or pay taxes on payments to statutory nonemployees.

Reporting payments to independent contractors and statutory nonemployees. If payments made to an independent contractor or a statutory nonemployee equal $600 or more during the year in the course of your trade or business, you must file with the IRS and provide the independent contractor a Form 1099-MISC, Miscellaneous Income.

Reporting payments to common-law employees. To report wages paid to a common-law employee, you must complete a Form W-2. The Form W-2 must show the total wages and other compensation paid, total wages subject to social security taxes, total wages subject to Medicare taxes, the amounts deducted for income, social security, and Medicare taxes, as well as any other information required on the statement. For information on preparing Form W-2, see the Instructions that come with Form W-2.

Reporting payments to statutory employees. To report wages paid to a statutory employee, complete a Form W-2. Report the same information that you reported for common-law employees. If the statutory employee has not elected to withhold income tax, this information does not have to be furnished. Also, the employer must check the box for "statutory employee" on Form W-2.

When hiring new employees, you are required to have the employee complete a Form W-4, Employee's Withholding Allowance Certificate, and a Form I-9, Employment Eligibility Verification Form. For more information on which payroll forms must be filed, see IRS Circular E, *Employer's Tax Guide.*

Office in the Home and Form 8829
It is not unusual for a person filing a Schedule C to use part of his or her home for business. If you use part of your home regularly and exclusively for business, you may be able to deduct certain operating and depreciation expenses on your home.

Requirements for claiming the deduction. You may deduct certain expenses for operating out of a part of your home only if that part of your home is used regularly and exclusively as:

1. Your principal place of business for any trade or business in which you engage (including administrative use, as further defined below), or
2. A place to meet or deal with your patients, clients, or customers in the normal course of your trade or business

The Taxpayer Relief Act of 1997 provided that for tax years beginning after December 31, 1998, a home office qualifies as the principal place of business if:

1. The office is used to conduct administrative or management activities of a trade or business, and
2. There is no other fixed location of the trade or business where you conduct substantial administrative or management activities.

Example. John Smith is a salesperson. His only office is a room in his house used regularly and exclusively to set up appointments and write up orders and other reports for the companies whose products he sells. John's tax year is the calendar year.

John's business is selling products to customers at various locations within the metropolitan area where he lives. To make these sales, he regularly visits the customers to explain the available products and to take orders. John makes only a few sales from his home office. John spends an average of 30 hours a week visiting customers and 12 hours a week working at his home office.

The essence of John's business as a salesperson requires him to meet with customers primarily at the customer's place of business. The home office activities are less important to John's business than the sales activities he performs when visiting customers. Nevertheless, John is entitled to deduct his home office expenses. You may also deduct certain expenses for operating out of a separate structure that is not attached to your home, if you use it regularly and exclusively for your trade or business. (See chapter 29, *Miscellaneous deductions*, for more about deducting these expenses.)

TAXSAVER

Even if you do not qualify for a business use of the home deduction, you may be allowed to take a depreciation deduction or elect a Section 179 deduction for furniture and equipment you use in your home for business or work as an employee.

If you use part of your home for business and meet the requirements discussed earlier, you must divide the expenses of operating out of your home between personal and business use. Some expenses are divided on the basis of square footage. Some of these are further divided on a time-usage basis. If neither of these methods is appropriate, you can choose any other reasonable method to figure the business part of the expense.

What to deduct. Some expenses you pay to maintain your home are directly related to its business use; others are indirectly related; some are unrelated. You can deduct direct expenses and part of your indirect expenses, both subject to certain limitations. If you are a cash-basis taxpayer, you can deduct only the expenses you pay during the tax year.

TAXALERT

The deduction for expenses related to a storage unit in the taxpayer's home that is regularly used for inventory of the taxpayer's business of selling products in which the home is the sole fixed location of the business has been expanded to cover product samples as well as inventory.

Taxpayers are not required to use the space *exclusively* for the storage of inventory or product samples in order to be eligible for the deduction. The new rule adds "product samples" to clarify the current rule, so taxpayers need not attempt to distinguish between inventory and product samples.

Example. Joe Smith is in the business of selling cosmetics. Joe's residence is the only location of his business. He uses space in the study of his home to store cosmetic samples. Joe may deduct the expenses related to the portion of his residence used to store the product samples. It does not matter if Joe uses the study for additional purposes.

Direct expenses. Direct expenses benefit only the business part of your home. They include a separate phone line installed for the business, painting, or repairs made to the specific area or room used for business. You can deduct direct expenses in full.

Indirect expenses. Indirect expenses are for keeping up and running your entire home. They benefit both the business and personal parts of your home. Examples of indirect expenses include:
- Real estate taxes
- Deductible mortgage interest
- Casualty losses
- Rent
- Utilities and services
- Insurance
- Repairs
- Security systems
- Depreciation

You can deduct the business percentage of your indirect expenses.

Figuring the business percentage. To figure deductions for the business use of your home, find the business percentage. You can do this by dividing the area used for business by the total area of your home. You may measure the area in square feet. To figure the percentage of your home used for business, divide the number of square feet of space used for business by the total number of square feet of space in your home. If the rooms in your home are about the same size, figure the business percentage by dividing the number of rooms used for business by the number of rooms in the home. You can also use any other reasonable method to determine the business percentage.

Example 1. Your home measures 1,200 square feet. You use one room that measures 240 square feet for business.

Therefore, you use one-fifth (240 ÷ 1,200), or 20%, of the total area for business.

Example 2. If the rooms in your home are about the same size, and you use one room in a 5-room house for business, you use one-fifth, or 20%, of the total area for business.

Real estate taxes. If you own your home, you can deduct part of the real estate taxes on your home as a business expense. To figure the business part of your real estate taxes, multiply the real estate taxes paid by the percentage of your home used for business.

Deductible mortgage interest. If you pay deductible mortgage interest, you can generally deduct part of it as a business expense. To figure the business part of your deductible mortgage interest, multiply this interest by the percentage of your home used in business. You can include interest on a second mortgage in this computation.

Casualty losses. If you have a casualty loss on your home or other property you use in business, you can deduct the business part of the loss as a business expense. Treat a casualty loss as an unrelated expense, a direct expense, or an indirect expense depending on the property affected.

In a partial destruction, the deductible loss is the decrease in fair market value of the property or the adjusted basis of the property, whichever is less. You must reduce this amount by any insurance or other reimbursement received.

If your business property is completely destroyed (becomes totally worthless), your deductible loss is the adjusted basis of the property, minus any salvage value and any insurance or other reimbursement you receive or expect to receive. Figure the loss without taking into account any decrease in fair market value.

Rent. If you rent, rather than own, a home and meet the requirements for business use of the home, you can deduct part of the rent you pay. To figure your deduction, multiply your rent payments by the percentage of your home used for business.

Utilities and services. Expenses for utilities and services, such as electricity, gas, trash removal, and cleaning services, are primarily personal expenses. However, if you use part of your home for business, you can deduct the business part of these expenses.

Telephone. The basic local telephone service charge, including taxes, for the first telephone line into your home is a nondeductible personal expense. However, charges for business long-distance phone calls on that line, as well as the cost of a second line into your home used exclusively for business, are deductible business expenses for the business use of your home. Deduct these charges separately on the appropriate schedule. Do not include them in your home office deduction.

Insurance. You can deduct the cost of insurance that covers the business part of your home.

Repairs. The cost of repairs and supplies that relate to your business, including labor (other than your own labor), is a deductible expense. For example, a furnace repair benefits the entire home. If you use 10% of your home for business, you can deduct 10% of the cost of the furnace repair.

Repairs keep your home in good working order over its useful life. Examples of common repairs are patching walls and floors, painting, wallpapering, repairing roofs and gutters, and mending leaks.

Security system. If you install a security system that protects all the doors and windows in your home, you can deduct the business part of the expenses you incur to maintain and monitor the system. You can also take a depreciation deduction for the part of the cost of the security system relating to the business use of your home.

Depreciation. The cost of property that can be used for more than 1 year, such as a building, a permanent improvement, or furniture, is a capital expenditure.

Land is not depreciable property. You generally cannot recover the cost of land until you dispose of it.

Permanent improvements. A permanent improvement increases the value of property, adds to its life, or gives it a new or different use. Examples of improvements are replacement of electric wiring or plumbing, a new roof, an addition, paneling, remodeling, or major modifications.

Depreciating your home. If you use part of your home for business, depreciate that part as nonresidential real property under the Modified Accelerated Cost Recovery System (MACRS). Under MACRS, nonresidential real property is depreciated using the straight-line method over 39 years.

To figure depreciation on the business part of your home, you need to know:

1. The business-use percentage of your home
2. The first month in your tax year for which you can deduct business use of your home expenses

3. The adjusted basis and fair market value of your home at the time you qualify for a deduction

Adjusted basis of home. The adjusted basis of your home is generally its cost plus the cost of any permanent improvements that you made to it minus any casualty losses deducted in earlier tax years.

When you change part of your home from personal to business use, your basis for depreciation is the business-use percentage times the lesser of:
1. The adjusted basis of your home (excluding land) on the date of change; or
2. The fair market value of your home (excluding land) on the date of change.

Unrelated expenses benefit only the parts of your home that you do not use for business. These include repairs to personal areas of your home, lawn care, and landscaping. You cannot deduct unrelated expenses. For more information, also see chapter 29, *Miscellaneous deductions*.

Recordkeeping. You do not have to use a particular method of recordkeeping, but you must keep records that provide the information needed to figure your deductions for the business use of your home. Your records must show the following:
1. The part of your home you use for business
2. That you use this part of your home exclusively and regularly for business as either your principal place of business or as the place where you meet or work with clients or customers in the normal course of your business
3. The depreciation and expenses for the business part of your home

Generally, you must keep your records for at least 3 years from the date the return was filed or 2 years from the date the tax was paid, whichever is later. Keep records that support your basis in your home for as long as they are needed to figure the correct basis of your home.

Deduction limit. If your gross income from the business use of your home equals or exceeds your total business expenses (including depreciation), you can deduct all of your expenses for the business use of your home. But if your gross income from the business is less than your total business expenses, your deduction for certain expenses for business use of your home is limited. The total of your deductions for otherwise nondeductible expenses, such as utilities, insurance, and depreciation (with depreciation taken last) cannot be more than your gross income from the business use of your home minus the sum of:
1. The business percentage of the otherwise deductible mortgage interest, real estate taxes, and casualty and theft loss, and
2. The business expenses that are not attributable to the business use of your home (e.g., salaries or supplies).

If you are self-employed, do not include in (2) above your deduction for half of your self-employment tax.

You can carry forward to your next tax year deductions over the current year's limit. These deductions are subject to the gross income limit from the business use of your home for the next tax year. The amount carried forward will be allowable only up to your gross income in the next tax year from the business in which the deduction arose, whether or not you live in the home during the year.

Figuring deduction limit and carryover. If you file Schedule C (Form 1040), figure your deduction limit on Form 8829, Expenses for Business Use of Your Home. Enter the amount from line 35 of Form 8829 on Schedule C, line 30.

Deductible mortgage interest. After you have figured the business portion of the mortgage interest on Form 8829, subtract that amount from total mortgage interest. The remainder is deductible on Schedule A; do not deduct any of the business portion on Schedule A. If the amount of interest allowed on Schedule A for home mortgage is limited, because it exceeds the maximum allowed (see chapter 24, *Interest expense*), the portion of the disallowed interest allocable to the business use of the home may be taken on Form 8829 (see instructions to line 16 of Form 8829 for further explanation).

Real estate taxes. If you file Schedule C, enter all your deductible real estate taxes on Form 8829. After you have figured the business portion of your taxes on Form 8829, subtract that amount from your total real estate taxes. The remainder is deductible on Schedule A; do not deduct any of the business part of real estate taxes on Schedule A.

Daycare facility. You can deduct expenses for using part of your home on a regular basis to provide daycare services if you meet the following requirements:
1. You must be in the trade or business of providing daycare for children, for persons age 65 or older, or for persons who are physically or mentally unable to care for themselves.
2. You must have applied for, been granted, or be exempt from having a license, certification, registration, or approval as a daycare center or as a family or group daycare home

under applicable state law. You do not meet this requirement if your application was rejected or your license or other authorization was revoked.

Meals. If you provide food for your daycare business, do not include the expense as a cost of using your home for business. Claim it as a separate deduction on your Schedule C. You can deduct 100% of the cost of food consumed by your daycare recipients and 50% of the cost of food consumed by your employees as a business expense. You cannot deduct the cost of food consumed by you and your family.

Do not deduct the cost of meals for which you were reimbursed under the Child and Adult Care Food Program administered by the U.S. Department of Agriculture. The reimbursements are not included in your income to the extent you used them to provide food for the eligible recipients.

TAXPLANNER

Beginning in 2013, the IRS provides a simplified method to determine your expenses for business use of your home. This new simplified option allows you an alternative to the calculation, allocation, and substantiation of actual expenses.

To calculate the allowable deduction using the simplified method, multiply the square footage of the home used as home office space (not to exceed 300 sq feet) by the prescribed rate of $5.00. (The IRS may adjust the $5.00 rate from time to time.) This means the most you can deduct using the new method is $1,500 per year.

You may choose either the simplified method or the actual expense method for any tax year. Once you use a method for a specific tax year, you cannot later change to the other method for that same year.

If you use the simplified method and you own your home, you cannot depreciate your home office. You can still deduct other qualified home expenses, such as mortgage interest and real estate taxes. You will not need to allocate these expenses between personal and business use. Instead, this allocation is required if you use the actual expense method. You'll claim these deductions on Schedule A, Itemized Deductions.

You can still fully deduct business expenses that are unrelated to the home if you use the simplified method. These may include costs such as advertising, supplies, and wages paid to employees.

You cannot use the simplified method if you are an employee with a home office who receives advances, allowances, or reimbursements for expenses related to your qualified business use of your home under a reimbursement or other expense allowance arrangement with your employer.

If you use more than one home with a qualified home office in the same year, you can use the simplified method for only one home in that year. However, you may use the simplified method for one and actual expenses for any others in that year.

TAXPLANNER

Retirement Plans

If you are self-employed, you can take an income tax deduction for certain contributions that you make for yourself to a retirement plan. You can also deduct a trustee's fees if contributions to the plan do not cover them.

TAXPLANNER

Under current law, small businesses, with 100 or fewer employees who collectively received a minimum of $5,000 in wages from the business in the preceding year, are eligible for a tax credit of 50% of the expenses to establish a new retirement plan. The maximum allowable credit is $500 for the first 3 years of the plan, beginning the year prior to the effective date of the plan. Deductible contributions plus the plan's earnings on them are tax-free until you receive distributions from the plan in later years. As a sole proprietor, you can deduct contributions made for your common-law employees, as well as contributions made for yourself. A common-law employee cannot take a deduction for your contributions.

The common types of plans a self-employed person may establish are Keogh plans, Simplified Employee Pension (SEP) plans, and SIMPLE plans.

Keogh plans. A Keogh (HR 10) plan is a retirement plan that can be established by a sole proprietor. The plan must be for the exclusive benefit of employees or their beneficiaries. As an employer, you can usually deduct, subject to limits, contributions you make to a Keogh plan, including those made for your own retirement. You can contribute up to 20% of your self-employment income to a defined contribution Keogh plan (up to a maximum of $52,000 in 2014), which may be deductible as described below. Even more may be contributed to a defined benefit Keogh plan, depending on your age.

Where to deduct on Form 1040. Take the deduction for contributions for yourself on line 28 of Form 1040. Deduct the contributions for your common-law employees on Schedule C.

Because the deduction for your contribution to a Keogh plan for your benefit is reported on Form 1040, line 28, not on Schedule C, the contribution does not reduce your self-employment income subject to tax.

Reporting requirements. As the Keogh plan administrator or the employer, you may have to file an annual return or report form by the last day of the seventh month following the end of the plan year (July 31 for calendar year filers).

Simplified Employee Pension (SEP). A simplified employee pension (SEP) is a written plan that allows an employer to make contributions toward an employee's retirement, and his or her own, if the employer is self-employed, without becoming involved in a more complex Keogh retirement plan.

For further information about SEPs, see chapter 17, *Individual retirement arrangements (IRAs)*.

SIMPLE retirement plan. Small businesses that normally employ 100 or fewer employees, who earned at least $5,000 in compensation in the preceding year, and do not maintain another qualified plan, may establish a Savings Incentive Match Plan for Employees (SIMPLE plan). A SIMPLE plan can be in the form of either an individual retirement arrangement (IRA) for each employee or part of a qualified cash or deferred arrangement (401(k) plan). Employees may make elective contributions of up to $12,000 for 2014 to a SIMPLE plan, and employers must make matching contributions. Employees are not taxed on account assets until distributions are made, and employers generally may deduct their contributions to the plan.

Individual retirement arrangements (IRAs). In addition to the retirement plans already discussed, a self-employed person may also make a contribution, which may or may not be deductible, to an individual retirement arrangement (IRA).

TAXALERT

The earnings on contributions generated by IRAs are generally not subject to tax. The distributions of deductible contributions and earnings from the plan, which are subject to certain limitations, may be taxable to you upon withdrawal.

For further information about IRAs, see chapter 17, *Individual retirement arrangements (IRAs)*.

For more information about tax credits for small businesses related to retirement plans, see IRS Publication 560, available at *www.irs.gov*.

Travel and Entertainment

Business travel and meals and entertainment expenses are deductible, subject to certain limits, assuming that these amounts are both ordinary and necessary, as defined earlier in the chapter.

For a self-employed person, the meals and entertainment expenses to be deducted are subject to the 50% limit. Also note there are certain documentation requirements, as discussed in chapter 27, *Car expenses and other employee business expenses*. (Chapter 27 also contains a more complete discussion of the deductibility of both travel and meals and entertainment expenses.)

Other Schedule C Deductions

Various other expenses not previously mentioned are allowed as a deduction on Schedule C. Examples of these expenses are advertising; commissions and fees; insurance (other than health); interest; legal and professional services; office expenses, including supplies and other items used in the office; general rent; repairs and maintenance; taxes; utilities; and any other business expense that can be classified as ordinary and necessary.

Sales of Business Property Used in Your Business

How Different Assets Are Treated

A sole proprietorship may have many assets. When sold, these assets must be classified as either depreciable personal property used in the business, real property used in the business, or property held for sale to customers, such as inventory or stock in trade or capital assets.

The gain or loss on each asset is figured separately. The sale of inventory results in ordinary income or loss and is reported on Schedule C. The sale of a capital asset results in a capital gain or loss and is reported on Schedule D. The sale of depreciable personal property and real property used in the business results in Section 1231 gains or losses and is reported on Form 4797. (For further information about Section 1231 transactions, see chapter 16, *Reporting gains and losses*.)

Any gain realized on sales and certain other dispositions of depreciable personal property and, under certain circumstances, depreciable real property, is treated as ordinary income to the extent of depreciation deductions taken prior to the sale. The amount of depreciation recapture is the lesser of (1) the gain recognized or (2) depreciation taken on the property. For more information, see chapters 13, *Basis of property*, 14, *Sale of property*, and 16, *Reporting gains and losses*.

Section 1231 business gain or loss. Once you have determined the gain or loss on personal and real property not subject to depreciation recapture, you must combine all gains and losses from the sale and disposition of Section 1231 property for the tax year including Section 1231 gains and losses reported to you through partnerships and S corporations in which you have an interest. In general, if all of your Section 1231 transactions resulted in a net gain, the gain is treated as a long-term capital gain. If all of your Section 1231 transactions resulted in a net loss, the loss is treated as an ordinary loss. See chapter 16, *Reporting gains and losses*, for a further discussion of how to treat Section 1231 gains and losses.

Recapture of net ordinary losses. A net Section 1231 gain is treated as ordinary income to the extent that it does not exceed your nonrecaptured net Section 1231 losses taken in prior years. Nonrecaptured losses are net Section 1231 losses deducted for your 5 most recent tax years that have not yet been applied (recaptured) against any net Section 1231 gains in a tax year beginning after 1984. Losses are recaptured, beginning with the earliest year subject to recapture.

Sale of the Entire Business

Because a sole proprietorship is not a separate entity, a sale of the business will be treated as if each asset in the business had been sold separately. The gain or loss on such a sale is the total of the gains or losses as separately computed for each individual asset.

Both the buyer and the seller of a group of assets constituting a trade or a business must report to the IRS on Form 8594 various information about the acquisition of assets, including the following:

1. The name of the buyer and seller of the assets
2. The fair market value of the assets transferred
3. The allocation of the sales price to the assets transferred
4. Whether the buyer purchased a license, covenant not to compete, or entered into a lease agreement, employment contract, management contract, or similar arrangement with the seller

Business Tax Credit

Tax credits are distinguished from deductions in that a deduction reduces taxable income and a credit reduces tax liability. Consequently, $1 in tax credit is more valuable than $1 in tax deduction.

Form 3800. The general business tax credit includes the following:

1. The investment credit (Form 3468)
2. The work opportunity credit (Form 5884)
3. The credit for increasing research activities (Form 6765)
4. The low-income housing credit (Form 8586)
5. The disabled access credit (Form 8826)
6. The credit for small employer pension plan start-up costs (Form 8881)

Form 3800 is filed to claim any of the general business credits listed on Part III, lines 1a through 4z. If your only source of credits listed on Form 3800 is from pass-through entities, you may not be required to complete the source credit form. Instead you may be able to report the credit directly on Form 3800. For more details, see the instructions for Form 3800.

Special Situations

Artists and Authors

The proper way for artists and authors to account for their expenses has been the topic of much debate in recent years. A special exception excludes authors and artists from the uniform capitalization rules for certain qualified creative expenses that they incur in their trade or business. As a result, these expenses can be currently deducted and not capitalized. A "qualified creative expense" is defined as any expense that is paid or incurred by an individual in the trade or business of being a writer or an artist and that would be allowable as a deduction for the taxable year.

Although you are allowed currently to deduct those expenses that are classified as qualified creative expenses, there are some expenses that need to be capitalized. Examples of such expenses include any expense related to printing, photographic plates, motion pictures, videotapes, and similar items.

There is an alternative way for an artist or an author to treat his or her qualified creative expenses. If the artist or author so chooses, he or she can capitalize all qualified creative costs. In the current year he or she is able to deduct 50% of the eligible costs and then deduct the remaining 50% ratably over the next 2 years. The reason one may choose this method over deducting all qualified creative expenses currently is that the meaning of a qualified creative cost is broader in this instance. It includes the costs of films, sound recordings, videotapes, and books. These expenses would otherwise be capitalized and amortized over their estimated useful lives.

Costs of Goods Sold

Part III of Schedule C is used to determine your cost of goods sold. If you make or buy goods to sell, you are entitled to deduct the cost of the goods sold on your tax return. One of the most important costs that must be determined is the cost of your inventory.

Inventories are required to be determined at the beginning and end of each tax year for manufacturers, wholesalers, retailers, and every other business that makes, buys, or sells goods to produce income. Inventories include goods held for sale in the normal course of business, work in process, and raw materials and supplies that will physically become a part of merchandise intended for sale.

Add to your beginning inventory the cost of inventory items purchased during the year, including all other items entering into the cost of obtaining or producing the inventory. From this total, subtract your inventory at the end of the year. The remainder represents the cost of goods sold during the tax period. It should not include selling expenses or any other expenses that are not directly related to obtaining or producing the goods sold.

Inventory methods. To determine the value of your inventory, you need a method for identifying the items in your inventory and a method for valuing these items. In general, there are three methods of identifying items in inventory: (1) specific identification; (2) first in, first out (FIFO); and (3) last in, first out (LIFO).

The specific identification method is used to identify the cost of each inventoried item by matching the item with its cost of acquisition in addition to other allocable costs, such as labor and transportation. This method is most often used by retailers of unique items.

If there is no specific identification of items with their costs, you must make an assumption to decide which items were sold and which remain in inventory. You make this identification by either the FIFO or the LIFO method.

The FIFO method assumes that the items purchased or produced first are the first items you sold, consumed, or otherwise disposed.

The LIFO method assumes that the items of inventory purchased or produced last are sold or removed from inventory first.

The FIFO method and the LIFO method produce different results in income, depending on the trend of price levels of the goods included in those inventories. In times of inflation, when prices are rising, LIFO will produce a larger cost of goods sold and a lower closing inventory. Under FIFO, the cost of goods sold will be lower and the closing inventory will be higher. However, in times of falling prices, LIFO will produce a smaller cost of goods sold and a higher closing inventory. Under FIFO, the reverse will be true.

Valuing inventory. Valuing the items in your inventory is a major factor in figuring your taxable income. The two common ways to value your inventory if you use the FIFO method are the specific-cost identification method and the lower-of-cost-or-market method.

Adopting LIFO method. To adopt the LIFO method, you are required to file Form 970, *Application to Use LIFO Inventory Method*, or a statement that has all the information required in Form 970. You must file the form (or the statement) with your timely filed tax return for the year in which you first use LIFO.

Once a method is selected you may not change to another method without the permission of the IRS. For a further discussion of inventory, see Publication 334, *Tax Guide for Small Business*.

How to Complete Schedule SE Line by Line, Briefly

Self-employed individuals filing Schedule C may be required to pay self-employment tax. Self-employment income and the related tax are discussed earlier in this chapter.

When completing Form 1040, Schedule SE, you must first determine whether you need to file the short Schedule SE form or the long Schedule SE form. You must use the long Schedule SE form if any of the following apply:

- You received wages or tips and the total of all of your wages (and tips) subject to social security, Medicare, or railroad retirement taxes plus your net earnings from self-employment are more than $117,000.
- You use either "optional method" to figure your net earnings from self-employment.
- You are a minister, a member of a religious order, or a Christian Science practitioner and you received IRS approval (by filing Form 4361) not to be taxed on your earnings from these sources, but you owe self-employment tax on other earnings.
- You had church employee income of $108.28 or more that was reported to you on Form W-2.
- You received tips subject to social security, Medicare, or railroad retirement taxes, but you did not report those tips to your employer.
- You reported wages on Form 8919, Uncollected Social Security and Medicare Tax on Wages.
- If none of these conditions exist, you are able to use the short Schedule SE form.

As a Schedule C filer, report Schedule C income on line 2 of Section A of the short Schedule SE form, or Section B of the long Schedule SE form (remember, do not include the income reported on Schedule C as a statutory employee).

Long Schedule SE Example

Peter Doyle is single. He is employed as a full-time Latin professor at a university. His wages from this job were $99,500. Dr. Doyle also gives lectures around the country on a freelance basis. His net profit from these lectures was $18,500, which he reported on Schedule C-EZ (Form 1040).

His net profit from lecturing and his wages total more than $117,000, so he must fill out Long Schedule SE.

1. On his Long Schedule SE, Doyle has no farm income, so he leaves line 1 blank.
2. Doyle enters the net profit from his Schedule C-EZ, $18,500.
3. Doyle has no farm income, so he enters the same amount on line 3, $18,500.
4a. Doyle multiplies the $18,500 by 92.35% (.9235) to get his net earnings and enters $17,085.
4b. Doyle did not elect an optional method, so he leaves this line blank.
5a-b. Doyle had no church employee income, so he leaves these lines blank.
6. Line 5b is blank, so Doyle enters the same amount he entered on line 4c, $17,085.
8a. Doyle enters his total wages, $99,500.
8b-c. These lines do not apply to him, so Doyle leaves them blank.
8d. Lines 8b and 8c are blank, so he enters the same amount he entered on line 8a, $99,500.
9. He subtracts line 8d ($99,500) from line 7 and enters the result, $17,500.
10. Doyle multiplies the smaller of line 6 ($17,085) or line 9 ($17,500) by 12.4% (.124) and enters the result, $2,119.
11. Doyle multiplies line 6 ($17,085) by 2.9% (.029) and enters the result, $495.
12. Doyle adds lines 10 and 11 and enters the total, $2,614, here and on line 56 of Form 1040 (not illustrated).
13. Doyle multiplies line 12 by 50% and enters the result ($1,307) on Line 13 of this schedule, and Line 27 of Form 1040. This is the amount of SE tax he can deduct.

Comprehensive Schedule C/Self-Employment Example

John Paul Jones is a self-employed comic book salesman. He does business as JPJ Comics. The majority of his business consists of retail sales of comic books. John Paul works out of his home, located at 6409 79th Street, Queens, New York 11379, where he has been running the business since January 1, 1994. One-fourth of his home is used solely for the purpose of running his business. John Paul accounts for his purchases and sales on the accrual method. All other income and expense items are accounted for by use of the cash method. He is also a professor of civil law studies and has $54,000 of W-2 wages in 2014. John Paul Jones had the following income and expenses during 2014:

Gross receipts from sales of comic books—accrual basis $35,000

Beginning inventory	2,200
Purchases	13,000
Ending inventory	2,700

Business subscriptions	350
Advertising	1,700
Legal fees	200
Supplies	1,200
Meals and entertainment	600
Travel	900
Telephone	300
Annual home insurance	900
Annual mortgage interest	6,000
Annual real estate taxes	4,000
Annual utilities	1,200
Basis of home purchase on 6/4/92	220,000
Amount attributable to land	40,000
Amount attributable to house	180,000

John Paul Jones has established a profit-sharing plan, providing for a maximum contribution of 25% of compensation. For 2014, he has made the maximum contribution before filing his tax return.

TAXORGANIZER

Records you should keep:
- Canceled checks, receipts, and other documents for evidence of expenses paid
- Any 1099-Misc forms provided to you from the operation of the business
- A record of time spent using your home office for business

		OMB No. 1545-0074

SCHEDULE SE
(Form 1040)

Department of the Treasury
Internal Revenue Service (99)

Self-Employment Tax

▶ Information about Schedule SE and its separate instructions is at *www.irs.gov/schedulese*.

▶ **Attach to Form 1040 or Form 1040NR.**

OMB No. 1545-0074

2014

Attachment
Sequence No. **17**

Name of person with **self-employment** income (as shown on Form 1040 or Form 1040NR)

Social security number of person
with **self-employment** income ▶

Before you begin: To determine if you must file Schedule SE, see the instructions.

May I Use Short Schedule SE or Must I Use Long Schedule SE?

Note. Use this flowchart **only if** you must file Schedule SE. If unsure, see *Who Must File Schedule SE* in the instructions.

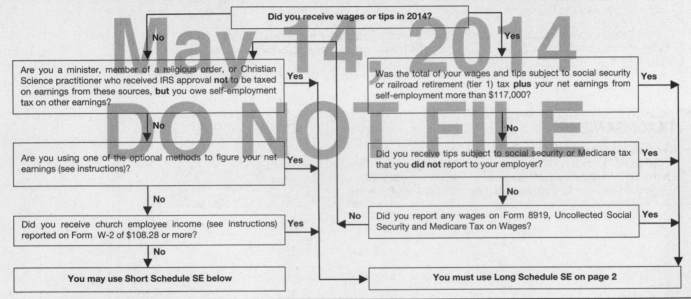

Section A—Short Schedule SE.   Caution. Read above to see if you can use Short Schedule SE.

1a	Net farm profit or (loss) from Schedule F, line 34, and farm partnerships, Schedule K-1 (Form 1065), box 14, code A	**1a**		
b	If you received social security retirement or disability benefits, enter the amount of Conservation Reserve Program payments included on Schedule F, line 4b, or listed on Schedule K-1 (Form 1065), box 20, code Z	**1b**	(	)
2	Net profit or (loss) from Schedule C, line 31; Schedule C-EZ, line 3; Schedule K-1 (Form 1065), box 14, code A (other than farming); and Schedule K-1 (Form 1065-B), box 9, code J1. Ministers and members of religious orders, see instructions for types of income to report on this line. See instructions for other income to report	**2**		
3	Combine lines 1a, 1b, and 2	**3**		
4	Multiply line 3 by 92.35% (.9235). If less than $400, you do not owe self-employment tax; do **not** file this schedule unless you have an amount on line 1b . . . . ▶	**4**		
	Note. If line 4 is less than $400 due to Conservation Reserve Program payments on line 1b, see instructions.			
5	**Self-employment tax.** If the amount on line 4 is:			
	• $117,000 or less, multiply line 4 by 15.3% (.153). Enter the result here and on **Form 1040, line 57,** or **Form 1040NR, line 55**			
	• More than $117,000, multiply line 4 by 2.9% (.029). Then, add $14,508 to the result. Enter the total here and on **Form 1040, line 57,** or **Form 1040NR, line 55**	**5**		
6	**Deduction for one-half of self-employment tax.** Multiply line 5 by 50% (.50). Enter the result here and on **Form 1040, line 27,** or **Form 1040NR, line 27**	**6**		

For Paperwork Reduction Act Notice, see your tax return instructions.   Cat. No. 11358Z   Schedule SE (Form 1040) 2014

Name of person with **self-employment** income (as shown on Form 1040 or Form 1040NR) Peter Doyle	Social security number of person with **self-employment** income ▶	001-12-2333

Section B—Long Schedule SE

Part I   Self-Employment Tax

Note. If your only income subject to self-employment tax is **church employee income,** see instructions. Also see instructions for the definition of church employee income.

A   If you are a minister, member of a religious order, or Christian Science practitioner **and** you filed Form 4361, but you had $400 or more of **other** net earnings from self-employment, check here and continue with Part I . . . . . . ▶ ☐

1a	Net farm profit or (loss) from Schedule F, line 34, and farm partnerships, Schedule K-1 (Form 1065), box 14, code A. **Note.** Skip lines 1a and 1b if you use the farm optional method (see instructions)	**1a**		
b	If you received social security retirement or disability benefits, enter the amount of Conservation Reserve Program payments included on Schedule F, line 4b, or listed on Schedule K-1 (Form 1065), box 20, code Z	**1b**	(	)
2	Net profit or (loss) from Schedule C, line 31; Schedule C-EZ, line 3; Schedule K-1 (Form 1065), box 14, code A (other than farming); and Schedule K-1 (Form 1065-B), box 9, code J1. Ministers and members of religious orders, see instructions for types of income to report on this line. See instructions for other income to report. **Note.** Skip this line if you use the nonfarm optional method (see instructions)	**2**	18,500	
3	Combine lines 1a, 1b, and 2	**3**	18,500	
4a	If line 3 is more than zero, multiply line 3 by 92.35% (.9235). Otherwise, enter amount from line 3	**4a**	17,085	
	Note. If line 4a is less than $400 due to Conservation Reserve Program payments on line 1b, see instructions.			
b	If you elect one or both of the optional methods, enter the total of lines 15 and 17 here . . .	**4b**		
c	Combine lines 4a and 4b. If less than $400, **stop**; you do not owe self-employment tax. **Exception.** If less than $400 and you had **church employee income,** enter -0- and continue ▶	**4c**	17,085	
5a	Enter your **church employee income** from Form W-2. See instructions for definition of church employee income . . . **5a**	**5b**		
b	Multiply line 5a by 92.35% (.9235). If less than $100, enter -0-	**5b**		
6	Add lines 4c and 5b	**6**	17,085	
7	Maximum amount of combined wages and self-employment earnings subject to social security tax or the 6.2% portion of the 7.65% railroad retirement (tier 1) tax for 2014	**7**	117,000	00
8a	Total social security wages and tips (total of boxes 3 and 7 on Form(s) W-2) and railroad retirement (tier 1) compensation. If $117,000 or more, skip lines 8b through 10, and go to line 11 **8a** 99,500			
b	Unreported tips subject to social security tax (from Form 4137, line 10) **8b**			
c	Wages subject to social security tax (from Form 8919, line 10) **8c**			
d	Add lines 8a, 8b, and 8c	**8d**	99,500	
9	Subtract line 8d from line 7. If zero or less, enter -0- here and on line 10 and go to line 11 ▶	**9**	17,500	
10	Multiply the **smaller** of line 6 or line 9 by 12.4% (.124)	**10**	2,119	
11	Multiply line 6 by 2.9% (.029)	**11**	495	
12	**Self-employment tax.** Add lines 10 and 11. Enter here and on **Form 1040, line 57,** or **Form 1040NR, line 55**	**12**	2,614	
13	**Deduction for one-half of self-employment tax.** Multiply line 12 by 50% (.50). Enter the result here and on **Form 1040, line 27,** or **Form 1040NR, line 27** **13** 1,307			

Part II   Optional Methods To Figure Net Earnings   (see instructions)

Farm Optional Method. You may use this method **only** if **(a)** your gross farm income[1] was not more than $7,200, **or (b)** your net farm profits[2] were less than $5,198.

14	Maximum income for optional methods	**14**	4,800	00
15	Enter the **smaller** of: two-thirds (2/3) of gross farm income[1] (not less than zero) **or** $4,800. Also include this amount on line 4b above	**15**		

Nonfarm Optional Method. You may use this method **only** if **(a)** your net nonfarm profits[3] were less than $5,198 and also less than 72.189% of your gross nonfarm income,[4] **and (b)** you had net earnings from self-employment of at least $400 in 2 of the prior 3 years. **Caution.** You may use this method no more than five times.

16	Subtract line 15 from line 14	**16**		
17	Enter the **smaller** of: two-thirds (2/3) of gross nonfarm income[4] (not less than zero) **or** the amount on line 16. Also include this amount on line 4b above	**17**		

[1] From Sch. F, line 9, and Sch. K-1 (Form 1065), box 14, code B.

[2] From Sch. F, line 34, and Sch. K-1 (Form 1065), box 14, code A—minus the amount you would have entered on line 1b had you not used the optional method.

[3] From Sch. C, line 31; Sch. C-EZ, line 3; Sch. K-1 (Form 1065), box 14, code A; and Sch. K-1 (Form 1065-B), box 9, code J1.

[4] From Sch. C, line 7; Sch. C-EZ, line 1; Sch. K-1 (Form 1065), box 14, code C; and Sch. K-1 (Form 1065-B), box 9, code J2.

Schedule SE (Form 1040) 2014

SCHEDULE C
(Form 1040)

Department of the Treasury
Internal Revenue Service (99)

Profit or Loss From Business
(Sole Proprietorship)

▶ Information about Schedule C and its separate instructions is at *www.irs.gov/schedulec.*
▶ **Attach to Form 1040, 1040NR, or 1041; partnerships generally must file Form 1065.**

OMB No. 1545-0074

2014

Attachment
Sequence No. **09**

Name of proprietor	Social security number (SSN)
John Paul Jones	111-22-3344

A	Principal business or profession, including product or service (see instructions)	B Enter code from instructions
	Retail sales of comic books	▶ 4 5 1 1 2 0

C	Business name. If no separate business name, leave blank.	D Employer ID number (EIN), (see instr.)
	JPJ Comics	1 3 2 9 9 9 9 0 9

E	Business address (including suite or room no.) ▶ **6409 79th St**
	City, town or post office, state, and ZIP code **Queens, NY 11379**

F Accounting method: (1) ☐ Cash (2) ☐ Accrual (3) ☑ Other (specify) ▶ **Hybrid**

G Did you "materially participate" in the operation of this business during 2014? If "No," see instructions for limit on losses   ☑ Yes ☐ No

H If you started or acquired this business during 2014, check here . . . . ▶ ☐

I Did you make any payments in 2014 that would require you to file Form(s) 1099? (see instructions) . . . ☐ Yes ☑ No

J If "Yes," did you or will you file required Forms 1099? . . . . ☐ Yes ☐ No

Part I   Income

1	Gross receipts or sales. See instructions for line 1 and check the box if this income was reported to you on Form W-2 and the "Statutory employee" box on that form was checked . . . . ▶ ☐	1	35,000
2	Returns and allowances	2	
3	Subtract line 2 from line 1	3	35,000
4	Cost of goods sold (from line 42)	4	12,500
5	**Gross profit.** Subtract line 4 from line 3	5	22,500
6	Other income, including federal and state gasoline or fuel tax credit or refund (see instructions) . . .	6	
7	**Gross income.** Add lines 5 and 6 . . . . ▶	7	22,500

Part II   Expenses. Enter expenses for business use of your home **only** on line 30.

8	Advertising	8	1,700	18	Office expense (see instructions)	18	
9	Car and truck expenses (see instructions)	9		19	Pension and profit-sharing plans .	19	
10	Commissions and fees .	10		20	Rent or lease (see instructions):		
11	Contract labor (see instructions)	11		a	Vehicles, machinery, and equipment	20a	
12	Depletion	12		b	Other business property . . .	20b	
13	Depreciation and section 179 expense deduction (not included in Part III) (see instructions)	13		21	Repairs and maintenance . . .	21	
				22	Supplies (not included in Part III) .	22	1,200
				23	Taxes and licenses	23	
				24	Travel, meals, and entertainment:		
14	Employee benefit programs (other than on line 19) . .	14		a	Travel	24a	900
15	Insurance (other than health)	15		b	Deductible meals and entertainment (see instructions)	24b	300
16	Interest:			25	Utilities	25	300
a	Mortgage (paid to banks, etc.)	16a		26	Wages (less employment credits) .	26	
b	Other	16b		27a	Other expenses (from line 48) . .	27a	350
17	Legal and professional services	17	200	b	**Reserved for future use** . . .	27b	

28	**Total expenses** before expenses for business use of home. Add lines 8 through 27a . . . . . ▶	28	4,950
29	Tentative profit or (loss). Subtract line 28 from line 7	29	17,550
30	Expenses for business use of your home. Do not report these expenses elsewhere. Attach Form 8829 unless using the simplified method (see instructions). **Simplified method filers only:** enter the total square footage of: (a) your home: _____ and (b) the part of your home used for business: _____ . Use the Simplified Method Worksheet in the instructions to figure the amount to enter on line 30	30	4,179
31	**Net profit or (loss).** Subtract line 30 from line 29. • If a profit, enter on both **Form 1040, line 12** (or **Form 1040NR, line 13**) and on **Schedule SE, line 2.** (If you checked the box on line 1, see instructions). Estates and trusts, enter on **Form 1041, line 3.** • If a loss, you **must** go to line 32.	31	13,371
32	If you have a loss, check the box that describes your investment in this activity (see instructions). • If you checked 32a, enter the loss on both **Form 1040, line 12,** (or **Form 1040NR, line 13**) and on **Schedule SE, line 2.** (If you checked the box on line 1, see the line 31 instructions). Estates and trusts, enter on **Form 1041, line 3.** • If you checked 32b, you **must** attach **Form 6198.** Your loss may be limited.	32a ☐ All investment is at risk. 32b ☐ Some investment is not at risk.

For Paperwork Reduction Act Notice, see the separate instructions.   Cat. No. 11334P   Schedule C (Form 1040) 2014

| Part III | Cost of Goods Sold (see instructions) |

33 Method(s) used to
value closing inventory:　**a** ☑ Cost　**b** ☐ Lower of cost or market　**c** ☐ Other (attach explanation)

34 Was there any change in determining quantities, costs, or valuations between opening and closing inventory?
If "Yes," attach explanation . . . . ☐ Yes　☑ No

35	Inventory at beginning of year. If different from last year's closing inventory, attach explanation . .	**35**	2,200
36	Purchases less cost of items withdrawn for personal use	**36**	13,000
37	Cost of labor. Do not include any amounts paid to yourself	**37**	
38	Materials and supplies	**38**	
39	Other costs	**39**	
40	Add lines 35 through 39	**40**	15,200
41	Inventory at end of year	**41**	2,700
42	**Cost of goods sold.** Subtract line 41 from line 40. Enter the result here and on line 4	**42**	12,500

| Part IV | **Information on Your Vehicle.** Complete this part **only** if you are claiming car or truck expenses on line 9 and are not required to file Form 4562 for this business. See the instructions for line 13 to find out if you must file Form 4562. |

43 When did you place your vehicle in service for business purposes? (month, day, year) ▶ _____ / _____ / _____

44 Of the total number of miles you drove your vehicle during 2014, enter the number of miles you used your vehicle for:

a Business _____　**b** Commuting (see instructions) _____　**c** Other _____

45 Was your vehicle available for personal use during off-duty hours? . . . . ☐ Yes　☐ No

46 Do you (or your spouse) have another vehicle available for personal use? . . . . ☐ Yes　☐ No

47a Do you have evidence to support your deduction? . . . . ☐ Yes　☐ No

b If "Yes," is the evidence written? . . . . ☐ Yes　☐ No

| Part V | **Other Expenses.** List below business expenses not included on lines 8–26 or line 30. |

Business subscriptions	350

48	**Total other expenses.** Enter here and on line 27a	**48**	

Schedule C (Form 1040) 2014

SCHEDULE SE (Form 1040) Department of the Treasury Internal Revenue Service (99)	**Self-Employment Tax** ▶ Information about Schedule SE and its separate instructions is at *www.irs.gov/schedulese*. ▶ Attach to Form 1040 or Form 1040NR.	OMB No. 1545-0074 20**14** Attachment Sequence No. **17**

Name of person with **self-employment** income (as shown on Form 1040 or Form 1040NR) John Paul Jones	Social security number of person with **self-employment** income ▶	111-22-3344

Before you begin: To determine if you must file Schedule SE, see the instructions.

May I Use Short Schedule SE or Must I Use Long Schedule SE?

Note. Use this flowchart **only if** you must file Schedule SE. If unsure, see *Who Must File Schedule SE* in the instructions.

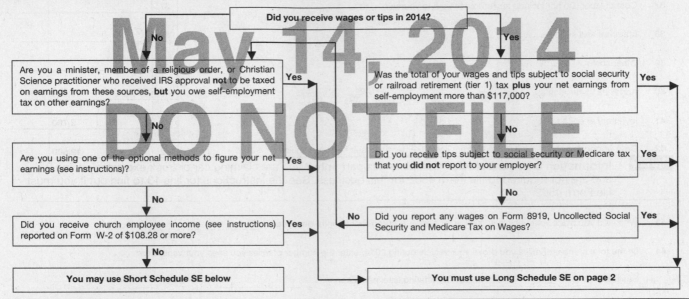

Section A—Short Schedule SE.   Caution.   Read above to see if you can use Short Schedule SE.

1a	Net farm profit or (loss) from Schedule F, line 34, and farm partnerships, Schedule K-1 (Form 1065), box 14, code A	**1a**		
b	If you received social security retirement or disability benefits, enter the amount of Conservation Reserve Program payments included on Schedule F, line 4b, or listed on Schedule K-1 (Form 1065), box 20, code Z	**1b** (		)
2	Net profit or (loss) from Schedule C, line 31; Schedule C-EZ, line 3; Schedule K-1 (Form 1065), box 14, code A (other than farming); and Schedule K-1 (Form 1065-B), box 9, code J1. Ministers and members of religious orders, see instructions for types of income to report on this line. See instructions for other income to report	**2**		
3	Combine lines 1a, 1b, and 2	**3**		
4	Multiply line 3 by 92.35% (.9235). If less than $400, you do not owe self-employment tax; **do not** file this schedule unless you have an amount on line 1b . . . . . . ▶	**4**		
	Note. If line 4 is less than $400 due to Conservation Reserve Program payments on line 1b, see instructions.			
5	**Self-employment tax.** If the amount on line 4 is: • $117,000 or less, multiply line 4 by 15.3% (.153). Enter the result here and on **Form 1040, line 57,** or **Form 1040NR, line 55** • More than $117,000, multiply line 4 by 2.9% (.029). Then, add $14,508 to the result. Enter the total here and on **Form 1040, line 57,** or **Form 1040NR, line 55**	**5**		
6	**Deduction for one-half of self-employment tax.** Multiply line 5 by 50% (.50). Enter the result here and on **Form 1040, line 27,** or **Form 1040NR, line 27**	**6**		

For Paperwork Reduction Act Notice, see your tax return instructions.   Cat. No. 11358Z   Schedule SE (Form 1040) 2014

Name of person with **self-employment** income (as shown on Form 1040 or Form 1040NR)	Social security number of person with **self-employment** income ▶	111-22-3344
John Paul Jones		

Section B—Long Schedule SE

Part I   Self-Employment Tax

Note. If your only income subject to self-employment tax is **church employee income,** see instructions. Also see instructions for the definition of church employee income.

A	If you are a minister, member of a religious order, or Christian Science practitioner **and** you filed Form 4361, but you had $400 or more of **other** net earnings from self-employment, check here and continue with Part I . . . . . . ▶			☐
1a	Net farm profit or (loss) from Schedule F, line 34, and farm partnerships, Schedule K-1 (Form 1065), box 14, code A. **Note.** Skip lines 1a and 1b if you use the farm optional method (see instructions)	**1a**		
b	If you received social security retirement or disability benefits, enter the amount of Conservation Reserve Program payments included on Schedule F, line 4b, or listed on Schedule K-1 (Form 1065), box 20, code Z	**1b**	(	)
2	Net profit or (loss) from Schedule C, line 31; Schedule C-EZ, line 3; Schedule K-1 (Form 1065), box 14, code A (other than farming); and Schedule K-1 (Form 1065-B), box 9, code J1. Ministers and members of religious orders, see instructions for types of income to report on this line. See instructions for other income to report. **Note.** Skip this line if you use the nonfarm optional method (see instructions)	**2**	13,371	
3	Combine lines 1a, 1b, and 2	**3**	13,371	
4a	If line 3 is more than zero, multiply line 3 by 92.35% (.9235). Otherwise, enter amount from line 3	**4a**	12,348	
	Note. If line 4a is less than $400 due to Conservation Reserve Program payments on line 1b, see instructions.			
b	If you elect one or both of the optional methods, enter the total of lines 15 and 17 here . . .	**4b**		
c	Combine lines 4a and 4b. If less than $400, **stop;** you do not owe self-employment tax. **Exception.** If less than $400 and you had **church employee income,** enter -0- and continue ▶	**4c**	12,348	
5a	Enter your **church employee income** from Form W-2. See instructions for definition of church employee income . . . **5a**	**5b**		
b	Multiply line 5a by 92.35% (.9235). If less than $100, enter -0-	**5b**		
6	Add lines 4c and 5b	**6**	12,348	
7	Maximum amount of combined wages and self-employment earnings subject to social security tax or the 6.2% portion of the 7.65% railroad retirement (tier 1) tax for 2014	**7**	117,000	00
8a	Total social security wages and tips (total of boxes 3 and 7 on Form(s) W-2) and railroad retirement (tier 1) compensation. If $117,000 or more, skip lines 8b through 10, and go to line 11 **8a** 54,000			
b	Unreported tips subject to social security tax (from Form 4137, line 10) **8b**			
c	Wages subject to social security tax (from Form 8919, line 10) **8c**			
d	Add lines 8a, 8b, and 8c	**8d**	54,000	
9	Subtract line 8d from line 7. If zero or less, enter -0- here and on line 10 and go to line 11 ▶	**9**	63,000	
10	Multiply the **smaller** of line 6 or line 9 by 12.4% (.124)	**10**	1,531	
11	Multiply line 6 by 2.9% (.029)	**11**	358	
12	**Self-employment tax.** Add lines 10 and 11. Enter here and on **Form 1040, line 57,** or **Form 1040NR, line 55**	**12**	1,889	
13	**Deduction for one-half of self-employment tax.** Multiply line 12 by 50% (.50). Enter the result here and on **Form 1040, line 27,** or **Form 1040NR, line 27** **13** 945			

Part II   Optional Methods To Figure Net Earnings (see instructions)

Farm Optional Method. You may use this method **only** if **(a)** your gross farm income[1] was not more than $7,200, **or (b)** your net farm profits[2] were less than $5,198.

14	Maximum income for optional methods	**14**		
15	Enter the **smaller** of: two-thirds (²/₃) of gross farm income[1] (not less than zero) or $4,800. Also include this amount on line 4b above	**15**	4,800	00

Nonfarm Optional Method. You may use this method **only** if **(a)** your net nonfarm profits[3] were less than $5,198 and also less than 72.189% of your gross nonfarm income,[4] **and (b)** you had net earnings from self-employment of at least $400 in 2 of the prior 3 years. **Caution.** You may use this method no more than five times.

16	Subtract line 15 from line 14	**16**	
17	Enter the **smaller** of: two-thirds (²/₃) of gross nonfarm income[4] (not less than zero) **or** the amount on line 16. Also include this amount on line 4b above	**17**	

[1] From Sch. F, line 9, and Sch. K-1 (Form 1065), box 14, code B.
[2] From Sch. F, line 34, and Sch. K-1 (Form 1065), box 14, code A—minus the amount you would have entered on line 1b had you not used the optional method.

[3] From Sch. C, line 31; Sch. C-EZ, line 3; Sch. K-1 (Form 1065), box 14, code A; and Sch. K-1 (Form 1065-B), box 9, code J1.
[4] From Sch. C, line 7; Sch. C-EZ, line 1; Sch. K-1 (Form 1065), box 14, code C; and Sch. K-1 (Form 1065-B), box 9, code J2.

Schedule SE (Form 1040) 2014

Form 8829

Department of the Treasury
Internal Revenue Service (99)

Expenses for Business Use of Your Home

▶ File only with Schedule C (Form 1040). Use a separate Form 8829 for each home you used for business during the year.

▶ Information about Form 8829 and its separate instructions is at *www.irs.gov/form8829*.

OMB No. 1545-0074

2014

Attachment
Sequence No. **176**

Name(s) of proprietor(s)

John Paul Jones

Your social security number

111-22-3344

Part I — Part of Your Home Used for Business

1	Area used regularly and exclusively for business, regularly for daycare, or for storage of inventory or product samples (see instructions)	1	200SF
2	Total area of home	2	800SF
3	Divide line 1 by line 2. Enter the result as a percentage	3	25 %

For daycare facilities not used exclusively for business, go to line 4. All others, go to line 7.

4	Multiply days used for daycare during year by hours used per day	4	hr.
5	Total hours available for use during the year (365 days x 24 hours) (see instructions)	5	8,760 hr.
6	Divide line 4 by line 5. Enter the result as a decimal amount	6	
7	Business percentage. For daycare facilities not used exclusively for business, multiply line 6 by line 3 (enter the result as a percentage). All others, enter the amount from line 3 ▶	7	25 %

Part II — Figure Your Allowable Deduction

		(a) Direct expenses	(b) Indirect expenses		
8	Enter the amount from Schedule C, line 29, **plus** any gain derived from the business use of your home, **minus** any loss from the trade or business not derived from the business use of your home (see instructions)			8	17,550

See instructions for columns (a) and (b) before completing lines 9–21.

		(a) Direct expenses	(b) Indirect expenses		
9	Casualty losses (see instructions)	9			
10	Deductible mortgage interest (see instructions)	10	6,000		
11	Real estate taxes (see instructions)	11	4,000		
12	Add lines 9, 10, and 11	12	10,000		
13	Multiply line 12, column (b) by line 7	13	2,500		
14	Add line 12, column (a) and line 13			14	2,500
15	Subtract line 14 from line 8. If zero or less, enter -0-			15	15,050
16	Excess mortgage interest (see instructions)	16			
17	Insurance	17	900		
18	Rent	18			
19	Repairs and maintenance	19			
20	Utilities	20	1,200		
21	Other expenses (see instructions)	21			
22	Add lines 16 through 21	22	2,100		
23	Multiply line 22, column (b) by line 7	23	525		
24	Carryover of prior year operating expenses (see instructions)	24			
25	Add line 22, column (a), line 23, and line 24			25	525
26	Allowable operating expenses. Enter the **smaller** of line 15 or line 25			26	525
27	Limit on excess casualty losses and depreciation. Subtract line 26 from line 15			27	14,525
28	Excess casualty losses (see instructions)	28			
29	Depreciation of your home from line 41 below	29	1,154		
30	Carryover of prior year excess casualty losses and depreciation (see instructions)	30			
31	Add lines 28 through 30			31	1,154
32	Allowable excess casualty losses and depreciation. Enter the **smaller** of line 27 or line 31			32	1,154
33	Add lines 14, 26, and 32			33	4,179
34	Casualty loss portion, if any, from lines 14 and 32. Carry amount to **Form 4684** (see instructions)			34	
35	**Allowable expenses for business use of your home.** Subtract line 34 from line 33. Enter here and on Schedule C, line 30. If your home was used for more than one business, see instructions ▶			35	4,179

Part III — Depreciation of Your Home

36	Enter the **smaller** of your home's adjusted basis or its fair market value (see instructions)	36	220,000
37	Value of land included on line 36	37	40,000
38	Basis of building. Subtract line 37 from line 36	38	180,000
39	Business basis of building. Multiply line 38 by line 7	39	45,000
40	Depreciation percentage (see instructions)	40	2.564 %
41	Depreciation allowable (see instructions). Multiply line 39 by line 40. Enter here and on line 29 above	41	1,154

Part IV — Carryover of Unallowed Expenses to 2015

42	Operating expenses. Subtract line 26 from line 25. If less than zero, enter -0-	42	
43	Excess casualty losses and depreciation. Subtract line 32 from line 31. If less than zero, enter -0-	43	

For Paperwork Reduction Act Notice, see your tax return instructions.   Cat. No. 13232M   Form **8829** (2014)

Chapter 39
Mutual funds

Note

ey.com/EYTaxGuide

Ernst & Young LLP will update the *EY Tax Guide 2015* website with relevant taxpayer information as it becomes available. You can also sign up for email alerts to let you know when changes have been made.

Introduction

A mutual fund is an investment created by "pooling" money from many investors and investing the money in stocks, bonds, short-term money market instruments, or other securities. A mutual fund will have a fund manager that buys and sells stocks, bonds, and other securities according to the style dictated by the fund's investment objectives. Reviewing a mutual fund's investment objective is an important consideration for any investor as the thousands of different mutual funds have different features, risks, and rewards. Aggressive growth funds, for example, are characterized by high risk and high potential return. These funds typically seek long-term capital appreciation and do not produce significant interest income or dividends. The objectives of balanced funds, on the other hand, are to conserve an investor's initial principal, pay current income through dividends, and promote the long-term growth of both principal and income. While aggressive growth funds generally invest only in stocks, balanced funds typically invest in both bonds and stocks. There are many other kinds of mutual funds–growth and income funds, bond funds, sector funds, index funds, and the like–all with different investing objectives and different strategies to achieve them. A general rule to keep in mind: The higher the potential reward from your investment, the greater risk of potential loss.

This chapter explains how differing distributions you may receive from a mutual fund are taxed, as well as the different methods by which you may calculate your gain or loss when you sell your mutual fund shares. It also discusses some of the expenses you may incur when investing in mutual funds.

TAXPLANNER

Kinds of Mutual Funds

A mutual fund is a regulated investment company generally created by "pooling" funds of investors to allow them to take advantage of a diversity of investments and professional management. The advantages that investment companies can offer you are numerous, including:
- Professional investment management of assets at a relatively low cost

Tax Breaks and Deductions You Can Use Checklist

Avoiding unexpected taxable income from a mutual fund. If you buy mutual fund shares right before a dividend distribution, you may be buying a tax liability. The share price you pay reflects this dividend right. For example, say that you buy 1,000 mutual fund shares for $20 a share shortly before the fund declares and pays a dividend of $4 per share. As a result of the dividend, the price per share will drop to $16. You will have to include the $4,000 ($4 per share × 1,000) dividend in your income even though there has been no increase in the overall value of your investment. If the investment had been delayed until after the dividend, the same $20,000 investment would have purchased 1,250 shares (at $16 per share) and this problem would have been avoided.

Tax-managed and index funds. A "tax-managed" mutual fund is a type of mutual fund where the fund's managers are required to employ a series of strategies designed to keep the investors' tax consequences to a minimum. Most large fund companies have tax-managed funds, and taxpayers often own these types of mutual funds in a taxable account (versus a tax-deferred account like a 401(k) or IRA). In addition to tax-managed funds, you might want to also consider stock index funds within a taxable account, which invest in the stocks making up a particular market index; for example, the Standard & Poor's index of 500 large

- Ownership in a diversified portfolio
- Potentially lower commissions, because the investment company buys and sells in large blocks
- Prospectuses and reports of various periodicals to assist people in readily accessing information needed to perform fund comparisons
- Other special services, such as dividend reinvestment plans, periodic withdrawal and investment plans, the ability to switch between funds by telephone or over the Internet, and in some cases, check-writing privileges

Investment Objectives

Mutual funds are classified according to their investment objectives. The following is a summary of common types of funds categorized by their investment objective.

Aggressive growth funds. These funds are characterized by high risk and high potential return. They typically seek capital appreciation and do not produce significant interest income or dividends.

Growth funds. Growth funds aim to achieve an increase in the value of their investments over the long term (capital gains) rather than paying dividends.

Growth and income funds. Also called "equity-income" and "total return" funds, these funds aim to balance the objectives of long-term growth and current income.

Balanced funds. These funds have three objectives: to conserve investors' initial principal, to pay high current income through dividends and interest, and to promote long-term growth of both principal and income. Balanced funds invest in both bonds and stocks.

Bond funds. Bond mutual funds invest primarily in bonds. Some funds may concentrate on short-term bonds, others on intermediate-term bonds, and still others on long-term bonds.

Sector funds. Sector funds invest in one industry, such as biotechnology or retail, and therefore do not offer the diversity you generally receive from a diversified growth mutual fund, which might invest a portion of the fund assets in a variety of sectors.

Index funds. Index mutual funds re-create a particular market index (e.g., the S&P 500). The holdings and the return should mirror that of the index.

Target date retirement funds. These funds invest in both stocks and bonds for specific long-term periods that you can match with your anticipated retirement date. Also referred to as life-cycle funds, they automatically rebalance their investment portfolios to a more conservative asset allocation as the participant approaches their retirement target date.

Money market funds. This is a type of mutual fund that is required by law to invest in low-risk securities. These funds have relatively low risk compared to other mutual funds and pay dividends that generally reflect short-term interest rates. Unlike a "money market deposit account" at a bank, money market funds are not federally insured.

Types of regulated investment companies

In addition to categorizing investment companies by their investment objectives, investment companies are classified by three types of capital structures:

- Closed-end funds
- Unit investment trusts
- Open-end funds

Closed-end funds. Closed-end investment companies have a set capital structure with a specified number of shares. For this reason, investors must generally purchase existing shares of closed-end funds from current stockholders. Investors who wish to liquidate their position in closed-end investment companies must sell their shares to other investors. Shares in closed-end funds are therefore traded on the open market just like the stock of publicly held corporations. As a result, closed-end funds have an additional risk that isn't present in open-end funds (discussed below)—their price does not necessarily equal their net asset value. Therefore, there is a risk that the fund's shares could sell for less than the value of the underlying investments. However, closed-end funds that are purchased at a discount from the value of the underlying investments can produce an opportunity for greater return.

Unit investment trusts. Unit investment trusts are a variation of closed-end funds. Unit investment trusts typically invest in a fixed portfolio of bonds that are held until maturity rather than managed and traded, as is the case with bond mutual funds. As an investor you purchase units that represent an ownership in the trust assets. Because the bonds are not actively traded, the annual fees charged for unit trusts may be lower than those charged by bond mutual funds. The unit trust collects the interest income and repayment of principal of the bonds held in the portfolio and distributes these funds to the unit holders. Unit investment trusts can provide you with a portfolio of bonds that have different maturity dates and an average holding period that meets your objectives. Cash flow is relatively predictable, because the intention is to hold the bonds until maturity.

Open-end funds. Commonly referred to as mutual funds, open-end funds differ from closed-end funds in that they do not have a fixed number of shares to issue. Instead, the number of shares outstanding varies as investors purchase and redeem them directly from the open-end investment company. An investor who wants a position in a particular mutual fund purchases the shares from the fund either through a brokerage firm or by contacting the fund company directly. Conversely, mutual fund shareholders who want to liquidate their position sell their shares back to the company. The value of a share in a mutual fund is determined by the net asset value (NAV). Funds compute NAV by dividing the value of the fund's total net assets by the number of shares outstanding.

Mutual Funds Fees

The costs associated with open-end fund shares resemble those for closed-end funds. Like closed-end funds, open-end funds bear the trading costs and investment management fees of the investment company. However, mutual fund investors may or may not be subject to a sales charge referred to as a "load."

Open-end mutual funds are classified by their type of load charge. These are:

* No-load funds
* 12b-1 funds
* Load funds

No-load funds. No-load funds don't impose a sales charge on their investors. Purchases and sales of shares in a no-load fund are made at the fund's NAV per share. Consequently, every dollar invested gets allocated to the fund for investment rather than having a portion permanently kept back to cover sales charges.

12b-1 funds. 12b-1 funds are a variation on no-load funds. While every dollar paid into the fund is committed to investment, the 12b-1 fund shareholders indirectly pay an annual fee to cover the fund's sales and marketing costs. This 12b-1 fee typically ranges from 0.1% to the maximum 1% of total fund net assets.

Note: The 12b-1 fee is assessed every year (instead of only once); thus, the longer you hold your 12b-1 fund shares, the greater the sales charge you will bear.

Load funds. Load funds charge the shareholder a direct commission at the time of purchase and/or when the shares are redeemed and may also assess ongoing 12b-1 fees. "Front-end loads" are charged to the investor at the time of purchase and can be as high as 8.5% of the gross amount invested. On the other hand, some load funds charge their shareholders the load at the time their shares are redeemed. This cost will be either a "back-end load" or a "redemption fee." A back-end load is based on the lesser of the initial cost or final value of the shares redeemed and may disappear after a certain number of years. A redemption fee is similar to a back-end load, but is based on the value of the shares you choose to redeem rather than your initial investment. It typically applies if the investor sells within a very short period of time (usually 30 to 90 days). The purpose of such fees is to discourage shareholders from short-term trading of fund shares.

All fees, loads, and charges reduce your investment return. Therefore, you should consider not only a fund's return, but all of the expenses that affect this return.

Foreign Stock Mutual Funds

Many stock mutual funds invest in foreign stocks. They are divided into the following categories:

* **Global or world funds.** These funds invest anywhere in the world, including the United States.
* **International or foreign funds.** Such funds invest anywhere in the world except the United States.
* **Emerging markets funds.** These funds invest in financial markets of a single developing country or a group of developing countries. A developing country is categorized by the prospect of economic growth and potential vulnerability to economic and political instability. These funds are sought by investors for the prospect of higher returns but generally carry additional risk.
* **Regional funds.** These invest in specific geographic areas, such as Europe, Latin America, or the Pacific Rim.
* **Country funds.** Funds of this sort invest entirely in a specific country. For the most part, single country funds are closed-end mutual funds that typically trade on either the New York Stock Exchange or the American Stock Exchange.
* **International index funds.** These are mutual funds that parallel the concept of a domestic equity index fund. They are designed and operated so that their portfolios mirror the composition of the market index after which the funds are named.

Foreign Bond Mutual Funds

In addition to foreign stock funds, numerous foreign bond funds are available for investment. Because economic conditions differ from country to country, interest rates vary as well. At any given time, you can usually find several countries with interest rates higher than those in the United States. There is a downside to consider, though. Overseas interest rates may be more attractive, but language barriers, differing regulations, and illiquid markets all increase the challenge of foreign investments. Fluctuating currency values, although a potential advantage, can work against you if the currency of your foreign investment loses value relative to the U.S. dollar.

companies. Since these funds stay invested only in the stocks making up the particular index, there are relatively few sales of stock from the portfolio and only a small amount of realized capital gain.

Useful Items

You may want to see:

Publication

☐ **550** Investment Income and Expenses

> ### TAXALERT
>
> Beginning with the 2011 tax year, the IRS requires all brokers to report adjusted cost basis in addition to gross proceeds for covered securities and also to report whether the related gain or loss is long-term or short-term. Regulated investment company (RIC) and dividend reinvestment plan (DRP) shares that are purchased or acquired after 2011 are classified as covered securities. See chapter 16, *Reporting gains and losses*, for further information on covered securities and the three-year implementation period for the these basis-reporting regulations.
>
> For RIC and DRP shares, brokers must report the adjusted cost basis in accordance with their default method unless a taxpayer notifies the financial institution in writing to use a different method.

> ### EXPLANATION
>
> Throughout this chapter, the term mutual fund is used in place of RIC when discussing the new basis reporting rules. However, a broker will determine if a mutual fund should be classified as an RIC and therefore be subject to the basis reporting requirements.

Tax Treatment of Distributions

> **Caution**
>
> *You may be treated as having received a distribution of capital gains even if the fund does not distribute them to you. See* Undistributed capital gains *under* Capital Gain Distributions.

A distribution you receive from a mutual fund may be an ordinary dividend, a qualified dividend, a capital gain distribution, an exempt-interest dividend, or a nondividend distribution. The fund will send you a Form 1099-DIV or similar statement telling you the kind of distribution you received. This section discusses the tax treatment of each kind of distribution, describes how to treat reinvested distributions, and explains how to report distributions on your return.

> ### TAXALERT
>
> As part of the Affordable Care Act, the Net Investment Income Tax (NIIT) on unearned income of individuals took effect for tax years beginning in 2013 and thereafter. For individuals, the NIIT is 3.8% of the lesser of: (1) "net investment income" or (2) the excess of modified adjusted gross income (MAGI) over $200,000 ($250,000 if married filing jointly; $125,000 if married filing separately). Net investment income subject to the tax is defined as investment income reduced by allocable deductions. Investment income includes dividends, capital gains distributions, and both short-term and long-term capital gains, as well as other items of income. The NIIT is payable regardless of whether you otherwise pay any regular income tax or are subject to alternative minimum tax on your income.

> ### TAXPLANNER
>
> **How mutual funds are taxed.** Which mutual fund or funds you choose will depend largely on your own investment objectives. One factor you should definitely consider is how your mutual fund investment will be taxed. Generally, a mutual fund is a conduit for tax purposes—that is, the fund does not ordinarily pay income taxes, but its shareholders do. Interest, dividends, gains, and losses are generally passed through to shareholders in a fund in the form of dividends and capital gains distributions. As a shareholder, you are liable for any taxes due on these distributions. Consequently, it can matter enormously how those gains and losses are taxed.
>
> **Dividends declared during the last quarter of one year but not paid until the next year.** Often, a mutual fund will declare a dividend in October, November, or December of one year but not pay it until January of the following year. Nevertheless, you are treated as having received the dividend in the year in which it was declared.
>
> *Example.* A fund declares a dividend in December 2014 payable to shareholders owning stock on that date. This is known as the record date. The dividend is not paid until January 2015. You are treated as having received the dividend on December 31, 2014.

Community property states. If you and your spouse live in a community property state and receive a distribution that is community income, one-half of the distribution is considered received by each of you. If you file separate returns, each of you must generally report one-half of any taxable distribution. For more information about community property, see Publication 555, *Community Property*.

If the distribution is not considered community income under state law and you and your spouse file separate returns, each of you must report your separate taxable distributions.

Share certificate in two or more names. If two or more persons, such as you and your spouse, hold shares as joint tenants, tenants by the entirety, or tenants in common, distributions on those shares are considered received by each of you to the extent provided by local law.

Tax-exempt mutual fund. Distributions from a tax-exempt mutual fund (one that invests primarily in tax-exempt securities) may consist of ordinary dividends, capital gain distributions, undistributed capital gains, or return of capital like any other mutual fund. These distributions generally are treated the same as distributions from a regular mutual fund. Distributions designated as exempt-interest dividends are not taxable. (See *Exempt-Interest Dividends*, later.)

All other distributions generally follow the same rules as a regular mutual fund. Regardless of what type of mutual fund you have (whether regular or tax-exempt), when you dispose of your shares (sell, exchange, or redeem), you usually will have a taxable gain or a deductible loss to report.

For more information on figuring taxable gains and losses see *Sales, Exchanges, and Redemptions*, later. Also see chapter 16, *Reporting Gains and Losses*, for further information.

Ordinary Dividends

Ordinary (taxable) dividends are the most common type of distribution from a mutual fund. They are paid out of earnings and profits and are ordinary income to you. This means they are not capital gains. You can assume that any dividend you receive on common or preferred stock is an ordinary dividend unless the mutual fund tells you otherwise. Ordinary dividends will be reported in box 1a of the Form 1099-DIV or on a similar statement you receive from the mutual fund.

> ### TAXALERT
> Dividend distributions from a mutual fund, such as dividends earned from the fund's investment securities, are generally treated as a net short-term capital gain for purposes of applying the capital gain tax rates for both the regular tax and the alternative minimum tax. In order to be eligible for the lower capital gain (versus ordinary) income tax rate, the mutual fund must hold the underlying stock for a specified time period. Each year, the mutual fund will be required to report to each shareholder the amount of dividends that qualify for the favorable capital gain and/or ordinary income tax treatment.

Qualified Dividends

Qualified dividends are ordinary dividends subject to the same 0%, 15%, or 20% maximum tax rate that applies to net capital gain. They will be shown in box 1b of Form 1099-DIV you receive.

Qualified dividends are subject to the 20% rate if your regular marginal tax rate is 39.6%. If your regular marginal tax rate is 25%, 28%, or 33%, then the tax rate on qualified dividends is 15%. If your regular marginal tax rate is either 10% or 15%, then qualified dividends are subject to a 0% tax rate.

To qualify for the 0%, 15%, or 20% maximum rate, all of the following requirements must be met:

1. The dividends must have been paid by a U.S. corporation or a qualified foreign corporation. See chapter 1 of Publication 550 for the definition of a qualified foreign corporation.
2. The dividends are not of the type excluded by law from the definition of a qualified dividend. See chapter 1 of Publication 550 for a list of these types of dividends.
3. You must meet the holding period requirement (discussed next).

Holding Period

You must have held the stock for more than 60 days during the 121-day period that begins 60 days before the ex-dividend date. The ex-dividend date is the first date following the declaration of a dividend on which the buyer of a stock is not entitled to receive the next dividend payment. When counting the number of days you held the stock, include the day you disposed of the stock, but not the day you acquired it. See chapter 1 of Publication 550 for more information about qualified dividends.

> ### TAXALERT
> Mutual funds that pass through dividend income to their shareholders must meet the holding period test for the dividend-paying stocks that they hold in order for the amounts they pay out to be reported as qualified dividends on Form 1099-DIV. In addition, investors must then meet the holding period test for the shares owned in the mutual fund in order for the qualified dividends reported to them to be taxed at the lower rates. If investors do not meet the holding period test, they cannot claim the lower tax rate on the qualified dividend income reported to them on Form 1099-DIV and must classify the qualified dividends as ordinary dividends.

Capital Gain Distributions

Capital gain distributions (also called capital gain dividends) are paid to you or credited to your account by mutual funds. They will be shown in box 2a of the Form 1099-DIV (or similar statement) you receive from the mutual fund.

Report capital gain distributions as long-term capital gains, regardless of how long you owned your shares in the mutual fund.

Undistributed capital gains of mutual funds. Some mutual funds keep their long-term capital gains and pay tax on them. You must treat your share of these gains as distributions, even though you did not actually receive them. However, they are not included on Form 1099-DIV. Instead, they are reported to you in box 1a of Form 2439, Notice to Shareholder of Undistributed Long-Term Capital Gains.

Form 2439 will also show how much, if any, of the undistributed capital gains is:
- Unrecaptured Section 1250 gain (box 1b),
- Gain from qualified small business stock (Section 1202 gain, box 1c), or
- Collectibles (28%) gain (box 1d).

The tax paid on these gains by the mutual fund is shown in box 2 of Form 2439.

Basis adjustment. Increase your basis in your mutual fund by the difference between the gain you report and the credit you claim for the tax paid.

Exempt-Interest Dividends

Exempt-interest dividends you receive from a mutual fund or other regulated investment company are not included in your taxable income. Exempt-interest dividends should be shown in box 8 of Form 1099-INT.

Information reporting requirement. Although exempt-interest dividends are not taxable, you must show them on your tax return if you have to file a return. This is an information reporting requirement and does not change the exempt-interest dividends to taxable income. See *Reporting tax-exempt interest* under *How to Report Interest Income* in chapter 1 of Publication 550 for more information.

Alternative minimum tax treatment. Exempt-interest dividends paid from specified private activity bonds may be subject to the alternative minimum tax. The exempt-interest dividends subject to the alternative minimum tax should be shown in box 11 of Form 1099-DIV. See Form 6251 and its instructions for more information.

Nondividend Distributions

A nondividend distribution is a distribution that is not paid out of the earnings and profits of a mutual fund. You should receive a Form 1099-DIV or other statement showing you the nondividend distribution. On Form 1099-DIV, a nondividend distribution will be shown in box 3. If you do not receive such a statement, you report the distribution as an ordinary dividend.

Basis adjustment. A nondividend distribution reduces the basis of your mutual fund. It is not taxed until your basis in your shares is fully recovered. This nontaxable portion is also called a return of capital; it is a return of your investment in the company. If you buy mutual funds investments in different lots at different times, and you cannot definitely identify the shares subject to the nondividend distribution, reduce the basis of your earliest purchases first.

When the basis of your shares has been reduced to zero, report any additional nondividend distribution you receive as a capital gain. Whether you report it as a long-term or short-term capital gain depends on how long you have held the mutual fund. See chapter 4 of Publication 550, *Holding Period*, for more information.

> ### EXAMPLE
> In 2000, Jane Smith bought shares in ABC Mutual Fund for $10 a share. In 2001, she received a return of capital distribution of $2 a share, which reduces her basis in each share by $2 to an adjusted basis of $8. In 2002, Jane received a return of capital of $4 per share, reducing her basis in each share from $8 to $4. In 2014, the return of capital distribution from the mutual fund is $5 a share. Jane will report the $1 excess per share as a long-term capital gain on Form 8949 and Schedule D.

Reinvestment of Distributions. Most mutual funds permit shareholders to automatically reinvest distributions in more shares in the fund, instead of receiving cash. If you use your dividends to buy more shares at a price equal to its fair market value, you must still report the dividends as income. This means that reinvested ordinary dividends and capital gain distributions generally must be reported as income. Reinvested exempt-interest dividends generally are not reported as income. Reinvested return of capital distributions are reported as explained under *Nondividend Distributions*, earlier. See *Keeping Track of Your Basis*, later, to determine the basis of the additional shares.

Money Market Funds. Report amounts you receive from money market funds as dividend income. Money market funds are a type of mutual fund and should not be confused with bank money market accounts that pay interest.

How To Report

Generally, you can use either Form 1040 or Form 1040A to report your dividend income. Report the total of your ordinary dividends on line 9a of Form 1040 or Form 1040A. Report qualified dividends on line 9b.

If you receive capital gain distributions, you may be able to use Form 1040A or you may have to use Form 1040. See *Capital gain distributions*, later. If you receive nondividend distributions required to be reported as capital gains, you must use Form 1040. You cannot use Form 1040EZ if you receive any dividend income.

Table 39-1, *Reporting Mutual Fund Distributions on Form 1040 or Form 1040A*, explains where on Form 1040 or Form 1040A or its related schedules to report distributions from mutual funds.

> ### EXPLANATION
> If your only capital gains are from mutual funds distributions, you should report them on line 13 of Form 1040 or line 10 of Form 1040A and not on Form 8949 or Schedule D. In addition, check the box on line 13 of Form 1040 that you are not required to file Form 8949 or Schedule D. Make sure you calculate the tax using the table in the instructions.

Foreign tax deduction or credit. Some mutual funds invest in foreign securities or other instruments. Your mutual fund may choose to allow you to claim a deduction or credit for the taxes it paid to a foreign country or U.S. possession. The fund will notify you if this applies to you. The notice will include your share of the foreign taxes paid to each country or possession and the part the dividend derived from sources in each country or possession.

Table 39-1.   **Reporting Mutual Fund Distributions on Form 1040 or 1040A**

If you receive	AND	Then report the distribution on	
		Form 1040 . . .	Form 1040A . . .
ordinary dividends (Form 1099-DIV, box 1a)	• your total ordinary dividends received are $1,500 or less, and • you did not receive any ordinary dividends as a nominee	line 9a	line 9a
	• your total ordinary dividends received are more than $1,500, or • you received ordinary dividends as a nominee	• line 9a, and • Schedule B, line 5	• line 9a, and • Schedule B, line 5
qualified dividends (Form 1099-DIV, box 1b)		• line 9b, and • Qualified Dividends and Capital Gain Tax Worksheet, line 2, or Schedule D Tax Worksheet, line 2, whichever applies	• line 9b, and • Qualified Dividends and Capital Gain Tax Worksheet, line 2
capital gain distributions (Form 1099-DIV, box 2a)	you do not have to file Form 1040, Schedule D	• line 13, and • Qualified Dividends and Capital Gain Tax Worksheet, line 3	• line 10, and • Qualified Dividends and Capital Gain Tax Worksheet, line 3
	you have to file Form 1040, Schedule D (see Schedule D instructions for line 13)	Schedule D, line 13	you must use Form 1040; you cannot use Form 1040A
Section 1250, 1202, or collectibles gain (Form 1099-DIV, box 2b, 2c, or 2d)		Schedule D (see the Schedule D instructions)	you must use Form 1040; you cannot use Form 1040A
nondividend distributions (Form 1099-DIV, box 3)		generally not reported*	generally not reported*
exempt-interest dividends (Form 1099-DIV, box 10)		line 8b	line 8b
undistributed capital gains (Form 2439, boxes 1a-1d)		Schedule D (see the Schedule D instructions)	you must use Form 1040; you cannot use Form 1040A

*Report any amount in any excess of your basis in your mutual fund shares on Form 8949. Use Part II if you held the shares more than one year. Use Part I if you held your mutual fund shares 1 year or less.

EXPLANATION

In most cases, you must complete Form 1116 if you choose to claim the credit for income tax paid to a foreign country. You do not have to complete Form 1116 if your total foreign taxes paid are $300 or less for the year ($600 if married filing jointly). You can claim the credit for the full amount of the taxes paid as long as your foreign income is all passive (e.g., interest, dividends, etc.). Under certain circumstances, however, it may be to your benefit to treat the tax as an itemized deduction on Schedule A (Form 1040).

For a discussion of the foreign tax credit and whether you should claim the credit or a tax deduction, see chapter 23, *Taxes you may deduct*.

Sales, Exchanges, and Redemptions

When you sell or exchange your mutual fund shares, or if they are redeemed (a redemption), you will generally have a taxable gain or a deductible loss. This also applies to shares of a tax-exempt mutual fund. Sales, exchanges, and redemptions are all treated as sales of capital assets. The amount of the gain or loss is the difference between your adjusted basis (defined later) in the shares and the amount you realize from the sale, exchange, or redemption.

In general, a sale is a transfer of shares for money only. An exchange is a transfer of shares in return for other shares. A redemption occurs when a fund reacquires its shares from you in exchange for money or other property.

TAXORGANIZER

When there is a sale, exchange, or redemption of your shares in a fund, keep the confirmation statement you receive. The statement shows the price you received for the shares and other information you need to report gain or loss on your return. Although brokers are required to track adjusted basis for mutual fund shares acquired after December 31, 2011, it is important to retain confirmation statements for all shares acquired prior to that date.

TAXSAVER

Exchanging funds in the same family. You will incur a taxable capital gain or loss when you exchange shares of one fund for shares in another, regardless of whether the new fund is in the same fund family. So, for example, if you exchange shares in ABC Growth Fund for shares in ABC Technology Fund, you will have to recognize a capital gain or loss. Any service fee charged for the exchange may be added to your basis of the shares you acquired.

You will not have to recognize a capital gain or loss, however, if the shares in one mutual fund are converted to the shares of another pursuant to a tax-free merger of the two funds, or if the redemption of your shares is treated as a dividend.

TAXORGANIZER

Information returns. If you sold your mutual fund shares through a broker during the year, you should receive, for each sale, a Form 1099-B, Proceeds From Broker and Barter Exchange Transactions, or substitute statement, from the broker. You should receive the statement by February 15 of the next year. It will show the gross proceeds from the sale. The IRS will also get a copy of Form 1099-B from the broker.

Use Form 1099-B (or substitute statement received from your broker) to complete Form 8949. If you sold a covered security in 2014, your broker will send you a Form 1099-B (or substitute statement) that shows your basis. This will help you complete Form 8949. Generally, a covered security is a security you acquired after 2010, with certain exceptions explained in the 2014 Instructions for Schedule D.

Taxpayer identification number. You must give the broker your correct taxpayer identification number (TIN). Generally, an individual will use his or her social security number as the TIN. If you do not provide your TIN, your broker is required to withhold tax at a rate of 28% on the gross proceeds of a transaction, and you may be penalized.

TAXPLANNER

Basis is a way of measuring your investment in property for tax purposes. You must know the basis of your property to determine whether you have a gain or loss on its sale of other disposition.

Mutual fund shares you buy normally have an original basis equal to its cost. If you obtain property in some way other than buying it, such as by gift or inheritance, its fair market value at the time you received it may be important in figuring the basis.

Keeping Track of Your Basis

Original basis. As explained in the following paragraphs, original basis depends on how you acquired your shares.

Adjusted basis. As described later under *Adjusted Basis*, your original basis is adjusted (increased or decreased) by certain events. You must keep accurate records of all events that affect basis so you can figure the proper amount of gain or loss.

Shares Acquired by Purchase

The original basis of mutual fund shares you bought is usually their cost or purchase price. The purchase price usually includes any commissions or load charges paid for the purchase.

Commissions and load charges. The fees and charges you pay to acquire or redeem shares of a mutual fund are not deductible. You can usually add acquisition fees and charges to your cost of the shares and thereby increase your basis. A fee paid to redeem the shares is usually a reduction in the redemption price (sales price).

You cannot add your entire acquisition fee or load charge to the cost of mutual fund shares if *all* of the following conditions apply.

1. You get a reinvestment right because of the purchase of the shares or the payment of the fee or charge.
2. You dispose of the shares within 90 days of the purchase date.
3. You acquire new shares in the same mutual fund or another mutual fund, for which the fee or charge is reduced or waived because of the reinvestment right you got when you acquired the original shares.

The amount of the original fee or charge in excess of the reduction in (3) is added to the cost of the original shares. The rest of the original fee or charge is added to the cost basis of the new shares (unless all three conditions above apply to the purchase of the new shares).

Shares Acquired by Reinvestment

Reinvestment right. This is the right to acquire mutual fund shares in the same or another mutual fund without paying a fee or load charge, or by paying a reduced fee or load charge.

The original cost basis of mutual fund shares you acquire by reinvesting your distributions is the amount of the distributions used to purchase each full or fractional share. This rule applies even if the distribution is an exempt-interest dividend that you do not report as income.

TAXORGANIZER

Dividend reinvestment plan. If you participate in a dividend reinvestment plan, you should keep a record of the dividends and of the shares purchased with the reinvestment. The reinvested dividends are part of your cost basis for the shares. You will need these records to figure your cost basis when you sell all or some of your shares. See *Identifying the Shares Sold*, later in this chapter.

Shares Acquired by Gift or Inheritance

Mutual fund shares received as a gift. If you receive a gift of mutual fund shares, your basis is determined by the donor's basis (or fair market value of the shares if this is less than the donor's basis). Your holding period is considered to have started on the same day that the donor's holding period started.

TAXALERT

For gifted mutual fund and DRP shares, a broker is required to report all covered securities to another broker in a written statement with all necessary information required for the receiving broker to meet basis reporting requirements. Mutual fund and DRP shares purchased or acquired on or after January 1, 2012, are covered securities.

TAXALERT

Inherited mutual fund shares. If you inherited mutual fund shares prior to 2010 or after 2010, your basis in the shares is:

1. The fair market value at the date of the decedent's death (or the alternate valuation date), or
2. The decedent's adjusted basis where the decedent received the shares as a gift in the year prior to the decedent's death.

This is known as "stepped-up basis." You are considered to have held the shares for more than 1 year (even if you disposed of the shares within 1 year after the decedent's death). Report the sale of mutual fund shares inherited before or after 2010 on Form 8949, Part II, line 3 and write "Inherited" in column (c) instead of the date you acquired the shares.

On the other hand, mutual fund shares acquired from a decedent who died in 2010 do not have an automatic increase in basis. Your basis will depend on whether or not the executor of the decedent's estate elected to have the estate tax apply to the decedent's estate. If the estate tax applied, then the shares you inherited qualify for the automatic step up in basis. If the executor chose not to have the estate tax apply, then your basis in the inherited shares is generally equal to the lesser of the fair market value of the property on the date of the decedent's death or the decedent's adjusted basis in the property. This is known as "carryover basis." If carryover basis applies, the executor may have also elected to make additional adjustments that could have increased the amount of basis in the shares you inherited. See *Property inherited from a decedent who died during 2010* in chapter 13, *Basis of property*.

Adjusted Basis

Addition to basis. Increase the basis in your shares by the difference between the amount of undistributed capital gain you include in income and the tax considered paid by you on that income.

The mutual fund reports the amount of your undistributed capital gain in box 1a of Form 2439 and any tax paid by the mutual fund in box 2. You should keep Copy C of all Forms 2439 to show increases in the basis of your shares.

Reduction of basis. You must reduce your basis in your shares by any nondividend distributions that you receive from the fund. The mutual fund reports the amount of any nondividend distributions on Form 1099-DIV, box 3. You should keep the form to show the decrease in the basis of your shares.

Basis cannot go below zero. Your basis cannot be reduced below zero. If your basis is zero, you must report the nondividend distribution on your tax return as a capital gain. Report this capital gain on Schedule D (Form 1040). Whether it is a long-term or short-term capital gain depends on how long you held the shares.

No reduction of basis. You do not reduce your basis for distributions from the fund that are exempt-interest dividends.

Identifying the Shares Sold

To figure your gain or loss when you dispose of mutual fund shares, you need to determine which shares were sold and the basis of those shares. If your shares in a mutual fund were acquired all on the same day and for the same price, figuring their basis is not difficult. However, shares are generally acquired at various times, in various quantities, and at various prices. Therefore, figuring your basis can be more difficult. You can choose to use either a cost basis or an average basis to figure your gain or loss. See Table 39-2, *Choosing a Basis Method*.

Table 39-2. **Choosing a Basis Method**

Basis Method	Advantages/Disadvantages
Specific identification	The most flexible way to determine your gains and losses. But there are important restrictions governing its use.
FIFO (first-in, first-out)	The simplest approach. But it may mean a large gain if your shares have appreciated significantly and you are redeeming only part of your account.
Average cost	The middle ground. A more modest tax burden than the FIFO method but more tedious calculations if you sell shares frequently.

Cost Basis
- You can figure your gain or loss using a cost basis only if you did not previously use an average basis for sale, exchange, or redemption of other shares in the same mutual fund. To figure cost basis, you can choose one of the following methods.
- Specific share identification, or
- First-in, first-out (FIFO)

> **TAXALERT**
> The IRS eliminated the average cost (double category) method for tracking basis effective April 1, 2011. Taxpayers who formerly used the double category method, must re-compute their basis as of April 1, 2011, by averaging the basis of all identical shares in an account regardless of holding period. Taxpayers must use the single category method or another elected method prospectively.

> **TAXALERT**
> For mutual fund and DRP shares acquired on or after January 1, 2012, financial institutions use their default method to determine adjusted basis unless the taxpayer selects another method. A taxpayer must notify their broker in writing if they wish to use another approved method.

It is important to remember that any mutual funds acquired before January 1, 2012, will be treated as a separate account from any mutual fund acquired on or after January 1, 2012. Therefore, if the average basis method has been elected for shares acquired after January 1, 2012, the average basis must be computed without regard to any shares acquired before January 1, 2012. A mutual fund company has the ability to elect on a shareholder-by-shareholder basis to treat all mutual fund shares held by the customer as covered securities without regard to when the securities were purchased. If this election applies, the average basis of a customer's mutual fund shares will be determined by taking into account all shares before, on, or after January 1, 2012.

Specific share identification. If you can adequately identify the shares you sold, you can use the adjusted basis of those particular shares to figure your gain or loss.

You will adequately identify your mutual fund shares, even if you bought the shares in different lots at various prices and times, if you:
1. Specify to your broker or other agent the particular shares to be sold or transferred at the time of the sale or transfer, and
2. Receive confirmation in writing from your broker or other agent within a reasonable time of your specification of the particular shares sold or transferred.

You continue to have the burden of proving your basis in the specified shares at the time of sale or transfer.

First-in, first-out (FIFO). If the shares were acquired at different times or at different prices and you cannot identify which shares you sold, use the basis of the shares you acquired first as the basis of the shares sold. In other words, the oldest shares still available are considered sold first. You should keep a separate record of each purchase and any dispositions of the shares until all shares purchased at the same time have been disposed of completely. Table 39-3, *How to Figure Basis of Shares Sold*, illustrates the use of the FIFO method to figure the cost basis of shares sold, compared with the use of the average basis method (discussed next).

Average Basis
You can figure your gain or loss using an average basis only if you acquired identical shares at various times and prices, or you acquired the shares after December 31, 2010, in connection with a dividend reinvestment plan, and you left the shares on deposit in an account handled by a custodian or agent who acquires or redeems those shares.

> **TAXPLANNER**
> Average basis is determined by averaging the basis of all shares of identical shares in an account regardless of how long you have held the shares. However, shares of mutual funds in a dividend reinvestment plan are not identical to shares of mutual funds with the same CUSIP number that are not in a dividend reinvestment plan. The basis of each share of identical mutual fund in the account is the aggregate basis of all shares of that mutual fund in the account divided by the aggregate number of shares.

Transition rule from double-category method. You may no longer use the double-category method for figuring your average basis. If you were using the double-category method for stock you acquired before April 1, 2011, and you sell, exchange, or otherwise dispose of that stock on or after April 1, 2011, you must figure the average basis of this stock by averaging together all identical shares of stock in the account on April 1, 2011, regardless of the holding period.

Election of average basis method for covered securities. To make the election to use the average basis method for your covered securities, you must send written notice to the custodian or agent who keeps the account. The written notice can be made electronically. You must also notify your broker that you have made the election. Generally, a covered security is a security you acquired after 2010, with certain exceptions explained in the 2014 Instructions for Schedule D.

You can make the election to use the average basis method at any time. The election will be effective for sales or other dispositions of stocks that occur after you notify the custodian or agent of your election. Your election must identify each account with that custodian or agent and each stock in that account to which the election applies. The election can also indicate that it applies to all accounts with a custodian or agent, including accounts you later establish with the custodian or agent.

Election of average basis method for noncovered securities. For noncovered securities, you elect to use the average basis method on your income tax return for the first taxable year that the election applies. You make the election by showing on your return that you used the average basis method in reporting gain or loss on the sale or other disposition.

Revoking the average basis method election. You can revoke an election to use the average basis method for your covered securities by sending written notice to the custodian or agent holding the stock for which you want to revoke the election. The election must generally be revoked by the earlier of 1 year after you make the election or the date of the first sale, transfer, or disposition of the stock following the election. The revocation applies to all the stock you hold in an account that is identical to the shares of stock for which you are revoking the election. After revoking your election, your basis in the shares of stock to which the revocation applies is the basis before averaging.

Beginning with shares acquired after December 31, 2011, a taxpayer may elect different cost-reporting methods for the same mutual fund shares held in different accounts with different brokers. For example, a taxpayer may elect to use specific identification in one account with one broker and the average method in another account with another broker, although the underlying mutual fund shares are identical. In addition, a taxpayer may make one election with a financial institution to cover all eligible accounts and future accounts. The election statement must clearly identify each account to which the election applies.

TAXALERT

Taxpayers may use the average method for shares acquired after December 31, 2010, through a DRP provided that at least 10% of every dividend paid is invested in identical stock. A DRP may also average the basis of stock acquired by reinvesting distributions that are not considered dividends such as capital gain distributions, nontaxable returns of capital, and cash in lieu of dividends.

EXAMPLE

You own two accounts in the aggressive fund issued by Company XYZ. You also own 200 shares of the bond fund issued by Company XYZ. If you elect to use average basis for the first account of the aggressive fund, you must use average basis for the second account. However, you may use cost basis for the bond fund.

Average basis method illustrated. Table 39-3 illustrates the average basis method of shares sold, compared with the use of the FIFO method to figure cost basis (discussed earlier).

Even though you include all unsold shares of identical stock in an account to compute average basis, you may have both short-term and long-term gains or losses when you sell these shares. To determine your holding period, the shares disposed of are considered to be those acquired first.

Tip

You may be able to find the average basis of your shares from information provided by the fund.

Table 39-3. **How to Figure Basis of Shares Sold**

This is an example showing two different ways to figure basis. It compares the cost basis using the FIFO method and the average basis method.

Date	Action	Share Price	No. of Shares	Total Shares Owned
02/04/13	Invest $4,000	$25	160	160
08/02/13	Invest $4,800	$20	240	400
12/13/13	Reinvest $300 dividend	$30	10	410
09/03/14	Sell $6,720	$32	210	200
COST BASIS (FIFO)	To figure the basis of the 210 shares sold on 09/03/14, use the share price of the first 210 shares you bought, namely, the 160 shares you purchased on 02/04/13 and 50 of those purchased on 08/02/13. $4,000 (cost of 160 shares on 02/04/13) + $1,000 (cost of 50 shares on 08/02/13) **Basis** = $5,000			
AVERAGE BASIS	To figure the basis of the 210 shares sold on 09/03/14, use the average basis of all 410 shares owned on 09/03/14. $9,100 (cost of 410 shares) ÷ 410 (number of shares) $22.20 (average basis per share) $22.20 × 210 **Basis** = $4,662			

EXAMPLE

You bought 400 identical shares in the LJO Mutual Fund: 200 shares on May 10, 2013, and 200 shares on May 9, 2014. On November 7, 2014, you sold 300 shares. The basis of all 300 shares sold is the same, but you held 200 shares for more than 1 year, so your gain or loss on those shares is long term. You held 100 shares for 1 year or less, so your gain or loss on those shares is short term.

Remaining shares. The average basis of the shares you still hold after a sale of some of your shares is the same as the average basis of the shares sold. The next time you make a sale, your average basis will still be the same, unless you have acquired additional shares (or have made a subsequent adjustment to basis).

TAXALERT

Shares received as gift. If your account includes shares that you received by gift, and the fair market value of the shares at the time of the gift was not more than the donor's basis, special rules apply. You cannot choose to use the average basis for the account unless you state in writing that you will treat the basis of the gift shares as the FMV at the time you acquire the shares. You must provide this written statement when you make the election to use the average basis method, as described under *Election of average basis method for covered securities* and *Election of average basis method for non-covered securities*, earlier, or when you transfer the gift shares to an account for which you have made the average basis method election, whichever is later. The statement must be effective for any gift shares identical to the gift shares to which the average basis method election applies that you acquire at any time and must remain in effect as long as the election remains in effect.

Gains and Losses

You figure gain or loss on the disposition of your shares by comparing the amount you realize with the adjusted basis of your shares. If the amount you realize is more than the adjusted basis of the shares, you have a gain. If the amount you realize is less than the adjusted basis of the shares, you have a loss.

Amount you realize. The amount you realize from a disposition of your shares is the money and value of any property you receive for the shares disposed of, minus your expenses of sale (such as redemption fees, sales commissions, sales charges, or exit fees).

Adjusted basis. Adjusted basis is explained under _Keeping Track of Your Basis_, earlier.

TAXALERT

Reporting information from Form 1099-B. If you sold property, through a broker, you should receive Form 1099-B or substitute statement from the broker. Use the Form 1099-B or substitute statement to complete Form 8949.

Report the gross proceeds shown in box 2 of Form 1099-B as the sales price in column (e) of either Part I, line 1, or Part II, line 3, of Form 8949, whichever applies. However, if the broker advises you, in box 2 of Form 1099-B, that gross proceeds (sales price) less commissions and option premiums were reported to the IRS, enter that net sales price in column (e) of either Part I, line 1, or Part II, line 3, of Form 8949, whichever applies.

Include in column (g) any expense of sale, such as broker's fees, commissions, state and local transfer taxes, and option premiums, unless you reported the net sales price in column (e). If you include an expense of sale in column (g), enter "O" in column (b).

All details on specific sales of mutual fund shares you made during the year are reported on Form 8949. Prior to 2011, such details were reported on Schedule D. You have to use a different copy of Form 8949 for each of the following conditions:

1. Basis was reported on Form 1099-B
2. Basis was NOT reported on Form 1099-B
3. Sale not reported on Form 1099-B

The totals from each Form 8949 flow to Schedule D and onward to Form 1040.

EXAMPLES

Example 1. Linda Jones sold 200 shares of Fund B for $5,000. She paid a $150 commission to the broker for handling the sale. Her Form 1099-B shows that the net sales proceeds, $4,850 ($5,000 – $150), were reported to the IRS. Report this amount in column (e) of Form 8949.

Example 2. Joe Green sold 100 shares of Fund KLM for $5,000. He paid a $50 commission to the broker for handling the sale. He bought the shares for $2,500. Joe's broker reported the gross proceeds of $5,000 to the IRS on Form 1099-B, so he must increase his basis in column (f) of Form 8949 to $2,550.

Holding Period

If you sold or traded mutual fund shares, you must determine your holding period. Your holding period determines whether any capital gain or loss was a short-term capital gain or loss or a long-term capital gain or loss.

Long-term or short-term. If you hold your shares more than one year, any capital gain or loss is a long-term capital gain or loss. If you hold your shares one year or less, any capital gain or loss is a short-term capital gain or loss.

To determine how long you held your shares, begin counting on the date after the day you acquired the property. The day you disposed of the property is part of your holding period.

EXAMPLE

Assume Lori Hill bought mutual fund shares on April 1, 2013, and sold it on April 1, 2014. Her holding period is not more than one year and, therefore she has a short-term capital gain or loss. If Lori sold the shares on April 2, 2014, her holding period is more than one year, and any gain or loss she recognized is treated as long-term.

Mutual fund shares received as a gift. If you receive a gift of mutual fund shares and your basis is determined by the donor's adjusted basis, your holding period is considered to have started on the same day that the donor's holding period started. If your basis is determined by the fair market value of the property, your holding period starts on the day after the date of the gift.

Loss on mutual fund held 6 months or less. If you hold stock in a mutual fund (or other regulated investment company) for 6 months or less and then sell it at a loss (other than under a periodic liquidation plan), special rules may apply.

Capital gain distributions received. The loss (after reduction for any exempt-interest dividends you received, as explained later) is treated as a long-term capital loss up to the total of any capital gain distributions you received and your share of any undistributed capital gains. Any remaining loss is short-term capital loss.

Reinvested distributions. If your dividends and capital gain distributions are reinvested in new shares, the holding period of each new share begins the day after that share was purchased. Therefore, if you sell both the new shares and the original shares, you might have both short-term and long-term gains and losses.

How to Figure Gains and Losses on Form 8949 and Schedule D

Separate your short-term gains and losses from your long-term gains and losses on all the mutual fund shares and other capital assets you disposed of during the year. Then determine your net short-term gain or loss and your net long-term gain or loss.

EXPLANATION

Net capital loss. If you have a net capital loss, your allowable capital loss deduction is the smaller of:
1. $3,000 ($1,500 if you are married and filing a separate return)
2. Your net capital loss

Enter your allowable loss on line 13 of Form 1040.

Example 1. Margaret has capital gains and losses for the year as follows:

	Short-term	Long-term
Gains	$700	$400
Losses	($800)	($2,000)

Margaret's deductible capital loss is $1,700, which she figures as follows:

Short-term capital losses	($800)
Subtract short-term capital gains	$700
Net short-term capital loss	($100)
Long-term capital losses	($2,000)
Subtract long-term capital gains	$400
Net long-term capital loss	($1,600)
Deductible capital loss	($1,700)

Example 2. Art and Karen file a joint return. Their capital gains and losses for the year are as follows:

Net short-term capital gain	$450
Net long-term capital loss	($5,600)
Deductible capital loss	($3,000)

Their net capital loss is $5,150 ($5,600 − $450). Because their net capital loss exceeds $3,000, the amount they can deduct for the current year is limited to $3,000; however, the capital loss carryover is $2,150.

Capital Losses

If your capital losses are more than your capital gains, you can claim a capital loss deduction. Report the deduction on line 13 of Form 1040, enclosed in parentheses.

Limit on deduction. Your allowable capital loss deduction, figured on Schedule D, is the lesser of:

$3,000 ($1,500 if you are married and file a separate return), or

Your total net loss as shown on line 16 of Schedule D.

You can use your total net loss to reduce your income dollar for dollar, up to the $3,000 limit.

Capital loss carryover. If you have a total net loss on line 16 of Schedule D that is more than the yearly limit on capital loss deductions, you can carry over the unused part to the next year and treat it as if you had incurred it in that next year. If part of the loss is still unused, you can carry it over to later years until it is completely used up.

When you figure the amount of any capital loss carryover to the next year, you must take the current year's allowable deduction into account, whether or not you claimed it and whether or not you filed a return for the current year.

When you carry over a loss, it remains long term or short term. A long-term capital loss you carry over to the next tax year will reduce that year's long-term capital gains before it reduces that year's short-term capital gains.

Figuring your carryover. The amount of your capital loss carryover is the amount of your total net loss that is more than the lesser of:

Your allowable capital loss deduction for the year, or

Your taxable income increased by your allowable capital loss deduction for the year and your deduction for personal exemptions.

If your deductions are more than your gross income for the tax year, use your negative taxable income in computing the amount in item (2).

Use the Capital Loss Carryover Worksheet at the end of chapter 16, *Reporting Gains and Losses*, to figure your capital loss carryover.

EXPLANATION

Bob and Gloria sold securities in 2014. The sales resulted in a capital loss of $7,000. They had no other capital transactions. Their taxable income was $26,000. On their joint 2014 return, they can deduct $3,000. The unused part of the loss, $4,000 ($7,000 − $3,000), can be carried over to 2015.

If their capital loss had been $2,000, their capital loss deduction would have been $2,000. They would have no carryover.

TAXSAVER

Use short-term losses first. When you figure your capital loss carryover, use your short-term capital losses first, even if you incurred them after a long-term capital loss. If you have not reached the limit on the capital loss deduction after using the short-term capital losses, use the long-term capital losses until you reach the limit.

Decedent's capital loss. A capital loss sustained by a decedent during his or her last tax year (or carried over to that year from an earlier year) can be deducted only on the final income tax return filed for the decedent. The capital loss limits discussed earlier still apply in this situation. The decedent's estate cannot deduct any of the loss or carry it over to following years.

Joint and separate returns. If you and your spouse once filed separate returns and are now filing a joint return, combine your separate capital loss carryovers. However, if you and your spouse once filed a joint return and are now filing separate returns, any capital loss carryover from the joint return can be deducted only on the return of the spouse who actually had the loss.

Investment Expenses

You can generally deduct the expenses of producing investment income. These include expenses for investment counseling and advice, legal and accounting fees, and investment newsletters. These expenses are deductible as miscellaneous itemized deductions to the extent that they exceed 2% of your adjusted gross income. See chapter 29 for further information.

TAXALERT

Publicly offered mutual funds. Most mutual funds are publicly offered. These mutual funds, generally, are traded on an established securities exchange. These funds do not pass investment expenses through to you. Instead, the dividend income they report to you in box 1a of Form 1099-DIV is already reduced by your share of investment expenses. As a result, you cannot deduct the expenses on your return. Include the amount from box 1a of Form 1099-DIV in your income.

Nonpublicly offered mutual funds. If you own shares in a nonpublicly offered mutual fund during the year, you can deduct your share of the investment expenses on your Schedule A (Form 1040) as a miscellaneous itemized deduction to the extent your miscellaneous deduction exceeds 2% of your adjusted gross income. Your share of the expenses will be shown in box 5 of Form 1099-DIV. A nonpublicly offered mutual fund is one that:
1. Is not continuously offered pursuant to a public offering.
2. Is not regularly traded on an established securities market.
3. Is not held by at least 500 persons at all times during the tax year.

Contact your mutual fund if you are not sure whether it is nonpublicly offered.

TAXSAVER

If you own shares in a publicly offered mutual fund, you do not have to pay tax on your share of the fund's expenses. There should be no entry in box 5 of Form 1099-DIV. However, expenses of a nonpublicly offered fund may be subject to tax. You should consult your tax advisor for details.

Expenses allocable to exempt-interest dividends. You cannot deduct expenses that are for the collection or production of exempt-interest dividends. Expenses must be allocated if they were partly for both taxable and tax-exempt income. One accepted method for allocating expenses is to divide them in the same proportion that your tax-exempt income from the mutual fund is to your total income from the fund.

Limit on Investment Interest Expense
The amount you can deduct as an investment interest expense may be limited. See chapter 24, *Interest Expense*.

Chapter 40

What to do if you employ domestic help

ey.com/EYTaxGuide

Note

ey.com/EYTaxGuide
Ernst & Young LLP will update the *EY Tax Guide 2015* website with relevant taxpayer information as it becomes available. You can also sign up for email alerts to let you know when changes have been made.

Introduction

If you have a domestic helper who qualifies as your employee, you may have to pay social security and Medicare taxes, as well as federal and state unemployment taxes. You may also have to withhold federal income tax. In general, a person who works in or around your house qualifies as your employee if you control his or her working conditions—pay, work schedule, conduct, and appearance. This chapter spells out what federal tax rules govern domestic help and advises you on how to comply with them.

Both you and your employee are subject to social security and Medicare taxes (together known as FICA) if you pay your employee $1,900 or more during any calendar year. If you have paid any employee $1,000 or more in any calendar quarter during the current or preceding year, you are also subject to federal unemployment taxes (called FUTA) on every employee during the current year.

Your employee may ask you to withhold federal income tax from compensation. If you agree, you must withhold the proper amount from each paycheck. This withholding must be remitted to the IRS at specified intervals.

Use Schedule H (Form 1040) to compute federal taxes for your household employees and attach it to your personal income tax return.

If you pay your income taxes late, you may owe penalties and interest on the taxes described in this chapter as well as on your personal income taxes.

This chapter only discusses the federal taxes applying to household employees. There may be additional taxes due depending on the state and city where the services are performed.

You may also be subject to federal and/or state rules regarding employees' pay and benefits. For example, state laws may dictate the maximum number of hours an employee may work, the amount to be paid for overtime, and/or the number of days of paid vacation and holidays to which the employee is entitled.

Even if your domestic employee does not have legal authorization to work in the United States, you are still liable for the payroll taxes discussed in this chapter.

Table 40-1. **Household Employer's Checklist**

You may need to do the following things when you have a household employee.

When you hire a household employee:	• Find out if the person can legally work in the United States. • Find out if you need to pay state taxes.
When you pay your household employee:	• Withhold social security and Medicare taxes. • Withhold federal income tax. • Decide how you will make tax payments. • Keep records.
By February 2, 2015:	• Get an employer identification number (EIN). • Give your employee Copies B, C, and 2 of Form W-2, Wage and Tax Statement.
By March 2, 2015 (March 31, 2015, if you file Form W-2 electronically):	• Send Copy A of Form W-2 to the Social Security Administration (SSA).
By April 15, 2015:	• File Schedule H (Form 1040), Household Employment Taxes, with your 2014 federal income tax return (Form 1040, 1040NR, 1040-SS, or Form 1041). If you do not have to file a return, file Schedule H by itself.

TAXPLANNER

The rules in this chapter relate to someone who works for you in the United States or who is a U.S. citizen or green card holder. If you are employing someone to work outside of the United States, you will need to investigate your responsibilities under the laws of that country.

Reminder

Social security and Medicare wage threshold is $1,900. The social security and Medicare wage threshold for household employees is $1,900 for 2014. This means that if you pay a household employee cash wages of less than $1,900 in 2014, you do not have to report and pay social security and Medicare taxes on that employee's 2014 wages. For more information, see *Social Security and Medicare Wages* in Publication 926, *Household Employer's Guide (For Wages Paid in 2014)*.

Employment Taxes for Household Employers

If you pay someone to come to your home and care for it, your dependent, or your spouse, you may be a household employer. If you are a household employer, you will need an employer identification number (EIN) and you may have to pay employment taxes. If the individuals who work in your home are self-employed, you are not liable for any of the taxes discussed in this section. Self-employed persons who are in business for themselves are not household employees. Usually, you are not a household employer if the person who cares for your dependent or spouse does so at his or her home or place of business.

EXCEPTION

Employees under the age of 18 at any time during the year are exempt from social security and Medicare taxes, regardless of how much they earn, provided household services are not their main job. If the employee is a student, providing household services is not considered to be his or her principal occupation.

TAXPLANNER

Paying the "nanny" tax. Employers are required to report the social security, Medicare, and federal unemployment taxes due on domestic workers' wages on the employers' Form 1040, Schedule H. The taxes can be paid through the employers' estimated tax payments. Alternatively, the employer could increase federal withholding on his or her own wages and pay these taxes on the domestic worker in that manner.

If you use a placement agency that exercises control over what work is done and how it will be done by a babysitter or companion who works in your home, that person is not your employee. This control could include providing rules of conduct and appearance and requiring regular reports. In this case, you do not have to pay employment taxes. But, if an agency merely gives you a list of sitters and you hire one from that list, the sitter may be your employee.

If you have a household employee you may be subject to:

1. Social security and Medicare taxes,
2. Federal unemployment tax, and
3. Federal income tax withholding.

Social security and Medicare taxes are generally withheld from the employee's pay and matched by the employer. Federal unemployment (FUTA) tax is paid by the employer only and provides for payments of unemployment compensation to workers who have lost their jobs. Federal income tax is withheld from the employee's total pay if the employee asks you to do so and you agree.

For more information on a household employer's tax responsibilities, see Publication 926 and Schedule H (Form 1040) and its instructions.

State employment tax. You may also have to pay state unemployment tax. Contact your state unemployment tax office for information. You should also find out whether you need to pay or collect other state employment taxes or carry workers' compensation and/or disability insurance. For a list of state unemployment tax agencies, visit the U.S. Department of Labor's website at *www.workforcesecurity.doleta.gov/unemploy/agencies.asp*.

Tax Breaks and Deductions You Can Use Checklist

Paying employment taxes. In most cases, you are required to collect and remit social security and Medicare taxes on wages paid to your domestic employee(s). Fortunately, the federal government allows you to make these payments along with your personal income tax payments—either through withholding or estimated taxes. You file Schedule H with your Form 1040 to report these amounts.

Are your employees working legally in the U.S.? Federal law requires you to verify that your new employees are eligible to work in the United States. You and your employee must complete USCIS (U.S. Citizenship and Immigration Services) Form I-9, Employment Eligibility Verification, and you should keep it for three years from the date of hire or one year from termination of employment, whichever is later. You can get Form I-9 at *www.uscis.gov*.

Federal employer identification number. If you employ someone to work in your home, you should apply for a federal employer identification number (EIN) to use when you file required forms. You can file for an EIN online. Go to *www.irs.gov* and enter keywords "Apply for an EIN Online" in the upper right-hand corner. For more information, see *Employer Identification Number* in this chapter.

EXPLANATION

You may be able to claim a child and dependent care credit for the expenses you incur for domestic help. See chapter 33, *Child and dependent care credit*, for more information.

Example

Janice is single and works to keep up a home for herself and her dependent father. Her adjusted gross income of $25,000 is entirely earned income. Her father was disabled and incapable of self-care for 6 months. To keep working, she paid a housekeeper $600 per month to care for her father, prepare lunch and dinner, and do housework. Her credit is as follows:

Total work-related expenses (6 × $600)	$3,600
Maximum allowable expenses	$3,000
Amount of credit (30% of $3,000)	$ 900

EXPLANATION

Employee or independent contractor? Whether or not a person who provides services in and around your house is your employee depends on the facts and circumstances of the situation. In general, a person is your employee if you control his or her working conditions and compensation. A person does not have to work for you full time to qualify as your employee.

Generally, workers are classified based on how they perform their work and their accountability for it. By definition, independent contractors are responsible for results, not how their tasks are accomplished. On the other hand, individuals who are instructed as to when, where, and how to complete their jobs would probably be considered employees. If you determine that your domestic helpers are employees, you must withhold and match social security and Medicare payments and may be subject to paying federal and state unemployment taxes as well.

To gain a better understanding of the distinction between an independent contractor and an employee, consider the person who mows your lawn. If the person works for an independent lawn service and is supervised by the lawn company that also provides its own equipment—all you provide is the grass—there's little question that the provider is an independent contractor. However, if a college student cuts your lawn using your mower, and you give specific instructions as to how and when to do the job, he or she will be considered your employee.

To enable you to determine whether a person is indeed an independent contractor, there are certain common indicators that can help. An independent contractor:

- Works for several homeowners
- Provides his or her own tools and supplies to perform the job
- Can bring in additional help if he or she deems necessary
- Determines how the results will be accomplished
- Is paid by the job, not by the hour
- Advertises his or her services
- May be fired at will
- Can set his or her own hours and leave when the job is completed

If you have reason to believe that a person is an independent contractor and not your employee, you should not withhold social security tax from his or her compensation. You may want to get a signed letter from this person indicating that he or she is an independent contractor and is responsible for his or her own employment taxes.

TAXPLANNER

Records you need. When you hire a household employee, make a record of that person's name and social security number exactly as it appears on his or her social security card. You will need this information when you remit social security, Medicare, federal unemployment, and withholding of federal income taxes.

An employee who does not have a social security number should apply for one using Form SS-5, Application for a Social Security Card. This form is available at all Social Security Administration offices, or on the Social Security Administration website at *www.socialsecurity.gov/online/ss-5.pdf*, as well as by calling 1-800-772-1213.

If your employee is not eligible to obtain a social security number, he or she may obtain an individual taxpayer identification number (ITIN) by filing Form W-7 with the IRS. The ITIN can be used on a tax return wherever a social security number should be used. You should note that the ITIN is for IRS records only. It does not change the employee's status with the USCIS or his or her entitlement to social security or other employment benefits.

Employer identification number (EIN). In order to pay federal taxes for your household employee, you will need an employer identification number (EIN). This is a nine-digit number issued by the IRS. It is not the same as your social security number. If you already have an EIN, use that number. If you do not have an EIN, you can apply for it online. Go to *www.irs.gov* and enter keywords "Apply for an EIN Online" in the upper right-hand corner. From this web page, you can access a web-based application that instantly processes requests and generates EINs in real time. Note that phone requests for domestic EIN numbers are no longer accepted. As of January 6, 2014, the IRS now refers all domestic EIN requests received by phone to the EIN Online Assistant. You can also apply for an EIN by fax or mailing in Form SS-4, Application for Employer Identification Number. Form SS-4 is available at *www.irs.gov/pub/irs-pdf/fss4.pdf*. If you choose to submit Form SS-4 you will need to send it to the IRS office listed in Table 40-2 for your location. If you need further information regarding the IRS process for issuing an EIN number, call or fax the IRS office in your area or refer to Publication 926, *Household Employer's Tax Guide*.

Social Security and Medicare Taxes (FICA)

If you pay a household employee cash wages of $1,900 or more during a calendar year, those wages are subject to social security and Medicare taxes. Cash wages include wages you pay by check or money order, but do not include the value of noncash items you give your household employee. Cash you give your employee in place of a noncash item, such as clothing or gifts, is included in cash wages. Payments in kind (meals, transportation, etc.) are not used to figure the $1,900 amount or to figure the taxes. Taxes are figured on all cash wage payments made to the employee during the year, regardless of when they were earned.

What is taxable compensation? Table 40-3 may help to clarify what is reportable income to your employee. Remember that state and local income tax and unemployment or disability and other employment tax rules may be different.

Family members. Social security and Medicare taxes do not apply to household services performed by your spouse or by your child under 21. However, social security and Medicare taxes apply to wages you pay your parents for household services if:

1. You are a surviving spouse or a divorced individual who hasn't remarried or have a spouse living in the home who has a mental or physical condition which results in the spouse's being incapable of caring for a child or stepchild for at least four continuous weeks in the quarter in which the service is performed; and
2. Your child or stepchild is living in the home; and
3. Your child or stepchild is under age 18 or has a mental or physical condition which requires the personal care of an adult for at least four continuous weeks in the calendar quarter in which the service is performed.

TAXALERT

If a person is an employee whom you pay a total of $1,900 or more per year, you have tax filing and payment responsibilities.

TAXALERT

Babysitters. If the babysitter watches your children in your house at the time you specify, IRS rulings conclude that the person is an employee. It's not enough to stop giving the sitter a ride home in an attempt to make him or her appear more independent. You would need to use sitters who watch children in their homes or other facilities during set business hours. Or you can rotate sitters to avoid paying anyone more than $1,900 per year. As previously noted, sitters under age 18 who are full-time students are exempt from social security and Medicare taxes.

Table 40-2.   IRS Offices for EIN Application

If your legal residence is located in:	Mail or Fax Form SS-4 to:
One of the 50 states or the District of Columbia	Internal Revenue Service Center Attn: EIN Operation Cincinnati, OH 45999 Fax-TIN: (859) 669-5760
If you have no legal residence, principal place of business, or principal office or agency in any state:	Internal Revenue Service Center Attn: EIN International Operation Cincinnati, OH 45999 Fax-TIN: (859) 669-5987

Paying the tax. You and your household employee each pay a share of the social security and Medicare taxes due on the employee's wages. For 2014, the social security tax rate applicable to your employee is 6.2% of wages received. The rate assessed to you as the employer contribution is an additional 6.2%. This combined tax rate of 12.4% applies only to the first $117,000 you paid each employee during calendar year 2014.

The Medicare tax rate is 1.45% for you and your employee each—a combined total of 2.9%. Under the Affordable Care Act (the comprehensive health care law that was passed in 2010 and upheld as constitutional by the U.S. Supreme Court in June 2012), higher income employees are subject to an additional 0.9% of Additional Medicare Tax on wages and other compensation over $200,000 for single filers and $250,000 for married taxpayers filing jointly ($125,000 if married filing separately). For married couples filing jointly, the additional tax is imposed on the combined wages of the employee and the employee's spouse. The 0.9% Additional Medicare Tax is imposed on the employee only; there is no employer share of Additional Medicare Tax. However the employer must withhold the additional 0.9% tax beginning in the pay period in which wages in excess of $200,000 are paid to an employee. For more information on Additional Medicare Tax, visit _irs.gov/Businesses/Small-Businesses-&-Self-Employed/Questions-and-Answers-for-the-Additional-Medicare-Tax_.

You must pay the total of these taxes (your employee's and your share) yourself if you do not deduct the employee's share from his or her wages. Any of the employee's share you pay is added income to the employee. This income must be included in box 1, _Wages, tips, other compensation_, on Form W-2, Wage and Tax Statement, but do not count it as cash wages for social security and Medicare purposes. You must also include the employee social security and Medicare taxes you pay in boxes 4 and 6 of the employee's Form W-2, even though the taxes were not actually withheld.

Table 40-3. **What Is Taxable Compensation?**

	Federal Income Tax	Social Security and Medicare (FICA)	Federal Unemployment Tax (FUTA)
Salary paid by cash, check, or other means	Yes	Yes	Yes
Cash bonus (overtime, holiday, etc.)	Yes	Yes	Yes
Cash gifts (holiday, birthday, wedding, etc.)	Yes	Yes	Yes
Gifts of property (holiday, birthday, etc.)[1]	Yes	Yes	Yes
Vacation Pay	Yes	Yes	Yes
Sign-on bonus	Yes	Yes	Yes
Value of meals & lodging on your premises as part of job and for your convenience	No	No	No
Car provided to employee for commutation	Yes	Yes	Yes
Car provided to employee to do work for you only	No	No	No
Cell phone[2]	Maybe	Maybe	Maybe
Value of public transit passes provided (up to $130 per month for 2014)[3]	No	No	No
Value of parking provided (up to $250 per month for 2014)	No	No	No
Insurance for employee's own car	Yes	Yes	Yes
Employee's medical insurance bills you pay	No	No	No
Uniforms you give to employee to wear on your premises	No	No	No
Cash uniform allowance	Yes	Yes	Yes
Value of vacation when nanny accompanies family to care for children	No	No	No
Employee's legal fees you pay	Yes	Yes	Yes
Employee's social security taxes you pay	Yes	No	Yes
Employee's income taxes you pay	Yes	Yes	Yes

[1] Taxable value is lesser of cost or fair market value. Certain gifts of nominal value may be excluded from income.

[2] See _Employer-provided cell phones_ later, for additional details.

[3] Payment of occasional transportation expense, if infrequent, reasonable in amount, and not based on hours worked, may be excluded from an employee's taxable wage. See De Minimis Transportation Benefits in Publication 15-B for more details.

TAXPLANNER

If you would rather pay your employee's share of social security and Medicare taxes without deducting it from wages, you may do so. Any portion you do pay, however, is added to the compensation to your employee, even though it does not constitute cash wages for social security and Medicare purposes. Although it may be easier if you pay your employee's share of social security and Medicare taxes, it does raise your cost. You should come to an agreement with your employee on this issue before he or she begins work.

Example. Meredith pays her full-time housekeeper a $15,000 salary. She also pays both the employer's share of the social security and Medicare taxes (7.65% of $15,000, or $1,147.50) and the employee's share (7.65% of $15,000, or $1,147.50). For federal income tax purposes, the housekeeper's total compensation for the year is $16,147.50 ($15,000 plus $1,147.50), even though only $15,000 is subject to social security and Medicare taxes.

TAXPLANNER

Employer-provided cell phones. Under guidance published by the IRS in 2011, when an employer provides an employee with a cell phone primarily for noncompensatory business reasons, the business and personal use of the cell phone is generally nontaxable to the employee. A common example of a noncompensatory business reason to provide a cell phone to a household employee might be the need to contact the employee at all times for work-related emergencies, such as the care and safety of a child or disabled person under the employee's care. This rule also applies to employer reimbursements of the employees' expenses for reasonable cell phone coverage as long as the reimbursement is done for noncompensatory business reasons.

This rule does not apply, however, to the compensatory provision of cell phones or reimbursements for cell phone use that are not primarily business related. In other words, if you provide a cell phone or reimburse cell phone expenses to your household employee in order to promote goodwill, boost morale, or attract a potential new employee, the reason for providing the benefit would be considered compensatory. Such arrangements are taxable cash or noncash income, depending on the way the benefit is provided to the employee.

These rules are complex. If you provide a cell phone or reimburse cell phone expenses to a household employee, see chapter 5, *Wages, salaries, and other earnings*, and Publication 15-B, *Employer's Tax Guide to Fringe Benefits*, for more information.

TAXPLANNER

If you and your employee agree that the employee will be responsible for his or her own share of the social security and Medicare taxes, you should also reach agreement on how it is to be paid. To minimize difficulties, you may want to start withholding immediately rather than wait until $1,900 has been earned each year. This avoids the problem of the employee having to pay you $145.35 (7.65% × $1,900) once the threshold has been met.

Federal Income Tax Withholding

If your household employee requests income tax withholding, and you agree, you must withhold an amount from each payment based on the information shown on Form W-4, Employee's Withholding Allowance Certificate, given to you by the employee. See chapter 5, *Wages, salaries, and other earnings*, for more information about Form W-4. Publication 15 (Circular E), *Employer's Tax Guide*, explains how to figure the amount to withhold.

TAXPLANNER

It is your decision whether or not to withhold income tax from your employee's compensation, even if withholding is requested by your employee. However, if you do withhold for an employee, everything that you pay your employee—whether cash or noncash—is income subject to withholding. Some of the more common forms of compensation for household employees are (1) salaries; (2) overtime and bonuses; (3) meals, unless provided in your home and for your convenience; and

(4) lodging, unless provided in your home, for your convenience, and as a condition of employment. As a general rule, if you have live-in domestic help, any meals and lodging you provide are not considered compensation. A car that you provide solely for use in transporting family members and doing household errands would not be considered compensation. However, a car provided to a domestic employee for his or her personal use (including getting to and from your house) would be considered income to him or her. Other forms of compensation include cash reimbursement for the employee's personal expenses, such as car insurance and vacation expenses. However, up to $130 per month in public transit passes and up to $250 per month for qualified parking can be provided to an employee without any federal tax effect. State tax laws may be different.

Any income tax withholding you pay for an employee without deducting it from the employee's wages is added income to the employee and subject to income, social security, and Medicare taxes.

Form W-4 and Publications 15 (which explains employer responsibilities and requirements), 15-A (which supplements and explains the Publication 15 information in greater detail), and 15-B (which explains the employment tax treatment of fringe benefits) can be requested by calling 1-800-TAX-FORM (1-800-829-3676) or downloaded at *www.irs.gov*.

TAXPLANNER

You can effectively receive the nonrefundable portion of the EIC through your paycheck by adjusting withholding, to the extent that you otherwise have positive tax liability.

Notice about the earned income credit (EIC). Copy B of the 2014 Form W-2, Wage and Tax Statement, has a statement about the EIC on the back. If you give your employee that copy by February 2, 2015, you do not have to give the employee any other notice about the EIC.

If you do not give your employee Copy B of the Form W-2, your notice about the EIC can be any of the following items.

1. A substitute Form W-2 with the same EIC information on the back of the employee's copy that is on Copy B of the Form W-2.
2. Notice 797, Possible Federal Tax Refund Due to the Earned Income Credit (EIC).
3. Your own written statement with the same wording as in Notice 797.

If a substitute Form W-2 is given on time but does not have the required EIC information, you must notify the employee within one week of the date the substitute Form W-2 is given. If Form W-2 is required but is not given on time, you must give the employee Notice 797 or your written statement about the 2014 EIC by February 2, 2015. If Form W-2 is not required, you must notify the employee by February 7, 2015.

You must give your household employee a notice about the EIC if you agree to withhold federal income tax from the employee's wages and the income tax withholding tables show that no tax should be withheld. Even if not required, you are encouraged to give the employee a notice about the EIC if his or her 2014 wages are less than $46,997 ($52,427 if married filing jointly).

You must notify any employees not having federal income tax withheld that they may be eligible for an income tax refund because of the earned income credit.

For more information about employment taxes, see Publication 926, *Household Employer's Tax Guide*.

Federal Unemployment Tax (FUTA)

Federal unemployment tax (FUTA) is for your employee's unemployment insurance. If you paid cash wages of $1,000 or more to household employees in any calendar quarter this year or last year, you are liable for FUTA for any employees you have this year. However, the tax does not apply to wages paid to your spouse, your parents, or your children under 21 years old.

Rate. The FUTA tax is 6.0% of your employee's FUTA wages. You may be able to take a credit of up to 5.4% against the FUTA tax, resulting in a net tax rate of 0.6%. Your credit for 2014 is limited unless you pay all the required contributions for 2014 to your state unemployment fund by April 15, 2015. The credit you can take for any contributions for 2014 that you pay after April 15, 2015, is limited to 90% of the credit that would have been allowable if the contributions were paid by April 15, 2015.

The tax is imposed on you as the employer. Unlike social security, Medicare, and federal income tax, federal unemployment tax is solely an employer's responsibility. It is an additional cost to you of having domestic help. You must not collect or deduct it from the wages of your employees.

When you hire a household employee, you should contact your state employment tax office to get information on how to file the state return and to get a state reporting number. The state will help you to figure the amount of tax you will pay the state. See the instructions to Schedule H for how to claim the credit.

Credit Reduction States. The 5.4% credit is reduced for wages paid in a credit reduction state (meaning that the states have not yet repaid loans they received from the federal government to pay unemployment claims). In 2013, 13 U.S. states and the U.S. Virgin Islands were designated by the U.S. Department of Labor as credit reduction states. The list of credit reduction states for 2014 has not yet been released, so it is unclear as of the date this book was published which states are affected. See the instructions for Schedule H (Form 1040) for additional information.

Example 1. Joaquin paid his housekeeper $3,000 in cash during the first quarter of 2014. He must pay federal unemployment tax (FUTA) for any employees he has during any part of 2014. Since he was liable for FUTA in 2014, any cash wages he pays to his employees in 2015 will also be subject to FUTA.

2014 Wages *for this employee* × FUTA rate	$3,000 × 6.0% = $ 180
Wages greater than $7,000 are not subject to FUTA	-0- = -0-
TOTAL FUTA TAX FOR 2014	$ 180
(before state unemployment credit)	

Example 2. Clement paid his housekeeper and sole employee $12,000 ($1,000 per month, paid monthly on the last day of each month) for all of 2014. Since FUTA is assessed only on the first $7,000 of cash compensation paid to each employee during the calendar year, Clement's FUTA liability (before any credit for state unemployment taxes) was $420.

2014 wages × the FUTA rate	$7,000 × 6.0% = $ 420
Wages greater than $7,000 are not subject to FUTA	-0- = -0-
TOTAL FUTA TAX FOR 2014	$ 420
(before state unemployment credit)	

Reporting and Paying Taxes on Wages Paid to Household Employees

Unless you own a business as a sole proprietor, you should report these taxes on Schedule H attached to your 2014 Form 1040. These taxes are added to your income taxes. The total must be paid during the course of the year. See chapter 4, *Tax withholding and estimated tax*.

If you are a sole proprietor who has non-household employees, you should be filing Form 940 (or 940-EZ) annually to report FUTA (unemployment taxes) and Form 941 quarterly (Form 944 annually for qualifying small businesses) to report and remit federal income tax and FICA (social security and Medicare) tax withholdings. The IRS gives sole proprietors the option of including withholdings and taxes paid for domestic employees with withholdings and taxes paid for non-domestic employees on Forms 940 and 941 or 944. Alternatively, sole proprietors can exclude domestic employees from Forms 940 and 941 or 944 and file Schedule H with their own income tax returns.

TAXALERT

The IRS notifies certain employers that they must file Form 944, Employer's ANNUAL Federal Tax Return, instead of Form 941, Employer's QUARTERLY Federal Tax Return. Form 944 is filed once a year, rather than quarterly as Form 941 is filed. Form 944 for calendar year 2014 will be due February 2, 2015. Employers that would otherwise be required to file Form 944 may opt out *for any reason*, if they want to file Form 941 quarterly instead of Form 944 annually. Complete details on the procedure for opting out of filing Form 944 are included in the Form 941 instructions, available at *www.irs.gov*. Employers who are required to file Form 944 have annual liability for social security, Medicare, and withheld income taxes of $1,000 or less. You cannot file Form 944 unless you have been notified by the IRS. However, if you believe you are eligible to file Form 944—and desire to do so in place of Form 941—you may opt in to filing Form 944 by contacting the IRS at 1-800-829-4933. If the IRS determines you are eligible to file Form 944, it will send you a written notice that your filing requirement has been changed. Note that you are ineligible to file Form 944 if you employ household employees only.

For more information about annual employment tax filing and deposit rules, see IRS Publication 15, Circular E, *Employer's Tax Guide*, available at *www.irs.gov*.

Whether or not you are a sole proprietor, once you withhold tax from an employee, you must remit the tax to the IRS. If you do not, you could be responsible for substantial fines and penalties.

Example. Paul and Irene Boyd employ Emily Whitney as a housekeeper and babysitter. Emily's weekly salary is $200, which is paid by Paul in cash each Friday. In addition, Irene pays Emily $50 for helping once a month on weekends when the Boyds entertain. Emily uses her own car to drive to and from the Boyd's home but is reimbursed weekly by Irene for gas to drive the children to school. Emily gives Irene a list of the actual miles driven and Irene pays her 56 cents per mile. Four times a year Paul pays $400 for Emily's medical insurance. Irene pays Emily's $300 vacation airfare in June and gives her a $500 bonus in December. Since Emily's annual compensation is expected to be over $1,900, the Boyds decide to deduct FICA from Emily's salary from the beginning of the year. Emily completes and provides to the Boyds a Form W-4. The Boyds agree to deduct income tax from Emily's compensation. Emily is a single person with no dependents. The Boyds will use the percentage method to calculate the federal withholding. See Publication 15, Circular E, *Employer's Tax Guide*, available at www.irs.gov, for instructions regarding the use of the percentage method and the 2014 Income Tax Withholding Tables. The state in which they reside has a flat income tax of 5% and total unemployment taxes of 9%–2% to be paid by Emily, and 7% to be paid by the Boyds on income up to $7,000. The Boyds' state of residence is not a credit reduction state for 2014.

Since Emily has provided documentation indicating how many miles were driven, for what purpose and when, and since the reimbursement is within the IRS guideline (the standard mileage rate is 56 cents per mile for business miles driven during 2014), Emily's reimbursement for gas is not taxable income to her. Also, since Emily does not have the option of receiving cash for the medical insurance premiums, the reimbursement for medical insurance is not taxable to her.

The worksheet in Table 40-4 summarizes the taxable compensation paid to Emily and the taxes required to be deducted from her pay. The Boyds would provide a Form W-2 to Emily showing taxable earnings of $11,800 and withholdings as indicated in Table 40-4. A copy would be sent to the Social Security Administration. They would report the federal income tax withholding and FICA and pay the required FUTA and their portion of social security and Medicare ($903) with their Form 1040, reflected on Schedule H. The state income tax and unemployment tax withholdings would be remitted as required by the state authorities. In addition, the Boyds would be liable for $490 of state unemployment tax, which would also be remitted as required, but not later than the due date for filing the Boyd's Form 1040. The employer is responsible for FUTA, which in this case would be $42 ($7,000 × 6.0%, less the 5.4% maximum credit).

The Boyds will have to either increase the withholding from their wages or increase their estimated tax payments by $2,846 in order to pay their household employee's federal taxes during the course of the year (total earnings of $11,800 × the total of employee and employer portions of social security [12.4%] and Medicare tax [2.9%] of 15.3%, plus $999 federal income tax, plus the net FUTA tax of $42).

Table 40-4. **Worksheet for Domestic Employee's Wages**

	Employee's Name: Emily Whitney			**Employee's Social Security Number**			**111-22-3333**
	Cash Paid Directly to Employee	**Non-Cash Amount**	**Total Earnings for W-2 Purposes**	**Social Security and Medicare Tax Deducted**	**Federal Income Tax Deducted**	**State Income Tax Deducted**	**State Unemployment Taxes Deducted**
January	$850		$850	$65	$68	$43	$17
February	$850		$850	$65	$68	$43	$17
March	$1,050		$1,050	$80	$84	$53	$21
April	$850		$850	$65	$68	$43	$17
May	$850		$850	$80	$84	$53	$21
June	$1,050	$300	$1,350	$88	$113	$58	$23
July	$850		$850	$65	$68	$43	$17
August	$1,050		$1,050	$80	$84	$53	$7
September	$850		$850	$65	$68	$43	
October	$850		$850	$65	$68	$43	
November	$1,050		$1,050	$80	$84	$53	
December	$1,350		$1,350	$103	$143	$68	
TOTAL	**$11,500**	**$300**	**$11,800**	**$903**	**$999**	**$590**	**$140**

TAXORGANIZER

Forms you will need. You will need the following federal tax forms if you employ household help:

- Schedule H
- Form W-2, Wage and Tax Statement
- Form W-3, Transmittal of Wage and Tax Statements
- Form W-4, Employees' Withholding Allowance Certificate

You will need to contact your state tax authorities for applicable state tax forms.

As an employer, you must keep records of any cash or noncash wages paid to your employee as well as any taxes withheld from those wages. Table 40-4 is designed to help you accumulate this information. You will need this information at year-end to prepare the employee's Form W-2, which must be given to the employee by January 31 of the following year. Even if you are preparing only one Form W-2, you also will need Form W-3, Transmittal of Wage and Tax Statements, to send copies to the Social Security Administration. The government copies must be sent by the last day of February of the following year.

TAXORGANIZER

Records you should keep:

- Employee's name and social security number exactly as it appears on the SSN card
- Employer identification number from the IRS
- Records of payments made to domestic help
- Copies of payroll tax forms (W-2, W-3, etc.) filed for domestic help

SCHEDULE H
(Form 1040)

Department of the Treasury
Internal Revenue Service (99)

Household Employment Taxes

(For Social Security, Medicare, Withheld Income, and Federal Unemployment (FUTA) Taxes)

▶ Attach to Form 1040, 1040NR, 1040-SS, or 1041.

▶ Information about Schedule H and its separate instructions is at *www.irs.gov/scheduleh.*

OMB No. 1545-1971

2014

Attachment
Sequence No. **44**

Name of employer	Social security number
PAUL BOYD	987-65-4321

Employer identification number

1	2	3	4	5	6	7	8	9

Calendar year taxpayers having no household employees in 2014 do not have to complete this form for 2014.

A Did you pay **any one** household employee cash wages of $1,900 or more in 2014? (If any household employee was your spouse, your child under age 21, your parent, or anyone under age 18, see the line A instructions before you answer this question.)

☑ **Yes.** Skip lines B and C and go to line 1.
☐ **No.** Go to line B.

B Did you withhold federal income tax during 2014 for any household employee?

☐ **Yes.** Skip line C and go to line 7.
☐ **No.** Go to line C.

C Did you pay **total** cash wages of $1,000 or more in **any** calendar **quarter** of 2013 or 2014 to **all** household employees? (**Do not** count cash wages paid in 2013 or 2014 to your spouse, your child under age 21, or your parent.)

☐ **No. Stop.** Do not file this schedule.
☐ **Yes.** Skip lines 1-9 and go to line 10.

Part I   Social Security, Medicare, and Federal Income Taxes

1	Total cash wages subject to social security tax	**1** 11,800	
2	Social security tax. Multiply line 1 by 12.4% (.124)	**2**	1,463
3	Total cash wages subject to Medicare tax	**3** 11,800	
4	Medicare tax. Multiply line 3 by 2.9% (.029)	**4**	342
5	Total cash wages subject to Additional Medicare Tax withholding . .	**5** 0	
6	Additional Medicare Tax withholding. Multiply line 5 by 0.9% (.009)	**6**	0
7	Federal income tax withheld, if any	**7**	999
8	**Total social security, Medicare, and federal income taxes.** Add lines 2, 4, 6, and 7	**8**	2,804

9 Did you pay **total** cash wages of $1,000 or more in **any** calendar **quarter** of 2013 or 2014 to **all** household employees? (**Do not** count cash wages paid in 2013 or 2014 to your spouse, your child under age 21, or your parent.)

☐ **No. Stop.** Include the amount from line 8 above on Form 1040, line 60a. If you are not required to file Form 1040, see the line 9 instructions.

☑ **Yes.** Go to line 10.

For Privacy Act and Paperwork Reduction Act Notice, see the instructions.   Cat. No. 12187K   **Schedule H (Form 1040) 2014**

Part II — Federal Unemployment (FUTA) Tax

		Yes	No
10	Did you pay unemployment contributions to only one state? (If you paid contributions to a credit reduction state, see instructions and check "No.") **10**	✓	
11	Did you pay all state unemployment contributions for 2014 by April 15, 2015? Fiscal year filers see instructions **11**	✓	
12	Were all wages that are taxable for FUTA tax also taxable for your state's unemployment tax? **12**	✓	

Next: If you checked the **"Yes"** box on **all** the lines above, complete Section A.

If you checked the **"No"** box on **any** of the lines above, skip Section A and complete Section B.

Section A

13 Name of the state where you paid unemployment contributions ▶ ANY STATE

14	Contributions paid to your state unemployment fund	**14**	490		
15	Total cash wages subject to FUTA tax			**15**	7,000
16	**FUTA tax.** Multiply line 15 by .6% (.006). Enter the result here, skip Section B, and go to line 25			**16**	42

Section B

17 Complete all columns below that apply (if you need more space, see instructions):

(a) Name of state	(b) Taxable wages (as defined in state act)	(c) State experience rate period		(d) State experience rate	(e) Multiply col. (b) by .054	(f) Multiply col. (b) by col. (d)	(g) Subtract col. (f) from col. (e). If zero or less, enter -0-.	(h) Contributions paid to state unemployment fund
		From	To					

18	Totals	**18**		
19	Add columns (g) and (h) of line 18 . . . . **19**			
20	Total cash wages subject to FUTA tax (see the line 15 instructions)	**20**		
21	Multiply line 20 by 6.0% (.060)	**21**		
22	Multiply line 20 by 5.4% (.054) **22**			
23	Enter the **smaller** of line 19 or line 22			
	(Employers in a credit reduction state must use the worksheet on page H-7 and check here) . ☐	**23**		
24	**FUTA tax.** Subtract line 23 from line 21. Enter the result here and go to line 25	**24**		

Part III — Total Household Employment Taxes

25	Enter the amount from line 8. If you checked the "Yes" box on line C of page 1, enter -0- . . .	**25**	2,804
26	Add line 16 (or line 24) and line 25	**26**	2,040
27	Are you required to file Form 1040?		

☑ **Yes. Stop.** Include the amount from line 26 above on Form 1040, line 60a. **Do not** complete Part IV below.

☐ **No.** You may have to complete Part IV. See instructions for details.

Part IV — Address and Signature— Complete this part **only** if required. See the line 27 instructions.

Address (number and street) or P.O. box if mail is not delivered to street address | Apt., room, or suite no.

City, town or post office, state, and ZIP code

Under penalties of perjury, I declare that I have examined this schedule, including accompanying statements, and to the best of my knowledge and belief, it is true, correct, and complete. No part of any payment made to a state unemployment fund claimed as a credit was, or is to be, deducted from the payments to employees. Declaration of preparer (other than taxpayer) is based on all information of which preparer has any knowledge.

▶ Employer's signature | Date

Paid Preparer Use Only

Print/Type preparer's name	Preparer's signature	Date	Check ☐ if self-employed	PTIN
Firm's name ▶			Firm's EIN ▶	
Firm's address ▶			Phone no.	

Schedule H (Form 1040) 2014

Chapter 41

U.S. citizens working abroad: Tax treatment of foreign earned income

ey.com/EYTaxGuide

Note

ey.com/EYTaxGuide

Ernst & Young LLP will update the *EY Tax Guide 2015* website with relevant taxpayer information as it becomes available. You can also sign up for email alerts to let you know when changes have been made.

Introduction

U.S. citizens and *resident aliens* are taxed on their worldwide income regardless of where it is earned, paid, or received. But U.S. citizens living abroad get certain tax benefits that are not available back home. *Employees* and *self-employed* individuals living abroad may elect to exclude up to $99,200 of their foreign-earned income from taxation in 2014. Employees and self-employed individuals may also exclude or deduct part of their housing costs from *taxable income*. This chapter tells you about the tax benefits you get from living abroad and what you have to do to qualify for them.

How to Qualify for the Foreign Earned Income Exclusion

You qualify for the foreign earned income exclusion if you are a U.S. citizen, you have a tax home in a foreign country, and you meet either the foreign residence test or the physical presence test, described below.

Generally, if you are a resident alien of the United States, you may qualify for the foreign earned income exclusion if you satisfy the physical presence test. This assumes that you continue your resident alien status while living outside the United States.

Tax home. Your tax home generally is the location of your principal place of employment, which may or may not coincide with the location of your family's residence. Among the factors that are important in determining whether or not your tax home is outside the United States are the anticipated duration of your overseas assignment and whether or not you will return to the same employment location in the United States. Under IRS guidelines, an anticipated short-term (1 year or less) assignment overseas, followed by a return to the same place of employment in the United States, would indicate that you do not have a tax home outside the United States.

If you meet either the foreign residence test or the physical presence test (discussed below) and have a tax home outside the United States, you are eligible for two exclusions—the foreign earned income exclusion and the foreign housing exclusion. Self-employed individuals are eligible for a housing deduction rather than the housing exclusion (see the discussion later in this chapter).

Foreign residence test. The foreign residence test requires that you be a "bona fide resident" of a foreign country (or more than one foreign country) for an uninterrupted period that includes an entire tax year. Whether or not you are a bona fide resident is a subjective question. The answer is determined by the facts and circumstances of your particular situation, including the purpose of your trip and the nature and length of your stay abroad, and your intent.

The following factors are considered by the IRS in determining your intent to be a "bona fide" resident in a specific place.
1. The type of quarters you occupy (hotel or rooming house, rented quarters, purchased quarters, or quarters furnished by your employer)
2. How long your family resided with you during the tax year
3. The length of the uninterrupted period of time during which you have been living outside the United States

4. The nature of any conditions or limitations concerning your employment agreement and the type and term of your visa to live/work in the foreign country
5. Whether you maintain a home in the United States and, if so, its rental status and the relationship of any tenants to you

If you make a statement to the authorities of a foreign country that you are not a resident of that country, and if you are not subject to tax by that country, you do not qualify as a bona fide resident of that country.

However, once you have met the foreign residence test for an entire tax year, your qualification is retroactive to the first day you established your bona fide residence. Occasional trips to the United States for business or vacation do not affect your qualification.

Example 1. You moved from the United States to a foreign country, arriving on September 15, 2014. You entered the country under a resident visa with your family for a 3-year assignment. You did not declare to the foreign authorities that you were not a resident of that country. You qualify as a bona fide resident of the foreign country if these facts remain the same through December 31, 2015. You may file your 2014 U.S. income tax return (or amend your original 2014 tax return) to claim the benefits of being a bona fide resident of a foreign country for the period September 15, 2014, through December 31, 2014.

Example 2. George has been a resident of the United Kingdom for 5 consecutive years. If he moves to France this year, he continues to be a bona fide resident of a foreign country. An uninterrupted period of bona fide residence may include residence in more than one foreign country in a given year.

Example 3. Amy moved to France with her family on June 15, 2013, for a job assignment of indefinite length. On December 3, 2014, she was transferred back to the United States. She did not satisfy the bona fide residence test in either year, since she did not maintain a bona fide residence in a foreign country for a period that includes a complete tax year. However, she may qualify for the foreign exclusions under the physical presence test (discussed below).

Physical presence test. This test simply requires that you be physically present in a foreign country (or countries) for 330 full days during any consecutive 12-month period. This is a purely objective test. There is no reference to your intentions or to any other factors that determine bona fide residence abroad.

Two important rules to keep in mind regarding this test are as follows:
1. A full day is a 24-hour period commencing at midnight. Thus, a day in which you travel *to or from the United States* is not a full day in a foreign country.
2. When you travel between *foreign countries*, the travel days will qualify as full days in a foreign country, provided that the time spent outside of either foreign country during the journey (i.e., time spent over international waters and/or time spent in the United States) is less than 24 hours.

TAXORGANIZER

Keep a calendar. Keep a record of your travel days in and out of the United States and retain it with your other important tax records. The calendar should be supported by airline tickets, stamped passports, or other evidence of arrival and departure dates.

The Foreign Earned Income Exclusion

If you qualify, you may elect to exclude a maximum of $99,200 in foreign earned income from your U.S. taxable income in 2014. The amount of the exclusion is indexed annually for inflation.

The amount of earned income you may exclude depends on either (1) the number of days during the year in which you were a bona fide resident of a foreign country or (2) the number of days you were physically present in a foreign country during a 12-month period. These are known as your "qualifying days." If you are out of the United States for the entire year, you may exclude all of your earned income up to the $99,200 limit. However, if you are out of the United States for only part of the year, you generally must prorate the exclusion based on your number of qualifying days during the taxable year.

Example. You were a bona fide resident of a foreign country for 300 days during 2014. The maximum amount of income you may exclude from U.S. taxes is 300/365 × $99,200, or $81,534. Your exclusion is, of course, limited by the amount of foreign income you earn. If you earn less than the maximum allowed, you may exclude only that lower amount.

Only foreign earned income is eligible for the exclusion. Earned income is income you receive for the performance of personal services. It does *not* include dividends, interest, capital gains, rental property income, and other kinds of unearned income. For example, interest paid on a bank account in the United Kingdom to a U.S. expatriate on assignment in London is not eligible for the exclusion, since it is not foreign *earned* income.

Earned income may be received in cash or as benefits-in-kind and includes the following:

- Salaries, wages, bonuses, commissions, overseas incentive premiums, and so on.
- A housing allowance. This may take the form of a cash payment to you, a cash payment by your employer directly to a landlord, or housing provided by your employer. When a cash payment is made, you must report the full amount as income. When housing is provided, your employer should furnish you with an estimate of its fair market value, which is used for income-reporting purposes.
- An automobile allowance. A cash allowance for an automobile should be included in your income. When an automobile is provided by your employer, an amount representing the value of its personal use to you should be included in your income.
- A cost-of-living allowance.
- An education allowance (e.g., for the cost of schooling your children).
- Home leave. The value of home leave benefits provided to you and your family is included in your income. However, if you spend a significant portion of your home leave on business, you may be justified in characterizing your portion of the trip as a business trip and thereby exclude your travel expenses from income.
- Rest and relaxation airfare.
- A moving expense reimbursement or allowance, in certain cases.
- A tax reimbursement or allowance.

Source of earned income. The source of earned income depends on the place where the services are rendered. If the services are performed in the United States, the income is considered U.S. source income. On the other hand, if the services are performed in a foreign country, the income is foreign source. For the income to be excluded on your tax return, the earned income must be from sources within a foreign country (or countries) and relate to services rendered in the current year.

How to compute your foreign source income. To compute your foreign source income for purposes of the foreign earned income exclusion, you must determine your earned income from sources outside the United States.

Foreign source earned income includes all income received for personal services performed outside the United States. The place of payment is irrelevant: a payment made into a U.S. bank account by a U.S.-based employer for services performed outside the United States is foreign source income. If you perform services both inside and outside the United States during the tax year, you must determine what portion of your income is from U.S. sources and what portion is from foreign sources.

Example 1. You received $50,000 for services performed in 2014. You worked a total of 240 days during the year, 235 days in the United Kingdom on foreign assignment and 5 days in the United States for a technical meeting. The source of your earned income is as follows:

$$\frac{5 \text{ days worked in the United States}}{240 \text{ days worked worldwide}} \times \$50,000 = \$1,042$$

$$\frac{235 \text{ days worked outside the United States}}{240 \text{ days worked worldwide}} \times \$50,000 = \$48,958$$

Your U.S. source income is $1,042, and your foreign source income is $48,958.

There are several other considerations to keep in mind when you are figuring out the source of your income:

1. If there has been a significant change in your rate of compensation during the year, it may be appropriate to allocate your compensation separately for the days worked and income earned in the respective periods.
2. If a payment is received during the year for services performed in a prior year, it may be appropriate to compute the foreign source portion of that payment based on the days worked in the prior year. It is not possible to exclude this prior year foreign source income using the current year's foreign earned income exclusion, but it might be possible to exclude some or all of the income on your current year's tax return to the extent that last year's exclusion was not fully used up.
3. Do not take into account vacation or holiday travel to the United States as part of your workday calculation.

Example 2. In 2013, you were eligible for the full $97,600 foreign earned income exclusion but only had $87,600 of foreign source earned income that was excluded on your 2013 tax return. Therefore, you have $10,000 of unused exclusion from 2013. In 2014, your compensation includes $12,000 of foreign source income earned in 2013 (in this case, a bonus payment). You are able to exclude $10,000 of the $12,000 of income on your 2014 tax return. The $10,000 exclusion is in addition to any exclusion you might have for foreign compensation earned and received in 2014.

The Foreign Housing Exclusion

If you qualify as a U.S. citizen living abroad, you may elect to exclude from your U.S. taxable income the excess of eligible housing costs over a "base housing amount." Eligible housing costs that an individual may exclude are limited to 30% of the foreign earned income exclusion ($29,760 for 2014). However, the IRS issues guidance periodically establishing higher maximum housing costs for certain geographic locations—as high as $114,300 for Hong Kong in 2014. This guidance can be found on the IRS website, _www.irs.gov_. The base housing amount is equal to 16% of the annual foreign earned income exclusion ($15,872 for 2014). The base housing amount is prorated by the ratio of the number of qualifying days to the total days in the year.

Example. You had $18,000 of qualified housing expenses in your 2014 qualifying period. Based on an allocation of your earned income, you determine that you had $98,000 of foreign source income. Furthermore, you had a qualifying period of 330 days in the tax year. The base housing amount is $15,872. Your housing exclusion is computed as follows:

1) Housing expenses	$18,000
2) Number of qualifying days	330
3) Total days in the tax year	365
4) Base housing amount	$15,872
5) 330/365 × $15,872	$14,350
6) Housing exclusion (line 1 – line 5)	$3,650

Assuming the same facts, you calculate your foreign earned income exclusion as follows:

1) Maximum foreign earned income exclusion	$99,200
2) Number of qualifying days	330
3) Total days in tax year	365
4) 330/365 × $99,200	$89,688
5) Total foreign source income	$98,000
6) Less: Housing exclusion	($3,650)
7) Total foreign source income available for exclusion	$94,350
8) Smaller of line 4 or 7	$89,688

Your foreign earned income exclusion is $89,688. In addition, your foreign housing exclusion is $3,650. Your total exclusion is $93,338.

Foreign housing deduction for self-employed individuals. If you are a self-employed individual and you do not have an employer to provide housing, you may deduct the cost of foreign housing, net of the base housing amount subject to the limitations discussed above, in computing your adjusted gross income. Your housing deduction is limited to the amount by which your foreign earned income exceeds your foreign earned income exclusion for that year.

If you are both an employee and a self-employed individual during the same tax year, see Publication 54, _Tax Guide for U.S. Citizens and Resident Aliens Abroad._

TAXPLANNER

When to elect the foreign earned income exclusion and the foreign housing exclusion. You elect and calculate the foreign earned income exclusion and the foreign housing exclusion separately using Form 2555 or, in some cases, Form 2555-EZ. The elections can be made on a tax return that you file on time, on an amended tax return, or on a late-filed tax return that is filed within 1 year of the original due date. The IRS also allows the elections to be made later under certain circumstances. When you are deciding whether or not to use the exclusions, you should take into account a number of factors, including the level of taxation in the foreign country in which you are living, the type of foreign assignment you are on, and your employer's policies concerning individuals on foreign assignment.

When you elect the foreign income exclusion, you are required to reduce your otherwise deductible expenses that are associated with the excluded income. Similarly, foreign taxes available for the foreign tax credit must also be reduced (see _Foreign Tax Credit_, later).

If you are living in a foreign country with a high tax rate, you may be better off forgoing the exclusions and claiming a larger foreign tax credit. In this case, forgoing the exclusions might result in a higher current tax liability but may also create larger foreign tax credits that you might be able to use in other years to offset tax on foreign source income. In countries with moderate or low tax rates, it is usually to your advantage to claim the exclusions. In any event, you should calculate your taxes with and without the exclusions to see which is more beneficial to you.

Once you elect the exclusion(s), you may revoke either or both of them by attaching a statement to your return or your amended return stating that you do not wish to claim the exclusion(s). Once revoked, you may not claim the exclusions again for the next 5 years without obtaining IRS approval.

Employer-Provided Meals and Lodging

Meals and lodging provided in kind by, or on behalf of, an employer to an employee or to his or her spouse or dependents are excluded from taxable income if certain requirements are met:

1. The meals are provided on the business premises of, and for the convenience of, the employer.
2. Lodging is furnished on the premises of, and for the convenience of, the employer, and the employee is required to accept this lodging as a condition of employment.

The IRS has taken a narrow view of the lodging exclusion. As a result, most employer-provided lodging is not excludable from your income. However, the exclusion applies if the employee resides in a camp that is provided by the employer because the employee's work site is in a remote area where satisfactory housing is not available on the open market. The camp has to be located as near as is practicable to the work site and should be furnished with a common area or enclave that is not available to the general public and normally accommodates 10 or more employees.

TAXALERT

You do not have to be living abroad to take advantage of this exclusion for employer-provided meals and lodging. All taxpayers are entitled to exclude the value of meals and lodging from taxable income when they are provided on the employer's premises for the employer's convenience and when the lodging must be accepted as a condition of employment.

Foreign Tax Credit

You may elect to claim a credit for foreign income taxes paid or accrued during the tax year, or you may claim the taxes paid as an itemized deduction. Generally, claiming a credit is more beneficial, since it results in a dollar-for-dollar reduction in your tax bill. The foreign tax credit on your U.S. return is limited to the lesser of (1) the actual foreign income taxes paid or accrued during the year (including carrybacks or carryforwards) or (2) the amount of U.S. tax attributable to foreign source taxable income for the year. The foreign tax credit is elected and calculated on Form 1116 (see **chapter 37**, _Other credits including the earned income credit_).

As mentioned above, if you elect either the foreign earned income exclusion or the foreign housing exclusion, the amount of foreign taxes that is available for credit is reduced.

Example 1. You had $98,000 of foreign source income and $18,000 of qualified housing expenses in 2014. The total amount you may exclude from your income is $93,338. (See the preceding _foreign housing exclusion example_ to learn how this number is calculated.) You paid $4,000 in foreign taxes for the year. You figure the amount that you must reduce foreign taxes available for foreign tax credit as follows:

$$\frac{\$93,338}{\$98,000} \times \$4,000 = \$3,810$$

Consequently, a maximum of $190 ($4,000 - $3,810) may be claimed as a foreign tax credit.

Example 2. You are an unmarried U.S. citizen currently residing in the United Kingdom. Your total gross income for the year is $140,000, all of which is compensation. You qualify for a foreign earned income exclusion of $99,200 and a housing exclusion of $2,500, for a total of $101,700. You spent 10% of your working days in the United States. You have $7,000 of itemized deductions, none of which directly relate to a particular class or source of income. The amount you may claim as a foreign tax credit is computed as follows:

Compensation from foreign sources (90% of $140,000)	$126,000
Deductions allocated to foreign source compensation: ($7,000 × 90%)	($6,300)
Less: Foreign earned income and housing exclusions	($101,700)
Foreign source taxable income	$18,000
U.S. source compensation (10% of $140,000)	$14,000
Balance of itemized deductions ($7,000 minus $6,300)	($700)
Total taxable income before personal exemptions	$31,300

The foreign tax credit limitation is calculated by determining the ratio of foreign source taxable income to total taxable income (as shown above). The ratio in the above example would be

$$\frac{\$18,000}{\$31,300} = 0.575$$

This ratio is then multiplied by the U.S. tax liability for the year to determine the maximum amount of foreign tax credit usable for the year. If we assume that the U.S. tax is $7,658, the maximum credit would be $4,403 (0.575 × $7,658).

Carryback and carryforward of foreign tax credit. Example 1 (above) shows how to determine the amount of foreign taxes that may be used as a credit. Example 2 (above) shows how to determine the maximum amount of foreign tax credit that may be currently used as a credit against your U.S. taxes. If the amount of the creditable foreign taxes paid or accrued in the current year exceeds the amount that may be used currently, you may carry back the excess one year. The remainder, if any, may be carried forward for up to ten years. The excess credit must be carried back first, and used in the preceding year if possible, before it can be carried forward.

TAXORGANIZER

Keep a copy of your foreign tax return and receipts for taxes paid in order to support the foreign tax credit calculations. This documentation may be needed if your return is audited by the IRS.

TAXPLANNER

Planning tips for individuals on international assignment. Here is a list of items you should consider in planning your tax affairs and preparing your tax return:

1. Sale of your principal residence. A taxpayer may claim an exclusion of up to $250,000 for single taxpayers ($500,000 for joint filers) once every 2 years if the taxpayer owned the residence and occupied it as a principal residence for at least 2 of the 5 years before the sale or exchange. The amount of excludable gain may be limited if the property was used as a vacation or rental property or if the property was left vacant (see chapter 15, *Selling your home*).

   There are no special rules for U.S. home sales by expatriates. If you have a significant gain built up in your home and you expect your assignment to last more than 3 years, you should give consideration to selling your home. Otherwise, if you decide to sell at a later date, you may fail the 2-year out of 5-year test and some or all of the exclusion may be lost (see chapter 15, *Selling your home*).

   Keep in mind that if you purchase your primary residence in a foreign country, the amount of any gain will be affected by changes in the foreign exchange rate. In addition, principal payments on a foreign mortgage may result in a taxable exchange gain.

2. Individual retirement arrangements (IRAs). An expatriate who contributes to an IRA (see chapter 17, *Individual retirement arrangements [IRAs]*) must have earned income in excess of the total of his or her foreign earned income and foreign housing exclusions if he or she elects to use the exclusions.

   If you are covered by a company pension plan, your modified adjusted gross income must be below a certain level for your IRA contribution to be tax deductible. Similarly, your modified adjusted gross income must be below a certain level in order to make a contribution to a traditional IRA or a Roth IRA. Note that for purposes of computing modified adjusted gross income, the foreign earned income exclusion and the foreign housing exclusion amounts must be disregarded. For a more detailed discussion of IRAs, please refer to chapter 17, *Individual retirement arrangements (IRAs)*.

3. Report of foreign bank and financial accounts. You should become familiar with the filing requirements of FinCEN Form 114 (formerly known as TD F 90-22.1), which is a form that is used to provide information concerning foreign bank and financial accounts if in the aggregate their value exceeds $10,000. Significant penalties apply for noncompliance.

4. Statement of specified foreign financial assets. You should also become familiar with the requirements of Form 8938. This form mandates reporting the highest fair market value of each foreign financial asset during the year for U.S. citizens and tax residents if the aggregate values of these assets exceed minimum thresholds. Examples of foreign financial assets include foreign bank and brokerage accounts, ownership interest in foreign companies/partnerships, bonds issued by a non-U.S. resident, ownership interest in a foreign trust, estate, or pension, or a derivative instrument with respect to the above assets. Minimum thresholds for 2014 reporting vary based on the taxpayer's filing status and residence abroad. Significant penalties apply for noncompliance. Although some reportable information will be identical to the Form 114 (described above), the Form 8938 represents a separate additional reporting obligation to the U.S. taxpayer. Further information can be found on the IRS website, *www.IRS.gov*.

TAXORGANIZER

Records you should keep:
- A calendar of travel days to track workdays and non-workdays in the United States, the assignment country, and any other country. The calendar can be supported by airline tickets, stamped passports, or other evidence documenting arrival and departure dates.
- A list of housing expenses in the host country
- A copy of your foreign tax returns and receipts for foreign taxes paid or accrued during the tax year, depending on the method used for claiming the foreign tax credit

Chapter 42
Foreign citizens living in the United States

Note

ey.com/EYTaxGuide

Ernst & Young LLP will update the *Ernst & Young Tax Guide 2015* website with relevant tax-payer information as it becomes available. You can also sign up for email alerts to let you know when changes have been made.

Introduction

Whether a U.S. citizen or not, almost everybody living in the United States is subject to U.S. income tax laws. Foreign nationals working in the United States are either resident aliens or non-resident aliens. Resident aliens, like U.S. citizens, are subject to U.S. tax on their worldwide income. Nonresident aliens are subject to U.S. tax only on certain types of their U.S. source income.

Some foreign citizens living in the United States are not taxed at all—at least not by the U.S. government. A foreign citizen residing in the United States who works for a foreign government doing normal diplomatic work is exempt from the U.S. tax laws, provided that U.S. government employees working in that foreign country are exempt from its tax laws. Tax treaties between the United States and some foreign countries contain numerous other exceptions that alter the normal domestic U.S. tax laws.

This chapter tells you how to determine if you are a resident alien or a nonresident alien and how you should calculate your tax.

Determining Your Status

Whether you are a resident alien or a nonresident alien is of critical importance when you compute how much U.S. income tax you will pay. Your residency status will determine your filing status, the tax rate schedule applicable to your income, and the amount of your income that will be subject to U.S. income tax. Under the tax rules, an alien must meet either one of the two following tests in order to be considered a resident of the United States for tax purposes:

1. **The green card test.** Have you been lawfully admitted to the United States for permanent residency? In other words, do you have a green card?
2. **The substantial presence test.** Have you been present in the United States for a substantial period of time? If you have been present in the United States for at least 31 days in the current year and if the total days you are present in the United States during the current year, plus one-third of the days present in the preceding calendar year, plus one-sixth of the days present in the second preceding calendar year, are equal to at least 183 days, you will meet the substantial presence test and be considered a resident alien in the current year.

Example 1. You were in the United States during 2014 for 75 days. During 2013, you spent 321 days in the U.S., which included 14 days of vacation. In 2012, you were in the United States for 30 days. Applying the three-year test to your travel to the U.S. results in 187 days. The days are counted as follows. One-sixth of the days in 2012 (five days), plus one-third of the days in 2013 (107 days—you may not exclude vacation days), plus the days in 2014 (75 days). You are therefore treated as a U.S. resident for 2014.

Example 2. You were in the United States during 2014 for 25 days. In 2013 you were present in the U.S. for 300 days and during 2012 you were in the United States for 360 days. Counting your days using the three-year test results in 185 days for 2014. However, because you were not in the U.S. during 2014 for at least 31 days, you do not meet the substantial presence test for 2014.

If you are considered a U.S. resident under the substantial presence test (and you were not a U.S. resident in the prior year), your residency period generally begins on the first day you were present in the United States in the current year. However, if you have a brief visit (or visits) to the United States, and the total days you spend in the United States during the visit (or visits) amount to 10 days or less, you may, under certain circumstances, ignore those days for purposes of determining when your residency period begins.

Example. You move to the United States on June 1, 2014, and spend a sufficient number of days in this country in 2014 to meet the substantial presence test. Prior to your actual arrival on June 1, you spent 10 days in the United States from February 2 through February 11 to house hunt and to meet with your U.S. employer while you maintained your tax home in a foreign country. Your U.S. residency period begins on June 1. In the event you had stayed in the United States until February 12 (11 days), your U.S. residency period would have begun on February 2.

A similar rule applies in the year in which your U.S. residency terminates. Your residency period generally ends on the 31st of December. However, if you can show that you have closer connections to a foreign country for the remainder of the year, your U.S. residency generally ends on the last day you are present in the United States. Visits to the United States totaling 10 days or less following your departure may be disregarded in determining the last day of your U.S. residency.

TAXPLANNER

To take advantage of this closer connection rule and terminate your residency on the last day you are present in the United States, you would be required to attach a statement to your U.S. tax return for that year detailing the facts that support your closer connection to a foreign country.

Example. In 2014, you lived in the United States continuously from January 1 through October 31, when you moved to a foreign country and established a closer connection to it. Generally, you are considered to be a resident of the United States through December 31. Your U.S. residency would be considered to terminate on October 31 if you established your closer connection to the foreign country by attaching a statement to your U.S. tax return. If you return to the United States on business trips or on vacation during November and December and spend 10 days or less in total in the United States, your residency period terminates on October 31. If you spend more than 10 days in total in the United States in November and December, your U.S. residency period will be extended beyond October 31. The actual termination date will depend on the specific dates of your visits. You would also want to take into consideration any tax treaty benefits that might be available to you.

TAXORGANIZER

Arrival and departure dates. To substantiate your arrival and departure dates to and from the United States, copies of travel tickets (airline, boat, etc.), stamped passports, and other relevant documentation should be retained in your tax files.

TAXPLANNER

Closer connection exception to substantial presence test. If you meet the substantial presence test described above, but you are present in the United States less than 183 days during the year, you should examine your ties to another country. You might qualify for an exception to the substantial presence test if you can demonstrate that your ties to another country are stronger than your ties to the United States. You must file a statement (IRS Form 8840) with your tax return supporting your claim, or, if no return is required, a statement alone must be filed with the IRS.

If your ties are weak and you want to try to strengthen them, consider:
1. Maintaining a home in that country
2. Obtaining a driver's license issued by that country
3. Joining a religious, political, or cultural organization in that country
4. Maintaining or establishing a membership in a social organization in that country
5. Having a bank account in that country
6. Having personal property in that country such as cars, clothing, or jewelry
7. Continuing to vote in that country

Example. Refer back to Example 1 in the section describing the substantial presence test. In the example, you meet the substantial presence test for 2014 because the total number of days in the three-year test is 187 (remember, if you have 183 days or more you are treated as a U.S. resident). However, because you were in the U.S. for fewer than 183 days during 2014, you may be able to be treated as a U.S. nonresident if you can establish a closer connection to another country than to the U.S. for all of 2014. For instance, if you and your family had moved back to your home country at the end of 2013, and, for all of 2014, your main employment was in your home country, your children attended school there, and you participated in social, religious, or cultural activities in your home country, etc., you may be able to demonstrate a closer connection to your home country than to the United States during 2014 even though you continued to come to the U.S. for a short time (75 days in the example) for business trips or vacations. If you can demonstrate the closer connection to your home country, you will be treated as a nonresident of the United States for 2014. Bear in mind that you will need to pay U.S. tax for 2014 following the rules of taxation for nonresidents (discussed later) and you will need to file Form 8840, listing all your facts and circumstances to show the IRS that you have a closer connection to your home country than to the United States.

If you spend a significant amount of time in the United States each year, you should carefully monitor the days to keep them below the 183-day threshold during the 3-year period considered under the substantial presence test to eliminate the requirement to file a statement of claiming a closer connection to another country. This generally means that you may be present in the United States for up to 121 days each year without triggering U.S. residence under the substantial presence test.

Election to Be Treated as a Resident

The tax law contains a rule that allows an alien to elect to be treated as a resident of the United States for tax purposes (a "first year election"), even though he or she does not meet the green card or substantial presence test. The first year election allows an alien with significant U.S. presence toward the end of year 1 and who meets the substantial presence test in year 2 to elect to be treated as a U.S. resident alien in year 1. The alien can only make this first year election after he or she has met the substantial presence test in year 2. This may require filing an extension for the year 1 tax return. This election will be advantageous to some aliens, such as those who incur significant expenses when they first arrive in the United States (such as mortgage interest, deductible mortgage points, and real estate taxes related to a purchased home in the United States), which would only be deductible for a resident. In addition, this election could also benefit married aliens who would otherwise be required to file using the married filing separate rates that apply to nonresidents. As U.S. residents under this election, they would be permitted to make a further election to be treated as residents for the entire year, thus permitting the filing of a joint return and the use of the more favorable joint return rates. An alien who meets the following criteria may make the election (see the following example):

1. Doesn't meet the green card or substantial presence tests for the current year,
2. Was not a resident alien in the prior year,
3. Meets the substantial presence test in the following year,
4. Is present in the United States for at least 31 consecutive days in the current year, and
5. Spends at least 75% of the days between the first of the 31 consecutive days and year-end in the United States. (Note: Up to 5 non-U.S. days will be counted as U.S. days for the purposes of this test.)

An alien who makes the election to be treated as a resident may also make a similar election on his or her tax return on behalf of dependent children if the children are not required to file tax returns on their own, assuming, of course, that the children also meet the requirements of the election. The filing of the election will enable an alien to take dependent exemptions for the children.

Example. Assume that an alien is present in the United States for the following periods:

7/4–8/15	43 days
9/16–11/25	71 days
12/16–12/31	16 days

During the testing period of July 4 through December 31, the individual is in the United States 130 days out of 181 days total. Including the 5 additional non-U.S. days that can be counted as

U.S. days, the individual is present in the United States on less than 75% of the days and cannot make the election for this period.

$$\frac{130 + 5}{181} = 74.6\%$$

However, since, during the testing period of September 16 through December 31, the individual was in the United States 87 days out of 107, which exceeds 75%, the individual could elect to be treated as a resident for the period of September 16 through December 31 (assuming that the other tests regarding the prior and subsequent years are also met).

TAXPLANNER

If you have or are planning to obtain a green card, you should be aware that you will generally be considered a resident alien from the date you receive the green card (or earlier depending on the substantial presence test) and that you will be subject to tax on all of your worldwide income. If you have substantial U.S. or foreign investment income, you may want to transfer the income-producing assets to somebody else, for example, a spouse or other close relative who is still living abroad. Before making any transfers, however, you should consult with a tax advisor to consider possible gift tax and foreign tax implications.

How Resident Aliens Are Taxed

Like U.S. citizens, resident aliens are subject to tax on the worldwide income they receive, regardless of its source. Resident aliens compute their taxable income and income tax liability the same way U.S. citizens do. They include the same items in income and are entitled to take the same deductions as U.S. citizens.

TAXPLANNER

Do not assume that nonresident alien filing status necessarily results in greater savings than resident alien status. Resident alien status may result in a lower U.S. tax if you can use the lower joint return rates (for married resident aliens), if you are eligible for greater itemized deductions, and/or if you can benefit from the foreign tax credit.

Income tax treaties. Income tax treaties may have the effect of overriding the provisions of U.S. law. Consult a tax advisor for details.

Generally, tax treaties are consulted when an individual is a dual resident, that is, a resident of both the United States and a foreign country under each country's tax rules. When a treaty is used to claim that an individual is a nonresident of the United States, the individual must file Form 1040-NR and attach Form 8833, Treaty-Based Return Position Disclosure, to the return, presenting facts to support his or her claim of not being a U.S. resident.

An election to be treated as a nonresident of the United States under a treaty will apply for all purposes in computing the individual's income tax liability for the dual residency period.

TAXPLANNER

Filing Form 1040-NR may influence the determination by the U.S. Department of Homeland Security as to whether you continue to qualify as a U.S. resident for immigration purposes if you hold a green card. Consult with an immigration lawyer to evaluate the impact of this tax position on your immigration situation. In addition, you should consult with a tax advisor so that you understand all the implications of a treaty-based nonresident filing position.

Report of Foreign Bank and Financial Accounts. If you become a resident of the United States, you should become familiar with the filing requirements of FinCEN Form 114 (formerly known as Form TD F 90-22.1), which is a form that is used to provide information concerning foreign bank and financial accounts if their aggregate value exceeds $10,000. Significant penalties apply for noncompliance.

Form 8938, *Statement of Specified Foreign Financial Assets.* You should also become familiar with the requirements of Form 8938. This form mandates reporting the highest fair market value of each foreign financial asset during the year for U.S. tax residents if the aggregate value of these assets exceeds a minimum threshold. Examples of foreign financial assets include foreign bank and brokerage accounts, ownership interest in foreign companies/partnerships, bonds issued by a non-U.S. resident, ownership interest in a foreign trust/estate/pension, or a derivative instrument with respect to the above assets. Minimum thresholds for 2014 reporting vary based on the taxpayer's filing status and residence abroad. Significant penalties apply for noncompliance. Although some reportable information will be identical to the Form 114 (described above), the Form 8938 represents a separate additional reporting obligation to the U.S. taxpayer. Further information can be found on the IRS website, *www.IRS.gov.*

TAXPLANNER

An alien's residency status may not be the same for all purposes. The definition discussed above applies for federal income tax laws. Different rules apply in determining residency for state income tax and for federal gift and estate tax purposes. Consult a tax advisor to find out more about how the residence rules are applied for these other taxes.

Rules for Individuals Giving Up U.S. Citizenship or U.S. Residency

The Heroes Earnings Assistance and Relief Tax Act of 2008 introduced significant changes to the tax rules for individuals giving up U.S. citizenship or U.S. residency. The law applies to individuals who relinquish U.S. citizenship or terminate long-term residency on or after June 17, 2008. Individuals who relinquished their U.S. citizenship or terminated their U.S. residency prior to this date are subject to a different set of rules. However, the current law refers to some of the prior rules when determining who is subject to the tax.

- According to the expatriation tax rules, a long-term resident is an individual who has held a green card for any part of eight of the 15 tax years ending with the year of expatriation. A year during which a green card holder was living outside the United States and filed a U.S. income tax return as a U.S. nonresident based upon an income tax treaty does not count toward the eight-year requirement.
- An expatriated individual continues to be treated as a U.S. citizen or long-term resident for U.S. tax purposes until he or she gives notice of an expatriating act or termination of his or her residency to the U.S. Secretary of State or the U.S. Secretary of Homeland Security, along with a statement containing information about his or her status. The statement provided has to comply with certain legal requirements, so you should consult an immigration attorney if you have decided to give up your U.S. citizenship or your U.S. green card.
- A U.S. citizen or long-term resident will be considered a "covered expatriate" subject to the expatriation tax rules unless the individual has an average annual U.S. federal income tax liability over the preceding five years of less than $157,000 (for 2014), and a net worth of less than $2 million. Limited exceptions apply. In addition, the expatriated individual has to certify that he or she has complied with all U.S. federal tax obligations for the preceding five years, and substantiate with documentation if requested by the IRS.

Covered expatriates are subject to a special exit tax. The tax—known as the mark-to-market exit tax—is calculated as if the covered expatriate sold all of his worldwide property for fair market value on the day before he gave up his citizenship or surrendered his green card. A gain of up to $600,000 (indexed annually for inflation; in 2014, this amount is $680,000) is excluded from tax. Furthermore, you are allowed to increase your basis in your property to its fair market value at the time you became a U.S. resident for purposes of calculating your gain or loss on property.

Special tax rules also apply to deferred compensation, specified tax deferred accounts, and interests in nongrantor trusts. Depending on the situation, deferred compensation may either be taxed under the normal income tax rules (although subject to a 30% withholding tax), or the present value of the accrued benefit or the value of the property may be taxed on the day prior to expatriation. The balance in specified tax-deferred accounts (e.g., traditional IRAs, 529 plans, and health savings accounts) is taxed as if received on the day prior to expatriation. Note that Roth IRAs are not considered tax-deferred accounts and are subject to the general mark-to-market exit tax rules described above. Distributions of property from nongrantor trusts to covered expatriates are subject to withholding tax. Furthermore, any distribution of appreciated property subjects the nongrantor trust to tax on the appreciation.

A covered expatriate is required to give IRS Form W-8CE to the payer of any of the items mentioned above. In addition, a covered expatriate must file IRS Form 8854 with the Internal Revenue Service with the income tax return for the year of departure and any following year in the event of a taxable distribution from one of the special income categories noted above.

Gifts and bequests from covered expatriates to U.S. citizens or residents are subject to tax at the highest gift tax rate (40% for 2014). Gifts below the annual exclusion amount ($14,000 for 2014) and certain other gifts are excluded from this tax. The tax is paid by the recipient of the gift or bequest.

TAXPLANNER

If you are contemplating terminating residency or relinquishing U.S. citizenship, consult your tax advisor and immigration attorney. The rules are very complex, and special filings may be required.

Dual-Status Aliens

A dual-status alien is a person who is considered a resident alien and a nonresident alien during the same tax year.

You are most likely to have dual status in the year of your arrival in or departure from the United States. You could, for example, be a resident alien until your departure from the United States. Thereafter, you would be a nonresident alien.

For purposes of computing your tax liability, different rules apply to the time when you are a resident alien and the time when you are a nonresident alien. However, it is necessary to fill out only one tax return. You are taxed on your worldwide income for the part of the year in which you are a resident alien. For the part of the year in which you are a nonresident alien, only certain types of your U.S. source income are taxed. Dual-status aliens who are married may not file a joint return or claim the standard deduction.

Exceptions. You may make a special election that may decrease your taxes for some years in which you have dual status. Dual-status aliens who are married have two other alternatives in the year in which they arrive in the United States:

1. **The Section 6013(h) election.** This election is available only in cases in which a U.S. citizen or resident alien is married to an individual who is a resident alien at the close of the tax year. An alien choosing this alternative is treated as a resident of the United States for the entire tax year. The most significant consequences of making this choice are:
   a. All income, whether from a U.S. or a foreign source, is subject to tax, including any income you had during the period in which you were not a resident of the United States. This income would have been exempt from U.S. taxes, or possibly taxed at a reduced rate, if you had not made the Section 6013(h) election.
   b. You may claim itemized deductions for the period in which you were not a resident of the United States, if such items would otherwise qualify for deduction. Some examples are foreign real property taxes, mortgage interest, and medical expenses.
   c. You may deduct, or elect to claim as a credit, foreign income taxes attributable to the period during which you were not a U.S. resident, which may substantially reduce or even eliminate U.S. income tax. Other benefits, however, like being able to file a joint return and thus be taxed at accordingly lower rates, are left intact. The result is that your net U.S. tax liability may be reduced.
2. **The Section 6013(g) election.** Under the Section 6013(g) election, a married couple may file a joint return as full-year residents of the United States if, at the end of the tax year, one spouse is a nonresident alien and the other is a citizen or resident alien of the United States.

The effects of making this election are the same as choosing the Section 6013(h) election, with one very significant distinction. The Section 6013(g) election is valid for all subsequent years in which you and your spouse qualify, including the year in which the resident alien leaves the United States. Once made, the Section 6013(g) election can be revoked. However, if you revoke the election, you cannot make another such election in the future. On the other hand, the Section 6013(h) election relates to only the year of the election and not later years. The election cannot be made if either spouse made the election in a prior year.

Example. You and your spouse became U.S. residents on April 1, 2014. Prior to your arrival in the United States, you earned $5,000 in wages and your spouse earned $1,000 in wages. Both of you also had $500 in joint interest income for the first 3 months of the year. Once in the United States, you earned $75,000 from April through December. Your spouse did not work in the United States. You had an additional $700 in joint interest income. Your itemized deductions equal the standard deduction. Your tax liabilities are computed as follows:

Alternative 1: Dual-status return, married filing separately (for period while a U.S. resident)

Salary	$75,000
Interest	350
Itemized deductions	(6,200)
Exemptions	(3,950)
Taxable income	$65,200
Tax	$12,156

You would not be taxed on your non-U.S. source income.

Alternative 2: Full-year election, joint return

Salary	$81,000
Interest	1,200
Standard deduction	(12,400)
Exemptions	(7,900)
Taxable income	$61,900
Tax	8,378

By electing to be treated as a resident alien for the entire tax year, you save $3,778 in federal income taxes. Note that your spouse could not be claimed as a dependent under Alternative 1, since your spouse had income during the U.S. residency period. Your spouse does not need to file a return under Alternative 1, since your spouse's income did not exceed the amount that requires you to file. (See chapter 1, *Filing information.*)

The $6,500 in income that you and your spouse had in your home country would probably be subject to tax there. If so, you would be eligible for the foreign tax credit if you filed under Alternative 2. The tax credit would further lower your taxes. See chapter 37, *Other credits including the earned income credit*, for a discussion of the foreign tax credit.

TAXORGANIZER

In order to claim exemptions for a resident alien's spouse and/or children who are not eligible to obtain a social security number, an individual taxpayer identification number (an "ITIN") is required for each person. Obtaining such a tax ID number no longer necessitates going to the social security office with the family. Rather, these numbers are now obtained directly from the IRS when the tax return is filed. Use Form W-7, *Application for IRS Individual Taxpayer Identification Number*, to apply for the ITIN.

How Nonresident Aliens Are Taxed

A nonresident alien is taxed as follows:

Compensation for services rendered in the United States or other income that is effectively connected with a U.S. trade or business is generally taxed at graduated rates, using the appropriate tax rate schedules. A nonresident alien may deduct certain expenses incurred in producing that income, such as business-related expenses and state and local income taxes. In addition, he or she may deduct casualty losses and qualifying charitable contributions. However, a nonresident alien may not claim the standard deduction.

Income that is effectively connected with a U.S. trade or business at the time it is earned will be considered "effectively connected" at the time it is received, even if receipt occurs in a different tax year.

A nonresident alien is generally able to claim a personal exemption only for himself or herself. However, a nonresident alien who is a resident of Mexico or Canada, or a national of the United States (such as certain American Samoans or Northern Mariana Islanders), is also entitled to claim personal exemptions for

1. A spouse, if the spouse had no gross income for U.S. tax purposes and was not the dependent of another taxpayer
2. Other dependents, if they meet the same requirements as a U.S. citizen.

In addition, certain tax treaties allow for personal exemptions for a spouse and dependents in specific cases.

A married nonresident alien is taxed under the "married filing separately" Tax Rate Schedule, which is the highest Tax Rate Schedule applicable to individuals.

You may not claim head of household status if you are a nonresident alien. A nonresident alien who is single would use the "unmarried" Tax Rate Schedule.

Dividends, interest, royalties, pensions, annuities, and other types of U.S. source income that are not effectively connected with a U.S. trade or business are usually subject to a flat 30% tax rate unless a tax treaty allows for a lower rate of tax. No deductions or exemptions are allowed against this income. Interest earned on U.S. bank accounts, as well as certain other investments (known as "portfolio" debt instruments), is exempt from U.S. taxes.

Gains and losses from the sale of capital assets, other than real property situated in the U.S., may be taxed in either of two ways. If the gains and losses are not connected with a trade or business in the United States, any gain (after deducting losses) is taxed at a 30% rate if the nonresident alien is in the United States for 183 days or more during the tax year. If a gain is derived from the sale of capital assets effectively connected with a trade or a business in the United States, it is taxed in the same manner as it would be for a U.S. citizen. Capital gains from the sale of real property located in the United States are considered to be connected with a U.S. trade or business and are subject to special U.S. tax laws. (For a more detailed discussion of the tax treatment of gains and losses, see IRS Publication 519, *U.S. Tax Guide for Aliens*.)

Foreign students. Foreign students who enter the U.S. under an "F," "M," or "Q" visa (academic or language student) or a "J" visa (educational and cultural exchange visitor) are generally nonresidents for U.S. income tax purposes, as long as they substantially comply with the terms of their visa.

TAXPLANNER

Foreign nationals who become U.S. residents. Foreign nationals who become U.S. residents are taxed on their worldwide income from the day on which they become residents. You may, however, take several steps before you become a U.S. resident in order to limit your U.S. tax liability. Consider the following:

1. If you anticipate receiving a payment of compensation for past services, such as a bonus, arrange to receive this payment before becoming a resident of the United States. If this payment is received after you become a U.S. resident alien, it will be taxable in full by the United States, even though the related services were rendered prior to coming to the United States. Review tax treaty and foreign tax credit rules for possible relief if the payment is received after becoming a U.S. tax resident.
2. If you anticipate incurring expenses that will be deductible for U.S. income tax purposes, such as mortgage points, interest, or certain charitable contributions, consider deferring these payments until after you are a resident of the United States.
3. If you sell shares in a foreign corporation for a gain prior to your arrival in the United States, the entire gain is not subject to U.S. tax. However, if you sell shares at a profit after you become a U.S. resident, the entire gain is subject to U.S. tax, even if the entire appreciation of the shares occurred before you became a U.S. resident. You should consider selling shares and other investments in which you have a profit before you become a U.S. resident. By the same token, if you hold an investment that has a loss and the entire loss was generated before you became a U.S. resident, but you did not realize the loss until after you took up residency, you may deduct the loss on your U.S. tax return, subject to the normal rules (see chapter 16, *Reporting gains and losses*, for more information).

4. If you receive a distribution from a government or private retirement plan after you have become a U.S. resident, the entire amount may be subject to U.S. tax. If at all possible, arrange to receive the payment before you become a U.S. resident, when it is not subject to U.S. tax. Review tax treaty and foreign tax credit rules for possible relief if a payment is received after becoming a U.S. tax resident.

5. If you sell your principal residence before becoming a U.S. resident, the proceeds are not normally subject to any U.S. tax. However, if you become a U.S. resident and elect to be taxed as a resident alien for the entire year to take advantage of lower joint filing rates (see *Exceptions*, earlier), you may end up paying tax on the sale of your principal residence, as well as tax on any exchange gain associated with the payoff of the mortgage. Be sure to consider this fact before you elect to be taxed as a resident alien for the entire year.

There is a $250,000 exclusion for single taxpayers ($500,000 for married taxpayers filing jointly) on the gain from the sale of a home if you have owned the home and lived in the home as your principal residence for 2 of the last 5 years. The use of the exclusion by foreign nationals who have ceased to be residents of the United States is permitted if the expatriation rules do not apply (see *Rules for Individuals Giving Up U.S. Citizenship or U.S. Residency*, earlier in this chapter). Given the fact that this area of law is complex, you should seek tax advice prior to disposing of your primary residence.

You may be able to take advantage of a "window between tax residencies," a situation in which certain income is never taxed. This requires analyzing the tax laws of your home country and the United States. A window may be created, for example, if you come from a country that does not tax income of its nonresident citizens.

Example. Humphrey Benson is a citizen of a country that does not tax its nonresident citizens, and he decides to move permanently to the United States. He owns securities that have appreciated by $10,000. On his move to the United States, Humphrey ceases being a resident of his home country and goes to a third country for 2 weeks. The tax rules in this third country are such that he is not subject to tax on sales of securities. While there, he sells all his securities. The result is that he does not have to pay any tax in his home country, in the United States, or in the third country.

TAXPLANNER
Minimizing your tax burden. The main point to remember is that the best time for you to minimize your U.S. tax burden is *before* you make an investment in the United States and *before* you become a U.S. resident.

Departing from the United States
Before you depart from the United States, you must obtain a certificate of compliance, indicating that you have satisfied your federal tax liability. This certificate, frequently referred to as a "sailing permit" or a "departure permit," is obtained by filing Form 1040-C or Form 2063. To get the permit, you must either pay all of the U.S. income tax due prior to departure or demonstrate that your departure from the United States will not impair the collection of the tax. The forms may be found on the IRS website (*www.irs.gov*). An exit permit is valid for only 30 days. If you postpone your departure, you probably have to apply for a new exit permit. See IRS Publication 519, *U.S. Tax Guide for Aliens*, for more details and for certain categories of individuals who are exempt from the "sailing permit" requirements.

TAXORGANIZER
Sailing permits. The IRS representative must see actual departure tickets in order to issue your "sailing permit." Make sure you bring these along to the IRS office. *A certificate of compliance is not a substitute for an annual income tax return.* A federal tax return still must be filed in accordance with regular filing procedures. Any payment in conjunction with the filing of Form 1040-C is treated as a payment on your annual tax return.

Note

ey.com/EYTaxGuide
Ernst & Young LLP will update the *EY Tax Guide 2015* website with relevant taxpayer information as it becomes available. You can also sign up for email alerts to let you know when changes have been made.

Introduction

The death of an individual can cause special tax problems, many of which are likely to be unfamiliar and puzzling to his or her survivors. Among other things, the deceased's will, along with state inheritance laws, can create a bewildering array of questions about how income is to be allocated and which deductions may be claimed and by whom.

This chapter helps you sort out such questions. It is most helpful to a survivor who has to deal with a relatively uncomplicated situation and a small estate. When the assets are large and the situation is complex, professional assistance is recommended.

Reminders

Consistent treatment of estate items. Beneficiaries must generally treat estate items the same way on their individual income tax returns as they are treated on the estate's income tax return. For more information, see How and When to Report under Distributions to Beneficiaries From an Estate in Publication 559, Survivors, Executors, and Administrators.

This chapter discusses the tax responsibilities of the person who is in charge of the property (estate) of an individual who has died (decedent). It also covers the following topics:

- Filing the decedent's final return.
- Tax effects on survivors.

This chapter does not discuss the requirements for filing an income tax return of an estate (Form 1041). For information on Form 1041, see Income Tax Return of an Estate—Form 1041 in Publication 559. This chapter also does not discuss the requirements for filing an estate tax return (Form 706). For information, see Form 706 and its instructions.

EXPLANATION

Though this chapter mainly discusses the filing requirement of a final individual income tax return for a decedent, an explanation of the various potential filing requirements may be helpful. Generally, upon an individual's death, there are three types of taxes that should be addressed: estate tax, gift tax, and income tax.

The estate tax is reported on Form 706, *U.S. Estate Tax Return*. Form 706 is a return that is generally based on the value of the net assets of the decedent's "estate" at the date of death. The filing deadline for Form 706 is nine months after the date of death, unless a six month extension of time to file is requested. Form 706 is generally required to be filed if the gross estate (the value of the estate without subtracting debts and liabilities) is over the applicable estate tax exemption.

In addition to an estate tax return, the decedent's personal representative may be required to file a gift tax return (Form 709) on the decedent's behalf. This return would report any gifts made by the decedent in the year of death and indicate the amount, if any, of gift tax due.

There are two possible income tax returns that may need to be filed: Form 1040, *U.S. Individual Income Tax Return*, and Form 1041, *U.S. Income Tax Return for Estates and Trusts*. Form 1040 is generally used to report all the income that the decedent earned and received prior to death. Any income that was earned and received after the date of death is generally reported by the estate (or the trust, if the asset was held in trust) and is reported on Form 1041. This chapter focuses mainly on Form 1040 issues.

Useful Items

You may want to see:

Publication

- ☐ **3** Armed Forces Tax Guide
- ☐ **559** Survivors, Executors, and Administrators

Form (and Instructions)

- ☐ **56** Notice Concerning Fiduciary Relationship
- ☐ **1310** Statement of Person Claiming Refund Due a Deceased Taxpayer
- ☐ **4810** Request for Prompt Assessment Under Internal Revenue Code Section 6501(d)

Personal Representative

A personal representative of an estate is an executor, administrator, or anyone who is in charge of the decedent's property.

Executor. An executor (or executrix) is named in a decedent's will to administer the estate (property owned and debts owed by the decedent) and distribute property as the decedent's last will and testament directs.

Administrator. An administrator (or administratrix) is appointed by the court if no will exists, if no executor was named in the will, or if the named executor cannot or will not serve.

Personal representative. In general, an executor and an administrator perform the same duties and have the same responsibilities. Because a personal representative for a decedent's estate can be an executor, administrator, or anyone in charge of the decedent's property, the term personal representative will be used throughout this chapter.

The surviving spouse may or may not be the personal representative, depending on the terms of the decedent's will or the court appointment.

Duties

The primary duties of a personal representative are to collect the decedent's assets, pay creditors (including any taxes due), and distribute the remaining assets to the heirs or other beneficiaries.

The personal representative also must perform the following duties:

1. Notify the IRS (as discussed below) that he or she is acting as the personal representative (or in a fiduciary capacity).
2. File any income tax and estate tax return when due. (See *Final Return for the Decedent*, later.)
3. Pay any tax determined up to the date of discharge from duties.
4. Provide the payers of any interest and dividends the name(s) and identification number(s) of the new owner(s). (See *Interest and Dividend Income [Forms 1099]*, later.)

For more information on the duties and responsibilities of the personal representative, see *Duties under Personal Representative* in Publication 559.

Notifying the IRS. If you are appointed to act in any fiduciary capacity for another, you must file a written notice with the IRS stating this. Form 56 can be used for this purpose. The instructions and other requirements are given on the back of the form.

Final Return for the Decedent

The same filing requirements that apply to individuals determine if a final income tax return must be filed for the decedent. Filing requirements are discussed in chapter 1, *Filing information*.

Filing to Get a Refund

A return should be filed to obtain a refund if tax was withheld from salaries, wages, pensions, or annuities, or if estimated tax was paid, even if a return is not required to be filed. See *Claiming a refund*, later. Also, the decedent may be entitled to other credits that result in a refund. See chapter 37, *Other credits including the earned income credit*, for additional information on refundable credits, and see chapter 35, *Child tax credit* for information on the child tax credit.

Determining income and deductions. The method of accounting regularly used by the decedent before death generally determines what income must be included and what deductions can be taken on the final return. Generally, individuals use one of two methods of accounting: cash or accrual.

Cash method. If the decedent used the cash method of accounting, include only the items of income actually or constructively received before death and deduct only the expenses the decedent paid before death. For an exception for certain medical expenses not paid before death, see *Decedent* in chapter 22, *Medical and dental expenses*.

Explanation

Examples of income actually or constructively received include such items as uncashed payroll and dividend checks, if they were received or were available to the decedent before death.

   Example. If the decedent's payroll check for June 1 through June 15 is available on Friday, June 14, but she fails to pick it up and dies on Sunday, June 16, the income is included on the decedent's final individual income tax return. However, if the decedent would not have been paid until Monday, June 17—that date appears on the check and that is the first day it could have been picked up—the income is reported as part of the estate and not on the final Form 1040. In the latter case, the income is called *income in respect of a decedent (IRD)* and is discussed in the following section.

   If the decedent was married and lived in a community property state—Arizona, California, Idaho, Louisiana, Nevada, New Mexico, Texas, Washington, or Wisconsin—half of the combined income and expenses of husband and wife up to the date of death may be attributable to the decedent. Wisconsin has a marital property law that is similar to community property law.

TAXSAVER

The person filing the decedent's final return may elect to include as income on that return all of the U.S. savings bond interest that had accumulated but had not been reported. If the decedent otherwise had low taxable income to report on his or her final return, this return could be the best one in which to recognize the interest income. To determine whether or not this is advantageous, you have to compare the tax rate of the decedent on the final individual income tax return with the tax rate of the recipient of the bonds. (For a further discussion of this point, see chapter 7, *Interest income*.)

Accrual method. If the decedent used the accrual method of accounting, report only those items of income that the decedent accrued, or earned, before death. Deduct those expenses the decedent was liable for before death, regardless of whether the expenses were paid.

Additional information. For more information on the cash and accrual methods, *see Accounting Methods* in chapter 1, *Filing information*.

Who must file the return? The personal representative (defined earlier) must file the final income tax return (Form 1040) of the decedent for the year of death and any returns not filed for preceding years. A surviving spouse, under certain circumstances, may have to file the returns for the decedent. See *Joint return*, later.

    Example. Samantha Smith died on March 21, 2015, before filing her 2014 tax return. Her personal representative must file her 2014 return by April 15, 2015. Her final tax return for 2015 is due April 15, 2016.

Explanation
If the decedent had not yet filed a return for the previous year, the personal representative or surviving spouse should prepare and file the return, just as the decedent would have. The only differences are (1) the personal representative signs the return (see *Signing the return*, later) and (2) the estimated tax payments that are due after the decedent died are not required to be made. If a joint return is being filed, see the discussion of estimated tax payments under *Joint return*, later.

    For the year of death, the decedent's final return covers income received and deductible items paid during the period from January 1 through the date of death (assuming that the decedent was a cash-basis taxpayer).

TAXSAVER

If the decedent was a member of the U.S. Armed Forces and died while in active service in a combat zone or from wounds, disease, or other injury received in a combat zone, the decedent's income tax liability is forgiven for the tax year in which death occurred.

    A decedent's income tax liability is also forgiven for any decedent who was either a military or civilian U.S. employee at death and died from wounds or injury incurred while a U.S. employee in a terrorist or military action outside the United States.

    For additional information, please seek advice from your tax advisor.

TAXSAVER

A surviving spouse may be able to reduce the tax on his or her income by filing a joint return with the decedent. Even if a taxpayer died on January 1 with no income earned by that date, the availability of joint tax rates to the surviving spouse could be beneficial. However, if the surviving spouse remarries before the end of the year, the decedent must file as married filing separately.

Filing the return. The word "DECEASED," the decedent's name, and the date of death should be written across the top of the tax return. In the name and address space, you should write the name and address of the decedent and, if a joint return, of the surviving spouse. If a joint return is not being filed, the decedent's name should be written in the name space and the personal representative's name and address should be written in the remaining space.

    Example. John Stone died in early 2014. He was survived by his wife, Jane. The top of their final joint return on Form 1040, which includes the required information, is illustrated below.

Signing the return. If a personal representative has been appointed, that person must sign the return. If it is a joint return, the surviving spouse must also sign it.

    If no personal representative has been appointed, the surviving spouse (on a joint return) should sign the return and write in the signature area "Filing as surviving spouse." See *Joint return*, later.

    If no personal representative has been appointed and if there is no surviving spouse, the person in charge of the decedent's property must file and sign the return as "personal representative."

Figure 43-A   **Surviving Spouse Filing Joint Return with Decedent**

| Form **1040** | Department of the Treasury—Internal Revenue Service (99) | | **2014** | OMB No. 1545-0074 | IRS Use Only—Do not write or staple in this space. |

U.S. Individual Income Tax Return

For the year Jan. 1–Dec. 31, 2014, or other tax year beginning _____ , 2014, ending _____ , 20 ___

See separate instructions.

Your first name and initial	Last name	Your social security number
John S	Stone	7 6 5 0 0 4 3 2 1

If a joint return, spouse's first name and initial	Last name	Spouse's social security number
Jane M	Stone	1 2 3 0 0 4 5 6 7

Home address (number and street). If you have a P.O. box, see instructions. | Apt. no.

1992 Oak St

▲ Make sure the SSN(s) above and on line 6c are correct.

City, town or post office, state, and ZIP code. If you have a foreign address, also complete spaces below (see instructions).

Sheridan, WY 82801

Foreign country name | Foreign province/state/county | Foreign postal code

Presidential Election Campaign
Check here if you, or your spouse if filing jointly, want $3 to go to this fund. Checking a box below will not change your tax or refund. ☐ You ☐ Spouse

Filing Status

Check only one box.

1 ☐ Single
2 ☑ Married filing jointly (even if only one had income)
3 ☐ Married filing separately. Enter spouse's SSN above and full name here. ▶
4 ☐ Head of household (with qualifying person). (See instructions.) If the qualifying person is a child but not your dependent, enter this child's name here. ▶
5 ☐ Qualifying widow(er) with dependent child

~~~~~~

Third Party Designee

Do you want to allow another person to discuss this return with the IRS (see instructions)? ☐ **Yes.** Complete below. ☐ **No**

Designee's name ▶ | Phone no. ▶ | Personal identification number (PIN) ▶

Sign Here

Joint return? See instructions. Keep a copy for your records.

Under penalties of perjury, I declare that I have examined this return and accompanying schedules and statements, and to the best of my knowledge and belief, they are true, correct, and complete. Declaration of preparer (other than taxpayer) is based on all information of which preparer has any knowledge.

Your signature	Date	Your occupation	Daytime phone number
Jane M. Stone	4/2/2015	**Engineer**	**555-111-2222**
Spouse's signature. If a joint return, **both** must sign.	Date	Spouse's occupation	If the IRS sent you an Identity Protection PIN, enter it here (see inst.)
Filling as surviving spouse			

Paid Preparer Use Only

Print/Type preparer's name	Preparer's signature	Date	Check ☐ if self-employed	PTIN

Firm's name ▶ | Firm's EIN ▶
Firm's address ▶ | Phone no.

www.irs.gov/form1040 | Form **1040** (2014)

If the personal representative is filing a claim for refund on Form 1040X, Amended U.S. Individual Income Tax Return, or Form 843, Claim for Refund and Request for Abatement, and the court certificate has already been filed with the IRS, attach Form 1310 and write "Certificate Previously Filed" at the bottom of the form.

Example. Mr. Green died before filing his tax return. You were appointed the personal representative for Mr. Green's estate and you file his Form 1040 for the prior year showing a refund due. You do not need Form 1310 to claim the refund if you attach a copy of the court certificate showing you were appointed the personal representative.

Important Tax-Related Actions to Take After a Death

Action	Comments
Obtain at least 10 death certificates from the local county clerk, mortuary, or funeral director.	The executor or personal representative (referred to as the "executor" in this chart) must file the death certificate with the estate tax return (Form 706) for the decedent. Also, death certificates will be needed to claim life insurance proceeds, change title to bank accounts, and transfer title to other assets. Death certificates usually will not be available until a week or two after the death.
Contact life insurance companies to claim the proceeds. The executor can usually find the telephone number on the most recent life insurance policy statement.	Contact the insurance company as soon as possible. The decedent's family may need the insurance proceeds for support.
Notify the Social Security Administration of the death. Also notify banks and investment brokers.	The telephone number for the Social Security Administration is 1-800-772-1213.
Contact an estate planning or probate attorney to determine what court filings are necessary.	Select an attorney who has at least 5 years of significant experience handling the administrations of estates. See the attorney as soon as possible after the death. Referrals to attorneys can be obtained from friends or relatives, or often from a local bar association referral service.
Contact an accountant regarding all tax filings that will be necessary.	The personal representative or surviving spouse must file a final income tax return for the decedent (Form 1040). No further estimated taxes for the decedent must be paid after the death of the decedent.
	The "probate estate" (if a probate is necessary) becomes a new taxpayer and the personal representative must file a tax return (Form 1041). The estate may select a fiscal year that may result in beneficial tax deferral.
	If the decedent funded a "revocable living trust" during life, that trust, which becomes irrevocable at death also becomes a new taxpayer and may also be required to file a Form 1041. However, in certain cases, the probate estate and the trust may file consolidated income tax returns.
Obtain an Employee Identification Number (EIN) for the estate.	The estate will need an EIN to file tax returns and to open a bank account. In addition, the estate will be required to get a new EIN if the funds from the estate are used to establish a trust. The IRS provides an online application with an interactive, interview-style questionnaire that will guide you through the application process. There is no charge to obtain an EIN. The estate's attorney or accountant can also help with this process.
Open an estate checking account as soon as possible—deposit all checks due to the decedent and pay all debts and expenses owed (including funeral expenses and taxes) from this account.	It is critical to keep accurate records. Do not commingle anyone else's income or expenses with the decedent's income and expenses, including income earned and expenses paid after date of death. The executor will need accurate information to file the decedent's final income tax return, the estate's and/or trust's income tax return, and the estate tax return.
Search through the decedent's desk, office, safe deposit box, and files to locate information that is needed for the tax returns.	Specifically, look for the following: will, codicils to the will and trust agreements; addresses and Social Security numbers of beneficiaries; checking, savings, money market, and CD statements; checkbook registers; brokerage statements; stock certificates; bonds; retirement plan and IRA benefit statements; life insurance and annuity policies; the last 3 years of state and federal income tax returns and all prior gift tax returns; property tax bill and deed for real estate; buy-sell or operating agreements for businesses; all outstanding bills (including last illness and funeral bills); and any undeposited checks.
Review the decedent's company retirement and benefit plans, as well as IRAs, with a tax advisor or attorney.	The beneficiary of these assets must make certain decisions regarding distributions from these plans and IRAs; the decisions made can have significant income tax consequences.

TAXPLANNER

To make sure that refunds are not delayed, attach Form 1310 to any return being filed for a decedent on which a refund is being claimed. This is true despite the fact that Form 1310 may not be required, as previously discussed.

Form 1310 can also be submitted to request that a refund check issued jointly to the decedent and surviving spouse be reissued to a surviving spouse.

When and Where to File

The final income tax return is due at the same time the decedent's return would have been due had death not occurred. The final return for a decedent who was a calendar year taxpayer is generally due April 15 following the year death occurred. However, when the due date falls on a Saturday, Sunday, or legal holiday, the return is filed timely if filed by the next business day.

TAXPLANNER

The personal representative or surviving spouse may request an extension of time to file the decedent's final income tax return by filing Form 4868, Application for Automatic Extension of Time To File U.S. Individual Income Tax Return. This will give an additional six months to file the return. Note that an extension of time to file does not mean an extension of time to pay tax. Hence, any tax liability owed must be paid in full by the due date of the return, excluding extensions. See *When Do I Have to File?* in chapter 1, *Filing information*.

You may obtain Form 4868 via the Internet by visiting the IRS website at *www.irs.gov*.

Generally, you must file the final income tax return of the decedent with the Internal Revenue Service Center for the place where you live. A tax return for a decedent can be electronically filed. A personal representative may also obtain an income tax filing extension on behalf of a decedent.

TAXPLANNER

A representative of a decedent's estate may be held personally liable by the IRS for later-discovered tax deficiencies if the representative has not retained enough of the estate's assets to pay those deficiencies. Therefore, many cautious representatives are slow to distribute the estate's assets to the heirs. Filing Form 4810, Request for Prompt Assessment Under Internal Revenue Code Section 6501(d), may shorten the period in which the IRS may hold the representative responsible for not paying enough tax, thereby potentially allowing the estate's assets to be distributed more promptly. However, the request may trigger an audit of those returns.

Joint return. Generally, the personal representative and the surviving spouse can file a joint return for the decedent and the surviving spouse. However, the surviving spouse alone can file the joint return if no personal representative was appointed before the due date for filing the joint return for the year of death. This also applies to the return for the preceding year if the decedent died after the close of the preceding tax year and before filing the return for that year. The income of the decedent that was includible on his or her return for the year up to the date of death (as explained under *Determining income and deductions*, earlier) and the income of the surviving spouse for the entire year must be included in the final joint return.

A joint return with the decedent cannot be filed for the year of death if the surviving spouse remarried before the end of the year of the decedent's death. The filing status of the decedent in this instance is married filing a separate return.

TAXPLANNER

If you are a surviving spouse and are filing a joint return with the decedent for 2014, you are not relieved of the obligation to make estimated tax payments for 2015 because of the death. See chapter 4, *Tax withholding and estimated tax*, for more information on estimated tax payments.

TAXSAVER

If the decedent was married, it is important to calculate whether the tax on a joint return would be less than the total tax on two separate returns.

Ordinarily, a joint return would result in the least overall tax for married couples, but only a complete computation will tell you for sure. Remember, the joint return will include all of the income and deductions of the survivor for the entire year, but those of the decedent are included only up to the date of death. If property was owned jointly with the surviving spouse, all of the income after death is required to be reported in the joint return, because it, along with the ownership of the property, passed to the surviving spouse by operation of law. However, if the property was not owned jointly and passed to an executor at death, the subsequent income on that property would be reported on the income tax return for the estate for which the executor is responsible, and not on the joint return.

Personal representative may revoke joint return election. A court-appointed personal representative may revoke an election to file a joint return that was previously made by the surviving spouse alone. This is done by filing a separate return for the decedent within one year from the due date of the return (including any extensions). The joint return made by the surviving spouse will then be regarded as the separate return of that spouse by excluding the decedent's items and refiguring the tax liability.

Relief from joint liability. In some cases, one spouse may be relieved of joint liability for tax, interest, and penalties on a joint return for items of the other spouse that were incorrectly reported on the joint return. If the decedent qualified for this relief while alive, the personal representative can pursue an existing request, or file a request, for relief from joint liability. The amount of time to request equitable relief depends on whether you have a balance due or are seeking a credit or refund:

- Balance Due—You generally must file Form 8857 10 years from the date the tax liability was assessed. In certain cases, the 10-year period is suspended. The amount of time the suspension is in effect will be added to the time remaining in the 10-year period.
- Credit or Refund—You generally must file Form 8857 within 3 years after the date the original return was filed or within 2 years after the date the tax was paid, whichever is later. But you may have more time to file if you live in a federally declared disaster area or you are physically or mentally unable to manage your financial affairs. For more information, see Publication 556, *Examination of Returns, Appeal Rights, and Claims for Refund*.

For information on requesting this relief, see Publication 971, *Innocent Spouse Relief*, and see *Filing a Joint Return* in chapter 2, *Filing status*.

How to Report Certain Income
This section explains how to report certain types of income on the final return. The rules on income discussed in the other chapters of this publication also apply to a decedent's final return. See chapters 5 through 16, if they apply.

Interest and dividend income (Forms 1099). A Form 1099 should be received for the decedent reporting interest and dividends earned before death. These amounts must be included on the decedent's final return. A separate Form 1099 should show the interest and dividends earned after the date of the decedent's death and paid to the estate or other recipient that must include those amounts on their respective return. You can request corrected Forms 1099 if these forms do not properly reflect the right recipient or amounts.

For example, a Form 1099-INT reporting interest payable to the decedent may include income that should be reported on the final income tax return of the decedent, as well as income that the estate or other recipient should report, either as income earned after death or as income in respect of a decedent (discussed later). For income earned after death, you should ask the payer for a Form 1099 that properly identifies the recipient (by name and identification number) and the proper amount. If that is not possible, or if the form includes an amount that represents income in respect of a decedent, report the interest, as shown next under *How to report*.

See *U.S. savings bonds acquired from decedent* in Publication 559 for information on savings bond interest that may have to be reported under income in respect of a decedent on the final return.

How to report. If you are preparing the decedent's final return and you have received a Form 1099-INT, Interest Income, for the decedent that includes amounts belonging to the decedent and to another recipient (the decedent's estate or another beneficiary), report the total interest shown on Form 1099-INT on Schedule 1 (Form 1040A) or on Schedule B (Form 1040). Next, enter a subtotal of the interest shown on Forms 1099 and the interest reportable from other sources for which you did not receive Forms 1099. Then, show any interest (including any interest you receive as a nominee) belonging to another recipient separately and subtract it from the subtotal. Identify this adjustment as a "Nominee Distribution" or other appropriate designation.

Report dividend income for which you received a Form 1099-DIV on the appropriate schedule using the same procedure.

Note: If the decedent received amounts as a nominee, you must give the actual owner a Form 1099, unless the owner is the decedent's spouse. See *General Instructions for Forms 1099, 1098, 5498, and W-2G* for more information on filing Forms 1099.

TAXPLANNER

No matter how hard you try, you may have difficulty getting the payers of dividends and interest to reflect properly the amounts attributable to the decedent prior to death and the amounts that are paid to the decedent's successor in interest. It is therefore imperative that you follow the example below carefully in order to avoid bothersome inquiries from the IRS.

Example 1. Marty died on June 30, 2014. Marty owned 50 shares of ABC Corporation and 75 shares of XYZ Corporation, both of which paid a $1 per share quarterly dividend on February 1, May 1, August 1, and November 1. Upon Marty's death, all shares were transferred to his estate. XYZ Corporation has properly issued two Forms 1099-DIV. One Form 1099-DIV identifies Marty as the recipient of $150 (the dividends paid to Marty prior to death, from January 1, 2014, to June 30, 2014), and the other identifies Marty's estate as the recipient of $150 (the dividends paid to the estate, from July 1, 2014, to December 31, 2014). ABC Corporation, however, issued only one Form 1099-DIV, naming Marty as the recipient of the entire year's dividend ($200).

On Marty's final return, you must report total dividends as indicated on all Forms 1099-DIV issued in Marty's name ($150 from XYZ Corporation and $200 from ABC Corporation) on line 5, Part II of Form 1040, Schedule B. Several lines above line 6, write "Subtotal" and enter $350. Below this subtotal, write "Nominee Distribution" and enter $100 (the dividends paid by ABC Corporation that belong to Marty's estate). Indicate the name and EIN of the nominee. Subtract the nominee distribution from the subtotal and report the net result of $250 on line 6. The same reporting procedure would apply to reporting interest. See the example below for an example of the language to put on Schedule B.

Example 2. John Johnson died on July 1, 2014. In January 2015, ABC Bank sent a Form 1099-INT to his executor reflecting interest paid during 2014 of $5,000. Because John was alive for only one-half of 2014, only one-half of the interest will be reported on his final Form 1040 for 2014. The other one-half of the interest will be reported on his estate's income tax return (Form 1041).

Schedule B of John's final Form 1040 should report the $2,500 of interest. Part I, line 1, should be completed as follows:

ABC Bank	$5,000
Less: Nominee distribution	($2,500)
(Estate of John Johnson: EIN: 00-0000000)	

Part 1, line 4, would show total interest income of $2,500.
The Form 1041 for the estate of John will report the other $2,500 of interest income.

TAXORGANIZER

You should keep a copy of the Forms 1099 that you receive as well as the tax worksheets showing pre- and post-death income for a minimum of three years.

Accelerated death benefits. Accelerated death benefits are amounts received under a life insurance contract before the death of the insured individual. These benefits also include amounts received on the sale or assignment of the contract to a provider of viatical settlements (life insurance payouts prior to death).

Generally, if the decedent received accelerated death benefits either on his or her life or on the life of another person, those benefits are not included in the decedent's income. This exclusion applies only if the insured was terminally or chronically ill. For more information, see *Accelerated death benefits* under *Gifts, Insurance, and Inheritances* in Publication 559.

Business income. This section discusses some of the business income that may have to be included on the final return.

Partnership income. The death of a partner closes the partnership's tax year for that partner. Generally, it does not close the partnership's tax year for the remaining partners. The decedent's distributive share of partnership items must be figured as if the partnership's tax year ended on the date the partner died. To avoid an interim closing of the partnership books, the partners can agree to estimate the decedent's distributive share by prorating the amounts the partner would have included for the entire partnership tax year.

On the decedent's final return, include the decedent's distributive share of partnership items for the following periods:

1. The partnership's tax year that ended within or with the decedent's final tax year (the year ending on the date of death); and
2. The period, if any, from the end of the partnership's tax year in (1) above to the decedent's date of death.

TAXALERT

A partnership's tax year closes with respect to a partner whose entire interest in the partnership is terminated by death. Therefore, the partnership income will have to be allocated between and reported by the decedent and the decedent's successor in interest. The final individual income tax return should include the decedent's share of partnership income and deductions for the partnership's tax year that ends within or with the decedent's last tax year (the year ending on the date of death). The final return must also include income for the period between the end of the partnership's last tax year and the date of death.

The income for the part of the partnership's tax year after the partner's death is reported by the estate or other person who has acquired the interest in the partnership.

Example. Jim, a partner in a law firm, died on December 1, 2014. The tax year for the partnership ends on June 30. Jim's partnership income of $100,000 for the fiscal year ending June 30, 2014, will be included on his final individual income tax return for 2014. In addition, Jim's final income tax return will also include his pro rata portion (154 days) of partnership income and deductions from July 1, 2014, to December 1, 2014, with the remainder to be reported to Jim's successor in interest.

TAXSAVER

Planning for partnership interests can save substantial amounts of income tax. For example, a partner should investigate the possibility of appointing his or her spouse as successor in interest to the partnership so that the income or loss for the year of death can flow onto the survivor's return and thus onto the joint return.

There is another way of ensuring the immediate transfer of the partnership interest to the spouse upon the partner's death so that the income or loss can be reported on the joint return. The spouses may own the partnership interest in joint tenancy. Be sure to check that the partnership will permit joint tenancy ownership. Also, if the executor has the assets and the legal authority to make an immediate distribution of the partnership interest to the spouse, all or a portion of the partnership income can be transferred to the final joint return. Prompt action may be necessary. Finally, consult with a tax advisor because there may be tax disadvantages to holding property in joint tenancy.

TAXPLANNER

If a decedent had an interest in a passive activity (e.g., a partnership or S corporation), the passive activity will be treated as though the activity was sold at death triggering the recognition of any suspended losses on the decedent's final individual tax return. However, these losses may have to be reduced depending on whether the interest received a step-up in basis. Generally, the remaining suspended losses may not be transferred to the partner's successor in interest. You should consult with your tax advisor for more information.

S corporation income. If the decedent was a shareholder in an S corporation, include on the final return the decedent's share of the S corporation's items of income, loss, deduction, and credit for the following periods:

1. The corporation's tax year that ended within or with the decedent's final tax year (the year ending on the date of death); and
2. The period, if any, from the end of the corporation's tax year in (1) above to the decedent's date of death.

Example. Julia Jones was a 20% partner in XYZ Partnership and a 20% shareholder in ABC Corporation, an S corporation. The tax year for both the partnership and the corporation ends on December 31. Julia died on October 1, 2014. Had she lived, Julia would have earned $100,000 of ordinary income in 2014 from the partnership and another $100,000 of ordinary income from the corporation.

Julia's final tax return for 2014 will include $75,070 (274 days) of income from ABC Corporation and $75,070 of income from XYZ Partnership. The remaining $24,930 of ABC Corporation income and the $24,930 from XYZ Partnership income will be included in the tax return of the successor in interest.

Self-employment income. Include self-employment income actually or constructively received or accrued, depending on the decedent's accounting method. For self-employment tax purposes only, the decedent's self-employment income will include the decedent's distributive share of a partnership's income or loss through the end of the month in which death occurred. For this purpose, the partnership income or loss is considered to be earned ratably over the partnership's tax year. For more information on how to compute self-employment income, see chapter 38, *Self-employment income: How to file Schedule C.*

Coverdell Education Savings Account (ESA). Generally, the balance in a Coverdell ESA must be distributed within 30 days after the individual for whom the account was established reaches age 30 or dies, whichever is earlier. The treatment of the Coverdell ESA at the death of an individual under age 30 depends on who acquires the interest in the account. If the decedent's estate acquires the interest, the earnings on the account must be included on the final income tax return of the decedent. If a beneficiary acquires the interest, see the discussion under *Income in Respect of a Decedent*, later.

The age 30 limit does not apply if the individual for whom the account was established, or the beneficiary that acquires the account, is an individual with special needs. This includes an individual who because of a physical, mental, or emotional condition (including a learning disability) requires additional time to complete his or her education.

For more information on Coverdell ESAs, see Publication 970, *Tax Benefits for Education.*

Archer MSA. The treatment of an Archer MSA, a Medicare Advantage MSA, or a Health Savings Account (HSA) at the death of the account holder depends on who acquires the interest in the account. If the decedent's estate acquires the interest, the fair market value of the assets in the account on the date of death is included in income on the decedent's final return.

If a beneficiary acquires the interest, see the discussion under *Income in Respect of a Decedent*, later. For more information on Archer MSAs, see Publication 969, *Health Savings Accounts and Other Tax-Favored Health Plans.*

Exemptions, Deductions, and Credits

Generally, the rules for exemptions, deductions, and credits allowed to an individual also apply to the decedent's final income tax return. Show on the final return deductible items the decedent paid (or accrued, if the decedent reported deductions on an accrual method) before death.

Exemptions. You can claim the decedent's personal exemption on the final income tax return. If the decedent was another person's dependent (for example, a parent's), you cannot claim the personal exemption on the decedent's final return.

Standard deduction. If you do not itemize deductions on the final return, the full amount of the appropriate standard deduction is allowed regardless of the date of death. For information on the appropriate standard deduction, see chapter 21, *Standard deduction.*

Itemized deductions. If the total of the decedent's itemized deductions is more than the decedent's standard deduction, the federal income tax will generally be less if you claim itemized deductions on the final return. See chapters 22 through 29 for the types of expenses that are allowed as itemized deductions.

Medical expenses. Medical expenses paid before death by the decedent are deductible, subject to limits, on the final income tax return if deductions are itemized. This includes expenses for the decedent as well as for the decedent's spouse and dependents.

For information on certain medical expenses that were not paid before death, see *Decedent* in chapter 22, *Medical and dental expenses.*

TAXPLANNER

Funeral burial and probate expenses are not deductible on the decedent's or estate's income tax return. However, these may be deducted on the decedent's estate tax return.

TAXSAVER

The executor or executrix may elect to either claim certain medical and dental expenses as deductions on the estate tax return or as deductions on the decedent's final income tax return. The tax should be computed both ways to see which results in more tax savings.

If an election is made to include the medical and dental expenses on the decedent's income tax return rather than on the federal estate tax return, the executor or executrix must attach a statement to the income tax return stating that he or she has not claimed the amount as an estate tax deduction and that the estate waives the right to claim the amount as a deduction.

TAXSAVER

When death is expected in the near future, proper planning can save tax dollars. Deductible expenses, such as interest expense and accounting fees that are due near the date of death may be paid before death or after death. Choose the time offering the greater tax benefit. If you arrange to pay the expenses before death, they are deductible on the decedent's final Form 1040 if deductions are itemized. If you arrange to pay them after death, they are deductible on the estate's income tax return. Limitations as to deductibility may apply.

Unrecovered investment in pension. If the decedent was receiving a pension or annuity (with an annuity starting date after 1986) and died without a surviving annuitant, you can take a deduction on the decedent's final return for the amount of the decedent's investment in the pension or annuity contract that remained unrecovered at death. The deduction is a miscellaneous itemized deduction that is not subject to the 2% limit on adjusted gross income. See chapter 29, *Miscellaneous deductions*.

Deduction for losses. A decedent's net operating loss deduction from a prior year and any capital losses (including capital loss carryovers) can be deducted only on the decedent's final income tax return. A net operating loss on the decedent's final income tax return can be carried back to prior years (see Publication 536, *Net Operating Losses (NOLs) for Individuals, Estates, and Trusts*). You cannot deduct any unused net operating loss or capital loss on the estate's income tax return.

TAXSAVER

Net operating losses (or carryover losses) from business operations and capital losses (or carryover losses) of the decedent may not be carried over to the returns of executors or heirs. However, if a joint return is filed for the year of death, these losses may be used to offset the survivor's income for the entire year. In this case, it may be advantageous for the surviving spouse to incur capital gains and/or other income and to offset them with the capital losses and/or net operating losses that cannot be carried forward past the year of the spouse's death.

Example. Your spouse died on June 30, 2014, with $10,000 in short-term capital losses from his personal account. Because the maximum capital loss that can be deducted in a year is $3,000, only $3,000 of those losses will be allowed on your 2014 joint return, with no carryover of the remaining $7,000. However, if you could recognize an additional $7,000 in gains before the end of the year, you could use your deceased spouse's remaining $7,000 of losses to offset the gains by filing a joint return. If you waited until a later year to recognize those gains, they would be fully taxable, unless you had incurred other losses to offset them.

Credits. Any of the tax credits discussed in this publication also apply to the final return if the decedent was eligible for the credits at the time of death. These credits are discussed in chapters 33 through 37.

Tax withheld and estimated payments. There may have been income tax withheld from the decedent's pay, pensions, or annuities before death, and the decedent may have paid estimated income tax. To get credit for these tax payments, you must claim them on the decedent's final return. For more information, see *Credit for Withholding and Estimated Tax* in chapter 4, *Tax withholding and estimated tax*.

Explanation

Exemption allowances, the standard deduction, and itemized deductions are not prorated over that part of the year during which a now deceased taxpayer was alive. However, exemptions claimed for dependents could be a problem if the decedent did not live long enough during the year to provide the required amount of support. In most situations, potential problems will be alleviated if the surviving spouse files a joint return with the decedent. See chapter 3, *Personal exemptions and dependents*, for more information.

Tax Effect on Others

This section contains information about the effect of an individual's death on the income tax liability of the survivors (including the widow or widower and any beneficiaries) and the estate. A survivor should coordinate the filing of his or her own tax return with the personal representative handling the decedent's estate. The personal representative can coordinate filing status, exemptions, income, and deductions so that the decedent's final return and the income tax returns of the survivors and the estate are all filed correctly.

Survivors. If you are a survivor, you may qualify for certain benefits when filing your own income tax return. This section addresses some issues that may apply to you.

Gifts and inheritances. Property received as a gift, bequest, or inheritance is not included in your income. However, if property you receive in this manner later produces income, such as interest, dividends, or rent, that income is taxable to you. If the gift, bequest, or inheritance you receive is the income from property, that income is taxable to you.

If you inherited the right to receive income in respect of a decedent, see *Income in Respect of a Decedent*, later.

TAXALERT

Property inherited from a decedent who died either before or after 2010. The cost basis of any asset distributed from the estate of a decedent who died either before or after 2010 (which he/she owned at death) via bequest or inheritance is "stepped up" to the fair market value at the date of the decedent's death or the alternate valuation date. See chapter 13, *Basis of property*, for more information.

Furthermore, the asset is deemed to be long-term capital gain property, so any capital appreciation on the asset above the fair market value on the date of the decedent's death will be taxed at the long-term capital gains tax rate.

Exception: If you or your spouse inherit property that you gave to the decedent within 1 year of that person's death, your basis in the asset is what the decedent's adjusted basis in the asset was immediately before his or her death.

Property inherited from a decedent who died during 2010. The Tax Relief, Unemployment Insurance Reauthorization, and Job Creation Act of 2010 (the Act) that was passed in late 2010 complicated the matter of determining the basis in assets that you receive from a decedent who died in 2010. The Act provided executors of estates of 2010 decedents with a choice: to select either a stepped-up basis for the assets left by the decedent or to use a carryover basis for the assets.

TAXALERT

Fees received by an executor or administrator for duties performed for an estate are includable in the gross income of the executor or administrator but are usually not subject to self-employment tax as long as you are not in the trade or business of being an executor or administrator.

However, a specific bequest to the executor is not treated as income. It is merely a gift to an heir who also happens to be serving as executor. Therefore, if you are the executor and an heir, you may consider declining to take a fee, in which case a larger portion of the estate will be available for distribution as a bequest that is not subject to income tax. Contact your tax advisor to assist you in determining which course of action is more beneficial.

Joint return by surviving spouse. A surviving spouse can file a joint return for the year of death and may qualify for special tax rates for the following two years. For more information, see *Qualifying Widow(er) With Dependent Child* in chapter 2, *Filing status*.

Explanation

After the two-year period following the date of death, a surviving spouse may still be able to qualify as a head of household and use the Tax Table and Tax Rate Schedules for head of household. While not as beneficial as joint return rates, they are better than those for single persons. See chapter 2, *Filing status*, for more details.

Decedent as your dependent. If the decedent qualified as your dependent for the part of the year before death, you can claim the exemption for the dependent on your tax return, regardless of when death occurred during the year.

Income In Respect of a Decedent

All income that the decedent would have received had death not occurred and that was not properly includible on the final income tax return, discussed earlier, is income in respect of a decedent.

How to Report. Income in respect of a decedent must be included in the income of one of the following.

- The decedent's estate, if the estate receives it.
- The beneficiary, if the right to income is passed directly to the beneficiary and the beneficiary receives it.
- Any person to whom the estate properly distributes the right to receive it.

Example 1. Frank Johnson owned and operated an apple orchard. He used the cash method of accounting. He sold and delivered 1,000 bushels of apples to a canning factory for $2,000, but did not receive payment before his death. The proceeds from the sale are income in respect of a decedent. When the estate was settled, payment had not been made and the estate transferred the right to the payment to his widow. When Frank's widow collects the $2,000, she must include that amount in her return. It is not to be reported on the final return of the decedent or on the return of the estate.

Example 2. Assume the same facts as in Example 1, except that Frank used an accrual method of accounting. The amount accrued from the sale of the apples would be included on his final return. Neither the estate nor the widow will realize income in respect of a decedent when the money is later paid.

Example 3. Cathy O'Neil was entitled to a large salary payment at the date of her death. The amount was to be paid in five annual installments. The estate, after collecting two installments, distributed the right to the remaining installments to you, the beneficiary. The payments are income in respect of a decedent. None of the payments were includible in Cathy's final return. The estate must include in its income the two installments it received, and you must include in your income each of the three installments as you receive them.

Transferring your right to income. If you transfer your right to income in respect of a decedent, you must include in your income the greater of:

- The amount you receive for the right, or
- The fair market value of the right at the time of the transfer.

Fair market value (FMV). FMV is the price at which the property would change hands between a willing buyer and a willing seller, neither having to buy or sell, and both having reasonable knowledge of all necessary facts.

Giving your right to income as a gift. If you give your right to receive income in respect of a decedent as a gift, you must include in your income the fair market value of the right at the time you make the gift.

Example. Tom has a right to receive a payment of $10,000 that represents income in respect of his deceased father (e.g., deferred compensation). He makes a gift of his right to receive the money. He would immediately have to recognize the $10,000 as income on his tax return.

Type of income. The character or type of income that you receive in respect of a decedent is the same as it would be to the decedent if he or she were alive. If the income would have been a capital gain to the decedent, it will be a capital gain to you.

Explanation

Installment obligations. If the decedent had sold property using the installment method and you have the right to collect the payments, use the same gross profit percentage the decedent would have used to figure the part of each payment that represents profit. Include in your income the same profit the decedent would have included had death not occurred. For more information on installment sales, see Publication 537, *Installment Sales*.

If you dispose of an installment obligation acquired from a decedent (other than by transfer to the obligor), the rules explained in Publication 537 for figuring gain or loss on the disposition apply to you.

Example. Andrew sold undeveloped real estate held as an investment in 2012 for $120,000, receiving a note payable in four annual installments of $30,000 each plus interest. Andrew's basis in the land was $40,000. Andrew died in 2013 before the first installment was due, and the note was transferred to Helen, Andrew's heir. Helen collected the first installment of the note, $30,000, later during 2013. When Helen was in need of additional cash in early 2014, she sold the note to a bank for its fair market value of $90,000. For 2013, Helen must recognize gain on the installment payment she received. Using the same gross profit percentage as the decedent's ($80,000/$120,000), she would recognize a $20,000 gain, computed as follows:

$$\$30,000 \times \$80,000 / \$120,000 = \$20,000$$

For 2014, Helen must recognize gain on the disposition of the installment obligation. The gain is the difference between her basis and the fair market value at the time of the disposition. Her basis in the obligation is the same as Andrew's ($40,000) less the payment of principal received by her in 2013 ($10,000). Hence, her gain is computed as follows:

$$\$90,000 - (\$40,000 - \$10,000) = \$60,000$$

Whether the gain recognized by Helen on her tax return is ordinary income or capital gain depends on what it would have been to Andrew had he lived to collect the payments.

Inherited IRAs. If a beneficiary receives a lump-sum distribution from a traditional IRA he or she inherited, all or some of it may be taxable. The distribution is taxable in the year received as income in respect of a decedent up to the decedent's taxable balance. This is the decedent's balance at the time of death, including unrealized appreciation and income accrued to date of death, minus any basis (nondeductible contributions). Amounts distributed that are more than the decedent's entire IRA balance (including taxable and nontaxable amounts) at the time of death are the income of the beneficiary.

If the beneficiary of a traditional IRA is the decedent's surviving spouse who properly rolls over the distribution into another traditional IRA, the distribution is not currently taxed. A surviving spouse can also roll over tax-free the taxable part of the distribution into a qualified plan, Section 403(b) annuity, or Section 457 plan.

Example. At the time of his death, Greg owned a traditional IRA. All of the contributions by Greg to the IRA had been deductible contributions. Greg's nephew, Mark, was the sole beneficiary of the IRA. The entire balance of the IRA, including income accruing before and after Greg's death, was distributed to Mark in a lump sum. Mark must include the total amount received in his income. The portion of the lump-sum distribution that equals the amount of the balance in the IRA at Greg's death, including the income earned before death, is income in respect of a decedent.

TAXALERT

Generally speaking, effective for distributions for calendar years beginning on or after January 1, 2003, a beneficiary may take distributions from an inherited IRA over his or her own life expectancy. For more information on inherited IRAs, see Publication 590, *Individual Retirement Arrangements (IRAs)*.

This rule also applies to Roth IRAs for post death distributions. For more information on Roth IRAs, see Publication 590.

Roth IRAs. Qualified distributions from a Roth IRA are not subject to tax. A distribution made to a beneficiary or to the Roth IRA owner's estate on or after the date of death is a qualified distribution if it is made after the 5-year tax period beginning with the first tax year in which a contribution was made to any Roth IRA of the owner.

Part of any distribution to a beneficiary that is not a qualified distribution may be includible in the beneficiary's income. Generally, the part includible is the earnings in the Roth IRA. Earnings attributable to the period ending with the decedent's date of death are income in respect of a decedent. Additional earnings are the income of the beneficiary.

TAXALERT

The Department of Defense provides a payment of $100,000 to the survivors of a soldier killed in the line of duty. In addition, certain uniformed service members are automatically insured in the event of death under the Service Members Group Life Insurance (SGLI). The Heroes Earnings Assistance and Relief Tax Act of 2008 provides that a recipient of a military death gratuity or SGLI proceeds can contribute the amounts received to a Roth IRA, and treat these amounts as "qualified rollover contributions." If death resulted from injuries occurring on or after October 7, 2001, and before June 17, 2008, the rollover must have been made no later than June 17, 2009. For payments received on account of death from injuries occurring on or after June 17, 2008, the rollover must be made within one year of the date of payment.

Coverdell Education Savings Account (ESA). If the decedent's spouse or other family member is the designated beneficiary of the decedent's account, the Coverdell ESA becomes that person's Coverdell ESA. It is subject to the rules discussed in Publication 970.

Any other beneficiary (including a spouse or family member who is not the designated beneficiary) must include in income the earnings portion of the distribution. Any balance remaining at the close of the 30-day period is deemed to be distributed at that time. The amount included in income is reduced by any qualified education expenses of the decedent that are paid by the beneficiary within one year after the decedent's date of death.

Archer MSA. If the decedent's spouse is the designated beneficiary of the account, the account becomes that spouse's Archer MSA. It is subject to the rules discussed in Publication 969.

Any other beneficiary (including a spouse who is not the designated beneficiary) must include in income the fair market value of the assets in the account on the decedent's date of death. This amount must be reported for the beneficiary's tax year that includes the decedent's date of death. The amount included in income is reduced by any qualified medical expenses for the decedent that are paid by the beneficiary within one year after the decedent's date of death.

Other income. For examples of other income situations concerning decedents, see *Specific Types of Income in Respect of a Decedent* in Publication 559.

Deductions in Respect of a Decedent

Items such as business expenses, income-producing expenses, interest, and taxes for which the decedent was liable but that are not properly allowable as deductions on the decedent's final income tax return will be allowed as a deduction to one of the following when paid.

- The estate; or
- The person who acquired an interest in the decedent's property (subject to such obligations) because of the decedent's death, if the estate was not liable for the obligation.

Explanation

Deductions in respect of a decedent are items that would normally be deductible by the decedent except that he or she had not paid them before death. Typical examples are real estate taxes, state income taxes, and interest expense.

TAXSAVER

Expenses in respect of a decedent are deductible on both the estate's income tax return (Form 1041) and the estate tax return (Form 706). The estate tax and income tax are two different taxes with two entirely unrelated sets of rules. Taking a deduction on one return does not preclude taking the same deduction on the other return. When death is anticipated, planning the best possible use of double deductions may yield significant tax savings. A professional who specializes in this area should be consulted.

Example. When Oscar died in 2014, he owed accrued interest of $100. The marginal estate tax rate for Oscar's estate is 40%, and the estate's marginal income tax rate is 28%. The deduction on the estate tax return is worth $40 (40% of $100) and the deduction on the estate's income tax return is worth $28. Consequently, $68 of the $100 liability is recovered through tax savings.

On the other hand, less tax savings would be realized if Oscar had paid the $100 of interest before he died. He would have been able to take the interest deduction on his personal income tax return, paying $28 less in taxes, assuming he was in the 28% bracket. When he died, he would have been net out-of-pocket $72, his estate would be $72 less, and therefore his estate tax would be reduced by $28.80 (40% of $72). Thus, if he had paid the expense, his total tax savings would have been $56.8—$28 of income tax and $28.80 of estate tax—instead of the $68 tax saved because he had not paid the interest before he died, thus allowing the double deduction.

Estate Tax Deduction

Income that a decedent had a right to receive is included in the decedent's gross estate and is subject to estate tax. This income in respect of a decedent is also taxed when received by the recipient (estate or beneficiary). However, an income tax deduction is allowed to the recipient for the estate tax paid on the income.

The deduction for estate tax can be claimed only for the same tax year in which the income in respect of a decedent must be included in the recipient's income. (This also is true for income in respect of a prior decedent.)

You can claim the deduction only as a miscellaneous itemized deduction on Schedule A (Form 1040). This deduction is not subject to the 2% limit on miscellaneous itemized deductions as discussed in chapter 29, *Miscellaneous deductions*.

If the income in respect of a decedent is capital gain income, you must reduce the gain, but not below zero, by any deduction for estate tax paid on such gain. This applies in figuring the following:

- The maximum tax on net capital gain.
- The 50% exclusion for gain on small business stock.
- The limitation on net capital losses.
  For more information, see *Estate Tax Deduction* in Publication 559.

TAXPLANNER

The deduction for federal estate tax attributable to income in respect of a decedent is complex. The good news is that the question does not arise if there is no federal estate tax on the decedent's estate. If the amount that each individual can leave estate-tax-free, $5.34 million in 2014, and the marital deduction is large enough to eliminate any federal estate tax liability, there cannot be an income tax deduction for federal estate tax.

If the estate incurs federal estate tax, the recipient of income in respect of a decedent may be entitled to an itemized deduction on his or her income tax return.

To determine the amount that can be deducted, you must first determine if the income and deductions in respect of the decedent result in net income. If so, you must then calculate the additional estate tax attributable to the net income in respect of a decedent.

To determine whether the items in respect of the decedent result in net income, you must deduct the total amount of deductions in respect of the decedent that appears on the estate tax return from the total amount of income in respect of a decedent that appears on that return. To calculate the additional estate tax, you must compare the actual estate tax with the estate tax that would have been paid if the net income in respect of a decedent had not been included. This amount is the deduction. The recipient's claim to the deduction is in the same proportion as his or her share in the total income in respect of a decedent.

Example. Assume that the estate tax return shows that the estate received salary income in respect of a decedent of $2,500 and had a deduction in respect of a decedent of $500 for unpaid real estate tax. The net of these two amounts is $2,000. Recomputation of the estate tax with $2,000 removed from the return shows that the estate tax caused by including these items is $740. If you, as one of two heirs of the estate, collect half of the $2,500 salary, you will be entitled to an income tax itemized deduction of half the $740, or $370.

TAXORGANIZER

Records you should keep:

- Power of appointment (or similar authorization to act as decedent's personal representative)
- Copies of decedent's wills, trust documents, and amendments to same
- Copies of decedent's death certificate
- Copies of all correspondence to and from attorneys, accountants, life insurers, and others related to administration of the estate
- Copies of all tax returns related to the decedent and copies of all source documents used to prepare these returns

Chapter 44

Estate and gift tax planning

ey.com/EYTaxGuide

Note

ey.com/EYTaxGuide
Ernst & Young LLP will update the *EY Tax Guide 2015* website with relevant taxpayer information as it becomes available. You can also sign up for email alerts to let you know when changes have been made.

Introduction

Although it is not possible to take it with you, with careful thought and astute planning it is possible to provide your heirs, loved ones, and friends with a significant portion of your wealth. This chapter discusses the estate tax, the gift tax, and the generation-skipping transfer tax. The chapter also contains some estate planning ideas and techniques that may help you in making your plans for the future.

Because both the tax laws and your goals and expectations constantly change as you go through life, you should periodically review your estate and gift tax plan. A review will help you (1) discover how your objectives may have changed; (2) assess whether your plan can still achieve your objectives; and (3) determine how legislative changes may affect existing plans and whether you can now accomplish your goals more effectively.

This chapter is intended as an introduction to estate and gift tax planning. You should seek professional advice, especially if your financial or family situation is complicated, if you own interests in closely held corporations or other illiquid assets, or if your spouse is not a U.S. citizen.

Getting Started

A periodic review of your personal financial plan makes sense. Filing an annual income tax return forces most taxpayers to look over their financial situation. Yet many—perhaps most—individuals allow years to go by without adequately considering changes in property titling, beneficiary designations, or key provisions in wills and trusts. To be on the safe side, you should periodically examine the following five basic tax and financial considerations:

1. Have there been any tax law changes, rulings, or other developments that might either adversely affect your present estate plan or offer an opportunity to pass more of your estate at a lower tax cost?
2. Does your estate have sufficient cash or other liquid assets to take care of debts, taxes, funeral expenses, and estate administration expenses?
3. Have there been any changes in your family's circumstances—births, adoptions, deaths, marriages, illness or disability, special schooling needs, and so on—that might call for revisions in your estate plan?
4. Is the current form of ownership of your assets and the current designations of beneficiaries still appropriate, meaning that the assets will pass to the right people in the right fashion? Are they appropriate for saving taxes (both income and estate) and expenses?
5. Should you initiate a plan to give some of your assets to your children, other family members, or charitable institutions? If you have already been making gifts, should you continue to do so? Which assets are now most appropriate for such a gift program?

Do You Need a Will?

A will is a legal document that specifies who receives what at your death and who will manage your estate. Even if you die without a will, you already have an estate plan of sorts. Generally, assets you own jointly with another person, such as a bank account, stock, personal residence, or business interest will pass to the surviving joint tenant. Where you have designated a particular beneficiary, as under an insurance policy or IRA, the asset will pass to the designated beneficiary. But assets you own in your name alone will be passed on in accordance with your state's laws if you die without a will.

If you die without a will—intestate is the legal term—state law determines how your estate is divided up among your surviving spouse, children, and parents—and what happens when there is no surviving spouse. However, state law may not conform to your wishes. Often, the biggest problem is not who will receive the property, but how and when they get it. Another important issue is the guardianship of minor children. If both parents die without a will that directs who will be guardian of a minor child, the court and the state social welfare department will make the decision. So, even if you do not have enough assets to pay federal estate tax, it's a good idea to draw up a will and a trust.

Estate Tax Fundamentals
Who Has to Pay Federal Estate Tax?

The American Taxpayer Relief Act (ATRA), which was enacted in early 2013, permanently set the estate tax exemption at $5.00 million indexed annually for inflation, and the top estate tax rate at 40%. The estate tax exemption for 2014 is $5.34 million. ATRA also made permanent the "portability" of the exemption between spouses, meaning the remaining exemption amount of one spouse can be passed on to the other at death. And, a spouse can still pass unlimited amounts to his or her surviving spouse without tax; that's known as the unlimited marital deduction.

TAXPLANNER

The significant estate tax exemption discussed above—exempting estates worth under $5.34 million for 2014 from tax and indexing that exemption for inflation—certainly makes estate tax planning easier for many Americans. But that should not lull you into thinking that planning is unnecessary. For starters, you may be worth more than you think. Despite the nationwide downturn in housing values with the bust of the housing bubble in 2007, many middle-class families still own homes that are worth much more than what they cost, and housing values have been rising in many areas. Moreover, even in this era of economic turmoil and heightened volatility in stock and bond prices, many investors still hold significant investment portfolios. And, in many cases, the proceeds of life insurance are also included in your taxable estate regardless of the beneficiary.

Even if your assets do not currently create a taxable estate, they might at the time of your death. Therefore, it is prudent to focus on strategies that help freeze the value of assets in your estate.

Table 44-1. Estate, Gift, and Generation-Skipping Transfer (GST) Tax Rates and Unified Credit

Exemption Amount Calendar Year	Estate, Gift, and GST Tax Exemption	Highest Estate, Gift, and GST Tax Rates
2014	$5.34 million for estate, gift, and GST tax	Estate, gift, and GST tax at 40%

What Is Included in Your Estate

Assets subject to estate tax. Federal estate tax is a levy on the transfer of property at death. Your gross estate will include the value of all property to the extent of your interest in it at the time of death. Following are types of property included in your gross estate:

Tangible personal property, real estate, and other assets. This category includes property you own in your own name that is passed at death by your will or by state intestacy laws. Such property is commonly referred to as the probate estate. Examples include real estate, stocks, bonds, furniture, personal effects, jewelry, works of art, an interest in a partnership, an interest in a sole proprietorship, a bank account, and a promissory note or other evidence of indebtedness you hold.

Jointly owned property. In general, one-half of the value of property owned jointly by a husband and wife will be included in the estate of the first spouse to die. The unlimited marital deduction allows the transfer of the property from the deceased to the surviving spouse without being subject to federal estate tax. Upon the survivor's death, however, the entire property will be subject to tax (assuming it is still held at the time of death). However, if two people who are not married own property jointly, the entire value of the property is included in the gross estate of the first to die, unless the estate can prove that all or part of the payment for acquiring the property was actually furnished by the other joint owner. If you and another joint owner acquired property by gift or inheritance, only your fractional share of the property is included.

Jointly held property passes to the other owner automatically on death without regard to whether or not you have a will. In many states, Transfer on Death (TOD) or Totten Trust accounts allow securities and bank accounts to pass directly to a beneficiary even if the property is not held in joint name.

Life insurance. Your gross estate will include life insurance proceeds that are received (1) by or for the benefit of your estate or (2) by other beneficiaries if you own all or part of the policies at the time of your death. "Ownership" includes the power to change the beneficiary of the policy, the right to cancel the policy and receive the cash value, the right to borrow against the policy, and the right to assign the policy, among other things.

TAXSAVER

You can transfer ownership of a life insurance policy to your children or to a trust for your family's benefit and reap significant estate tax advantages. To be effective in keeping the proceeds out of your estate, the gift must be made more than three years before death. The three-year waiting period can be avoided for a newly purchased policy if proper steps are taken to have someone else (e.g., a trustee of an irrevocable life insurance trust) apply for the policy and own it from its inception. These types of irrevocable life insurance trusts can be structured so that your contributions each year to the trust can qualify for the annual gift tax exclusion (explained below). Setting up such a trust can be an effective way to remove the insurance proceeds from your estate, thereby reducing your estate tax.

Employee benefits. The value of payments from qualified pension plans, IRAs, and other qualified or nonqualified retirement plans payable to surviving beneficiaries or the estate of an employee (or the owner, in the case of a Keogh/HR 10 plan) generally is included in your gross estate.

Certain gifts and gift tax paid within three years of death. Gifts of property made during your lifetime are generally not included in your gross estate, but must be figured in the estate tax calculation if they exceed the $14,000 annual gift tax exclusion (discussed later). However, life insurance proceeds are included in your estate if the policies or ownership of the policies were given away within three years of your death. Also included is any gift tax you have paid within three years of your death. Lifetime gifts in which you retain some interest (e.g., a life income interest) or control (e.g., voting rights in closely held stock given as a gift) will be included in your gross estate.

Allowable deductions and exclusions. Deductions are allowed for funeral and estate administration expenses, and debts–such as unpaid mortgages–and other indebtedness on property included in the gross estate. Also allowed are special deductions such as the marital deduction and the charitable deduction. (See later sections for more details on the marital deduction.)

Funeral and administration expenses. Deductible funeral expenses include burial costs, costs for a burial lot, costs for future care of a grave site, and so on. Deductible administration costs include executor's commissions, attorney's fees, accounting fees, appraisal fees, and court costs.

Other deductible estate expenses. To be deductible, debts must be enforceable personal obligations of the decedent, such as mortgages or personal bank loans, auto loans, credit card balances, utility bills, and so on. The deductible amount also includes any interest accrued on such debt at the date of death. Transfers made under a marital property settlement because of a divorce may be treated as estate expenses. Taxes are also deductible debts if they are accrued and unpaid at date of death. Deductible taxes include accrued property taxes, gift taxes unpaid at death, and income taxes.

Valuing estate property. Property is included in an estate at its "fair market value," which is the price at which property would change hands between a willing buyer and a willing seller. Property that trades on an established market may be valued easily. For example, publicly traded stocks and bonds are valued based on the average of the high and low selling price on the date of death (or, if elected, the date six months after death). However, interests in closely held businesses or partnerships must generally be appraised, taking into account the business's assets, earning capacity, and other factors. An accountant can assist you in obtaining the appropriate appraisal of your business interests for estate or gift tax valuation purposes.

Your gross estate is valued as of the date of your death or six months later (also known as the alternative valuation date), whichever your personal representative elects. An election to value the estate six months after the date of death will generally apply to all assets in the estate, but is available only if the election results in a decrease in your gross estate and estate tax liability.

The amount remaining after subtracting any allowable deductions is your taxable estate. The federal estate tax is computed on this amount. Gifts made after 1976 are also factored in and can increase the marginal tax bracket of the estate.

If You Are the Beneficiary of an Estate

Property acquired from a decedent generally gets a new basis. Basis is generally the cost of an asset or the amount you will use to figure your tax when you sell the asset. In most cases, the new basis is the fair market value at date of death or alternative valuation date, whichever is used for estate tax purposes. If the new basis is greater than the old basis, this is known as your "stepped-up" basis.

How Your Estate Is Taxed

Tax rates. The federal estate tax is progressive, ranging from a marginal rate of 18% to 40% in 2014. The 40% top rate will apply to estates larger than $5.34 million.

Credits and Exemptions

Your estate can claim certain credits and exemptions before figuring the amount of federal estate tax owed. These items include:

Estate tax exemption. Each individual is entitled to an estate tax exemption. For 2014, the exemption is $5.34 million. In other words, no federal estate tax will be assessed on the first $5.34 million of an individual's combined taxable gifts and transfers at death. To the extent that the exemption has been used to offset gifts the decedent made during his or her lifetime, the exemption against the estate tax is reduced. While you should have your estate plan reviewed on a regular basis, it is especially important to be sure it is drafted to take advantage of the estate tax exemption available under the law in existence at the time of your death.

Example. Mary had an estate valued at $5.34 million at the time of her death in 2014. Two years before she died, she gave her son Bill a gift of $340,000 to help him buy a house. Instead of an estate tax exemption of $5.34 million, only $5 million of Mary's estate will qualify for the exemption.

The marital deduction. One of the most significant tax-saving provisions of the law is the marital deduction. As its name implies, it is a special deduction available only to married persons, where the spouse receiving the assets is a U.S. citizen. An estate is allowed an unlimited deduction for the value of property transferred to the spouse of the deceased. Thus, in effect, the marital deduction permits a couple to postpone paying any estate tax until the surviving spouse dies.

TAXSAVER

Most married individuals who have or will have taxable estates will want to take advantage of both the estate tax exemption and the unlimited marital deduction. The marital deduction is only available for U.S. citizen spouses and will reduce the federal estate tax to zero for the estate of the first spouse to die. The coordinated use of the exemption and the marital deduction is usually accomplished by transferring property in a special type of trust, often called a bypass trust. These trusts, which are used to take full advantage of a spouse's estate tax exemption, typically provide income and discretionary distributions of principal to the deceased's surviving spouse. The amount that goes into these trusts is typically determined by a formula that puts the maximum possible amount into the trust without generating federal estate tax in the deceased spouse's estate. Assets in excess of the remaining exemption either pass to the surviving spouse outright or remain in a form of trust that will qualify for the estate tax marital deduction. The advantage of the bypass trust is that its assets will not be included in the surviving spouse's estate at his or her death, regardless of the amount in that trust at that time.

Portability. If a spouse passes away during 2014, the surviving spouse can add to his or her own exemption whatever amount of the exemption—up to $5.34 million if death occurred during 2014—the deceased had not used during his or her lifetime. In order to take advantage of this option, an election must be made with a timely filed estate tax return for the deceased spouse, even though the estate of the deceased spouse many not be large enough to require the filing of an estate tax return.

A surviving spouse will be able to use the deceased spouse's unused exemption for lifetime transfers as well as his own at death. However, portability does not extend to the generation-skipping transfer (GST) tax exemption.

Prior to the availability of portability, a typical plan for an estate in excess of the estate tax exemption equivalent would be to fund a bypass trust with the decedent's remaining unused amount of estate tax exemption equivalent. By funding the bypass trust at the death of the first spouse, the full, remaining amount of the estate tax exemption plus future appreciation would not be included and taxed in the estate of the surviving spouse. If an estate plan did not fund a bypass trust, all assets transferred to the surviving spouse under the marital deduction upon the decedent's death would be includable in the surviving spouse's estate. Therefore, the full value of the exemption of the deceased could go unused and possibly be lost. Even though no estate tax would be due upon the death of the first spouse, a larger estate tax would be due upon the death of the surviving spouse.

Under the portability rules, there would still be no tax due on the first-to-die. However the deceased's exemption would not be "wasted." Instead, any of the deceased's unused exemption carries over to the surviving spouse. While the portability rules provide relief in the ability to use a deceased's unused exemption, the funding of a bypass trust should continue to be considered in an estate plan. First, the funding of a bypass trust at the death of the first spouse removes the exemption equivalent amount <u>and</u> the associated future appreciation from the surviving spouse's estate. Second, the traditional benefits of using a trust, such as creditor protection, should be considered as well as the possibility of the surviving spouse remarrying and the potential inability to use the first deceased spouse's unused exemption amount. Third, the bypass trust may be needed to assure that the children of a deceased spouse's prior marriage are not disinherited by the surviving "new" spouse. Finally, portability is not allowed for GST tax exemptions, so a surviving spouse would not be able to use the unused GST tax exemption of the first-to-die.

The following examples explain how an estate or gift tax exemption can be transferred from a deceased spouse to a surviving spouse.

Example 1. Assume that Husband 1 dies in 2014, having made taxable transfers of $3 million and having no taxable estate. An election is made on Husband 1's estate tax return to permit his Wife to use Husband 1's deceased spousal unused exclusion amount. As of Husband 1's death, the Wife has made no taxable gifts. Thereafter, Wife's applicable exclusion amount is $7.68 million (her $5.34 million basic exclusion amount plus $2.34 million deceased spousal unused exclusion amount from Husband 1), which she may use for lifetime gifts or for transfers at death.

Example 2. Assume the same facts as in Example 1, except that Wife subsequently marries Husband 2. Husband 2 also predeceases Wife, having made $4 million in taxable transfers and having no taxable estate. An election is made on Husband 2's estate tax return to permit Wife to use Husband 2's deceased spousal unused exclusion amount. Although the combined amount of unused exclusion of Husband 1 and Husband 2 is $3.68 million ($2.34 million for Husband 1 and $1.34 million for Husband 2), only Husband 2's $1.34 million unused exclusion is available for use by Wife, because the deceased spousal unused exclusion amount is limited to the lesser of the basic exclusion amount ($5.34 million) or the unused exclusion of the last deceased spouse of the surviving spouse (here, Husband 2's $1.34 million unused exclusion). Thereafter the Wife's applicable exclusion amount is $6.68 million (her $5.34 million basic exclusion amount plus $1.34 million deceased spousal unused exclusion amount from Husband 2), which she may use for lifetime gifts or for transfers at death.

Example 3. Assume the same facts as in Examples 1 and 2, except that Wife predeceases Husband 2. Following Husband 1's death, Wife's applicable exclusion amount is $7.68 million (her $5.34 million basic exclusion amount plus $2.34 million deceased spousal unused exclusion amount from Husband 1). Wife made no taxable transfers and has a taxable estate of $3 million. An election is made on Wife's estate tax return to permit Husband 2 to use Wife's deceased spousal unused exclusion amount, which is $4.68 million (Wife's $7.68 million applicable exclusion amount less her $3 million taxable estate). Husband 2's applicable exclusion amount is increased by $4.68 million (i.e., the amount of deceased spousal unused exclusion amount of Wife).

State death tax considerations. Most states impose some kind of inheritance or estate tax. In some states, the estate tax is simply the amount of the federal credit for state death taxes. However, since the federal state death tax credit had been eliminated for decedents dying in 2005 through 2009, there would be no state estate tax. To avoid this result, many states enacted estate taxes that are not tied to the federal credit. In addition, some states revised their tax laws to set their estate tax exemption at an amount that is less than the federal estate tax exemption. Furthermore, some states do not allow an unlimited marital deduction, as the federal government does. Consequently, in many states it is possible to have a taxable estate for state estate tax purposes but not for federal purposes. In these states, state death tax considerations may influence how your estate plan should be structured.

Foreign death tax credit. A credit is allowed against the federal estate tax for any death taxes actually paid to a foreign country, Puerto Rico, or the Virgin Islands on property that is also subject to the federal estate tax. The credit is limited to the U.S. tax attributable to the property taxed by the foreign country.

Credit for tax on prior transfers. Under certain circumstances a credit is allowed against the federal estate tax for part or all of any estate tax paid on property transferred to the present decedent from a prior estate.

TAXSAVER

Your property can be left to a special type of trust that benefits a spouse who is not a U.S. citizen. The trust enables estate tax on the property to be postponed until the property is distributed out of the trust or the surviving spouse dies. This type of trust is called a Qualified Domestic Trust (QDOT). It permits property to qualify for the marital deduction if certain requirements—which provide that the property will eventually be subject to estate tax—are met.

EXAMPLE

Here is an example of a computation of the gross estate, the taxable estate, and the estate tax due for an unmarried individual who is assumed to die in 2014 as a resident of a state that has no estate tax. We assume that the estate tax laws for 2014, including the $5.34 million exemption, will be in place. The assets of the individual are listed in Step 1 below.

Step 1: Computing the gross estate

Cash	$1,400,000
Marketable securities	3,750,000
Residence	900,000
Personal property	350,000
Deferred compensation	300,000
Ordinary life insurance	1,000,000
Group-term insurance	300,000
Gross estate	$8,000,000

Step 2: Computing the taxable estate

The executor of the estate will subtract from the total value of the gross estate all those deductions allowable under the tax law, including the mortgage and any charitable bequest the individual made at his death.

Gross estate	$8,000,000
Deductions:	
Funeral expenses	(20,000)
Estate administration expenses	(80,000)
Debts	(900,000)
Mortgages	(400,000)
Marital deduction	-0-
Charitable deductions	(1,000,000)
Total deductions	(2,400,000)
Taxable estate	$5,600,000

Step 3: Computing the federal estate tax

To determine the amount of federal estate tax, calculate the tentative estate tax on the taxable estate, then reduce that amount by the estate tax exemption credit (the unified credit) to arrive at the net federal estate tax.

Gross estate	$8,000,000
Deductions	(2,400,000)
Taxable estate	$5,600,000
Tentative estate tax	$2,185,800
Reduced by the unified credit	$2,081,800
Federal estate tax	$104,000

The Fundamentals of the Gift Tax

You might think that the government would make it easy to give money away to non-charitable recipients. In some respects it does. You can give up to $14,000 annually ($28,000 if your spouse consents) in 2014 to as many individuals as you want without paying any gift tax. But, above that amount, gifts consume the lifetime gift tax exemption amount of $5.34 million and then can result in gift tax. The reason is that without such a tax, people could escape death taxes—assuming they were willing to give away a large portion of their property before death.

TAXALERT

Under the current tax law, the highest gift tax rate for 2014 is 40%.

Any gift you give above the annual amount that is exempt from tax is, in effect, included in your estate when you die. The value of the gift is not the value at the date of your death, but the value at the time you gave the gift. In addition, there are some special rules. A gift of a life insurance policy, for example, made within three years of your death will be included in your gross estate at its full face value. Any gift tax you pay on gifts made within three years of your death is also added to the value of your taxable estate. Nevertheless, giving gifts can substantially reduce your overall estate tax, as well as fulfill other desires. But gift-giving does require careful planning—and the commitment to make the gifts before it is too late.

Tax Basis to the Recipient of a Gift

In general, the basis of appreciated property acquired by gift is the donor's basis for tax purposes. If a gift tax return was filed, the recipient—or donee—should examine it for information regarding the donor's basis, the holding period, and the amount of depreciation. The basis of gifts received after 1976 is increased by the amount of the federal gift tax attributable to the difference between the donor's basis and the gift's fair market value, if higher as of the date of gift.

How to Give Tax-Free Gifts

The gift tax annual exclusion. As noted above, in 2014 you may give up to $14,000 to as many individuals as you want without incurring any gift tax (the annual gift exclusion amount is indexed for inflation). And, if your spouse joins in making the gift (by signing a consent on a gift tax return), you may give $28,000 to each person annually without paying any tax. But this annual gift tax exclusion applies only to gifts of "present interests"—items that can be used, possessed, and enjoyed presently. Examples of a gift of a present interest include gifts of money, holiday presents, and so forth.

Gifts of "future interests" do not qualify for the annual exclusion. Gifts of future interests include remainder interests, reversions, or any other interest that will not give the recipient the right to possess, enjoy, or profit from the gift until some future date or time. There is an exception for gifts in trust to minors, which are subject to special rules that may allow an otherwise future interest to qualify for the annual exclusion.

Gifts to pay medical or educational expenses. In addition to the annual exclusion, an unlimited gift tax exclusion is available to pay someone's medical or educational expenses. The beneficiary does not have to be your dependent or even related to you, although payment of a grandchild's education expenses is perhaps the most common use of the exclusion. Also, contributions to a qualified tuition program (QTP) or a Section 529 plan will be eligible for the regular $14,000 exclusion. (See *Qualified Tuition Programs* under *Giving Gifts to Minors*, later.)

TAXSAVER

In order for a gift to be exempt from taxes, you must make the payment directly to the medical or educational institution providing the service. The beneficiary of the gift should not actually receive the payment. In addition, educational expenses include only tuition. Room and board, books, and other fees will not qualify for the unlimited exclusion, although they can, of course, qualify for the annual gift tax exclusion.

TAXSAVER

You can reduce your taxable estate substantially through a planned annual gifting program. All gifts within the exclusion limits are exempt from federal estate taxes. In addition, outright gifts that qualify for the annual exclusion are also protected from generation-skipping transfer taxes (see below). Obviously, you cannot hope to significantly reduce your estate tax by making gifts in a single year. But the estate tax savings can be substantial if you embark upon a carefully planned gift-giving program that extends for a number of years before your death.

TAXSAVER

A donor who makes contributions to a qualified tuition program (commonly known as a "Section 529 plan") in excess of the $14,000 annual exclusion amount may elect to recognize the contributions for gift tax purposes ratably over the five-year period starting with the year of the contributions. This means a donor can make a $70,000 tax-free contribution in one year—or $140,000 if the donor is married and the donor's spouse consents to gift-splitting. If the donor dies before the end of the five-year period, the portion of the contribution allocable to the period after the donor's date of death is included in the donor's gross estate.

TAXSAVER

Another major tax advantage of making a gift is that future appreciation in the gift's value and after-tax income earned on the property are not included in your estate. Example: Suppose you give stock worth $50,000 to your children now. If you die in 10 years and the stock is worth $130,000, the $80,000 of appreciation will not be included in your estate. Nor will you (or your estate) include any dividends paid on the stock after the gift.

Gift tax charitable contribution deduction. An unlimited gift tax deduction is available for gifts to qualified charitable organizations.

The gift tax marital deduction. The gift tax marital deduction allows you to transfer unlimited amounts of property during your lifetime to your spouse without gift tax.

Property can be transferred outright or in trust. Also, a gift of a lifetime income interest in property to your spouse can qualify for the marital deduction, if it is structured properly. You should consult with your tax advisor.

TAXSAVER

The gift tax marital deduction can help you lower the taxes on your estate. Consider that in order for one spouse to make full use of his or her estate tax exemption, it may be desirable to make gifts to that spouse so that he or she will have an estate at least equal to the estate tax exemption equivalent. Since the gift tax marital deduction allows you to make unlimited tax-free transfers to your spouse, you can build up your spouse's assets without worrying that your gifts will be taxable.

Some words of caution: The unlimited marital deduction is not allowed for gifts to a spouse who is not a U.S. citizen, although tax-free transfers of up to $144,000 (in 2014; this amount is adjusted annually for inflation) are permitted each year. (See the section on _Marital Deduction_ under _Estate Tax Fundamentals_, earlier in this chapter.) Furthermore, the amount of the gift tax marital deduction for a particular state may differ from the federal amount. It is therefore vital to get professional advice before making any significant gifts.

**Example: Giving gifts without paying gift tax.** This example illustrates how you can set up a substantial gift program and avoid paying any gift tax. Note, however, that part of the $5.34 million gift tax exemption is being used.

During 2014, James made outright gifts of $200,000 to his wife, Helen, and $60,000 to each of his three children, for a total of $380,000.

James incurred no gift tax on Helen's gift because of the unlimited marital deduction. James and Helen were entitled to a total of $84,000 in annual exclusions (based on $28,000 for each child) because they elected to treat one-half of those gifts as made by Helen. That still leaves, however, a taxable gift of $96,000 to the three children. Since James and Helen have elected to treat the one-half of the gifts made by James as made by Helen, each parent has made $48,000 in taxable gifts. By applying a portion of their respective gift tax exemptions, James and Helen can entirely eliminate paying gift tax. Assuming that this was their first gift using their exemptions, they will have reduced the remaining assets that will be considered tax-free for taxable gifts made in future years from $5.34 million to $5,292,000 each.

Giving Gifts to Minors

Before a parent or grandparent gives a gift to a minor child, certain legal and practical matters need to be considered. Because a child typically cannot manage his or her own affairs and because parents usually do not want to give young children unfettered control over gift property, some special arrangements need to be made. The tax law, too, poses some challenges since only gifts of a "present interest"–property for the beneficiary's immediate enjoyment–qualify for the annual gift tax exclusion, $14,000 in 2014. Furthermore, state laws frequently discourage outright gifts to minors. Many states commonly prohibit or discourage the registration of securities in the name of a minor and impose supervisory restrictions upon the sale of a minor's property. Consequently, gifts to minors can take different forms and have different tax consequences.

Outright gifts. The $14,000 annual gift tax exclusion is available for these gifts unless the property being given as a gift is a "future interest." Income from the property is taxed to the minor, and the property is included in the minor's estate if he or she should die. However, because of the "kiddie tax," which requires that a child's unearned income over a certain threshold, $2,000 for tax year 2014, be taxed at the parent's rate until the child reaches age 19 (or age 24 if a student), your child may actually be taxed at your rates on any income he or she receives from the property.

Guardianship. A guardianship is an arrangement whereby property is under a guardian's legal control subject to formal (and possibly burdensome) accounting to a court. The gift, income, and estate tax consequences are the same as for outright gifts. Thus, such gifts also qualify for the $14,000 (in 2014) gift tax exclusion.

Custodial arrangements. To overcome the legal disability minors have in owning property outright, all 50 states, the District of Columbia, and the Virgin Islands have adopted the Uniform

Gifts (or Transfers) to Minors Act. Under this act, a custodian may hold both cash and securities for a minor until he or she reaches adulthood. Securities may be registered in the name of any bank, trust company, or adult as custodian for the minor. Custodial gifts to minors are considered completed gifts for gift tax purposes, and such gifts are eligible for the annual gift tax exclusion. The income from the gift property during the custodial period is taxable to the minor (subject to kiddie tax provisions). However, if you use the income for your minor child's maintenance and support, it is taxable to you because you are the person legally obligated to support the minor.

TAXSAVER

Generally, you should not act as custodian of your own gifts to your minor child. If you do and die before your child becomes an adult, the value of the custodial account maintained for your child's benefit will be included in your estate. Instead, your spouse may be the custodian. If you and your spouse both make gifts to your minor child, in essence splitting your gifts to take advantage of the annual gift tax exclusion, you should consider making a third party the custodian for the child.

Present interest trust. Special rules enacted by Congress provide a method of making gifts to minors that qualify for the annual exclusion. Specifically, a gift to a qualifying trust established for an individual under the age of 21 will be considered a gift of a present interest and qualify for the annual gift tax exclusion. The trust instrument must provide that the gift property and its income:

- May be expended for the benefit of the beneficiary before reaching age 21, and
- To the extent not so expended, will pass to the beneficiary upon becoming age 21.

If the child dies before reaching age 21, the funds must be payable to the child's estate or as the child may designate under a general power of appointment. This rule applies to trusts for children under the age of 21, even if a state law has reduced the age of majority to age 19 or 18.

Crummey trust. This is a type of trust to which you can transfer property and have the gift qualify for the annual gift tax exclusion. The distinguishing characteristic of a Crummey trust (which takes its name from a court case) is that it gives the beneficiary the annual right to demand distributions from the trust equal to the lesser of the amount of the contributions to the trust during the year or some specified amount (e.g., $5,000 or 5% of the trust's value). The beneficiary (or legal guardian) must be notified of the power to withdraw from the trust, although the power is permitted to lapse or terminate after a short period of time, such as 30 days. To the extent the beneficiary (or legal guardian) has the right to demand distribution of the year's contribution, that contribution is considered a "present interest" and, therefore, qualifies for the annual gift tax exclusion. If the beneficiary fails to make a demand during the window period, after being notified that a contribution was made, the right lapses for that year's contributions. If the right lapses without the beneficiary exercising the withdrawal power, the beneficiary may (depending on the terms of the trust) be deemed to have made a taxable gift back to the trust to the extent that his or her withdrawal power exceeded $5,000 or 5% of the trust's value.

A Crummey trust is very flexible. The trustee can be required to accumulate income until the child reaches a specified age above age 21. The trustee also can be restricted to using trust assets and income for specific purposes (e.g., college expenses). The trust is useful as a vehicle for permanently removing assets from the parents' gross estates.

Totten trust. An "In Trust For" or so-called Totten Trust is created when a donor deposits his or her own money into a bank account for the benefit of a minor and names himself or herself as trustee. Under the laws of certain states, this is an informal and revocable arrangement. Upon the donor-trustee's death, the funds avoid probate and pass directly to the minor. However, the trust is not considered a separate entity for tax purposes because the donor retains complete control over any property in the trust. Accordingly, the donor will be taxed on the income as if the trust were not in existence. Also, assets in the trust account will be included in the donor's estate.

Qualified tuition programs (Section 529 plans). Section 529 plans allow a donor to either buy tuition credits or contribute to a special higher-education savings account for a designated beneficiary. A donor can leverage the 2014 gift tax exclusion of $14,000 under a special gift tax rule that allows the donor to recognize any contribution to a qualified tuition program in excess of the annual exclusion amount as if it were made ratably over five years. This permits a donor to contribute up to $70,000 in one year—or $140,000 if gift-splitting with spouse—per beneficiary, free of gift tax.

Although the funds in a Section 529 account are treated as a completed gift, you can retain ownership and control over them. This unique provision allows you to decide when to distribute funds to the beneficiary. Subject to certain guidelines, you can even substitute a different beneficiary or revoke the account and take back the funds.

Earnings in the account are permitted to grow on a tax-deferred basis. In addition, under current law, no federal income tax is imposed on the earnings, provided that the funds are used to pay for qualifying higher education expenditures. Although contributions to Section 529 plans are not deductible for federal income tax purposes, a number of states offer a deduction against state income tax for contributions made to their programs.

Do You Need to File a Gift Tax Return?

Only individuals are required to file a gift tax return. If a trust, estate, partnership, or corporation makes a gift, the individual beneficiaries, partners, or stockholders are considered donors and may be liable for the gift tax. If a donor dies before filing a return, the donor's executor must file the gift tax return.

Although you may have made gifts during the year, you do not need to file a gift tax return so long as you meet all of the following requirements:

1. You made no gifts during the year to your spouse;
2. You gave no more than $14,000 in 2014 during the year to any one recipient; and
3. All of the gifts you made were of present interests.

Additionally, except in limited circumstances, you do not have to file a gift tax return solely to report gifts to your spouse (regardless of the amount of these gifts and regardless of whether the gifts are present or future interests).

You must file a gift tax return, however, if:

- Your spouse is not a U.S. citizen and the total gifts you made to your spouse during 2014 exceed $145,000;
- You make any gift of a terminable interest to your spouse that does not meet certain exceptions;
- You make a Qualified Terminable Interest Property election;
- You gave gifts to any donee, other than your spouse, which are not fully excluded under the $14,000 annual exclusion. Thus, you must file a gift tax return to report any gift of a future interest (regardless of amount) or to report gifts to any donee that total more than $14,000 for the year; or
- You elect to split gifts with your spouse (regardless of the amount of the gifts).

If you are required to file a gift tax return, use Form 709, United States Gift Tax Return.

When to File the Gift Tax Return

The gift tax return is an annual return. In general, you must file a gift tax return on or after January 1 but not later than April 15 (without extensions) of the year following the calendar year when the gifts were made. If the donor of the gifts died during the year in which the gifts were made, the executor must file the donor's gift tax return not later than the earlier of (1) the due date (with extensions) for filing the donor's estate tax return; or (2) April 15 of the year following the calendar year when the gifts were made. If no estate tax return is required to be filed, the due date for the gift tax return (without extensions) is April 15.

Extension of time to file. You can extend the time to file the gift tax return in either of two ways. First, you can request an extension by filing Form 8892 if you are not extending your Form 1040. Second, any extension of time to file your income tax return will also extend the time to file your gift tax return.

TAXPLANNER

Like the income tax return, an extension to file a gift tax return does not extend the time to pay the gift tax due. If you want an extension of time to pay the gift tax, you must make a separate request using Form 8892-V.

Gift Tax Return—Form 709

Form 709 is used to report transfers subject to the federal gift tax (as well as the generation-skipping transfer tax, not discussed here) and also to compute the tax, if any, due on those transfers. A married couple cannot file a joint Form 709, even if the spouses elect gift-splitting. Instead, both the donor spouse and the consenting spouse must each file a separate gift tax return, unless either of two situations is met:

Situation 1. During the calendar year:
- Only one spouse made any gifts;
- The total value of these gifts to each third-party donee does not exceed $28,000; and
- All of the gifts were of present interests.

Situation 2. During the calendar year:
- Only one spouse (the donor spouse) made gifts of more than $14,000, but not more than $28,000 to any third-party donee;

- The only gifts made by the other spouse (the consenting spouse) were gifts of not more than $14,000 to third-party donees other than those to whom the donor spouse made gifts; and
- All of the gifts by both spouses were of present interests.

If either of these two situations is met, only the donor spouse must file a return and the consenting spouse signifies consent on that return.

TAXORGANIZER
Records you should keep:
- All gift tax returns filed by you and your spouse

The Generation-Skipping Transfer Tax

An additional tax may apply to gifts or bequests that skip a generation. For example, a gift of property directly from a grandparent to a grandchild (which effectively "skips" the intervening generation) would be subject to the generation-skipping transfer (GST) tax.

The reason for the tax is simple. It's designed to impose the equivalent of the gift or estate tax that would have been paid if the intervening generation had received the gift or bequest. So for a direct gift from a grandparent to a grandchild, the GST tax represents the amount of tax that would have been paid if the property had first been transferred to the child, who then died leaving the property to the grandchild.

The generation-skipping transfer tax is stiff. Under current law, the top tax rate on GST tax transfers in 2014 is 40%. It will be payable in addition to any estate or gift tax otherwise payable as a result of the transfer. Fortunately, most individuals will escape paying it. First, an outright gift under $14,000 from a grandparent to a grandchild ($28,000 if made with the consent of a spouse) that qualifies for the annual gift tax exclusion is exempt from this tax. Gifts into trusts from a grandparent for the benefit of a grandchild do not always qualify for the GST tax annual exclusion, even when the gift qualifies for the regular gift tax annual exclusion. The trust terms must meet certain elements to qualify. Furthermore, each individual is entitled to an aggregate GST tax exemption for lifetime gifts and transfers at death.

TAXSAVER

A wealthy individual can maximize his or her opportunity to avoid the imposition of the GST tax on transfers to grandchildren and later generations by allocating the $5.34 million exemption for gifts during his or her lifetime.

If your living descendants are already well provided for, you may want to consider establishing a "dynasty trust." As its name implies, the trust can benefit future descendants by sheltering assets from estate, gift, and GST taxes for several generations.

How to Use Trusts

A trust is one of the most useful personal financial planning tools available. A trust is an arrangement under which one person or institution holds legal title to real or personal property for the benefit of another person or persons, usually under the terms of a written document setting forth the rights and responsibilities of all parties. Its primary virtue is that it can hold property for the benefit of other persons, now or in the future, and often avoid some taxes that otherwise would have to be paid.

Revocable trusts. A revocable trust (also known as a "living trust") is created during your lifetime, and you may amend or revoke it at any time. The trust instrument stipulates how the assets held by the trust are to be managed during your lifetime. This type of trust can also act very much like a will; the trust instrument can include instructions about how the assets in the trust should be distributed after your death.

What distinguishes a revocable trust from other kinds of trust arrangements is that you keep the power to reclaim the trust assets or contribute additional property to the trust at any time and for any reason. Thus, in effect, if you set up a revocable trust you really have not committed yourself to anything—at least until you die and the trust becomes irrevocable. For all practical purposes, you continue to own the trust property; the trust merely gets legal title. Since you keep complete control over the trust and its assets, the property held in it will be included in your gross estate for estate tax purposes. Also, all income and deductions attributable to the property in the trust will be included on your income tax return. On the other hand, you will not be liable for any gift tax when you contribute assets to the trust. This is the case even though the trust names the beneficiaries who will inherit the property upon your death. However, a gift will occur if you give up your power to revoke or amend the trust, or if income or principal is actually paid to someone else.

Essentially, there are no tax advantages gained by establishing a revocable trust. But there can be some real financial and administrative advantages, including:

Avoiding probate and ancillary administration. Revocable trust assets pass to the beneficiaries you name in the trust document and are not controlled by your will. This cuts out the costs and delays arising from the probate process, but first check the laws in your state. Many states have streamlined the probate process and reduced the associated costs. Also, unlike probate, with a revocable trust the identity and instructions for distributing estate property are not part of the public record. Further, if you own real property in a state other than your state of domicile, a revocable trust will avoid the ancillary probate administration in that state that would otherwise be required.

Avoiding legal guardianship. If you become incapacitated, the assets kept in your living trust would be managed by a trustee you named in the trust document. Otherwise, the determination of whether and to what extent you are disabled or incompetent and who is going to handle your affairs could be left to public, and potentially costly, guardianship proceedings. A durable power of attorney can also be an effective tool for prearranging the management of your affairs in the event you become incapacitated.

Irrevocable trusts. An irrevocable trust may not be changed or revoked after its creation. It is usually created to remove property and its future income and appreciation from the estate of the creator of the trust. A present interest trust and a Crummey trust, both of which are discussed above, are irrevocable trusts. You might also use an irrevocable trust if you want to make a gift to someone but want to prevent the assets from being spent too quickly. An irrevocable trust also can be used to protect assets you give from your beneficiary's creditors.

However, property placed in an irrevocable trust will not be removed from your estate if you retain certain interests or powers in the trust—such as an interest that entitles you to receive the income from the trust for the rest of your life or the power to determine which beneficiaries will receive distributions. In addition, any transfer to an irrevocable trust will be subject to gift tax to the extent you relinquish control over the property. If someone else will receive the current income from the trust, or if it is a present income trust, the $14,000 annual gift tax exclusion in 2014 can shield at least part of the property transferred to the trust from gift tax.

Besides saving you estate tax, irrevocable trusts created for your children can cut your income taxes. The amount of income tax savings depends on how much other income your children already receive and whether the "kiddie tax" applies to them. Also, there are very strict rules that limit the amount of control you or your spouse may keep over the trust in order for you not to include the trust's income on your tax return. The income from the trust will be taxed to you if the trust is used to pay for an item that you are legally obligated to provide as support for the beneficiary.

Relief from financial responsibility. If desired, an independent trustee can be used immediately to relieve you of the details of managing your property and investments, record-keeping chores, and the preparation and filing of income tax returns.

Living trusts have some drawbacks and are not suited for everyone:

- Expect to pay legal fees and other expenses, such as recording fees, to set up the trust and transfer property to it. You will also owe recurring trustee and administrative charges if you use a corporate trustee rather than managing the trust yourself.
- You will not necessarily save on other legal, accounting, and executor's fees paid to handle your estate. Whether your assets are held in a living trust or pass through probate, the same sort of work will generally be needed to value your assets, prepare federal and state tax returns, settle creditors' claims, and resolve disputes among beneficiaries.

TAXSAVER

Two reminders: (1) If you establish a living trust, be sure that any property covered by the trust is legally titled in the trust's name. This is a straightforward, but often overlooked, point. (2) After setting up a living trust, you must remember to conduct your personal business affairs regarding the transferred assets through the trust. This is not difficult but can be a burden. Property held outside the trust at your death will be subject to probate—except for life insurance proceeds (payable to a beneficiary other than your estate) and property held jointly with right of survivorship, which by law would avoid probate.

How to Raise Cash to Pay Estate Taxes

In many instances, the estate of an owner of a closely held business–or for that matter, any estate–may not have sufficient cash to pay all the estate's obligations, including estate taxes. Without sufficient liquidity, the estate may be forced to sell a portion of the business to raise the necessary cash. But there are special rules for the estates of owners of closely held businesses. The techniques described below can help alleviate these problems.

Stock Redemptions to Pay Death Taxes

A special tax provision (Section 303 of the Internal Revenue Code) allows certain redemptions or partial redemptions of closely held stock to be treated as a sale or exchange, not as a dividend. Since the estate's basis in the decedent's stock will be the stock's fair market value at the date of death, only post-death appreciation will be taxed upon the redemption and only up to the maximum long-term capital gains tax rate (generally 20% for sales and exchanges).

TAXALERT

To qualify for what is called a Section 303 redemption, the value of all the stock of the corporation included in the decedent's gross estate must exceed 35% of the decedent's adjusted gross estate. The adjusted gross estate is the gross estate less the allowable deductions for funeral and administration expenses, debts, the family owned business deduction, and certain losses (but before any charitable deduction or marital deduction). A qualifying redemption under Section 303 is limited in amount to the sum of the following items:

- Federal and state death taxes,
- Funeral expenses, and
- Estate administration expenses.

TAXALERT

The advantages of sale and exchange treatment under Section 303 may be somewhat diminished under the tax law, which taxes certain qualified dividends at the lower capital gains (vs ordinary income) rate. As long as the redemption by the estate results in qualified dividend treatment, the estate would generally be taxed at 20% on post-death appreciation without meeting the Section 303 requirements.

TAXSAVER

An estate does not actually have to be illiquid in order to qualify for this special redemption. The estate may redeem stock up to the maximum amount referred to above, if the estate otherwise has sufficient liquid assets to take care of its expenses and taxes.

Installment Payment of Estate Tax

The estate taxes attributable to a decedent's closely held business can be paid over a 14-year period if certain conditions are met. This 14-year payout offers a very favorable interest rate plus a 5-year deferral on the first installment of estate taxes. The deferral provision only applies to an "interest in a closely held business." To qualify, the value of the closely held business must exceed 35% of the adjusted gross estate. The amount of estate tax that qualifies for a deferred payout is limited to the portion of the total tax that is attributable to the decedent's business interest. Thus, if the decedent's qualifying stock constitutes 62% of the adjusted gross estate, then 62% of the total estate tax liability may be deferred.

Even though none of the tax attributable to the closely held business interest is paid for five years, the interest on the tax for the first four years must be paid annually. Starting in the fifth year, the estate tax due plus interest may be paid in up to 10 yearly installments.

The interest rate charged on the deferred estate tax attributable to the first $1.430 million (in 2014) in value of the closely held business interest is 2%. An interest rate equal to 45% of the rate applicable to tax underpayments applies to the deferred estate tax in excess of that amount.

Concerns Regarding Community Property

Community property is most often property acquired by spouses while they are married and domiciled in a community property state. But not all property acquired during the marriage is community property. If one spouse individually receives a gift or inheritance, it is not community property but rather is "separate property" owned solely by the recipient. Property acquired or otherwise owned by each spouse prior to marriage is also considered separate property.

Community property and marital property are treated differently from non-community property when someone dies. In a non-community property state, the basis of the decedent's property is increased or decreased for tax purposes to fair market value as of the date generally of the decedent's death. However, when one spouse in a community property state dies, the basis of *both* spouses' interest in all community property is stepped up or down, that is, increased or decreased to the fair market value at date of death.

Estate Planning—Steps to Take Now

Here's a useful checklist of estate planning measures you should consider:

- Review with your spouse your current financial situation and your entire personal financial plan (including plans for your retirement as well as plans for the years after one of you has died).
- If any adult member of your family does not have a will, or if any wills have not been reviewed within the last three years, contact your attorney. This is especially important because of the frequency of tax law changes.
- Compile a list documenting where all your important financial and legal papers are located. Inform all appropriate persons of your list. If you have not already done so, be sure your spouse or whomever you designate as your personal representative knows your attorney, accountant, trust officer, broker, insurance advisor, and other appropriate individuals.
- Compile information on the cost and approximate purchase date of all your assets, including your residence.
- To reduce federal estate taxes, consider assigning ownership rights of your group term life insurance to children, a trust, or other appropriate recipient.
- Review whom you have designated as a beneficiary for your employee retirement or Keogh plan and other employee benefits.
- Review how your assets will be passed on to your beneficiaries.
- Make sure that you have provided for the legal guardianship and personal custody of your minor children.
- Review your will or any trust you have set up with your attorney. In particular, you and your spouse should check the provisions in your wills that pertain to what would happen to your estates if both of you died at the same time. Have you, for example, properly divided your assets to take maximum advantage of the marital deduction and the estate tax exemption?
- If you and your spouse do not have durable powers of attorney, health care proxies, or living wills, consider having them drawn up soon.

If the answer to any of the following questions is yes, you may need professional assistance to help you determine whether there are tax problems on the horizon. Remember: A "yes" answer is a warning flag, but not necessarily a signal that there is a problem.

Are you:

- Making significant cash gifts to members of your family that are likely to continue indefinitely?
- Planning to make gifts to grandchildren within the next few years? In your will?
- Anticipating a significant inheritance? Is your spouse?
- A non-U.S. citizen? Is your spouse?

Do you:

- Hold assets jointly with your spouse, other than your residence and a working banking account?
- Have a simple will that leaves all property you own at the date of your death outright to your spouse?
- Own any real property in a state other than the state of your residence?
- Have a child or other relative with a serious medical problem who may require special consideration in your will or trust instrument?
- Have substantially more or less property than your spouse?

Have you:

- Moved your residence to a different state since you last executed your will?
- Named your estate as the beneficiary of your life insurance or your retirement plan benefits?

Chapter 45
Everything you need to know about e-filing

Note

ey.com/EYTaxGuide
Ernst & Young LLP will update the *EY Tax Guide 2015* website with relevant taxpayer information as it becomes available. You can also sign up for email alerts to let you know when changes have been made.

Introduction

E-filing has been a tremendous success and is now the standard method for filing tax returns. More than one billion returns have been e-filed with the IRS since 1990. For the 2013 filing season (for 2012 tax returns), 82% (over 118,000,000 returns) were filed electronically, exceeding the record set in 2012 of over 113,000,000. This includes over 46,000,000 returns filed from home computers. Returns are still being filed for the 2014 filing season as of the time this is written, but the totals so far are approximately 3 million e-filed returns ahead of last year at this time.

E-filing can offer a number of advantages. It's easy, efficient, and eliminates filling out paper forms line by line. If you owe additional taxes, you can e-file and authorize an electronic funds withdrawal, pay by credit or debit card, or pay by enrolling in the Electronic Federal Tax Payment System (EFTPS). The electronic funds withdrawal and EFTPS payment options are offered for free; however, you should expect to pay a convenience fee if you pay your taxes by credit or debit cards. Generally, you receive electronic proof of submission within 48 hours of when the IRS has received your return. Your return can be quickly and automatically checked for certain errors and some missing information. Approximately 89 percent of returns are accepted the first time they are transmitted. If you are entitled to a refund, you can typically get it in less than half the time it takes for paper filers to get their refunds. Your chance of being audited does not differ whether you e-file or file a paper tax return. Finally, your bank account information, as well as your other tax return information, is safeguarded.

E-filing is becoming mandatory for many additional types of returns and in more states and cities. Starting January 1, 2012, the IRS began mandating many paid tax return preparers to electronically file federal income tax returns prepared and filed for individuals, trusts, and estates if they anticipate filing 11 or more Forms 1040, 1040A, 1040EZ and 1041 during the year. The states vary in requirements for e-filing or electronic payments of taxes.

While e-filing is available for all individual income tax returns, except those who must file Form 1040NR, it might not be right for you. This may be true if you prefer the familiarity of paper and pen or if you're simply not comfortable with computers and the Internet. If that is the case, although your paid tax preparer must follow the new federal e-file mandate, you still have an option to file your tax return on paper if you choose. Consult your tax preparer to discuss your options. If you prefer to opt out of e-filing your federal return or if there is a particular reason why your tax preparer cannot e-file your return, Form 8948, Preparer Explanation for Not Filing Electronically, must be attached to your paper-filed tax return by your tax preparer explaining why the return is not being e-filed. If you do not use a paid preparer, the form is not needed.

Additionally, the following states allow resident taxpayers to web-file tax returns directly via their state website or use Free File: Alabama, Arizona, Arkansas, California, Colorado, Connecticut, District of Columbia, Delaware, Georgia, Hawaii, Idaho, Illinois, Indiana, Iowa, Kansas, Kentucky, Louisiana, Massachusetts, Maryland, Maine, Michigan, Minnesota, Missouri, Montana,

Nebraska, New Hampshire, New Jersey, New Mexico, New York, North Carolina, North Dakota, Ohio, Oklahoma, Oregon, Pennsylvania, Rhode, Island, South Carolina, Tennessee, Utah, Vermont, Virginia, West Virginia, and Wisconsin. You may consider using the online method of filing directly rather than using tax preparation software if you are familiar with the rules and requirements of filing your state tax return. Almost all states offer e-file through the use of tax preparation software. Consult your tax preparer or your tax software provider for a listing of eligible states.

This chapter discusses the three options available for e-filing and which one, if any, might be right for you.

Information You'll Need to E-File

Whether you decide to e-file or not, your first step is to get all of your tax information together. That way you'll save time and won't have to stop in the middle of preparing your return to find a missing document. Here's what you'll need:

- Social security numbers for yourself, your spouse, and any dependents.
- Forms W-2, W-2G, and 1099-R from all employers or payers are required for yourself and your spouse. If you are filing electronic returns using a personal computer, you enter the data from the forms into the electronic filing software. Unlike paper tax returns, you don't have to attach Forms W-2, Forms W-2G and Forms 1099-R. However, if you choose to use an "authorized IRS *e-file* Provider" (explained later), you must provide Forms W-2, Forms W-2G, and Forms 1099-R to the authorized IRS *e-file* provider before the provider is allowed to transmit the electronic return to the IRS. It is not required that you separately send these forms to the IRS.
- Forms 1099 for interest, dividends, retirement, or other income, or any Forms 1099 with income tax withholding.
- Schedules K-1 from passthrough entities including partnerships, S corporations, estates or trusts.
- Expense receipts for itemized deductions (Schedule A).
- Receipts and records for other income or expenses, including business income and expenses, if you are a sole proprietor.
- Checking and/or savings account numbers and the routing number for your financial institution (for a faster refund, or to pay electronically).
- A copy of your prior year tax return.

Note: For a brief explanation of some of the details of e-filing, also see *Filing Information, Does My Return Have to Be on Paper?* in chapter 1, *Filing information*.

Signing Your Electronic Tax Return

You will sign your electronic return by using a Self-Select PIN (see discussion later) for filing a completely paperless return. This allows you to confirm your identity with a five-digit PIN and your prior year's adjusted gross income (AGI). Or if you filed electronically last year, you can use the same PIN that you used to file last year's return. In most cases it is unnecessary to mail anything to the IRS when using e-file to transmit your return. In certain cases, the IRS will require you to mail Form 8453, U.S. Individual Income Tax Transmittal for an IRS *e-file* Return, along with the supporting documents. See the *Supporting Documents* section for more information.

Self-Select PIN

The Self-Select PIN (Personal Identification Number) method allows you to electronically sign your e-filed return by selecting a five-digit PIN as your signature. The five-digit PIN can be any five numbers except all zeroes. You can use your PIN whether you do your own taxes using a personal computer (described later) or have a tax professional prepare them for you.

You create your own PIN. You do not register the PIN with the IRS before filing or need to contact the IRS to get it. When you use one of the commercially available tax software packages on your personal computer that support the Self-Select PIN option, you will be guided through the process of entering your own PIN. If you use a tax professional, the preparer will help you and will require that you sign an e-filing authorization form in that process. If filing a joint return, a PIN is needed for each taxpayer. The IRS has a web-based application called "Electronic Filing PIN Help" that provides taxpayers with a PIN to be used when they cannot locate their prior year AGI or prior year PIN; refer to *www.irs.gov* for more information.

The following taxpayers are eligible to use the Self-Select PIN method:

- Taxpayers who are eligible to file Form 1040, Form 1040A, Form 1040EZ, and Form 1040-SS(PR) for Tax Year 2014.
- Taxpayers who did not file for Tax Year 2013, but have filed previously.
- Taxpayers who are age 16 or older on or before December 31, 2014, who have never filed a tax return.

- Taxpayers under age 16, filing as "primary" taxpayers, who have filed previously. A primary taxpayer is the taxpayer whose name appears on the first name line of the return.
- Taxpayers under age 16, filing as "secondary" taxpayers (spouse), who filed in the immediate prior year. A secondary taxpayer is the person whose name appears in the spouse's name line of the return.
- Military personnel residing overseas with an APO/FPO address.
- U.S. citizens and resident aliens residing in the U.S. Possessions of the Virgin Islands, Puerto Rico, American Samoa, Guam and Northern Marianas, or with a foreign country address.
- Taxpayers filing a Form 4868 (extension of time to file) or Form 2350 (extension for certain U.S. citizens living abroad).
- Those who are filing on behalf of deceased taxpayers.
- Taxpayers filing Form 8453, U.S. Individual Income Tax Transmittal for an IRS e-file Return, with required attachments.
  The following taxpayers are not eligible to use the Self-Select PIN method:
- Primary taxpayers under age 16 who have never filed.
- Secondary taxpayers (spouse) under age 16 who did not file in the immediate prior year.

Supporting Documents

The IRS requires a select list of supporting documents to be mailed in hard copy, unless they are being attached to the electronic file for your tax return as pdf documents. If you need to file any of the following forms or schedules, you may need to include a copy with Form 8453 (with the appropriate boxes checked) and send the package to the IRS after your e-filed return has been acknowledged and accepted by the IRS. Refer to Form 8453 for specific documents that must be attached in support of the following forms if you or your preparer is not able to attach them to your return as pdf documents:

- Form 1098-C, Contributions of Motor Vehicles, Boats, and Airplanes (or equivalent contemporaneous written acknowledgment)
- Form 2848, Power of Attorney (POA) and Declaration of Representative (or POA that states the agent is granted authority to sign the return)
- Form 3115, Application for Change in Accounting Method
- Form 3468, Investment Credit (if Historic Preservation Certificate is required)
- Form 4136, Credit for Federal Tax Paid on Fuels (if attachments are required to support the Biodiesel or Renewable Diesel Mixture Credit)
- Form 5713, International Boycott Report
- Form 8283, Noncash Charitable Contributions (if Section A statement or qualified appraisal is required or if using Section B)
- Form 8332, Release of Claim to Exemption for Children of Divorced or Separated Parents
- Form 8858, Information Return of U.S. Persons With Respect to Foreign Disregarded Entities
- Form 8864, Biodiesel and Renewable Diesel Fuels Credit
- Form 8885, Health Coverage Tax Credit
- Form 8949, Sales and Other Dispositions of Capital Assets (or a statement with the same information), if you elect not to report your transactions electronically on Form 8949 8864
- Only the attachments listed on Form 8453 should be attached and mailed to the IRS in support of your federal tax return.
- All attachments not listed on Form 8453 must be attached to your return using a pdf of the document, or portable document attachments. Your tax preparer will handle inserting these attachments for you before they transmit your tax return.

Transmission and Acceptance Process

After you sign the return using a Self-Select PIN, the electronic record of your tax return is transmitted to the IRS for processing. Once received at the IRS, the return is automatically checked by computers for errors and missing information. If it cannot be processed, it is sent back to the transmitter to clarify any necessary information. After correction, the transmitter retransmits the return to the IRS.

Within 48 hours of electronically sending your return to the IRS, the IRS sends an acknowledgment to the transmitter stating the return is accepted for processing. This is your proof of filing and assurance that the IRS has your return information. As long as your return was transmitted by the filing deadline, your return will be considered to have been timely filed, even if errors need to be corrected after the filing deadline and the errors are corrected in the specified calendar days (see more below). If you e-filed using your personal computer and have any of the items listed above under _Supporting Documents_, you need to mail the documents along with the completed Form 8453 to the IRS within three business days after receiving the acknowledgment. If a tax preparer e-filed your return, the preparer is responsible for sending Form 8453 to the IRS on your behalf within three business days after receiving the acknowledgment.

Errors/Rejections

Validation checks are built into return preparation software to catch errors in the process of preparing tax returns. Also, the IRS performs automatic checks when a return is initially e-filed and will "reject" the return if there are any errors or inconsistencies. If the IRS rejects an e-filed return, you will receive electronic notification of the items causing the return to be rejected. You should promptly correct the issues and resubmit the return for e-file within 5 calendar days. It is critical that you monitor the e-file transmission until you receive the acknowledgment indicating the IRS has accepted your return in order to ensure your return is considered to be timely filed. Both your tax return preparation software and the IRS will provide assistance to resolve rejection notifications and facilitate acceptance of your e-filed return. However, in the rare event that you are unable to resolve the issues listed in the rejection notification, you will be required to submit the return in paper format. In order to timely file a paper return, you must file it by the later of the due date of the return (including extensions) or ten calendar days after the date the IRS rejects it. Because of the many validation checks built into both the return preparation software and the IRS *e-file* process to locate errors before the final return is allowed to be transmitted, the error rate on e-filed returns is dramatically lower than on paper-filed returns; thereby reducing the chance of IRS notices. Approximately 89 percent of returns are accepted the first time they are transmitted.

Refunds

If you're due a refund and e-file, you can generally expect to receive it in approximately three weeks from the acknowledgment date—or even as fast as 10 days if you e-file and choose direct deposit. The direct deposit method will enable you to direct your refund into up to three separate checking, savings, or other accounts (i.e., individual retirement arrangement (IRA), health savings account (HSA), Archer MSA, Coverdell education savings account (ESA), or TreasuryDirect® online account) by providing the routing information for your financial institution and your bank account numbers. You can also request that your refund be used to buy up to $5,000 in paper U.S. Series I savings bonds. These requests are made using Form 8888, Allocation of Refund (Including Savings Bond Purchases).

Making Tax Payments

If you owe additional taxes, you can make payment in one of four convenient ways:

Option 1: By authorizing an electronic funds withdrawal from a checking or savings account. For electronic funds withdrawal, you include the routing information for your financial institution and your bank account number on Form 1040 when you file electronically. You can designate the exact date (up to and including April 15) that you want the payment to be withdrawn (by the Department of Treasury financial agents) from either your checking or savings account at your bank or other financial institution,

Option 2: By credit card (American Express®, Discover®, MasterCard®, or Visa®) or debit card (Visa®, NYCE®, Pulse®, ACCEL® or Star® Debit Card), or Bill Me Later®, a PayPal® Service. This payment is facilitated by a third-party payment processor that you choose at IRS.gov, and a convenience fee will be payable to that processor,

Option 3: By mailing a check or money order (made payable to the United States Treasury) using Form 1040-V, Payment Voucher, or

Option 4: By enrolling in the Electronic Federal Tax Payment System (EFTPS), which is a secure government website that allows users to make federal tax payments and schedule tax payments in advance conveniently 24/7 via the Internet or phone. For more information on EFTPS go to the IRS website (*www.irs.gov*) and choose **"EFTPS"** under **"Filing & Payment"** on the right-hand side of the website. To enroll in the EFTPS program or to make an electronic payment go to the EFTPS site (*www.eftps.gov/*). Note that you must enroll in the program before you utilize it. EFTPS allows individuals to schedule tax payments up to 365 days in advance of their due date, and modifications to those payments can be made up to 2 business days in advance of the scheduled payment date. Payments must be scheduled at least one calendar day prior to the tax due date by 8:00 p.m. Eastern.

One of the advantages of Options 1, 2, and 4 is that you receive an immediate acknowledgment when the IRS accepts your payment. A downside of using a credit or debit card is that the credit or debit card companies will charge a separate convenience fee for this service, in addition to any interest that might be charged on any outstanding credit card balance.

When to File and Pay Any Tax Due

If you use a tax professional, they can file your return electronically anytime during the filing season provided they have sufficient information from you to submit a complete and accurate return. However, sending the payment for a balance due by April 15 is still your responsibility.

Your tax professional should advise you of the amount of any balance due by April 15, as well as provide you with Form 1040-V, the voucher to transmit your payment to the IRS so that it is properly posted to your account, or discuss with you the alternative options to transmit your payment electronically, as mentioned above. If you are not using a tax professional, you may file electronically as soon as you are ready and will receive a confirmation from the IRS within 48 hours of receipt of your return. All balance-due payments, regardless of method of payment, must be authorized or sent to the IRS by April 15 to avoid late payment penalties or interest charges.

E-File for Your State Tax Returns
The option to e-file your state return (Federal/State e-file) is an extension of IRS *e-file* and is allowed in most states and the District of Columbia. However, not all Authorized IRS *e-file* providers offer this service. Your Authorized IRS *e-file* Provider can tell you if they participate in the Federal/State e-file program.

Extra Fees for E-Filing
The IRS does not charge a fee for electronic filing. However, some Authorized IRS *e-file* Providers (or Electronic Return Originators, "EROs") charge a fee for providing this service to their clients while others may offer it free of charge. This fee cannot be based on any figure from the tax return. Fees vary depending upon the tax professional you choose and the specific services you request.

With IRS *e-file*, you can prepare your own return and pay a professional only to transmit it electronically, or you can pay to have your return both prepared and transmitted. Whichever you choose, shop around for a tax professional who offers the services you need at a cost acceptable to you.

Methods of E-Filing
There are three basic methods to e-file your tax return: using a tax professional, using your personal computer, and the IRS "Free File" option. We'll explain each of these methods in detail.

Tax Professional
Tax professionals who are accepted into the electronic filing program are called "Authorized IRS *e-file* Providers." In many cases, the tax professional is also the ERO who is authorized to file your return electronically with the IRS. If you've prepared your own return and are simply using a tax professional to transmit the return, the tax professional will need to convert the return into the appropriate format for e-filing.

Many tax professionals are mandated by the IRS to e-file eligible returns for their clients. To find a tax professional to file your return electronically, search online for the Authorized IRS *e-file* Provider nearest you, or look in your local telephone directory under "Tax Return Preparation" for an Authorized IRS *e-file* Provider that meets your needs. Also, look for the "Authorized IRS *e-file* Provider" sign or decal in storefront windows.

Personal Computer
Instead of using the services of a tax professional, you can quickly and conveniently e-file your return using a personal computer. To do this you can:
• Purchase commercially available software,
• Download software from an Internet site and prepare your return offline, or
• Prepare and file your return online. Some vendors offer websites to complete your entire return online and then transmit it.

Note: The IRS cannot compete with private enterprise and does not offer free e-file software or direct filing. A number of companies, tested and approved by the IRS, do offer free use of their software and free filing, while others will charge nominal fees. Terms and conditions vary among companies and you are advised to review the information on each company's website and choose the product that is right for you.

Who can file using a personal computer? Anyone can use this method of filing. Obviously, access to the Internet through a personal computer is necessary. Software can be purchased, downloaded from the Internet, or accessed online.

Using this method, you prepare your tax return on a personal computer and transmit the information to the IRS. You can transmit up to five returns using tax preparation software, which enables you to prepare returns for family and friends with the same software and computer used for your return.

To actually e-file your return, the tax preparation software first converts your tax data into a format that meets IRS specifications and then transmits the electronic file to the IRS. The IRS checks the return and notifies the transmitter (who then informs you) whether the return has been accepted or rejected. If your return is not accepted, the electronic return transmitter will provide you with customer support to correct your return and resubmit it.

Signing your return. You can sign the return using the Self-Select PIN if you meet the eligibility requirements described earlier in this chapter. If you do not meet the eligibility requirements, you will need to authenticate yourself using other information, such as your prior-year Adjusted Gross Income (AGI). The IRS does not require you to mail your Form W-2 or any other form in hard copy, unless you are filing an item listed previously in the Supporting Documents section. Following the completion of your return, you should maintain copies of all items used in preparation and, if applicable, copies of any documents sent to the IRS.

Extra fees for e-filing a tax return from a personal computer. The IRS does not charge a fee for e-filing using a personal computer. However, an electronic return transmitter offering this service to taxpayers may charge a fee for transmission. Check out the IRS *e-file* Partners or Online Filing Software Companies listed at *www.irs.gov* to learn about free and low-cost e-file opportunities.

Payment methods and refunds. The same payment methods available by using a tax professional are available with e-filing from a personal computer—check or money order, electronic funds withdrawal, credit or debit card, and EFTPS. Refunds should be in your savings or checking account within 2 weeks if you choose direct deposit or in about 3 weeks if you choose a paper check. If you combine e-file with direct deposit, you could receive your refund in as few as 10 days.

If you have additional questions, you can also contact the IRS's toll-free customer service at 1-800-829-1040. Be prepared for long hold times as tax deadlines approach.

IRS Free File
This program began in 2003 and is a popular e-filing method.

Through a public-private partnership between the IRS and the tax software industry (i.e., Free File Alliance, LLC), you may access free, online tax preparation and electronic filing services through *www.irs.gov*. Eligible taxpayers may prepare and file their federal income tax returns using online software provided by the Free File Alliance companies—not the IRS.

The partnership agreement calls for the Free File Alliance to provide free tax preparation and filing to at least 70% of all taxpayers. Each participating software company has its own eligibility requirements, but none offer Free File to taxpayers with an Adjusted Gross Income of more than $57,000.

The difference between Free File and the first two methods is that the entire filing process takes place online—there is no need to visit a tax professional or purchase or download software. You just input data while you're on the provider's website to complete your return.

Privacy and security concerns. Your tax information and data will be protected when using a company's website. To ensure your data's safety, the IRS requires participating companies to obtain both privacy and security seal certifications. These certification programs, administered by third-party providers, certify your tax return information is protected from unauthorized access during the tax preparation process. Be sure your personal computer is protected by installing and updating antivirus software.

In addition:
- Tax return preparation is accomplished using proprietary software approved by the IRS; transmittal is through the established IRS *e-file* system.
- Alliance companies must comply with all federal rules and regulations on taxpayer privacy for paying and free customers. These rules prohibit use of tax return data for purposes not specifically authorized by the taxpayer.
- The IRS monitors the progress of each of the companies. If any problems develop, the companies are required to alert the IRS. If appropriate, the IRS will remove the company from the *www.irs.gov* website until the problem is resolved.

For more information, you should visit the company's privacy and security policy located on the company's website.

Step 1. How to Get Started: You start at the IRS website (*www.irs.gov*) and choose "freefile" under "Filing & Payment" on the right-hand side of the website. Click on "Option 2: Browse the list of Free File companies." The program can also be accessed through the IRS website at the following link: *http://apps.irs.gov/app/freeFile/jsp/index.jsp*. You will go to a *www.irs.gov* Free File page where you may start your search for a Free File company.

Step 2. Determine Your Eligibility: You must first determine your eligibility for using a particular company. Each company has a simple description of its eligibility criteria for using its free service.

Step 3. Link to Free File Company Service: After choosing a company, click on the company's name, which sends you directly to the company's website (you will be notified you are leaving *www.irs.gov* and being sent to a commercial website). Follow the instructions on that company's website to begin the preparation of your tax return.

Alternatively, if you are having trouble choosing by scanning the list of Free File companies, you may want to use the interactive help tool. Choose "Option 2-Get Help finding a Free File company" to narrow down the possible companies offering free preparation and e-filing for you. Answer the questions on the website and click "Submit."

If you are uncertain about your answers to these questions, you may want to view the complete list of companies and their services. The accuracy of the results is dependent on the accuracy of the information you provide in the tool.

Step 4. If You Do Not Qualify for the Selected Company's Free Offer: You may want to check other Free File company offers by accessing the _www.irs.gov_ Free File page. If you are on the company's website, look for the link that takes you back to _www.irs.gov_ and search for another Free File service. Go back and scan the listing of free company services as described in Step 3.

If you do **not** qualify for the company's free offer but continue with the preparation and e-filing process with this company, be aware you will be charged a fee for preparing and e-filing your federal tax return.

Example. If you select a company whose free services are provided to individuals with an adjusted gross income (AGI) of $57,000 or less and, based on your tax data, the company determines your AGI exceeds the $57,000 limit, you will be notified that you will be charged a fee. It is important you understand each of the company's eligibility criteria (which can be reviewed at the IRS Free File page as discussed above) before selecting a company. You may find the fee for returns not eligible for Free File on each company's website along with additional details of the company's offer, such as fees for state tax returns, if any, and a listing of tax forms the company supports. Access the company's website directly from the IRS Free File page by clicking on the company name (you will be notified you are leaving _www.irs.gov_ and being sent to a commercial website).

Step 5. Prepare and E-File Your Federal Income Tax Return on a company's website: The company's software prepares and e-files your income tax returns using proprietary processes and systems over the Internet. Electronically filed returns are transmitted by the company to the IRS using the established e-file system. An acknowledgment file, notifying you that the return has been either accepted or rejected, is sent via e-mail from the company.

Refunds and payments using Free File are handled the same way as they are for the other e-filing options.

Free File Fillable Forms. The IRS has a program called "Free File Fillable Forms." This program opens up free online filing to everyone regardless of income level by providing the online equivalent of a paper return. All forms needed to prepare and electronically file your federal income tax return are available (state return forms are not available). The program can be accessed through the IRS website at the following link: _https://www.freefilefillableforms.com/#/fd_.

Once you access the program, you may select the federal income Free File Fillable Forms and schedules you plan to submit, fill in the tax data, perform basic mathematical calculations, sign electronically, print for recordkeeping, and e-file your return. Most federal forms are available and can be used by 1040, 1040A, or 1040EZ filers. Please note, this program does not include questions or guidance that could assist you in preparation of your return. Free File Fillable Forms is most helpful to those who are familiar with the tax law, know what forms they need to use, and do not need assistance to complete their tax returns. If you are not comfortable with this method, you may want to access the _www.irs.gov_ Free File home page and check out the list of companies that offer free tax preparation assistance and e-filing services via the Free File program explained previously.

Chapter 46

If your return is examined

ey.com/EYTaxGuide

Note

ey.com/EYTaxGuide
Ernst & Young LLP will update the EY Tax Guide 2015 website with relevant taxpayer information as it becomes available. You can also sign up for email alerts to let you know when changes have been made.

Introduction

This chapter is probably not for you. Overall, the IRS examines only a small fraction of all tax returns that are filed. However, if you are contacted by the IRS about your tax return, this material may be very important to you. Just how important will depend on how carefully your return was prepared and the sources and amount of your income.

An IRS examination is nothing to be feared, if you have kept accurate records to support your deductions and all of your income has been reported. In most cases, IRS audits are rather routine. In fact, in about 25% of the cases, the IRS makes no changes or issues a refund. Whatever the result, you won't do yourself much good by making things difficult for the IRS. An IRS examiner has the legal power to force a taxpayer to produce books and records to complete the examination. The best strategy is almost invariably one of concluding the examination as quickly as possible by providing the facts needed and by meeting deadlines.

On the other hand, an IRS examination is nothing to take lightly. You should be prepared, and that preparation starts with keeping receipts and records, followed by careful preparation of your return. The IRS examiner must follow certain rules in conducting the examination. Since you'd be well advised to know what they are, this chapter tells you about them.

You will find a summary of your rights as a taxpayer at the beginning of this chapter. It may be especially helpful in cases that involve the delinquent payment of assessed taxes. This chapter tells you about your rights when your return is examined. You should know these rights, since they affect you and your pocketbook.

The first part of this section explains some of your most important rights as a taxpayer. The second part explains the examination, appeal, collection, and refund processes.

IRS Declaration of Taxpayer Rights

Protection of your rights. IRS employees will explain and protect your rights as a taxpayer throughout your contact with us.

Privacy and confidentiality. The IRS will not disclose to anyone the information you give us, except as authorized by law. You have the right to know why we are asking you for information, how we will use it, and what happens if you do not provide requested information.

Professional and courteous service. If you believe that an IRS employee has not treated you in a professional, fair, and courteous manner, you should tell that employee's supervisor. If the supervisor's response is not satisfactory, you do have the right to elevate your request for a further review with the Territory Manager or can write to the IRS director for your area or the center where you file your return.

Representation. You may either represent yourself or, with proper written authorization, have someone else represent you in your place. Your representative must be a person allowed to practice before the IRS, such as an attorney, certified public accountant, or enrolled agent. If you are in an interview and ask to consult such a person, then we must stop and reschedule.

You can have someone accompany you at an interview. You may make sound recordings of any meetings with our examination, appeal, or collection personnel, provided you tell us in writing 10 days before the meeting. Be sure you have received our confirmation and approval to record prior to the meeting.

Payment of only the correct amount of tax. You are responsible for paying only the correct amount of tax due under the law—no more, no less. If you cannot pay all of your tax when it is due, you may be able to make monthly installment payments. If you are unable to pay the full amount of taxes when due, interest and failure to pay penalties will continue to accrue until the balance is paid in full.

Help with unresolved tax problems. The Taxpayer Advocate Service can help you if you have tried unsuccessfully to resolve a problem with the IRS. Your local Taxpayer Advocate can offer you special help if you have a significant hardship as a result of a tax problem. For more information, call toll free 1-877-777-4778 (1-800-829-4059 for TTY/TDD) or write to the Taxpayer Advocate at the IRS office that last contacted you.

Appeals and judicial review. If you disagree with us about the amount of your tax liability or certain collection actions, you have the right to ask the Appeals Office to review your case. You may also ask a court to review your case.

Relief from certain penalties and interest. The IRS will waive penalties when allowed by law if you can show you acted reasonably and in good faith or relied on the incorrect advice of an IRS employee. We will waive interest that is the result of certain errors or delays caused by an IRS employee. While the IRS can waive or remove penalties based on reasonable cause, removal of most penalties is automatic if it is the first time you have incurred any penalties. You just have to ask the IRS to waive them. If you are not certain if you have had a penalty assessed on a prior return, you can contact the IRS and request an account transcript or ask the IRS assistor to check the account(s) for you and provide you with that information. There is no charge for this service. You can visit an IRS office where taxpayer assistance walk-in services are available or call the IRS on 1-800-829-1040 regarding individual tax returns and 1-800-829-4933 for business returns.

Examinations, Appeals, Collections, and Refunds

Examinations (Audits)

We accept most taxpayers' returns as filed. If we inquire about your return or select it for examination, it does not suggest that you are dishonest. The inquiry or examination may or may not result in more tax. We may close your case without change; or, you may receive a refund.

The process of selecting a return for examination usually begins in one of two ways. First, we use computer programs to identify returns that may have incorrect amounts. These programs may be based on information returns, such as Forms 1099 and W-2, on studies of past examinations, or on certain issues identified by compliance projects. Second, we use information from outside sources that indicates that a return may have incorrect amounts. These sources may include newspapers, public records, and individuals. If we determine that the information is accurate and reliable, we may use it to select a return for examination.

Publication 556, *Examination of Returns, Appeal Rights, and Claims for Refund*, explains the rules and procedures that we follow in examinations. The following sections give an overview of how we conduct examinations.

By mail. We handle many examinations and inquiries by mail. We will send you a letter with either a request for more information or a reason why we believe a change to your return may be needed. You can respond by mail or you can request a personal interview with an examiner. If you mail us the requested information or provide an explanation, we may or may not agree with you, and we will explain the reasons for any changes. Please do not hesitate to write to us about anything you do not understand.

By interview. If we notify you that we will conduct your examination through a personal interview, or you request such an interview, you have the right to ask that the examination take place at a reasonable time and place that is convenient for both you and the IRS. If our examiner proposes any changes to your return, he or she will explain the reasons for the changes. If you do not agree with these changes, you can meet with the examiner's supervisor.

Repeat examinations. If we examined your return for the same items in either of the 2 previous years and proposed no change to your tax liability, please contact us as soon as possible so we can see if we should discontinue the examination. The procedure only applies to individual returns and may not apply to returns with Schedule C business operations.

The Examination Process
The IRS examines returns for accuracy or correctness of income, exemptions, credits, deductions, and losses. Indeed, the IRS can examine any line item on the return.

Who Gets Audited?
The odds that your return will be examined by the IRS are, in fact, quite low. According to the most recent Treasury tables, the IRS examined only approximately 1% of all individual returns, down from about 5% in the mid-1960s. The odds shift substantially, depending on your income level and types of income. There are several ways in which your return can be selected by the IRS for audit which are explained in more detail later. But the majority of returns are selected based on a review of the income reported and deductions/expenses taken and their reasonableness in comparison to the norm. In other words does the item(s) look out of line compared to the normal or average amounts on other returns.

TAXALERT
In 2007, the IRS received Congressional permission to study individual returns in order to update the criteria it uses to select which tax returns it will audit. Less than 50,000 returns out of the 132 million individual returns filed were sampled in the IRS study, known as the National Research Program (NRP). The results of the study allowed the IRS to update the statistical models it uses to assess the audit potential of various types of returns. The bottom line for individuals is that as a result of the study, the criteria the IRS uses to assess the potential for errors and adjustments on filed tax returns has been updated and could increase your chances of being audited.

TAXPLANNER
While IRS statistical models impact your chances of being audited, here is a list of some items or circumstances that also frequently draw the IRS's attention:
- Reported income does not agree with information on information returns, Forms 1099, and W-2 filed by the payor with the IRS.
- Married taxpayers filing separately. Many such taxpayers do not report items consistently between returns (e.g., itemized deductions, zero bracket, or standard deduction amount elections).
- Returns with significant items that may trigger alternative minimum tax (e.g., significant miscellaneous itemized deductions and state, local, and property taxes).
- Taxpayers who may receive substantial cash payments in the normal course of business (e.g., doctors, lawyers, retail establishments, waiters, etc.).
- Deductions that seem unusually large compared to your income level.
- Total Schedule C (business income) gross receipts of $100,000 or more. According to one recent study, the IRS has concluded that individuals filing Schedule C are most likely not to report all business income or receipts.
- Large business expenses in relation to your income.
- A return submitted by an accountant or a tax preparer who is on an IRS list of problem preparers because they have repeatedly violated the law. The IRS has the power to conduct an examination of virtually all returns prepared by preparers who have been determined to be unscrupulous or have a proven history of filing returns with errors claiming large refunds.
- Complex investment or business transactions without clear explanations.
- Schedule F (farm) losses, particularly where the taxpayer has significant salary income.

- Earned income credit. Because there is the perception of potential abuse in this area, returns claiming the earned income credit are more closely scrutinized.
- Taxpayers' returns that fall in an area included in the IRS Market Segment Specialization Program (MSSP) such as automobile dealers, taxi services, air charters, attorneys, gas retailers, and others in a series of businesses or occupations that the IRS believes to need examination attention.

In addition, a local IRS office may undertake an Information Gathering Project (IGP) to more specifically focus on issues or types of returns they have reason to believe represent local compliance problems.

TAXALERT

The IRS is also realigning its audit resources to focus on key areas of noncompliance with the tax laws. This strategy represents a new direction for the agency's compliance effort. The new approach will focus on high-risk areas of noncompliance. The IRS effort will generally focus first on tax shelter or abusive scheme promoters and then on participants in these various schemes. The initiative will feature new and enhanced efforts in several priority areas, including:

- Offshore credit card users
- High-risk, high-income taxpayers
- Abusive schemes and promoter investigations
- High-income nonfilers
- Unreported income

The strategy reflects a new way of doing business at the IRS. Several of these efforts—such as the National Research Program, described earlier in this chapter, and the credit card initiative—reflect innovative approaches to tackle long-standing tax problems.

Fairness If Your Return Is Examined

Only a small percentage of filed returns are actually examined by the IRS. But, even if your return is selected for examination, it does not suggest that you are dishonest. The inquiry or examination may or may not result in more tax. Your case may be closed without change or you may even receive a refund. The mission of the IRS is to determine the correct tax liability for returns examined, regardless of the outcome.

Courtesy and consideration. You are entitled to courteous and considerate treatment from IRS employees at all times. If you ever feel that you are not being treated with fairness, courtesy, and consideration by an IRS employee, you should ask to speak to the employee's supervisor. Publication 1, Your Rights as a Taxpayer, explains the many rights you have as a taxpayer. You can get free publications by calling 1-800-829-3676 or view them online at www.irs.gov/pub/irs-pdf/p1.pdf.

Your rights as a taxpayer. While the Taxpayer Bill of Rights does not break new legal ground, it does create a single document that informs you of your rights. It is useful to review it to be aware of the rights you have. A summary of the most important points follows.

Pay only the required tax. You have the right to plan your business and personal finances in such a way that you will pay the least tax that is due under the law. You are liable only for the correct amount of tax. The purpose of the IRS is to apply the law consistently and fairly to all taxpayers.

Privacy and confidentiality. You have the right to have your tax case kept confidential. Under the law, the IRS must protect the privacy of your tax information. However, if a lien or a lawsuit is filed, certain aspects of your tax case will become public record. People who prepare your return or represent you must also keep your information confidential.

You also have the right to know why the IRS is asking you for the information, exactly how the agency will use it, and what might happen if you do not give it. You also have the right to ask the question, "Why was my return selected for audit?" In most cases, however, the examiner will not know exactly why the return was selected, particularly if the return was selected as a result of an IRS computer-based statistical screening program that singles out certain items on your return.

Examination of Returns

An examination usually begins when the IRS notifies you that your return has been selected. The IRS will tell you which records you will need. The initial contact can come in the form of a phone call followed by a confirmation letter or just a letter notifying you of the examination. If you gather your records and organize them before the examination, it can help speed the examination along with the least amount of effort.

How returns are selected. The IRS selects returns for examination by several methods.

1. **Discriminant Function System (DIF).** A computer program, developed under the National Research Program (NRP) called the Discriminant Function System (DIF) is used to preliminarily select most returns for further review and possible audit. Basically, DIF assigns a numerical value to certain items on your return. If the total of all the values equals or exceeds a minimum set by the IRS, the computer will single out the return for a possible audit. IRS agents or tax auditors will then check the return to see if it is worth the IRS's time to conduct an audit. This will depend on, among other things, staffing in your IRS district office. Even if your return is selected for an audit, it is likely that only specific items, such as charitable contributions or employee business expenses, would be examined, not your entire return.

   It's a closely guarded secret what weight DIF assigns to which items. Some things this computer program is on the lookout for include:
   - Large amounts of income not subject to withholding
   - More deductions than seem to be reasonable for your income level
   - Claims for an unusual number of dependency deductions as compared to withholding and other items on the return
   - Discrepancies such as a change of address combined with deductions claimed for owning a residence when you have not reported that you sold your old residence

   The DIF system is being used less as a selection source in recent years, especially in the case of Schedule C filers.

2. **Random selection.** Some returns are selected at random. The IRS uses the results of examining these returns to update and improve its selection process.

3. **Claims for credits and refunds.** The IRS also selects returns by examining claims for credit or refund and by matching information documents, such as Forms W-2 and the 1099 series, with returns.

4. **Information from outside sources.** Your return can be selected as a result of information received from other sources on potential noncompliance with the tax laws or inaccurate filing. This information can come from a number of sources, including the media, public records, or possibly informants. The information is evaluated for reliability and accuracy before it is used as the basis of an examination or investigation.

5. **The Market Segment Specialization Program (MSSP) and other special projects.** In 1991, the Internal Revenue Service began a project in the Los Angeles District Office focusing on developing highly trained revenue agents for a particular business market segment. Prior to this initiative, the IRS had not been training their revenue agents to be specialists within any certain business market segment. From that LA initiative, the IRS has expanded the program to cover more business market segments and has formally named the program the Market Segment Specialization Program (MSSP). The following is a list of these market segments:

Air charter	Construction/general building
Alaska commercial fishing	contractors
Alaska placer gold mining	Construction industry
Architectural services	Cooperative housing corporations
Artists and art galleries	Drywallers
Attorneys	Electronic components
Auto body and repair industry	Emergency care clinics
Auto dealerships	Employment tax–pizza drivers
Aviation tax	Entertainment industry:
Bail bondsmen	Contracts–audit applications
Bankruptcy	Foreign athletes and entertainers
Beauty shops/barber shops	Motion pictures/television
Bed & breakfast	Music (Nashville)
Building maintenance services	Theater–live performances
Cable TV	Escort service
Car washing and detailing	Farmers
Casino gambling	Federal excise tax, coal mining
Check cashing establishments	Financial institutions
Child care	Foreign tourism
Citrus industry	Form 1042S withholding agents
Commercial baking	Furniture manufacturing
Community banks	Garden supplies
Computers, electronics, & high	Garment industry
tech industry	Gas retailers

General livestock	Port of Houston
Golf courses	Poultry
Grain and milo growers	Printing
Grocery stores	Real estate agents/brokers
Health care	Real estate developers
Insurance agencies	Recycling
IRC Section 936 corporations	Reforestation
Jewelry dealers	Rehabilitation credit
Laundromat	Rent to own
Lawsuits, awards and settlements	Restaurants/bars/eating places
Life insurance	Retail industry
Liquor stores	Retail liquor industry
Low-income housing credit	RTC project (forgiveness
Manufacturing industry	of debt)
Masonry and concrete industry	Scrap metal
Ministers	Seafood purchases
Mobile cart vendors	Shareholder loans
Mortuaries	Sports franchises
Music industry	Swine farm industry
Nursing/rest homes	Taxicabs
Offshore captive insurance co.	Timber sales
Oil and gas operators	Tobacco
Passive activity losses	Tour bus industry
Pawn shops	Trucking industry
Petroleum contamination cleanup	Used auto dealers
Pizza parlors	Veterinary medicine
Plastic surgeons	Wine industry

The scope of the MSSP will affect virtually every taxpayer who has a Schedule C attached to his or her return whose business operations come under one of the many business market segments. Once a business market segment is identified, the IRS issues detailed audit guidelines to their specialists as a guide to conduct an audit of the tax return. These guidelines will detail various issues and practices within a market segment that should be scrutinized by all revenue agents for potential adjustment. The IRS has issued formal audit guidelines to their examiners with respect to 27 market segments, including, but not limited to, gas retailers, attorneys, trucking, mortuaries, air charters, bed and breakfasts, taxicabs, the music industry, foreign athletes and entertainers, architectural services, bars and restaurants, mobile food vendors, resolution trust corporations, the wine industry, passive activity losses, and the rehabilitation credit.

In addition, the IRS initiates compliance projects on an area-by-area basis to identify areas of noncompliance which could also lead to your return being selected for examination. For example, one area examined all the drywall contractors in a major metro area and claims to have found widespread underreporting of gross receipts as well as nonfilers. Another area selected returns of individuals who had renegotiated loans and examined them to determine if they were subject to tax because an indebtedness had been forgiven.

Verification methods for proper payment. Besides the methods identified earlier that are used to select returns for examination and check the accuracy and proper reporting of tax, the IRS also uses several other methods and techniques to attempt to verify that the proper amount of tax is being paid by taxpayers:

1. **Document perfection.** Every return is checked for mathematical, tax calculation, and clerical errors in initial processing. If a mistake is discovered, a recalculation of the tax due and a notice of explanation are sent to the taxpayer. This procedure is not an audit or examination of your tax return—an important distinction.

   The IRS determines whether the return is in "processible form." The law lets the IRS avoid payment of interest on any refund until the return contains the taxpayer's name, address, identifying number, and required signature. Furthermore, the return must be on the permitted form and contain sufficient information to permit the mathematical verification of the tax liability shown on the return.

   The IRS has carried this to extremes by sending tax returns back to taxpayers for failing to check a box, not attaching all required forms, and not making alternative minimum tax computations when it is obvious no such action is due. While the IRS concentrates on refund returns with small errors that permit them to avoid large refunds, it has also sent balance-due returns back after depositing any checks attached. If the return is not perfected and returned before the due date, the IRS says the return is delinquent. The IRS has lost this issue in the Tax Court but persists in its position.

2. **Document-matching program.** The IRS matches the information supplied by your bank, your employer, and others on Forms W-2 and 1099 and other information documents with the information supplied on your return. If an item is omitted from your return or conflicts with what is reported to the IRS, the IRS computer will generate a notice that recalculates your tax with corrections for the omitted income or overstated deduction.

    The Revenue Reconciliation Act of 1989 repealed the section of the tax law that gave the IRS the presumption of being correct in asserting a negligence penalty if you fail to report correctly relevant amounts reflected on information returns. The change applies to returns filed after December 31, 1989. It is probable that the IRS will continue to assert not only the negligence penalty but also the substantial understatement penalty. This procedure does not technically constitute a formal examination.

3. **Economic reality audits.** Once an examination is started, the IRS instructs their examiners to examine the taxpayer, not just the return. This means that all information on the return and any additional internal information or documentation the IRS has access to is considered to assess an individual's financial status, particularly if the return includes a Schedule C or Schedule F business or farm operation. This often involves an examination of the taxpayer's lifestyle as an additional check on whether the taxpayer had unreported income. Areas of inquiry may include standard of living, accumulated wealth, economic history, business environment, and potential nontaxable income.

    Since the passage of the Internal Revenue Service Restructuring and Reform Act of 1998, economic reality audits have been severely restricted. These audit techniques were extremely intrusive and their use has been limited to situations where the IRS already has indications of unreported income. However, if the IRS does have indications of unreported income or if a taxpayer's income appears to be insufficient to support his or her lifestyle, the examiner is authorized to dig deeper into the apparent discrepancy or issue. In these cases, the examiners have been instructed to discuss their concerns with the taxpayer and give him or her an opportunity to explain and/or resolve any discrepancies. However, due to the potential serious nature of this type of issue, the well-informed taxpayer should consider contacting a tax advisor. Because of the delicate balance between what is and what is not a proper subject of inquiry of the IRS examiner, some care should be exercised.

    If your return reflects losses from Schedule C or F operations that reduce overall income to near or below zero, there is a good chance the auditor will consider an economic reality type of examination. If the auditor begins questioning personal living expense amounts, bank account and loan balances at the beginning and end of the year, you can probably assume that an economic reality audit is under way. If this is the case, the auditor will be working toward determining all sources of funds, both taxable and non-taxable (i.e., gifts, loans, etc.), as well as all personal and business expenses incurred during the year. The auditor will then compare the total amount spent during the year to the total sources of funds, and if the expenditures exceed the identified sources of funds, the auditor is within his or her authority to propose adding the difference to income as "unreported income." If that does happen, you would be advised to seek assistance from your tax preparer or other representative.

Arranging the examination. Many examinations are handled by mail. However, if the IRS notifies you that your examination is to be conducted through a personal interview, or if you request an interview, you have the right to ask that the examination take place at a reasonable time and place that are convenient for both you and the IRS. If the time or place the IRS suggests is not convenient, the examiner will try to work out something more suitable. However, the IRS will make the final determination on how, when, and where an examination takes place. The difference between the correspondence and office audit is as follows:

Correspondence audit. After a tax return is initially selected for examination, the IRS may first conduct a correspondence audit, requesting that documentation of a specific item on your tax return be submitted by mail. If it is more convenient, you may request that the audit be held at the IRS's local district office. However, by law, the IRS has the right to make the final decision on where and how an examination will be conducted, as long as it is not unreasonable in exercising its discretion. The Taxpayer Bill of Rights directed the IRS to publish regulations defining reasonable time and place. These regulations were published in temporary form, effective June 4, 1990.

Office audit. If the examination is conducted at an IRS office, its scope may be expanded to cover all questionable items. Although correspondence audits may be resolved more quickly than examinations conducted at an IRS office, there is no rule of thumb for which type of audit would be more beneficial to you. However, it is generally to your disadvantage to request that a correspondence audit be changed to an office audit or a field audit. Correspondence audits are limited in scope. If you request an interview audit at an IRS office or an audit at your place of business, you open up the opportunity for the examiner to question other items.

The easier you make the IRS's job, the less the amount of time required to conclude the audit and the greater the likelihood that you will avoid any arbitrary adjustments.

An examination verifies the accuracy of your tax liability on a specific item as reported on a tax return, claim, or other filing. An examination is generally limited to the study of those matters bearing directly on the tax question at hand. The IRS has the authority to examine information that may not appear to be directly related to your tax liability. For example, the IRS may study your living expenses to determine if your reported income can support your lifestyle or whether you may have unreported income.

Transfers to another district. Generally, your individual return is examined in the IRS district office nearest your home. However, not all offices have examination facilities. Your business return is examined where your books and records are maintained. If the place of examination is not convenient, you may ask to have the examination done in another office or transferred to a different district.

Representation. Throughout the examination, you may represent yourself, have someone else accompany you, or, with proper written authorization, have someone represent you in your absence. If you want to consult an attorney, an enrolled agent, a CPA, or any other person permitted to represent a taxpayer during an examination, the auditor has the latitude to schedule the audit appointment to allow sufficient time for you to contact your tax preparer or representative to assist you with the audit. If the examination has started and you become uncomfortable with the way the audit appears to be going, you still have time to consult with your tax preparer or representative, even if you have not had them involved in the process previously. The IRS can stop and reschedule the interview or appointment. The IRS will generally not suspend the interview if you are there because of an administrative summons.

If you use Form 8821, Tax Information Authorization, to name a representative for you, the representative is only authorized to receive information and cannot fully represent you by taking action on the information. If you use Form 2848, Power of Attorney, to name your representative, the representative is fully authorized to represent you and take any action necessary, including signing an agreement for a deficiency or overassessment of tax to conclude the case. The latest revision of the Form 2848 is dated 07/2014.

In recent years, some districts and some examiners have been very aggressive in demanding that the taxpayer, even though represented by a qualified practitioner with a power of attorney, appear personally to answer questions. This practice was admittedly to probe for unreported income and to establish if the taxpayer's lifestyle might suggest other problems in compliance with tax laws. The Taxpayer Bill of Rights now specifies that the IRS "may not require a taxpayer to accompany the representative in the absence of an administrative summons," and a properly qualified practitioner with a power of attorney is authorized to represent a client in any interview without the taxpayer's presence, except for criminal cases or matters involving the integrity of an IRS employee. Furthermore, the law specifies that "if a taxpayer clearly states at any time during an interview," except where an administrative summons has been enforced or accepted, "that the taxpayer wishes to consult with an attorney, certified public accountant, enrolled agent, enrolled actuary, or any other person permitted to represent the taxpayer," the IRS "shall suspend such interview, regardless of whether the taxpayer may have answered one or more questions."

TAXPLANNER

Do you need professional help? The answer is: It depends on the issues involved and your ability to represent yourself. If the amounts involved are small, it may not be worth it to pay for an advisor's time. If your return was prepared by a certified public accountant or a lawyer, you will want to inquire whether his or her fee included representing you at an audit. If it didn't and you want him or her to represent you, you should agree on a fee at the beginning of the process. You will certainly want an accountant or a lawyer to represent you if (1) the law involved in the audit is unclear or complicated, (2) highly technical supporting information may be required, (3) you think other issues may come up, or (4) you are too nervous or emotionally involved to handle the matter yourself.

Tape recording meetings with the IRS. You can generally make an audio recording of an interview with an IRS examination officer. Your request to record the interview should be made in writing. You must notify the IRS at least 10 days before the meeting and bring your own recording equipment. The IRS also can record an interview. If the IRS initiates the recording, it will notify you 10 days before the meeting, and you can get a copy of the recording at your expense.

Repeat examinations. The IRS tries to avoid repeat examinations of the same items, but sometimes this happens. If the IRS examined your tax return for the same items in either of the 2 previous years and proposed no change to your tax liability, you should contact the IRS as soon as possible so that the agency can see if it should discontinue the examination.

Generally, in connection with auditing your return for a particular year, the IRS may inspect your books only once. But there may be a second examination if you request it or if the IRS notifies you in writing that an additional audit is necessary. A further investigation could be considered necessary simply if the IRS suspects that additional tax is owed. You may refuse the IRS's request to make a second examination. In fact, if you do not object, you have, in effect, given your consent for the examination to take place. If you refuse to produce records, the IRS must issue a summons. If you still resist, the IRS will be forced to obtain court assistance to enforce the summons.

The ban on second examinations does not apply:

1. When the original audit, although prolonged and characterized by IRS staffing changes, is still going on.
2. When the examination is not considered an examination as such (e.g., when the IRS contacts you to verify the amount of dividends or interest on your return because that figure does not match what was otherwise reported).
3. When the second examination is for a different kind of tax (e.g., employment or excise tax, instead of income tax) than was dealt with in the first examination.
4. When a mere visual inspection of the return has taken place, not an examination of your books and records.
5. In cases involving the year of deduction of a net operating loss carryback (or similar type of carryback).
6. In cases in which there have been involuntary conversions and the taxpayer has not recomputed the tax liability after the replacement period has expired.

In summary, it is difficult for the IRS to justify a second examination of your books and records for the same year, but if there is a legitimate reason to do so, the IRS is usually within its rights. However, if your return has been examined and you have received a final closing letter indicating that no changes were made nor any additional tax or refund was due, the IRS is required to undertake a formal re-opening of the return for examination. Permission for such a formal re-opening is difficult for an examiner to obtain. In any case, it is important that you keep all correspondence from the IRS, especially if your return was examined.

Explanation of changes. If the IRS proposes any changes to your return, it will explain the reasons for the changes. It is important that you understand the reasons for any proposed change. You should not hesitate to ask about anything that is unclear to you.

Agreement with changes. If you agree with the proposed changes, you may sign an agreement form and pay any additional tax you may owe. You must pay interest on any additional tax. If you pay when you sign the agreement, the interest is generally figured from the due date of your return to the date you paid.

The IRS uses misleading language when it describes this consent form as an "agreement form." When you sign a Form 870 or Form 4549, you are simply permitting the IRS to make its assessment of tax without waiting 90 days, as required by law, and you are forfeiting your right to go to the Tax Court. You are not bound to follow the IRS position in subsequent years and may even file a claim for a refund for the years covered by the Form 870 after the tax has been paid.

If you do not pay the additional tax when you sign the agreement, you will receive a bill. The interest on the additional tax is generally figured from the due date of your return to the billing date. However, you will not be billed for more than 30 days' additional interest, even if the bill is delayed. Also, you will not have to pay any additional interest or penalties if you pay the amount due within 10 days of the billing date.

If you are due a refund, the IRS can refund your money more quickly if you sign the agreement form. You will be paid interest on the refund.

An IRS examiner's authority. An IRS examiner has virtually unlimited authority to determine the facts. Since most examination issues concern factual matters, the examiner has considerable discretion in accepting secondary evidence and in deciding what constitutes acceptable proof. On technical legal issues, though, he or she must adhere to established IRS policy. Therefore, even if certain court cases support your argument, the examiner must disallow it if the IRS has decided not to follow the precedents established by these cases.

In theory, IRS examiners are also not permitted to trade off items, letting you take one deduction in return for disallowing another. In practice, negotiations with the IRS are commonplace.

An important reminder. IRS examiners are under considerable pressure to close cases by reaching an agreement at the initial examination. An agent is given high marks for explaining the IRS position in a convincing manner. Contrary to popular belief, examiners are not rated by the amount of money they bring in or by the number of cases they close.

While all examination reports have a chance of being reviewed, except for cases that fall into a mandatory review category, the review is on a sample basis, so only a small percentage of cases are actually reviewed. The mandatory categories include cases involving refunds in excess of $2 million, tax shelters, NRP, and fraud. All unagreed cases are subject to a limited review on receipt of a protest asking for an Appeals hearing. This review is primarily focused on perfecting the IRS case based on your arguments in the protest. An examination of your return is not complete, however, until you receive a "closing" letter from the IRS. Even if the agent completes the examination and you agree and pay any tax due, the examination results will still be reviewed by the examiner's manager or further up the line by a "quality reviewer." These reviewers can still send the case back to the agent to correct any problem identified.

Appeals

If you do not agree with the examiner's proposed changes, you can appeal them to the Appeals Office of the IRS. Most differences can be settled without expensive and time-consuming court trials. Your appeal rights are explained in detail in both Publication 5, *Your Appeal Rights and How to Prepare a Protest If You Don't Agree*, and Publication 556, *Examination of Returns, Appeal Rights, and Claims for Refund.*

If you do not wish to use the Appeals Office or disagree with its findings, you may be able to take your case to the U.S. Tax Court, U.S. Court of Federal Claims, or the U.S. District Court where you live. If you take your case to court, the IRS will have the burden of proving certain facts if you kept adequate records to show your tax liability, cooperated with the IRS, and meet certain other conditions. If the court agrees with you on most issues in your case and finds that our position was largely unjustified, you may be able to recover some of your administrative and litigation costs. You will not be eligible to recover these costs unless you tried to resolve your case administratively, including going through the appeals system, and you gave us the information necessary to resolve the case.

EXPLANATION

Appealing the Examination Findings

If you and the IRS auditor reach an agreement on the issue under examination, the auditor will be on your side if his or her report is reviewed by his or her boss.

If you do not agree with the examiner's report, you can meet with the examiner's supervisor to discuss your case further. If you still do not agree after receiving the examiner's findings, you have the right to appeal them. The examiner will explain your appeal rights and give you a copy of Publication 5, *Your Appeal Rights and How to Prepare a Protest If You Don't Agree*. This free publication explains your appeal rights in detail and tells you exactly what to do if you want to appeal.

The IRS now offers fast-track mediation services to help taxpayers resolve many disputes. Most cases that are not docketed in any court qualify for fast-track mediation. Mediation can take place as early as the conference you requested with the examiner's supervisor. The process involves an Appeals Officer who has been trained in mediation.

If you disagree with the IRS. If you and the IRS examiner disagree over the proper interpretation of a point of law, either you or the examiner may request technical advice from the IRS national office. Technical advice will be given only if the issue is unusual or complex, or if there is a lack of uniformity within the IRS about its treatment. If you ask for technical advice and the examiner denies the request, you may appeal to the Territory Manager and Area Director for your area. If he or she also denies the request and you disagree with the denial, all data will be forwarded to the national office for review. Action on the disputed issue generally will be suspended until it is decided whether or not technical advice will be issued.

Technical disagreements may be resolved by taking them to the agent's supervisor. However, this course of action is not recommended unless you are absolutely certain you are correct. The supervisor could point out an alternative position that might be more favorable to the examining agent.

Appeals. There is a single level of administrative appeal within the IRS. You make your appeal about the findings of the examiner to the Appeals Office in your region. Appeals conferences are conducted as informally as possible.

If you want an appeals conference, address your request to your Area Director according to the instructions in the IRS letter to you. Your case will be forwarded to the Appeals Office, which will arrange for a conference at a convenient time and place. You or your representative should be prepared to discuss all disputed issues and to present your views at this meeting in order to save the time and expense of additional conferences. Most differences are resolved at this level.

If agreement is not reached at your appeals conference, you may, at any stage of the proceedings, take your case to court. See _Appeals to the Courts_, later.

Written protests. Along with your request for a conference, you may be required to file a written protest with your District Director.

You do not have to file a written protest if:

1. The proposed increase or decrease in tax, or claimed refund, is not more than $25,000 for any of the tax periods involved.
2. Your examination was conducted by correspondence or in an IRS office by a tax auditor.

To request an appeal, follow the instructions in the letter to you by sending a letter requesting Appeals consideration, indicating the changes you don't agree with and the reasons why you don't agree.

If a written protest is required, you should send it within the period granted in the letter that you received with the examination report. Your protest should contain all of the following:

1. A statement that you want to appeal the findings of the examiner to the Appeals Office
2. Your name and address and a daytime phone number
3. The date and symbols from the letter, showing the adjustments and findings you are protesting
4. The tax periods or years involved
5. An itemized schedule of the adjustments with which you do not agree and why you do not agree
6. A statement of facts supporting your position in any issue with which you do not agree
7. A statement outlining the law or other authority on which you rely

You must sign the written protest, stating that it is true, under penalties of perjury as follows:

"Under the penalties of perjury, I declare that I have examined the facts stated in this protest and in any accompanying schedules and, to the best of my knowledge and belief, they are true, correct, and complete."

If your representative submits the protest for you, he or she may substitute a declaration stating the following:

1. That he or she prepared the protest and accompanying documents
2. Whether he or she knows personally that the statement of facts contained in the protest and accompanying documents is true and correct

Representation. You may represent yourself at your appeals conference, or you may be represented by an attorney, a certified public accountant, or a person enrolled to practice before the IRS.

If your representative attends a conference without you, he or she may receive or inspect confidential information only if a power of attorney or a tax information authorization has been filed. Form 2848, Power of Attorney and Declaration of Representative, or Form 8821, Tax Information Authorization, or any other properly written power of attorney or authorization may be used for this purpose.

You may also bring witnesses to support your position. You should consider consulting an attorney specializing in tax law before you do this.

Bargaining with the IRS. Whereas an IRS examiner must follow established IRS policy on statutory and procedural points, the appeals officer may bargain with you. He or she may consider whether litigation is worthwhile (hazards of litigation), given the strength of the views at odds with the IRS's position. If you make an unsuitable good faith settlement offer, the appeals officer may reject it but indicate a settlement he or she would recommend be accepted. In arriving at a figure, the appeals officer may calculate the chances of the IRS prevailing in court. Generally, however, the IRS will not settle a case just because it is a nuisance to continue to pursue it.

Appeals officers do not have final settlement authority in all cases and for all issues. Accordingly, it is good practice in negotiating a settlement to ask the appeals officer if any part of a settlement proposed is subject to a supervisory review.

If no agreement can be reached at the appeals conference, you have two options:

1. Pay the additional tax generated by the disputed issue and sue for the refund of this payment in your District Court or the U.S. Court of Federal Claims (formerly the U.S. Claims Court; see _Appeals to the Courts_, later).
2. Wait for the arrival of your closing letter and select a course of action at that point. If you do not pay the disputed amount, you will receive from the IRS a notice of deficiency, which is also known as a 90-day letter. This notice authorizes you to file a petition in the U.S. Tax Court without first having to pay the tax. A Tax Court suit may not be filed before receipt of the 90-day letter.

TAXPLANNER

Partnerships and S corporations. Special procedures apply to certain partnerships and S corporations. The amount of any adjustment is determined at the partnership or S corporation level. The procedures are complex, regular statutory notices are not issued, and you should consult a professional if you want to contest a partnership or S corporation issue raised in the examination of your return.

Appeals to the Courts

Depending on whether you first pay the disputed tax, you can take your case to the U.S. Tax Court, the U.S. Court of Federal Claims, or your U.S. District Court. These courts are entirely independent of the IRS. However, a U.S. Tax Court case is generally reviewed by an Appeals Office before it is heard by the Tax Court. You must file a petition with the Tax Court in order to obtain a pre-trial settlement opportunity with Appeals. As always, you can represent yourself or have someone admitted to practice before the court represent you.

Tax Court. If your case involves a disagreement over whether you owe additional income tax, estate tax, gift tax, windfall profit tax on domestic crude oil, certain excise taxes of private foundations, public charities, qualified pension and other retirement plans, or real estate investment trusts, you may take it to the U.S. Tax Court. For you to appeal your case to the Tax Court, the IRS must first issue a formal letter, called a notice of deficiency. You have 90 days from the date this notice is mailed to you to file a petition with the Tax Court (150 days if it is addressed to you outside the United States). If you do not file your petition within the 90 or 150 days, you lose your opportunity to appeal to the Tax Court.

Generally, the Tax Court hears cases only if the tax has not been assessed and paid; however, you may pay the tax after the notice of deficiency has been issued and still petition the Tax Court for review. You must be sure that your petition to the Tax Court is filed on time. If it is not, the proposed liability will be automatically assessed against you. Once the tax is assessed, a notice of tax due (a bill) will be sent to you, and you may no longer take your case to the Tax Court. Once the assessment has been made, collection of the full amount due may proceed, even if you believe that the assessment was excessive. Publication 594, _What You Should Know About the IRS Collection Process_, explains IRS collection procedures.

If you filed your petition on time, the Tax Court will schedule your case for trial at a location that is convenient to you. You may represent yourself before the Tax Court, or you may be represented by anyone admitted to practice before the Tax Court.

If your case involves a dispute of not more than $50,000 for any 1 tax year, the Tax Court provides a simple alternative for resolving disputes. At your request, and with the approval of the Tax Court, your case may be handled under the small case procedures, whereby you can present your own case to the Tax Court for a binding decision. If your case is handled under this procedure, the decision of the Tax Court is final and cannot be appealed. You can get more information about the small case procedures and other Tax Court matters from the U.S. Tax Court, 400 Second Street, N.W., Washington, D.C. 20217.

TAXALERT

Representing yourself. Since many taxpayers represent themselves in small cases, the IRS has a very high win record. Filing your own petition may not be a good idea, especially if the amount is substantial to you. In any event, be careful in following the instructions _to the letter_, especially regarding the date for filing, the required fee, and the address of the Tax Court. The date of mailing a petition to the Tax Court is the filing date, but you should use certified mail and carefully retain the receipt with a legible postmark.

District Court and U.S. Court of Federal Claims. Generally, the District Court and the U.S. Court of Federal Claims hear tax cases only after you have paid the tax and have filed a claim for a credit or a refund. As explained later under *Claims for Refunds*, you may file a claim for a credit or a refund with the IRS if, after you pay your tax, you believe that the tax is incorrect or too high. If your claim is rejected, you will receive a notice of disallowance of the claim, unless you signed a Form 2297, Waiver of Statutory Notification of Claim Disallowance. If the IRS has not acted on your claim within 6 months from the date on which you filed it, you may then file suit for refund. You must file suit for a credit or a refund no later than 2 years after the IRS disallows your claim or a Form 2297 is issued.

You may file your credit or refund suit in your U.S. District Court or in the U.S. Court of Federal Claims. However, the U.S. Court of Federal Claims does not have jurisdiction if your claim was filed after July 18, 1984, and is for credit or refund of a penalty that relates to promoting an abusive tax shelter or to aiding and abetting the understatement of tax liability on someone else's return.

For information about procedures for filing suit in either court, contact the Clerk of your U.S. District Court or the Clerk of the U.S. Court of Federal Claims. The addresses of the District Courts and the U.S. Court of Federal Claims are in Publication 556, *Examination of Returns, Appeal Rights, and Claims for Refund.*

Before you file suit. Here are some of the factors that you might want to consider before you decide to file your suit in Tax Court, District Court, or the U.S. Court of Federal Claims:

1. Which court has most recently arrived at favorable rulings on similar disputed issues.
2. The amount of tax involved. You may file a suit in Tax Court without paying the IRS the amount it claims you owe. If the tax has already been paid and you wish to file suit to obtain a refund, the U.S. District Court and the U.S. Court of Federal Claims are your only choices. However, to stop the accumulation of interest, you can at any time make a deposit in the nature of a cash bond of the tax that an examiner says you owe. Note: Such a remittance must be clearly labeled as a deposit. If you are successful in an appeal, you will draw no interest on the deposits returned. A deposit does not prevent you from going to the Tax Court. Once you file a suit in Tax Court, you may then pay the alleged tax deficiency and your suit will not be thrown out of court. If you do make the payment at this point in the process, you will not be liable for interest charges past the payment date. If you win, the government will then owe you interest from the date on which you made the payment. A deposit will be converted to a payment of the tax when you file a petition with the Tax Court. It is important to distinguish between payments of tax and deposits to stop the accumulation of interest.
3. Jury trials are available only in the District Courts. If your case rests on a question of equity, rather than on a finer point of tax law, a jury might be more responsive to your arguments. Remember, however, that both parties may appeal a District Court or a Tax Court decision.
4. A representative who is not an attorney may appear before the Tax Court if admitted to practice before that court.
5. Filing a suit before the Tax Court suspends the statute of limitation for assessment on the tax return that you are contesting. Consequently, if the IRS chooses, it could raise new issues and assert additional tax while your case is pending in court.
6. You're more likely to avoid embarrassing publicity before the Court of Federal Claims. The U.S. Court of Federal Claims is located in Washington, D.C. There is a U.S. District Court near your hometown. The Tax Court tries cases on a circuit-riding basis in most major cities.
7. You may file suit in Tax Court within 90 days (150 days if outside the United States) after the IRS issues a statutory notice of deficiency. You have more time to file before the U.S. District Court and the U.S. Court of Federal Claims.
8. In Tax Court, attorneys from the Office of Chief Counsel represent the IRS. In District Court and U.S. Court of Federal Claims, attorneys from the Tax Division of the Department of Justice will oppose your case.
9. Tax Court and District Court cases are appealed to the Circuit Court of Appeals and then to the Supreme Court. U.S. Court of Federal Claims decisions may be appealed to the Court of Appeals for the Federal Circuit and then to the Supreme Court.
10. Any court of the United States may now award attorney's fees and other costs for cases initiated after December 31, 1985, including certain costs incurred in an administrative appeal if the IRS's position was not substantially justified.

Recovering litigation expenses. If the court agrees with you on most of the issues in your case and finds the IRS's position to be largely unjustified, you may be able to recover some of your litigation expenses from the IRS. But to do this, you must have used up all the administrative remedies available to you within the IRS, including going through the appeals system. You may also be able to recover administrative expenses from the IRS. Free Publication 556, *Examination of Returns, Appeal Rights, and Claims for Refund*, explains your appeal rights.

The Taxpayer Bill of Rights corrects an inequity in prior law by permitting the courts to award costs, not only for litigating but also for administrative proceedings once a taxpayer's administrative appeal rights have been exhausted and a "notice of decision" by the IRS or a statutory notice of deficiency has been issued, whichever occurs earlier. The prior law had been interpreted to permit recovery only after the IRS's attorneys had taken a position before the courts. To recover, a taxpayer must substantially prevail through a determination in an administrative proceeding, after the point specified previously, or in a court of law and must establish that the position of the United States in the proceeding was not substantially justified. In collection matters, when neither notice is issued, only litigation costs are recoverable.

Reasonable administrative costs include the following:

- Fees or charges imposed by the IRS
- Reasonable expert witness fees
- Reasonable costs of studies and analyses
- Costs associated with engineering or test reports
- Reasonable fees (generally not in excess of $150 per hour) for a qualified representative of the taxpayer in connection with the administrative action

Collections

Publication 594, *What You Should Know About the IRS Collection Process*, explains your rights and responsibilities regarding payment of federal taxes. It describes:

- What to do when you owe taxes. It describes what to do if you get a tax bill and what to do if you think your bill is wrong. It also covers making installment payments, delaying collection action, and submitting an offer in compromise.
- IRS collection actions. It covers liens, releasing a lien, levies, releasing a levy, seizures and sales, and release of property.

Your collection appeal rights are explained in detail in Publication 1660, *Collection Appeal Rights*.

Innocent spouse relief. Generally, both you and your spouse are responsible, jointly and individually, for paying the full amount of any tax, interest, or penalties due on your joint return. However, if you qualify for innocent spouse relief, you may be relieved of all or part of the joint liability. To request relief, you must file Form 8857, Request for Innocent Spouse Relief, no later than 2 years after the date on which the IRS first attempted to collect the tax from you. The 2-year period for filing your claim may start if the IRS applies your tax refund from one year to the taxes that you and your spouse owe for another year. For more information on innocent spouse relief, see Publication 971, *Innocent Spouse Relief*, and Form 8857.

Potential Third Party Contacts

Generally, the IRS will deal directly with your or your duly authorized representative. However, the IRS can and will sometimes talk with other persons if it needs information that you have been unable to provide, or to verify information it has received. If the IRS intends to contact third parties for information on you, they are required to give notice to you that they intend to do so. The examiner may contact other persons, such as a neighbor, bank, employer, or employees to verify or gather information needed to complete the examination. The law prohibits the IRS from disclosing any more information than is necessary to obtain or verify the information it is seeking. The IRS's need to contact other persons may continue as long as there is activity in your case. If the IRS does contact other persons, you may have a right to request a list of those contacted.

Claims for Refunds

You may file a claim for refund if you think you paid too much tax. You must generally file the claim within 3 years from the date you filed your original return or 2 years from the date you paid the tax, whichever is later. The law generally provides for interest on your refund if it is not paid within 45 days of the date you filed your return or claim for refund. Publication 556, *Examination of Returns, Appeals Rights, and Claims for Refund*, has more information on refunds.

If you were due a refund but you did not file a return, you must file within 3 years from the date the return was originally due to get that refund.

EXPLANATION

If you believe that tax, penalty, or interest was unjustly charged, you have rights that can remedy the situation.

Claims for refund. Once you have paid your tax, you have the right to file a claim for a credit or refund if you believe the tax is too much. Be aware that informal claims that mention vague and general future possibilities to justify a refund will not be considered valid. The procedure for filing a claim is explained in chapter 1, *Filing information*.

If you do file a claim, you should keep all support or documentation used when the claim was prepared. In the event you are notified by the IRS that the claim will be examined, you will need to provide the documentation to support the claim upon request. The IRS will not allow time for you to gather the documentation requested. The IRS's position is that if you filed a claim, you had to have had a basis for filing that claim and that should have constituted adequate support at that time. Therefore, you should not need more time to gather documentation. You will generally be given only one opportunity to provide the requested information and if you can't provide it within a reasonable amount of time, the claim will be disallowed and you will not receive the requested refund.

Some courts have held that an informal claim for a refund will, under certain circumstances, prevent the statutory period from expiring before you can accumulate and submit all your data. An informal claim should be in writing, should notify the IRS that a right to a refund is being asserted, and should tell as fully as possible the reasons why you feel the refund would be valid. A formal claim for the refund filed on official IRS forms should be made as soon as practical thereafter.

If you file with the wrong IRS center. If you file an amended return with the wrong IRS Service Center, it is under no obligation to forward that return to the correct Service Center. If you do not hear from the IRS within 6 months of filing Form 1040X, you should make a point of contacting it to determine the source of the delay.

Claims (Form 1040X) should always ask for a specific dollar amount or "for such greater amount as is legally refundable" to ensure that you receive a refund of interest and interest on such interest where appropriate.

Cancellation of penalties. You have the right to ask that certain penalties (but not interest, as discussed later) be canceled (abated) if you can show reasonable cause for the failure that led to the penalty (or can show that you exercised due diligence, if that is the standard for the penalty).

If you relied on wrong advice from IRS employees given to you by phone, the agency will cancel certain penalties that may result. But you have to show that your reliance on the advice was reasonable.

Reduction of interest. If the IRS's error caused a delay in your case, and this is grossly unfair, you may be entitled to a reduction of the interest that would otherwise be due. Only delays caused by procedural or mechanical acts that do not involve exercising judgment or discretion qualify. If you think the IRS caused such a delay, please discuss it with the examiner and file a claim.

TAXSAVER

If the IRS makes an error. If the IRS made an error, sent you a refund check, and then made you pay interest when you repaid it, you can strike back. According to the Tax Reform Act of 1986, the IRS may not charge you interest from the date of the erroneous refund to the date they demanded you repay it. The law has also given the IRS the discretion to refund or abate excessive interest that you may have paid on an underpayment of your tax if an IRS employee was dilatory or made an error in processing it. To qualify, you must not have caused the error in any way. The erroneous refund must have been less than $50,000. Use Form 843 to file your claim.

Past-Due Taxes

The Taxpayer Bill of Rights recognized that taxpayers occasionally may have problems paying taxes due on their returns because of unanticipated changes on examination or other unexpected difficulties. To ensure fair treatment, the Taxpayer Bill of Rights made some changes in how notices are issued, how much time is allowed for payment, how taxpayers can get help, and so on. The key provisions relating to past-due taxes are as follows:

1. The period from when the IRS provides written notice to a taxpayer to the first permissible date on which the IRS can levy on bank accounts, wages, and so on is increased from 10 days to 30 days. The IRS also cannot levy on property on any day on which the person appears before the IRS in response to a summons, unless the IRS determines the collection of the tax is in jeopardy. In addition, financial institutions are required to hold accounts garnished by the IRS for 21 days after receipt of the notice of levy.

2. The IRS established a formal system for the appeal of liens similar to that existing in the income tax deficiency area. The appeals procedures are printed on the notice of lien. See Publication 1660, *Collection Appeal Rights*.

3. The IRS now has the legal right to enter into installment agreements with taxpayers so that they can more easily pay delinquent taxes. The agreement will remain in effect unless the taxpayer has provided inaccurate information, does not pay an installment when it is due, fails to respond to a reasonable request for updated financial information, or the collection of the balance is in jeopardy. In addition, the IRS may only modify or terminate an agreement if the taxpayer's financial condition has significantly changed. Notification of the reason for the action has to be given at least 30 days prior to any action.

4. The Taxpayer Advocate is authorized to issue a taxpayer assistance order (TAO) in any situation in which the taxpayer is suffering or about to suffer a significant hardship as a result of the manner in which the IRS laws are being administered. During the period in which the order is in effect, the statute of limitations is suspended and any further IRS action is halted. Only the Commissioner, Deputy Commissioner, or Taxpayer Advocate can modify or rescind the order. The Taxpayer Advocate administers the IRS Problem Resolution Program, which was created to resolve problems not remedied through normal operating channels.

One avenue for possible resolution of issues is to contact the Taxpayer Advocate Service (TAS). In 1996, the Taxpayer Bill of Rights established the Office of the Taxpayer Advocate and described its function as:

1. To assist taxpayers in resolving problems with the Internal Revenue Service;
2. To identify areas in which taxpayers have problems in dealings with the Internal Revenue Service;
3. To the extent possible, propose changes in the administrative practices of the IRS to mitigate those identified problems; and,
4. To identify potential legislative changes which may be appropriate to mitigate such problems.

Taxpayers who have tried, unsuccessfully, to resolve a pending issue with the IRS may be able to receive assistance from the Office of the Taxpayer Advocate. Generally, the Taxpayer Advocate can help a taxpayer if, due to the administration of tax laws, the taxpayer:

a. Is experiencing economic harm or significant cost;
b. Has experienced a delay of more than 30 days to resolve a tax issue; or,
c. Has not received a response or resolution to the problem by the date promised by the IRS.

To receive assistance, the taxpayer must provide the following information:

a. Name, address, and social security number (or Employer Identification Number);
b. Telephone number and best time to call; and,
c. A description of the problem or hardship, detail on previous attempts to resolve the problem, and the office(s) contacted if known.

The Office of the Taxpayer Advocate will provide qualifying taxpayers with:

a. An assigned case advocate's contact number;
b. An impartial and independent review of the problem and updates on progress;
c. Advice on preventing future federal tax problems.

The Taxpayer Advocate is not designed to assist taxpayers in avoiding valid tax liabilities or to interfere with the normal examination or collection process within the IRS. But, it can assist if the IRS is not following procedural guidelines or there is a significant financial hardship as a result of the IRS actions. The IRS has designed Form 911, Application for Taxpayer Assistance Order (TAO), for requesting Taxpayer Advocate assistance in instances when there is significant financial hardship.

Chapter 47

Planning ahead for 2015 and beyond

ey.com/EYTaxGuide

Note

ey.com/EYTaxGuide
Ernst & Young LLP will update the *EY Tax Guide 2015* website with relevant taxpayer information as it becomes available. You can also sign up for email alerts to let you know when changes have been made.

Introduction

In contrast to 2013, in which there were major tax changes, 2014 has lacked significant developments in the tax legislative landscape—although that may change late in the year if Congress returns for a post-election "lame duck" session. There are several reasons for the hiatus, among them midterm elections in November, a challenging political climate, and world events that have competed for Washington's attention.

   This relative paralysis in Washington has made it difficult for taxpayers to plan ahead for their 2014 tax returns. One of the areas of greatest uncertainty is the fate of "tax extenders," a group of 55 individual and business tax provisions that expired at the end of 2013. These provisions span a broad range of deductions and exclusions relevant to many taxpayers. In years past, Congress has extended them on a temporary basis, sometimes retroactively. As of this writing, those expired provisions do not apply for 2014, although there is an expectation that following the elections, Congress may retroactively extend them at least temporarily. If that happens, taxpayers should revisit their tax planning as soon as they can. For updated information on new tax legislation that is enacted after this book is published, see our website, *ey.com/EYTaxGuide*.

   In late 2013 and early 2014, there was widespread talk of overhauling the U.S. tax code. Both Senate Finance Committee Chairman Max Baucus (D-MT) and House Ways and Means Committee Chairman Dave Camp (R-MI) each released tax reform discussion drafts and solicited feedback. However, Baucus' departure from the Senate in early 2014 to become the U.S. ambassador to China and Camp's pending retirement from the House has left these efforts in limbo.

   Given all these uncertainties, it is even more important for taxpayers to start planning at the beginning of each year and regularly update their planning as new tax legislation is passed and their own personal circumstances change. This chapter presents a summary of tax planning ideas to help you get started.

One tax-related carryover item from 2013 is ongoing implementation of the Affordable Care Act (ACA), the comprehensive health care legislation enacted in 2010. The ACA's "individual shared responsibility payment," otherwise known as the "individual mandate," began to apply in 2014. Also, effective January 1, 2014, refundable tax credits became available for many individuals to purchase coverage through state or federal exchanges—although there have since been questions raised by conflicting U.S. Appeals Court decisions regarding whether these tax credits are available to individuals through the federally facilitated exchanges. Millions of people who have purchased insurance through these exchanges could be affected, and the issue could end up before the U.S. Supreme Court. See the discussion about the _Affordable Care Act (ACA) Individual Provisions_ later in this chapter for more information that can help you understand these issues.

Another area of activity stems from the U.S. Supreme Court's June 2013 ruling on the federal Defense of Marriage Act (DOMA). The Court ruled that the DOMA provisions limiting the definition of marriage to the union of one man and one woman and defining a spouse as a person of the opposite sex for federal law purposes was unconstitutional. The decision has significant tax implications for single-sex couples, and the issue continues to play out in the states. See _Same-Sex Marriages: Tax Changes after the U.S. Supreme Court Ruling on the Defense of Marriage Act (DOMA)_, later in this chapter for more information.

Year-End and Ongoing Tax Planning Considerations

Tax planning needs to be an ongoing process; one that takes into consideration both the continually evolving political, fiscal, and legislative environment and changes in your own personal circumstances, needs, and goals. The following section outlines a number of tax planning ideas that may help you reduce not only this year's tax bill but your tax liability in future years.

Prepare a Tax Projection

The first step in tax planning is to project what you will pay in taxes this year. Determine your estimated marginal tax rate—the percentage of tax you will pay on your last dollar of income (meaning the tax bracket your last dollar of income falls into, and therefore the highest tax rate you pay). Then, think about whether your marginal tax rate will likely go up or down next year. In doing so, consider the significant difference between the tax rate on your ordinary income (up to 39.6% in 2014, plus, if applicable, 3.8% Net Investment Income Tax (NIIT) on Net Investment Income (NII)) and the rate on your long-term capital gains and qualified dividends (generally 15%, with the highest tax rate at 20% for taxpayers who are otherwise subject to the 39.6% marginal rate on ordinary income, plus, if applicable, 3.8% NIIT on gains and dividends treated as NII).

Consider building out your tax projection to cover the next few years, not just to see what your overall taxable income could be, but to gain a deeper perspective on the composition of that income and how future tax law changes could affect it. You should also look at your investment asset allocation and asset location. The former is about what you own. The latter is about where and in what types of accounts you own your investments. Take care not to make short-term, tax-driven decisions today that may undermine your overall financial goals tomorrow. By doing these analyses and assessments, you can effectively position yourself to determine what, if any, adjustments you should consider for tax and investment planning.

Tax planning often, but not always, involves deferring income and accelerating deductions. It can also involve shifting income to a person in a lower tax bracket and repositioning an appropriate portion of your portfolio from investments that generate ordinary taxable income to those that may create capital gains and produce tax-exempt income. Generally, you want to recognize income in years in which your tax rate is comparatively low and pay deductible expenses when your tax rate is comparatively high. Only when you understand your current situation can you evaluate whether the tax law provides any incentives for taking action this year.

Ways to Postpone or Reduce Income Subject to Tax

Defer interest income. Consider purchasing a short-term certificate of deposit (CD) that matures in the following year. None of the interest earned will be subject to tax in the year you bought the CD, provided any interest received this year would be penalized by the issuer of the CD. Buying tax-deferred U.S. Treasury securities, such as Series EE or Series I bonds, is another way to defer interest income.

Evaluate the effect of the lower tax rate for qualified dividends. For taxpayers subject to the 25%, 28%, 33%, or 35% tax brackets on ordinary income, qualified dividend income—but not interest income—is taxed at a top income tax rate of 15%. For high-income taxpayers who are otherwise in the 39.6% regular income tax bracket (i.e., in 2014, taxable incomes over $406,750 for individual filers, $432,200 for heads of households, $457,600 married filing jointly, and $228,800 if married filing separately), the tax rate is 20% on qualified dividends. Qualified dividends received by taxpayers in the 10% and 15% tax brackets are taxed at a zero rate. These preferential tax rates on qualified dividend income apply to both the regular tax and the alternative minimum tax. The lower tax rates for qualified dividends means that you should consider dividends, as well as long-term capital gains (discussed next) when evaluating the tax considerations in a year-end sale of stock. A number of tests must be met for a dividend to qualify for the reduced tax rates. See *Qualified Dividends* in chapter 8, *Dividends and other corporate distributions*, for more information.

Qualify for the lower long-term capital gains rates. The maximum federal income tax rate on gains from sales of most types of investments held longer than 12 months is 15% for taxpayers who are otherwise subject to the 25%, 28%, 33%, or 35% tax brackets on ordinary income. Net long-term capital gains are taxed at a maximum rate of 20% for high income taxpayers who are otherwise in the 39.6% regular income tax bracket (i.e., in 2014, taxable incomes over $406,750 for individual filers, $432,200 for heads of households, $457,600 if married filing jointly, and $228,800 if married filing separately). The rate on net capital gains received by taxpayers in the 10% and 15% tax brackets is zero. The 12-month period begins the day after you buy the property. When selling securities, ignore the settlement date. The trade date determines the date of disposition.

Identify shares of stock and mutual funds that you want to sell to maximize tax benefits. If you want to sell shares that you purchased at different times, select those in which you have a high tax basis in order to reduce taxable gain or increase a tax loss that can be used to offset other taxable income.

Use your capital losses. If you had capital gains this year, consider offsetting those gains by selling property in which you have unrealized capital losses. You can offset capital losses against capital gains dollar for dollar. You can also use capital losses in excess of capital gains to offset up to $3,000 of ordinary income (for example, wages, interest, etc.) each year. Doing so may save you nearly $1,200 in federal income tax (if you are in the top tax bracket). Any unused capital losses are carried forward for use in future tax years.

Take a capital loss on worthless securities. If you have investments that became worthless during the past year, the tax code treats you as having realized a loss as of the last day of the year. This rule applies only if the investments have no value; even if your investments are worth only pennies, they will not be considered worthless for tax purposes. To ensure that you can utilize the loss on an investment that has dramatically declined in value but is not worthless, sell the investment to an unrelated party before the end of this year.

Don't be caught by the "wash-sale" rule. If you sell securities to realize a tax loss, make sure you do not purchase the same or substantially similar securities within 30 days before or after the date of sale. If you do, you will not be able to claim the loss on this year's tax return.

Properly time your year-end investments in mutual funds. Mutual funds generally make distributions to investors holding shares on a record date near year-end. If you want to invest in a fund, but would be subject to tax on such a distribution (that is, your investment will not be held in a 401(k) or other tax-deferred or tax-exempt vehicle), wait until after the record date before making your purchase. If you plan to sell a substantial interest in a mutual fund near year-end, consult with your tax advisor as to how the sale might affect whether dividends from that fund are qualified dividends (subject to the 15% maximum federal tax rate).

Review how investments are allocated among taxable and tax-deferred accounts. Distributions from tax-deferred accounts, such as traditional 401(k) plans, are taxed at ordinary income tax rates. This is true even if the income in those accounts consists of long-term capital gains and qualified dividends that would otherwise have been eligible for the reduced federal income tax rates described earlier in this section. From a tax perspective, it may be beneficial to hold investments that generate long-term capital gains and qualified dividends in taxable accounts, while holding investments that generate short-term gains, interest, and other ordinary taxable income in your tax-deferred accounts. Since there may be significant investment and tax considerations involved in shifting assets, speak with your tax advisor before taking any action.

Review your stock options. Don't overlook your options or option shares when you do your year-end tax planning. There may be opportunities to avoid or minimize regular income tax or alternative minimum tax (AMT) by taking action this year.

Use flexible spending plans. These plans permit you to pay for eligible health care and dependent care expenses with pretax wages. The amounts you contribute to these plans are not subject to federal income, Social Security, or Medicare taxes. If your employer sponsors this type of plan and you contributed to it during the year, make sure you incur sufficient qualifying expenses by year-end or you will forfeit any unused funds. Your employer may provide you with an option to either use unspent funds to cover expenses incurred up to 2½ months following the end of the plan year (March 15th of the following year for plan years ending on December 31st) or to roll over up to $500 to the next plan year (without reducing your maximum allowed contribution for the new plan year). But your employer cannot offer both options.

Properly characterize alimony. Alimony payments are deductible to the payer and includable in the income of the person who receives them. When the recipient is in a low tax bracket, there may be a net tax benefit that the payer and recipient can share. This will occur only if the payments can be properly characterized as alimony rather than a property settlement or child support. Before you finalize a divorce or separation agreement, discuss with your tax advisor whether a portion of any payments may be deductible alimony.

Review the use of deferred compensation agreements. If you and your employer are willing to defer a portion of your future earnings, you may be able to use a written deferred compensation agreement to defer tax. To obtain the tax benefit, you must accept some risk that you may not receive the payments and be subject to strict rules on when the compensation can be paid. Using certain irrevocable trusts to fund the deferred compensation can minimize certain risks, though it will not protect against the risk that the deferred income may be subject to the claims of your employer's creditors.

Speak with your tax advisor if you are currently using, or considering entering into, this type of agreement, as the tax rules governing these arrangements are complex. Failure to adhere to these rules may trigger current income tax on amounts deferred, as well as substantial penalties and interest.

Review the special rules for inherited property. Most investment property you inherit will be valued for capital gains purposes as of the date of death. In almost all situations, if inherited property is sold for a price above this value, the gain will qualify for taxation at long-term capital gains rates. This is true no matter how long you or the person from whom you inherited the property held it.

Ways to Accelerate Income

Accelerating income can be the better tax-planning approach if you expect that your tax rate this year will be significantly lower than your rate in the near future. If you were not working for a portion of the current year or anticipate a substantial increase in income next year, you may be in a higher tax bracket next year. If you're in such a situation, consider the following:

- **Redeem savings bonds.** If you have not reported interest earned on Series EE savings bonds in prior years, you can redeem the bonds and report all the accrued interest in the current year.
- **Accelerate IRA distributions.** If you are 59½ or older and have a traditional Individual Retirement Account (IRA), you may be able to increase your income for this year without penalty by making withdrawals from the account. Consult with your tax advisor before making withdrawals.
- **Exercise stock options.** If you own non-qualified stock options, consider whether, from an investment perspective, this might be a good year to exercise those options. Exercising appropriate options will generate taxable income. Regular taxable income is generally not triggered on the exercise of incentive stock options (ISOs), although do keep in mind that exercising ISOs could trigger AMT liability.

Make the Most of Your Deductions

Identify all above-the-line deductions. There are a number of "above-the-line" deductions that are available whether or not you claim itemized deductions on your tax return. These deductions are particularly valuable because they reduce your AGI, which can help increase the value of other tax breaks. Above-the-line deductions include deductions for moving expenses, self-employed health insurance premiums, and Keogh, SEP, and SIMPLE plan contributions.

Bunch your itemized deductions. Each year you are entitled to take either your itemized deductions or the appropriate standard deduction on your return. Review your tax returns for the last few years. If your itemized deductions have been approximately the same as the allowable standard deduction, you may be able to save taxes by "bunching" your itemized deductions in alternate years.

Properly establish deductions. If you pay deductible expenses by check, make sure the checks are delivered on or before the end of the year. If you send checks by mail, they will be deemed to have met this deadline if mailed by December 31st. If you pay with a standard credit card, the charge date controls. You need not pay the credit card bill before year-end to take the deduction this year.

Evaluate when to incur discretionary medical expenses. Only unreimbursed medical expenses in excess of 10.0% (7.5% if either you or your spouse are age 65 or older) of your AGI may be claimed as a deduction. (For purposes of the AMT, medical expenses are deductible only to the extent that they exceed 10% of AGI, regardless of your age.) If you have the choice to incur medical expenses either this year or next, consider whether bunching these expenses into the same year is feasible and can surpass the threshold. For the year you estimate your medical expenses paid will beat the threshold, consider making additional purchases of discretionary (but not purely cosmetic) medical products and services before year-end. Allowable expenditures include those for prescription drugs, eyeglasses, hearing aids, laser eye surgery, weight-loss programs to combat medically diagnosed obesity, smoking cessation programs, annual physicals, health insurance programs, and certain payments and insurance premiums related to long-term care services. The IRS has ruled that the costs of medically necessary equipment (for example, crutches), supplies (for example, bandages), and diagnostic devices (such as blood pressure monitors), even if not prescribed by a physician, can be deducted as medical expenses.

Consider accelerating deductible tax payments. To increase your deduction for state or local income taxes, you need to make estimated tax payments or increase withholdings on or before year-end. Most state and local property taxes and foreign income taxes are also deductible. If you have control over any of these taxes, consider paying them before year-end, unless you think you'll be subject to the AMT.

Maximize the residential interest expense deduction. Interest on loans used to acquire, construct, or substantially improve your principal residence and one other residence is, within statutory limits, deductible if paid during the year. (See *Amount deductible*, in the *Home Mortgage Interest* section of chapter 24, *Interest expense*, for more information about the applicable limits.) Interest on an additional $100,000 of home equity indebtedness is also deductible. You may be able to accelerate deductions to this year by making the mortgage or home equity loan payment due in January on or before the end of the current year.

If you are considering refinancing an existing mortgage, you should note that only a portion, if any, of prepaid interest in the form of "points" may be deductible in the year you refinance. For this reason, you may want to look at a "no-points" loan if you are refinancing.

Generally, you can deduct the entire amount you pay as points if the loan is used to buy or improve your principal residence and the loan is secured by that home. If you satisfy the requirements for deductibility, try to close on the loan before year-end so you can deduct all the points on this year's tax return.

Deduct a greater amount of certain capital expenditures. Business owners may be able to save on this year's taxes by making certain capital expenditures before year-end. While capital expenditures (such as furniture or equipment) must ordinarily be depreciated over a set period of time, Section 179 of the tax code allows you to deduct all or part of the cost—up to specified yearly limits—of certain qualifying property in the year in which the property is purchased and placed into service, rather than capitalizing the cost and depreciating it over its life. This means that you can deduct all or part of the cost up front in one year rather than taking depreciation deductions spread out over many years. You must decide for each item of qualifying property whether to deduct (subject to the yearly limit) or capitalize and depreciate its cost.

Eligible property includes tangible personal property (i.e., tangible property that is not real property) and certain other specified tangible property. See Publication 946, *How to Depreciate Property*, for further information.

Specified limits. The maximum Section 179 deduction available for qualifying property placed into service during 2014 is $25,000 (down from $500,000 in 2013). The allowable deduction is reduced dollar for dollar once the cost of qualifying property placed into service during 2014 exceeds $200,000 (down from $2 million in 2013). Unlike 2013, the definition of Section 179 property does not include certain qualified real qualified leasehold improvement property, qualified restaurant property, or qualified retail improvement property. At the time this book was published, Congress had been considering legislation that would extend the higher limits that had expired at the end of 2013 at least through 2014; perhaps even permanently, but no such extension had yet been passed. For updated information on tax law changes that occur after this book was published, see our website, *ey.com/EYTaxGuide*.

Make year-end charitable gifts. Make your contributions in the most tax-efficient manner. In addition to cash, gifts of property (such as clothing, equipment, or investment securities) can qualify for a charitable deduction.

You can claim a charitable deduction for contributions of clothing and household items (for example, furniture, furnishings, electronics, appliances, linens, and similar items) only if the item is in good used condition or better. An exception to this general rule permits a deduction if the amount claimed for the item is more than $500 and a qualified appraisal is obtained.

If investment securities you have held more than one year have appreciated, donate the actual securities, not the proceeds from selling them, to charity. You get a charitable deduction for the value of the securities and avoid paying income tax and, if applicable, the 3.8% NIIT, on the appreciation. This strategy can be even more valuable if you donate property, such as a collectible, that would not qualify for the 15% (20% for high-income taxpayers who are otherwise in the 39.6% regular income tax bracket) maximum federal tax rate on long-term gains (gains on collectibles are taxed at 28%). However, a deduction for the fair market value of appreciated tangible personal property donated to charity is allowed only if the charity uses the property as part of its exempt function (for example, a gift of modern art to a museum).

If investment securities are worth less than your cost, it is usually better to sell them and donate the proceeds. The charity will receive the same value, and you will recognize a capital loss that may be used to offset other income.

You may also want to pre-fund charitable gifts for the next few years. By establishing a private foundation or contributing to a donor-advised fund, you can obtain the full charitable tax deduction this year, while you retain the ability to identify one or more charitable organizations as recipients in the future.

Consider the Impact of the AMT

The AMT was designed to ensure that the highest-income taxpayers pay at least a minimum amount of income tax. The AMT is an alternative income tax calculation that limits or disallows certain deductions, credits, and exclusions available under regular income tax to arrive at AMT income subject to tax at 26% or 28% rates. It is effectively a separate tax system with its own allowable deductions and exclusions, many of which are different than those allowed for regular income tax purposes. You might be subject to AMT if:

- Long-term capital gains and/or qualified dividends are likely to be a substantial portion of your total income for the year;
- You claim large deductions for state and local taxes or large miscellaneous itemized deductions;
- You pay interest on a mortgage and the loan proceeds have not been used to buy, construct, or improve your home;
- You exercised, or will exercise, incentive stock options this year.

To the extent AMT is triggered by adding back designated itemized deductions and other so-called "exclusion items" that reduce your taxable income for regular tax purposes but are not allowed for determining alternative minimum taxable income, consider the following to help minimize the impact of the AMT:

- Postponing the payment and recognition of such deductions to a tax year in which you will not be subject to the AMT. Shifting these deductions to a non-AMT year can save you up to 39.6% of the deduction claimed, assuming you are in the top tax bracket. On the other hand, these deductions forfeit their tax benefits if they are recognized in an AMT year.
- Accelerating income into the AMT year until your regular tax is equal to your AMT attributable to itemized deductions and other exclusion items. This accelerated income would be taxed at the 26% or 28% AMT rates, albeit a year earlier than it would otherwise be subject to regular income tax at higher tax rates.

See _Alternative Minimum Tax_, in chapter 31, _How to figure your tax_, for a detailed discussion about the AMT.

Review Available Education Incentives

Investigate Coverdell Education Savings Accounts. Contributions to Coverdell accounts grow tax-free when distributions are used to pay qualifying educational expenses. You can use these accounts to pay for elementary and secondary school expenses as well as for higher education expenses. You can even use the accounts to purchase a computer or pay for Internet service for your child. The maximum annual contribution for each designated beneficiary is now $2,000. Unfortunately, the ability to make contributions is phased out at higher income levels.

Contribute to a qualified tuition (Section 529) plan. You can help your child, grandchild, or other individual save for higher education by making a gift to him or her through a qualified tuition plan. These plans are commonly called Section 529 plans, a name that references the section of the Internal Revenue Code that authorized the plans. There are two general categories of Section 529 plans: prepaid plans (which involve the purchase of tuition credits or certificates) and college savings plans (in which contributions are made to an account that is invested in mutual funds or other financial instruments).

College savings plans are the most rapidly growing type of Section 529 plans. As with a Coverdell account, earnings in these plans can grow tax-free when distributions are used to pay qualifying educational expenses; that is, no federal income tax is imposed when distributions are used to pay qualifying higher education expenses. Unlike the Coverdell program (and most other tax incentive programs for education), you may make contributions to a college savings plan regardless of the amount of your income.

While contributions to Coverdell accounts are capped at $2,000 annually, you can at any time contribute a lump sum to a college savings plan in an amount that may be sufficient to pay the entire future college expenses of the designated beneficiary. Contributions are not deductible on your federal income tax return but may be deductible on your state income tax return. Under a special gift-tax rule, you can make a contribution of up to $70,000 per beneficiary ($140,000 for a married couple who elect gift-splitting) this year without paying gift tax or using any portion of your lifetime gift tax exemption.

There are many meaningful differences among the available Section 529 plans, and many states offer incentives of their own. Consult with your tax advisor to get help in determining which option may be best for you.

IRA and Other Retirement Account Contributions

You do not have to make contributions to traditional IRA and Keogh plans by year-end to offset current-year income. There are, however, a number of important year-end considerations related to contributions to these and other retirement plans.

Determine if you satisfy income limits for contributions. See if you are eligible to make a deductible contribution to a traditional IRA (for 2014: $5,500; $6,500 if you're at least age 50 by the end of the year) or to make a nondeductible contribution to a Roth IRA. If you are an active participant in a qualified plan, you cannot deduct contributions to a traditional IRA if your income exceeds certain amounts. (See *What's New*, in chapter 17, *Individual retirement accounts (IRAs)*, for the modified AGI limits applicable for 2014.)

Regardless of whether you are an active participant in a qualified plan, you can make an un-reduced contribution to a Roth IRA if you are single and, for 2014, your modified AGI is under $114,000, or if you are married and filing jointly and your modified AGI is under $181,000. Your maximum allowable contribution to a Roth IRA is phased out depending on the amount of your modified adjusted gross income and your filing status. (See *What's New*, in chapter 17, *Individual retirement accounts (IRAs)*, for the modified AGI limits applicable for 2014.)

Evaluate converting to a Roth IRA. Unlike distributions from a traditional IRA, qualified distributions from a Roth IRA are not subject to tax (i.e., the funds are not withdrawn until age 59½ and at least five years from the date of conversion. Tax-free distributions may also be made under other circumstances such as disability.) You will have to pay income taxes currently on the taxable amounts converted, except to the extent it includes nontaxable amounts (e.g., after-tax contributions).

Fully fund your workplace 401(k) account. For 2014, your 401(k) plan may allow you to save up to $17,500 of your salary ($23,000 if you will be at least age 50 by year-end) on a pretax basis. Unlike IRA contributions, 401(k) deferrals for the current year may only be made during this year. If you have a 401(k) plan, make sure you have deferred the maximum amount that is allowable under your plan, and that you can afford, before year-end.

Consider contributing to a Roth 401(k), if available. Employers can offer participants in their company's 401(k) plan the ability to designate some or all of their 401(k) contributions as "Roth 401(k)" contributions. These contributions do not reduce current taxable wages, but, if certain requirements are met, all future earnings from investments held in a Roth 401(k) account can be distributed completely tax-free. The requirements for this tax treatment are similar to those that apply to Roth IRAs. However, unlike with Roth IRAs, the ability to contribute to a Roth 401(k) account is not limited by your AGI. Your tax advisor can help you evaluate whether, based on your particular situation, contributing to a Roth 401(k) account may be more beneficial than making pre-tax contributions to a traditional 401(k).

Establish a solo 401(k). This type of 401(k) allows self-employed individuals with no employees (or who work with their spouse) and limited income to save more than traditional retirement plans allow and take advantage of tax-deductible contributions. With a solo 401(k) plan, you can make the full allowable employee contribution and match that with an additional employer contribution of not more than 25% of your income, with a combined maximum limit (exclusive of special catch-up contributions) of $54,000 in 2014 (this limit is adjusted annually for inflation).

Retirement Distribution Planning

Retirement assets make up the largest component of wealth for a significant number of individuals. Many taxpayers do not realize, however, that making the right distribution choices can substantially reduce taxes and even significantly enhance the lifestyle that they can enjoy in retirement.

Take advantage of the rules on required minimum distributions. The tax laws mandate when you must begin taking taxable distributions from your retirement plans and how much you must take out each year. Under the IRS final rules, the amount you must take from your plans each year may be minimized with proper planning. Speak with your tax advisor to see if you can enjoy tax benefits by deferring a portion of these taxable distributions.

Consider the effect of taking a lump-sum distribution. If you are retired and were born before 1936, discuss with your tax advisor whether you should take a lump-sum distribution from your retirement plan.

Evaluate if you should take a distribution in company stock. There may be tax advantages in taking a taxable lump-sum distribution of your company's stock from your retirement plan. You will have to pay current income tax on the distribution, but generally, the taxable amount will be the cost of the stock when it was added to your account. Subsequent increases in the stock's value will not be taxed until you sell the stock. When you do sell, all or part of the increase will be taxed at the capital gains rate.

Retirement distribution planning can be complex, because it requires an understanding of the tax law, your retirement plans, and your individual needs and goals. If you plan on retiring in the near future, or even if you are already retired, speak with your tax advisor as to whether you should consider a retirement distribution checkup.

More Year-End Ideas

Adjust tax withholdings. If you have not remitted enough tax to cover your anticipated tax liability, you may be subject to underpayment penalties. These penalties are assessed based on payments throughout the year, so you may not be able to avoid the penalties by simply paying the amount due with your return. Consider increasing withholdings from your wages, because withheld taxes are considered to have been paid evenly throughout the year. Therefore, by increasing your withholdings near the end of the current year, you can avoid penalties that would otherwise have been imposed due to an underpayment of taxes earlier in the year.

Increase support to qualify for personal exemptions. Review the amount of support you have provided to your dependents. If necessary, pay additional expenses to ensure that you meet the support test that allows you to claim an exemption for dependents on your return. Each exemption you claim can reduce your taxable income by up to $3,950. (However, the amount of each personal exemption claimed is phased out at higher income levels.) In 2014, the personal exemption amount begins to phase out when AGI reaches $254,200 for single filers, $305,050 for married couples who file jointly and qualifying widow(er)s, $279,650 for taxpayers filing as head of household, and $152,525 for married filing separately.

ACA Individual Provisions

Requirement to Obtain Health Care Coverage or Pay a Penalty Tax

In addition to the 3.8% NIIT and 0.9% Additional Medicare Tax that were enacted under the ACA and took effect beginning in 2013 (these taxes are discussed in multiple other chapters of this book), the ACA required most U.S. citizens and legal residents to have health insurance (meeting "minimal essential coverage" requirements, described later) beginning in January 2014 or face a penalty tax.

The ACA's many provisions are scheduled to take effect between 2010 and 2018. In broad terms, the mission of the ACA has been twofold: to extend affordable medical insurance coverage to a larger proportion of the U.S. population and to increase the efficiency of the nation's health care delivery system. While the content of the ACA is broad in scope and dense in detail, our discussion in this book is confined to features of the law with near-term implications for U.S. individual taxpayers. Keep in mind that many details associated with carrying out the provisions of the ACA are subject to further clarification and possible legislative change. The following summarizes what is known as of the date this book went to press and its potential relevance to your federal income taxes.

Individual Mandate

Beginning in 2014, with limited exceptions (listed below), the ACA requires most individuals to maintain "minimum essential coverage." This is commonly referred to as the individual mandate. If individuals fail to get this coverage, they will be subject to a tax for any months in which they, their spouses, or dependents lack such health care coverage. This "penalty" is referred to in the law as a "shared responsibility payment."

Exceptions. The individual mandate does not apply to the following groups of people:
- Individuals who cannot afford coverage (defined as individuals for whom a required contribution for the lowest-priced minimum essential coverage available would cost more than 8% of their household income)
- Individuals whose household income does not exceed the threshold for filing a federal income tax return
- Members of certain Indian tribes
- Individuals who are incarcerated
- Individuals who have a qualifying religious exemption
- Members of qualifying health care sharing ministries

- Individuals who are not legally present in the United States
- Individuals who have a gap in coverage for a continuous period of three months or less (an exemption that may only be used for one period without coverage in any given year)
- Individuals who are granted a certified hardship exemption through the Health Insurance Marketplace[1] (Marketplace)

Note that even if an individual is exempt from the requirement to maintain minimum essential coverage for himself or herself, the individual may still be subject to a penalty for dependents who lack coverage, unless the dependents also qualify for an exemption.

Minimum essential coverage. An individual may obtain minimum essential coverage from several sources, including (though not limited to):
- Employer-sponsored health plans (including "grandfathered" plans, COBRA, and retiree coverage)
- Government-sponsored programs (e.g., Medicare, most Medicaid coverage, CHIP, TRICARE, etc.)
- Individual market insurance, including a qualified health plan offered in the Health Insurance Marketplace

Affordability test. For the purpose of the individual mandate, an individual's coverage is generally deemed to be affordable if the required premium for minimum essential coverage does not exceed 8% of household income. (See *definition of household income in the text that follows*.)

Importantly, access to employer-sponsored coverage plays a critical role in determining the criteria for affordability.

An employee's own coverage under an employer-sponsored health plan is deemed to be affordable if his or her required contribution for the lowest-cost, self-only coverage[2] is no more than 8% of household income.[3] If the employee's spouse or dependents (including any individual for whom the employee may claim a personal exemption deduction under Internal Revenue Code Section 151) are eligible for coverage under his or her employer-sponsored health plan, then coverage for these individuals, assuming they are not otherwise exempt from the individual mandate, is considered affordable if the employee's required contribution for the lowest-cost option that would provide minimum essential coverage to his or her family members is not more than 8% of the family's household income.

For an employee who is eligible for minimum essential coverage under an employer-sponsored health plan, the affordability of the employee's coverage is based on the individual's required contributions under the employer plan, even if the employee has access to minimum essential coverage from an alternate source. However, if an employee is not eligible for minimum essential health coverage under an employer-sponsored health plan, then the affordability test is based on the cost of individual coverage that could be purchased through the Health Insurance Marketplace.

If a family member is eligible for coverage under an employer-sponsored health plan by reason of a relationship to the employee, but the employee is not able to claim the person as a dependent on his or her tax return, then the affordability test for family members will not apply to that person. In this case, affordability will be determined without regard to coverage available by relationship to the employee. If the only other coverage available to the family member is coverage purchased through the Health Insurance Marketplace, the cost of that coverage in

---

[1.] The Health Insurance Marketplace (also commonly referred to as the Marketplace or Exchange) is a cornerstone of the ACA. It brings together individuals shopping for coverage with private insurers offering "qualified health plans." Qualified health plans are those certified by the Marketplace as meeting coverage requirements established under the ACA. The Marketplace includes health insurance exchanges that serve residents in each state. Each state's Marketplace will be administered by the state, the federal government, or through a partnership between the state and federal governments. A recent number of challenges to the provision of subsidies to federally (as opposed to state) run exchanges is working its way through the court system. In July 2014, two separate circuit courts came to the exact opposite conclusions, one court supporting the subsidy and the other court rejecting the subsidy (this court has since decided to rehear the case). It is anticipated this debate may continue to the Supreme Court. The IRS continues operating under the presumption the federal exchange subsidy will withstand legal challenge.

[2.] The Treasury Department has released Notice 2013-54 explaining how employer-sponsored health reimbursement arrangements (HRA) will be applied to determine whether coverage is affordable for purposes of the individual mandate.

[3.] To determine whether coverage is affordable for purposes of the individual mandate, household income is increased by any exclusion from gross income for any portion of the required contribution for health coverage made by the employee through a salary reduction arrangement.

relation to the individual's household income (rather than the employee's household income) will determine whether the family member is eligible for affordable coverage. If the family member is not exempt from the individual mandate and fails to maintain minimum essential coverage, the family member, not the employee, is liable for the penalty. Such a circumstance may arise in the case of an employee's adult child. An employee generally may not claim a child as a dependent on his or her tax return after the child reaches age 19 (or age 24, if the child is a qualifying student), although an employer may offer health care coverage for the benefit of an employee's child until age 26.

With respect to the individual mandate, it should also be noted that a former employee who is eligible for a continuation of minimum essential coverage under COBRA or an employer-sponsored retiree health plan is treated as being eligible for coverage under the plan for purposes of the affordability test only if the individual actually enrolls in such coverage.

For married couples, if both spouses work and are eligible for minimum essential health coverage through their respective employers, the affordability test applies to each spouse based on his or her required contribution for the lowest-cost, self-only coverage offered by his or her own employer. Assuming that they file a joint return, they would be jointly liable for their dependents. They would owe a penalty for their dependent children if the children are eligible for affordable family coverage under the employer-sponsored health plan of either parent and the parents fail to maintain minimum essential coverage for the children through any available resource.

Household income. For purposes of the individual mandate under the ACA, household income is defined to include the modified adjusted gross income (MAGI) of the taxpayer plus the combined MAGI of all others for whom the taxpayer is allowed a deduction, and who were required to file a tax return. In turn, MAGI is equal to AGI as reported on line 37 of IRS Form 1040 and increased by tax-exempt interest income and foreign earned income. The definition of household income for purposes of the individual mandate is the same as the definition of "household income" for purposes of the premium tax credit (discussed later) with the exception that MAGI is not increased by the nontaxable portion of Social Security benefits.

Shared Responsibility Payment ("the penalty")

The tax for failing to obtain minimum essential coverage (unless an exception applies) went into effect as of January 1, 2014, and will continue to be phased in over the three years covering 2014 through 2016. After 2016, it will be reviewed annually and periodically adjusted for inflation.

The tax is typically referred to as a shared responsibility payment or an individual penalty. The penalty is equal to the higher of a flat dollar amount or a percentage of income.

- Flat dollar amount. The annual flat-dollar amount used to determine the tax for each individual without coverage in 2014 is $95 per adult and $47.50 per child, but capped at $285 per household. The annual flat-dollar amount used to determine the tax for each individual without coverage in 2015 is $325 per adult and $162.50 per child, capped at $975 per household. The annual flat-dollar amount used to determine the tax for each individual without coverage in 2016 is $695 per adult and $347.50 per child, capped at $2,085 per household. For purposes of the penalty, a child is an individual under the age of 18.
- Percentage of income. The percentage used to determine the applicable tax for 2014 is 1% of income in excess of the threshold for filing an income tax return in 2014. The applicable percentage of income rises to 2.0% in 2015 and to 2.5% in 2016.

The tax under the percentage-of-income provision is determined by subtracting the taxpayer's personal exemption(s) and standard deduction from household income, as defined earlier. The net result is then multiplied by the applicable percentage. You will owe 1/12th of the annual payment for each month you or your dependent(s) do not have coverage or do not qualify for an exemption.

The greater of these two amounts (not to exceed the national average cost of bronze-level coverage,[4] for the relevant family size, offered through the Marketplace) is divided by 12, and then

---

[4.] Through the Health Insurance Marketplace, individuals in the United States generally will have access to qualified health plans that offer coverage at four levels of "actuarial value" (that is, the percentage of costs for covered plan benefits expected to be paid by the insurer for a standard population). The levels of coverage are categorized as follows:

Category	Actuarial value
Bronze	60%
Silver	70%
Gold	80%
Platinum	90%

multiplied by the number of months for which the penalty is applicable. For 2014, the annual national average cost for a bronze-level health plan available through the Marketplace is $2,448 per individual ($204 per month per individual) with a maximum of $12,240 for a family with five or more members ($1,020 per month per family of five or more).

You will not need to make the shared responsibility payment until you file your 2014 federal income tax return in 2015. If you owe a shared responsibility payment, the IRS may offset that liability against any tax refund that may be due to you. The law prohibits the IRS from using liens or levies to collect any owed individual shared responsibility payments.

TAXPLANNER

Should You Obtain Coverage through the Health Insurance Marketplace?

During the annual Open Enrollment[5] or if you qualify for a Special Enrollment Period,[6] you may be eligible to purchase health insurance coverage through the Health Insurance Marketplace.[7] If you are eligible, your decision as to whether to purchase coverage through the Marketplace should be based on the following key considerations:

- **Do you have employer-sponsored health insurance coverage?**

  If so, you may not be eligible to benefit from either the premium tax credit (discussed in the text that follows) or cost-sharing subsidies available to those with low to moderate household income to help pay for the cost of qualified health coverage purchased through the Marketplace.

  Additionally, you'll want to take into account the tax and other potential financial benefits of participating in employer-sponsored coverage. Employers often make a contribution toward the cost of an employee's coverage and may also subsidize coverage for an employee's eligible spouse and children. Also, premiums paid by both the employer and employee for coverage under an employer-sponsored plan are generally tax-free to the employee.

- **Will you be able to claim a tax deduction or adjustment to income for premiums that you pay for health insurance coverage?**

  Premiums paid for health insurance coverage purchased in the private market or through the Health Insurance Marketplace are paid for with after-tax dollars, though in some situations may be claimed as an adjustment to income or qualify to be taken as an itemized deduction (as described in greater detail later in this text). If you take the premium as an itemized deduction, the ability to reduce your level of taxable income based on the health care expenses that you pay (including insurance premiums) will be determined in part by how high your qualifying medical expenses are in relation to your AGI. This assumes that you itemize your deductions, rather than claim the standard deduction. It's therefore important to consider the net cost of coverage when evaluating your alternatives.

[5.] The Open Enrollment period for 2015 coverage is November 15, 2014, to February 15, 2015.

[6.] The special enrollment period is a time period outside of Open Enrollment where you can enroll in a health plan through the Marketplace. In the Marketplace, you qualify for a special enrollment period 60 days following certain life events:
  - Marriage or divorce
  - Birth of a child, adoption of a child, or placing a child for adoption or foster care
  - Moving your residence, gaining citizenship, leaving incarceration
  - Losing other health coverage (e.g., loss of job-based coverage, COBRA expiration, aging out of a parent's plan, etc.)
  - Gaining status as a member of an Indian tribe
  - Change in income or household status affecting the eligibility for the premium tax credit or cost-sharing reductions for those already enrolled in the Marketplace

  Voluntarily ending coverage does not qualify you for a special enrollment period. For example, if you have enrolled in COBRA continuation coverage, terminating your COBRA coverage early would not grant a special enrollment period.

[7.] Lawful residents will have the opportunity to shop for coverage through the Health Insurance Marketplace operating in their state of residence. For the 2015 plan year, the earliest date of coverage through the Marketplace is January 1, 2015. During enrollment, if you enroll between the 1st and 15th days of the month, your coverage starts on the first day of the next month. If between the 16th and the last day of the month, your coverage starts on the first day of the second following month. For example, if you enroll in the Marketplace on January 16th, your coverage starts on March 1st.

- **How does coverage available to you through other sources compare with that offered through the Health Insurance Marketplace?**

  The answer to this question is not just a matter of choosing the coverage with a less expensive annual premium. Depending on the scope of coverage offered, selecting a plan with a higher premium could potentially (although not necessarily) result in a lower level of overall health care costs, taking into account deductibles, co-payments, and out-of-pocket maximums. You also need to factor in the tax and financial benefits described above. Beyond the numbers, you'll want to compare plan features and benefits to assess which coverage provides access to your preferred health care providers as well as health care services and consumer support important to you and your family members.

Premium Tax Credits

The ACA provides financial assistance to eligible individuals who participate in qualified health plans through the Health Insurance Marketplace. This comes in the form of premium tax credits and cost-sharing subsidies intended to help make health insurance coverage more affordable, by reducing premiums and out-of-pocket expenses (e.g., deductibles, coinsurance, and co-payments). This text will discuss the premium tax credits made available under the ACA.

Premium tax credits limit the premium paid for coverage through the Marketplace for individuals and families who qualify for assistance and enroll in coverage at one of the four "metal levels."[8] The credit places a cap on premiums paid for health care insurance coverage based on a percentage of household income. The percentage, in turn, is based on the amount of household income in relation to the federal poverty level (FPL). The amount of the premium tax credit is equal to the lesser of:

- The premium for the qualified health plan in which the individual or the family enrolls through the Marketplace; or
- The premium for the second lowest-cost silver-level plan available to the individual or family through the Marketplace reduced by the individual's or family's share of premiums set on a sliding scale limiting the contributions as follows:

Income Level	Premium as a percent of income	
	2014	**2015**
100%-133% of FPL	2% of income	2.01% of income
133%-150% of FPL	3%-4% of income	3.02%-4.02% of Income
150%-200% of FPL	4%-6.3% of income	4.02%-6.34% of income
200%-250% of FPL	6.3%-8.05% of Income	6.34%-8.10% of income
250%-300% of FPL	8.05%-9.5% of income	8.10%-9.56% of Income
300%-400% of FPL	9.5% of income	9.56% of income

Federal poverty level (FPL) guidelines. For those who enroll in coverage through the Health Insurance Marketplace, premium tax credits will generally be available to people whose household income falls between 100% and 400% of the FPL. For 2014, the applicable range of household income lies between $11,670 and $46,680 for an individual and between $23,850 and $95,400 for a household of four. Note that these thresholds apply to the 48 contiguous states as well as the District of Columbia. The corresponding thresholds are different for Alaska and Hawaii.

Household income. For purposes of the premium tax credit, household income is defined to include the MAGI of the taxpayer plus the combined MAGI of all others for whom the taxpayer is allowed a deduction, and were required to file a tax return. In turn, MAGI is equal to AGI as reported on line 37 of IRS Form 1040 and increased by tax-exempt interest income, foreign earned income, and Social Security benefits that are otherwise excludible from gross income. This is distinguished from the definition of household income for purposes of the individual mandate (discussed earlier).

Lack of access to minimum essential coverage. Only those individuals who don't have access to minimum essential coverage from another source are eligible to receive premium tax credits. Generally speaking, employer-sponsored health insurance coverage will meet the definition of minimum essential coverage under the ACA. This means that most people who have access to employer-sponsored health insurance coverage, as well as the employee's eligible spouse and dependents, won't qualify to receive premium tax credits unless the employer-sponsored coverage is classified as "unaffordable" or fails to provide "minimum value."

---

8. Coverage through the Marketplace will generally be classified by one of four "metal levels" to include bronze, silver, gold, and platinum. Each metal category has its own actuarial value as indicated in a preceding footnote.

Definition of "minimum value." Under the provisions of the ACA, an employer-sponsored plan is said to provide minimum value if it covers, on average, at least 60% of total allowed costs.

Definition of "unaffordable." An employer-sponsored plan is considered to be unaffordable if the portion of the annual premium that the employee must pay (whether by salary reduction or other means) for self-only coverage is greater than 9.5% of household income[9] in 2014, adjusted to 9.56% for 2015. Note that this same threshold applies for determining the affordability of employer-sponsored coverage for the employee's spouse or other eligible dependents. In other words, for purposes of determining whether family members are eligible to receive premium tax credits, the cost of family coverage isn't taken into account; the only relevant factor is whether or not the cost of self-only coverage is affordable to the employee.

For individuals who do qualify to receive premium tax credits, the tax credits are advanceable. This means that the U.S. Department of the Treasury will make payments directly to the health plan as an offset against the individual's premium costs during the plan year. Alternatively, the tax credits are also refundable in those cases where qualifying individuals prefer to wait until they file their federal income tax returns to receive the benefit of the credit. Individuals benefiting from the premium tax credit must file a federal tax return; married couples must file jointly.

Note that the premium tax credit is based on a projection of the household's income, which by definition is susceptible to over- or understatement. The premium tax credit will be "trued-up," or reconciled, when filing the household's tax return. Here, actual household income for the year will be used to determine the credit the individual or family was entitled to receive. If advanced payments were made in excess of the credit due, then the overpayment must be repaid to the federal government, subject to limits for those with household income below 400% of the federal poverty level. On the other hand, if payments made in advance were less than the credit due, then the difference will be included in the taxpayer's refund or applied against federal tax owed for the year.

---

[9] IRC Section 36B proposed regulations, entitled "Minimum Value of Employer-Sponsored Plans and Other Rules Regarding the Health Insurance Premium Tax Credit," provide that amounts newly available for the current plan year under a Health Reimbursement Arrangement (HRA) that is integrated with an eligible employer-sponsored plan and that an employee may use to pay premiums or for cost sharing are counted for purposes of determining affordability. In addition, the proposed regulations provide that affordability of an employer-sponsored plan is determined assuming the employee fails to satisfy the requirements of a wellness program that offers incentives that affect the cost of premiums, except with regard to incentives that relate to tobacco use. In the latter case, an employer-sponsored plan that charges a higher initial premium for tobacco users will be determined based on the premium that is charged to nontobacco users, or tobacco users who complete a related wellness program, such as participating in a smoking cessation program.

TAXPLANNER

Only those individuals who don't have access to minimum essential coverage from another source, such as an employer-sponsored health plan or government program (e.g., Medicare, Medicaid, CHIP, TRICARE, etc.), and whose household income is between 100% and 400% of the FPL, are eligible to receive premium tax credits and other forms of assistance for purchase of coverage through the Health Insurance Marketplace.

However, if coverage available through employment is either "unaffordable" or fails to provide "minimum value," the employee and his or her family members may qualify for an exception that permits receipt of the benefit of premium tax credits and potentially other forms of assistance to help purchase coverage through the Marketplace.

Furthermore, if a family member is eligible for coverage under an employer-sponsored health plan by reason of a relationship to the employee, but the employee is not able to claim the person as a dependent on his or her tax return, then the family member is treated as having access to minimum essential coverage under such plan only for months the family member is enrolled in the plan. Thus, access to minimum essential coverage under this condition does not itself preclude the family member from potentially qualifying for the premium tax credit.

Additionally, for the purpose of determining eligibility for the premium tax credit, former employees with access to continuation of employer-sponsored coverage under COBRA are treated as having access to minimum essential coverage only for months when the individual is actually enrolled in COBRA coverage. Proposed regulations apply this rule to retirees with access to employer-sponsored retiree health care coverage as well.

Deductibility of Health Insurance Marketplace Premiums

As previously indicated, the premiums you pay for insurance coverage through the Marketplace (as well as private coverage and employer-sponsored coverage that is not deducted from your paycheck on a pre-tax basis) can potentially be claimed as a deduction on IRS Form 1040, Schedule A ("Itemized Deductions"), assuming that you do not elect to use the standard deduction applicable to your tax filing status.

Specifically, the premiums can be included in the calculation of the qualified medical expenses that you pay during the year for yourself, your spouse, and other eligible dependents. You can claim a deduction for your qualified medical expenses as an itemized deduction to the extent that they exceed 10% of your AGI. However, if you or your spouse is age 65 or older, you can still claim a deduction for your qualified medical expenses as an itemized deduction to the extent that they exceed 7.5% of your AGI through the 2016 tax year. (For AMT purposes, however, the threshold is 10% of AGI, regardless of your age.) See chapter 22, *Medical and dental expenses*, for more information.

For insurance premium payments to be counted as qualified medical expenses, the policy must be purchased to cover medical care (e.g., hospitalization, prescription drugs, surgical services, dental care, etc.). If the policy provides benefits or services beyond medical care, you can only include the portion of the premium that is used to pay for the health care coverage provided by the policy. This, in turn, requires that the portion of the premium attributable to medical care coverage be clearly stated in the insurance contract or a separate statement that provides adequate documentation.

Deduction for the self-employed. Self-employed persons may be able to deduct the premiums they pay for health insurance coverage obtained for themselves, their spouses, and dependents. This includes a child under the age of 27 at the end of 2014, even if the child is not claimed as a dependent. If eligible, the deduction would be reflected as an adjustment to income on Form 1040, line 29, resulting in a decline in AGI as well as taxable income. However, this adjustment to income does not reduce income subject to self-employment tax.

TAXPLANNER
How Can You Pay for Out-of-Pocket Health Care Expenses in 2015?

- **Health care flexible spending arrangement (health care FSA).** If your employer offers a health care FSA, the amount of your salary that you contribute into it, and withdrawals you make to pay for qualified medical expenses for yourself, your spouse, and your dependents, are not included in taxable income. The net effect is that your savings in income taxes effectively reduces the cost of your out-of-pocket medical expenses. Contributions are made throughout the year up to a maximum of $2,500 per spouse whose employer offers a health care FSA. However, if you fail to use up the balance in your health care FSA by the end of the plan year, you will forfeit any unspent funds. Your employer may provide you with an option to either use unspent funds to cover expenses incurred up to 2½ months following the end of the plan year (March 15th for plan years ending on December 31st) or to roll over up to $500 to the next plan year (without reducing your maximum allowed contribution for the new plan year). An employer cannot offer both options.

- **Health Savings Account (HSA).** An HSA is an account created for individuals who are covered under high-deductible health plans to save and pay for qualified medical expenses. If you are eligible for an HSA, contributions can be made by you or any other person, including your employer or a family member. Contributions can be made by the individual either directly or through payroll reductions, subject to an annual limit. In 2014, an individual can contribute up to $3,300 to an HSA and families may contribute up to $6,550. For 2015, these limits are $3,350 and $6,650, respectively. For each spouse age 55 or older, you can make an additional $1,000 "catch-up" contribution. Individuals age 65 or older or who have enrolled in Medicare cannot make contributions. Contributions to an HSA, other than through employer contributions, are deductible as an "above-the-line" adjustment to gross income, whether or not you itemize deductions. Contributions made by an employer through payroll reduction are excludable from income for purposes of income, Social Security, and Medicare taxes.

  These contributions can be invested so that they grow over time, and balances can be withdrawn free of federal income taxes if the proceeds are used to pay for qualified medical expenses. Unlike the health care FSA described above, any funds left over in an HSA by the end of the year are not automatically forfeited. These funds can be carried forward and used to pay for qualified medical expenses in subsequent years.

- **Limited-purpose health flexible spending arrangement (limited-purpose FSA).** A limited-purpose FSA operates in a manner similar to a health care FSA. However, distributions from a limited-purpose FSA can only be used for eligible dental, vision, and preventive care expenses (as defined by the employer under IRS guidelines) in order to qualify for favorable tax treatment. These plans are designed specifically to work in conjunction with an HSA, as IRS regulations do not permit contributions to an HSA if you participate in a health care FSA.

- **Health reimbursement arrangement (HRA).** An HRA is an employer-sponsored plan that permits employees to pay for medical costs using funds contributed by the employer. These funds may be used to pay for health insurance premiums as well as other expenses. The amounts reimbursed to the employee are generally excludable from taxable income. Unused funds may be carried forward for use in future years. Most commonly, employers make these plans available in conjunction with a high-deductible health plan (HDHP).
- **Medical expense deduction.** You can also pay for out-of-pocket medical expenses through your existing savings or anticipated cash inflows and account for such payments as a medical expense deduction on your federal income tax return. However, you must itemize deductions on Form 1040, Schedule A, and you may deduct only the amount by which qualifying medical expenses for yourself, your spouse, and your dependents exceed 10% of your adjusted gross income (the applicable threshold is currently 7.5% if you or your spouse is age 65 or older).

Same-Sex Marriages: Tax Changes after the U.S. Supreme Court Ruling on the Defense of Marriage Act (DOMA)

In late June 2013, the U.S. Supreme Court ruled that the provision of the federal Defense of Marriage Act (DOMA) that limited the definition of marriage to the union of one man and one woman and defined a spouse to be a person of the opposite sex who is a husband or wife for purposes of applying federal laws (such as federal tax laws and federal benefit programs) was unconstitutional. This decision did not change federal tax law, but it presented broad implications on federal tax compliance and planning for same-sex married couples.

Following the Supreme Court decision, the IRS issued Revenue Ruling 2013-17 in late August 2013, which addressed a spectrum of federal income and gift and estate tax issues. (The IRS subsequently issued additional guidance in 2013 and 2014 for employers and employees making claims for refund or adjustments of Social Security/Medicare taxes and income tax withholding resulting from *Windsor* and the holdings of the revenue ruling for any period between tax years 2011 and 2013, as well as to employers on the application—including retroactive application—of the *Windsor* decision to qualified retirement plans.)

Overall, Revenue Ruling 2013-17 holds that same-sex couples who legally married in a state (including the District of Columbia) or foreign jurisdiction that recognizes same-sex marriages will be treated as married for U.S. federal tax purposes. The ruling applies a "place-of-celebration" standard, which means that couples who were married in a jurisdiction recognizing same-sex marriages are treated as married even if they reside in a jurisdiction that does not recognize same-sex marriage.

As of September 10, 2014, same-sex marriages are recognized in 19 states and the District of Columbia as follows:

State	Effective date
California	Re-established June 2013
Connecticut	November 12, 2008
District of Columbia	March 3, 2010
Delaware	July 1, 2013
Hawaii	December 2, 2013
Illinois	June 1, 2014
Iowa	April 24, 2009
Maine	December 29, 2012
Maryland	January 1, 2013
Massachusetts	May 17, 2004
Minnesota	August 1, 2013
New Hampshire	January 1, 2010
New York	July 24, 2011
New Jersey	October 21, 2013
New Mexico	December 19, 2013
Oregon	May 19, 2014
Pennsylvania	May 20, 2014
Rhode Island	August 1, 2013
Vermont	September 1, 2009
Washington	December 9, 2012

Under this ruling, same-sex couples are treated as married for all federal tax purposes, including income, gift, and estate taxes.

The ruling applies for all federal tax purposes for which marriage is a factor, including filing status, claiming personal and dependency exemptions, taking the standard deduction, contributing to an IRA, and employee benefits.

Exception: The ruling further holds that, for federal tax purposes, registered domestic partners, individuals who enter into a civil union or other similar formal relationship are not treated as a married couple.

At the same time that the Revenue Ruling was issued, the IRS posted "Answers to Frequently Asked Questions for Individuals of the Same Sex Who Are Married Under State Law" and "Answers to Frequently Asked Questions for Registered Domestic Partners and Individuals in Civil Unions." These FAQs provide additional guidance on the federal tax implications of the ruling.

There are widespread federal income, gift, and estate tax implications for same-sex married couples from the IRS ruling. For example, because of the ruling, you may be able to amend previously filed income, gift, and estate returns, which could yield significant tax savings. For estate and gift planning purposes, the ability for same-sex spouses to be considered "married" is a highly significant tax savings development. Indeed, same-sex married couples, as well as same-sex couples contemplating marriage, should consider undertaking a comprehensive review of their income tax and wealth transfer planning goals and objectives.

Other key implications of the IRS ruling include the following:

How does the revenue ruling affect federal income tax returns?

Same-sex married spouses are required to file their federal income tax return using either married filing jointly or married filing separately filing status.

However, individuals who are in registered domestic partnerships, civil unions, or other similar formal relationships that are not marriages under state law are not considered as married or spouses for federal tax purposes. Such couples may not file a federal return using a married filing jointly or separately filing status.

Should same-sex married spouses amend previously filed federal income tax returns?

Same-sex spouses have the option to amend previously filed tax returns for any previous tax year for which the statute of limitations for filing an amended return has not yet expired using either married filing jointly or separately filing status. Same-sex married couples should calculate their combined income tax liability that would have been due had they been able to file using either married filing status. They should consider amending returns for tax years if filing jointly or as married filing separately would have resulted in a lower tax liability than the total of the tax liabilities reported on the individual returns they previously filed.

A taxpayer generally may file a claim for refund for three years from the date the return was filed or two years from the date the tax was paid, whichever is later. Same-sex spouses who were legally married (i.e., in a domestic or foreign jurisdiction whose laws authorized same-sex marriage) during a tax year for which the statute of limitations for filing an amended tax return is now closed may be able to pursue refunds through judicial means. Couples should consult with appropriate tax counsel about their options.

What actions should same-sex married spouses consider taking for federal gift and estate tax purposes?

The marital deduction for spousal gifts and bequests now applies to married same-sex spouses. Therefore, any individual who had previously reported a taxable gift to a same-sex spouse or any individual who received a taxable bequest from a same-sex spouse should consider filing an amended gift or estate tax return to request a refund for any return for which the statute of limitations remains open.

Furthermore, under the Supreme Court decision, DOMA's definition of a spouse was declared unconstitutional from the time the law was passed. Therefore, an affected individual may be able to pursue a refund of overpaid gift and estate tax through judicial means, if the statute of limitations for requesting a refund is closed. Couples should consult with appropriate tax counsel about their options. In addition, same-sex married spouses should now seek legal counsel regarding the need to update their estate planning documents.

What are some other planning areas same-sex couples should consider?

A same-sex couple that is not currently married should evaluate for income tax purposes whether marriage will improve or in some cases disadvantage the taxpayers; that is, due to the marriage penalty (see the *EXPLANATION* regarding the *Marriage tax penalty* in chapter 2, *Filing status*). Since marital status affects over 200 sections of the Internal Revenue Code and accompanying regulations, a case-by-case analysis is needed for each same-sex married couple. Here is list of some of the other issues affected:

- Naming the spouse as a qualified beneficiary on a retirement account and allowing the spouse to "roll over" the account into his or her qualified retirement account
- Community property treatment of income
- Application of Internal Revenue Code Section 1041(a) on the transfer of property subject to a qualified marriage settlement agreement, which allows the tax-free transfer of appreciated property between U.S. resident spouses upon divorce
- The $25,000 offset for passive activity losses for rental real estate
- Applying the adoption tax credit (previously, same-sex spouses could each claim the credit)
- Gift and estate tax marital deduction
- Electing portability of a deceased spouse's unused applicable lifetime exemption amount
- Simplifying the basis and contribution determinations for jointly owned property
- Splitting of lifetime gifts
- Applying the retained interest rules on transfers to related persons, which treat certain restricted transfers of property between related persons as a completed taxable gift of the property, while transfers between unrelated persons may not be a taxable gift at all
- Availability of certain Social Security, Medicare, and Medicaid benefits
- Applying the thresholds for the tax penalties and health insurance subsidies available under the ACA

Finally, if a same-sex partner is legally a spouse, there may also be ramifications under the ACA. Dependents, but not spouses, are required to be offered coverage in order to avoid the shared responsibility payment penalty tax. Spouses who are offered coverage, however, may not be eligible for premium tax credits for coverage through state exchanges. For more information about the requirements to obtain health care coverage or pay a penalty tax, see *Affordable Care Act (ACA) Individual Provisions*, earlier in this chapter.

What is the impact on state and local tax?

With few exceptions (e.g., New Jersey and Pennsylvania), federal taxable wages (Form W-2, box 1) are currently the starting point for determining state taxable income. For states that do not recognize the validity of same-sex marriages, the effect of the IRS revenue ruling that legally married, same-sex couples are married regardless of the jurisdiction where they now reside is unclear. For states that do not recognize same-sex marriages and do not treat same-sex spouses as spouses for state tax law purposes, a change in the state tax law likely will be necessary. Further, where states choose to depart from following the federal treatment, the "place-of-celebration" rule set forth in Revenue Ruling 2013-17 will result in conflicts between the filing status on federal and state/local income tax returns.

Since the Supreme Court decision and IRS revenue ruling were issued, affected states have been assessing how these issues will be resolved. Taxpayers, including their employers, will need to respond to a flurry of changes in withholding allowance certificate procedures and Form W-2 reporting requirements.

Inflation Adjustments for 2015

Each year a number of tax benefits and income limitations for tax benefits are indexed for inflation. Some of the items typically adjusted annually for inflation include:

1. Tax rate tables
2. Standard deduction
3. Personal exemption
4. Income limitations for the child tax credit, the education credits, interest on education loans and the adoption credit
5. Medical savings accounts
6. Contribution limits to qualified retirement plans and IRAs

As of the date this book went to press, the inflation adjustments for 2015 had not yet been published. The 2015 adjustments will be posted on *ey.com/EYTaxGuide* after the IRS announces them.

Chapter 48
2014 Tax rate schedules

ey.com/EYTaxGuide

Note

ey.com/EYTaxGuide

Ernst & Young LLP will update the *EY Tax Guide 2015* website with relevant taxpayer information as it becomes available. You can also sign up for email alerts to let you know when changes have been made.

Introduction

This chapter contains the 2014 final Tax Rate Schedules that taxpayers with taxable income of $100,000 or more must use. The 2014 Tax Tables must be used by taxpayers with taxable income of less than $100,000. Those Tax Tables can be found at *www.irs.gov/pub/irs-pdf/i1040tt.pdf*.

Schedule X—If your filing status is Single

If your taxable income is: Over–	But not over–	The tax is:		of the amount over–
$0	$9,075	....	10%	$0
9,075	36,900	$907.50	+15%	9,075
36,900	89,350	5,081.25	+25%	36,900
89,350	186,350	18,193.75	+28%	89,350
186,350	405,100	45,353.75	+33%	186,350
405,100	406,750	117,541.25	+35%	405,100
406,750	....	118,118.75	+39.6%	406,750

Schedule Y-1—If your filing status is Married filing jointly or Qualifying widow(er)

If your taxable income is: Over–	But not over–	The tax is:		of the amount over–
$0	18,150	....	10%	$0
18,150	73,800	$1,815.00	+15%	18,150
73,800	148,850	10,162.50	+25%	73,800
148,850	226,850	28,925.00	+28%	148,850
226,850	405,100	50,765.00	+33%	226,850
405,100	457,600	109,587.50	+35%	405,100
457,600	....	127,962.50	+39.6%	457,600

Schedule Y-2—If your filing status is Married filing separately

If your taxable income is: Over–	But not over–	The tax is:		of the amount over–
$0	$9,075	....	10%	$0
9,075	36,900	$907.50	+15%	9,075
36,900	74,425	5,081.25	+25%	36,900
74,425	113,425	14,462.50	+28%	74,425
113,425	202,550	25,382.50	+33%	113,425
202,550	228,800	54,793.75	+35%	202,550
228,800	....	63,981.25	+39.6%	228,800

Schedule Z—If your filing status is Head of household

If your taxable income is:		The tax is:		
Over–	But not over–			of the amount over–
$0	$12,950	....	10%	$0
12,950	49,400	$1,295.00	+15%	12,950
49,400	127,550	6,762.50	+25%	49,400
127,550	206,600	26,300.00	+28%	127,550
206,600	405,100	48,434.00	+33%	206,600
405,100	432,200	113,939.00	+35%	405,100
432,200	....	123,424.00	+39.6%	432,200

Index

Symbols

5% owners, 258
12b-1 funds, 865
401(k) plans, 134, 235-236, 250, 253-254, 257
403(b) plans, 235, 250, 253, 257
457(b) plans, 235, 236, 250, 253

A

Abandonment of home, 384
Academic periods, 778
Accelerated Cost Recovery System (ACRS), 226
Accelerated death benefits, 281, 921
Accelerated income, 324-325, 971
Accidental death benefits, 129
Accountable plans, 663-665
Accounting methods, 21-24, 226, 837-839
Accounting periods, 21, 50, 126
Account statements, 35
Accreditation fees, professional, 708
Accrual method, 24, 167, 184, 838
Accrued leave payment, 124, 142
Accuracy-related penalties, 40-41
Acknowledgment of charity, 595-596
Acquisition indebtedness, 548
ACRS (Accelerated Cost Recovery System), 226
Active participation, rental real estate activity, 228-229
Additional child tax credit, 774, 775
Address, change of, 6, 36, 111
Adjusted basis, 320-324, 349, 384, 386-387, 613, 623, 873, 875, 879
Adjusted gross income (AGI):
   earned income credit, 807-808
   education-related adjustments, 475-484
   IRS e-*file* and, 14
   itemized deductions, 545, 570, 711
   limits, 52
   medical and dental expenses, 510, 512, 513
   moving expenses, 485
   phaseout of exemptions, 85-86
   reporting educational expenses, 685
   Self-Select PIN and, 14
   tuition, 674
Adjusted qualified higher educational expenses, 174
Administrators, 8, 138, 914
Adoption:
   credits, 774, 791-792, 811
   employer-provided benefits, 128-129
   exception for personal exemptions, 64
   expenses, 708, 792
   medical and dental expenses of, 514-515
   as qualifying child for exemptions, 65
   as qualifying relative for exemptions, 76
   without social security numbers, 87
Adoption taxpayer identification number (ATIN), 6, 25, 87, 750
Advance commissions, 122
Advance payment of income, 24, 122
Advance rent, 210-211
Affordable Care Act (ACA), 4, 975-984. *See also* Net investment income tax (NIIT)
   additional taxes, 299, 301, 309, 866
   dividends, 187, 197
   Medicare tax, 89-90, 728
   pensions, 100
AFTC (Armed Forces Tax Council), 16
Age test, 65, 811
AGI, *see* Adjusted gross income
Airline employees, 325
Alaska permanent fund dividends, 205, 296, 561
Aliens:
   alien status waiver, 139
   child and dependent care credit, 756
   credit for elderly or disabled, 768
   dual-status, 908-909

earned income credit, 808-809
estimated tax, 106
filing requirements, 10
foreign nationals who become U.S. residents, 910-911
joint returns for married couples, 51
nonresident, 909-911
resident, 906-909
spouses filing under head of household status, 54
taxpayer identification number for, 6
without social security numbers, 87
Alimony, 296, 461-474, 971
Allocated tips, 151-154
Allocating basis, 326
Allocation of interest, 558, 565-567
Allowances, 122, 663
Alternative fuel vehicle refueling property credit, 789
Alternative minimum tax (AMT), 721-728, 973
   adjustments and tax preference items, 724-728
   capital gain rates, 401, 416
   for children, 745
   depreciable property, 225
   divorce and, 47
   figuring, 717-718
   home equity loan interest and, 546
   medical expenses, 513, 517
   more information, 728
   mutual funds, 869
   overview, 721
   refund of credit, expiration of, 726
   standard deduction versus itemizing, 504-505, 507
   stock sales and, 370
Alternative motor vehicle credit, 792-793
Amended returns, 37-39
American opportunity credit, 64, 71, 777, 780
American Taxpayer Relief Act of 2012 (ATRA), 717
   estate tax, 931
   and net investment income, 234
Amount realized, 384
AMT, *see* Alternative minimum tax
Annual wage, guaranteed, 292
Annuities, 234-261
   cost, 241-242
   defined, 253
   designated Roth accounts, 236, 241
   disability pensions, 236
   early distributions tax, 255
   earned income credit, 820
   estimated tax, 237
   excess accumulation tax, 258-261
   foreign employment contributions, 242
   General Rule, 243-244
   how to report, 241
   joint return, 241
   loans, 237-238
   lump-sum distributions, 245-247
   more than one program, 236, 241
   nonperiodic payments taxation, 245-247
   overview, 234-235
   periodic payments taxation, 242-244
   purchased, 237
   qualified plans for self-employed individuals, 237
   railroad retirement benefits, 237
   retired public safety officers, 236
   rollovers, 248-255
   sale of, 369
   section 457 deferred compensation plans, 236
   Simplified Method, 242-244
   starting dates and distribution, 243-244
   survivors, 261
   taxes on payments, 177
   tax-free exchange, 241
   trades of, 355
   unrecovered investment in, 705
   withholding, 99-103, 237
Annuity contracts, interest on, 164
Annulments, 46, 472

Appeals, audits, 953-954, 961-965
Appraisals, 349, 519, 583, 610, 613
Archer MSAs (Archer Medical Savings Accounts), 126, 306, 923
Armed Forces, *see* Military personnel
Armed Forces Tax Council (AFTC), 16
Artists, 671, 686, 853
Assumption of mortgage, 319
ATIN, *see* Adoption taxpayer identification number
At risk limitations, 309-310
At-risk rules, 227, 283
Attachments, 26
Audits, 953-967
   appeals, 953-954, 961-965
   collections, 953-954, 965
   confidentiality, 952
   correspondence audit, 958
   discriminant function system, 956
   document-matching program, 957-958
   economic reality audits, 958
   examination of returns, 955-961
   examiner's authority, 960-961
   explanation of changes, 960
   fairness if return is examined, 955
   interview, 953-954
   IRS declaration of taxpayer rights, 952-953
   litigation expenses, 964-965
   mail, 953
   market segmentation specialization program, 956-957
   office audit, 959
   overview, 952, 954
   partnerships, 963
   past-due taxes, 966-967
   payment of correct amount, 953
   privacy, 952
   professional and courteous service, 952-953
   refunds, 953-954, 965-966
   relief from penalties and interest, 953
   repeat examinations, 954, 960
   representation, 953, 959, 962
   S corporations, 963
   third party contacts, 965
   transfer to another district, 959
   verification methods, 957-958
   who gets audited, 954-955
   written protest, 962
Authors, 853
Automatic extensions, 6, 17, 18
Automatic investment services, 335, 372
Automobile expenses, *see* Cars and car expenses
Average basis:
   capital gains, 410-411
   mutual funds, 873, 876-878
Awards, 123, 164, 297, 306-308

B

Babysitting, 122, 887
Back pay awards, 122
Backup withholding, 104, 113, 159, 192
Bad check penalty, 43
Bad debt, 373-378, 840-841
Balance due, figuring, 721
Bankruptcy, 301, 368-371
Bargain sales, 325, 589
Bar review courses, 680
Bartering, 276
Basis, 317-338
   adjusted, 320-324
   capital gains, 410-411
   cost, 318-320
   costs that increase, 320-322
   decreases to, 322-324
   determining for home sale, 385-387
   figuring received, 353
   inherited property, 329-332

Basis (*continued*)
  involuntary conversions, 325-327
  mutual funds, 870, 872-878
  nontaxable exchanges, 327-328
  overview, 317
  partnerships, 282-283
  property changed from personal to business or
    rental use, 332
  property received as gift, 328-329
  property received for services, 324-325
  property transferred from a spouse, 328
  recordkeeping, 33, 34
  replacement property, 379
  required in bad debt, 374
  S corporation, 284-285
  stocks and bonds, 201, 203, 332-338
  taxable exchanges, 325
Bearer CDs, 183
Below-market loans, 165-167
Beneficiaries of estates or trusts, 158, 191-192,
    298, 933
Bicycle commuting, qualified, 132, 629
Birth of child, 58, 66-67, 76, 749, 812
Blind taxpayers, 97, 504-505, 508
Bona fide loans, 374-375
Bonds, 332-338. *See also* Savings bonds
  amortizable premium on taxable, 704
  basis of, 318
  capital assets, 358-362
  convertible, 345, 353
  determining if decedent or estate should redeem,
    171-172
  gift to child, interest reporting responsibility, 170
  identifying sold, 333-334
  interest, 158
  market discount, 183
  municipal, 77-78, 177-178, 534
  mutual fund shares, 334
  OID on debt instruments, 335
  overview, 333
  premiums, 335, 568
  retirement, 250
  Series E, Series EE, and Series I, 158
  sold between interest dates, 176-177
  state issued, 177-179
  stripped coupon, 180
  traded flat, 165
  zero-coupon, 181-182
Bonuses, 123, 307
Breach of employment contract, damages for, 690
Breast-feeding supplies, 12
Bribes, 296
Brokers' commissions, 427, 429
Bureau of Justice Assistance payments, 313
Burglar alarms, 612
Business bad debts, 375-377, 689
Business days, 638
Business interest expense, 565
Business-producing property, 609, 618
Business property, 471

C

Cafeteria plans, 141, 520-521
Calendar tax year, 837
Calendar year, 21
Camp, cost of sending children to, 754
Campaigns, 296, 706
Canada, children in, 75
Canceled debt, 276-279
Canceling leases, payment for, 211
Capital assets, 358-362
Capital expenditures, 840
Capital expenses, 82-83, 518, 519
Capital gains and losses, 358-379
  in 2014, 135
  capital and noncapital assets, 358-362
  capital asset treatment for self-created musical
    works, 359-360
  capital or ordinary gain or loss, 358
  carryovers, 414, 881-882
  character of gain or loss, 358

deposit in insolvent or bankrupt financial institution,
    368-371
  discounted debt instruments, 360-368
  holding period, 371-373
  investment property, 359
  limit on deduction, 413
  municipal bonds, 177-178
  nonbusiness bad debts, 373-378
  overview, 358, 413
  personal use property, 359
  reporting, 202, 403-418
  rollover of gain from publicly traded securities, 379
  small business, 970
  tax rates, 414-418
  treatment on taxable part of lump-sum
    distributions, 247
  undistributed capital gains, 200, 800, 869, 874
  wash sales, 378-379
Capital gain distributions, 200-201, 561, 739,
    868-869
Capital gain property, 570, 587-589
Capitalized interest, 478
Car allowances, 665-667
Cars and car expenses, 651-656
  advertising display on, 650
  charitable contribution deductions, 579, 583-584,
    586, 598
  commuter highway, 132
  deducting, 494, 523
  license fees, 543
  losses, 611
  plug-in electric vehicle credit, 789
  reporting, 668
  sales taxes on, 654
  self-employed persons, 841
  transportation to school, 681-682
Car pools, 296, 650
Carryovers, 414, 592-593, 881-882
Carryover basis rules, 331
Cash, 350, 594-596
Cash method, 21-24, 167, 183-184, 838
Cash rebates, 296
Casualty and theft losses, 22, 599-623
  adjusted basis, 613
  business property, 848
  casualty, 601-604
  decrease in fair market value, 609-613
  deductions, 617-621, 701
  gain from reimbursement, 609
  of income-producing property, 704
  insurance and other reimbursements, 297,
    613-616
  leased property, 609
  loss on deposits, 605-607
  overview, 599-600
  proof of loss, 607-608
  reporting gains and losses, 621-623
  single casualty on multiple properties, 616-617
  theft, 604-605
Catch-up contributions, 134
C corporations, 189, 340, 401
Cell phones, employer-provided, 889
Certificates of deposit (CDs), 162-163, 182-183
Certified public accountant (CPA), 680
Chambers of commerce, dues to, 691
Charitable contributions, *see* Contributions, charitable
Charitable remainder trusts, 586
Charity benefit events, 576-577
Checks, 23, 111, 590, 659
Child and dependent care credit, 746-766
  amount of, 762
  dollar limit, 761-762
  earned income limit, 759-761
  earned income test, 750-751
  employment taxes for household employers,
    763-764
  figuring, 757-762
  how to claim, 763
  joint return test, 755
  overview, 746-747, 757
  provider identification test, 756
  qualifying person test, 749-750
  work-related expenses, 752-759

Child born alive exemption, 67
Child care expenses, 83
Childcare providers, 121-122
Children. *See also* Adoption; Investment income
  birth of, 58, 66-67, 76, 749, 812
  in Canada or Mexico, 75
  capital asset gifts to, 401-402
  credits for care expenses, 733
  death of, 58, 66-67, 76, 749, 812
  filing requirements for those under age 19, 9
  income from property given to, 160
  kidnapped, 54, 58, 67, 74, 812
  married, 56
  medical and dental expenses of, 514-515
  of person not required to file returns, 74-75
  place of residence and personal exemptions, 64
  qualifying to file as head of household, 55, 56
  school transportation, 309
  social security benefits, 263
Child support, 297, 467-469
Child tax credit, 63, 773-776
Chronically ill individuals, 143, 281
Church employees, 820
Civil penalties, 39
Civil unions, 7, 47-48
Claim of right, repayments under, 705
Clergy, 137-138, 301, 820
Clerical help, 701
Closing costs on home, 386
Clothing, 583, 586, 698-699
Club dues, 642-643, 706
Coins, 359, 447
Collectibles, 416, 447
College professors, research expenses of, 698
Combat zone, 6, 20, 809
Combined penalties, 40
Commodity futures, 365
Common-law employees, 845
Common-law marriage, 61
Community income, 7
Community property, 332, 426, 760, 810, 944
Community property states, 53, 867
Commuting expenses, 650, 706-707
Compensatory damages, 295
Complex trust, 298, 299
Computers, depreciation on, 690, 691, 701
Condemnations, 164, 354, 390, 398
Condominiums, 210
Conservation reserve program (CRP) payments, 811
Conservator, court-appointed, 27
Constructive receipt, 121
Constructive receipt, of income, 22, 23
Consumer Product Safety Commission (CPSC), 603-604
Contract price, 345
Contributions, charitable, 569-598
  of $250 or more, 594
  acknowledgment of, 595-596
  amount of, 595
  appraisal fees, 583
  athletic events, 575-576
  benefits received, 575-577
  boats, 586
  capital gain property, 570
  car expenses, 579, 598
  cash, 594-596
  charity benefit events, 576-577
  clothing and household items, 583, 586
  conventions, 579
  deductions, 572-580, 583, 590-593, 938
  exceptions, 584
  expenses paid for students, 577-578
  fair market value, 573-574, 576-577, 586
  foreign charitable organizations, 572
  foster parents, 579
  future interests in tangible personal property, 586
  how to report, 598
  to individuals, 580-581
  intellectual property, 575
  large quantities, 586
  membership fees or dues, 577
  noncash, 596-597
  to nonqualified organizations, 581

Differential wage payments, 92, 123, 140
Difficulty-of-care payments, 302-303
Direct deposit refunds, 6, 13-15, 28, 429
Direct expenses, 847
Direct rollovers, 100-102, 249, 251-252
Disability, individuals with:
    dependent care expenses, 523-524
    exceptions to ownership and use tests, 389-390
    impairment-related work expenses of, 671
    public assistance benefits, 292
    qualifying child for exemptions, 66
Disability benefits, 295, 810
Disability income, 771
Disability payments, 121, 272, 810
    conditions for exclusion, 142
    deduction for repaid, 263, 272-274
    due to terrorist attack, 313
Disability pensions, 141-142, 236
Disabled, credit for, 733, 767-772
    under age 65, 768, 769-770
    disability income, 771
    eligibility, 768-772
    exceptions, 768
    figured by IRS, 771-772
    figuring, 772
    head of household, 769
    income limits, 771
    married persons, 768
    overview, 767
    permanent and total disability, 770
    physician's statement, 770
    qualified individuals, 768-772
    U.S. citizen or resident alien, 768
Disaster areas:
    losses, 621-622
    replacement period, 325-326
Disaster mitigation payments, 276-277, 293
Disaster preparedness, 34
Disaster relief, 276-277, 292-293, 614, 615
Disclosure, 41
Discounted debt instruments, 360-368
    notes of individuals, 362
    overview, 360
    short-term government obligations, 360
    short-term nongovernment obligations, 360
    tax-exempt state and local government bonds, 360-361
Discounted mortgage loan, 277
Discriminant function system, 956
Dishonored payment penalty, 30
Dislocation allowance, military personnel, 493
Disregard, 40
Distance test, moving expenses, 487-492
Distributed capital gains, 200-201
Distributions:
    defined, 189-190
    early distributions tax, 255-258
    involuntary, 246
    mutual funds, 866-871, 880
    and net investment income, 234
    nondividend in mutual funds, 869-870
    rolling over, 245
Dividends, 187-190
    Alaska permanent fund, 205
    backup withholding, 192
    basis adjustment, 201
    beneficiaries of estates or trusts, 191-192
    capital gain distributions, 200-201
    distributions of stock and stock rights, 202-203
    exempt-interest, 161, 204
    expenses related to, 207
    forms, 192-193, 205-206
    how to report, 205-208
    insurance policies, 204
    interest on insurance, 163
    interest on VA, 162
    liquidating distributions, 202
    money market funds, 199-200
    mutual funds, 868
    ordinary, 195-200
    overview, 187-190
    patronage dividends, 204

qualified, 195-196
received in January, 194
social security number, 192
stock certificate in two or more names, 192
on stock sold, 193-194
tax on investment income of certain children, 190-191
that are actually interest, 162
used to buy more stock, 197-199
veterans' insurance, 204
Dividend reinvestment plans (DRPs), 187, 197-199, 333, 335, 703
Divorce decree, 68-69
Divorced taxpayers, 46-47, 50
    child and dependent care credit, 750
    with children with investment income, 737
    earned income credit, 815-816
    estimated tax credit for 2014, 114-115
    exemptions when filing, 62
    home mortgage interest deduction, 551
    IRA transfers incident to, 440
    medical and dental expenses of children, 515
    qualifying child of, 67-69, 73-74
    tax deductions, 541
    use of home after, 391
Documentary evidence of employee expenses, 658-659
Document-matching program, 23, 957-958
Dollar limit, work-related expenses for child and dependent care credit, 761-762
DOMA (Defense of Marriage Act), 982-983
Domestic help, see Household employees
Domestic partners, 7
Donation of use of property, 222
Double-category method, 876
Down payment assistance, 298
Drought, 601
DRPs, see Dividend reinvestment plans
Dual-status aliens, 10, 51, 908-909
Due dates, filing, 37
Dwelling units, 218-221-225

E

Early distributions, 255-258, 441-442, 449-451, 458
Earned income, 740, 759-761, 809
Earned income advance payment, 890
Earned income credit (EIC), 804-826
    adjusted gross income, 807-808
    age limits, 817
    community property, 810
    conservation reserve program payments, 810
    dependents of others, 817-818
    disability benefits, 810
    disability insurance payments, 810
    earned income, 809
    figuring, 819-821
    filing, 732, 733
    forms, 809-810, 820-826
    household employees, 890
    improper claim made in prior year, 806
    increase in earned income amount, 804-805
    inmate earnings, 810
    investment income limit, 809
    married filing separately status, 808
    nontaxable combat pay election, 809
    nontaxable military pay, 811
    overview, 804-805
    qualifying child, 806, 811-817
    residence in United States, 819
    Schedule EIC, 821, 822
    self-employed persons, 809
    social security number, 808
    statutory employees, 809
    taxpayer cannot be qualifying child of another person, 818-819
    U.S. citizen or resident alien all year, 808-809
    wages, salaries, and tips, 809
    workfare payments, 810
    worksheet for, 820-825
Earned income test, 750-751

Earthquakes, 601, 603
Easements, 324, 344
Economic reality audits, 958
Educational expenses, 442, 779-780
Educational institutions, 174, 778
Education credits, 85, 777-787
    academic period, 778
    dependent's expenses, 779
    double benefit, 781
    eligibility for, 778-779
    overview, 777-778
    paid with borrowed funds, 781
    qualified education expenses, 779-786
    refunds, 782
    student withdrawal from class, 781
    tax-free educational assistance, 781-782
Education loans, 279, 564
Education-related AGI adjustments, 475-484
Education savings accounts, 81
Education Savings Bond Program, 155, 173-175
Education savings bonds, 155
Educator expenses, 477, 483-484, 691
E-filing, 6, 13-18, 945-951
EFTPS (Electronic Federal Tax Payment System), 18
EHLP (Emergency Homeowners' Loan Program), 293
EIC, see Earned income credit
EIN (employer identification number), 887
Elderly, credit for, 733, 767-772
    under age 65, 768, 769-770
    disability income, 771
    eligibility, 768-772
    exceptions, 768
    figured by IRS, 771-772
    figuring, 772
    head of household, 769
    income limits, 771
    married persons, 768
    overview, 767
    permanent and total disability, 770
    physician's statement, 770
    qualified individuals, 768-772
    U.S. citizen or resident alien, 768
Elective deferrals, 119, 238-240
Electronic Federal Tax Payment System (EFTPS), 18
Electronic payment options, 111
Electronic records, 33, 34
Eligible rollover distributions (ERDs), 100-102, 237, 248, 251-252
Emancipated child, 68
Embezzlement income, 304
Emergency disaster fund, 614
Emergency Homeowners' Loan Program (EHLP), 293, 551
Emotional distress compensation, 297
Employee achievement award, 123, 307
Employee benefits, 932
Employee compensation, 120-137
    advance commissions and other earnings, 122
    allowances and reimbursements, 122
    awards, 123
    bonuses, 123
    childcare providers, 121-122
    differential wage payments, 123
    Form W-2, 121
    fringe benefits, 126-133
    government cost-of-living allowances, 123
    nonqualified deferred compensation plans, 124
    note received for services, 124
    overview, 120-122
    restricted property, 136-137
    retirement plan contributions, 133-134
    severance pay, 124
    sick pay, 124
    social security and Medicare taxes paid by employer, 124
    stock appreciation rights, 125
    stock options, 134-136
Employee expenses, 651-656. See also Household employees
    car expenses, 651-656
    education expenses, 685-686
    entertainment expenses, 639-646

Forms: (*continued*)
  8453, 14
  8606, 48, 423, 434, 438, 446
  8615, 157, 190–191, 740–745
  8814, 158, 191
  8829, 846–850, 862
  8839, 128
  8853, 281
  8867, 806
  8889, 127
  8938, 155–156
  8939, 373
  8949, 402–403, 881
  8960, 245
  for exemptions, 61
  File Fillable, 13
  RRB-1099, 262
  SS-4, 305
  SSA-1099, 262, 263
  substitute, 21
  W-2, 21, 26, 112–113, 121, 126
  W-2c, 113
  W-2G, 103, 112, 113, 303
  W-4, 92, 93, 96, 98
  W-4P, 101
  W-4S, 99
  W-4V, 103
  W-7, 6
Foster care, 65, 69, 80, 302–303, 579, 811
Found property, 303
401(k) plans, 134, 235–236, 250, 253–254, 257
403(b) plans, 235, 250, 253, 257
457(b) plans, 235, 236, 250, 253
Fractional shares, 203
Fraud, 42
Free file fillable forms, 951
Free tour, 303
Fringe benefits, 126–133, 325, 627
Frivolous tax submissions, 6, 42
Frozen deposits, 164–165, 306
FSA (Flexible Spending Account), 120
Full retirement age, 274
Full-time students, 9, 66, 738
FUTA (federal unemployment tax), 890–891
Future production sale, 291

G

Gains and losses. *See also* Capital gains and losses
  capital gain tax rates, 414–418
  from casualties or thefts, 621–623
  from disposition of depreciable property, 227
  figuring on sale of property, 349–353
  Form 1099-B transactions, 407, 408
  Form 1099-CAP transactions, 407
  Form 1099-S transactions, 407–408
  home sale, 383–387
  installment sales, 406
  long-term, 372, 409–412
  lot sales, 367–368
  mutual funds, 879–882
  nominees, 408–409
  overview, 400–402
  passive activity, 406–407
  postponed, 379
  qualified small business stock, 370–371
  from reimbursement, 609
  reporting, 400–418
  sale expenses, 409
  sale of property bought at various times, 409
  short-term, 409
  total net gain or loss, 413
Gambling gains and losses, 103, 303, 689, 704–705
Game-related student expenses, 482
Gaming Industry Tip Compliance Agreement Program, 150
Garnished wages, 23
Gas, royalties from, 290
Gems, 359
General Rule, 235, 243–244, 562
General sales taxes, 531–532
Generation-skipping transfer (GST) taxes, 514, 941

Genuine debt, 374–375
GI Bill, tuition payments and allowances under, 83
Gifts, 646–647
  cash, 614
  Crummey trust, 939
  custodial, 938–939
  as income, 304
  to minors, 938–939
  mutual fund shares, 874, 880
  for opening accounts, 163
  outright, 938
  present interest trust, 939
  property received as, 328–329
  qualified tuition programs, 939–940
  to reduce debt held by public, 32
  tax-free, 936–939
  tips and gratuities versus, 148
  Totten trust, 939
  year-end, 972–973
Gift loans, 166–167
Gift taxes, 543, 936–939
Gold, 359
Golden parachute payments, 720
"Good faith" payment, 31
Government obligations, short-term, 360
Grandfathered debt, 547
Grantor trust, 300
Green card test, 903
Gross income, 7–8, 77, 278
Gross profit, 345
Gross rental income, 224–225
Group-term life insurance, 129–131, 720
GST (generation-skipping transfer) taxes, 514, 941
Guaranteed annual wage, 292
Guaranteed payments in annuity contract, 243

H

Half-time student enrollment, 477
HAMP (home affordable modification program), 293
Handicapped persons, *see* Disability, individuals with
Hardest Hit Fund, 293, 551
Hardship distributions, 251
HDHP (High Deductible Health Plan), 121, 128
Head of household, 47, 54–57, 769
Health Care and Education Reconciliation Act of 2010, 401
Health coverage tax credit, 789, 802
Health flexible spending arrangement (health FSA), 126–127
Health insurance:
  benefits, 295
  employer-sponsored, 521
  premiums of qualifying relative, 83
  self-employed persons, 529–530, 845
Health Insurance Marketplace, 789, 799
Health reimbursement arrangement (HRA), 127, 521, 524
Health savings accounts (HSAs), 121, 127–128, 511, 720, 923
Health spa expenses, 707
High Deductible Health Plan (HDHP), 121, 128
Hobbies, 304, 482, 701
Holders of tax credit bonds, credit for, 793–794
Holding period, 195–196, 371–373, 868, 879–880
Holiday gifts, 129
Holocaust restitution payments, 141
Home, 221–224
Home acquisition debt limit, 52
Home affordable modification program (HAMP), 293
Home equity loans, 548
Home for the aged payments, 80
Home improvement loans, 554
Homeless shelters, 812, 819
Home mortgage interest, 52, 546–558
  amount deductible, 547–552
  Form 1098, 557–558
  overview, 546
  points, 552–557
  premiums, mortgage interest, 557–558
  reporting, 567
Home office, 651, 692–696, 846–850

Homeowners' association charges, 543
Home rehabilitation grants, 294
Home sale, 380–399
  acquired in like-kind exchange, 398
  business use or rental of home, 393–397
  excluding gain, 387–393
  expatriates, 398
  figuring gain or loss, 383–387
  home destroyed or condemned, 398
  home mortgage interest deduction, 550
  home relinquished in like-kind exchange, 398
  as income, 308
  main home, 382–383
  overview, 380–381
  postponed gain from, 324
  recapturing federal mortgage subsidy, 398–399
  reporting, 397–398
  sale of remainder interest, 398
Home security system, 707
Hosts and hostesses, 279
"Hours of service" limits, 641–642
Household employees, 884–895
  babysitters, 887
  earned income credit, 890
  employer identification number, 887
  employment taxes, 891–893
  "nanny tax," 855
  overview, 884–885
  recordkeeping, 886, 893
  reporting and paying taxes on wages paid to, 891
  social security and Medicare wage threshold, 855
  state employment tax, 855
  taxable compensation, 887
  withholding, 91
Housekeepers, 62
HRA, *see* Health reimbursement arrangement
HSAs, *see* Health savings accounts
HUD (Department of Housing and Urban Development), 603–604
Hydrogen refueling property credit, 793

I

Identity theft, 43
Illegal income, reporting, 304
Impairment-related work expenses, 528–529, 671, 686, 705
Improvements on property, 214, 226, 320–322
Incentive items, 163, 304
Incentive stock options (ISOs), 135, 334
Income:
  accelerated, 324–325
  accounting method for, 21–24
  advance payment of, 24
  in basic records, 34
  distributions from IRA, 440
  identifying, 33
  including recapture of alimony in, 471
  limits for credit for elderly or disabled, 771
  repayments of, 703
  tax-exempt expenses, 709
Income aid payment, repayment of, 698
Income-producing property, 568, 609, 618, 704
Income tax treaties, 196
Incomplete expense deduction records, 660
Independent contractors, 845
Indian fishing rights, 305
Indian tribal governments, 533, 571
Indirect expenses, 847
Indirect transactions, 357
Individual filing requirements, 4, 5, 7–8
Individual retirement arrangements (IRAs), 53, 162, 421–460, 902
  deductions, 429–433
  direct deposit of tax refunds, 428–429
  distributions delivered outside US, 446
  distributions from for charity, 570
  early distributions, 257–258
  expatriates, 902
  fees, 688
  inherited, 434–435
  Kay Bailey Hutchison Spousal, 429